# THE
# ORGANIZATIONAL
# BEHAVIOR
# READER

6th Edition

# THE ORGANIZATIONAL BEHAVIOR READER

Edited by

**David A. Kolb**
*Case Western Reserve University*

**Joyce S. Osland**
*University of Portland*

**Irwin M. Rubin**
*Temenos, Inc.*

PRENTICE HALL, Englewood Cliffs, New Jersey 07632

The Organizational behavior reader  /  edited by David A. Kolb, Joyce S.
   Osland, Irwin M. Rubin. -- 6th ed.
        p.     cm..
      Can be used as a companion to the editor's text, Organizational
   behavior  (6th ed.,  c1995), or as a stand-alone text.
      Includes bibliographical references.
      ISBN 0-13-186487-4
      1. Psychology, Industrial.  2.  Organizational behavior.     I. Kolb,
   David A.,  1939–      .  II.  Osland, Joyce.  III.  Rubin, Irwin M.,  1939–        .

   HF5548.8.K552   1995b
   158.7—dc20                                                   94–47064
                                                                    CIP

Production Editor: Pencil Point Studio: Suzanne Visco
Senior Project Manager: Alana Zdinak
Acquisitions Editor: Natalie Anderson
Interior Design: Pencil Point Studio
Cover Design: Pencil Point Studio
Design Director: Linda Fiordilino/Patricia Wosczyk
Copy Editor: Pencil Point Studio:Barbara Visco/Rita Pinkus
Proofreader: Pencil Point Studio: Kerime Toksu/E.G. Sauters
Permissions Editor: Pencil Point Studio: Suzanne Visco
Manufacturing Buyer: Vincent Scelta
Assistant Editor: Lisamarie Brassini
Editorial Assistant: Nancy Proyect

Cover art: Pencil Point Studio/Marles Najaka
Technical art: Pencil Point Studio: Patricia Amirante

© 1995, 1991, 1984, 1979, 1974, 1971 by Prentice Hall, Inc.
A Simon and Schuster Company
Englewood Cliffs, New Jersey 07632

Printed in the United States of America

10  9  8  7  6  5  4   3  2  1

ISBN 0-13-186487-4

Prentice-Hall International (UK) Limited, *London*
Prentice-Hall of Australia Pty.  Limited, *Sydney*
Prentice-Hall Canada Inc., *Toronto*
Prentice-Hall Hispanoamericana, S.A., *Mexico*
Prentice-Hall of India Private Limited, *New Delhi*
Prentice-Hall of Japan, Inc., *Tokyo*
Simon & Schuster Asia Pte.  Ltd., *Singapore*
Editora Prentice-Hall do Brasil, Ltda., *Rio de Janeiro*

# Contents

# PART III: LEADERSHIP AND MANAGEMENT

# Preface

This book is intended as a source of primary material in organizational behavior for the student of management at all three levels—undergraduate, graduate, and in-service. There are represented here the works of scholars and practitioners who have contributed to our understanding of human behavior on the individual, group, and organizational level. In this revised edition we have attempted to portray a balanced view of the field of organizational behavior including basic ideas and concepts, new approaches developed in current research, and emerging perspectives that suggest the future shape of the field.

The articles in this volume fall into one or more of the following categories:

(1) classic articles which, though written years ago, are still the best representative of their genre;

(2) lucid overviews of the theories about a particular subject matter;

(3) descriptions of recently developed theories; and

(4) practical guides for managers.

We have tried throughout the volume to provide a balance of research reports and theoretical essays that were readable enough to be understood by the beginning student and at the same time sufficiently weighty to be of help to the active manager who wants an overview of the field. Based on feedback from our students and from colleagues who have used the book, this volume is considerably different from previous editions. Our colleagues, graduates, and doctoral students in the Department of Organizational Behavior at Case Western Reserve University have been particularly helpful in shaping this fifth edition of the book by sharing their views of our field and by their suggestions of readings. In particular we would like to thank Gail Ambuske, Barbara Bird, Gene Bocialetti, Richard Boyatzis, Pamela Johnson, Rebecca Jordan, Karen Locke, Michael Manning, Eric Neilsen, William Pasmore, Asbjorn Osland, Paul Sears, Michael Sokoloff, and Sue Taft for their contributions to this volume. Don McCormick of Antioch College West was especially generous with his suggestions and teaching expertise.

This book is designed to be used with the text/workbook *Organizational Behavior: An Experiential Approach to Organizational Behavior* by the same authors. The articles contained herein form a complete package with the exercises and theory contained in the workbook, allowing the student to go through all the phases of the experiential learning process.

Although designed as a companion volume, this collection of readings stands on its own and should be useful to teachers, managers, and consultants for the breadth of viewpoints and the wealth of data that it provides about the field of organizational behavior.

David A. Kolb
Joyce S. Osland
Irwin M. Rubin

# 1

# The Psychological Contract and Organizational Socialization

THE IMPACT OF CHANGING VALUES ON ORGANIZATIONAL LIFE—THE LATEST UPDATE
*Richard E. Boyatzis*
*Florence R.  Skelly*

THE PARADOX OF "CORPORATE CULTURE":
RECONCILING OURSELVES TO SOCIALIZATION
*Richard Pascale*

## THE IMPACT OF CHANGING VALUES ON ORGANIZATIONAL LIFE—THE LATEST UPDATE

*Richard E. Boyatzis*
*Florence R. Skelly*

Decisions as to which organizations to join and our willingness to stay are determined by our values. They will determine how much effort we exert once in a job.  An individual's capability, or competencies, will have significant impact on his/her effectiveness in a job, but capability alone will not assure effectiveness.  The person must want to be effective and choose to use his/her capability. The willingness to use one's capability can be called commitment.  Our values will determine how much commitment we feel toward an organization, or the products and services we offer.  Values also affect relationships among people working in an organization.  People who grew up in different eras or cultures often must work together and depend on each other.  Their differing values, or beliefs on the importance of work, loyalty, entitlements, responsibilities, winning, and life are fertile ground for sowing the seeds of dissension and conflict, as well as those of identity and cooperation.

   The compatibility we see between our values and those inherent in the culture of the organization in which we work is the basis for a social or psychological contract with the organization. As with a legal contract, our psychological contract with the organization lists what we expect to give and what we expect to get from the organization.  It reflects our beliefs, or assumptions, about work and life.  Embedded in the contract are limits to what we will do and descriptions of conditions that

   The authors wish to thank Madelyn Hochstein, Arthur White and Daniel Yankelovich for their insights, support, and contribution to the research over the years.

we view as fair, exciting, and desirable, as well as those we view as unfair, boring, and unpleasant. This contract is seldom written and often not even discussed, but it carries far more than the power of law, it carries the power of our commitment.

The culture of an organization in which we work, as well as the larger societal context within which our organization exists create a climate, or context, for our individual values. This social context will affect development and changes in our personal values. The context may be supportive and encouraging, or hostile and frustrating, or irrelevant and apathetic. Emerson, in his essay *Art* (cf. Schlesinger, 1986) said, "No man can quite emancipate himself from his own age and country, or produce a model in which the education, the religion, the politics, usages, and arts of his time shall have no share."

To explore aspects of our organizational context and the psychological contract, we must first examine the larger societal context in which most of us have grown and entered the workforce. In this paper, current trends will be discussed in light of past values of the workforce of the United States. The excitement, synergy, and conflict that may result from people with diverse values working in the same organization will be discussed.

## EMERGING VALUES IN THE UNITED STATES

To understand the values presently expressed in the workforce and the emerging trends, an historical context of the past fifty years is important. The following descriptions of the values of the American people are based upon annual, national surveys conducted within the United States over the past thirty-five years, surveys conducted within numerous organizations,[1] and historical documents. The values of the American people can be described in terms of themes. The dominant values cannot be presumed to reflect every individual but these themes do describe the sentiment of the larger segments, if not the majority of the population.

### The Late 1940s to the Early 1960s

As the United States emerged from World War II, the national agenda became the pursuit of economic growth. Government, business, and the public all subscribed to it. Stimulated by government funding of technology and industrial expansion during the war, business moved to continue this expansion.

Upward mobility was the dominant goal in life during this period. It was measured by the acquisition of material possessions. Business provided a wide array of new consumer goods, as well as providing well-paying jobs in technology and industry. The government supported growth through housing subsidies to veterans. The resulting expansion of the construction and housing industries provoked growth in the appliance industry and other derivative industries (such as the automotive industry) and development of small businesses in the suburbs. The government supported massive increases in education through the GI Bill. Thus, the government was the initial funding agent of this expansion in many ways.

In the 1950s, the social climate exemplified a commitment to the American dream, realizable by such traditional American values as hard work, sacrifice and allegiance to family. Dedicated to upward mobility—into the middle class—Americans were preoccupied with home ownership, acquisition of cars and other major possessions which signaled middle-class status. Success in achieving this goal was seen to depend on a series of self-denials that are central to the Puritan tradition; stifle

[1]The authors wish to acknowledge the work and contributions of their colleagues at the DYG (ie., the Daniel Yankelovich Group, Inc., of Elmsford, NY), what was then called Yankelovich, Skelly & White, Inc. prior to 1985, and McBer and Company, Inc.

one's expressive desires in favor of conformity; deny oneself pleasure in favor of duty and work; deny the present in favor of the future; deny the self in favor of others. This credo of self-denial created a tight social structure which was unidimensional in terms of what the good life and success were all about: a good job with a future, enough money to educate the children and to buy the requisite material possessions for the newly-owned homes. Children flourished in abundance: the 1950s were the heart of the baby boom about which so much has been written. Regardless of one's personal views of husband and wife roles (i.e., in 1950's terms, the man as breadwinner and the woman as superwife, mother, and housekeeper), commitment to family and to traditional family roles was seen as a precondition for success.

The mix worked. By the end of the 1950s, the United States had achieved worldwide economic leadership in technology, business theory, and industrial capability. About 70% of the populace formed a true middle class, the largest in the history of the world. This group owned homes, cars, and other trappings of material well-being. The era marked the birth of rock and roll. Many films were musicals. Heroes were military or industrial leaders. The concept of unlimited economic growth was accepted by the public, the government, and business alike. There was a widespread belief that the American dream would never die!

By the end of the 1950s we also were shifting to a "psychology of affluence," the belief that our economic struggles were over and that middle-class status or better was achievable by all. It was in the context of the psychology of affluence that the vast changes in values during the 1960s and 1970s flourished.

## The Mid-1960s to Late 1970s

The next era occurred as the national agenda shifted from an economic one to a social agenda, under the psychology of affluence. A major thrust developed to correct the adverse affects of technology and industrialization. The positive contributions of these elements were recognized, but now the negative aspects were of interest and concern. Efforts to clean up and protect the environment (e.g., air, water, waste disposal, land use, etc.) became driving concerns, as well as the focus on the dehumanizing effects of industrial work on people. Worker happiness emerged as an important issue while productivity was more or less assumed. The public began to assert its moral heritage in a new way; a fix-it agenda developed.

Assuming affluence, society moved to expand the middle class and improve the quality of the middle-class lifestyle. Target groups were identified for catch-up efforts: minorities, the handicapped, and the elderly. Improvements in education and medical care were sought not only for the target groups, but for everyone.

As part of this egalitarian movement, there was an increasing sense that business was to blame for the inequities. Pressure was applied to make business more accountable to the people. At the same time, corporate ownership was spread over a greater number of stockholders, moving the basic nature of corporate ownership away from family ownership to "public" ownership. Conglomerates emerged as vehicles to stabilize growth in earnings per share and cash flow. This introduced the era of professional management. It also introduced the ultimate power of Wall Street in determining the criteria and assessing the performance of corporations, thereby replacing the customer. Assessments based on financial measures superseded assessments based on product quality or innovation.

A growing concern about the rigidity of values earlier embraced as part of the Protestant Ethic appeared first among up-scale youth, then other youth, then the older wealthy, and eventually the less well-off. The goal became self-fulfillment. Pale versions of hedonism emerged as people searched for the full, rich, high-quality life. The focus on the self replaced the focus on self-denial. People were asked to "turn on and tune out." Flower power and Woodstock were associated with a shift in music. Even the Beatles' music, which coincided with the beginning of the era, started by asking the eternal question, "Does she love you?" and through the decade changed to describing the ethereal pleasures of being in "Strawberry fields forever."

Pluralism and introspection replaced conformity. The "me" was placed above concern for social units and the future. A sense of entitlements spread quickly. The introspection industry of psychotherapy and personal growth experiences grew from a few hundred million a year to over two billion dollars a year by the middle of this era. Consumer preferences turned to things that were "cold, white, and lite," as seen in the shift from scotch and bourbon to gin and vodka, butter to margarine, beef to chicken, from full-bodied to light beer, and "chilled" anything. The women's movement originally drew its momentum from this agenda. Self-fulfillment and the new focus of self-realization became a driving force for the women's movement of the 1960s and 1970s. It began with upper-middle-class women who did not want to be constrained by the sex role distinctions of the earlier eras. They found an ideological justification (i.e., egalitarianism) for this quest and the society moved toward blurring of the sexes. The redefinition of the family to include "people living together" by the National Association of Home Economists was a further reflection of the changing roles of husband and wife.

New non-institutional elements of the public became the cutting edge in setting the social agenda (i.e., Ralph Nader et al.). Their mission was, in their eyes, to identify problems for fixing and to find the warts, not to work out solutions. The methods were assumptive, moralistic, loud, and theatrical. Business became the villain. Government became the major actor, assuming such roles as watch dog and implementor of programs in addition to its funding role via such legislation and agencies as the Occupational Safety and Health Act, Equal Employment Opportunity Commission, Clean Air Act, Coastal Zone Management Act of 1972, Noise Control Act, Federal Insecticide, Fungicide and Rodenticide Act.

The heroes had become anti-heroes, like television's Jim Rockford and Lieutenant Columbo. Although business and government were no longer as united as they had been in the 1950s, there was still a spirit of optimism and confidence. The activists believed that if we could identify the problems, we as a society had the means to correct them.

The second half of the era of the social, fix-it agenda had a different mood. The remarkable economic success of Japan was a rebuke to American industry, especially in autos and consumer electronics. Now accused of shortsightedness and inadequate commitment to research and development, American business was blamed for a faltering U.S. role in world trade. The OPEC nations made the dependence on foreign powers evident and threatened many assumed aspects of our lives, such as our beliefs that personal automobiles, driving, and use of unlimited amounts of electrical energy were our birthright.

The restoration of the environment had met with some, but only limited, success. The costs were staggering. Inequity still existed. The Great Society did not end poverty, and evidence of racial discrimination persisted. The national debt rose and inflation increased to what were then considered alarming rates. There was a decline in savings and an increase in consumption, fed through the increased use of credit instruments and easier availability of credit cards.

The search for self-fulfillment proved frustrating for many who discovered that the path to happiness still remained hidden. Crime was increasing, as was child abuse, divorce, pornography and such. Many felt these were manifestations of self-expressionism gone too far. Popular music took a demonic shift with groups like the Doors. Science fiction and horror films had changed from non-human, amorphous entities as earlier villains in *The Blob* or plants in *The Day of the Triffids* to decidedly human and violent villains in *Texas Chainsaw Massacre*. In context of the observation that the mood of the country is reflected in the ups and downs of skirt length, further evidence of the depressing mood was the increasing popularity of the maxi-skirt.

4

New theories of management emerged as popular with an anti-authority tenor, with bottoms-up planning and organizational climate sessions. Communications efforts were seen as a panacea. There was a decrease in personal commitment to organizations and an alarming decrease in respect for managers. Professionalism, and loyalty to one's field, discipline, profession, or self replaced loyalty to the organization. Job hopping became a desirable activity and a sign of being on the "fast track" rather than its earlier interpretation as being a sign of instability or a character flaw.

If the first half of the era (i.e., the mid 1960s to mid 1970s) of the social, fix-it agenda grew out of a reaction to the narrowness of the social outlook under a flowering economy of the 1950s, the second half of the era (i.e., the mid to late 1970s) was a reaction to the breadth and diversity of social commitments in a constricted economy. We had lost the war on poverty declared in the Great Society of President Johnson. We had lost the war in Vietnam. We had lost the war on inflation (remember the Whip Inflation Now program of President Ford). We had lost our trust and respect for the Presidency (i.e., under President Nixon), and the very government that we had viewed as our protector (e.g., President Carter's inability to release Americans in Iran). Fear, followed by disbelief, followed by anger were the reactions to the realities of the late 1970s and our entry into the 1980s. We were treated to the humiliation of America every night on television news and in newspapers and magazines. We were held hostage in Iran, at the gas pump, and in the global marketplace.

## The Late 1970s Through the 1980s: Competitive Pragmatism

The reaction to the anger and sense of growing helplessness of the late 1970s with its increasing complexity resulted in the emergence of a new agenda of "competitive pragmatism." People wanted to win and, in the context of limited opportunities, the mood shifted to a feeling that, "I want mine." There was an acceptance of limits and the notion that we cannot do, be, or have everything. Therefore, people wanted to be strategic and get competitive. If pragmatism can be considered an American contribution to the field of philosophy, then this agenda of competitive pragmatism can be seen as a practical perspective rather than an ideological one. It was neither the Protestant Ethic of self-denial nor the social, fix-it agenda. People built blended personal agendas, balancing family, financial progress, occupational success, and personal health.

The strategic will to win transcended individuals and emerged in corporations in forms of strategic consolidation, divestments, and a return to the core business. As Peters and Waterman (1982) said, "stick to your knitting." Cost-effectiveness became a god to be worshiped. The reduction of overhead and elimination of costs, especially people that were now being considered "unnecessary," resulted in substantial dislocations of the workforce.

At the same time, within many organizations, competitive pragmatism was converted by individuals into a desire for meritocracy, characterized by compensation and reward systems based on performance rather than longevity or egalitarianism. Organizations were restructured to increase speed and flexibility in decision making. Hierarchies were flattened, and bureaucratic, functional forms of organization structure gave way to decentralization and smaller, strategic business units.

If corporate America could not respond, people were willing to by-pass large organizations that had previously symbolized growth, success, and stability (Kinkead, 1988). Temporary work has become an accepted activity *(Wall Street Journal,* 1987). Entrepreneurship and the excitement of small business was reborn in a workforce that, on the whole, did not remember such earlier eras in America. Even social activists embraced competitive pragmatism and shifted their tactics to taking actions that would result in some accomplishment, even if smaller than desired, instead of taking moralistic stands reminiscent of the 1960s and 1970s.

In the marketplace, consumers became "smart" and turned to quality in an effort to maximize their personal price/performance curve. Self-directed investment vehicles took hold with the by-pass of investment houses and the increase in discount brokerage houses which enabled people to do their own research and make their own investment decisions. Even in pension programs, the IRA, Keough, and 401K became important aspects of a person taking care of himself/herself rather than depending on Social Security and company or union pension programs. As people accepted the necessity of making "trade-offs" and being strategic about things that matter the most, health and physical fitness became a preoccupation. Consciousness about our bodies, the delicate interdependence of our internal physical systems, the effect of nutrition and exercise combined with advances in medical technology and skyrocketing costs to make health a strategic issue. The only way to "beat" increasing costs of health care was to take steps now to prevent illness or anticipate future potential problems.

With competitive pragmatism and the strategic will to win came an increased importance of pride in performance and identification with winning social entities. This emerged as another theme, the importance of belonging to an identifiable group or organization that reflects values in which we believe. If we were to be strategic and competitive and "cheering" for our team, which team was it? We were searching for a social context. The marriage to divorce ratio reversed for the first time in many years, reflecting a new popularity of marriage as a desirable form of relationship. Church and temple membership increased. The number of professional, occupational, civic, or interest/hobby centered clubs, associations, and organizations expanded.

In the corporate world, people asked for vision. They wanted their leaders to describe and explain what the organization "stood for" and what beliefs we share. Corporate philosophy statements began appearing in annual reports and image advertisements, while previously they were, if at all, relegated to wall posters inside of organizations or employee newsletters. This theme was occasionally mis-interpreted as a hunger for ideology rather than what appeared to be more a case of the search for identity and social context.

At a community level, the development of self-help groups appeared to aid in stemming the increase in crime (i.e., Crime Watch groups), reducing costs (i.e., food buying cooperatives), and volunteerism in helping to clean up neighborhoods, parks, and support community institutions. Even in architecture, what has been called neo-traditional community design appeared to catch public attention (i.e., communities like Seaside in Florida in which the layout of the town incorporates public space for people to congregate and other similar features).

The revival of the importance of the nuclear family was another manifestation of this theme that appeared in the mid-1980s (Miller, 1987). The most popular television shows were family situation shows, like *The Cosby Show* and *Family Ties.* Women who had moved into the labor force eagerly in the 1960s and 1970s began to rethink their roles as superwomen, capable of both a job and the major responsibility for running the home. While not economically able to leave the labor force, many began to think of part-time work or of entrepreneurial ventures which they could manage out of their own homes, thereby controlling their hours.

Regional parochialism and nationalism became apparent early in the 1980s as economic, political, and social forces and technology were making the world "smaller" and removing perceived boundaries. This blending of institutional, regional, and national boundaries may have contributed to the speed and strength of this theme. The desire to identify with a relatively local entity (i.e., become increasingly parochial) might have been a reaction to greater globalization. If I am increasingly a part of everything, how do I sustain a sense of my identity and difference and uniqueness? Events like the 1984 Olympics and the invasion of Grenada became strong symbols of our success and pride far beyond the impact of similar events in earlier eras. The power of state governments had increased steadily during this era.

Even companies had been demanding cultural compatibility in the services or goods they purchased. For example, parts manufacturers and consultants were asked to provide "customized" rather than generic, off-the-shelf products or services.

Another theme began to emerge in the mid-1980s which was not as clearly tied to competitive pragmatism nor the desire to belong to something in which you can believe; it was the increased importance of formalism and style. There had been an increase in formal weddings, showers, and related events, with the corresponding increase in bridal registrations and purchases of china, crystal, and formal silverware. The "power shower" as an extravagant event was in store for parents to be (*Wall Street Journal,* 1988). Etiquette was again seen as important. At first for young women, then for young men and older people, and then as a practice in corporate America, people were attending etiquette schools and training programs. It was possible that this theme was a manner of distinguishing a person from others, and in that way manifesting a competitive edge in the social arena. That is, "I will use style and form as a way of showing that I am a winner."

The links to the strategic will to win and articulation of belonging to a group that has certain beliefs may be clearer in what appeared to be the version of this theme in the late 1980s, the growing sense of morality in the United States. The number of embarrassments, scandals, and exposés indicate an increase in moralistic fervor. The Wall Street insider traders were "bad," a number of television evangelists had been exposed as "bad," individuals working in or for the White House had been prosecuted as having been "bad," and of course there was the condemnation of sexual deviations from the norm which was evident in the fear of and reaction to AIDS. If this was a form of "moral" strategic will to win, or moral competitive pragmatism, then we could expect more of it in the 1990s

The era, whose reflective value themes began to appear in the late 1970s but did not attain widespread recognition until the early 1980s, can be described as having competitive pragmatism as its agenda. In reaction to the excesses attributed to the self-fulfillment orientation and the relative failures and extreme costs of the social, fix-it agenda, the agenda of the 1980s seemed to be a desire to "be smart so I can get my share within a context of limitations." This agenda appeared to be shared by the public, business, and government. Because of the very nature of the agenda itself, conflicts emerged. There was all too often an assumption of zero-sum (i.e., "I win, you lose" or "You win, I lose"), and therefore, attempts to be strategically competitive resulted in conflicts.

## The 1990s: Social Pragmatism

The competitive pragmatism of the earlier period has evolved into a sincere desire to take back control and rearrange our priorities. Because there is both a spirit of hope that we must tackle tough issues, while at the same time a cynicism about whether anything will actually change, the themes of the 1990s could be called social pragmatism.

A new sense of empowerment is emerging in numerous forms. One form is political, as evident in the Perot phenomenon. This alternative to the two parties gained a following which continues to function even after the election. Memories of recent third party attempts, John Anderson in the 1970s and the Eugene McCarthy in the late 1960s, were short-lived and ended with their candidate's loss in the elections. The Perot-backed party continues to be a vocal presence on the national and political scene.

As consumers, we have a continuing concern for quality, but with an increased sensitivity to the value of the goods (i.e., the cost of the quality). The social pragmatism appears to be focusing on determining the relative values of goods. In the same way organizations are looking for "critical-path activities" that add value in their reengineering or reinventing efforts, consumers are looking to goods, methods of shopping, and places to shop that reflect the greatest return (i.e., the greatest value). The return to popularity of American cars, from the Saturn and Taurus to the minivan, may represent the trend as applied to automobiles. There is an increasing belief that the alphabet-soup of technology (e.g., FAXes, TVs, VCRs, CDs, PCs, and MODEMS) can help us solve problems efficiently.

In work organizations, we see a strong, new trend emerging—a change in what we expect from work. Resulting from downsizing, restructuring, and overhead reductions, there is an increasing unwillingness to commit to work beyond the requirements of a job. People are searching for more autonomy and the independence it provides. The nature of the employee relationship between a worker and employer has changed: our jobs are not for our life nor does our employer deserve loyalty.

A surprising realization, reversing the increased belief in meritocracy from the 1980s, is that we do not believe that we will be rewarded for learning and the development of new skills. Technology is increasingly seen as a substitute for the "wit-and-wisdom" valued in earlier periods. Quality programs and continuous improvements are seen as leading to continuous downsizing. The contingent and part-time labor force is increasing in size and nature. Our increased closeness to our customer or product may come at the expense of our closeness to the organization. Our desire to be a part of mission/vision driven organizations (Osborne and Gaebler, 1992; Hammer and Chiampy, 1993) creates a conflict with the flexibility and continuous change necessary in today's organizations.

Human resource staff, in this time of shrinking size and budgets, are often preoccupied with not raising people's expectations that cannot be met. The low-key introduction of new human resource development programs, made in the spirit of "let's not raise a fuss," is dramatically different than the pomp, ceremony, and "unveiling" of new programs in the early to mid-1980s. It is not surprising, therefore, that the social pragmatism continues to feed a hunger of going into one's own business and increase the desirability in working for small companies.

Despite attempts to label it as a return to 1960's values, we are realizing and accepting a role for government, especially in the economy. The 1992 elections confirmed a trend that began in the 1988 presidential elections—people want the government to address certain shared problems. The primary focus is job creation. Efforts to protect certain industries, reduce foreign trade barriers, and rebuild the infrastructure are popular economic stimuli. The same amount of money may be spent as the reductions in the military budget, with the corresponding loss of jobs, base-closings, and reduction in procurements. But the new spending seems to reflect a consensus as a better place to spend money. It is actually more reminiscent of programs and the role of government in the 1950s than in the 1960s.

While the role of government is becoming legitimized, there is a shift in social policy. The shift appears to be away from a sense of entitlements driving social policy to the idea of reciprocity. You give back some of what you have gotten. If you have benefited, you lend a helping hand. This can be seen in the popularity of the National Service plan in exchange for collegiate student loans, welfare in exchange for training to help people get meaningful employment, and increased popularity and donations to groups such as Habitat for Humanity (i.e., they build or rebuild houses for people who could not otherwise afford them but require at least two hundred hours of "sweat equity" from the perspective of the home-owner).

The emergent social policy is not dramatically different from some of the pragmatic thinking of the 1980s. It may be more activist, but still carries a cost-benefit approach rather than a moral imperative. We can expect the debate about programs to concern how much we can afford to spend rather than the value of the concept. People want to do something about homelessness, poverty, and general education, but are not sure what we can effectively accomplish.

Even in the international arena, we can see the pragmatism emerge in the small, reluctant steps taken to intervene in the Bosnian-Serbian war. We succeeded in the Persian Gulf war, even though many were unsure why we were leading the fight, but we were willing to engage Iraq for a limited period of time. Then we failed in Somalia. With the removal of the singular arch-enemy (i.e., Soviet, imperialistic communism), questions of involvement in regional conflicts are increasingly asked in pragmatic terms. What can we accomplish? At what cost?

We now see the definition of success and the "Good Life" in terms of quality rather that what you own. Good relationships are important. Marriage continues to be of increasing interest ( a trend first appearing in the mid-1980s). In the area of AIDS, we see a reversal in the trend as to the age of marriage, with people getting married at an earlier age.

People are defining success as including a healthy, clean environment and less stressful lifestyle. The limitation on our commitment to our work organization helps. All implications in the consumer area are that non-status brands will become more acceptable than in the 1980s. With less emphasis on consumption, an increased effort at debt reduction and savings can be expected. The health consciousness of the 1980s continues, but with some modifications. There is a strong commitment to looking good, even if it involves significant investment of time and money. But in some areas, such as eating, sacrifice for the sake of health may not be as popular. We also see a dramatic increase in interest in non-traditional, non-Western, spiritual approaches to health and fitness.

The importance of the nuclear family began as a trend in the mid-1980s and continues to gain strength, as it expands to incorporate children. Even though the morally-toned position of the Republican Convention in 1992 was rejected by many, there is an increased focus on the family and children. Women in dual roles are increasingly refocusing on the family rather than their careers, and even men are showing more interest in the family. Sex roles continue to be blurred, as some men want more of a relationship with children and some wives earn more than their husbands. Even with changing sex roles, children are still linked more to women than men. Single parent households are more frequent and seen as difficult.

As a reaction to the parental absence of the dual career parents, or parents active outside the home, there now appears to be a return to the concept of parental child-rearing as desirable. The people over thirty are worried about all of the disruptions to their family. The people over thirty are not as willing to put their families second to careers and advancement, somewhat as a reaction to their upbringing.

As part of this theme, the home is becoming more central to people's lives. We can expect more and more time to be spent at home and in activities in and around the home. Increased working at home coupled with the increased threats of crime, stress, traffic, and hassle outside of the home, suggest that we will be seeking to conduct more activities from the home, as well as having more free time at home.

## ALTERNATING CYCLES AND THE FUTURE

The approximate fifteen year duration of these eras is supported by the observations and theory of Arthur M. Schlesinger, Jr., in his book, *The Cycles of American History* (1986), in which he reported that he and his father hypothesized that the cycles of intent, or what is called value orientation in this article, appeared to be twelve to sixteen years in duration.

### Philosophical Roots

Schlesinger (1986) described the duality of the American tradition as a continual alternating cycle between envisioning our intent as an experiment or destiny. The sense of America being an experiment is rooted in the Calvinist ethos of Providential History. He explained that this belief contends that all secular communities are finite and problematic, therefore they flourish and decay. The "experiment" is a test against the hypothesis of inevitable decay.

From George Washington to Abraham Lincoln, the experiment has been repeatedly proposed. In his first Inaugural Address, President Washington commented on the American opportunity, "The preservation of the sacred fire of liberty and the destiny of the republican model of government are justly considered, perhaps, as deeply, as finally, staked on the experiment entrusted to the hands of the American people." Lincoln, in his first message to Congress asked whether all republics had an inherent and fatal weakness. At Gettysburg, Lincoln asked whether any nation "conceived in liberty and dedicated to the proposition that all men are created equal can long endure?"

According to Schlesinger (1986), the sense of America having a destiny is rooted in the Calvinist ethos via Augustine and the concept of redemptive history. That is, all people were close to God but some were closer. The purpose of life is for the journey of the elect to salvation and beyond the limits of our history. John Winthrop had said to the first New Englanders that they were "as a city upon a hill, with all eyes upon them." With a sacred mission and a sanctified destiny for people yearning to be free, it is not surprising that Americans periodically feel like The Chosen, or at least the recently chosen in the sight of God.

## The Duality

The alternation between experiment and destiny, Schlesinger (1986) wrote, is also reflected in alternating cycles of 1) self-critical realism, with its focus on things that need to be changed and 2) ideal-oriented messianism, with its focus on "what might be." The pattern is also reflected in alternating concerns with social and political innovation or individual-rights oriented conservatism, and the alternative attempts to increase plurality and diversity or contain it. He described this as cycles of public purpose and private interest.

Each cycle, he contended, flows out of the conditions and contradictions of the last cycle. Each period of public purpose appeared to be ushered in with a detonating social or political issue. These cycles have remained relatively consistent in theme and duration since 1776 and the founding of the nation.

The first era described earlier in this article, **the late 1940s to early 1960s, was a private interest-oriented period** focused on the economic agenda of growth through materialism. Although this interpretation of the dominant theme, agenda, and duration differs from Schlesinger's (1986) to some degree, the description of this era as a private interest oriented period is consistent. The following **social, fix-it agenda of the mid-1960s through the late 1970s appeared to be a public purpose-oriented period** in which the attempts were made to experiment with changes in most aspects of life. Following these cycles, **the competitive pragmatism agenda of the 1980s appeared to be a private interest oriented** agenda that drew energy from the desire to fulfill our destiny.

The themes and mood of the 1990s reflect a shift of priorities. Some of which could be seen as early as the 1988 presidential election (e.g., a 1988 survey showed an increase in the number of people who saw a positive role for government in their lives). **The social pragmatism of the 1990s appears to be a public purpose-oriented agenda** directed at changing some of the negative consequences of the earlier period (i.e., crime, runaway deficits, homelessness, etc.), adapting to some of the apparently immutable changes (i.e., give less commitment to your work organization because it will give less to you), but be realistic about it.

The detonating issue, heralding the current public purpose oriented agenda, seems to be the loss of the American dream. The people entering the workforce during this period, called the X-Generation by Douglas Coupland, or the 13th Generation by Howe and Strauss (1993), are "...the only generation born since the Civil War to come of age unlikely to match their parents' economic fortunes; and the only ones born this century to grow up personifying (to others) not the advance, but the decline of their society's greatness" (Howe and Strauss, 1993, p. 7). Added to their sense of frustration and emerging cynicism, is the increasing threat experienced by most of the population. The general condition of life in the U.S, as evident in the daily news, shows unsafe streets, unstable intimate and family relationships (even if you can find one), uncertain jobs at all levels in organizations, inaccessible health care for many while new, incurable diseases appear, insufficient housing, and inadequate education and preparation for work. Even the sense of hope generated by having the White House and Congress of the same political party has been tainted with what appears to be inevitable, parochial protectionism and compromises threatening the original intention of various initiatives. No longer is the threat the image of a soldier in a distant country eager to hurl nuclear warheads at us, but the seemingly nice person who lives in the nearby neighborhood who cuts the workforce in your company, or the "kids" down the street who may be playing with real guns.

The typical duration of the cycles would suggest that this era will continue until about 2005 to 2008. Since each of the cycles reviewed in this article have been increasingly subject to forces of the entire world, the periodicity and potency of each cycle may vary.

## Dominant Values of Each Generation

The dominant values of each generation of Americans appear to be closely related to the agenda and themes of the era in which they grew up. Schlesinger (1986) believed that the thirty year cycle for return to a similar type of dominant concern (i.e., public purpose or private interest) had a relationship to the number of years it takes for people to grow up, enter the workforce, achieve voting age and political consciousness to vote, and to reach positions of power in organizations from which to launch efforts consistent with the personal orientation of the individual. Of course, such generalizations should only be considered when describing and considering behaviors and beliefs of large groups of people. Each person may have his own variations, and certainly entire groups of people will share beliefs and behaviors that are not consistent with nor similar to the majority or the "dominant trends."

# THE IMPACT ON ORGANIZATIONAL LIFE

There appear to be three basic ways in which these value trends have an impact on life in organizations. First, the values a person holds influence his/her desire to join and stay with a particular organization. Second, once in the organization, the degree of value compatibility affects a person's use of discretionary effort, and therefore, determines the extent to which the person uses his/her capability or competencies. Third, since people appear to hold the beliefs consistent with the era in which they grew up (especially through adolescence), there will be inevitable conflicts as managers, subordinates, and colleagues find themselves interacting but having substantially different values about the nature of work and life. These can be considered conflicts among various cultures (i.e., correctly stated it would be sub-cultures) or generation gaps.

## Joining and Staying

There are many factors that influence how a person chooses an organization for which to work. During times of high unemployment and for those people in society having a difficult time finding jobs, the mere availability or offer of compensated work may be enough to justify joining an organization. For many, the reasons get complicated as the person's sense of efficacy increases. Whether as a result of increasing education, skill development, or higher expectations about the meaning of work, people appear more interested than before in what the organization stands for and aspects of its culture, climate, and values (Kiechel, 1988). This expectation is a result of the value theme of "belonging through believing," of looking for a social, organizational context.

In a study of what members of the workforce viewed as the most important qualities of a job, Yankelovich and Immerwahr (1983) found that 88% felt that "working with people who treat me with respect" and 87% felt that "interesting work" were very important. In addition, 83–84% of the respondents felt that "recognition for good work," "the chance to develop skills, abilities, and creativity," "working for people who listen if you have ideas about how to do things," and "having a chance to think for myself rather than just carry out instructions" all rated significantly higher than concerns about job security or financial incentives (i.e., 68% and 64%, respectively). The point is that an increasing number of people feel that they have some choice in what organization to join (or they have the expectation that they should have such a choice) and that the factors influencing the choice are linked to complex forces emphasizing value compatibility more than in previous periods. In the job-finding patterns of the 1990s people seem willing to make short-term sacrifices, often involving part-time or temporary work, until they can find "the organization" that they want to join.

People may need more of a sense of belonging to their work organization than previously as a result of certain demographic trends. For example, more Americans are living alone than ever before, a ninety percent increase since 1970 *(Time,* December 12, 1985, page 41). The percentage of one-person households reached 24% of all households in 1986. The 1993 SCAN (i.e., the DYG annual, national survey) showed that the single lifestyle is not only acceptable to many, but now often considered desirable. In part due to people staying single longer (i.e., postponing the age of marriage), increased longevity, increased widowhood and divorces, there is increased pressure on the workplace as a source of context and social meaning.

Some reaction to this trend is expected in living patterns. For example, elderly are sharing homes at an increasing rate rather than living alone. Although some of this is for purposes of safety and economic necessity, social contact and context is also a factor. Given that the number of 20–29 year old men exceeded the number of 18–27 year old women in 1985, a return to romance, courting, and monogamous concerns expressed through increased marriages is expected in the coming years *(NYT,* June 15, 1988).

The new women's dilemma, reflected in the conclusion that full-time work and full-time family responsibilities require more than is humanly possible, and the return to the nuclear family lead to new criteria for women in considering joining an organization. Possibilities for flexible work design and creation of meaningful part-time work become central in choosing an organization with which to have a career. The organization's policies and practices regarding day care are also an issue to which the test of value compatibility is applied.

The importance of the values of the organization, which is really the values reflected in the culture and climate of the organization, also increases with the diversity of the workforce. With increased pluralism of the workforce, people will continue to find it difficult to assume compatibility with co-workers based on visible similarities. Therefore, people will be forced to look at ideas, values, and products and services.

As people seek to determine their compatibility with the organization, the consistency of an organization's value positions will be under increased scrutiny. Speeches by the CEO emphasizing ethics and conducting ethics training programs will be embarrassments if the newspapers reveal bribery, fraud, or kickback schemes in government contracts. Similarly, an organizational commitment to innovation will be studied to see if it reflects a belief in increased sales, or new markets, or R&D. Consistency will be used as an indication of the veracity of an organization's values.

A longer range problem for the American scene is revealed in the aging of the workforce. As the "baby-bust" or 13th Generation enters and then dominates the workforce in the years ahead, there will be labor shortages, especially in jobs requiring advanced skills. There are already such shortages appearing in certain regions and specific job markets. As this occurs, organizations will be forced to attract people and compete for employees. The recruiting appeal will take many forms, but it can be expected that one consistent theme will be to "pitch" the values of the organization (i.e., its culture and climate) as a distinguishing feature, making it a better place to work than other organizations.

## Giving Your All

Yankelovich (1981) contended that a person's commitment to the organization would be the key factor in determining how much discretionary effort the person used in those jobs that allowed a person to exercise discretion in how he/she performed and acted. In other words, commitment to the organization determined the degree to which a person would use his/her capabilities or competencies. A person's commitment to an organization was, in large part, a function of the degree of value compatibility between the person and the organization. In a survey of about 1,500 managers who were members of the American Management Association, Schmidt and Posner (1983) compared managers who shared their organization's values to a low, moderate, or high degree. They found that managers with highly shared values had: "greater feelings of personal success; stronger feelings of organizational commitment; clearer perspectives on ethical dilemmas; lower levels of work/home stress; better understanding of others' values; greater commitment to organizational goals; higher regard in general for other organizational stakeholders; and different perception of important personal qualities" (Schmidt and Posner, 1983, page 13). These findings are consistent with earlier studies on the consequences of increased commitment and the use of discretionary effort (Yankelovich, 1981; Yankelovich and Immerwahr, 1983).

A startling and dramatic increase in perceived underutilization of the workforce emerged in the 1985 national survey, entitled *Signal,* by Yankelovich, Skelly, and White Inc. When asked if people could increase the quantity and quality of their job output if conditions were ideal in their organization, 79% and 73% said, "Yes," respectively. Fifty one percent (51%) said they could increase the quantity of their output by more than 20% if conditions were ideal in their organization. This represented a dramatic increase over the 32% answering the same question in the prior year. The perception of underutilization has been reported by other national surveys of the workforce in the mid-1980s by The Opinion Research Corporation and The Hay Group. People reported that they not only have the ability to do more but they even have an idea of how to go about doing it, but conditions in the organization did not induce, encourage, or stimulate them to give their maximum effort.

The values reflected in an organization's culture and climate are conveyed to employees in many ways. The rewards and incentives for performance are a major source of information about values. Given the theme of competitive pragmatism dominant in the late 1970s and throughout the 1980s, manifested in the desire for increased meritocracy in organizations, it can be expected that an increasing proportion of today's workforce wants rewards and incentives related to performance, not longevity, equality, or need.

The continuation of the 1980s theme of "In a world of constricting benefits, I want mine," is appearing in the demands and expectations of the 13th Generation. As Bret Easton Ellis said, in his *New York Times* article, "The Twentysomethings: Adrift in a Pop Landscape," they want to be the "unambiguous winners" (cf. Howe and Strauss, 1993). Their socialization through Beavis and Butthead, Bart Simpson, and comedy clubs emphasize a cynical attitude towards organizations, and a lack of faith that rewards will come to those who labor hard and wait. There is no value-based rallying point or cause (e.g., earlier groups had the Vietnam War or civil rights) through which to exchange moral rewards for effort. In addition, the continual, world-wide personal contact with tragedy is building a hard-edge on their expectations about life. Exposure to bombs over Baghdad, flies on the face of malnourished children in Somalia, centennial floods along the Mississippi River, crushed freeways from earthquakes in San Francisco and Los Angeles, and roofless homes from hurricanes in Florida, the Carolinas, and the Gulf of Mexico do not encourage a caring, safe, unbounded, and hopeful image of life.

Complicating the dynamics of rewards in organizations, this generation has a shorter time focus on personal matters (in contrast to their concern about the environment which is a long-term view). Video games, MTV, channel surfing, and even gourmet fast food via the microwave have resulted in a sense of wanting JITR—just-in-time-rewards. The pressure for quicker rewards is challenging human resource management systems and managers to be inventive, appropriate, and timely in their dispensing of rewards for performance. Without them, the 13th Generation will not give their all to the organization, and may even save their creative energy for pursuits outside of the organization.

Other ways, beyond rewards, that values are conveyed to employees include the method and frequency of communication about the condition of the organization. The visibility and accessibility of top management, the organization structure, the physical condition, attractiveness, and comfort of the work setting communicate the shared beliefs of the organization.

In addition to giving your all to the company (i.e., maximizing discretionary effort), value compatibility between the employees and the organization affects the degree to which people give their all to the product. The recent popularity of quality and customer service concepts are an indication that, as customers or managers, we all want people to give more of themselves to the product or service they offer. Attempts to engage a person's discretionary effort applied to product or service quality will involve similar activities as attempts to stimulate and maintain a person's commitment to the organization.

The competitive pragmatism agenda also appears to increase people's desire to work for those organizations that are "winning" There is a desire to feel proud of the organization. Pride in performance of the organization extends beyond the desire for a context (i.e., belonging through believing) to acknowledged signs of an organization's success.

## Conflicting Cultures in the Workplace

If a person's dominant work ethic (i.e., his/her basic orientation to work and its place in life) is shaped during his/her childhood and adolescent years, then inevitable conflicts will arise in work organizations when people from different eras work with and for each other. Managers and leaders set the climate and sometimes the culture of an organization and manage the modifications. This may be explicit or implicit, but it occurs. So what happens when people who embraced or grew to believe in the competitive pragmatism agenda of the 1980s work for managers who embraced or grew to believe in the ethic of self-fulfillment and the social, fix-it agenda of the 1960s and early 1970s, or those who believe in the work ethic of self-denial and the economic growth agenda of the 1950s?

Considering the age distribution of the current workforce, four major value eras are represented. First, the 49–75 year olds who grew up during the era of the economic growth have the ethic of self-denial. They valued and may still value upward mobility. On the whole, they are non-introspective and have a respect for authority. The dominant belief is that people should work hard and have patience, "you will get your turn." This cadre of the workforce can be called prebaby-boomers. Howe and Strauss (1993) called them the Silent Generation. They value commitment to a company or organization, have relatively singular views of leadership, and expect obedience and loyalty as repayment for efforts on another's behalf.

Second, the 39–48 year olds grew up with the ethic of self-fulfillment during the era of the social, fix-it agenda. They tend to be self-absorbed and do not respond to authority with any automatic respect. This cadre of the workforce has pluralistic models of how to "beat the system." They tend to be more people oriented than older managers and accept concepts like flextime as necessary to respond to varying needs of the workforce. They tend to have a more balanced view of their own life than older managers, including ideas like holistic health and compromising job demands and family demands. They can be called early baby-boomers.

Third, the 29–38 year olds grew up with the ethic of self-fulfillment, but in the context of a constricting economy during the latter part of the social, fix-it agenda era. The disappointments and frustration of this era emerge in this group's desire to win. Actually, it appears to be almost an intense desire not to lose. They seek and have self-knowledge. They are cynical of authority, not team players, and willing to by-pass corporate America. This cadre can be called the late baby-boomers. Like the early baby-boomers, they are self–rather than other– oriented, competitive, pluralistic, and rejectors of authority. Unlike their slightly older colleagues, they want the romance of ideology in terms of belonging or identifying with an organization or groups through shared beliefs. This latter group appears willing to commit to a social or organizational context, if he/she feels it is a "winning" or successful organization.

A fourth cadre, the X-Generation, twentysomethings, or 13th Generation grew up in the era of the competitive pragmatism agenda. Their priorities are likely to be centered on strategic positioning, creating their personal blended agendas—but they are highly driven to "get their share."

The first source of conflict that appears among these cadres concerns the degree to which a person expects work to be fun and fulfilling versus a blend of obligation and challenge. In most organizations, the higher level managers believe in the ethic of self-denial (especially in service of the organization's benefit). They have been in the organization longer and tend to have risen to higher levels. When these managers encounter people from the early boomer cadre, they see them as selfish, self-absorbed, and often ungrateful and immature. Meanwhile, the early boomer cadre look upon the pre-boomers as reactionary devotees of the status quo who are attempting to exploit the people coming along because of archaic notions of paying one's dues and demanding loyalty to the organization.

An odd coalition may occur between the cadres of the workforce we are calling pre-boomers and the later boomers. Both are competitive and feel pressure to not lose. They appreciate the reality that life may not yield pleasant experiences nor fulfilling ones. Although emerging from different value trends, they both have the desire to win. That common agenda may result in a coalition. Of course, this delicate coalition is split apart when and if the organization does not succeed. The late boomer cadre will move out of the organization without looking back while the pre-boomers will stick with the organization through the tough times.

The cadre which appears to be caught in the most conflict are the older pre-boomers. If they have not reached their personal apogees, the path ahead is full of disappointment and battles. Hierarchies are flattened, middle management jobs eliminated, and the sources of authority and material symbols of success that this cadre has worked to attain are being deleted. If people in this position feel defensive and threatened, it is with good reason. The assumptions, based upon their values, with which they labored over the years are being invalidated. The psychological contract with which they joined and entered the organization is broken.

The early boomers appear to be seeking new vehicles for self-fulfillment. As careers have gone stale and organizational mobility is blocked by older managers, they have sought retraining and are returning to educational institutions for advanced degrees. The proliferation of Masters and Doctoral degree programs is, in part, an indication of the thirst of this cadre for continuing self-development. As a contrast, significant numbers of the 13th Generation seem to be collecting college and graduate degrees the way others used to collect merit badges, in the Girl or Boy Scouts, as a way to package themselves as desirable assets to be acquired by an organization (i.e., to get a job).

As this group of older, early-boomers reaches financial maturity and attains positions of influence in organizations, they can be expected to become advocates for public purpose, social agendas. The projected political conservatism and resistance to change by corporate management will mutate into new forms. Differences in the comfort with and willingness to accept diversity and pluralism of each of these cadres of the workforce will predict future conflict. The conflicts can be expected to shift, sometime in the future, from differences based upon notions of authority or who is right and wrong to differences based upon pragmatic concepts of who can win, or make it, or succeed.

Along with this shift toward a value-based agenda of the early-boomers, the late-boomers had their obsession with values and desire for back to basics (i.e., a sense of yearning for the simple life). As these tendencies of the Baby-boomers encounter the cynicism of the 13th Generation, another conflict emerges. The twentysomethings have already placed limits on their efforts on behalf of the organization (i.e., work will not automatically take second place to family issues). It is as if they are saying to their older colleagues, "Lighten up! We all want to win and be excited, but don't be so serious all the time."

The twentysomethings are computer users. Earlier cadres are labeled as computer literate or illiterate, friendly or unfriendly. These distinctions do not make sense to the 13th Generation. They have grown up with menu-driven TV's, videogames, and educational programs that are operated by remote control, a joy stick, or a mouse. Information access and use will be an area of potential conflict, as one cadre assumes computer usage and others must adapt.

For those of any of the cadres who are frustrated to the point of anger, comparisons to each other may lead to increased prejudicial judgments. In some ways the balanced agenda of the 13th Generation represent the image of the way the early Baby-boomers wanted to live, but could not escape the power of their socialization toward hard work and sense of responsibility to their organizations. In contrast, angry twentysomethings look at them and feel, "Every phase of life has been fine, even terrific, when Boomers entered it—and a wasteland when they left it" (Howe and Strauss, 1993, p. 43). Rather than looking to the older generation for guidance, we can expect the attitude that the older generations are out of date. Graduate students look at a book published ten years earlier and now claim it is not relevant, after all, "This is the 90s!"

Before concluding this section of the article, several thoughts about individuals who are conspicuously variant from their cadre are necessary. Aspects of a person's ethnoreligious background and family can have a profound effect on shifting him/her into a different value era. For example, children of immigrants who come from ethnoreligious cultures valuing self-reliance and assuming God's blessing on those who succeed, may appear caught in a cusp between the ethic of self-denial and the current notions of competitive pragmatism. In a quite different way, a person may have found emotional and spiritual resonance with a reference group embracing a particular era's dominant values. Maintaining close ties with this reference group over the years, and possibly excluding alternate emergent value trends, may result in a person being "fixed in time." That is, the individual may dedicate himself/herself to a particular set of values with a missionary zeal. If this set of values were not a part of the dominant agenda of the era within which he/she grew up, then this person would appear considerably different from his/her cohort.

## Concluding Comment

Each of us will inevitably work with others who have different values, having emerged from our formative years with different assumptions about life and work, and a wide variety of expectations concerning desirable conditions in the workplace. Understanding, acceptance, and learning about the diversity is a crucial start. Each of us is both product and producer of our age and social context. To work effectively in organizations with others, the challenge is to be able to hold onto our own beliefs and not feel wimpy or noncommittal while at the same time remaining open to the diversity and its possibilities.

## REFERENCES

Hammer, M., and Chiampy, J., *Reengineering the Corporation: A Manifesto for Business Revolution*, New York: Harper Business, 1993.

Howe, N., and Strauss, B., *13th Generation: Abort, Retry, Ignore, Fail?*, New York: Vintage Books, 1993.

Kiechel, W. III, "Love, Don't Lose, the Newly Hired," *Fortune,* June 6, 1988, pp. 271–274.

Kinkead, G., "The New Independents," *Fortune*, April 25, 1988, pp. 66–80.

McCarthy, M. J., "On Their Own: In Increasing Numbers, White Collar Workers Leave Steady Positions," *Wall Street Journal*, Vol. 68, No. 25, October 13, 1987.

Miller, T.A.W. (ed.), *The Public Pulse*, New York: The Roper Organization, 1987. *New York Times,* June 5, 1988.

Osborne, D., and Gaebler, T., *Reinventing Government: How the Entrepreneurial Spirit is Transforming the Public Sector*, New York: Plume Book, 1992.

Peters, T. J., and Waterman, R. H. Jr., *In Search of Excellence: Lessons from America's Best Run Corporations*, New York: Harper & Row, 1982.

Ratan, S., "Generational Tension in the Office: Why Busters Hate Boomers," *Fortune,* October 4, 1993, pp. 56–70.

Schlesinger, A. M., Jr., *The Cycles of American History*, Boston: Houghton Mifflin, 1986.

Schmidt, W.H., and Posner, B. Z., *Managerial Values in Perspective*, New York: American Management Associations Survey Report, 1983.

*Time Magazine*, December 12, 1985, page 41.

*Wall Street Journal*, April 28, 1988, page 1.

*Wall Street Journal*, September 2, 1986, page 27.

Yankelovich, D., and Immerwahr, J., *Putting the Work Ethic Back to Work: A Public Agenda Report on Restoring America's Competitive Vitality,* New York: The Public Agenda Foundation; 1983.

Yankelovich, D., *New Rules: Searching for Self-Fulfillment in a World Turned Upside Down,* New York: Random House, 1981.

# THE PARADOX OF "CORPORATE CULTURE": RECONCILING OURSELVES TO SOCIALIZATION

*Richard Pascale*

An assistant controller at IBM is rehearsed for a stand-up presentation with flip charts—the principal means of formal communication. Each presentation gets "probed"—IBM's secret weapon for training and assessing young professionals. A manager states: "You're so accustomed to being probed you're almost unaware of it. IBM bosses have an uncanny way of pushing, poking, having a follow-up question, always looking for the hidden ball. It's a rigorous kind of self-discipline we impose on ourselves for getting to the heart of problems. It's also management's way of assessing potential and grooming subordinates for the next job. Senior management spends most of its time 'probing.'"[1]

- An MBA joining Bain and Company, the management consulting firm is surprised by the incredible number of meetings he must attend—company meetings, recruiting meetings, officer meetings, office meetings, case team meetings, and near-mandatory participation on sports teams and attendance at social events. The objective is to build cohesiveness, participation, and close identification with the firm. There are a set of imperatives for working at Bain: "don't compete directly with peers," "make major conceptual contributions without being a prima donna," "demonstrate an ability to build on others' ideas." In aggregate, these features of Bain's culture are viewed as the underpinnings of success—both internally and with clients.[2]

- An applicant for an entry-level position in brand management at Procter and Gamble experiences an exhaustive application and screening process. His or her interviewer is one of an elite cadre who have been selected and trained extensively via lectures, video tapes, films, practice interviews, and role plays. P&G regards this as a crucial task: it predestines the creative and managerial resources on which the institutes' future depends. The applicant is interviewed in depth for such qualities as his or her ability to "turn out high volumes of excellent work," "identify and understand problems," and "reach thoroughly substantiated and well reasoned conclusions that lead to action." The applicant receives two interviews and a general knowledge test, before being flown back to Cincinnati for three more one-on-one interviews and a group interview at lunch. Each encounter seeks corroborating evidence of the traits which P&G believes correlate highly with "what counts" for institutional excellence. Notwithstanding the intensity of this screening process, the recruiting team strives diligently to avoid overselling P&G, revealing both its pluses and minuses. P&G actually *facilitates* an applicant's de-selection, believing that no one knows better than the candidate whether the organization meshes with his or her own objectives and values.[3]

- Morgan Guaranty, a bank so profitable and well run that most other bankers use it as a model, competes fiercely for bright and aggressive talent. Once recruited, an extraordinary amount of institutional energy is invested into molding these strong and talented individuals into the Morgan "collegian" style. All employees go through a one year training program that tests their intellect, endurance, and that requires teamwork as an essential factor of survival. Constant evaluation assesses interpersonal skills as well as analytical abilities. "The spirit of camaraderie and togetherness" is an explicit objective of entry level indoctrination. Once on the job, frequent rotations provide cross-training and necessitate building an ever-growing network of relationships. Performance evaluations are based not solely upon one's own boss's opinion but upon inputs from every major department with which one interacts. One learns quickly that to succeed one must succeed through the team. Overt political battles are taboo and conflict is resolved directly but never disagreeably. States one officer: "The Morgan traits provide a basic grammar of understanding that enables divergent elements of our organization to speak a common language."[4]

The common thread of these examples is the systematic means by which firms bring new members into their culture. The technical term is "socialization". It encompasses the process of being made a member of a group, learning the ropes, and being taught how one must communicate and interact to get things done. Mention the term "socialization" and a variety of unsavory images come to mind. Some equate it to the teaching of socialism—an incorrect interpretation—but even when correctly understood as the imposition of social conformity, the concept makes most of us cringe. Americans, dedicated by constitution and conviction to the full expression of individuality, regard "socialization" as alien and vaguely sinister. This taboo causes us to undermanage the forces for cohesion in organizations.

The debate between "individuality" and "socialization," like politics or religion, evokes a strong emotional response. Due perhaps to our hypersensitivity to the topic, most corporations avoid the issue. Most American managers know relatively little about the precise process through which strong culture firms "socialize" There is little written on the subject. Business schools give the subject a passing wink. In fact, business schools find themselves in a particular dilemma since, in extolling management as a profession, they foster the view that a cadre of "professional managers" can move from firm to firm with generic skills that enable them to be effective in each. This runs squarely against the requirements of a strong culture. MIT's Edgar Schein states: "I believe that management education, particularly graduate (business schools), are increasingly attempting to train professionals, and in this process are socializing the students to a set of professional values which are, in fact, in a severe and direct conflict with typical organizational values."[5] It is not surprising that many businesses have become disenchanted with MBAs in line management positions because of their tendency to skip from one firm to the next. It is certainly of interest that most strong culture firms, if they hire MBAs at all, insist on starting them from the ground up and promote exclusively from within. There are no significant MBA programs in Japan and Japanese students earning MBAs in the U.S. are sent primarily for language skills and the cross-cultural experience.[6]

Consider the fad that currently surrounds the subject of "organizational culture." Many adherents lose enthusiasm when brought face-to-face with the stark reality that "creating a strong culture" is a nice way of saying that an organization's members have to be more comprehensively socialized. Most American firms are culturally permissive. We are guided by a philosophy—initially articulated by Locke, Hobbes, and Adam Smith—which holds that individuals who are free to choose make the most efficient decisions. The independence of the parts makes a greater sum. Stemming from this tradition, American organizations allow members to do their own thing to a remarkable degree. Trendy campaigns "to become a strong culture" encounter resistance when a organization's members are asked to give up their idiosyncrasies and some of their individuality for the common good. The end result is usually the status quo.

Of course, some firms do openly worry about their "culture." Many, however, often err on the side of fostering "pseudo-cultures." (There are numerous examples in Silicon Valley.) Issuing "company creeds" or hosting rituals like "Friday night beer busts" may project the aura of corporate culture, but such elements alone do not facilitate organizational effectiveness. Real changes in style cannot prevail without a carefully thought through and interlocking socialization process.

The crux of the dilemma is this: We are intellectually and culturally opposed to the manipulation of individuals for organizational purposes. At the same time, a certain degree of social uniformity enables organizations to work better. The less we rely on informal social controls, the more we must inevitably turn to formal financial controls and bureaucratic procedures. U.S. firms that have perfected and systematized their processes of socialization tend to be a disproportionate majority of the great self-sustaining firms which survive from one generation to the next. Virtually none of these companies discuss "socialization" directly. It occurs as an exercise of the left hand—something that just happens "as the way we do things around here." When we examine any particular aspect (e.g., how the firm recruits, the nature of its entry level training, its reward systems, and so forth), little stands out as unusual. But when the pieces are assembled, what emerges in firms as different as AT&T is from P&G, as Morgan Guaranty is from IBM or Delta Airlines, is an awesome internal consistency which powerfully shapes behavior.

## STEPS OF SOCIALIZATION

It is time to take socialization out of the closet. If some degree of socialization is an inescapable necessity for organizational effectiveness, the challenge for managers is to reconcile this with the American insistence upon retaining the latitude for independent action. The solution is neither mind control nor manipulation. It is neither necessary nor desirable to oscillate from extreme individualism to extreme conformity. We can learn from those who have mastered the process. A practical middle road is available. Strong culture firms that have sustained themselves over several generations of management reveal remarkable consistency across seven key steps.

*Step One.* Careful selection of entry-level candidates. Trained recruiters use standardized procedures and seek specific traits that tie to success in the business. Never oversell a new recruit. Rely heavily on the informed applicant deselecting himself if the organization doesn't fit with his personal style and values.

The earlier Procter and Gamble illustration captures the crucial aspect.[7] Recruitment is the organizational equivalent of "romance." Hiring someone is like marriage—and a broken engagement is preferable to a messy divorce. Recruiters are expected to get deeper than first impressions. Their skill and intuition are developed by intensive training. A great deal of thought is given to articulating precisely and concretely the traits that count. The format for recording these traits is standardized. From the recruit's point of view, the extensive screening sends a signal: "You've got to be special to join." The screening process causes one to reveal oneself and causes most to wonder if they are good enough to get in. This increases receptivity for the second stage.

*Step Two.* Humility-inducing experiences in the first months on the job precipitate self-questioning of prior behavior, beliefs, and values. A lowering of individual self-comfort and self-complacency promotes openness toward accepting the organization's norms and values.

Most strong culture companies get the new hire's attention by pouring on more work than can possibly be done. IBM and Morgan Guaranty socialize extensively through training where "you work every night until 2:00 a.m. on your own material and then help others."[8] Procter and Gamble achieves the same result via "upending experiences," sometimes requiring a new recruit to color in a sales territory map—a task for which the novitiate is clearly overqualified.[9] These experiences convey a metamessage: "While you're smart in some ways, you're in kindergarten as far as what you know about this organization." One learns to be humble. Humility tends to flourish under certain conditions; especially long hours of intense work that bring you to your limits. When vulnerability is high, one also becomes close to one's colleagues—and cohesiveness is intensified in pressure-cooker

20

environments where little opportunity is given to re-establish social distance and regain one's bearings. At the investment banking firm Morgan Stanley, one is expected to work 12-to-14 hour days and most weekends. Lunches are confined to the firm cafeteria and limited to thirty minutes; trainees are censured for taking lunch outside.[10] Near identical patterns of long hours, exhausting travel schedules, and extensive immersion in case work are true at the major consulting firms and law practices. Socialization is a little like exercise—it's easier to reconcile yourself to it when you're young.

*Step Three.* In-the-trenches training leads to mastery of one of the core disciplines of the business. Promotion is inescapably tied to a proven track record.

The first phase of socialization aims to attract the right trainees predisposed toward the firm's culture. The second instills enough humility to evoke self-examination; this facilitates "buying" into the firm's values. Increasingly, the organizational culture becomes the relevant universe of experience. Having thus opened one's mind to the company's way of doing business, the task is now to cement this new orientation. The most effective method for doing so is via extensive and carefully reinforced field experience. While IBM hires some MBAs and a few older professionals with prior work experience, almost all go through the same training and start at the same level. It takes six years to grow an IBM marketing representative, twelve years for a controller. McKinsey consultants and Morgan Stanley analysts must likewise earn their way up from the ranks. The gains from such an approach are cumulative. When all trainees understand there is one step by step career path, it reduces politics. There is no quick way to jump ranks and reach the top. Because the evaluation process has a long time horizon, short term behavior is counterproductive. Cutting corners catches up with you. Relationships, staying power, and a consistent proven track record are the inescapable requirements of advancement. Those advancing, having been grown from within, understand the business not as financial abstraction but as a hands on reality. Senior managers can communicate with those at the lowest ranks in the "short hand" of shared experience.

*Step Four.* Meticulous attention is given to systems measuring operational results and rewarding individual performance. Systems are comprehensive, consistent, and triangulate particularly on those aspects of the business that are tied to competitive success and corporate values.

Procter and Gamble measures three "what counts" factors that have been found to drive brand success. These factors are Building Volume; Building Profit; and Planned Change (defined as changes which, simply put, increase effectiveness or otherwise add satisfaction to a job).[11] Operational measures track these factors using Nielsen market share indices as well as traditional financial yardsticks. All performance appraisals are tied to milestones which impact on these factors. Promotions are determined by success against these criteria plus successful demonstration of management skills.

Another example of comprehensive, consistent, and interlocking systems are those used at IBM to track adherence to its value of "respecting the decency of the individual." This is monitored via climate surveys; "Speak-up!" (a confidential suggestion box); open door procedures; skip-level interviews; and numerous informal contacts between senior-level managers and employees.[12] The Personnel Department moves quickly when any downward changes are noted in the above indices. In addition, managers are monitored for percent performance appraisals completed on time and per-cent of employees missing the required one week a year of training. All first-level managers receive an intensive two-week course in people management and each managerial promotion results in another week-long refresher. These systems provide a near "fail-safe" network of checks and double checks to ensure adherence to IBM's core value of respecting individual dignity.

Included in IBM's mechanisms for respecting the individual is a device known as the "Penalty Box."[13] Often a person sent to the "penalty box" has committed a crime against the culture—for example, harsh handling of a subordinate, overzealousness against the competition, gaming the reporting system. Most penalty box assignments involve a lateral move to a less desirable location —a branch manager in Chicago might be moved to a nebulous staff position at headquarters. For an outsider, penalty box assignments look like normal assignments, but insiders know they are off the track. Penalty boxes provide a place for people while the mistakes they've made or the hard feelings they've created are gradually forgotten-and while the company looks for a new useful position. The mechanism is one among numerous things IBM does that lend credence to employees' benefits that the firm won't act capriciously and end a career. In the career of strong, effective managers, there are times when one steps on toes. The penalty box is IBM's "half-way house" enabling miscreants to contemplate their errors and play another day. (Don Estridge, maverick pioneer of IBM's success in personal computers and currently head of that division, came from the penalty box.)

**Step Five.** Careful adherence to the firm's transcendent values. Identification with common values enables employees to reconcile personal sacrifices necessitated by their membership in the organization.[14]

Of all the steps this is perhaps most essential. It is the foundation of trust between organization and individual. Values also serve as the primary safeguard against our great fear that highly socialized organizations will degenerate into an Orwellian nightmare.[15] Much of our resistance to socialization stems from the suspicion that corporations are fundamentally amoral and their members, once socialized, will pursue inappropriate goals. There are, in fact, significant checks and balances in American society against the extremes of social manipulation. Government, the media, and various other stakeholders such as consumers, environmentalists, and unions become powerfully vocal when corporations cross the line of decorum. And of the great self-sustaining institutions, all over a half century old, little evidence exists of major transgressions despite their strongly socialized cultures. These corporations avoid the undesirable extremes by continually recommitting themselves to shared values that keep them in tune with society.

Placing one's self "at the mercy" of an organization imposes real costs. There are long hours of work, missed weekends, bosses one has to endure, criticism that seems unfair, job assignments and rotations that are inconvenient or undesirable. The countervailing force for commitment under these circumstances is the organization's set of transcendent values which connect *its* purpose with significant higher order human values,—such as serving mankind, providing a first-class product for society, or developing people. Prior to joining Delta Airlines, candidates hear endlessly about the "Delta family feeling." Numerous anecdotes illustrate that Delta's values require sacrifices: management takes pay cuts during lean times; senior flight attendants and pilots voluntarily work fewer hours per week in order to avoid laying off more junior employees.[16] Candidates who accept employment with Delta tend to accept this quid pro quo, believing that the restrictions on individual action comprise a reasonable trade-off. Delta'a family philosophy is deemed worthy enough to make their sacrifices worthwhile. The organization, in turn, needs to honor its values and continually reaffirm their importance. To the outsider, the fuss IBM makes over "respecting the dignity of the individual," the intensity with which Delta Airlines expresses "the Delta family feeling," may seem like overzealousness. But for those within, these values represent a deeply felt mission. Their credibility and constancy is essential to the socialization transaction.

***Step Six.*** Reinforcing folklore provides legends and interpretations of watershed events in the organization's history that validate the firm's culture and its aims. Folklore reinforces a code of conduct for "how we do things around here."

All firms have their stories. The difference among firms that socialize well is that the morals of the stories all tend to "point north." Procter and Gamble fires one of their best brand managers for overstating the features of a product. The moral: ethical claims come ahead of making money. Morgan Stanley canonizes partners with legendary skills at "cutting a deal." One of the richest legacies of folklore was found within the former Bell system where numerous stories and anecdotes extolled employees who made sacrifices to keep the phones working.

The Bell folklore was so powerful and widely shared that when natural disaster struck, all elements of a one million member organization were able to pull together, cut corners, violate procedures, make sacrifices against measurement criteria—all in the interest of restoring phone service. This occurred despite extensive bureaucratic obstacles and illustrates how folklore, when well understood, can legitimize special channels for moving an organization in a hurry.[17]

***Step Seven.*** Consistent role models and consistent traits are associated with those recognized as on the fast track.

Nothing communicates so powerfully to younger professionals within an organization than having peers or superiors who share common qualities and who are formally or informally recognized as winners. Far more can be taught by examples than can ever be conveyed in a classroom. The protege watches the role model make presentations, handle conflict, write memos and replicates as closely as possible the traits that seem to work most effectively.

Strong culture firms regard role models as the most powerful ongoing "training program" available. Because other elements of the culture are consistent, those emerging as role models are consistent. Morgan Stanley carefully selects its high potential cadre for the combination of energy, aggressiveness, and team play that the organization requires.[18] Procter and Gamble exhibits extraordinary consistency among its brand managers across traits such as tough mindedness, motivational skills, enormous energy, and ability to get things done through others.[19]

Unfortunately most firms leave the emergence of role models to chance. Some on the fast track seem to be whizzes at analysis, others are skilled with people, others seem astute at politics: the result for those below is confusion as to what it *really* takes to succeed. The set of companies, formerly parts of the Bell System, have a strong need to become more market oriented and aggressive. Yet the Bell culture continues to discriminate against candidates for the high-potential list who, against the backdrop of the older monopoly culture, are "too aggressive."[20]

The seven dimensions of socialization, while not surprising when examined individually, tend to be overlooked and undermanaged. Many companies can point to isolated aspects of their organizational practices that follow these patterns but rarely is each of the seven factors managed as a concerted and well-coordinated effort. Rarer yet is the firm where all seven hang together. Indeed, it is *consistency* across all seven elements of the socialization process that results in a strong cohesive culture that lasts over time.

# THE CASE FOR SOCIALIZATION

All organizations require a certain degree of order and consistency. To achieve this, they either utilize *explicit* procedures and formal controls or *implicit social* controls. Great firms tend to do an artful job of blending both. American firms, in aggregate, tend to rely on formal controls. The result is that management often appears to be over-steering, rigid, and bureaucratic. A United Technologies executive states: "I came from the Bell system. Compared to AT&T, this is a weak culture and there is little socialization. But, of course there is still need for controls. So they put handcuffs on you, shackle you to every nickel, track every item of inventory, monitor every movement in production, and head count. They control you by balance sheet."[21]

An inordinate amount of energy in American companies is invested in fighting "the system." (We often find ourselves playing games to work around it.) When an organization instills a strong, consistent set of implicit understandings, it is effectively establishing a common law to supplement its statutory laws. This enables us to interpret formal systems in the context for which they were designed, to use them as tools rather than straitjackets. An IBM manager states: "Socialization acts as a fine-tuning device: it helps us make sense out of the procedures and quantitative measures. Any number of times I've been faced with a situation where the right thing for the measurement system was 'X' and the right thing for IBM was 'Y'. I've always been counseled to tilt toward what was right for IBM in the long term and what was right for our people. They pay us a lot to do that. Formal controls, without coherent values and culture are too crude a compass to steer by."[22]

Organizations that socialize effectively manage a lot of internal ambiguity. This tends to free up time and energy; more goes toward getting the job done and focusing on external things like the competition and the customer. "At IBM you spend 50% of your time managing the internal context," states a former IBMer, now at ITT, "at most companies it's more like 75%."[23] A marketing manager at Atari states: "You can't imagine how much time and energy around here goes into politics. You've got to determine who's on first base this month in order to figure out how to obtain what you need to get the job done. There are no rules. There are no clear values. Bushnell and Kassar stood for diametrically opposite things. Your bosses are constantly changing. I've had 4 in 18 months. We're spread out over 43 buildings over a 20-mile radius and we're constantly reorganizing. All this means that you never had time to develop a routine way for getting things done at the interface between your job and the next guy's. Without rules for working with one another, a lot of people get hurt, get burned out, are never taught the 'Atari way' of doing things because there isn't an 'Atari way.'"[24]

The absence of cultural rules makes organizational life capricious. This is so because success as middle and senior managers not only requires managing the substance of the business, but increasingly involves managing one's role and relationships. When social roles are unclear, no one is speaking the same language; communication and trust break down. Remember, the power to get things done in corporations seldom depends on formal titles and formal authority alone. In great measure, it depends on a person's track record and reputation, knowledge, and a network of relationships. In effect, the power to implement change and execute effectively relies heavily on one's *social* currency, something a person accumulates over time. Strong culture firms *empower* employees helping them build this social currency by providing continuity and clarity. Organizations which do not facilitate this process incur a cost.

Continuity and clarity also yield great dividends in reducing career anxiety. The ebbs and flows of career fortunes attract close scrutiny in organizations. Mixed signals surrounding such things as rewards, promotions, career paths, criteria for being on the "fast track" or a candidate for termination, inevitably generate a lot of gossip, game playing, and counter productive expenditure of energy. Some might feel that these elements can be entirely resolved by the explicit provisions in the policy manual. Fact is, many of the criteria of success for middle and senior level positions are implicit. It is almost impossible to articulate in writing the nuances and shared understandings that govern the rise or demise of executives. The rules tend to be communicated and enforced via relatively subtle cues. When the socialization process is weak, the cues tend to be poorly or inconsistently communicated.[25]

Look carefully at career patterns in most companies. Ambitious professionals strive to learn the ropes but there are as many "ropes" as there are individuals who have, by one means or another, made their way to the top. So one picks an approach and if by coincidence it coincides with how your superiors do things, you're on the fast track. Far more prevalent, however, the approach that works with one superior is offensive to another. "As a younger manager, I was always taught to touch bases and solicit input before moving ahead," a manager of a Santa Clara electronics firm states. "It always worked. But at a higher level with a different boss, my base touching was equated with 'being political.' Unfortunately, the organization doesn't forewarn you when it changes signals. A lot of good people leave owing to misunderstandings over things of this kind. The human cost in weakly socialized organizations tends to go unrecognized."[26]

What about the cost of conformity? A senior vice-president of IBM states: "Conformity among IBM employees has often been described as stultifying in terms of dress, behavior, and lifestyle. There is, in fact, strong pressure to adhere to certain norms of superficial behavior, and much more intensely to the three tenets of the company philosophy: 1) respect for the dignity of the individual, 2) providing first-rate customer service, and 3) excellence. These are the bench marks. Between them there is wide latitude for divergence in opinions and behavior." A Procter and Gamble executive adds: "There is a great deal of consistency around here in how certain things are done and these are rather critical to our sustained success. Beyond that, there are very few hard and fast rules. People on the outside might portray our culture as imposing lock-step uniformity. It doesn't feel rigid when you're inside. It feels like it accommodates you. And best of all, you know the game you're in—you know whether you're playing soccer or football; you can find out very clearly what it takes to succeed and you can bank your career on that."[27]

It is useful to distinguish between norms that are central to the core factors that drive business success and social conventions that signal commitment and belonging. The former set is most essential as it ensures consistency around certain crucial activities that link to a firm's strategy. At IBM, people, customers, and excellence have priority. As noted earlier, IBM's format for stand-up presentations and its style of "probing" are seen as vital to keeping the culture on its toes. Bain, Morgan Guaranty, and Procter & Gamble each imposes variations on this theme.

The second set of norms are, in effect, organizational equivalents of a handshake. They are social conventions that make it easier for people to be comfortable with one another. One need not observe all of them, but as some conventions count more than others, one strives to reassure the organization that one is on the team. The important aspect of this second set of social values is that, like a handshake, they are usually not experienced as oppressive. Partly, this is because adherence is only skin deep. (Most of us don't feel our individualism is compromised by shaking hands.) In addition, these social conventions are usually self-evident to prospective members and self-selection eliminates many whose integrity would be violated by observing them.

# MISCONCEPTIONS

The aim of socialization is to establish a base of attitudes, habits, and values that foster cooperation, integrity, and communication. The most frequently advanced objection is that the companies who do so will lose innovativeness over the long haul. The record does not bear this out. Many of the companies who socialize most extensively are the ones that have lasted over many generations—at least prima face evidence of sufficient innovation to cope with the changing environment. Further consider 3M or Bell Labs. Both socialize extensively and both are highly innovative institutions— and they remain so by fostering social rules that *reward* innovation. Another misconception is that socialization necessarily occurs at the expense of maintaining a desirable amount of internal competition. Again, IBM, P&G, major consulting firms, law practices, and outstanding financial institutions like Morgan Stanley are illustrations of strong culture firms where internal competition tends to be healthy but intense. There is, of course, an ever present danger of strong culture firms becoming incestuous and myopic—the "General Motors syndrome." Most opponents of socialization rally around this argument. But what is learned from the firms that have avoided these pitfalls is that they consciously minimize the downside of socialization by cultivating *obsessions*—not just *any* obsession, but ones that serve to continually wrench attention from internal matters to the world outside. The four most common "obsessions" are quality, competition, customer service, and productivity.

FIGURE 1   Seven Steps of Socialization

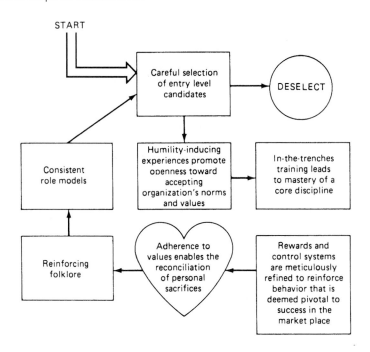

**FIGURE 2  Compute Your "Socialization" Score**

Respond to the items below as they apply to the handling of professional employees. Upon completion, compute the total score.  For comparison, scores for a number of strong, intermediate, and weak culture firms are to be found below.

|  | Not true of this company |  |  | Very true of this company |  |
|---|---|---|---|---|---|
| 1. Recruiters receive at least one week of intensive training. | 1 | 2 | 3 | 4 | 5 |
| 2. Recruitment firms identify several key traits deemed crucial to the firm's success, traits are defined in concrete terms and interviewer records specific evidence of each trait. | 1 | 2 | 3 | 4 | 5 |
| 3. Recruits are subject to at least four in depth interviews. | 1 | 2 | 3 | 4 | 5 |
| 4. Company actively facilitates de-selection during the recruiting process by revealing minuses as well as plusses. | 1 | 2 | 3 | 4 | 5 |
| 5. New hires work long hours, are exposed to intensive training of considerable difficulty and/or perform relatively menial tasks in the first four months. | 1 | 2 | 3 | 4 | 5 |
| 6. The intensity of entry level experience  builds cohesiveness among peers in each entering class. | 1 | 2 | 3 | 4 | 5 |
| 7. All professional employees in a particular discipline begin in entry level positions regardless of prior experience or advanced degrees. | 1 | 2 | 3 | 4 | 5 |
| 8. Reward systems and promotion criteria require mastery of a core discipline as a precondition of advancement. | 1 | 2 | 3 | 4 | 5 |
| 9. The career path for professional employees is relatively consistent over the first six to ten years with the company | 1 | 2 | 3 | 4 | 5 |
| 10. Reward systems, performance incentives, promotion criteria and other primary measures  of success reflect a high degree of congruence. | 1 | 2 | 3 | 4 | 5 |
| 11. Virtually all professional employees can identify and articulate the firm's shared values (i.e., th purpose or mission that ties the firm to society, the customer or it's employees). | 1 | 2 | 3 | 4 | 5 |
| 12. There are very few instances when actions of management appear to violate the firm's espoused values. | 1 | 2 | 3 | 4 | 5 |
| 13. Employees frequently make personal sacrifices for the firm out of commitment to the firm's shared values. | 1 | 2 | 3 | 4 | 5 |
| 14. When confronted with trade-offs between systems measuring short-term results and doing what's best for the company in the long-term, the firm usually decides in favor of the long-term. | 1 | 2 | 3 | 4 | 5 |
| 15. This organization fosters mentor-protégé relationships. | 1 | 2 | 3 | 4 | 5 |
| 16. There is considerable similarity among high potential candidates in each particular discipline. | 1 | 2 | 3 | 4 | 5 |

Compute your score: _____

For comparative purposes:

|  | Scores |  |
|---|---|---|
| Strongly Socialized Firms. . . . . | 65–80. . . . . . | IBM, P&G, Morgan Guaranty |
|  | 55–64. . . . . . | ATT, Morgan Stanley, Delta Airlines |
|  | 45–54. . . . . . | United Airlines, Coca Cola |
|  | 35–44. . . . . . | General Foods, Pepsi Co. |
|  | 25–34. . . . . . | United Technologies, ITT |
| Weakly Socialized Firms. . . . . . | Below 25. . . . . | Atari |

Each demands an external focus and serves as a built-in way of maintaining vigilance. Positive examples are McDonald's obsessive concern for quality control, Toyota's for productivity, IBM's for customer service, and Morgan Stanley's for competition. These "obsessions" contribute to a lot of fire drills and are regarded as overkill by some. But they also serve as an organizational equivalent of calisthenics. They maintain organizational alertness and muscle tone for the day when real change is required. It should be noted that organizations which tend to be obsessive over internal matters, such as Delta's with "the family feeling," may be riding for a fall.[28]

The underlying dilemma of socialization is so sensitive to core American values that it is seldom debated. When discussed, it tends toward a polarized debate—especially from members of the media and academics who, as a subset of the U.S. population, tend to be among the most preoccupied with individualism and individual rights. A central premise of this essay is that such polarization generates more heat than light. We will do better if we can advance beyond the extremes of the argument.

Revolutions begin with an assault on awareness. It is time to deal more clearmindedly with this crucial aspect of organizational effectiveness. Between our *espoused* individualism and the *enacted* reality in most great companies lies a zone where organizational and individual interests overlap, if we can come to grips with our ambivalence about socialization we will undoubtedly make our organizations more effective. Equally important, we can reduce the human costs that arise today as many stumble along ineffectually on careers within companies that lack a sufficient foundation of social rules. This insufficiency is only partly the result of ignorance. In equal measure it derives from our instinctive resistance to social controls—even when some measure of them may be in our own best interest.

## REFERENCES

1. Interview with Skip Awalt, Director of Management Development, IBM, Armonk, NY, May 26, 1982.
2. Interviews with Bain Consultants, 1983. Also, see: "Those Who Can't, Consult," *Harpers* (November 1982), pp. 8–17.
3. N. Kaible, Recruitment and Socialization at Procter and Gamble, Stanford Graduate School of Business, Case II S-BP-236, May 1984.
4. Interviews with professional staff, Morgan Guaranty Trust, New York, 1982.
5. Edgar H. Schein, "Organizational Socialization," in Kolb, Rubin, and McIntire, eds., *Organizational Psychology* (Englewood Cliffs, NJ: Prentice Hall, 1974), pp. 1–15.
6. Richard Pascale and Anthony Athos, *The Art of Japanese Management* (New York, NY: Simon & Schuster, 1981).
7. Kaible, op. cit., pp. 2-6.
8. Interview with recent trainees of IBM's sales development program, Palo Alto, CA, May 1982.
9. Kaible, op. cit., p. 10.
10. Interviews with professional staff, Morgan Stanley, New York, March 1983.
11. Kaible, op. cit., p. 16. See also "Readiness Criteria for Promotion to Assistant Brand Manager," unpublished P&G internal document #0689A, pp. 1–2.
12. Interview with Skip Await, IBM, op. cit. See also T. Rohan, "How IBM Stays Non Union," *Industry Week,* November 26, 1979, pp. 85–96.

13. Interviews with IBM managers, Palo Alto, CA, April 13, 1983.

14. See Pascale and Athos, op. cit., Chapter Seven.

15. See for example Zimbardo, "To Control a Mind," *The Stanford Magazine* (Winter 1983), pp. 59–64.

16. J. Guyon, "Family Feeling at Delta Creates Loyal Workers," *Wall Street Journal*, July 17, 1980, p. 13.

17. Interviews with executives of AT&T, Basking Ridge, NJ, February 1982.

18. Interview with professional staff, Morgan Guaranty, Palo Alto, CA, April 1983.

19. Kaible, op. cit., p. 16.

20. Interview with line executives of Northwestern Bell, Omaha, NE, March 1982.

21. Interview with executives, Pratt & Whitney Division, United Technologies, NY, January 1981.

22. Interview with IBM Marketing and Production managers, Palo Alto, CA, op. cit.

23. Ibid.

24. Interview with product development managers, Atari, Santa Clara, CA, April 1983.

25. Pascale and Athos, op. cit., Chapters 3 & 4.

26. Interview with a production manager of Rolm, Santa Clara, CA, January 1983.

27. Interview with IBM marketing and production managers, Palo Alto, CA. op. cit.

28. M. Loeb, "Staid Delta Air Tries to Stem Losses by Following Other Carriers' Moves," *Wall Street Journal*, July 10, 1983.

# 2
# Theories of Managing People

THE MANAGER'S JOB: FOLKLORE AND FACT
*Henry Mintzberg*

MASTERING COMPETING VALUES:
AN INTEGRATED APPROACH TO MANAGEMENT
*Robert E. Quinn*

THE HUMAN SIDE OF ENTERPRISE
*Douglas M. McGregor*

## THE MANAGER'S JOB: FOLKLORE AND FACT

*Henry Mintzberg*

If you ask a manager what he does, he will most likely tell you that he plans, organizes, coordinates, and controls. Then watch what he does. Don't be surprised if you can't relate what you see to these four words.

When he is called and told that one of his factories has just burned down, and he advises the caller to see whether temporary arrangements can be made to supply customers through a foreign subsidiary, is he planning, organizing, coordinating, or controlling? How about when he presents a gold watch to a retiring employee? Or when he attends a conference to meet people in the trade? Or on returning from that conference, when he tells one of his employees about an interesting product idea he picked up there?

The fact is that these four words, which have dominated management vocabulary since the French industrialist Henri Fayol first introduced them in 1916, tell us little about what managers actually do. At best, they indicate some vague objectives managers have when they work.

The field of management, so devoted to progress and change, has for more than half a century not seriously addressed *the* basic question: What do managers do? Without a proper answer, how can we teach management? How can we design planning or information systems for managers? How can we improve the practice of management at all?

Considering its central importance to every aspect of management, there has been surprisingly little research on the manager's work, and virtually no systematic building of knowledge from one group of studies to another. In seeking to describe managerial work, I conducted my own research and also scanned the literature widely to integrate the findings of studies from many diverse sources with my own. These studies focused on two very different aspects of managerial work. Some were concerned with the characteristics of the work—how long managers work, where, at what pace and with what interruptions, with whom they work, and through what media they communicate. Other studies were more concerned with the essential content of the work—what activities the managers actually carry out, and why. Thus, after a meeting, one researcher might note that the manager spent 45 minutes with three government officials in their Washington office, while another might record that he presented his company's stand on some proposed legislation in order to change a regulation.

A few of the studies of managerial work are widely known, but most have remained buried as single journal articles or isolated books. Among the more important ones I cite (with full references in the footnotes) are the following:

- Sune Carlson developed the diary method to study the work characteristics of nine Swedish managing directors. Each kept a detailed log of his activities. Carlson's results are reported in his book *Executive Behavior*. A number of British researchers, notably Rosemary Stewart, have subsequently used Carlson's method. In *Managers and Their Jobs*, she describes the study of 160 top and middle managers of British companies during four weeks, with particular attention to the differences in their work.

- Leonard Sayles's book *Managerial Behavior* is another important reference. Using a method he refers to as "anthropological," Sayles studied the work content of middle- and lower-level managers in a large U.S. corporation. Sayles moved freely in the company collecting whatever information struck him as important.

- Perhaps the best-known source is *Presidential Power*, in which Richard Neustadt analyzes the power and managerial behavior of Presidents Roosevelt, Truman, and Eisenhower. Neustadt used secondary sources—documents and interviews with other parties—to generate his data.

- Robert H. Guest, in *Personnel,* reports on a study of the foreman's working day. Fifty-six U.S. foremen were observed and each of their activities recorded during one eight-hour shift.

- Richard C. Hodgson, Daniel J. Levinson, and Abraham Zaleznik studied a team of three top executives of a U.S. hospital. From that study they wrote *The Executive Role Constellation*. (These researchers addressed in particular the way in which work and socioemotional roles were divided among the three managers.)

- William F. Whyte, from his study of a street gang during the Depression, wrote *Street Corner Society*. His findings about the gang's leadership, which George C. Homans analyzed in *The Human Group,* suggest some interesting similarities of job content between street gang leaders and corporate managers.

My own study involved five American CEOs of middle—to large-sized organizations—a consulting firm, a technology company, a hospital, a consumer goods company, and a school system. Using a method called "structural observation," during one intensive week of observation for each executive I recorded various aspects of every piece of mail and every verbal contact. My method was designed to capture data on both work characteristics and job content. In all, I analyzed 890 pieces of incoming and outgoing mail and 368 verbal contacts.

Our ignorance of the nature of managerial work shows up in various ways in the modern organization—in the boast by the successful manager that he never spent a single day in a management training program; in the turnover of corporate planners who never quite understood what it was the manager wanted; in the computer consoles gathering dust in the back room because the managers never used the fancy on-line MIS some analyst thought they needed. Perhaps most important, our ignorance shows up in the inability of our large public organizations to come to grips with some of their most serious policy problems.

Somehow, in the rush to automate production, to use management science in the functional areas of marketing and finance, and to apply the skills of the behavioral scientist to the problem of worker motivation, the manager—that person in charge of the organization or one of its subunits—has been forgotten.

My intention in this article is simple: to break the reader away from Fayol's words and introduce him to a more supportable, and what I believe to be a more useful, description of managerial work. This description derives from my review and synthesis of the available research on how various managers have spent their time.

In some studies, managers were observed intensively ("shadowed" is the term some of them used); in a number of others, they kept detailed diaries of their activities; in a few studies, their records were analyzed. All kinds of managers were studied—foremen, factory supervisors, staff managers, field sales managers, hospital administrators, presidents of companies and nations, and even street gang leaders. These "managers" worked in the United States, Canada, Sweden, and Great Britain. In the ruled insert on page 31 is a brief review of the major studies that I found most useful in developing this description, including my own study of five American chief executive officers.

A synthesis of these findings paints an interesting picture, one as different from Fayol's classical view as a cubist abstract is from a Renaissance painting. In a sense, this picture will be obvious to anyone who has ever spent a day in a manager's office, either in front of the desk or behind it. Yet, at the same time, this picture may turn out to be revolutionary, in that it throws into doubt so much of the folklore that we have accepted about the manager's work.

I first discuss some of this folklore and contrast it with some of the discoveries of systematic research—the hard facts about how managers spend their time. Then I synthesize these research findings in a description of ten roles that seem to describe the essential content of all managers' jobs. In a concluding section, I discuss a number of implications of this synthesis for those trying to achieve more effective management, both in classrooms and in the business world.


## SOME FOLKLORE AND FACTS ABOUT MANAGERIAL WORK

There are four myths about the manager's job that do not bear up under careful scrutiny of the facts.

1. **Folklore.** *The manager is a reflective, systematic planner.* The evidence on this issue is overwhelming, but not a shred of it supports this statement.

   **Fact.** *Study after study has shown that managers work at an unrelenting pace, that their activities are characterized by brevity, variety, and discontinuity, and that they are strongly oriented to action and dislike reflective activities.* Consider this evidence:

- Half the activities engaged in by the five chief executives of my study lasted less than nine minutes, and only 10% exceeded one hour.[1]  A study of 56 U.S. foremen found that they averaged 583 activities per eight-hour shift, an average of 1 every 48 seconds.[2] The work-pace for both chief executives and foremen was unrelenting. The chief executives met a steady stream of callers and mail from  the moment they arrived in the morning until they left  in  the evening.  Coffee breaks and lunches were inevitably work related, and ever-present subordinates seemed to usurp any free moment.
- A diary study of 160 British middle and top managers found that they worked for a half hour or more without interruption only about once every two days.[3]
- Of the verbal contacts of the chief executives in my study,  93% were arranged on an ad hoc basis. Only 1% of the executives' time was spent in open-ended observational tours. Only 1% out of 368 verbal contacts was unrelated to a specific issue and could be called general planning. Another researcher finds that "*in not one single case* did a manager report the obtaining of important external  information from a general conversation or other undirected personal communication."[4]
- No study has found important patterns in the way managers schedule their time.  They seem to jump from issue to issue, continually responding to the needs of the moment.

Is this the planner that the classical view describes? Hardly.  How, then, can we explain this behavior? The manager is simply responding to the pressures of his job.  I found that my chief executives terminated many of their own activities, often leaving meetings before the end, and interrupted their desk work to call in subordinates.  One president not only placed his desk so that he could look down a long hallway but also left his door open when he was alone—an invitation for sub-ordinates to come in and interrupt him.

Clearly, these managers wanted to encourage the flow of current information.  But more signif-icantly, they seemed to be conditioned by their own work loads.  They appreciated the opportunity cost of their own time, and they were continually aware of their ever-present obligations—mail to be answered, callers to attend to, and so on.  It seems that no matter what he is doing, the manager is plagued by the possibilities of what he might do and what he must do.

When the manager must plan, he seems to do so implicitly in the context of daily actions, not in some abstract process reserved for two weeks in the organization's mountain retreat.  The plans of the chief executives I studied seemed to exist only in their heads—as flexible, but often specific intentions.  The traditional literature notwithstanding, the job of managing does not breed reflective planners; the manager is a real-time responder to stimuli, an individual who is conditioned by his job to prefer live to delayed action.

2.  **Folklore**.  *The effective manager has no regular duties to perform.*  Managers are constantly being told to spend more time planning and delegating, and less time seeing customers and engaging in negotiations.  These are not, after all, the true tasks of the manager.  To use the popular analogy, the good manager, like the good conductor, carefully orchestrates everything in advance, then sits back to enjoy the fruits of his labor, responding occasionally to an unforeseeable exception.

But here again the pleasant abstraction just does not seem to hold up.  We had better take a closer look at those activities managers feel compelled to engage in before we arbitrarily define them away.

***Fact.***   In addition to handling exceptions managerial work involves performing a *number of regular duties, including ritual and ceremony, negotiations, and processing of soft information that links the organization with its environment.*  Consider some evidence from the research studies:

- A study of the work of the presidents of small companies found that they engaged in routine activities because their companies could not afford staff specialists and were so thin on operating personnel that a single absence often required the president to substitute.[5]

- One study of field sales managers and another of chief executives suggest that it is a natural part of both jobs to see important customers, assuming the managers wish to keep those customers.[6]

- Someone, only half in jest, once described the manager as that person who sees visitors so that everyone else can get his work done.  In my study, I found that certain ceremonial duties—meeting visiting dignitaries, giving out gold watches, presiding at Christmas dinner—were an intrinsic part of the chief executive's job.

- Studies of managers' information flow suggest that managers play a key role in securing "soft" external information (much of it available only to them because of their status) and in passing it along to their subordinates.

3.   ***Folklore.***   *The senior manager needs aggregated information, which a formal management information system best provides.*  Not too long ago, the words *total information system* were everywhere in the management literature.  In keeping with the classical view of the manager as that individual perched on the apex of a regulated, hierarchical system, the literature's manager was to receive all his important information from a giant, comprehensive MIS.

But lately, as it has become increasingly evident that these giant MIS systems are not working—that managers are simply not using them—the enthusiasm has waned.  A look at how managers actually process information makes the reason quite clear.  Managers have five media at their command—documents, telephone calls, scheduled and unscheduled meetings, and observational tours.

***Fact.***   *Managers strongly favor the verbal media—namely telephone calls and meetings.*  The evidence comes from every single study of managerial work.  Consider the following:

- In two British studies, managers spent an average of 66% and 80% of their time in verbal (oral) communication.[7]  In my study of five American chief executives, the figure was 78%.

- These five chief executives treated mail processing as a burden to be dispensed with.  One came in Saturday morning to process 142 pieces of mail in just over three hours, to "get rid of all the stuff." This same manager looked at the first piece of "hard" mail he had received all week, a standard cost report, and put it aside with the comment, "I never look at this."

- These same five chief executives responded immediately to 2 of the 40 routine reports they received during the five weeks of my study and to 4 items in the 104 periodicals.  They skimmed most of these periodicals in seconds, almost ritualistically.  In all, these chief executives of good-sized organizations initiated on their own—that is, not in response to something else—a grand total of 25 pieces of mail during the 25 days I observed them.

An analysis of the mail the executives received reveals an interesting picture—only 13% was of specific and immediate use.  So now we have another piece in the puzzle: not much of the mail provides live, current information—the action of a competitor, the mood of a government legislator, or the rating of last night's television show.  Yet this is the information that drove the managers, interrupting their meetings and rescheduling their workdays.

Consider another interesting finding. Managers seem to cherish "soft" information, especially gossip, hearsay, and speculation. Why? The reason is its timeliness; today's gossip may be tomorow's fact. The manager who is not accessible for the telephone call informing him that his biggest customer was seen golfing with his main competitor may read about a dramatic drop in sales in the next quarterly report. But then it's too late.

To assess the value of historical, aggregated, "hard" MIS information, consider two of the manager's prime uses for his information—to identify problems and opportunities[8] and to build his own mental models of the things around him (e.g., how his organization's budget system works, how his customers buy his product, how changes in the economy affect his organization, and so on!). Every bit of evidence suggests that the manager identifies decision situations and builds models not with the aggregated abstractions an MIS provides, but with specific tidbits of data.

Consider the words of Richard Neustadt, who studied the information collecting habits of Presidents Roosevelt, Truman, and Eisenhower:

> "It is not information of a general sort that helps a President see personal stakes; not summaries, not surveys, not the *bland amalgams*. Rather…it is the odds and ends of *tangible detail* that pieced together in his mind illuminate the underside of issues put before him. To help himself he must reach out as widely as he can for every scrap of fact, opinion, gossip, bearing on his interests and relationships as President. He must become his own director of his own central intelligence."[9]

The manager's emphasis on the verbal media raises two important points:

First, verbal information is stored in the brains of people. Only when people write this information down can it be stored in the files of the organization—whether in metal cabinets or on magnetic tape—and managers apparently do not write down much of what they hear. Thus the strategic data bank of the organization is not in the memory of its computers but in the minds of its managers.

Second, the manager's extensive use of verbal media helps to explain why he is reluctant to delegate tasks. When we note that most of the manager's important information comes in verbal form and is stored in his head, we can well appreciate his reluctance. It is not as if he can hand a dossier over to someone; he must take the time to "dump memory"—to tell that someone all he knows about the subject. But this could take so long that the manager may find it easier to do the task himself. Thus the manager is damned by his own information system to a "dilemma of delegation"— to do too much himself or to delegate to his subordinates with inadequate briefing.

4. ***Folklore.*** *Management is, or at least is quickly becoming, a science and a profession.* By almost any definitions of *science* and *profession*, this statement is false. Brief observation of any manager will quickly lay to rest the notion that managers practice a science. A science involves the inaction of systematic, analytically determined procedures or programs. If we do not even know what procedures managers use, how can we prescribe them by scientific analysis? And how can we call management a profession if we cannot specify what managers are to learn? For after all, a profession involves "knowledge of some department of learning or science" (*Random House Dictionary*).[10]

***Fact.*** *The managers' programs—to schedule time, process information, make decisions, and so on—remain locked deep inside their brains.* Thus, to describe these programs, we rely on words like *judgment* and *intuition*, seldom stopping to realize that they are merely labels for our ignorance.

I was struck during my study by the fact that the executives I was observing—all very competent by any standard—are fundamentally indistinguishable from their counterparts of a hundred years ago (or a thousand years ago, for that matter). The information they need differs, but they seek it in the same way—by word of mouth. Their decisions concern modern technology, but the procedures they use to make them are the same as the procedures of the nineteenth-century manager. Even the computer, so important for the specialized work of the organization, has apparently had no influence on the work procedures of general managers. In fact, the manager is in a kind of loop, with increasingly heavy work pressures but no aid forthcoming from management science.

Considering the facts about managerial work, we can see that the manager's job is enormously complicated and difficult. The manager is overburdened with obligations, yet he cannot easily delegate his tasks. As a result, he is driven to overwork and is forced to do many tasks superficially. Brevity, fragmentation, and verbal communication characterize his work. Yet these are the very characteristics of managerial work that have impeded scientific attempts to improve it. As a result, the management scientist has concentrated his efforts on the specialized functions of the organization, where he could more easily analyze the procedures and quantify the relevant information.[11]

But the pressures of the manager's job are becoming worse. Where before he needed only to respond to owners and directors, now he finds that subordinates with democratic norms continually reduce his freedom to issue unexplained orders, and a growing number of outside influences (consumer groups, government agencies, and so on) expect his attention. And the manager has had nowhere to turn for help. The first step in providing the manager with some help is to find out what his job really is.

## BACK TO BASIC DESCRIPTION OF MANAGERIAL WORK

Now let us try to put some of the pieces of this puzzle together. Earlier, I defined the manager as that person in charge of an organization or one of its subunits. Besides chief executive officers, this definition would include vice presidents, bishops, foremen, hockey coaches, and prime ministers. Can all of these people have anything in common? Indeed they can. For an important starting point, all are vested with formal authority over an organizational unit. From formal authority comes status, which leads to various interpersonal relations, and from these comes access to information. Information, in turn, enables the manager to make decisions and strategies for his unit.

The manager's job can be described in terms of various "roles," or organized sets of behaviors identified with a position. My description, shown in Exhibit I, comprises ten roles. As we shall see, formal authority gives rise to the three interpersonal roles, which in turn give rise to the three informational roles; these two sets of roles enable the manager to play the four decisional roles.

### Interpersonal Roles

Three of the manager's roles arise directly from his formal authority and involve basic interpersonal relationships.

1. First is the *figurehead* role. By virtue of his position as head of an organizational unit, every manager must perform some duties of a ceremonial nature. The president greets the touring dignitaries, the foreman attends the wedding of a lathe operator, and the sales manager takes an important customer to lunch.

The chief executives of my study spent 12% of their contact time on ceremonial duties; 17% of their incoming mail dealt with acknowledgments and requests related to their status. For example, a letter to a company president requested free merchandise for a crippled schoolchild; diplomas were put on the desk of the school superintendent for his signature.

Duties that involve interpersonal roles may sometimes be routine, involving little serious communication and no important decision making. Nevertheless, they are important to the smooth functioning of an organization and cannot be ignored by the manager.

EXHIBIT I   The Manager's Roles

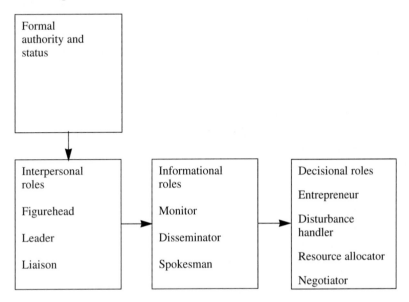

2.   Because he is in charge of an organizational unit the manager is responsible for the work of the people of that unit. His actions in this regard constitute the *leader* role. Some of these actions involve leadership directly—for example, in most organizations the manager is normally responsible for hiring and training his own staff.

In addition, there is the indirect exercise of the leader role. Every manager must motivate and encourage his employees, somehow reconciling their individual needs with the goals of the organization. In virtually every contact the manager has with his employees, subordinates seeking leadership clues probe his actions: "Does he approve?" "How would he like the report to turn out?" "Is he more interested in market share than high profits?"

The influence of the manager is most clearly seen in the leader role. Formal authority vests him with great potential power; leadership determines in large part how much of it he will realize.

3.   The literature of management has always recognized the leader role, particularly those aspects of it related to motivation. In comparison, until recently it has hardly mentioned the *liaison* role, in which the manager makes contacts outside his vertical chain of command. This is remarkable in light of the finding of virtually every study of managerial work that managers spend as much time with peers and other people outside their units as they do with their own subordinates —and, surprisingly, very little time with their own superiors.

In Rosemary Stewart's diary study, the 160 British middle and top managers spent 47% of their time with peers, 41% of their time with people outside their unit, and only 12% of their time with their superiors. For Robert H. Guest's study of U.S. foremen, the figures were 44%, 46%, and 10%. The chief executives of my study averaged 44% of their contact time with people outside their organizations, 48% with subordinates, and 7% with directors and trustees.

The contacts the five CEOs made were with an incredibly wide range of people: subordinates; clients, business associates, and suppliers; and peers—managers of similar organizations, government and trade organization officials, fellow directors on outside boards, and independents with no relevant organizational affiliations. The chief executives' time with and mail from these groups is shown in Exhibit II. Guest's study of foremen shows, likewise, that their contacts were numerous and wide ranging, seldom involving fewer than 25 individuals, and often more than 50.

As we shall see shortly, the manager cultivates such contacts largely to find information. In effect, the liaison role is devoted to building up the manager's own external information system—informal, private, verbal, but, nevertheless, effective.

## Informational Roles

By virtue of his interpersonal contacts, both with his subordinates and with his network of contacts, the manager emerges as the nerve center of his organizational unit. He may not know everything, but he typically knows more than any member of his staff.

EXHIBIT II   The Chief Executives' Contacts

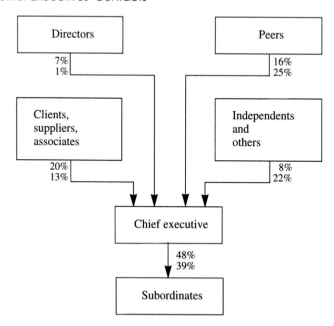

Note: The top figure indicates the proportion of total contact time spent with each group and the bottom figure, the proportion of mail from each group.

Studies have shown this relationship to hold for all managers, from street gang leaders to U.S. presidents. In *The Human Group*, George C. Homans explains how, because they were at the center of the information flow in their own gangs and were also in close touch with other gang leaders, street gang leaders were better informed than any of their followers.[12] And Richard Neustadt describes the following account from his study of Franklin D. Roosevelt:

"The essence of Roosevelt's technique for information-gathering was competition. 'He would call you in,' one of his aides once told me, 'and he'd ask you to get the story on some complicated business, and you'd come back after a couple of days of hard labor and present the juicy morsel you'd uncovered under a stone somewhere, and *then* you'd find out he knew all about it, along with something else you *didn't* know. Where he got this information from he wouldn't mention, usually, but after he had done this to you once or twice you got damn careful about *your* information.'"[13]

We can see where Roosevelt "got this information" when we consider the relationship between the interpersonal and informational roles. As leader, the manager has formal and easy access to every member of his staff. Hence, as noted earlier, he tends to know more about his own unit than anyone else does. In addition, his liaison contacts expose the manager to external information to which his subordinates often lack access. Many of these contacts are with other managers of equal status, who are themselves nerve centers in their own organizations. In this way, the manager develops a powerful data base of information.

The processing of information is a key part of the manager's job. In my study, the chief executives spent 40% of their contact time on activities devoted exclusively to the transmission of information; 70% of their incoming mail was purely informational (as opposed to request for action). The manager does not leave meetings or hang up the telephone in order to get back to work. In large part, communication is his work. Three roles describe these informational aspects of managerial work.

1. As *monitor*, the manager perpetually scans his environment for information, interrogates his liaison contacts and his subordinates, and receives unsolicited information, much of it as a result of the network of personal contacts he has developed. Remember that a good part of the information the manager collects in his monitor role arrives in verbal form, often as gossip, hearsay, and speculation. By virtue of his contacts, the manager has a natural advantage in collecting this soft information for his organization.

2. He must share and distribute much of this information. Information he gleans from outside personal contacts may be needed within his organization. In his *disseminator* role, the manager passes some of his privileged information directly to his subordinates, who would otherwise have no access to it. When his subordinates lack easy contact with one another, the manager will sometimes pass information from one to another.

3. In his *spokesman* role, the manager sends some of his information to people outside his unit—a president makes a speech to lobby for an organization cause, or a foreman suggests a product modification to a supplier. In addition, as part of his role as spokesman, every manager must inform and satisfy the influential people who control his organizational unit. For the foreman, this may simply involve keeping the plant manager informed about the flow of work through the shop.

The president of a large corporation, however, may spend a great amount of his time dealing with a host of influences. Directors and shareholders must be advised about financial performance; consumer groups must be assured that the organization is fulfilling its social responsibilities; and government officials must be satisfied that the organization is abiding by the law.

## Decisional Roles

Information is not, of course, an end in itself; it is the basic input to decision making. One thing is clear in the study of managerial work: the manager plays the major role in his unit's decision-making system. As its formal authority, only he can commit the unit to important new courses of action; and as its nerve center, only he has full and current information to make the set of decisions that determines the unit's strategy. Four roles describe the manager as decision-maker.

1. As *entrepreneur*, the manager seeks to improve his unit, to adapt it to changing conditions in the environment. In his monitor role, the president is constantly on the lookout for new ideas. When a good one appears, he initiates a development project that he may supervise himself or delegate to an employee (perhaps with the stipulation that he must approve the final proposal).

There are two interesting features about these development projects at the chief executive level. First, these projects do not involve single decisions or even unified clusters of decisions. Rather, they emerge as a series of small decisions and actions sequenced over time. Apparently, the chief executive prolongs each project so that he can fit it bit by bit into his busy, disjointed schedule and so that he can gradually come to comprehend the issue, if it is a complex one.

Second, the chief executives I studied supervised as many as 50 of these projects at the same time. Some projects entailed new products or processes; others involved public relations campaigns, improvement of the cash position, reorganization of a weak department, resolution of a morale problem in a foreign division, integration of computer operations, various acquisitions at different stages of development, and so on.

The chief executive appears to maintain a kind of inventory of the development projects that he himself supervises—projects that are at various stages of development, some active and some in limbo. Like a juggler, he keeps a number of projects in the air; periodically, one comes down, is given a new burst of energy, and is sent back into orbit. At various intervals, he puts new projects on-stream and discards old ones.

2. While the entrepreneur role describes the manager as the voluntary initiator of change, the *disturbance handler* role depicts the manager involuntarily responding to pressures. Here change is beyond the manager's control. He must act because the pressures of the situation are too severe to be ignored: a strike looms, a major customer has gone bankrupt, or a supplier reneges on his contract.

It has been fashionable, I noted earlier, to compare the manager to an orchestra conductor, just as Peter F. Drucker wrote in *The Practice of Management*:

> "The manager has the task of creating a true whole that is larger than the sum of its parts, a productive entity that turns out more than the sum of the resources put into it. One analogy is the conductor of a symphony orchestra, through whose effort, vision and leadership individual instrumental parts that are so much noise by themselves become the living whole of music. But the conductor has the composer's score; he is only an interpreter. The manager is both composer and conductor."[14]

Now consider the words of Leonard R. Sayles, who has carried out systematic research on the manager's job:

> "[The manager] is like a symphony orchestra conductor, endeavoring to maintain a melodious performance in which the contributions of the various instruments are coordinated and sequenced, patterned and paced, while the orchestra members are having various personal difficulties, stage hands are moving music stands, alternating excessive heat and cold are creating audience and instrument problems, and the sponsor of the concert is insisting on irrational changes in the program."[15]

In effect, every manager must spend a good part of his time responding to high-pressure disturbances. No organization can be so well run, so standardized, that it has considered every contingency in the uncertain environment in advance. Disturbances arise not only because poor managers ignore situations until they reach crisis proportions, but also because good managers cannot possibly anticipate all the consequences of the actions they take.

3. The third decisional role is that of *resource allocator*. To the manager falls the responsibility of deciding who will get what in his organizational unit. Perhaps the most important resource the manager allocates is his own time. Access to the manager constitutes exposure to the unit's nerve center and decision-maker. The manager is also charged with designing his unit's structure, that pattern of formal relationships that determines how work is to be divided and coordinated.

Also, in his role as resource allocator, the manager authorizes the important decisions of his unit before they are implemented. By retaining this power, the manager can ensure that decisions are interrelated; all must pass through a single brain. To fragment this power is to encourage discontinuous decision making and a disjointed strategy.

There are a number of interesting features about the manager's authorizing others' decisions. First, despite the widespread use of capital budgeting procedures—a means of authorizing various capital expenditures at one time— executives in my study made a great many authorization decisions on an ad hoc basis. Apparently, many projects cannot wait or simply do not have the quantifiable costs and benefits that capital budgeting requires.

Second, I found that the chief executives faced incredibly complex choices. They had to consider the impact of each decision on other decisions and on the organization's strategy. They had to ensure that the decision would be acceptable to those who influence the organization, as well as ensure that resources would not be overextended. They had to understand the various costs and benefits as well as the feasibility of the proposal. They also had to consider questions of timing. All this was necessary for the simple approval of someone else's proposal. At the same time, however, delay could lose time, while quick approval could be ill considered and quick rejection might discourage the subordinate who had spent months developing a pet project.

One common solution to approving projects is to pick the man instead of the proposal. That is, the manager authorizes those projects presented to him by people whose judgment he trusts. But he cannot always use this simple dodge.

4. The final decisional role is that of *negotiator*. Studies of managerial work at all levels indicate that managers spend considerable time in negotiations: the president of the football team is called in to work out a contract with the holdout superstar; the corporation president leads his company's contingent to negotiate a new strike issue; the foreman argues a grievance problem to its conclusion with the shop steward. As Leonard Sayles puts it, negotiations are a "way of life" for the sophisticated manager.

These negotiations are duties of the manager's job; perhaps routine, they are not to be shirked. They are an integral part of his job, for only he has the authority to commit organizational resources in "real time," and only he has the nerve center information that important negotiations require.

## The Integrated Job

It should be clear by now that the ten roles I have been describing are not easily separable. In the terminology of the psychologist, they form a gestalt, an integrated whole. No role can be pulled out of the framework and the job be left intact. For example, a manager without liaison contacts lacks external information. As a result, he can neither disseminate the information his employees need nor make decisions that adequately reflect external conditions. (In fact, this is a problem for the new person in a managerial position, since he cannot make effective decisions until he has built up his network of contacts.)

Here lies a clue to the problems of team management.[16] Two or three people cannot share a single managerial position unless they can act as one entity. This means that they cannot divide up the ten roles unless they can very carefully reintegrate them. The real difficulty lies with the informational roles. Unless there can be full sharing of managerial information—and, as I pointed out earlier, it is primarily verbal—team management breaks down. A single managerial job cannot be arbitrarily split, for example, into internal and external roles, for information from both sources must be brought to bear on the same decisions.

To say that the ten roles form a gestalt is not to say that all managers give equal attention to each role. In fact, I found in my review of the various research studies that

> …sales managers seem to spend relatively more of their time in the interpersonal roles, presumably a reflection of the extrovert nature of the marketing activity;
> …production managers give relatively more attention to the decisional roles, presumably a reflection of their concern with efficient work flow;
> …staff managers spend the most time in the informational roles, since they are experts who manage departments that advise other parts of the organization.

Nevertheless, in all cases the interpersonal, informational, and decisional roles remain inseparable.

## TOWARD MORE EFFECTIVE MANAGEMENT

What are the messages for management in this description? I believe, first and foremost, that this description of managerial work should prove more important to managers than any prescription they might derive from it. That is to say, *the manager's effectiveness is significantly influenced by his insight into his own work*. His performance depends on how well he understands and responds to the pressures and dilemmas of the job. Thus managers who can be introspective about their work are likely to be effective at their jobs. The ruled insert on page 43 offers 14 groups of self-study questions for managers. Some may sound rhetorical; none is meant to be. Even though the questions cannot be answered simply, the manager should address them.

Let us take a look at three specific areas of concern. For the most part, the managerial logjams—the dilemma of delegation, the data base centralized in one brain, the problems of working with the management scientist—revolve around the verbal nature of the manager's information. There are great dangers in centralizing the organization's data bank in the minds of its managers. When they leave, they take their memory with them. And when subordinates are out of convenient verbal reach of the manager, they are at an informational disadvantage.

1. Where do I get my information, and how? Can I make greater use of my contacts to get information? Can other people do some of my scanning for me? In what areas is my knowledge weakest, and how can I get others to provide me with the information I need? Do I have powerful enough mental models of those things I must understand within the organization and in its environment?

2. What information do I disseminate in my organization? How important is it that my subordinates get my information? Do I keep too much information to myself because dissemination of it is time-consuming or inconvenient? How can I get more information to others so they can make better decisions?

3. Do I balance information collecting with action taking? Do I tend to act before information is in? Or do I wait so long for all the information that opportunities pass me by and I become a bottleneck in my organization?

4. What pace of change am I asking my organization to tolerate? Is this change balanced so that our operations are neither excessively static nor overly disrupted? Have we sufficiently analyzed the impact of this change on the future of our organization?

5. Am I sufficiently well informed to pass judgment on the proposals that my subordinates make? Is it possible to leave final authorization for more of the proposals with subordinates? Do we have problems of coordination because subordinates in fact now make too many of these decisions independently?

6. What is my vision of direction for this organization? Are these plans primarily in my own mind in loose form? Should I make them explicit in order to guide the decisions of others in the organization better? Or do I need flexibility to change them at will?

7. How do my subordinates react to my managerial style? Am I sufficiently sensitive to the powerful influence my actions have on them? Do I fully understand their reactions to my actions? Do I find an appropriate balance between encouragement and pressure? Do I stifle their initiative?

8. What kind of external relationships do I maintain, and how? Do I spend too much of my time maintaining these relationships? Are there certain types of people whom I should get to know better?

9. Is there any system to my time scheduling, or am I just reacting to the pressures of the moment? Do I find the appropriate mix of activities, or do I tend to concentrate on one particular function or one type of problem just because I find it interesting? Am I more efficient with particular kinds of work at special times of the day or week? Does my schedule reflect this? Can someone else (in addition to my secretary) take responsibility for much of my scheduling and do it more systematically?

10. Do I overwork? What effect does my work load have on my efficiency? Should I force myself to take breaks or to reduce the pace of my activity?

11. Am I too superficial in what I do? Can I really shift moods as quickly and frequently as my work patterns require? Should I attempt to decrease the amount of fragmentation and interruption in my work?

12. Do I orient myself too much toward current, tangible activities? Am I a slave to the action and excitement of my work, so that I am no longer able to concentrate on issues? Do key problems receive the attention they deserve? Should I spend more time reading and probing deeply into certain issues? Could I be more reflective? Should I be?

13. Do I use the different media appropriately? Do I know how to make the most of written communication? Do I rely excessively on face-to-face communication, thereby putting all but a few of my subordinates at an informational disadvantage? Do I schedule enough of my meetings on a regular basis? Do I spend enough time touring my organization to observe activity at first hand? Am I too detached from the heart of my organization's activities, seeing things only in an abstract way?

14. How do I blend my personal rights and duties? Do my obligations consume all my time? How can I free myself sufficiently from obligations to ensure that I am taking this organization where I want it to go? How can I turn my obligations to my advantage?

1. *The manager is challenged to find systematic ways to share his privileged information.* A regular debriefing session with key subordinates, a weekly memory dump on the dictating machine, the maintaining of a diary of important information for limited circulation, or other similar methods may ease the logjam of work considerably. Time spent disseminating this information will be more than regained when decisions must be made. Of course, some will raise the question of confidentiality. But managers would do well to weigh the risks of exposing privileged information against having subordinates who can make effective decisions.

If there is a single theme that runs through this article, it is that the pressures of his job drive the manager to be superficial in his actions—to overload himself with work, encourage interruption, respond quickly to every stimulus, seek the tangible and avoid the abstract, make decisions in small increments, and do everything abruptly.

2. *Here again, the manager is challenged to deal consciously with the pressures of superficiality by giving serious attention to the issues that require it, by stepping back from his tangible bits of information in order to see a broad picture, and by making use of analytical inputs.* Although effective managers have to be adept at responding quickly to numerous and varying problems, the danger in managerial work is that they will respond to every issue equally (and that means abruptly) and that they will never work the tangible bits and pieces of informational input into a comprehensive picture of their world.

As I noted earlier, the manager uses these bits of information to build models of his world. But the manager can also avail himself of the models of the specialists. Economists describe the functioning of markets, operations researchers simulate financial flow processes, and behavioral scientists explain the needs and goals of people. The best of these models can be searched out and learned.

In dealing with complex issues, the senior manager has much to gain from a close relationship with the management scientists of his own organization. They have something important that he lacks—time to probe complex issues. An effective working relationship hinges on the resolution of what a colleague and I have called "the planning dilemma."[17] Managers have the information and the authority; analysts have the time and the technology. A successful working relationship between the two will be effected when the manager learns to share his information and the analyst learns to adapt to the manager's needs. For the analyst, adaptation means worrying less about the elegance of the method and more about its speed and flexibility.

It seems to me that analysts can help the top manager especially to schedule his time, feed in analytical information, monitor projects under his supervision, develop models to aid in making choices, design contingency plans for disturbances that can be anticipated, and conduct "quick-and-dirty" analysis for those that cannot. But there can be no cooperation if the analysts are out of the mainstream of the manager's information flow.

3. *The manager is challenged to gain control of his own time by turning obligations to his advantage and by turning those things he wishes to do into obligations.* The chief executives of my study initiated only 32% of their own contacts (and another 5% by mutual agreement). And yet to a considerable extent they seemed to control their time. There were two key factors that enabled them to do so.

First, the manager has to spend so much time discharging obligations that if he were to view them as just that, he would leave no mark on his organization. The unsuccessful manager blames failure on the obligations; the effective manager turns his obligations to his own advantage. A speech is a chance to lobby for a cause; a meeting is a chance to reorganize a weak department; a visit to an important customer is a chance to extract trade information.

Second, the manager frees some of his time to do those things that he—perhaps no one else— thinks important by turning them into obligations. Free time is made, not found, in the manager's job; it is forced into the schedule. Hoping to leave some time open for contemplation or general planning is tantamount to hoping that the pressures of the job will go away. The manager who wants to innovate initiates a project and obligates others to report back to him; the manager who needs certain environmental information establishes channels that will automatically keep him informed; the manager who has to tour facilities commits himself publicly.

## THE EDUCATOR'S JOB

Finally, a word about the training of managers. Our management schools have done an admirable job of training the organization's specialists—management scientists, marketing researchers, accountants, and organizational development specialists. But for the most part they have not trained managers.[18]

Management schools will begin the serious training of managers when skill training takes a serious place next to cognitive learning. Cognitive learning is detached and informational, like reading a book or listening to a lecture. No doubt much important cognitive material must be assimilated by the manager-to-be. But cognitive learning no more makes a manager than it does a swimmer. The latter will drown the first time he jumps into the water if his coach never takes him out of the lecture hall, gets him wet, and gives him feedback on his performance.

In other words, we are taught a skill through practice plus feedback, whether in a real or a simulated situation. Our management schools need to identify the skills managers use, select students who show potential in these skills, put the students into situations where these skills can be practiced, and then give them systematic feedback on their performance.

My description of managerial work suggests a number of important managerial skills—developing peer relationships, carrying out negotiations, motivating subordinates, resolving conflicts, establishing information networks and subsequently disseminating information, making decisions in conditions of extreme ambiguity, and allocating resources. Above all, the manager needs to be introspective about his work so that he may continue to learn on the job.

Many of the manager's skills can, in fact, be practiced, using techniques that range from role playing to videotaping real meetings. And our management schools can enhance the entrepreneurial skills by designing programs that encourage sensible risk taking and innovation.

No job is more vital to our society than that of the manager. It is the manager who determines whether our social institutions serve us well or whether they squander our talents and resources. It is time to strip away the folklore about managerial work, and time to study it realistically so that we can begin the difficult task of making significant improvements in its performance.

# REFERENCES

1. All the data from my study can be found in Henry Mintzberg, *The Nature of Managerial Work* (New York: Harper & Row, 1971).
2. Robert H. Guest, "Of Time and the Foreman," *Personnel*, May 1986, p. 478.
3. Rosemary Stewart, *Managers and Their Jobs* (London: Macmillan, 1967); see also Sune Carlson, *Executive Behavior* (Stockholm: Strombergs, 1951), the first of the diary studies.
4. Francis J. Aguilar, *Scanning the Business Environment* (New York: Macmillan, 1967), p. 102.
5. Unpublished study by Irving Choran, reported in Mintzberg, *The Nature of Managerial Work*.
6. Robert T. Davis, *Performance and Development of Field Sales Managers.* (Boston: Division of Research, Harvard Business School, 1957); George H. Copeman, *The Role of the Managing Director* (London: Business Publications, 1963).
7. Stewart, *Managers and Their Jobs*; Tom Burns, "The Directions of Activity and Communication in a Departmental Executive Group," *Human Relations* 7, no. 1 (1954): 73.
8. H. Edward Wrapp, "Good Managers Don't Make Policy Decisions," HBR September–October 1967, p. 91: Wrapp refers to this as spotting opportunities and relationships in the stream of operating problems and decisions; in his article Wrapp raises a number of excellent points related to this analysis.
9. Richard E. Neustadt, *Presidential Power* (New York: John Wiley, 1960), pp. 153–154: italics added.
10. For a more thorough, though rather different, discussion of this issue, see Kenneth R. Andrews, "Toward Professionalism in Business Management," HBR March–April 1969, p. 49.
11. C. Jackson Grayson, Jr., in "Management Science and Business Practice," HBR July–August 1973, p. 41, explains in similar terms why, as chairman of the Price Commission, he did not use those very techniques that he himself promoted in his earlier career as a management scientist.
12. George C. Homans, *The Human Group* (New York: Harcourt, Brace & World, 1959), based on the study by William F. Whyte entitled *Street Corner Society*, rev. ed. (Chicago: University of Chicago Press, 1955).
13. Neustadt, *Presidential Power*, p. 157.
14. Peter F. Drucker, *The Practice of Management* (New York: Harper & Row, 1954), pp. 341–342.
15. Leonard R. Sayles, *Managerial Behavior* (New York: McGraw-Hill, 1964), p. 162.
16. See Richard C. Hodgson, Daniel J. Levinson, and Abraham Zaleznik, *The Executive Role Constellation* (Boston: Division of Research, Harvard Business School, 1965), for a discussion of the sharing of roles.
17. James S. Hekimian and Henry Mintzberg, "The Planning Dilemma," *The Management Review*, May 1968, p. 4.
18. See 1. Sterling Livingston, "Myth of the Well-Educated Manager," HBR January–February 1971, p. 79.

# MASTERING COMPETING VALUES:
# AN INTEGRATED APPROACH TO MANAGEMENT

*Robert E. Quinn*

It was awful. Everything was always changing and nothing ever seemed to happen. The people above me would sit around forever and talk about things. The technically right answer didn't matter. They were always making what I thought were wrong decisions, and when I insisted on doing what was right, they got pissed off and would ignore what I was saying. Everything was suddenly political. They would worry about what everyone was going to think about every issue. How you looked, attending cocktail parties—that stuff to me was unreal and unimportant.

I went through five and a half terrible years. I occasionally thought I had reached my level of incompetence, but I refused to give up. In the end, the frustration and pain turned out to be a positive thing because it forced me to consider some alternative perspectives. I eventually learned that there were other realities besides the technical reality.

I discovered perception and long time lines. At higher levels what matters is how people see the world, and everyone sees it a little differently. Technical facts are not as available or as important. Things are changing more rapidly at higher levels, you are no longer buffered from the outside world. Things are more complex, and it takes longer to get people on board. I decided I had to be a lot more receptive and a lot more patient. It was an enormous adjustment, but then things started to change. I think I became a heck of a lot better manager.

## THE CONCEPT OF MASTERY

If there is such a thing as a master of management, what is it that differentiates the master from others? The answer has to do with how the master of management sees the world.

Most of us learn to think of the concept of organization in a very static way. Particularly at the lower levels, organizations seem to be characterized by relatively stable, predictable patterns of action. They appear to be, or at least we expect them to be, the product of rational-deductive thinking. We think of them as static mechanisms designed to accomplish some single purpose.

One of the most difficult things for most of us to understand is that organizations are dynamic. Particularly as one moves up the organizational ladder, matters become less tangible and less predictable. A primary characteristic of managing, particularly at higher levels, is the confrontation of change, ambiguity, and contradiction. Managers spend much of their time living in fields of perceived tensions. They are constantly forced to make tradeoffs, and they often find that there are no right answers. The higher one goes in an organization, the more exaggerated this phenomenon becomes. One-dimensional bromides (care for people, work harder, get control, be innovative) are simply half-truths representing single domains of action. What exists in reality are contradictory pressures, emanating from a variety of domains. This fact is important because much of the time the choice is not between good and bad, but between one good and another or between two unpleasant alternatives. In such cases the need is for complex, intuitive decisions, and many people fail to cope successfully with the resulting tension, stress, and uncertainty. This is well illustrated by the initial failure and frustration of the engineer who was quoted earlier.

*Source:* Adapted from *Beyond Rational Management* by Robert Quinn, Jossey-Bass, Inc., 1988. With permission of author and publisher.

The people who come to be masters of management do not see their work environment only in structured, analytic ways. Instead, they also have the capacity to see it as a complex, dynamic system that is constantly evolving. In order to interact effectively with it, they employ a variety of different perspectives or frames. As one set of conditions arises, they focus on certain cues that lead them to apply a very analytic and structured approach. As these cues fade, they focus on new cues of emerging importance and apply another frame, perhaps this time an intuitive and flexible one. At another time they may emphasize the overall task, and at still another they may focus on the welfare of a single individual.

Because of these shifts, masters of management may appear to act in paradoxical ways. They engage the contradictions of organizational life by using paradoxical frames. Viewed from a single point in time, their behaviors may seem illogical and contradictory. Yet these seeming contradictions come together in a fluid whole. Things work out well for these people.

The ability to see the world in a dynamic fashion does not come naturally. It requires a dramatic change in outlook, a redefinition of one's world view. It means transcending the rules of mechanistic logic used for solving well-defined problems and adopting a more comprehensive and flexible kind of logic. It is a logic that comes from experience rather than from textbooks. It requires a change not unlike a religious conversion.

## THE EVOLUTION OF MASTERY

Dreyfus, Dreyfus, and Athanasion (1986) provide a five-stage model that describes the evolution from novice to expert.

*In the novice stage people learn facts and rules.*   The rules are learned as absolutes that are never to be violated. For example, in playing chess people learn the names of the pieces, how they are moved, and their value. They are told to exchange pieces of lower value for pieces of higher value. In management, this might be the equivalent of the classroom education of an M.B.A.

*In the advanced beginner stage, experience becomes critical.*   Performance improves somewhat as real situations are encountered. Understanding begins to exceed the stated facts and rules. Observation of certain basic patterns leads to the recognition of factors that were not set forth in the rules. A chess player, for example, begins to recognize certain basic board positions that should be pursued. The M.B.A. discovers the basic norms, values, and culture of the workplace on the first job.

*The third stage is competence.*   Here the individual has begun to appreciate the complexity of the task and now recognizes a much larger set of cues. The person develops the ability to select and concentrate on the most important cues. With this ability competence grows. Here the reliance on absolute rules begins to disappear. People take calculated risks and engage in complex trade-offs. A chess player may, for example, weaken board position in order to attack the opposing king. This plan may or may not follow any rules that the person was ever taught. The M.B.A. may go beyond the technical analysis taught in graduate school as he or she experiments with an innovation of some sort. Flow or excellence may even be experienced in certain specific domains or subareas of management, as in the case of the engineer at the beginning of the article who displayed technical brilliance.

*In the proficiency stage, calculation and rational analysis seem to disappear, and unconscious, fluid, and effortless performance begins to emerge.*   Here no one plan is held sacred. The person learns to unconsciously "read" the evolving situation. Cues are noticed and responded to, and attention shifts to new cues as the importance of the old ones recedes. New plans are triggered as emerging patterns call to mind plans that worked previously. Here there is a holistic and intuitive grasp of the situation. Here we are talking, for example, about the top 1 percent of all chess players, the people with the ability to intuitively recognize and respond to change in board positions. Here the M.B.A. has become an effective, upper-level manager, capable of meeting a wide variety of demands and contradictions.

*Experts, those at the fifth stage, do what comes naturally.* They do not apply rules but use holistic recognition in a way that allows them to deeply understand the situation. They have maps of the territory programmed into their heads that the rest of us are not aware of. They see and know things intuitively that the rest of us do not know or see (many dimensions). They frame and reframe strategies as they read changing cues (action inquiry). Here the manager has fully transcended personal style. The master manager seems to meet the contradictions of organizational life effortlessly.

## THE NEED FOR MORE COMPLEX THEORY

In their popular book, *In Search of Excellence*, Peters and Waterman (1982) seek to discover what differentiates excellent companies from ordinary ones. Embedded in their work is an observation that is quite consistent with our observations. They conclude that managers in excellent companies have an unusual ability to resolve paradox, to translate conflicts and tensions into excitement, high commitment, and superior performance. In reviewing the book, Van de Ven (1983) applauds this insight and notes a grave inadequacy in the theories generated by administrative researchers. He argues that while the managers of excellent companies seem to have a capacity for dealing with paradox, administrative theories are not designed to take this phenomenon into account. In order to be internally consistent, theorists tend to eliminate contradiction. Hence, there is a need for a dynamic theory that can handle both stability and change, that can consider the tensions and conflicts inherent in human systems. Among other things, the theory would view people as complex actors in tension-filled social systems, constantly interacting with a "fast-paced, ever-changing array of forces" (Van de Ven, 1983, p. 624). The theory would center on transforming leadership that focuses on "the ethics and value judgments that are implied when leaders and followers raise one another to higher levels of motivation and morality" (p. 624).

For most of us, discovering the contradictory nature of organizing is not easy. We have biases in how we process information, and we prefer to live in certain kinds of settings. Our biases are further influenced by our organizational experience at both the functional and cultural levels. At the functional level, for example, accountants and marketing people tend to develop very different assumptions about what is "good." At the cultural level, there is often a set of values that conveys "how we do things around here." Because these values tend to be so powerful, it is very difficult to see past them. It is difficult to recognize that there are weaknesses in our own perspective and advantages in opposing perspectives. It is particularly difficult to realize that these various perspectives must be understood, juxtaposed, and blended in a delicate, complex, and dynamic way. It is much more natural to see them as either/or positions in which one must triumph over the other.

## A COMPETING VALUES MODEL

In the late seventies and early eighties, many of my colleagues and I became interested in the issue of organizational effectiveness. We were asking the question, What are the characteristics of effective organizations? Many studies were done in which people set out to measure the characteristics of organizations. These measures were then submitted to a technique called factor analysis. It produced lists of variables that characterized effective organizations. The problem was that these variables differed from one study to another. It seemed that the more we learned, the less we knew.

My colleague, John Rohrbaugh, and I therefore tried to reframe the question. Instead of asking what effective organizations looked like, we decided to ask how experts think about effective organizations. This would allow us to get to the assumptions behind the studies and perhaps make sense of what was causing the confusion. In a series of studies (Quinn and Rohrbaugh, 1983), we had organizational theorists and researchers make judgments regarding the similarity or dissimilarity between pairs of effectiveness criteria. The data were analyzed using a technique called multidimensional scaling. Results of the analyses suggested that organizational theorists and researchers share an implicit theoretical framework, or cognitive map (Figure 1).

Note that the two axes in the figure create four quadrants. The vertical axis ranges from flexibility to control, the horizontal axis ranges from an internal to an external focus. Each quadrant of the framework represents one of the four major models in organizational theory. The human relations model, for example, stresses criteria such as those in the upper-left quadrant: cohesion and morale, along with human resource development. The open systems model stresses criteria such as those in the upper-right quadrant. These include flexibility and readiness as well as growth, resource acquisition, and external support. The rational goal model stresses the kind of criteria found in the lower-right quadrant, including planning and goal setting and productivity and efficiency. The internal process model is represented in the lower-left quadrant. It stresses information management and communication, along with stability and control.

FIGURE 1   Competing Values Framework: Effectiveness

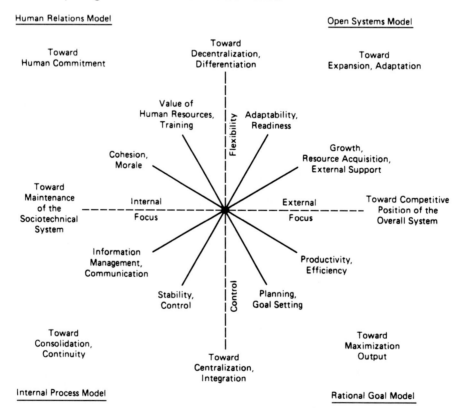

Each model has a polar opposite. The human relations model, which emphasizes flexibility and internal focus, stands in stark contrast to the rational goal model, which stresses control and external focus. The open systems model, which is characterized by flexibility and external focus, runs counter to the internal process model, which emphasizes control and internal focus. Parallels among the models are also important. The human relations and open systems models share an emphasis on flexibility. The open systems and rational goal models have an external focus (responding to outside change and producing in a competitive market). The rational goal and internal process models are rooted in the value of control. Finally, the internal process and human relations models share an internal focus (concern for the human and technical systems inside the organization).

Each model suggests a mode or type of organizing. The two sets of criteria in each quadrant also suggest an implicit means-ends theory that is associated with each mode. Thus, the rational goal model suggests that an organization is a rational economic firm. Here planning and goal setting are viewed as a means of achieving productivity and efficiency. In the open systems model we find the adhocracy, where adaptability and readiness are viewed as a means to growth, resource acquisition, and external support. In the internal process model is the hierarchy, where information management and communication are viewed as a means of arriving at stability and control. In the human relations quadrant we find the team. Here cohesion and morale are viewed as a means of increasing the value of human resources.

This scheme is called the competing values framework because the criteria seem to initially carry a conflictual message. We want our organizations to be adaptable and flexible, but we also want them to be stable and controlled. We want growth, resource acquisition, and external support, but we also want tight information management and formal communication. We want an emphasis on the value of human resources, but we also want an emphasis on planning and goal setting. The model does not suggest that these oppositions cannot mutually exist in a real system. It suggests, rather, that these criteria, values, and assumptions are oppositions in our minds. We tend to think that they are very different from one another, and we sometimes assume them to be mutually exclusive. In order to illustrate this point we will consider how values manifest themselves and, in so doing, consider some applied examples.

## HOW VALUES MANIFEST THEMSELVES

In recent years much has been written about culture in organizations. When we think of the manifestation of values in organizations, it is their cultures that we are thinking of. Simply put, culture is the set of values and assumptions that underlie the statement, "This is how we do things around here." Culture at the organizational level, like information processing at the individual level, tends to take on moral overtones. While cultures tend to vary dramatically, they share the common characteristic of providing integration of effort in one direction while often sealing off the possibility of moving in another direction. An illustration may be helpful.

In October 1980 *Business Week* ran an article contrasting the cultures at J.C. Penney and PepsiCo. At Penney's the culture focuses on the values of fairness and long-term loyalty. Indeed, a manager was once chewed out by the president of the company for making too much money! To do so was unfair to the customers, and at Penney's one must never take advantage of the customer. Customers are free to return merchandise with which they are not satisfied. Suppliers know that they can establish stable, long-term relationships with Penney's. Employees know that if their ability to perform a given job begins to deteriorate, they will not find themselves out on the street; rather, an appropriate alternative position will be found for them.

The core of the company's culture is captured in "The Penney Idea." Although it was adopted in 1913, it is a very modern-sounding statement, consisting of seven points: "To serve the public, as nearly as we can, to its complete satisfaction; to expect for the service we render a fair remuneration and not all the profit the traffic will bear; to do all in our power to pack the customer's dollar full of value, quality, and satisfaction; to continue to train ourselves and our associates so that the service we give will be more and more intelligently performed; to improve constantly the human factor in our business; to reward men and women in our organization through participation in what the business produces; to test our every policy, method, and act in this wise: 'Does it square with what is right and just?' "

The culture at PepsiCo is in stark contrast to that at Penney's. After years as a sleepy company that took the back seat to Coca-Cola, PepsiCo underwent a major change by adopting a much more competitive culture. This new culture was manifest both externally and internally. On the outside PepsiCo directly confronted Coca-Cola. In bold ads customers were asked to taste and compare the products of the two companies. Internally, managers knew that their jobs were on the line and that they had to produce results. There was continuous pressure to show improvement in market share, product volume, and profits. Jobs were won or lost over a "tenth of a point" difference in these areas.

Staffs were kept small. Managers were constantly moved from job to job and expected to work long hours. The pressure never let up. During a blizzard, for example, the chief executive officer found a snowmobile and drove it to work. (This story is told regularly at PepsiCo.) Competitive team and individual sports are emphasized, and people are expected to stay in shape. The overall climate is reflected in the often repeated phrase, "We are the marines not the army."

The differences between these two companies could hardly be greater. Reading this account, you have probably concluded that one culture is more attractive than the other, and you would expect others to agree with your choice. But it is very likely that if you visited PepsiCo and spoke of "The Penney Idea," you would be laughed at. If you tried to press it upon PepsiCo employees, they would probably become incensed. Likewise, if you visited Penney's and described or tried to press upon them the values of PepsiCo, they would have the same reaction. You would be violating sacred assumptions.

Interestingly, the major problem at PepsiCo was seen as the absence of loyalty. Coca-Cola's response to the PepsiCo attack, for example, was to hire away some of PepsiCo's best "Tigers," and they were, because of the constant pressure, willing to go. (PepsiCo's rate of tenure is less than one-third of the rate at Penney's.) And what, according to *Business Week*, was the major problem at Penney's? Lack of competitiveness. Despite a reputation as one of the best places to work, and despite intense employee and customer loyalty, Penney's had been rapidly losing market share to KMart. Some critics expressed doubt that Penney's could respond to the challenge.

What is happening here? The surface conclusion is that two opposite cultures exist. Penney's reflects the human relations model in that the company seems to resemble a team, clan, or family. PepsiCo reflects the rational goal model in that it appears to be an instrumental firm. The strength of one is the weakness of the other. While this conclusion is true, there is a deeper insight to be gained. I will later return to this interesting contrast after considering the transformation of values.


## INEFFECTIVENESS

The competing values framework consists of juxtaposed sets of organizational effectiveness criteria. Each of these "good" criteria can become overvalued by an individual and pursued in an unidimensional fashion. When this zealous pursuit of a single set of criteria takes place, a strange inversion can result. Good things can mysteriously become bad things. In Figure 2, I show how criteria of effectiveness, when pursued blindly, become criteria of ineffectiveness. These latter criteria are depicted in the negative zone on the outside of the diagram.

## FIGURE 2 The Positive and Negative Zones

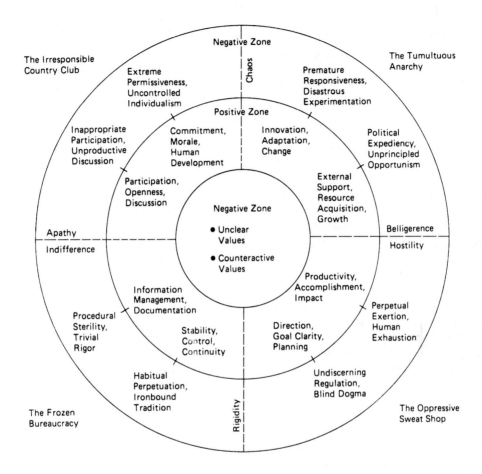

The structure of this model parallels the competing values framework of effectiveness. The axes, however, are negatively, rather than positively, labeled. Thus, the vertical dimension ranges from chaos (too much flexibility and spontaneity) to rigidity (too much order and predictability). The horizontal dimension ranges from belligerence and hostility (too much external focus and too much emphasis on competition and engagement) to apathy and indifference (too much internal focus and too much emphasis on maintenance and coordination within the system). Each quadrant represents a negative culture with negative effectiveness criteria. Embedded within these quadrants are eight criteria of ineffectiveness.

In the upper-left quadrant is the irresponsible country club. In this quadrant, human relations criteria are emphasized to the point of encouraging laxity and negligence. Discussion and participation, good in themselves, are carried to inappropriate lengths. Commitment, morale, and human development turn into extreme permissiveness and uncontrolled individualism. Here, administrators are concerned only with employees, to the exclusion of the task.

In the upper-right quadrant is the tumultuous anarchy. In this quadrant, there is so much emphasis on the open systems criteria of effectiveness that disruption and discontinuity result. Emphasis on insight, innovation, and change turn into premature responsiveness and disastrous experimentation. Concern for external support, resource acquisition, and growth turn into political expediency and unprincipled opportunism. Here, administrators are concerned only with having a competitive advantage and show no interest in continuity and control of the work flow.

In the lower-right quadrant is the oppressive sweatshop. In this quadrant, there is too much emphasis on the criteria of effectiveness associated with the rational goal model. Effort, productivity, and emphasis on profit or impact of service turn into perpetual exertion and human exhaustion. Here, we see symptoms of burnout. Concern for goal clarification, authority, and decisiveness turn into an emphasis on strict regulation and blind dogma. There is no room for individual differences; the boss has the final say.

Finally, in the lower-left quadrant is the frozen bureaucracy. Here, there is too much concern with internal processes. The organization becomes atrophied as a result of excessive measurement and documentation; it becomes a system of red tape. Control measures, documentation, and computation turn into procedural sterility and trivial rigor. Everything is "by the book." The emphasis on stability, control, and continuity lead to the blind perpetuation of habits and traditions. Procedures are followed because "we've always done it this way"; there is no room for trying something new.

## STRENGTH BECOMING WEAKNESS

Let us return to PepsiCo and J.C. Penney. Earlier I said that introducing the culture of one company into the other would be highly conflictual. Further, I pointed out that each culture had weaknesses. Now we can see that their very strengths put them at risk.

Because of the inability of the PepsiCo culture to tolerate the values in the human resource quadrant, the company is in danger of moving into the negative zone on the right side of Figure 2. Because of the inability of the J.C. Penney culture to more fully absorb the values on the right side of the figure, the company is in danger of moving into the negative zone on the left side of the figure. The more fully that each company pushes a particular set of positive values, without tending to the opposite positive values, the greater the danger to it.

The major point here is that everything in the two outer circles is related. The more that success is pursued around one set of positive values, the greater will be the pressure to take into account the opposite positive values. If these other values are ignored long enough, crisis and catastrophe will result.

## STAYING IN THE POSITIVE ZONE: MASTERING PARADOX

Staying in the positive zone requires high levels of complex thought. Consider, for example, the stereotypical entrepreneur, like Steve Jobs of Apple Computer. Entrepreneurs are typically very creative and action oriented. They are usually not very sympathetic to the values in the hierarchy quadrant. When they build a new organization they often try to avoid hierarchy. Unfortunately, if their initial vision is successful, and their new company expands rapidly, the growth (an indicator of success) stimulates a need for hierarchical coordinating mechanisms (often seen as an indication of failure). This phenomenon is often called the formalization crisis. Many successful entrepreneurs are forced, like Steve Jobs, to leave their company because they cannot comprehend the paradox or manage the competing values. For this reason, it is instructive to consider Bill Gates of Microsoft.

54

Microsoft is the second largest software company in the world. Run by Bill Gates, who is still in his early thirties, Microsoft has been best known for its widely used MS DOS system. But in 1987 Gates was successful in convincing IBM to adopt its newest product, called Windows, for use in IBM's new line of personal computers. Upon completion of the agreement analysts began to predict that within twelve months Microsoft would become the largest software company in the world.

In many ways, Gates is the stereotypical entrepreneur. He is a technical genius with a burning mission. He feels a drive to bring the power of computing to the masses. His company is marked by considerable flexibility and excitement. The median age of the work force is thirty-one. People work long days, with Gates himself setting the example with an early morning to midnight routine. There are frequent picnics, programmers set their own hours, dress is casual, and the turnover rate is less than 10 percent.

The company has grown rapidly. From 1980 to 1981, Gates watched his company go from 80 to 125 employees and saw profits double to $16 million. The market value of the company now exceeds $2 billion. Given our earlier cases, all these indicators would lead us to worry about Gates and his ability to meet the demands for formalization.

In fact, however, Gates has already faced the formalization crisis and has come off well. What were the keys to this success? First, he made a very significant decision to bring in professional managers and to focus his own energies on technology. He seemed to grasp an important paradox that eludes most entrepreneurs: to have power means one must give up power. Maintaining a primary focus on technology, however, does not mean that he has abandoned the tasks of leadership. Instead, he has taken the time to learn the principles of law, marketing, distribution, and accounting and apply them in his work. He also has the paradoxical capacity of simultaneously caring and being tough. For example, dissatisfied with the performance of Microsoft's president, Gates removed him from office after only one year. But not long after, Gates was invited to be the best man at the wedding of the former president.

Perhaps the best summary of Gates and his abilities comes from one of his colleagues: "Bill Gates is very good at evaluating situations as they change." This, of course, is a key characteristic for staying in the positive zone.

Figure 2 has some important implications for management. It suggests that managers need to stay in the positive zone, that is, they need to pursue the seemingly "competing" positive values in the middle circle while also being careful to stay out of the external negative zone. They must maintain a dynamic, creative tension. Over time they must, like Bill Gates, be able to frame and reframe, that is, to move from one set of competing values to another.

## SOME IMPLICATIONS FOR MANAGEMENT

The notions of mastery and competing values suggest a more complex and dynamic approach to management. The novice-like "rules" taught in the textbooks are misleading in that they usually represent only one of the competing perspectives or polarities embedded in organizational life. Theory X is not inherently better than theory Y. Change is not inherently better than the status quo. Productivity is not inherently better than cohesion and morale.

The challenge for experienced managers is threefold: the first is far more difficult than it sounds, to recognize and appreciate the positive (and the negative) aspects of all areas of the competing values framework; second, to assess and work on the roles and skills associated with each area (these are identified in Quinn, 1988); third, to analyze the present organizational moment, with all its dilemmas, and trust one's ability to integrate and employ the skills appropriate to that moment. Together these three steps are key points in the process of mastering management.

# THE HUMAN SIDE OF ENTERPRISE

*Douglas M. McGregor*

## PREVIEW

**A.** Theory X is a set of propositions of the conventional view of management's task in harnessing human energy to organizational requirements.
   1. It is management's responsibility to organize the elements of productive enterprise—money, materials, equipment, people—in the interest of economic ends.
   2. To fit the needs of the organization, the behavior of people must be directed, motivated, controlled and modified or else they would be passive.
   3. Additional briefs behind this conventional view show the worker to be indolent by nature, lacking ambition, inherently self-centered, resistant to changes, and gullible.
   4. To accomplish its task, management uses these assumptions as guidelines and ranges its possibilities between "hard" or "strong" and "soft" or "weak" approaches.
   5. Since difficulties exist between the hard and soft approach, the current view is "firm" but "fair."
**B.** Although social scientists do not deny that the worker's behavior is similar to what the management perceives, they feel that this behavior is not a consequence of the worker's inherent nature, but rather the result of the nature of industrial organizations, of management philosophy, policy, and practice.
**C.** The subject of motivation is supposedly the best way of indicating the inadequacy of the conventional concepts of management.
   1. At the lowest level in the hierarchy of individual needs are the *physiological needs.*
   2. The next higher level of needs are called *safety needs.*
   3. When the worker's physiological needs and safety needs are satisfied, his other behavior is motivated by *social needs.*
   4. Above the social needs are two kinds of *egoistic needs:* (a) those that relate to one's *self-esteem,* and b) those that relate to one's *reputation.* Unlike the lower needs these are rarely satisfied.
   5. Finally there are needs for *self-fulfillment.*
**D.** Just as deprivation of physiological needs has behavioral consequences, the same is true for higher level needs.
**E.** In the carrot-and-stick approach, management can provide or withhold the means for satisfying the worker's physiological and safety needs.
   1. But today the philosophy of management by direction and control is inadequate to motivate, because the human needs under the carrot-and-stick approach are important motivators of behavior.
**F.** Theory Y is based on more adequate assumptions about human nature and human motivation and therefore has broader dimensions.
   1. Responsibility lies with management for organizing the elements of productive enterprise in the interest of economic ends.
   2. People have become passive or resistant to organizational needs because of their experience in organizations.

*Source:* Reprinted by permission of the publisher from *Management Review,* November 1957. © 1957 by the American Management Association, New York. All rights reserved.

3. Management should enable people to recognize and develop motivational characteristics.

4. By arranging organizational conditions and methods of operation, management's task is to allow people to achieve their own goals by directing their own best efforts towards organizational objectives.

5. Peter Drucker calls this process "management by objectives" in contrast to management by control.

**G.** The major difference associated with these theories is that Theory X places exclusive reliance upon external control of human behavior, while Theory Y relies heavily on self-control and self-direction.

**H.** The ideas associated with Theory Y are being applied slowly but with success.

1. Sears Roebuck and Company is an example where decentralization in the organization and delegation of duties is consistent with what the theory proposes.

2. IBM and Detroit Edison are pioneers in job enlargement.

3. The Scanlon Plan illustrates the ideas of participative and consultative management.

4. Most conventional programs of performance appraisal within management ranks reveal consistency with Theory X, although a few companies are taking steps in the direction of Theory Y.

**I.** Until full implementation of Theory Y is successful, only management that has confidence in human capacities and is itself directed towards organizational objectives rather than towards the preservation of personal power can grasp its implications.

It has become trite to say that industry has the fundamental know-how to utilize physical science and technology for the material benefit of mankind, and that we must now learn how to utilize the social sciences to make our human organizations truly effective. To a degree, the social sciences today are in a position like that of the physical sciences with respect to atomic energy in the thirties. We know that past conceptions of the nature of man are inadequate and, in many ways, incorrect. We are becoming quite certain that under proper conditions, unimagined resources of creative human energy could become available within the organizational setting.

We cannot tell industrial management how to apply this new knowledge in simple, economic ways. We know it will require years of exploration, much costly development research, and a substantial amount of creative imagination on the part of management to discover how to apply this growing knowledge to the organization of human effort in industry.

# MANAGEMENT'S TASK: THE CONVENTIONAL VIEW

The conventional conception of management's task in harnessing human energy to organizational requirements can be stated broadly in terms of three propositions. In order to avoid the complications introduced by a label, let us call this set of propositions "Theory X":

1. Management is responsible for organizing the elements of productive enterprise—money, materials, equipment, people—in the interest of economic ends.

2. With respect to people, this is a process of directing their efforts, motivating them, controlling their actions, modifying their behavior to fit the needs of the organization.

3. Without this active intervention by management, people would be passive—even resistant—to organizational needs. They must therefore be persuaded, rewarded, punished, controlled—their activities must be directed. This is management's task. We often sum it up by saying that management consists of getting things done through other people.

Behind this conventional theory there are several additional beliefs—less explicit, but widespread:

4.   The average man is by nature indolent—he works as little as possible.
5.   He lacks ambition, dislikes responsibility, prefers to be led.
6.   He is inherently self-centered, indifferent to organizational needs.
7.   He is by nature resistant to change.
8.   He is gullible, not very bright, the ready dupe of the charlatan and the demagogue.

The human side of economic enterprise today is fashioned from propositions and beliefs such as these. Conventional organization structures and managerial policies, practices, and programs reflect these assumptions.

In accomplishing its task—with these assumptions as guides—management has conceived of a range of possibilities.

At one extreme, management can be "hard" or "strong." The methods for directing behavior involve coercion and threat (usually disguised), close supervision, tight controls over behavior. At the other extreme, management can be "soft" or "weak." The methods for directing behavior involve being permissive, satisfying people's demands, achieving harmony. Then they will be tractable, accept direction.

This range has been fairly completely explored during the past half century, and management has learned some things from the exploration. There are difficulties in the "hard" approach. Force breeds counter-forces: restriction of output, antagonism, militant unionism, subtle but effective sabotage of management objectives. This "hard" approach is especially difficult during times of full employment.

There are also difficulties in the "soft" approach. It leads frequently to the abdication of management—to harmony, perhaps, but to indifferent performance. People take advantage of the soft approach. They continually expect more, but they give less and less.

Currently, the popular theme is "firm but fair." This is an attempt to gain the advantages of both the hard and the soft approaches. It is reminiscent of Teddy Roosevelt's "speak softly and carry a big stick."

## IS THE CONVENTIONAL VIEW CORRECT?

The findings which are beginning to emerge from the social sciences challenge this whole set of beliefs about man and human nature and about the task of management. The evidence is far from conclusive, certainly, but it is suggestive. It comes from the laboratory, the clinic, the schoolroom, the home, and even to a limited extent from industry itself.

The social scientist does not deny that human behavior in industrial organization today is approximately what management perceives it to be. He has, in fact, observed it and studied it fairly extensively. But he is pretty sure that this behavior is *not* a consequence of man's inherent nature. It is a consequence rather of the nature of industrial organizations, of management philosophy, policy, and practice. The conventional approach of Theory X is based on mistaken notions of what is cause and what is effect.

Perhaps the best way to indicate why the conventional approach of management is inadequate is to consider the subject of motivation.

# PHYSIOLOGICAL NEEDS

Man is a wanting animal—as soon as one of his needs is satisfied, another appears in its place. This process is unending. It continues from birth to death.

Man's needs are organized in a series of levels—a hierarchy of importance. At the lowest level, but pre-eminent in importance when they are thwarted, are his *physiological needs*. Man lives for bread alone, when there is no bread. Unless the circumstances are unusual, his needs for love, for status, for recognition are inoperative when his stomach has been empty for a while. But when he eats regularly and adequately, hunger ceases to be an important motivation. The same is true of the other physiological needs of man—for rest, exercise, shelter, protection from the elements.

*A satisfied need is not a motivator of behavior!* This is a fact of profound significance that is regularly ignored in the conventional approach to the management of people. Consider your own need for air: Except as you are deprived of it, it has no appreciable motivating effect upon your behavior.

# SAFETY NEEDS

When the physiological needs are reasonably satisfied, needs at the next higher level begin to dominate man's behavior—to motivate him. These are called *safety needs*. They are needs for protection against danger, threat, deprivation. Some people mistakenly refer to these as needs for security. However, unless man is in a dependent relationship where he fears arbitrary deprivation, he does not demand security. The need is for the "fairest possible break." When he is confident of this, he is more than willing to take risks. But when he feels threatened or dependent, his greatest need is for guarantees, for protection, for security.

The fact needs little emphasis that, since every industrial employee is in a dependent relationship, safety needs may assume considerable importance. Arbitrary management actions, behavior which arouses uncertainty with respect to continued employment or which reflects favoritism or discrimination, unpredictable administration of policy—these can be powerful motivators of the safety needs in the employment relationship *at every level*, from worker to vice president.

# SOCIAL NEEDS

When man's physiological needs are satisfied and he is no longer fearful about his physical welfare, his *social needs* become important motivators of his behavior—needs for belonging, for association, for acceptance by his fellows, for giving and receiving friendship and love.

Management knows today of the existence of these needs, but it often assumes quite wrongly that they represent a threat to the organization. Many studies have demonstrated that the tightly knit, cohesive work group may, under proper conditions, be far more effective than an equal number of separate individuals in achieving organizational goals.

Yet management, fearing group hostility to its own objectives, often goes to considerable lengths to control and direct human efforts in ways that are inimical to the natural "groupiness" of human beings. When man's social needs—and perhaps his safety needs, too—are thus thwarted, he behaves in ways which tend to defeat organizational objectives. He becomes resistant, antagonistic, uncooperative. But this behavior is a consequence, not a cause.

# EGO NEEDS

Above the social needs—in the sense that they do not become motivators until lower needs are reasonably satisfied—are the needs of greatest significance to management and to man himself. They are the *egoistic needs*, and they are of two kinds:

1. Those needs that relate to one's self-esteem—needs for self-confidence, for independence, for achievement, for competence, for knowledge.

2. Those needs that relate to one's reputation—needs for status, for recognition, for appreciation, for the deserved respect of one's fellows.

Unlike the lower needs, these are rarely satisfied; man seeks indefinitely for more satisfaction of these needs once they have become important to him. But they do not appear in any significant way until physiological, safety, and social needs are all reasonably satisfied.

The typical industrial organization offers few opportunities for the satisfaction of these egoistic needs to people at lower levels in the hierarchy. The conventional methods of organizing work, particularly in mass-production industries, give little heed to these aspects of human motivation. If the practices of scientific management were deliberately calculated to thwart these needs, they could hardly accomplish this purpose better than they do.

# SELF-FULFILLMENT NEEDS

Finally—a capstone, as it were, on the hierarchy of man's needs—there are what we may call the *needs for self-fulfillment*. These are the needs for realizing one's own potentialities, for continued self-development, for being creative in the broadest sense of that term.

It is clear that the conditions of modern life give only limited opportunity for these relatively weak needs to obtain expression. The deprivation most people experience with respect to other lower-level needs diverts their energies into the struggle to satisfy *those* needs, and the needs for self-fulfillment remain dormant.

# MANAGEMENT AND MOTIVATION

We recognize readily enough that a man suffering from a severe dietary deficiency is sick. The deprivation of physiological needs has behavioral consequences. The same is true—although less well recognized—of deprivation of higher-level needs. The man whose needs for safety, association, independence, or status are thwarted is sick just as surely as the man who has rickets. And his sickness will have behavioral consequences. We will be mistaken if we attribute his resultant passivity, his hostility, his refusal to accept responsibility to his inherent "human nature." These forms of behavior are *symptoms* of illness—of deprivation of his social and egoistic needs.

The man whose lower-level needs are satisfied is not motivated to satisfy those needs any longer. For practical purposes they exist no longer. Management often asks, "Why aren't people more productive? We pay good wages, provide good working conditions, have excellent fringe benefits and steady employment. Yet people do not seem to be willing to put forth more than minimum effort."

The fact that management has provided for these physiological and safety needs has shifted the motivational emphasis to the social and perhaps to the egoistic needs. Unless there are opportunities at *work* to satisfy these higher-level needs, people will be deprived, and their behavior will reflect this deprivation. Under such conditions, if management continues to focus its attention on physiological needs, its efforts are bound to be ineffective.

People *will* make insistent demands for more money under these conditions. It becomes more important than ever to buy the material goods and services which can provide limited satisfaction of the thwarted needs. Although money has only limited value in satisfying many higher-level needs, it can become the focus of interest if it is the *only* means available.

## THE CARROT-AND-STICK APPROACH

The carrot-and-stick theory of motivation (like Newtonian physical theory) works reasonably well under certain circumstances. The *means* for satisfying man's physiological and (within limits) his safety needs can be provided or withheld by management. Employment itself is such a means, and so are wages, working conditions, and benefits. By these means the individual can be controlled so long as he is struggling for subsistence.

But the carrot-and-stick theory does not work at all once man has reached an adequate subsistence level and is motivated primarily by higher needs. Management cannot provide a man with self-respect, or with the respect of his fellows, or with the satisfaction of needs for self-fulfillment. It can create such conditions that he is encouraged and enabled to seek such satisfactions for *himself*, or it can thwart him by failing to create those conditions.

But this creation of conditions is not "control." It is not a good device for directing behavior. And so management finds itself in an odd position. The high standard of living created by our modern technological know-how provides quite adequately for the satisfaction of physiological and safety needs. The only significant exception is where management practices have not created confidence in a "fair break"—and thus where safety needs are thwarted. But by making possible the satisfaction of low-level needs, management has deprived itself of the ability to use as motivators the devices on which conventional theory has taught it to rely on—rewards, promises, incentives, or threats and other coercive devices.

The philosophy of management by direction and control—*regardless of whether it is hard or soft*—is inadequate to motivate because the human needs on which this approach relies are today unimportant motivators of behavior. Direction and control are essentially useless in motivating people whose important needs are social and egoistic. Both the hard and the soft approach fail today because they are simply irrelevant to the situation.

People, deprived of opportunities to satisfy at work the needs which are important to them, behave exactly as we might predict—with indolence, passivity, resistance to change, lack of responsibility, willingness to follow the demagogue, unreasonable demands for economic benefits. It would seem that we are caught in a web of our own weaving.

## A NEW THEORY OF MANAGEMENT

For these and many other reasons, we require a different theory of the task of managing people based on more adequate assumptions about human nature and human motivation. I am going to be so bold as to suggest the broad dimensions of such a theory. Call it "Theory Y," if you will.

1.  Management is responsible for organizing the elements of productive enterprise—money, materials, equipment, people—in the interest of economic ends.

2.  People are *not* by nature passive or resistant to organizational needs. They have become so as a result of experience in organizations.

3.  The motivation, the potential for development, the capacity for assuming responsibility, the readiness to direct behavior toward organizational goals are all present in people.  Management does not put them there.  It is a responsibility of management to make it possible for people to recognize and develop these human characteristics for themselves.

4.  The essential task of management is to arrange organizational conditions and methods of operation so that people can achieve their own goals *best* by directing *their own* efforts toward organizational objectives.

This is a process primarily of creating opportunities, releasing potential, removing obstacles, encouraging growth, providing guidance.  It is what Peter Drucker has called "management by objectives" in contrast to "management by control."  It does *not* involve the abdication of management, the absence of leadership, the lowering of standards, or the other characteristics usually associated with the "soft" approach under Theory X.

## SOME DIFFICULTIES

It is no more possible to create an organization today which will be a full, effective application of this theory than it was to build an atomic power plant in 1945.  There are many formidable obstacles to overcome.

The conditions imposed by conventional organization theory and by the approach of scientific management for the past half century have tied men to limited jobs which do not utilize their capabilities, have discouraged the acceptance of responsibility, have encouraged passivity, have eliminated meaning from work.  Man's habits, attitudes, expectations—his whole conception of membership in an industrial organization—have been conditioned by his experience under these circumstances.

People today are accustomed to being directed, manipulated, controlled in industrial organizations and to finding satisfaction for their social, egoistic, and self-fulfillment needs away from the job.  This is true of much of management as well as of workers.  Genuine "industrial citizenship"—to borrow again a term from Drucker—is a remote and unrealistic idea, the meaning of which has not even been considered by most members of industrial organizations.

Another way of saying this is that Theory X places exclusive reliance upon external control of human behavior, while Theory Y relies heavily on self-control and self-direction.  It is worth noting that this difference is the difference between treating people as children and treating them as mature adults.  After generations of the former, we cannot expect to shift to the latter overnight.

## STEPS IN THE RIGHT DIRECTION

Before we are overwhelmed by the obstacles, let us remember that the application of theory is always slow.  Progress is usually achieved in small steps.  Some innovative ideas which are entirely consistent with Theory Y are today being applied with some success.

## Decentralization and Delegation

There are ways of freeing people from the too-close control of conventional organization, giving them a degree of freedom to direct their own activities, to assume responsibility, and, importantly, to satisfy their egoistic needs. In this connection, the flat organization of Sears, Roebuck and Company provides an interesting example. It forces "management by objectives," since it enlarges the number of people reporting to a manager until he cannot direct and control them in the conventional manner.

## Job Enlargement

This concept, pioneered by I.B.M. and Detroit Edison, is quite consistent with Theory Y. It encourages the acceptance of responsibility at the bottom of the organization; it provides opportunities for satisfying social and egoistic needs. In fact, the reorganization of work at the factory level offers one of the more challenging opportunities for innovation consistent with Theory Y.

## Participation and Consultative Management

Under proper conditions, participation and consultative management provide encouragement to people to direct their creative energies toward organizational objectives, give them some voice in decisions that affect them, provide significant opportunities for the satisfaction of social and egoistic needs. The Scanlon Plan is the outstanding embodiment of these ideas in practice.

## Performance Appraisal

Even a cursory examination of conventional programs of performance appraisal within the ranks of management will reveal how completely consistent they are with Theory X. In fact, most such programs tend to treat the individual as though he were a product under inspection on the assembly line.

A few companies—among them General Mills, Ansul Chemical, and General Electric—have been experimenting with approaches which involve the individual in setting "targets" or objectives for *himself* and in a *self*-evaluation of performance semiannually or annually. Of course, the superior plays an important leadership role in this process—one, in fact, which demands substantially more competence than the conventional approach. The role is, however, considerably more congenial to many managers than the role of "judge" or "inspector" which is usually forced upon them. Above all, the individual is encouraged to take a greater responsibility for planning and appraising his own contribution to organizational objectives; and the accompanying effects on egoistic and self-fulfillment needs are substantial.

## APPLYING THE IDEAS

The not infrequent failure of such ideas as these to work as well as expected is often attributable to the fact that a management has "bought the idea" but applied it within the framework of Theory X and its assumptions.

Delegation is not an effective way of exercising management by control. Participation becomes a farce when it is applied as a sales gimmick or a device for kidding people into thinking they are important. Only the management that has confidence in human capacities and is itself directed toward organizational objectives rather than toward the preservation of personal power can grasp the implications of this emerging theory. Such management will find and apply successfully other innovative ideas as we move slowly toward the full implementation of a theory like Y.

## THE HUMAN SIDE OF ENTERPRISE

It is quite possible for us to realize substantial improvements in the effectiveness of industrial organizations during the next decade or two. The social sciences can contribute much to such developments; we are only beginning to grasp the implications of the growing body of knowledge in these fields. But if this conviction is to become a reality instead of a pious hope, we will need to view the process much as we view the process of releasing the energy of the atom for constructive human ends—as a slow, costly, sometimes discouraging approach toward a goal which would seem to many to be quite unrealistic.

The ingenuity and the perseverance of industrial management in the pursuit of economic ends have changed many scientific and technological dreams into commonplace realities. It has now become clear that the application of these same talents to the human side of enterprise will not only enhance substantially these materialistic achievements, but will bring us one step closer to "the good society."

# 3

# Individual and Organizational Learning

R&D ORGANIZATIONS AS LEARNING SYSTEMS
*Barbara Carlsson*
*Peter Keane*
*J. Bruce Martin*

THE LEADER'S NEW WORK: BUILDING LEARNING ORGANIZATIONS
*Peter M. Senge*

BUILDING A LEARNING ORGANIZATION
*David A. Garvin*

# R&D ORGANIZATIONS AS LEARNING SYSTEMS

*Barbara Carlsson*
*Peter Keane*
*J. Bruce Martin*

In comparison with the relatively systematic, logical, and planned process of some organizations, R&D processes often appear to be disorderly and unpredictable—difficult, if not impossible, to manage. However, the hypothesis that the primary output of R&D is *knowledge* (incorporated in formulas and specifications) suggests that its major process is *learning*. We have confirmed that, when R&D activities are viewed as part of a learning process, much of what appears disorderly is seen to have an underlying order. Furthermore, we have determined that this perspective is useful for describing, understanding, and improving the R&D process.

Linear models of technical innovation may be useful in describing key steps in the R&D process and in documenting projects after the fact but are not particularly helpful in understanding the process

*Source*: Reprinted by permission of the authors and publisher from *Sloan Management Review*, Spring, 1976.

The authors are indebted to David A. Kolb, whose work has provided the foundation for this paper, and to Richard Beckhard, who introduced us to Kolb and encouraged our work.

in real time. Linear models can describe what happened but not how it happened, and tend to reinforce the belief in a kind of orderliness which does not exist (see Figure 1).[1]

FIGURE 1   Linear Models of Technical Innovation

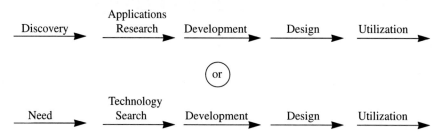

The model we *have* found to be descriptive of the way learning occurs in R&D organizations is based on D. A. Kolb's work on individual experiential learning.[2] Kolb postulates a four-step repetitive cycle, which provides the framework for the model shown in Figure 2. This cycle is summarized as follows:

> Immediate concrete experience is the basis for observation and reflection. These observations are assimilated into a "theory" from which new implications for action can be deduced. These implications, or hypotheses, then serve as guides in acting to create new experiences.[3]

We have generalized Kolb's work, which focuses on the individual learning process, to the organizational learning process.

Kolb's learning process requires orientations that are polar opposites: active and reflective; concrete and abstract. The shifting orientation results in four kinds of activity, each of which is required at some stage of the learning process.

1. *Divergence* (concrete and reflective). This kind of activity is required to seek background information and sense opportunities, investigate new patterns, recognize discrepancies and problems, and generate alternatives. Literature Browsing and Brainstorming are techniques which may be used to aid this kind of activity.

2. *Assimilation* (abstract and reflective). This kind of activity is required to develop theory, compare alternatives, establish criteria, formulate plans and hypotheses, and define problems. Grounded Theory techniques are designed to aid this kind of activity.[4]

3. *Convergence* (abstract and active). This kind of activity is required to select among alternatives, focus efforts, evaluate plans and programs, test hypotheses, and make decisions. Venture Analysis techniques are designed to aid this kind of activity.

---

[1]This paper is no exception. The relatively orderly description of our research bears little resemblance to the actual cycling and recycling, false starts, definition and redefinition of hypotheses and objectives which occurred. However, Harvard Business School Professor Charles J. Christenson has described God as "using an inelegant method to design the world but cleaning up His approach in the published version." At least we are in good company.

[2]See Kolb [6].

[3]See Kolb [6], p. 2

[4]See Glaser and Strauss [3].

FIGURE 2   The Learning Model

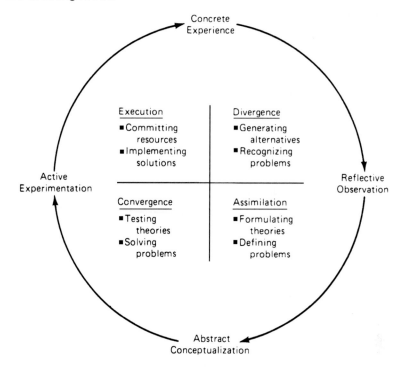

4.   Execution[5] (concrete and active).  This kind of activity is required to advocate positions or ideas, set objectives, commit to schedules, commit resources, and implement decisions.  PERT and Critical Path Scheduling are techniques frequently used to aid this kind of activity.

Organizations differ in their capabilities for performing the tasks associated with each of the stages.  There are predictable strengths associated with an appropriate skill level in each stage and there are predictable weaknesses associated with either an excess or a deficiency in any stage.  Figure 3 on page 69 outlines some of these strengths and weaknesses.

## EXPERIMENTAL VALIDATION

In a series of experiments, we have demonstrated that the Learning Method provides a useful description of the R&D process in a way which permits strengths and weaknesses to be assessed, identifies bottlenecks, and provides cues to remedial action.  We asked R&D managers what factors inhibited

---

[5]We have chosen the term "Execution" rather than "Accommodation," the more precise term used by Kolb, as the label for this stage of the Learning Model.  We have found that the term "Accommodation" is frequently misunderstood because of its connotations of passivity and compromise.

innovation in their individual areas. We found that most of their responses fit into the patterns of strengths of weaknesses predicted in Figure 3 on the following page. The following are a few examples.

| Comment | Corresponding Strength or Weakness |
| --- | --- |
| "We're not idea poor, but we do need people to push ideas." | Strength in divergence<br>Lack of execution |
| "Timetables are sometimes too tight to let people explore." | Excessive execution<br>Too little divergence |
| "We execute well; we need to develop ideas." | Sufficient execution<br>Too little divergence |
| "We allow ourselves to be diffuse; we need more focus." | Lack of convergence |
| "We lack conceptualization–fitting all the elements into a full concept." | Lack of assimilation |
| "We lack good ideas." | Lack of divergence |

These data not only suggest that major elements of the R&D process can be expressed in terms of the Learning Model, but also confirm that organizations can develop "flat spots" which may be described in terms of the Learning Model.

In another experiment, we devised a scheme for scoring biweekly progress reports which are written by professional members of our organizations.[6] For each report, this scoring scheme provided a measure of the effort in each stage of the learning process. We applied this scoring scheme to several series of reports written by individual staff members. Our findings, which are summarized below, support our hypothesis that the Learning Model is descriptive of the dynamics of R&D projects.

1.   Most of the subjects appeared to be following a clockwise sequence through the stages of the Learning Model; that is, a report scoring relatively high in Assimilation was likely to be followed by a report high in Execution, etc.

2.   A researcher who had no familiarity with the content of the reports or with the authors could from the scores alone predict with accuracy the strengths and weaknesses of the projects. For example, from a series of scores indicating consistently high levels of Assimilation and Execution, and consistently low levels of Divergence and Convergence, one of the researchers correctly predicted that the project would be suffering from a lack of creativity (Divergence) and lack of focusing and testing of hypotheses (Convergence) prior to execution of new activities, and that these deficiencies could result in executions that failed without adding to understanding.

3.   The effect of management interventions could be observed in the scores. For example, late in the project cited above there was a sharp but temporary shift into the Convergence stage. Although we observed the shift, we did not know its cause. Subsequent discussions with the manager revealed that the shift was the result of his probing questions about their research design, and confirmed his fear that the effect of his action had been only temporary.

[6]The scoring system was quite complex and specific to the particular reports which were being evaluated. The system consisted essentially of assigning each sentence to a stage of the Learning Model, and totaling the number of sentences in each stage. We are grateful to Sherry Ewald and Paula Miller for their efforts in the sometimes arduous task of scoring the documents.

Figure 3    Strengths and Weaknesses

Concrete<br>Experience

| | | | |
|---|---|---|---|
| **Execution** | | **Divergence** | |
| Strength: | Accomplishment<br>Goal-orientated action | Strength: | Generation of<br>alternatives<br>Creativity |
| Excess: | Trivial improvements<br>Tremendous accom-<br>plishment of the<br>wrong thing | Excess: | Paralyzed by<br>alternatives |
| Deficiency: | Work not completed<br>on time<br>Not directed to goals | Deficiency: | Inability to recognize<br>problems/opportunities<br>Idea poor |

Active                                                             Reflective

Experimentation                                             Observation

| | | | |
|---|---|---|---|
| **Convergence** | | **Assimilation** | |
| Strength: | Design<br>Decision making | Strength: | Planning<br>Formulating theory |
| Excess: | Premature closure<br>Solving the wrong<br>problem | Excess: | Castles in the air<br>No practical<br>application |
| Deficiency: | No focus to work<br>Theories not tested<br>Poor experimental<br>design | Deficiency: | No theoretical basis<br>for work<br>Unable to learn from<br>mistakes |

Abstract<br>Conceptualization

In a third experiment we collected historical data on the progress of a project and extended the data into real time by periodic interviews with members of the project team. We found that key steps in the progress of the project could be interpreted as representing a clockwise sequence through the Learning Model as shown in Figure 4. A list of the activities involved with the project (corresponding to the numbers on the diagram) and a list of the information inputs which occurred during the project (corresponding to the letters on the diagram) follow Figure 4. Critical examination of this analysis by other project managers and their higher-level R&D managers confirmed that the model represented the realities of the project. The higher-level managers were particularly reassured by the sense of order given to a set of events that had not seemed nearly so orderly at the time.

We have subsequently analyzed other projects in the same manner and found less orderly progression around the model. We found instances of stages being skipped, of project teams "stuck" in a stage, and even instances of reverse (i.e., counterclockwise) movement through the stages. The managers involved generally agreed that the pictures were accurate and that the deviations indicated problems deserving of management attention.

69

## USE OF THE MODEL

We can testify to the usefulness of the Learning Model from our own experience. Our individual strengths are in different stages of the model and our efforts to work together often involved more conflict that the task seemed to warrant. As we learned more about the Learning Model, we each developed an appreciation of the contributions of the other members of our group. Our working relationships are greatly improved; now if we find ourselves pulling in different directions, we refer to the Model for resolution.

FIGURE 4 Project History in Terms of the Learning Model

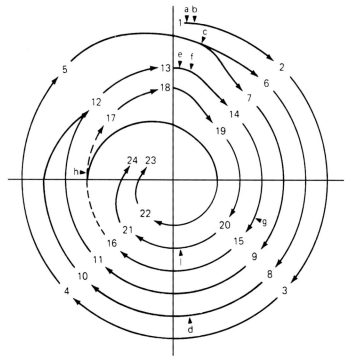

List of the Activities for Figure 4

1. Planning activity initiated by a management question: "What businesses should this division be in?"
2. Generation of nine alternatives.
3. Establishment of criteria for selection made jointly with marketing.
4. Evaluation of the nine alternatives against the criteria resulting in the selection of three projects to pursue.
5. Assignment of staff to activate three projects, one of which is the subject of this study.
6. Identifying the options for positioning the product in the market.
7. Identifying the potential process routes to making the product.
8. Establishing the criteria for deciding the competitive targets.
9. Examining standing criteria in the division for choice of processes, and weighting flexibility higher than normal for this project.
10. Deciding on the specific objective for this product.

11. Choosing the process route to be developed.
12. Making the product and placing a consumer test.
13. Obtaining consumer test results that confirmed that the product targets had been met.
14. Generation of alternatives for obtaining a more favorable economic position in the marketplace.
15. Analyzing the alternatives from the standpoint of the user.
16. Selection of the specific target and the attribute to be optimized.
17. Making the product and placing a consumer test. (The path from 16 to 17 is shown as a broken line because the work was incomplete, i.e., the consumer test was placed without having the optimum product.)
18. Obtaining and analyzing consumer test results which were worse than predicted.
19. Generation of alternatives for the project in view of the outcome of the consumer test.
20. Reexamination of criteria.
21. Optimizing product/process variables.
22. Specifying the process details for the test market production and trimming costs to fit within the appropriation. (The path from "h" to 22 is shown as a solid line, because the intervening steps were obviously taken even though they were not specified as activities, e.g., each item of cost was questioned and trimmed if not justified.)
23. Meeting specific requirements for the test market plant.
24. Meeting product and placing next consumer test.

List of the Information Inputs for Figure 4

a. Management input—desire to capitalize on a new technology and desire to be of service to society.
b. Consumer input—a generally recognized, unmet consumer need.
c. Technical input—temporary transfer in of a scientist familiar with the new technology.
d. Marketing input—desired product target.
e. Economic input—cost estimate for test market plant much higher than expected.
f. Management input—in view of the projected costs, the business opportunity is seen as unattractive.
g. Marketing input—proposal for new product targets.
h. Management input—appropriation for test market (much lower than original estimate).
i. Management input—top management confirmation of overall market strategy and requirements.

In the course of our experiments, we have exposed the Learning Model to a large number of R&D managers and project team members, and have received responses suggesting that the Model also has been useful to them. Sharing the Learning Model with others in our organization has been most productive when we have communicated the *concept*, and allowed others to discover applications for themselves. Kolb has developed a Learning Style Inventory which we have found very useful in these discussions.[7] The Learning Style Inventory is a brief pencil-and-paper test which give the subject an indication of his preference for activity in each of the stages of the Learning Model. Members of work teams who shared their individual results have invariably found important differences among

[7]Kolb [5] describes the development of the Learning Style Inventory, which has been published in Kolb, Rubin, and McIntyre [7].

themselves, and usually came quickly to understand how these differences in "Learning Style" have influenced their process of working together. Individuals who prefer Execution are likely to be impatient with Assimilation, and Divergers are likely to find Convergers stodgy and stifling of creativity. An understanding of individual differences has generally led to an interest in understanding the Learning Model, which has in turn led to the kinds of learning and applications reported below.

One project team had been having difficulty in understanding why the character of their interactions with each other shifted sharply from meeting to meeting. In some meetings they found themselves open to new ideas, free to raise questions, and valuing the inputs of other members. In other meetings they found themselves rejecting new ideas, making few significant comments on each other's work, and generally rejecting those ideas which were offered. After being exposed to the Learning Model, they realized that the first condition prevailed when the project was in a Divergence stage, and the latter occurred when the project required Convergence or Execution.

Discussions with the manager of the same project team provided the basis for a new concept of the role of the project manager. A traditional manager's role has been viewed primarily as one of planning, organizing, directing and controlling. When organizations are viewed as learning systems, the manager's role can be viewed as one of providing leadership in the learning process. The following observations developed out of our conversations with the manager of this team.

1.   When the development of a product is going smoothly, the manager's role will involve thinking and planning about the next stage, and will be 90° to 135° ahead of that of the team members. For example, if the team is engaged in Execution, the manager will be thinking about the possible alternatives for the project when the results of Execution are known; if the team is engaged in idea generation, the manager's role will involve thinking about the criteria for solution. By concentrating on what is to come, the manager exerts a useful pull on the project.

2.   In time of crisis, when the team is finding it difficult to move through the learning cycle, the role requires the manager to move into the same stage as the project team. For example, the manager may work with the team to develop theories to explain an unexpected result or to help in the pilot plan when there is a critical deadline.

3.   The manager must take care that he does not move too far ahead of the project team, thus not only losing sensitivity to their current problems but also confusing them with regard to the path they should take. The manager should avoid pulling the team *across* the Model instead of *around* it.

This same manager used his knowledge of the work team process and his understanding of his role of leadership in the learning process to devise a special plan for supporting the work of one of the team members. The team member had come forward with a proposal to investigate some leads which might result in options which would be alternative or supplemental to those which the team was soon to execute. The manager recognized the merits of the proposal but also recognized that the team member was proposing to involve himself deeply in the Divergence stage of the Model, while the rest of the team was involved in the Convergence of the rest of the team: "I built a fence around the Divergence quadrant and told him to stay in it and the others to stay out." He thus encouraged and supported the team member's independent pursuit of the learning process until it came into phase with the learning process of the rest of the team.

In still another instance, a group of technical information specialists found the model useful in suggesting ways they could increase their effectiveness in providing technical information to project teams. They realized that the information needs of project teams vary according to the stage of the learning process as shown below.[8]

---

[8]Thomas J. Allen (private communications) has suggested that the information needs of R&D projects vary with the kind of project (e.g., research, service, engineering) and with the maturity of the project.

| Stage | Activity | Information Need |
|---|---|---|
| Divergence | Generation of alternatives | Specific Alternatives |
| | Creativity | Stimulation of the process of generating alternatives (e.g., information about Brainstorming) |
| | Problem/opportunity sensing | State of the art |
| | | State of the world |
| Assimilation | Planning | Policy |
| | Formulating theory | Planning methodology |
| | | Strategy models |
| | Establishing criteria | Evaluation criteria |
| Convergence | Interpretation of data | Screening/selection techniques |
| | Narrowing down alternatives | |
| | Design of experiments | Experimental design |
| | Evaluation of outcome | |
| Execution | Execution of plan | Feedback on results (Monitoring techniques) |
| | Implementation of decision | |
| | Goal setting | Information on need |

## IMPLICATIONS FOR MANAGEMENT OF R&D

The Learning Model provides a basis for several kinds of action which can be taken by management to improve the R&D process.

*Staffing decisions can be made in light of the Learning Model.* The assignment of individuals with requisite skills in each of the stages of the learning process should result in improving that process. The balance of skills required is likely to shift over the course of a project. In the earliest cycles through the learning process (e.g., during concept and prototype development), skills in the Divergence and Assimilation stages are likely to be most critical. Later (e.g., when the design is fixed and engineering specifications are being prepared) skills in Convergence and Execution become most critical. Shifts in assignment of individuals during the project life may, in some instances, not only improve the progress of the project, but also permit individuals to have assignments which match their preferences and abilities.[9]

*Organization policies and reward systems can be used to support an appropriate balance of learning activities.* It is our observation (which is supported by research reported by Kolb[10]) that organizations and professional disciplines often develop values which favor activity in one learning stage over the others. When these values are out of balance with the needs of the organization the kinds of problems outlined in Figure 3 can result. Managers can help restore appropriate balance.

---

[9]We caution against the assumption that the learning preferences of individuals are fixed. It has been our observation that for many individuals learning style preference is highly situational.

[10]See Kolb [6].

*Specific problems can be identified and strategies for remedial action suggested by reference to the Learning Model.* The most common specific problems, we expect, will arise when an individual or team is either stuck in or deficient in a learning stage. Some of the techniques which can be used in these situations are shown in Figure 5.

FIGURE 5   Intervention Strategies

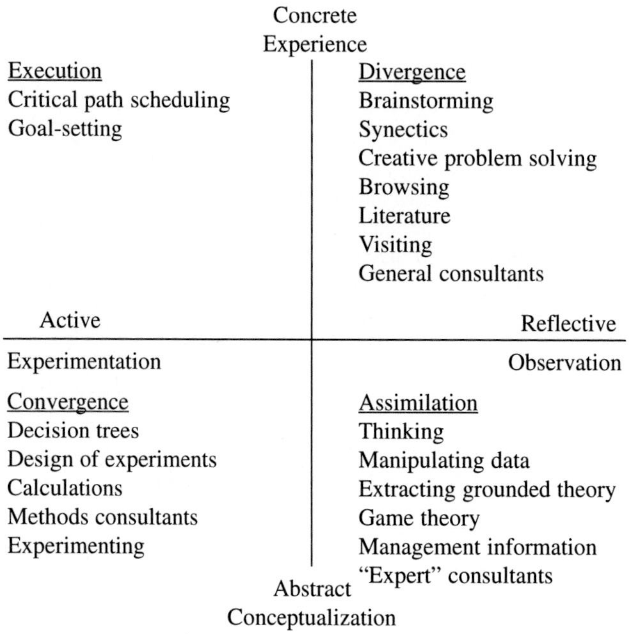

```
                              Concrete
                             Experience
        Execution                 │    Divergence
        Critical path scheduling  │    Brainstorming
        Goal-setting              │    Synectics
                                  │    Creative problem solving
                                  │    Browsing
                                  │    Literature
                                  │    Visiting
                                  │    General consultants

        Active                    │                    Reflective
    Experimentation ──────────────┼──────────────────── Observation

        Convergence               │    Assimilation
        Decision trees            │    Thinking
        Design of experiments     │    Manipulating data
        Calculations              │    Extracting grounded theory
        Methods consultants       │    Game theory
        Experimenting             │    Management information
                                  │    "Expert" consultants
                             Abstract
                          Conceptualization
```

## IMPLICATIONS BEYOND R&D ORGANIZATIONS

We believe the experience of the technical information specialists can be generalized to many other support organizations. For example, management science groups are sometimes seen as only helpful in decision making (Convergence), and even then only when risks can be quantified and defined.[11] Another view suggests that management science can provide benefits much more broadly.[12] We believe that the ability of management scientists to provide these benefits is dependent upon their sensitivity to the stage of the learning cycle of the organization (or individuals) they are supporting. The table below relates Hammond's categories of benefits to the corresponding stages of the Learning Model.

[11]For example, see Arcand [1].
[12]For example, see Hammond [4].

| Potential Benefits of Management Science* | Corresponding Stage of the Learning Model |
|---|---|
| 1. Provides a structure for a situation which is initially relatively unstructured to the manager. | Assimilation |
| 2. Extends the decision maker's information processing ability. | Divergence |
| 3. Facilitates concept formation. | Assimilation |
| 4. Provides cues to the decision maker. | Assimilation/Convergence |
| 5. Stimulates the collection, organization, and utilization of data which might not otherwise be collected. | Divergence |
| 6. Frees from mental set. | Divergence/Assimilation |

*The list of benefits is taken directly from Hammond [4], pp. 9–11.

While our research and applications have been almost entirely within R&D systems, we believe the Learning Model has parallel applications in other kinds of systems. The importance of the Model to an organization will be proportionate to the importance of production of new knowledge as an organizational goal. To the extent that technical, social, and political turbulence is forcing even the most stable organizations and institutions to adopt a learning orientation if they are to survive, we expect the Learning Model to be increasingly useful.[13]

## REFERENCES

1. Arcand, C. G., "Bureaucratic Innovation: The Failure of Rationality," *Chemtech*, 1975, pp. 710–714.
2. Bennis, W. G., and Slater, P. E., *The Temporary Society,* New York: Harper & Row, 1968.
3. Glaser, B. B., and Strauss, A. L., *The Discovery of Grounded Theory: Strategies for Qualitative Research*, Chicago: Aldine Publishing Company, 1967.
4. Hammond, J. S. "The Roles of the Manager and Management Scientist in Successful Implementation." *Sloan Management Review*, Winter 1974, pp. 1-24.
5. Kolb, D. A., *The Learning Style Inventory: Technical Manual*, Boston, Mass.: McBer and Co., 1976.
6. Kolb, D. A., Rubin, I. M., and McIntyre, J. M., *Organization Psychology: An Experiential Approach*, 2nd ed. Englewood Cliffs, N.J.: Prentice-Hall, 1974, pp. 23–25.
7. Schein, E. H., *Organizational Psychology*, Englewood Cliffs, N.J.: Prentice-Hall, 1965.
8. Schon, D. A., *Beyond the Stable State,* New York: Random House, 1971.

[13]For example, see Bennis and Slater [2], Schon [8], and the discussion of the "adaptive-coping cycle" appearing in Schein [7].

# THE LEADER'S NEW WORK: BUILDING LEARNING ORGANIZATIONS

*Peter M. Senge*

Human beings are designed for learning. No one has to teach an infant to walk, or talk, or master the spatial relationships needed to stack eight building blocks that don't topple. Children come fully equipped with an insatiable drive to explore and experiment. Unfortunately the primary institutions of our society are oriented predominately toward controlling rather than learning, rewarding individuals for performing for others rather than for cultivating their natural curiosity and impulse to learn. The young child entering school discovers quickly that the name of the game is getting the right answer and avoiding mistakes—a mandate no less compelling to the aspiring manager.

"Our prevailing system of management has destroyed our people," writes W. Edwards Deming, leader in the quality movement.[1] "People are born with intrinsic motivation, self-esteem, dignity, curiosity to learn, joy in learning. The forces of destruction begin with toddlers—a prize for the best Halloween costume, grades in school, gold stars, and up on through the university. On the job, people, teams, divisions are ranked—reward for the one at the top, punishment at the bottom. MBO, quotas, incentive pay, business plans, put together separately, division by division, cause further loss, unknown and unknowable."

Ironically, by focusing on performing for someone else's approval, corporations create the very conditions that predestine them to mediocre performance. Over the long run, superior performance depends on superior learning. A Shell study showed that, according to former planning director Arie de Geus, "a full one-third of the Fortune ' 500' industrials listed in 1970 has vanished by 1983."[2] Today, the average lifetime of the largest industrial enterprises is probably less than *half* the average lifetime of a person in an industrial society. On the other hand, de Geus and his colleagues at Shell also found a small number of companies that survived for seventy-five years or longer. Interestingly, the key to their survival was the ability to run "experiments in the margin," to continually explore new businesses and organizational opportunities that create potential new sources of growth.

If anything, the need for understanding how organizations learn and accelerating that learning is greater today than ever before. The old days when a Henry Ford, Alfred Sloan, or Tom Watson *learned for the organization* are gone. In an increasingly dynamic, interdependent, and unpredictable world, it is simply no longer possible for anyone to "figure it all out at the top." The old model, "the top thinks and the local acts," must now give way to integrating thinking and acting at all levels. While the challenge is great, so is the potential payoff. "The person who figures out how to harness the collective genius of the people in his or her organization," according to former Citibank CEO Walter Wriston, "is going to blow the competition away."

## Adaptive Learning and Generative Learning.

The prevailing view of learning organizations emphasizes increased adaptability. Given the accelerating pace of change, or so the standard view goes, "the most successful corporation of the 1990s," according to *Fortune* magazine, "will be something called a learning organization, a consummately adaptive enterprise."[3] As the Shell study shows, examples of traditional authoritarian bureaucracies that responded too slowly to survive in changing business environments are legion.

But increasing adaptiveness is only the first stage in moving toward learning organizations. The impulse to learn in children goes deeper than desire to respond and adapt more effectively to environmental change. The impulse to learn, at its heart, is an impulse to be generative, to expand our capability. This is why leading corporations are focusing on *generative* learning, which is about creating, as well as *adaptive* learning, which is about coping.[4]

The total quality movement in Japan illustrates the evolution from adaptive to generative learning. With its emphasis on continuous experimentation and feedback, the total quality movement has been the first wave in building learning organizations. But Japanese firms' view of serving the customer has evolved. In the early years of total quality, the focus was on "fitness to standard," making a product reliably so that it would do what its designers intended it to do and what the firm told its customers it would do. Then came a focus on "fitness to need," understanding better what the customer wanted and then providing products that reliably *met* those needs. Today, leading edge firms seek to understand and meet the "latent need" of customers—what customers might truly value but have never experienced or would never think to ask for. As one Detroit executive commented recently, "You could never produce the Mazda Miata solely from market research. It required a leap of imagination to see what the customer *might* want."[5]

Generative learning, unlike adaptive learning, requires new ways of looking at the world, whether in understanding customers or in understanding how to better manage a business. For years, U.S. manufacturers sought competitive advantage in aggressive controls on inventories, incentive against overproduction, and rigid adherence to production forecasts. Despite these incentives, their performance was eventually eclipsed by Japanese firms who saw the challenges of manufacturing differently. They realized that eliminating delays in the production process was the key to reducing instability and improving cost, productivity, and service. They worked to build networks of relationships with trusted suppliers and to redesign physical production processes so as to reduce delays in materials procurement, production setup, as in—process inventory—a much higher-leverage approach to improving both cost and customer loyalty.

As Boston Consulting Group's George Stalk has observed, the Japanese saw the significance of delays because they see the process of order entry, production scheduling, materials procurement, production, and distribution *as an integrated system.* "What distorts the system so badly is time," observed Stalk—the multiple delays between events and responses. "These distortions reverberate throughout the system, producing disruptions, waste, and inefficiency."[6] Generative learning requires seeing the systems that control events. When we fail to grasp the systematic source of problems, we are left to "push on" symptoms rather than eliminate underlying causes. The best we can ever do is adaptive learning.

## The Leaders New Work

"I talk with people all over the country about learning organizations, and the response is always very positive," says William O'Brien, CEO of the Hanover Insurance companies. "If this type of organization is so widely preferred, why don't people create such organizations? I think the answer is leadership. People have no real comprehension of the type of commitment it requires to build such an organization."[7]

Our traditional view of leaders—as special people who set the direction, make the key decisions, and energize the troops—is deeply rooted in an individualistic and nonsystemic worldview, especially in the West, leaders are *heroes*—great men (and occasionally women) who rise to the fore in times of crisis. So long as such myths prevail, they reinforce a focus on short-term events and charismatic heroes rather than on systematic forces and collective learning.

Leadership in learning organizations centers on subtler and ultimately more important work. In a learning organization, leaders' roles differ dramatically from that of the charismatic decision maker. Leaders are designers, teachers, stewards. These roles require new skills: the ability to build shared vision, to bring to the surface and challenge prevailing mental models, and to foster more systematic patterns of thinking. In short, leaders in learning organizations are responsible for *building organizations* where people are continually expanding their capabilities to shape their future—that is, leaders are responsible for learning.

## CREATIVE TENSION: THE INTEGRATING PRINCIPLE

Leadership in a learning organization starts with the principle of creative tension.[8] Creative tension comes from seeing clearly where we want to be, our "vision," and telling the truth about where we are, our "current reality." The gap between the two generates a natural tension (see Figure 1).

Creative tension can be resolved in two basic ways: by raising current reality toward the vision, or by lowering the vision toward current reality. Individuals, groups, and organizations who learn how to work with creative tension learn how to use the energy it generates to move reality more reliably toward their visions.

The principle of creative tension has long been recognized by leaders. Martin Luther King, Jr., once said, "Just as Socrates felt that it was necessary to create a tension in the mind, so that individuals could rise from the bondage of myths and half truths...so must we...create the kind of tension in society that will help men rise from the dark depths of prejudice and racism."[9]

FIGURE 1   The Principle of Creative Tension

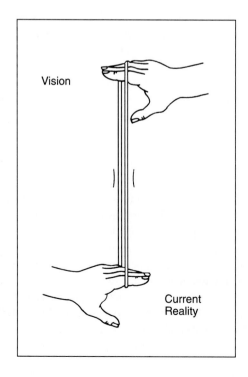

Without vision there is no creative tension. Creative tension cannot be be generated from current reality alone. All the analysis in the world will never generate a vision. Many who are otherwise qualified to lead fail to do so because they try to substitute analysis for vision. They believe that, if only people understood current reality, they would surely feel the motivation to change. They are then disappointed to discover that people "resist" the personal and organizational changes that must be made to alter reality. What they never grasp is that the natural energy for changing reality comes from holding a picture of what might be that is more important to people than what is.

But creative tension cannot be generated from vision alone; it demands an accurate picture of current reality as well. Just as King had a dream, so too did he continually strive to "dramatize the shameful conditions" of racism and prejudice so that they could no longer be ignored. Vision without an understanding of current reality will more likely foster cynicism than creativity. The principle of creative tension teaches that *an accurate picture of current reality is just as important as a compelling picture of a desired future.*

Leading through creative tension is different than solving problems. In problem solving, the energy for change comes from attempting to get away from an aspect of current reality that is undesirable. With creative tension the energy for change comes from the vision, from what we want to create, juxtaposed with current reality. While the distinction may seem small, the consequences are not. Many people and organizations find themselves motivated to change only when their problems are bad enough to cause them change. This works for a while, but the change process runs out of steam as soon as the problems driving the change become less pressing. With problem solving, the motivation for change is extrinsic. With creative tension, the motivation is intrinsic. This distinction mirrors the distinction between adaptive and generative learning.

## NEW ROLES

The traditional authoritarian image of the leader as "the boss calling the shots" has been recognized as oversimplified and inadequate for some time. According to Edgar Schein, "Leadership is intertwined with culture formation." Building an organization's culture and shaping its evolution is the "unique and essential function" of leadership.[10] In a learning organization, the critical roles of leadership— designer, teacher, and steward—have antecedents in the ways leaders have contributed to building organizations in the past. But each role takes on a new meaning in the learning organizations and, as will be seen in the following sections, demands new skills and tools.

### Leader as Designer

Imagine that your organization is an ocean liner and that you are "the leader." What is your role?

I have asked this question of groups of managers many times. The most common answer, not surprisingly, is "the captain." Others say, "The navigator, setting the direction." Still others say, "The helmsman, actually controlling the direction," or, "The engineer down there stroking the fire, providing energy," or, "The social director, making sure everybody's enrolled, involved, and communicating." While these are legitimate leadership roles, there is another which, in many ways, eclipses them all in importance. Yet rarely does anyone mention it.

The neglected leadership role is the *designer* of the ship. No one has a more sweeping influence than the designer. What good does it do for the captain to say, "Turn starboard 30 degrees," when the designer has built a rudder that will only turn to port, or which takes six hours to turn to starboard? It's fruitless to be the leader in an organization that is poorly designed.

The functions of design, or what some have called "social architecture," are rarely visible; they take place behind the scenes. The consequences that appear today are the result of work done long in the past, and work today will show its benefits far in the future. Those who aspire to lead out of a desire to control, or gain fame, or simply to be at the center of the action, will find little to attract them to the quiet design work of leadership.

But what, specifically, is involved in organizational design? "Organizational design is widely misconstrued as moving around boxes and lines," says Hanover's O'Brien. "The first task of organization design concerns designing the governing ideas of purpose, vision, and core values by which people will live." Few acts of leadership have a more enduring impact on an organization than building a foundation of purpose and core values.

In 1982, Johnson & Johnson found itself facing a corporate nightmare when bottles of its best-selling Tylenol were tampered with resulting in several deaths. The corporation's immediate response was to pull all Tylenol off the shelves of retail outlets. Thirty-one million capsules were destroyed, even though they were tested and found safe. Although the immediate cost was significant, no other action was possible given the firm's credo. Authored almost forty years earlier by president Robert Wood Johnson, Johnson & Johnson's credo states that permanent success is possible only when modern industry realizes that:

- service to its customers comes first;
- service to its employees and management comes second;
- service to the community comes third; and
- service to its stockholders, last.

Such statements might seem like motherhood and apple pie to those who have not seen the way a clear sense of purpose and values can affect key business decisions. Johnson & Johnson's crisis management in this case was based on that credo. It was simple, it was right, and it worked.

If governing ideas constitute the first design task of leadership, the second design task involves the policies, strategies, and structures that translate guiding ideas into business decisions. Leadership theorist Philip Selznick calls policy and structure the "institutional embodiment of purpose."[11] "Policy making (the rules that guide decisions) ought to be separated from decision making," says Jay Forrester.[12] "Otherwise, short-term pressures will usurp time from policy creation."

Traditionally, writers like Selznick and Forrester have tended to see policy making and implementation as the work of a small number of senior managers. But that view is changing. Both the dynamic business environment and the mandate of the learning organization to engage people at all levels now make it clear that this second design task is more subtle. Henry Mintzberg has argued that strategy is less a rational plan arrived at in the abstract and implemented throughout the organization than an "emergent phenomenon." Successful organizations "craft strategy" according to Mintzberg, as they continually learn about shifting business conditions and balance what is desired and what is possible.[13] The key is not getting the right strategy but fostering strategic thinking. "The choice of individual action is only part of the policymaker's need," according to Mason and Mitroff.[14] "More important is the need to achieve insight into the nature of the complexity and to formulate concepts and world views for coping with it."

Behind appropriate policies, strategies, and structures are effective learning processes; their creation is the third key design responsibility in learning organizations. This does not absolve senior managers of their strategic responsibilities. Now, they are not only responsible for ensuring that an organization have well-developed strategies and policies, but also for ensuring that processes exist whereby these are continually improved.

In the early 1970s, Shell was the weakest of the big seven oil companies. Today, Shell and Exxon are arguably the strongest, both in size and financial health. Shell's ascendence began with frustration. Around 1971 members of Shell's "Group Planning" in London began to foresee dramatic change and unpredictability in world oil markets. However, it proved impossible to persuade managers that the stable world of steady growth in oil demand and supply they had known for twenty years was about to change. Despite brilliant analysis and artful presentation, Shell's planners realized, in the words of Pierre Wack, that they "had failed to change behavior in much of the Shell organization."[15] Progress would probably have ended there, had the frustration not given way to a radically new view of corporate planning.

As they pondered this failure, the planner's view of their basic task shifted: "We no longer saw our task as producing a documented view of the future business environment five or ten years ahead. Our real target was the microcosm (the 'mental model') of our decision makers." Only when the planners reconceptualized their basic task as fostering learning rather than devising plans did their insights begin to have an impact. The initial tool used was "scenario analysis," through which planners encouraged operating managers to think through how they would manage in the future under different possible scenarios. It mattered not that the managers believed the planners' scenarios absolutely, only that they became engaged in ferreting out the implications. In this way, Shell's planners conditioned managers to be mentally prepared for a shift from low prices to high prices and from stability to instability. The results were significant. When OPEC became a reality, Shell quickly responded by increasing local operating company control (to enhance maneuverability in the new political environment), building buffer stocks, and accelerating development of non-OPEC sources—actions that its competitors took much more slowly or not at all.

Somewhat inadvertently, Shell planners had discovered the leverage of designing institutional learning processes, whereby, in the words of former planning director De Geus, "Management teams change their shared mental models of their company, their markets, and their competitors."[16] Since then, "planning as learning" has become a byword at Shell, and Group Planning has continually sought out new learning tools that can be integrated into the planning process. Some of these are described below.

## Leader as Teacher

"The first responsibility of a leader," writes retired Herman Miller CEO Max de Pree, "is to define reality."[17] Much of the leverage leaders can actually exert lies in helping people achieve more accurate, more insightful, and more *empowering* views of reality.

Leader as teacher does *not* mean leader as authoritarian expert whose job it is to teach people the "correct" view of reality. Rather, it is about helping everyone in the organization, oneself included, to gain more insightful views of current reality. This is in line with a popular emerging view of *leaders* as coaches, guides, or facilitators.[18] In learning organizations, this teaching role is developed further by virtue of explicit attention to people's mental models and by the influence of the system's perspective.

The role of leader as teacher starts with bringing to the surface people's mental models of important issues. No one carries an organization, a market, or a state of technology in his or her head. What we carry in our heads are assumptions. These mental pictures of how the world works have a significant influence on how we perceive problems and opportunities, identify courses of action, and make choices.

One reason that mental models are so deeply entrenched is that they are largely tacit. Ian Mitroff, in his study of General Motors, argues that an assumption that prevailed for years was that, in the United States, "Cars are status symbols. Styling is therefore more important than quality."[19] The Detroit automakers didn't say, "We have a mental model that all people care about is styling." Few actual managers would even say publicly that all people care about is styling. So long as the view remained unexpressed, there was little possibility of challenging its validity or forming more accurate assumptions.

But working with mental models goes beyond revealing hidden assumptions. "Reality," as perceived by most people in most organizations, means pressures that must be borne, crises that must be reacted to, and limitations that must be accepted. Leaders as teachers help people *restructure their views of reality* to see beyond the superficial conditions and events into the underlying causes of problems—and therefore to see new possibilities for shaping the future.

Specifically, leaders can influence people to view reality at three distinct levels: events, patterns of behavior, and systemic structure.

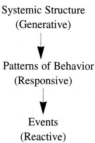

Systemic Structure
(Generative)

Patterns of Behavior
(Responsive)

Events
(Reactive)

The key question becomes *where do leaders predominantly focus their own and their organization's attention?*

Contemporary society focuses predominantly on events. The media reinforces this perspective, with almost exclusive attention to short-term, dramatic events. This focus leads naturally to explaining what happens in terms of those events: "The Dow Jones average went up sixteen points because high fourth-quarter profits were announced yesterday."

Pattern-of-behavior explanations are rarer, in contemporary culture, than event explanations, but they do occur. "Trend analysis" is an example of seeing patterns of behavior. A good editorial that interprets a set of current events in the context of long-term historical changes is another example. Systemic, structural explanations go even further by addressing the questions, "What causes the patterns of behavior?"

In some sense, all three levels of explanation are equally true. But their usefulness is quite different. Event explanations—who did what to whom—doom their holders to a reactive stance toward change. Pattern-of-behavior explanations focus on identifying long-term trends and assessing their implications. They at least suggest how, over time, we can respond to shifting conditions. Structural explanations are the most powerful. Only they address the underlying causes of behavior at a level such that patterns of behavior can be changed.

By and large, leaders of our current institutions focus their attention on events and patterns of behavior, and, under their influence, their organizations do likewise. That is why contemporary organizations are predominantly reactive, or at best responsive—rarely generative. On the other hand, leaders in learning organizations pay attention to all three levels, but focus especially on systemic structure; largely by example, they teach people throughout the organization to do likewise.

## Leader as Steward

This is the subtlest role of leadership. Unlike the roles of designer and teacher, it is almost solely a matter of attitude. It is an attitude critical to learning organizations.

While stewardship has long been recognized as an aspect of leadership, its source is still not widely understood. I believe Robert Greenleaf came closest to explaining real stewardship, in his seminal book *Servant Leadership*.[20] There, Greenleaf argues that "The servant leader is servant *first*...It begins with the natural feeling that one wants to serve, to serve *first*. This conscious choice brings one to aspire to lead. That person is sharply different from one who is leader *first,* perhaps because of the need to assuage an unusual power drive or to acquire material possessions."

Leaders' sense of stewardship operates on two levels: stewardship for the people they lead and stewardship for the larger purpose or mission that underlies the enterprise. The first type arises from a keen appreciation of the impact one's leadership can have on others. People can suffer economically, emotionally, and spiritually under inept leadership. If anything, people in a learning organization are more vulnerable because of their commitment and sense of shared ownership. Appreciating this naturally instills a sense of responsibility in leaders. The second type of stewardship arises from a leader's sense of personal purpose and commitment to the organization's larger mission. People's natural impulse to learn is unleashed when they are engaged in an endeavor they consider worthy of their fullest commitment. Or, as Lawrence Miller puts it, "Achieving return on equity does not, as a goal, mobilize the most noble forces of our soul." [21]

Leaders engaged in building learning organizations naturally feel part of a larger purpose that goes beyond their organization. They are part of changing the way businesses operate, not from a vague philanthropic urge, but from a conviction that their efforts will produce more productive organizations, capable of achieving higher levels of organizational success and personal satisfaction than more traditional organizations. Their sense of stewardship was succinctly captured by George Bernard Shaw when he said,

> This is the true joy in life, the being used for a purpose you consider a mighty one, the being a force of nature rather than a feverish, selfish clod of ailments and grievances complaining that the world will not devote itself to making you happy.

# NEW SKILLS

New leadership roles require new leadership skills. These skills can only be developed, in my judgment, through a lifetime commitment. It is not enough for one or two individuals to develop these skills. They must be distributed widely throughout the organization. This is one reason that understanding the disciplines of a learning organization is so important. These disciplines embody the principles and practices that can widely foster leadership development.

Three critical areas of skills (disciplines) are building shared vision, surfacing and challenging mental models, and engaging in systems thinking.[22]

## Building Shared Vision

How do individual visions come together to create shared visions? A useful metaphor is the hologram, the three-dimensional image created by interacting light sources.

If you cut a photograph in half, each half shows only part of the whole image. But if you divide a hologram, each part, no matter how small, shows the whole image intact. Likewise, when a group of people come to share a vision for an organization, each person sees an individual picture of the organization at its best. Each shares responsibility for the whole, not just for one piece. But the component pieces of the hologram are not identical. Each represents the whole image from a different point of view. It's something like poking holes in a window shade; each hole offers a unique angle for viewing the whole image. So, too is each individual's vision unique.

When you add up the pieces of a hologram, something interesting happens. The image becomes more intense, more lifelike. When more people come to share a vision, the vision becomes more real in the sense of a mental reality that people can truly imagine achieving. They now have partners, co-creators; the vision no longer rests on their shoulders alone. Early on, when they are nurturing an individual vision, people may say it is "my vision." But, as the shared vision develops, it becomes both "my vision" and "our vision."

The skills involved in building shared vision include the following:

- **Encouraging Personal Vision.** Shared visions emerge from personal visions. It is not that people only care about their own self-interest—in fact, people's values usually include dimensions that concern family, organization, community, and even the world. Rather, it is that people's capacity for caring is personal.

- **Communicating and Asking for Support.** Leaders must be willing to continually share their own vision, rather than being the official representative of the corporate vision. They also must be prepared to ask, "Is this the vision worthy of your commitment?" This can be difficult for a person used to setting goals and presuming compliance.

- **Visioning as an Ongoing Process.** Building shared vision is a never-ending process. At any one point there will be a particular image of the future that is predominant, but that image will evolve. Today, too many managers want to dispense with the "vision business" by going off and writing the Official Vision Statement. Such statements almost always lack the vitality, freshness, and excitement of a genuine vision that comes from people asking, "What do we really want to achieve?"

- **Blending Extrinsic and Intrinsic Visions.** Many energizing visions are extrinsic—that is, they focus on achieving something relative to an outsider, such as a competitor. But a goal that is limited to defeating an opponent can, once the vision is achieved, easily become a defensive posture. In contrast, intrinsic goals like creating a new type of product, taking an established product to a new level, or setting a new standard for customer satisfaction can call forth a new level of creativity and innovation. Intrinsic and extrinsic visions need to coexist; a vision solely predicated on defeating an adversary will eventually weaken an organization.

- **Distinguishing Positive from Negative Visions.** Many organizations only truly pull together when their survival is threatened. Similarly, most social movements aim at eliminating what people don't want: for example, anti-drugs, anti-smoking, or anti-nuclear arms movements. Negative visions carry a subtle message of powerlessness: people will only pull together when there is sufficient threat. Negative visions also tend to be short term. Two fundamental sources of energy can motivate organizations: fear and aspiration. Fear, the energy source behind negative visions, can produce extraordinary changes in short periods, but aspiration endures as a continuing source of learning and growth.

## Surfacing and Testing Mental Models

Many of the best ideas in organizations never get put into practice. One reason is that new insights and initiatives often conflict with established mental models. The leadership task of challenging assumptions without invoking defensiveness requires reflection and inquiry skills possessed by a few leaders in traditional controlling organizations.[23]

- **Seeing Leaps of Abstraction.** Our minds literally move at lightning speed. Ironically, this often slows our learning, because we leap to generalizations so quickly that we never think to test them. We then confuse our generalizations with the observable data upon which they are based, treating the generalizations as if they were data. The frustrated sales rep reports to the home office that "customers don't really care about quality, price is what matters," when what actually happened was that three consecutive large customers refused to place an order unless a larger discount was offered. The sales rep treats her generalization, "customers care only about price," as if it were absolute fact rather than an assumption (very likely an assumption reflecting her own views of customers and the market). This thwarts future learning because she starts to focus on how to offer attractive discounts rather than probing behind the customers' statements. For example, the customers may have been so disgruntled with the firm's delivery or customer service that they are unwilling to purchase again without larger discounts.

- **Balancing Inquiry and Advocacy.** Most managers are skilled at articulating their views and presenting them persuasively. While important, advocacy skills can become counterproductive as managers rise in responsibility and confront increasingly complex issues that require collaborative learning among different, equally knowledgeable people. Leaders in learning organizations need to have both inquiry and advocacy skills.[24]

Specifically, when advocating a view, they need to be able to:
   –explain the reasoning and data that led to their view;
   –encourage others to test their view (e.g., Do you see gaps in my reasoning? Do you disagree with the data upon which my view is based?); and
   –encourage others to provide different views (e.g., Do you have either different data, different conclusions, or both?).
When inquiring into another's views, they need to:
   –actively seek to understand the other's view, rather than simply restating their own view and how it differs from the other's view; and
   –make their attributions about the other and the other's view explicit (e.g., Based on your statement that...; I am assuming that you believe...; Am I representing your views fairly?).
If they reach an impasse (others no longer appear open to inquiry), they need to:
   –ask what data or logic might unfreeze the impasse, or if an experiment (or some other inquiry) might be designed to provide new information.

- **Distinguishing Espoused Theory from Theory in Use.** We all like to think that we hold certain views, but often our actions reveal deeper views. For example, I may proclaim that people are trustworthy, but never lend friends money and jealously guard my possessions. Obviously, my deeper mental model (my theory in use), differs from my espoused theory. Recognizing gaps between espoused views and theories in use (which often requires the help of others) can be pivotal to deeper learning.

- **Recognizing and Defusing Defensive Routines.** As one CEO in our research program puts it, "Nobody ever talks about an issue at the 8:00 business meeting exactly the same way they talk about it at home that evening or over drinks at the end of the day." The reason is what Chris Argyris calls "defensive routines," entrenched habits used to protect ourselves from the embarrassment and threat that come with exposing our thinking. For most of us, such defenses began to build early in life in response to pressures to have the right answers in school or at home. Organizations add new levels of performance anxiety and thereby amplify and exacerbate this defensiveness. Ironically, this makes it even more difficult to expose hidden mental models, and thereby lessens learning.

The first challenge is to recognize defensive routines, then to inquire into their operation. Those who are best at revealing and defusing defensive routines operate with a high degree of self-disclosure regarding their own defensiveness (e.g., I notice that I am feeling uneasy about how this conversation is going. Perhaps I don't understand it or it is threatening to me in ways I don't yet see. Can you help me see this better?).

# Systems Thinking

We all know that leaders should help people see the big picture. But the actual skills whereby leaders are supposed to achieve this are not well understood. In my experience, successful leaders often are "systems thinkers" to a considerable extent. They focus less on day-to-day events and more on underlying trends and forces of change. But they do this almost completely intuitively. The consequence is that they are often unable to explain their intuitions to others and feel frustrated that others cannot see the world the way they do.

One of the most significant developments in management science today is the gradual coalescence of managerial systems thinking as a field of study and practice. This field suggests some key skills for future leaders:

- **Seeing Interrelationships, Not Things, and Processes, Not Snapshots.** Most of us have been conditioned throughout our lives to focus on things and to see the world in static images. This leads us to linear explanations of systemic phenomenon. For instance, in an arms race each party is convinced that the other is the cause of problems. They react to each new move as an isolated event, not as part of a process. So long as they fail to see the interrelationships of these actions, they are trapped.

- **Moving Beyond Blame**. We tend to blame each other or outside circumstances for our problems. But it is poorly designed systems, not incompetent or unmotivated individuals, that cause most organizational problems. System thinking shows us that there is no outside—that you and the cause of your problems are part of a single system.

- **Distinguishing Detail Complexity from Dynamic Complexity**. Some types of complexity are more important strategically than others. Detail complexity arises when there are many variables. Dynamic complexity arises when cause and effect are distant in time and space, and when the consequences over time of interventions are subtle and not obvious to many participants in the system. The leverage in most management situations lies in understanding dynamic complexity, not detail complexity.

- **Focusing on Areas of Higher Leverage**. Some have called systems thinking the "new dismal science" because it teaches that most obvious solutions don't work—at best, they improve matters in the short run, only to make things worse in the long run. But there is another side to the story. Systems thinking also shows that small, well-focused actions can produce significant, enduring improvements, if they are in the right place. Systems thinkers refer to this idea as the principle of "leverage." Tackling a difficult problem is often a matter of seeing where the high leverage lies, where a change—with a minimum of effort—would lead to lasting, significant improvement.

- **Avoiding Symptomatic Solutions**. The pressures to intervene in management systems that are going awry can be overwhelming. Unfortunately, given the linear thinking that predominates in most organizations, interventions usually focus on symptomatic fixes, not underlying causes. This results in only temporary relief, and it tends to create still more pressures later and for further, low leverage intervention. If leaders acquiesce to these pressures, they can be sucked into an endless spiral of increasing intervention. Sometimes the most difficult leadership acts are to refrain from intervening though popular quick fixes and to keep the pressure on everyone to identify more enduring solutions.

While leaders who can articulate systemic explanations are rare, those who can will leave their stamps on an organization. One person who had this gift was Bill Gore, the founder and longtime CEO of W.L. Gore and Associates (makers of Gore Tex and other synthetic fiber products). Bill Gore was adept at telling stories that showed the organization's core values of freedom and individual responsibility required particular operating policies. He was proud of his egalitarian organization, in which there were (and still are) no "employees," only "associates," all of whom own shares in the company and participate in its management. At one talk, he explained the company's policy of controlled growth: "Our limitation is not financial resources. Our limitation is the rate at which we can bring in new associates. Our experience has been that if we try to bring in more than a 25 percent per year increase, we begin to bog down. Twenty-five percent per year growth is a real limitation; you can do much better than that with an authoritarian organization." As Gore tells the story, one of the associates, Esther Baum, went home after this talk and reported the limitation to her husband. As it happened, he was an astronomer and mathematician at Lowell Observatory. He said, "That's a very interesting figure." He took out his pencil and paper and calculated and said, "Do you realize that in only fifty-seven and a half years, everyone in the world will be working for Gore?"

Through the story, Gore explains the systemic rationale behind a key policy, limited growth rate-a policy that undoubtedly caused a lot of stress in the organization. He suggests that, at larger rates of growth, the adverse effects of attempting to integrate too many new people too rapidly would begin to dominate. (This is the "limits to growth" systems archetype explained below.) The story also reaffirms the organization's commitment to creating a unique environment for its associates and illustrates the types of sacrifices that the firm is prepared to make in order to remain true to its vision. The last part of the story shows that, despite the self-imposed limit, the company is still very much a growth company.

The consequences of leaders who lack systems thinking skills can be devastating. Many charismatic leaders manage almost exclusively at the level of events. They deal in visions and in crises, and little in between. Under the leadership, an organization hurtles from crisis to crisis. Eventually, the worldview of people in the organization becomes dominated by events and reactiveness. Many, especially those who are deeply committed, become burned out. Eventually, cynicism comes to pervade the organization. People have no control over their time, let alone their destiny.

Similar problems arise with the "visionary strategist," the leader with vision who sees both patterns of change and events. This leader is better prepared to manage change. She or he can explain strategies in terms of emerging trends, and thereby foster a climate that is less reactive. But such leaders still impart a responsive orientation rather than a generative one.

Many talented leaders have rich, highly systemic intuitions but cannot explain those intuitions to others. Ironically, they often end up being authoritarian leaders, even if they don't want to, because only they see the decisions that need to be made. They are unable to conceptualize their strategic insights so that these can become public knowledge, open to challenge and further improvement.

## NEW TOOLS

Developing the skills described above requires new tools—tools that will enhance leaders' conceptual abilities and foster communication and collaborative inquiry. What follows is a sampling of tools starting to find use in learning organizations.

### Systems Archetypes

One of the insights of the budding, managerial systems-thinking field is that certain types of systemic structures recur again and again. Countless systems grow for a period, then encounter problems and cease to grow (or even collapse) well before they have reached intrinsic limits to growth. Many other systems get locked in  runaway vicious spirals where every actor has to run faster and faster to stay in the same place. Still others lure individual actors into doing what seems right locally, yet which eventually causes suffering for all.[25]

Some of the system archetypes that have the broadest relevance include:

- **Balancing Process with Delay.** In this archetype, decision makers fail to appreciate the time delays involved as they move toward a goal. As a result, they overshoot the goal and may even produce recurring cycles. Classic example: Real estate developers who keep starting new projects until the market has gone soft, by which time an eventual glut is guaranteed by the properties still under construction.

- **Limits to Growth.** A reinforcing cycle of growth grinds to a halt, and may even reverse itself, as limits are approached. The limits can be resource constraints, or external or internal responses to growth. Classic examples: Product life cycles that peak prematurely due to poor quality or service, the growth and decline of communication in a management team, and the spread of a new movement.

- **Shifting the Burden.** A short-term "solution" is used to correct a problem, with seemingly happy immediate results. As this correction is used more and more, fundamental long-term corrective measures are used less. Over time, the mechanisms of the fundamental solution may atrophy or become disabled, leading to an even greater reliance on the symptomatic solution. Classic example: Using corporate human resource staff to solve local personnel problems, thereby keeping managers from developing their own interpersonal skills.

- **Eroding Goals.** When all else fails, lower your standards. This is like "shifting the burden," except that the short-term solution involves letting a fundamental goal, such as quality standards or employee morale standards, atrophy. Classic example: A company that responds to delivery problems by continually upping its quoted delivery times.

- **Escalation.** Two people or two organizations, who each see their welfare as depending on a relative advantage over the other, continually react to the other's advances. Whenever one side gets ahead, the other is threatened, leading it to act more aggressively to reestablish its advantage, which threatens the first, and so on. Classic examples: Arms race, gang warfare, price wars.

- **Tragedy of the Commons.**[26] Individuals keep intensifying their use of a commonly available but limited resource until all individuals start to experience severely diminishing returns. Classic examples: Sheepherders who keep increasing their flocks until they overgraze the common pasture; divisions in a firm that share a common salesforce and compete for the use of sales reps by upping their sales targets, until the salesforce burns out from overextension.

- **Growth and Underinvestment.** Rapid growth approaches a limit that could be eliminated or pushed into the future, but only by aggressive investment in physical and human capacity. Eroding goals or standards cause investment that is too weak, or too slow, and customers get increasingly unhappy, slowing demand growth and thereby making the needed investment (apparently) unnecessary or impossible. Classic example: Countless once-successful growth firms that allowed product or service quality to erode, and were unable to generate enough revenues to invest in remedies.

The Archetype Template is a specific tool that is helping managers identify archetypes operating in their own strategic areas (see Figure 2).[27] The template shows the basic structural form of the archetype but lets managers fill in the variables of their own situation. For example, the shifting the burden template involves two balancing processes ("B") that compete for control of a problem symptom. The upper, symptomatic solution provides a short-term fix that will make the problem symptom go away for a while. The lower, fundamental solution provides a more enduring solution. The side-effect feedback ("R") around the outside of the diagram identifies unintended exacerbating effects of the symptomatic solution, which, over time, make it more and more difficult to invoke the fundamental solution.

FIGURE 2 "Shifting the Burden" Archetype Template

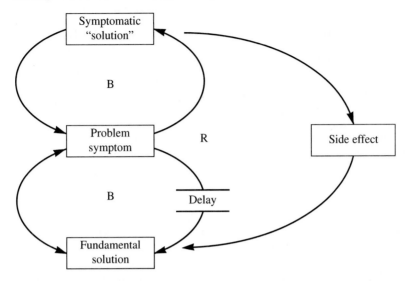

In the "shifting the burden" template, two balancing processes (B) compete for control of a problem symptom. Both solutions affect the symptom, but only the fundamental solution treats the cause. The symptomatic "solution" creates the additional side effect (R) of deferring the fundamental solution, making it harder and harder to achieve.

Several years ago, a team of managers from a leading consumer goods producer used the shifting the burden archetype in a revealing way. The problem they focused on was financial stress, which could be dealt with in two different ways: by running marketing promotions (the symptomatic solution) or by product innovation (the fundamental solution). Marketing promotions were fast. The company was expert in their design and implementation. The results were highly predictable. Product innovation was slow and much less predictable, and the company had a history over the past ten years of product-innovation mismanagement. Yet only through innovation could they retain a leadership position in their industry, which had slid over the past ten to twenty years. What the managers saw clearly was that the more skillful they became at promotions, the more they shifted the burden away from product innovation. But what really struck home was when one member identified the unintended side effect: the last three CEOs had all come from advertising function, which had become the politically dominant function in the corporation, thereby institutionalizing the symptomatic solution. Unless the political values shifted back toward product and process innovation, the managers realized, the firm's decline would accelerate—which is just the shift that had happened over the past several years.

## Charting Strategic Dilemmas

Management teams typically come unglued when confronted with core dilemmas. A classic example was the way U.S. manufacturers faced the low cost–high quality choice. For years, most assumed that it was necessary to choose between the two. Not surprisingly, given the short-term pressures perceived by most managements, the prevailing choice was low cost. Firms that chose high quality usually perceived themselves as aiming exclusively for high quality, high price market niche. The consequences of this perceived either-or choice have been disastrous, even fatal, as U.S. manufacturers have encountered increasing international competition from firms that have chosen to consistently improve quality and cost.

In a recent book, Charles Hampden-Turner presented a variety of tools for helping management teams confront strategic dilemmas creatively.[28] He summarizes the process in seven steps:

- **Eliciting the Dilemmas.** Identifying the opposed values that form the "horns" of the dilemma, for example, cost as opposed to quality, or local initiative as opposed to central coordination and control. Hampden-Turner suggests that humor can de a distinct asset in this process since "the admission that dilemmas even exist tends to be difficult for some companies."

- **Mapping.** Locating the opposing values as two axes and helping managers identify where they see themselves, or their organization, along the axes.

- **Processing.** Getting rid of nouns to describe the axes of the dilemma. Present participles formed by adding "ing" convert rigid nouns into processes that imply movement. For example, central control versus local control becomes "strengthening national office" and "growing local initiatives." This loosens the bond of implied opposition between the two values. For example, it becomes possible to think of "strengthening national services" from which local branches can benefit.

- **Framing/Contextualizing.** Further softening the adversarial structure among different values by letting "each side in turn be the frame or context for the other." This shifting of the "figure-ground" relationship undermines any implicit attempts to hold one value as intrinsically superior to the other, and thereby to become mentally closed to creative strategies for continuous improvement of both.

- **Sequencing.** Breaking the hold of static thinking. Very often, values like low cost and high quality appear to be in opposition because we think in terms of a point in time, not in terms of an ongoing process. For example, a strategy of investing in a new process technology and developing a new production-floor culture of worker responsibility may take time and money in the near term, yet reap significant long-term financial rewards.

- **Waving/Cycling.** Sometimes the strategic path toward improving both values involves cycles where both values will get "worse" for a time. Yet, at a deeper level, learning is occurring that will cause the next cycle to be at a higher plateau for both values.

- **Synergizing.** Achieving synergy where significant improvement is occurring along all axes of all relevant dilemmas. (This is the ultimate goal, of course.) Synergy, as Hampden-Turner points out, is a uniquely systemic notion, coming from the Greek *Syn-ergo* or "work together."

## "The Left-Hand Column": Surfacing Mental Models

The ideas that the mental models can dominate business decisions and that these models are often tacit and even contradictory to what people espouse can be very threatening to managers who pride themselves on rationality and judicious decision making. It is important to have tools to help managers discover for themselves how their mental models operate to undermine their own intentions.

One tool that has worked consistently to help managers see their own mental models in action is the "left-hand column" exercise developed by Chris Argyris and his colleagues. This tool is especially helpful in showing how we leap from data to generalization without testing the validity of our generalizations.

When working with managers, I start this exercise by selecting a specific situation in which I am interacting with other people in a way that is not working, that is not producing the learning that is needed. I write out a sample of the exchange, with the script on the right-hand side of the page. On the left-hand side, I write what I am thinking but not saying at each stage in the exchange (see sidebar).

The left-hand column exercise not only brings hidden assumptions to the surface, it shows how they influence behavior. In the example, I make two key assumptions about Bill: he lacks confidence and he lacks initiative. Neither may be literally true, but both are evident in my internal dialogue, and both influence the way I handle the situation. Believing that he lacks confidence, I skirt the fact that I've heard the presentation was a bomb. I'm afraid that if I say it directly, he will lose what little confidence he has, or he will see me as unsupportive. So I bring up the subject of the presentation obliquely. When I ask Bill what we should do next, he gives no specific course of action. Believing he lacks initiative, I take this as evidence of his laziness; he is content to do nothing when action is definitely required. I conclude that I will have to manufacture some form of pressure to motivate him, or else I will simply have to take matters into my own hands.

---

## The Left-Hand Column: An Exercise

Imagine my exchange with a colleague, Bill, after he made a big presentation to our boss on a project we are doing together. I had to miss the presentation, but I've heard that it was poorly received.
**Me:** How did the presentation go?
**Bill:** Well, I don't know. It's really too early to say. Besides, we're breaking new ground here.
**Me:** Well, what do you think we should do? I believe that the issues you were raising were important.
**Bill:** I'm not so sure. Let's just wait and see what happens.
**Me:** You may be right, but I think we may need to do more than just wait.

   Now, here is what the exchange looks like with my "left-hand column":

| What I'm Thinking | What Is Said |
| --- | --- |
| Everyone says the presentation was a bomb. | **Me:** How did the presentation go? |
| Does he really not know how bad it was? Or is he not willing to face up to it? | **Bill:** Well, I don't know. It's too early to say. Besides we're breaking new ground here. |
|  | **Me:** Well, what do you think we should do? I believe that the issues you were raising are important. |
| He really is afraid to see the truth. If he only had more confidence, he could probably learn from a situation like this. | **Bill:** I'm not so sure. Let's just wait and see what happens. |
| I can't believe he doesn't realize how disastrous that presentation was to our moving ahead. | **Me:** You may be right, but I think we may need to do more than just wait. |
| I've got to find some way to light a fire under the guy. |  |

The exercise reveals the elaborate webs of assumptions we weave, within which we become our own victims. Rather than dealing directly with my assumptions about Bill and the situation, we talk around the subject. The reasons for my avoidance are self-evident: I assume that if I raised my doubts, I would provoke a defensive reaction the would only make matters worse. But the price of avoiding the issue is high. Instead of determining how to move forward to resolve problems, we end our exchange with no clear course of action. My assumptions about Bill's limitations have been reinforced. I resort to a manipulative strategy to move things forward.

The exercise not only reveals the need for skills in surfacing assumptions, but that we are the ones most in need of help. There is no one right way to handle difficult situations like my exchange with Bill, but any productive strategy revolves around a high level of self-disclosure and willingness to have my views challenged. I need to recognize my own leaps of abstraction regarding Bill, share the events and reasoning that are leading to my concern over the project, and be open to Bill's views on both. The skills to carry on such conversations without invoking defensiveness take time to develop. But if both parties in a learning impasse start by doing their own left-hand column exercise and sharing them with each other, it is remarkable how quickly everyone recognizes their contribution to the impasse and progress starts to be made.

## Learning Laboratories: Practice Fields for Management Teams

One of the most promising new tools is the learning laboratory or "microworld": constructed microcosms of real-life settings in which management teams can learn how to learn together.

The rationale behind learning laboratories can be best explained by analogy. Although most management teams have great difficulty learning (enhancing their collective intelligence and capacity to create), in other domains team learning is the norm rather than the exception—team sports and the performing arts, for example. Great basketball teams do not start off great. They learn. But the process by which these teams learn is, by and large, absent from modern organizations. The process is a continual movement between practice and performance.

The vision guiding current research in management learning laboratories is to design and construct effective practice fields for management teams. Much remains to be done, but the broad outlines are emerging.

First, since team learning in organizations is an individual-to-individual and individual-to-system phenomenon, learning laboratories must combine meaningful business issues with meaningful interpersonal dynamics. Either alone is incomplete.

---

### Learning at Hanover Insurance

*Hanover Insurance has gone from the bottom of the property and liability industry to a position among the top 25 percent of U.S. insurance companies over the past twenty years, largely through the efforts of CEO William O'Brien and his predecessor, Jack Adam. The following comments are excerpted from series of interviews Senge conducted with O'Brien as background for his book.*

*Senge:* Why do you think there is so much change occurring in management and organizations today? Is it primarily because of increased competitive pressures?
*O'Brien:* That's a factor, but not the most significant factor. The ferment in management will continue until we find models that are more congruent with human nature.

---

One of the great insights of modern psychology is the hierarchy of human needs. As Maslow expressed this idea, the most basic needs are food and shelter. Then comes belonging. Once these three basic needs are satisfied, people begin to aspire toward self-respect and esteem, and toward self-actualization—the fourth—and fifth-order needs.

Our traditional hierarchical organizations are designed to provide for the first three levels, but not the fourth and fifth. These first three levels are now widely available to members of industrial society, but our organizations do not offer people sufficient opportunities for growth.

*Senge:* How would you asses Hanover's progress to date?

*O'Brien:* We have been on a long journey away from traditional hierarchical culture. The journey began with everyone understanding some guiding ideas about purpose, vision, and values as a basis for participative management. This is a better way to begin building a participative culture than by simply "letting people in on decision making." Before there can be meaningful participation, people must share certain values and pictures about where we are trying to go. We discovered that people have real need to feel that they're part of an ennobling mission. But developing shared visions and values is not the end, only the beginning.

Next we had to get beyond mechanical, linear thinking. The essence of our jobs as managers is to deal with "divergent" problems—problems that have no simple answer. "Convergent" problems—problems that have a "right" answer—should be solved locally. Yet we are deeply conditioned to see the world in terms of convergent problems. Most managers try to force-fit simplistic solutions and undermine the potential for learning when divergent problems arise. Since everyone handles the linear issues fairly well, companies that learn how to handle divergent issues will have a great advantage.

The next basic stage in our progression was coming to understand inquiry and advocacy. We learned that real openness is rooted in people's ability to continually inquire into their own thinking. This requires exposing yourself to being wrong—not something that most managers are rewarded for. But learning is very difficult if you cannot look for errors or incompleteness in your own ideas.

What all this builds to is the capability throughout an organization to manage mental models. In a locally controlled organization, you have the fundamental challenge of learning how to help people make good decisions without coercing them into making particular decisions. By managing mental models, we create "self-concluding" decisions—decisions that people come to themselves—which will result in deeper conviction, better implementation, and the ability to make better adjustments when the situation changes.

*Senge:* What concrete steps can top managers take to begin moving toward learning organizations?

*O'Brien:* Look at the signals you send through the organization. For example, one critical signal is how you spend your time. It's hard to build a learning organization if people are unable to take the time to think through important matters. I rarely set up an appointment for less than one hour. If the subject is not worth an hour, it shouldn't be on my calendar.

*Senge*: Why is this so hard for so many managers?

*O'Brien:* It comes back to what you believe about the nature of your work. The authoritarian manager has a "chain gang" mental model: "The speed of the boss is the speed of the gang. I've got to keep things moving fast, because I've got to keep people working." In a learning organization, the manager shoulders an almost sacred responsibility: to create conditions that enable people to have happy and productive lives. If you understand the effects the ideas we are discussing can have on the lives of people in your organization, you will take the time.

Second, the factors that thwart learning about complex business issues must be eliminated in the learning lab. Chief among these is the inability to experience the long-term, systemic consequences of key strategic decisions. We all learn best from experience, but we are unable to experience the consequences of many important organizational decisions. Learning laboratories remove this constraint through system dynamics simulation games that compress time and space.

Third, new learning skills must be developed. One constraint on learning is the inability of managers to reflect insightfully on their assumptions, and to inquire effectively into each other's assumptions. Both skills can be enhanced in a learning laboratory, where people can practice surfacing assumptions in a low-risk setting. A note of caution: It is far easier to design an entertaining learning laboratory than it is to have an impact on real management practices and firm traditions outside the learning lab. Research on management simulations has shown that they often have greater entertainment value than the educational value. One of the reasons appears to be that many simulations do not offer deep insights into systemic structures causing business problems. Another reason is that they do not foster new learning skills. Also, there is no connection between experiments in the learning lab and real life experiments. These are significant problems that research on laboratory design is now addressing.

## DEVELOPING LEADERS AND LEARNING ORGANIZATIONS

In a recently published retrospective on organization development in the 1980s, Marshall Sashkin and N. Warner Burke observe the return of an emphasis on developing leaders who can develop organizations.[29] They also note Schein's critique that most top executives are not qualified for the task of developing culture.[30] Learning organizations represent a potentially significant evolution of organizational culture. So it should come as no surprise that such organization will remain a distant vision until the leadership capabilities they demand are developed. "The 1990s may be the period," suggest Sashkin and Burke, "during which organization development and ( a new sort) of management development are reconnected."

I believe that this new sort of management development will focus on the roles, skills, and tools for leadership in learning organizations. Undoubtedly, the ideas offered above are only a rough approximation of this new territory. The sooner we begin seriously exploring the territory, the sooner the initial map can be improved-and the sooner we will realize an age-old vision of leadership.

> The wicked leader is he who the people despise.
> The good leader is he who the people revere.
> The great leader is he who the people say, "We did it ourselves."
> —Lao Tsu

## REFERENCES

1. P. Senge, *The Fifth Discipline: The Art and Practice of the Learning Organization* (New York: Doubleday/Currency, 1990).
2. A. P. de Geus, "Planning as Learning," *Harvard Business Review,* March–April 1988, pp.70–74.
3. B. Domain, *Fortune*, 3 July 1989, pp. 48–62.

4. The distinction between adaptive and generative learning has its roots in the distinction between what Argyris and Schon have called their "single-loop" learning, in which individuals or groups adjust their behavior relative to fixed goals, norms, and assumptions, and "double-loop" learning, in which goals, norms, and assumptions, as well as behavior, are open to change (e.g., see C. Argyris and D. Schon, *Organizational Learning: A Theory-in-Action Perspective* [Reading, Massachusetts: Addison-Wesley, 1978]).

5. All unattributed quotes are from personal communications with the author.

6. G. Stalk, Jr., "Time: The Next Source of Competitive Advantage," *Harvard Business Review*, July–August 1988, pp. 41-51.

7. Senge (1990).

8. The principle of creative tension comes from Robert Fritz' work on creativity. See R. Fritz, *The Path of Least Resistance* (New York: Ballantine, 1989) and *Creating* (New York: Ballantine, 1990).

9. M. L. King, Jr., "Letter from Birmingham Jail," *American Visions*, January–February 1986, pp. 52–59.

10. E. Schein, *Organizational Culture and Leadership* (San Francisco: Jossey-Bass, 1985). Similar views have been expressed by many leadership theorists. For example, see: P. Selznick, *Leadership in Administration* (New York: Harper & Row, 1957); W. Bennis and B. Nanus, *Leaders* (New York: Harper & Row, 1985); and N. M. Tichy and M. A. Devanna, *The Transformational Leader* (New York: John Wiley & Sons, 1986).

11. Selznick (1957).

12. J. W. Forrester, "A New Corporate Design," *Sloan Management Review* (formerly *Industrial Management Review*), Fall 1965, pp. 5–17.

13. See, for example, H. Mintzberg, "Crafting Strategy," *Harvard Business Review,* July–August 1987, pp. 66–75.

14. R. Mason and I. Mitroff, *Challenging Strategic Planning Assumptions* (New York: John Wiley & Sons, 1981), p. 16.

15. P. Wack, "Scenarios: Uncharted Waters Ahead," *Harvard Business Review*, September–October 1985, pp. 73–89.

16. de Geus (1988).

17. M. de Pree, *Leadership Is an Art* (New York: Doubleday, 1989) p. 9.

18. For example, see T. Peters and N. Austin, *A Passion for Excellence* (New York: Random House, 1985); and J. M. Kouzes and B. Z. Posner, *The Leadership Challenge* (San Francisco: Jossey-Bass, 1987).

19. I. Mitroff, *Break-Away Thinking* (New York: John Wiley & Sons, 1988), pp. 66–67.

20. R. K. Greenleaf, *Servant Leadership: A Journey into the Nature of Legitimate Power and Greatness* (New York: Paulist Press, 1977).

21. L. Miller, *American Spirit: Visions of a New Corporate Culture* (New York: William Morrow, 1984), p. 15.

22. These points are condensed from the practices of the five disciplines examined in Senge (1990).

23. The ideas below are based to a considerable extent on the work of Chris Argyris, Donald Schon, and their Action Science colleagues: C. Argyris and D. Schon, *Organizational Learning: A Theory-in-Action Perspective* (Reading, Massachusetts: Addison-Wesley, 1978); C. Argyris, R. Putnam, and D. Smith, *Action Science* (San Francisco: Jossey-Bass, 1985); C. Argyris, *Strategy Change and Defensive Routines* (Boston: Pitman, 1985); and C. Argyris, *Overcoming Organizational Defenses* (Englewood Cliffs, New Jersey: Prentice-Hall, 1990).

24. I am indebted to Diana Smith for the summary points below.

25. The system archetypes are one of several systems diagramming and communication tools. See D. H. Kim, "Toward Learning Organizations: Integrating Total Quality Control and Systems Thinking" (Cambridge, Massachusetts: MIT Sloan School of Management, Working Paper No. 3037-89-BPS, June 1989).

26. This archetype is closely associated with the work of ecologist Garrett Hardin, who coined its label: G. Hardin, "The Tragedy of the Commons," *Science*, 13 December 1968.

27. These templates were originally developed by Jennifer Kemeny, Charles Kiefer, and Michael Goodman of Innovation Associates, Inc., Farmingham, Massachusetts.

28. C. Hampden-Turner, *Charting the Corporate Mind* (New York: The Free Press, 1990).

29. M. Sashkin and W. W. Burke, "Organization Development in the 1980s" and "An End-of-the-Eighties Retrospective," in *Advances in Organization Development,* ed. F. Masarik (Norwood, New Jersey: Ablex, 1990).

30. E. Schein (1985).

# BUILDING A  LEARNING ORGANIZATION

*David A. Garvin*

Continuous improvement programs are sprouting up all over as organizations strive to better themselves and gain an edge. The topic list is long and varied, and sometimes it seems as though a program a month is needed just to keep up. Unfortunately, failed programs far outnumber successes, and improvement rates remain distressingly low. Why? Because most companies have failed to grasp a basic truth. Continuous improvement requires a commitment to learning.

How, after all, can an organization improve without first learning something new? Solving a problem, introducing a product, and reengineering a process all require seeing the world in a new light and acting accordingly. In the absence of learning, companies—and individuals—simply repeat old practices. Change remains cosmetic, and improvements are either fortuitous or short-lived.

A few farsighted executives—Ray Stata of Analog Devices, Gordon Forward of Chaparral Steel, Paul Allaire of Xerox—have recognized the link between learning and continuous improvement and have begun to refocus their companies around it. Scholars too have jumped on the bandwagon, beating the drum for "learning organizations" and "knowledge-creating companies." In rapidly changing businesses like semiconductors and consumer electronics, these ideas are fast taking hold. Yet despite the encouraging signs, the topic in large part remains murky, confused, and difficult to penetrate.

# MEANING, MANAGEMENT, AND MEASUREMENT

Scholars are partly to blame. Their discussions of learning organizations have often been reverential and utopian, filled with near mystical terminology. Paradise, they would have you believe, is just around the corner. Peter Senge, who popularized learning organizations in his book *The Fifth Discipline*, described them as places "where people continually expand their capacity to create the results they truly desire, where new and expansive patterns of thinking are nurtured, where collective aspiration is set free, and where people are continually learning how to learn together."[1] To achieve these ends, Senge suggested the use of five "component technologies": systems thinking, personal mastery, mental models, shared vision, and team learning. In a similar spirit, Ikujiro Nonaka characterized knowledge-creating companies as places where "inventing new knowledge is not a specialized activity…it is a way of behaving, indeed, a way of being, in which everyone is a knowledge worker."[2] Nonaka suggested that companies use metaphors and organizational redundancy to focus thinking, encourage dialogue, and make tacit, instinctively understood ideas explicit.

Sound idyllic? Absolutely. Desirable? Without question. But does it provide a framework for action? Hardly. The recommendations are far too abstract, and too many questions remain unanswered. How, for example, will managers know when their companies have become learning organizations? What concrete changes in behavior are required? What policies and programs must be in place? How do you get from here to there?

Most discussions of learning organizations finesse these issues. Their focus is high philosophy and grand themes, sweeping metaphors rather than the gritty details of practice. Three critical issues are left unresolved; yet each is essential for effective implementation. First is the question of *meaning*. We need a plausible, well-grounded definition of learning organizations; it must be actionable and easy to apply. Second is the question of *management*. We need clearer guidelines for practice, filled with operational advice rather than high aspirations. And third is the question of *measurement*. We need better tools for assessing an organization's rate and level of learning to ensure that gains have in fact been made.

Once these "three Ms" are addressed, managers will have a firmer foundation for launching learning organizations. Without this groundwork, progress is unlikely, and for the simplest of reasons. For learning to become a meaningful corporate goal, it must first be understood.

# WHAT IS A LEARNING ORGANIZATION?

Surprisingly, a clear definition of learning has proved to be elusive over the years. Organizational theorists have studied learning for a long time; the accompanying quotations suggest that there is still considerable disagreement (see the insert "Definitions of Organizational Learning"). Most scholars view organizational learning as a process that unfolds over time and link it with knowledge acquisition and improved performance. But they differ on other important matters.

Some, for example, believe that behavioral change is required for learning; others insist that new ways of thinking are enough. Some cite information processing as the mechanism through which learning takes place; others propose shared insights, organizational routines, even memory. And some think that organizational learning is common, while others believe that flawed, self-serving interpretations are the norm.

How can we discern among this cacophony of voices yet build on earlier insights? As a first step, consider the following definition:

A learning organization is an organization skilled at creating, acquiring, and transferring knowledge, and at modifying its behavior to reflect new knowledge and insights.

This definition begins with a simple truth: new ideas are essential if learning is to take place. Sometimes they are created de nova, through flashes of insight or creativity; at other times they arrive from outside the organization or are communicated by knowledgeable insiders. Whatever their source, these ideas are the trigger for organizational improvement. But they cannot by themselves create a learning organization. *Without accompanying changes in the way that work gets done, only the potential for improvement exists.*

Definitions of Organizational Learning

---

**Scholars have proposed a variety of definitions of organizational learning.  Here is a small sample:**

Organizational learning means the process of improving actions through better knowledge and understanding. C. Marlene Fiol and Marjorie A. Lyles, "Organizational Learning," *Academy of Management Review*, October 1985.

An entity learns if, through its processing of information, the range if its potential behaviors is changed. George P. Huber, "Organizational Learning: The Contributing Processes and the Literature," *Organization Science*, February 1991.

Organizations are seen as learning by encoding inferences from history into routines that guide behavior. Barbara Levitt and James G. March, "Organizational Learning," *American Review of Sociology,* Vol. 14, 1988.

Organizational Learning is a process of detecting and correcting error. Chris Argyris, "Double-Loop Learning in Organizations," *Harvard Business Review*, September–October 1977.

Organizational learning occurs through shared insights, knowledge, and mental models...(and) builds on past knowledge and experience—that is, on memory. Ray Strata, "Organizational Learning—The Key to Management Innovation," *Sloan Management Review,* Spring 1989.

---

This is a surprisingly stringent test for it rules out a number of obvious candidates for learning organizations. Many universities fail to qualify, as do many consulting firms. Even General Motors, despite its recent efforts to improve performance, is found wanting. All of these organizations have been effective at creating or acquiring new knowledge but notably less successful in applying that knowledge to their own activities. Total quality management, for example, is now taught at many business schools, yet the number using it to guide their own decision making is very small. Organizational consultants advise clients on social dynamics and small-group behavior but are notorious for their own infighting and factionalism. And GM, with a few exceptions (like Saturn and NUMMI), has had little success in revamping its manufacturing practices, even though its managers are experts on lean manufacturing, JIT production, and the requirements for improved quality of work life.

Organizations that do pass the definitional test—Honda, Corning, and General Electric come quickly to mind—have, by contrast, become adept at translating new knowledge into new ways of behaving. These companies actively manage the learning process to ensure that it occurs by design rather than by chance. Distinctive policies and practices are responsible for their success; they form the building blocks of learning organizations.

## BUILDING BLOCKS

Learning organizations are skilled at five main activities: systematic problem solving, experimentation with new approaches, learning from their own experience and past history, learning from the experiences and best practices of others, and transferring knowledge quickly and efficiently throughout the organization. Each is accompanied by a distinctive mind-set, tool kit, and pattern of behavior. Many companies practice these activities to some degree. But few are consistently successful because they rely largely on happenstance and isolated examples. By creating systems and processes that support these activities and integrate them into the fabric of daily operations, companies can manage their learning more effectively.

1.    Systematic problem solving. This first activity rests heavily on the philosophy and methods of the quality movement. Its underlying ideas, now widely accepted, include:

- Relying on the scientific method, rather than guesswork, for diagnosing problems (what Deming calls the "Plan, Do, Check, Act" cycle, and others refer to as "hypothesis-generating, hypothesis-testing techniques).
- Insisting on data, rather than assumptions, as background for decision making (what quality practitioners call "fact-based management").
- Using simple statistical tools (histograms, Pareto charts, correlations, cause-and-effect diagrams) to organize data and draw inferences.

Most training programs focus primarily on problem-solving techniques, using exercises and practical examples. These tools are relatively straightforward and easily communicated; the necessary mind-set, however, is more difficult to establish. Accuracy and precision are essential for learning. Employees must therefore become more disciplined in their thinking and more attentive to details. They must continually ask, "How do we know that's true?" recognizing that close enough is not good enough if real learning is to take place. They must push beyond obvious symptoms to assess underlying causes, often collecting evidence when conventional wisdom says it is unnecessary. Otherwise, the organization will remain a prisoner of "gut facts" and sloppy reasoning, and learning will be stifled.

Xerox has mastered this approach on a company-wide scale. In 1983, senior managers launched the company's Leadership Through Quality initiative; since then, all employees have been trained in small-group activities and problem-solving techniques. Today a six-step process is used for virtually all decisions (see the insert "Xerox's Problem-Solving Process"). Employees are provided with tools in four areas: generating ideas and collecting information (brainstorming, interviewing, surveying); reaching consensus (list reduction, rating forms, weighted voting); analyzing and displaying data (cause-and-effect diagrams, force-field analysis); and planning actions (flow charts, Gantt charts). They then practice these tools during training sessions that last several days. Training is presented in "family groups," members of the same department or business-unit team, and the tools are applied to real problems facing the group. The result of this process has been a common vocabulary and a consistent, companywide approach to problem solving. Once employees have been trained, they are expected to use the techniques at all meeting, and no topic is off-limits. When a high-level group was formed to review Xerox's organizational structure and suggest alternatives, it employed the very same process and tools.[3]

# Xerox's Problem-Solving Process

| Step | Questions to Be Answered | Expansion/ Divergence | Contraction/ Convergence | What's Needed to Go to the Next Step |
|------|--------------------------|-----------------------|--------------------------|--------------------------------------|
| 1. Identify and select problem | What do we want to change? | Lots of problems for consideration | One problem statement, one "desired state" agreed upon | Identification of the gap "Desired state" described in observable terms |
| 2. Analyze problem | What's preventing us from reaching the "desired state?" | Lots of potential causes identified | Key cause(s) identified and verified | Key cause(s) documented and ranked |
| 3. Generate potential solutions | How *could* we make the change? | Lots of ideas on how to solve the problem | Potential solutions clarified | Solution list |
| 4. Select and plan the solution | What's the *best* way to do it? | Lots of criteria for evaluating potential solutions  Lots of ideas on how to implement and evaluate the selected solution | Criteria to use for evaluating solution agreed upon  Implementation and evaluation plans agreed upon | Plan for making and monitoring the change  Measurement criteria to evaluate solution effectiveness |
| 5. Implement the solution | Are we following the plan? | | Implementation of agreed on contingency plans (if necessary) | Solution in place |
| 6. Evaluate the solution | How well did it work? | | Effectiveness of solution agreed upon  Continuing problems (if any) identified | Verification that the problem is solved, or  Agreement to address continuing problems |

2.    Experimentation. This activity involves the systematic searching for and testing of new knowledge. Using the scientific method is essential, and there are obvious parallels to systematic problem solving. But unlike problem solving, experimentation is usually motivated by opportunity and expanding horizons, not by current difficulties. It takes two main forms: ongoing programs and one-of-a-kind demonstration projects.

*Ongoing programs* normally involve a continuing series of small experiments, designed to produce incremental gains in knowledge. They are the mainstay of most continuous improvement programs and are especially common on the shop floor. Corning, for example, experiments continually with diverse raw materials and new formulations to increase yields and provide better grades of glass. Allegheny Ludlum, a specialty steelmaker, regularly examines new rolling methods and improved technologies to raise productivity and reduce costs.

Successful ongoing programs share several characteristics. First they work hard to ensure a steady flow of new ideas, even if they must be imported from outside the organization. Chaparral Steel sends its first-line supervisors on sabbaticals around the globe, where they visit academic and industry leaders, develop an understanding of new work practices and technologies, then bring what they've learned back to the company and apply it to daily operations. In large part as a result of the initiatives, Chaparral is one of the five lowest cost steel plants in the world. GE's Impact Program originally sent manufacturing managers to Japan to study factory innovations, such as quality circles and kanban cards, and then apply them in their own organization; today Europe is the destination, and productivity improvement practices the target. The program is one reason GE has recorded productivity gains averaging nearly 5% over the last four years.

Successful ongoing programs also require an incentive system that favors risk taking. Employees must feel that the benefits of experimentation exceed the costs; otherwise, they will not participate. This creates a difficult challenge for managers, who are trapped between two perilous extremes. They must maintain accountability and control over experiments without stifling creativity by unduly penalizing employees for failures. Allegheny Ludlum has perfected this juggling act: it keeps expensive, high-impact experiments off the scorecard used to evaluate managers but requires prior approvals from four senior vice presidents. The result has been a history of productivity improvements annually averaging in 7% to 8%.

Finally, ongoing programs need managers and employees who are trained in the skills required to perform and evaluate experiments. These skills are seldom intuitive and must usually be learned. They cover a broad sweep: statistical methods, like design of experiments, that efficiently compare a large number of alternatives; graphical techniques, like process analysis, that are essential for redesigning work flows; and creativity techniques, like storyboarding and role playing, that keep novel ideas flowing. The most effective training programs are tightly focused and feature a small set of techniques tailored to employees' needs. Training in design of experiments, for example, is useful for manufacturing engineers, while creativity techniques are well suited to development groups.

Demonstration projects are usually larger and more complex than ongoing experiments. They involve holistic, systemwide changes, introduced at a single site, and are often undertaken with the goal of developing new organizational capabilities. Because these projects represent a sharp break from the past, they are usually designed from scratch, using a "clean slate" approach. General Foods' Topeka plant, one of the first high-commitment work systems in this country, was a pioneering demonstration project initiated to introduce the idea of self-managing teams and high levels of worker autonomy; a more recent example, designed to rethink small-car development, manufacturing, and sales, is GM's Saturn Division.

Demonstration projects share a number of distinctive characteristics:

- They are usually the first projects to embody principles and approaches that the organization hopes to adopt later on a larger scale. For this reason, they are more transitional efforts than endpoints and involve considerable "learning by doing." Mid-course corrections are common.
- They implicitly establish policy guidelines and decision rules for later projects. Managers must therefore be sensitive to the precedents they are setting and must send strong signals if they expect to establish new norms.
- They often encounter severe tests of commitment from employees who wish to see whether the rules have, in fact, changed.
- They are normally developed by strong multifunctional teams reporting directly to senior management. (For projects targeting employee involvement or quality of work life, teams should be multilevel as well.)
- They tend to have only limited impact on the rest of the organization if they are not accompanied by explicit strategies for transferring learning.

All of these characteristics appeared in a demonstration project launched by Copeland Corporation, a highly successful compressor manufacturer, in the mid-1970s. Matt Diggs, then the new CEO, wanted to transform the company's approach to manufacturing. Previously, Copeland had machined and assembled all products in a signal facility. Costs were high, and quality was marginal. The problem, Diggs felt, was too much complexity.

At the outset, Diggs assigned a small, multifunctional team the task of designing a "focused factory" dedicated to a narrow, newly developed product line. The team reported directly to Diggs and took three years to complete its work. Initially, the project budget was $10 million to $12 million; that figure was repeatedly revised as the team found, through experience and with Digg's prodding, that it could achieve dramatic improvements. The final investment, a total of $30 million, yielded unanticipated breakthroughs in reliability testing, automatic tool adjustments, and programmable control. All were achieved through learning by doing.

The team set additional precedents during the plant's start-up and early operations. To dramatize the importance of quality, for example, the quality manager was appointed second-in-command, a significant move upward. The same reporting relationship was used at all subsequent plants. In addition, Diggs urged the plant manager to ramp up slowly to full production and resist all efforts to proliferate products. These instructions were unusual at Copeland, where the marketing department normally ruled. Both directives were quickly tested; management held firm, and the implications were felt throughout the organization. Manufacturing's stature improved, and the company as a whole recognized its competitive contribution. One observer commented, "Marketing had always run the company, so they couldn't believe it. The change was visible at the highest levels, and it went down hard."

Once the first focused factory was running smoothly—it seized 25% of the market in two years and held its edge in reliability for over a decade—Copeland built four more factories in quick succession. Diggs assigned members of the initial project to each factory's design team to ensure that early learnings were not lost; these people later rotated into operating assignments. Today focused factories remain the cornerstone of Copeland's manufacturing strategy and a continuing source of its cost and quality advantages.

Whether they are demonstration projects like Copeland's or ongoing programs like Allegheny Ludlum's, all forms of experimentation seek the same end: moving from superficial knowledge to deep understanding. At its simplest, the distinction is between knowing how things are done and knowing why they occur. Knowing how is partial knowledge; it is rooted in norms of behavior, standards of practice, and settings of equipment. Knowing why is more fundamental; it captures underlying cause-and-effect relationships and accommodates exceptions, adaptations, and unforeseen events. The ability to control temperatures and pressures to align grains of silicon and form silicon steel is an example of knowing how; understanding the chemical and physical process that produces the alignment is knowing why.

Further distinctions are possible, as the insert "Stages of Knowledge" suggests. Operating knowledge can be arrayed in a hierarchy, moving from limited understanding and the ability to make few distinctions to more complete understanding in which all contingencies are anticipated and controlled. In this context, experimentation and problem solving foster learning by pushing organizations up the hierarchy, from lower to higher stages of knowledge.

3. Learning from past experience. Companies must review their successes and failures, assess them systematically, and record the lessons in a form that employees find open and accessible. One expert has called this process the "Santayana Review," citing the famous philosopher George Santayana, who coined the phrase "Those who cannot remember the past are condemned to repeat it." Unfortunately, too many managers today are indifferent, even hostile, to the past, and by failing to reflect on it, they let valuable knowledge escape.

Scholars have suggested that production and operating knowledge can be classified systematically by level or stage of understanding. At the lowest levels of manufacturing knowledge, little is known other than the characteristics of a good product. Production remains an art, and there are few clearly articulated standards or rules. An example would be Stradivarius violins. Experts agree that they produce vastly superior sound, but no one can specify precisely how they were manufactured because skilled artisans were responsible. By contrast, at the highest levels of manufacturing knowledge, all aspects of production are known and understood. All materials and processing variations are articulated and accounted for, with rules and procedures for every contingency. Here an example would be a "lights out," fully automated factory that operates for many hours without any human intervention.

In total, this framework specifies eight stages of knowledge. From lowest to highest, they are:

1. Recognizing prototypes (what is a good product?)
2. Recognizing attributes within prototypes (ability to define some conditions under which process gives good output).
3. Discriminating among attributes (which attributes are important? Experts may differ about relevance of patterns; new operators are often trained through apprenticeships).
4. Measuring attributes (some key attributes are measured; measures may be qualitative and relative).
5. Locally controlling attributes (repeatable performance; process designed by expert, but technicians can perform it).
6. Recognizing and discriminating between contingencies (production process can be mechanized and monitored manually).
7. Controlling contingencies (process can be automated).
8. Understanding procedures and controlling contingencies (process is completely understood).

*Adapted from work by Ramchandran Jaikumar and Roger Bohn.[9]*

A study of more than 150 new products concluded that "the knowledge gained from failures [is] often instrumental in achieving subsequent successes....In the simplest terms, failure is the ultimate teacher."[4] IBM's 360 computer series, for example, one of the most popular and profitable ever built, was based on the technology of the failed Stretch computer that preceded it. In this case, as in many others, learning occurred by chance rather than by careful planning. A few companies, however, have established processes that require their managers to periodically think about the past and learn from their mistakes.

Boeing did so immediately after its difficulties with the 737 and 747 plane programs. Both planes were introduced with much fanfare and also with serious problems. To ensure that the problems were not repeated, senior managers commissioned a high-level employee group, called Project Homework, to compare the development processes of the 737 and 747 with those of the 707 and 727, two of the company's most profitable planes. The group was asked to develop a set of "lessons learned" that could be used on future projects. After working for three years, they produced hundreds of recommendations and an inch-thick booklet. Several members of the team were then transferred to the 757 and 767 start-ups, and guided by experience, they produced the most successful, error-free launches in Boeing's history.

Other companies have used a similar retrospective approach. Like Boeing, Xerox studied its product development process, examining three troubled products in an effort to understand why the company's new business initiatives failed so often. Arthur D. Little, the consulting company, focused on its past successes. Senior management invited ADL consultants from around the world to a two-day "jamboree," featuring booths and presentations documenting a wide range of the company's most successful practices, publications, and techniques. British Petroleum went even further and established the post-project appraisal unit to review major investment projects, write up case studies, and derive lessons for planners that were then incorporated into revisions of the company's planning guidelines. A five-person unit reported to the board of directors and reviewed six projects annually. The bulk of the time was spent in the field interviewing managers.[5] This type of review is now conducted regularly at the project level.

At the heart of this approach, one expert has observed, "is a mind-set that…enables companies to recognize the value of productive failure as contrasted with unproductive success. A productive failure is one that leads to insight, understanding and thus an addition to the commonly held wisdom of the organization. An unproductive success occurs when something goes well, but nobody knows how or why."[6] IBM's legendary founder, Thomas Watson, Sr., apparently understood the distinction well. Company lore has it that a young manager, after losing $10 million in a risky venture, was called into Watson's office. The young man, thoroughly intimidated, began by saying, "I guess you want my resignation." Watson replied, "You can't be serious. We just spent $10 million educating you."

Fortunately, the learning process need not be so expensive. Case studies and post-project reviews like those of Xerox and British Petroleum can be performed with little cost other than managers' time. Companies can also enlist the help of faculty and students at local colleges or universities; they bring fresh perspectives and view internships and case studies as opportunities to gain experience and increase their own learning. A few companies have established computerized data banks to speed up the learning process. At Paul Revere Life Insurance, management requires all problem-solving teams to complete short registration forms describing their proposed projects if they hope to qualify for the company's award program. The company then enters the forms into its computer system and can immediately retrieve a listing of other groups of people who have worked or are working on the topic, along with a contact person. Relevant experience is then just a telephone call away.

4. Learning from others. Of course, not all learning comes from reflection and self-analysis. Sometimes the most powerful insights come from looking outside one's immediate environment to gain a new perspective. Enlightened managers know that even companies in completely different businesses can be fertile sources of ideas and catalysts for creative thinking. At these organizations, enthusiastic borrowing is replacing the "not invented here" syndrome. Milliken calls the process SIS, for "Steal Ideas Shamelessly"; the broader term for it is benchmarking.

According to one expert, "benchmarking is an ongoing investigation and learning experience that ensures that the best industry practices are uncovered, analyzed, adopted, and implemented."[7] The greatest benefits come from studying practices, the way that work gets done, rather than results, and from involving line managers in the process. Almost anything can be benchmarked. Xerox, the concept's creator, has applied it to billing, warehousing, and automated manufacturing. Milliken has been even more creative: in an inspired moments, it benchmarked Xerox's approach to benchmarking.

Unfortunately, there is still considerable confusion about the requirements for successful benchmarking. Benchmarking is not "industrial tourism," a series of ad hoc visits to companies that have received favorable publicity or won quality awards. Rather, it is a disciplined process that begins with a thorough search to identify best-practice organizations, continues with careful study of one's own practices and performance, progresses through systematic site visits and interviews, and concludes with an analysis of results, development of recommendations, and implementation. While time-consuming, the process need not be terribly expensive. AT&T's Benchmarking Group estimates that a moderate-sized project takes four to six months and incurs out-of-pocket costs of $20,000 (when personnel costs are included, the figure is three to four times higher).

Benchmarking is one way of gaining an outside perspective; another, equally fertile source of ideas is customers. Conversations with customers invariably stimulate learning; they are, after all, experts in what they do. Customers can provide up-to-date product information, competitive comparisons, insights into changing preferences, and immediate feedback about service and patterns of use. And companies need these insights at all levels, from the executive suite to the shop floor. At Motorola, members of the Operating and Policy Committee, including the CEO, meet personally and on a regular basis with customers. At Worthington Steel, all machine operators make periodic, unescorted trips to customers' factories to discuss their needs.

Sometimes customers can't articulate their needs or remember even the most recent problems they have had with a product or service. If that's the case, managers must observe them in action. Xerox employs a number of anthropologists at its Palo Alto Research Center to observe users of new document products in their offices. Digital Equipment has developed an interactive process called "contextual inquiry" that is used by software engineers to observe users of new technologies as they go about their work. Milliken has created "first-delivery teams" that accompany the first shipment of all products; team members follow the product through the customer's production process to see how it is used and then develop ideas for further improvement.

Whatever the source of outside ideas, learning will only occur in a receptive environment. Managers can't be defensive and must be open to criticism or bad news. This is a difficult challenge, but it is essential for success. Companies that approach customers assuming that "we must be right, they have to be wrong" or visit other organizations certain that 'they can't teach us anything" seldom learn very much. Learning organizations, by contrast, cultivate the art of open, attentive listening.

5. Transferring knowledge. For learning to be more than a local affair, knowledge must spread quickly and efficiently throughout the organization. Ideas carry maximum impact when they are shared broadly rather than held in a few hands. A variety of mechanisms support this process, including written, oral, and visual reports, site visits and tours, personnel rotation programs, education and training programs, and standardization programs. Each has distinctive strengths and weaknesses.

Reports and tours are by far the most popular mediums. Reports serve many purposes: they summarize findings, provide checklists of dos and don'ts, and describe important processes and events. They cover a multitude of topics, from benchmarking studies to accounting conventions to newly discovered marketing techniques. Today written reports are often supplemented by video-tapes, which offer greater immediacy and fidelity.

Tours are an equally popular means of transferring knowledge, especially for large, multidivisional organizations with multiple sites. The most effective tours are tailored to different audiences and needs. To introduce its managers to the distinctive manufacturing practices of New United Motor Manufacturing Inc. (NUMMI), its joint venture with Toyota, General Motors developed a series of specialized tours. Some were geared to upper and middle managers, while others were aimed at lower ranks. Each tour described the policies, practices, and systems that were most relevant to that level of management.

Despite their popularity, reports and tours are relatively cumbersome ways of transferring knowledge. The gritty details that lie behind complex management concepts are difficult to communicate second-hand. Absorbing facts by reading them or seeing them demonstrated is one thing; experiencing them personally is quite another. As a leading cognitive scientist has observed, "It is very difficult to become knowledgeable in a passive way. Actively experiencing something is considerably more valuable than having it described."[8] For this reason, personnel rotation programs are one of the most powerful methods of transferring knowledge.

In many organizations, expertise is held locally: in a particularly skilled computer technician, perhaps, a savvy global brand manager, or a division head with a track record of successful joint ventures. Those in daily contact with these experts benefit enormously from their skills, but their field of influence is relatively narrow. Transferring them to different parts of the organization helps share the wealth. Transfers may be from division to division, department to department, or facility to facility; they may involve senior, middle, or first-level managers. A supervisor experienced in just-in-time production, for example, might move to another factory to apply the methods there, or a successful division manager might transfer to a lagging division to invigorate it with already proven ideas. The CEO of Time Life used the latter approach when he shifted the president of the company's music division, who had orchestrated several years of rapid growth and high profits through innovative marketing, to the presidency of the book division, where profits were flat because of continued reliance on traditional marketing concepts.

Line to staff transfers are another option. These are most effective when they allow experienced managers to distill what they have learned and diffuse it across the company in the form of new standards, policies, or training programs. Consider how PPG used just such a transfer to advance its human resource practices around the concept of high-commitment work systems. In 1986, PPG constructed a new float-glass plant in Chehalis, Washington; it employed a radically new technology as well as innovations in human resource management that were developed by the plant manger and his staff. All workers were organized into small, self-managing teams with responsibility for work assignments, scheduling, problem solving and improvement, and peer review. After several years running the factory, the plant manager was promoted to director of human resources for the entire glass group. Drawing on his experiences at Chehalis, he developed a training program geared toward first-level supervisors that taught the behaviors needed to manage employees in a participative, self-managing environment.

As the PPG example suggests, education and training programs are powerful tools for transferring knowledge. But for maximum effectiveness, they must be linked explicitly to implementation. All too often, trainers assume that new knowledge will be applied without taking concrete steps to ensure that trainees actually follow through. Seldom do trainers provide opportunities for practice, and few programs consciously promote the application of their teachings after employees have returned to their jobs.

Xerox and GTE are exceptions. As noted earlier, when Xerox introduced problem-solving techniques to its employees in the 1980s, everyone, from the top to the bottom of the organization, was taught in small departmental or divisional groups led by their immediate superior. After an introduction to concepts and techniques, each group applied what they learned to a real-life work problem. In a similar spirit, GTE's Quality: The Competitive Edge program was offered to teams of business-unit presidents and the managers reporting to them. At the beginning of the 3-day course, each team received a request from a company officer to prepare a complete quality plan for their unit, based on the course concepts, within 60 days. Discussion periods of two to three hours were set aside during the program so that teams could begin working on their plans. After the teams submitted their reports, the company officers studied them, and then the teams implemented them. This GTE program produced dramatic improvements in quality, including a recent semifinalist spot in the Baldrige Awards.

The GTE example suggests another important guideline: knowledge is more likely to be transferred effectively when the right incentives are in place. If employees know that their plans will be evaluated and implemented—in other words, that their learning will be applied—progress is far more likely. At most companies, the status quo is well entrenched; only if manager and employees see new ideas as being in their own best interest will they accept them gracefully. AT&T has developed a creative approach that combines strong incentives with information sharing. Called the Chairman's Quality Award (CQA), it is an internal quality competition modeled on the Baldrige prize but with an important twist: awards are given not only for absolute performance (using the same 1,000-point scoring system as Baldrige) but also for improvements in scoring from the previous year. Gold, silver, and bronze Improvement Awards are given to units that have improved their scores 200, 150, and 100 points, respectively. These awards provide the incentive for change. An accompanying Pockets of Excellence program simplifies knowledge transfer. Every year, it identifies every unit within the company that has scored at least 60% of the possible points in each award category and then publicizes the names of these units using written reports and electronic mail.

# MEASURING LEARNING

Managers have long known that "if you can't measure it, you can't manage it." This maxim is as true of learning as it is of any other corporate objective. Traditionally, the solution has been "learning curves" and "manufacturing progress functions." Both concepts date back to the discovery, during the 1920s and 1930s, that the costs of airframe manufacturing fell predictably with increases in cumulative volume. These increases were viewed as proxies for greater manufacturing knowledge and most early studies examined their impact on the costs of direct labor. Later studies expanded the focus, looking at total manufacturing costs and the impact of experience in other industries, including shipbuilding, oil refining, and consumer electronics. Typically, learning rates were in the 80% to 85% range (meaning that with a doubling of cumulative production, costs fell to 80% to 85% of their previous level), although there was wide variation.

Firms like the Boston Consulting Group raised these ideas to a higher level in the 1970s. Drawing on the logic of learning curves, they argued that industries as a whole faced "experience curves," costs and prices that fell by predictable amounts as industries grew and their total production increased. With this observation, consultants suggested, came an iron law of competition. To enjoy the benefits of experience, companies would have to rapidly increase their production ahead of competitors to lower prices and gain market share.

Both learning and experience curves are still widely used, especially in the aerospace, defense, and electronics industries. Boeing, for instance, has established learning curves for every work station in its assembly plant; they assist in monitoring productivity, determining work flows and staffing levels, and setting prices and profit margins on new airplanes. Experience curves are common in semi-conductors and consumer electronics, where they are used to forecast industry costs and prices.

For companies hoping to become learning organizations, however, these measures are incomplete. They focus on only a single measure of output (cost or price) and ignore learning that affects other competitive variables, like quality, delivery, or new product introductions. They suggest only one possible learning driver (total production volumes) and ignore both the possibility of learning in mature industries, here output is flat, and the possibility that learning might be driven by other sources, such as new technology or the challenge posed by competing products. Perhaps most important, they tell us little about the sources of learning or the levers of change.

Another measure has emerged in response to these concerns. Called the "half-life" curve, it was originally developed be Analog Devices, a leading semiconductor manufacturer, as a way of comparing internal improvement rates. A half-life curve measures the time it takes to achieve a 50% improvement in a specified performance measure. When represented graphically, the performance measure (defect rates, on-time delivery, time to market) is plotted on the vertical axis, using a logarithmic scale, and the time scale (days, months, years) is plotted horizontally. Steeper slopes then represent faster learning.

The logic is straightforward. Companies, divisions, or departments that take less time to improve must be learning faster than their peers. In the long run, their short learning cycles will translate into superior performance. The 50% target is a measure of convenience; it was derived empirically from studies of successful improvement processes at a wide range of companies. Half-life curves are also flexible. Unlike learning and experience curves, they work on any output measure, and they are not confined to costs or prices. In addition, they are easy to operationalize, they provide a simple measuring stick, and they allow for ready comparison among groups.

Yet even half-life curves have an important weakness: they focus solely on results. Some types of knowledge take years to digest, with few visible changes in performance for long periods. Creating a total quality culture, for instance, or developing new approaches to product development are difficult systemic changes. Because of their long gestation periods, half-life curves or any other measures focused solely on results are unlikely to capture any short-run learning that has occurred. A more comprehensive framework is needed to track progress.

Organizational learning can usually be traced through three overlapping stages. The first step is cognitive. Members of the organization are exposed to new ideas, expand their knowledge, and begin to think differently. The second step is behavioral. Employees begin to internalize new insights and alter their behavior. And the third step is performance improvement, with changes in behavior leading to measurable improvements in results: superior quality, better delivery, increased market share, or other tangible gains. Because cognitive and behavioral changes typically precede improvements in performance, a complete learning audit must include all three.

Surveys, questionnaires, and interviews are useful for this purpose. At the cognitive level, they would focus on attitudes and depth of understanding. Have employees truly understood the meaning of self-direction and teamwork, or are the terms still unclear? At PPG, a team of human resource experts periodically audits every manufacturing plant, including extensive interviews with shop-floor employees, to ensure that the concepts are well understood. Have new approaches to customer service been fully accepted? At its 1989 Worldwide Marketing Managers' Meeting, Ford presented participants with a series of hypothetical situations in which customer complaints were in conflict with short-term dealer or company profit goals and asked how they would respond. Surveys like these are the first step toward identifying changed attitudes and new ways of thinking.

To assess behavioral changes, surveys and questionnaires must be supplemented by direct observation. Here the proof is in the doing, and there is no substitute for seeing employees in action. Domino's Pizza uses "mystery shoppers" to assess managers' commitment to customer service at its individual stores; L.L. Bean places telephone orders with its own operators to assess service levels. Other companies invite outside consultants to visit, attend meetings, observe employees in action, and then report what they have learned. In many ways, this approach mirrors that of examiners for the Baldrige Award, who make several-day site visits to semifinalists to see whether the companies' deeds match the words on their applications.

Finally, a comprehensive learning audit also measures performance. Half-life curves or other performance measures are essential for ensuring that cognitive and behavioral changes have actually produced results. Without them, companies would lack a rationale for investing in learning and the assurance that learning was serving the organization's ends.

## FIRST STEPS

Learning organizations are not built overnight. Most successful examples are the products of carefully cultivated attitudes, commitments, and management processes that have accrued slowly and steadily over time. Still, some changes can be made immediately. Any company that wishes to become a learning organization can begin by taking a few simple steps.

The first step is to foster an environment that is conducive to learning. There must be time for reflection and analysis, to think about strategic plans, dissect customer needs, assess current work systems, and invent new products. Learning is difficult when employees are harried or rushed; it tends to be driven out by the pressures of the moment. Only if top management explicitly frees up employees' time for the purpose does learning occur with any frequency. That time will be doubly productive if employees possess the skills to use it wisely. Training in brainstorming, problem solving, evaluating experiments, and other core learning skills is therefore essential.

Another powerful lever is to open up boundaries and stimulate the exchange of ideas. Boundaries inhibit the flow of information; they keep individuals and groups isolated and reinforce preconceptions. Opening up boundaries, with conferences, meetings, and project teams, with other cross organizational levels or linking the company and its customers and suppliers, ensures a fresh flow of ideas and the chance to consider competing perspectives. General Electric CEO Jack Welch considers this to be such a powerful stimulant of change that he has made "boundarylessness" a cornerstone of the company's strategy for the 1990s.

Once managers have established a more supportive, open environment, they can create learning forums. These are programs or events designed with explicit learning goals in mind, and they can take a variety of forms: strategic reviews, which examine the changing competitive environment and the company's product portfolio, technology, and market positioning; systems audits, which review the health of large, cross-functional processes and delivery systems; internal benchmarking reports, which identify and compare best-in-class activities within the organization; study missions, which are dispatched to leading organizations around the world to better understand their performance and distinctive skills; and jamborees or symposiums, which bring together customers, suppliers, outside experts, or internal groups to share ideas and learn from one another. Each of these activities fosters learning by requiring employees to wrestle with new knowledge and consider its implications. Each can also be tailored to business needs. A consumer goods company, for example, might sponsor a study mission to Europe to learn more about distribution methods within the newly unified Common Market, while a high-technology company might launch a systems audit to review its new product development process.

Together these efforts help to eliminate barriers that impede learning and begin to move learning higher on the organizational agenda. They also suggest a subtle shift in focus, away from continuous improvement and toward a commitment to learning. Coupled with a better understanding of the "three Ms," the meaning, management, and measurement of learning, this shift provides a solid foundation for building learning organizations.

## REFERENCES

1. Peter M. Senge, *The Fifth Discipline* (New York: Doubleday, 1990), p. 1.
2. Ikujiro Nonaka, "The Knowledge-Creating Company," *Harvard Business Review*, November–December 1991, p. 97.
3. Robert Howard, "The CEO as Organizational Architect: An Interview with Xerox's Paul Allaire," *Harvard Business Review*, September–October 1992, p. 106.
4. Modesto A. Maidique and Billie Jo Zirger, "The New Product Learning Cycle," *Research Policy,* Vol. 14, No. 6 (1985), pp. 299, 309.
5. Frank R. Gulliver, "Post-Project Appraisals Pay," *Harvard Business Review*, March–April 1987, p. 128.
6. David Nadler, "Even Failures Can Be Productive," *New York Times,* April 23, 1989, Sec. 3, p. 3.
7. Robert C. Camp, *Benchmarking: The Search for Industry Best Practices that Lead to Superior Performance* (Milwaukee: ASQC Quality Press, 1989), p. 12.
8. Roger Schank, with Peter Childers, *The Creative Attitude* (New York: Macmillan, 1988), p. 9.
9. Ramchandran Jaikumar and Roger Bohn, "The Development of Intelligent Systems for Industrial Use: A Conceptual Framework," *Research on Technological Innovation, Management and Policy,* Vol. 3 (1986), pp. 182–188.

# 4
# Individual Motivation and Organizational Behavior

WORK MOTIVATION: THEORY AND PRACTICE
*Raymond A. Katzell*
*Donna E. Thompson*

MOTIVATION: A DIAGNOSTIC APPROACH
*David A. Nadler*
*Edward E. Lawler III*

THAT URGE TO ACHIEVE
*David C. McClelland*

## WORK MOTIVATION: THEORY AND PRACTICE

*Raymond A. Katzell*
*Donna E. Thompson*

In recent years, work motivation has emerged as an increasing topic of concern for American society. This heightened interest is due, in part, to the flagging productivity of our organizations. Demographic changes have further underscored the need for innovative approaches to developing, motivating, and retaining valuable human resources. There is no longer an endless supply of qualified individuals either for unskilled entry-level positions or for technical or more highly skilled jobs (Szilagyi & Wallace, 1983). Moreover, changes have occurred in what American workers want out of jobs and careers and, for that matter, out of their lives in general (Katzell, 1979; Lawler, 1985). Demographic projections for the increased diversity of the American workforce in the 1990s and beyond are also raising the additional problems of matching motivational practices to the needs and values of diverse subgroups of employees (Thompson & DiTomaso, 1988).

Interest in work motivation among psychologists and other behavioral scientists who study organizations has escalated dramatically as well. In fact, probably no other subject has received more attention in recent journals and textbooks of organizational behavior (Cooper & Robertson, 1986). Current reviews of that literature amply document the extensive empirical research that has been done and the theories that have been formulated (e.g., Landy & Becker, 1987; Locke & Henne, 1986; Pinder, 1984).

In this article we endeavor to bring together major theories, research, and applications on the subject of motivation for work performance. Work motivation is defined as a broad construct pertaining to the conditions and processes that account for the arousal, direction, magnitude, and maintenance effort in a person's job. We begin by briefly summarizing and classifying key theories. Seven key strategies for improving work motivation are then distilled from this classification. Various programs are described for implementing those strategies, with the aim of creating work situations in which workers are both better satisfied and more productive. Last, we suggest some future directions for research and practice.

Reprinted with permission of the authors.

# THEORIES OF WORK MOTIVATION

The early theories of work motivation can be characterized as simplistic. One view was that the key to motivating people at work was a behavioral version of the carrot and stick: Pay people for being good workers and punish or fire them, for being otherwise. That was a basic tenet of so-called scientific management (Taylor, 1911). In contrast was the notion that a happy worker is a good worker, a notion that has been criticized as the core of the naive "human relations" movement (Perrow, 1972). Eventually, the validity of both of these formulations was called into question by empirical findings. For example, it was noted that workers respond to incentives and disincentives other than money and even the keeping of a job (Hertzberg, Mausner, & Snyderman, 1959; Roethlisberger & Dickson, 1939), and the basic assumption of the human relations movement was challenged by the typically low correlations between job satisfaction and job performance (Brayfield & Crockett, 1955).

To deal with such deficiencies, other students of work motivation have since proposed a variety of other theoretical approaches, which we summarize in the following subsections. The list is not meant to be exhaustive, but rather indicative of major classes of theories that have received considerable attention from researchers and scholars interested in work motivation. Although there may be differences in the specific formulations of different theorists within a category, we believe it is more useful here to emphasize common or related ideas. Readers interested in extensions or variations of the theories, as well as citations of the original literature, can consult the general reviews cited earlier.

Although theories of work motivation have been categorized in various ways, we have chosen to classify them broadly as either dealing with exogenous causes or endogenous processes. We believe this conceptualization facilitates the examination of what is known about the conditions and practices affecting work motivation. Exogenous theories focus on motivationally relevant independent variables that can be changed by external agents. Thus, exogenous variables (e.g., organizational incentives and rewards and social factors such as leader and group behavior) represent action levers or handles that can be used by policymakers (or experimenters, for that matter) to change the motivation of workers. Endogenous theories, in turn, deal with process or mediating variables (expectancies, attitudes, etc.) that are amenable to modification only indirectly in response to variation in one or more exogenous variables.

## Exogenous Theories

*Motive/need theory.* People have certain innate or acquired propensities to seek out or avoid certain kinds of stimuli. These propensities, called motives or needs, influence behavior and are major determinants of performance. Various theories differ in content regarding the number of basic needs or sets of needs proposed and in whether needs are arranged in some hierarchical order.

*Incentive/reward theory.* Incentives consist of features of the work situation (e.g., what the supervisor says and does) that lead the workers to associate certain forms of behavior (e.g., high quality of product) with a reward (e.g., praise). Disincentives are stimuli that conversely evoke avoidance, or refraining, such as a company policy that docks pay when employees are absent. Incentives are therefore important in attracting and holding employees and in directing behavior. Rewards are stimuli that satisfy one or more motives and therefore arouse positive psychological states that serve to encourage and maintain the behavior that produced them.

*Reinforcement theory.* People are motivated to perform well when there have been positive consequences of good performance. Conversely, ineffective behavior should not be positively reinforced or should be punished. The effects of reinforcement depend heavily on the schedule according to which reinforcers are delivered. Hence, more attention is devoted to schedules than to properties of the reinforcers.

*Goal theory*.　The basic proposition of goal theory is that people will perform better if goals are defined that are difficult, specific, and attractive.　People need feedback to continue to perform at high levels.　Commitment to a goal may be increased by money or another concrete reward or by participating in setting the work goals.

*Personal and material resource theory*.　Constraints on workers' abilities or opportunities to attain their work goals are demotivating.　In the extreme, such constraints can lead to apathy or learned helplessness.　Conversely, conditions that facilitate goal attainment are positively motivating.　These constraints and facilitators can be personal (such as skill level) or material (such as equipment).

*Group and norm theory*.　People are motivated to perform well when their work group facilitates and approves of it.　The dynamics of formal and informal work groups often include the development of cohesiveness, the emergence of norms regarding behavior, particularly about how much work is appropriate, and the conformity of individual members to these norms.　The work group develops and maintains adherence to norms through the use of social rewards and sanctions.　Working in the presence of other group members is itself a source of arousal, especially if the other members are perceived as monitoring or evaluating one's performance.　People are also prone to absorb the attitudes and behavioral dispositions of other group members.

*Sociotechnical system theory*.　People are motivated to perform well when the work system is designed so that conditions for effective personal, social, and technological functioning are harmonizing. The work should be meaningful, challenging, and diversified, and workers should have skills, autonomy, and resources to do it well.

## Endogenous Theories

*Arousal/activation theory*.　Arousal/activation theories focus on internal processes that mediate the effects of conditions of work on performance.　Physiological and affective states are the two types of mediators that have received the most attention.

*Expectancy-valence theory*.　People are motivated when they expect that effort will result in good performance, which in turn will be instrumental in attaining valued outcomes.　Equity theory people are motivated by their need for fair treatment.　Justice consists of balance between a worker's inputs in a given situation (e.g., ability, seniority) and its outcomes (e.g., money, promotions).　Equity exists when output/input ratios for the individual employee and the reference source (e.g., co-worker, profession) are equal.

*Attitude theory*.　People who have favorable attitudes towards their jobs, work, and/or organizations will be more highly motivated to remain in and perform their jobs.　The principle of cognitive consistency also implies that people will act in ways that accord with their attitudes.　Two major work-related attitudes are job satisfaction (affect associated with one's job) and job involvement (how important the job is to the incumbent).

*Intention/goal theory*.　A person's performance is determined by the goals to which he or she is committed.　The goals may be self-set or accepted from those set by others.　Intentions are cognitive representations of goals to which the person is committed.　People who are committed to specific, hard goals perform at higher levels than people who have easier or vaguer goals.

*Attribution/self-efficacy theory*.　Although attributions and self-efficacy represent two somewhat different theoretical strands, they can be merged in their implications for work motivation. Attribution theory is concerned with explanations that people have for why particular events occur or why people behave as they do.　If people think that the causes of their performance are stable, internal, and intentional, successful performance will affect their self-efficacy beliefs favorably.　People with perceptions of greater self-efficacy and higher self-esteem are more likely to have higher performance standards and goals, have expectations of better performance, have more favorable job attitudes, and show greater willingness to put forth effort on challenging tasks.

*Other cognitive theories.* With the exception of arousal/activation theory, the endogenous theories of motivation summarized above feature various cognitive processes. Several other cognitive formulations have recently been advanced. Because they have not yet been the target of extensive research and application in work situations, we simply note them here. They include social cognition, social information processing, and control theory (see Ilgen & Klein, 1989).

## EXOGENOUS THEORIES: SEVEN MOTIVATIONAL IMPERATIVES

Although endogenous theories help explain what is going on in motivation, it is the exogenous theories that suggest "action levers" that can be employed to change work motivation. Seven key strategies for improving work motivation can be distilled from the exogenous theories. Table 1 presents these motivational imperatives. Each of the columns corresponds to an exogenous construct. Within each column, the motivational imperative or principle implied by the related exogenous theory is summarized and illustrative programs that have been used to fulfill the imperative are listed. Space prevents us from discussing all of the specific programs that organizations have used with some degrees of success, or even all that are listed in Table 1. In this section, we briefly describe some of the more widely employed programs that have been used to implement the motivational imperatives. For purpose of illustration, we also describe in greater detail one example relating to each of the seven imperatives.

TABLE 1   Approaches to Improving Work Motivation

| | Exogenous variables | | | | | | |
|---|---|---|---|---|---|---|---|
| Imperative and programs | 1. Personal motives | 2. Incentives and rewards | 3. Reinforcement | 4. Goal-setting techniques | 5. Personal and material resources | 6. Social and group factors | 7. Socio-technical systems |
| Motivational imperative | Workers' motives and values must be appropriate for their jobs | Make jobs attractive, interesting, and satisfying | Effective performance must be positively reinforced, but not ineffective performance | Work goals must be clear, challenging, attainable, attractive | Provide needed resources and eliminate constraints to performance | Interpersonal and group processes must support goal attainment | Personal, social, and technological parameters must be harmonious |
| Illustrative programs | Personnel selection Job previews Motive training Socialization | Financial compensation Promotion Participation Job security Career development Considerate supervision Job enrichment Benefits Flexible hours Recognition "Cafeteria" plans | Financial incentive plans Behavioral analysis Praise and criticism Self-management | Goal setting Management by objectives Modeling Quality circles Appraisal and feedback | Training and development Coaching and counseling Equipment Technology Supervision Methods improvement Problem solving groups | Division of labor Group composition Team development Sensitivity training Leadership Norm building | Quality of work-life programs Socio-technical systems designs Organizational development Scanlon plan |

113

## Personal Motives and Values

The motivational imperative inherent in motive/need theory is that it is important to ensure that workers have been motivated and values are relevant to the types of organization and to the jobs in which they are placed. It should be noted that the theoretical and practical value of the construct of personal motives has been questioned (e.g., Salancik & Pfeffer, 1978). Nevertheless, this theory remains central to two basic strategies for improving work motivation: a) selecting workers whose motives match the situation (personnel selection), and b) developing those motives in them (motive training).

*Personnel selection.* In an extensive, long-term effort to assess managerial potential, measures of various personal characteristics were obtained from junior managers at AT&T in an assessment center by such techniques as paper-and-pencil tests, projective tests, interviews, and observed group exercises (Bray, Campbell, & Grant, 1974). Among the findings was that 64% of the initial 61 assessees who had been predicted to reach the middle management in fact did so eight years later; that figure may be contrasted with only 32% of 62 assessees reaching middle management who had been predicted not to do so.

Not all of the measures in this study address motivational characteristics. But among those qualities that predicted success in attaining the middle-management level were need for advancement, energy, primacy of work, inner work standards, range of interests, and need for security (inverse relationship). Summarizing the qualities deemed essential to managerial success in the study, Bray and Grant (1966) pointed to the importance of motivation to perform well, desire for rapid advancement, independence of the approval of others, and lesser concern with security, in addition to having the requisite intellectual, administrative, and social abilities.

Howard and Bray (1988) subsequently reported a 20-year follow-up of a total of 266 assessees in the AT&T program. Motivational dimensions again proved to be prominent in predicting career advancement and success 20 years later—specifically, the dimensions of advancement or achievement motivation and work involvement. This study also shed light on motivational factors predictive of staying with or voluntarily leaving the company: Stayers scored, on average, significantly higher on need for security, company value orientation, work involvement, and tolerance for delayed gratification but showed less urgent need for advancement.

*Job previews.* Another program designed to implement the motivational imperative of fitting workers' motives to the job provides candidates with realistic job previews. Although results have not always been positive, there have been numerous instances of reduction in later turnover when organizations provided applicants with realistic previews of what their job would be like, via brochures, films, and even reports of previous employee attitude surveys, thereby furnishing a basis for self-selection (Wanous, 1980).

*Motive training.* The second broad strategy, that of changing motives by training, is based on the premise that some of the motives pertinent to work behavior are at least partly learned and therefore subject to change. For example, McClelland and Winter (1969) demonstrated that achievement motivation can be strengthened through training, with favorable consequences for job success. Training women to be more assertive and dominant in work relationships is another application of this approach (O'Donnell & Colby, 1979).

## Incentives and Rewards

The imperative that follows from incentive/reward theory is that jobs and their associated perquisites must be designed so as to be attractive, interesting, and satisfying to workers. When a national sample of 1,500 workers was asked about the importance to them of various features of a job, the highest ratings were assigned to the rewards of interesting work, good pay, availability of needed resources, having sufficient authority, and friendly and cooperative co-workers (Survey Research Center, University of Michigan, 1971). Having control over one's working life appears to be becoming increasingly salient as well (Katzell, 1979; Lawler, 1985).

Enlightened employers and unions endeavor to create working conditions and policies that provide such rewards. It is important to note, however, that the best of such programs can be undercut if they are administered inequitably. The motivational role of equity was noted among the endogenous theories summarized earlier. Its importance extends even to administering nonmonetary rewards such as status (Greenberg, 1988).

*Job enrichment.* Job enrichment is one kind of innovative program designed to fulfill the imperative of making jobs attractive, interesting, and satisfying. Many behavioral scientists have advanced the thesis that diversified, challenging jobs are more satisfying and intrinsically motivating than simpler, more routine ones (e.g., Hackman & Oldham, 1975, 1980; Herzberg, 1966). A number of attempts to implement this thesis have been reported; in the aggregate they show that effects of job enrichment on attitudes are usually favorable, whereas effects on performance, although often positive, are less consistent (Stone, 1986).

A program undertaken with 90 clerical workers in a large quasi-federal agency illustrates this approach (Orpen, 1979). The employees were divided into two groups, one in which no changes were made. The jobs of the employees in the other group were enriched by increasing skill variety, task identity and significance, autonomy, and feedback, these being core dimensions of job scope proposed by Hackman and Oldham (1975). Measures of attitudes, quality and quantity of job performance, turnover, and the absenteeism were obtained before, during, and after the experimental period, which lasted six months. The resulting job performance of employees in the experimental group differed little from that of employees in the comparison group. However, not only were job attitudes significantly better among the employees whose jobs had been enriched, but absenteeism and turnover declined. The positive effects were stronger among employees having stronger needs for personal growth and achievement, as hypothesized by Hackman and Oldham (1975).

This study underscores the importance of person-environment fit (Pervin, 1968), in this case fitting the rewards to the employees. Furthermore, we are reminded that job performance depends on factors in addition to improved motivation Resources and methods for doing the job are also important, so changes in job design are not likely to improve performance unless the new procedures are at least as efficient as the old ones (Fein, 1971). It is also worth noting that reactions to job characteristics depend on social cues as well as on their objective properties (Griffin, Bateman, Wayne, & Head, 1987).

Of course, the variety of incentives and rewards reflected in various organizational practices is enormous. Examples in addition to job enrichment include financial compensation, promotion, merit rating, benefit programs, considerate supervision, and recognition awards. Because there are individual differences in what people regard as desirable in their jobs, Lawler (1987) espoused the idea of having a package of rewards and benefits from which individuals could choose the combination most suitable for them. Such so-called "cafeteria" plans have been found to be workable and useful in industry (Cohn, 1988).

## Reinforcement

Some behavioral psychologists would question the inclusion of reinforcement in a list of motivational factors, preferring to consider it as a description of how behavior is shaped by its consequences. However, inasmuch as it can account for the arousal, direction, and maintenance of effort, students of work motivation often view it literally as a motivational mechanism.

The imperative that derives from this motivational element is that effective performance should be positively reinforced in order to be maintained in the future. Conversely, ineffective behavior should not be rewarded, and a case can even be made for the judicious use of aversive reinforcement, or punishment, in organizations (Arvey & Ivancevich, 1980). In contrast to rewards and incentive theory, the emphasis here is not on the nature of the reinforcers as much as on their linkage to performance.

*Behavior analysis.*   In a quasi-experiment in a wholesale bakery by Komaki, Berwick, and Scott (1978), the targeted behavior consisted of specific practices or conditions that an analysis of previous accidents suggested would avert injuries.  The employees were given instructions on what constituted safe and unsafe practices, were shown a record of their performance of each during a baseline period, and were encouraged to improve their incidence of safe practices from the approximately 70% level during the baseline period, to 90%.  Safe performance was then reinforced by feedback via regularly posting the percentage of safe incidents observed for each group as a whole and by having the supervisors comment favorably to individual employees when they saw them performing certain selected acts safely.  The percentage of safe practices increased markedly during the 8–11 week intervention periods— from 70% to 96% in one department and from 78% to 98% in the other.  Within a year, the lost-time accident rate stabilized at the relatively low figure of below 1 per million work-hours, less than one-fifth the accident rate during the year preceding the initiation of the program.  Although the intervention introduced training, goal setting, and observation in addition to reinforcement, the fact that performance subsided to prointervention levels during a reversal period and later improved again when reinforcement was resumed points to reinforcement as the principal causal mechanism.

*Financial reinforcement programs.*   Traditionally, financial compensation is often administered in a noncontingent way, or the contingency involves just coming to work regularly enough and performing well enough to avoid discharge.  Another problem occurs when the appropriate contingent rewards are indeed administered but their contingency is not clearly understood, because an awareness that rewards are contingent appears to contribute to their effectiveness (Feder & Ferris, 1981).  However, a number of systems have been devised for tying financial remuneration more directly to performance.  Incentive pay systems link the workers' remuneration to some concrete measure of output, such as sales or parts completed.  Research data, on average, support the beneficial effects of such techniques on performance (Locke, Feren, McCaleb, Shaw, & Denny, 1980).  Guzzo, Jette, and Katzell (1985) reported wide variations in those effects, from excellent to negligible.  Possibilities for these variations include a) differences in coping with such problems as measuring performance and providing a sufficiently large pay supplement, and b) situational differences that have been occurring that make incentive plans based on individual or small-group performance less congruent with contemporary social values (Lawler, 1987).

More consistent with the emerging organizational climate and culture are plans that accept the reality of employees as influential participants in the organization and that relate their compensation to performance either of the whole organization or of its major subdivisions.  There are basically three types of such plans:  profit sharing; employee stock ownership; and gain sharing, in which the supplemental payments depend on production improvements rather than profits.  The advantages of the latter are that changes in production are more directly attributable to employee performance and can be calculated more frequently.  Hammer (1988) provided a review of these various plans as a framework for understanding their effects.  Comprehensive organization-wide plans, such as the Scanlon Plan, typically involve a number of nonfinancial motivational factors as well, so they may be regarded as a type of "quality of work-life" program, to be described later (Katzell & Yankelovich, 1975).

*Nonfinancial reinforcers.*   Such reinforcers may also be made contingent on performance.  Examples include time off, opportunity to obtain additional vacation time, and posting of individual performance data, in addition to feedback and praise that were described earlier.

*Self-management.*   Another approach to reinforcement adapts the practice of self-management from clinical psychology (Stuart, 1977).  Target-setting, monitoring, and feedback reinforcement are here the responsibility of the individual employee rather than of a mentor or supervisor (e.g., Frayne & Latham, 1987).

A criticism of extrinsic reinforcement is that it may reduce intrinsic motivation to do the job (Deci, 1972). However, there are two rejoinders to that criticism: a) No one has shown that in actual employment situations use of extrinsic reinforcement reduces total motivation to work; and b) designing work so that it is maximally self-reinforcing and intrinsically rewarding is not inconsistent with the basic notion of rewarding good performance (Farr, 1976; Hamner, 1974). This, in fact, appears to be the way in which organizational reward systems are moving.

## Goal Theory

The motivational imperatives that follow from goal theory are that the goals of work should be specific, clear, attractive, and difficult but attainable. Feedback or knowledge of results of goal attainment is useful for maintaining the motivational force of goals (Locke, Cartledge, & Koepel, 1968).

*Goal-setting programs.* A field experiment by Pritchard, Jones, Roth, Stuebing, and Ekeberg (1988) demonstrates how a program of goal setting and feedback can favorably affect productivity and attitudes. The experiment was conducted with five groups of Air Force personnel totaling approximately 80 individuals over the course of study. One group repaired electronic equipment, and the other four were engaged in storage and distribution of materials and supplies. Productivity measures were compiled over a baseline period of 8 to 9 months. For the next 5 months, the groups received only feedback on their productivity. For the following 5 months, each group participatively set difficult but attainable productivity goals for itself. On average, productivity improved 50% over baseline during the 5-month feedback period, which the experimenters pointed out probably involved informal goal setting by the groups as well. When formal goal setting was added to feedback, productivity improved an additional 25%. Significant improvements were also found in measures of job satisfaction and morale, but not in turnover intentions. Taken together, the results strongly support the positive motivational effects of setting specific, difficult but attainable goals, coupled with feedback on performance.

Although in this case formal goal setting followed feedback and was done participatively and at the group level, other studies have shown positive results when goals are assigned or set on an individual basis and when formal feedback follows, rather than precedes, goal setting (see reviews by Licke, Shaw, Saari, & Latham, 1981, and Tubbs, 1986). It should be also noted that the positive effects of goal setting are sometimes only temporary (Ivancevich, 1976; Quick, 1979).

*Management by objectives.* Positive results have also been reported for other types of programs that aim to improve motivation through goals. For example, although specific practices vary, management by objectives (MBO) programs typically entail an element of participative negotiation between a supervisor and a subordinate in the setting of work goals, plus considerations of what might help the subordinate attain them, and feedback on past performance, which can also incorporate praise and criticism. Reviewing experience with MBO, Carroll and Tosi (1973) concluded that setting hard goals results in better performance only for employees who have self-confidence and expect to achieve the goals—contingencies that probably moderate the effects of all goal setting treatments. It is also important that the employee be committed to the goals, a condition that is fostered by ensuring that the goals are acceptable, which the participative nature of MBO helps to accomplish (Locke, Latham, & Erez, 1988).

Goals are imparted as features of several other practices of human resource management, including job descriptions, training, performance appraisal, participative management, quality circles, and incentive pay plans. Although such practices are not usually undertaken mainly as goal-setting techniques, we should recognize that their worth may depend in large measure on how well they serve that function (Locke et al., 1980).

# Personal and Material Resources

There is recent evidence that inadequate resources can adversely affect the attitudes and emotions of workers (e.g., Eisenberg, Huntington, Hutchison, & Sowa, 1986; Freedman & Phillips, 1985; O'Connor et al., 1984). Katzell and Thompson (1986) found in a path analysis of their complex motivational model that the adequacy of resources had a significant direct effect on the perceived level of extrinsic rewards and thereby indirectly affected morale and work effort. Such findings indicate that resource adequacy does affect motivation.

The motivational imperative that derives from this thesis is manifestly that workers need to have the personal, social, and material resources that facilitate performing their work and attaining their goals. The specific programs and interventions that can contribute to that end are countless. Katzell and Guzzo (1983) reviewed 10 years of literature reporting behavioral science interventions aimed at improving various aspects of worker performance. Of the 206 reports, 83% found improvement in at least one objective aspect of performance, and 72% also found improvements in worker attitudes. Many interventions, such as training, had obvious implications for resource improvement and corresponded to facilitators discussed by various contributors to the volume by Schoorman and Schneider (1988). Unfortunately for our purpose, few of the studies expressly traced effects on specific motivational processes. However, the fact that the majority of the studies showed improvements in both attitudes and performance is again suggestive of the involvement of motivational factors, as is the fact that several of the types of intervention were derived specifically from motivational theory, including appraisal and feedback, MBO, goal setting, financial incentives, and job design.

# Social and Group Factors

The motivational imperative that derives from social and group theories is that interpersonal and group processes must support members' goal attainment. A number of programs have been devised with the aim of improving the motivational climate afforded by groups.

*Division of labor.* An instructive example is offered by a quasi-experimental field study reported by Fisher (1981). The work of production employees in a major corporation was traditionally done via an assembly line. The intervention involved reorganizing employees into five semi-autonomous work teams that were supplied with the responsibility and information they needed to manage their work. The resulting dramatic improvements in production and costs were maintained over a 4-year follow-up period. This study illustrates the motivational benefits of restructuring the traditional division of labor in one or more of the following ways summarized by Walton (1976): setting up self-managing work teams, giving teams responsibility for whole tasks rather than special fragments, and/or encouraging flexibility of job responsibilities among group members.

*Group composition.* Another approach to improving the motivational climate of work groups involves composing groups so that the members are more likely to work well together. Perhaps the most systematic program for applying this insight was devised by Schutz (1966). His research lent support to the theory that a good motivational fit involves matching people whose interpersonal needs complemented each other (e.g., by ensuring that group members who need friendship and affection are balanced by group members disposed to offer such rewards; that those who are passive are matched with others inclined to be assertive; and so forth). In addition to creating groups with need complementarity, establishing groups whose members have similar attitudes and demographic characteristics has also been found to be favorable for work performance (Turban & Jones, 1988).

*Team Development.* Team development is another group-centered approach. These programs can be broadly categorized as a) group goal setting and norm building; b) group problem solving; c) interpersonal and intergroup relations; and d) role negotiation concerned with clarifying and improving

118

allocation of responsibilities among group members (Beer, 1976; Woodman & Sherwood, 1980). Team development programs often contain more than one of these features. (See Sundstrom, DeMeuse, and Futrell, this issue, pp.120–133.)

*Leadership.* Programs for selecting and developing people who can function effectively as leaders can be useful for improving the performance and attitudes of group members (Guzzo et al., 1985). Good leaders can help to create the conditions noted above that enhance the motivational effects of group membership (Locke, 1974; Yukl, 1989).

## Sociotechnical Systems

We have noted that interventions in field situations generally are unable to focus the exogenous changes on a single motivational construct, although the programs we have cited so far were typically aimed at one or another of the six other constructs we identified. An alternative strategy exists that deliberately involves several or all of the exogenous constructs in an orchestrated set of changes. Although these changes are not necessarily introduced simultaneously, the ultimate objective is to develop systems of exogenous variables that harmonizes the individual, social, and technical parameters of the organization. This type of intervention has variously been termed sociotechnical, system-wide, or quality of work life (QWL).

For example, Goodman (1979) reported on a wide-ranging QWL intervention guided by sociotechnical principles at a mining company. The changes, which involved miners and supervisors in one section of the mine, included such features as increased training, improved internal communication, shared responsibility for decisions among workers and managers, job rotation, and incentive pay. Compared with another section of the mine, the experimental section showed improved job attitudes but only slight improvements in performance. However, another well-known system-wide intervention, this one in a garment factory, conversely resulted in marked improvements in performance but relatively slight changes in attitudes (Marrow, Bowers, & Seashore, 1967; Seashore & Bowers, 1970). Reviews of a number of system-wide interventions by Guzzo and Bondy (1983) and Katzell, Beinstock, and Faerstein (1977) showed that such changes often result in improvements in both performance and attitudes and generally have stronger effects than do more limited changes.

## SUMMARY AND CONCLUSIONS

The vast body of research and theory that we have endeavored to summarize here points to a number of practices that can raise the level of motivation of people in work organizations. We have formed these into the following seven imperatives: a) Ensure that workers' motives and values are appropriate for the jobs on which they are placed; b) make jobs attractive to and consistent with workers' motives and values; c) define work goals that are clear, challenging, attractive, and attainable; d) provide workers with the personal and material resources that facilitate their effectiveness; e) create supportive social environments; f) reinforce performance; and g) harmonize all of these elements into a consistent sociotechnical system.

Rational, and even self-evident, as these principles may seem, it is no secret that most organizations have far to go in implementing them. For example, it has been reported that fewer than one-third of employees surveyed perceive that their compensation is based on their performance (Plawin & Suied, 1988). Perhaps acknowledging the principles is one thing, but acting on them—implementing them—is quite another. This obstacle to utilization may stem from either or both of two sources. One is that the technology for applying the principles may not be known. Alternatively, there may be barriers to employing the technology. We refer here to well-known issues of resistance to social and institutional change: vested interests, conflicts of interest, tradition, threats to power or privilege, and so forth. The strategies and tactics for coping with resistance to change in themselves constitute a set of technologies known collectively as organizational development and conflict management; because those are discussed in other articles in this issue, we do not endeavor to treat them here.

It is also possible that the alleged obviousness of the principles is largely a matter of hindsight, as is so often the case with psychological pronouncements. People may not really appreciate the salience of these principles or, if they do, may not know how to apply them. We hope that dissemination of the principles and practices summarized in the present article will help overcome those reasons for suboptimum motivational conditions in organizations.

However, although it is evident that much has been learned about work motivation, we still have far to go in advancing our understanding of its ingredients and in perfecting techniques for applying that understanding. On the scientific front, agendas deserving further attention include the following:

1. Clarify the conceptualization of the key constructs and improve their operationalization. To illustrate, it is apparent that job involvement is an important element in work motivation. However, it seems that job involvement is actually not a unitary construct but reflects both state and trait factors (Rabinowitz & Hall, 1977). Moreover, although as a construct it can be differentiated from job satisfaction and organizational commitment, operational measures of the three are excessively correlated (Brooke, Russell, & Price, 1988).

2. Develop integrative theories. Mitchell (1982) and others have suggested that the various theories of motivation are individually incomplete and that it would be desirable to integrate them in a comprehensive framework. Katzell and Thompson (in press) described a model that combines virtually all of the constructs cited in Table 1. Landy and Becker (1987) argued that the motivational dynamics of such diverse outcomes as job satisfaction, choice behavior, and production are likely to be quite different and therefore lend themselves to less extensive middle-range theories. Another approach to middle-range theory construction would be to fit various theories to differences in situations, such as properties of individuals (Mayes, 1978) or of work settings (Staw, 1977).

3. Perform empirical research to test the developments resulting from each of the preceding two agenda items.

4. Pay more attention to individual differences. Theories of and research on work motivation have generally focused on environmental determinants of attitudes and performance; even theories of personal motives have emphasized person-environment fit. More attention to habitual or even biological dispositions of the individual that may to some degree determine his or her attitudes and energy levels in all work situations is warranted (Arvey, Bouchard, Segal, & Abraham, 1989; Staw, Bell, & Clausen, 1986; Staw & Ross, 1985).

In addition to these and undoubtedly other needed advances in the science of work motivation, there is a need to develop or improve the technology for improving work motivation. Specific areas needing development are so numerous that we can but suggest a few for illustration:

1. What can be done to increase the attractiveness of and commitment to work goals (Hollenbeck & Klein, 1987)?

2. How can job involvement be increased? Some of these methods may involve changing the characteristics of work and its context, whereas others may have to address the personal dispositions of workers (Rabinowitz & Hall, 1977).

3. How can sociotechnical systems be designed that include most, if not all, of the other six motivational imperatives in orchestrated combination with the technical requirements of the work? The difficulty of this charge is illustrated by a recent set of articles in a special issue of the Journal of Applied Behavioral Science ("Innovations in Designing," 1986).

4. How can policymakers be convinced of the desirability and feasibility of applying those motivational imperatives? How can barriers to their adoption be removed?

Projections concerning the not-too-distant future world of work also pose challenges and opportunities for the psychological scientist and practitioner. Here are a few that have motivational implications:

1. As employing organizations undergo frequent changes via downsizing, mergers, acquisitions, new product lines, and so forth, what can replace old-fashioned loyalty and identification as sources of commitment for employees? What will substitute for a sense of long-term continuity and security in their careers?

2. How can the postindustrial society satisfy the newer generation of workers who increasingly value actualization and self-expression relative to traditional bread-and-butter rewards, and who seem to be seeking a better balance between their work and nonwork lives?

3. What are the implications of high technology—computers, robots, telecommunications—for the design of jobs and teams and for selection, training, and careers of workers and managers?

4. What are implications of changes in sex roles and family patterns for the connections between work and nonwork?

5. How can employers adapt their motivational policies and practices to a work force that is increasingly diverse in terms of gender, age, ethnicity, and culture?

We submit that success in coping with these and similar challenges would contribute much to creating a more productive and happier society.

## REFERENCES

Arvey, R. D., Bouchard, T. J., Jr., Segal, N. L., & Abraham, L. M. (1989). Job satisfaction: Environmental and genetic components. *Journal of Applied Psychology, 74,* 187-192.

Arvey, R. D., & Ivancevich, J. M. (1980). Punishment in organizations: A review, propositions, and research suggestions. *Academy of Management Review, 5,* 123–132.

Beer, M. (1976). The technology of management development. In M. D. Dunnette (Ed.), *Handbook of industrial and organizational Psychology* (pp. 937–993). Chicago: Rand McNally.

Bray, D. W., Campbell, R. J., & Grant, D. L. (1974). *Formative years in business.* New York: Wiley.

Bray, D. W., & Grant, D. L. (1966). The assessment center in the measurement of potential for business management. *Psychological Monographs: General and Applied, 80,* 53.

Brayfield, A. H., & Crockett, W. H. (1955). Employee attitudes and employee performance. *Psychological Bulletin, 52,* 396–424.

Brooke, P., Jr., Russell, D. W. , & Price, J. L. (1988). Discriminant validation of measures of job satisfaction, job involvement and organizational commitment. *Journal of Applied Psychology,* 1988, 139–145.

Carroll, S. J., & Tosi, H. L. (1973). *Management by objectives*: *Applications and research.* New York: Macmillan.

Cohn, B. (1988, August 1). A glimpse of the 'flex' future. *Newsweek,* pp. 38–39.

Cooper, C. L., & Robertson, I. T. (1986). Editorial foreword. In *International review of industrial and organizational psychology* (pp.ix–xi). Chichester, England: Wiley.

Deci, E. L. (1972). The effects of contingent and non-contingent rewards and controls on intrinsic motivation. *Organizational Behavior and Human Performance, 8,* 217–229.

Eisenberger, R., Huntington, R., Hutchinson, S., & Sowa, D. (1986). Perceived organizational support. *Journal of Applied Psychology, 71,* 500–507.

Farr, J. L. (1976). Task characteristics, reward contingency, and intrinsic motivation. *Organizational Behavior and Human Performance, 16,* 292–307.

Feder, D. B., & Ferris, G. R. (1981). Integrating O.B. mod with cognitive approaches to motivation. *Academy of Management Review, 6,* 115–125.

Fein, M. (1971). *Motivation for work.* New York: American Institute of Industrial Engineers.

Fisher, M. S. (1981). Work teams: A case study. *Personnel Journal*, 60, 42–45.

Frayne, C. A., & Latham, G. P. (1987). Application of social learning theory to employee self-management of attendance. *Journal of Applied Psychology*, 72, 387–392.

Freedman, S. M., & Phillips, J. S. (1985). The effects of situational performance constraints on intrinsic motivation and satisfaction: The role of perceived competence and self-determination. *Organizational Behavior and Human Decision Processes*, 35, 397–416.

Goodman, P. S. (1979). *Assessing organizational change: The Rushton quality of work experiment.* New York: Wiley–Interscience.

Greenberg, J. (1988). Equity and workplace status: A field experiment. *Journal of Applied Psychology*, 73, 606–613.

Griffin, R. W., Bateman, T. S., Wayne, S. V., & Head, T. C. (1987). Objective and social factors as determinants of task perceptions and responses: An integrated perspective and empirical investigation. *Academy of Management Journal*, 30, 501–523.

Guzzo, R. A., & Bondy, J. S. (1983). *A guide to worker productivity experiments in the United States*, 1976–1981. New York: Pergamon.

Guzzo, R. A., Jette, R. D., & Katzell, R. A. (1985). The effects of psychologically based intervention programs on worker productivity: A meta-analysis. *Personnel Psychology*, 38, 275–292.

Hackman, J. R. and Oldham, G. R., (1975). The development of the job diagnostic survey. *Journal of Applied Psychology*; 60, 159–170.

Hackman, J. R., & Oldham, G. R. (1980). *Work redesign.* Reading, MA: Addison-Wesley.

Hammer, T. H. (1988). New developments in profit sharing, gain-sharing, and employee ownership. In J. P. Campbell & R. J. Campbell (Eds.), *Productivity in organizations* (pp. 328–366). San Francisco: Jossey-Bass.

Hamner, W. C. (1974). Reinforcement theory and contingency management in organizational settings. In H. L. Tosi & W. C. Hamner (Eds.), *Organizational behavior and management: A contingency approach* (pp. 86–112). Chicago: St. Clair.

Herzberg, F. (1966). *Work and the nature of man.* Cleveland, OH: World.

Herzberg, F., Mausner, B., & Snyderman, B. B. (1959). *The motivation to work.* New York: Wiley.

Hollenbeck, J. R., & Klein, H. J. (1987). Goal commitment and the goal-setting process: Problems, prospects, and proposals for future research. *Journal of Applied Psychology*, 72, 212–220.

Howard, A., & Bray, D. W. (1988). *Managerial lives in transition.* New York: Guilford Press.

Ilgen, D. R., & Klein, H. J. (1989). Organizational behavior. *Annual Review of Psychology*, 40, 327–352.

Innovations in designing high performance systems [Special issue]. (1986). *Journal of Applied Behavioral Science*, 22(3).

Ivancevich, J. M. (1976). The effects of goal setting on performance and job satisfaction. *Journal of Applied Psychology*, 61, 605–612.

Katzell, R. A. (1979). Changing attitudes toward work. In C. Kerr & J. M. Rosow (Eds.), *Work in America: The decade ahead* (pp. 35–57.) New York: Van Nostrand Reinhold.

Katzell, R. A., Bienstock, P., & Faerstein, P. H. (1977). *A guide to worker productivity experiments in the United States: 1971–1975.* Scarsdale, NY: Work in America, Inc.

Katzell, R. A., & Guzzo, R. A. (1983). Psychological approaches to productivity improvement. *American Psychologist*, 38, 468–472.

Katzell, R. A., & Thompson, D. E. (1986). *Empirical research on a comprehensive theory of work motivation.* Paper presented at the 21st International Congress of Applied Psychology, Jerusalem, Israel.

Katzell, R. A., & Thompson, D. E. (in press). An integrative model of work attitudes, motivation, and performance. *Human Performance*.

Katzell, R. A., & Yankelovich, D. (1975). *Work, productivity and job satisfaction*. New York: Psychological Corporation.

Komaki, J., Berwick, K. D., & Scott, L. R. (1978). A behavioral approach to occupational safety: Pinpointing and reinforcing safe performance in a food manufacturing plant. *Journal of Applied Psychology*, 63, 434–445.

Landy, F. J., & Becker, W. S. (1987). Motivation theory reconsidered. In L. Cummings & B. M. Staw (Eds.), *Research in organizational behavior* (Vol. 9, pp. 1–38). Greenwich, CT: JAI Press.

Lawler, E. E., III. (1985). Education, management style, and organizational effectiveness. *Personnel Psychology*, 38, 1–26.

Lawler, E. E., III. (1987). Pay for performance: A motivational analysis. In H. Nalbantian (Ed.), *Incentives, cooperation, and risk sharing* (pp. 84–86). Totowa, NJ: Rowman & Littlefield.

Locke, E. A. (1974). The supervisor as "motivator": His influence on employee performance and satisfaction. In B. M. Bass, R. Cooper, & J. A. Haas (Eds.), *Managing for accomplishment* (pp. 57–67). Lexington, MA: Lexington Books.

Locke, E. A., Cartledge, N., & Koepel, J. (1986). Motivational effects of knowledge of results: A goal setting phenomenon. *Psychological Bulletin*, 70, 474–485.

Locke, E. A., Feren, D. D. B, McCaleb, V. M., Shaw, K. N., & Denny, A. T. (1980). The relative effectiveness of four methods of motivating employee performance. In K. D. Duncan, M. M. Gruneberg, & D. Wallis (Eds.), *Changes in working life* (pp. 363–388). New York: Wiley.

Locke, E. A., & Henne, D. (1986). Work motivation theories. In C. L. Cooper & I. T. Robertson (Eds.), *International review of industrial and organizational psychology* (pp. 1–35). Chichester, England: Wiley.

Locke, E. A., Latham, G. P., & Erez, M. (1988). The determinants of goal commitment. *Academy of Management Review*, 13, 23–39.

Locke, E. A., Shaw, K. N., Saari, L. M., & Latham, G. P. (1981). Goal setting and task performance: 1969–1980. *Psychological Bulletin*, 90, 125–152.

Marrow, A. J., Bowers, D. G., & Seashore, S. E. (1967). *Management by participation*. New York: Harper & Row.

Mayes, B. T. (1978). Some boundary conditions in the application of motivation models. *Academy of Management Review*, 3, 51–58.

McClelland, D. C., & Winter, D. G. (1969). *Motivating economic achievement*. New York: Free Press.

Michell, T. R. (1982). Motivation: New directions for theory, research, and practice. *Academy of Management Review,* 7, 80–88.

O'Connor, E. J., Peters, L. H., Pooyan, A., Weekley, J., Frank, B., & Erenkrantz, B. (1984). Situational constraint effects on performance, affective reactions and turnover: A field replication and extension. *Journal of Applied Psychology*, 64, 663–672.

O'Donnell, M., & Colby, L. (1979). Developing managers through assertiveness training. *Training*, 16, 36–37.

Orpen, C. (1979). The effects of job enrichment on employee satisfaction, motivation, involvement, and performance. *Human Relations,* 32, 189–217.

Perrow, C. (1972). *Complex organizations*. Glenview, IL: Scott, Foresman.

Pervin, L. A. (1968). Performance and satisfaction as a function of individual-environment fit. *Psychological Bulletin*, 69, 56–68.

Pinder, C. C. (1984). *Work motivation*. Glenview, IL: Scott, Foresman.

Plawin, P., & Suied, M. (1988, December). Can't get no satisfaction. *Changing Times*, p. 106.

Pritchard, R. D., Jones, S. D., Roth, P. L., Stuebing, K. K., & Ekeberg, S. E. (1988). Effects of group feedback, goal setting, and incentives on organizational productivity. *Journal of Applied Psychology*, 73, 337–358.

Quick, J. C. (1979). Dyadic goal-setting and role stress: A field study. *Academy of Management Journal*, 22, 242–252.

Rabinowitz, S., & Hall, D. T. (1977). Organizational research on job involvement. *Psychological Bulletin*, 84, 265–288.

Roethlisberger, F. J., & Dickson, W. J. (1939). *Management and the worker*. Cambridge, MA: Harvard University Press.

Salancik, G. R., & Pfeffer, J. (1978). A social informational processing approach to job attitudes and task design. *Administrative Science Quarterly*, 23, 224–253.

Schoorman, F. D., & Schneider, B. (1988). *Facilitating work effectiveness*. Lexington, MA: Lexington Books.

Schutz, W. (1966). *The interpersonal underworld*. Palo Alto, CA: Consulting Psychologists Press.

Seashore, S. E., Bowers, D. G. (1970). Durability of organizational change. *American Psychologist*, 25, 227–233.

Staw, B. M. (1977). Motivation in organizations: Toward synthesis. In B. M. Staw (Ed.), *Psychological foundations of organizational behavior* (pp. 77–89). Santa Monica, CA: Goodyear.

Staw, B. M., & Bell, N. E., & Clausen, J. A. (1986). The dispositional approach to job attitudes. *Administrative Science Quarterly*, 31, 35–77.

Staw, B. M., & Ross, J. (1985). Stability in the midst of change: A dispositional approach to job attitudes. *Journal of Applied Psychology*, 70, 469–480.

Stone, E. F. (1986). Job scope-job satisfaction and job-scope-job performance relationships. In E. A. Locke (Ed.), *Generalizing from laboratory to field settings* (pp. 189–206). Lexington, MA: Lexington Books.

Stuart, R. B. (1977). *Behavioral self-management*. New York: Brunner-Mazel.

Sundstrom, E., DeMeuse, K. P., & Futrell, D. (1990). Work teams: Applications and effectiveness. American Psychologist, 45, 120–133.

Survey Research Center, University of Michigan. (1971). *Survey of working conditions*. Washington, DC: U.S. Government Printing Office.

Szilagyi, A. D., & Wallace, M. J. (1983). *Organizational behavior and human performance*. Glenview, IL: Scott, Foresman.

Taylor, F. W. (1911). *The principles of scientific management*. New York: Harper.

Thompson, D. E., & DiTomaso, N. (Eds.). (1988). *Ensuring minority success in corporate management*. New York: Plenum.

Tubbs, M. E. (1986). Goal-setting: A meta-analytic examination of the empirical evidence. *Journal of Applied Psychology,* 71, 474–483.

Turban, D. B., Jones, A. P. (1988). Supervisor-subordinate similarity: Types, effects, and mechanisms. *Journal of Applied Psychology*, 73, 228–234.

Walton, R. E. (1976). Innovative restructuring of work. In J. M. Rosow (Ed.), *The worker and the job* (pp. 145–178). Englewood Cliffs, NJ: Prentice-Hall.

Wanous, J. P. (1980). *Organizational entry: Recruitment, selection, and socialization of newcomers*. Reading, MA: Addison-Wesley.

Woodman, R. W., & Sherwood, J. J. (1980). The role of team development in organizational effectiveness: A critical review. *Psychological Bulletin*, 88, 166–186.

Yukl, G. A. (1989). *Leadership in organizations* (2nd ed.). Englewood Cliffs, NJ: Prentice-Hall.

# MOTIVATION: A DIAGNOSTIC APPROACH

*David A. Nadler*
*Edward E. Lawler III*

- What makes some people work hard while others do as little as possible?
- How can I, as a manager, influence the performance of people who work for me?
- Why do people turn over, show up late to work, and miss work entirely?

These important questions about employees' behavior can only be answered by managers who have a grasp of what motivates people. Specifically, a good understanding of motivation can serve as a valuable tool for *understanding* the causes of behavior in organizations, for *predicting* the effects of any managerial action, and for *directing* behavior so that organizational and individual goals can be achieved.

## EXISTING APPROACHES

During the past twenty years, managers have been bombarded with a number of different approaches to motivation. The terms associated with these approaches are well known—"human relations," "scientific management," "job enrichment," "need hierarchy," "self-actualization," etc. Each of these approaches has something to offer. On the other hand, each of these different approaches also has its problems in both theory and practice. Running through almost all of the approaches with which managers are familiar are a series of implicit but clearly erroneous assumptions.

*Assumption 1: All employees are alike.* Different theories present different ways of looking at people, but each of them assumes that all employees are basically similar in their makeup. Employees all want economic gains, or all want a pleasant climate, or all aspire to be self-actualizing, etc.

*Assumption 2: All situations are alike.* Most theories assume that all managerial situations are alike, and that the managerial course of action for motivation (for example, participation, job enlargement, etc.) is applicable in all situations.

*Assumption 3: One best way.* Out of the other two assumptions there emerges a basic principle that there is "one best way" to motivate employees.

When these "one best way" approaches are tried in the "correct" situation they will work. However, all of them are bound to fail in some situations. They are therefore not adequate managerial tools.

*Source*: J. R. Hackman and E. E. Lawler, *Perspectives on Behavior in Organizations.* New York: McGraw-Hill, 1977.

# A NEW APPROACH

During the past ten years, a great deal of research has been done on a new approach to looking at motivation. This approach, frequently called "expectancy theory," still needs further testing, refining, and extending. However, enough is known that many behavioral scientists have concluded that it represents the most comprehensive, valid, and useful approach to understanding motivation. Further, it is apparent that it is a very useful tool for understanding motivation in organizations.

The theory is based on a number of specific assumptions about the causes of behavior in organizations.

*Assumption 1:* *Behavior is determined by a combination of forces in the individual and forces in the environment.* Neither the individual nor the environment alone determines behavior. Individuals come into organizations with certain "psychological baggage." They have past experiences and a developmental history which has given them unique sets of needs, ways of looking at the world, and expectations about how organizations will treat them. These all influence how individuals respond to their work environment. The work environment provides structures (such as a pay system or a supervisor) which influence the behavior of people. Different environments tend to produce different behavior in similar people just as dissimilar people tend to behave differently in similar environments.

*Assumption 2:* *People make decisions about their own behavior in organizations.* While there are many constraints on the behavior of individuals in organizations, most of the behavior that is observed is the result of individuals' conscious decisions. These decisions usually fall into two categories. First, individuals make decisions about *membership behavior*—coming to work, staying at work, and in other ways being a member of the organization. Second, individuals make decisions about the amount of *effort* they will direct *towards performing their jobs*. This includes decisions about how hard to work, how much to produce, at what quality, etc.

*Assumption 3*: *Different people have different types of needs, desires, and goals.* Individuals differ on what kinds of outcomes (or rewards) they desire. These differences are not random; they can be examined systematically by an understanding of the differences in the strength of individuals' needs.

*Assumption 4:* *People make decisions among alternative plans of behavior based on their perceptions (expectancies) of the degree to which a given behavior will lead to desired outcomes.* In simple terms, people tend to do those things which they see as leading to outcomes (which can also be called "rewards") they desire and avoid doing those things they see as leading to outcomes that are never desired.

In general, the approach used here views people as having their own needs and mental maps of what the world is like. They use these maps to make decisions about how they will behave, behaving in those ways which their mental maps indicate will lead to outcomes that will satisfy their needs. Therefore, they are inherently neither motivated nor unmotivated; motivation depends on the situation they are in, and how it fits their needs.

# THE THEORY

Based on these general assumptions, expectancy theory states a number of propositions about the process by which people make decisions about their own behavior in organizational settings. While the theory is complex at first view, it is in fact made of a series of fairly straightforward observations about behavior. (The theory is presented in more technical terms in Appendix A.) Three concepts serve as the key building blocks of the theory:

*Performance-outcome expectancy.* Every behavior has associated with it, in an individual's mind, certain outcomes (rewards or punishments). In other words, the individual believes or expects that if he or she behaves in a certain way, he or she will get certain things.

Examples of expectancies can easily be described. An individual may have an expectancy that if he produces ten units he will receive his normal hourly rate while if he produces fifteen units he will receive his hourly pay rate plus a bonus. Similarly an individual may believe that certain levels of performance will lead to approval or disapproval from members of her work group or from her supervisor. Each performance can be seen as leading to a number of different kinds of outcomes and outcomes can differ in their types.

*Valence.* Each outcome has a "valence" (value, worth, attractiveness) to a specific individual. Outcomes have different valences for different individuals. This comes about because valences result from individual needs and perceptions, which differ because they in turn reflect other factors in the individual's life.

For example, some individuals may value an opportunity for promotion or advancement because of their needs for achievement or power, while others may not want to be promoted and leave their current work group because of needs for affiliation with others. Similarly, a fringe benefit such as a pension plan may have great valence for an older worker but little valence for a young employee on his first job.

*Effort-performance expectancy.* Each behavior also has associated with it in the individual's mind a certain expectancy or probability of success. This expectancy represents the individual's perception of how hard it will be to achieve such behavior and the probability of his or her successful achievement of that behavior.

For example, you may have a strong expectancy that if you put forth the effort, you can produce ten units an hour, but that you have only a fifty-fifty chance of producing fifteen units an hour if you try.

Putting these concepts together, it is possible to make a basic statement about motivation. In general, the motivation to attempt to behave in a certain way is greatest when:

a. The individual believes that the behavior will lead to outcomes (performance outcome expectancy).
b. The individual believes that these outcomes have positive value for him or her (valence).
c. The individual believes that he or she is able to perform at the desired level (effort performance expectancy).

Given a number of alternative levels of behavior (ten, fifteen, and twenty units of production per hour, for example) the individual will choose that level of performance which has the greatest motivational force associated with it, as indicated by the expectancies, outcomes, and valences.

In other words, when faced with choices about behavior, the individual goes through a process of considering questions such as, "Can I perform at that level if I try?" "If I perform at that level, what will happen?" "How do I feel about those things that will happen?" The individual then decides to behave in that way which seems to have the best chance of producing positive, desired outcomes.

# A General Model

On the basis of these concepts, it is possible to construct a general model of behavior in organizational settings (see Figure 1). Working from left to right in the model, motivation is seen as the force on the individual to expend effort. Motivation leads to an observed level of effort by the individual. Effort, alone, however, is not enough. Performance results from a combination of the effort that an individual puts forth *and* the level of ability which he or she has (reflecting skills, training, information, etc.). Effort thus combines with ability to produce a given level of performance. As a result of performance, the individual attains certain outcomes. The model indicates this relationship in a dotted line, reflecting the fact that sometimes people perform but do not get desired outcomes. As this process of performance-reward occurs, time after time, the actual events serve to provide information which influences the individual's perceptions (particularly expectancies) and thus influences motivation in the future.

FIGURE 1    The Basic Motivation-Behavior Sequence

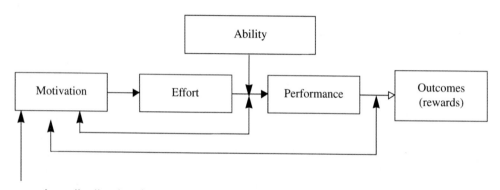

A person's motivation is a function of:    a. Effort-to-performance expectancies
b. Performance-to-outcome expectancies
c. Perceived valence of outcomes

Outcomes, or rewards, fall into two major categories. First, the individual obtains outcomes from the environment. When an individual performs at a given level he or she can receive positive or negative outcomes from supervisors, coworkers, the organization's rewards systems, or other sources. These environmental rewards are thus one source of outcomes for the individual. A second source of outcomes is the individual. These include outcomes which occur purely from the performance of the task itself (feelings of accomplishment, personal worth, achievement, etc.). In a sense, the individual gives these rewards to himself or herself. The environment cannot give them or take them away directly; it can only make them possible.

## Supporting Evidence

Over fifty studies have been done to test the validity of the expectancy-theory approach to predicting employee behavior.[1] Almost without exception, the studies have confirmed the predictions of the theory. As the theory predicts, the best performers in organizations tend to see a strong relationship between performing their jobs well and receiving rewards they value. In addition they have clear performance goals and feel they can perform well. Similarly, studies using the expectancy theory to predict how people choose jobs also show that individuals tend to interview for and actually take those jobs which they feel will provide the rewards they value. One study, for example, was able to correctly predict for 80 percent of the people studied which of several jobs they would take.[2] Finally, the theory correctly predicts that beliefs about the outcomes associated with performance (expectancies) will be better predictors of performance than will feelings of job satisfaction since expectancies are the critical causes of performance and satisfaction is not.

## Questions about the Model

Although the results so far have been encouraging, they also indicate some problems with the model. These problems do not critically affect the managerial implications of the model, but they should be noted. The model is based on the assumption that individuals make very rational decisions after a thorough exploration of all the available alternatives and on weighing the possible outcomes of all these alternatives. When we talk to or observe individuals, however, we find that their decision processes are frequently less thorough. People often stop considering alternative behavior plans when they find one that is at least moderately satisfying, even though more rewarding plans remain to be examined.

People are also limited, in the amount of information they can handle at one time, and therefore the model may indicate a process that is much more complex than the one that actually takes place. On the other hand, the model does provide enough information and is consistent enough with reality to present some clear implications for managers who are concerned with the question of how to motivate the people who work for them.

## Implications for Managers

The first set of implications is directed toward the individual manager who has a group of people working for him or her and is concerned with how to motivate good performance. Since behavior is a result of forces both in the person and in the environment, you as manager need to look at and diagnose both the person and the environment. Specifically, you need to do the following:

*Figure out what outcomes each employee values.* As a first step, it is important to determine what kinds of outcomes or rewards have valence for your employees. For each employee you need to determine "what turns him or her on." There are various ways of finding this out, including a) finding out employees' desires through some structured method of data collection, such as a questionnaire, b) observing the employees' reactions to different situations or rewards, or c) the fairly simple act of asking them what kinds of rewards they want, what kind of career goals they have, or "what's in it for them." It is important to stress here that it is very difficult to change what people want, but fairly easy to find out what they want. Thus, the skillful manager emphasizes diagnosis of needs, not changing the individuals themselves.

*Determine what kinds of behavior you desire.*   Managers frequently talk about "good performance" without really defining what good performance is.  An important step in motivating is for you yourself to figure out what kinds of performances are required and what are adequate measures or indicators of performance (quantity, quality, etc.).  There is also a need to be able to define those performances in fairly specific terms so that observable and measurable behavior can be defined and subordinates can understand what is desired of them (e.g., produce ten products of a certain quality standard— rather than only produce at a high rate).

*Make sure desired levels of performance are reachable.*   The model states that motivation is determined not only by the performance-to-outcome expectancy, but also by the effort-to-performance expectancy.  The implication of this is that the levels of performance which are set as the points at which individuals receive desired outcomes must be reachable or attainable by these individuals.  If the employees feel that the level of performance required to get a reward is higher than they can reasonably achieve, then their motivation to perform well will be relatively low.

*Link desired outcomes to desired performances.*   The next step is to directly, clearly, and explicitly link those outcomes desired by employees to the specific performances desired by you.  If your employee values external rewards, then the emphasis should be on the rewards systems concerned with promotion, pay, and approval.  While the linking of these rewards can be initiated through your making statements to your employees, it is extremely important that employees see a clear example of the reward process working in a fairly short period of time if the motivating "expectancies" are to be created in the employees' minds.  The linking must be done by some concrete public acts, in addition to statements of intent.

If your employee values internal rewards (e.g., achievement), then you should concentrate on changing the nature of the person's job, for he or she is likely to respond well to such things as increased autonomy, feedback, and challenge, because these things will lead to a situation where good job performance is inherently rewarding.  The best way to check on the adequacy of the internal and external reward system is to ask people what their perceptions of the situation are. Remember it is the perceptions of people that determine their motivation, not reality.  It doesn't matter for example whether you feel a subordinate's pay is related to his or her motivation. Motivation will be present only if the subordinate sees the relationship.  Many managers are misled about the behavior of their subordinates because they rely on their own perceptions of the situation and forget to find out what their subordinates feel.   There is only one way to do this: ask. Questionnaires can be used here, as can personal interviews.

*Analyze the total situation for conflicting expectancies.*   Having set up positive expectancies for employees, you then need to look at the entire situation to see if other factors (informal work groups, other managers, the organization's reward systems) have to set up conflicting expectancies in the minds of the employees. Motivation will only be high when people see a number of rewards associated with good performance and few negative outcomes.  Again, you can often gather this kind of information by asking your subordinates.  If there are major conflicts, you need to make adjustments, either in your own performance and reward structure, or in the other sources of rewards or punishments in the environment.

*Make sure changes in outcomes are large enough.*   In examining the motivational system, it is important to make sure that changes in outcomes or rewards are large enough to motivate significant behavior.  Trivial rewards will result in trivial amounts of effort and thus trivial improvements in performance.  Rewards must be large enough to motivate individuals to put forth the effort required to bring about significant changes in performance.

*Check the system for its equity.* The model is based on the idea that individuals are different and therefore different rewards will need to be used to motivate different individuals. On the other hand, for a motivational system to work it must be a fair one—one that has equity (not equality). Good performers should see that they get more desired rewards than do poor performers, and others in the system should see that also. Equity should not be confused with a system of equality where all are rewarded equally, with no regard to their performance. A system of equality is guaranteed to produce low motivation.

## Implications for Organizations

Expectancy theory has some clear messages for those who run large organizations. It suggests how organizational structures can be designed so that they increase rather than decrease levels of motivation or organization members. While there are many different implications, a few of the major ones are as follows:

*Implication 1: The design of pay and reward systems.* Organizations usually get what they reward, not what they want. This can be seen in many situations, and pay systems are a good example.[3] Frequently, organizations reward people for membership (through pay tied to seniority, for example) rather than for performance. Little wonder that what the organization gets is behavior oriented towards "safe," secure employment rather than effort directed at performing well. In addition, even where organizations do pay for performance as a motivational device, they frequently negate the motivational value of the system by keeping pay secret, therefore preventing people from observing the pay-to-performance relationship that would serve to create positive, clear, and strong performance-to-reward expectancies. The implication is that organizations should put more effort into rewarding people (through pay, promotion, better job opportunities, etc.) for the performances which are desired, and that to keep these rewards secret is clearly self-defeating. In addition, it underscores the importance of the frequently ignored performance evaluation or appraisal process and the need to evaluate people based on how they perform clearly defined specific behaviors, rather than on how they score on ratings of general traits such as "honesty," "cleanliness," and other, similar terms which frequently appear as part of the performance appraisal form.

*Implication 2: The design of tasks, jobs, and roles.* One source of desired outcomes is the work itself. The expectancy-theory model supports much of the job enrichment literature, in saying that by designing jobs which enable people to get their needs fulfilled, organizations can bring about higher levels of motivation.[4] The major difference between the traditional approaches to job enlargement or enrichment and the expectancy-theory approach is the recognition by expectancy theory that different people have different needs and, therefore, some people may not want enlarged or enriched jobs. Thus, while the design of tasks that have more autonomy, variety, feedback, meaningfulness, etc., will lead to higher motivation in some, the organization needs to build in the opportunity for individuals to make choices about the kind of work they will do so that not everyone is forced to experience job enrichment.

*Implication 3: The importance of group structures.* Groups, both formal and informal, are powerful and potent sources of desired outcomes for individuals. Groups can provide or withhold acceptance, approval, affection, skill training, needed information, assistance, etc. They are a powerful force in the total motivational environment of individuals. Several implications emerge from the importance of groups. First, organizations should consider the structuring of at least a portion of rewards around group performance rather than individual performance. This is particularly important where group members have to cooperate with each other to produce a group product or service, and where the individual's contribution is often hard to determine. Second, the organization needs to

131

train managers to be aware of how groups can influence individual behavior and to be sensitive to the kinds of expectancies which informal groups set up and their conflict or consistency with the expectancies that the organization attempts to create.

*Implication 4: The supervisor's role.* The immediate supervisor has an important role in creating, monitoring, and maintaining the expectancies and reward structures which will lead to good performance. The supervisor's role in the motivation process becomes one of defining clear goals, setting clear reward expectancies, and providing the right rewards for different people (which could include both organizational rewards and personal rewards such as recognition, approval, or support from the supervisor). Thus, organizations need to provide supervisors with an awareness of the nature of motivation as well as the tools (control over organizational rewards, skill in administering those rewards) to create positive motivation.

*Implication 5: Measuring motivation.* If things like expectancies, the nature of the job, supervisor-controlled outcomes, satisfaction, etc., are important in understanding how well people are being motivated, then organizations need to monitor employee perceptions along these lines. One relatively cheap and reliable method of doing this is through standardized employee questionnaires. A number of organizations already use such techniques, surveying employees' perceptions and attitudes at regular intervals (ranging from once a month to once every year and-a-half) using either standardized surveys or surveys developed specifically for the organization. Such information is useful both to the individual manager and to top management in assessing the state of human resources and the effectiveness of the organization's motivational systems.[5]

*Implication 6: Individualizing organizations.* Expectancy theory leads to a final general implication about a possible future direction for the design of organizations. Because different people have different needs and therefore have different valences, effective motivation must come through the recognition that not all employees are alike and that organizations need to be flexible in order to accommodate individual differences. This implies the "building in" of choice for employees in many areas, such as reward systems, fringe benefits, job assignments, etc., where employees previously have had little say. A successful example of the building in of such choice can be seen in the experiments at TRW and the Educational Testing Service with "cafeteria fringe-benefits plans" which allow employees to choose the fringe benefits they want, rather than taking the expensive and often unwanted benefits which the company frequently provides to everyone.[6]

## SUMMARY

Expectancy theory provides a more complex model of man for managers to work with. At the same time, it is a model which holds promise for the more effective motivation of individuals and the more effective design of organizational systems. It implies, however, the need for more exacting and thorough diagnosis by the manager to determine a) the relevant forces in the individual, and b) the relevant forces in the environment, both of which combine to motivate different kinds of behavior. Following diagnosis, the model implies a need to act—to develop a system of pay, promotion, job assignments, group structures, supervision, etc.—to bring about effective motivation by providing different outcomes for different individuals.

Performance of individuals is a critical issue in making organizations work effectively. If a manager is to influence work behavior and performance, he or she must have an understanding of motivation and the factors which influence an individual's motivation to come to work, to work hard, and to work well. While simple models offer easy answers, it is the more complex models which seem to offer more promise. Managers can use models (like expectancy theory) to understand the nature of behavior and build more effective organizations.

# APPENDIX A: THE EXPECTANCY
# THEORY MODEL IN MORE TECHNICAL TERMS

A person's motivation to exert effort towards a specific level of performance is based on his or her perceptions of associations between actions and outcomes. The critical perceptions which contribute to motivation are graphically presented in Figure 2. These perceptions can be defined as follows:

a. The effort-to-performance expectancy (E→P): This refers to the person's subjective probability about the likelihood that he or she can perform at a given level, or that effort on his or her part will lead to successful performance. This term can be thought of as varying from 0 to 1. In general, the less likely a person feels that he or she can perform at a given level, the less likely he or she will be to try to perform at that level. A person's E→P probabilities are also strongly influenced by each situation and by previous experience in that and similar situations.

b. The performance-to-outcomes expectancy (P→O) and valence (V): This refers to a combination of a number of beliefs about what the outcomes of successful performance will be and the value or attractiveness of these outcomes to the individual. Valence is considered to vary from + 1 (very desirable) to - 1 (very undesirable) and the performance-to-outcomes probabilities vary from + 1 (performance sure to lead to outcome) to 0 (performance not related to outcome). In general, the more likely a person feels that performance will lead to valent outcomes, the more likely he or she will be to try to perform at the required level.

c. Instrumentally: As Figure 2 indicates, a single level of performance can be associated with a number of different outcomes, each having a certain degree of valence. Some outcomes are valent because they have direct value or attractiveness. Some outcomes, however, have valence because they are seen as leading to (or being "instrumental" for) the attainment of other "second level" outcomes which have direct value or attractiveness.

FIGURE 2   Major Terms in Expectancy Theory

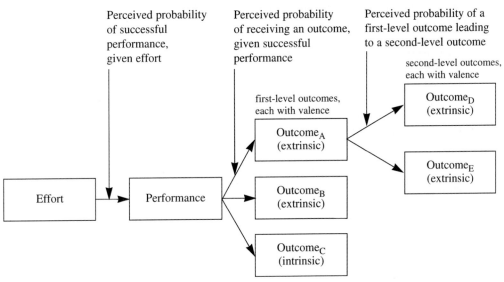

Motivation is expressed as follows:  M • [E→P] x ≤ [(P • O) (V)]

d. Intrinsic and extrinsic outcomes: Some outcomes are seen as occurring directly as a result of performing the task itself and are outcomes which the individual thus gives to himself (i.e., feelings of accomplishment, creativity, etc.). These are called "intrinsic" outcomes. Other outcomes that are associated with performance are provided or mediated by external factors (the organization, the supervisor, the work group, etc.). These outcomes are called "extrinsic" outcomes.

Along with the graphic representation of these terms presented in Figure 2, there is a simplified formula for combining these perceptions to arrive at a term expressing the relative level of motivation to exert effort towards performance at a given level. The formula expresses these relationships:

a. The person's motivation to perform is determined by the P→O expectancy multiplied by the valence (V) of the outcome. The valence of the first order outcome subsumes the instrumentalities and valences of second order outcomes. The relationship is multiplicative since there is no motivation to perform if either of the terms is zero.

b. Since a level of performance has multiple outcomes associated with it, the products of all probability-times-valence combinations are added together for all the outcomes that are seen as related to the specific performance.

c. This term (the summed P→O expectancies times valences) is then multiplied by the E→P expectancy. Again the multiplicative relationship indicates that if either term is zero, motivation is zero.

d. In summary, the strength of a person's motivation to perform effectively is influenced by (1) the person's belief that effort can be converted into performance, and (2) the net attractiveness of the events that are perceived to stem from good performance.

So far, all the terms have referred to the individual's perceptions which result in motivation and thus an intention to behave in a certain way. Figure 3 is a simplified representation of the total model, showing how these intentions get translated into actual behavior.[7] The model envisions the following sequence of events:

a. First, the strength of a person's motivation to perform correctly is most directly reflected in his or her effort—how hard he or she works. This effort expenditure may or may not result in good performance, since at least two factors must be right if effort is to be converted into performance. First, the person must possess the necessary abilities in order to perform the job well. Unless both ability and effort are high, there cannot be good performance. A second factor is the person's perception of how his or her effort can best be converted into performance. It is assumed that this perception is learned by the individual on the basis of previous experience in similar situations. This "how to do it" perception can obviously vary widely in accuracy, and—where erroneous perceptions exist—performance is low even though effort or motivation may be high.

b. Second, when performance occurs, certain amounts of outcomes are obtained by the individual. Intrinsic outcomes, not being mediated by outside forces, tend to occur regularly as a result of performance, while extrinsic outcomes may or may not accrue to the individual (indicated by the wavy line in the model).

FIGURE 3 Simplified Expectancy Theory Model of Behavior

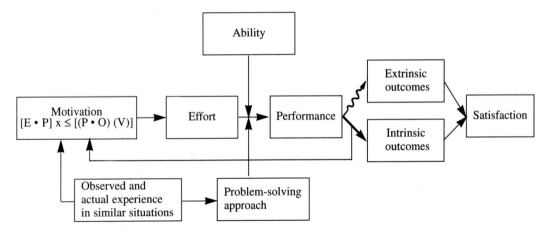

c. Third, as a result of the obtaining of outcomes and the perceptions of the relative value of the outcomes obtained, the individual has a positive or negative affective response (a level of satisfaction or dissatisfaction).

d. Fourth, the model indicates that events which occur influence future behavior by altering the E→P, P→O, and V perceptions. This process is represented by the feedback loops running from actual behavior back to motivation.

## REFERENCES

1. For reviews of the expectancy theory research see Mitchell, T. R. Expectancy models of job satisfaction, occupational preference and effort. A theoretical methodological, and empirical appraisal. *Psychological Bulletin,* 1974, 81, 1053–1077. For a more general discussion of expectancy theory and other approaches to motivation see Lawler, E.E. *Motivation in work organizations.* Belmont Calif.: Brooks/Cole, 1973.
2. Lawler, E. E., Kuleck, W. J., Rhode, J. G., & Sorenson, J. F. Job choice and postdecision dissonance. *Organizational Behavior and Human Performance,* 1975, 13, 133–145.
3. For a detailed discussion of the implications of expectancy theory for pay and reward systems, see Lawler, E. E. *Pay and organizational effectiveness: A psychological view.* New York: McGraw-Hill, 1971.
4. A good discussion of job design with an expectancy theory perspective is in Hackman, J. R., Oldham, G. R., Janson, R., & Purdy, K. A new strategy for job enrichment. *California Management Review.* Summer, 1975, p. 57.
5. The use of questionnaires for understanding and changing organizational behavior is discussed in Nadler, D. A. *Feedback and organizational development: Using databased methods.* Reading, Mass.: Addison-Wesley, 1977.
6. The whole issue of individualizing organizations is examined in Lawler, E. E. The individualized organization: Problems and promise. *California Management Review,* 1974, 17(2), 31–39.
7. For a more detailed statement of the model see Lawler, E. E. Job attitudes and employee motivation: Theory, research and practice. *Personnel Psychology,* 1970, 23, 223–237.

# THAT URGE TO ACHIEVE

*David C. McClelland*

Most people in this world, psychologically, can be divided into two broad groups. There is that minority which is challenged by opportunity and willing to work hard to achieve something, and the majority which really does not care all that much.

For nearly twenty years now, psychologists have tried to penetrate the mystery of this curious dichotomy. Is the need to achieve (or the absence of it) an accident, is it hereditary, or is it the result of environment? Is it a single, isolatable human motive, or a combination of motives—the desire to accumulate wealth, power, fame? Most important of all, is there some technique that could give this will to achieve to people, even whole societies, who do not now have it?

While we do not yet have complete answers for any of these questions, years of work have given us partial answers to most of them and insights into all of them. There is a distinct human motive, distinguishable from others. It can be found, in fact tested for, in any group.

Let me give you one example. Several years ago, a careful study was made of 450 workers who had been thrown out of work by a plant shutdown in Erie, Pennsylvania. Most of the unemployed workers stayed home for a while and then checked back with the United States Employment Service to see if their old jobs or similar ones were available. But a small minority among them behaved differently: the day they were laid off, they started job-hunting.

They checked both the United States and the Pennsylvania Employment Office: they studied the "Help Wanted" sections of the papers; they checked through their union, their church, and various fraternal organizations; they looked into training courses to learn a new skill; they even left town to look for work, while the majority when questioned said they would not under any circumstances move away from Erie to obtain a job. Obviously the members of that active minority were differently motivated. All the men were more or less in the same situation objectively: they needed work, money, food, shelter, job security. Yet only a minority showed initiative and enterprise in finding what they needed. Why? Psychologists, after years of research, now believe they can answer that question. They have demonstrated that these men possessed in greater degree a specific type of human motivation. For the moment let us refer to this personality characteristic as "Motive A" and review some of the other characteristics of the persons who have more of the motive than other persons.

Suppose they are confronted by a work situation in which they can set their own goals as to how difficult a task they will undertake. In the psychological laboratory, such a situation is very simply created by asking them to throw rings over a peg from any distance they may choose. Most persons throw more or less randomly, standing now close, now far away, but those with Motive A seem to calculate carefully where they are most likely to get a sense of mastery. They stand nearly always at moderate distances, not so close as to make the task ridiculously easy, nor so far away as to make it impossible. They set moderately difficult, but potentially achievable goals for themselves, where they objectively have only about a 1-in-3 chance of succeeding. In other words, they are always setting challenges for themselves, tasks to make them stretch themselves a little.

*Source*: Reprinted by permission from THINK Magazine, published by IBM, © 1966 by International Business Machines Corporation, and from the author.

But they behave like this only if *they* can influence the outcome by performing the work themselves. They prefer not to gamble at all. Say they are given a choice between rolling dice with one in three chances of winning and working on a problem with a one-in-three chance of solving in the time allotted, they choose to work on the problem even though rolling the dice is obviously less work and the odds of winning are the same. They prefer to work at a problem rather than leave the outcome to chance or to others.

Obviously they are concerned with personal achievement rather than with the rewards of success per se, since they stand just as much chance of getting those rewards by throwing the dice. This leads to another characteristic the Motive A persons show—namely, a strong preference for work situations in which they get concrete feedback on how well they are doing, as one does, say in playing golf, or in being a salesman, but as one does not in teaching, or in personnel counseling. A golfer always knows his score and can compare how well he is doing with par or with his own performance yesterday or last week. A teacher has no such concrete feedback on how well he is doing in "getting across" to his students.

## THE *n* ACH PERSON

But why do certain persons behave like this? At one level the reply is simple: because they habitually spend their time thinking about doing things better. In fact, psychologists typically measure the strength of Motive A by taking samples of a person's spontaneous thoughts (such as making up a story about a picture they have been shown) and counting the frequency with which he mentions doing things better. The count is objective and can even be made these days with the help of a computer program for content analysis. It yields what is referred to technically as an individual's *n* Ach score (for "need for Achievement"). It is not difficult to understand why people who think constantly about "doing better" are more apt to do better at job-hunting, to set moderate achievable goals for themselves, to dislike gambling (because they get no achievement satisfaction from success), and to prefer work situations where they can tell easily whether they are improving or not. But why some people and not others come to think this way is another question. The evidence suggests it is not because they are born that way, but because of special training they get in the home from parents who set moderately high achievement goals but who are warm, encouraging and nonauthoritarian in helping their children reach these goals.

Such detailed knowledge about one motive helps correct a lot of commonsense ideas about human motivation. For example, much public policy (and much business policy) is based on the simpleminded notion that people will work harder "if they have to." As a first approximation, the idea isn't totally wrong, but it is only a half-truth. The majority of unemployed workers in Erie "had to" find work as much as those with higher *n* Ach, but they certainly didn't work as hard at it. Or again, it is frequently assumed that *any* strong motive will lead to doing things better. Wouldn't it be fair to say that most of the Erie workers were just "unmotivated"? But our detailed knowledge of various human motives shows that each one leads a person to behave in *different ways*. The contrast is not between being "motivated" or "unmotivated" but between being motivated toward A or toward B or C, etc.

A simple experiment makes the point nicely: subjects were told that they could choose as a working partner either a close friend or a stranger who was known to be an expert on the problem to be solved. Those with higher *n* Ach (more "need to achieve") chose the experts over their friends, whereas those with more *n* Ach (the "need to affiliate with others") chose friends over experts. The latter were not "unmotivated"; their desire to be with someone they liked was simply a stronger motive than their desire to excel at the task. Other such needs have been studied by psychologists. For instance, the need for Power is often confused with the need for Achievement because both may lead to "out-standing" activities. There is a distinct difference. People with a strong need for Power want to command attention, get recognition, and control others. They are more active in political life and tend to busy themselves primarily with controlling the channels of communication both up to the top and down to the people so that they are more "in charge." Those with high *n* Power are not as concerned with improving their work performance daily as those with high *n* Ach.

It follows, from what we have been able to learn, that not all "great achievers" score high in *n* Ach. Many generals, outstanding politicians, great research scientists do not, for instance, because their work requires other personality characteristics, other motives. A general or a politician must be more concerned with power relationships, a research scientist must be able to go for long periods without the immediate feedback the person with high *n* Ach requires, etc. On the other hand, business executives, particularly if they are in positions of real responsibility or if they are salesmen, tend to score high in *n* Ach. This is true even in a Communist country like Poland: apparently there, as well as in a private enterprise economy, a manager succeeds if he is concerned about improving all the time, setting moderate goals, keeping track of his or the company's performance, etc.

## MOTIVATION AND HALF-TRUTHS

Since careful study has shown that common sense notions about motivation are at best half-truths, it also follows that you cannot trust what people tell you about their motives. After all, they often get their ideas about their own motives from common sense. Thus a general may say he is interested in achievement (because he has obviously achieved), or a businessman that he is interested only in making money (because he has made money), or one of the majority of unemployed in Erie that he desperately wants a job (because he knows he needs one); but a careful check of what each one thinks about and how he spends his time may show that each is concerned about quite different things. It requires special measurement techniques to identify the presence of *n* Ach and other such motives. Thus what people say and believe is not very closely related to these "hidden" motives which seem to affect a person's "style of life" more than his political, religious or social attitudes. Thus *n* Ach produces enterprising men among labor leaders or managers, Republicans or Democrats, Catholics or Protestants, capitalists or Communists.

Wherever people begin to think often in *n* Ach terms, things begin to move. Men with higher *n* Ach get more raises and are promoted more rapidly, because they keep actively seeking ways to do a better job. Companies with many such men grow faster. In one comparison of two firms in Mexico, it was discovered that all but one of the top executives of a fast growing firm had higher *n* Ach scores than the highest scoring executive in an equally large but slow-growing firm. Countries with many such rapidly growing firms tend to show above-average rates of economic growth. This appears to be the reason why correlations have regularly been found between the *n* Ach content in popular literature (such as popular songs or stories in children's textbooks) and subsequent rates of national economic growth. A nation which is thinking about doing better all the time (as shown in its popular literature) actually does do better economically speaking. Careful quantitative studies have shown this to be true in Ancient Greece, in Spain in the Middle Ages, in England from 1400–1800, as well as among contemporary nations, whether capitalist or Communist, developed or underdeveloped.

Contrast these two stories for example. Which one contains more *n* Ach? Which one reflects a state of mind which ought to lead to harder striving to improve the way things are?

*Excerpt from story A* (4th grade reader): "Don't Ever Owe a Man—The world is an illusion. Wife, children, horses and cows are all just ties of fate. They are ephemeral. Each after fulfilling his part in life disappears. So we should not clamor after riches which are not permanent. As long as we live it is wise not to have any attachments and just think of God. We have to spend our lives without trouble, for is it not time that there is an end to grievances? So it is better to live knowing the real state of affairs. Don't get entangled in the meshes of family life."

*Excerpt from story B* (4th grade reader): "How I Do Like to Learn—I was sent to an accelerated technical high school. I was so happy I cried. Learning is not very easy. In the beginning I couldn't understand what the teacher taught us. I always got a red cross mark on my papers. The boy sitting next to me was very enthusiastic and also an outstanding student. When he found I could not do the problems he offered to show me how he had done them. I could not copy his work. I must learn through my own reasoning. I gave his paper back and explained I had to do it myself. Sometimes I worked on a problem until midnight. If I couldn't finish, I started early in the morning. The red cross marks on my work were getting less common. I conquered my difficulties. My marks rose. I graduated and went on to college."

Most readers would agree, without any special knowledge of the *n* Ach coding system, that the second story shows more concern with improvement than the first, which comes from a contemporary reader used in Indian public schools. In fact the latter has a certain Horatio Alger quality that is reminiscent of our own McGuffey readers of several generations ago. It appears today in textbooks of Communist China. It should not, therefore, come as a surprise that a nation like Communist China, obsessed as it is with improvement, tended in the long run to outproduce a nation like India, which appears to be more fatalistic.

The *n* Ach level is obviously important for statesmen to watch and in many instances to try to do something about, particularly if a nation's economy is lagging. Take Britain, for example. A generation ago (around 1925) it ranked fifth among 25 countries where children's readers were scored for *n* Ach—and its economy was doing well. By 1950 the n Ach level had dropped to 27th out of 39 countries well below the world average—and today, its leaders are feeling the severe economic effects of this loss in the spirit of enterprise.

## ECONOMICS AND *n* ACH

If psychologists can detect *n* Ach levels in individuals or nations, particularly before their effects are widespread, can't the knowledge somehow be put to use to foster economic development? Obviously detection or diagnosis is not enough. What good is it to tell Britain (or India for that matter) that it needs more *n* Ach, a greater spirit of enterprise? In most such cases, informed observers of the local scene know very well that such a need exists, though they may be slower to discover it than the psychologist hovering over *n* Ach scores. What is needed is some method of developing *n* Ach in individuals or nations.

Since about 1960, psychologists in my research group at Harvard have been experimenting with techniques designed to accomplish this goal, chiefly among business executives whose work requires the action characteristics of people with high *n* Ach. Initially, we had real doubts as to whether we could succeed, partly because like most American psychologists we have been strongly influenced by the psychoanalytic view that basic motives are laid down in childhood and cannot really be changed later, and partly because many studies of intensive psychotherapy and counseling have shown minor if any long-term personality effects.   On the other hand we were encouraged by the nonprofessionals: those enthusiasts like Dale Carnegie, the Communist ideologue or the Church missionary, who felt they could change adults and in fact seemed to be doing so.   At any rate we ran some brief (7 to 10 days) "total push" training courses for businessmen, designed to increase their $n$ Ach.

## FOUR MAIN GOALS

In broad outline the courses had four main goals:  1) They were designed to teach the participants how to think, talk and act like a person with high $n$ Ach, based on our knowledge of such people gained through 17 years of research.   For instance, individuals learned how to make up stories that would code high in $n$ Ach (i.e., how to think in $n$ Ach terms), how to set moderate goals for themselves in the ring toss game (and in life).  2) The courses stimulated the participants to set higher but carefully planned and realistic work goals for themselves over the next two years.   Then we checked back with them every six months to see how well they were doing in terms of their own objectives. 3) The courses also utilized techniques for giving the participants knowledge about themselves.  For instance, in playing the ring toss game, they could observe that they behaved differently from others— perhaps in refusing to adjust a goal downward after failure.  This would then become a matter for group discussion and the man would have to explain what he had in mind in setting such unrealistic goals.  Discussion could then lead on to what a person's ultimate goals in life were, how much he cared about actually improving performance v. making a good impression or having many friends. In this way the participants would be freer to realize their achievement goals without being blocked by old habits and attitudes. 4) The courses also usually created a group *esprit de corps* from learning about each other's hopes and fears, successes and failures, and from going through an emotional experience together, away from everyday life, in a retreat setting.  This membership in a new group helps a person achieve his goals, partly because he knows he has their sympathy and support and partly because he knows they will be watching to see how well he does.  The same effect has been noted in other therapy groups like Alcoholics Anonymous.  We are not sure which of these course "inputs" is really absolutely essential—that remains a research question—but we are taking no chances at the outset in view of the general pessimism about such efforts, and we wanted to include any and all techniques that were thought to change people.

The courses have been given: to executives in a large American firm, and in several Mexican firms; to underachieving high school boys; and to businessmen in India from Bombay and from a small city—Kakinada in the state of Andhra Pradesh.  In every instance save one (the Mexican case), it was possible to demonstrate statistically, some two years later, that the men who took the course— had done better (made more money, got promoted faster, expanded their businesses faster) than comparable individuals who did not take the course or who took some other management course.

Consider the Kakinada results, for example.  In the two years preceding the course 9 men, 18 percent of the 52 participants, had shown "unusual" enterprise in their businesses.  In the 18 months following the course 25 of the individuals, in other words nearly 50 percent, were unusually active. And this was not due to a general upturn of business in India.  Data from a control city, some forty-five miles away, show the same base rate of "unusually active" men as in Kakinada before the course—namely, about 20 percent.  Something clearly happened in Kakinada: the owner of a small radio shop started a chemical plant; a banker was so successful in making commercial loans in an enterprising way that he was promoted to a much larger branch of his bank in Calcutta; the local political leader accomplished his goal (it was set in the course) to get the federal government to deepen the harbor and make it into an all-weather port; plans are far along for establishing a steel rolling mill, etc. All this took place without any substantial capital input from the outside. In fact, the only costs were for four 10-day courses plus some brief follow-up visits every six months. The men are raising their own capital and using their own resources for getting business and industry moving in a city that had been considered stagnant and unenterprising.

The promise of such a method of developing achievement motivation seems very great. It has obvious applications in helping underdeveloped countries, or "pockets of poverty" in the United States, to move faster economically. It has great potential for businesses that need to "turn around" and take a more enterprising approach toward their growth and development. It may even be helpful in developing more $n$ Ach among low-income groups. For instance, data show that lower-class African-Americans have a very low level of $n$ Ach. This is not surprising. Society has systematically discouraged and blocked their achievement striving. But as the barriers to upward mobility are broken down, it will be necessary to help stimulate the motivation that will lead them to take advantage of new opportunities opening up.

## EXTREME REACTIONS

But a word of caution: Whenever I speak of this research and its great potential, audience reaction tends to go to opposite extremes. Either people remain skeptical and argue that motives can't really be changed, that all we are doing is dressing Dale Carnegie up in fancy "psychologese," or they become converts and want instant course descriptions by return mail to solve their local motivational problems. Either response is unjustified. What I have described here in a few pages has taken 20 years of patient research effort, and hundreds of thousands of dollars in basic research costs. What remains to be done will involve even larger sums and more time for development to turn a promising idea into something of wide practical utility.

## ENCOURAGEMENT NEEDED

To take only one example, we have not yet learned how to develop $n$ Ach really well among low-income groups. In our first effort—a summer course for bright underachieving 14-year-olds—we found that boys from the middle class improved steadily in grades in school over a two-year period, but boys from the lower class showed an improvement after the first year followed by a drop back to their beginning low grade average (see the accompanying chart). Why? We speculated that it was because they moved back into an environment in which neither parents nor friends encouraged achievement or upward mobility. In other words, it isn't enough to change a man's motivation if the environment in which he lives doesn't support at least to some degree his new efforts. African-Americans striving to rise out of the ghetto frequently confront this problem: they are often faced by skepticism at home and suspicion on the job, so that even if their $n$ Ach is raised, it can be lowered again by the heavy odds against their success. We must learn not only to raise $n$ Ach but also to find methods of instructing people in how to manage it, to create a favorable environment in which it can flourish.

Many of these training techniques are now only in the pilot testing stage. It will take time and money to perfect them, but society should be willing to invest heavily in them in view of their tremendous potential for contributions to human betterment.

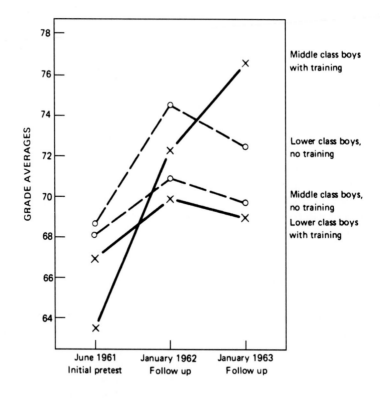

In a Harvard study, a group of underachieving 14-year-olds was given a six-week course designed to help them do better in school.

Some of the boys were also given training in achievement motivation, or *n* Ach (solid lines). As graph reveals, the only boys who continued to improve after a two-year period were the middle-class boys with the special *n* Ach training.

Psychologists suspect the lower-class boys dropped back, even with *n* Ach training, because they returned to an environment in which neither parents nor friends encouraged achievement.

# 5
# Ethics and Values

AMERICA'S PROBLEMS AND NEEDED REFORMS:
CONFRONTING THE ETHIC OF PERSONAL ADVANTAGE
   *Terence R. Mitchell*
   *William G. Scott*

CHANGING UNETHICAL ORGANIZATIONAL BEHAVIOR
   *Richard P. Nielsen*

## AMERICA'S PROBLEMS AND NEEDED REFORMS: CONFRONTING THE ETHIC OF PERSONAL ADVANTAGE

*Terence R. Mitchell*
*William G. Scott*

Mikhail Gorbachev summarized the troubles that beset the Soviet Union as bureaucratic paralysis, economic stagnation, and moral decay.[1] Gorbachev's list of Soviet ills must ring familiar bells in Americans' ears. Books, surveys, TV specials, and editorial commentary all assault us with a common theme: America is in trouble, it is in decline.

Headlines tell the story: "Defense Bribery Rampant"; "Greenhouse Effects Loom"; "Racism Rears Ugly Head"; "Troubled Seas: Global Red Tides"; "Whatever Happened to Ethics"; "A Growing Gap Between Rich and Poor"; "Something's Rotten in Government"; "Commonplace Violence is Legacy of Our Drug Culture"; "Acid Rain Imperils Sea Life"; "Ethical Lapses Mark Reagan Administration"[2]—and the beat goes on. We assert that no one in our national leadership has made particularly dramatic or serious efforts to argue and act for fundamental reforms. Perhaps they believe things are not truly that bad, and that this country is not in danger. That assessment is a delusion and the purpose of this article is to present commentary and conclusions that support our call for America to change its values and behavior.

First, we describe the threats—the major signs of decay in the physical, social, and moral fabric of our society. Next, we focus on American values, particularly those that compare the ethic of personal advantage, which is an ethic of self-interested, outcome-oriented, individualism.[3] We believe this ethic is the cause of American decay. Finally, we suggest reforms that America's managerial leadership must undertake to address these problems and change these values.

*Source*: Terrence, R. Mitchell and William G. Scott, "America's Problems and Needed Reforms: Confronting the Ethic of Personal Advantage," *Academy of Management Executive*, 1990, Vol. 4, No. 3, pp. 23–35. Copyright © 1990. Reprinted with permission.

# AMERICA'S BLIGHT

Three major problems are disabling society. They reflect actions that undermine the physical, social, and moral foundations of the Republic, and to some extent are the tangible outcomes of the ethic of personal advantage.

## Environmental Decay

The physical deterioration of our environment is apparent everywhere. Our oceans are being threatened by red tides of algae that consume large quantities of oxygen in the water resulting in the death of numerous aquatic life forms. Red tides are now being linked to industrial discharges, sewage, fertilizer runoff, and pollutants in the air. Acid rain is a major concern as areas of the Atlantic Coast and the Northeast Seaboard report the loss of marine life, damage to forests and lakes, and even the erosion of buildings. We have far more toxic waste than we can effectively handle. The Great Lakes are threatened by industrial effluent and municipal sewage. Alaska's oil development has caused far more environmental damage than the government predicted—and on and on—with the sobering fact that the dreaded "Greenhouse Effect" has finally arrived. Wild swings in temperature are predicted, increased cancer rates, the globe covered with clouds, and many coastlines in completely obliterated by water. Also, there appears to be great holes in the ozone layer of the planet which have been created by burning fossil fuels, cutting down our forests, releasing large amounts of nitrous oxide from fertilizers and car emissions, and the use of chlorofluorocarbons in product design industrial processes.

Beyond this, we continue to use up the Earth's natural resources at an alarming rate—far outstripping our ability to replace them. Environmental pillage is not a pretty picture, especially since many American business and government leaders bear considerable responsibility for this state.

## Those Who Are Lost

Just as numerous as the environmental abuses are the social problems that confronts us: crimes, drug abuse, poverty, discrimination, physical and sexual abuses, and wide-spread alienation. There are different ways that one can aggregate or categorize these problems and it is not easy to reduce them to a common denominator. However, one overwhelming related fact is that there is an increasing number of people who are simply disconnected from our society. They are America's "invisible" people, whose existence provides a sharp contrast between the advantaged and disadvantaged in our cities. The gap between rich and poor is widening.

Based on the 1980 census, there are now more than 30 million people living below the poverty level. These people are defined as the "underclass"—generally uneducated, unemployed, poor, and more likely to use drugs or engage in criminal activity than the rest of the population. There is a greater percentage of minorities in this group than in the population as a whole and they tend to live in the core of most major cities in the United States. Types of jobs available for the underclass are being reduced, the quality of their education is getting worse, and the use of drugs is increasing as is its associated violence.

The most disturbing fact about the situation is that these people seem to have permanently dropped out of American society. Government welfare seems not to help and is viewed by some as institutionalizing dependency. In short, we are faced with a potentially catastrophic situation of human degradation. Many of our inner cities are unsafe and dirty and filled with grief. The invisible people are increasingly isolated from mainstream America and their numbers are growing larger.

# Leaderless and Corrupt

We believe the most serious threat to our society is American leaders' lack of stewardship of which the S&L debacle is a recent egregious example. Management abuses of trust are everywhere and some say the lack of moral leadership is America's number one problem. Over the last few years, we have had major stock scandals, connections between organized crime and banks, "golden parachutes," greenmail operations, and the proliferation of junk bonds that threaten the stability of the banking system. We witnessed the E.F. Hutton check-kiting practices, General Electric's contract frauds, and insider trading scandals. More recently there was the WedTech contract favoritism issue, stock manipulation by GAF Corporation, allegations of influence peddling at HUD, racketeering and fraud indictments at Drexel, Burnham, Lambert, and of course Irangate plus the Defense Department procurement probe which has uncovered indications of rampant bribery. In an issue focusing on these ethical violations in both the private and public sector, *Time* magazine (May 25, 1987) said, "White Collar scams abound, insider trading, money laundering, greenmail, greed combined with technology has made stealing more tempting than ever. Result: pinstriped outlaw." Discussing the public sector, *Time* said "a relentless procession of forlorn faces assaults the nations' moral equanimity, characters linked in the public mind not by any connection between their diverse dubious deeds but by the fact that each in his or her own way has somehow seemed to betray the public trust."[4]

Whether corruption is now more, the same as, or less than it has been in the past is impossible to say and pointless to argue about. Corruption is wrong regardless of how extensive it is. But the coverage given to miscreant managers by the media has heightened America's awareness of wrong doing by those in power, leaving us with an alienated distrusting populace.

Survey after survey has shown decreasing trust in the leadership of American institutions.[5] Such decreases in confidence have historically preceded major social upheavals and, on occasion, revolutionary changes in government. It is a serious problem and one which, again, we believe is partly reflected by the values that are propagated and sustained by the individuals who lead American institutions. We turn now to an investigation of those values.

# VALUES THAT SERVE THE SELF

The data for the problems cited above are fairly easy to acquire as well as interpret. People may differ on the degree to which they consider these problems to be serious but there is little doubt about the problems themselves. The evidence is massive that we, as a society, are degrading our physical environment, have a significant portion of our population that is alienated from the rest of society, and have engaged in widely reported amounts of fraud, crime, and unethical behavior.

Our investigation of the literature on values also presents a fairly clear picture. Since we are discussing problems that are widespread, we need to consider generalized values: that is, values that are held by a significant number of individuals and powerful groups in our own society. Therefore, our research for this article began with an extensive search of the psychological, sociological, management, and popular literature about values.

We identified three types of articles. First, there are numerous empirical surveys of values that are reported in the scientific and popular press.[6] Second, there are many books of social criticism that summarize various positions related to values.[7] Finally, there are scholarly literature reviews, published in journals or books of readings that attempt to integrate or give an overall perspective on the topic.[8]

Our conclusion after this review was that three major sets of opposing values recur constantly as central themes in the literature. These values are 1) a present versus a future orientation, 2) an instrumental as opposed to a substantive focus, and 3) an emphasis on individualism contrasted with community. Each value in the three sets is in constant tension with the one to which it is paired. However, the emphasis on these values now reflects a present, instrumental, individualistic orientation and that this orientation is associated with the problems discussed previously. That is, these values are reflected in behavior that maximizes personal advantage in the short run and discounts the long run costs of disregarding ethics, the underclass, and the environment. In the following sections, each of these values is discussed as well as its relationship to these problems. To greater or lesser extent, the problems of America's blight have the effect of personal advantage as their common denominator.

## LIVING IN THE PRESENT

"We have a deadly obsession with short-term success." "National Mood: Grab It Now." These and other editorial comments reflect a pervasive phenomenon in American society: a preoccupation with maximizing individual return or impact in the short run. According to Richard Darnum, Director of the Office of Management and Budget, "this affliction is endemic to our society and pervasive in our public policy."

One of the most obvious indicators of this mood is called the "New Careerism." Over the last twenty years there has been an increasing tendency for people to stay in jobs for shorter periods of time and be less committed to them. A survey by the Hay Group (1986–1987) indicated that over 40 percent of employees say they expect to leave their current employer within 3 years or less. In positions of power (management, supervisor, professional) these figures were over 50 percent. The average length of stay in top level positions of the government is 18 months. The report on business education by Porter and McKibbin laments the lack of loyalty of present MBA's to their organizations.[9]

Numerous books and articles discuss the issue and its consequences (e.g., Bolles, "What Color Is My Parachute," Korda, "Power," Lasch, "The Culture of Narcissism," Lear, "Our Fragile Tower of Greed") Summaries of these works highlight both the values and the outcomes of the new careerism. The basic principles are reflected by statements such as "stay mobile," "don't stay more than two to three years in one job," "look at the growth curve," "learn what you can from your boss and move on," "maximize your influence immediately," "have an impact now."

What are the downsides of this perspective? The most frequently discussed are 1) lack of job involvement and commitment, 2) increased turnover, 3) poor interpersonal relations, 4) self-absorption, and 5) unethical behavior.

These observed behaviors are supported by interviews, surveys, and editorial commentary as well as hard data on turnover, attitudes of employee discontent, and the cost and frequency of unethical actions and criminal activity. One author suggests that individuals work carefully at their job—but always keep a resume out. A second suggests that its okay to be dishonest to help your career if you can get away with it. A third argues that "winning images are more important than types of competence." In short, this preoccupation with current payoffs contributes to the type of behavior that disregards the environment, the well-being of others, and leadership integrity. "Our culture has been weaned from a respect for other values to the worshiping of instant gratification."[10]

### The Ends Are All That Matter

The idea that ends justify the means is the underlying value of instrumental behavior—that people are more concerned with the outcomes of their actions than the substantive nature of the process or the experience. Acquiring wealth for the purpose of consumption is the end, and the means to get it are unimportant.

146

The current literature on values emphasizes this instrumental perspective. For example, a major survey of the American work force found that extrinsic outcomes such as pay, benefits, and security were as important or more important than the employees' satisfaction with the work itself. Another concluded that work was merely an annoyance to be suffered for the sake of weekend retail therapy. In summary, people value work an as activity that is instrumental for extrinsic rewards.[11]

One of the most influential popular books about American values is *Habits of the Heart*.[12] While the authors' basic theme focuses on our third value—individualism—the role of instrumentalism is also recognized. The authors highlight the "dominant American tradition of thinking about success" and, along with other books, elaborate on the role of the large corporation and its managers as propagating this perspective.

> The emphasis is on results, efficiency, effectiveness, and success at any cost. A recent survey of 6,000 business managers showed that, of eleven values, the top two in importance were organizational effectiveness and high productivity and the bottom two were value to the community and service to the public.

In a separate study of 803 public officials at the GS-15 level, the same researchers found effectiveness and productivity were first and third while service to the public and community were seventh and eight.[13] One of the most articulate and comprehensive statements of the instrumental position argues that market-driven societies, that are managerial in orientation, reinforce instrumental values and behaviors.[14] Substantive experiences and variety are suppressed through an explicit reward system that places performance above all else. Concerns about the environment, the disadvantaged, and morality are left floundering in the wake of the pursuit of the bottom line.

## A Loss of Community

Individualism is probably the easiest value to document, partly because the American tradition has been grounded in it. As we mentioned earlier, however, each of these values is in tension with an opposite. In this case, community was also important in the American ethos. As our society has become more mobile, transitory, secular, and urban, community values are less prominent leaving Bellah et al. in *Habits of the Heart* to conclude that "individualism may have grown cancerous" and is "threatening the survival of freedom itself."

We are described as a self-serving society, one where the individual is continually exhorted to "look out for number one." Again, the headlines assault us: "Society based on trust won't work when everyone cheats"; "Kids seem morally adrift in a me-first world"; "Hypocrisy, betrayal and greed unsettle the nation's soul." The common theme is that Americans simply have lost their sense of commitment to community. Bellah et al. discuss this theme in detail from a historical perspective and from the data that emerged from their interviews. They suggest that "individualism has been at the very core of American culture" and what is missing a sense of "calling"—a way of seeing our actions as entwined with a higher purpose serving a larger community.

Other authors argue that this form of individualism based on the ethic of personal advantage is mostly a result of the organizational and managerial systems that need reform.[15] Data from surveys are also clear. In fact, the Posner and Schmidt studies mentioned previously demonstrated not only how the instrumental values of personal advantage were most important but that the community beliefs were least important—in both the public and private sectors. One study with public employees even showed that public service was rated in a negative manner.

As a society that highly regards the present over the future, ends over means, and self over community, we are confronted with the degradation of our environment, decay of our social fabric, and a decline of our moral fiber. solving these problems appears to be irreconcilable with our current values. Social and personal constraints provided by family and religion have all but disappeared, yet somehow we need to elevate our concern for the future and for the substantive experience found in community.

## SUGGESTED REFORMS

We have argued that a number of behavioral problems can be tied to underlying values. By focusing on immediate self-interest and using any means to attain that goal, some of the behaviors that follow include a disregard for the environment (who cares, I won't be here), other parts of the social community (it's their problem, not mine), and the letter and spirit of the law (everybody's doing it, why not me). We recognize that behaviors are caused by multiple factors. Values are only one. We believe that we have both a value problem and a behavior problem.

The point, substantiated by dissonance theory, is that values and behavior are part of a reciprocal causation system: values cause behavior and behavior shapes values. Thus, to change values, we can focus on ways to directly change them or indirectly change them by altering behavior. Similarly, changes in behavior can be effected through reinforcement techniques or indirectly through changes in attitudes and values.

As there are many problems and values in America, so also are there many avenues for reform. The ones we selected are aimed at educational institutions, management, and organizations. As their power is ubiquitous so also is their responsibility for many social ills. Thus, reforms pertaining to education, legal oversight, and organizational change are all necessary, but overriding emphasis is placed on the transformation in the nature of management itself.

### Moral Discourse and Moral Character

Our first reform aims at changing values through moral development. The research on this topic has repeatedly emphasized that higher levels of development reflect the ability to understand and empathize with perspectives different and perhaps more complex than one's own. Such new perspectives can help one to transcend the self-centeredness of the ethic of personal advantage. We believe that one of the main objectives of education is the development of students' moral character. Business schools are not exempted from this obligation. The question is how to proceed on the pedagogical front.

Currently, it is popular to treat ethical and moral issues as problems to be solved. The tendency in business schools is to consider them, in Edmond Pincoffs' words, as quandaries.[16] Quandary ethics concern tangible and concrete moral dilemmas of business life. Students are asked to address ethical matters through analyzing case studies, engaging in role playing, or solving critical incidents. These techniques are often buttressed with lectures by professors, talks by guest speakers, and selected readings from moral philosophy classics.

Quandary ethics is attractive to business educators because it is instrumental; it draws upon familiar teaching techniques; and it promises a quick-fix educational solution for the "need to do something" about the ethical shortcomings of management. However, quandary ethics is rule-driven, based upon value systems that do not have an a priority face validity, eg., what makes Utilitarianism more or less valid than, say, Kant's categorical imperatives? The problem is that once a value system is widely accepted, its rules assume the status of an act of God. Thus, while rules are often necessary for ethical behavior, they are seldom sufficient because they do little to enhance moral character. The step beyond quandary ethics in schools of business curricula is moral discourse.

Moral discourse is a process of rhetorical engagement by students and professors in free and open forums of conversations and debate. One tries to persuade others of the truth of his or her point of view on moral issues. In the process, widely divergent opinions are expressed and each individual is exposed to alternative propositions about values. The whole point is to provide knowledge of moral options and the opportunity to choose among different value systems. In the academic atmosphere of modern business schools, in which bottom-line thinking is supreme, the chance that such forums afford for students to hear something different is essential to their moral development. Students need to know that people make decisions using guidelines other than those suggested by expected value and maximization.

While ethics courses may have a place in the business school curriculum, they have to be more than a mere appendage to a student's program. Wharton, for example, has ethics "modules" in some of their core MBA courses. Other schools have full-term ethics courses that have the same status as a core course. The importance of an ethics course integrated into a school's curriculum cannot be stressed too strongly. But these are matters of pedagogical form, not function. The function of ethics courses should be to instill an open, moral, loving, humane, and broadly informed mentality, so that student's may come to see life's trials and business's ethical challenges as occasions to live through with integrity and courage. Ethics courses must attempt to heighten moral character.

But this is asking a great deal of a college course. Beyond formal courses, business schools should encourage and support informal enclaves of moral discourse—forums where honorable people gather to seek moral truth and the appropriate means for applying the truth. These forums should be separate from official business school programs, and financially independent. They should be loosely structured without attendance requirements, a specific course of study, or rigid scheduling. They should "float," convening on those occasions when the interests and the purpose of the participants dictate that they should.[17]

Finally, the reform of business education must involve the larger professional academic community. It should encourage major professional associations and professional journals to deal with moral philosophy reflectively and speculatively, not simply as an exercise in positive science or theoretical model-building. Papers submitted to journals should not be accepted merely on the basis of their ideological conformity to orthodox management values. Rather, diversity should be sought by sensitive and intelligent editorial leadership. Above all, an independent national institute for the study of moral philosophy in business should be established. The Academy of Management, the American Society for Public Administration, the American Assembly of Collegiate Schools of Business, in addition to many other professional associations in health care, education, and social work should transcend their narrow perspectives and support such a joint undertaking.

The reform of business education through moral discourse does not downgrade existing programs that prepare students for jobs. Rather, it redresses an imbalance by giving added weight to the ethical and moral aspects of the development of student character. In Mary Parker Follet's words, we need leaders who "do not conceive their tasks as that of fulfilling purposes, but also that of finding ever larger purposes to fulfill and more fundamental values to be reached."[18] We hope that these values will represent a greater concern for the long-run health of our institutions, an enriched substantive life within these institution, and an enhanced sense of what constitutes ethically appropriate behavior.

# The Legal Climate

A second set of needed reforms exist in the legal arena. Rules and laws are necessary (but not sufficient) conditions for change. Changing rules and laws is a direct attempt to influence behavior. If you behave appropriately, you are rewarded, if you behave inappropriately, the penalties should be clear, severe, and quickly administered. The direct linking of consequences to action is a very strong regulator of behavior especially when appropriate and inappropriate behaviors are clearly stated and the former is rewarded while the latter is punished. While most of what follows concerns ways to restrict inappropriate behavior we also argue that systems of reward for appropriate actions are important as well. Individuals and organizations that act unselfishly in the long-run interests of others should be recognized and rewarded.

Many laws have been passed already; laws that regulate and protect the environment, laws that provide some surcease to the underclass, and the laws aimed at stemming corruption and unfair privilege. The Clear Air Act, The National Environmental Policy Act, and The Federal Water Pollution Act can be mentioned in connection with the first instance. The Environmental Protection Agency (EPA) was established to enforce these laws and to recommend new policies to protect the environment. This attention to environmental issues is laudable. However, most experts agree that the EPA has been slow to interpret legislation, slow to act and enforce the existing legislation, and remiss in being proactive regarding new threats to the environment. To some extent, these inadequacies can be attributed to a lack of federal funding and a lack of political support from the administration. The main need, however, is for cooperation between the public and private sector.

Laws exist to protect the economically and socially disadvantaged. The minimum wage guarantees an income floor. Public assistance is obviously designed to provide income to the unemployed, as social security does for the elderly and retired. The former, however, often is seen as an incentive not to work and the latter is insufficient to maintain a reasonable standard of living. But these are economic solutions to the problems of the underclass. There is also the need for more training, education, jobs, health care, protection from crime and drug abuse, and care for the mentally troubled. Manpower programs help train and educate, EEOC regulations help to deter discrimination and create opportunity, and OSHA is concerned with worker safety. Better enforcement is required, however, in addition to new legislation. Most observers of the Reagan years would agree that the emphasis on the "safety net" has declined dramatically. The underclass is worse off now than it was ten years ago.

Finally, there is a substantial body of law designed to thwart corrupt behavior. Securities law deals with trading stock and some of the prohibitions against insider trading, takeovers, use of junk bonds, and withholding disclosure. Anti-trust law has the potential to curb certain takeovers and price collusion. There are limitations on Political Action committees as well as consulting opportunities after public service. The Ethics in Government Act has curtailed some of the more obvious abuses of public officials. ERISA was designed to regulate the use of employee pensions and the Foreign Corrupt Practices Act was designed to prohibit bribery and payoffs as well as increase various reporting requirements. State corporation law regulates various activities such as the composition of boards of directors and state constitutional law has been interpreted to limit the right to fire. RICO, although designed to deal with racketeering, has been used to control other types of corruption.

The difficulty with these legal remedies to the American blight is generally the same difficulty faced by most statutory regulations: they create rules that in turn breed more rules as ways are sought to circumvent the original ones. A society that relies on laws to enforce desired behavior inevitably becomes rule-laden. Some behavioral changes may be achieved but without the spirit needed for fundamental reform.

Laws do not necessarily change values unless two other conditions exist. First, laws must be perceived by the public as serving the needs of justice. Law without justice is a fundamental paradox of our times.19 Second, if justice can be accomplished, then the probability is raised that the public will support the spirit of the law—especially if enforcement is fair, consistent, and expeditious.

Reform in the way that executives in business and government are held accountable for their decisions and actions is more relevant on the legal front. Since managers have the privilege of power, they should be accountable for its use. Private sector managers historically have been protected from accountability by the prudent business judgment rule and managers in government jobs by sovereign immunity. It is almost impossible to establish personal managerial culpability in either civil or criminal actions. Virtually no legal standards for assessing managerial malpractice, malfeasance, or nonfeasance exist. The most promising reforms may be achieved at this level in the judicial process.

We are not suggesting that every decision made by managers or civil servants be subject to retrospective consideration, taken with the benefit of hindsight. We believe that unethical behavior conducted by people who know that their actions are a violation of federal or state laws or violate public trust and social responsibility should be held accountable. Such actions most always involve the determination of the accused's intentions. Like it or not, judgements about those intentions can be determined only in the court system. Consequently, increased litigation may be the price of individual executive accountability.

## Organizational Governance and Due Process

Our final set of reforms are aimed at values and behavior that exist within the organizational context.

America has been characterized as a sea of freedom filled with islands of organizational despotism. This metaphor implies a difference between the rights and liberties enjoyed by Americans as citizens versus rights and liberties denied them as employees of organizations.20 We believe that such a disparity exists and should be an object of reform: that is, reform of organizational governance and systems of due process within organizations. Such reforms are both a challenge to the willful abuse of power that we claim has created America's blight and a way to increase a sense of shared community.

Our first recommendation is to consider the federal model as a worthy ideal of governance. Similar to our national forms of governance, organizational federalism requires the separation of governance powers, a system of checks and balances among the organization's functional units, and shared sovereignty among all the participants. This does not fit the prescription of orthodox management, and its apologists argue that the federal model is impractical, inefficient, and unsuited to meet the realities of world competition. We counter that the models of organizational governance now in use have not been dazzling in their practicality, efficiency, or grasp of reality.

So what about unorthodox organizational governance? Henry Mintzberg described a system called professional bureaucracy—a design that seems best suited to complex organizations that employ highly skilled and experienced people.21 These organizations, structured around modules of expertise, permit people greater freedom in determining the nature and performance of their jobs. Universities, law and public accounting firms, general hospitals, and social work agencies, all use this design.

The freedom of professionals in federalized organizations is no doubt good for them and often good for their employers. The problem is that the federal model tends not to extend to employees who are less qualified and who lack the support of professional associations. Can federal principles of reform be applied to them as well? The answer is that they can, but only if there is reform in those organizational due process systems that guarantees the rights and freedoms to all employees that they enjoy as citizens.

Systems of due process, commonly called procedural and substantive, are administrative devices for implementing corrective and distributive justice. Procedural due process provides the means for redressing grievances if an employee believes that his or her rights have been abridged. Substantive due process secures employee interests, and is concerned with just distribution of organizational resources. These forms of due process are analogous, respectively, to the judicial and legislative functions of government.

A great deal has been written about the theory and practice of due process in organizations.[22] Many companies report having management-inititated grievance systems (MIGS) for settling employee disputes over rights. There are also numberless employee participation schemes that involve employees in resource allocation decisions. However, all of these programs, plans, and administrative devices do not add up to real protection of employee rights and interest. Ninety-nine percent of all MIGS do not include outside arbitration. More alarming, most MIGS are secret administrative proceedings, and those who have an interest in cases brought to appeal never know if justice was done. MIGS are not independent of management executive authority or subject to the scrutiny of outside independent judgment.

Furthermore, management does not permit employees to participate in substantive due process activities with anything like a grant of power, necessary to make it meaningful in negotiating their interests. Participation in decision-making is largely a manipulative technique and not an exercise in power equalization. In short, management's executive authority dominates the legislative action in organizations.

We propose two reforms of organizational due process systems. First, procedural due process has to be an independent judicial function in organizations. Second, cooperative employee ownership of organizations is the only real way to put teeth into substantive due process. Let us elaborate.

For MIGS to be a truly independent judicial function, several minimum standards must be met: 1.) Impartial third party arbitration as a final and binding step. 2.) Hearing boards composed of representatives drawn widely from company employees, and from citizens at large in the community. 3.) Provision of adequate legal counsel at no cost for employees. 4.) Open hearings so that all employees who are interested in a case may attend. 5.) Establishment of an independent trust fund by the organization to pay the costs of the judicial system.

Substantive due process requires power equalization among those who divide the resource pie if there is to be distributive justice. Some view West Germany's codetermination laws as a way to achieve power equalization. Others see stronger unions as the answer. But cooperative employee ownership of organizations may be a more effective approach to power equalization. As things stand now, the absentee owners of American corporations are unable to intervene on behalf of their employees' interests even if they want to do so. This might be different if employees themselves were owners of the organization.

## CONCLUSION

Prospective costs of these reform proposals may seem inordinately high, and if implemented they may jeopardize America's competitiveness in the global economy. Yet this is not certain. Changes that could make a difference in ending America's blight could also unleash an undreamed of prosperity for all. One thing is certain, America's condition is not benefiting our international economic position. However, there is even a larger issue to be faced than an economic cost-benefit analysis. Competing values are at stake. The potential benefits to America are great if standards other than efficiency and dollars are used to measure our notions of a good society. American welfare can also be thought of in terms of enhanced citizen virtue, justice, and humane organizations.

Certain reforms we suggest have been recognized and some limited changes attempted. But these changes are fragmented and only scratch the surface. What is needed is a more comprehensive, proactive, set of reforms that target value and behavior changes simultaneously. We are skeptical about spontaneous support of such reforms if they continue to be proposed piecemeal. Values and action go together, and it is unlikely that reform will appear except under certain extraordinary conditions.

These conditions, however, are happening—in China, the Soviet Union, the Baltic States, and Eastern Europe—where the moral authority of old ideas and worn-out leadership are being challenged. What is the key ingredient that may lead eventually to successful change? We believe that it is courageous leadership that risks raising social, political, and economic issues to the level of national debate, since both our problems and values are entwined and interdependent. To respond to this challenge successfully requires a managerial and political leadership commitment that has not occurred in this country since the "New Deal" led by Franklin D. Roosevelt in 1933. Modern times require a modern leadership vision, one coached in specific values and reforms that stress substantiveness over instrumentality, community over personal advantage, and the long-term over the short-term.

Some believe it is already too late. MacIntyre concluded *After Virtue* by stating that "the new dark ages are already upon us" and that "the barbarians have been governing us for quite some time."[23] Perhaps MacIntyre is right. But, for the moment, we argue that a national agenda led by enlightened managers could implement a program to change our course. Individual leaders do make a difference. Their autonomous moral choices can invigorate America so that we are not consigned to a decline in our physical surroundings, our concern for community, and the moral fabric of our society.

# ENDNOTES

1. M. Gorbachev, *Perestroika: New Thinking for Our Country and the World* (New York: Harper and Row, 1987).
2. The headlines come from numerous papers but mostly from the *New York Times*. Throughout this article, we note numerous headlines but we do not have the space to provide a full citation for each one. Interested readers may contact the authors for these citations.
3. See D. K. Hart, "The Fatal Flaw in Theory Y," in K. Kolenda (Ed.), *Organizations and Ethical Individualism* (New York: Greenwood, Praeger, 1988).
4. Evidence for this statement can be found in N. H. Snyder, "Leadership: The Essential Quality for Transforming United States Businesses," *Advanced Management Journal*, Spring 1986, 15–18.
5. A good reference is S. M. Lipset and W. Schneider, *The Confidence Gap: Business, Labor, and Government in the Public Mind* (New York: The Free Press, 1983); as well as T. R. Mitchell, and W. G. Scott, "Leadership Failures, the Distrusting Public and Prospects of the Administrative State," *Public Administration Review*, November–December 1987, 445–452.
6. See *Achieving Competitive Advantage Through the Effective Management of People,* (Philadelphia: The Hay Group, 1986–1987); and G. W. England and J. Musimi, "Work centrality in Japan and the United States," *Journal of Cross Culture Psychology*, December 1986, 359–416; and B. Z. Posner and W. H. Schmidt, "Values and the American Manager: An Update," *California Management Review*, Spring 1984, 202–216; and W. H. Schmidt and B. Z. Posner, "Values and Expectations of Federal Senior Executives, *Public Administration Review,* September–October 1986, 447–454; and F.D. Sturdevant, J. L. Ginter, and A. G. Sawyer, "Managers' Conservatism and Corporate Performance," *Strategic Management Journal*, January/March 1985, 17–38; and S. J. Yeager, J. Rabin, and T. Vocino, "Professional Values of Public Servants in the United States," *American Review of Public Administration*, Winter, 1982, 402–412.
7. See W. H. Whyte, Jr., *The Organization Man* (New York: Andron Books, 1957); A. MacIntyre, *After Virtue* (Notre Dame: University of Notre Dame Press, 1981); and P. D. Anthony, *The*

*Idealogy of Work* (United Kingdom: Tavestock, 1977); R. N. Bellah, R. Masden, W. M. Sullivan, A. Swidler, and S. M. Tripton, *Habits of the Heart* (Berkeley, CA: University of California Press 1985); C. Lasch, *The Culture of Narcissism* (New York: Warner Books, 1979); S. M. Peck, *The Different Drum: Community Making and Peace,* (New York: Simon & Shuster, 1987); and W.G. Scott and D. K. Hart, *Organizational Values in America* (New Brunswick, N.J.: Transaction Books, 1989).

8. See R. .J. Aldag, and A. P. Brief, Task Design and Employee Motivation, (Glenview, Ill: Scott, Foresman & Co., 1979); M. R. Blood, "Work Values and Job Satisfaction," *Journal of Applied Psychology,* 1969, 53, 456–459; G. S. Howard, "The Role of Values in the Science of Psychology," *American Psychologist,* 1985, 40, 255–265; W. R. Nord, A. P. Brief, J. M. Atieh, and E. M. Doherty, "Work Values and the Conduct of Organizational Behavior," in B. M. Staw and L. L. Cummings (Eds.), *Research in Organizational Behavior,* Vol. 10 (Greenwich, Conn.: JAI Press, 1988), 1–42; and J. T. Spence, "Achievement American Style: The Rewards and Costs of Individualism," *American Psychologist,* 1985, 40, 1285–1295.

9. L. W. Porter and L. E. McKibbin, *Management Education and Development: Drift or Thrust into the 21st Century?* (New York: McGraw-Hill Book Co., 1988).

10. The following articles and books discuss this perspective: H. Edelhertz and T. D. Overcast, *White Collar Crime: An Agenda for Research* (Lexington, MA: Lexington Books, 1982); D. C. Feldman, "The New Careerism: Origins, Tenets and Consequences, *The Industrial Psychologist,* Spring 1986, 39–44; N. Lear, "Our Fragile Tower of Greed and Debt," *The Washington Post,* 1988, C1.

11. See W. A. Schiemann and B. S. Morgan, *Managing Human Resources: Employee Discontent and Declining Productivity* (Princeton, N.J.: Opinion Research Corp, 1983); J. H. Goldthorpe, D. Lockwood, F. Bechhofer, and J. Platt, *The Affluent Worker in the Class Structure* (Cambridge, England: Cambridge University Press, 1969); M. Fein, "Motivation for Work," In R. Dubin (Ed.), *Handbook of Work, Organization and Society* (Chicago Rand McNally: 1976), 465–530; and R. Jackall, *Workers in a Labyrinth* (New York: Universe Books, 1976).

12. Bellah et al., op cit.

13. Posner & Schmidt, op. cit. and Schmidt & Posner, op. cit.

14. A. G. Ramos, *The New Science of Organization* (Toronto: University of Toronto Press, 1981).

15. MacIntyre, op. cit. and Peck, op. cit.

16. E. L. Pincoffs, *Quandaries and Virtues: Against Reductivism in Ethics* (Lawrence, KS: University of Kansas Press, 1986).

17. For a discussion of how one such forum worked, see W. G. Scott and T. R. Mitchell, "Markets and Morals in Management Education," *Selection,* Autumn 1986, 3, 3–8.

18. Quoted in L. M. Lane, "Karl Weick's Organizing: The Problem of Purpose and the Search for Excellence," *Administration and Society,* May 1986, 132–133.

19. A session at the 1989 national meetings of the Academy of Management was devoted to this issue, see R. Bies and S. Sitkin, "Law without Justice: When Formalization Eclipses Fairness in the Work Place," Session 234, August 15.

20. W. G. Scott, "The Management Governance Theories of Justice and Liberty," *Journal of Management,* Summer 1988, 14, 277–298.

21. H. Mintzberg, *Structure in Fives: Designing Effective Organizations* (Englewood Cliffs, NJ: Prentice-Hall, 1983).

22. W. G. Scott, T. R. Mitchell, and N. S. Peery, "Organizational Governance," in P. C. Nystrom and W. Starbuck (Eds.), *Handbook of Organizational Design,* 2 (Oxford, England: Oxford University Press, 1981), 135–151.

23. MacIntyre, op. cit., 244–245.

# CHANGING UNETHICAL ORGANIZATIONAL BEHAVIOR

*Richard P. Nielsen*

*To be or not to be: that is the question:*
*Whether 'tis nobler in the mind to suffer*
*The slings and arrows of outrageous fortune,*
*Or to take arms against a sea of troubles,*
*And by opposing end them?*

William Shakespeare, *Hamlet*

What are the implications of Hamlet's question in the context of organizational ethics? What does it mean to be ethical in an organizational context? Should one suffer the slings and arrows of unethical organizational behavior? Should one try to take arms against unethical behaviors and by opposing, end them?

The consequences of addressing organizational ethics issues can be unpleasant. One can be punished or fired, one's career can suffer, or one can be disliked, considered an outsider. It may take courage to oppose unethical and lead ethical organizational behavior.

How can one address organizational ethics issues? Paul Tillich, in his book, *The Courage to Be,* recognized, as Hamlet did, that dire consequences can result from standing up to and opposing unethical behavior. Tillich identified two approaches: being as an individual and being as a part of a group.[1]

In an organizational context, these two approaches can be interpreted as follows: 1) Being as an individual can mean intervening to end unethical organizational behaviors by working against others and the organizations performing the unethical behaviors; and 2) being as a part can mean leading an ethical organizational change by working with others and the organization. These approaches are not mutually exclusive; rather, depending on the individual, the organization, the relationships, and the situation, one or both of these approaches may be appropriate for addressing ethical issues.

## BEING AS AN INDIVIDUAL

According to Tillich, the courage to be as an individual is the courage to follow one's conscience and defy unethical and/or unreasonable authority. It can even mean staging a revolutionary attack on that authority. Such an act can entail great risk and require great courage. As Tillich explains, "The anxiety conquered in the courage to be…in the productive process is considerable, because the threat of being excluded from such a participation by unemployment or the loss of an economic basis is what, above all, fate means today."[2]

*Source*: Richard P. Nielsen, "Changing Unethical Organizational Behavior," *The Academy of Management Executive*, 1989, Vol. 3, No. 2, pp. 123–130. Copyright ©1989. Reprinted by permission.

According to David Ewing, retired executive editor of the *Harvard Business Review*, this type of anxiety is not without foundation.

> There is very little protection in industry for employees who object to carrying out immoral, unethical or illegal orders from their superiors. If the employee doesn't like what he or she is asked to do, the remedy is to pack up and leave. This remedy seems to presuppose an ideal economy, where there is another company down the street with openings for jobs just like the one the employee left.[3]

How can one be as an individual, intervening against unethical organizational behavior? Intervention strategies an individual can use to change unethical behavior include: 1) secretly blowing the whistle within the organization; 2) quietly blowing the whistle, informing a responsible higher-level manager; 3) secretly threatening the offender with blowing the whistle; 4) secretly threatening a responsible manager with blowing the whistle outside the organization; 5) publicly threatening a responsible manager with blowing the whistle; 6) sabotaging the implementation of the unethical behavior; 7) quietly refraining from implementing an unethical order or policy; 8) publicly blowing the whistle within the organization; 9) conscientiously objecting to an unethical policy or refusing to implement the policy; 10 )indicating uncertainty about or refusing to support a cover-up in the event that the individual and/or organization gets caught; 11) secretly blowing the whistle outside the organization; or 12) publicly blowing the whistle outside the organization. Cases of each are considered below.

## Cases

1. *Secretly blowing the whistle within the organization.* A purchasing manager for General Electric secretly wrote a letter to an upper-level manager about his boss, who was soliciting and accepting bribes from subcontractors. The boss was investigated and eventually fired. He was also sentenced to six months' imprisonment for taking $100,000 in bribes, in exchange for which he granted favorable treatment on defense contracts. [4]

2. *Quietly blowing the whistle to a responsible higher-level manager.* When Evelyn Grant was first hired by the company with which she is now a personnel manager, her job included administering a battery of tests that, in part, determined which employees were promoted to supervisory positions. Grant explained:

> There have been cases where people will do something wrong because they think they have no choice. Their boss tells them to do it, and so they do it, knowing it's wrong. They don't realize there are ways around the boss...When I went over his [the chief psychologist's] data and analysis, I found errors in assumptions as well as actual errors of computation...I had two choices: I could do nothing or I could report my findings to my supervisor. If I did nothing, the only persons probably hurt were the ones who "failed" the test. To report my findings, on the other hand, could hurt several people, possibly myself.

She spoke to her boss, who quietly arranged for a meeting to discuss the discrepancies with the chief psychologist. The chief psychologist did not show up for the meeting; however, the test battery was dropped. [5]

3. *Secretly threatening the offender with blowing the whistle.* A salesman for a Boston-area insurance company attended a weekly sales meeting during which the sales manager instructed the salespeople, both verbally and in writing, to use a sales technique that the salesman considered unethical. The salesman anonymously wrote the sales manager a letter threatening to send a copy of the unethical sales instructions to the Massachusetts insurance commissioner and the Boston Globe newspaper unless the sales manager retracted his instructions at the next sales meeting. The sales manager did retract the instructions. The salesman still works for the insurance company. [6]

4. *Secretly threatening a responsible manager with blowing the whistle outside the organization.* A recently hired manager with a San Francisco Real Estate Development Company found that the construction company his firm had contracted with was systematically not giving minorities opportunities to learn construction management. This new manager wrote an anonymous letter to a higher-level real estate manager threatening to blow the whistle to the press and local government about the contractor unless the company corrected the situation. The real estate manager intervened, and the contractor began to hire minorities for foremen-training positions.[7]

5. *Publicly threatening a responsible manager with blowing the whistle.* A woman in the business office of a large Boston-area university observed that one middle-level male manager was sexually harassing several women in the office. She tried to reason with the office manager to do something about the offensive behavior, but the manager would not do anything. She then told the manager and several other people in the office that if the manager did not do something about the behavior, she would blow the whistle to the personnel office. The manager then told the offender that if he did not stop the harassment, the personnel office would be brought in. He did stop the behavior, but he and several other employees refused to talk to the woman who initiated the actions. She eventually left the university.[8]

6. *Sabotaging the implementation of the unethical behavior.* A program manager for a Boston-area local social welfare organization was told by her superior to replace a significant percentage of her clients who received disability benefits with refugee Soviet Jews. She wanted to help both the refugees and her current clients; however, she thought it was unethical to drop current clients, in part because she believed such an action could result in unnecessary deaths. Previously, a person who had lost benefits because of what the program manager considered unethical "bumping" had committed suicide: He had not wanted to force his family to sell their home in order to pay for the medical care he needed and qualify for poverty programs. After her attempts to reason with her boss failed, she instituted a paperwork chain with a partially funded federal agency that prevented her own agency from dropping clients for nine months, after which time they would be eligible for a different funding program. Her old clients received benefits and the new refugees also received benefits. In discussions with her boss, she blamed the federal agency for making it impossible to drop people quickly. Her boss, a political appointee who did not understand the system, also blames the federal agency office.[9]

7. *Publicly blowing the whistle within the organization.* John W. Young, the chief of NASA's astronaut office, wrote a 12-page internal memorandum to 97 people after the Challenger explosion that killed seven crew members. The memo listed a large number of safety-related problems that Young said had endangered crews since October 1984. According to Young, "If the management system is not big enough to stop the space shuttle program whenever necessary to make flight safety corrections, it will not survive and neither will our three space shuttles or their flight crews." The memo was instrumental in the decision to broaden safety investigations throughout the total NASA system. [10]

8. *Quietly refraining from implementing an unethical order/policy.* Frank Ladwig was a top salesman and branch manager with a large computer company for more than 40 years. At times, he had trouble balancing his responsibilities. For instance, he was trained to sell solutions to customer problems, yet he had order and revenue quotas that sometimes made it difficult for him to concentrate on solving problems. He was responsible for signing and keeping important customers with annual revenues of between $250,000 and $500,000 and for aggressively and conscientiously representing new products that had required large R&D investments. He was required to sell the full line of products and services, and sometimes he had sales quotas for products that he believed were not a good match for the customer or appeared to perform marginally. Ladwig would quietly not sell those products, concentrating on selling the products he believed in. He would quietly explain the characteristics of the questionable products to his knowledgeable customers and get their reactions, rather than making an all-out sales effort. When he was asked by his sales manager why a certain product was not moving, he explained what the customers objected to and why. However, Ladwig thought that a salesman or manager with an average or poor performance record would have a difficult time getting away with this type of solution to an ethical dilemma. [11]

9. *Conscientiously objecting to an unethical policy or refusing to implement it.* Francis O'Brien was a research director for the pharmaceutical company Searle & Co. O'Brien conscientiously objected to what he believed were exaggerated claims for the Searle Copper 7 intrauterine contraceptive. When reasoning with upper-level management failed, O'Brien wrote them the following:

> *Their continued use, in my opinion, is both misleading and a thinly disguised attempt to make claims which are not FDA approved...Because of personal reasons I do not consent to have my name used in any press release or in connection with any press release. In addition, I will not participate in any press conference.*

O'Brien left the company ten years later. Currently, several lawsuits are pending against Searle, charging that its IUD caused infection and sterility. [12]

10. *Indicating uncertainty about or refusing to support a cover-up in the event that the individual and/or organization gets caught.* In the Boston office of Bear Stearns, four brokers informally worked together as a group. One of the brokers had been successfully trading on insider information, and he invited the other three to do the same. One of the three told the others that such trading was not worth the risk of getting caught, and if an investigation ever occurred, he was not sure he would be able to participate in a cover-up. The other two brokers decided not to trade on the insider information, and the first broker stopped at least that type of insider trading. [13]

11. *Secretly blowing the whistle outside the corporations.* William Schwartzkopf of the Commonwealth Electric Company secretly and anonymously wrote a letter to the Justice Department alleging large-scale, long-time bid rigging among many of the largest U.S. electrical contractors. The secret letter accused the contractors of raising bids and conspiring to divide billions of dollars of contracts. Companies in the industry have already paid more than $20 million in fines to the government in part as a result of this letter, and they face millions of dollars more in losses when the victims sue. [14]

12. *Publicly blowing the whistle outside the organization.* A. Earnest Fitzgerald, a former high-level manager in the U.S. Air Force and Lockheed CEO, revealed to Congress and the press that the Air Force and Lockheed systematically practiced a strategy of underbidding in order to gain Air Force contracts for Lockheed, which then billed the Air Force and received payments for cost overruns on the contracts. Fitzgerald was fired for his trouble, but eventually received his job back. The underbidding/cost overruns, on at least the C-5/A cargo plane, were stopped. [15]

# LIMITATIONS OF INTERVENTION

The intervention strategies described above can be very effective, but they also have some important limitations.

1. *The individual can be wrong about the organization's actions.* Lower-level employees commonly do not have as much or as good information about ethical situations and issues as higher-level managers. Similarly, they may not be as experienced as higher-level managers in dealing with specific ethical issues. The quality of experience and information an individual has can influence the quality of his or her ethical judgments. To the extent that this is true in any given situation, the use of intervention may or may not be warranted. In Case 8, for example, if Frank Ladwig had had limited computer experience, he could have been wrong about some of the products he thought would not produce the promised results.

2. *Relationships can be damaged.* Suppose that instead of identifying with the individuals who want an organization to change its ethical behavior, we look at these situations from another perspective. How do we feel when we are forced to change our behavior? Further, how would we feel if we were forced by a subordinate to change, even though we thought that we had the position, quality of information, and/or quality of experience to make the correct decisions? Relationships would probably be, at the least, strained, particularly if we made an ethical decision and were nevertheless forced to change. If we are wrong, it may be that we do not recognize it at the time. If we know we are wrong, we still may not like being forced to change. However, it is possible that the individual forcing us to change may justify his or her behavior to us, and our relationship may actually be strengthened.

3. *The organization can be hurt unnecessarily.* If an individual is wrong in believing that the organization is unethical, the organization can be hurt unnecessarily by his or her actions. Even if the individual is right, the organization can still be unnecessarily hurt by intervention strategies.

4. *Intervention strategies can encourage "might makes right" climates.* If we want "wrong" people, who might be more powerful now or in the future than we are, to exercise self-restraint, then we may need to exercise self-restraint even when we are "right." A problem with using force is that the other side may use more powerful or effective force now or later. Many people have been punished for trying to act ethically both when they were right and when they were wrong. By using force, one may also contribute to the belief that the only way to get things done in a particular organization is through force. People who are wrong can and do use force, and win. Do we want to build an organization culture in which force plays an important role? Gandhi's response to "an eye for an eye" was that if we all followed that principle, eventually everyone would be blind.

# BEING AS A PART

While the intervention strategies discussed above can be very effective, they can also be destructive. Therefore, it may be appropriate to consider the advantages of leading an ethical change effort (being as a part) as well as intervening against unethical behaviors (being as an individual).

Tillich maintains that the courage to be as a part is the courage to affirm one's own being through participation with others. He writes,

> The self affirms itself as participant in the power of a group, of a movement....Self-affirmation within a group includes the courage to accept guilt and its consequences as public guilt, whether one is responsible or whether somebody else is. It is a problem of the group which has to be expiated for the sake of the group, and the methods of punishment and satisfaction...are accepted

by the individual…In every human community, there are outstanding members, the bearers of the traditions and leaders of the future. They must distance in order to judge and to change. They must take responsibility and ask questions. This unavoidably produces individual doubt and personal guilt. Nevertheless, the predominant pattern is the courage to be a part in all members of the…group…The difference between the genuine Stoic and the neocollectivist is that the latter is bound in the first place to the collective and in the second place to the universe, while the Stoic was first of all related to the universal Logos and secondly to possible human groups.…The democratic-conformist type of the courage to be as a part was in an outspoken way tied up with the idea of progress. The courage to be as a part in the progress of the group to which one belongs.[16]

## Leading Ethical Change

A good cross-cultural conceptualization of leadership is offered by Yoshino and Lifson: "The essence of leadership is the influential increment over and above mechanical compliance with routine directives of the organization."[17] This definition permits comparisons between and facilitates an understanding of different leadership styles through its use of a single variable: created incremental performance. Of course, different types of leadership may be more or less effective in different types of situations; yet, it is helpful to understand the "essence" of leadership in its many different cultural forms as the creation of incremental change beyond the routine.

For example, Yoshino and Lifson compare generalizations (actually overgeneralizations) about Japanese and American leadership styles:

> In the United States, a leader is often thought of as one who blazes new trails, a virtuoso whose example inspires awe, respect, and emulation. If any individual characterizes this pattern, it is surely John Wayne, whose image reached epic proportions in his own lifetime as an embodiment of something uniquely America. A Japanese leader, rather than being an authority, is more of a communications channel, a mediator, a facilitator, and most of all, a symbol and embodiment of group unity. Consensus building is necessary in decision making, and this requires patience and an ability to use carefully cultivated relationships to get all to agree for the good of the unit. A John Wayne in this situation might succeed temporarily by virtue of charisma, but eventually the inability to build strong emotion-laden relationships and use these as a tool of motivation and consensus building would prove fatal.[18]

A charismatic, "John Wayne type" leader can inspire and/or frighten people into diverting from the routine. A consensus-building, Japanese-style leader can get people to agree to divert from the routine. In both cases, the leader creates incremental behavior change beyond the routine. How does leadership (being as a part) in its various cultural forms differ from the various intervention (being as an individual) strategies and cases discussed above? Some case data may be revealing.

## Cases

1. *Roger Boisjoly and the Challenger Launch.*[19] In January 1985, after the postflight hardware inspection of Flight 52C, Roger Boisjoly strongly suspected that unusually low temperatures had compromised the performance effectiveness of the O-ring seals on two field joints. Such a performance compromise could cause an explosion. In March 1985, laboratory tests confirmed that low temperature did negatively affect the ability of the O-rings to perform this sealing function. In June 1985, the postflight inspection of Flight 51B revealed serious erosion of both primary and backup seals that, had it continued, could have caused an explosion.

These events convinced Boisjoly that a serious and very dangerous problem existed with the O-rings. Instead of acting as an individual against his supervisors and the organization, for example, by blowing the whistle to the press, he tried to lead a change to stop the launching of flights with unsafe O-rings. He worked with his immediate supervisor, the director of engineering, and the organization in leading this change. He wrote a draft of a memo to Bob Lund, vice-president of engineering, which he first showed and discussed with his immediate supervisor to "maintain good relationships." Boisjoly and others developed potential win-win solutions, such as investigating remedies to fix the O-rings and refraining from launching flights at too-low temperature. He effectively established a team to study the matter, and participated in a teleconference with 130 technical experts.

On the day before the Challenger launch, Boisjoly and other team members were successful in leading company executives to reverse their tentative recommendation to launch because the overnight temperature were predicted to be too low. The company recommendation was to launch only when temperatures were above 53 degrees. To this point, Boisjoly was very effective in leading a change toward what he and other engineering and management people believed was a safe and ethical decision.

However, according to testimony from Boisjoly and others to Congress, the top managers of Morton Thiokol, under pressure from NASA, reversed their earlier recommendation not to launch. The next day, Challenger was launched and exploded, causing the deaths of all the crew members. While Boisjoly was very effective in leading a change within his own organization, he was not able to counteract subsequent pressure from the customer, NASA.

2. *Dan Phillips and Genco, Inc.*[20] Dan Phillips was a paper products group division manager for Genco, whose upper-level management adopted a strategy whereby several mills, including the Elkhorn Mill, would either have to reduce costs or close down. Phillips was concerned that cost cutting at Elkhorn would prevent the mill from meeting government pollution-control requirements, and that closing the mill could seriously hurt the local community. If he reduced costs, he would not meet pollution-control requirements; if he did not reduce costs, the mill would close and the community would suffer.

Phillips did not secretly or publicly blow the whistle, nor did he sabotage, conscientiously object, quietly refrain from implementing the plan, or quit; however, he did lead a change in the organization's ethical behavior. He asked research and development people in his division to investigate how the plant could both become more cost efficient and create less pollution. He then asked operations people in his division to estimate how long it would take to put such a new plant design on line, and how much it would cost. He asked cost accounting and financial people within his division to estimate when such a new operation would achieve a break even payback. Once he found a plan that would work, he negotiated a win-win solution with upper-level management: in exchange for not closing the plant and increasing its investment in his division, the organization would over time benefit from lower costs and higher profitability. Phillips thus worked with others and the organization to lead an inquiry and adopt an alternative ethical and cost-effective plan.

3. *Lotus and Brazilian Software Importing.*[21] Lotus, a software manufacturer, found that in spite of restrictions on the importing of much of its software to Brazil, many people there were buying and using Lotus software. On further investigation, the company discovered that Brazilian businessmen, in alliance with a Brazilian general, were violating the law by buying Lotus, software in Cambridge, Massachusetts, and bringing it into Brazil.

Instead of blowing the whistle on the illegal behavior, sabotaging it, or leaving Brazil, Lotus negotiated a solution: In exchange for the Brazilians' agreement to stop illegal importing, Lotus helped set them up as legitimate licensed manufacturers and distributors of Lotus products in Brazil. Instead of working against them and the Lotus salespeople supplying them, the Lotus managers worked with these people to develop an ethical, legal, and economically sound solution to the importing problem.

And in at least a limited sense, the importers may have been transformed into ethical managers and business people. This case may remind you of the legendary "old West," where government officials sometimes negotiated win-win solutions with "outlaw gunfighters," who agreed to become somewhat more ethical as appointed sheriffs. The gunfighters needed to make a living, and many were not interested in or qualified for such other professions as farming or shop-keeping. In some cases, ethical behavior may take place before ethical beliefs are assumed.

4. *Insurance company office/sales manager and discrimination.*[22] The sales-office manager of a very large Boston-area insurance company tried to hire female salespeople several times, but his boss refused to permit the hires. The manager could have acted against his boss and the organization by secretly threatening to blow the whistle or actually blowing the whistle, publicly or secretly. Instead he decided to try to lead a change in the implicit hiring policy of the organization.

The manager asked his boss why he was not permitted to hire a woman. He learned that his boss did not believe women made good salespeople and had never worked with a female salesperson. He found that reasoning with his boss about the capabilities of women and the ethics and legality of refusing to hire women was ineffective.

He inquired within the company about whether being a woman could be an advantage in any insurance sales areas. He negotiated with his boss a six-month experiment whereby he hired on a trial basis one woman to sell life insurance to married women who contributed large portions of their salaries to their home mortgages. The woman he hired was not only very successful in selling this type of life insurance, but became one of the office's top salespeople. After this experience, the boss reversed his policy of not hiring female salespeople.

## Limitations to Leading Ethical Organizational Change

In the four cases described above, the individuals did not attack the organization or people within the organization, nor did they intervene against individuals and/or the organization to stop an unethical practice. Instead, they worked with people in the organization to build a more ethical organization. As a result of their leadership, the organizations used more ethical behaviors. The strategy of leading an organization toward more ethical behavior, however, does have some limitations. These are described below.

1. In some organizational situations, ethical win-win solutions or compromises may not be possible. For example, in 1975 a pharmaceutical company in Raritan, New Jersey decided to enter a new market with a new product.[23] Grace Pierce, who was then in charge of medical testing of new products, refused to test a new diarrhea drug product on infants and elderly consumers because it contained high levels of saccharin, which was feared by many at the time to be a carcinogen. When Pierce was transferred, she resigned. The drug was tested on infant and elderly consumers. In this case, Pierce may have been faced with an either-or situation that left her little room to lead a change in organizational behavior.

Similarly, Errol Marshall, with Hydraulic Parts and Components, Inc.,[24] helped negotiate the sale of a sub-contract to sell heavy equipment to the U.S. Navy while giving $70,000 in kickbacks to two materials managers of Brown & Root, Inc., the project's prime contractor. According to Marshall, the prime contractor "demanded the kickbacks...It was cut and dried. We would not get the business otherwise." While Marshall was not charged with any crime, one of the upper-level Brown & Root managers, William Callan, was convicted in 1985 of extorting kickbacks, and another manager, Frank DiDomenico, pleaded guilty to extorting kickbacks from Hydraulic Parts & Components, Inc. Marshall has left the company. In this case, it seems that Marshall had no win-win alternative to paying the bribe. In some situations it may not be possible to lead a win-win ethical change.

2.    Some people do not understand how leadership can be applied to situations that involve organizational-ethics issues. Also, some people—particularly those in analytical or technical professions, which may not offer much opportunity for gaining leadership experience—may not know how to lead very well in any situation. Some people may be good leaders in the course of their normal work lives, but do not try to lead or do not lead very well when ethical issues are involved. Some people avoid discussing ethical, religious, and political issues at work.

For example, John Geary was a salesman for U.S. Steel when the company decided to enter a new market with what he and others considered an unsafe new product.[25] As a leading salesman for U.S. Steel, Geary normally was very good at leading the way toward changes that satisfied customer and organizational needs. A good salesman frequently needs to coordinate and spearhead modification in operations, engineering, logistics, products design, financing, and billing/payment that are necessary for a company to maintain good customer relationships and sales. Apparently, however, he did not try to lead the organization in developing a win-win solutions, such as soliciting current orders for a later delivery of a corrected product. He tried only reasoning against selling the unsafe product and protested its sale to several groups of upper-level engineers and managers. He noted that he believed the product had a failure rate of 3.6% and was therefore both unsafe and potentially damaging to U.S. Steel's longer-term strategy of entering higher technology/profit margin businesses. According to Geary, even though many upper-level managers, engineers, and salesmen understood and believed him, "the only desire of everyone associated with the project was to satisfy the instructions of Henry Wallace (the sales vice-president). No one was about to buck this man for fear of his job."[26] The sales vice-president fired Geary, apparently because he continued to protest against sale of the product.

Similarly, William Schwartzkopf of Commonwealth Electric Co.[27] did not think he could either ethically reason against or lead an end to the large-scale, long-time bid rigging between his own company and many of the largest U.S. electrical contractors. Even though he was an attorney and had extensive experience in leading organizational changes, he did not try to lead his company toward an ethical solution. He waited until he retired from the company, then wrote a secret letter to the Justice Department accusing the contractors of raising bids and conspiring to divide billions of dollars of contracts among themselves.

Many people—both experienced and inexperienced in leadership—do not try to lead their companies toward developing solutions to ethical problems. Often, they do not understand that it is possible to lead such a change; therefore, they do not try to do so—even though as the cases here show, many succeed when they do try.

3. Some organizational environments—in both consensus-building and authoritarian types of cultures—discourage leadership that is noncomforming. For example as Robert E. Wood, former CEO of the giant internation retailer Sears, Roebuck, has observed, "We stress the advantages of the free enterprise system, we complain about the totalitarian state, but in our individual organizations we have created more or less a totalitarian system in industry, particularly in large industry."[28] Similarly, Charles W. Summers, in a *Harvard Business Review* article, observes, "Corporate executives may argue that…they recognize and protect…against arbitrary termination through their own internal procedures. The simple fact is that most companies have not recognized and protected that right."[29]

David Ewing concludes that "It [the pressure to obey unethical and illegal orders] is probably most dangerous however, as a low-level infection. When it slowly bleeds the individual conscience dry and metastasizes insidiously, it is most difficult to defend against. There are no spectacular firings or purges in the ranks. There are no epic blunders. Under constant and insistent pressure, employees simply give in and conform. They become good 'organization people.'"[30]

Similar pressures can exist in participative, consensus-building types of cultures. For example, as mentioned above, Yoshino and Lifson write, "A Japanese leader, rather than being an authority, is more of a communications channel, a mediator, a facilitator, and most of all, a symbol and embodiment of group unity. Consensus building is necessary to decision making, and this requires patience and an ability to use carefully cultivated relationships to get all to agree for the good of the unit."[31]

The importance of the group and the position of the group leaders as a symbol of the group are revealed in the very popular true story, "Tale of the Forty-Seven Ronin." The tale is about 47 warriors whose lord is unjustly killed. The Ronin spend years sacrificing everything, including their families, in order to kill the person responsible for their leader's death. Then all those who survive the assault killed themselves.

Just as authoritarian top-down organizational cultures can produce unethical behaviors, so can participative, consensus-building cultures. The Japanese novelist Shusaku Endo, in his *The Sea and Poison*, describes the true story of such a problem.[32] It concerns an experiment cooperatively performed by the Japanese Army, a medical hospital, and a consensus-building team of doctors on American prisoners of war. The purpose of the experiment was to determine scientifically how much blood people can lose before they die.

Endo describes the reasoning and feelings of one of the doctors as he looked back at this behavior:

"At the time nothing could be done…If I were caught in the same way, I might, I might just do the same thing again…We feel that getting on good terms ourselves with the Western Command medical people, with whom Second [section] is so cosy, wouldn't be a bad idea at all. Therefore we feel there's no need to ill-temperedly refuse their friendly proposal and hurt their feelings…Five doctors from Kando's section most likely will be glad to get the chance…For me the pangs of conscience…were from childhood equivalent to the fear of disapproval in the eyes of others—fear of the punishment which society would bring to bear.

…To put it quite bluntly, I am able to remain quite undisturbed in the face of someone else's terrible suffering and death…I am not writing about these experiences as one driven to do so by his conscience…all these memories are distasteful to me. But looking upon them as distasteful and suffering because of them are two different matters. Then why do I bother writing? Because I'm strangely ill at ease. I, who fear only the eyes of others and the punishment of society, and whose fears disappear when I am secure from these, am now disturbed…I have no conscience, I suppose. Not just me, though. None of them feel anything at all about what they did here." The only emotion in his heart was a sense of having fallen as low as one can fall.[33]

# WHAT TO DO AND HOW TO BE

In light of the discussion of the two approaches to addressing organization ethics issues and their limitations, what should we do as individuals and members of organizations? To some extent that depends on the circumstances and our own abilities. If we know how to lead, if there's time for it, if the key people in authority are reasonable, and if a win-win solution is possible, one should probably try leading an organizational change.

If, on the other hand, one does not know how to lead, time is limited, the authority figures are unreasonable, a culture of strong conformity exists, and the situation is not likely to produce a win-win outcome, then the chances of success with a leadership approach are much lower. This may leave one with only the choice of using one of the intervention strategies discussed above. If an individual wishes to remain an effective member of the organization, then one of the more secretive strategies may be safer.

But what about the more common, middle range of problems? Here there is no easy prescription. The more win-win potential the situation has, the more time there is, the more leadership skills one has, and the more reasonable the authority figures and organizational cultures are, the more likely a leadership approach is to succeed. If the opposite conditions exist, then forcing change in the organization is the likely alternative.

To a large extent, the choice depends on an individual's courage. In my opinion, in all but the most extreme and unusual circumstances, one should first try to lead a change toward ethical behavior. If that does not succeed, then mustering the courage to act against others and the organization may be necessary. For example, the course of action that might have saved the Challenger crew was for Boisjoly or someone else to act against Morton Thiokol, its top managers, and NASA by blowing the whistle to the press.

If there is an implicitly characteristic American ontology, perhaps it is some version of William James' 1907 Pragmatism, which, for better or worse, sees through a lens of interactions the ontologies of being as an individual and being as a part. James explains our situation as follows:

*What we were discussing was the idea of a world growing not integrally but piecemeal by the contributions of its several parts. Take the hypothesis seriously and as a live one. Suppose that the world's author put the case to you before creation, saying: "If I am going to make a world not certain to be saved, a world the perfection of which shall be conditional merely, the condition being that each agent does its own 'level best,' I offer you the chance of taking part in such a world. Its safety, you see, is unwarranted. It is a real adventure, with real danger, yet it may win through. It is a social scheme of co-operative work genuinely to be done. Will you join the procession? Will you trust yourself and trust the other agents enough to face the risk?...Then it is perfectly possible to accept sincerely a drastic kind of universe from which the element of "seriousness" is not to be expelled. Who so does so, it seems to me, a genuine pragmatist. He is willing to live on a scheme of uncertified possibilities which he trusts; willing to pay with his own person, if need be, for the realization of the ideals which he frames. What now actually are the other forces which he trusts to co-operate with him, in a universe of such a type? They are at least his fellow men, in the stage of being which our actual universe has reached.[34]*

In conclusion, there are realistic ethics leadership and intervention action strategies. We can act effectively concerning organizational ethics issues. Depending upon the circumstances including our own courage, we can choose to act and be ethical both as individuals and as leaders. Being as a part and leading ethical change is the more constructive approach generally. However, being as an individual intervening against others and organizations can sometimes be the only short- or medium-term effective approach.

## NOTES

1. Paul Tillich, *The Courage to Be*. New Haven, CT: Yale University Press, 1950.
2. See Endnote 1, page 159.
3. David Ewing, *Freedom Inside the Organization*. New York: McGraw-Hill, 1977.
4. The person blowing the whistle in this case wishes to remain anonymous. See also Elizabeth Neuffer, "GE Managers Sentenced for Bribery," *The Boston Globe*, July 26, 1988, p. 67.
5. Barbara Ley Toffler, *Tough Choices: Managers Talk Ethics*. New York: John Wiley, 1986, pp. 153–169.
6. Richard P. Nielsen, "What Can Managers Do about Unethical Management?" *Journal of Business Ethics*, 6, 1987, 153–161. See also Nielsen's "Limitations of Ethical Reasoning as an Action Strategy," *Journal of Business Ethics*, 7, 1988, pp. 625–733, and "Arendt's Action Philosophy and the Manager as Eichmann, Richard III, Faust or Institution Citizen," *California Management Review*, 26, 3, Spring 1984, pp. 191–201.
7. The person involved wishes to remain anonymous.
8. The person involved wishes to remain anonymous.
9. See Endnote 6.
10. R. Reinhold, "Astronauts' Chief Says NASA Risked Life for Schedule," *The New York Times*, 36, 1986, p. 1.
11. Personal conversation and letter with Frank Ladwig, 1986. See also Frank Ladwig and Associates' *Advanced Consultative Selling for Professionals*. Stonington, CT.
12. W. G. Glaberson, "Did Searle Lose Its Eyes to a Health Hazard?" *Business Week*, October 14, 1985, p. 120–122.
13. The person involved wishes to remain anonymous.
14. Andy Pasztor, "Electrical Contractors Reel under Charges That They Rigged Bids," *The Wall Street Journal*, November 29, 1985, pp. 1, 14.
15. A. Ernest Fitzgerald, *The High Priests of Waste*. New York: McGraw-Hill, 1977.
16. See Endnote 1, pp. 89, 93.
17. M. Y. Yoshino and T. B. Lifson, *The Invisible Link: Japan's Saga Shosha and the Organization of Trade*. Cambridge, MA: MIT Press, 1986.
18. See Endnote 17, p. 178.
19. Roger Boisjoly, address given at Massachusetts Institute of Technology on January 7, 1987. Reprinted in *Books and Religion*, March/April 1987, 3–4, 12–13. See also Caroline Whitbeck, "Moral Responsibility and the Working Engineer," *Books and Religion*, March/April 1987, 3, 22–23.

20. Personal conversation with Ray Bauer, Harvard Business School, 1975. See also R. Ackerman and Ray Bauer, *Corporate Social Responsiveness*. Reston, VA: Reston Publishing, 1976.
21. The person involved wishes to remain anonymous.
22. The person involved wishes to remain anonymous.
23. David Ewing, *Do It My Way or You're Fired*. New York: John Wiley, 1983.
24. E. T. Pound, "Investigators Detect Pattern of Kickbacks for Defense Business," *The Wall Street Journal*, November 14, 1985, pp. 1, 25.
25. See Endnote 23. See also Geary vs. U.S. Steel Corporation, 319 A. 2nd 174, Supreme Court of Pa.
26. See Endnote 23, p. 86.
27. See Endnote 14.
28. See Endnote 3, p. 21.
29. C. W. Summers, "Protecting All Employees against Unjust Dismissal," *Harvard Business Review*, 58, 1980, pp. 132–139.
30. See Endnote 3, pp. 216–217.
31. See Endnote 17, p. 187.
32. Shusaku Endo, *The Sea and Poison*. New York: Taplinger Publishing Company, 1972. See also Y. Yasuda, *Old Tales of Japan*. Tokyo: Charles Tuttle Company, 1947.
33. See Endnote 32.
34. William James, *Pragmatism: A New Name for Some Old Ways of Thinking*. New York: Longmans, Green and Co., 1907, p. 290, 297–298.

# 6
# Personal Growth, Career Development, and Work Stress

ON THE REALIZATION OF HUMAN POTENTIAL:
A PATH WITH A HEART
>  Herbert A. Shepard

CAREER GRIDLOCK: BABY BOOMERS HIT THE WALL
>  Douglas T. Hall
>  Judith Richter

STRESS IN ORGANIZATIONS
>  Robert L. Kahn
>  Philippe Byosiere

## ON THE REALIZATION OF HUMAN POTENTIAL: A PATH WITH A HEART

*Herbert A. Shepard*

### A VISION UNFULFILLED

The central issue is a life fully worth living. The test is how you feel each day as you anticipate that day's experience. The same test is the best predictor of health and longevity. It is simple.

If it's simple, why doesn't everyone know it? The answer to that question is simple, too. We have been brought up to live by rules that mostly have nothing to do with making our lives worth living; some of them in fact are guaranteed not to. Many of our institutions and traditions introduce cultural distortions into our vision, provide us with beliefs and definitions that don't work, distract us from the task of building lives that are fully worth living, and persuade us that other things are more important.

The human infant is a life-loving bundle of energy with a marvelous array of potentialities, and many vulnerabilities. It is readily molded. If it is given a supportive environment, it will flourish and continue to love its own life and the lives of others. It will grow to express its own gifts and uniqueness, and to find joy in the opportunity for doing so. It will extend these talents to the world and feel gratified from the genuine appreciation of others. In turn, it will appreciate the talents of others and encourage them, too, to realize their own potential and to express their separate uniqueness.

*Source: Working with Careers* by Michael B. Arthur, Lotte Barilyn, Daniel J. Levinson, and Herbert A. Shepard. Columbia University School of Business, 1984.

But if a child is starved of a supportive environment, it will spend the rest of its life trying to compensate for that starvation. It becomes hungry for what it has been denied, and compulsively seeks to satisfy perceived deficiencies. In turn, these perceived deficiencies become the basis for measuring and relating to others. As Maslow pointed out, such deficiency motivation does not end with childhood (Maslow, 1962; Maslow and Chang, 1969). Rather, the struggle makes a person continually dependent on and controllable by any source that promises to remove the deficiencies.

## Deficiency Motivation in Operation

Frequently we refer to deficiency motivation in terms of needs: needs for approval, recognition, power, control, status; needs to prove one's masculinity, or smartness, or successfulness in other's eyes—and in one's own eyes, which have been programmed to see the world in terms of one's deficiencies. An emphasis on such needs can lead to a denial of individual uniqueness and may make us vulnerable to exploitation. In either case, the outcome for the individual can be devastating, and the rich promise of human potential remains unfulfilled.

*Denial of Uniqueness.* The way this process takes place can be illustrated by a fable, "The School for Animals":

> Once upon a time the animals got together and decided to found a school. There would be a core curriculum of six subjects: swimming, crawling, running, jumping, climbing and flying. At first the duck was the best swimmer, but it wore out the webs of its feet in running class, and then couldn't swim as well as before. And at first the dog was the best runner, but it crash landed twice in flying class and injured a leg. The rabbit started out as the best jumper, but it fell in climbing class and hurt its back. At the end of the school year, the class valedictorian was an eel, who could do a little bit of everything, but nothing very well.

The school for animals, of course, is much like our schools for people. And the notion of a common, unindividualized curriculum has permeated the whole fabric of our society, bringing with it associated judgments about our worth as human beings. It is all too easy for uniqueness to go unrecognized, and to spend a lifetime trying to become an eel.

*Exploitation of Uniqueness.* A second, perhaps subtler way that deficiency motivation can operate is illustrated by the story of the cormorant. Dr. Ralph Siu, when asked what wisdom the ancient oriental philosophers could contribute to modern man in modern organizations on how to preserve his mental health, developed a list of "advices." One of them was as follows:

> Observe the cormorant in the fishing fleet. You know how cormorants are used for fishing. The technique involves a man in a rowboat with about half a dozen or so cormorants, each with a ring around the neck. As the bird spots a fish, it will dive into the water and unerringly come up with it. Because of the ring, the larger fish are not swallowed but held in the throat. The fisherman picks up the bird and squeezes out the fish through the mouth. The bird then dives for another, and the cycle repeats itself.
>     Observe the cormorant...Why is it that of all the different vertebrates the cormorant has been chosen to slave away day and night for the fisherman? Were the bird not greedy for fish, or not efficient in catching it, or not readily trained, would society have created an industry to exploit the bird? Would the ingenious device of a ring around its neck, and the simple procedure of squeezing the bird's neck to force it to regurgitate the fish have been devised? Of course not
>
> (Siu, 1971).

169

The neo-Taoist alerts us to how the cormorant's uniqueness is exploited by the fisherman for his own selfish use. Similarly, human motives can get directed to making others prosper, but not always in a way that benefits the person providing the talent. Human life can too easily parallel that of the captive cormorant.

## Institutions and Deficiency Motivation

Let us stay with Dr. Siu's cormorant story a little longer. His advice continues:

> Greed, talent, and capacity for learning, then, are the basis of exploitation. The more you are able to moderate and/or hide them from society, the greater will be your chances of escaping the fate of the cormorant...It is necessary to remember that the institutions of society are geared to making society prosper, not necessarily to minimize suffering on your part. It is for this reason, among others, that the schools tend to drum into your mind the high desirability of those characteristics that tend to make society prosper—namely, ambition, progress, and success. These in turn are valued in terms of society's objectives, All of them gradually but surely increase your greed and make a cormorant out of you (Siu, 1971).

The further point here is even more far-reaching: that the institutions and organizations in which we spend our lives collude with one another in causing denials, deflections, or distortions of human potential. In particular, three sets of institutions—parents, schools, and organizations—demand consideration.

*Parents.* First, parents, sincerely concerned for their children's ability to survive in the world, unwittingly ignore their individuality and measure their offspring's progress by a simple set of common standards. What parents are not delighted to be able to say that their children are ambitious, talented, and have a great capacity for learning? It is something to boast about, rather than something to hide. Outside confirmation of achievement earns love and recognition, its absence draws disapproval. Any evidence of "A" student behavior is immediately rewarded. Lesser performance calls for added effort so that deficiencies can be corrected. Much of this parental energy is targeted toward helping children qualify for an occupational future that will in no way reflect their true interests and abilities. The expression or suppression of talent is externally defined, and parents stand as the most immediate custodians of society's standards and its dogma.

*Schools.* In our schools, the ideal is the "Straight A" student. It is this student who is most sought after, either at the next stage of institutional learning, or by employers from the world of work. What "Straight A" means is that the student has learned to do a number of things at a marketable level of performance, regardless of whether the student has any interest in or innate talent for the activity, and regardless of whether it brings pain, joy, or boredom. The reward is in the grade, not the activity. On the one hand, schools collaborate with parents to reinforce this concern over grades as ends in themselves. On the other, as Dr. Siu points out, the school's objectives are to serve the needs of society, not necessarily those of the student. Once more, a person's uniqueness is not valued for its own sake. Schools are selective about the talents they identify, and represent outside interests in the talents that they choose to develop.

*Organizations.* Lastly, in organizations, the continued external denial or manipulation of talent has its direct career consequences. Organizations have implicit ways of teaching about careers, regardless of whether they have explicit career planning and development programs. Reward systems are geared to common deficiencies—needs for status, approval, power—and a career consists of doing the right things to move up the ladder. A vice president of one company counselled his subordinates: "The work day is for doing your job; your overtime is for your promotion."

In many companies the message about careers is very clear: not only is your career more important than the rest of your life, it is more important than your life. In one large corporation, great emphasis was placed on moving young professionals and managers through many company functions as their preparation for general management responsibility, The career plan was well understood: "When you're rotated, don't ask if it's up, down or sideways; the time to worry is when you stop rotating." In such companies, successful careers are based on working hard at any job you are given whether you like it or not, and on conforming to the organization's unwritten rules and to the expectations of your superiors in such matters as office manners, dress, presentation style, language, and prejudices.

Do these paths have "heart"? Do they provide for the expression of human potential and facilitate individual growth? For some, as much through good luck as good management, they do. But perhaps a greater number ultimately lose their way, and get labeled as suffering from "burnout" or "retiring on the job."

In one company that recruits only top graduates, that devotes a great deal of managerial time to tracking their performance, that moves each one along at what is judged to be an appropriate pace into jobs that are judged to be suited to his or her talents and potentials, the amount of burnout observed in mid-career management ranks became a matter of concern. As a result, the company offered career planning workshops to mid-career managers, the main objective of which was, according to one executive: "…to revitalize them by reminding them that in an ultimate sense each of them is in business for himself!"

For deficiency-motivated people, moving up the hierarchy of management is likely to be such a compelling need that they may desert careers that did have some heart for them. In an informal survey of industrial research scientists conducted by the author some years ago, it was possible to identify the ones for whom their career path had a heart, by their response to the question: "What is your main goal over the next two or three years?" Some responded in such terms as: "Some equipment I've tried to get for three years has finally made it into this year's budget. With it, I can pursue some very promising leads." Others responded in such terms as: "I hope to become a department head." But the second group seemed to have lost its zest. Many of them enjoyed their work and had no real desire to leave it in order to direct the work of others. They were just singing the preferred organizational song.

Don Juan, in teaching Carlos Casteneda about careers, asserted that to have a path of knowledge, a path with a *heart*, made for a joyful journey and was the only conceivable way to live. But he emphasized the importance of thinking carefully about our paths before we set out on them. For by the time a man discovers that his path "has no heart," the path is ready to kill him. At that point, he cautions, very few men stop to deliberate, and leave that path (Castaneda, 1968). For example, in a life/career planning workshop for the staff of a mid-west military research laboratory, a 29-year-old engineer confessed that he was bored to death with the laboratory work, but his eyes lit up at the prospect of teaching physical education and coaching athletic teams at the high school level. He emerged with a career plan to do just that, and to do it in his favorite part of the country, northern New England. He resolved to do it immediately upon retirement from his civil service job as an engineer—at age 65, a mere 36 years away!

Thus, all these institutions—parents, schools, and organizations—are suspect when they attempt to give career guidance. Suspect if, like the school for animals, they discourage uniqueness and enforce conformity. Suspect if, like the fisherman with his cormorant, they harness talent only to serve their vested interests. Suspect if they address only the development of a career, so that the rest of life becomes an unanticipated consequence of the career choice. Suspect if they stress only the how-to's of a career and not its meaning in your life. And suspect, too, if they describe a career as a way to make a living, and fail to point out that the wrong career choice may be fatal. In sum, suspect because they are not concerned with whether a life is fully worth living.

# A FRAMEWORK FOR UNDERSTANDING HUMAN POTENTIAL

An outcome of people's experience with society and its institutions is that many adults cannot remember, if they ever knew, what their unique talents and interests were. They cannot remember what areas of learning and doing were fulfilling for them, what paths had heart. These have to be discovered and rediscovered.

For many, the relationship between formal schooling and subsequent occupation needs to be re-examined. In adult life/career planning workshops, the author has found that of the things participants actually enjoy doing, less than 5% are things they learned in school as part of formal classroom work. A related outcome is that adults distinguish between work and play. Work is something you have to be "compensated" for, because it robs you of living. Play is something you usually have to pay for, because your play is often someone else's work. Children have to be taught these distinctions carefully, for they make no sense to anyone whose life is fully worth living. As one philosopher put it:

> A master in the art of living draws no sharp distinction between his work and his play, his labor and his leisure, his mind and his body, his education and his recreation. He scarcely knows which is which. *He simply pursues his vision of excellence* through whatever he is doing and leaves others to determine whether he is working or playing. To himself he always seems to be doing both.

But pursuing a vision of excellence is not always simple. What does "vision of excellence" mean? How do you acquire your own? We can be reasonably sure that it has little to do with getting A's, excelling against others in competition, or living up to someone else's standards. It is one's own unique vision. It will not emerge in school, if each person must be comparable to every other person so that grades and rank can be assigned. Such a system defines individuality as differences in degree, not in kind. Consider, too, the word "genius." To most of us it means a person with a high IQ. But differences in IQ are differences of degree, whereas the notion of "unique" makes it impossible to rank and compare.

In the search for your own unique vision, you need a different definition of "genius," one closer to the dictionary definition as "the unique and identifying spirit of a person or place." By this definition, your genius consists of those of your talents that you love to develop and use. These are the things that you can now or potentially could do with excellence, which are fulfilling in the doing of them; so fulfilling that if you also get paid to do them, it feels not like compensation, but like a gift.

## Discovering Genius and Developing Autonomy

Discovering your genius may be easy or difficult. At some level of your being you already know it; you are fortunate if it is in your conscious awareness. If not, there are several routes to discovery, and many sources of pertinent information.

The first source is *play*. Make a list of the things you enjoy doing and find the common themes. Observe what you do when you are not obliged to do anything. What activities are you likely to engage in? What catches your eye when you thumb through a magazine? When you are in an unfamiliar environment, what interests you, what catches your attention? What are the contents of your fantasies and daydreams? What do you wish you were doing? Your sleep-dreams are also important. Record them, for some of them contain important wishes that you may want to turn into plans.

The second source is your own *life history*. Record in some detail the times in your past when you were doing something very well and enjoying it very much. What themes or patterns of strength, skill, and activity pervade most of those times? What were the sources of satisfaction in them?

The third source is *feedback* from others. What do those who know you have to say about your strengths and talents? As they see it, what seems to excite you, give you pleasure, engage you? And if you can find people who knew you when you were a child, can they recall what used to capture your attention and curiosity, what activities you enjoyed, what special promise and talents you displayed?

The fourth source is *psychological instruments*, which provide a variety of ways of helping you to organize and interpret your experience. There are many such instruments that can provide you with clues to your interests, strengths, and sources of satisfaction. Perhaps the most valuable is the Myers-Briggs Type Indicator, which is based on the insights of the psychologist Carl Jung. A recent book, based on these ideas, identifies four basic temperaments, four quite different ways of approaching life (Keirsey and Bats, 1978). One of these is oriented to tradition and stability in the world, and devoted to making systems work and to the maintenance of order. The second type loves action, freedom, excitement, and the mastery of skills. The third type is oriented to the future and to mastery of the unknown. The fourth loves to work in the service of humanity and bring about a better world. One can learn to perform competently in activities that do not fit one's temperament, and to some extent one must, but it always feels like "work." In contrast, if the activities are in accord with one's temperament, it feels more like "play." It follows that your temperament is one of the important components of your genius.

As you take these four routes, you may find the same messages about yourself over and over again—and you may also find a few surprises and contradictions. In general, the truth strategy you employ is the one enunciated in *Alice in Wonderland:* "What I tell you three times is true." You may emerge from the search with some hunches to explore further; you may emerge with certainty about a new direction to take; or you may simply affirm what you already knew—confirming or disconfirming the life and career choices you have already made. This discovery or affirmation of your genius is a first step, but it needs also to be nourished and developed, and you need to learn how to create the conditions that will support you in practicing it. The second step then, is to acquire the resources you need in order to build a world for yourself that supports you in the pursuit and practice of your genius. The process of acquiring these resources can be called the *development of autonomy*—learning the skills needed to build that world.

Consider the following case:

Jerome Kirk, a well-known sculptor, discovered his genius through play, though not until his late twenties. Alone on an island off the Maine coast for a week, he amused himself by fashioning sculptures out of driftwood. It was a dazzling experience. But his education had prepared him for work in the field of personnel administration. For the following twenty years he developed his skill as a sculptor, "while earning a living" as a personnel administrator—and he was quite successful in this profession. After twenty years, his sculptures matched his own vision of excellence, he was a recognized artist, and the income from his art was sufficient to enable him to devote all his time to it. It was the realization of a dream. His comment: "I was good in the personnel field, but I never really enjoyed it. It wasn't me. And now I'm utterly convinced that if a person really loves something, and focuses his energy there, there's just no way he can fail to fulfill his 'vision of excellence.'"

The point of this story is not to idealize the creative arts. For others, discovery of genius would take them in a different direction, perhaps toward greater interaction with people rather than away from it. But the story does illustrate the qualities that get released when a person discovers his or her genius. Passion, energy, and focus all came as a natural by-product of Kirk's discovery. These were the qualities needed to develop the autonomy that ultimately allowed Kirk to realize his dream. They were inspired by the knowledge of his genius that he carried within him. The same qualities will be evident in any person who has discovered his or her genius, whether it is in sculpture or in the leadership of organizations (Vaill, 1982).

## Living Out Your Potential

You began your life as a bundle of life-loving energy with a marvelous array of potentialities. As you grew up you learned to do many things and not to do other things. Some of these things were good for you, some bad for you, some good for others, some bad for others. Out of the things you learned, you fashioned an identity, a self-image. Thus, your self-image is a cultural product, and the distortion it contains may prevent you from recognizing yourself anymore as a bundle of life-loving energy with a marvelous array of potentialities. Acquiring a renewed identity, an identification with what is truly wonderful about yourself and therefore worth nourishing and loving, is not an easy task. It requires a lot of unlearning and letting go, as well as new learning and risk-taking.

How can you tell when you have achieved this goal? What can you feel from communion with others that confirms your own life as fully worth living? What should living out your potential mean in relationship to the outer world? Three qualities are critical indications that you have achieved a life fully worth living. They can be called tone, resonance, and perspective. Tone refers to feeling good about yourself, resonance to feeling good about your relationships, and perspective to feeling good about the choices in your life. To experience these qualities consistently is to know that you are living life well. Once again, though, our society interferes with and disguises the messages that we receive. Therefore, it is necessary not only to grasp the essence of these qualities, but also to recognize and to separate oneself from the distortions of them that our culture imposes.

*Tone.* Tone refers to your aliveness as an organism. When you think of good muscle tone, you think of a relaxed alertness, a readiness to respond. As used here, the term tone refers to your entire being, your mental and emotional life as well as your muscle and organ life. Hence anxiety is as much the enemy of tone as drugs or being overweight. Lowen expressed this idea as follows:

> A person experiences the reality of the world only through his body....If the body is relatively unalive, a person's impressions and responses are diminished. The more alive the body is, the more vividly does he perceive reality and the more actively does he respond to it. We have all experienced the fact that when we feel particularly good and alive, we perceive the world more sharply....The aliveness of the body denotes its capacity for feeling. In the absence of feeling, the body goes "dead" insofar as its ability to be impressed by or respond to situations is concerned....It is the body that melts with love, freezes with fear, trembles in anger, and reaches for warmth and contact. Apart from the body these words are poetic images. Experienced in the body, they have a reality that gives meaning to existence (Lowen, 1967).

But the self-images we forge on our journey through society's institutions often deprive us of our ability to maintain tone. We are no longer in touch with our bodies or with our genuine feelings, and our self-images have been distorted.

174

One of the most common distortions is to comprise your self-image out of some role or roles you play in society. Great actors and actresses use their capacity for total identification with another human being as a basis for a great performance, but their self-image is not that of a person portrayed. That costume is removed at the end of each performance. Cornelia Otis Skinner declared that the first law of the theater is to love your audience. She meant, of course, that the actor or actress, rather than the character portrayed, must love the audience. You cannot love the audience unless you love yourself, and yourself is not a role. Thus, it is vitally important to recognize your roles as costumes you wear for particular purposes, and not to let them get stuck to you. Your prospects at retirement from your profession or organization will otherwise be for a very short life.

A second common distortion is to make your head (your brain) your self-image, and the rest of you part of your environment. Cutting your body into two segments places enormous stress on it, and your tone will suffer severely. "You don't exist within your body. Your body is a person" (Lowen, 1967). A third distortion is to make your gender your self-image. The sexual-reproductive aspects of people are among their most wonderful potentialities, but to identify with your gender leads you to spend the first years of your life learning some bad habits that you spend the rest of your life trying to liberate yourself from.

Other common distortions include being the public relations representative of your family (often forced on boys and girls), being an underdog, a clown, or a representative of superior values. All such distortions will exact their price by robbing you of tone: by causing you to eat too much or drink too much or worry too much or keep your body in continuous stress, and miss the joy of being alive.

***Resonance.*** The second quality for living out your genius is your capacity for resonance. This involves an enhanced, stimulated, and yet relaxed vitality that you can experience in interaction with particular others and particular environments. Discovering those others and those environments that are able to provide resonance can be one of the most fulfilling aspects of the journey through a life fully worth living. The word resonance is chosen rather than the word love, with which it has much in common, because the very meaning of love has become distorted in our society. It has become a commodity in short supply, a marketable item, a weapon used to control others; it is difficult to distinguish love from exploitation or imprisonment.

The term resonance is chosen for other reasons as well. It conveys the notion of being "in tune" with other people and environments; it suggests the synergy and expansion of tone when your energy has joined with the energy of others. It also implies harmony. Harmony is a beautiful arrangement of different sounds, in contrast to mere noise, which is an ugly arrangement. Resonance, as used here, implies people's capacity to use their differences in ways that are beautiful rather than ugly.

The world you build that supports you in the pursuit of your genius is not worth living in if it lacks resonance. But once again, your capacity to build and maintain resonant relationships, and to transform dead or noisy relationships into resonant ones, may have been damaged. To regain that capacity first requires that you become aware of the cultural forces that have damaged it, and robbed you of the potential resonance in your life.

Perhaps the greatest distortion to resonance that we face comes from our intensely adversarial society. Almost everything is perceived in competitive, win-lose, success-failure terms. "Winning isn't everything. It's the *only* thing!" We have been encouraged to believe that the world is our enemy. One must be either on the defensive or offensive, or both at once. One must conquer, control, exploit, or be conquered, controlled, exploited. One must fight or run away. As a result one experiences others and is experienced by them either as hostile, aggressive, aloof, or as frightened, shy, withdrawn. Under these circumstances, resonance is hard to come by and short-lived. For many people, win-lose competitiveness does not dominate all aspects of their lives, but is induced by particular kinds of situations—and destroys the potential resonance and synergy of those situations.

For example, many seminars and staff meetings bring in thoughts of winning or losing, succeeding or failing, proving oneself or making points. These displace the potential resonance and synergy that can evolve when a group works creatively together, building on one another's thoughts, stimulating each other's ideas, and mixing work and laughter.

Three further cultural themes that can cripple the capacity for resonance are materialism, sexism, and violence. Materialism is defined as the tendency to measure one's self-worth by the number and kinds of possessions one has, and the tendency to turn experiences into things so that they can be possessions. Collectibles are a way of "life." Sexism is defined as the tendency to turn sexual relationships and partners into materials, and to use sexual labels to sum oneself and others up—gay, macho, or liberated. Morality and fidelity have lost all but their sexual meanings. Lastly, "Violence is as American as apple pie." We have more guns than people. Our folk heroes were violent men.

Various combinations of adversarial, materialistic, sexist, and violent themes are commonly destructive of resonance in intimate relationships, such as marriage. Jealousy, possessiveness, and feelings of being exploited can dominate the relationship and the partners become each other's prisoners and jailers. But if they are able to free themselves of these distortions, the relationship can be transformed and resonance restored. If you think of any intimate relationships as consisting of three creatures: yourself, the other person, and the couple, you can see that the phrase "a life fully worth living" applies to each. It follows that you would reserve for the couple only those things that are growthful and fulfilling for it. In pursuing the other aspects of your life, your partner can be a resource to you, and you a resource to your partner. Rather than being each other's jailers, you become the supporters of each other's freedom—and this will enhance your resonance. An application of this principle is not difficult for most parents to grasp: your delight in seeing your child leading a fulfilling life as a result of the support you provided. Cultural distortions make it more difficult to understand that the principle applies equally to intimate relationships among adults.

*Perspective.* The third important quality of a worthwhile life is the perspective necessary to guide choices and to inform experience. If you have only one way of looking at the situation you are in, you have no freedom of choice about what to do. And if you have only one framework for understanding your experience, all of your experiences will reinforce that framework. If your outlook is adversarial, you will interpret whatever happens as evidence that the world is hostile, and your choices will be limited to fighting or running away. If you fight, it will confirm your belief that the world is hostile. If you run away, you will know that you were wise to do so. If your perspective is differentiated—if you can see, for example, the potential of a new relationship to be either collaborative or adversarial—you enlarge your range of choices. Thus, if you are aware of "the multiple potential of the moment," you will usually be able to make a choice that will make the next moment better for you and for the others in the situation.

The cultural distortions that lock you into a limited undifferentiated perspective, which lead you to make self-destructive choices, are the same ones that interfere with your tone and self-image, or your capacity for resonance. The messages of adversarialism, materialism, and sexism seek to dictate to you how you should see the world. And your life roles, as defined by other people, are an all too convenient set of prescriptions for your behavior. Take heed of your own feelings, ask what may be causing them, and whether cultural forces are at work. That such distortions are blocking your access to a useful perspective is evidenced whenever you find yourself humorless. The essence of humor is a sudden shift in point of view. To be without humor is to be dying, and laughter is one of the most valuable sources of health and well-being on the journey called a life fully worth living (Cousins, 1979).

Thus tone, resonance, and perspective are the signs that you have discovered your genius and have developed the autonomy to live by it, rather than by society's dictates.

# PROSPECTS FOR CHANGE

The foregoing pages have offered a framework for understanding human potential, parts of which may be familiar, parts of which may be new. In some ways the categories of genius, autonomy, tone, resonance, and perspective are arbitrary, and they should only be used when they fit your purposes. And, clearly, these aspects of life are not separable. The expression of genius needs autonomy. Poor tone, low resonance, and limited perspective almost always have a confirming effect upon one another, and serve to limit autonomy. The essential point is to work in a direction that will begin to free human potential, and to rid it of its cultural fetters.

## A Role for Institutions

The view presented here is critical of the way society's institutions impose cultural distortions on people, and prevent them from finding a path with a heart. Does this mean that, for the well-being of all of us, our institutions should refrain from showing any interest in careers? Does it mean that there can be no institution with a vested interest in people having a life that is fully worth living?

I believe the answer to both questions is no. Two concurrent forces are operating to change the culture quite rapidly. One of these is the dawning realization in many American organizations that the theories of management and organization on which our society has operated in the past have failed us, and will not serve us in the future. They have failed because they have regarded human beings as part of a social machine and have treated as irrelevant individual spirit and well-being. Nor have these theories capitalized on individuals' needs and capacities to work harmoniously with each other. This realization of past failure is bringing about a transformation in industrial organizations, and non-industrial organizations will eventually catch up. The second force for change is technological progress, especially the rapid development of electronic communications and computers. The more that routine operations are performed by machines, the more demand there is that the non-routine operations be performed with excellence. This kind of excellence in human performance can only be attained by persons who are fully alive and operating in the area of their genius. Only if the path has a heart will it sustain excellence.

When the aerospace industry was in its infancy, the technical challenge, and hence the need for creativity and teamwork, was immense. One of the most successful companies recognized this fully in its organizational structure and culture. It invented new organizational forms that were suited to its mission and the capacities of its members to work together creatively. In the process, it created most of the principles and processes that are in use today in what has come to be called organization development. Among other things, it offered its members Life and Career Planning workshops, to help them identify their talents and interests. The approach was somewhat different from the one outlined in this paper, but its intent was the same. The spirit of these workshops was summed up in the way the company introduced them: "What you do with your life and career is your responsibility. But because you are a member of this company, the company shares some of that responsibility with you. Perhaps it's 80% yours, 20% the company's. This workshop is the company's effort to contribute towards its 20%." In a similar spirit, another company offers workshops based on their version of Dalton and Thompson's career-stages model, to help employees identify their position on the path, understand their potential more clearly, and find ways of fulfilling it (Dalton, Thompson, and Price, 1977).

These companies have a vested interest in having their members rediscover their genius. Our hope for changing the order of things is that more and more organizations will follow their example. But we must insist that their interventions be explicitly on their members' behalf. And their processes must seek to liberate people from their cultural surroundings—including organizational cultures—rather than to reaffirm their dependencies. Then their example can be picked up by the schools, who can help others much earlier in their lives. Parents, in turn, will come to appreciate the freedom of spirit that they can encourage in their own children. The path with a heart is also the path to improving our institutions. Let our teaching about careers stand for nothing less.

# CAREER GRIDLOCK: BABY BOOMERS HIT THE WALL

*Douglas T. Hall*
*Judith Richter*

It would appear that the baby boomers have finally arrived. After enduring overcrowded public schools in the '50s and '60s, competing for admission and surviving mass education "megaversities" and the turmoil of war in the '60s and '70s, and then competing for jobs in recessions in the '70s and '80s, most are now in their 30s and comfortably established in careers. Now it's the employers' turn to adapt to the baby boom, as this group composes almost 55 percent of the United States labor force.[1] Indeed, in 1988, a well-publicized member of the baby boom generation was elected Vice President of the United States.

Have the baby boomers really "made it"? They happen to have "arrived" during a period of unprecedented restructuring of American industry, with widespread workforce reductions, streamlining, and reorganizations, all aimed at generating greater output from fewer people. Where have all the opportunities gone? How should top management respond to the concerns of this large cluster of new arrivals at midcareer?

Consider the case of Mary Jackson (not her real name, as will be the case with the other baby boomers' names used). After competing with a large number of other bright college graduates 15 years ago, she was accepted into a training program at AT&T. She did outstanding technical work and struggled to get on the managerial track. Finally, after being turned down for a long-hoped-for promotion, she consulted a senior person for advice. He pointed out that the competition for management slots was becoming severe (the result of multiple workforce reductions at AT&T), that being turned down did not mean that she would never make it into management, and that she should be patient and wait for the next round of promotions.

Reconsidering her chances in light of the large number of candidates for the next round of promotions, Mary decided to step out of the race. She is now successfully running her own consulting firm. She also found that the exit from corporate life provides greater balance for marriage and family.

Unfortunately, the effort to stand out leads most baby boomers to feel that their work is taking up too much of their lives. A recent Fortune article called this group "the workaholic generation."[2] Work-family balance, which has been a visible management issue lately, is a major problem for members of the baby boom generation. Their attempts to restore balance, either by dropping out, cutting back to "mommy track" or "daddy track" involvement, or simply by continuing to operate at a higher level of conflict and stress, have become a major management "story" of the 1990s.

*Source*: Douglas T. Hall and Judith Richter, "Career Gridlock: Baby Boomers Hit the Wall," *Academy of Management Executive*, 1990, Vol. 4, No. 3, pp. 23–35. Copyright © 1990. Reprinted with permission.

# The Missing View: Impact of the Baby Boom on Managerial Careers

Mary Jackson, Fred Revitch, and Brett Johnson are all members of the post-World War II baby boom generation, and they are dealing with issues of how to achieve fulfillment both at work and at home.

Significant media attention has been placed on the baby boom in recent years, even before the 1988 election campaign. *Time* announced in a cover story, "The Baby Boomers Turn 40" (May 19, 1986). The *Boston Globe* wondered about "Middle Managers with No Place To Go" (February 9, 1988). A movie was titled "Baby Boom," and then it became a television series. Several other series were targeted at baby boomers such as "thirtysomething" and "L.A. Law." As *The Wall Street Journal* put it in 1989, "Marketers have been in love with the baby boom for years now."[3]

Do the baby boomers look as distinctive in the workplace as they do in the marketplace? Should organizational career paths be redefined? This article examines these questions and attempts to determine the implications of the baby boom for the management of organizations.

## A Profile of the Baby Boomers at Work

What are the distinctive values and concerns which characterize people like Mary Jackson and the other baby boom employees? Based upon our own interviews, and other studies, we have identified the following profile of the baby boom:

1. *A strong concern for basic values.* Not only are there particular values which baby boomers tend to hold, but the issue of values *per se* is important to baby boomers. Whereas older generations may have been more concerned with achievements, success, status, or power for their own sake, baby boomers are more likely to question *why* they are seeking success and what the *personal meaning* of success is to them.

2. *A sense of freedom to act on values.* Baby boomers have a greater sense of freedom to act out their values than previous age groups. In a sense, this is the corporate extension of the 1960's campus rallying cry, "Do it." Now we see a generation of professional and managerial employees who, without making loud corporate protests, are more likely than their predecessors to behave in ways that are congruent with their values.

This quality of independence manifests itself in various ways: a computer specialist who would not even interview in one company because it did a lot of military contract work, the manager who turned down a promotion because it would require four days' travel each week and keep him away from his year-old son, and countless "whistle blowers" who report corporate fraud, at the expense of their careers. For example, Walker Williams, former head of human resources of Westin Hotels, estimates that when the telephone rings, and an employee is told, "We need you in Atlanta in 15 minutes, no questions, just go," half of the people will not go. He estimated that in a few years, 90 percent will say no.

Channeling humanistic values into a professional career is exemplified in the work of Susan McCrea. After completing her undergraduate degree, she wanted to "make health care more accessible to all people in the world." She wanted to influence domestic health care policy, so she took a job with the State of Minnesota as a state health planner. However, she left the public sector after concluding that health care policy didn't necessarily influence health care delivery systems. She went first to an HMO (health maintenance organization), and then became an independent marketing consultant to HMOs and nonprofit health organizations. She later earned an MBA in health care to increase her earning potential and to improve her professional credentials. She is now assistant to the president of a major Boston medical center, responsible for marketing and planning. She feels satisfied that she is able to influence organizational policies and practices in a way that is consistent with her social values.

3. *A focus on self.* Concern for values and consistency between values and behavior is related to a strong sense of self-awareness. Dr. Phyllis Horner, an internal personnel consultant at Ford Motor Company, reports that this group's definition of professionalism includes one's own determination of the source of one's self-concept. Finding one's work in life, then, becomes a way to find and express one's self-identity. Dr. Horner refers to this focus on self as a "healthy narcissism."

4. *Need for autonomy and questioning authority.* Implementing a self-concept and living out one's values require a certain level of freedom. Indeed, the need for freedom and the impatience with formal hierarchical authority is probably the most distinctive single feature of the baby boom group. Donald Kanter and Philip Mirvis, using a national probability sample of United States workers, found that only 22 percent reported trust in management, even though 70 percent are generally satisfied with their jobs, and 55 percent are satisfied with their job rewards (pay, promotion prospects, benefits, etc.). Although these data include workers of all ages, the authors cited the baby boomers' disillusionment as a major influence on workforce morale. When they sorted their data by age, they found a "relatively high level" of cynicism reported by the baby boomers. Kanter and Mirvis describe the importance of workers' age in this low trust of management:

> "These data suggest to us that a central problem is human resource management in 1985 is workers' response to authority in general. A young, hostile, cynical workforce that holds high opinions of itself…is not easy to manage, efficient, loyal, or (probably) very receptive to change." [4]

To be more positive, what qualities would baby boomers value in a leader? In a creative research design, William G. Dyer and Jeffrey H. Dyer conducted a survey of what they called the "M*A*S*H Generation" (1,000 people born in the late 1950s and early 1960s). The purpose was to identify the kinds of organizational processes and conditions that people associated with the hospital organization in the TV show M*A*S*H, which was extremely popular among baby boomers. Dyer and Dyer concluded that the show's Colonel Sherman Potter most clearly fits baby boomers' image of the effective boss:

> "He is the only one they identify as having the trait of leadership. Specifically, they want to work under a superior who treats subordinates with respect and is concerned about their welfare and tries to understand them. They list the important personal characteristics of the leader as being broadmindedness, competence, maturity, and fairness."[5]

5. *Less concern with advancement.* Related to the baby boomers' questioning of authority is a weaker desire to become part of it. There appears to be less of a driving passion to move up the hierarchy among this group. For example, Ann Howard and James A. Wilson compared motivation profiles for two groups of AT&T managers, one hired in the 1950s and the other in the 1970s (baby boomers). In terms of intrinsic motivation to achieve and perform well on the job, there were no significant differences between the two groups. The big difference came in their desires for upward mobility, expressed in a variety of measures (e.g., a questionnaire measuring desires for upward mobility, needs for dominance, expectations for a higher position in the next five years). Although both groups wanted a challenging job and a middle manager's salary in the following five years, 54 percent of the 1950s sample indicated a desire to advance to a middle management position while only 34 percent of the 1970s cohort chose that outcome. Howard and Wilson concluded that, "By and large, the [1970s] recruits were inclined neither to push their way up the organization hierarchy nor

to lead others. In short, the new managers weren't motivated to act like managers." Based on this AT&T research and his own interviews, Walter Kiechel concludes,

"They don't like telling others what to do any more than they like being told. No respecters of hierarchy, they don't want to get to the top just because it's the top."[6]

These conclusions are supported by Miner and Smith's finding that the motivation to manage has declined among college students between 1960 and 1980.[7] Similarly, Driver reports a drop in what he calls "linear" (i.e., advancement) career motives for college students in the 1960s and early 1970s (although Driver finds that this trend has now reversed for the post-baby boom group).[8] Although challenging work and financial rewards are still very important to baby boomers, they may be less willing than other groups to assume higher-level managerial responsibilities to attain these rewards. (This may help explain the appeal to baby boomers of investment banking, real estate development, and entrepreneurship, activities in which financial rewards are high but organizational management responsibilities are relatively low.)

6. *Crafting: In-place career development.* Perhaps related to this lower need for advancement is the baby boomer's orientation to high quality in the current job. In this highly educated, highly principled group, utilizing one's potential (i.e., self-actualization) is not only an important need but a basic value. To perform poorly produces dissatisfaction and guilt.

An Opinion Research Corporation study found that by the late 1970s, concerns for self-fulfillment and personal growth had become pervasive in the work force as a result of the addition of the baby boomers.[9] As one person described his need for growth, "How do I keep myself growing even if my company isn't interested in that?" Walter Kiechel, who called boomers the workaholic generation, asks, "Why do they work so hard? Because they love it, they say, often using the words 'fun,' 'creative,' and 'stimulating' to describe the experience…Work is also where they perform, as an athlete performs, winning the applause of the crowd."[10]

This concern for craft in one's work shows up in the baby boomers' preference for professional work, as identified by Raelin (see Endnote 14). The critical motivation is the intrinsic reward which comes from crafting one's work, and doing a high-quality job in the service of a useful purpose.

7. *Entrepreneurship.* If the baby boomer values achievement and autonomy but does not want to submit to authority or exercise it, what career and organization design options are left open? One option is to become an entrepreneur. A study of 9,000 graduates of the Harvard Business School found that the peak age for entrepreneurship is in the early 30s (30 percent of the entrepreneurs studied start at this age). People in their early 30s represent the peak of the baby boom cohort.

Howard Stevenson of the Harvard Business School's entrepreneurship project, sees entrepreneurship as a way of expressing the counter-culture values of the 1960s and 1970s.[11] Warren Bennis views it as an expression of selfhood which is a major legacy of the 1960s, and he predicts a major growth in self-employment over the next 10 years (10 percent of the United States working population is now self-employed). Bennis refers to this phenomenon as the "Big Chill" factor (named after the movie): if there is a hero, he or she is played by an entrepreneur.[12]

8. *Concern for work/family balance: The total life perspective.* The baby boom group is getting into parenting in a big way. Part of the concern for the self is an awareness of one's personal and family life. Even though work is important, as we have just said, there is a sense among baby boomers that "I work to live; I don't live to work."

The baby boom has done well occupationally, despite the dire forecasts referred to earlier, and this work success may spill over into private life. Louise Russell found that, although crowded, the baby boom cohort has not suffered educationally because of its size. More of its members were educated than any previous generation, and more money was spent on education per student than ever before. Furthermore, despite the negative effects of their numbers, Russell concluded that baby boomers are still earning real income as high as, or higher than, any previous generation.[13]

Further evidence of the occupational success of this group is found in Joseph Raelin's analysis of what he calls "the 60s generation." Raelin uses census data to show that an unusually high proportion of the '60s generation's members are in professions. Similar findings were reported by Werner and Stillman and by Mills.[14]

There is a sense of costs and benefits of various life and career options (eg., "Can I really have a truly statisfying career and a truly satisfactory parenting experience?"). There is an ability to make trade-offs and establish balance between work and family concerns.

The fact that the baby boomer manager/professional cohort has a large proportion of women is a significant factor in this concern for family. We refer to this balanced, autonomous work life, in which the employee takes major responsibility, as the protean career. In the remaining sections, we consider how organizations can cope with these growing numbers of protean baby boomers.

## Guidelines: Toward More Effective Utilization of Baby Boom Potential

There seems to be great potential in the "problems" represented by the baby boom. They are exceptionally well-educated, value-driven, independent and quality-oriented. In response to these qualities, what steps might management take to tap this potential? Let us detail some recommendations about how an organization might yield the maximum benefit from its baby boom managers and employees.

1. *Concern for Values: Replace the "Promotion Culture" with a "Psychological Success" Culture.* Since values are so important to the baby boomer, corporate cultures must be changed to accommodate these new career orientations. As Dave Cornett, a human resources consultant at DuPont said, "The continuous upward mobile employee is a thing of the past. The key for DuPont is to make the current position as rewarding and exciting as possible." In our work with organizations, we have repeatedly heard comments such as, "I personally would like to make a lateral move, but everyone else around here would see that as a mark of failure." Every organization has a career culture which acts as a powerful source of resistance to the changes we just recommended. How might these career cultures be modified to produce an organizational transformation?

Strategic human resource development has been advocated as a way to implement changes in how an organization nurtures its talent.[15] The culture of an organization is reinforced by forces at three levels: the top strategic level is translated into design through managerial systems and programs (the middle level), and put into action at the implementation (bottom) level.

Human resource policies that affect employees' personal growth (e.g., policies on promotion from within, cross-training and cross-functional moves, using key management jobs for developmental purposes, holding managers accountable for subordinate development, and a strong internal succession planning process) are key to human resource development.

We believe that the corporate career culture is changed by promoting dialogue on and establishing clear policies, endorsed and acted upon by top management, which promote more diverse and flexible forms of career growth. Time and energy should be directed at these basic development policies before work is put into managerial-level activities (such as training managers in new forms of career management) or implementation-level changes (such as career workshops). While the latter activities are worthwhile, their effects are multiplied if supportive human resource policies are in place first.

More organizations are engaging in these new practices all the time. Companies, such as DuPont, IBM, and Johnson and Johnson, have committees or task forces on work/family issues, that raise awareness and create significant change in career management practices. DuPont's task force on career and family issues was made up of a cross-section of levels and job functions so that the total work force was represented. The task force met with groups of employees, identified key issues, commissioned a major employee survey, and recommended explicit policies and implementation strategies, that are currently being adopted. Conscious use of organizational development values and processes were important in the success of this process, according to Faith Wohl, co-chair of the task force.

2. *Freedom To Act on Values: Support More Protean or Self-Directed Careers.* Organizational careers must be reframed to reflect the notion that "up is not the only way," to use the words of author Beverly Kaye.[16] Career paths are becoming more differentiated and self-directed— i.e., more protean. As another part of the culture change process, these protean career paths should be more widely communicated and valued. Employees need to have the option of periodically changing direction, so they are not locked into one single, long-term, career plan. As Will Cookta, personnel director for Beringer Ingelheim Pharmaceuticals, put it, "We want our company to look at multiple options, not just up-or-out or up-or-you're-a-jerk. We need to crack the culture."

To tap the great diversity of the baby boom group in a leaner organization, there must be a range of career paths from which to choose: functional specialist (growth within a discipline), consultant, local generalist (rotational, lateral movement, while remaining in one location), fast-track or slow-track into management, project management, permanent part-timer, job specialist (career development within a specific job position), and multipath option (the freedom to move from one of the paths to another). These different career forms are already available in many organizations. However, they are often used on a case-by-case basis, without the realization that they represent the career preferences of large numbers of baby boomers and the needs of contemporary organizations. They need to be legitimized (or "blessed") by the culture as valued and respected careers.

How might we move toward these differentiated career paths to provide opportunities for more protean careers? The following approaches are being taken in some organizations:

- *Articulate a policy that the career is the individual's responsibility.* This is a radical departure for many organizations that take a more paternalistic approach to career development ("Trust us"). Ford Motor Company has made this change, and employees are assisted through training workshops in asserting more personal control over their careers.[17] It may mean supporting the employee in saying "no" to the company at times. The end result in giving the employee more self-control, however, is often better choices and greater employee commitment to their own decisions.

- *Encourage the manager's self-assessment.* To crack the upward-mobility career culture, managers and executives require special attention. Managers need to become more self-aware and self-directed. A realistic self-assessment is important to a manager's self-directed career choices. Even in an era of widespread career planning, this self-assessment is still a relatively new activity in company-run management education programs. (It is more often done for lower-level employees.) Each person needs to take a good honest look at his or her own skills, interests, and values, compared to those required of fast-trackers. DuPont's Individual Career Management program (ICM), for example, helps employees assess their values, skills, and interests and then develop an action plan for work directions that express these personal preferences.

- *Promote early rotational (lateral) moves.* To give an employee a sense of the wide range of available career paths, there should be opportunities for lateral, cross-functional, moves early in the career. This prevents people from becoming stuck in a dead-end career path and makes rotational moves a realistic option later in the career. Periodic rotation creates a wide range of skills which can be used for general management or to produce a well-rounded specialist.

According to Goodyear career counselor Laura Bettinger, Goodyear employees submit applications for lateral moves, stating their skills, experience, and the position sought. Managers submit lists of openings and the human resource department serves as an internal placement broker. This lateral pool program has a positive reputation, and many people apply, creating competition for open slots.

- *Discourage career planning; stress "work planning."* While we have stressed the need for activities like self-assessment, we have not specifically recommended career planning. *Organizations should not encourage long-term career planning.*

In view of the volatile nature of today's organizational environments, it is difficult for both organizations and individuals to do effective long-term planning. What may be more realistic is to encourage people to assess their own values, interests, skills, and lifestyle needs in relation to various work options that are available. The focus is on identifying the type of work the person would like to do over the next few years, without trying to worry about the rest of his or her career.

Self-assessment is different than setting a long-term plan for a career with a complete set of specific goals and stepping stones. Given the turbulence in the environments of today's organizations, the latter is unrealistic. Using solid, realistic self-understanding and skills the individual is empowered to recognize and use career opportunities as they arise. Shorter-term work plans, combined with a longer-term sense of personal direction, is required.

Indeed, a shorter-term focus fits well with that of most employers. As Joe Robinson, budget manager for First Union Corporation, said, "I've noticed in job interviews that nobody asks what you plan to be doing five to ten years from now. They only talk about one-year plans."

- *Define career growth as the development and use of new skills and abilities.* One concrete way to reinforce the notions of work planning and up-is-not-the-only-way is to communicate the idea that growth in the career is the development and use of new skills and abilities. For most people, and in particular for intrinsically-motivated, growth-oriented baby boom managers, the important experience in the career is learning and growing, not necessarily ascending the hierarchy, as mentioned earlier. However, top management must legitimize this concept and set a policy facilitating career-long growth. For example, Chrysler encourages employees to establish stretch goals for their current positions, an activity that is supported by a pay-for-performance program. These practices are combined with development of new learning through periodic job changes (e.g., rotational moves, in-place changes in responsibility).

3. *Focus On the Self: Self-Development and Lifelong Learning in the Work Itself.* Almost 30 years ago, Chris Argyris raised the issue of whether the needs of psychologically healthy individuals could be congruent with the goals of the employing organization.[18] Today, it seems clear that the answer is, yes, the *effective* organization can find ways to make human need satisfaction and organizational goal attainment compatible. The move to participative and team leadership practices in today's downsized and delayered organization is probably the most important change in management circles today, and it certainly fits well with the self-directed, authority-questioning values of the baby boom cohort.[19] This is the "silver lining" which can be seen in the wake of severe corporate cutbacks and restructuring.

John Morley, personnel manager at Kodak, described an example of this delayering, in which a vice president of operations moved up to replace an executive vice president who retired. However, there was no replacement for the vice president. This one move impacted ten levels in the company. While these changes do produce frustrations, they also result in greater spans of control and responsibility for lower levels managers and employees. To support this increased responsibility, managers are trained to coach and develop their employees. These in-place development activities are supported by a pay-for-performance program.

Creating small, autonomous work units, such as the small project team that developed IBM's personal computer has great potential. Autonomous work teams, described in Tracy Kidder's *The Soul of a New Machine,* created a new computer at Data General. Project engineers and managers (in their 20s and 30s, primarily) often would work late into the night and through the weekend, motivated by the "pinball theory": if you win the game, you get to play it again (i.e., you get another project, with greater significance and more resources). The rewards came from learning and solving complex problems, so that good performance demanded the development of new knowledge and skills.[20]

The autonomy and intrinsic challenges associated with these new leadership styles provides the employee with a greater opportunity for self-development. Another way to think of this is as in-place career development. The smart manager attempts to give employees freedom to generate their own solutions to work problems and to implement them in their own ways. Not only does this autonomy provide a way to tap employees' creativity and motivation most effectively, but it is often virtually demanded by the wider spans of control resulting from eliminating layers of management. Managers who try to supervise too closely soon realize that they are overworked to the point of burnout. Permitting greater employee freedom is congruent with the high-autonomy and self-related values of the baby boom manager. More stress on life-long learning is a natural by-product of restructured leaner, organizations.

4. *Concern for Autonomy: More Flexibility and Diversity.* As organizations face the need for more flexible human resource policies, flexibility in employee work arrangements needs to be extended. This is especially important for women. A growing number of women and men in their mid-to-late thirties are beginning to conclude that they cannot have it all (career, marriage, and family) and are opting for marriage and family. For women, this often happens after an attempt to resume working after the first baby is born. The realization comes that a) they have already proven to themselves that they can be successful in the career, b) life is short, and c) at this time in their life they would rather be home raising the family. At this point, many women are opting out of organizational careers. Our hunch is that in five to ten years, they will be back at a different form of work. For women to continue rising in the ranks of management, organizations are going to have to find even more flexible arrangements to accommodate them.[21]

How might this greater flexibility be attained? One method is to use more permanent part-time jobs. As organizations are forced to make part-time work available to recruit and retain qualified employees (especially working mothers), part-time work is becoming more common in professional and managerial positions. It has always been an option for hourly and clerical employees. Parental leaves, with a phased re-entry period, are becoming longer and more flexible. Flextime is also widespread and a boon to working parents. Similarly, "flexplace" (working in the home) is becoming more available thanks to computer technology and a more liberal corporate culture. Baby boomers who are well established in their careers and are now part of management have more leverage to negotiate work arrangements. Given the choice of being flexible or losing a valued manager or professional, many organizations have opted for flexibility. This was the work/family balance track that Felice Schwartz recommended in her widely-quoted *Harvard Business Review* article, "Management, Women and the New Facts of Life."[22] However, if the organization has not been confronted by baby boom managers with this choice, this flexibility is not freely offered.

Moving to part-time work has to be done carefully and on a job-by-job basis, as not all jobs are conducive to part-time schedules. One organizational inducement, however, is that part-time managers and professionals usually contribute full-time involvement.

Corporate timetables must be adjusted to let part-timers rise at a more gradual rate. In the Westin Hotel organizations, for example, employees' needs and career preferences are included as part of the potential assessment process. The company uses different development strategies for employees who report they are geographically mobile and for those who are not. "When we know what they want to do, we won't try to sell the person on a move they don't want. In the past, managers could staff a position with exactly who they wanted. Now we will have to change the company's expectations," reported Walker Williams, former head of Westin's human resources.

5. *Less Concern for Advancement: More Diversity in Career Paths.* In contrast to earlier eras when people had to conform to the structure of the work place, the structure of assignments can be more responsive to people's needs. As industries become more competitive and new technologies widely available, the competitive edge is often obtained through the flexible use and development of people.

For example, a construction firm founded by two baby-boom Harvard graduates rapidly acquired a reputation for building individualized, high-quality, bright, airy, aesthetic, energy-efficient townhouses in the Cambridge area. (These townhouses are in great demand by their fellow baby boomers.) How do they maintain the quality of their work as the number of projects expands? They use fairly simple designs and simple, high-quality materials that are easy to install and are not labor-intensive. Since the Boston work force is so unpredictable, they adjust the structure of their designs to fit the capabilities of the available workforce resulting in a high level of quality.

Consulting is another way to retain a valued professional or manager in a more autonomous role. An employee who needs large blocks of time off can be hired on a retainer basis, and used for specific projects and problems. This keeps the employee involved and up to date so re-entering the organization on a full-time basis if his or her personal situation changes is made easier.

Organization structures are also being made more flexible by differentiated career paths. Not everyone aspires to be president of the company. There are, of course, high potential young people who have senior executive aspirations, and they need to be moved across a variety of specialties, to learn the complete business. However, many other talented people aspire to be the best within their particular specialty:

> *"Not everyone needs to be a high potential achiever. For many people, being the food and beverage director at the Plaza Hotel would be a lifelong fulfillment. We need to establish different disciplines (e.g., personnel, front office, maintenance) as career objectives and create specialized career paths within them." (Walker Williams, Westin Corporation )*

Monsanto found that the focus on more specialized career paths fits well in a leaner organization with slower overall corporate growth. There is a need to invest more creativity and energy in specific businesses and plant locations. According to Charles Arnold:

*"With less corporate mobility, there is a need to emphasize the employees' identification with their own unit or location. This does not mean that some employees will not be asked to move around the corporation, but it does mean that broad corporate career programs are being de-emphasized, and specialization is OK."*

Local identification is a way to provide more freedom, and to nurture creativity and innovation with less bureaucracy, but within the context of a world-wide organization. It also places more stress on development within the current assignment.

Greater differentiation in career development paths means that development is being encouraged in the following directions:

- within the present job (in-place development)
- within the present function (or specialty or discipline)
- within the present geographic location (which could include cross-functional rotational moves within that location)
- across functions and locations (i.e., corporate mobility for high-potential employees)

6. *Crafting: Reward Quality of Performance, Not Potential.* In the management and professional ranks in most organizations, there is a tendency to pay for potential rather than performance. For example, if two people are both performing at the same level, and if one person is a 25-year-old "high potential" manager and the other is 40 years old and seen as plateaued, the younger "hi-po" person usually gets larger salary increases, and the older manager feels unrewarded for his or her performance. The organization suffers a tremendous loss in motivation by linking pay to future promotions.

Many organizations, such as Eli Lilly, are now seeking ways to identify and reward performance excellence, regardless of the person's age or career stage. One-time cash awards can be given for outstanding achievements (and in some cases they can simply be honorific awards and still be effective). In addition to helping de-couple promotion and rewards, such excellence awards fit nicely with the baby boomer's appreciation of quality and craftsmanship.

7. *Entrepreneurship: Encourage It in the Organization's Interest.* We recommend two strategies for using baby boomers' entrepreneurial potential. The first, and preferable, route is to harness energy in the service of organizational change. When baby boom managers or professionals become restless and start thinking about starting up their own venture, find a "start up" activity for them in your own organization. This could be a project assignment (either full-time or part of the current job) to explore the creation of a new product, service, or process. The person would be responsible for gathering resources, forming coalitions with key supporters, and championing the idea. In Rosabeth Kanter's terms, he or she would be expected to be a "change master."

News columnist Ellen Goodman has commented on how much corporate vitality and renewal is lost when baby boom entrepreneurs (whom she calls "corporate misfits, blue-jeaned [people] in three-piece corporations") leave to start up their own ventures.

*"The new breed are among the liveliest most exciting business people I meet. I don't want to read failure into their personal success, but few are starting the next IBM. Few will become the employers of hundreds of thousands. And as they leave larger companies, those workplaces are diminished. They lose another agent for change. More to the point, as these entrepreneurs walk out the door, one by one, American corporations lose another source of ideas, of innovation, of energy.*

*And sometimes, after I have heard these success stories, I wonder how many of their old colleagues and bosses ever realize the gap left by another "misfit" who dropped a pair of old floppy wing tips beside the exit door."*[23]

As newly restructured organizations attempt to tap the commitment and involvement of all employees to produce "high-performance systems," the entrepreneurial spirit of baby boom employees is a perfect resource to tap more systematically.

A second strategy is to support baby boomers in exploring entrepreneurial activities outside the organization. Often, helping the individual gather realistic information on starting up one's own business, leads to a decision that the cost and risks are too high. For example, a computer professional in her early 30s was interested in starting a company to make and sell high-quality hand-sewn craft items. Her company, through a career exploration seminar, supported her in interviewing people who had started similar businesses. She also interviewed people in various parts of her own firm to get more realistic information about future career opportunities there. She concluded that even the most successful entrepreneurs in her area of interest were putting in longer hours than she was currently and making less money. At the same time, she found an opportunity to start up a new line of products in her current firm. (In a similar case, a 30-year-old software manager who initially wanted to get into real estate development talked it over with his senior management, and they agreed to let him redesign his current job to include new venture activity, with a sizeable incentive compensation arrangement.)

But what if exploration had led these managers to leave rather than stay? We argue that it is in the company's interest to support a person in a decision to leave, if that would be the best fit for her or him. If managers feel coerced to stay, eventually their performance suffers, and they eventually have to leave anyway.

We also recommend that a company keep its door open to allow baby boomers to return if they ever become dissatisfied with working on their own. Many firms, however, have a policy of not hiring ex-employees. To us, this seems self-punitive for the firm, since this strong performer would just go to work for the competition, if she were barred from rejoining her old employer.

Thus, our message is, fan this entrepreneurial spirit. Use it to help restructure and vitalize the organization, and support individuals in finding a good fit for their own form of entrepreneurship, either inside or outside the firm. Chances are, a good thorough search will lead them to stay and to use this energy on the organization's behalf.

8. *Concern for Balance: More Organizational Sensitivity to the Employee's Home Life.* While many organizations recognize that a manager's personal and family life affect work and career decisions, there is reluctance to do anything to assist with strains between work and family life. This arises out of a sincere desire not to intrude in the manager's personal life.

However, sometimes the organization already is intruding on the person's private life to a considerable extent (i.e., through disruptive relocations, demanding work schedules, job stress). There are ways to assist the manager in dealing with work-home conflicts in ways which maintain privacy and enhance autonomy and coping skills. A few possibilities are listed below:[24]

- Establishing corporate dialogue on work-family balance. The critical step is to make this a "discussable" topic in the organization and to establish mechanisms to work on it. The experience of firms like DuPont and Stride Rite have shown that a representative task force or committee is effective in creating this dialogue.
- Management training sessions in managing the work-home interaction. One pharmaceutical company does this in a three hour seminar, using company cases and a sharing of managers' learnings about how best to deal with work-home conflicts. In this extremely popular seminar, managers consider both what they can do for themselves and to help subordinates.

EXHIBIT I

| Summary of Baby Boom Characteristics and Recommended Organizational Actions | |
| --- | --- |
| Profile of Baby Boom Characteristics | Recommended Organizational Action |
| 1. Concern for basic values | 1.a. Replace promotion culture with psychological success culture<br>b. Examine, change corporate career criteria<br>c. Focus on corporate ethics |
| 2. Freedom to act on values | 2.a. Support protean career paths<br>b. More lateral mobility<br>c. De-couple rewards and the linear career path |
| 3. Focus on self | 3. Build on-going development into the job through:<br>• Self-development<br>• Life-long learning |
| 4. Need for autonomy | 4. More flexible careers |
| 5. Less concern with advancement | 5. More diversity in career paths.<br>More change:<br>• within present job<br>• within present function<br>• within present location<br>• across function and locations |
| 6. Crafting | 6. Reward quality performance, not potential |
| 7. Entrepreneurship | 7.a. Create internal entrepreneurial assignments<br>b. Encourage employee career exploration (internally and externally) |
| 8. Concern for work/home balance | 8.a. More organizational sensitivity to home life<br>b. Training for managing the work-home interface<br>c. Inclusion of spouse in career discussions<br>d. Career assistance for employed spouse<br>e. Flexible benefits to help meet family needs (e.g., child care, elder care, care for sick children)<br>f. More flexible work arrangements |

- After-hours workshops for managers and spouses to share problems and solutions in specific family topics (e.g., coping with a move, the first child, adolescents).

- Including the spouse in discussions about an impending relocation.

- Job search assistance to a career spouse during a relocation. This is often done through informal personnel networks in the new location or by making the firm's outplacement consultants available to the spouse. What is critical is expanding the organization's sphere of perceived responsibility to include the spouse and family, as well as the employee.

- Including spouses in more social events or conferences to share the benefits of corporate life.

There are numerous ways the manager's private life could by insulated more from the stresses of the job. Older managers accept the intrusion of work into family life; baby boom managers do not.

Exhibit I summarizes these profile characteristics and provides recommendations. The need to provide support and opportunities for greater self-awareness and empowerment is the common thread through the recommendations.

## Conclusion

The basic career and personal values of the baby boom manager are congruent with today's changing management practices and philosophy—as long as we can recognize and be comfortable with the paradoxical idea that the more self-control the manager has over his or her career, the more control (in the form of information and predictability) the organization has as well. The dark side of the baby boom and the downsized organization is that there are too many good people available for too few management slots. But the bright side is that a lot of good baby boomers have their own sense of where they want to head with their protean careers. While the number of ways of achieving promotional (vertical) success is finite (and shrinking), the number of ways of achieving psychological (vertical) success is infinite. The more an organization can match its human resource management practices to this new protean career orientation, the more effective it will be in tapping the potential of the baby boom.

## ENDNOTES

1. See Walter Kiechel III, "The Workaholic Generation," *Fortune,* April 10, 1989, 50–62.
2. *Ibid.*
3. David Wessel, "One Sure Fact: Baby Boomers Are Aging," *The Wall Street Journal,* January 3, 1989, Bl.
4. Donald L. Kanter and Philip H. Mirvis, "Managing Jaundiced Workers," Working Paper, Boston University School of Management, 1985, 12. This work is also reported in D. L. Kanter and P. H. Mirvis, *The Cynical Americans* (San Francisco: Jossey-Bass, 1989).
5. William G. Dyer and Jeffrey H. Dyer, "The M*A*S*H Generation: Implications for Future Organizational Values," *Organizational Dynamics,* Summer 1984, *13,* 78.
6. This research is reported in Ann Howard and James A. Wilson, "Leadership in a Declining Work Ethic," *California Management Review,* Summer 1982, Vol. XXIV, *4,* 33. See also Kiechel, *op cit.,* 50.
7. See J. Miner and N. Smith, "Decline and Stabilization of Managerial Motivation over a 20-year Period," *Journal of Applied Psychology,* 1982, *67,* 297–305. More data on the lower levels of advancement motivation among baby boomers, compared to the previous generation, are reported in an excellent longitudinal AT&T study, Ann Howard and Douglas W. Bray, *Managerial Lives in Transition* (New York, Guilford, 1988).
8. See Michael J. Driver, "Careers: A Review of Personal and Organizational Research," in C. L. Cooper and I. Robertson (Eds.), *International Review of Industrial Psychology 1988* (London: John Wiley & Sons, Ltd., 1988), 245–277.
9. See M. R. Cooper, B. S. Morgan, P. M. Foley, and L. B. Kaplan, "Changing Employee Values: Deepening Discontent," *Harvard Business Review,* 1979, *57,* 117–125.
10. See Kiechel, *op. cit.,* 51–52.

11. Howard Stevenson, "Entrepreneurship," presentation at Academy of Management.

12. Warren G. Bennis, "Leadership," presentation at Academy of Management, Boston, 1984. These ideas are elaborated in Bennis's book *Leaders* (co-authored with Burt Nanus, (New York: Harper & Row, 1985).

13. See Louise B. Russell, *The Baby Boom Generation and the Economy* (Washington, DC: The Brookings Institute, 1982), 1. Another excellent source is Landon Jones, *Great Expectations: America and the Baby Boom Generation* (New York: Ballantine Books, 1980).

14. See Joseph A. Raelin, "The 60's Kids in the Corporation: More than Just 'Daydream Believers,'" *The Academy of Management Executive*, February 1987, 21–30. The Mills survey is reported in D. Quinn Mills, *Not Like Our Parents* (New York: William Morrow and Company, 1987). See also, Rex Werner and Deanne Stillman, *The Woodstock Census* (New York: Viking Press, 1979).

15. See, for example, D. T. Hall, "Human Resource Development and Organizational Effectiveness," in C. J. Fombrun, N. M. Tichy, and M. A. Devanna, *Strategic Human Resource Development* (New York: John Wiley & Sons, 1984), 159–181; D. T. Hall, "Dilemmas in Linking Succession Planning to Individual Executive Learning," *Human Resource Planning*, 1986, *25*, 235–265; and D. T. Hall, and J. G. Goodale, *Human Resource Management: Strategy, Design, and Implementation* (Glenview, IL: Scott, Foresman, 1986).

16. See Beverly Kaye, *Up Is Not the Only Way* (Englewood Cliffs, NJ: Prentice-Hall, 1982).

17. This work was reported in Phyllis C. Horner, "Career Development in Traditional Manufacturing Organizations," Career Division Workshop presentation, Academy of Management Meetings, Boston, August 11, 1984.

18. This idea was originally reported in Chris Argyris, *Personality and Organization* (New York: Harper, 1957). It is now showing up in practice as a trend in organizational career programs. See, for example, Manuel London and Steven A. Stumpf, "Individual and Organizational Career Development in Changing Times," in Douglas T. Hall and Associates, *Career Development in Organizations* (San Francisco: Jossey-Bass, 1985), 21–49, for more discussion of this guideline and the others which follow.

19. For more discussion on how cutting-edge organizations are designing their career systems to better match individual and corporate career needs, see Thomas Gutteridge, "Organizational Career Development Systems: The State of the Practice," in Douglas T. Hall and Associates, *op cit.*, 50–94.

20. See Tracy Kidder, *The Soul of a New Machine* (Boston: Little, Brown and Company, 1981).

21. See Felice N. Schwartz, "Management Women and the New Facts of Life," *Harvard Business Review*, 1989, *67*, 65–82; Douglas T. Hall and Judith Richter, "Balancing Work Life and Home Life: What Can Organizations Do to Help?" *Academy of Management Executive,* 1988, *2*, 213–223; and Douglas T. Hall, "Promoting work/family balance: An organization change approach," *Organizational Dynamics*, Winter, 1990, *18*, 5–18.

22. See Schwartz, *op. cit.*

23. Ellen Goodman, "Corporate "Misfits," *Boston Globe*, November 1, 1988, 13.

24. For more discussion on work-home balance, see Hall and Richter, *op. cit.*, and Hall, "Promoting work/family balance," *op. cit.*

25. See, for example, the work of Raelin, Jones, Russell, Mills, and Werner & Stillman referred to in Notes 13 and 14. See also the work on student values in the 1960s reported in Douglas T. Hall, "Potential for Career Growth," *Personnel Administration,* May–June, 1971, 18–30; Douglas T. Hall, "Humanizing Organizations: The Potential Impact of New People and Emerging Values Upon Organizations," in H. Meltzer and F. R. Wickert (Eds.), *Humanizing Organizational Behavior* (Springfield, IL: Charles C. Thomas, 1976), 158–174; S. E. Seashore and T. Barnowe, "Collar Color Doesn't Count," *Psychology Today,* August 1972, 53–54, 80–82; L.D. Johnston, J. G. Backman, and P. M. O'Malley, "Monitoring the Future: Questionnaire Responses from the Nation's High School Seniors, 1979" (Ann Arbor, MI: Institute for Social Research, University of Michigan, 1979); D. Yankelovich, "Putting the New Work Ethic to Work" (New York: The Public Agenda Foundation, September 1983); P. Renwick, and E. E. Lawler III, "What You Really Want from Your Job," *Psychology Today,* May 1978, 53–58, 60, 65, 118; R. A. Easterlin, *Birth and Fortune: The Impact of Numbers on Human Welfare* (New York: Basic Books, 1980); "Americans change," *Business Week,* February 20, 1978, 65–66; D. Quinn Mills, *Not Like Our Parents: A New Look at How the Baby Boom Generation Is Changing America:* (New York William Morrow and Company, 1987); and Martin M. Greller and David M. Nee, *From Baby Boom to Baby Bust* (Reading, MA: Addison-Wesley, 1989).

• The authors gratefully acknowledge the helpful comments of Marcy Crary, Kathy Kram, and anonymous reviewers, as well as the support of the Human Resources Policy Institute of the Boston University School of Management and that of its Director, Fred Foulkes.

## Study Methodology

*We define career as a series of work-related experiences (events and the person's reactions to those events) which occur over the span of the person's work life.* Note that this definition says nothing about advancement to a certain level, nothing about success as defined by salary or other external measures. In fact, surveys of work values in the contemporary work force indicate that the most important kind of success to most people is what we call *psychological success*: the achievement of those goals which the individual values most. To some people, psychological success might be measured in terms of professional competence, to others, family rewards, and to still others, fame and public recognition. To understand the career situation as it is perceived by members of the baby boom group in today's leaner organization, we need to consider their *values*, as well as career strategies.

Our information comes from three sources. One source was research literature on baby boomers.[25] A second source is the numerous seminars and workshops, both for MBA students and corporate managers, on self-assessment and career planning which we have offered over the last 15 years. The participants in these seminars have been predominantly members of the baby boom cohort, and many of the issues raised have been related to career stage concerns of this group. Finally, although we did not intend for this to be an empirical article, we did interview 20 managers in the baby boom group and 25 human resource executives in companies noted for progressive human resource practices (e.g., Monsanto, DuPont, Westin, Kodak, Florida Power and Light, AT&T, Corning Glass) to obtain more in-depth examples of how individuals and organizations are being affected by this demographic phenomenon. While somewhat limited, our own data are useful for illustrative purposes, and they are consistent with trends in the research literature.

# STRESS IN ORGANIZATIONS

*Robert L. Kahn*
*Philippe Byosiere*

In recent years, the amount of attention and research devoted to organizational stress has expanded rapidly. In a Gallup poll that sampled over 200 large and small companies, the personnel and medical directors reported that 25% of their employees suffered from anxiety or stress-related disorders (cited in Stewart, 1990). This article presents what researchers have learned about the relationship between organizational antecedents to stress and the stressors they generate, the perception and appraisal of those stressors by individuals, the short-term responses that are evoked, and the effects of long-term exposure. We have also included the moderating effects of individual differences and interpersonal relationships at each step in this casual chain.

The term *stress* has been in the English language for a long time and has still earlier origins in Latin as a verb meaning to injure, molest, or constrain. During the 18th and 19th centuries, the major uses of the term identified it as a force of pressure exerted upon a material object or person, a usage that is close to the more precise definition that developed in science and engineering. This precision of definition was not carried into medicine and biology when the concept of stress was first borrowed in the first half of the 19th century. Today we still talk about stress as both an external pressure or demand *and* its internal result.

For example, Selye (1936, 1982), whose influential writings on stress span almost half a century, wrote in 1936 (p. 3) and reiterated in 1982 (p. 7) that "*stress is the nonspecific* (that is, common) *result of any demand upon the body,* be the effect mental or somatic." Since his days as a medical student, Seyle had been intrigued by the fact that "diverse noxious agents" seemed to generate the same physiological responses, which he described as involving enlargement and discoloration of the adrenal glands, intense shrinkage of the thymus and lymph nodes, and concomitant development of bloody stomach ulcers. In subsequent research, he described more fully the complex biochemical sequence that he called the *general adaptation syndrome* (GAS) or stress response. However, Seyle (1982) also referred to the psychological stress induced in laboratory rats by external pressure. Thus, in the fields of organizational behavior and psychology, we are interested in both the externally induced organizational stress experienced by employees and their stress response.

## EUSTRESS AND DISTRESS

To regard every organizational demand on the persons as stressors, and somehow therefore undesirable, would be naive and unsatisfactory. It would imply that the preferred state of the human being is inactivity, which we know to be untrue. People seek activity, including the kinds of activities that use abilities they value and, not infrequently, activities that challenge those abilities and require the acquisition of new ones. Therefore, in his later years, Seyle (1982) put increasing

*Source*: This article is an excerpt from "Stress in Organizations," in Marvin D. Dunnette and Leaette M. Hough (Eds.), *Handbook of Industrial and Organizational Psychology*, Vol. 3 (Palo Alto, CA: Consulting Psychologists Press, Inc., 1992), pp. 571–650.

emphasis on the distinction between good stress and bad stress or, as he called them *eustress* and *distress*. He refers to eustress also as the stress of fulfillment. These definitions, which are less than precise, are part of a Seyle script about human nature that is part demonstrated fact, part assumption, and perhaps part faith. The key elements begin with the assertion that human beings are by nature intended to work—that is, to set tasks and attempt to complete them successfully. Doing so involves demands on the mind and body, and exposure to these demands evokes that sequence of physiological changes that Seyle called the general adaptation syndrome. To that extent, distressing and eustressing stressors (stimuli) would seem to be similar in their effects. The difference seems to lie in the prospects for fulfillment or achievement. Without such challenges and opportunities to use existing capacities successfully, muscles atrophy and mental abilities diminish. With them, the inevitable processes of wear and tear continue, but they cannot be avoided in any case. The idea is not to avoid the stress of life, but to maximize the eustress component.

Many organizational variables become stressors under conditions of both deprivation and excess. Examples in organizational life come easily to mind— too much work or too little, supervision that is too detailed or conversely too general, required interaction with colleagues that is too frequent or too infrequent. French, Caplan, and Harrison (1982) found that strain (an index of overall psychological strain) was likely to occur when the job was either too complex or too simple for the individual's preference. The pattern was similar for role ambiguity, responsibility for persons, work load, and overtime; too much and too little of these variables led to increased strain scores. Strain is also related to life events, events like job loss, moving, divorce, etc. that tend to cluster at the onset of disease.

## A THEORETICAL MODEL OF STRESS

There are several theoretical models of stress (Elliot & Eisdorfer, 1982; McGrath, 1976; Lazarus & Folkman, 1984; Dohrenwend et al, 1982; Ivancevich & Mattson, 1980; Levi, 1981; Frankenhauser, 1989; and French & Kahn, 1962). However, the model which we will utilize for the remainder of this article is shown in Figure 1.

Five elements are identified as comprising a causal sequence that leads from organizational characteristics to specific stressors, from stressors to the perceptual and cognitive processes that constitute appraisal of threat, and then to the immediate responses generated by threat appraisal— physiological, psychological, and behavioral; these lead, finally, to the ramifying or long-term consequences of stress for the individual and for the organization. The solid arrows indicate causal relationships, either hypothesized or demonstrated, depending on the specific variables in question.

This model includes factors, such as enduring properties of the person (demographic and personality) and of the situation, that moderate or mediate the causal sequence in the model. The model acknowledges the possibility that stressors may have effects without involving the processes of perception and cognition that usually intervene. Toxicologists and epidemiologists are perhaps more concerned with such effects than are psychologists, but we should recognize the fact that all experiences that are ultimately damaging are not perceived as such at the time of exposure.

FIGURE 1    Theoretical Framework for the Study of Stress in Organizations

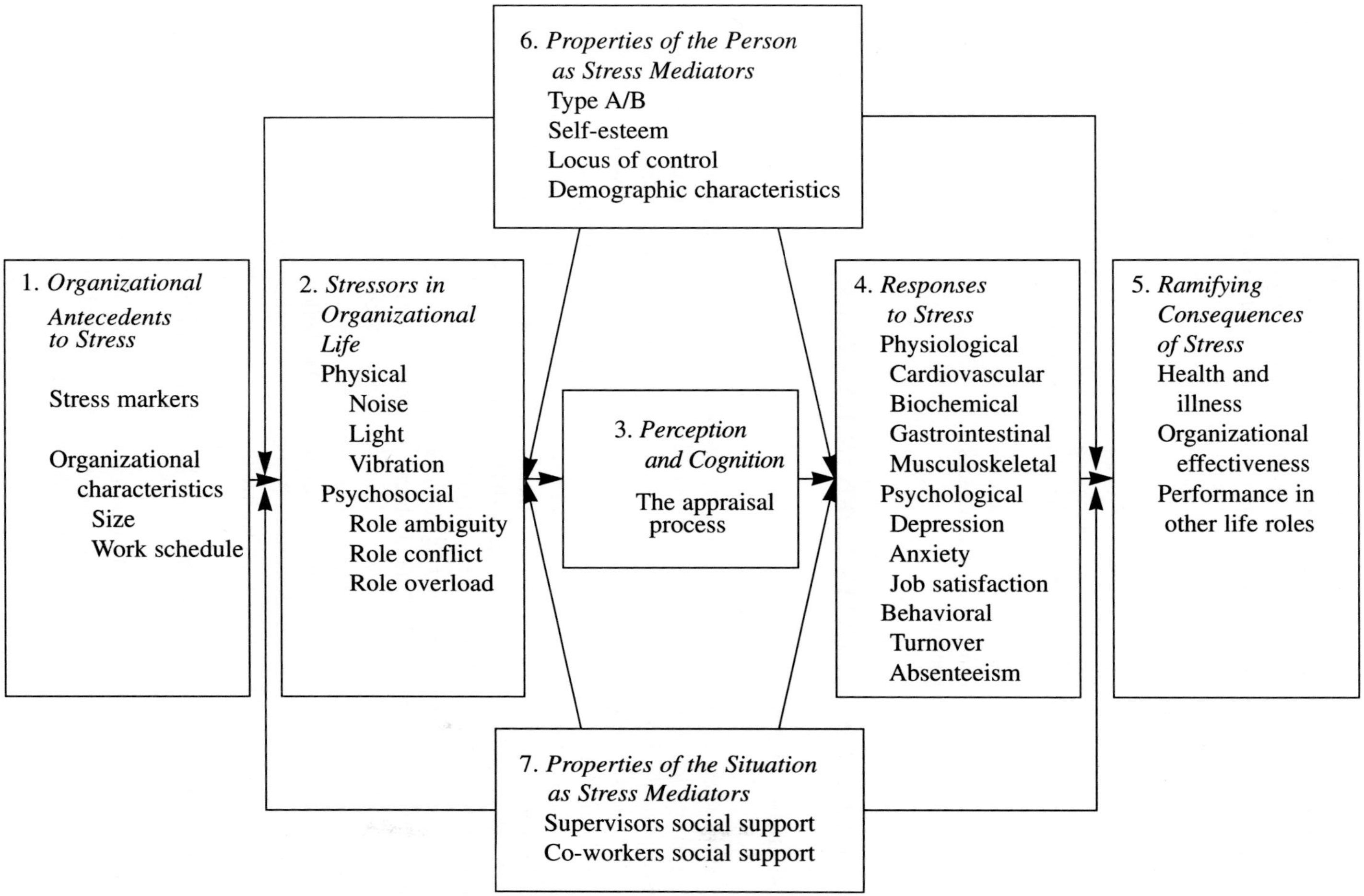

1. *Organizational Antecedents to Stress*

Stress markers

Organizational characteristics
Size
Work schedule

2. *Stressors in Organizational Life*
Physical
Noise
Light
Vibration
Psychosocial
Role ambiguity
Role conflict
Role overload

3. *Perception and Cognition*
The appraisal process

4. *Responses to Stress*
Physiological
Cardiovascular
Biochemical
Gastrointestinal
Musculoskeletal
Psychological
Depression
Anxiety
Job satisfaction
Behavioral
Turnover
Absenteeism

5. *Ramifying Consequences of Stress*
Health and illness
Organizational effectiveness
Performance in other life roles

6. *Properties of the Person as Stress Mediators*
Type A/B
Self-esteem
Locus of control
Demographic characteristics

7. *Properties of the Situation as Stress Mediators*
Supervisors social support
Co-workers social support

# EMPIRICAL FINDINGS

Our review of empirical research on stress will concentrate on studies that have explicit relevance to organizational theory and practice, either because they were conducted in organizational settings or because they attempted to deal with organizational problems. The following discussion of research findings is organized around eight main topics, the first seven of which correspond to the categories in Figure 1:

- Organizational antecedents to stress
- Stressors in organizational life
- Perception and cognition: the appraisal process
- Responses to stress: physiological, psychological, and behavioral
- Ramifying consequences of stress: health and illness; organizational effectiveness; performance in other life roles
- Properties of the person as stress mediators
- Properties of the situation as stress mediators
- Prevention and intervention

# ORGANIZATIONAL ANTECEDENTS TO STRESS

## Social Indicators as Stress Markers

Some of the stress caused by organizations can be measured by social indicators. This is a research strategy associated almost exclusively with Harvey Brenner and his colleagues. They have demonstrated repeatedly that for many large populations, regional and national, there are substantial and plausibly lagged correlations between economic conditions and health. The social indicators used in these analyses include economic growth, economic instability, and unemployment levels. These in turn are associated with such criterion variables as institutionalization rates, suicides, and various health indicators. For a review of these studies, see Brenner and Mooney (1983).

Brenner's more recent work ( Brenner, 1987a, 1987b) extends this research in several ways. He replicates and extends the basic findings relating economic change and mortality in nine industrialized countries— Australia, Canada, England and Wales, Denmark, Federal Republic of Germany, Finland, France, Sweden, and the United States. Unemployment and business failures predict mortality from heart disease, with a one-year to four-year lag and with controls on such variables as alcohol consumption and cigarette smoking. In eight of the nine countries the greater the economic growth, the lower the mortality rates from heart disease. We believe that the Brenner data are important and deserve to be accepted; however, the task of specifying the causal mechanisms through which these gross economic changes affect health and mortality remains to be completed.

## Organizations as Stress-generators:  Systems and Subsystems

Organizational size has been hypothesized as a source of stress, although the link has not been specified. Moreover, the evidence is thin and inconsistent. Kahn et al. (1964), in a national survey in which workers estimated the size of their employing firms, found a significant relationship between size and reported job tension. The connection between the two was presumed to involve increased formalization and bureaucratization in larger organizations. However, a Dutch investigation into the relationship of company size to stress and strain found that reported incidence of stressors was greatest in medium-sized as opposed to large companies (Reiche & Van Dijkhuizen, 1979). Research that has investigated the effects of formalization on work stressors, however, has produced few significant findings (Pearce, 1981). Ironically, the most consistent of them is a negative relationship between formalization and role ambiguity, which means that the more formalized the organization the less role ambiguity is experienced by employees (House and Rizzo, 1972; Morris, Steers, & Koch, 1978; Rizzo, House, & Listzman, 1970; Rogers & Molnar, 1976).

Although specific causal connections remain to be demonstrated, evidence continues to accumulate slowly that links phenomena at the organizational level to experienced stress at the individual level. For example, a comparative study of employees in eight organizations of comparable technology tested the hypothesis that illness was actually an organizational phenomenon (Schmitt, Colligan, & Fitzgerald, 1980). There were significant differences in the between-company variance revealed in the data, and the company means on such variables as work pressure and dissatisfaction with personnel policies were associated with frequency of reported physical symptoms. A more rigorous longitudinal study compared private and semipublic savings banks in Belgium with respect to the incidence of coronary heart disease among male bank clerks, matched by age and sex and free of the disease at the beginning of the 10-year study. Incidence of sudden deaths and nonfatal myocardial infarctions was significantly higher in the private banks than in the semipublic banks by a margin of 50 percent after major individual coronary risk functions were controlled by multiple logistic analysis. The causal factors behind these findings were not identified, and the possibility that they are entirely reflective of self-selection (different types of individuals choosing a particular type of organization) cannot be ruled out. Nevertheless, the hypothesis that organizational determinants cause illness remains plausible.

Differences of this kind between organizations lead one to wonder to what extent similar differences can be demonstrated between subunits of single organizations. One such study (Parasuraman & Alutto, 1981) found that the five subsystems of a food-processing firm (production, production-supportive, maintenance, adaptive, and managerial) differed significantly in type and magnitude of reported stressors. People in subunits that reported more stressors experienced more stress and lower job satisfaction.

Recent research on the stresses associated with reductions in organizational size (Sutton & D'Aunno, 1989) raises the possibility that change at the organizational level may be an important generator of stressors, even when size itself is not. Most of the research on organizational downsizing has been qualitative, however, and does not include health indicators as outcome variables.

## Role Characteristics as Antecedents to Stress

Stress can vary according to one's hierarchial position within an organization and proximity to the boundaries of the organization. For example, people in boundary spanning roles, who serve as liaisons with external organizations or between different departments, sometimes report greater stress (Bartunek & Reynolds, 1983; Miles, 1976; Miles & Perreault, 1976).

The data on the relationship between hierarchal position and role stress are mixed and can only be understood in the context of the particular organization. In a study that compared upper-, middle-, and lower-level managers, a curvilinear relationship was reported, with stress highest among the middle-level managers (Ivancevich, Matteson, & Preston, 1982), a finding consistent with their reported satisfaction levels and their physiological measures. Other studies, usually conducted in single companies, have not replicated this pattern but have shown that as the hierarchical level increases so do both the type and magniude of reported stresors (Parasuraman & Allutto, 1981).

## Occupations as Antecedents to Stress

Some occupations are apparently more stressful than others. For example, occupations characterized by high levels of demand (e.g., lifting) and low levels of control (autonomy) were associated with elevated risks of myocardial infarction in a Swedish study of 118 occupational groups (Alfredsson & Theorell, 1983). Air traffic controllers are usually cited as a high stress occupation. Studies of air traffic controllers, some involving comparison groups in other occupations and some involving comparisons across airports with different traffic densities, identified responsibility for the welfare of others in combination with heavy and variable work load and irregular work-rest cycles as occupation-determined stressors (Rose, Jenkins, Hurst, & Apple-Levi, 1978).

A large scale study (French, Caplan, & Harrison, 1982) found consistent stressor patterns that differentiated blue collar from white collar occupations. The unskilled blue collar occupations scored lowest in complexity and responsibility. People in those occupations reported a greater discrepancy between their preferences regarding complexity and responsibility at work and the way their jobs really were.

## Work-Related Events

Stressful life events have figured prominently in health-oriented social research, at least since the initial work of Holmes and Rahe (1967), and job loss has always been prominent in the roster of such events. Whether we regard job loss as a stressor in itself or as an organizational antecedent to other stressors, such as economic deprivation and status reduction, is essentially a matter of definitional preference.

While work is a source of stress, it is also a source of both material and psychological gratification. The importance of these gratifications becomes most apparent when work is denied. The study of Michigan plant closings by Cobb and Kasl (1977) is an interesting example. Workers in plants that did not close were compared with those in plants that were marked for closing. Five waves of data were collected over a two-year period, spanning the entire event sequence beginning with rumors and threats to actual job loss and (in most cases) reemployment. Physiological measures were collected along with self-reported information. The research results show that the costs of unemplyment are physical as well as economic and psychological. They also show that the threat of unemployment triggers some physiological changes long before actual job loss occurs and that most physical indicators return to normal after new job stability is attained. Indeed, some people show net gains as a consequence of a job loss. For most, however, involuntary loss of a job is an event that generates stressors and consequent strains, directly and indirectly. Recent field experiments by Vinokur, Price, and Caplan (in press) and their colleagues demonstrate the possibility of reducing such strains by means of counseling, role playing, and peer support.

## Stressors in Organizational Life

We use the term stressors to designate stimuli generated on the job that have negative consequences, physical or psychological, for significant proportions of people exposed to them. We have found more than 250 research reports published in the last 16 years, that measure job-generated stressors and specific associated strains or effects. The findings are heavily clustered around two conceptual categories:

*Task content and related characteristics.* These include such dimensions as simplicity-complexity, variety-monotony, shift work, and physical conditions at work.

*Role properties.* These refer primarily to the social aspects of the job, and include supervisory and peer relations, lack of autonomy, as well as the familiar concepts of role conflict, ambiguity, and overload.

# Perception and Cognition: The Appraisal Process

The acknowledgment of appraisal as an important cognitive element in the stress sequence has come about largely through the theoretical conviction and experimental research of Lazarus and Folkman (1984). Perceived stressfulness increases with the importance of the event and the uncertainty of the outcome.

The argument for the importance of the appraisal process (Lazarus and Folkman, 1984) begins with the fact of individual differences; different people react differently to stressors that are objectively the same. Furthermore, the stressors encountered in real life are often embedded in complex situations, and successful coping requires analysis of both positive and negative situational aspects to reach some overall judgment of potential gain or loss and to decide upon a course of action.

Appraisal thus goes beyond perception; it is "the process of categorizing an encounter, and its various facets, with respect to its significance for well-being" (Lazarus & Folkman, 1984, p. 31).

## Responses to Stress

Our model of stress distinguishes three major categories of possible responses to stress; physiological responses, psychological responses, and behavioral responses. Physiological responses to stress are found in measures of heart rate, blood pressure, and catecholamine levels (epinephrine and norepinephrine) as well as gastric symptoms.

There are numerous psychological responses to stress, such as anxiety, burnout, depression, dissatisfaction with job and life, fatigue, strain, etc.

Behavioral responses to stress consist of degradation/disruption of the work role itself (e.g., decreased job performance), aggressive behavior at work (e.g., stealing, spreading rumors, etc.), flight from the job (absenteeism, turnover, strikes, etc.), degradation /disruption of other life roles (e.g., spouse abuse), and self-damaging behaviors (alcohol use, smoking, accidents).

## Ramifying Consequences of Stress

Job stress has potential consequences that go far beyond the immediate experience of stress and its associated response. Some such ramifications involve performance—performance of the individual on the job and in other life roles and, by extension, performance of the organization as a whole. Other ramifications involve the health of the individual, as affected by prolonged exposure to physical stressors or noxiants and through responses to prolonged or recurrent psychosocial stressors.

The effects of work-generated stress on individual health are best demonstrated with respect to coronary heart disease. Job stressors of various kinds—cyclic overload, threat of job loss, and role conflict and ambiguity, for example are associated with such risk factors as elevated cholesterol levels (Friedman, Rosenman, & Carroll, 1958), elevations in blood pressure (Kasl & Cobb, 1970), and increased heart rate (French & Caplan, 1970).

## Properties of the Person as Stress Mediators

The recognition of individual differences in resistance to stress must be among the oldest insights into the complexities of human behavior. Kahn, Wolfe, Quinn, and Snoek (1964) reported that the effects of role conflict and ambiguity were moderated or conditioned by such personality characteristics as flexibility-rigidity, introversion-extroversion, and emotional sensitivity. The Type A behavior pattern intensifies the effects of various job stressors (Ganster, 1987) when it is accompanied by hostility and anger (Williams, 1989). Self-esteem and loss of control also moderate the stress that people experience.

## Properties of the Situation as Stress Mediators

Our model of stress and strain stipulates the possibility that certain properties of the situation, as well as enduring characteristics of the individual, can moderate or buffer the effects of a stressor. In principle, the buffering effect can occur between any pair of variables in the stress-strain sequence. Thus, the buffering variable can reduce the tendency of organizational properties to generate specific stressors, alter the perceptions and cognitions evoked by such stressors, moderate the responses that follow the appraisal process, or reduce the health-damaging consequences of such responses.

Social support at work and from one's supervisor buffers the effects of stress. Sutton and Kahn (1987), on the basis of research outside the organizational context, have proposed three other situational variables as potential buffers against stress: a) the extent to which the onset of a stressor is predictable, b) the extent to which it is understandable, and c) the extent to which aspects of the stressor are controllable by the person who must experience it.

## Prevention and Intervention

Recent years have seen a great deal of activity directed at the management of stress and its ramifying effects on health. To organizational psychologists, however, the activity pattern is disappointing in several respects. First, it is concentrated disproportionately on reducing the effects of stress rather than reducing the presence of stressors at work. Second, perhaps as a consequence, the main target of intervention has been the individual rather than the organization; the effort has been directed at increasing individual resistance to stressors generated at work. Third, the surge of practitioner activity in the domain of stress management has not been accompanied by a commensurate increase in serious research; most programs have not been evaluated in that sense. Finally, the programs in stress management that are sold to companies are seldom tailored to the specific needs of the company.

Murphy (1986) describes three classes of intervention programs. *Employee assistance programs* attempt to repair damage already done, usually by abuse of alcohol and other substances. *Stress management programs* train individuals in techniques for reducing their physiological and psychological responses to stress. *Stress reduction* programs are few and deal with aspects of control—increased participation in decision making, autonomy on the job itself, and control over one's work schedule.

We conclude that stress programs are probably cost effective, regardless of their mode. Nevertheless, there is too little research to permit systematic comparisons of effectiveness by program type. The content of most programs, with their emphasis on individualized approaches and stress management, reflects the concerns of managerial and white collar employees rather than those of blue collar populations. The one study that makes such comparisons (Neale, Singer, Schwartz, & Schwartz, 1982) shows that blue collar workers, at least those who are members of labor unions, more often point to physical and technological aspects of work as sources of stress, and propose remedies that involve organizational policies, government actions, and labor contracts.

# BIBLIOGRAPHY

Alfredsson, L., & Theorell, T. (1983). Job characteristics of occupations and myocardial infarction risk: Effect of possible confounding factors. *Social Science and Medicine, 17(20)*, 1497–1503.

Bartunek, J. M., & Reynolds, C. (1983). Boundary-spanning and public accountant role stress. *Journal of Social Psychology, 121(1)*, 65–72.

Brenner, M. H, (1987a). Economic change, alcohol consumption, and heart disease mortality in nine industrialized countries. *Social Science and Medicine, 25(2)*, 119–132.

Brenner, M. H., (1987b). Relation of economic change to Swedish health and social well-being, 1950–1980. *Social Science and Medicine, 25(2)*, 183–195.

Brenner, M. H., & Mooney, A. (1983). Unemployment and health in the context of economic change. *Social Science and Medicine, 17(16)*, 1125–1138.

Cobb, S., & Kasl, S. V. (1977). *Termination: The consequences of job loss.* U.S. Department of Health, Education and Welfare. Washington, DC: U.S. Government Printing Office.

Dohrenwend, B. S., Krasnoff, L., Askenasy, A. R., & Dohrenwend, B. P. (1982). The Psychiatric Epidemiology Research Interview Life Events Scale. In L. Golderger & S. Breznitz (Eds.), *Handbook of Stress* (pp. 332–363). New York: Free Press.

Dohrenwend, B., Pearlin, L., Clayton, P., Hanburg, B., Riley, R., & Rose, R. M. (1982). Report on stress and life events. In G. Elliott & C. Eisodorfer (Eds.), *Stress and human health.* New York: Springer.

Elliott, G. R., & Eisendorfer, C. (Eds.). (1982). *Stress and human health: Analysis and implications of research.* New York: Springer-Verlag.

Frankenhaeuser, M., Lundberg, U., Fredrikson, M., Melin, B., Tuomisto, M., Myrster, A., Hedman, M., Bergman-Losman, B., & Wallin, L. (1989). Stress on and off the job as related to sex and occupational status in white-collar workers. *Journal of Organizational Behavior, 10*, 321–346.

French, J. R. P., Jr., & Caplan, R. D. (1970). Psychosocial factors in coronary heart disease. *Industrial Medicine, 29(9)*, 383–397.

French, J. R. P., Jr., Caplan, R. D., & Harrison, R.V. (1982). *The mechanisms of job stress and strain.* Chichester, England: Wiley.

French, J. R. P., Jr., & Kahn, R. L. (1962). A programmatic approach to studying the industrial environment and mental health. *Journal of Social Issues, 18(3)*, 1–47.

Friedman, M., Roseman, R., & Carroll, V. (1958). Changes in the serum cholesterol and blood clotting time in men subjected to cyclic variation of occupational stress. *Circulation, XVII*, 852–861.

Ganster, D. C. (1987). Type A behavior and occupational stress. Job Stress: From theory to suggestion [Special issue]. *Journal of Organizational Behavior Management, 8(2)*, 61–84.

Holmes, T. H., & Rahe, R. H (1967). The social readjustment rating scale. *Journal of Psychosomatic Research, 11*, 213–218.

House, R. J., & Rizzo J. R. (1972). Role conflict and ambiguity as critical variables in a model of organizational behavior. *Organizational Behavior and Human Performance, 16*, 467–505.

Ivancevich, J. M., & Matteson, M. T. (1980). *Stress and work: A managerial perspective.* Glenview, IL: Scott Foresman.

Ivancevich, J., Matteson, M., & Preston, C. (1982). Occupational stress, type A behavior, and physical well-being. *Academy of Management Journal, 25(2)*, 373–391.

Kahn, R. L., Wolfe, D. M., Quinn, R. P., & Snoek, J. D. (1964). *Organizational stress: Studies in role conflict and ambiguity.* New York: Wiley.

Lazarus, R. S., & Folkman, S. (1984). S*tress, appraisal, and coping.* New York: Springer.

Levi, L. (1981). *Preventing work stress.* Reading, MA: Addison-Wesley.

McGrath, J. E. (1976). Stress and behavior in organizations. In M. D. Dunnette (Ed.), *Handbook of industrial and organizational psychology.* Chicago: Rand McNally.

Miles, R. H. (1976). Role requirements as sources of organizational stress. *Journal of Applied Psychology, 61(2),* 172–179.

Miles, R., & Perreault, W. (1976). Organizational role conflict: Its antecedents and consequences. *Organizational Behavior and Human Performance, 17(1),* 19–44.

Morris, J. H., Steers, R. M., & Koch, J. L. (1978). *Influence of organizational structure on role conflict and ambiguity for three occupational groupings* (Tech. Rep. Paper 16). University of Oregon Graduate School of Management.

Murphy, L. R. (1984). Occupational stress management: A review and appraisal. *Journal of Occupational Psychology, 57(1),* 1–15.

Neale, M. S., Singer, J., Schwartz, G. E., & Scwartz, J. (1982). *Conflicting perspectives on stress reduction in occupational settings: A systems approach to their resolution* (Report to NIOSH on P.O. No. 82–1058). Cincinnati, OH.

Parasuraman, S., & Alutto, I. A. (1981). An examination of the organizational antecedents of stressors at work. *Academy of Management Journal, 24(1),* 48–67.

Pearce, J. L. (1981). Bringing some clarity to role ambiguity research. *Academy of Management Review, 6(4),* 665–674.

Reiche, H. M., & Van Dijkhuizen, N. (1979). Company size, hierarchy and personality: Do they influence feelings of stress and strain? *Tijdschrift voor Psychologie, 7(1–2),* 58–75.

Rizzo, J. R., House, R. J., & Lisztman, S. I. (1970). Role conflict and ambiguity in complex organizations. *Administrative Science Quarterly, 15,* 150–163.

Rogers, D. L., & Molnar, J. (1976). Organizational antecedents of role conflict and ambiguity in top-level administrators. *Administrative Science Quarterly, 23(4),* 598–610.

Rose, R. M., Jenkins, C. D., Hurst, M. W., & Apple-Levin, M. (1978). *Air traffic controller health study* (Federal Aviation Authority Report FAA-AM 78, 39). Washington, DC: Department of Transportation.

Schmitt, N., Colligan, M. J., & Fitzgerald, M. (1980). Unexplained physical symptoms in eight organizations: Individual and organizational analyses. *Journal of Occupational Psychology, 53(4),* 305–317.

Seyle, H. (1982). History and present status of the stress concept. In L. Goldberger & S. Breznitz (Eds.), *Handbook of stress* (pp. 7–17). New York: Free Press.

Stewart, T. A. (1990). Do you push your people too hard? *Fortune,* October 22, p. 121.

Sutton, R. I., D'Aunno, T. (1989). Decreasing organizational size: Untangling the effects of people and money. *Academy of Management Review, 14,* 194–212.

Vinokur, A., Price, R. H., & Caplan, R. D. (in press). From field experiments to program implementation: Assessing the potential outcomes of an experimental program for the unemployed. *American Journal of Community Psychology.*

Williams, R. (1989). The trusting heart: Great news about type A behavior. New York: Times Books.

# 7

# Interpersonal Communication

ACTIVE LISTENING
*Carl R. Rogers*
*Richard E. Farson*

COMMUNICATION: THE USE OF TIME, SPACE AND THINGS
*Anthony G. Athos*

DEFENSIVE COMMUNICATION
*Jack R. Gibb*

## ACTIVE LISTENING

*Carl R. Rogers*
*Richard E. Farson*

### THE MEANING OF ACTIVE LISTENING

One basic responsibility of the supervisor or manager is the development, adjustment, and integration of individual employees. He tries to develop employee potential, delegate responsibility, and achieve cooperation. To do so, he must have, among other abilities, the ability to listen intelligently and carefully to those with whom he works.

There are, however, many kinds of listening skills. The lawyer, for example, when questioning a witness, listens for contradictions, irrelevancies, errors, and weaknesses. But this is not the kind of listening skill we are concerned with. The lawyer usually is not listening in order to help the witness adjust, cooperate, or produce. Our emphasis will be on listening skills of the supervisor or manager that will help employees gain a clearer understanding of their situations, take responsibility, and cooperate with each other.

*Source*: Reprinted by special permission of the Industrial Relations Center of the University of Chicago and the authors.

## Two Examples

The kind of listening we have in mind is called "active listening." It is called "active" because the listener has a very definite responsibility. He does not passively absorb words which are spoken to him. He actively tries to grasp the facts and the feelings in what he hears, and he tries, by his listening, to help the speaker work out his own problems.

To get a clearer picture of what active listening means, let us consider two different approaches to the same work problem. The example is set in the printing industry, but the behavior of the men could surface in any organization.

EXAMPLE NO. 1

| | |
|---|---|
| FOREMAN: | Hey, Al, I don't get this rush order. We can't handle any 50,000 run today. What do they think we are? |
| SUPERVISOR: | But that's the order. So get it out as soon as you can. We're under terrific pressure this week. |
| F: | Don't they know we're behind schedule already because of that press breakdown? |
| S: | Look, Kelly, I don't decide what goes on upstairs. I just have to see that the work gets out and that's what I'm gonna do. |
| F: | The guys aren't gonna like this. |
| S: | That's something you'll have to work out with them, not me. |

EXAMPLE NO. 2

| | |
|---|---|
| F: | Hey, Ross, I don't get this rush order. We can't handle any run of 50,000 today. What do they think we are? |
| S: | They're pushing you pretty hard, aren't they Kelly? |
| F: | They sure are and I'm getting sore. We were just about back to schedule after the press breakdown. Now this comes along. |
| S: | As if you didn't have enough work to do, huh? |
| F: | Yeah. I don't know how I'm going to tell the pressman about this. |
| S: | Hate to face him with a rush order now, is that it? |
| F: | I really do. Joe is under a real strain today. Seems like everything we do around here is rush, rush, rush! |
| S: | I guess you feel it's unfair to load anything more on him today. |
| F: | Well, yeah. I know there must be plenty of pressure on everybody to get the work out, but—well, Joe doesn't deserve all the rush orders. But, if that's the way it is—I guess I'd better get the word to him and see how I can rearrange the work flow. |

There are obviously many differences between these two examples. The main one, however, is that Ross, the supervisor in the second example, is using the active listening approach. He is listening and responding in a way that makes it clear that he appreciates both the meaning and the feeling behind what Kelly is saying.

Active listening does not necessarily mean long sessions spent listening to grievances, personal or otherwise. It is simply a way of approaching those problems which arise out of the usual day-to-day events of any job.

To be effective, active listening must be firmly grounded in the basic attitudes of the user. We cannot employ it as a technique if our fundamental attitudes are in conflict with its basic concepts. If we try, our behavior will be empty and sterile, and our associates will be quick to recognize such behavior. Until we can demonstrate a spirit which genuinely respects the potential worth of the individual, which considers his rights and trusts his capacity for self-direction, we cannot begin to be effective listeners.

## What We Achieve by Listening

Active listening is an important way to bring about changes in people. Despite the popular notion that listening is a passive approach, clinical and research evidence clearly shows that sensitive listening is a most effective agent for individual personality change and group development. Listening brings about changes in people's attitudes toward themselves and others, and also brings about changes in their basic values and personal philosophy. People who have been listened to in this new and special way become more emotionally mature, more open to their experiences, less defensive, more democratic, and less authoritarian.

When people are listened to sensitively, they tend to listen to themselves with more care and make clear exactly what they are feeling and thinking. Group members tend to listen more to each other, become less argumentative, more ready to incorporate other points of view. Because listening reduces the threat of having one's ideas criticized, the person is better able to see them for what they are and is more likely to feel that his contributions are worthwhile.

Not the least important result of listening is the change that takes place within the listener himself. Besides the fact that listening provides more information about people than any other activity, it builds deep, positive relationships and tends to alter constructively the attitudes of the listener. Listening is a growth experience.

## HOW TO LISTEN

The goal of active listening is to bring about changes in people. To achieve this end, it relies upon definite techniques—things to do and things to avoid doing. Before discussing these techniques, however, we should first understand why they are effective. To do so, we must understand how the individual personality develops.

## The Growth of the Individual

Through all of our lives, from early childhood on, we have learned to think of ourselves in certain, very definite ways. We have built up pictures of ourselves. Sometimes these self-pictures are pretty realistic but at other times they are not. For example, an average, overweight lady may fancy herself a youthful, ravishing siren, or an awkward teenager regard himself as a star athlete.

All of us have experiences which fit the way we need to think about ourselves. These we accept. But it is much harder to accept experiences which don't fit. And sometimes, if it is very important for us to hang on to this self-picture, we don't accept or admit these experiences at all.

These self-pictures are not necessarily attractive. A man, for example, may regard himself as incompetent and worthless. He may feel that he is doing his job poorly in spite of favorable appraisals by the organization. As long as he has these feelings about himself he must deny any experiences which would seem not to fit this self-picture, in this case any that might indicate to him that he is competent. It is so necessary for him to maintain this self-picture that he is threatened by anything which would tend to change it. Thus, when the organization raises his salary, it may seem to him only additional proof that he is a fraud. He must hold onto this self-picture, because, bad or good, it's the only thing he has by which he can identify himself.

This is why direct attempts to change this individual or change his self-picture are particularly threatening. He is forced to defend himself or to completely deny the experience. This denial of experience and defense of the self-picture tend to bring on rigidity of behavior and create difficulties in personal adjustment.

The active-listening approach, on the other hand, does not present a threat to the individual's self-picture. He does not have to defend it. He is able to explore it, see it for what it is, and make his own decision as to how realistic it is. He is then in a position to change.

If I want to help a man or woman reduce defensiveness and become more adaptive, I must try to remove the threat of myself as a potential changer. As long as the atmosphere is threatening, there can be no effective communication. So I must create a climate which is neither critical, evaluative, nor moralizing. The climate must foster equality and freedom, trust and understanding, acceptance and warmth. In this climate and in this climate only does the individual feel safe enough to incorporate new experiences and new values into his concept of himself. Active listening helps to create this climate.

## What to Avoid

When we encounter a person with a problem, our usual response is to try to change his way of looking at things—to get him to see his situation the way we see it, or would like him to see it. We plead, reason, scold, encourage, insult, prod–anything to bring about a change in the desired direction, that is, in the direction we want him to travel. What we seldom realize, however, is that under these circumstances we are usually responding to *our own* needs to see the world in certain ways. It is always difficult for us to tolerate and understand actions which are different from the ways in which *we* believe *we* should act. If, however, we can free ourselves from the need to influence and direct others in our own paths, we enable ourselves to listen with understanding, and thereby employ the most potent available agent of change.

One problem the listener faces is that of responding to demands for decisions, judgments, and evaluations. He is constantly called upon to agree or disagree with someone or something. Yet, as he well knows, the question or challenge frequently is a masked expression of feelings or needs which the speaker is far more anxious to communicate than he is to have the surface questions answered. Because he cannot speak these feelings openly, the speaker must disguise them to himself and to others in an acceptable form. To illustrate, let us examine some typical questions and the type of answers that might best elicit the feeling beneath them.

These responses recognize the questions but leave the way open for the employee to say what is really bothering him. They allow the listener to participate in the problem or situation without shouldering all responsibility for decisionmaking or actions. This is a process of thinking *with* people instead of *for* or *about* them.

Passing judgment, whether critical or favorable, makes free expression difficult. Similarly, advice and information are almost always seen as efforts to change a person and thus serve as barriers to his self-expression and the development of a creative relationship. Moreover, advice is seldom taken and information hardly ever utilized. The eager young trainee probably will not become patient just because he is advised that, "The road to success is a long, difficult one, and you must be patient." And it is no more helpful for him to learn that "only one out of a hundred trainees reach top management positions."

| Employee's Question | Listener's Answer |
|---|---|
| Just who is responsible for getting this job done? | Do you feel that you don't have enough authority? |
| Don't you think talent should count more than seniority in promotions? | What do you think are the reasons for your opinion? |
| What does the boss expect us to do about those broken-down machines? | You're tired of working with worn-out equipment, aren't you? |
| Don't you think my performance has improved since the last review? | Sounds as if you feel your work has picked up over these last few months. |

Interestingly, it is a difficult lesson to learn that *positive evaluations* are sometimes as blocking as negative ones. It is almost as destructive to the freedom of a relationship to tell a person that he is good or capable or right, as to tell him otherwise. To evaluate him positively may make it more difficult for him to tell of the faults that distress him or the ways in which he believes he is not competent.

Encouragement also may be seen as an attempt to motivate the speaker in certain directions or hold him off rather than as support. "I'm sure everything will work out O. K." is not a helpful response to the person who is deeply discouraged about a problem.

In other words, most of the techniques and devices common to human relationships are found to be of little use in establishing the type of relationship we are seeking here.

## What to Do

Just what does active listening entail, then? Basically, it requires that we get inside the speaker, that we grasp, from his point of view, just what it is he is communicating to us. More than that, we must convey to the speaker that we are seeing things *from his point of view*. To listen actively, then, means that there are several things we must do.

*Listen for Total Meaning.*    Any message a person tries to get across usually has two components: the content of the message and the *feeling* or attitude underlying this content. Both are important, both give the message *meaning*. It is this total *meaning* of the message that we must try to understand. For example, a secretary comes to her boss and says: "I've finished that report." This message has obvious factual content and perhaps calls upon the boss for another work assignment. Suppose, on the other hand, that the secretary says: "Well! I'm finally finished with your damn report!" The factual content is the same, but the total meaning of the message has changed—and changed in an important way for both supervisor and worker. Here sensitive listening can facilitate the work relationship in this office. If the boss were to respond by simply giving his secretary some letters to type, would the secretary feel that she had gotten her total message across? Would she feel free to talk to her boss about the difficulty of her work? Would she feel better about the job, more anxious to do good work on her next assignment?

Now, on the other hand, suppose the supervisor were to respond, "Glad to get that over with, huh?" or "That was a rough one, wasn't it?" or "Guess you don't want another one like that again," or anything that tells the worker that he heard and understands. It doesn't necessarily mean that her next work assignment need be changed or that he must spend an hour listening to the worker complain about the problems she encountered. He may do a number of things differently in the light of the new information he has from the worker—but not necessarily. It's just that extra sensitivity on the part of the supervisor that can transform an average working climate into a good one.

*Respond to Feelings.* In some instances the content is far less important than the feeling which underlies it. To catch the full flavor or meaning of the message one must respond particularly to the feeling component. If, for instance, our secretary had said, "I'd like to pile up all those carbons and make a bonfire out of them!" responding to content would be obviously absurd. But to respond to her disgust or anger in trying to work with the report recognizes the meaning of this message. There are various shadings of these components in the meaning of any message. Each time the listener must try to remain sensitive to the total meaning the message has to the speaker. What is she trying to tell me? What does this mean to her? How does she see this situation?

*Note All Cues.* Not all communication is verbal.The speaker's words alone don't tell us everything he is communicating. And hence, truly sensitive listening requires that we become aware of several kinds of communication besides verbal. The way in which a speaker hesitates in his speech can tell us much about his feelings. So too can the inflection of his voice. He may stress certain points loudly and clearly, and he may mumble others. We should also note such things as the person's facial expressions, body posture, hand movements, eye movements, and breathing. All of these help to convey his total message.

## What We Communicate by Listening

The first reaction of most people when they consider listening as a possible method for dealing with human beings is that listening cannot be sufficient in itself. Because it is passive, they feel, listening does not communicate anything to the speaker. Actually, nothing could be farther from the truth.

By consistently listening to a speaker you are conveying the idea that: "I'm interested in you as a person, and I think that what you feel is important. I respect your thoughts, and even if I don't agree with them, I know that they are valid for you. I feel sure that you have a contribution to make. I'm not trying to change you or evaluate you. I just want to understand you. I think you're worth listening to, and I want you to know that I'm the kind of person you can talk to."

The subtle but most important aspect of this is that it is the *demonstration* of the message that works. Although it is most difficult to convince someone that you respect him by *telling* him so, you are much more likely to get this message across by really *behaving* that way—by actually *having* and *demonstrating* respect for this person. Listening does this most effectively.

Like other behavior, listening behavior is contagious. This has implications for all communications problems, whether between two people, or within a large organization. To insure good communication between associates up and down the line, one must first take the responsibility for setting a pattern of listening. Just as one learns that anger is usually met with anger, argument with argument, and deception with deception, one can learn that listening can be met with listening. Every person who feels responsibility in a situation can set the tone of the interaction, and the important lesson in this is that any behavior exhibited by one person will eventually be responded to with similar behavior in the other person.

It is far more difficult to stimulate constructive behavior in another person but far more valuable. Listening is one of these constructive behaviors, but if one's attitude is to "wait out" the speaker rather than really listen to him, it will fail. The one who consistently listens with understanding, however, is the one who eventually is most likely to be listened to. If you really want to be heard and understood by another, you can develop him as a potential listener, ready for new ideas, provided you can first develop yourself in these ways and sincerely listen with understanding and respect.

## Testing for Understanding

Because understanding another person is actually far more difficult than it at first seems, it is important to test constantly your ability to see the world in the way the speaker sees it. You can do this by reflecting in your own words what the speaker seems to mean by his words and actions. His response to this will tell you whether or not he feels understood. A good rule of thumb is to assume that one never really understands until he can communicate this understanding to the other's satisfaction.

Here is an experiment to test your skill in listening. The next time you become involved in a lively or controversial discussion with another person, stop for a moment and suggest that you adopt this ground rule for continued discussion. Before either participant in the discussion can make a point or express an opinion of his own, he must first restate aloud the previous point or position of the other person. This restatement must be in his own words (merely parroting the words of another does not prove that one has understood, but only that he has heard the words). The restatement must be accurate enough to satisfy the speaker before the listener can be allowed to speak for himself.

You might find this procedure useful in a meeting where feelings run high and people express themselves on topics of emotional concern to the group. Before another member of the group expresses his own feelings and thought, he must rephrase the *meaning* expressed by the previous speaker to that person's satisfaction. All the members in the group should be alert to the changes in the emotional climate and the quality of the discussion when this approach is used.

## PROBLEMS IN ACTIVE LISTENING

Active listening is not an easy skill to acquire, it demands practice. Perhaps more important, it may require changes in our own basic attitudes. These changes come slowly and sometimes with considerable difficulty. Let us look at some of the major problems in active listening and what can be done to overcome them.

## The Personal Risk

To be effective in active listening, one must have a sincere interest in the speaker. We all live in glass houses as far as our attitudes are concerned. They always show through. And if we are only making a pretense of interest in the speaker, he will quickly pick this up, either consciously or subconsciously. And once he does, he will no longer express himself freely.

Active listening carries a strong element of personal risk. If we manage to accomplish what we are describing here—to sense the feelings of another person, to understand the meaning his experiences have for him, to see the world as he sees it we risk being changed ourselves. For example, if we permit ourselves to listen our way into the life of a person we do not know or approve of—to get the meaning that life has for him we risk coming to see the world as he sees it. We are threatened when we give up, even momentarily, what we believe and start thinking in someone else's terms. It takes a great deal of inner security and courage to be able to risk one's self in understanding another.

For the manager, the courage to take another's point of view generally means that he must see *himself* through another's eyes—he must be able to see himself as others see him. To do this may sometimes be unpleasant, but it is far more *difficult* than unpleasant. We are so accustomed to viewing ourselves in certain ways—to seeing and hearing only what we want to see and hear—that it is extremely difficult for a person to free himself from the need to see things his way.

Developing an attitude of sincere interest in the speaker is thus no easy task. It can be developed only by being willing to risk seeing the world from the speaker's point of view. If we have a number of such experiences, however, they will shape an attitude which will allow us to be truly genuine in our interest in the speaker.

## Hostile Expressions

The listener will often hear negative, hostile expressions directed at himself. Such expressions are always hard to listen to. No one likes to hear hostile words or experience hostility which is directed against them. And it is not easy to get to the point where one is strong enough to permit these attacks without finding it necessary to defend himself or retaliate.

Because we all fear that people will crumble under the attack of genuine negative feelings, we tend to perpetuate an attitude of pseudo-peace. It is as if we cannot tolerate conflict at all for fear of the damage it could do to us, to the situation, to the others involved. But of course the real damage is done by the denial and suppression of negative feelings.

## Out-of-Place Expressions

Expressions dealing with behavior that is not usually acceptable in our society also pose problems for the listener. These out-of-place expressions can take the extreme forms that psychotherapists hear—such as homicidal fantasies or expressions of sexual perversity. The listener often blocks out such expressions because of their obvious threatening quality. At less extreme levels, we all find unnatural or inappropriate behavior difficult to handle. Behavior that brings on a problem situation may be anything from telling an "off-color" story in mixed company to seeing a man cry.

In any face-to-face situation, we will find instances of this type which will momentarily, if not permanently, block any communication. In any organization, expressions of weakness or incompetency will generally be regarded as unacceptable and therefore will block good two-way communication. For example, it is difficult to listen to a manager tell of his feelings of failure in being able to "take charge" of a situation in his department because *all* administrators are supposed to be able to "take charge."

## Accepting Positive Feelings

It is both interesting and perplexing to note that negative or hostile feelings or expressions are much easier to deal with in any face-to-face relationship than are positive feelings. This is especially true for the manager because the culture expects him to be independent, bold, clever, and aggressive and manifest no feelings of warmth, gentleness, and intimacy. He therefore comes to regard these feelings as soft and inappropriate. But no matter how they are regarded, they remain a human need. The denial of these feelings in himself and his associates does not get the manager out of a problem of dealing with them. The feelings simply become veiled and confused. If recognized they would work for the total effort; unrecognized, they work against it.

## Emotional Danger Signals

The listener's own emotions are sometimes a barrier to active listening. When emotions are at their height, when listening is most necessary, it is most difficult to set aside one's own concerns and be understanding. Our emotions are often our own worst enemies when we try to become listeners. The more involved and invested we are in a particular situation or problem, the less we are likely to be willing or able to listen to the feelings and attitudes of others. That is, the more we find it necessary to respond to our own needs, the less we are able to respond to the needs of another. Let us look at some of the main danger signals that warn us that our emotions may be interfering with our listening.

*Defensiveness.* The points about which one is most vocal and dogmatic, the points which one is most anxious to impose on others—these are always the points one is trying to talk oneself into believing. So one danger signal becomes apparent when you find yourself stressing a point or trying to convince another. It is at these times that you are likely to be less secure and consequently less able to listen.

*Resentment of Opposition.* It is always easier to listen to an idea which is similar to one of your own than to an opposing view. Sometimes, in order to clear the air, it is helpful to pause for a moment when you feel your ideas and position being challenged, reflect on the situation, and express your concern to the speaker.

*Clash of Personalities.* Here again, our experience has consistently shown us that the genuine expression of feelings on the part of the listener will be more helpful in developing a sound relationship than the suppression of them. This is so whether the feelings be resentment, hostility, threat, or admiration. A basically honest relationship, whatever the nature of it, is the most productive of all. The other party becomes secure when he learns that the listener can express his feelings honestly and openly to him. We should keep this in mind when we begin to fear a clash of personalities in the listening relationship. Otherwise, fear of our own emotions will choke off full expression of feelings.

## Listening to Ourselves

To listen to oneself is a prerequisite to listening to others. And it is often an effective means of dealing with the problems we have outlined above. When we are most aroused, excited, and demanding, we are least able to understand our own feelings and attitudes. Yet, in dealing with the problems of others, it becomes most important to be sure of one's own position, values, and needs.

The ability to recognize and understand the meaning which a particular episode has for you, with all the feelings which it stimulates in you, and the ability to express this meaning when you find it getting in the way of active listening, will clear the air and enable you once again to be free to listen. That is, if some person or situation touches off feelings within you which tend to block your attempts to listen with understanding, begin listening to yourself. It is much more helpful in developing effective relationships to avoid suppressing these feelings. Speak them out as clearly as you can, and try to enlist the other person as a listener to your feelings. A person's listening ability is limited by his ability to listen to himself.

# ACTIVE LISTENING AND ORGANIZATION GOALS

"How can listening improve productivity?"

"We're in business, and it is a rugged, fast, competitive affair. How are we going to find time to counsel our employees?"

"We have to concern ourselves with organizational problems first."

"We can't afford to spend all day listening when there is work to do."

"What's morale got to do with service to the public?"

"Sometimes we have to sacrifice an individual for the good of the rest of the people in the organization."

Those of us who are trying to advance the listening approach in organizations hear these comments frequently. And because they are so honest and legitimate, they pose a real problem. Unfortunately, the answers are not so clearcut as the questions.

## Individual Importance

One answer is based on an assumption that is central to the listening approach. That assumption is: the kind of behavior which helps the individual will eventually be the best thing that could be done for the work group. Or saying it another way: the things that are best for the individual are best for the organization. This is a conviction of ours, based on our experience in psychology and education. The research evidence from organizations is still coming in. We find that putting the group first, at the expense of the individual, besides being an uncomfortable individual experience, does *not* unify the group. In fact, it tends to make the group less a group. The members become anxious and suspicious.

We are not at all sure in just what ways the group does benefit from a concern demonstrated for an individual, but we have several strong leads. One is that the group feels more secure when an individual member is being listened to and provided for with concern and sensitivity. And we assume that a secure group will ultimately be a better group. When each individual feels that he need not fear exposing himself to the group, he is likely to contribute more freely and spontaneously. When the leader of a group responds to the individual, puts the individual first, the other members of the group will follow suit, and the group comes to act as a unit in recognizing and responding to the needs of a particular member. This positive, constructive action seems to be a much more satisfying experience for a group than the experience of dispensing with a member.

## Listening and Productivity

As to whether or not listening or any other activity designed to better human relations in an organization actually makes the organization more productive—whether morale has a definite relationship to performance is not known for sure. There are some who frankly hold that there is no relationship to be expected between morale and productivity—that productivity often depends upon the social misfit, the eccentric, or the isolate. And there are some who simply choose to work in a climate of cooperation and harmony, in a high-morale group, quite aside from the question of achievement or productivity.

A report from the survey Research Center at the University of Michigan on research conducted at the Prudential Life Insurance Company lists seven findings related to production and morale. First-line supervisors in high-production work groups were found to differ from those in low-production groups in that they:

1. Are under less close supervision from their own supervisors.
2. Place less direct emphasis upon production as the goal.

3. Encourage employee participation in the making of decisions.
4. Are more employee-centered.
5. Spend more of their time in supervision and less in straight production work.
6. Have a greater feeling of confidence in their supervisory roles.
7. Feel that they know where they stand with the company.

After mentioning that other dimensions of morale, such as identification with the company, intrinsic job satisfaction, and satisfaction with job status, were not found significantly related to productivity, the report goes on to suggest the following psychological interpretation:

> People are more effectively motivated when they are given some degree of freedom in the way in which they do their work when every action is prescribed in advance. They do better when some degree of decision-making about their jobs is possible than when all decisions are made for them. They respond more adequately when they are treated as personalities than as cogs in a machine. In short if the ego motivation of self-determination, of self-expression, of a sense of personal worth can be tapped, the individual can be more effectively energized. The use of external sanctions, or pressuring for production may work to some degree, but not to the extent that the more internalized motives do. When the individual comes to identify himself with his job and with the work of his group, human resources are much more fully utilized in the production process.

The survey Research Center has also conducted studies among workers in other industries. In discussing the results of these studies, Robert L. Kahn writes:

> In the studies of clerical workers, railroad workers, and workers in heavy industry, the supervisors with the better production records gave a larger proportion of their time to supervisory functions, especially to the interpersonal aspects of their jobs. The supervisors of the lower-producing sections were more likely to spend their time in tasks which the men themselves were performing, or in the paper-work aspects of their jobs.

## Maximum Creativeness

There may never be enough research evidence to satisfy everyone on this question. But speaking from an organizational point of view, in terms of the problem of developing resources for productivity, the maximum creativeness and productive effort of the human beings in the organization are the richest untapped source of power available. The difference between the maximum productive capacity of people and that output which the organization is now realizing is immense. We simply suggest that this maximum capacity might be closer to realization if we sought to release the motivation that already exists within people rather than try to stimulate them externally.

This releasing of the individual is made possible first of all by listening, with respect and understanding. Listening is a beginning toward making the individual feel himself worthy of making contributions, and this could result in a very dynamic and productive organization. Profit making organizations are never too rugged or too busy to take time to procure the most efficient technological advances or to develop rich sources of raw materials. But technology and materials are but paltry resources in comparison with the resources that are already within the people in the organization.

G. L. Clements, of Jewel Tea Co., Inc., in talking about the collaborative approach to management says:

> We feel that this type of approach recognizes that there is a secret ballot going on at all times among the people in any business. They vote for or against their supervisors. A favorable vote for the supervisor shows up in the cooperation, teamwork, understanding, and production of the group. To win this secret ballot, each supervisor must share the problems of his group and work for them.

The decision to spend time listening to employees is a decision each supervisor or manager has to make for himself. Managers increasingly must deal with people and their relationships rather than turning out goods and services. The minute we take a man from work and make him a supervisor he is removed from the basic production of goods or services and now must begin relating to men and women instead of nuts and bolts. People are different from things and our supervisor is called upon for a different line of skills completely. These new tasks call for a special kind of person. The development of the supervisor as a listener is a first step in becoming this special person.

# COMMUNICATION: THE USE OF TIME, SPACE, AND THINGS[1]

*Anthony G. Athos*

It was amazing to me to discover how many ways we have of talking about time. We have time, keep time, buy time, and save time; we mark it, spend it, sell it, and waste it; we kill time, pass time, give time, take time, and make time. With so many ways of dealing with time in the English language, we must be as sensitive to it as Eskimos are to snow, for which they have many words and no small respect.

Our American[2] concepts of time are that it is continuous, irreversible, and one-dimensional. Recent movies that shuffle the sequence of events so that they do not proceed in the same order as they "do" in "real" time, including flash aheads as well as the old standard flashbacks, are effective in disturbing us into powerful experiencing precisely because they deny our long-standing assumptions about time. We often seem to experience tomorrow as spatially in front of us and yesterday as almost literally behind us. With some effort we might be able to think of today as the space we were just in and the space we will very soon be in as we walk in a straight line. "Now" is even harder for many Americans, and it seems we experience it as the space filled by our bodies.

*Source*: Reprinted by permission of the author and publisher from A. G. Athos and J. Gabarro, *Interpersonal Behavior* (Englewood Cliffs, N.J.: Prentice-Hall, Inc., 1978).

[1]Some of the ideas in this chapter were developed in a lecture given by Anthony G. Athos which was first published in *Behavior in Organizations: A Multidimensional View*, by A. G. Athos and R. E. Coffey, Prentice-Hall, Englewood Cliffs, N.J., 1968. The author is greatly indebted to the stimulation of Edward T. Hall's *The Silent Language* (Premier Paperback, 1961) and *The Hidden Dimension* (Doubleday, 1966). Hall's work is much recommended to those who find that this brief discursive introduction stimulates further interest in a different and more systematic approach.

[2]"United States" and "America" refer here to the whole country, ignoring the considerable differences in the "cultures" of Hawaii, Alaska, Texas, and other parts of the whole.

Perhaps that is why such interesting variations exist in different parts of the United States in orientations toward time. My personal experience in New England leads me to see people here as more oriented toward the past and the future than toward the present. Southern Californians seem more present- and future-oriented, with some important emphasis upon now (and thus greater familiarity with their bodies). The Latin Americans I know seem more past- and future-oriented. My point here is that we differ in our experiencing of time (as contrasted with our ways of thinking about it), focusing upon different aspects of it. Yet there is a tendency for us to assume that it is linear "in" space: i.e., as a "straight line" from the past through the present into the future.

Of course, those who live more in touch with nature, say, farmers or resort operators, might also see time as cyclical. The earth makes its daily round of the sun; the seasons, like circles, "each mark to the instant their ordained end" and cycle again. And many of us, on an island vacation, for example, "unwind" like a corkscrew from what we left behind, slowly lose our concerns for tomorrow, and relax into letting days happen so that each merges with the one before and into the one after as an experienced, continuous present. The loosening delight of such vacations is in contrast with our more usual patterns, wherein our concerns about time can easily become compulsive.

## Accuracy

I can recall being in Athens, Greece, and asking my Greek cousin "How long does it take to walk from here to the library?" I was staying with her family and I wanted to spend the afternoon at the library and leave there in time to get back home for a 6 P.M. appointment with an American friend. She said, "Not long." I replied with some irritation "No. I need to know, so I can stay there as long as possible. How long does it take?" She shrugged and said "It's a short walk." I said with a frown "Come on. I want to know exactly. How long?" With great exasperation she finally dismissed me with "A cigarette!" Well, I felt a bit defeated, if a little amused, for to her a 10- or even 20-minute error in estimate would have been simply irrelevant. Any greater precision would confine her. Yet we want to know *exactly*. Our concern for accuracy is enormous. Where else but in the Western industrialized world would watches get advertised as not being off more than a few seconds a month? Where else would people literally have timepieces strapped to their bodies so they can be sure they "keep on time"? Because of our concern for accuracy, the way we use time in our culture "talks" to other people.

Many men can remember the first time they ever drove to pick up someone for a date. It's not surprising that many of us got there a bit early and drove around the block a while so as not to communicate our anxiety or eagerness too openly. To arrive at 7:00 for a 7:30 date is to "tell" the other about these feelings and may result in "seeming" naive, unless the boy can explain it away. To arrive at 8:00 for a 7:30 date "says" you feel somewhat indifferent, and a decent explanation is required if the evening is to make any sense at all. Similarly, it is not uncommon for professors to assume that a student who is frequently late for class "doesn't care." Most get angry as a result. Students tend to assume that professors who are late to class also don't care very much. Time thus often "tells" caring, whether accurately or not.

We also use time to tell how we feel and see others in terms of relative status and power. If the President of the United States called you to Washington to talk with him next Tuesday at 3 P.M., it is unlikely that you would arrange your flight to arrive at National Airport at 2 P.M. You would most likely want very much to be sure you were at the White House no later than 3 P.M., and might very well get to Washington on Monday to be certain nothing would go wrong. Because of the great difference between the status of the President and the rest of us, we would likely feel that any inconvenience in waiting ought to be ours.

The same can be true in companies. If the president of a large organization calls a young salesman to his office for a 3 P.M. meeting, the chances are awfully good that the salesman will arrive before 3 P.M., even if he walks around the block for an hour, so as not to arrive "too early."

Imagine two men who are executives in the same large company, whose respective status is virtually the same but who are very competitive in many ways. One calls the other on the phone, and asks him to come to his office for a meeting at 1 P.M. that afternoon. (Notice that one is initiating, which generally indicates higher status; that he is specifying the place and the time, which diminishes the other's influence on those decisions; and that the "invitation" comes only a few hours before the intended meeting, which may imply that the other has nothing more important to do.) The chances are good that the second man will not arrive before or even at 1 P.M. for the meeting, unless his compulsiveness about time in general is so great that it overcomes his feelings about being "put down" (in which case he has lost a round in the competition and may be searching for a "victory" during the meeting). He might well arrive late, perhaps 5 minutes, which is enough to irritate but not openly insult, and then offer either no apology or only a very casual one. The way he handles time in this setting will communicate to the first executive, and so he may plan his response as carefully as a choreographer plans a ballet. Yet little of the process may be fully conscious for him. As Hall says in the title of his book, these are often truly silent languages for many of us.

The longer people are kept waiting, the worse they feel. If the young salesman who was invited to his company president's office for a 3 P.M. meeting arrives at a "respectful" 2:50 and is told by the secretary to have a seat, he remains relatively comfortable until 3 P.M. If the secretary waits until 3:10 to phone the president and remind him the salesman is there, she may communicate (i.e., the salesman may "hear") that she thinks a 10-minute wait is about all she can handle without feeling that the salesman will be feeling the first pangs of being unwanted. If she hangs up the phone and says "He'll be right with you" and the clock continues to tick until 3:25, she might feel impelled to say something about how busy the president is today (i.e., "Don't feel bad. It's nothing personal."). By 3:45 the salesman is likely to be somewhat angry, since he is likely to assume that the president doesn't really care about seeing him. If the president comes out of his office (note this use of space) to get the salesman and apologizes for being late and explains why (especially if the explanation includes information about "the top" that the salesman is not usually aware of), the salesman may "forgive" his boss ("That's all right. I don't mind at all. Your time is more important than mine.") and all can go well. If the president buzzes his secretary and tells her to send the salesmen in, and then proceeds directly to the business at hand, the salesman is likely to be torn between the anger he feels and the fear of expressing it, which may affect their meeting without either knowing why. In short, then, the longer a person is kept waiting, the more "social stroking" is required to smooth ruffled feathers. Awareness of the process can reduce its power to discomfort when you are on the receiving end, and can increase your skills at helping others to realize when you were not deliberately, with intent, trying to "put them down." Being "thoughtless" and thus "hurting other's feelings" is all too often just what we call it: thoughtless. Thinking about our uses of time can, after an awkward self-consciousness, lead to an increase in intuitive, out-of-awareness skill in dealing with self and others.

Using time to manipulate or control others is common, even if we who do so are unaware of it. I once hired a gardener on a monthly contract to care for my yard. When we were discussing the arrangements, I felt somewhat uncertain that he would do all I wanted done or do it to my satisfaction. My feelings of mistrust were expressed by focusing upon time. I wanted to know precisely what day of the week he would come and how many hours he would stay. He seemed to understand and said "Thursday. Four hours."

Well, he actually did come on Thursday once in a while, but he also came on every other day of the week except Sunday and Monday. He never to my knowledge stayed four hours even when I happened to be home. I was sure I was being "taken" until it occurred to me the yard had never looked so good and everything really needing to be done was done.

The gardener apparently thought in terms of planting and cutting and fertilizing cycles. He felt his duty was to the yard, not to me. He sent me bills about every three or four months and then he often had to ask me what I owed him. He trusted me completely to pay him what he deserved. He worked in terms of seasons of the year, and I was trying to pin him down to an hourly basis. My attempt to replace my mistrust with the brittle satisfaction of controlling another person, in time, would eventually have led him to quit or me to fire him. I was lucky to see what was happening, and I left him alone. We got along fine.

Time is viewed as both precious and personal, and when we allow someone to structure our time, it is usually in deference to his or her greater status or power. This is especially true when we would rather be doing something else, as is the case with some employees in many organizations who "put in their time" from nine to five. Many people today are looking for an opportunity to "do their own thing" (when they can figure out what that is) and their reluctance to be controlled vis-à-vis a dimension as personal as time is reflected in such questions as "How much of your time is yours?", "Did you take time to smell the flowers?", and "Do you own your life?" "Private time" (such as weekends) is often "intruded upon" by work, with the notable exception of the Pacific Northwest, where it is generally regarded more strongly as "non-work" time.

The use of time to define relationships can also be seen in most marriages. How many Americans do you know who work through the dinner hour or into the night without calling their spouses? By contrast, people in other cultures often handle the time of their arrival home differently. In Greece I found that dinner was served at my uncle's house whenever he came home—and that might be anywhere from 6 to 9 P.M. This variation in the use of time, as well as my dealing with the gardener, introduces still another major notion about time.

## Scarcity

We seem to see time as a limited resource for each person, so we think that what they choose to do with what time they have is a signal about how they feel about us. You are already experienced with the application of this notion. We all have feelings about how frequently we "ought" to see certain persons in order to express a "suitable" amount of affection. Take visits home to see your parents. Some students go home every weekend, some only on vacations, some only on holidays, some every few years, and some never. But almost all parents are pleased, assuming they like their children, to find their offspring choose to visit them rather than do something else. There is a mutual exclusivity operating here. If you go home to see your parents, they know you did so at the expense of some other option. If your other options were attractive, they hear you care enough about your relationship with them to forego some other pleasure. Simply choosing to "spend your time" with them is thus a gift of sorts and a signal about your sentiments. The same is true with other people, of course, especially subordinates in an organization.

Even when the choice of how or with whom we spend our time is not really our own, others may "hear" a communication about our feelings. If you and two other persons begin to meet after class once a week for a beer and then you take a part-time job that forces you to go directly from class to work, your absence in the pub will be "understood" as out of your control (given the choice you made to work). But the loss of interaction must be made up elsewhere or your friends will probably feel that you "withdrew."

Some people are really tough on this one. You may have three final exams to study for and a broken leg, and like most professors some friends will insist you come to the appointed meeting and bring your leg with you. And yet there need be no unreasonable demands involved for misunderstandings to occur. Perfectly reasonable people can think we don't care for them because we do something else rather than see them. They can misjudge the importance to us of the something else and be ignorant of the conditions that made it important. A supervisor who spends more time per day with one subordinate because the tasks being done temporarily require closer supervision may communicate to other subordinates, especially if time with them is temporarily reduced, that the supervisor "cares" more about what the one subordinate is doing, and perhaps will come to care more about that person than them. There may be more than a little truth in this. Sociologists have noted that it is not uncommon for positive sentiment to increase as the frequency of interaction increases, albeit with several important exceptions (including the problem of formal authority).

We sometimes experience with new friends an increase in frequency of interaction that accelerates beyond a point of equilibrium, given the importance the relationship comes to have for one or both persons. Then, if one person begins to withdraw a bit in order to adjust the frequency of contact to the kind and amount of sentiment, the other person—especially if she/he is desirous of more frequent interaction—tends to feel hurt. This hurt can lead them to react by further reducing or demanding increases in the frequency of contact, and until someone says openly what they are feeling, the cycle can proceed to the destruction of the relationship.

The scarcity of time for a person at a given moment is also his/her "cost" of time. When two people "spend" time together in any activity, communication will be strained and difficult unless the time being spent has approximately the same value for each participant. This is obvious when we by chance meet a friend in the street or hallway; if one begins to chat and the other is in a hurry, the encounter is bound to be a little awkward even if the person "short of time" explains why.

Our notion that time is scarce fits most Americans' feelings that things should be ordered, and that earlier is better than later. First born, first position, number two man, fourteenth in a class of 655, top 10 percent all assume meaning because of their position.

Early promotions in business or an advanced degree in two years instead of three are seen as praiseworthy, even if some run right by what they are trying to catch. These notions of time sequence are not inborn; they are culturally conditioned. Edward Hall reports that it takes the average child a little more than twelve years to master time and the concepts of order. I am constantly reminded of this by my young daughter, who recently asked: "But how long away is Friday?"

The point of this is, again, that time is seen as scarce, and thus whom you choose to "give your time to" is a way of measuring your sentiments. Just being more aware of this can help you recognize the usefulness of simply saying, out loud, what the meaning of your choice is for you. And, of course, such awareness also helps prevent you from assuming (without awareness of the assumption) the meanings of other persons without checking their intent.

## Repetition

Finally, time has meaning for us in terms of repetition of activities. Some of our personal rhythms are so intimate and familiar to us that we are unaware of them. Most of us eat three meals a day, for example, not two, not five. The culture assumes that lunch is at noon for the most part, and this was probably defined originally in response to what people experienced in terms of hunger. But the convention also becomes a structure to which we adapt and with which we become familiar. When we experience an interruption of our pattern, we often become irritated. I can recall, for example, that I found it difficult to adjust to a change in schedule on my first teaching job. For several years as a doctoral candidate, I had had coffee at 10 o'clock with a group of congenial colleagues. The coffee hour became one of the central social functions of my day, in addition to a means of getting some caffeine into my reluctantly awakening body. When I began teaching I had a 9 o'clock and a 10 o'clock class three days a week, and I was troubled by the 10 o'clock class and adjusted by bringing a cup of coffee into class with me. The pattern was so well developed and so valued within me that I was willing to "break a norm" (and, in fact, a rule) against food in the classrooms in order to have my 10 o'clock coffee. It sounds like a small matter, and in one sense it is, but it makes my point even if it is a trivial example. There are daily cycles we are used to, and while there are many we share, there are others relatively unique to each of us. The closer to the body any repetitions of activity come, the more important they are to us.

Take seasons of the year, for example. In areas that have weather rather than climate, say, New England rather than southern California, the use of time varies from season to season as activities change. People in Boston not only put away their silver and use their stainless steel in August, but they give different kinds of parties with different time rules than they do in winter. In general, the rules are relaxed, more variety is "allowed," and time is less carefully measured for meaning.

Our rhythms are also influenced by our feasts and holidays and rituals. Christmas, Easter, Rosh Hashonah, Chanukah, Father's Day, Thanksgiving, Memorial Day, and the like, all have their "time" in the year. It has been hypothesized that Christ was really born in August, and the December celebration of his birth came about because the people in northern Europe had long had a pagan winter festival which they were used to. In any event, we are accustomed to certain activities and feelings in connection with each "special day."

Take Christmas, for example. Most business people know there will be less work done just prior to and after Christmas than is usual. People experience a need for closeness, for family, for ritual, for the nostalgia of past Christmases, for gift giving and midnight services. They eat more and drink more and even get fond of their old Aunt Minny. It is a time set aside for warmth, affection, children, family, friends, and ritual.

The Greeks, however, celebrate their Easter much as we do our Christmas, and mark their Christmas almost as casually as we do our Easter. If you were to spend Christmas in Athens, you would likely sense something was missing. If you were there on Easter, you would get a "bonus." If you were in the United States working on a job that peaked in volume between December 20 and January 3, say in a post office, and you had to work long hours, the chances are you would feel quite resentful. The rhythms of our days, our weeks, our months, our years are all deeply familiar to us even if we are unaware of them. Any serious disruption of any of them is felt as deprivation. Just being aware of this can help you in many ways—planning changes, for example. Can you see why major changes in work design or location or personnel are particularly resented during the Christmas holidays?

Then, for students (and nowadays nearly everyone in the country spends at least twelve years as one, and more are spending sixteen or even eighteen), certain rhythms that matter are established. Where else in our culture do people get promoted every year for anything better than dreadful work? Where else can people choose their bosses (professors) so as to avoid certain ones, and where else can they drop one of them with no penalty after several weeks work? If you look at the assumptions students naturally take with them to work from school, you can see why the yearly immigration of graduates into business is such a trauma for both students and companies. Subculture shock is what it is.

A subsummary may help here. Basically, all I am saying is that time is important to us in many ways, that *when* you do what you do says things to others about what you feel, and that the "rules" about time vary from setting to setting. If you will just watch for one day what is going on in your life vis-à-vis time, I think you will see some interesting things. How you and others use time to communicate would make a terrific din if "talking" with time made noise.

# SPACE

Space is a language just as expressive as time. Indeed, as hinted above, it is hard to separate it from the language of time, but it is useful to try.

## More Is Better Than Less

The chances are good that you have seen various business organizations. The chances are even better that you found the size of offices related to the status of people there. It is rare indeed to find a company president occupying a smaller office than his subordinates, and it is not uncommon to find the top person ensconced in a suite of rooms. One of the ways we "tell" about the importance of people is by the amount of space we assign to them. Space, like time, is a scarce and limited resource.

I recall a distinguished senior professor returning to school after a long and nearly fatal illness. He was being moved from his old office to a new one in an air-conditioned new building, largely because the dean of his school believed the air conditioning would be of help to him. The professor may have thought he "heard" something else, for as I passed his office one day I found him on his hands and knees measuring his new office with a 12-inch ruler. It was a good deal smaller than his prior office, and from how he behaved later I think he was "learning" that his illness had diminished his importance to the school, so that he was reduced to a small office. It would be amusing if it were not so painful.

Another time I was being toured through a new and beautiful office building of a large corporation. The president's office was handsome indeed, but when I was taken next door to the executive vice president's office, I realized that the VP had a larger and recognizably more stunning space in which to work. I later asked my guide, an officer of the company, if the president and executive vice president had been vying for power. He looked surprised and defensively asked "Why do you ask?" I told him what I saw in the use of space. He laughed and said "Another theory bites the dust! The VP's office is better because he has charge of sales in this district and his office is our best example of what we can do for customers."

A year later the VP and president came into open conflict in seeking the support of the board of directors, and the VP left the organization. Of course, the offices were not "the" cause. But they were a signal that something was off. There are few organizations that can accept incongruence in the use of space when it communicates so clearly to hundreds of employees. In the company mentioned, I heard later, a frequent question in the executive ranks prior to the VP's departure was: "Who is running this place?"

Of course, we observe this in everyday life. We want larger houses on more land. We want lots with a view. (Although I notice few people with a picture window looking out at the view. What we want, I suspect, is mostly the illusion of an enlargement of our space.) Yet other people are more comfortable in smaller spaces. Latin people love to be awed by cathedrals and vistas in parks, but they seem to enjoy being "hugged" by smaller rooms at home and at work. The smaller space apparently is associated with warmth and touch and intimacy, while larger spaces are associated with status and power and importance. Perhaps this is why entering a huge office intimidates many of us. We almost physically inflate the person who occupies it. In any event there is a strong tendency in organizational subcultures to relate the amount of space assigned to individuals to their formal status or organizational height. Check this out around school or in any business. When the pattern does not hold, something interesting may be going on.

# Private Is Better Than Public

As a doctoral candidate I was first given a desk in a large room with many other desks, then was "upgraded" to a cubicle with 6-foot walls and an open top, then to a private office. It was minuscule, but I could close it and be alone or private within it. When I began working as a professor, I shared an office with two others, then I shared it with one other, and now once again I have my own private office, roughly twice as big as my last one. Sequence and size are what matter here. It is "better" to have your own space than to share it, and it is "better" if it can be closed off for privacy than if it is open to the sight or hearing of others. And each "advantage" was distributed by rank, and by seniority within rank.

We use much the same thinking about country clubs or pools or university clubs. By excluding some others, on whatever criteria, we make it feel more private to us. And we apparently like that. The very process of exclusion marks the boundaries of our space both physically and socially, and, of course, psychologically. When we say that a person is "closed," we mean that we are excluded from him/her and vice versa. Thus, the process of defining the extent to which our various spaces are private is complex. As we set our boundaries we also exclude. And we need our own space, as we also at times need to be "open." Yet in organizations, it is clearly the rule that private offices are better than public ones. To go from a large but public office to a smaller but private one is a mixed blessing, but often the balance is favorable. For we are not like Miss Garbo who wants to be alone, but we do want to be able to be alone or private when we wish.

A powerful illustration of the value we place on privacy took place in the 1920s. A coal company in West Virginia owned the houses in which its miners lived. When the miners struck, the company took the doors off the houses. It is not hard to imagine the wrath of the miners. Another example is the automobile company that took the doors off the men's room stalls in the 1950s to discourage workers for long toilet breaks. The response in this instance was also very strong, and understandably so. When a space is designed for activity that is close to our body, we value its privacy all the more. Our free-flowing modern houses almost always have doors on at least two rooms, the bedroom and the bathroom. Perhaps that infamous "key to the executive men's room" is of more utility than arbitrary status.

Given the importance we attach to privacy, the way we use the space we have "talks" to others. If we have a private office and shut its door to speak with someone, we announce a message to that person and to those outside. We are saying "This conversation is important and not to be overheard or casually interrupted." Neither the person nor those outside know whether the news is good or bad, but they do know that you care about it and they may make unwarranted assumptions. For we close off our space for more private or personal behavior. Whether it is angry or loving, we intend to focus importantly.

# Higher Is Better Than Lower

A few years ago I watched my three-year-old daughter playing "I'm the king of the castle" with friends. They laughingly fought each other for position at the top of a small steep hill. Each wanted to be on top, to be higher up than the others in this instance, quite literally, in space. When they grow up, I fell to musing, they'll jockey for height with less laughter and more discomfort.

Perhaps our desire to be higher rather than lower is inherited from our primitive ancestors or perhaps it comes from such childlike games, or rather from the important business of being little for so long, and thus less powerful than we might wish. In any event, houses higher on the hill, from Hong Kong to Corning, are "better" (and usually more expensive) than those below. The view is often cited as the reason, but I doubt it. It's more likely a residue of our childhood that probably reaches back in evolution far beyond the Greeks, who built the Acropolis on a sharp-rising rock for protection as much as grandeur. Much as dogs still circle about before they lie to sleep (a still visible link to their wild forebears, who circled to crush tall grass into a kind of nest), we seek height for reasons in large part lost to us.

We move up in organizations, or "climb the ladder." We go up to the head office and down to the shop. We call the wealthiest people the upper classes and the poorest the lower classes. Much of our imagery for what we value is in terms of up and down. People from Boston go "down" to Maine, although it is north of Boston. Allegedly this is because early travelers were referring to tides, but it also fits the notion of some Bostonians that Boston is the apex from which one can only go down.

On a more concrete level, the ground-floor walk-in legal aid centers that have opened their doors in deprived neighborhoods are less frightening to prospective clients partly because of their ground-level location. Here again space speaks. To be higher than you is to be better than you.

## Near Is Better Than Far

Really, this one can be just the reverse of what it says. It depends upon whether sentiments are positive or negative. Near is better if the sentiments are positive. Far is better if the sentiments are negative.

In a business organization, it is not uncommon for the offices near the boss to be more highly valued than those farther away. If the chief executive officer is on the third floor, the others on that floor are also assumed to be privileged. They are closer to the top person and thus have more opportunities for informal interaction, as well as the formal designation of spatial assignment near the boss's space.

The same principle holds at formal dinner parties, where nearness to the host is valued. The farther down the table one is placed, the lower one's status at the dinner. In branch organizations that cover large territories a common problem is that each branch develops internal loyalties greater than the loyalty to the head office. The distance from the center of the organization impedes communication.

Thus when the sentiments are positive, being near is better than being far away. As I mentioned, the reverse can also be true. People prefer to increase distance when their sentiments are negative.

## In Is Better Than Out

We seem to assume that people who work inside are better than those who work outside, perhaps because of the respective associations with mental and manual work. Baseball teams prefer to be in their own field, their most familiar space. Often when we are uneasy or anxious we move to our own space. In it we feel more secure.

The basic difference between in-out and near-far is that the former works from a specific point while the latter is a matter of degree. But they are closely related. For example, a few years ago a wedding was to take place in the side chapel off the main seating area of a church. The number of guests exceeded the number of seats in the chapel. So decisions needed to be made about who sat in the chapel and who sat outside it. There were thus created two "classes" of guests: those sitting inside and those sitting outside, yet within each class there was a sliding scale at work. How close to the front of your class were you seated? I can tell you those who sat at the back of the school class felt like relative "outsiders." Certainly, they were not among the "in" group.

Naturally these five dimensions of space are related. An office that is smaller but private and near an important executive may be highly desirable in spite of its size. When you consider the impact of space, you must look at the possible influence of each of the five dimensions and how they can balance each other in specific settings, as well as how they influence the use of time as a language.

# Interpersonal Space

On a more personal level we have another silent language related to space. We have the general notion that we own the space around us, much like an invisible bubble. Others are to stay outside the bubble except when powerful feelings—of intimacy or anger—are being expressed. Touch is especially to be avoided in our culture, with the same exceptions. How many times have you sat next to a stranger in a movie theater and jockeyed for the single armrest? Since touching is out, it often ends up under the arm of the bolder person, who risks touch.

I recall an amusing yet painful incident at a recent cocktail party. A woman, newly arrived from Israel, was talking with an American male of Swedish descent. Her conception of the proper distance from her face to his was about half the distance he apparently felt comfortable with. She would step in, he would step back. She virtually chased him across the room before they both gave up. She dismissed him as "cold." He saw her as "pushy." Each had a different notion of the appropriateness of distance given their relationship, and neither could feel comfortable with the other's behavior.

When someone with a different notion of the use of interpersonal space steps into our bubble we feel either uncomfortable and crowded, aggressed upon and threatened, or expectant of affection. Getting that close in the United States is for many a hit-or-kiss affair.

In addition, in our mouthwashed, deodorant-using culture the idea of smelling another's body or breath is often thought to be repugnant. The experience is avoided except in lovemaking, and even there many perfume away all traces of personal odor. Yet some people enjoy being close enough to others in public settings to feel their body warmth and smell their natural odors, and they touch others more often that we do. When we meet such people we have a terrible time because they "say" things, in the way they use space, that we do not appreciate or understand. They, in turn find us as difficult as we find them.

Yet within this huge country there are many subgroups with variations in their use of interpersonal space. Men walking down the street in the Italian district of Boston often do so arm-in-arm, something one would seldom, if ever, see around most universities in the Boston area. And in any large business organization, you can see the effects of variations in the use of space complicating relationships. A warm, expressive executive who feels comfortable touching the arm or shoulder of a subordinate may make him exceedingly uncomfortable if he is the nontouch, keep-your-distance type. You can watch your own behavior here to see how you use your own space and how you react to others who behave differently. Just being aware of it helps a great deal.

Since the American experience of smell, body warmth, and touch is so poorly developed, most of what we say to each other using these media does not take place in our awareness. But it does take place. Communication by smell, largely a chemical process, is far more extensive than we think. Edward Hall reports that in discussing olfactory messages with a psychoanalyst, a skillful therapist with an unusual record of success, he learned that the therapist could clearly distinguish the smell of anger in patients at a distance of 6 feet or more. Schizophrenic patients are reputed to have a characteristic odor and Dr. Kathleen Smith of St. Louis has demonstrated that rats readily distinguish between the smell of a schizophrenic and a nonschizophrenic. If chemical messages are this powerful, one wonders how many of what we consider to be well-hidden feelings are being "telegraphed" by the smells we are unable to disguise.

If smell as a communicator is out of awareness, how much more so is the skin as a major sense organ. Yet the skin has remarkable thermal characteristics and apparently has an extraordinary capacity both to emit and detect infrared heat. Under stress or strong emotion, we can send out thermal messages which can be "read" by perceptive individuals (usually spouses, lovers, or children) who can get within 2 feet. Getting "red in the face" in anger or embarrassment or sexual arousal is so common we hardly think about it. Yet the coloration of skin talks, too.

In summary, remember that people use space to say things they are often unaware of, but highly responsive to. To the extent that you can become more aware of your own behavior and that of others, you can be more skillful at "saying" what you mean to others and "hearing" what they mean. It is a fascinating exploration.

## THINGS

This aspect of communication is so easily grasped that I will just briefly present 10 rather obvious generalizations. Each points to what I see as a major assumption operating in our culture. Each naturally has exceptions, and each interacts with the others much as the various dimensions of space modify outcome, and relate to time.

1. *Bigger is better than smaller.* Until recently, the automobile has been a good example in the United States. Except for small sports cars, bigger cars (which, see below, are often more expensive) were generally regarded as better than smaller.
2. *More is better than fewer.* Two cars, houses, etc., are better than one.
3. *Clean is better than dirty.* The American fetish under attack.
4. *Neat and orderly is better than messy and disorderly.* A clean desk may communicate efficiency, while a messy one may "say" you are disorganized in many settings.
5. *Expensive is better than cheap.* Original works of art are "better" than reproductions.
6. *Unique is better than common.* Ditto.
7. *Beautiful is better than ugly.* Ditto.
8. *Accurate is better than inaccurate.* Back to Acutron.
9. *Very old or very new is better than recent.* Victorian furnishings are now becoming "old" enough to be of increasing value after 60 years of being "recent."
10. *Personal is better than public.* One's own object, say, chair or desk, is valued as a possession. In offices, as in homes, the boss or host often has "his" chair and others usually stay out of it. The news photo of a student sitting in the chair of the president of Columbia University during the 1969 uprising was used so often because it showed someone breaking this "rule."

## SUMMARY

Just as the various aspects of space are interrelated (remember the small but private office near the boss?) and influence the uses of time as language, so, too, do both overlap with our use of things. If that same office near the boss has an expensive, one-of-a-kind Persian rug and antique furniture, it can become even more valued, even though it is small.

The way we and others use time and space and things talks. If you are deaf to the messages, you miss much of the richness of what is being said by you and others. If you start "listening" consciously, you can begin to appreciate more of the subtle languages that are in use and thus gradually increase your personal intuitive skill in being with other persons in and out of organizations.

# REFERENCES

Hall, Edward, J. *The Silent Language.* New York: Premier Paperback, 1961.

Hall, Edward J. *The Hidden Dimension.* New York: Doubleday, 1966.

Sommer, Robert. *Personal Space: The Behavioral Basis of Design.* Englewood Cliffs, N.J.: Prentice-Hall, 1966.

Steele, Fred I. *Physical Settings and Organization Development.* Reading, Mass.: Addison-Wesley, 1973.

# DEFENSIVE COMMUNICATION

*Jack R. Gibb*

One way to understand communication is to view it as a people process rather than as a language process. If one is to make fundamental improvement in communication, he must make changes in interpersonal relationships. One possible type of alteration—and the one with which this paper is concerned—is that of reducing the degree of defensiveness.

## DEFINITION AND SIGNIFICANCE

"Defensive behavior" is behavior which occurs when an individual perceives threat or anticipates threat in the group. The person who behaves defensively, even though he also gives some attention to the common task, devotes an appreciable portion of his energy to defending himself. Besides talking about the topic, he thinks about how he appears to others, how he may be seen more favorably, how he may win, dominate, impress or escape punishment, and/or how he may avoid or mitigate a perceived or anticipated attack.

Such inner feelings and outward acts tend to create similarly defensive postures in others; and, if unchecked, the ensuing circular response becomes increasingly destructive. Defensive behavior, in short, engenders defensive listening, and this in turn produces postural, facial, and verbal cues which raise the defense level of the original communicator.

Defensive arousal prevents the listener from concentrating upon the message. Not only do defensive communicators send off multiple value, motive, and affect cues, but also defensive recipients distort what they receive. As a person becomes more and more defensive, he becomes less and less able to perceive accurately the motives, the values, and the emotions of the sender. The writer's analysis of tape recorded discussions revealed that increases in defensive behavior were correlated positively with losses in efficiency in communication.[1] Specifically, distortions became greater when defensive states existed in the groups.

The converse also is true. The more "supportive" or defense reductive the climate the less the receiver reads into the communication distorted loadings which arise from projections of his own anxieties, motives, and concerns. As defenses are reduced, the receivers become better able to concentrate upon the structure, the content, and the cognitive meanings of the message.

*Source*: Reprinted from the *Journal of Communication*, XI, No. 3 (September 1961), 141–48, by permission of the author and the publisher.

[1]J. R. Gibb, "Defense Level and Influence in Small Groups," in *Leadership and Interpersonal Behavior*, ed. L. Petrullo and B. M. Bass (New York: Holt, Rinehart & Winston, 1961), pp. 66–81.

# CATEGORIES OF DEFENSIVE
# AND SUPPORTIVE COMMUNICATION

In working over an eight-year period with recordings of discussions occurring in varied settings, the writer developed the six pairs of defensive and supportive categories presented in Table 1. Behavior which a listener perceives as possessing any of the characteristics listed in the left-hand column arouses defensiveness, whereas that which he interprets as having any of the qualities designated as supportive reduces defensive feelings. The degree to which these reactions occur depend upon the personal level of defensiveness and upon the general climate in the group at the time.[2]

TABLE 1  Categories of Behavior Characteristic of Supportive
and Defensive Climates in Small Groups

| Defensive Climates | Supportive Climates |
| --- | --- |
| 1. Evaluation | 1. Description |
| 2. Control | 2. Problem orientation |
| 3. Strategy | 3. Spontaneity |
| 4. Neutrality | 4. Empathy |
| 5. Superiority | 5. Equality |
| 6. Certainty | 6. Provisionalism |

## Evaluation and Description

Speech or other behavior which appears evaluative increases defensiveness. If by expression, manner of speech, tone of voice, or verbal content the sender seems to be evaluating or judging the listener, then the receiver goes on guard. Of course, other factors may inhibit the reaction. If the listener thinks that the speaker regards him as an equal and is being open and spontaneous, for example, the evaluativeness in a message will be neutralized and perhaps not even perceived. This same principle applies equally to the other five categories of potentially defense–producing climates. The six sets are interactive.

Because our attitudes toward other persons are frequently, and often necessarily, evaluative, expressions which the defensive person will regard as nonjudgmental are hard to frame. Even the simplest question usually conveys the answer that the sender wishes or implies the response that would fit into his value system. A mother, for example, immediately following an earth tremor that shook the house, sought for her small son with the question: "Bobby, where are you?" The timid and plaintive "Mommy, I didn't do it" indicated how Bobby's chronic mild defensiveness predisposed him to react with a projection of his own guilt and in the context of his chronic assumption that questions are full of accusation.

Anyone who has attempted to train professionals to use information-seeking speech with neutral affect appreciates how difficult it is to teach a person to say even the simple "Who did that?" without being seen as accusing. Speech is so frequently judgmental that there is a reality base for the defensive interpretations which are so common.

[2]J. R. Gibb, "Sociopsychological Processes of Group Instruction," in *The Dynamics of Instructional Groups*, ed. N. B. Henry (Fifty-ninth Yearbook of the National Society for the Study of Education, Part II, 1960), pp. 115–35.

When insecure, group members are particularly likely to place blame, to see others as fitting into categories of good or bad, to make moral judgments of their colleagues, and to question the value, motive, and affect loadings of the speech which they hear. Since value loadings imply a judgment of others, a belief that the standards of the speaker differ from his own causes the listener to become defensive.

Descriptive speech, in contrast to that which is evaluative, tends to arouse a minimum of uneasiness. Speech acts which the listener perceives as genuine requests for information or as material with neutral loadings is descriptive. Specifically, presentations of feelings, events, perceptions, or processes which do not ask or imply that the receiver change behavior or attitude are minimally defense–producing. The difficulty in avoiding overtone is illustrated by the problems of news reporters in writing stories about unions, Communists, Negroes, and religious activities without tipping off the "party" line of the newspaper. One can often tell from the opening words in a news article which side the newspaper's editorial policy favors.

## Control and Problem Orientation

Speech which is used to control the listener evokes resistance. In most of our social intercourse someone is trying to do something to someone else—to change an attitude, to influence behavior, or to restrict the field of activity. The degree to which attempts to control produce defensiveness depends upon the openness of the effort, for a suspicion that hidden motives exist heightens resistance. For this reason attempts of non-directive therapists and progressive educators to refrain from imposing a set of values, a point of view, or a problem solution upon the receivers meet with many barriers. Since the norm is control, non-controllers must earn the perceptions that their efforts have no hidden motives. A bombardment of persuasive "messages" in the fields of politics, education, special causes, advertising, religion, medicine, industrial relations, and guidance has bred cynical and paranoidal responses in listeners.

Implicit in all attempts to alter another person is the assumption by the change agent that the person to be altered is inadequate. That the speaker secretly views the listener as ignorant, unable to make his own decisions, uninformed, immature, unwise, or possessed of wrong or inadequate attitudes is a subconscious perception which gives the latter a valid base for defensive reactions.

Methods of control are many and varied. Legalistic insistence on detail, restrictive regulations and policies, conformity norms, and all laws are among the methods. Gestures, facial expressions, other forms of non-verbal communication, and even such simple acts as holding a door open in a particular manner are means of imposing one's will upon another and hence are potential sources of resistance.

Problem orientation, on the other hand, is the antithesis of persuasion. When the sender communicates a desire to collaborate in defining a mutual problem and in seeking its solution, he tends to create the same problem orientation in the listener; and, of greater importance, he implies that he has no predetermined solution, attitude, or method to impose. Such behavior is permissive in that it allows the receiver to set his own goals, make his own decisions, and evaluate his own progress—or to share with the sender in doing so. The exact methods of attaining permissiveness are not known, but they must involve a constellation of cues, and they certainly go beyond mere verbal assurances that the communicator has no hidden desires to exercise control.

## Strategy and Spontaneity

When the sender is perceived as engaged in a stratagem involving ambiguous and multiple motivations, the receiver becomes defensive. No one wishes to be a guinea pig, a role player, or an impressed actor, and no one likes to be the victim of some hidden motivation. That which is concealed, also, may appear larger than it really is, with the degree of defensiveness of the listener determining the perceived size of the suppressed element. The intense reaction of the reading audience to the material in the *Hidden Persuaders* indicates the prevalence of defensive reactions to multiple motivations behind strategy. Group members who are seen as "taking a role, " as feigning emotion, as toying with their colleagues, as withholding information, or as having special sources of data are especially resented. One participant once complained that another was "using a listening technique" on him!

A large part of the adverse reaction to much of the so-called human relations training is a feeling against what are perceived as gimmicks and tricks to fool or to "involve" people, to make a person think he is making his own decision, or to make the listener feel that the sender is genuinely interested in him as a person. Particularly violent reactions occur when it appears that someone is trying to make a stratagem appear spontaneous. One person has reported a boss who incurred resentment by habitually using the gimmick of "spontaneously" looking at his watch and saying. "My gosh, look at the time—I must run to an appointment." The belief was that the boss would create less irritation by honestly asking to be excused.

Similarly, the deliberate assumption of guilelessness and natural simplicity is especially resented. Monitoring the tapes of feedback and evaluation sessions in training groups indicates the surprising extent to which members perceive the strategies of their colleagues. This perceptual clarity may be quite shocking to the strategist, who usually feels that he has cleverly hidden the motivational aura around the "gimmick."

This aversion to deceit may account for one's resistance to politicians who are suspected of behind-the-scenes planning to get his vote; to psychologists whose listening apparently is motivated by more than the manifest or content-level interest in his behavior, or to the sophisticated, smooth, or clever person whose "one-upmanship" is marked with guile. In training groups the role-flexible person frequently is resented because his changes in behavior are perceived as strategic maneuvers.

Conversely, behavior which appears to be spontaneous and free of deception is defense reductive. If the communicator is seen as having a clean id, as having uncomplicated motivations, as being straightforward and honest, and as behaving spontaneously in response to the situation, he is likely to arouse minimal defense.

## Neutrality and Empathy

When neutrality in speech appears to the listener to indicate a lack of concern for his welfare, he becomes defensive. Group members usually desire to be perceived as valued persons, as individuals of special worth, and as objects of concern and affection. The clinical, detached, person-is-an-object-of-study attitude on the part of many psychologist-trainers is resented by group members. Speech with low affect that communicates little warmth or caring is in such contrast with the affect-laden speech in social situations that it sometimes communicates rejection.

Communication that conveys empathy for the feelings and respect for the worth of the listener, is particularly supportive and defense reductive. Reassurance results when a message indicates that the speaker identifies himself with the listener's problems, shares his feelings, and accepts his emotional reactions at face value. Abortive efforts to deny the legitimacy of the receiver's emotions by assuring the receiver that he need not feel bad, that he should not feel rejected, or that he is overly anxious, though often intended as support giving, may impress the listener as lack of acceptance. The combination of understanding and empathizing with the other person's emotions with no accompanying effort to change him apparently is supportive at a high level.

The importance of gestural behavior cues in communicating empathy should be mentioned. Apparently spontaneous facial and bodily evidences of concern are often interpreted as especially valid evidence of deep-level acceptance.

## Superiority and Equality

When a person communicates to another that he feels superior in position, power, wealth, intellectual ability, physical characteristics, or other ways, he arouses defensiveness. Here, as with the other sources of disturbance, whatever arouses feelings of inadequacy causes the listener to center upon the affect loading of the statement rather than upon the cognitive elements. The receiver then reacts by not hearing the message, by forgetting it, by competing with the sender, or by becoming jealous of him.

The person who is perceived as feeling superior communicates that he is not willing to enter into a shared problem-solving relationship, that he probably does not desire feedback, that he does not require help, and/or that he will be likely to try to reduce the power, the status, or the worth of the receiver.

Many ways exist for creating the atmosphere that the sender feels himself equal to the listener. Defenses are reduced when one perceives the sender as being willing to enter into participative planning with mutual trust and respect. Differences in talent, ability, worth, appearance, status, and power often exist, but the low defense communicator seems to attach little importance to these distinctions.

## Certainty and Provisionalism

The effects of dogmatism in producing defensiveness are well known. Those who seem to know the answers, to require no additional data, and to regard themselves as teachers rather than as co-workers tend to put others on guard. Moreover, in the writer's experiment, listeners often perceived manifest expressions of certainty as connoting inward feelings of inferiority. They saw the dogmatic individual as needing to be right, as wanting to win an argument rather than solve a problem, and as seeing his ideas as truths to be defended. This kind of behavior often was associated with acts which others regarded as attempts to exercise control. People who were right seemed to have low tolerance for members who were "wrong"—i.e., who did not agree with the sender.

One reduces the defensiveness of the listener when he communicates that he is willing to experiment with his own behavior, attitudes, and ideas. The person who appears to be taking provisional attitudes, to be investigating issues rather than taking sides on them, to be problem solving rather than debating, and to be willing to experiment and explore tends to communicate that the listener may have some control over the shared quest or the investigation of the ideas. If a person is genuinely searching for information and data, he does not resent help or company along the way.

## CONCLUSION

The implications of the above material for the parent, the teacher, the manager, the administrator, or the therapist are fairly obvious. Arousing defensiveness interferes with communication and thus makes it difficult—and sometimes impossible—for anyone to convey ideas clearly and to move effectively toward the solution of therapeutic, educational, or managerial problems.

# 8
# Interpersonal Perception

COMMUNICATION REVISITED
*Jay Hall*

THE THINKING ORGANIZATION:
HOW PATTERNS OF THOUGHT DETERMINE ORGANIZATIONAL CULTURE
*Evelyn Pitre*
*Henry P. Sims, Jr.*

## COMMUNICATION REVISITED

*Jay Hall*

High on the diagnostic checklist of corporate health is communication; and the prognosis is less than encouraging. In a recent cross-cultural study,[1] roughly 74 percent of the managers sampled from companies in Japan, Great Britain, and the United States cited communication breakdown as the single greatest barrier to corporate excellence.

Just what constitutes a problem of communication is not easily agreed upon. Some theorists approach the issue from the vantage point of information bits comprising a message; others speak in terms of organizational roles and positions of centrality or peripherality; still others emphasize the directional flows of corporate data. The result is that more and more people are communicating about communication, while the achievement of clarity, understanding, commitment, and creativity—the goals of communication—becomes more and more limited.

More often than not, the communication dilemmas cited by people are not communication problems at all. They are instead *symptoms* of difficulties at more basic and fundamental levels of corporate life. From a dynamic standpoint, problems of communication in organizations frequently reflect dysfunctions at the level of *corporate climate*. The feelings people have about where or with whom they work—feelings of impotence, distrust, resentment, insecurity, social inconsequence, and all the other very human emotions—not only define the climate which prevails but the manner in which communications will be managed. R. R. Blake and Jane S. Mouton[2] have commented upon an oddity of organizational life: when management is effective and relationships are sound, problems of communication tend not to occur. It is only when relationships among members of the organization are unsound and fraught with unarticulated tensions that one hears complaints of communication breakdown. Thus, the quality of relationships in an organization may dictate to a great extent the level of communication effectiveness achieved.

*Source*: ©1973 by the Regents of the University of California. Reprinted from the *California Management Review*, Vol. 15, No. 3. By permission of The Regents.

# INTERPERSONAL STYLES
# AND THE QUALITY OF RELATIONSHIPS

The critical factor underlying relationship quality in organizations is in need of review. Reduced to its lowest common denominator, the most significant determinant of the quality of relationships is the interpersonal style of the parties to a relationship. The learned, characteristic, and apparently preferred manner in which individuals relate to others in the building of relationships—the manner in which they monitor, control, filter, divert, give, and seek the information germane to a given relationship—will dictate over time the quality of relationships which exist among people, the emotional climate which will characterize their interactions, and whether or not there will be problems of communication. In the final analysis, individuals are the human links in the corporate network, and the styles they employ interpersonally are the ultimate determinants of what information goes where and whether it will be distortion-free or masked by interpersonal constraints.

The concept of interpersonal style is not an easy one to define; yet, if it is to serve as the central mechanism underlying the quality of relationships, the nature of corporate climate, managerial effectiveness, and the level of corporate excellence attainable, it is worthy of analysis. Fortunately, Joseph Luft[3] and Harry Ingham two behavioral scientists with special interests in interpersonal and group processes—have developed a model of social interaction which affords a way of thinking about interpersonal functioning, while handling much of the data encountered in everyday living. The Johari Window, as their model is called, identifies several interpersonal styles, their salient features and consequences, and suggests a basis for interpreting the significance of style for the quality of relationships. An overview of the Johari model should help to sharpen the perception of interpersonal practices among managers and lend credence to the contention of Blake and Mouton that there are few communication problems as such, only unsound relationships. At the same time, a normative statement regarding effective interpersonal functioning and, by extension, the foundations of corporate excellence may be found in the model as well. Finally, the major tenets of the model are testable under practical conditions, and the latter portion of this discussion will be devoted to research on the managerial profile in interpersonal encounters. The author has taken a number of interpretive liberties with the basic provisions of the Johari Awareness model. While it is anticipated that none of these violate the integrity of the model as originally described by Luft, it should be emphasized that many of the inferences and conclusions discussed are those of the author, and Dr. Luft should not be held accountable for any lapses of logic or misapplications of the model in this paper.

# THE JOHARI WINDOW:
# A GRAPHIC MODEL OF INTERPERSONAL PROCESSES

As treated here, the Johari Window is essentially an information processing model; interpersonal style and individual effectiveness are assessed in terms of information processing tendencies and the performance consequences thought to be associated with such practices. The model employs a four celled figure as its format and reflects the interaction of two interpersonal sources of information—Self and Others—and the behavioral processes required for utilizing that information. The model, depicted in Figure 1, may be thought of as representing the various kinds of data available for use in the establishment of interpersonal relationships. The squared field, in effect, represents a personal space. This in turn is partitioned into four regions, with each representing a particular combination or mix of relevant information and having special significance for the quality of relationships. To fully appreciate the implications that each informational region has for interpersonal effectiveness, one must consider not only the size and shape of each region but also the reasons for its presence in the interpersonal space. In an attempt to "personalize" the model, it is helpful to think of oneself as the *Self* in the relationship for, as will be seen presently, it is what the *Self* does interpersonally that has the most direct impact on the quality of resulting relationships. In organizational terms, it is how the management-Self behaves that is critical to the quality of corporate relationships.

FIGURE 1   The Johari Window: A Model of Interpersonal Processes

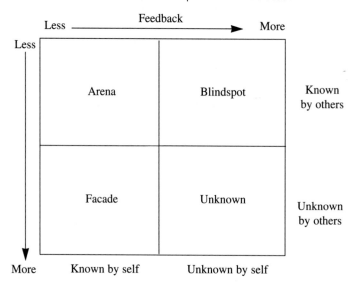

Figure 1 reveals that the two informational sources, Self and Others, have information which is pertinent to the relationship and, at the same time, each lacks information that is equally germane. Thus, there is relevant and necessary information which is *Known by the Self*, *Unknown by the Self*, *Known by Others* and *Unknown by Others*. The Self/Other combinations of known and unknown information make up the four regions within the interpersonal space and, again, characterize the various types and qualities of relationships possible within the Johari framework.

Region I, for example, constitutes that portion of the total interpersonal space which is devoted to mutually held information. This Known by Self–Known by Others facet of the interpersonal space is thought to be the part of the relationship which, because of its shared data characteristics and implied likelihood of mutual understanding, controls interpersonal productivity. That is, the working assumption is that productivity and interpersonal effectiveness are directly related to the amount of mutually held information in a relationship. Therefore, the larger Region I becomes, the more rewarding, effective, and productive the relationship. As the informational context for interpersonal functioning, Region I is called the "Arena."

Region II, using the double classification approach just described, is that portion of the interpersonal space which holds information Known by Others but Unknown by the Self. Thus, this array of data constitutes an interpersonal handicap for the Self, since one can hardly understand the behaviors, decisions, or potentials of others if he doesn't have the data upon which these are based. Others have the advantage of knowing their own reactions, feelings, perceptions, and the like while the Self is unaware of these. Region II, an area of hidden unperceived information, is called the "Blindspot." The Blindspot is, of course, a limiting factor with respect to the size of Region I and may be thought of, therefore, as inhibiting interpersonal effectiveness.

Region III may also be considered to inhibit interpersonal effectiveness, but it is due to an imbalance of information which would seem to favor the Self; as the portion of the relationship which is characterized by information Known by the Self but Unknown by Others, Region III constitutes a protective feature of the relationship for the Self. Data which one perceives as potentially prejudicial to a relationship or which he keeps to himself out of fear, desire for power, or whatever, make up the "Facade." This protective front, in turn, serves a defensive function for the Self. The question is not one of whether a Facade is necessary but rather how much Facade is required realistically; this raises the question of how much conscious defensiveness can be tolerated before the Arena becomes too inhibited and interpersonal effectiveness begins to diminish.

Finally, Region IV constitutes that portion of the relationship which is devoted to material neither known by the self nor by other parties to the relationship. The information in this Unknown by Self-Unknown by Others area is thought to reflect psychodynamic data, hidden potential, unconscious idiosyncrasies, and the database of creativity. Thus, Region IV is the "Unknown" area which may become known as interpersonal effectiveness increases.

Summarily, it should be said that the information within all regions can be of any type—feeling data, factual information, assumptions, task skill data, and prejudices—which are relevant to the relationship at hand. Irrelevant data are not the focus of the Johari Window concept: just those pieces of information which have a bearing on the quality and productivity of the relationship should be considered as appropriate targets for the information processing practices prescribed by the model. At the same time, it should be borne in mind that the individuals involved in a relationship, particularly the Self, control what and how information will be processed. Because of this implicit personal control aspect, the model should be viewed as an open system which is *dynamic* and amendable to change as personal decisions regarding interpersonal functioning change.


# BASIC INTERPERSONAL PROCESSES:
# EXPOSURE AND FEEDBACK

The dynamic character of the model is critical; for it is the movement capability of the horizontal and vertical lines which partition the interpersonal space into regions which gives individuals control over what their relationships will become. The Self can significantly influence the size of his Arena in relating to others by the behavioral processes he employs in establishing relationships. To the extent that one takes the steps necessary to apprise others of relevant information which he has and they do not, he is enlarging his Arena in a downward direction. Within the framework of the model, this enlargement occurs in concert with a reduction of one's Facade. Thus, if one behaves in a non-defensive, trusting, and possibly risk taking manner with others, he may be thought of as contributing to increased mutual awareness and sharing of data. The process one employs toward this end has been called the "Exposure" process. It entails the open and candid disclosure of one's feelings, factual knowledge, wild guesses, and the like in a conscious attempt to share. Frothy, intentionally untrue, diversionary sharing does not constitute exposure; and, as personal experience will attest, it does nothing to help mutual understanding. The Exposure process is under the direct control of the Self and may be used as a mechanism for building trust and for legitimizing mutual exposures.

The need for mutual exposures becomes apparent when one considers the behavioral process required for enlarging the Arena laterally. As a behavior designed to gain reduction in one's Blindspot, the Feedback process entails an active solicitation by the Self of the information he feels others might have which he does not. The active, initiative-taking aspect of this solicitation behavior should be stressed, for again the Self takes the primary role in setting interpersonal norms and in legitimizing certain acts within the relationship. Since the extent to which the Self will actually receive the Feedback he solicits is contingent upon the willingness of others to expose their data, the need for a climate of mutual exposures becomes apparent. Control by the Self of the success of his Feedback-seeking behaviors is less direct therefore than in the case of self-exposure. He will achieve a reduction of his Blindspot only with the cooperation of others; and his own prior willingness to deal openly and candidly may well dictate what level of cooperative and trusting behavior will prevail on the part of other parties to the relationship.

Thus, one can theoretically establish interpersonal relationships characterized by mutual understanding and increased effectiveness (by a dominant Arena) if he will engage in exposing and feedback soliciting behaviors to an optimal degree. This places the determination of productivity and amount of interpersonal reward—and the quality of relationships—directly in the hands of the Self. In theory, this amounts to an issue of interpersonal competence; in practice, it amounts to the conscious and sensitive management of interpersonal processes.

## INTERPERSONAL STYLES AND MANAGERIAL IMPACTS

While one can theoretically employ Exposure and Feedback processes not only to a great but to a similar degree as well, individuals typically fail to achieve such an optimal practice. Indeed, they usually display a significant preference for one or the other of the two processes and tend to overuse one while neglecting the other. This tendency promotes a state of imbalance in interpersonal relationships which, in turn, creates disruptive tensions capable of retarding productivity. Figure 2 presents several commonly used approaches to the employment of Exposure and Feedback processes.

FIGURE 2  Interpersonal Styles as Functions of Exposure Use and Feedback Solicitation

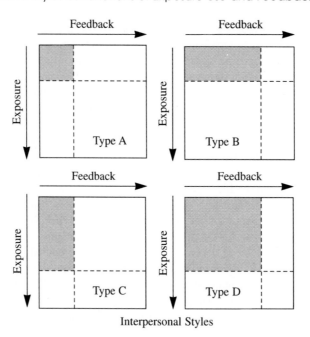

Interpersonal Styles

Each of these may be thought of as reflecting a basic interpersonal style—that is, fairly consistent and preferred ways of behaving interpersonally. As might be expected, each style has associated with it some fairly predictable consequences.

*Type A.* This interpersonal style reflects a minimal use of both Exposure and Feedback processes; it is a fairly impersonal approach to interpersonal relationships. The Unknown region dominates under this style; and unrealized potential, untapped creativity, and personal psychodynamics prevail as the salient influences. Such a style would seem to indicate withdrawal and an aversion to risktaking on the part of its user; interpersonal anxiety and safety-seeking are likely to be prime sources of personal motivation. Persons who characteristically use this style appear to be detached, mechanical, and uncommunicative. They may often be found in bureaucratic highly structured organizations of some type where it is possible, and perhaps profitable, to avoid personal disclosure or involvement. People using this style are likely to be reacted to with more than average hostility, since other parties to the relationship will tend to interpret the lack of Exposure and Feedback solicitation largely according to their own needs and how this interpersonal lack affects need fulfillment.

Subordinates whose manager employs such a style, for example, will often feel that his behavior is consciously aimed at frustrating them in their work. The person in need of support and encouragement will often view a Type A manager as aloof, cold, and indifferent. Another individual in need of firm directions and plenty of order in his work may view the same manager as indecisive and administratively impotent. Yet another person requiring freedom and opportunities to be innovative may see the Type A interpersonal style as hopelessly tradition-bound and as symptomatic of fear and an overriding need for security. The user of Type A behaviors on a large scale in an organization reveals something about the climate and fundamental health of that organization. In many respects, interpersonal relationships founded on Type A uses of Exposure and Feedback constitute the kind of organizational ennui about which Chris Argyris[4] has written so eloquently. Such practices are, in his opinion, likely to be learned ways of behaving under oppressive policies of the sort which encourage people to act in a submissive and dependent fashion. Organizationally, of course, the result is lack of communication and a loss of human potentials; the Unknown becomes the dominant feature of corporate relationships, and the implications for organizational creativity and growth are obvious.

*Type B.* Under this approach, there is also an aversion to Exposure, but aversion is coupled with a desire for relationships not found in Type A. Thus, Feedback is the only process left in promoting relationships and it is much overused. An aversion to the use of Exposure may typically be interpreted as a sign of basic mistrust of self and others, and it is therefore not surprising that the Facade is the dominant feature of relationships resulting from neglected Exposure coupled with overused Feedback. The style appears to be a probing supportive interpersonal ploy and, once the Facade becomes apparent, it is likely to result in a reciprocal withdrawal of trust by other parties. This may promote feelings of suspicion on the part of others: such feelings may lead to the manager being treated as a rather superficial person without real substance or as a devious sort with many hidden agendas.

Preference for this interpersonal style among managers seems to be of two types. Some managers committed to a quasi-permissive management may employ Type B behaviors in an attempt to avoid appearing directive. Such an approach results in the manager's personal resources never being fully revealed or his opinions being expressed. In contrast—but subject to many of—the same inadequacies—is the use of Type B behaviors in an attempt to gain or maintain one's personal power in relationships. Many managers build a facade to maintain personal control and an outward appearance of confidence. As the Johari model would suggest, however, persons who employ such practices tend to become isolated from their subordinates and colleagues alike. Lack of trust predominates and consolidation of power and promotion of an image of confidence may be the least likely results of Type B use in organizations. Very likely, the seeds of distrust and conditions for covert competitiveness—with all the implications for organizational teamwork—will follow from widespread use of Type B interpersonal practices.

*Type C.* Based on an overuse of Exposure to the neglect of Feedback, this interpersonal style may reflect ego-striving and/or distrust of others' competence. The person who uses this style usually feels quite confident of his own opinions and is likely to value compliance from others. The fact that he is often unaware of his impact or of the potential of others' contributions is reflected in the dominant Blindspot which results from this style. Others are likely to feel disenfranchised by one who uses this style; they often feel that he has little use for their contributions or concern for their feelings. As a result, this style often triggers feelings of hostility, insecurity, and resentment on the part of others. Frequently, others will learn to perpetuate the manager's Blindspot by withholding important information or giving only selected feedback; as such, this is a reflection of the passive aggressiveness and unarticulated hostility which this style can cause. Labor-management relations frequently reflect such Blindspot dynamics.

The Type C interpersonal style is probably what has prompted so much interest in "listening" programs around the country. As the Johari model makes apparent, however, the Type C over-use of Exposure and neglect of Feedback is just one of several interpersonal tendencies that may disrupt communications. While hierarchical organizational structure or centrality in communication nets and the like may certainly facilitate the use of individual Type C behaviors, so can fear of failure, authoritarianism, need for control, and over-confidence in one's own opinions; such traits vary from person to person and limit the utility of communication panaceas. Managers who rely on this style often do so to demonstrate competence; many corporate cultures require that the manager be *the* planner, director, and controller and many managers behave accordingly to protect their corporate images. Many others are simply trying to be helpful in a paternalistic kind of way; others are, of course, purely dictatorial. Whatever the reasons, those who employ the Type C style have one thing in common: their relationships will be dominated by Blindspots and they are destined for surprise whenever people get enough and decide to force feedback on them, solicited or not.

*Type D.* Balanced Exposure and Feedback processes are used to a great extent in this style; candor, openness, and a sensitivity to others' needs to participate are the salient features of the style. The Arena is the dominant characteristic, and productivity increases. In initial stages, this style may promote some defensiveness on the part of others who are not familiar with honest and trusting relationships; but perseverance will tend to promote a norm of reciprocal candor over time in which creative potential can be realized.

Among managers, Type D practices constitute an ideal state from the standpoint of organizational effectiveness. Healthy and creative climates result from its widespread use, and the conditions for growth and corporate excellence may be created through the use of constructive Exposure and Feedback exchanges. Type D practices do not give license to "clobber," as some detractors might claim; and, for optimal results, the data explored should be germane to the relationships and problems at hand, rather than random intimacies designed to overcome self-consciousness. Trust is slowly built, and managers who "experiment with Type D processes should be prepared to be patient and flexible in their relationships. Some managers, as they tentatively try out Type D strategies, encounter reluctance and distrust on the part of others, with the result that they frequently give up too soon, assuming that the style doesn't work. The reluctance of others should be assessed against the backdrop of previous management practices and the level of prior trust which characterizes the culture. Other managers may try candor only to discover that they have opened a Pandora's box from which a barrage of hostility and complaints emerges. The temptation of the naive manager is to put the lid back on quickly; but the more enlightened manager knows that when communications are opened up after having been closed for a long time, the most emotionally laden issues—ones which have been the greatest sources of frustration, anger, or fear—will be the first to be discussed. If management can resist cutting the dialogue short, the diatribe will run its course as the emotion underlying it is drained off, and exchanges will become more problem centered and future oriented. Management intent will have been tested and found worthy of trust, and creative unrestrained interchanges will occur. Organizations built on such practices are those headed for corporate climates and resource utilization of the type necessary for true corporate excellence. The manager's interpersonal style may well be the catalyst for this reaction to occur.

Summarily, the Johari Window model of interpersonal processes suggests that much more is needed to understand communication in an organization than information about its structure or one's position in a network. People make very critical decisions about what information will be processed, irrespective of structural and network considerations. People bring with them to organizational settings propensities for behaving in certain ways interpersonally. They prefer certain interpersonal styles, sharpened and honed by corporate cultures, which significantly influence—if not dictate entirely—the flow of information in organizations. As such, individuals and their preferred styles of relating one to another amount to the synapses in the corporate network which control and coordinate the human system. Central to an understanding of communication in organizations, therefore, is an appreciation of the complexities of those human interfaces which comprise organizations. The work of Luft and Ingham, when brought to bear on management practices and corporate cultures, may lend much needed insight into the constraints unique to organizational life which either hinder or facilitate the processing of corporate data.

# RESEARCH ON THE MANAGERIAL PROFILE: THE PERSONNEL RELATIONS SURVEY

As treated here, one of the major tenets of the Johari Window model is that one's use of Exposure and Feedback soliciting processes is a matter of personal decision. Whether consciously or unconsciously, when one employs either process or fails to do so he has decided that such practices somehow serve the goals he has set for himself. Rationales for particular behavior are likely to be as varied as the goals people seek; they may be in the best sense of honest intent or they may simply represent evasive logic or systems of self-deception. The *purposeful* nature of interpersonal styles remains nevertheless. A manager's style of relating to other members of the organization is never simply a collection of random, unconsidered acts. Whether he realizes it or not, or admits it or denies it, his interpersonal style *has purpose* and is thought to serve either a personal or interpersonal goal in his relationships.

Because of the element of decision and purposeful intent inherent in one's interpersonal style, the individual's inclination to employ Exposure and Feedback processes may be assessed. That is, his decisions to engage in open and candid behaviors or to actively seek out the information that others are thought to have may be sampled, and his Exposure and Feedback tendencies thus measured. Measurements obtained may be used in determining the manager's or the organization's Johari Window configuration and the particular array of interpersonal predilections which underlie it. Thus, the Luft-Ingham model not only provides a way of conceptualizing what is going on interpersonally, but it affords a rationale for actually assessing practices which may, in turn, be coordinated to practical climate and cultural issues.

Hall and Williams have designed a paper-and-pencil instrument for use with managers which reveals their preferences for Exposure and Feedback in their relationships with subordinates, colleagues, and superiors. The *Personnel Relations Survey*[5] as the instrument is entitled, has been used extensively by industry as a training aid for providing personal feedback of a type which "personalizes" otherwise didactic theory sessions on the Johari, on one hand, and as a catalyst to evaluation and critique of ongoing relationships, on the other hand. In addition to its essentially training oriented use, however, the *Personnel Relations Survey* has been a basic research tool for assessing current practices among managers. The results obtained from two pieces of research are of particular interest from the standpoint of their implications for corporate climates and managerial styles.

***Authority Relationships and Interpersonal Style Preferences.*** Using the *Personnel Relations Survey*, data were collected from 1000 managers. These managers represent a cross-section of those found in organizations today; levels of management ranging from company president to just above first-line supervisor were sampled from all over the United States. Major manufacturers and petroleum and food producers contributed to the research, as well as a major airline, state and federal governmental agencies, and nonprofit service organizations.

Since the *Personnel Relations Survey* addresses the manner in which Exposure and Feedback processes are employed in one's relationships with his subordinates, colleagues, and superiors, the data from the 1000 managers sampled reveal some patterns which prevail in organizations in terms of downward, horizontal, and upward communications. In addition, the shifting and changing of interpersonal tactics as one moves from one authority relationship to another is noteworthy from the standpoint of power dynamics underlying organizational life. A summary of the average tendencies obtained from managers is presented graphically in Figure 3.

Of perhaps the greatest significance for organizational climates is the finding regarding the typical manager's use of Exposure. As Figure 3 indicates, one's tendency to deal openly and candidly with others is directly influenced by the amount of power he possesses relative to other parties to the relationship. Moving from relationships with subordinates in which the manager obviously enjoys greater formal authority, through colleague relationships characterized by equal authority positions, to relationships with superiors in which the manager is least powerful, the plots of Exposure use steadily decline. Indeed, a straight linear relationship is suggested between amount of authority possessed by the average manager and his use of candor in relationships.

While there are obvious exceptions to this depiction, the average managerial profile on Exposure reveals the most commonly found practices in organizations which, when taken diagnostically, suggest that the average manager in today's organizations has a number of "hang-ups" around authority issues which seriously curtail his interpersonal effectiveness. Consistent with other findings from communication research, these data point to power differences among parties to relationships as a major disruptive influence on the flow of information in organizations. A more accurate interpretation, however, seems to be that it is not power differences as such which impede communication, but the way people *feel* about these differences and begin to monitor, filter, and control their contributions in response to their own feelings and apprehensions.

Implications for overall corporate climate may become more obvious when the data from the Exposure process are considered with those reflecting the average manager's reliance on Feedback acquisition. As Figure 3 reveals, Feedback solicitation proceeds differently. As might be expected, there is less use of the Feedback process in relationships with subordinates than there is of the Exposure process. This variation on the Type C interpersonal style, reflecting an overuse of Exposure to some neglect of Feedback, very likely contributes to subordinate feelings of resentment, lack of social worth, and frustration. These feelings—which are certain to manifest themselves in the *quality* of subordinate performance if not in production quantity—will likely remain as hidden facets of corporate climate, for a major feature of downward communication revealed in Figure 3 is that of managerial Blindspot.

FIGURE 3    Score Plots on Exposure and Feedback for the "Average" Manager from a
              Sample of 1,000 Managers in the United States

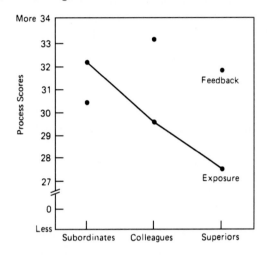

Relationships at the colleague level appear to be of a different sort with a set of dynamics all their own. As reference to the score plots in Figure 3 will show, the typical manager reports a significant preference for Feedback seeking behaviors over Exposure in his relationships with his fellow managers. A quick interpretation of the data obtained would be that, at the colleague level, everyone is seeking information but very few are willing to expose any. These findings may bear on a unique feature of organizational life—one which has serious implications for climate among corporate peers. Most research on power and authority relationships suggests that there is the greatest openness of equal power. Since colleague relationships might best be considered to reflect equal if not shared distributions of power, maximum openness coupled with maximum solicitation of others' information might be expected to characterize relationships among management co-workers. The fact that a fairly pure Type B interpersonal style prevails suggests noise in the system. The dominant Facade which results from reported practices with colleagues signifies a lack of trust of the sort which could seriously limit the success of collaborative or cooperative ventures among colleagues. The climate implications of mistrust are obvious, and the present data may shed some light on teamwork difficulties as well as problems of horizontal communication so often encountered during inter-departmental or inter-group contacts.

Interviews with a number of managers revealed that their tendencies to become closed in encounters with colleagues could be traced to a competitive ethic which prevailed in their organizations. The fact was a simple one: "You don't confide in your 'buddies' because they are bucking for the same job you are! Any worthwhile information you've got, you keep to yourself until a time when it might come in handy." To the extent that this climate prevails in organizations, it is to be expected that more effort goes into Facade building and maintenance than is expended on the projects at hand where colleague relationships are concerned.

Superiors are the targets of practices yielding the smallest, and therefore least productive, Arena of the three relationships assessed in the survey. The average manager reports a significant reluctance to deal openly and candidly with his superior while favoring the Feedback process as his major interpersonal gambit; even the use of Feedback, however, is subdued relative to that employed with colleagues. The view from high in organizations is very likely colored by the interpersonal styles addressed to them; and, based on the data obtained, it would not be surprising if many members of top management felt that lower level management was submissive, in need of direction, and had few creative suggestions of their own. Quite aside from the obvious effect such an expectation might have on performance reviews, a characteristic reaction to the essentially Type B style directed at superiors is, on their part, to invoke Type C behaviors. Thus, the data obtained call attention to what may be the seeds of a self-reinforcing cycle of authority-obedience-authority. The long-range consequences of such a cycle, in terms of relationship quality and interpersonal style, has been found to be corporate-wide adoption of Type A behaviors which serve to depersonalize work and diminish an organization's human resources.

Thus, based on the present research at least, a number of interpersonal practices seem to characterize organizational life which limit not only the effectiveness of communication within, but the attainment of realistic levels of corporate excellence without. As we will see, which style will prevail very much depends upon the individual manager.

***Interpersonal Practices and Managerial Styles.*** In commenting upon the first of their two major concerns in programs of organization development, Blake and Mouton[6] have stated: "The underlying causes of communication difficulties are to be found in the character of supervision. . . . The solution to the problem of communication is for men to manage by achieving production and excellence through sound utilization of people." To the extent that management style is an important ingredient in the communication process, a second piece of research employing the Johari Window and Managerial grid models in tandem may be of some interest to those concerned with corporate excellence.

Of the 1,000 managers sampled in the *Personnel Relations Survey*, 384 also completed a second instrument, the *Styles of Management Inventory*,[7] based on the Managerial Grid (a two-dimensional model of management styles).[8] Five "anchor" styles are identified relative to one's concern for production vis-à-vis people, and these are expressed in grid notation as follows: 9,9 reflects a high people concern; 5,5 reflects a moderate concern for each; 9,1 denotes high production coupled with low people concerns, while 1,9 denotes the opposite orientation; 1, 1 reflects a minimal concern for both dimensions. In an attempt to discover the significance of one's interpersonal practices for his overall approach to management, the forty individuals scoring highest on each style of management were selected for an analysis of their interpersonal styles. Thus, 200 managers—forty each who were identified as having dominant managerial styles either 9,9; 5,5; 9,1; 1,9; or 1,1—were studied relative to their tendencies to employ Exposure and Feedback Processes in relationships with their subordinates. The research question addressed was: How do individuals who prefer a given managerial style differ in terms of their interpersonal orientations from other individuals preferring other managerial approaches?

The data were subjected to a discriminant function analysis and statistically significant differences were revealed in terms of the manner in which managers employing a given dominant managerial style also employed the Exposure and Feedback processes. The results of the research findings are presented graphically in Figure 4. As a bar graph of Exposure and Feedback scores reveals, those managers identified by a dominant management style of 9,9 displayed the strongest tendencies to employ both Exposure and Feedback in their relationships with subordinates. In addition, the Arena which would result from a Johari plotting of their scores would be in a fairly good state of balance, reflecting about as much use of one process as of the other. The data suggest that the 9,9 style of management—typically described as one which achieves effective production through the sound utilization of people—also entails the sound utilization of personal resources in establishing relationships. The Type D interpersonal style which seems to be associated with the 9,9 management style is fully consistent with the open and unobstructed communication which Blake and Mouton view as essential to the creative resolution of differences and sound relationships.

The 5,5 style of management appears, from the standpoint of Exposure and Feedback employment, to be a truncated version of the 9,9 approach. While the reported scores for both processes hover around the fiftieth percentile, there is a noteworthy preference for Exposure over Feedback. Although a Johari plotting of these scores might also approach a Type D profile, the Arena is less balanced and accounts for only 25 percent of the data available for use in a relationship. Again, such an interpersonal style seems consistent with a managerial approach based on expediency and a search for the middle ground.

As might be expected, the 9,1 managers in the study displayed a marked preference for Exposure over Feedback in their relationships with subordinates. This suggests that managers who are maximally concerned with production issues also are given to an overuse of Exposure—albeit not maximum Exposure—and this is very likely to maintain personal control. In general, a Type C interpersonal style seems to underlie the 9,1 approach to management; and it is important that such managerial practices may be sustained by enlarged Blindspots.

FIGURE 4    A Comparison of Exposure and Feedback Use among Managers with Different Dominant Managerial Styles

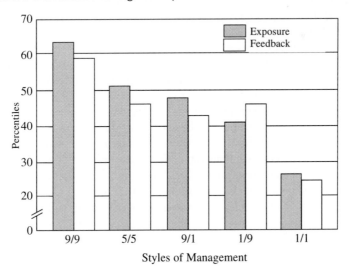

Considering the opposing dominant concerns of the 1,9 manager as compared to the 9,1, it is not too surprising to find that the major interpersonal process of these managers is Feedback solicitation. As with the 9,1 style, the resulting Arena for 1,9 managers is not balanced; but the resulting tension likely stems from less than desired Exposure, leading to relationships in which the managerial Facade is the dominant feature. The Type B interpersonal style may be said to characterize the 1,9 approach to management, with its attendant effects on corporate climate.

Finally, the use of Exposure and Feedback processes reported by those managers identified as dominantly 1,1 is minimal. A mechanical impersonal approach to interpersonal relationships which is consistent with the low profile approach to management depicted under 1,1 is suggested. The Unknown region apparently dominates relationships, and hidden potential and untapped resources prevail. The consequences of such practices for the quality of relationships, climates, and communication effectiveness have already been described in the discussion of Type A interpersonal behaviors.

In summary, it appears that one's interpersonal style is a critical ingredient in his approach to management. While the uses of Exposure and Feedback reported by managers identified according to management style seem to be quite consistent with what one might expect, it is worthy to mention that the test items comprising the *Personnel Relations Survey* have very little, if anything, to do with production versus people concerns. Rather, one's willingness to engage in risk-taking disclosures of feelings, impressions, and observations coupled with his sensitivity to others' participative needs and a felt responsibility to help them become involved via Feedback solicitation were assessed. The fact that such purposive behaviors coincide with one's treatment of more specific context-bound issues like production and people would seem to raise the question: Which comes first, interpersonal or managerial style? The question is researchable, and management practices and information flow might both be enhanced by the results obtained.

## CORPORATE CLIMATE AND PERSONAL DECISIONS

The major thesis of this article has been that interpersonal styles are at the core of a number of corporate dilemmas: communication breakdowns, emotional climates, the quality of relationships, and even managerial practices have been linked to some fairly simple dynamics between people. The fact that the dynamics are simple should not be taken to mean that their management is easy—far from it. But, at the same time, the fact that individuals can and do change their interpersonal style—and thereby set in motion a whole chain of events with corporate significance—should be emphasized. A mere description of one's interpersonal practices has only limited utility, if that is as far as it goes. The value of the Johari Window model lies not so much with its utility for assessing what is but, rather, in its inherent statement of what might be.

Although most people select their interpersonal styles as a *reaction* to what they anticipate from other parties, the key to effective relationships lies in "proaction"; each manager can be a norm setter in his relationships if he will but honestly review his own interpersonal goals and undertake the risks necessary to their attainment. Organizations can criticize their policies—both formal and unwritten— in search for provisions which serve to punish candor and reward evasiveness while equating solicitation of data from others with personal weakness. In short, the culture of an organization and the personal and corporate philosophies which underlie it may be thought of as little more than a *decision product* of the human system. The quality of this decision will directly reflect the quality of the relationships existing among those who fashion it.

If the model and its derivations make sense, then corporate relationships and managerial practices based on candor and trust, openness and spontaneity, and optimal utilization of interpersonal resources are available options to every member of an organizational family. As we have seen, power distributions among people may adversely influence their interpersonal choices. Management styles apparently constrain individuals, but the choice is still there. Type A practices require breaking away from the corporate womb into which one has retreated; personal experiments with greater Exposure and Feedback, however anxiety producing, may be found in the long-run to be their own greatest reward. For the manager locked into Type B behaviors, the task is more simple; he already solicits Feedback to an excellent degree. Needed is enough additional trust in others—whether genuine or forced—to allow a few experiences with Exposure. Others may be found to be less fragile or reactionary than one imagined. Learning to listen is but part of the task confronting managers inclined toward Type C styles; they must learn to seek out and encourage the exposures of others. This new attention to the Feedback process should not be at the expense of Exposure, however. Revamping Type C does not mean adopting Type B. These are all forms of low-risk high-potential-yield personal experiments. Whether they will ever be undertaken and their effects on corporate excellence determined depends upon the individual; the matter is one of personal decision.

## REFERENCES

1. R. R. Blake and Jane S. Mouton, *Corporate Excellence Through Grid Organization Development* (Houston, Texas: Gulf Publishing Co., 1968), p. 4.
2. *Ibid.*, pp. 3–5.
3. Joseph Luft, *Of Human Interaction* (Palo Alto, California: National Press Books, 1969), *passim.*
4. C. Argyris, *Interpersonal Competence and Organizational Effectiveness* (Homewood, Illinois: Dorsey, 1962), *passim.*
5. J. Hall and Martha S. Williams, *Personnel Relations Survey* (Conroe, Texas: Teleometrics International, 1967).
6. R. R. Blake and Jane S. Mouton, *op. cit.*, p. 5.
7. J. Hall, J. B. Harvey, and Martha S. Williams, *Styles of Management Inventory* (Conroe, Texas: Teleometrics International, 1963).
8. R. R. Blake and Jane S. Mouton, *The Managerial Grid* (Houston, Texas: Gulf Publishing Co., 1964), *passim.*

# THE THINKING ORGANIZATION: HOW PATTERNS OF THOUGHT DETERMINE ORGANIZATIONAL CULTURE

*Evelyn Pitre*
*Henry P. Sims, Jr.*

*Thursday evening, 7:30 P.M. In his office on the seventh floor, Michael G. Smith, new CEO of Avant-Garde Computer, Inc. (AGC), examines the most recent sales report. The message is depressing: sales have leveled off in the past year. AGC is a small and innovative young company located in the Silicon Valley. Founded eight years ago, AGC's specialization is engineering graphics design software. The founder, an engineer himself, had successfully marketed two highly specialized software packages for mechanical and electronic design. Two years ago, the need for capital became acute, and the founder sold AGC to a very large multinational corporation.*

*Michael G. Smith was appointed CEO by the consortium. He recognizes the difficulty of AGC's current situation, but he is optimistic that he can revive the company. His strategy would be to broaden AGC's market by adapting and offering its graphics products to other end-user specialists besides engineers, and to add a counseling service to educate and orient clients to graphics applications. However, he foresees that the members of AGC's team would not be thrilled by his view of the future, since they are concerned solely with the engineering applications of the company's products. Quite honestly, he really does not know how to introduce these major strategic changes without losing either the team's spirit or the team.*

Michael's problem is more common than one might think. Each time a manager sets out to change someone else's point of view about a task, a decision, an orientation, or a strategy, he or she would be asking the same set of "how to" questions that trouble Michael. How can I introduce this change in the most effective manner? Is our corporate culture sympathetic or antagonistic to this change?

The difficulties associated with changing individual attitudes and behaviors have been addressed through literature on resistance to change. From an organizational viewpoint, resistance to change takes on an entirely different perspective. At that level, change impacts on more than individual attitudes and behaviors. Indeed, aggregate patterns of thoughts, attitudes, and behaviors throughout an organization will either reinforce the proposed change, or, more likely, severely impede its progress. Therefore, changing an entire organization frequently entails changing patterns of thought that are deeply rooted among large numbers of people. Like Michael, many CEOs have faced the difficulty of turning around an organization from one way of thinking to another.

Fortunately, a new stream of theory and research has emerged that promises to help executives understand how to change organizπation-wide patterns of thought. The ideas, generally known as organizational social cognition, originate from the science of cognitive psychology, which studies the process of how humans think. The term cognition derives from the Greek word "cognos"—to think —and the term social cognition refers mainly to how we think about other people in social situations. For Michael, our CEO, the main issue is how the people in his organization think of themselves with regard to their product/market interface.

A recent book, *The Thinking Organization*,[1] draws on developments in organizational social cognition to provide new knowledge to executives who face the challenge of changing organizational patterns of thought.

*Source: National Productivity Review, Autumn 1987, pp. 340–347.*

The book is based on the assumption that the way people think and organize their thoughts in their organizational life is likely to influence the direction of organizational culture. Therefore, in this article we draw upon ideas from *The Thinking Organization* to introduce fundamentals of social cognition; namely the notions of schema and symbol, and to suggest how they can be used to facilitate organizational change. From a managerial viewpoint, greater understanding of how people think could be an important asset that might determine the success or failure of change.

## FUNDAMENTALS OF SOCIAL COGNITION

Obviously, organizations do not think, but people within them do. Since organizations are an aggregation of people, a "thinking organization" can be viewed as an aggregate of people's thoughts and representations. This metaphor is used by Henry Sims and Dennis Gioia, who argue that "organizations are products of the thought and action of their members,"[2] and who "explore how people in organizations think about their experiences and how they act in conjunction with their thoughts."[3] The way we think is not yet fully understood. Nevertheless, scholars are beginning to derive some knowledge about how cognitions and symbols are created and used, and how these cognitions and symbols lead to behaviors and actions.

### Person schemas or categories

A person is said to cognitively abstract and simplify the multitude of information encountered in day-to-day life in order to capture the inherent organization of the world. Various ideas have emerged regarding how people reorganize that information. One common type of cognitive process is a categorization procedure by which a person mentally classifies an object or another person.

When first encountering a person, an individual mentally matches that person with cognitive structures that have previously been created from long-standing experience and interaction with the world. A cognitive structure, sometimes called a "schema," is a mental representation or system of organization, usually expressed through language or imagery. The cognitive schema used in categorization is called a "category." A particularly vivid representation of a category is sometimes called a "prototype." A common example used in cognitive psychology is the label "bird," which calls forth a mental schema with attributes like "feathers," "beak," "flying," etc.

One particular type of social schema is a person category, which stands in contrast to an object category. The boundaries of a person category are not as well defined. Indeed, it is easier to judge an object as a member of a "chair" or "shirt" category than it is to adequately categorize a person as an "extrovert" or an employee as a "bad supervisor." Social categorization always involves a "fuzzier set." That is why, in an attempt to simplify the categorization process of individuals, cognitive prototypes emerge.

Social categorization is a fairly common event for managers. Formal decisions such as selection and appraisal, as well as more informal day-to-day activities, are based on that process. For example, our own research has shown that when a potential employee matches the prototype of a category, like an extroverted person for a salesperson job, that person is more likely to be preferred to fill the job,[4] even though on the basis of objective information, others could fill the job as well or better.

Executives build prototypes of good and bad performers (person schema) that they use to select or appraise employees. A prototype of a good employee, for example, might be someone who is always on time, who meets and outdoes standards, who is willing to occasionally do something extra, etc.

The main advantage of social categorization is that it is efficient. That is, the cognitions involved in categorization allow us to process mentally a potentially overwhelming amount of information relatively quickly. It is a way to simplify chaos, to order our perceptions. Categorization is not very "effortful." It is a short cut.

However, executives should be aware that social categorization also has disadvantages. One is the fact that people, when asked to reconstruct social information about someone, tend to add to their description information that fits their schema even if it may not be a true characteristic of the individual described. This process is called "gap filling," because we are able to fill in information that we do not truly possess. On the one hand, gap filling allows a person to form an impression from only a few cues, yet can also lead to overgeneralization and false impressions.

Another problem with social categories is that they are particularly resistant to evidence that is inconsistent with them. That is, they "persist stubbornly" even when specific situations, persons, or behaviors contradict them.[5] Typically, people explain the persistence by claiming that the inconsistency is the exception that confirms the rule. Further, we tend to selectively seek out and attend to information that supports our prototypes and to ignore or discount disconfirming evidence. Thus, managers judging employees may, at least for a while, continue to favorably appraise a once good employee despite systematic evidence of decline in performance.

Prototypes also typically have an emotional component deeply entwined within the schema. For example, we might have a particular prototype of how a supervisor for our company should appear and act. An individual who matches or conforms to this prototype would evoke an unconscious positive effect. A supervisor who consistently violates our conventional viewpoints of appropriate supervisory behavior is likely to evoke an unconscious negative effect.

This connection between emotion and cognitive structure is one reason that individuals may not be able to recognize bias brought on by their own emotional response, but sincerely believe their viewpoints are "objective" and "rational." Also, the emotional component is one reason that mere exposure to contradictory information is not enough to change the pattern of thought.

Most of all, it is important to understand that this resistance is not overt or deliberate but is a subtle, usually unconscious cognitive response.

## Event schemas or scripts

Another type of cognitive organization is "event schemas," also called "scripts." Executives usually have clear cognitive structures regarding which behaviors are appropriate under certain conditions. When these behaviors are linked together into sequences of behavior, the cognitive organization that describes the sequence is known as an event schema, or script. For example, because of their long experience, most executives have well-formed and relatively detailed scripts concerning how performance appraisals should be conducted. An event schema is a cognitive organization of appropriate sequential behaviors in a specific situation. Event schemas are constructed as a result of doing something in a certain way over and over again. Religious rites (an Irish Catholic mass or a funeral in Louisiana); habits (morning rituals or superstitious ones); everyday life routines (driving a car or eating in a restaurant); and work-related situations (job interviewing, negotiating, or sales calls) are all examples of event schemas.

An event schema usually allows a person to act automatically in a given circumstance, freeing him or her of unnecessary cognitive burdens. Managers who do not have to think about the procedure of interviewing (including what questions to ask) can concentrate their energy on evaluating candidates and their responses. For example, secretaries who are good typists can perform efficiently when typing from a Dictaphone and yet, when asked, may not be able to recall the content of what they have just typed.

Special kinds of event schemas known as metascripts are used to organize rules and procedure. In decision-making processes and problem-solving strategies, metascripts are used as guidelines for integrating apparently unrelated information under uncertainty. Through plausible reasoning (a special kind of reasoning used under conditions of uncertainty) and schematic information processing, it is said that managers can take action "despite several kinds of ignorance."[6] Managers using metascripts as guidelines for their actions have a basis for their decisions despite uncertainty and lack of information.

## Role schemas

In organizational settings, a further type of schema is of particular importance. Who a person is within a given company and situation represents a "person-in-situation" or "role" schema. A role schema is a representation of a category or person playing a specific role in a given situation. A doctor informing a patient of a bad prognosis, a manager scolding an employee who is frequently late, and a board of directors deciding on a joint venture with another company are all examples of role schemas.

Person-in-situation schemas are based on knowledge of social norms usually linked with a specific role. For example, a worker in a steel plant is not expected to work in a three-piece suit but is expected to conform to policies of his company regarding safety behavior, including the wearing of safety clothing. As another example, the status and authority of an executive can be recognized by his or her display of a socially accepted set of behaviors in a given situation. He or she is the one who is supposed to be responsible, who controls outputs, who evaluates performance, and so on.

As with other types of schemas, role schemas free individuals of extensive and laborious information processing. Also, information contained in a role schema is usually richer, more detailed, and more completely intertwined than in other types of schema and, therefore, potentially less connected to the true characteristics of a given person in a given situation. That is, there is more potential for false gap filling through the intricacy of a role schema. There is a high probability of biases associated with role schemas.

## Self schemas

The last type of schema consists of information organized around the self. "Self-schemas" are generalizations about the self abstracted from the present situation and past experiences. Individuals build representations of themselves based on their perception of themselves (physical characteristics), or their traits (psychological characteristics), and their acts (behavioral characteristics).

For example, an employee who has a negative self-schema because he perceives himself as short, shy, and bungling may believe that he will not be able to perform a new task adequately. The odds are that his behaviors will confirm his apprehensions and will reinforce his self-schema. This influence of self-schema on behaviors is called self-fulfilling prophecy. Self-schemas are notoriously inaccurate or incomplete.

## Symbols

Symbolic processes are also an important part of individuals' cognitive representation of the world. In an attempt to assign meaning to the environment and to communicate understanding to others, individuals use words or images to convey a rich and complex message. Organizations and other social institutions are rich in symbolic processes.

"Symbols" are traditionally defined as words or images that represent something else. To "roll out the red carpet" is a symbolic representation of respect shown to an important guest. The Congressional Medal of Honor is a symbolic representation of bravery and courage. Individuals, for personal convenience or through social agreement, transform realities into symbols whose meaning transcends the boundaries of the reality itself.

Symbols can be used to describe the reality to others, but most of all, they act as "energy savers." They are mental short cuts used to amalgamate informal rules, situational information, emotional content, and other apparently unrelated information into a succinct representation. Organization officials do not have to express explicitly their gratitude toward a retiring partner if they organize a reception, invite his or her friends, and offer a gift. The whole package symbolizes their recognition of his or her contribution. Symbols are a very efficient way to deal with a large amount of complex information.

Another way by which symbols are energy savers is their capacity to alleviate tension or stress. Symbolic rituals, such as the "meal after the show" for actors and actresses or the involvement of some employees in sports tournaments sponsored by their company, are examples of the venting functions of symbols.

Symbols also serve as excellent retrieval cues, since they are more easily remembered than the information they represent and can trigger a flood of memories. Awards, trophies, or diplomas represent years of effort, battles, and incremental progress toward a goal. Executives also have symbolic representations of power and authority, which are frequently conveyed through titles, appearance, and dress. Those symbols imply or convey knowledge far beyond the immediate attributes associated with them.

Symbolization is also a process by which complexities of environments are reduced and simplified. In social contexts, like organizations, symbols are widely used. Indeed, symbols quickly communicate the ideology or the philosophy of the enterprise, spread values and the sense of what is important for the organization, and help identify organizational hierarchy and power. Highly symbolic action can be used to develop shared meanings that facilitate commitment and concerted action. Allocation of resources, bigger budgets, a personal secretary, and a carpet in one's office are all common symbolic representations of organizational power. In personnel-related policies, for example, publicity about a successful team effort can tell other employees much about an organization's ideology and culture.

Symbols are also an essential part of the socialization process. New employees must identify "the rules" as quickly as possible. Informal rules are frequently represented by symbols. Stories about daring behavior, past practical jokes, bosses' feats, and so on, rapidly tell the newcomer what is important, what is permitted, what is valued, who is to be respected, etc. Most of all, executives should think about the potential of deliberately managing symbols as a means to influence organizational culture.

## ORGANIZATIONAL CULTURAL CHANGE

Organizational culture is a broad, complex, and sometimes confusing concept. Most writers use the term to represent a system of rules, norms, and symbols on which members agree and which is a basis for action. But organizational culture can also be viewed from a social cognition perspective.

Each individual employee has patterns of thought (schemas, symbols) that are highly idiosyncratic. But some patterns are shared by the vast majority within a given organization. The technical term for a shared pattern of thought is "consensual." This means that people in an organization, for example, who shared notions of how a meeting is to be conducted, have a consensual script about the appropriate sequence of behaviors. Also, employees of an organization typically have fairly consistent ideas about how an executive should appear and behave—an example of a consensual person-in-situation schema.

Organizational culture is the result of a convergence of employee schemas and symbols. But culture is also a cause. That is, once created or implemented and shared, organizational culture provides justifications or reasons for employees and managers to decide, behave, plan, and perform the way they do. In most organizations, there is also some degree of shared understanding about the fundamental nature and strategies of the organization, and this is also a type of consensual pattern of thought. For example, Michael Smith, the CEO in our introductory case, took over a company when the label of "engineering application" was the currently operative consensual pattern that identified the company. In this case, schemas and symbols represent a culture that is internally focused, with major emphasis on the development of a technically excellent product. In contrast, Michael, with his broader experiences, sees the need for an externally-focused, marketing-oriented strategy, where the product would be oriented to a wider application base and then could be fine-tuned to the needs of specific customers. Like many executives who wish to reorient a department or a company, Michael is faced with the problem of dealing with a deeply entrenched consensual pattern of thought.

Changes of culture are typically not evolutionary, but revolutionary. Crisis is a typical prerequisite for cultural change. In the AGC example, the take-over of the company and the arrival of Michael as new CEO, along with the dismal business outlook, may provide the necessary conditions for organizational cultural transition to take place. Other potential times of transitions would be sharp periods of recession, technological breakthroughs, changes in the management team, and all sorts or managerial crises. Under those circumstances, the confidence of organizational employees in the veracity and applicability of previously shared patterns of thought can be unfrozen, thus paving the way for a new consensual pattern of thought. Nevertheless, it is important to remember that those patterns are very persistent and quite resistant to disconfirmatory information.

Understanding consensual schemas and symbols are of crucial importance in any attempt to change an organizational structure. The essence of cultural change is the replacement of one consensual pattern with another. The challenge to Michael is to replace an internally-oriented engineering schema with an externally-oriented marketing schema.

## Steps toward change

How this replacement might be accomplished is not an easy question to answer. What are the specific actions that Michael can take? Here are some suggestions that revolve around the idea of replacing one consensual schema with another.

First, it is important to recognize, define, and articulate the current consensual pattern of thought. For Michael, especially, since he is new, this might entail extensive conversations with the staff and customers to obtain information about how they view the company. Another approach might be to bring important members of the staff together and ask questions like: What are we? What do we stand for? What is our current strength? Clearly, the main value of this first step would be to help define and understand a baseline from which a change effort can be mounted.

Then, it may be useful to organize and list the so-called rational factors that currently constrain the company. What are the impediments and disadvantages of the present way of doing things? Why is the current situation inadequate to accomplish what needs to be done? However, it is important at this stage to remember that information alone is not sufficient to create change. For example, Michael would be disappointed if he depended solely on an objective argument about the inadequacies of engineering elegance to meet market demands.

Another step is an analysis of the emotional factors that might stand in the way of change. One should perform an analysis of who will be threatened. Will some perceive the possibility that they may suffer a loss of power or prestige? Understanding the emotional bases of resistance to change will be helpful. Most of all, a realization that the resistor may not be fully aware of the underlying reasons that are causing his or her resistance, and an awareness that the resistance is not necessarily malevolent, will help one to be patient and understanding.

Perhaps the most important step is to institute a process of reevaluation. A top-down transmittal of information and orders is not likely to be successful. A bottom-up effort of analysis and examination of alternatives has a better chance of succeeding. Additional information from outsiders might be very appropriate at this stage.

For example, Michael might learn from John Scully, CEO of Apple Computer, who instituted a re-evaluation of Apple's way of thinking soon after he assumed the chairmanship. He brought together key corporate executives for an extended retreat to reevaluate the coordination and direction among the divergent, and some thought confusing, Apple product line. This was a difficult and extended process, but it was ultimately successful in creating a coherent direction for the organization.

Another important step is selecting and choosing the actors who will carry out the change. Several alternatives are available. The frontal assault would be attempting to directly change the patterns of thought of the existing staff. Sometimes this will work, especially if the organization is really seen to be in crisis. A second alternative would be to select those individuals who seem to be most sympathetic to new ideas and empower them with authority and responsibility for change.

A third alternative would entail importing new key individuals from outside. One CEO who wanted to make a radical shift in product technology went to the extreme of creating a new and separate legal entity to compete directly with his old organization. When queried about this rather unusual strategy, he stated that he felt the old organization was "too married" to the old technology.

Whichever alternative is chosen, the key element is the development and implementation of new consensual patterns of thought.

Michael would also be wise to utilize specific symbolic action as a part of his change effort. As one example, he might, with some publicity, establish a new task force charged with the assignment of developing a new strategic marketing thrust. He might emphasize, especially through his own actions, the importance of adapting the company' systems to unique customer needs, and ensure that these actions are given wide visibility in the organization. The point here is to create highly visible examples that vividly convey the new pattern of thinking.

Finally, sometime well into the change implementation phase, Michael should try to "close the loop" by attempting to articulate and publicize a coherent strategy that will solidify the new consensual pattern of thought.

## CONCLUSION

In changing an organization's culture, it has been said that leadership is of prime importance, especially the leader's "vision." Vision means the capability to formulate and articulate new patterns of thought that can be shared by all to propel the organization toward new horizons. If we view organizational culture as consensual patterns of thought, then management and control of those patterns can be used to create, implement, or change an organizational culture. Personal schemas, event schemas, role schemas, and symbolic representations should be objects of focus.

The major goal is to hammer together a new consensual pattern of values. Again using the examples of AGC, one can predict that Michael Smith will have more success in changing AGC's set of values if he can systematically demonstrate what he believes in and diffuse it throughout the organization. The creation of new symbols and patterns of thought are realistic ways to change an organizational culture.

## NOTES

1. H. P. Sims, Jr., and D. A. Gioia, *The Thinking Organization: Dynamics of Organizational Social Cognition* (San Francisco: Jossey-Bass, 1986).
2. *Ibid.*, p. 1.
3. *Ibid.*, p. 2.
4. A. J. Jaccoud, D. A. Gioia, and H. P. Sims, Jr., "Schema-Based Categorization and Personnel Decisions," *Proceeding: National Academy of Management Meeting,* 1984, pp. 274–78.
5. S. T. Fiske and S. E. Taylor, *Social Cognition* (New York: Random House, 1984).
6. D. J. Isenberg, "The Structure and Process of Understanding Implication for Managerial Action," in H. P. Sims, Jr., and D. A. Gioia, *op. cit.,* pp. 238–62.

# 9
# Group Dynamics and Self-Managed Work Teams

GROUPTHINK RECONSIDERED
*Glen Whyte*

WORK TEAMS
APPLICATIONS AND EFFECTIVENESS
*Eric Sundstrom*
*Kenneth P. DeMeuse*
*David Futrell*

## GROUPTHINK RECONSIDERED

### *Glen Whyte*

Several authors (e.g., Bazerman, Giuliano & Appelman, 1984; Janis, 1972, 1982; Jervis, 1976; Staw, 1981; Tuchman, 1984) have written about groups' pursuit of disadvantageous policies after the risks of doing so have become apparent. Janis (1972, 1982) and Tuchman (1984) in particular focused on a variety of historically noteworthy decision fiascoes that moved them to speculate about why people in authority frequently act contrary to enlightened self-interest by making decisions that are likely to be counterproductive. Examples of such decisions include, among others, the American failure in Vietnam, the Kennedy administration's decision to invade Cuba at the Bay of Pigs, and the Watergate cover-up. The critical question from an analytical point of view is whether or not any pattern can be recognized from decisions of this sort, or are these simply difficult decisions that unfortunately went awry?

This paper will advance and integrate some theoretical determinants of excessive risk taking in group decision making, the consequences of which have been described as fiascoes. *Risk*, as it is used here, refers to the probability and the value of the outcomes associated with an act. A risky decision is one that rejects a certain outcome in favor of a gamble of equal or lower expected value. To qualify for inclusion in the analysis, the particular course of action pursued must have been recognized as excessively risky or ill-advised at the time the decision was made, feasible alternative courses of action must have existed, and the policy or decision in question must have been the product of group discussion. More contemporary examples include the decision to launch the space shuttle *Challenger* and the Iran-Contra affair. The examples cited in this article represent instances of

*Source*: Glen Whyte, "Groupthink Reconsidered," *Academy of Management Review*, 1989, Vol. 14, No. 1, pp. 40–56. Copyright ©1989. Reprinted by permission.

defective decision making by a few policy makers in which the option pursued had only a low probability of success. Consequently, the primary focus of this paper is on the process by which a decision is reached rather than on the ultimate consequences of the decision, to which process is not always tightly coupled (Janis, 1982).

Many examples of decision fiascoes are characterized by the group's inability to change a failing policy (Staw, 1981), but other examples such as the Watergate cover-up or the launch of the space shuttle *Challenger* were choices about a specific isolated event rather than about the fate of an entire course of action. It is suggested that similar theoretical mechanisms underlie risky decision making, regardless of whether the policy was clearly mistaken at the outset or whether its flaws became apparent only as commitment mounted.

Consider, for example, the decision of the Kennedy administration to invade Cuba at the Bay of Pigs in 1963. As a policy decision, the Bay of Pigs fiasco ranks among the worst blunders ever committed by an American administration. The groupthink hypothesis has been invoked as a major causal factor to explain this and other notorious examples of bad decision making (Janis, 1972, 1982). *Groupthink* refers to "a mode of thinking that people engage in when they are deeply involved in a cohesive in-group, when the members' striving for unanimity overrides their motivation to realistically appraise alternative courses of action" (Janis, 1982, p. 9). Janis identified eight main symptoms of groupthink: a) an illusion of invulnerability, b) an illusion of morality, c) rationalization, d) stereotyping, e) self-censorship, f) an illusion of unanimity, g) direct pressure on dissidents, and h) reliance upon self-appointed mindguards. By facilitating the development of shared illusions and related norms, these symptoms are used by groups to maintain esprit de corps during difficult times. The price paid to maintain group cohesiveness, however, is a decline in mental efficiency, reality testing, moral judgment, and ultimately it leads to a decline in the quality of decision making.

The groupthink hypothesis is a less-than-comprehensive explanation for why groups may make excessively risky decisions. The main theme of groupthink is concurrence seeking. But concurrence seeking generally occurs in group decision making, and it is not unique to groups that perform poorly such as President Kennedy's team in 1963. The task, after all, of a decision-making group is to produce consensus from the initial preferences of its members. Consensus, moreover, is typically obtained around preferences that are initially dominant within the group, although groupthink sheds no light on what these initial preferences might be.

This is unfortunate because knowledge of the dominant point of view of group members at the onset of discussion, combined with knowledge of the nature of the task and the alternatives being considered, can enable researchers to make accurate predictions about the ultimate choice of the group (Kerr, 1982). Increasingly, evidence suggests that the probability that various alternatives will be chosen arising from even complex decisions can be determined with a high degree of accuracy (e.g., Davis, 1980; Kerr & MacCoun, 1985). This can be accomplished by relying on social decision schemes (Davis, 1973), which relate the initial distribution of member preferences to the group's decision. In the case of the kind of decisions under discussion, which are judgmental tasks, the best fitting social decision scheme is a majority social combinatory process (Laughlin & Adamopoulous, 1982). That is, groups in these circumstances tend to select the option supported by the majority at the outset of group discussion, and they tend to do so regardless of the presence or absence of groupthink.

An additional gap in the groupthink hypothesis is that it does not take into account some of the current research on group dynamics. One of the most intensively researched phenomena in social psychology during recent years describes the tendency for collective judgment that is the product of group discussion to magnify the dominant initial inclination of group members. This phenomenon, group polarization, is demonstrated in the field by the excessive risk seeking observed in decision fiascoes such as the Bay of Pigs invasion. Group polarization implies that when individual members of a group are generally disposed toward risk before group discussion, it is reliable that the decision of the group will be even riskier than that of the average group member. Janis (1982) briefly acknowledged group polarization, but the phenomenon was not integrated into the theory of group-think because such integration is dependent on knowledge of the initial preferences of group members.

This paper develops an alternative explanation of decision fiascoes and explains certain theoretical devices that address the limitations of an approach founded on group dynamics. Such theoretical devices include framing effects (Kahneman & Tversky, 1981), risk seeking in the domain of losses (Kahneman & Tversky, 1979), and group polarization (Myers & Lamm, 1976).

More specifically, it is suggested that decision fiascoes are the product of a choice that is framed to appear as one in the domain of losses. Given such a frame, risk seeking preferences usually are elicited (Kahneman & Tversky, 1979). In group decision making, pressures for uniformity will militate toward a choice that is consistent with the initial risky preferences of a majority of members. Group discussion will also amplify the extent to which the group prefers the risky option via the process of polarization. The net effect of these processes is such that groups whose members frame the choice as one between losses will evidence a normatively inappropriate preference for risk even more frequently and to a greater degree than would their average member.

## THE ASPIRATION-LEVEL CONCEPT

The key concept in the model of excessively risky group behavior advanced here is derived from the general notion of an aspiration level. Although this notion is not new, it has been reemphasized in recent models of risky decision-making behavior (e.g., Fishburn, 1977; Kahneman & Tversky, 1979).

The aspiration level concept is important because it helps us to understand attitudes toward risk that contradict the prevailing view about risk attitude in management science research. In the prevailing view, the aspiration level concept is ignored and decision makers are assumed to be uniformly risk averse (Payne, Laughhunn, & Crum 1980). Results from many studies plus field observations (e.g., Janis, 1982; Tuchman, 1984) indicated that such a view is inadequate (Payne et al. 1980). The consensus emerging from a variety of studies is that *risk preference* is more accurately described as a mixture of risk seeking when individuals choose between losses and *risk aversion* when individuals choose between gains.

This characterization of risk preference has been discussed in detail by Kahneman and Tversky (1979) in their explication of prospect theory. More specifically, to be risk seeking is to reject a certain outcome in favor of a gamble with equal or lower expected value. To be risk averse is to prefer a certain outcome to a gamble with an equal or greater expected value. An example of risk seeking in the domain of losses would be the rejection of a certain loss of $60 in favor of a gamble with a 60 percent chance of a $100 loss and a 40 percent chance of no loss at all. An example of risk aversion in the domain of gains would be the acceptance of a $60 gain over a gamble with a 60 percent chance of a $100 gain and a 40 percent chance of no gain whatsoever. Loss aversion is consistent with both risk seeking in the domain of losses and risk aversion in the domain of gains.

Prospect theory differs in two critical ways from the preeminent theory of decision making under risk, the expected utility model. These differences are particularly relevant to the present analysis. First, prospect theory relies on the certainty effect, which implies that a given decrease in the probability of an event will have most effect on judgment when the event is initially considered inevitable, rather than merely possible. The certainty effect promotes risk seeking in choices between losses by exaggerating the distastefulness of losses that are certain, relative to those that are less sure. When choices are made between gains, the certainty effect leads to risk aversion because the attractiveness of positive gambles is diminished relative to sure things.

Second, the manner in which people regard risky options is described in terms of what is referred to as a value function. The value function represents the relation between objectively defined gains and losses and the subjective value a person places on such gains and losses. The value function also implies that people evaluate the outcomes of decisions in terms of gains or losses relative to a subjectively appropriate reference point. Consequently, the selection of that point can have strong and predictable effects on the perceived attractiveness of outcomes because objectively identical options may be evaluated or framed as either gains or losses depending on where the reference point is set.

When a decision maker observes an event and frames a subsequent related decision as a choice between losses, he or she has moved on the value function from Point A to Point B. This is precisely the case when a decision maker is faced with a dilemma in which one option is perceived to be the acceptance of a certain loss and the other would be to possibly avoid those losses at the cost of potentially increasing them. At Point B, further losses do not loom as large in terms of value as do comparable gains. As a result, an individual at Point B is inclined to risk further losses in order to obtain possible gains. Compared to a person at Point A, a person at Point B is more likely to engage in risk-seeking behavior. This situation is graphically described in Figure 1 in terms of the value function.

For example, consider an entrepreneur who has lost $1,000 and now is facing a choice between a sure gain of $500 and an even chance to earn $1,000 or nothing. Unless the entrepreneur has adapted to his or her losses, the choice is likely to be considered as one between a sure loss of $500 and a 50 percent chance of a $1,000 loss, rather than as a choice between a sure gain of $500 and a 50 percent chance of a $1,000 gain. As suggested in prospect theory, the former characterization promotes the seeking of risk and a resultant preference for the gamble, whereas the latter characterization does not. A person who has not come to terms with his other losses and, hence, who has not yet shifted his or her reference point to reflect the status quo is likely to engage in more adventurous behavior than normal (Kahneman & Tversky, 1979).

Framing effects may explain the occurrence of decision fiascoes because many of these decisions share a common structure. Decisions that lead to fiascoes are most naturally framed, whether appropriately or not, as a choice between two or more unattractive options. One option typically involves the immediate recognition of the permanence of an aversive state of affairs. The other option or options entail potentially an even worse situation combined with the possibility that the aversive state of affairs may be avoided. That is, the reference level suggested by the problem leads to the choice being interpreted by those empowered to make it as one between losses, rather than as one between gains or between that status quo versus a potential loss or gain. Typically, the consequence of a person's framing the choice in this manner is the elicitation of risk-seeking preferences, at least at the individual level of analysis. The following will suggest why this may also be true at the group level.

## PRODUCTS OF GROUP INTERACTION

*Uniformity Pressures.* The task of a decision-making group is to produce a group position from the initial preferences of its members through the sharing of beliefs, information, and arguments. Although unanimity about the choice is usually unlikely at first, social interaction provides the means by which mutual influence can lead to group convergence and, ultimately, consensus. The socially mediated change that may be necessary if consensus is to be attained can occur through either normative or informational influence (Stasser, Kerr, & Davis, 1980). Normative influence produces conformity in the group through the desire to comply with the expectations or feelings of others. Informational influence occurs when one person relies on another for information about reality. Both modes of influence usually are responsible for socially mediated change because most exchanges communicate information and expectations (Stasser et al., 1980).

FIGURE 1    The Value Function of Prospect Theory

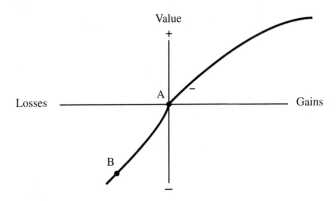

Note: From "Prospect Theory: An Analysis of Decision under Risk" by D. Kahneman and A. Tversky, 1979, *Econometrica*, 47, p. 279. Copyright 1979 by Econometrica. Reprinted by permission.

The observation that a group's discussion of a problem generates pressures toward uniformity is hardly novel. These pressures result in a tendency for group members to move toward majority positions, even in the absence of external pressure to reach unanimity and independent of the correctness of the majority position (Janis, 1982). The tendency for a member's responses to conform more closely to that of the group after exposure to group discussion has been demonstrated in a variety of contexts, and it has played a significant role in many historic fiascoes. As such, uniformity pressures should form an integral part of any theoretical model that attempts to describe the group process that culminates in a decision fiasco.

The strength of the tendency for group members to conform to the view dominant in the group is contingent on several factors, but it is more powerful under two conditions (Ferrell, 1985). The first condition is uncertainty about the appropriate response, and it is characteristic of decision fiascoes. Rarely in these circumstances is there an obvious correct choice. As a result, group members will be compelled to seek information from others about the selection of the appropriate choice. The second condition that encourages individual conformity to the view of the group is the need to maintain a good relationship with other group members. The organizational context in which most decisions of broad-ranging consequence occur will ensure that this condition is also operative. An organizational setting should induce concerns about social desirability, continued membership in the group, and a desire to maintain the group as a functioning entity.

An important determinant of the direction and extent of normative and informational influence and, hence, of the likelihood that a group will adopt a given alternative is the number of proponents that the alternative has at the outset of group discussion. Assume that a five-person group is required to choose between two options. One option entails a certain loss, and the other entails a potential loss of equal expected value to the certain loss. Assume further that the five group members have been drawn randomly from a population in which 80 percent of individuals are risk seeking in the domain of losses. Such an assumption is tenable in light of previous research (e.g., Toland & O'Neil, 1984) that suggests that approximately this percentage of individuals exhibits an aversion to certain losses in relation to losses of equal or even lower expected value that are less sure.

Based on these assumptions, 94 percent of such five-person groups will contain a majority or more of members who prefer the risky option over the certain loss. Given knowledge of the group decision rule, which is the degree of consensus required for a group decision, and knowledge of the initial preferences of individual group members, it can be determined if the group will attain sufficient consensus in order to make a decision. If majority rule prevails, it is apparent that 94 percent of the groups will have satisfied this criterion at the outset and will prefer the risky option over the certain loss.

Although minority viewpoints can be influential under certain conditions, conformity to the majority view is the dominant form of behavior (Moscovici, 1984). This should particularly be the case with the kind of decision which has been associated with fiascoes in the past. This type of decision is a judgmental task of medium to high uncertainty, for which there is no objectively correct choice. There is strong support for the notion of majority process as characterizing the manner in which groups tend to attain consensus in these circumstances (Davis, 1982; Kerr, 1982). Such evidence supports the notion that reliance on a group, as opposed to an individual, decision process to resolve a judgmental task in the domain of losses will increase the frequency with which the risky option will be preferred.

*Group Polarization.* In addition to pressures for uniformity, another well-established product of group interaction is relevant to the occurrence of decision fiascoes. For more than two decades it has been observed that social interaction in small groups can result in group polarization, the tendency for group discussion to enhance the point of view initially dominant within the group. More specifically, the change effect that groups have on individuals in decision-making tasks can be described as a phenomenon in which "the average post-discussion response will tend to be more extreme in the same direction as the average of the pregroup responses....Note that polarization refers to an increase in the extremity of the average response of the subject population responses" (Myers & Lamm, 1976, p. 603).

In the area of risk taking, several studies employing choice dilemmas and other methodologies confirm that a group will be inclined to be more risky than its average member was before participation in group discussion, when that average member had an initial preference for risk (e.g., Burnstein, 1969; Deets & Hoyt, 1970; Doise, 1969; Runyan, 1974; Zaleska, 1974, 1976). Observations in the field also are consistent with the changes implied by the polarization effect (Myers, 1982).

Because group polarization has been well documented, attention has shifted to the processes that are responsible for its occurrence, and two related theories are most commonly advanced (Isenberg, 1986; Myers, 1982). Interpersonal comparison explanations describe polarization in the language of social motivation. Group members alter their views in a manner calculated to maintain an image of social desirability because people need to perceive of and present themselves in a favorable light. Informational influence theories, in contrast, suggest that polarization occurs because the preponderance of arguments and facts adduced during discussion tend to be supportive of the dominant initial position and will therefore reinforce it. Also operative are the biases toward information that are consistent with one's position: the fact that such attention will generate even more arguments in favor of the initially preferred position and the tendency to become committed to a position after espousing support for it (Ferrell, 1985).

It is suggested that group polarization relates to the occurrence of a decision fiasco in the following way. When a required choice is perceived to be between a sure loss and the possibility of a larger loss of equal or even lower expected value, the majority of group members are likely to initially prefer the risky option over the certain loss. Polarization is then hypothesized to occur. That is, the effect of social interaction will be to amplify the dominant initial preference for risk that characterizes individual group members. As a result, a group choice between losses should evidence an even more extreme preference for risk than the average of group members' preferences prior to discussion. The difference in risk preference may not be large, but it should be reliable (Myers & Lamm, 1976).

This increased propensity for risk in choices between a certain loss and a potential loss of equal or lower expected value will manifest itself in at least one of three ways: (a) holding constant the probability of failure if action is taken and the amount of certain loss if no action is taken, groups will be willing to risk even greater potential losses than will individuals to avoid a certain loss; (b) holding constant both the amount and probability of loss if action is taken, groups will be inclined to prefer the action option to a lower value of certain loss than will individuals; (c) holding constant both the certain loss in the event that no action is taken and the potential loss in the event that action occurs, but is unsuccessful, groups will find the potential loss option to be preferable at a higher level of probability of loss if action is taken than will individuals.

## RELATION TO GROUPTHINK

Irving Janis (1972, 1982) laid the basis for a theory of the causes and effects of groupthink, "a collective pattern of defensive avoidance" (Janis & Mann, 1977, p.129). Janis described several shared characteristics of cohesive decision-making groups that have been responsible for some policy debacles. The following quotation from Janis and Mann (1977, p. 130) is a good example.

> Many historic fiascoes can be traced to defective policy making on the part of government leaders who receive social support from their in-group of advisors. A series of historic fiascoes by Janis (1972) suggests that the following four groups of policy advisors, like Kimmel's in-group of naval commanders, were dominated by concurrence seeking or groupthink and displayed characteristic symptoms of defensive avoidance: 1) Neville Chamberlains' inner circle, whose members supported the policy of appeasement of Hitler during 1937 and 1938, despite repeated warnings and events that it would have adverse consequences; 2) President Truman's advisory group, whose members supported the decision to escalate the war in North Korea despite firm warnings by the Chinese Communist government that U.S. entry into North Korea would be met with armed resistance from the Chinese; 3) President Kennedy's inner circle, whose members supported the decision to launch the Bay of Pigs invasion of Cuba despite the availability of information indicating that it would be an unsuccessful venture and would damage U.S. relations with other countries; 4) President Johnson's close advisors, who supported the decision to escalate the war in Vietnam despite intelligence reports and other information indicating that this course of action would not defeat the Vietcong or the North Vietnamese and would entail unfavorable political consequences within the United States. All these groupthink dominated groups were characterized by strong pressures toward uniformity, which inclined their members to avoid raising controversial issues, questioning weak arguments, or calling a halt to soft-headed thinking.

There also is evidence that groupthink was at work in the Nixon entourage, which was responsible for the Watergate cover-up, although there is some question of the cohesiveness of this group (Janis, 1982).

To add a contemporary flavor to the discussion, consider the tragedy of the space shuttle *Challenger*. This situation was the product of a flawed decision as much as it was a failure of technology. The pressures on the National Aeronautics and Space Administration (NASA) to launch the space shuttle at the earliest opportunity were intense, despite evidence that this course of action was inadvisable. A decision to delay the launch was undesirable from NASA's perspective because of the impact it would have on political and public support for the program. In contrast, a successful launch would have appeased the public and the politicians alike, and it would have amounted to another major achievement. NASA engineers claimed that pressure to launch was so intense that authorities routinely dismissed potentially lethal hazards as acceptable risks, reducing such bureaucratic safeguards as the flight readiness review to a meaningless exercise (McConnell, 1987).

Strong pressures for uniformity also characterize the process surrounding the flawed decisions of the Reagan administration to exchange arms for hostages with Iran and to continue commitment to the Nicaraguan Contras in the face of several congressional amendments limiting or banning aid. For example, the Tower commission report censured Secretary of State Shultz and Defense Secretary Weinberger for not presenting their objections to the arms-for-hostages deal with a sufficient degree of vigor. Also, President Reagan's former national security advisor Robert McFarlane testified before the joint congressional panel investigating the arms-for-hostages deal and the diversion of funds to the Contras that he had reservations about the policies of the Reagan administration. McFarlane, however, said he erred in "not having the guts to stand up and tell the President that.....Because if I'd done that, [CIA Director] Bill Casey, [former U.N. ambassador] Jeanne Kirkpatrick, and [Defense Secretary} Cap Weinberger would have said, 'I was some kind of commie, you know'" ("It Was," 1987, p. 19).

The foregoing examples can be described with some degree of accuracy as situations in which groups were faced with a negative deviation from a neutral reference point or, in other words, there would be a sure loss unless action was taken. That is, the groups were at Point B on the value function illustrated in Figure 1. In some cases, as in the example of American escalation in the Vietnam War, the U.S. government was responsible for finding itself in this situation. Not all of the deviations from the neutral reference point, however, were attributable to the action of the group that responded to the situation with a decision fiasco. For example, the U.S. government was not directly responsible for the appearance of Castro's regime on America's doorstep. Nor is it easy to characterize the negative deviation from the neutral reference level in terms of resources. For example, the existence of Castro's government did not directly lead to the incurring of costs by the Kennedy administration. Yet the appearance of a communist regime so close to the United States was perceived by anticommunist American policy makers as a decrease in the level of U.S. national security to which they were unwilling or unable to adapt.

Similarly, the situation faced by Nixon's group subsequent to the discovery of the Watergate burglary was such that the likelihood of their escaping detection for various illegal activities had been decreased to an intolerably low level. Their choices were admitting responsibility for the burglary of the Watergate building that was conducted in order to plant eavesdropping equipment in the national headquarters of the Democratic party or fabricating an illegal cover-up. A cover-up entailed the possibility of success, but it also entailed additional grievous consequences in the event of its probable failure.

The decision to launch the *Challenger* also can be described as a choice in the domain of losses. To delay the launch an additional time entailed certain unfortunate consequences for the space shuttle program. Those consequences, however, could possibly have been avoided by the decision to launch, although such a choice entailed additional risks and, hence, additional potential losses.

Understandably, the arms-for-hostages deal also was perceived by those who made it as the product of a choice between losses. The status quo—American nationals held by terrorist groups—was a certain loss to which it would be difficult to adapt. The striking of an arms deal with Iran created the possibility that those losses could be averted, although it was likely that the deal would fail and add to American woes. An important additional element in the trade was also consistent with the view that U.S. decision makers adopted a decision frame for this act consistent with a choice in the domain of losses. The strategic importance of Iran led U.S. policy makers to attempt to reestablish American influence in Iran and "to restore something resembling normal relations with that country" (Tower, Muskie, & Scowcroft, 1987, p. B1).

Finally, consider the decision of the Reagan administration to continue to support the Nicaraguan Contras in the face of a congressional ban on such activity. The administration was attempting to maintain the Contras during a period in which aid was denied by Congress, even though the program of support might eventually have been judged illegal. Apparently, the collapse of the Contra movement was an aversive state of affairs to which White House decision makers were unwilling or unable to adapt. According to President Reagan, without U.S. support for the Contras, the Soviets would gain a dangerous toehold in Central America. Shortly after Congress prohibited aid to the Contras in April, 1985, President Reagan described his congressional opponents as "voting to have a totalitarian Marxist-Leninist government here in the Americas, and there's no way for them to disguise it. So, we're not going to give up" (Hamilton & Inouye, 1987, p. 48). The preferred alternative was the development of a covert program to encourage aid for the Contras, which, if successful, would sustain the Contras until additional congressional funding could be obtained. If discovered, however, such activity could lead to indictments for participation in broad conspiracy to evade the restrictions on military aid, and it could also imperil future congressional support for the Contras. In testimony before the Congressional Committee, former national security adviser Rear Admiral John Poindexter states: "Very frankly, we were willing to take some risks in order to keep the Contras alive…until we could eventually win the legislative battle" (Hamilton & Inouye, 1987, p. 42).

More generally, the initial events that produced the loss or the deviation from the neutral reference point in the preceding examples produced a decision frame for subsequent, related decisions that can be roughly described as follows. One possible subsequent choice becomes the acceptance of losses, whether they are in terms of wasted resources, a decrease in the level of national security, or the admittance of complicity in illegal activity. The other choice, to put it in the boldest relief possible, is to engage in risky behavior. Through such behavior a group may regain what has been lost in the past and return to the neutral reference point. However, such behavior also includes the possibility of exacerbating the situation and of further movement away from the neutral reference point. When decision makers are presented with a decision frame of this description, there is substantial empirical support in laboratory studies employing the method of hypothetical and real choices that the risky option will be preferred, even when it is normatively unacceptable to do so (Kahneman & Tversky, 1979, 1984). In addition, the polarizing effect of group discussion will tend to push the group in the direction of even greater risk and, hence, frequently even greater propensity for error. Figure 2 diagrams the relationships among the processes described.

## DISCUSSION

Evidence to support the foregoing analysis is far from complete, and it is subject to multiple interpretations. Yet evidence also suggests that for each of the fiascoes discussed by Janis, the frame adopted by decision makers led them to perceive their decision as between certain loss and potentially greater losses. For example, a major reason for the Bay of Pigs invasion that was offered by informed insiders and the president was the political costs of doing nothing (Schlesinger, 1965). In addition, Truman ran the significant risk of war with Communist China by crossing the 38th parallel into North Korea in part because he favored unification of North and South Korea (Neustadt, 1976). In doing that, the decision to stop at the border amounted to the acceptance of a certain loss. The greater danger of war with China was less than certain and as a result more attractive than accepting the failure of the unification policy.

The failure to fortify the defenses at Pearl Harbor was also most likely seen as the avoidance of certain losses at the expense of potentially greater losses. Kimmel and his group of advisers often discussed at length whether to go on full alert, but they were keenly aware that an alert could only have been put into effect "at the cost of interrupting ongoing training programs and the high priority mission

FIGURE 2   Proposed Structure of a High-Risk Group Decision

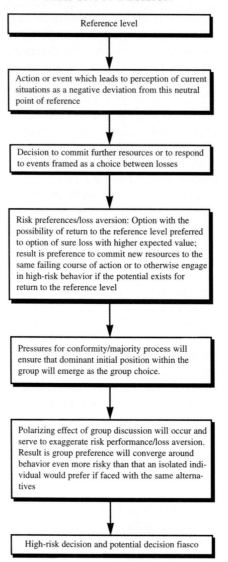

PROPOSED STRUCTURE OF A HIGH-
RISK GROUP DECISION

Reference level

Action or event which leads to perception of current situations as a negative deviation from this neutral point of reference

Decision to commit further resources or to respond to events framed as a choice between losses

Risk preferences/loss aversion: Option with the possibility of return to the reference level preferred to option of sure loss with higher expected value; result is preference to commit new resources to the same failing course of action or to otherwise engage in high-risk behavior if the potential exists for return to the reference level

Pressures for conformity/majority process will ensure that dominant initial position within the group will emerge as the group choice.

Polarizing effect of group discussion will occur and serve to exaggerate risk performance/loss aversion. Result is group preference will converge around behavior even more risky than that an isolated individual would prefer if faced with the same alternatives

High-risk decision and potential decision fiasco

of supplying personnel and equipment to United States outposts close to Japan" (Janis, 1982). The option the group elected to pursue contained "less probable, but more damaging eventualities" (Wohlsetter, 1962).

As in other cases there has been a lack of well-authenticated details about the way the president and his inner circle carried out their decision-making process leading to the escalation of the Vietnam War. However, there has been some support for the view that American policy makers perceived their choice to be in the domain of losses and, hence, were engaged in loss aversion. For example, Ellsberg (1971) argued that President Johnson and his advisers regarded their motions not as "last steps" but rather as "holding actions, adequate to avoid defeat in the short run but long shots so far as ultimate success was concerned" (p. 257).

British Prime Minister Neville Chamberlain chose the path of appeasement in response to Hitler's demands, thereby facilitating the outbreak of world war. The decision to agree to Hitler's demands also was the product of a choice in the domain of losses. Chamberlain's private letters and diaries contain several references to his view that the high-risk appeasement policy was chosen in order to save Britain from the perils of otherwise certain war (Janis, 1982).

Finally, it is likely that the Watergate cover-up, undertaken by the White House to prevent knowledge of the link between criminal activities and the Committee to Reelect the President, was the product of a decision framed to appear as a choice in the domain of losses. Nixon was involved in the cover-up once the arrests were made in the Watergate burglary, and he was clear in discussions with his aides that necessary steps should be taken to avoid otherwise certain damage to his reelection campaign (Janis, 1982).

In support of the analysis offered here, note that a variety of researchers have confirmed that the alternative framing of objectively identical decisions can elicit different preferences and can affect attitudes toward risk (e.g., Bazerman, 1983; Levin, Johnson, Russo, & Deldin, 1985; McNeil, Pauker, Sox, & Tversky, 1982; Nealse, Huber, & Northcraft, 1987; Schelling, 1981; Slovic, Fischoff, & Lichtenstein, 1982; Tversky & Kahneman 1981, 1986). Also, risk seeking in choices between losses, which is suggested to underlie the occurrence of decision fiascoes, is a robust form of behavior, and this is consistent with the findings of several social scientists (e.g., Fishburn & Kochenberger, 1979; Hershey & Shoemaker, 1980; Payne et al., 1980; Slovic et al., 1982). This pattern of preference has been observed in choices involving other than financial outcomes, including the duration of pain (Eraker & Sox, 1981) and the loss of human life (Fischoff, 1983; Tversky, 1977). Although it is not possible to say whether it is wrong to seek risk when choosing between losses, it is evident that such a preference, particularly when exacerbated by the polarizing effect of group discussion, often will lead to undesirable outcomes.

Prospect theory was founded on people's reactions to monetary outcomes of varying probabilities, yet this paper advocates the application of prospect theory to situations in which outcomes are not necessarily quantitative and in which the probabilities associated with various outcomes are less than certain. In this regard, Kahneman and Tversky commented (1979, p. 288):

*[Prospect] theory is readily applicable to choices involving other attributes [than monetary out-comes], e.g., quality of life or the number of lives that could be lost or saved as a consequence of a policy decision. The main properties of the proposed value function for money should apply to other attributes as well. In particular, we expect outcomes to be coded as gains or losses, relative to a neutral reference point, and losses to loom larger than gains. The theory can also be extended to the typical situation of choice, where the probabilities of outcomes are not explicitly given. In such situations, decision weights must be attached to particular events rather than to stated probabilities, but they are expected to exhibit the essential properties that were ascribed to the weighting function.*

An assumption implicit in this analysis is that decision makers often will share a common frame when making a particular decision. Evidence suggests that people tend to rely upon the reference level suggested or implied by the statement of the problem in order to evaluate options (Kahneman & Tversky, 1984; McNeil et al., 1982; Thaler, 1980). Additional factors thought to influence framing include norms, habits, and expectations (Tversky & Kahneman, 1986). Another assumption contained in this analysis for which there is support is that groups will amplify the behavioral tendencies on which prospect theory is founded (McGuire, Kiesler, & Siegel, 1987). These results parallel the findings that group judgments are even more susceptible to the preference reversal phenomenon than those of individuals (Slovic & Lichtenstein, 1983).

Regarding the malady of groupthink, prospect polarization is relevant to, and has predictive utility for, the notion of a concurrence-seeking tendency. Although groupthink posits that such a tendency exists, it is not possible to discern the option toward which such a tendency will be directed, except to say that it will move in the direction of the initial majority. Yet groupthink provides no insight into what that initial majority position will be. Prospect theory implies, however, that when the choice facing a group is framed as one in the domain of losses, a majority of group members will prefer the risky option. It is then reasonable to suggest by reliance on the notions of group polarization and pressures for uniformity that in a choice between losses, concurrence seeking will move most easily toward risk taking. In other words, consensus will be most easily maintainable in the direction of risk and away from the acceptance of a certain loss.

On the one hand, prospect polarization provides leverage with which to discern and predict what the dominant initial preference within the group will be and what will happen to it during the course of group interaction. Groupthink, on the other hand, illuminates the means by which the convergence of the stated views of group members occurs. Using groupthink to explain policy debacles provides only a partial explanation. Although the tendency of group members to conform and the convergence of group members' views around an option can be explained by groupthink, the theory sheds no light on why the group view coalesces around the particular policy option that it does. Prospect polarization can be used to fill this void in the groupthink hypothesis.

Group polarization implies that group pressures toward uniformity will be in the direction of the policy option that is somewhat more extreme than the point of view initially dominant within the group. This point of view can in turn be predicted by knowledge of the decision frame adopted by decision makers. In the context of a choice in the domain of losses and as a result of group interaction, conditions favorable to the occurrence of the distinct processes of group convergence around a high-risk option and group polarization will be established. Unless the tendencies of groups to succumb to these separate and subtle processes are overcome, for example, by systematically approaching the decision-making task, it is likely that consensus around a risky choice will be attained. It is also likely that the option chosen will be even riskier than the choice of an individual acting in isolation and facing the identical situation.

If an option is initially preferred by a majority in a group of decision makers and group discussion serves to heighten that preference, then it is highly likely that this option will be chosen (Stasser et al., 1980). Groupthink symptoms, when they exist, should serve to harden the already existing resolve of individuals in the group to embark upon this initially preferred course of action, regardless of whether or not it makes good sense to do so. Further, groupthink may have an effect by limiting the number of ways available for group members to frame the subject of the decision. But according to this analysis, groupthink is not the proximate cause of any given decision fiasco. That role is accorded to the decision frame initially adopted by decision makers. It we think about the Bay of Pigs invasion, the Watergate cover-up, American involvement in the Vietnam War, or the Challenger disaster, it becomes increasingly clear that "the adoption of a decision frame is an ethically significant act" (Kahneman & Tversky, 1981, p. 458).

# IMPLICATIONS

Several implications flow from the approach to decision fiascoes adopted here. These implications address the results of the few studies designed to test the groupthink model, and they suggest alternative route by which to proceed with theory building and future research.

Previous researchers have attempted to examine the effect of those antecedent conditions that were argued by Janis to be necessary for the occurrence of groupthink. Although several antecedent conditions were identified, only group cohesiveness and leader behavior are group-level constraints that identify groupthink as a group, rather than an individual, phenomenon (Leana, 1985). Several studies have found that cohesiveness is not an important antecedent condition of groupthink. Directive leader behavior, however, significantly influences the frequency of groupthink symptoms (Courtwright, 1978; Flowers, 1977; Leana, 1985). These findings are at variance with the groupthink model, but they are consistent with an emphasis on the manner in which the problem is framed at the outset of group discussion, either as a result of directive leadership practices or otherwise.

More generally, this paper links in a theoretically coherent way concepts from cognitive and social psychology and then attempts to demonstrate their relevance for important real-life events. Several testable hypotheses also can be generated from the foregoing analysis of decision fiascoes. Most fundamental, such an approach implies that groups, as well as individuals, will be subject to framing effects. In addition, groups, as well as individuals, should be loss averse, which leads to risk-seeking choices in the domain of losses. Furthermore, groups should be subject to framing effects, and they should manifest a tendency to seek risk in the domain of losses more frequently, and to a greater degree, than individuals. That is, choices made in a social context should be more pronounced, more narrowly distributed, and more consistent with prospect theory than choices made by individuals acting in isolation. A test of prospect theory at the group level of analysis is an important first step in testing the validity of the model advocated here.

Further research is also required on the extent to which the value function is readily applicable to choices that are more than unidimensional. Most policy decisions of consequence do not simply involve choices in which either money or lives may be lost, but involve a variety of potential costs and benefits. What, for example, does the value function look like when decision makers are simultaneously concerned about several issues such as preserving national security, maximizing global influence, and balancing domestic political concerns? Most complex choices are multidimensional. In these circumstances, do decision makers choose as if they possess an aggregate value function, or do they respond to the value function involving that attribute of the situation that is most salient for them? The answer is not yet clear.

Another area that requires attention is derived from the concern in prospect theory with decision making under risk. Prospect theory was based on individual responses to gambles, in which the probabilities and potential losses and gains were precisely specified. Most decisions, however, are made under conditions of uncertainty, in which the amounts at risk and the probabilities of loss or gain are not explicit. Theoretically, there is no reason why prospect theory cannot be extended to the more typical situation of choice under conditions of uncertainty. More compelling would be empirical evidence, currently lacking, which demonstrates this. There is, however, some data suggesting that in the domain of losses, choices under risk and under uncertainty do not differ (Cohen, Jaffray, & Said, 1987).

Further issues requiring investigation are why and how the neutral reference level of prospect theory changes over time to become more consistent with the objective characteristics of the situation. In other words, what determines which reference level will be used to evaluate the outcomes of choice? In some cases, the reference level is a state to which one is accustomed, although it is possible for the reference level to be determined by aspirations (Tversky & Kahneman, 1981). Factors such as the way the problem is presented, personal and cultural values, expectations, and leader behavior also influence the framing of decisions, yet the precise roles of these variables and the ways in which they interact are not well understood. Absent from prospect theory is a formal theory of framing, which makes it difficult to predict the type of frame that decision makers will adopt in a given situation.

Although laboratory studies may be the best way to address some of the issues, the full range of behavioral research methods, including comparative case studies and field experiments in natural settings, could be used to further refine and test the theoretical position advanced here. It is not enough to tailor individual-level explanations for group phenomena to take into account the social context. Ultimately, such explanations must be applicable in the presence of structural attributes of organizations designed to minimize individual limitations in information-processing capability.

In a different vein, there are a number of ways to reduce the occurrence of decision fiascoes. Many of these suggestions, such as those designed to counteract defensive avoidance (Janis & Mann, 1977) and those used to reduce group insularity and directive leadership practices (Janis, 1982), are appropriate regardless of whether or not cognitive or motivational explanations are emphasized. An approach based on prospect theory, however, implies a fundamentally different approach to reduce the incidence of poor decision making. One general hypothesis relates to the effects of training, and it can be stated as follows: Knowledge about the causes and consequences of framing effects will facilitate high quality decision making. More specifically, decision makers should be encouraged to frame a decision problem in a variety of ways in order to investigate the stability of preferences. Perhaps most useful, decision makers should be instructed not to evaluate decision problems in terms of gains or losses from a neutral reference point, as they are inclined to do. Instead, they should be taught to formulate a decision problem in terms of final states or assets, as business students are encouraged to do (Kahneman & Tversky, 1984). Whether any of these strategies will be effective when employed in real decision-making groups faced with important problems has yet to be empirically validated.

The explanation advanced here for the pursuit of policies that have a high risk of failure is not meant to be confined to military or political decisions. It is equally applicable to business decision making, and it is consistent with the previously advanced view (e.g., Singh, 1986) that firms that are performing below target or reference level are more likely to pursue risky options than those that are not (Fiegenbaum & Thomas, 1988). Naturally, the result of the pursuit of such policies is failure in the majority of cases, combined with scattered success.

## CONCLUSION

This article has argued that groupthink, although relevant, is an incomplete explanation for the occurrence of decision fiascoes. Reliance upon prospect polarization to understand excessive risk seeking in group decision making implies that egregious errors in group judgment are not solely the product of group dynamics. Rather, they also are the product of the way group members frame decisions and choose between alternatives. A theory of decision fiascoes, and a theory of choice in general, cannot be descriptively adequate and at the same time ignore the effects of the framing of decisions.

# REFERENCES

Abelson, R. P., and Levi, A. (1986) Decision making and decision theory. In G. Lindzey & E. Aronson (Eds.), *The handbook of social psychology* (3rd ed., pp. 231–309). New York: Random House.

Bazerman, M. (1983) Negotiator judgment. *American Behavior Scientist, 27*, 211–228.

Bazerman, M., Guiliano, T., & Appleman, A. (1984) Escalation of commitment in individual and group decision making. *Organizational Behavior and Human Performance, 33*, 141–152.

Burnstein, E. (1969) An analysis of group decisions involving risk ("The risky shift"). *Human Relations, 22*, 381–395.

Cohen, M., Jaffray, J., & Said, T. (1987) Experimental comparison of individual behavior under uncertainty for gains and for losses. *Organizational Behavior and Human Decision Processes, 39*, 1–22.

Courtwright, J. (1978) A laboratory investigation of groupthink. *Communications Monographs, 45*, 229–246.

Davis, J. (1973) Group decision and social interaction: A theory of social decision schemes. *Psychological Review, 80*, 97–125.

Davis, J. (1980) Group decisions and procedural justice. In M. Fishbein (Ed.), *Progress in social psychology* (pp. 98–125). Hillsdale, NJ: Erlbaum.

Davis, J. (1982) Social interaction as a combinational process in group decision making. In H. Brandstatter, J. Davis, & G. Stocker-Kreichgauer (Eds.), *Group decision making* (pp. 27–58). New York: Academic Press.

Deets, M., & Hoyt, G. (1970) Variance preferences and variance shifts in group investment decisions. *Organizational Behavior and Human Performance, 5*, 378–386.

Doise, W. (1969) Jugement collectif et prise de risque des petits groups [Risk taking in small group decision making]. *Psychologie Française, 14*, 87–95.

Ellsberg, D. (1971) The quagmire myth and the stalemate machine. *Public Policy, 19*, 217–274.

Eraker, S. E., & Sox, H. C. (1981) Assessment of patients' preferences for therapeutic outcomes. *Medical Decision Making, 1*, 29–39.

Ferrell, W. (1985) Combining individual judgments. In G. Wright (Ed.), *Behavioral decision making* (pp. 111–145). New York: Plenum Press.

Fiegenbaum, A., & Thomas, H. (1988) Attitudes toward risk and the risk return paradox: Prospect theory explanations. *Academy of Management Journal, 31*, 86–106.

Fischoff, B. (1983) Predicting frames. *Journal of Experimental Psychology: Learning, Memory, and Cognition, 9*, 103–116.

Fishburn, P. C. (1977) Mean-risk analysis with risk associated with below target returns. *American Economic Review, 67*, 116–126.

Fishburn, P. C. & Kochenberger, G. A. (1979), Two piece Von Newmann-Morgenstern utility functions. *Decision Sciences, 10*, 503–518.

Flowers, M. (1977) A laboratory test of some implications of Janis's groupthink hypothesis. *Journal of Personality and Social Psychology, 1*, 288–299.

Hamilton, L., & Inouye, D. (1987) *Report of the Congressional Committees Investigating the Iran-Contra Affairs* (H. Rept. No. 100–433) Washington, DC: Government Printing Office.

Hershey, J. C., & Schoemaker, P. (1980) Risk taking and problem context in the domain of losses: An expected utility analysis. *Journal of Risk and Insurance, 47*, 111–132.

Isenberg, D. (1986) Group polarization: A critical review and meta-analysis. *Journal of Personality and Social Psychology, 50,* 1141–1151.

It was my idea—Dropping his didn't know defense, Reagan takes credit. (1987, May 25) *Newsweek,* pp. 16–19.

Janis, I. L. (1972) *Victims of groupthink.* Boston: Houghton Mifflin.

Janis, I. L. (1982) *Groupthink.* Boston: Houghton Mifflin.

Janis, I. L., & Mann, L. (1977) *Decision making: A psychological analysis of conflict, choice, and commitment.* New York: Free Press.

Jervis, R. (1976) Perception and misperception in international politics. Princeton: Princeton University Press.

Kahneman, D., & Tversky, A. (1979) Prospect theory: an analysis of decisions under risk. *Econometrica, 47,* 263–291.

Kahneman, D., & Tversky, A. (1981) The framing of decisions and the psychology of choice. *Science, 211,* 453–458.

Kahneman, D., & Tversky, A. (1984) Choices, values, and frames. *American Psychologist, 39,* 341–350.

Kerr, N. (1982) Social transition schemes: Model, method and applications. In H. Brandstatter, J. Davis, & G. Stocker-Kreichgauer (Eds.), *Group decision making* (pp. 59–79). London: Academic Press.

Kerr, N., & MacCoun, R. (1985) The effects of jury size and polling method on the process and product of jury deliberation. *Journal of Personality and Social Psychology, 48,* 349–363.

Laughlin, P., & Adamopoulos, J. (1982) Social decision schemes on intellective tasks. In H. Brandstatter, J. Davis, & G. Stocker-Kreichgauer (Eds.), *Group decision making* (pp. 81–94). London: Academic Press.

Leana, C. (1985) A partial test of Janis' groupthink model: Effects of group cohesiveness and leader behavior on defective decision making. *Journal of Management, 11* (1), 5–17.

Levin, I., Johnson, R., Russo, C., & Deldin, P. (1985) Framing effects in judgment tasks with varying amounts of information. *Organizational Behavior and Human Decision Processes, 36,* 362–377.

McConnell, M. (1987) *Challenger: A major malfunction.* New York: Doubleday.

McGuire, T., Kiesler, S., & Siegel, J. (1987) Group and computer mediated discussion effects in risk decision making. *Journal of Personality and Social Psychology, 52,* 917–930.

McNeil, B., Pauker, S., Sox, H., & Tversky, A. (1982) On the elicitation of preferences for alternative therapies. *New England Journal of Medicine, 306,* 1259–1262.

Moscovici, S. (1984) Social influence and conformity. In G. Lindzey & E. Aronson (Eds.), *The handbook of social psychology* (3rd ed., pp. 347–412). New York: Random House.

Myers, D. (1982) Polarizing effects of social interaction. In H. Brandstatter, J. Davis, & G. Stocker-Kreichgauer (Eds.), *Group decision making* (pp. 125–161). London: Academic Press.

Myers, D. G., & Lamm, H. (1976) The group polarization phenomenon. *Psychological Bulletin, 83,* 602–627.

Neale, M., Huber, V., & Northcraft, G. (1987) The framing of negotiations: Contextual versus task frames. *Organizational Behavior and Human Decision Processes, 39,* 228–241.

Neustadt, R. (1976) *Presidential power: The politics of leadership with reflections on Johnson and Nixon.* New York: Wiley.

Payne, J. W., Laughhunn, D. J., & Crum, R. (1980) Translation of gambles and aspiration level effects in risky choice behavior. *Management Science, 26,* 1039–1060.

Runyan, D. (1974) The group risk shift effect as a function of emotional bonds, actual consequences, and extent of responsibility. *Journal of Personality and Social Psychology, 27*, 297–300.

Schelling, T. (1981) Economic reasoning and the ethics of policy. *Public Interest, 63*, 37–61.

Schlesinger, A. (1965) *A thousand days*. Boston: Houghton Mifflin.

Singh, J. V. (1986) Performance, slack, and risk taking in organizational decision making. *Academy of Management Journal, 29*, 562–585.

Slovic, P., Fischoff, B., & Lichtenstein, S. (1982) Response made, framing and information processing effects in risk assessment. In R. Hogarth (Ed.), *New directions for methodology of social and behavioral science: Question framing and response consistency* (pp. 21–36). San Francisco: Jossey Bass.

Slovic, P., & Lichtenstein, S. (1983) Preference reversals: A broader perspective. *American Economic Review, 73*, 596–605.

Stasser, G., Kerr, N. L., & Davis, J. H. (1980) Influence processes in decision making groups: A modeling approach. In P. B. Paulus (Ed.), *Psychology of group influence* (pp. 431–477). Hillsdale, NJ: Erlbaum.

Staw, B. (1981) The escalation of commitment to a course of action. *Academy of Management Review, 6*, 577–587.

Thaler, R. (1980) Toward a positive theory of consumer choice. *Journal of Economic Behavior and Organization, 1*, 39–60.

Toland, A., & O'Neill, P. (1983) A test of prospect theory. *Journal of Economic Behavior and Organization, 4*, 53–56.

Tower, J., Muski, E., & Scowcroft, B. (1987) *Report of the President's Special Review Board*. Washington, DC: Government Printing Office.

Tuchman, B. (1984) *The march of folly*. New York: Knopf.

Tversky, A. (1977) On the elicitation of preferences: Descriptive and prescriptive considerations. In D. Bell, R. Kenney, & H. Raiffa (Eds.), *Conflicting objectives in decisions* (pp. 209–222). New York: Wiley.

Tversky, A., & Kahneman, D. (1981) The framing of decisions and the psychology of choice. *Science, 211*, 453–458.

Tversky, A., & Kahneman, D. (1981) Rational choice and the framing of decisions. *Journal of Business, 59*, S251–S278.

Wohlsetter, R. (1962) *Pearl Harbor: Warning and decision*. Stanford: Stanford University Press.

Zaleska, M. (1974) The effects of discussion on group and individual choices among bets. *European Journal of Social Psychology, 4*, 229–250.

Zaleska, M. (1976) Majority influence on group choices among bets. *Journal of Personality and Social Psychology, 33*, 8–19.

# WORK TEAMS
# APPLICATIONS AND EFFECTIVENESS

*Eric Sundstrom*
*Kenneth P. De Meuse*
*David Futrell*

The terms *work team* and *work group* appear often in today's discussions or organizations. Some experts claim that to be effective modern firms need to use small teams for an increasing variety of jobs. For instance, in an article subtitled "The Team as Hero," Reich (1987) wrote,

> If we are to compete in today's world, we must begin to celebrate collective entrepreneurship, endeavors in which the whole of the effort is greater than the sum of individual contributions. We need to honor our teams more, our aggressive leaders and maverick geniuses less. (p. 78)

Work teams occupy a pivotal role in what has been described as a management transformation (Walton, 1985), paradigm shift (Ketchum, 1984), and corporate renaissance (Kanter, 1983). In this management revolution, Peters (1988) advised that organizations use "multi-function teams for *all* development activities" (p. 210) and "organize *every function* into ten- to thirty-person, largely self-managing teams" (p. 296). Tornatzky (1986) pointed to new technologies that allow small work groups to take responsibility for whole products. Hackman (1986) predicted that, "organizations in the future will rely heavily on member self-management" (p. 90). Building blocks of such organizations are self-regulating work teams. But far from being revolutionary, work groups are traditional; "the problem before us is not to invent more tools but to use the ones we have" (Kanter, 1983, p. 64).

In this article, we explore applications of work teams and propose an analytic framework for team effectiveness. Work teams are defined as interdependent collections of individuals who share responsibility for specific outcomes for their organizations. In what follows, we first identify applications of work teams and then offer a framework for analyzing team effectiveness. Its facets make up topics of subsequent sections: organizational context, boundaries, and team development. We close with issues for research and practice.

## APPLICATIONS OF WORK TEAMS

Two watershed events called attention to the benefits of applying work teams beyond sports and military settings: the Hawthorne studies (Homans, 1950) and European experiments with autonomous work groups (Kelly, 1982). Enthusiasm has alternated with disenchantment (Bramel & Friend, 1987), but the 1980s have brought a resurgence of interest.

Unfortunately, we have little evidence on how widely work teams are used or whether their use is expanding. Pasmore, Francis, Haldeman, and Shani (1982) reported that introduction of autonomous work groups was the most common intervention in 134 experiments in manufacturing firms. Production teams number among four broad categories of work team applications: a) advice and involvement, b) production and service, c) projects and development, and d) action and negotiation.

## Advice and Involvement

Decision-making committees traditional in management now are expanding to first-line employees. Quality control (QC) circles and employee involvement groups have been common in the 1980s, often as vehicles for employee participation (Cole, 1982). Perhaps several hundred thousand U. S. employees belong to QC circles (Ledford, Lawler, & Mohrman, 1988), usually first-line manufacturing employees who meet to identify opportunities for improvement. Some make and carry out proposals, but most have restricted scopes of activity and little working time, perhaps a few hours each month (Thompson, 1982). Employee involvement groups operate similarly, exploring ways to improve customer service (Peterfreund, 1982). QC circles and employee involvement groups at times may have been implemented poorly (Shea, 1986), but they have been used extensively in some companies (Banas, 1988).

## Production and Service

Teams use technology to generate products or services, as in assembly, maintenance, construction, mining, commercial airlines, sales, and others. These usually consist of first-line employees working together full-time, sometimes over protracted periods, with freedom to decide their division of labor. For example, at Volvo in Kalmar, Sweden, teams of 15 to 20 employees assemble and install components in an unfinished automobile chassis conveyed by motorized carriers (Katz & Kahn, 1978). They elect their own leaders and divide their tasks, but have output quotas. Such teams have been called autonomous (Cummings, 1978), self-managing (Hackman, 1986), or self-regulating (Pearce & Ravlin, 1987) and have been used in factories at Sherwin-Williams (Poza & Markus, 1980), General Foods (Walton, 1977), and Saab (Katz & Kahn, 1978).

## Projects and Development

Groups of white-collar professionals such as researchers, engineers, designers, and programmers often collaborate on assigned or original projects. Their cycles of work may be longer than in production and service, and outputs may be complex and unique. They may have a mandate of innovation more than implementation, broad autonomy, and an extended team life span. An example is a team of engineers, programmers, and other specialists who design, program, and test prototype computers (Kidder, 1981). However, their performance may be difficult to assess because the value of their one-of-a-kind outputs, like studies and patents, may only be apparent long after the work is finished.

## Action and Negotiation

Sports teams, military combat units, flight crews, surgery teams, musical groups, and others are highly skilled specialist teams cooperating in brief performance events that require improvisation in unpredictable circumstances. They often have elaborate, specialized roles for members. Their missions usually call for outcomes such as negotiating a contract or winning a competition, as in military units (Dyer, 1984), or in executing a safe flight, as in flight crews (Foushee, 1984).

Other applications do not easily fit the types mentioned so far. Examples include some management teams (Bushe, 1987), transition teams for corporate mergers, and start-up teams. However, differences among applications can perhaps best be addressed through an analytic framework.

# FRAMEWORK FOR ANALYSIS

Figure 1 depicts work team effectiveness as dynamically interrelated with organizational context, boundaries, and team development. It incorporates an ecological perspective (Sundstrom & Altman, 1989) and the premise that work teams can best be understood in relation to external surroundings and internal processes. The main facets—organizational context, boundaries, and team development—reflect current research, theory, and applied literature on work teams.

## Organizational Context

Relevant features of the organization external to the work team, such as reward systems and training resources, comprise its context. Since the late 1970s, the external factors seen as relevant to group operation have grown from a few selected "inputs" to a long list of factors discovered in practice (Ketchum, 1984) and research (Pasmore et al., 1982). Models of work groups now incorporate many aspects of organizational context (Cummings, 1981; Gladstein, 1984; Hackman, 1987; Kolodny & Kiggundu, 1980; Pearce & Ravlin, 1987; Shea & Guzzo, 1987a, 1987b). Such factors can augment team effectiveness by providing resources needed for performance and continued viability as a work unit.

## Boundaries

An ecological view depicts boundaries as both separating and linking work teams within their organizations (Alderfer, 1987; Friedlander, 1987). Yet group boundaries are difficult to describe concisely, because they subsume so many aspects of the relationship of group and organization. By *boundaries* we mean features that a) differentiate a work unit from others (Cherns, 1976); b) pose real or symbolic barriers to access or transfer of information, goods, or people (Katz & Kahn, 1978); or c) serve as points of external exchange with other teams, customers, peers, competitors, or other entities (Friedlander, 1987).

Boundaries at least partly define how a group needs to operate within its context to be effective. If the boundary becomes too open or indistinct, the team risks becoming isolated and losing its identity. If its boundary is too exclusive, the team might lose touch with suppliers, managers, peers, or customers (Alderfer, 1987).

## Team Development

This facet reflects the premise that over time, teams change and develop new ways of operating as they adapt to their contexts. Some features of team development, such as norms and roles, can be seen as structural. Yet it is difficult to identify aspects of groups stable enough to be called structure. We prefer to err by depicting groups as too dynamic rather than too static. Temporal patterns in group processes may be tied to effectiveness during even brief work sessions (Sundstrom, Bobrow, Fulton, Blair, & McClane, 1988). So we use the term *team development* to include what has been called group structure as well as interpersonal processes.

# Team Effectiveness

Figure 1 shows effectiveness as consisting of performance and viability. This two-part definition agrees with some earlier approaches, but is more inclusive than those based only on output. Shea and Guzzo (1987b) defined group effectiveness as "production of designated products or services per specification" (p. 329). This overlooks the possibility that a team can "burn itself up" through unresolved conflict or divisive interaction, leaving members unwilling to continue working together (Hackman & Oldham, 1980, p. 169). We favor a broad definition that accounts for members' satisfaction and the group's future prospects as a work unit by incorporating *team viability*. At a minimum, this entails members' satisfaction, participation, and willingness to continue working together. A more demanding definition might add cohesion, intermember coordination, mature communication and problem-solving, and clear norms and roles—all traditionally identified with team maturity. *Performance* means acceptability of output to customers within or outside the organization who receive team products, services, information, decisions, or performance events (such as presentations or competitions).

Effectiveness is defined globally to apply to a variety of work teams, consistent with current thinking (Goodman, Ravlin, & Argote, 1986). However, Goodman (1986) argued for fine-grained criteria of effectiveness such as "quality, quantity, downtime, satisfaction, group stability over time" (p. 145). Perhaps global and fine-grained approaches can be merged by measuring specific, local criteria and combining them into general indexes for cross-team comparisons, as in the method pioneered by Pritchard, Jones, Roth, Stuebing, and Ekeberg (1988).

FIGURE 1   Ecological Framework for Analyzing Work Team Effectiveness

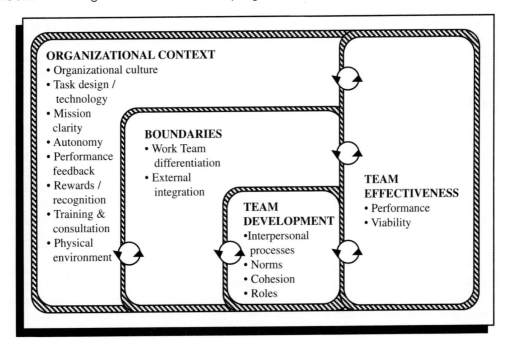

## Interrelationships

The framework is deliberately vague about causal and temporal dynamics, reflecting the premise that team effectiveness is more a process than an end-state. We depart from McGrath's (1964) "input-process-output" approach (e.g., Gladstein, 1984), which now is even questioned by former proponents. For instance, Hackman (1987) suggested that groups evaluate their collective performance as they work, and evaluations affect group processes, which influence subsequent performance. This can yield "self-reinforcing spirals of increasing effectiveness" after initial success—perhaps a "synergy bonus" (Hall & Watson, 1971). However, negatively reinforcing spirals of decreasing effectiveness can also create "processes losses" (Steiner, 1972).

Adjacent facets of the framework are linked by circular symbols intended to show *reciprocal interdependence* (Thompson, 1967). For instance, one indicates that boundaries influence effectiveness, which alters the boundaries, which further influence effectiveness. Ambiguity about temporal dynamics begs the question of developmental processes in work teams, which we address after discussing organizational context and boundaries in relation to team effectiveness.

# ORGANIZATIONAL CONTEXT AND WORK TEAM EFFECTIVENESS

Figure 1 lists eight aspects of organizational context distilled from several sources, including Cummings and Molloy's (1977) analysis of 16 experiments on autonomous work-groups. Present in more than half of the studies with favorable outcomes were six "action levers": autonomy; technical-physical features such as new equipment or facilities; task variety; information or feedback; pay or rewards; interpersonal interventions. Present in three or more successful experiments were: training; work-unit support, such as maintenance or technical help; and altered organizational structure as in widened span of supervisor control or fewer levels of authority. Other potentially important context features are mission clarity (Hardaker & Ward, 1987) and organizational culture (Cummings, 1981).

## Organizational Culture

Culture in an organization refers to collective values and norms (Rousseau & Cooke, 1988). Those that favor innovation (Cummings, 1981) or incorporate shared expectations of success (Shea & Guzzo, 1987a) may especially foster team effectiveness. For instance, Peters and Waterman's (1982) "excellent" companies valued such things as superior quality and service, attention to detail, and support of innovation. Firms that report success in applying work teams have had similar cultures, often guided by philosophies of top managers (Galagan, 1986; Poza & Markus, 1980; Walton, 1977). But culture may be more a property of work units than a pervasive feature of whole organizations (James, James, & Ashe, in press).

Organizational culture probably figures most prominently in the effectiveness of work teams least clearly defined as work units. For example, new production teams may look to the wider culture for values and norms. In organizations moving toward self-management, values consistent with team autonomy may foster self-direction (Hackman, 1986). Failed quality circles may have experienced confusion about their purposes (Shea, 1986) and looked in vain for guidance from organizational culture.

## Task Design and Technology

If the research literature on small groups agrees on one point, it is the importance of the task (McGrath, 1984), a major source of differences among work teams. For instance, committees spend large shares of their time in problem-solving meetings, whereas surgery teams spend much of their time together in carefully sequenced operations. Team tasks differ on broad categories of activity, such as generating solutions versus executing action plans (McGrath, 1984); technical versus interpersonal demands (Herold, 1978); difficulty (Shaw, 1981); number of desired outcomes and trade-offs among them (Campbell, 1988); intermember communications (Naylor & Dickenson, 1969); coordination requirements (Nieva, Fleishman, & Reick, 1978); task divisibility (Steiner, 1972); subtask demands (Roby & Lanzetta, 1958); and dependence of team outcomes on performance by all members (Steiner, 1972).

Task design and social organization depend to a degree on technology—and may even be largely determined by it. For example, coal mining changed with the advent of mechanized conveyors and coal cutters (Trist, Higgins, Murray, & Pollack, 1963). Earlier methods permitted miners to work independently, but new technology created specialized tasks that required miners to synchronize efforts in small teams. Some technologies allow team members to master all tasks; others carry tasks so complex that each member can master only one, as in musical groups and space shuttle crews. Here technology dictates a social organization of individual roles.

Optimal fit among task, technology, and social organization calls for "logical subdivision of the technical process into operating subunits of reasonable size that can become partially independent" (Ketchum, 1984, p. 247). Ideally, teams produce whole products (Cummings, 1981), and do tasks designed for significance, skill, and variety (Hackman & Oldham, 1980); responsibility for outcomes (Hackman, 1986); challenge (Cummings, 1981); member interdependence (Shea & Guzzo, 1987b); learning, and recognition (Pasmore et al., 1982). Technology can be crucial, as in mining and harvesting crews whose output depends on equipment design, maintenance, down-time, and other factors (Goodman, Devadas, & Hughson, 1988; Kolodny & Kiggundu, 1980).

For work teams who repeatedly do the same work-cycle (which often happens in manufacturing), task difficulty may depend on predictability of inputs (Cummings, 1981) or outcomes (Campbell, 1988). Work teams faced with unpredictable inputs or uncertain outcomes may perform best in contexts that foster decentralized communication (Tushman, 1979) and flexible internal coordination (Argote, 1982; Susman, 1970).

## Mission Clarity

Team effectiveness may depend on having a clearly defined mission or purpose within the organization (Shea & Guzzo, 1987b). It may entail expectations regarding output, quality, timing, and pacing— and perhaps expectations for anticipating and designing new procedures as the task changes (Hackman, 1986). Communication of a team's mission throughout the organization especially may help teams whose work is closely linked to or synchronized with that of other work units (e.g., Galagan, 1986; Pearce & Ravlin, 1987).

## Autonomy

Central to work team design and management, autonomy is usually described by reference to three categories: a) *Semi-autonomous* groups are supervisor-led (Cherry, 1982); b) *self-regulating* or self-managing groups elect their leaders and control their division of labor (Pearce & Ravlin, 1987); and c) *self-designing* teams have authority over their definitions as work units and external relations (Hackman, 1987).

Team autonomy depends on the role of leader (Hackman & Walton, 1986) and on how authority is distributed. A team can have a manager, administrator, leader, supervisor, facilitator, director, coordinator, spokesperson, or chairperson—or several of these. Division of leadership among manager(s) and members may vary with team longevity and maturity. Manz and Sims (1987) recommended that managers foster self-management by acting as "un-leaders." Eventually a team may develop its own leadership capabilities if given a progressively less prominent leader role (Glickman et al., 1987).

## Performance Feedback

Practitioners agree that team effectiveness depends on accurate, timely feedback on performance (Ketchum, 1984; Kolodny & Kiggundu, 1980) despite limited research evidence (Dyer, 1984). Koch's (1979) study of sewing machine operator groups found increased product quality but decreased satisfaction after the introduction of specific goals with systemic feedback. Nadler, Camman, and Mirvis (1980) had mixed success with a feedback system in retail banks in which performance was not tied to work-unit rewards. Pritchard et al. (1988) used goal-setting and feedback (with team incentives) to bring about improved performance and satisfaction in aviation maintenance teams.

Performance feedback requires dependable measurement systems. These are probably most feasible in teams with repetitive, quantifiable output and short cycles of work, such as coal mining crews and assembly teams. Feedback may be more difficult in teams with longer cycles of work and/or one-of-a-kind outputs, such as project and development teams.

## Rewards and Recognition

Team performance may hinge on desirable consequences to individual members contingent on the whole team's performance—or *outcome interdependence*. Outcomes can include public recognition and praise for team successes, team celebrations, or individual rewards such as preferred work assignments, desirable schedules, or money. Shea and Guzzo (1987b) tested the effects of cash performance incentives on retail sales teams. Contrary to prediction, rewards did not bring increases in team sales, but members' evaluations of customer service rose and the organization showed higher sales overall. In contrast, Pritchard et al. (1988) did find increased performance (and satisfaction) in aviation maintenance units after introducing a group incentive plan based on time off.

## Training and Consultation

Traditional among prescriptions for work team effectiveness are training and consultation on team tasks and interpersonal processes. But apart from a few case studies we know little about the appropriate content or design of team training programs (Dyer, 1984). Key interpersonal skills may include "un-leadership" (Manz & Sims, 1987). An approach to technical skills in production groups, often called "cross-training," provides training and incentives for learning new skills in teams whose members can rotate jobs (Poza & Markus, 1980).

## Physical Environment

Inter-member communication and cohesion may depend on the extent to which informal, face-to-face interaction is fostered by proximity of work-stations and gathering places (Sundstrom, 1986; see also Stone & Luchetti, 1985). Territories can reinforce group boundaries (Miller, 1959) and foster or inhibit external exchange. When tasks call for external coordination, exchange can be aided by reception and conference rooms. In cases in which group processes are easily disrupted, effectiveness may be aided by enclosed group working areas. So, physical environments are central to group boundaries (Sundstrom & Altman, 1989).

## BOUNDARIES AND WORK TEAM EFFECTIVENESS

The framework in Figure 1 suggests that group boundaries mediate between organizational context and team development and are tied to effectiveness. By defining the relation of a work team and its organization, boundaries also help define what constitutes effectiveness for the team in its particular context (Sundstrom & Altman, 1989). Besides doing its task, a work team has to satisfy requirements of the larger system and maintain enough independence to perform specialized functions (Berrien, 1983). So one key aspect of the group-organization boundary is *integration* into the larger system through coordination and synchronization with suppliers, managers, peers, and customers. When a team's mission requires a high degree of external integration or linkage, effectiveness depends on the pace and timing of exchanges with other work units, as in a production team that gets materials from the preceding team and provides the next operation with materials for its work. When one team falls behind, the whole system suffers (Kolodny & Dresner, 1986). In cases in which team performance depends less on timing and synchronization with counterpart work units, effectiveness may be more a function of internal group processes.

A second key aspect of group-organization boundaries is *differentiation* (Lawrence & Lorsch, 1969), or the degree of specialization, independence, and autonomy of a work team in relation to other work units. Differentiation of a work team in an organization can occur when the mission requires special expertise or facilities, or isolation from contamination and interference, as in a surgery team. Team effectiveness can hinge on the ability to isolate certain activities from outside interference, such as sensitive operations, problem-solving meetings, or practice sessions. A team can be differentiated from other work units through exclusive membership, extended working time or team life span, or exclusive access to physical facilities such as surgery suites or product testing laboratories.

Demands for external integration and differentiation inherent in the relationship of a team and the surrounding organization can be seen as partly specifying what constitutes team effectiveness. A taxonomy by Sundstrom and Altman (1989) uses integration and differentiation to identify four types of work groups whose boundaries create different demands for effectiveness, shown in Table 1. The types correspond with the four applications of work teams mentioned earlier: a) advice and involvement groups; b) production and service teams; c) project and development teams; and d) action and negotiation teams. An example of a team low on both external integration and differentiation—an advice and involvement group—is a quality control circle. Differentiation is minimal in that membership is often broadly representative, working time is limited, and the group may have only a temporary meeting room. External integration is also minimal: Within broad limits a QC circle can proceed at its own pace with few requirements for synchronization with other work units. Its work may call for external communication, but the task imposes few constraints on timing or turn-around. In contrast, the organizational context of action and negotiation teams often demands both external differentiation and integration, which dictate conditions for team effectiveness. For example, a cockpit crew consists of qualified experts who work in specialized, limited-access facilities (their cockpits), and performance depends on their ability to work without distraction or interference. They carry out complex performance events (flights) that call for activities closely synchronized with those of other work units (ground crew, cabin crew, control tower, and other cockpit crews). High levels of external differentiation and integration may make such teams sensitive to particular features of organizational context, such as training and technology, which in turn might enter into team development.

TABLE 1  Applications of Work Teams: Differentiation, External Integration, Work-Cycles, and Outputs

| Applications and examples | Work-team differentiation | External integration | Work cycles | Typical outputs |
|---|---|---|---|---|
| **Advice/Involvement**<br>Committees<br>Review panels, boards<br>Quality control circles<br>Employee involvement groups<br>Advisory councils | **Low** differentiation<br>Inclusive or representative membership; Often short group life span and/or limited working time. | **Low** integration<br>Often few demands for synchronization with other work units; external exchange can be minimal; work cycle may not be repeated. | Work cycles can be brief or long; one cycle can be team life span. | Decisions<br>Selections<br>Suggestions<br>Proposals<br>Recommendations |
| **Production/service**<br>Assembly teams<br>Manufacturing crews<br>Mining teams<br>Flight attendant crews<br>Data processing groups<br>Maintenance crews | **Low** differentiation:<br>Variable membership requirements; sometimes high turnover; variable team life span; often special facilities. | **High** integration<br>Externally paced work usually synchronized with suppliers and customers inside and outside the organization. | Work-cycles typically repeated or continuous process; cycles often briefer than team life span. | Food, chemicals<br>Components<br>Assemblies<br>Retail sales<br>Customer service<br>Equipment repairs |
| **Project/development**<br>Research groups<br>Planning teams<br>Architect teams<br>Engineering teams<br>Development teams<br>Task forces | **High** differentiation:<br>Members usually expert specialists; task may require specialized facilities; Sometimes extended team life span. | **Low** integration<br>Often internally paced project with deadline; little synchronization inside organization; task can require much external communication. | Work cycles typically differ for each new project; one cycle can be team life span. | Plans, designs<br>Investigations<br>Presentations<br>Prototypes<br>Reports, findings |
| **Action/negotiation**<br>Sports teams<br>Entertainment groups<br>Expeditions<br>Negotiating teams<br>Surgery teams<br>Cockpit crews | **High** differentiation:<br>Exclusive membership of expert specialists; specialized training and performance facilities; Sometimes extended team life span. | **High** integration:<br>Performance events closely synchronized with counterparts & support units inside the organization. | Brief performance events, often repeated under new conditions, requiring extended training and/or preparation. | Combat missions<br>Expeditions<br>Contracts, lawsuits<br>Concerts<br>Surgical operations<br>Competitions |

## External Integration: Coordination With Suppliers, Managers, Peers, Staff, and Customers

External integration represents the way a team fits into the larger organization, or the external demands inherent in its boundary. A team's work can be seen as a process of receiving materials or information from suppliers; transforming or adding value in cooperation with managers, peers, and staff; and delivering output to team customers. (A team's customer can be inside the organization, like a packaging and shipping department in a factory.) The need for coordination with external agents is related to a team's work cycle. As shown in Table 1, teams with high levels of external integration (whose relationships with their organizations require close external synchronization) may tend to repeat their work cycles. For example, production teams generate the same or similar outputs over and over again. Teams with less external synchronization may tend toward single cycles of work that extend over long periods, yielding one-of-a-kind outputs. In some project teams, the work cycle equals the team life span; when the project is finished the team disbands. Such work units are more "loosely coupled" with counterparts than production teams (Weick, 1982). Teams facing demands for both external integration and differentiation tend to have two kinds of work cycles: brief, repeated performance events that require synchronization with support staff or competitors, and longer cycles of independent preparation. For maximum effectiveness, boundaries may need to be managed differently during the two types of work cycles.

## External Differentiation: Definition as a Work Unit

A work team is differentiated from its organizational context to the extent that it comprises an identifiable collection of people working in a specific place, over the same time period, on a unique task. Besides the task, aspects of differentiation important to effectiveness are membership, temporal scope, and territory. Together these features help define the team boundary (what distinguishes it from other work units).

1. *Membership: Composition, turnover, and size.* Basic to the definition of a work team is the identity of individuals treated as members by both group and organization. Research has traditionally asked what mix of individual traits, in what size group, yields greatest effectiveness. The following question is less often asked: Who decides the composition and size of a work team? Especially in organizations developing a participative style of management, the question is inevitable. An answer that might apply in some circumstances is to give members a substantial role in deciding team composition (Smith, 1981), at least from among qualified individuals. An early study of construction crews whose members chose their own team-mates did find them more productive than other crews (Van Zelst, 1952). Recently, Tziner and Vardi (1982) demonstrated a technique for using mutual preferences to form teams.

A second, seldom-asked question concerns turnover among members. In groups that meet only once or twice, like some problem-solving groups, turnover may be inconsequential. In longer lived groups, particularly those comprised of skilled specialists, the loss or gain of a member might require substantial adjustment by the group; at the least, socialization of new members is necessary (Moreland & Levine, 1988). Relevant research is scarce, but Dyer (1984) described a study of bomber crews in the Korean conflict in which crew performance was inversely related to personnel changes.

Group composition has seldom been studied in actual work teams, despite evidence of its importance. For instance, one study found that in military tank crews composed of soldiers with uniformly high ability, performance far exceeded what was expected from individuals' abilities (Tziner & Eden, 1985). Crews with uniformly low ability fell far short of expectations based on individual ability. In other words, these crews showed a "synergy" effect due to composition.

Among different types of groups in Table 1, links of composition with team effectiveness may hinge on different issues. In advice/involvement groups, such as committees and advisory boards, performance may depend on heterogeneity of task-related abilities or specialties, as suggested by research on group problem solving (Goodman et al., 1986). But such groups often have short life spans and limited time to work, so members' social skills could help determine how much talent is applied to the problem (Hackman, 1987). Among resources for assessing interpersonal skills a method called SYMLOG may offer promise (Bale, Cohen, & Williamson, 1979) as a vehicle for selecting potential team members with behavior profiles associated with team effectiveness.

In other types of teams with longer life spans, effectiveness may be related more to personal compatibility among members—especially when groups work for long periods in confined quarters. A taxonomy of personality traits relevant to team composition is outlined by Driskell, Hogan, and Salas (1988). Research on airliner flight crews supports selection of teams for personal compatibility (Foushee, 1984).

As for team size, current literature yields a consistent guideline: the smallest possible number of people who can do the task (Hackman, 1987). In the laboratory, group performance declines with the addition of extra members beyond the required minimum (Nieva et al., 1978). This could reflect added difficulty of coordinating more members (Steiner, 1972) or "social loafing" in larger groups (Latane, Williams, & Harkins, 1979). Laboratory research also suggests that increasing group size brings lower cohesion (McGrath, 1984). Similar findings emerge in two studies of work teams (Gladstein, 1984; O'Reilly & Roberts, 1977).

2. *Temporal scope: Team life span and working time.* The longer a work team exists and the more time its members spend cooperating, the greater its temporal scope (McGrath, 1984) and differentiation as a work-unit (Sundstrom & Altman, 1989). Effectiveness may improve over time (Heinen & Jacobson, 1976), but eventually may decline (Shonk & Shonk, 1988). For example, a study of research and development groups found that team longevity associated with isolation from key information sources was important to technical performance (Katz, 1982). Little is known about temporal aspects of group functioning (McGrath & Kelly, 1986).

3. *Team territories.* Practitioners emphasize the importance to a work team of having its own "turf" (Ketchum, 1981). Even teams who need no special facilities may rely on their physical environments for identity and management of external relations. Especially in teams whose missions demand both external integration and differentiation, territories may aid effectiveness (Sundstrom & Altman, 1989).

## TEAM DEVELOPMENT AND EFFECTIVENESS

Figure 1 lists four developmental features: interpersonal processes, norms, cohesion, and roles. These can be seen as aspects of developmental sequences in teams and as foci of efforts to aid team development and process interventions.

## Developmental Sequences

Some theories suggest that groups develop through a series of phases culminating in effective performance. Perhaps best known is Tuckman's (1965) model: "Forming, storming, norming, performing," and later, "adjourning" (Tuckman & Jensen, 1977). The model is supported by studies of training and laboratory groups (Heinen & Jacobson, 1976; Moreland & Levine, 1988) that may not necessarily generalize to work teams.

Gersick's (1988) "punctuated equilibrium" model suggests that groups exhibit long stable periods interspersed with relatively brief, revolutionary changes. Unlike Tuckman's model, it assumes that development depends on external relations. This model comes out of observations of eight project groups, each responsible for a specific product, with an external reporting relationship and a deadline. Initial periods of inertia lasted half of the allotted time, followed by *midpoint transitions:* They "dropped old patterns, re-engaged with outside supervisors, adopted new perspectives on their work, and made dramatic progress" (Gersick, 1988, p. 16). Transitions occurred halfway through the calendars, regardless of group life span (7 days to 6 months). Stable phases followed. Seven of eight finished on time, though effectiveness varied; thus the model seems to describe relatively effective project teams.

A recent model by Glickman et al. (1987) builds on both Tuckman's and Gersick's models. Support for it comes from 13 U.S. Navy gunnery teams studied during training, which showed a progression from "teamwork," or intermember coordination, to "taskwork." However, whether teams follow a fixed developmental sequence or show different temporal patterns in varied organizational contexts remains a question for future research. Considering the variety of relationships between work teams and organizational contexts, it seems unlikely that a single sequence can describe the development of all kinds of teams. Perhaps, as suggested by McGrath, Futoran, and Kelly (1986), each team has to deal with certain developmental issues, but the order of precedence depends on the circumstances.

## Aspects of Team Development

Longitudinal theories suggest that groups develop norms, cohesion, and roles.

1. *Norms.* Since the Hawthorne studies (Roethlisberger & Dickson, 1939) linked performance with group norms, their importance for work groups has been obvious, but elusive. Practitioners (e.g., Bassin, 1988) recommended that effective teams have norms and rules of behavior agreed on by all members. Hackman (1987) identified norms about performance as a desirable design feature of groups and implied that they can be externally influenced. Foushee (1984) reported some success in altering norms in flight crews through videotaped flight simulations and feedback about interpersonal styles. But other research suggests that work groups develop unique norms, even at odds with their organization (e.g., Richards & Dobyns, 1957). Organizational culture may provide a vehicle for external influence over group norms. "Charters" drafted by team members and managers around team mission and organizational goals may incorporate both imposed and developed norms.

2. *Cohesion.* This crucial ingredient of team viability has been found to be correlated with communication and conformity to group norms (McGrath, 1984). Besides small group size, conditions found favorable to cohesion include similar attitudes (Terborg, Castore, & DeNinno, 1976) and physical proximity of workspaces (Sundstrom, 1986). Context factors likely to foster cohesion include external pressure (Glickman et al., 1987) and rewards for team performance (Shea & Guzzo, 1987a).

The link of cohesion with performance may depend on group norms. Stogdill (1972) examined 34 work groups and found cohesion positively correlated with performance in 12, inversely correlated in 11, and unrelated in the remaining groups. Cohesion apparently amplified norms favoring both high and low production. During routine operations, Goodman (1986) found that group cohesion was unrelated to production, but in uncertain working conditions cohesive groups were more productive.

The seemingly optimal combination of cohesion and a norm of high performance may not always be ideal. Janis (1971) claimed that cohesive groups under pressure can make poor decisions through *groupthink*, a complex process in which groups exhibit a variety of dysfunctional decision making "symptoms" such as disregarding new information to protect an apparent consensus. This may occur in autonomous groups (Liebowitz & De Meuse, 1982; Manz & Sims, 1982), especially high-ranking teams who make decisions with little outside help. Examples are task forces, committees, and some project teams. When group tasks require external synchronization, peer work units may check tendencies toward groupthink. But the potential for groupthink bolsters Manz and Sims's (1982) recommendation for training in group decision making.

3. *Roles.* Roles are sufficiently basic to work groups to be considered one of their defining features (Alderfer, 1987). However, even in teams with a high degree of specialization, members may rotate roles if possible (Susman, 1970).

For the much-studied role of leader, past research has identified two leadership functions—task and interpersonal (McGrath, 1984). But in light of a trend toward self-management, leadership may be increasingly expected of team members (Manz & Sims, 1987). It may be more equally shared by members as their team develops over time. Consistent with this idea, Schriesheim (1980) found that in utility crews with low cohesion, leaders' initiation of structure was correlated with role clarity, satisfaction, and self-rated performance. In cohesive groups the same criteria were correlated instead with leader consideration.

## Team Development Intervention Studies

In efforts designed to improve team functioning called *team development* (Beckhard, 1969) or *team-building* (Dyer, 1977), consultants meet with groups to diagnose interpersonal processes and facilitate development of the team. Their interventions reflect several decades of research and practice (Hall & Williams, 1970) and vary depending on the combination of consultant, team, and organization (Liebowitz & De Meuse, 1982). At least four types of team interventions can be identified (e.g., Beer, 1980), as follows:

1. *Interpersonal processes.* This intervention involves candid discussion of relationships and conflicts among team members, often directed toward resolving "hidden agendas." This approach assumes that teams operate best with mutual trust and open communication; it attempts to build group cohesion (Kaplan, 1979).

2. *Goal-setting.* This approach involves clarifying the team's general goals and specific objectives, sometimes by defining subtasks and establishing timetables. Often combined with performance measurement and feedback, this type of intervention has a record of successful application in organizations (Locke, Shaw, Saari, & Latham, 1982).

3. *Role definition.* This intervention entails clarifying individual role expectations, group norms, and shared responsibility of team members (Bennis, 1966).

4. *Problem-solving.* In this approach, task-related processes are clarified within the group, such as identifying problems, causes, and solutions; choosing solutions; and developing and implementing action plans (Buller & Bell, 1986).

Intervention studies often report improved communication, cohesion, or other signs of viability (De Meuse & Liebowitz, 1981; Kaplan, 1979; Woodman & Sherwood, 1980a). The few that measure performance tend to report mixed results and are sometimes flawed by a lack of control groups. Woodman and Sherwood (1980b) concluded that findings from goal-setting interventions are more interpretable than others, leading them to place greater confidence in goal setting.

We examined empirical research on team development interventions published since 1980 in selected journals.[1] Table 2 shows the 13 studies we found, with type of team, intervention (interpersonal, goal setting, role definition, and problem solving), and results classified under headings of performance or team viability. Most studies used multiple approaches to team development, often combining an interpersonal approach with others. Most research designs had control groups, yielding results more interpretable than in earlier reviews. Teams include advisory groups, production and service teams, project groups, and action teams, a broad mix that could reflect an expanding use of workgroups. The table may overrepresent successful team development interventions, as failures are probably less likely to be published.

Interventions had mixed success, as in prior studies. Performance improved in 4 out of 9 cases in which it was measured. Aspects of viability improved in 8 out of 10 studies using interpersonal approaches, although some studies found adverse effects. Overall, Table 2 suggests that in *some circumstances* team development interventions may have enhanced work group effectiveness.

An ecological perspective suggests a reason why team development interventions do not always succeed: they usually focus only on internal team processes. This strategy might be more effective if coupled with a focus on external relations.

## ISSUES FOR RESEARCH AND PRACTICE

Current literature leaves many unanswered questions on work teams. But we see a handful of issues that deserve particular attention in future research and practice.

### Organizational Contexts and Differences Among Work Teams

An ecological view calls attention to the variety of relationships between work teams and their larger organizations. Such differences call into question our longstanding assumptions that the small group represents a single entity and that one model can fit all groups. Unfortunately, current research evidence gives little basis for testing these assumptions. Indeed, if the psychology of small groups dealt with a kind of animal, we could not be sure whether it was one or several species, what habitats it occupied, or what distinguished its subspecies. Work teams very well could represent several different types of social units that share superficial similarities. This might account for the persistent difficulty in arriving at generalizations about small groups. For researchers, an obvious next step is to study the *demographics of work groups*, or the prevalence of various applications of work teams and their organizational contexts. Another is to study specific applications of work teams in depth, through longitudinal case studies (e.g., Hackman, 1989).

[1] This review covers research published after the reviews by DeMeuse and Liebowitz (1981) and Woodman and Sherwood (1980a) through the end of 1988. Research-oriented journals included in our review were *Academy of Management Journal, Academy of Management Review, Administrative Science Quarterly, Group and Organization Studies, Human Relations, Journal of Applied Behavioral Science, Journal of Applied Psychology, Journal of Occupational Psychology, Organizational Behavior* and *Human Decision Processes*, and *Personnel Psychology*. Practitioner-oriented journals included in our review were *California Management Review, Harvard Business Review, Personnel, Personnel Administrator, Personnel Journal*, and *Training and Development Journal*.

TABLE 2   Thirteen Intervention Studies of Team Development, 1980–1988

| Study | Teams | Interventions | Performance | Viability |
|---|---|---|---|---|
| Morrison & Surges (1980) | Top management team in state government | Interpersonal, role definition | — | Increased communication collaboration, role clarity. |
| Porras & Wilkins (1980) | Cafeteria food service teams | Interpersonal, problem-solving | Little change in costs, output, or profit. | Decreased job satisfaction, commitment. |
| Woodman & Sherwood (1980a) | Student project groups | Problem-solving, goal-settings | No effect on grades. | Better problem solving, participation; no change in satisfaction. |
| Boss & McConkie (1981) | Government employee groups | Interpersonal | — | Better communication and goal-setting immediately after intervention. More turnover, grievances. Poorer climate. |
| Paul & Gross (1981) | City maintenance crews | Problem-solving, role definitions | Increased service efficiency; no change in customer satisfaction. | Higher job satisfaction. No change in absences, turnover. Faster resolution of employee grievances. |
| Boss (1983) | (not reported) | Interpersonal, role definition | Higher ratings of group effectiveness. | Increased participation, involvement, trust. |
| Hughes, Rosenbach, & Clover (1983) | Air force cadet teams | Interpersonal, role definition, goal-settings | Higher ratings of group performance, trust. | Higher cohesiveness, group satisfaction. No change in goal commitment, job clarity. |
| Eden (1985) | Army combat units | Interpersonal, role definition, goal-setting | No change in team performance ratings. | No change in satisfaction, communication, peer relations, coordination. |
| Buller & Bell (1986) | Mining crews | Problem-solving | Little change in quality or quantity of ore-mined. | Better work techniques, communication. |
| Eden (1986) | Army combat units | Interpersonal, role definition, goal-setting | No change in ratings of combat readiness. | Improved teamwork, conflict handling, planning. No change in cohesion, involvement, support, job clarity. |
| Miller & Phillip (1986) | Engineering project groups | Interpersonal, problem-solving | Project completed $30 million under budget. | Enhanced cooperation, trust, communication, morale. |
| Mitchell (1986) | Student project groups | Interpersonal | — | Better interpersonal relations. |
| Margerison, Davies, & McCann (1987) | Airliner cockpit crews | Interpersonal, problem-solving | — | Better communication, interpersonal relations. |

Differences among work teams pose an immediate practical challenge for management. Some teams, such as those in production and service, tend to be synchronized with counterpart work units and customers. So management of external relations might be more critical to their effectiveness than internal team dynamics. Others, such as project teams, have missions calling for creativity and innovation. They may need special help in applying group processes to their resources. Team managers need to be sensitive to such differences when making decisions on such issues as team training and consultation, physical environments, performance measurement and feedback systems, reward systems, and other contextual features.

## Organizational Context of Work Team Effectiveness

Practitioners and theorists agree fairly well on features of organizational context that foster team effectiveness, but these remain to be studied. Near the top of our agenda for empirical research is an assessment of the role of specific context factors in work team effectiveness, such as organizational culture, technology and task design, mission clarity, autonomy, rewards, performance feedback, training and consultation, and physical environment. This list of contextual factors could be a practical checklist for managers of work teams. However, the challenge is to create an optimal mix of context features for each particular group. One context factor could make the difference, as in a project team whose members need to develop a mission statement before they can even start working.

## Boundaries and Their Management

Team development practitioners have long emphasized the importance of group boundaries (e.g., Alderfer, 1987). Up to now, boundaries have had little role in a small group research literature dominated by laboratory studies. Yet in an organizational context, boundaries may be critical to work team effectiveness. An ecological approach suggests that the group boundary needs continual management to ensure that it becomes neither too sharply delineated nor too permeable, so that the team neither becomes isolated nor loses its identity. At the same time, boundary management calls for maintenance of conditions that promote needed external synchronization and coordination. The physical environment may figure prominently in boundary management (Sundstrom & Altman, 1989). However, practitioners can hope for little guidance from current research evidence. It remains for researchers to study the processes through which work teams maintain external integration and differentiation needed for effectiveness.

## Team Development

As lamented in 1966 by McGrath and Altman, longitudinal processes in work groups are still poorly understood. Pending basic, empirical studies of temporal sequences in actual, intact work teams, we can only speculate how predictors of effectiveness relate to team development. Future research needs to examine work teams in their natural contexts at multiple points in time, to look for developmental stages analogous to infancy, adolescence, maturity, and old age. Lacking such research, our theories can only continue to generalize from the laboratory or use "black boxes" to describe team development. Fortunately, some researchers are now using innovative methods to study developmental processes in teams, such as the qualitative approach by Gersick (1988), the case study approach by Hackman (1989), and the quantitative methods by Glickman and colleagues (1987). However, practitioners may have to wait a while longer for a compelling model of team development that can serve as a guide for managing and facilitating work teams. Evidence for such a model could grow out of action research in which work groups are systematically monitored over time, perhaps in conjunction with team development interventions. A trend toward applying work teams could provide many real-world research opportunities, for instance in companies reorganizing around work teams after a merger or an acquisition.

# Team Effectiveness: Definition and Measurement

Of course, progress in studying and managing work teams depends on having a well-accepted, measurable criterion of effectiveness. Although many experts agree that effectiveness includes more than performance, the "more" remains an issue. A convincing empirical basis for defining and measuring what we have labeled *team viability* may point to certain, specific interpersonal skills requisite to effective team membership. These skills, in turn, could be used in the selection and the training of team members.

As for performance, measurement has traditionally relied on specific criteria such as tons of coal extracted by mining teams, sales revenues produced by sales teams and manager ratings of project teams. Such specific, local criteria allow cross-team comparisons only if converted into dependable, global indexes. The innovative method of Pritchard and colleagues (1988) sets a valuable precedent by merging specific indicators into an index of percentage of maximum capability.

In conclusion, an ecological view emphasizes the role of organizational context, boundaries, and team development in work team effectiveness. Our selective review of current literature points to features of organizational context and aspects of group-organization boundaries likely to make them salient. Researchers and practitioners need to look beyond a group's internal processes to the prescriptions for effectiveness inherent in the relationship between the work team and the organization.

# REFERENCES

Alderfer, C. P. (1987). An intergroup perspective on group dynamics. In J. Lorsch (Ed.), *Handbook of organizational behavior* (pp. 190–222). Englewood Cliffs, NJ: Prentice-Hall.

Argote, L. (1982). Input uncertainty and organizational coordination in hospital emergency units. *Administrative Science Quarterly, 27,* 420–434.

Bales, R. F., Cohen, S. P., & Williamson, S. A. (1970). *SYMLOG.* New York: Holt, Rinehart & Winston.

Banas, P. (1988). Employee involvement: A sustained labor/management initiative at Ford Motor Company. In J. P. Campbell & R. J. Campbell (Eds.), *Productivity in organizations* (pp. 388–416). San Francisco: Jossey-Bass.

Bassin, M. (1988). Teamwork at General Foods: New and improved. *Personnel Journal, 67* (5), 62–70.

Beckhard, R. (1969). *Organization development: Strategies and models.* Reading, MA: Addison-Wesley.

Beer, M. (1980). *Organization change and development: A systems view.* Santa Monica, CA: Goodyear.

Bennis, W. (1966). *Changing organizations.* New York: McGraw-Hill.

Berrien, F. K. (1983). A general systems approach to organizations. In M. Dunnette (Ed.), *Handbook of industrial and organizational psychology* (pp. 41–62). New York: Wiley.

Boss, R. W. (1983). Team building and the problems of regression: The personal management interview as an intervention. *Journal of Applied Behavioral Science, 19,* 67–83.

Boss, R. W., & McConkie, M. L. (1981). The destructive impact of a positive team-building intervention. *Group and Organization Studies, 6,* 45–56

Bramel, D., & Friend, R. (1987). The work group and its vicissitudes in social and industrial psychology. *Journal of Applied Behavioral Science, 23,* 233–253.

Buller, P. F., & Bell, C. H., Jr. (1986). Effects of team building and goal setting on productivity: A field experiment. *Academy of Management Journal, 29,* 305–328.

Bushe, G. R. (1987). Temporary or permanent middle-management groups? Correlates with attitudes in QWL change projects. *Group and Organization Studies, 12*, 23–37.

Campbell, D. J. (1988). Task complexity: A review and analysis. *Academy of Management Review, 13* (1), 40–52.

Cherns, A. (1976). The principles of sociotechnical design. *Human Relations, 29*, 783–792.

Cherry, R. L. (1982). The development of General Motors' team-based plants. In R. Zager & M. P. Rosow (Eds.), *The innovative organization* (pp. 21–43). New York: Pergamon.

Cole, R. E. (1982). Diffusion of participatory work structures in Japan, Sweden, and the United States. In P. S. Goodman & Associates (Eds.), *Change in organizations* (pp. 166–225). San Francisco: Jossey-Bass.

Cummings, T. G. (1978). Self-regulating work groups: A socio-technical synthesis. *Academy of Management Review, 3*, 624–634.

Cummings, T. G. (1981). Designing effective work-groups. In P. C. Nystrom & W. Starbuck (Eds.), *Handbook of organizational design* (Vol. 2, pp. 250–271). Oxford: Oxford University Press.

Cummings, T. G., & Molloy, E. S. (1977). *Improving productivity and the quality of work life.* New York: Praeger.

De Meuse, K. P., & Liebowitz, S.J. (1981). An empirical analysis of team-building research. *Group & Organization Studies, 6*, 357–378.

Driskell, J. E., Hogan, R., & Salas, E. (1988). Personality and group performance. *Review of Personality and Social Psychology, 14*, 91–112.

Dyer, J. L. (1984). Team research and team training: A state-of-the-art review. In F. A. Muckler (Ed.), *Human factors review: 1984* (pp. 285–323). Santa Monica, CA: Human Factors Society.

Dyer, W. G. (1977). *Team building.* Reading, MA: Addison-Wesley.

Eden, D. (1985). Team development: A true field experiment at three levels of rigor. *Journal of Applied Psychology, 70*, 94–100.

Eden, D. (1986). Team development: Quasi-experimental confirmation among combat companies. *Group and Organization Studies, 11*, 133–146.

Foushee, H. C. (1984). Dyads and triads at 35,000 feet: Factors affecting group process and aircrew performance. *American Psychologist, 39*, 885–893.

Friedlander, F. (1987). The ecology of work groups. In J. Lorsch (Ed.), *Handbook of organizational behavior* (pp. 301–314). Englewood Cliffs, NJ: Prentice-Hall.

Galagan, P. (1986). Work teams that work. *Training and Development Journal, 11*, 33–35.

Gersick, C. J. G. (1988). Time and transition in work teams: Toward a new model of group development. *Academy of Management Journal, 31*, 9–41.

Gladstein, D. L. (1984). Groups in context: A model of task group effectiveness. *Administrative Science Quarterly, 29*, 499–517.

Glickman, A. S., Zimmer, S., Montero, R. C., Guerette, P. J., Campbell, W. J., Morgan, B., & Salas, E. (1987). *The evolution of teamwork skills: An empirical assessment with implications for training* (Tech. Report 87–016). Orlando, FL: Office of Naval Research, Human Factors Division.

Goodman, P. S. (1986). Impact of task and technology on group performance. In P. S. Goodman and Associates (Eds.), *Designing effective work groups* (pp. 120–167). San Francisco: Jossey-Bass.

Goodman, P. S., Devadas, R., & Hughson, T. L. G. (1988). Groups and productivity: Analyzing the effectiveness of self-managing teams. In J. P. Campbell & R. J. Campbell (Eds.), *Productivity in organizations* (pp. 295–327). San Francisco: Jossey-Bass.

Goodman, P. S., Ravlin, E. C., & Argote, L. (1986). Current thinking about groups: Setting the stage for new ideas. In P. S. Goodman & Associates (Eds.), *Designing effective work groups* (pp. 1–33). San Francisco: Jossey-Bass.

Hackman, J. R. (1986). The psychology of self-management in organizations. In M. S. Pallak & R. Perloff (Eds.), *Psychology and work* (pp. 89–136). Washington DC: American Psychological Association.

Hackman, J. R. (1987). The design of work teams. In J. Lorsch (Ed.), *Handbook of organizational behavior* (pp. 315–342). New York: Prentice-Hall.

Hackman, J. R. (1989). *Groups that work (and those that don't).* San Francisco: Jossey-Bass.

Hackman, J. R., & Oldham, G. R. (1980). *Work redesign.* Reading, MA: Addison-Wesley.

Hackman, J. R., & Walton, R. E. (1986). Leading groups in organizations. In P. S. Goodman & Associates (Eds.), *Designing effective work groups* (pp. 72–119). San Francisco: Jossey-Bass.

Hall, J. S., & Watson, W. (1971). The effects of a normative intervention on group decision-making performance. *Human Relations, 23,* 299–317.

Hall, J. S., & Williams, M. S. (1970). Group dynamics training and improved decision making. *Journal of Applied Behavioral Science, 6,* 39–68.

Hardaker, M., & Ward, B. K. (1987). Getting things done: How to make a team work. *Harvard Business Review, 65,* 112–119.

Heinen, J. S., & Jacobson, E. J. (1976). A model of task group development in complex organizations and a strategy of implementation. *Academy of Management Review, 1,* 98–111.

Herold, D. M. (1978). Improving the performance effectiveness of groups through a task-contingent selection of intervention strategies. *Academy of Management Review, 4,* 315–325.

Homans, G. C. (1950). *The human group.* New York: Harcourt, Brace & World.

Hughes, R. L., Rosenbach, W. E., & Clover, W. H. (1983). Team development in an intact, ongoing work group: A quasi-field experiment. *Group & Organization Studies, 8,* 161–186.

James, L. R., James, L. A., & Ashe, D. K. (in press). The meaning of organizations: An essay. In B. Schneider (Eds.), *Frontiers in industrial and organizational psychology,* Greenwich, CT: JAI Press.

Janis, I. L. (1971). *Victims of groupthink.* Boston: Houghton Mifflin.

Kanter, R. M. (1983). *The change masters.* New York: Simon & Schuster.

Kaplan, R. E. (1979). The conspicuous absence of evidence that process consultation enhances task performance. *Journal of Applied Behavioral Science, 15,* 346–360.

Katz, D., & Kahn, R. L. (1978). *The social psychology of organizations* (2nd ed.). New York: Wiley.

Katz, R. (1982). The effects of group longevity on project communication and performance. *Administrative Science Quarterly, 27,* 81–104.

Kelly, L, (1982). *Scientific management, job redesign, and work performance.* London: Academic Press.

Ketchum, L. (1981). How to start and sustain a work redesign program. *National Productivity Review, 1,* 75–86.

Ketchum, L. (1984). How redesigned plants *really* work. *National Productivity Review, 3,* 246–254.

Kidder, T. (1981). *The soul of a new machine.* New York: Avon Books.

Koch, J. L. (1979). Effects of goal specificity and performance feedback to work groups on peer leadership, performance, and attitudes. *Human Relations, 33,* 819–840.

Kolodny, H. F., & Dresner, B. (1986). Linking arrangements and new work designs. *Organizational Dynamics, 14* (3), 33–51.

Kolodny, H. F., & Kiggundu, M. N. (1980). Towards the development of a sociotechnical systems model in woodlands mechanical harvesting. *Human Relations, 33,* 623–645.

Latane, B., Williams, K., & Harkins, S. (1979). Many hands make light the work: The causes and consequences of social loafing. *Journal of Personality and Social Psychology, 37,* 822–832.

Lawrence, P. R., & Lorsch, J. W. (1969). *Developing organizations: Diagnosis and action.* Reading, MA: Addison-Wesley.

Ledford, G. E., Lawler, E. E., & Mohrman, S. A. (1988). The quality circle and its variations. In J. P. Campbell & R. J. Campbell (Eds.), *Productivity in organizations* (pp. 255–294). San Francisco: Jossey-Bass.

Liebowitz, S. J., & De Meuse, K. P. (1982). The application of team building. *Human Relations, 35,* 1–18.

Locke, E. A., Shaw, K. N., Saari, L. M., & Latham, G. P. (1982). Goal setting and task performance: 1969–1980. *Psychological Bulletin, 90,* 125–152.

Manz, C. C., & Sims, H. P. (1982). The potential for "groupthink" in autonomous work groups. *Human Relations, 35,* 773–784.

Manz, C. C., & Sims, H. P. (1987). Leading workers to lead themselves: The external leadership of self-managing work teams. *Administrative Science Quarterly, 32,* 106–128.

Margerison, C., Davies, R., & McCann, D. (1987). High-flying management development. *Training and Development Journal, 41,* 38–41.

McGrath, J. E. (1964). *Social psychology: A brief introduction.* New York: Holt, Rinehart & Winston.

McGrath, J. E. (1984). *Groups: Interaction and performance.* Englewood Cliffs, NJ: Prentice-Hall.

McGrath, J. E., & Altman, I. (1966). *Small group research: A synthesis and critique of the field.* New York: Holt, Rinehart & Winston.

McGrath, J. E., Futoran, G. C., & Kelly, J. R. (1986). *Complex temporal patterning in interaction and task performance: A report of progress in a program of research on the social psychology of time* (Technical Report No. 86–1). Urbana-Champaign: University of Illinois, Psychology Department.

McGrath, J. E., & Kelly, J. R. (1986). *Time and human interaction: Toward a social psychology of time.* New York: Guilford Press.

Miller, B. W., & Phillip, R. C. (1986). Team building on a deadline. *Training and Development Journal, 40,* 54–57.

Miller, E. J. ·(1959). Technology, territory, and time: The internal differentiation of complex production systems. *Human Relations, 12,* 245–272.

Mitchell, R. (1986). Team building by disclosure of internal frames of reference. *Journal of Applied Behavioral Science, 22,* 15–28.

Moreland, R. L., & Levine, J. M. (1988). Group dynamics over time: Development and socialization in small groups. In J. E. McGrath (Ed.), *The social psychology of time* (pp. 151–181). Beverly Hills, CA: Sage.

Morrison, P., & Sturges, J. (1980). Evaluation of organization development in a large state government organization. *Group and Organization Studies, 5,* 48–64.

Nadler, D. A., Cammann, C., & Mirvis, P. H. (1980). Developing a feedback system for work units: A field experiment in structural change. *Journal of Applied Behavioral Science, 16,* 41–62.

Naylor, J. C., & Dickenson, T. L. (1969). Task structure, work structure, and team performance, *Journal of Applied Psychology, 53,* 167–177.

Nieva, V. F., Fleishman, E. A., & Rieck, A. (1978). *Team dimensions: Their identity, their measurement, and their relationships* (Technical report, Contract No. DAHC19–78–C–001). Washington DC: Advanced Research Resources Organizations.

O'Reilly, C. A., & Roberts, K. H. (1977). Task group structure, communication, and effectiveness in three organizations. *Journal of Applied Psychology, 62,* 674–681.

Pasmore, W., Francis, C., Haldeman, J., & Shani, A. (1982). Sociotechnical systems: A North American reflection on empirical studies of the seventies. *Human Relations, 35,* 1179–1204.

Paul, C. F., & Gross, A. C. (1981). Increasing productivity and morale in a municipality: Effects of organization development. *Journal of Applied Behavioral Science, 17,* 59–78.

Pearce, J. A., & Ravlin, E. C. (1987). The design and activation of self-regulating work groups. *Human Relations, 40,* 751–782.

Peterfruend, S. (1982). "Face–to-face" at Pacific Northwest Bell. In R. Zager & M. P. Rosow (Eds.), *The innovative organization* (pp. 21–43). New York: Pergamon.

Peters, T. J. (1988). *Thriving on chaos.* New York: Knopf.

Peters, T. J., & Waterman, R. H. (1982). *In search of excellence.* New York: Warner.

Porras, J. I., & Wilkins, A. (1980). Organization development in a large system: An empirical assessment. *Journal of Applied Behavioral Science, 16,* 506–534.

Poza, E. J., & Marcus, M. L. (1980). Success story: The team approach to work-restructuring. *Organizational Dynamics, 8,* 3–25.

Pritchard, R. D., Jones, S., Roth, P., Stuebing, K., & Ekeberg, S. (1988). Effects of group feedback, goal setting, and incentives on organizational productivity. *Journal of Applied Psychology, 73* (2), 337–358.

Reich, R. B. (1987). Entrepreneurship reconsidered: The team as hero. *Harvard Business Review, 65* (3), 77–83.

Richards, C. B., & Dobyns, H. F. (1957). Topography and culture: The case of the changing cage. *Human Organization, 16,* 16–20.

Roby, T. B., & Lanzetta, J. T. (1958). Considerations in the analysis of group tasks. *Psychological Bulletin, 35* (2), 88–101.

Roethlisberger, F. J., & Dickson, W. J.(1939). *Management and the worker.* Cambridge, MA: Harvard University Press.

Rosseau, D. M., & Cooke, R. A. (1988, August). *Cultures of high reliability: Behavioral norms aboard a U.S. Aircraft carrier.* Paper presented at the meeting of the Academy of Management, Anaheim, CA.

Schriesheim, J. F. (1980). The social context of leader–subordinate relations. *Journal of Applied Psychology, 65,* 183–194.

Shaw, M. E. (1981). *Group dynamics* (3rd ed.). New York: McGraw-Hill.

Shea, G. P. (1986). Quality circles: The danger of bottled change. *Sloan Management Review, 27,* 33–46.

Shea, G. P., & Guzzo, R. A. (1987a). Group effectiveness: What really matters? *Sloan Management Review, 3,* 25–31.

Shea, G. P., & Guzzo, R. A. (1987b). Groups as human resources. In K. M. Rowland & G. R. Ferris (Eds.), *Research in personnel and human resources management* (Vol. 5, pp. 323–356). Greenwich, CT: JAI Press.

Shonk, W., & Shonk, J. H. (1988). What business teams can learn from athletic teams. *Personnel, 65,* 76–80.

Smith, R. (1981). Let your employees choose their co-workers. *Society for Advancement of Management Advanced Management Journal, 46,* 27–36.

Steiner, I. D. (1972). *Group process and productivity.* New York: Academic Press.

Stogdill, R. M. (1972). Group productivity, drive, and cohesiveness. *Organizational Behavior and Human Performance, 8,* 26–43.

Stone, P., & Luchetti, R. (1985). Your office is where you are. *Harvard Business Review, 63* (2), 102–117.

Sundstrom, E., (1986). *Work places.* New York: Cambridge University Press.

288

Sundstrom, E., & Altman, I. (1989). Physical environments and work-group effectiveness. In L. L. Cummings & B. Staw (Eds.), *Research in organizational behavior* (Vol. 11, pp. 175–209). Greenwich, CT: JAI Press.

Sundstrom, E., Bobrow, W., Fulton, K., Blair, L. Y., & McClane, W. E. (1988, June). *Interpersonal processes in small group performance*. Paper presented at the 11th International Conference on Groups, Networks, and Organizations, Nags Head, NC.

Susman, G. I. (1970). The impact of automation on work group autonomy and task specialization. *Human Relations, 23*, 567–577.

Terborg, J. R., Castore, C., & DeNinno, J. A. (1976). A longitudinal field investigation of the impact of group composition on group performance and cohesion. *Journal of Personality and Social Psychology, 34*, 782–790.

Thompson, J. D. (1967). *Organizations in action.* New York: McGraw-Hill.

Thompson, P. C. (1982). Quality circles at Martin Marietta Corporation, Denver Aerospace/Michoud Division. In R. Zager & M. Rosow (Eds.), *The innovative organization* (pp. 3–20). New York: Pergamon.

Tornatzky, L. G. (1986). Technological change and the structure of work. In M. S. Pallak & R. Perloff (Eds.), *Psychology and work* (pp. 89–136). Washington, DC: American Psychological Association.

Trist, E. L., Higgins, G. W., Murray, H., & Pollock, A. B. (1963). *Organizational choice.* London: Tavistock Publications.

Tuckman, B. W. (1965). Developmental sequence in small groups. *Psychological Bulletin, 63*, 384–389.

Tuckman, B. W., & Jensen, M. (1977). Stages of small-group development revisited. *Group & Organization Studies, 2,* 419–427.

Tushman, M. L. (1979). Impacts of environmental variability on patterns of work related communications. *Academy of Management Journal, 23*, 482–500.

Tziner, A., & Eden, D. (1985). Effects of crew composition on crew performance: Does the whole equal the sum of the parts? *Journal of Applied Psychology, 70*, 85–93.

Tziner, A., & Vardi, Y. (1982). Effects of command style and group cohesiveness on the performance effectiveness of self-selected tank crews. *Journal of Applied Psychology, 67*, 769–775.

Van Zelst, R. H. (1952). Sociometrically selected work teams increase production. *Personnel Psychology, 5*, 175–185.

Walton, R. E. (1977). Work innovation at Topeka: After six years. *Journal of Applied Behavioral Science, 13*, 422–433.

Walton, R. E. (1985). From control to commitment in the workplace. *Harvard Business Review, 63* (2), 76–84.

Weich, K. (1982). Management of organizational change among loosely coupled elements. In P. S. Goodman & Associates (Eds.), *Change in organizations* (pp. 375–408). San Francisco: Jossey-Bass.

Woodman, R. W., & Sherwood, J. J. (1980a). Effects of team development intervention: A field experiment. *Journal of Applied Behavioral Science, 16*, 211–227.

Woodman, R. W., & Sherwood, J. J. (1980b). The role of team development in organizational effectiveness: A critical review. *Psychological Bulletin, 88*, 166–186.

# 10
# Problem Management

MANAGING CREATIVITY: A JAPANESE MODEL
*Min Basadur*

OF BOXES, BUBBLES, AND EFFECTIVE MANAGEMENT
*David K. Hurst*

# MANAGING CREATIVITY: A JAPANESE MODEL

*Min Basadur*

## Claiming an Unstable Future

The rapidly accelerating rate of technological and environmental change demands much greater organizational adaptability than in the more stable past. Attempting behavioral change has turned out to be very difficult for many North American organizations because they have, by and large, developed along bureaucratic, non-flexible, and non-adaptive lines. Recent research has indicated that people at all organizational levels in North American business and industry can learn to think more creatively, to discover and solve important interfunctional problems, and to innovate new products and new methods faster, all of which results in greater organizational adaptability.[1] Simply put, creativity in organizations is a continuous search for and solving of problems and a creating and implementing of new solutions for the betterment of the organization, its customers, and its members.

Much has been written about the recent business success of Japanese corporations. It is often implied that superior management methods are the key. At the same time, the Japanese are viewed as not being truly creative. They are accused of being very good at copying and nothing more. For example, it is pointed out they have not produced many Nobel laureates, nor have they made many basic science discoveries. It could be argued that this is because they have not yet had the world class training needed by their scientists. Some observers believe the Japanese will soon begin producing Nobel laureates by making world-class training available. This belief is based on the fact that Japanese students are being sent to top North American institutions to learn mathematics and science from the current "masters," much like North American students went to learn from the European masters in the 19th century.

*Source: Academy of Management Executive,* © 1992, Vol. 6, No. 2, pp. 29–41.

The Japanese may already be better students of creativity than North Americans. They appear to be ahead of North Americans in implementing new ideas about management from the behavioral sciences which our own managers find difficult to accept. These new ideas include improved manufacturing and service management methods for higher quality, efficiency, and flexibility, such as "Just in Time" (J.I.T.), "Statistical Process Controls" (S.P.C.), and "Quality Circles" (Q.C.C.).

Many of these ideas originated in North America in the 1940s and 1950s but have never really caught on and were left in the classroom. Attempts to apply them in the workplace have often failed. Rather than admit we just don't want to change, North American managers have found it easier to assume that there is something mysterious about Japanese culture that permits new approaches to management to work over there but not here. This article examines the ways in which management ideas that originated in North America are being applied in Japan.

## Finding Out About Japanese Creativity

A bilingual Japanese colleague of mine set up open-ended interviews with five major Japanese companies including second and third visits in cases when it was necessary to probe more deeply. Comparisons were made with North American firms on emerging themes. To facilitate comparisons, data were gathered during the same time period from eleven leading North American companies. These data were obtained by a combination of questionnaire, in-depth interviews, and shop floor visits. The data from the Japanese and North American companies were organized along emerging themes, similarities, contrasts. For example, would Japanese styles of creativity favor problem finding activity more than their North American counterparts? Another purpose was to see if Japanese organizations understood creativity as the process pictured in Exhibit I and do they try to implement the model.

The model in Exhibit I provides a framework for speculation about Japanese management practices. Creativity in organizations is a continuous finding and solving of problems and a creating and implementing of new solutions. *Problem finding* activity means continuously identifying new and useful problems to be solved. This may include finding new product or service opportunities by anticipating new customer needs, discovering ways to improve existing products, services, procedures and processes or finding opportunities to improve the satisfaction and well-being of organizational members. Finally, problem finding includes defining such new problems and opportunities accurately and creatively. *Problem solving* activity means developing new, useful, imaginative solutions to found problems. *Solution implementing* activity means successfully installing such new solutions into the ongoing life of the organization.[2]

Problem finding may be the key to Japanese management success. The more emphasis placed on problem finding, the less is needed for solving and implementation. Solutions are more on target and successful implementation is facilitated. This is especially true when hierarchically lower level employees are invited to participate in the problem finding phase. Ownership and commitment are increased by early inclusion in change making. It takes less time to implement solutions when those affected have been permitted to participate from the beginning in finding and defining the problem and developing the solution.

Trained by traditional business schools in the "scientific management" approach originally identified by Frederick Taylor, most North American managers do not understand the importance of involving employees in early problem finding activities. They assume they are the only ones who know what needs to be done or that they can solve problems faster or better on their own. When these managers attempt to impose their solutions on their subordinates, there can be resentment and subordinates are often left uncommitted. Solutions fail either due to inadequate problem definition or lack of ownership. The same managers are likely to to repeat the cycle over and over again hoping to find one solution that will finally be accepted and do some good. Such haphazard problem solving activity wastes human resources and detracts from managerial productivity. Training in creative problem solving is designed to improve upon these inadequate attitudes and behaviors but it is difficult to get many North American organizations to provide such training and to get it used on the job.

Organizations often view training as a luxury to be initiated only when business is good and the pressure is off. It is regarded as an educational experience serving as a reward for people having done a good job, rather than to change attitudes and behaviors. The training is not seen as something that can genuinely change and improve the way work is done. As a result, many management methods are rejected after a short trial period even when they have worked well elsewhere, notably in Japan. The real reason for rejection is often a lack of desire or willpower to make significant changes. Since change is the essence of creativity, the ability to foster change is a major indicator worth observing when comparing management practices in Japan and North America.

EXHIBIT I   Creative Activity in an Organization

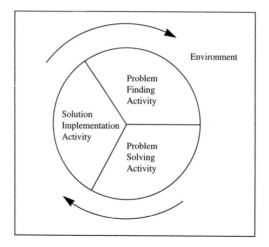

## Problem Finding Is Emphasized

The first Japanese company visited was a large international consumer electronics firm. Discussions were held with several senior R&D managers about managing this function. While there were many similarities to North American R&D management, one major difference that emerged was that newly hired R&D scientists and engineers always start their careers with six months in the sales department. The company wants them to learn first hand at the beginning of their careers about the needs and problems of their customers. In the long run, their jobs will focus on meeting those needs and solving those problems. For the next eighteen months, the new hires gradually work their way back to R&D through stints in various other functions including manufacturing and engineering. This suggests an interesting organizational emphasis on inducing problem finding behavior (anticipating and sensing customer needs) through structural means (job placement and rotation).

The remaining four companies visited were world-class manufacturers of car parts and scale measurement instruments. This time the interviews were with manufacturing and personnel managers and centered on the nature of their Employee Suggestion Systems (E.S.S.). It is not uncommon for employees of top Japanese companies to conceive and implement between forty and one hundred new suggestions per person, per year on average. This figure might amaze most North Americans managers since leading U.S. companies consider themselves lucky to obtain an average of about two suggestions per person, per year (see Table 1). The rest of this article explains not only how it is possible to achieve the Japanese levels, but also the theoretical rationale and comprehensive organizational benefits.

The interviews were in-depth, open-ended question and answer sessions, and shop floor visits. The collected data reveals that the primary objectives of the E.S.S. are motivation, job satisfaction, and group interaction. There is an infrastructure which guarantees that all three phases of creativity are completed. Individuals are encouraged to find problems with their work and improve their own jobs. Suggestions are submitted only after the solution has been demonstrated to work successfully. All suggestions are accepted and given credit. Monetary awards for most ideas are small.

Quality circle activity provides a reservoir of problems to aid individual problem finding activity, and smart managers learn how to get individuals to select problems of strategic importance to solve. Employees are trained that suggestions desired include new and improved products as well as methods. Individuals are encouraged to ask co-workers for help in problem solving. If individuals or informal teams cannot solve certain problems, they are referred to a quality circle team or the engineering department for help.

Group-oriented quality circles work supportively with the individually oriented Employee Suggestion System in other ways as well. The team gets credit every time one of its members submits a suggestion. Major celebrations are held by top management each year-end honoring teams and individual members of teams who have performed well in their suggestion work. All new employees are trained the first day on the job about the importance of the E.S.S. and how it works. Managers and supervisors are trained to work closely with subordinates to help them find and solve problems, implement their solutions, and provide plenty of positive feedback throughout.

TABLE 1   Leading Japanese Companies

| Company | # Of Suggestions | # Of Employees | Per/Employee |
|---|---|---|---|
| MATSUSHITA | 6,446,935 | 81,000 | 79.6 |
| HITACHI | 3,618,014 | 57,051 | 63.4 |
| MAZDA | 3,025,853 | 23,929 | 126.5 |
| TOYOTA | 2,648,710 | 55,578 | 47.6 |
| NISSAN | 1,393,745 | 48,849 | 38.5 |
| NIPPON DENSO | 1,393,745 | 33,192 | 41.6 |
| CANON | 1,076,356 | 13,788 | 78.1 |
| FUJI ELECTRIC | 1,022,340 | 10,226 | 99.6 |
| TOHOKU OKI | 734,044 | 881 | 833.2 |
| JVC | 728,529 | 15,000 | 48.6 |
| TYPICAL LEADING U.S. COMPANY | 21,000 | 9,000 | 2.3 |

Reference: Japan Human Relations Association, April, 1988: "The Power of Suggestion."

# R&D Is Everybody's Business

In all four companies, suggestions for improving both procedures and products are encouraged. Employees are trained from the first day on the job that "R&D is everybody's business." For example, in one company of 9,000 employees, 660,000 employee suggestions were received in one year. Of these, 6,000 were suggestions for new products or product improvements and the remainder were suggestions for new methods. New methods are improvements to the work itself—simplifying jobs, accelerating procedures and work flow, and so on.

# Problems Are Golden Eggs

In the companies studied, creative activity is deliberately induced on the job in a manner that is consistent with Exhibit I. On the first day on the job, new employees are trained that problems (discontents) are really "golden eggs." In other words, it is good to identify problems. One should be constructively "discontented" with one's job and with company products and seek ways to improve them. In some of the companies, the "golden eggs" are posted on large sheets of paper in the work area. Employees are then encouraged to interact with their co-workers to solve such problems and demonstrate that their solutions can be implemented.

In North America there is a real reluctance to identify problems. Employees, especially managers, often don't want anybody to know they've got problems because they are seen as a sign of weakness and poor performance. Subordinates soon pick up this attitude and adopt a problem avoidance approach to their work ("it didn't happen on my shift" and "that's not our problem"). This leads to neglect of important interfunctional opportunities for improvement and customer needs.

In these Japanese firms not only are people taught, but there is also a structured mechanism for causing problem finding activity. Workers are provided with problem finding cards. If dissatisfied with something about one's job, the worker writes the discontent on the card and posts it up on a wall poster in the column marked "problems." Workers post their problems, their "golden eggs," their discontents, so other people can see them. If others notice a problem posted which is of interest to them, they will join forces to help solve it.

Group interaction is stimulated and people work together on the problems they select. Later they can write their solutions in the second column beside the problem on the wall poster. There is a third column for implementation documentation. When all three columns are complete, and the individual or small team has done the problem finding and the problem solving and has shown that the solution works, then it can be said that a suggestion has been completed, but not until then. This suggestion can now be submitted.

# Implementation Before Submission and All Suggestions Accepted

Although not all suggestions are actually implemented, all of them are accepted. In other words, when all three phases of the creative process are completed (problem found, problem solved, solution shown to be implementable) by the employees themselves, a suggestion has been created and is accepted. About ninety-six percent of the suggestions end up being put into practice.

An "idea" is not a "suggestion" until it has gone through all three stages of the creative process modeled in Exhibit I. Every suggestion receives a monetary award. The vast majority of the suggestions are small $5 (500 yen) ideas. These are accepted and assigned the award by the supervisor on the spot. The suggestions that are more creative and significant are evaluated by a committee against multiple criteria including creativity and contribution to goals; they receive bigger awards of up to $10,000 and more.

The main objective is to accept all ideas and encourage the little ones as well as the big ones. It is the process of getting involved in one's work that counts, not the quality of any single idea. The goal is to have thinking workers and a spirit of never-ending improvement. Of the small ratio (about four percent) of accepted suggestions that do not get implemented right away, most are the kind that require skills beyond the scope of the suggesters. The team leader or the supervisor can get additional help from other departments for these ideas. Also, it may be found that the implementation of a suggestion is not timely or is inappropriate in the bigger picture. In this case, the idea is not implemented, but is given credit anyway. This is the way the system is supposed to operate and works very well in actual practice.

Employees are told they are expected to create new ideas. Some companies even establish informal goals per person per month. Each formal work group has a team leader, who ensures that daily production is met and new ideas keep flowing at the same time. The team leader communicates, coordinates, and gets help across the organization as needed. This prevents the work group from worrying unduly about maintaining daily production and saying "we don't have time to work on new ideas." Workers are given overtime as needed to complete their suggestions. The overtime is usually aimed at implementation work. Much of the problem finding and problem solving work is done continuously in people's minds off the job as well as on the job. When people are creatively involved in their work, ideas about new problems and solutions can occur to them at any time.

## Coaching, Positive Feedback, and Facilitator Skills Emphasized for Managers

The secret to making this process work begins with getting people to take ownership of problem finding as well as evaluation and implementation. Employees learn to accept evaluation and implementation of their ideas as part of their jobs. Their supervisors and managers support them and help them to be successful throughout the process. This includes helping the employee evaluate a potential suggestion's worthiness and how to make it work.

The boss is trained to be an encourager and coach, providing positive feedback at every opportunity. The system is structured to make sure such coaching and feedback occurs. A supervisor will help a new employee find a "golden egg" and develop a suggestion as part of the orientation process. Employees are given coaching on the appropriateness of "golden eggs" to be posted and positive feedback on all contributions.

On larger projects, the team leader and supervisor make sure that additional time (including overtime) and other resources are made available to workers as needed. Also, teams routinely make presentations to the rest of the organization during working hours, typically in the company cafeteria. The plant manager acts as a master of ceremonies, giving praise, recognition, and expert commentary as each project is presented. Suggestions which require higher level consideration for awards or implementation enter a formal system of evaluation and feedback. The suggestions are given feedback and positive recognition by design at several stages of this formal process.

Managers are not permitted to submit suggestions—that is, to get directly involved in the Employee Suggestion System; however, they are trained to get indirectly involved. For example, if a manager happens to think up an idea, rather than submit it, he or she is trained to figure out what problem that idea is trying to solve. The manager then goes down into the ranks and seeks out someone willing to post that problem. The group, or anybody in the group, can solve it themselves, probably with a different solution. This is how problem ownership is built.

Managers learn how to "dump problems into the fray" and let the ownership grow. This contrasts with the old-fashioned scientific management approach which designates management as "thinkers" and labor as "doers," which is not very scientific at all because thinking is done from the top down and wastes the minds of the workers. Worse yet, changes are usually sprung on the work force suddenly and are resisted.

First line supervisors find themselves stuck in the middle—expected to support the change but facing an unwilling, untrusting, and unaccepting group of subordinates who feel no ownership for the change. According to this research, Japanese managers are trained to facilitate change, not impose it. The Employee Suggestion System provides an excellent tool to accomplish this facilitative approach.

## Motivation Is the Outcome

When the top managers of these leading companies were asked what the primary objective of their Employee Suggestion System was, none of them said new products or new methods. Furthermore, none of them said lower costs, or higher profits. In fact, none of them mentioned any final economic outcomes. In contrast, all of them said *motivated* people.

These Japanese organizations believe that workers get motivated when they get a chance to be creative on the job. Employees enjoy coming to work. This is what the Japanese call "cheerfulness" and we call "job satisfaction." This creative activity also stimulates group interaction. People help each other solve problems which provides the opportunity for genuine team building.

People find real reasons to work together and feel good about their accomplishments, monetary awards, and the fact that their work team gets credit for their individual suggestions. Individual awards, especially larger ones, are shared with the team. The team decides how much the individual gets and how much they keep for their "activity fund." The activity fund is accumulated by the work teams to fund personal development, recreation, physical education, and other growth activities. The fund grows from quality circle awards and employee suggestion awards. Individuals get recognition and the team gets recognition.

All of the companies said they have found that when people are given the opportunity to engage in creative activity (as it has been described here), they become very motivated. This causes them to want to participate even more in creative activity. It also causes them to work harder on performing their normal routine jobs better—more quality, more quantity, and lower cost. This is consistent with increasing organizational efficiency and short-term organizational effectiveness. Exhibit II[3] models this simple management process.

## Consistency with Motivation Research

Organizational research conducted by P. E. Mott showed that effective organizations have three major simultaneous characteristics: efficiency, adaptability, and flexibility.[3] Efficiency is the ability to organize for routine production. Every organization is turning out some kind of product (a needed good or service).

Efficient organizations are customer focused; they know their customer and product. Over the years they have developed good routines for making their product the best they can with current technology. They produce a high quantity, quality product, and maintain a high output over input ratio (low cost) during production.

EXHIBIT II   Japanese Model

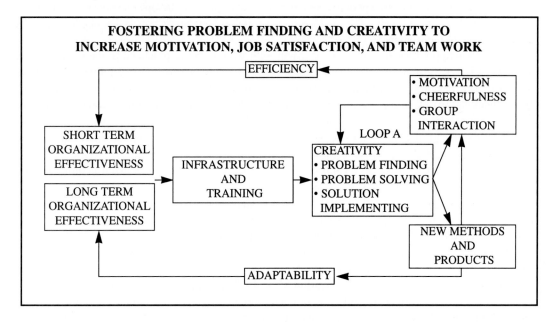

**FOSTERING PROBLEM FINDING AND CREATIVITY TO INCREASE MOTIVATION, JOB SATISFACTION, AND TEAM WORK**

Effective organizations are also able to respond and react to sudden temporary changes or interruptions. They can deal with unexpected disruptions and get back quickly to their normal routine without getting stuck in red tape. Flexibility is a way of preserving efficiency. Flexibility and efficiency are both necessary in the short run.

Adaptability is a longer range characteristic and refers to an organization's capacity to continually and intentionally change its routines and find new and better ways to do the work. Adaptable organizations anticipate problems and develop timely solutions. They stay abreast of new methods and technologies that may be applicable to the organization. The organization's members accept good, new ideas and make sure new solutions and techniques get installed and maintained. Acceptance of new ideas is widespread across all organizational departments.

The creative process of problem finding, problem solving and solution implementation becomes more vital as the amount of change confronting the organization increases. Up until recently, many organizations could be effective by concentrating only on efficiency and flexibility. Today, adaptability is equally important because of the rapidly accelerating rate of change. Adaptability is crucial for long-term effectiveness.

Motivating people by providing the opportunity for creative activity is consistent with the motivation literature in industrial and organizational psychology. One major category of motivational theories are the *need* theories. Two important motivational need sets are the need for competence and the need for curiosity and activity. These two needs and related motives provide the most direct explanation of how creativity is a means for motivating people.[4]

People have a desire to master their environment. Such mastery is intrinsically pleasurable and independent of outside rewards. This need for competence is aroused when people are faced with new challenging situations and dissipates after repeated mastery of the task. The concept of intrinsic motivation is also consistent with the notion that curiosity, activity, and exploration are enjoyed for their own sake. This was discovered in early animal research and in later studies on humans.

People develop negative attitudes toward repetitive tasks and report experiencing fatigue and boredom. Berlyne suggests that people adapt to certain levels of stimulation and take action to reduce discrepancies from these levels. The implication is similar to Herzberg's notion that challenging jobs are motivating in themselves.

Other motivation theories are also consistent with what is being practiced in the companies in this study. Herzberg proposes that the way to motivate most people is by redesigning their jobs so the work itself provides opportunity for growth, challenge, stimulation, learning, and recognition.[5] McClelland has advanced the need for achievement as the primary driving force motivating organizational members.[6] By giving employees the opportunity to find challenging problems, solve them, and implement solutions, the Employee Suggestion System taps into both the forces of intrinsically rewarding work and the need for achievement. According to Maslow, offering employees the opportunity to satisfy their higher level needs for self-esteem and for self-actualization through work accomplishment is the best way to motivate them.[7]

The Japanese Employee Suggestion System is a straightforward example of how these two highest level needs can be met. People are provided with the opportunity to use their creativity. They seek out work-related challenges of interest to themselves, then find success and recognition in developing implementable solutions that are welcomed and celebrated by the organization.

Motivation theory has not remained static since the 1950s and 1960s. Deci and Ryan provided a comprehensive review of intrinsic motivation.[8] Locke and Latham showed that when people are given a chance to set their own goals (the problem-anticipating aspect of problem finding) and the more specifically they state those goals (the problem definition aspect of problem finding), the more motivated they are to achieve those goals.[9]

The Japanese may not yet be at the forefront of initiating theoretical research, but their ability to apply motivation theory is impressive and far more than simple copying. As Japanese students continue to learn from the "masters," the time will come when their research informs our practice.

The vast majority of North American business and industry is still organized and managed on the scientific management concept made popular by Frederick Taylor in 1911.[10] One of the main premises of scientific management is that people at work are motivated by one dominant factor— money. This is the concept of "economic man." In spite of research showing that most people at work are multi-motivated (money does play a role but in a complex way), most managers continue to manage by simplistic, economic formulae.

The motivating factor in most North American employee suggestion systems is extrinsic, usually money. A few employees suggest a few big ideas that save the company large sums of money and win major cash awards for themselves. Most people don't participate.

In contrast, Japanese employee suggestion systems emphasize a large number of small ideas and everyone participates. There are small monetary awards for each implementable suggestion shared by the participating members. Larger awards are given for ideas of greater scope, but the vast majority of suggestions win small awards. The real awards, as far as employees are concerned, are the feelings of accomplishment, recognition, and growth.

## Top Down Impetus and Strategic Alignment

In the Japanese companies interviewed, training and a well-developed infrastructure are used to make creative activity important. They are also used to align creative activity strategically with important organizational goals as an everyday routine. Managers are trained to help their employees find, solve, and implement problems and solutions.

As clear company goals are articulated by top management and specific departmental objectives and subgoals are developed, these are communicated downward to guide individuals and teams in their selection of problems. This results in a close alignment of E.S.S. activity with strategic corporate needs. Managers who are skillful in the E.S.S. learn how to influence their subordinates toward including problems which are related to specific goals and objectives for their departments.

The reward system reinforces the importance of creative activity to the company. Not only does the E.S.S. provide extrinsic and intrinsic rewards for employees, but their managers' performance appraisals are also based in part on their ability to get their subordinates to perform well in the E.S.S.

In the Japanese companies I visited, Management by Objectives (M.B.O.) is integrated with the Employee Suggestion System. Typically, the manager's objectives will include helping people create and implement suggestions. This emphasis on getting subordinates involved in creating new ideas is part of the long-range process of management. The belief is that if people are encouraged to use their thinking power on a habitual daily basis, major tangible benefits will accrue to the organization in the long run.

Quality circle (Q.C.C.) group activity also serves to help align E.S.S. activity with strategic goals Q.C.C.work is a concentrated attack on major "theme" problems identified by upper management. These themes are assigned about every six months. A bonus of Q.C.C. activity is that it also provides a regular forum for spontaneous discussion of spinoff problems during Q.C.C. team meetings. The Q.C.C. infrastructure serves as a deliberate reservoir for problem finding to fuel the Employee Suggestion System program. Both the group-oriented Quality Circles and the individually oriented Employee Suggestion System are sparked by top management involvement. Not only is top management instrumental in setting direction and relevant goals, it also works hard insuring that such goals are followed up. Celebrations are hosted at the end of the year by presidential level management for teams which have performed well in Q.C.C. and E.S.S. activity.

## Job Redesign, Enrichment, and Adaptability

Proactive creative activity leads to a continuous supply of new methods and new products. This is synonymous with Mott's definition of organizational adaptability. Not only are new problems deliberately anticipated and solved, but also acceptance of the new solutions by employees is virtually assured because the employees are finding and solving their own problems and implementing their own changes. They have high ownership of the solutions and are redesigning their own jobs. This is consistent with a well-documented axiom of organizational psychology: "People don't resist change; they do resist being changed."

Herzberg's research on job satisfaction suggests that motivation can be achieved best by factors intrinsic to the work itself, such as responsibility and opportunity for growth and achievement. The validity of job enrichment, which is based on Herzberg's dual factor theory is supported by the findings reported in this article. Many companies have tried to redesign employee jobs to make them more intrinsically rewarding, however, evaluation of research results have been inconsistent. This may be because employees do not participate in it. The Japanese model goes one step further by letting employees be creative and allowing them to enrich their own jobs. Perhaps this is the missing link for North American companies who have tried other approaches to job enrichment and failed.

## Teamwork and Individual Work Harmonized

When individuals start working together on problems of common interest, solve them, and implement solutions together, group cohesiveness develops. Cohesiveness is an important factor in group productivity. The E.S.S. encourages small, informal teams to develop. People who want to work together on problems of common interest join up. The attraction contributes to cohesiveness. Group cohesiveness is also built more formally through the Quality Circle approach. Even though Q.C.C. activity is, in theory, voluntary, in actual practice everybody is a member of a quality circle team because it is the same as their functional work unit team.

One of the firms stressed that in their experience Q.C.C. didn't work well alone and neither did E.S.S., but together they worked very well. The firm recommended that both be used for best results.

The Quality Circle (Q.C.C.) system provides opportunities for group performance, recognition, and initiative. The Employee Suggestion System (E.S.S.) adds opportunities for individual performance, recognition, and initiative. Q.C.C. activity is highly structured and uses analytical problem solving tools such as fishboning and root cause analysis. The team must stick to the theme and not pursue other problems or ideas. Prior to the introduction of E.S.S., this restriction bothered many people. If one were sitting in a Quality Circle working on the assigned theme and suddenly thought up an idea to solve a totally unrelated problem, it would be frustrating to not be permitted to voice the idea.

The Employee Suggestion System provides an outlet for finding, solving, and implementing solutions to off-theme problems. The team gets credit for every suggestion that one of their team members submits individually and there is little conflict between the E.S.S. and Q.C.C. systems.

In contrast, attempts by some North American companies to install group-based Q.C.C. systems have run into conflict with long-established individual-based suggestion systems. These companies have not yet figured out how to integrate the two systems.

## How Do North American Systems Compare?

One key to the success of the Japanese Employee Suggestion System is the emphasis on problem finding. In North America, promotions and rewards go more often to people who appear not to have many problems. Managers don't feel they have enough time for problem finding. They feel they are too busy doing their "regular work" which often means fire-fighting activity and meeting short-term cost and profit goals. They want their people feeling the same way, and put focus on solutions, not problems. While the term "constructive discontent" is something that is often given lip service in North American organizations, the Japanese companies studied in this research are promoting and implementing it through simple structural methods.

Most North American suggestion systems use the suggestion box approach. Employees dump ideas in the suggestion box without the responsibility of evaluating them first or explaining just what the problem is that they are trying to solve. Managers evaluate the ideas and the employee waits to hear the judgment. Usually, the wait is long and most ideas are rejected. Managers find it onerous to judge so many suggestions and worry about the amount of change they represent. Many suggestions are difficult to understand since they have neither been discussed, nor shared with other employees. There is no incentive to share an idea with anybody for reasons such as the boss may not want to hear about new changes, other employees will want to share in the award, or someone may claim it as their own idea. The main incentive is to make lots of money for the individual submitting the suggestion. Small ideas are not worth the effort.

Teamwork, job satisfaction, and motivation are all secondary. In addition, many employees of North American companies do not receive awards for suggestions to improve their own job. They are rewarded only for ideas that are outside their own job. This goes against all the rules of motivation theory.

Finally, in many traditional North American companies, new product ideas are considered the job of R&D departments exclusively. Suggestion systems are concerned only with methods and procedures to save money or increase efficiency. New product ideas are not encouraged from employees of other departments and usually there are no organizational mechanisms to facilitate their emergence or development.

## Discovering How and Why Japanese Organizations Induce Creativity

The major discovery of this research is that Japanese organizations demonstrate a great deal of knowledge about inducing employee creativity through deliberate structural means. They believe they derive important benefits in doing so. This study indicates that top Japanese organizations recognize, emphasize, support, and induce problem finding which is elevated to at least equal priority as problem solving and solution implementation. They recognize all three as separate important activities which is consistent with research that suggests that all three activities need to be nurtured and managed to achieve organizational creativity.

TABLE 2   Contrasting Elements Summary Employee Suggestion Systems

|  | New (Japanese) | Traditional (North American) |
|---|---|---|
| Culture | * Group & individual synchronized | * Individual |
| Core objectives | * Thinking workers | * Breakthrough |
|  | * Never ending improvement | * Produce savings |
|  | * Individual growth |  |
|  | * Communications |  |
|  | * Decision making | * Improve safety |
| Management | * Primary responsibility | * Secondary at best |
| Area of suggestion | * Within your job & your workplace | * Outside of your job or your * workplace |
| Evaluation | * Simple | * Very structured |
|  | * Quick answers | * Slow answers |
|  | * Supervisor responsibility | * Evaluator responsibility |
|  | * Lots of suggester involvement | * Little suggester involvement |
|  | * Most accepted | * Most rejected |
| Communication | * Employee to supervisor | * Employee to evaluator |
|  | * Employee to employee | to supervision to management |
| Awards | * Intrinsic | * Extrinsic |

They have devised structural means through the way they place R&D hires and their Employee Suggestion Systems to induce creativity throughout the organization.

Through managing the Employee Suggestion System, the Japanese companies in our study implement what theory and literature suggest needs to be done to induce creative behavior, to get creative input in the organization, and to motivate members of the organization. By doing so, they get tangible creative output like short-term costs savings and new products and procedures. They also reap other important benefits, the most important being motivated, committed people who enjoy their jobs, participate in teamwork, and get fully involved in advancing the company goals.

## ENDNOTES

The author would like to acknowledge Professor Mitsuru Wakabayashi, associate professor, Dept. of Educational Psychology, Nagoya University, Dr. Bruce Paton , vice president, Internal Consulting, Frito-Lay, Inc., and Jim O'Neal, president of Northern European Operations, Pepsi-Co Foods International for their help in laying the groundwork for this research.

1. For discussion and supporting data on organizational creativity see the author's following research. M. S. Basadur, G. B. Graen, and S. G. Green, "Training in Creative Problem Solving: Effects on Ideation and Problem Finding and Solving in an Industrial Research Organization," in *Organizational Behavior and Human Performance, 30*, 1982, 41–70; M. S. Basadur, "Needed Research in Creativity for Business and Industrial Applications," in S. G. Isaksen (ed.), *Frontiers of Creativity Research: Beyond the Basics* (Buffalo, NY: Bearly, 1987); M. S. Basadur, G. B. Graen, and T. A. Scandura, "Training Effects on Attitudes Toward Divergent Thinking Among Manufacturing Engineers," in *Journal of Applied Psychology*, Vol. 71, No. 4, 1986, 612–617.

2. For more information concerning the creative process in organizations, see M. S. Basadur, G. B. Graen, and M. Wakabayashi, "Identifying Individual Differences in Creative Problem Solving Style," in *Journal of Creative Behavior*, Vol. 24, No. 2, 1990, 111–131; M. S. Basadur, "Managing the Creative Process in Organizations," in M .J. Runco (ed.), *Problem Finding, Problem Solving and Creativity* (New York: Ablex, 1991, in press). The latter is also available from the author as McMaster University Faculty of Business Research and Working Paper Series, No. 357, April 1991.

3. See P. E. Mott, *The Characteristics of Effective Organizations* (New York, NY: Harper and Row, 1972); M. S. Basadur, "Impacts and Outcomes of Creativity in Organizational Settings," in S.G. Isaksen, M.C. Murdock, R. L. Firestein, and D. J. Treffinger (eds.), *The Emergence of a Discipline: Nurturing and Developing Creativity,* Volume II (New York: Ablex, 1991; in press). The latter is also available as McMaster University Faculty of Business Research and Working Paper Series, No. 358, April 1991.

4. For more discussion on human needs and related motives see D. E. Berlyne, "Arousal and Reinforcement," in D. Levine (ed.), *Nebraska Symposium on Motivation*, (Lincoln, NE: University of Nebraska Press, 1967) and R. W. White, "Motivation reconsidered: The concept of competence,"*Psychological Review*, 66 (5), 297–333.

5. For further discussion on motivation see F. Herzberg, B. Mausner, and B. Snyderman, *The Motivation to Work* (2nd ed.) (New York, NY: Wiley, 1959).

6. See D. C. McClelland, *Personality* (New York, NY: Dryden Press, 1951).

7. See A. H. Maslow, *Motivation and Personality* (New York, NY: Harper and Row, 1954).

8. See E. L. Deci and R.M. Ryan, *Intrinsic Motivation and Self-determination in Human Behavior* (New York, NY: Plenum Press, 1985).

9. See E. A. Locke and G. P. Latham, "Work Motivation and Satisfaction: Light at the End of the Tunnel," *Psychological Science,* Vol. 1, No. 4, July 1990, 240–246.

10. For review of scientific management see F. W. Taylor, *Principles of Scientific Management* (New York, NY: Norton, reprinted 1967, originally published in 1911).

# OF BOXES, BUBBLES,
# AND EFFECTIVE MANAGEMENT

*David K. Hurst*

Harvard Business Review
Soldiers Field Road
Boston, Massachusetts 02163

Dear Editors:

We are writing to tell you how events from 1979 on have forced us, a team of four general managers indistinguishable from thousands of others, to change our view of what managers should do. In 1979 we were working for Hugh Russel Inc., the fiftieth largest public company in Canada. Hugh Russel was an industrial distributor with some $535 million in sales and a net income of $14 million. The organization structure was conventional: 16 divisions in four groups, each with a group president reporting to the corporate office. Three volumes of corporate policy manuals spelled out detailed aspects of corporate life, including our corporate philosophy. In short, in 1979 our corporation was like thousands of other businesses in North America.

During 1980, however, through a series of unlikely runs, that situation changed drastically. Hugh Russel found itself acquired in a 100% leveraged buyout and then merged with a large, unprofitable (that's being kind!) steel fabricator, York Steel Construction, Ltd. The resulting entity was York Russel Inc., a privately held company except for the existence of some publicly owned preferred stock which obliged us to report to the public.

As members of the acquired company's corporate office, we waited nervously for the ax to fall. Nothing happened. Finally, after about six weeks, Wayne (now our president) asked the new owner if we could do anything to help the deal along. The new chairman was delighted and gave us complete access to information about the acquirer.

It soon became apparent that the acquiring organization had little management strength. The business had been run in an entrepreneurial style with hundreds of people reporting to a single autocrat. The business had, therefore, no comprehensive plan and, worse still, no money. The deal had been desperately conceived to shelter our profits from taxes and use the resulting cash flow to fund the excessive debt of the steel fabrication business.

Our first job was to hastily assemble a task force to put together a $300 million bank loan application and a credible turnaround plan. Our four-member management team (plus six others who formed a task force) did it in only six weeks. The merged business, York Russel, ended up with $ 10 million of equity and $275 million of debt on the eve of a recession that turned out to be the worst Canada had experienced since the Great Depression. It was our job then to save the new company, somehow.

Conceptual frameworks are important roads to managers' perceptions, and every team should have a member who can build them. Before the acquisition, the framework implicit in our organization was a "hard," rational model rather like those Thomas Peters and Robert Waterman describe.[1] Jay Galbraith's elaborate model is one of the purest examples of the structure-follows-strategy school.[2] The model clearly defines all elements and their relationships to each other, presumably so that they can be measured (see the *Exhibit*).

EXHIBIT I   The hard and soft model and how they work together

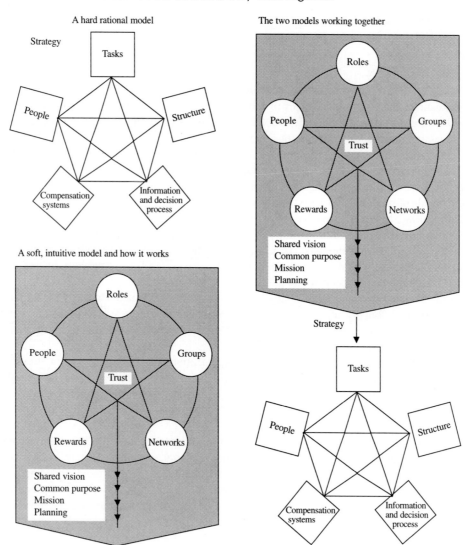

Because circumstances changed after the acquisition, our framework fell apart almost immediately. Overnight we went from working for a growth company to working for one whose only objective was survival. Our old decentralized organization was cumbersome and expensive; our new organization needed cash, not profits. Bankers and suppliers swarmed all over us, and the quiet life of a management-controlled public company was gone.

Compounding our difficulties, the recession quickly revealed all sorts of problems in businesses that up to that time had given us no trouble. Even the core nuggets offered up only meager profits, while merest rates of up to 25% quickly destroyed what was left of the balance sheet.

In the heat of the crisis, the management team jelled quickly. At first each member muddled in his own way, but as time went by, we started to plan a new understanding of how to be effective. Even now we do not completely understand the conceptual framework that has evolved, and maybe we never will. What follows is our best attempt to describe to you and your readers what guides us today.

Yours truly,

The management team

## TWO MODELS ARE BETTER THAN ONE

The hard, rational model isn't wrong; it just isn't enough. There is something more. As it turns out, there is a great deal more.

At York Russel we have had to develop a "soft," intuitive framework that offers a counterpart to every element in the hard, rational framework. As the exhibit shows and the following sections discuss, in the soft model, roles are the counterparts of tasks, groups replace structure, networks operate instead of information systems, the rewards are soft as opposed to hard, and people are viewed as social animals rather than as rational beings.

That may not sound very new. But we found that the key to effective management of not only our crisis but also the routine is to know whether we are in a hard "box" or a soft "bubble" context. By recognizing the dichotomy between the two, we can choose the appropriate framework.

| ☐ | **TASKS** | ... & ... | ○ | **ROLES** |
|---|---|---|---|---|
| ☐ | Static | | ○ | Fluid |
| ☐ | Clarity | | ○ | Ambiguity |
| ☐ | Content | | ○ | Process |
| ☐ | Fact | | ○ | Perception |
| ☐ | Science | | ○ | Art |

These are some of our favorite words for contrasting these two aspects of management. Here's how we discovered them.

The merger changed our agenda completely. We had new shareholders, a new bank, a new business (the steel fabrication operations consisted of nine divisions), and a new relationship with the managers of our subsidiaries, who were used to being left alone to grow. The recession and high interest rates rendered the corporation insolvent. Bankruptcy loomed large. Further, our previously static way of operating became very fluid.

In general, few of us had clear tasks, and for the most part we saw the future as ambiguous and fearful. We found ourselves describing what we had to do as roles rather than as tasks. At first our descriptions were crude. We talked of having an "inside man" who deals with administration, lawyers, and bankers versus an "outside man" who deals with operations, customers, and suppliers. Some of us were "readers," others "writers," some "talkers," and others "listeners." As the readers studied the work of behavioral science researchers and talked to the listeners, we found more useful classifications. Henry Mintzberg's description of managers' work in terms of three roles—interpersonal (figurehead, leaders, liaison), informational (monitor, disseminator, spokesperson), and decisional—helped us see the variety of the job.[3] Edgar Schein's analysis of group roles helped us concentrate on the process of communication as well as on what was communicated.[4]

The most useful framework we used was the one Ichak Adize developed for decision-making roles.[5] In his view, a successful management team needs to play four distinct parts. The first is that of producer of results. A *producer* is action oriented and knowledgeable in his or her field; he or she helps compile plans with an eye to their implementability. The *administrator* supervises the system and manages the detail. The *entrepreneur* is a creative risk taker who initiates action, comes up with new ideas, and challenges existing policies. And the *integrator* brings people together socially and their ideas intellectually, and interprets the significance of events. The integrator gives the team a sense of direction and shared experience.

According to Adize, each member must have some appreciation of the others' roles (by having some facility in those areas), and it is essential that they get along socially. At York Russel the producers (who typically come out of operations) and administrators (usually accountants) tend to be hard box players, while the entrepreneurs tend to live in the soft bubble. Integrators (friendly, unusually humble MBAs) move between the hard and the soft, and we've found a sense of humor is essential to being able to do that well.

The key to a functioning harmonious group, however, has been for members to understand that they might disagree with each other because they are in two different contexts. Different conceptual frameworks may lead people to different conclusions based on the same facts. Of the words describing tasks and roles, our favorite pair is "fact" versus "perception." People in different boxes will argue with each other over facts, for facts in boxes are compelling—they seem so tangible. Only from the bubble can one see them for what they are: abstractions based on the logical frameworks, or boxes, being used.

| ☐ STRUCTURE | ... & ... | ○ GROUPS |
|---|---|---|
| ☐ Cool | | ○ Warm |
| ☐ Formal | | ○ Informal |
| ☐ Closed | | ○ Open |
| ☐ Obedience | | ○ Trust |
| ☐ Independence | | ○ Autonomy |

Our premerger corporation was a pretty cold place to work. Senior management kept control in a tight inner circle and then played hardball (in a hard box, of course) with the group presidents. Managers negotiated budgets and plans on a win-lose basis; action plans almost exclusively controlled what was done in the organization. Top managers kept a lot of information to themselves. People didn't trust each other very much.

The crises that struck the corporation in 1980 were so serious that we could not have concealed them even if we had wanted to. We were forced to put together a multitude of task forces consisting of people from all parts of the organization to address these urgent issues, and in the process, we had to reveal everything we knew, whether it was confidential or not.

We were amazed at the task forces' responses: instead of resigning en masse (the hard box players had said that people would leave the company when they found out that it was insolvent), the teams tackled their projects with passion. Warmth, a sense of belonging, and trust characterized the groups; the more we let them know what was going on, the more we received from them. Confidentiality is the enemy of trust. In the old days strategic plans were stamped "confidential." Now we know that paper plans mean nothing if they are not in the minds of the managers.

Division managers at first resented our intrusion into their formal, closed world. "What happened to independence?" they demanded. We described the soft counterpart—autonomy—to them. Unlike independence, autonomy cannot be granted once and for all. In our earlier life, division personnel told the corporate office what they thought it wanted to hear. "You've got to keep those guys at arm's length" was a typical division belief. An autonomous relationship depends on trust for its nourishment. "The more you level with us," we said, "the more we'll leave you alone." That took some getting used to.

But in the end autonomy worked. We gave division managers confidential information, shared our hopes and fears, and incorporated their views in our bubble. They needed to be helped out of their boxes, not to abandon them altogether but to gain a deeper appreciation of and insight into how they were running their businesses. Few could resist when we walked around showing a genuine interest in their views. Because easy access to each other and opportunities for communication determine how groups form and work together, we encouraged managers to keep their doors open. We called this creation of opportunities for communication by making senior management accessible "management by walking around." Chance encounters should not be left to chance.

Although the primary objective of all this communication is to produce trust among group members, an important by-product is that the integrators among us have started to "see" the communication process.[6] In other words, they are beginning to understand why people say what they say. This ability to "see" communication is elusive at times, but when it is present, it enables us to "jump out of the box"—that is, to talk about the frameworks supporting conclusions rather than the conclusions themselves. We have defused many potential confrontations and struck many deals by changing the context of the debate rather than the debate itself.[7]

Perhaps the best example of this process was our changing relationship with our lead banker. As the corporation's financial position deteriorated, our relationship with the bank became increasingly adversarial. The responsibility for our account rose steadily up the bank's hierarchy (we had eight different account managers in 18 months), and we received tougher and tougher "banker's speeches" from successively more senior executives. Although we worried a great deal that the bank might call the loan, the real risk was that our good businesses would be choked by overzealous efforts on the part of individual bankers to "hold the line."

Key to our ability to change the relationship was to understand why individuals were taking the position they were. To achieve that understanding we had to rely on a network of contacts both inside and outside the bank. We found that the bank had as many views as there were people we talked to. Fortunately, the severity of the recession and the proliferation of corporate loan problems had already blown everyone out of the old policy "boxes." It remained for us to gain the confidence of our contacts, exchange candid views of our positions, and present options that addressed the corporation's problems in the bank's context and dealt with the bank's interests.

The "hard" vehicle for this was the renegotiation of our main financing agreements. During the more than six month negotiating process, our relationship with the bank swung 180 degrees from confrontation to collaboration. The corporation's problem became a joint bank-corporation problem. We had used the bubble to find a new box in which both the corporation and the bank could live.

| ☐ **INFORMATIONAL PROCESSES** ... & ... | ○ **NETWORKS** |
|---|---|
| ☐ Hard | ○ Soft |
| ☐ Written | ○ Oral |
| ☐ Know | ○ Feel |
| ☐ Control | ○ Influence |
| ☐ Decision | ○ Implementation |

Over the years our corporation has developed some excellent information systems. Our EDP facility is second to none in our industry. Before the acquisition and merger, when people talked about or requested information, they meant hard, quantitative data and written reports that would be used for control and decision making. The crisis required that we make significant changes to these systems. Because, for example, we became more interested in cash flow than earnings per share, data had to be aggregated and presented in a new way.

The pivotal change, however, was our need to communicate with a slew of new audiences over which we had little control. For instance, although we still have preferred stock quoted in the public market, our principal new shareholders were family members with little experience in professional management of public companies. Our new bankers were in organizational turmoil themselves and took 18 months to realize the horror of what they had financed. Our suppliers, hitherto benign, faced a stream of bad financial news about us and other members of the industry. The rumor mill had us in receivership on a weekly basis.

Our plant closures and cutbacks across North America brought us into a new relationship with government, unions, and the press. And we had a new internal audience: our employees, who were understandably nervous about the "imminent" bankruptcy.

We had always had some relationship with these audiences, but now we saw what important sources of information they were and expanded these networks vastly.[8] Just as we had informed the division managers at the outset, we decided not to conceal from these other groups the fact that the corporation was insolvent but worthy of support. We made oral presentations supported by formal written material to cover the most important bases.

To our surprise, this candid approach totally disarmed potential antagonists. For instance, major suppliers could not understand why we had told them we were in trouble before the numbers revealed the fact. By the time the entire war story was news, there was no doubt that our suppliers' top managers, who tended not to live in the hard accounting box, were on our side. When their financial specialists concluded that we were insolvent, top management blithely responded, "We've known that for six months."

Sharing our view of the world with constituencies external to the corporation led to other unexpected benefits, such as working in each other's interests. Our reassurance to customers that we would be around to deliver on contracts strengthened the relationship. Adversity truly is opportunity!

Management by walking around was the key to communicating with employees in all parts of the company. As a result of the continual open communication, all employees appreciated the corporation's position. Their support has been most gratifying. One of our best talker-listeners (our president) tells of a meeting with a very nervous group of employees at one facility. After he had spent several hours explaining the company's situation, one blue-collar worker who had been with the company for years took him aside and told him that a group of employees would be prepared to take heavy pay cuts if it would save the business. It turns out that when others hear this story it reinforces *their* belief in the organization.

We have found that sharing our views and incorporating the views of others as appropriate has a curious effect on the making and the implementing of decisions. As we've said, in our previous existence the decisions we made were always backed up by hard information; management was decisive, and that was good. Unfortunately, too few of these "good" decisions ever got implemented. The simple process of making the decision the way we did often set up resistance down the line. As the decision was handed down to consecutive organizational levels, it lost impetus until eventually it was unclear whether the decision was right in the first place.

Now we worry a good deal less about making decisions; they arise as fairly obvious conclusions drawn from a mass of shared assumptions. It's the assumptions that we spend our time working on. One of our "producers" (an executive vice president) calls it "conditioning" and indeed it is. Of course, making decisions this way requires that senior management build networks with people many layers down in the organization. This kind of communication is directly at odds with the communication policy laid down in the premerger corporation, which emphasized direct-line reporting.

A consequence of this network information process is that we often have to wait for the right time to make a decision. We call the wait a "creative stall." In the old organization it would have been called procrastination, but what we're doing is waiting for some important players to come "on-side" before making an announcement.[9] In our terms, you "prepare in the box and wait in the bubble."

Once the time is right, however, implementation is rapid. Everyone is totally involved and has given thought to what has to be done. Not only is the time it takes for the decision to be made and implemented shorter than in the past but also the whole process strengthens the organization rather than weakening it through bitterness about how the decision was made.

| ☐ **PEOPLE** | . . . & . . . | ○ **PEOPLE** |
|---|---|---|
| ☐ Rational | | ○ Social |
| ☐ Produce | | ○ Create |
| ☐ Think | | ○ Imagine |
| ☐ Tell | | ○ Inspire |
| ☐ Work | | ○ Play |

In the old, premerger days, it was convenient to regard employees as rational, welfare-maximizing beings; it made motivating them so much easier and planning less messy.

But because the crisis made it necessary to close many operations and terminate thousands of employees, we had to deal with people's social nature. We could prepare people intellectually by sharing our opinions and, to some extent, protect them physically with severance packages, but we struggled with how to handle the emotional aspects. Especially for long service employees, severing the bond with the company was the emotional equivalent of death.

Humor is what rescued us. Laughter allows people to jump out of their emotional boxes or rigid belief structures. None of us can remember having laughed as much as we have over the past three years. Although much of the humor has inevitably been of the gallows variety, it has been an important ingredient in releasing tension and building trust.

Now everyone knows that people are social as well as rational animals. Indeed, we knew it back in the premerger days, but somehow back then we never came to grips with the social aspect, maybe because the rational view of people has an appealing simplicity and clarity. Lombard's Law applied to us—routine, structured tasks drove out nonroutine, unstructured activities.[10]

| □ **COMPENSATION SYSTEMS** ...& ... | ○ **REWARDS** |
|---|---|
| □ Direct | ○ Indirect |
| □ Objective | ○ Subjective |
| □ Profit | ○ Fun |
| □ Failure | ○ Mistake |
| □ Hygiene | ○ Motivator |
| □ Managing | ○ Caring |

In our premerger organization, the "total compensation policy" meant you could take your money any way you liked—salary, loans, fringes, and so forth. Management thought this policy catered to individual needs and was, therefore, motivating. Similarly, the "Personnel Development Program" required managers to make formal annual reviews of their employees' performances. For some reason, management thought that this also had something to do with motivation. The annual reviews, however, had become a meaningless routine, with managers constrained to be nice to the review subject because they had to work with him or her the next day.

The 1981 recession put a stop to all this by spurring us to freeze all direct compensation. Profit-based compensation disappeared; morale went up.

The management team discussed this decision for hours. As the savings from the freeze would pay for a few weeks' interest only, the numbers made no sense at all. Some of us prophesied doom. "We will lose the best people," we argued. Instead, the symbolic freeze brought the crisis home to everyone. We had all made a sacrifice, a contribution that senior management could recognize at a future time.

Even though the academics say they aren't scientifically valid, we still like Frederick Herzberg's definition of motivations (our interpretations of them are in parentheses):[11]

Achievement (what you believe you did).
Recognition (what others think you did).
Work itself (what you really do).
Responsibility (what you help others do).
Advancement (what you think you can do).
Growth (what you believe you might do).

## THE NEW FRAMEWORK AT WORK

The diagram of the soft model in the exhibit shows our view of how our management process seems to work. When the motivating rewards are applied to people playing the necessary roles and working together in groups that are characterized by open communication and are linked to networks throughout the organization, the immediate product is a high degree of mutual trust. This trust allows groups to develop a shared vision that in turn enhances a sense of common purpose. From this process people develop a feeling of having a mission of their own. The mission is spiritual in the sense of being an important effort much larger than oneself. This kind of involvement is highly motivating. Mission is the soft counterpart of strategy.

| | STRATEGY | ... & ... | | MISSION |
|---|---|---|---|---|
| ☐ | Objectives | | ○ | Values |
| ☐ | Policies | | ○ | Norms |
| ☐ | Forecasts | | ○ | Vision |
| ☐ | Clockworks | | ○ | Frameworks |
| ☐ | Right | | ○ | Useful |
| ☐ | Target | | ○ | Direction |
| ☐ | Precise | | ○ | Vague |
| ☐ | Necessary | | ○ | Sufficient |

Listed are some of our favorite words for contrasting these two polarities. We find them useful for understanding why clear definition of objectives is not essential for motivating people. Hard box planners advocate the hard box elements and tend to be overinvested in using their various models, or "clockworks" as we call them. Whether it's a Boston Consulting Group matrix or an Arthur D. Little life-cycle curve, too often planners wind them up and managers act according to what they dictate without looking at the assumptions, many of which may be invalid, implicit in the frameworks.

We use the models only as take-off points for discussion. They do not have to be right, only useful. If they don't yield genuine insights we put them aside. The hard box cannot be dispensed with. On the contrary, it is essential—but not sufficient.

The key element in developing a shared purpose is mutual trust. Without trust, people will engage in all kinds of self-centered behavior to assert their own identities and influence coworkers to their own ends. Under these circumstances, they just won't hear others, and efforts to develop a shared vision are doomed. Nothing destroys trust faster than hard box attitudes toward problems that don't require such treatment.

Trust is self-reproductive. When trust is present in a situation, chain reactions occur as people share frameworks and exchange unshielded views. The closer and more tightly knit the group is, the more likely it is that these reactions will spread, generating a shared vision and common purpose.

Once the sense of common purpose and mission is established, the managing group is ready to enter the hard box of strategy (see the right-hand side of the exhibit). Now the specifics of task, structure, information, and decision processes are no longer likely to be controversial or threatening. Implementation becomes astonishingly simple. Action plans are necessary to control hard box implementation, but once the participants in the soft bubble share the picture, things seem to happen by themselves as team members play their roles and fill the gaps as they see them. Since efforts to seize control of bubble activity are likely to prove disastrous, it is most fortunate that people act spontaneously without being "organized." Paradoxically, one can achieve control in the bubble only by letting go—which gets right back to trust.

In the hard box, the leadership model is that of the general who gives crisp, precise instructions as to who is to do what and when. In the soft bubble, the leadership model is that of the shepherd, who follows his flock watchfully as it meanders along the natural contours of the land. He carries the weak and collects the strays, for they all have a contribution to make. This style may be inefficient, but it is effective. The whole flock reaches its destination at more or less the same time.[12]

| ☐ **BOXES** | ...&... | ○ **BUBBLES** |
|---|---|---|
| ☐ Solve | | ○ Values |
| ☐ Sequential | | ○ Norms |
| ☐ Left Brain | | ○ Vision |
| ☐ Serious | | ○ Frameworks |
| ☐ Explain | | ○ Useful |
| ☐ Rational | | ○ Direction |
| ☐ Conscious | | ○ Unconscious |
| ☐ Learn | | ○ Remember |
| ☐ Knowledge | | ○ Wisdom |
| ☐ Lens | | ○ Mirror |
| ☐ Full | | ○ Empty |
| ☐ Words | | ○ Pictures |
| ☐ Objects | | ○ Symbols |
| ☐ Description | | ○ Parable |

Thought and language are keys to changing perceptions. Boxes and bubbles describe the hard and soft thought structures, respectively. Boxes have rigid, opaque sides; walls have to be broken down to join boxes, although if the lid is off one can jump out. Bubbles have flexible, transparent sides that can easily expand and join with other bubbles. Bubbles float but can easily burst. In boxes problems are to be solved; in bubbles they are dissolved. The trick is to change the context of the problem, that is, to jump out of the box. This technique has many applications.

We have noticed a number of articles in your publication that concern values and ethics in business, and some people have suggested that business students be required to attend classes in ethics. From our view of the world, sending students to specific courses is a hard box solution and would be ineffective. Ethical behavior is absent from some businesses not because the managers have no ethics (or have the wrong ones) but because the hard "strategy box" does not emphasize them as being valuable. The hard box deals in objectives, and anyone who raises value issues in that context will not survive long.

In contrast, in the "mission bubble' people feel free to talk about values and ethics because there is trust. The problem of the lack of ethical behavior is dissolved.

We have found bubble thinking to be the intellectual equivalent of judo; a person does not resist an attacker but goes with the flow, thereby adding his strength to the other's momentum. Thus when suppliers demanded that their financial exposure to our lack of creditworthiness be reduced, we agreed and suggested that they protect themselves by supplying goods to us on consignment. After all, their own financial analysis showed we couldn't pay them any money! In some cases we actually got consignment deals, and where we didn't the scheme failed because of nervous lawyers (also hard box players) rather than reluctance on the part of the supplier.

Bubble thought structures are characterized by what Edward de Bono calls lateral thinking.[13] The sequential or vertical thought structure is logical and rational; it proceeds through logical stages and depends on a yes-no test at each step. De Bono suggests that in lateral thinking the yes-no test must be suspended, for the purpose is to explore not explain, to test assumptions not conclusions.

We do the same kind of questioning when we do what we call "humming a lot." When confronted with what initially appears to be an unpalatable idea, an effective manager will say "hmm" and wait until the idea has been developed and its implications considered. Quite often, even when an initial idea is out of the question, the fact that we have considered it seriously will lead to a different, innovative solution.

We have found it useful to think of the action opposite to the one we intend taking. When selling businesses we found it helpful to think about acquiring purchasers. This led to deeper research into purchasers' backgrounds and motives and to a more effective packaging and presentation of the businesses to be sold. This approach encourages novel ideas and makes the people who generate them (the entrepreneurs) feel that their ideas, however "dumb," will not be rejected out of hand.

In hard box thought structures, one tends to use conceptual frameworks as lenses, to sit on one side and examine an object on the other. In bubble structures, the frameworks are mirrors reflecting one's own nature and its effect on one's perceptions; object and subject are on the same side. In the hard box, knowledge is facts, from learning; in the bubble knowledge is wisdom, from experience.

Bubble thought structures are not easily described in words. Language itself is a box reflecting our cultural heritage and emphasizing some features of reality at the expense of others. Part of our struggle during the past three years has been to unlearn many scientific management concepts and develop a new vocabulary. We have come up with some new phases and words: management by walking around, creative stall, asking dumb questions, jumping out of the box, creating a crisis, humming a lot, and muddling. We have also attached new meanings to old words such as fact and perception, independence and autonomy, hard and soft, solve and dissolve, and so forth.

## THREE YEARS LATER

What we have told you about works in a crisis. And we can well understand your asking whether this approach can work when the business is stable and people lapse back into boxes. We have developed two methods of preventing this lapse.

1. If there isn't a crisis, we create one. One way to stir things up is familiar to anyone who has ever worked in a hard box organization. Intimidation, terror, and the use of raw power will produce all the stress you need. But eventually people run out of adrenaline and the organization is drained, not invigorated.

In a bubble organization, managers dig for opportunities in a much more relaxed manner. During the last three years, for instance, many of our divisions that were profitable and liquid were still in need of strategic overhaul. During the course of walking around, we unearthed many important issues by asking dumb questions.

The more important of the issues that surface this way offer an opportunity to put a champion (someone who believes in the importance of the issue) in charge of a team of people who can play all the roles required to handle the issue. The champion then sets out with his or her group to go through the incremental development process-developing trust, building both a hard box picture and a shared vision, and, finally, establishing strategy. By the time the strategy is arrived at, the task force disciples have such zeal and sense of mission that they are ready to take the issue to larger groups, using the same process.

Two by-products of asking dumb questions deserve mention. First, when senior management talks to people at all levels, people at all levels start talking to each other. Second, things tend to get fixed before they break. In answering a senior manager's casual question, a welder on the shop floor of a steel fabrication plant revealed that some critical welds had failed quality tests and the customer's inspector was threatening to reject an entire bridge. A small ad hoc task force, which included the inspector (with the customer's permission), got everyone off the hook and alerted top management to a potential weakness in the quality control function.

Applying the principles in other areas takes years to bear fruit. We are now using the process to listen to customers and suppliers. We never knew how to do this before. Now it is clear that it is necessary to create an excuse (crisis) for going to see them, share "secrets," build trust, share a vision, and capture them in your bubble. It's very simple, and early results have been excellent. We call it a soft revolution.

2. Infuse activities that some might think prosaic with real significance. The focus should be on people first, and always on caring rather than managing. The following approach works in good times as well as bad:

> Use a graphic vocabulary that describes what you do.
>
> Share confidential information, personal hopes, and fears to create a common vision and promote trust.
>
> Seize every opportunity (open doors, management by walking around, networks) to make a point, emphasize a value, disseminate information, share an experience, express interest, and show you care.
>
> Recognize performance and contribution of as many people as possible. Rituals and ceremonies—retirements, promotions, birthdays—present great opportunities.
>
> Use incentive programs whose main objective is not compensation but recognition.

We have tried to approach things this way, and for us the results have been significant. Now, we are a very different organization. Of our 25 divisions, we have closed 7 and sold 16. Five of the latter were bought by Federal Industries, Ltd. of Winnipeg. Some 860 employees including us, the four members of the management team, have gone to Federal. These divisions are healthy and raring to go. Two divisions remain at York Russel, which has changed its name to YRI-YORK, Ltd.

Now we face new questions, such as how one recruits into a management team. We know that we have to help people grow into the team, and fortunately we find that they flourish in our warm climate. But trust takes time to develop, and the bubble is fragile. The risk is greatest when we have to transplant a senior person from outside, because time pressures may not allow us to be sure we are compatible. The danger is not only to the team itself but also to the person joining it.

Our new framework has given us a much deeper appreciation of the management process and the roles effective general managers play. For example, it is clear that while managers can delegate tasks in the hard box rather easily—perhaps because they can define them—it's impossible to delegate soft bubble activities. The latter are difficult to isolate from each other because their integration takes place in one brain.

Similarly, the hard box general management roles of producer and administrator can be formally taught, and business schools do a fine job of it. The soft roles of entrepreneur and integrator can probably not be taught formally. Instead, managers must learn from mentors. Over time they will adopt behavior patterns that allow them to play the required roles. It would seem, however, that natural ability and an individual's upbringing probably play a much larger part in determining effectiveness in the soft roles than in the hard roles; it is easier to teach a soft bubble player the hard box roles than it is to teach the soft roles to a hard box player.

In the three-year period when we had to do things so differently, we created our own culture, with its own language, symbols, norms, and customs. As with other groups, the acculturation process began when people got together in groups and trusted and cared about each other.[14]

In contrast with our premerger culture, the new culture is much more sympathetic toward and supportive of the use of teams and consensus decision making. In this respect, it would seem to be similar to oriental ways of thinking that place a premium on the same processes. Taoists, for instance, would have no trouble recognizing the polarities of the hard box and the soft bubble and the need to keep a balance between the two.[15]

| ☐ **HEAVEN** | ...&... | ○ **EARTH** |
|---|---|---|
| ☐ Yang | | ○ Yin |
| ☐ Father | | ○ Mother |
| ☐ Man | | ○ Woman |

These symbols are instructive. After all, most of us grew up with two bosses: father usually played the hard box parts, while mother played the soft, intuitive, and entrepreneurial roles. The family is the original team, formed to handle the most complex management task ever faced. Of late, we seem to have fired too many of its members—a mistake we can learn from.

## TOWARD A MANAGERIAL THEORY OF RELATIVITY

The traditional hard box view of management, like the traditional orientation of physics, is valid (and very useful) only within a narrow range of phenomena. Once one gets outside the range, one needs new principles. In physics, cosmologists at the macro level as well as students of subatomic particles at the micro level use Einstein's theory of relativity as an explanatory principle and set Newton's physics aside.[16] For us, the theory in the bubble is our managerial theory of relativity. At the macro level it reminds us that how management phenomena appear depends on one's perspective and biases. At the micro level we remember that all jobs have both hard and soft components.

This latter point is of particular importance to people like us in the service industry. The steel we distribute is indistinguishable from anyone else's We insist on rigid standards regarding how steel is handled, what reporting systems are used, and so forth. But hard box standards alone wouldn't be enough to set us apart from our competitors. That takes service, a soft concept. And everyone has to be involved. Switchboard operators are in the front line; every contact is an opportunity to share the bubble. Truck drivers and warehouse workers make their own special contribution—by taking pride in the cleanliness of their equipment or by keeping the inventory neat and accessible.

With the box and bubble concept, managers can unlock many of the paradoxes of management and handle the inherent ambiguities. You don't do one or the other absolutely; you do what is appropriate. For instance, the other day in one of our operations the biweekly payroll run deducted what appeared to be random amounts from the sales representatives' pay packets. The branch affected was in an uproar. After taking some hard box steps to remedy the situation, our vice president of human resources seized the opportunity to go out to the branch and talk to the sales team. He was delighted with the response. The sales force saw that he understood the situation and cared about them, and he got to meet them all, which will make future contacts easier. But neither the hard box nor soft bubble approach on its own would have been appropriate. We need both. As one team member put it, "You have to find the bubble in the box and put the box in the bubble." Exactly.

The amazing thing is that the process works so well. The spirit of cooperation among senior managers is intense, and we seem to be getting "luckier" as we go along. When a "magic" event takes place it means that somehow we got the timing just right.[17] And there is great joy in that.

# REFERENCES

1. Thomas I. Peters and Robert H. Waterman, *In Search of Excellence* (New York: Harper and Row, 1981), p. 29.
2. For the best of the hard box models we have come across, see Jay R. Galbraith, *Organization Design* (Reading, Mass.: Addison-Wesley, 1977).
3. Henry Mintzberg, "The Manager's Job: Folklore and Fact," *HBR,* July–August, 1975, p. 49.
4. Edgar H. Schein, *Process Consultation: Its Role in Organization Development* (Reading, Mass.: Addison-Wesley, 1969).
5. Ichak Adize, *How to Solve the Mismanagement Crisis* (Los Angeles, MDOR Institute, 1979).
6. Edgar H. Schein's *Process Consultation*, p. 10, was very helpful in showing us how the process differs from the content.
7. Getting consensus among a group of managers poses the same challenge as negotiating a deal. *Getting to Yes* by Robert Fisher and William Ury (Boston: Houghton Mifflin, 1981) is a most helpful book for understanding the process.
8. For discussion of the importance or networks, see John P. Kotter, "What Effective General Managers Really Do," *HBR,* November–December 1982, p. 156.
9. For discussion of a "creative stall" being applied in practice, see Stratford P. Sherman, "Muddling to Victory at Geico," *Fortune,* September 5, 1983, p. 66.
10. Louis B. Barnes, "Managing the Paradox of Organizational Trust," *HBR,* March–April 1981, p. 107.
11. In "One More Time: How Do You Motivate Employees?" *HBR*, January–February 1968, p. 53.
12. For another view of the shepherd role, see the poem by Nancy Esposito, "The Good Shepherd," *HBR,* July–August 1983, p. 121.
13. See Edward de Bono, *The Use of Lateral Thinking* (London: Jonathan Cape, 1967) and *Beyond Yes and No* (New York: Simon and Schuster, 1972).
14. To explore the current concern with creating strong organizational cultures in North American corporations, see Terrence E. Deal and Alan A. Kennedy, *Corporate Cultures* (Reading, Mass.: Addison-Wesley, 1982).
15. For discussion of Tao and some applications, we highly recommend Benjamin Hoff, The *Tao of Pooh* (New York: E. P. Dutton, 1982), p. 67; also Allen Watts, *Tao: The Watercourse Way* (New York: Pantheon Books, 1975).
16. Frity of Capra, *The Tao of Physics* (London: Fontana Paperbacks, 1963).
17. Carl Jung developed the concept of synchronicity to explain such events. See, for example, Ira Progoff, *Jung Synchronicity and Human Destiny–Non-Causal Dimensions of Human Experience* (New York: Julian Press, 1973). For an excellent discussion of Jung's work and its relevance to our times, see Laurens van de Post, *Jung and the Story of Our Time* (New York: Random House, 1975).

# 11
# Intergroup Conflict and Negotiation

MANAGING CONFLICT AMONG GROUPS
  *L. David Brown*

INGROUP AND INTERGROUP RELATIONS:  EXPERIMENTAL ANALYSIS
  *Musafer Sherif*
  *Carolyn W. Sherif*

NEGOTIATING WITH "ROMANS"—PART 2
  *Stephen E. Weiss*

## MANAGING CONFLICT AMONG GROUPS

### L. David Brown

Conflict among groups is extremely common in organizations, although it often goes unrecognized. Managing conflict among groups is a crucial skill for those who lead modern organizations.  To illustrate:

> Maintenance workers brought in to repair a production facility criticize production workers for overworking the machinery and neglecting routine maintenance tasks.  The production workers countercharge that the last maintenance work was improperly done and caused the present breakdown.  The argument results in little cooperation between the two groups to repair the breakdown, and the resulting delays and misunderstandings ultimately inflate organization-wide production costs.
>
> A large manufacturing concern has unsuccessful negotiations with a small independent union, culminating in a bitter strike characterized by fights, bombings, and sabotage.  The angry workers, aware that the independent union has too few resources to back a protracted battle with management, vote in a powerful international union for the next round of negotiations. Management prepares for an even worse strike, but comparatively peaceful and productive negotiations ensue.
>
> Top management of a large bank in a racially mixed urban area commits the organization to system-wide integration.  Recruiters find several superbly qualified young black managers, after a long and highly competitive search, to join the bank's prestigious but all-white trust division and yet, subsequently, several leave the organization.  Since virtually all the managers in the trust division are explicitly willing to integrate, top management is mystified by the total failure of the integration effort.

*Source*:  Prepared specifically for this volume.

These cases are all examples of conflict or potential conflict among organizational groups that influence the performance and goal attainment of the organization as a whole. The cases differ in two important ways.

First, the extent to which the potential conflict among groups is *overt* varies across cases: conflict is all too obvious in the labor-management situation; it is subtle but still evident in the production-maintenance relations; it is never explicit in the attempt to integrate the bank's trust division. It is clear that *too much* conflict can be destructive, and much attention has been paid to strategies and tactics for reducing escalated conflict. Much less attention has been paid to situations in which organizational performance suffers because of *too little* conflict, or strategies and tactics for making potential conflicts more overt.

Second, the cases also differ in the *defining characteristics* of the parties: the production and maintenance groups are functionally defined; the distribution of power is critical to the labor and management conflict; the society's history of race relations is important to the black-white relations in the bank. Although there has been much examination of organizational conflict among groups defined by function, there has been comparatively little attention to organizational conflicts among groups defined by *power differences* (e.g., headquarters-branch relations, some labor-management relations) or by *societal history* (e.g., religious group relations, black-white relations, male-female relations).

It is increasingly clear that effective management of modern organizations calls for dealing with various forms of intergroup conflict: too little as well as too much conflict, and history-based and power-based as well as function-based conflicts. This paper offers a framework for understanding conflict among groups in the next section, and suggests strategies and tactics for diagnosing and managing different conflict situations.

## CONFLICT AND INTERGROUP RELATIONS

### Conflict: Too Much or Too Little?

Conflict is a form of interaction among parties that differ in interests, perceptions, and preferences. Overt conflict involves adversarial interaction that ranges from mild disagreements through various degrees of fighting. But it is also possible for parties with substantial differences to act as if those differences did not exist, and so keep potential conflict from becoming overt.

It is only too clear that it is possible to have *too much* conflict between or among groups. Too much conflict produces strong negative feelings, blindness to interdependencies, and uncontrolled escalation of aggressive action and counteraction. The obvious costs of uncontrolled conflict have sparked a good deal of interest in strategies for conflict reduction and resolution.

It is less obvious (but increasingly clear) that it is possible to have *too little* conflict. Complex and novel decisions, for example, may require pulling together perspectives and information from many different groups. If group representatives are unwilling to present and argue for their perspectives, the resulting decision may not take into account all the available information. The Bay of Pigs disaster during the Kennedy Administration may have been a consequence of too little conflict in the National Security Council, where critical information possessed by representatives of different agencies was suppressed to preserve harmonious relations among them (Janis, 1972).

In short, moderate levels of conflict—in which differences are recognized and extensively argued—are often associated with high levels of energy and involvement, high degrees of information exchange, and better decisions (Robbins, 1974). Managers should be concerned, in this view, with achieving levels of conflict that are *appropriate* to the task before them, rather than concerned about preventing or resolving immediately all intergroup disagreements.

# Conflict among Groups

Conflict in organizations takes many forms. A disagreement between two individuals, for example, may be related to their personal differences, their job definitions, their group memberships, or all three. One of the most common ways that managers misunderstand organizational conflict, for example, is to attribute difficulties to "personality" factors, when it is, in fact, rooted in group memberships and organizational structures. Attributing conflict between production and maintenance workers to their personalities, for example, implies that the conflict can be reduced by replacing the individuals. But if the conflict is, in fact, related to the differing goals of the two groups, *any* individual will be under pressure to fight with members of the other group, regardless of their personal preferences. Replacing individuals in such situations without taking account of intergroup differences will *not* improve relations.

Groups are defined in organizations for a variety of reasons. Most organizations are differentiated horizontally, for example, into functional departments or product divisions for task purposes. Most organizations also are differentiated vertically into levels or into headquarters and plant groups. Many organizations also incorporate in some degree group definitions significant in the larger society, such as racial and religious distinctions.

A good deal of attention has been paid to the relations among groups of relatively equal power, such as functional departments in organizations. Much less is known about effective management of relations between groups of unequal power or those having different societal histories. But many of the most perplexing intergroup conflicts in organizations include all three elements—functional differences, power differences, and historical differences. Effective management of the differences between a white executive from marketing and a black hourly worker from production is difficult indeed, because so many issues are likely to contribute to the problem.

Intergroup relations, left to themselves, tend to have a regenerative, self-fulfilling quality that makes them extremely susceptible to rapid escalation. The dynamics of escalating conflict, for example, have impacts within and between the groups involved. *Within* a group (i.e., within the small circles in Figure 1), conflict with another group tends to increase cohesion and conformity to group norms (Sherif, 1966; Coser, 1956) and to encourage a world view that favors "us" over "them" (Janis, 1972; Deutsch, 1973). Simultaneously, *between-groups* (i.e., the relations between the circles in Figure 1) conflict promotes negative stereotyping and distrust (Sherif, 1966), increased emphasis on differences (Deutsch, 1973), decreased communications (Sherif, 1966), and increased distortion of communications that do take place (Blake and Mouton, 1961). The *combination* of negative stereotypes, distrust, internal militancy, and aggressive action creates a vicious cycle: "defensive" aggression by one group validates suspicion and "defensive" counteraggression by the other, and the conflict escalates (Deutsch, 1973) unless it is counteracted by external factors. A less well understood pattern, in which positive stereotypes, trust, and cooperative action generates a benevolent cycle of increasing cooperation may also exist (Deutsch, 1973).

To return to one of the initial examples, both the maintenance concern with keeping the machines clean and the production concern with maximizing output were organizationally desirable. But those concerns promoted a negative maintenance stereotype of production ("too lazy to clear the machines") and a production stereotype of maintenance ("want us to polish the machine, not use it") that encouraged them to fight. Part A of Figure 1 illustrates the overt but not escalated conflict between the parties.

Introducing power differences into intergroup relations further suppresses communications among the groups. The low-power group is vulnerable, and so must censor communication—such as dissatisfaction—that might elicit retaliation from the high-power group. In consequence, the high-power group remains ignorant of information considered sensitive by the low-power group. The longterm consequences of this mutually reinforcing fear and ignorance can be either escalating oppression—a peculiarly destructive form of too little conflict—or sporadic eruptions of intense and unexpected fighting (Brown, 1978).

The fight between the small independent union and the large corporation described at the outset illustrates the potential for outbursts of violent conflict when the parties are separated by large differences in power. The small union felt unable to influence the corporation at the bargaining table, and so used violence and guerrilla tactics to express its frustration and to influence management without exposing the union to retaliation. Part B of Figure 1 illustrates the positions of the parties and the quality of their conflict.

Conflicts among groups that involve societal differences may be even more complicated. Differences rooted in societal history are likely to be expressed in a network of mutually reinforcing social mechanisms—political, economic, geographic, educational—that serve to *institutionalize* the differences. Societal differences do not necessarily imply power differences between the groups, but very frequently the effect of institutionalization is to enshrine the dominance of one party over another. Relations among such groups within organizations are strongly influenced by the larger society. Organizational tensions may be the result of environmental developments that the organization cannot control. In addition, differences associated with histories of discrimination or oppression may involve strong feelings and entrenched stereotypes that can lead to explosive conflict. Societal differences in organizations call for careful management that permits enough overt conflict so the differences are understood, but not so much that they are exacerbated.

The failure to integrate the trust division illustrates the problem of managing institutionalized racism. The black recruits had all the technical skills for success, but they could not join the all-white clubs or buy a house in the all-white suburbs where their colleagues lived, played, and learned the social ropes of the trust business. Nor could they challenge top-level decisions to keep them away from the oldest (and richest) clients ("who might be racist and so take their business elsewhere"). But the failure to face the potential conflicts—among members of the organization and between the organization and its clients—in essence made it impossible for the black managers to become full members. This situation is diagrammed in Part C of Figure 1.

## MANAGING CONFLICT AMONG GROUPS

### Diagnosing the Conflict

Diagnosis is a crucially important and often-neglected phase of conflict management. Since conflict problems are often not recognized until after they have become acute, the need for immediate relief may be intense. But intervention in a poorly understood situation is not likely to produce instant successes. On the contrary, it may make the situation worse.

The manager of conflict should at the outset answer three questions about the situation:

1. At what level or levels is the conflict rooted (e.g., personal, interpersonal, intergroup, etc.)?
2. What role does he/she play in the relations among the parties?
3. What is a desirable state of relations among the parties?

FIGURE 1   Varieties of Intergroup Conflict

A.  Functional
Differences:
Maintenance and
Production

M = Maintenance
P = Production
◄─► = Overt Conflict

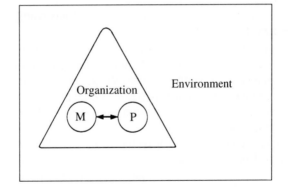

B.  Power
Differences:
Management and
Labor

Mt = Management
L = Labor
◄─► = Escalated
Conflict

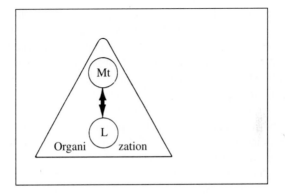

C.  Societal
Differences:
Black and
White Managers

W = Management
B = Labor
◄--► = Covert
Conflict

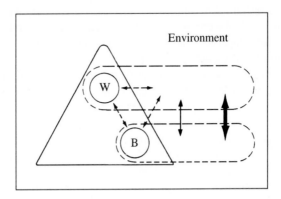

321

A conflict may be the result of an individual, an interpersonal relationship, an intergroup relationship, or a combination of the three. If the manager understands the contributions of different levels, he/she can respond appropriately. It is generally worthwhile to examine the conflict from *each* of these perspectives early in the diagnosis.

The position of the manager vis-à-vis the parties is also important. Managers who are themselves parties to the dispute are likely to be biased, and almost certainly will be perceived by their opponents as biased. Actual bias requires that the manager be suspicious of his/her own perceptions and strive to empathize with the other party; perceived bias may limit the manager's ability to intervene credibly with the other party until the perception is dealt with. Conflict managers who are organizationally superior to the parties may not be biased in favor of either, but they are likely to have poor access to information about the conflict. For such persons special effort to understand the parties' positions may be necessary. Third parties that are respected and seen as neutral by both sides are in perhaps the best position to intervene, but they are a rare luxury for most situations. In any case, awareness of one's position vis-à-vis the parties can help the manager avoid pitfalls.

Finally, a conflict manager needs to develop a sense of what is too much and what is too little conflict among the parties—when is intervention merited, and should it increase or decrease the level of conflict? Relations among groups may be diagnosed in terms of attitudes, behavior, and structure, and each of those categories have characteristic patterns associated with too much and too little conflict.

*Attitudes* include the orientations of groups and group members to their own and other groups—the extent to which they are aware of group interdependencies, the sophistication of group representatives about intergroup relations, and the quality of feelings and stereotypes within groups. Too much conflict is characterized by blindness to interdependencies, naiveté about the dynamics and costs of conflict, and strong negative feelings and stereotypes. Too little conflict, in contrast, is marked by blindness to conflicts of interests, naiveté about the dynamics and costs of collusion, and little awareness of group differences.

*Behaviors* include the ways in which groups and their members act—levels of cohesion and conformity within groups, the action strategies of group representatives, the extent to which interaction between the groups is marked by escalating conflict or cooperation. Too much conflict often involves monolithically conforming groups, rigidly competitive action strategies, and escalating aggression among the groups. Too little conflict is associated with undefined or fragmented groups, unswervingly cooperative action strategies, and collusive harmony and agreement in place of examination of differences.

*Structures* are underlying factors that influence interaction in the long term—the larger systems in which parties are embedded, structural mechanisms that connect the parties, group boundaries and long-term interests, and regulatory contexts that influence interaction. Too much conflict is promoted by undefined or differentiated larger systems, lack of integrative mechanisms that link the groups, clearly defined and conflicting group interests and identities, and few rules or regulations to limit conflict. Too little conflict is encouraged by a shared larger system that suppresses conflict, no mechanisms to promote examination of differences, vague definitions of conflicting group interests and identities, and regulations that discourage overt conflict.

These diagnostic categories and the earmarks of too much and too little conflict are summarized in Table 1. Attitudinal, behavioral, and structural aspects of intergroup relations tend to interact with and support one another. The result is a tendency to escalate either the conflict or the collusion until some external force exerts a moderating effect. Thus, intergroup relations are volatile and capable of rapid escalatory cycles, but they also offer a variety of leverage points at which their self-fulfilling cycles may be interrupted by perceptive managers.

TABLE 1  Diagnosing Conflict among Groups

| Area of Concern | General Issue | Symptoms of Too Much Conflict | Symptoms of Too Little Conflict |
|---|---|---|---|
| Attitudes | Awareness of similarities and differences | Blind to interdependence | Blind to conflicts of interest |
| | Sophistication about intergroup relations | Unaware of dynamics and costs of conflicts | Unaware of dynamics and cost of collusion |
| | Feelings and perceptions of own and other group | Elaborated stereotypes favorable to own and unfavorable to other group | Lack of consciousness of own group and differences from the other group |
| Behavior | Behavior within groups | High cohesion and conformity; high mobilization | Fragmentization; mobilization |
| | Conflict management style of groups | Over competitive style | Over competitive style |
| | Behavior between groups | Aggressive, exploitative behavior; preemptive attack | Avoidance of conflict; appeasement |
| Structure | Nature of larger system | Separate or underdefined common larger system | Shared larger system that discourages conflict |
| | Regulator context for interaction | Few rules to limit escalation | Many rules that stifle differences |
| | Relevant structural mechanisms | No inhibiting third parties available | No third parties to press differences |
| | Definition of groups and their goals | Impermeably bounded groups obsessed with own interests | Unbounded groups aware of own interests |

## Intervention

Intervention to promote constructive conflict may involve *reducing* conflict in relations with too much or *inducing* conflict in relations with too little. In both cases, intervention involves efforts to disrupt a cyclical process produced by the interaction of attitudes, behavior, and structure. Interventions may start with any aspect of the groups' interaction, although long-term change will probably involve effects in all of them. More work has been done on the problem of reducing conflict than on inducing it—but conflict-reduction strategies often have the seeds of conflict induction within them.

Changing *attitudes* involves influencing the ways in which the parties construe events. Thus *altering group perceptions of their differences or similarities* may influence their interaction. Sherif (1966), for example, reports reduction in intergroup conflicts as a consequence of introducing superordinate goals that both groups desired but whose achievement required cooperation; emphasizing interdependencies may reduce escalated conflict. On the other hand, inducing conflict may require deemphasizing interdependencies and emphasizing conflicts of interest. Attitudes may also be changed by *changing the parties' understanding of their relations*. Increased understanding of the dynamics of intergroup conflict and its costs, for example, may help participants reduce their unintentional contributions to escalation (e.g., Burton, 1969). By the same token, increased understanding may help parties control the development of collusion (Janis, 1972). *Feelings and stereotypes may also be changed* by appropriate interventions. Sharing discrepant perceptions of each other has helped depolarize negative stereotypes and reduce conflict in a number of intergroup conflicts (e.g., Blake, Shepard, and Mouton, 1964), and consciousness raising to clarify self and other perceptions may help to increase conflict in situations where there is too little. Attitude-change interventions, in short, operate on the ways in which the parties understand and interpret the relations among the groups.

Changing *behaviors* requires modifying ways in which group members act. *Altering within-group behavior*, for example, may have a substantial impact on the ways in which the groups deal with each other. When members of a highly cohesive group confront explicitly differences that exist *within* the group, their enthusiasm for fighting with outside groups may be reduced. Similarly, an internally fragmented group that becomes more cohesive may develop an increased appetite for conflict with other groups (Brown, 1977). A second behavior-changing strategy is to *train group representatives to manage conflict more effectively.* Where too much conflict exists, representatives can be trained in conflict-reduction strategies, such as cooperation induction (Deutsch, 1973) or problem solving (Filley, 1975). Where the problem is too little conflict, the parties might benefit from training in assertiveness or bargaining skills. A third alternative is to *monitor between-group behavior,* and so influence escalations. Third parties trusted by both sides can control escalative tendencies or lend credibility to reduction initiatives by the parties that might otherwise be distrusted (Walton, 1969). Similarly, conflict induction may be an outcome of third-party "process consultation" that raises questions about collusion (Schein, 1969). Behavior-change strategies, in summary, focus on present activities as an influence on levels of conflict, and seek to move those actions into more constructive patterns.

*Changing structures* involve altering the underlying factors that influence long-term relations among groups. A common alternative is to *invoke larger system interventions.* Conflict between groups in the same larger system is often reduced through referring the question at issue to a higher hierarchical level (Galbraith, 1971). A similar press for conflict induction may be created when too little conflict results in lowered performance that catches the attention of higher levels. A related strategy for managing conflict is to *develop regulatory contexts* that specify appropriate behaviors. Such regulatory structures can limit conflict by imposing rules on potential fights, as collective bargaining legislation does on labor-management relations. Changes in regulatory structures can also loosen rules that stifle desirable conflict. A third strategy is the *development of new interface mechanisms* that mediate intergroup relations. Integrative roles and departments may help to reduce conflict among organizational departments (Galbraith, 1971), while the creation of ombudsmen or "devil's advocates" can help surface conflict that might otherwise not become explicit (Janis, 1972). Another possibility is *redefinition of group boundaries and goals,* so the nature of the parties themselves is reorganized. Redesigning organizations into a matrix structure, for example, in effect locates the conflicted interface within an individual to ensure that effective management efforts are made (Galbraith, 1971). Alternatively, too little conflict may call for clarifying group boundaries and goals so the differences among them become more apparent and more likely to produce conflict. Structural interventions typically demand heavier initial investments of time and energy, and they may take longer to bear fruit than attitudinal and behavioral interventions. But they are also more likely to produce long-term changes.

These strategies for intervention are summarized in Table 2. This sample of strategies is not exhaustive, but it is intended to be representative of interventions that have worked with groups that are relatively equal in power and whose differences are primarily related to the organization's task. The introduction of power differences and societal differences raises other issues.

**TABLE 2** Intervening in Conflict among Groups

| Area of Concern | General Issue | Symptoms of Too Much Conflict | Symptoms of Too Little Conflict |
|---|---|---|---|
| Attitudes | Clarify differences and similarities | Emphasize interdependence | Emphasize conflict of interest |
| | Increased sophistication about intergroup relations | Clarify dynamics and costs of escalation | Clarify costs and dynamics of collusion |
| | Change feelings and perceptions | Share perceptions to depolarize stereotypes | Consciousness raising about group and others |
| Behavior | Modify within-group behavior | Increase expression of within-group differences | Increase within-group cohesion and consensus |
| | Train group representative to be more effective | Expand skills to include cooperative strategies | Expand skills to include assertive, confrontive strategies |
| | Monitor between group behavior | Third-party peacemaking | Third-party process consultation |
| Structure | Invoke larger system interventions | Refer to common hierarchy | Hierarchical pressure for better performance |
| | Develop regulatory contexts | Impose rules on interaction that limit conflict | Deemphasize rules that stifle conflict |
| | Create new interface mechanisms | Develop integrating roles of groups | Create "devils advocates" or ombudsmen |
| | Redefine group boundaries and goals | Redesign organization to emphasize task | Clarify group boundaries and goals to increase differentiation |

## Power Differences

Relations between high-power and low-power groups are worth special examination because of their potential for extremely negative outcomes. The poor communications that result from fear on the part of the low-power group and ignorance on the part of the high-power group can result in either extreme oppression (too little conflict) or unexpected explosions of violence (too much).

It is understandable that high-power groups prefer too little conflict to too much, and that low-power groups are anxious about the risks of provoking conflict with a more powerful adversary. But organizations that in the short run have too little conflict often have too much in the long term. Inattention to the problems of low-power groups requires that they adopt highly intrusive influence strategies in order to be heard (e.g., Swingle, 1976). So the comfort of avoiding conflict between high- and low-power groups may have high costs in the long run.

Managing conflict between high- and low-power groups requires dealing in some fashion with their power differences, since those differences drastically affect the flow of information and influence among the parties. A prerequisite to conflict management interventions may well be *evening the psychological odds*, so that both groups feel able to discuss the situation without too much risk. Evening the odds does not necessarily mean power equalization, but it does require trustworthy protection (to reduce the fear of low-power groups) and effective education (to reduce the ignorance of high-power groups). Given psychological equality, interventions related to attitudes, behavior, and structure that have already been discussed may be employed to promote constructive levels of conflict (e.g., Brown, 1977). It should be noted that for different powerful groups the boundary between too much and too little conflict is easily crossed. Managers may find themselves oscillating rapidly between interventions to induce and interventions to reduce conflict between such groups.

To return once again to an initial example, the history of fighting and violence between the small union and the corporation led the latter's managers to expect even worse conflict when faced by the international union. But voting in the international in effect evened the odds between labor and management. Violent tactics considered necessary by the small union were not necessary for the international, and the regulatory structure of collective bargaining proved adequate to manage the conflict subsequently.

## Societal Differences

Organizations are increasingly forced to grapple with societal differences. These differences are typically not entirely task-related; rather, they are a result of systemic discrimination in the larger society. Group members enter the organization with sets toward each other with which the organization must cope to achieve its goals. Societal differences are most problematic when they involve histories of exploitation (e.g., blacks by whites, women by men), and successful conflict management of such differences requires more than good intentions.

Managing societal differences in organizations may call for evening the odds, as in managing power differences, since societal differences so often include an element of power asymmetry. But coping with societal differences may also require more, since the effect of institutionalization is to ensure that the differences are preserved. *Invoking pressures from the environment* may be required even to get members of some groups into the organization at all. External forces such as federal pressure for "equal opportunity" and expanding educational opportunities for minorities can be used to press for more attention to societally based conflicts within organizations. Organizations may also develop *internal counterinstitutions* that act as checks and balances to systemic discrimination. A carefully designed and protected "communications group," which includes members from many groups and levels, can operate as an early warning system and as a respected third party for managing societal intergroup tensions in an organization (Alderfer, 1977).

The bank's failure to integrate the trust department turned largely on institutionalized racism. The decision to hire black managers was made partly in response to environmental pressure, and so overcame the initial barrier to letting blacks into the division at all. But once into the division, no mechanisms existed to press for overt discussion of differences. Without that discussion, no ways could be developed for the black managers to scale the insurmountable barriers facing them. The bank colluded with its supposedly racist clients by protecting them from contact with the new recruits. Although the first step—recruiting the black managers—was promising, trust division managers were unable to make the differences discussable or to develop the mechanisms required for effective management of the black-white differences in the division.

326

# CONCLUSION

It may be helpful to the reader to summarize the major points of this argument and their implications. It has been argued that relations among groups in organizations can be characterized by too much or too little conflict, depending on their task, the nature of their differences, and the degree to which they are interdependent. This proposition suggests that *conflict managers should strive to maintain some appropriate level of conflict,* rather than automatically trying to reduce or resolve all disagreements. Effective management of intergroup conflict requires both understanding and appropriate action. Understanding intergroup conflict involves diagnosis of attitudes, behaviors, structures, and their interaction. *Effective intervention to increase or decrease conflict requires action to influence attitudes, behaviors, and structures grounded in accurate diagnosis.*

Power differences between groups promote fear and ignorance that result in reduced exchange of information between groups and the potential for either explosive outbursts of escalated conflict or escalating oppression. Evening the odds, at least in psychological terms, may be a prerequisite to effective intervention in such situations. *Managers must cope with fear, ignorance, and their consequences to effectively manage conflicts between unequally powerful groups.*

Societal differences institutionalized in the larger society may further complicate relations among groups in organizations by introducing environmental events and long histories of tension. Managing such differences may require invocation of environmental pressures and the development of counterinstitutions that help the organization deal with the effects of systemic discrimination in the larger society. *Environmental developments produce the seeds for organizational conflicts, but they also offer clues to their management.*

The importance of effective conflict management in organizations is increasing, and that development is symptomatic of global changes. We live in a rapidly shrinking, enormously heterogeneous, increasingly interdependent world. The number of interfaces at which conflict may occur is increasing astronomically, and so are the stakes of too much or too little conflict at those points. If we are to survive—let alone prosper—in our onrushing future, we desperately need skilled managers of conflict among groups.

# REFERENCES

Alderfer, C. P. Improving Organizational Communication Through Long-Term Intergroup Intervention. *Journal of Applied Behavioral Science,* 13, 1977, 193–210.

Blake, R. R., and Mouton, J. S. Reactions to Intergroup Competition Under Win-Lose Conditions. *Management Science,* 4, 1961.

Blake, R. R., Shepard, H. A., and Mouton, J. S. *Managing Intergroup Conflict in Industry.* Ann Arbor, Mich.: Foundation for Research on Human Behavior, 1964.

Brown, L. D. Can Haves and Have-Nots Cooperate? Two Efforts to Bridge a Social Gap. *Journal of Applied Behavioral Science,* 13, 1977, 211–224.

Brown, L. D. Toward a Theory of Power and Intergroup Relations, in *Advances in Experiential Social Process,* edited by C. A. Cooper and C. P. Alderfer. London: Wiley, 1978.

Burton, J. W. *Conflict and Communication: The Use of Controlled Communication in International Relations.* London: Macmillan, 1969.

Coser, L. A. *The Functions of Social Conflict.* New York: Free Press, 1973.

Deutsch, M. *The Resolution of Conflict.* New Haven, Conn.: Yale University Press, 1973.

Filley, A. C. *Interpersonal Conflict Resolution.* Glenview, Ill.: Scott, Foresman, 1975.

Galbraith, J. R. *Designing Complex Organizations.* Reading, Mass.: Addison-Wesley, 1971.

Janis, I. *Victims of Groupthink.* Boston: Houghton-Mifflin, 1972.

Lawrence, P. R., and Lorsch, J. W. *Organization and Environment.* Boston: Harvard Business School, 1967.

Robbins, S. P. *Managing Organizational Conflict.* Englewood Cliffs, N.J.: Prentice Hall, 1974.

Schein, E. G. *Process Consultation.* Reading, Mass.: Addison-Wesley, 1969.

Sherif, M. *In Common Predicament.* Boston: Houghton-Mifflin, 1966.

Swingle, P. G. *The Management of Power.* Hillsdale, N.J.: Erlbaum Associates, 1976.

Walton, R. *Interpersonal Peacemaking.* Reading, Mass.: Addison-Wesley, 1969.

# INGROUP AND INTERGROUP RELATIONS: EXPERIMENTAL ANALYSIS

*Musafer Sherif*
*Carolyn W. Sherif*

The development and effects of ingroup and outgroup delineation in a situation that fostered rivalry were examined in an experimental study of boys in a summer camp setting. By structuring the boys' activities the experiments were able to observe the effects of intergroup competitive tournaments and frustrating events on intergroup hostility. Hostile clashes were observed, but despite the high level of intergroup aggression, procedures were found that had the effect of reducing the level of conflict.

When individuals who have established relationships are brought together to interact in group activities with common goals, they produce a group structure that contains hierarchical statuses and roles.

If two ingroups thus formed are brought into functional relationships in conditions of competition and group frustration, attitudes and appropriate hostile actions in relation to the outgroup and its members will arise and will be standardized and shared in varying degrees by group members.

To test these motions three separate experiments were conducted in the natural setting of a boys' summer camp. The subjects were 11- to 12-year-old boys who had similar family backgrounds but had no previous acquaintance with the other boys in the camp.

The specific hypotheses tested during the three-week camp sessions in the three experiments were as follows.

## Group Formation

*Hypothesis 1.* When individuals participate in group formation, their initially formed friendship choices will be switched to favor members of their new group.

*Hypothesis 2.* When a collectivity of individuals, unknown to one another, interact together in activities that have a common goal and appeal and require their concerted effort, over time a group will form and will be evidenced by 1) differential roles and statuses and 2) norms regulating group behavior.

---

*Source*: Abstracted from *Social Psychology*, Chap. 11 (New York: Harper & Row, 1969).

# Intergroup Conflict

*Hypothesis 3.* When two established groups participate in competitive activities that only one may win, over time friendly competition will turn into intergroup hostility.

*Hypothesis 4.* During competitive activities unfavorable attitudes and conceptions (stereotypes) of the outgroup will form, resulting in lack of communication or contact between groups.

*Hypothesis 5.* Conflict between the groups serves to increase ingroup unity.

*Hypothesis 6.* Ingroup unity and pride is shown by the members' overestimation of the ingroup's achievement and lower estimates of outgroup performance.

*Hypothesis 7.* Interaction between groups (i.e., conflict) will produce changes in the ingroup's organization and practices.

# Conflict Reduction

*Hypothesis 8.* Activities that both groups' members participate in as individuals and that require no interdependency do not reduce intergroup conflict.

*Hypothesis 9.* When groups must work together toward a goal that is highly appealing to each group but cannot be attained by one group alone, they will cooperate.

*Hypothesis 10.* Cooperation between the groups toward a series of superordinate goals serves to reduce the social distance and negative impressions of the outgroup and thus reduces intergroup conflict.

In all three experiments the data were collected by trained observers who acted in roles of camp leaders and made daily ratings on the developing relationships among the boys in terms of the amount of effective initiative each boy showed (a measure of status). Informal interview notes also determined whom the boys considered to be their current best friends (sociometric measure). The camp leaders did not initiate or guide camp activities, and gave advice only when directly asked by the boys. Every effort was made to keep the boys naive about the experimental nature of the camp.

At the beginning of camp the boys were free to choose companions in the camp activities. Following the formation of these small friendship circles, the boys in the first two experiments (1949 and 1953) were split into two groups in such a way that in each group two-thirds of the best friends were in different groups. In the 1954 study this stage of group formation began when Ss were divided into two groups according to the matched size and skills of the individual boys. During the week the groups in all three experiments had little contact with each other and separately engaged in appealing and cooperative activities (i.e., cooking, transporting canoes). At the end of the week (1949 and 1953 experiments) the boys were asked who their best friends were. As shown in Figure 1, Hypothesis 1 was confirmed—the boys switched their friendship choices to group members.

Gradually, as expected in Hypothesis 2, the experiments' two groups formed into a definite group organization involving differentiated roles according to the boys' individual talents and status positions. The highest status boy showed effective initiative in many activities and assumed a leadership position. Also, as predicted, each group developed norms peculiar to the group. For example, in the 1954 study one group developed a norm of toughness to such an extent that members refused to report any injury to camp leaders. The other group, however, created a norm that emphasized the importance of being good (no swearing, praying before meals). Gradually, as the groups formed, nicknames were given to individual members, and each group developed a little culture consisting of secrets, private jokes and vocabulary, and secret hiding places. Further, each group developed ways of punishing those members who violated group norms. The groups then named themselves in order to be distinguished

FIGURE 1 Friendship Choices Before and After Group Formation

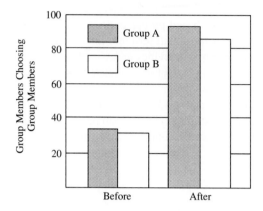

from the other groups—the Red Devils and the Bull Dogs (1949), Panthers and Pythons (1953), and Rattlers and Eagles (1954). Thus the criteria for group formation as described in Hypothesis 2 seem to be satisfied.

In order to begin to examine *inter*group relations in the three experiments, it was arranged for the two groups to compete in a tournament of games. Prizes were to be given to the victorious group and individual prizes to the winning group's members. The tournament in each experiment began with a spirit of friendly competition. However, as the games progressed, the sense of good sportsmanship vanished. For example, after the Red Devils (1949) had experienced a losing streak they began accusing the proud Bull Dogs of playing dirty.

After the tournament the camp leaders planned a purposely frustrating situation that appeared to have been devised by one group. A party was held for both groups in order to bury the hatchet. Through the camp leaders' careful timing (not suspected by the boys), the Red Devils arrived at the party before the Bull Dogs and were thus able to enjoy the best of the assorted refreshments. On arrival the Bull Dogs realized that they had been left the less delectable food and immediately started to insult and taunt the Red Devils.

A series of hostile clashes followed, including food wars, sneak raids on each other's cabins, and hate posters displayed around camp. Gradually the hostility on both sides took on quite a premeditated and scheming character (i.e., collecting and hiding caches of green apples for ammunition). Thus, as predicted (Hypotheses 3 and 4), out of the competitive nature of the tournament rose intergroup hostility. Further, as evidenced by the posters and name calling, derogatory images and stereotypes of the outgroup (the beginning of prejudice) were formed and led to great social distance between groups. Also, boys described ingroup members in favorable terms (brave and tough) but rated outgroup members unfavorably (sneaky, smart alecks).

In order to test the predictions about a group's achievement estimation, a game of bean toss was arranged and a prize was offered to the group that not only collected the most beans but also judged the game's outcome most accurately. Figure 2 indicates judgment errors in the boys' estimates of the amount collected by ingroup and outgroup members. As expected (Hypothesis 6), the members of one group tended to overestimate their group's achievement and underestimate the performance of the other group. Winners tended to make larger errors.

FIGURE 2   Average Errors in Estimating Performance for Ingroup and Outgroup

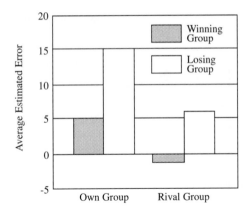

Sociometric measures taken after the tournament further supported Hypothesis 5. The conflict between the groups tended to increase group unity, and friendship choices were made almost exclusively within the ingroup. The hostility also served to produce the expected organizational changes within the groups (Hypothesis 7). In the Eagles the leader role changes hands from peacetime (group formation) to this period of conflict. In another group a low status bully found himself in the leadership role when the intergroup conflict began. To an outside observer these intelligent, well adjusted, middle class boys would probably be described as violent, disturbed, or delinquent.

Now, to the constructive phase of these experiments. How can we reduce the intergroup conflict? As expected (Hypothesis 8), activities such as moviegoing or shooting firecrackers that had appeal but no need for cooperation between groups did not reduce hostility. Therefore, superordinate goals were created (i.e., goals that are important to both groups but cannot be attained by only one group), such as finding a fault in a water supply line and pooling money to see a desired movie. After a series of these cooperative activities, the amount of intergroup conflict was reduced (Hypothesis 10) and members began to act friendlier. Interviews reflected this change in attitudes. Many friendship choices were now made from the outgroup, and negative ideas about outgroup members rapidly dissipated (Figure 3).

Can we dismiss these findings as being true only among children and not applicable in the sphere of adults? Current research (Blake, Shepard & Mouton, 1964) suggests that we most definitely cannot. Adults in human relations workshops were divided into two groups, given problems, and asked to find better solutions than the other group could devise. The events that occurred faithfully replicated the Sherifs' findings. The competitive activities engendered hostility between groups, but cooperative activities dissipated the hostility. Perhaps nations can coexist peacefully if they develop goals that are mutually meaningful and beneficial and can be realized only if the nations jointly cooperate.

FIGURE 3   Friendship Choices Before and After Series of Subordinate Goals

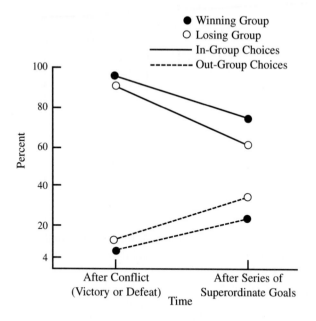

Figure 11.21b (p. 263) in *Social Psychology* by Muzafer Sherif and Carolyn W. Sherif (Harper & Row, 1969).

## REFERENCE

Blake, R. R.; Shepard, H. A.; and Mouton, Jane S. 1964. *Managing intergroup conflict in industry.* Houston, Texas: Gulf Publishing.

# NEGOTIATING WITH "ROMANS"—PART 2

*Stephen E. Weiss*

Managers are increasingly called on to negotiate with people from other cultures. Cross-cultural negotiation need not be as frustrating nor as costly as it is often made out to be; it can be a productive and satisfying experience. Which of these outcomes a manager achieves depends in part on the negotiation strategies taken in response to—or better, in anticipation of—the counterpart's plans and behavior. There are eight culturally responsive strategies for a manager to consider (see Figure 1).[1]

Clearly, the quality of a negotiation outcome and a manager's satisfaction with it also depend on how well he or she chooses and implements one of these approaches.

*Source*: Reprinted from "Negotiating With 'Romans'—Part 2" by Stephen E. Weiss, *Sloan Management Review*, Spring 1994, pp. 85–99, by permission of publisher. Copyright 1994 by the Sloan Management Review Association. All rights reserved.

This article presents five steps for selecting a culturally responsive strategy and then offers various tips for implementation, such as making the first move, monitoring feedback, and modifying the approach. These guidelines reflect four basic, ongoing considerations for a strategy: its *feasibility* for the manager, its fit with the counterpart's likely approach and therefore its capacity to lead to *coherent interaction*, its *appropriateness* to the relationship and circumstances at hand, and its *acceptability* in light of the manager's values. There are challenges involved in all of these efforts, and they are pointed out below rather than ignored or belittled, as happens in much cross-cultural negotiation literature. Thus, from this article, managers stand to gain both an operational plan and the heightened awareness necessary to use a culturally responsive negotiation strategy effectively.

## SELECTING A STRATEGY

Every negotiator is advised to "know yourself, the counterpart, and the situation."[2] This advice is useful but incomplete, for it omits the relationship—the connection—between the negotiator and the counterpart.[3] (For clarity, the negotiator from the "other" culture will be called the "counterpart" in this article.) Different types of relationships with counterparts and even different phases of a relationship with a particular counterpart call for different strategies.

For the cross-cultural negotiator, the very presence of more than one culture complicates the process of understanding the relationship and "knowing" the counterpart. In contrast to the "within-culture" negotiator, the cross-cultural negotiator cannot take common knowledge and practices for granted and thereby simply concentrate on the individual. It becomes important to actively consider the counterpart in two respects: as a member of a group and as an individual.

The right balance in these considerations is not easily struck. An exclusive emphasis on the group's culture will probably lead the negotiator off the mark because individuals often differ from the group average. Members of the same group may even differ very widely on certain dimensions. At the same time, the degree of variation tolerated between group members is itself an aspect of culture. For example, Americans have traditionally upheld the expression, "He's his own man," while Japanese believed that "the protruding nail is hammered down." The cross-cultural negotiator should thus consider both the counterpart's cultural background and individual attributes, perhaps weighting them differently according to the culture involved, but mindful always that every negotiation involves developing a relationship with a particular individual or team.[4]

> *For years, Japanese managers have come to one of my classes each term to negotiate with graduate students so the students can experience negotiating first-hand and test the often stereo-typical descriptions they have read about Japanese negotiating behavior. I deliberately invite many Japanese, not just one or two. The students invariably express surprise when the Japanese teams "deviate" from the Japanese negotiating script, as the students understand it, and when differences appear in the behavior of various Japanese teams.*

The five steps for selecting a culturally responsive negotiation strategy take into account these complexities:

1. Reflect on your culture's negotiation script.
2. Learn the negotiation script of the counterpart's culture.
3. Consider the relationship and circumstances.
4. Predict or influence the counterpart's approach.
5. Choose your strategy.

These steps take minutes or months, depending on the parties and circumstances involved. Each step will probably not require the same amount of time or effort. Furthermore, the sequencing of the steps is intended to have an intuitive, pragmatic appeal for an American negotiator, but it should not be treated rigidly. Some steps will be more effective if they are coupled or treated iteratively. Nor should these efforts start at the negotiation table when time, energy, resources, and introspection tend to be severely limited. Every one of these steps merits *some* attention by every cross-cultural negotiator before the first round of negotiation.

It is important to remember that the procedure represented by these five steps is itself culturally embedded, influenced by the author's cultural background and by that of the intended audience (American negotiators).[5] Not all counterparts will find the pragmatic logic herein equally compelling. As two Chinese professionals have observed, "In the West, you are used to speaking out your problems....But that is not our tradition," and "In our country, there are so many taboos. We're not used to analytic thinking in your Western way. We don't dissect ourselves and our relationships."[6] Even with this procedure, culture continues to influence what we do and how we do it.

One way to deal with this inescapable cultural bias is to acknowledge it and remain aware of the continual challenges of effectively choosing and implementing a strategy. Often these challenges do not stand out—books on international negotiation have not addressed them—yet they can hamper, even ruin, a negotiator's best efforts. Each step below thus includes a list of cautions for cross-cultural negotiating.

FIGURE 1    Culturally Responsive Strategies and Their Feasibility

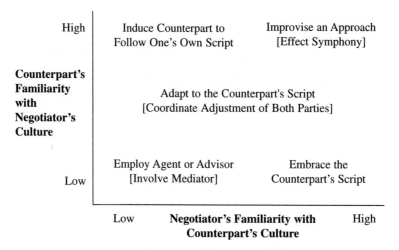

Brackets indicate a joint strategy, which requires deliberate consultation with counterpart. At each level of familiarity, a negotiator can consider feasible the strategies designated at that level and any lower level.

# 1. Reflect on Your Culture's Negotiation Script

Among members of our "home"group, we behave almost automatically.[7] We usually have no impetus to consider the culture of the group because we repeatedly engage in activities with each other without incident or question. It is easy to use these "natural," taken-for-granted ways in a cross-cultural situation—too easy.

FIGURE 2   Negotiator Profile

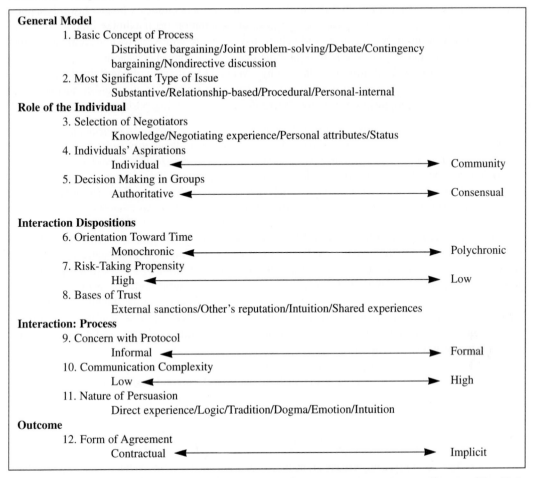

**General Model**
   1. Basic Concept of Process
            Distributive bargaining/Joint problem-solving/Debate/Contingency
            bargaining/Nondirective discussion
   2. Most Significant Type of Issue
            Substantive/Relationship-based/Procedural/Personal-internal
**Role of the Individual**
   3. Selection of Negotiators
            Knowledge/Negotiating experience/Personal attributes/Status
   4. Individuals' Aspirations
            Individual ⟵————————————————⟶ Community
   5. Decision Making in Groups
            Authoritative ⟵————————————————⟶ Consensual

**Interaction Dispositions**
   6. Orientation Toward Time
            Monochronic ⟵————————————————⟶ Polychronic
   7. Risk-Taking Propensity
            High ⟵————————————————⟶ Low
   8. Bases of Trust
            External sanctions/Other's reputation/Intuition/Shared experiences
**Interaction: Process**
   9. Concern with Protocol
            Informal ⟵————————————————⟶ Formal
   10. Communication Complexity
            Low ⟵————————————————⟶ High
   11. Nature of Persuasion
            Direct experience/Logic/Tradition/Dogma/Emotion/Intuition
**Outcome**
   12. Form of Agreement
            Contractual ⟵————————————————⟶ Implicit

*Source*: Adapted from S. E. Weiss with W. Stripp, *Negotiating with Foreign Business Persons* (New York: New York University Graduate School of Business Administration, Working Paper #85-6, 1985), p. 10.

*A book on international negotiation published by the U.S. State Department displays the flags of six nations on its front cover. On initial copies of the book, the French flag appeared in three bands of red, white, and blue. The actual French flag is blue, white, and red.[8]*

A cross-cultural negotiator should construct a thoughtful, systematic profile of his or her culture's negotiation practices, using personal knowledge and other resources. Let's say you want to develop an "American negotiator profile." There is a vast amount of research and popular literature on negotiation in the United States.[9]  For insights about American culture more broadly, consider both Americans' self-examinations and outsiders' observations.[10]  Then organize this information into the profile represented in Figure 2.[11]  The profile consists of four topic areas: the general model of the negotiation process, the individual's role, aspects of interaction, and the form of a satisfactory agreement.  The left side of the ranges in Figure 2 generally fit the American negotiator profile (e.g., the basic concept is distributive bargaining, the most significant issues are substantive ones,  negotiators are chosen for their knowledge, individual aspirations predominate over community needs, and so forth).

This profile should also uncover the values that support these tendencies. For instance, distributive bargaining implies certain attitudes toward conflict and its handling (direct), toward business relationships (competitive), and toward the purpose of negotiation (to maximize individual gains). Since some of your group's tendencies and values may not align with your own, develop a personal profile as well. Doing so does not require probing deeply into your unconscious. Simply ask yourself, "What do I usually do at times like this? Why? What do I gain from doing it this way?" These kinds of questions resemble those used in basic negotiation training to distinguish an underlying interest from a bargaining position, namely, "What does this bargaining position do for me? Why?"

> *In the mid 1980s, a white American banker planned to include an African-American analyst on his team for a forthcoming visit to white clients in South Africa. When they learned about this, the clients intimated their preference that she not attend. While the banker wanted to serve his clients, he also had strong feelings about including the analyst and about basing qualifications on merit. She was the best analyst on his staff. The banker's values swayed his decision: he told his clients that he would not make the trip without this analyst on his team.[12]*

Developing cultural and personal profiles is an ongoing task. Instead of writing them up once and moving on, return to them and refine them as you gain experience and understanding. The value of such a process is considerable. It increases your self-awareness; it helps you explain your expectations and behavior to a counterpart; it prepares you to make decisions under pressure; it allows you to compare your culture to another on a holistic rather than fragmented basis; it helps you determine a counterpart's level of familiarity with your culture; its products—profiles—can be used in future negotiations with other cultural groups; it motivates interest in other cultures; and it enables you to act consistently and conscientiously.

This process demands a good deal of effort, especially at the outset (note the cautions in Table 1). But as a negotiator, you will find such reflection to be a good basis for developing a cross-cultural negotiation strategy.

---

TABLE 1    Cautions: Understanding Your Own Culture's Script

- Beware of psychological and group biases, such as denial and "groupthink."
- Probe for assumptions and values; they are seldom identified explicitly in day-to-day life.
- Don't become rigidly wedded to your own ways.
- Take time during negotiations to step out of the action and reflect on your behavior.

---

## 2. Learn the Negotiation Script of the Counterpart's Culture

This step applies to both the negotiator highly familiar with a counterpart's culture and the one who knows next to nothing about it.[13] The highly familiar negotiator should review what he or she knows and gather additional information to stay current. The uninitiated negotiator should begin to construct a negotiator profile from the ground up. Ideally, this process involves learning in the active sense: developing the ability to use the counterpart's cultural and personal negotiation scripts, as well as "knowing" the scripts and related values.

Learning these scripts enhances the negotiator's ability to anticipate and interpret the counterpart's behavior. Even a negotiator with low familiarity who is likely to employ an agent needs some information in order to interact effectively with the agent and to assess the agent's performance. Although few negotiators learn everything about a counterpart before negotiation, advance work allows for assimilation and practice, provides a general degree of confidence that helps the negotiator to cope with the unexpected, and frees up time and attention during the negotiation to learn finer points.

Again, the negotiator profile framework is a good place to start. Try especially to glean and appreciate the basic concept of negotiation because it anchors and connects the other dimensions. Without it, a negotiator, as an outsider, cannot comprehend a counterpart's actions; they appear bizarre or whimsical. Moreover, if you focus merely on tactics or simple "do and don't"-type tips and reach a point in a transaction for which you have no tip, you have no base—no sense of the "spirit of the interaction"—to guide you through this juncture. For instance, the "spirit" of French management has been described like this:

> *French managers see their work as an intellectual challenge requiring the remorseless application of individual brainpower. They do not share the Anglo-Saxon view of management as an interpersonally demanding exercise, where plans have to be constantly "sold" upward and downward using personal skills. The bias is for intellect rather than for action.[14]*

Continuing with this example, let's say you are preparing to negotiate with a French counterpart. You may find information about French negotiation concepts and practices in studies by French and American researchers and in natives' and outsiders' popular writings.[15] In addition to general nonfiction works on French culture, novels and films can convey an extraordinary sense of interactions among individuals and groups.[16] Other sources include intensive culture briefings by experts and interviews with French acquaintances, colleagues, and compatriots familiar with French culture, and, in some cases, even the counterpart.

Here, as in reflections on your own culture, make sure to consider core beliefs and values of the culture. Keep an eye on the degree of adherence to them as well as their substantive content.

> *A Frenchman involved in the mid-1980s negotiations between AT&T and CGE over a cross-marketing deal revealed his own culture's concern for consistency in thought and behavior as he discussed AT&T's conduct. He described the AT&T representatives' style as "very strange" because they made assurances about "fair" implementation while pushing a "very tough" contract.*

Moving from information gathering to assimilation and greater familiarity with a culture usually requires intensive training on site or in seminars.[17] Some Japanese managers, for example, have been sent overseas by their companies for three to five years to absorb a country's culture before initiating any business ventures. When the time comes, familiarity may be assessed through tests of language fluency, responses to "critical incidents" in "cultural assimilator" exercises, and performance in social interactions in the field.[18]

Whether or not you have prior experience working with a particular counterpart or other inside information, try to explore the counterpart's own negotiation concepts, practices, and values. They can be mapped in a negotiator profile just as you mapped your own values.

This entire undertaking poses challenges for every negotiator, regardless of the strategy ultimately chosen. One of the highest hurdles may be the overall nature of the learning itself. Learning about another culture's concepts, ways, and values seems to hinge on the similarity between that culture and one's own. Learning is inhibited when one is isolated from members of that culture (even if one is living in their country) and "may fail to occur when attitudes to be learned contradict deep-seated personality orientations (e.g., authoritarianism), when defensive stereotypes exist, or at points where home and host cultures differ widely in values or in conceptual frame of reference."[19] Other significant challenges can be seen in Table 2. Remember that, ultimately, you have access to different strategies for whatever amount of learning and level of familiarity you attain.

- Don't be too quick to identify the counterpart's home culture. Common cues (name, physical appearance, language, accent, and location) may be unreliable. The counterpart probably belongs to more than one culture.
- Beware of the Western bias toward "doing." In Arab, Asian, and Latin groups, ways of being (e.g., comportment, smell), feeling, thinking, and talking can more powerfully shape relationships than doing.
- Try to counteract the tendency to formulate simple, consistent, stable images. Not many cultures are simple, consistent, or stable.
- Don't assume that all aspects of the culture are equally significant. In Japan, consulting all relevant parties to a decision *(nemawashi)* is more important than presenting a gift *(omiyage)*.
- Recognize the forms for interactions involving outsiders may differ from those for interactions between compatriots.
- Don't overestimate your familiarity with your counterpart's culture. An American studying Japanese wrote New Year's wishes to Japanese contacts in basic Japanese characters but omitted one character. As a result, the message became "Dead man, congratulations."

## 3. Consider the Relationship and Circumstances

Negotiators and counterparts tend to behave differently in different relationships and contexts.[20] One does not, for instance, act the same way as a seller as one does as a buyer. So a negotiator should not count on the same strategy to work equally well with every counterpart from a given cultural group (even if the counterparts have the same level of familiarity with the negotiator's culture) or, for that matter, with the same counterpart all the time. The peaks and valleys that most relationships traverse require different strategies and approaches. In the same vein, circumstances suggest varying constraints and opportunities.

To continue your preparations for a negotiation, consider particular facets of your relationship with the counterpart and the circumstances. The most important facets on which to base strategic choices have not yet been identified in research and may actually depend on the cultures involved. Furthermore, laying out a complete list of possibilities goes beyond the scope of this article.[21] But the following considerations (four for relationships, four for circumstances) seem significant.

*Life of the Relationship.* The existence and nature of a prior relationship with the counterpart will influence the negotiation and should figure into a negotiator's deliberations. With no prior contact, one faces a not-yet personal situation; general information and expectations based on cultural scripts will have to do until talks are under way. Parties who have had previous contact, however, have experienced some form of interaction. Their expectations concerning the future of the relationship will also tend to influence negotiation behavior.[22] In sum, the negotiator should acknowledge any already established form of interaction, assess its attributes (e.g., coherence) and the parties' expectations of the future, and decide whether to continue, modify, or break from the established form. These decisions will indicate different culturally responsive strategies.

*Fit of Respective Scripts.* Having completed steps 1 and 2, you can easily compare your negotiator profiles, both cultural and individual, with those of the counterpart. Some culture comparisons based on the negotiator profile in Figure 2 have already been published.[23] Noting similarities as well as differences will enable you to identify those aspects of your usual behavior that do not need to change (similarities) and those aspects that do (major differences) if you choose a strategy that involves elements of both your negotiation script and the counterpart's (e.g., the adapt strategy). The number and kinds of differences will also suggest how difficult it would be to increase your level of familiarity with the counterpart's culture or to use certain combinations of strategies.

Do not allow such a comparison to mislead you. Some people overemphasize differences. Others, focusing on superficial features, overestimate similarities and their understanding of another culture (e.g., when Americans compare American and Canadian cultures). The cautions in Table 3 can help you stay on track.

Of course, a negotiator highly familiar with the counterpart's culture who plans to adapt an embrace strategy, operating wholly within that culture, has less need for these comparisons.

***Balance of Power.*** It may seem that power would have a lot to do with the choice of strategy. A more powerful party could induce the other to follow his or her cultural script. A less powerful party would have to embrace the other's script. A balance of power might suggest an adapt or improvise strategy.

But the issue is not so simple. The tilt of the "balance" is not easily or clearly determined; parties often measure power using different scales.[24] Indeed, forms of power, their significance, and appropriate responses are all culturally embedded phenomena.[25] Furthermore, it makes little sense to rely on power and disregard a counterpart's familiarity with one's culture when one's goal is coherent interaction. This is not to say that one could not benefit from an imbalance of power *after* choosing a culturally responsive strategy or in other areas of negotiation. Still, since power is culturally based and Americans have a general reputation for using it insensitively, American negotiators should be extremely careful about basing the strategy decision on power.

***Gender.*** Consider the possible gender combinations in one-on-one cross-cultural relationships: female negotiator with female counterpart, male negotiator with male counterpart, male negotiator with female counterpart, and female negotiator with male counterpart. Within most cultures, same-gender and mixed relationships entail different negotiating scripts. There are few books on negotiation designated for American women, but communication research has shown that men tend to use talk to negotiate status, women tend to use it to maintain intimacy, and they are often at cross-purposes when they talk to each other.[26] The debates over how American women should act in male-dominated workplaces further substantiate the existence of different scripts. In a sense, gender groups have their own cultures, and mixed interaction within a national culture is already cross-cultural.

---

TABLE 3  Cautions: Considering the Relationship and Circumstances

- Pay attention to the similarities *and* differences, in kind and in magnitude, between your negotiator profiles and those of the counterpart.
- Be careful about judging certain relationship aspects as major (big picture issues) and minor (fine details). The dichotomy, let alone the particular contents of the two categories, is not used in all cultures.
- Consider the relationship from the counterpart's perspective.
- Identify the relationship factors and circumstances most significant to you and the counterpart.
- Beware of the use and abuse of power.
- Discover the "wild cards" either party may have.
- Remember that the relationship will not remain static during negotiation.

---

Mixed interaction across national and other cultures holds even greater challenges. One of the primary determinations for a woman should be whether a male counterpart sees her first as a foreigner and second as a woman, or vice versa. According to some survey research, Asian counterparts see North American businesswomen as foreigners first.[27] The opposite may be true in parts of France. Edith Cresson, former French prime minister, once said, "Anglo-Saxons are not interested in women as women. For a [French] woman arriving in an Anglo-Saxon country, it is astonishing. She says to herself, 'What is the matter?'"[28] Thus, although current information about negotiating scripts for other countries tends to be based on male-male interactions, complete culturally-based negotiator profiles should include gender-based scripts.

Whether your negotiation involves mixed or same-gender interaction, try to anticipate the counterpart's perception of the gender issue and review your core beliefs. Gender-based roles in France, for instance, may appear so antithetical (or laudable) that you will not entertain (or will favor) the embrace strategy.

With regard to circumstances, the second part of step 3, there are at least four relevant considerations.

***Opportunity for Advance Coordination.*** Do you have—or can you create—an opportunity beforehand to coordinate strategy with your counterpart? If so, consider the joint strategies. If not, concentrate at the outset on feasible, unilateral strategies.

***Time Schedule.*** Time may also shape a negotiator's choice in that different strategies require different levels of effort and time. For the negotiator with moderate familiarity of the counterpart's culture but an inside track on a good agent, employing an agent may take less time than adapting to the counterpart's script. The time required to implement a strategy also depends on the counterpart's culture (e.g., negotiations based on the French script generally take longer than the American script). And time constrains the learning one can do to increase familiarity. Imagine the possibilities that open up for a diligent negotiator when discussions are scheduled as a series of weekly meetings over a twelve-month period instead of as one two-hour session.

***Audiences.*** Consider whether you or the counterpart will be accompanied by other parties, such as interpreters, advisors, constituents, and mass media. Their presence or absence can affect the viability and effectiveness of a strategy. If no one else will attend the meeting, for instance, you have no one to defer to or involve as a mediator at critical junctures.

*During the early months of the ITT-CGE telecommunications negotiations in 1985 and 1986, fewer than ten individuals were aware of the talks. That permitted the parties to conduct discussions in ways not possible later, when over a hundred attorneys, not to mention other personnel, became involved. At the same time, that choice may have ruled out the initial use of some culturally responsive strategies.*

***Wild Cards.*** Finally, you should assess your own and the counterpart's capacities to alter some relationship factors and circumstances. Parties may have extra-cultural capabilities such as financial resources, professional knowledge, or technical skills that expand their set of feasible options, bases for choice, or means of implementation.

*During the GM-Toyota joint venture negotiation in the early 1980's, Toyota could afford to and did hire three U.S. law firms simultaneously for a trial period in order to compare their advice and assess their compatibility with the company. After three months, the company retained one of the firms for the duration of the negotiations.*

# 4. Predict or Influence the Counterpart's Approach.

The last step before choosing a strategy is to attempt to determine the counterpart's approach to the negotiation, either by predicting it or by influencing its selection. For the effectiveness of a culturally responsive strategy in bringing about coherent interaction depends not only on the negotiator's ability to implement it but also on its complementarity with the counterpart's strategy. Embracing the counterpart's script makes little sense if the counterpart is embracing your script. Further, reliable prediction and successful influence narrow the scope of a negotiator's deliberations and reduce uncertainty. And the sooner the prediction, the greater the time available for preparation. While these concerns relate to the parties' relationship (step 3), they have a direct impact on interaction that merits a separate step.

Assuming that your counterpart will not ignore cultural backgrounds and that each of you would adopt only a unilateral strategy, you can use Figure 3 to preview all possible intersections of these strategies.[29] They fall into three categories: complementary, potentially but not inherently complementary, and conflicting. Thus the figure shows the coherence of each strategy pair.

Among these pairs, adapt-adapt and improvise-improvise might seem inherently complementary. The catch is that parties can adapt or improvise in conflicting ways. Of all the potentially complementary cells, the improvise-improvise interaction may, however, be the most likely to become coherent, given the nature of the improvise strategy and the capabilities it entails.

Not all of the strategies in Figure 3 will be available to you in every situation. Remember that in addition to potential coherence, your choice will be based on your familiarity with the counterpart's culture, the counterpart's familiarity with yours, appropriateness, and acceptability.

***Prediction.*** Sometimes a counterpart will make this step easy by explicitly notifying you of his or her strategy in advance of your talks. If the counterpart does not do that, there may be telling clues in the counterpart's prenegotiation behavior, or other insiders (associates or subordinates) may disclose information.

Without direct and reliable information, you are left to predict the counterpart's strategy choice on the basis of his or her traits and motivations. Some counterparts will have a rational, task-directed orientation. Strategy research based on this perspective shows that counterparts seeking to coordinate their actions with a negotiator often select the course of action most prominent or salient to both parties (e.g., choosing a river as a property boundary).[30] Other counterparts will focus on what is socially proper. Indeed, whether a counterpart even responds to the cross-cultural nature of the interaction may vary with his or her cosmopolitanism. A cosmopolitan counterpart may lean toward adapt and improvise strategies, whereas a counterpart having little experience with other cultures may be motivated primarily by internal, cultural norms. In the latter case, the counterpart's negotiator profile may be used to predict some behavior. For example, the internally focused individual from a culture with high communication complexity (reliance on nonverbal and other contextual cues for meaning), which often correlates with low risk-taking propensity, would be more likely to involve a mediator than to coordinate adjustment (which is too explicit) or to embrace or improvise (which are too uncertain).[31]

*Influence.* Whether or not you can predict a counterpart's strategy choice, why not try to influence it? If you predict a strategy favorable to you, perhaps you can reinforce it; if unfavorable, change it; and if predicted without certainty, ensure it. Even if prediction proves elusive, it behooves you to try to influence the counterpart.

The first task in this process is to determine your own preferred strategy based on the criteria in step 5. This may appear to be jumping ahead, but choosing and influencing go hand in hand. They will go on throughout negotiation, for new information will come to light and necessitate reassessments.

Once you have chosen a strategy, use the matrix in Figure 3 to locate interaction targets. Your prime targets should be the coherent (complementary) combinations, followed by the potentially coherent ones. For example, if you intend to employ an agent, influence the counterpart to use the induce strategy.

Some negotiators may also contemplate targeting conflicting strategies. In this line of thinking, a conflict could bring out the parties' differences so dramatically as to provide valuable lessons and "working" material for both the negotiator and counterpart. Influencing the counterpart to pursue a strategy that conflicts with one's own (or selecting one by oneself if the counterpart has already set a strategy) might establish that one is not a negotiator who can be exploited. However, these effects lie outside of our main purposes of demonstrating responsiveness to cultural factors and establishing a coherent form of interaction. Furthermore, such conflict often confuses, causes delays, and provokes resentment. (Note also the other cautions in Table 4).

FIGURE 3    The Inherent Coherence of Parties' Culturally Responsive Strategies

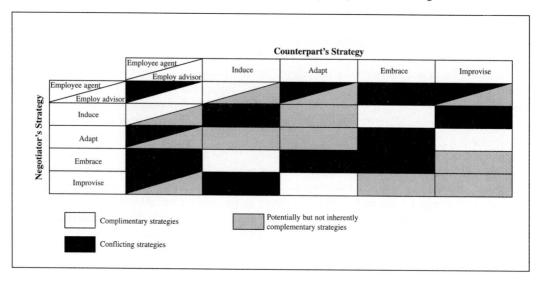

With respect to means of influence, Americans sometimes preemptively take action, such as using English in conversation without inquiring about a non-American counterpart's wishes or capabilities, but there are other, often more mutually satisfactory, ways to influence a counterpart. They range from direct means, such as explicitly requesting a counterpart to choose a particular strategy, to tacit means, such as disclosing one's level of familiarity with the counterpart's culture, revealing one's own strategy choice, or designating a meeting site likely to elicit certain types of conduct. For example, in 1989, then U.S. Secretary of State James Baker hosted his Soviet counterpart Eduard Shevardnadze in Jackson Hole, Wyoming, instead of Washington, D.C. Prenegotiation communications may also be carried out by advance staff or through back channels. As you evaluate these options, bear in mind that their effectiveness will probably differ according to the counterpart's culture and personal attraction to you. [32]

## 5. Choose Your Strategy

When you have completed the previous steps, it is time to choose a strategy or a combination of strategies. Four selection criteria emerge from these steps. The strategy must be feasible given the counterpart and cultures involved; able to produce a coherent pattern of interaction, given the counterpart's likely approach; appropriate to the relationship and circumstances; and acceptable, ideally but not necessarily, to both parties. These criteria apply to the prenegotiation choice of strategy, but you may also use them to assess your strategy during negotiation.

A possible fifth criterion would be your degree of comfort with a strategy. Even negotiators highly familiar with two cultures' scripts favor one script over another in certain circumstances. So if the four criteria above do not direct you to only one right strategy, consider, at the the end, which of the remaining strategies you would be most comfortable implementing.

Apply the four criteria in order, for their sequence is deliberate and designed for negotiators with a pragmatic orientation (e.g., Americans). Feasibility, after all, appears first. Acceptability appears later because the value judgment it involves impedes deliberation in cross-cultural situations when used early.[33] (Note that counterparts from other cultural groups may prefer to use a list that begins with appropriateness or acceptability.)

Each criterion deserves attention. Feasibility and coherence considerations may narrow your choices down to one unilateral strategy, yet you should still check that choice for its appropriateness, given the relationship and circumstances, and its consonance with core beliefs and values. For a negotiation scheduled to take place over many years, for example, the negotiator might look at strategy that is potentially but not inherently complementary to the counterpart's (see Figure 3) or at combinations or progressions of strategies. For a negotiation where the negotiator cannot narrow strategy options by reliability predicting the counterpart's strategy, the negotiator may actually have to rely on the last two criteria. And when a negotiator wishes to consider joint strategies, relationship factors and circumstances are essential to consult. In sum, the support of all four criteria for a particular strategy choice should give you confidence in it.

Occasionally, criteria may conflict. Feasibility and coherence point to an embrace strategy for a counterpart's induce strategy, but the negotiator may find aspects of the counterpart culture's script unacceptable (e.g., *fatwa*, Iran's death threat.) Or the embrace-induce strategy pairing may have worked well in a cross-cultural relationship for years, but now you expect your counterpart to be at least moderately familiar with your culture. The resolution of such conflicts begs for further research. In the meantime, you may want to defer to your core beliefs and values. Values define the very existence of your home group and your membership in it; by ignoring or violating them you risk forfeiting your membership.[34]

TABLE 4   Cautions:  Predicting or Influencing the Counterpart's Approach

- Try to discern whether the counterpart's culture categorically favors or disfavors certain strategies.
- Don't fixate on "what's typical" for someone from the counterpart's cultural group.
- Recognize the difficulty in accurately assessing the counterpart's familiarity with your culture's negotiating script.
- Heed the line, however fuzzy, between influencing and "meddling"—a U.S. diplomat was detained in Singapore in 1988 for interfering in internal affairs.*
- Track changes in the counterpart's strategic choices over time.
- Don't focus so obsessively on parties' strategies that you ignore the richness of the relationship or the context.

*F. Deyo, *Dependent Development and Industrial Order* (New York: Praeger, 1981), p. 89.

As an example of strategy selection based on all four criteria, consider an American, Smith, who is preparing for a confidential, one-on-one meeting with a Frenchman he has never met before, Dupont.

*Smith once lived in France and, as the meeting is being held in Dupont's Paris office, his gut feeling is to speak in French and behave according to Dupont's culture—that is, to use an embrace strategy. However, he takes the time to evaluate his options. Smith realizes that he is no longer familiar enough with French language and culture to use an embrace strategy, and the short lead time prevents him from increasing his familiarity. With a moderate level of familiarity, he has five feasible strategies: employ an agent or adviser, involve a mediator, induce Dupont to follow his script, adapt to Dupont's script, or coordinate adjustment by both parties. Smith does some research and learns that Dupont has only a moderate level of familiarity with American negotiation practices. That rules out the induce strategy. The relationship and circumstances make an agent or mediator inappropriate. An adapt strategy would be hit-or-miss because Smith has no cues from previous face-to-face interaction and only one meeting is planned. Overall, the best strategy choice is to coordinate adjustment.*

A complicated situation will require more complex considerations.  (See also the cautions on choosing a strategy in Table 5.)  But the five steps above—reflect, learn, consider, predict, and choose—constitute a sound and useful guide for strategy selection.

TABLE 5   Cautions:  Choosing a Strategy

- Don't assume the counterpart will use the same criteria or order you to (e.g., efficiency is not a universal concern).
- Watch out for parties' miscalculations and conflicting impressions (e.g., the counterpart's assessments of your respective levels of cultural familiarity may differ from yours).
- Proceed carefully when criteria conflict; further research may help.
- Don't treat an embrace strategy, by mere definition, as costly or a concession.

## Implementing Your Strategy

The full value of the most carefully selected strategy rests on effective implementation, a formidable task in the general fluidity of negotiations and especially in the multifaceted process of most cross-cultural negotiations. It is here, in a negotiation's twists and turns, that a negotiator deals head on with distinctions between the counterpart's attributes as an individual and as a member of a cultural group. Simply adhering to one's own plan of action is difficult—and may become undesirable. For the negotiator must ensure that the strategy complements the counterpart's approach and enables the two of them to establish and maintain a coherent form of interaction.

Whatever the chosen culturally responsive strategy, a negotiator may enhance the effectiveness of first moves and ongoing efforts by generally respecting the counterpart and his or her group's culture and by demonstrating empathy (both of which may take different forms for different cultures). These qualities, among others, have been recommended in the literature on cross-cultural competence and are consistent with cultural responsiveness.[35] They do not necessitate lowering one's substantive negotiation goals.[36]

## First Moves

The strategies of employ agent, embrace, and induce entail complete, existing scripts for negotiation. Pursuing one of these strategies essentially involves following the script associated with it. The adapt strategy involves modifications of your own script, at least some of which should be determined beforehand. With the improvise strategy, you ought to give some advance thought to a basic structure even if much of the path will emerge as you travel on it. Thus you have a starting point for each of the five unilateral strategies.

These strategies assume that when a counterpart recognizes your strategy, he or she will gravitate toward its corresponding script.[37] The counterpart wants to understand you and to be understood; that is what occurs in *coherent* interaction. If you have accurately assessed the counterpart's level of familiarity with your culture and ability to use a particular script, and if the counterpart recognizes the strategy you are using, you stand a better chance of achieving coherence.

Should you make the first strategic move or wait until the counterpart does? This decision affects the transition from preliminary "warm-up" discussions to negotiation of business matters. It depends, in part, on whether you need to gather more information about the counterpart's strategic intentions and abilities. This would matter when both parties have at least moderate familiarity with each other's cultures and have more than one unilateral strategy they can realistically choose, and when you have chosen a strategy (e.g., adapt, improvise) that relies on cues from the counterpart. The decision over timing also depends on whether you need to make the strategy you have chosen distinguishable from another one (e.g., improvise from adapt) and want to clearly establish this strategy at the outset. (Note that if a negotiator has chosen to employ an agent or has successfully influenced the counterpart, then timing should not be an issue.) In sum, to decide on timing, you should weigh the benefits of additional information against the costs of losing an opportunity to take leadership and set the tone of the the interaction, a loss that includes being limited in your strategy options by the counterpart's strategy choice.

The three joint strategies are explicit and coordinated by definition. Once parties have decided to use a joint strategy, first moves consist of fleshing out particulars. Which mediator? What kinds of adjustments? What basic structure will underlie improvisation? These discussions may require the intermediate use of one of the five unilateral strategies.

Parties coordinating adjustment might consider trading off their respective priorities among the twelve cultural aspects in the negotiator profiles. If your counterpart values certain interpersonal conduct (protocol) more than the form of the agreement, for example, and you value the latter more than the former, the two of you could agree to adhere to a certain protocol and, on agreement, to draw up a comprehensive legal document. This pragmatic approach will probably appeal more to Western counterparts than to Asian ones, however, particularly if the Asian counterparts have only low or moderate cultural familiarity. So take this approach with caution rather than presuming that it will always work.

Whichever joint strategy you adopt, pursue it visibly in your moves. Especially in first-time encounters, a counterpart reads these moves as indications of one's integrity ("sincerity," in Japan) and commitment to coordination.

## Ongoing Efforts

A cross-cultural negotiator has myriad concerns and tasks, including vigilant attention to the cautions in the tables presented thus far. Still, as negotiations proceed, one's most important task is concentrating on interaction with the counterpart. Parties' actions and reactions evidence adherence to and departures from a given negotiation script, fill out the incomplete scripts associated with some strategies (i.e., adapt, improvise, effect symphony), and determine the ultimate effectiveness of every one of the eight culturally responsive strategies. These interactions occur so quickly that analyzing them makes them seem fragmented and in "slow motion." Nevertheless, some analysis can have tremendous value.

As you negotiate, shift most of your attention from the counterpart's culture to the counterpart as an individual. Specifically, monitor feedback from him or her, be prepared to modify, shift, or change your strategy, and develop *this* relationship.

**Monitor Counterpart's Feedback.** A counterpart's reactions to your ideas and conduct provide critical information about the counterpart personally and about the effectiveness of your chosen strategy with this particular individual. As you use that information to make continual adjustments and to evaluate your strategy, you may want to return to the four criteria of feasibility, coherence, appropriateness, and acceptability.

Some verbal and nonverbal cues transcend cultures in signaling positive or negative reception to a negotiator's use of a certain script. They range from a counterpart's statements ("Things are going well." "We don't do things that way") to a tightening of the corner of the mouth and cocked head, which convey contempt.[38]

> In one film of the "Going International" series, an American manager urges his Saudi counterpart to expedite delivery of supplies from the docks to the hospital building site. He points out that the supplies have already sat at the dock for a week just because of paperwork, he personally is "in a crisis," "nobody works here" on Thursday and Friday (it is now Tuesday), and during the upcoming Ramadan observance "things really slow down." At various points during these remarks, the Saudi does not respond at all to a direct question, perfunctorily sets aside a written schedule he receives, and looks disparagingly at the American's shoes. In the end, the Saudi states, "Mr. Wilson, my people have been living for many years without a hospital. We can wait two more weeks."[39]

Admittedly a counterpart's statements can be more or less honest or truthful, and the gradations are often fuzzy to an outsider. A number of cultures distinguish between saying what is socially acceptable (*tatemae* in Japanese) and saying what is truly on one's mind (*honne*). Other standards may also differ across cultures.

Many cues (e.g., silence) do not carry consistent meaning from culture to culture. Generally, individuals learn the culturally specific meanings as they become familiar with a culture. Negotiator profiles include some cues and imply others under dimensions such as "communication complexity" and "nature of persuasion." A negotiator can use these cues when he or she embraces the counterpart's culture.

Then again, some singularly powerful cues are very subtle. (See other cautions for strategy implementation in Table 6.)

*In the 1950s, an American couple—the lone foreigners—at a Japanese wedding banquet in Tokyo were socializing and dining like everyone else. All of a sudden, everyone else finished eating and left the reception. Residents of Japan for many years, the Americans concluded later that a signal had been sent at some point, and they had not even detected it.*

In cross-cultural interactions that do not involve embracing or inducing, or when a negotiator cannot clearly decipher the counterpart's strategy, nonuniversal cues are disconcertingly difficult to detect and interpret correctly. You can handle ambiguous cues (e g., the hesitation of a counterpart who has so far been loquacious) by keeping them in mind until additional cues and information convey and reinforce one message. Other ambiguous cues may be decoded only by asking the counterpart; alternatively, they remain unclear. Dealing with these cues is a very real and ongoing challenge.

**Be Prepared to Modify, Shift, or Change.** Even the well-prepared negotiator faces some surprises and some negative feedback in a negotiation. You want to be nimble enough to respond effectively. "Modifying" refers to refining implementation of a strategy without abandoning it; "shifting" refers to moving from one strategy to another within a previously planned combination of strategies; and "changing" refers to abandoning the strategy for another, unplanned one.

Making alterations is relatively easy with some counterparts.

*For the first round of the 1980–1981 Ford-Toyota talks, Ford negotiators employed a bilingual Japanese staffer from their Japan office. The Toyota team, apparently confident in their English language abilities, suggested that Ford not bring the interpreter to subsequent meetings, so that the negotiators could "talk directly." Ford negotiators obliged and changed their approach.*

On other occasions, one may have to explain modifications, shifts, and changes before they are made in order to minimize the odds of being perceived as unpredictable or deliberately disruptive. One may also deflect criticism by directly or indirectly associating these actions with changes in circumstances, the subject on the agenda, phase of the discussion, or, when negotiating as part of a team, personnel. For ideas about specific modifications to make, other than those prompted by your counterpart, review the counterpart's negotiator profile. Changes in strategy should be shaped by both a negotiator's culturally relevant capabilities and the strategy being abandoned. You may go relatively smoothly from an adapt to a coordinate adjustment strategy, for example, but not from inducing to embracing or from involving a mediator to employing an agent.

Over time, some movement between strategies may occur naturally (e.g., adapt to coordinate adjustment), but a *shift* as defined here involves a preconceived combination, or sequence, of strategies (e.g., coordinate adjustment, then effect symphony). A negotiator could plot a shift in strategies for certain types of counterpart feedback, variation in circumstances or relationship factors, or, especially during a long negotiation, for a jump in his or her level of cultural familiarity.

> TABLE 6  Cautions: Implementing Your Strategy

- Remember that cross-cultural interaction can be creative and satisfying, not always taxing.
- Stay motivated.
- Separate your observations of the counterpart's behavior from your interpretations and conclusions about his or her intentions.
- Notice the changes as well as the constants in the counterpart's behavior over time.
- Try to pick up even the subtle clues.
- Give some thought to whether the counterpart might be feigning low familiarity with your culture and language.
- Don't get in too deep; don't unwittingly lead the counterpart to think your familiarity with his or her culture is higher than it actually is.
- Accept some of the limitations that the counterpart's culture may impose on outsiders; not all limitations can be surmounted no matter how well or long you try.
- Balance your responsiveness to cultural factors with your other aspirations and needs as a negotiator.

**Develop *This* Relationship.**    Pragmatic Americans may view the cultivation of a relationship with the counterpart primarily as an instrument for strategy implementation. Concentrating on coherent interaction and a satisfactory relationship usually does enhance a culturally responsive strategy's effectiveness. But the strategy should also—even primarily—be seen as serving the relationship.

> *Riding describes the views of Mexican negotiators when they returned home from Washington after the negotiations over Mexico's insolvency in 1982: " 'We flew home relieved but strangely ungrateful,' one Mexican official recalled later. 'Washington had saved us from chaos, yet it did so in an uncharitable manner.' Even at such a critical moment, the substance and style of the relationship seemed inseparable."*[40]

Many of your non-American counterparts will be accustomed to an emphasis on relationships. Indeed, greater attention to relationship quality may be the most common distinction between negotiators from American and non-American cultures.

Developing a relationship with a particular counterpart requires an attentiveness to its life and rhythms. The form of your interaction can evolve across different scripts and approaches, especially after many encounters. There is also the potential for culturally driven conflict, which you should be willing to try to resolve.

Clearly, such a relationship should be treated dynamically, whether time is measured in minutes or in months. In that light, you can continuously learn about the counterpart and the counterpart's culture *and* educate the counterpart about you and your culture. Over a long period, you may experiment with a counterpart's ways in noncritical areas (at low risk) to develop skills within and across culturally responsive strategies. In this way, you can expand the number of feasible strategies, giving both you and the counterpart more flexibility in the ways you relate to each other.

## TOWARD CROSS-CULTURAL NEGOTIATING EXPERTISE

> *A friend of mine, a third-generation American in Japan who was bilingual in Japanese and English, used to keep a file of items that one must know…to function in Japan.…[He] never stopped discovering new things; he added to the file almost every day.*[41]

Over the years, many cross-cultural negotiators have essentially asked, "What happens when you're in Rome, but you're not Roman?" The most common advice available today was first offered 1,600 years ago: "Do as the Romans do." Yet these days, a non-Roman in Rome meets non-Romans as well as Romans and encounters Romans outside of Rome. The more we explore the variety of parties' capabilities and circumstances and the more we question the feasibility, coherence, appropriateness, and acceptability of "doing as Romans do," the more apparent the need becomes for additional culturally responsive strategies.

The range of strategies presented here provides every negotiator, including one relatively unfamiliar with a counterpart's culture, with at least two feasible options. Combinations of strategies further broaden the options.

If there is "something for everyone" here, the value of developing and sustaining cross-cultural expertise should still be clear. That includes high familiarity with a "Roman" culture—knowing the cognitive and behavioral elements of a Roman negotiating script and being able to use the script competently. The negotiator at the high familiarity level enjoys the broadest possible strategic flexibility for negotiations with Romans and the highest probability that, for a particular negotiation, one strategy will solidly meet all four selection criteria.

A negotiator can also gain a great deal from learning about more than one other culture. For lack of space I have concentrated on negotiations between two individuals, each belonging to one cultural group, but most cross-cultural negotiations involve more than two cultures: most individuals belong to more than one group; negotiations often occur between teams that have their own team cultures in addition to the members' ethnic, national, and organizational backgrounds; and multiparty, multicultural negotiations occur as well. In short, the non-Roman highly familiar with culture A still encounters cultures B, C, and D. Even though a negotiator may need to focus only on the one culture that a counterpart deems predominant at any one point in time, there are several to explore and manage across time, occasions, and people.[42]

*As soon as he was assigned to GM's Zurich headquarters in the mid-1980s, Lou Hughes, one of GM's main representatives in the GM-Toyota negotiations of the early 1980s, began taking German lessons because GM's main European plant was located in Germany. Now president of GM Europe, Hughes' effectiveness as an executive has been attributed in part to his cultural sensitivity and learning.[43]*

In the process of exploring other cultures, one may discover an idea or practice useful for all of one's negotiations.

*Another American negotiator in the GM-Toyota talks was so impressed with the Toyota negotiators' template for comparing parties' proposals that he adopted it and has relied on it since for his negotiations with others.*

It is in this spirit of continuous learning that this article has presented culturally responsive strategies, selection criteria, key steps in the choice process, and implementation ideas. If negotiators with a moderate amount of cross-cultural experience have the most to gain from these tools, first-time negotiators have before them a better sense of what lies ahead, and highly experienced negotiators can find some explanation for the previously unexplained and gain deeper understanding. In addition, the culture-individual considerations and ongoing challenges highlighted throughout the article will serve all cross-cultural negotiators. Perhaps we can all travel these paths more knowingly, exploring and building them as we go.

# REFERENCES

1. S. E. Weiss, "Negotiating with 'Romans'—Part 1," *Sloan Management Review,* Winter 1994, pp. 51–61. All examples that are not referenced come from personal communications or the author's experiences.

2. See J. K. Murnighan, *Bargaining Games: A New Approach to Strategic Thinking in Negotiations* (New York: William Morrow and Co., 1992), p. 22.

3. G. T. Savage, J. D. Blair, and R. L. Sorenson, "Consider Both Relationships and Substance When Negotiating Strategically," *The Executive* 3 (1989): 37–47; and S. E. Weiss, "Analysis of Complex Negotiations in International Business: The RBC Perspective," *Organization Science* 4 (1993): 269–300.

4. Attending to both culture and the individual has also been supported by: S. H. Kale and J. W. Barnes, "Understanding the Domain of Cross-National Buyer-Seller Interactions," *Journal of International Business Studies* 23 (1992): 101–132.

5. To speak of an "American culture" is not to deny the existence of cultures within it that are based on ethnic, geographic, and other boundaries. In fact, the strategies described in Part 1 of this article and the five steps described here can be applied to these cross-cultural negotiations as well. These ideas deserve the attention of those, for example, who are concerned about diversity in the workplace.

6. C. Thubron, *Behind the Wall* (London: Penguin, 1987), pp. 158, 186–187.

7. See R. Keesing as quoted in: W. B. Gudykunst and S. Ting-Toomey, *Culture and Interpersonal Communication* (Newbury Park, California: Sage, 1988), p. 29.

8. H. Binnendijk, ed., *National Negotiating Styles* (Washington, D.C.: Foreign Service Institute, U.S. Department of State, 1987).

9. For a review of popular books, see: S. Weiss-Wik, "Enhancing Negotiator's Successfulness: Self-Help Books and Related Empirical Research," *Journal of Conflict Resolution* 27 (1983): 706–739. For a recent research review, see: P. .J. D. Carnevale and D. G. Pruitt, "Negotiation and Mediation," *Annual Review of Psychology* 43 (1992): 531–582.

10. For self-examinations, see G. Althen, *American Ways: A Guide for Foreigners in the United States* (Yarmouth, Maine: Intercultural Press, 1988); E. T. Hall and M. R. Hall, *Understanding Cultural Differences* (Yarmouth, Maine: Intercultural Press, 1990); and E. C. Stewart and M. J. Bennett, *American Cultural Patterns* (Yarmouth, Maine: Intercultural Press, 1991). The views of outsiders include: A. de Tocqueville, *Democracy in America, 1805–1859* (New York: Knopf, 1980); L. Barzini, *The Europeans* (Middlesex, England: Penguin, 1983), pp. 219–253; and Y. Losoto, "Observing Capitalists at Close Range," *World Press Review,* April 1990, pp. 38–42.

11. The original framework appeared in: S. E. Weiss with W. Stripp, "Negotiating with Foreign Business Persons: An Introduction for Americans with Propositions on Six Cultures" (New York: New York University Graduate School of Business Administration, Working Paper No. 85–6, 1985).

12. Although I am not certain, my recollection is that the clients relented, and the bank team made the trip to South Africa. The point, however, is that the banker took a stand on an issue that struck values dear to him. Other examples include whether or not to make "questionable payments" and how to handle social settings in France and in Japan when one is allergic to alcohol or cigarette smoke. On payments, see: T. N. Gladwin and I. Walter, *Multinationals under Fire* (New York: John Wiley & Sons, 1980), p. 306. On smoking, see: W. E. Schmidt, "Smoking Permitted: Americans in Europe Have Scant Protection," *New York Times*, 8 September 1991, p. 31. On the other hand, some customs, while different, may not be abhorrent or worth contesting. An American male unaccustomed to greeting other men with "kisses" (the translation itself projects a bias) might simply go along with an Arab counterpart who has initiated such a greeting.

13. Murnighan (1992), p. 28; and Kale and Barnes (1992), p. 122.
14. J. L. Barsoux and P. Lawrence, "The Making of a French Manager," *Harvard Business Review*, July–August 1991, p. 60.
15. For example, for each of the four categories respectively, see: D. Chalvin, *L'entreprise négociatrice* (Paris: Dunod, 1984) and C. Dupont, *La négociation: conduite, théorie, applications,* 3rd ed. (Paris: Dalloz, 1990); N. C. G. Campbell et al., "Marketing Negotiations in France, Germany, the United Kingdom, and the United States," *Journal of Marketing* 52 (1988): 49–62; and G. Fisher, *International Negotiation: A Cross-Cultural Perspective* (Yarmouth, Maine: Intercultural Press, 1980); L. Bellenger, *La négociation* (Paris: Presses Universitaires de France, 1984); and A. Jolibert and M. Tixier, *La négociation commerciale* (Paris: Les éditions ESF, 1988); and Hall and Hall (1990).
16. Nonfiction writings include: J. Ardagh, *France Today* (London: Penguin, 1987); L. Barzini (1983); S. Miller, *Painted in Blood*: *Understanding Europeans* (New York: Atheneum, 1987); and T. Zeldin, *The French* (New York: Vintage, 1983). Fictional works include the classics by Jean-Paul Sartre and Andre Malraux and, more recently, A. Jardin, *Le Zébre* (Paris: Gallimard, 1988).
17. I will leave to others the debate over the effectiveness of training focused on "skills" versus other types of training. Somewhat surprisingly, some research on individuals' perceived need to adjust suggests that "interpersonal" and documentary training have comparable effects. See: P. C. Earley, "Intercultural Training for Managers," *Academy of Management Review* 30 (1987): 685–698. Note also that a number of negotiation seminars offered overseas do not directly increase familiarity with negotiation customs in those countries. These seminars import and rely on essentially American concepts and practices.
18. On cultural assimilator exercises, see: R. W. Brislin et al., *Intercultural Interactions: A Practical Guide* (Beverly Hills, California: Sage, 1986).
19. J. Watson and R. Lippitt, *Learning across Cultures* (Ann Arbor, Michigan: University of Michigan Press, 1955), as quoted in: A. T. Church, "Sojourner Adjustment," *Psychological Bulletin* 91 (1982): 544.
20. See Savage, Blair, and Sorenson (1989), p. 40. The following all include relationship factors (e.g., interest interdependence, relationship quality, concern for relationship) in their grids for strategic selection: R. Blake and J. S. Mouton, *The Managerial Grid* (Houston, Texas: Gulf, 1964); Gladwin and Walter (1980); and K. W. Thomas and R. H. Kilmann, *Thomas-Kilmann Conflict Mode Instrument* (Tuxedo, New York: Xicom, Inc., 1974).
21. For more extensive lists, see: Weiss (1993).
22. D. G. Pruitt and J. Z. Rubin, *Social Conflict: Escalation, Stalemate, and Settlement* (New York: Random House, 1986), pp. 33–34.
23. Weiss with Stripp (1985); F. Gauthey et al., *Leaders sans frontiéres* (Paris: McGraw-Hill, 1988), p. 149–156, 158; and R. Moran and W. Stripp, *Dynamics of Successful International Business Negotiations* (Houston, Texas: Gulf, 1991).
24. P. H. Gulliver, *Disputes and Negotiations* (New York: Academic, 1979), pp. 186–190, 200–207.
25. G. Hofstede, *Culture's Consequences* (Beverly Hills: Sage, 1984).
26. The literature on women and negotiation includes: M. Gibb-Clark, "A Look at Gender and Negotiations," *The Globe and Mail*, 24 May 1993, p. B7; J. Ilich and B. S. Jones, *Successful Negotiating Skills for Women* (New York: Playboy Paperbacks, 1981); and C. Watson and B. Kasten, "Separate Strengths? How Men and Women Negotiate" (New Brunswick, New Jersey: Rutgers University, Center for Negotiation and Conflict Resolution, Working Paper). On gender-based communication, see: D. Tannen, *You Just Don't Understand* (New York: William Morrow and Co., 1990).

27. N. J. Adler, "Pacific Basin Managers: Gaijin, Not a Woman," *Human Resource Management* 26 (1987): 169–191. This corresponds with the observation that "the different groups a person belongs to are not all equally important at a given moment." See: K. Lewin, *Resolving Social Conflicts* (New York: Harper & Row, 1948), p. 46 according to: Gudykunst and Ting-Toomey (1988), p. 201.

28. A. Riding, "Not Virile? The British are Stung," *New York Times*, 20 June 1991, p. A3. See the disguises used by a female American reporter in: S. Mackey, *The Saudis: Inside the Desert Kingdom* (New York: Meridian, 1987). On the other hand, the all-woman New York City-based firm of Kamsky and Associates has been widely recognized for their business deals in the People's Republic of China. See also: C. Sims, "Mazda's Hard-driving Saleswoman," *New York Times*, 29 August 1993, Section 3, p. 6; and M. L. Rossman, *The International Business Woman* (New York: Praeger, 1987).

29. This interaction format draws on a game theoretic perspective and borrows more directly from: T. A. Warschaw, *Winning by Negotiation* (New York: McGraw-Hill, 1980), p. 79.

30. T. C. Schelling, *The Strategy of Conflict* (New York: Oxford University Press, 1960), p. 53–58. The prominence of many courses of action would seem, however, to rest on assumptions that are culturally based and thus restricted rather than universal.

31. On risk-taking propensity, see: Gudykunst and Ting-Toomey (1988), pp. 153–160.

32. For discussions of similarity-attraction theory and research, see: K. R. Evans and R. F. Beltramini, "A Theoretical Model of Consumer Negotiated Pricing: An Orientation Perspective," *Journal of Marketing* 51 (1987): 58–73; J. N. P. Francis, "When in Rome? The Effects of Cultural Adaptation on Intercultural Business Negotiations," *Journal of International Business Studies* 22 (1991): 403–428; and J. L. Graham and N. J. Adler, "Cross-Cultural Interaction: The International Comparison Fallacy," *Journal of International Business Studies* 20 (1989): 515–537.

33. N. Dinges, "Intercultural Competence," in *Handbook of Intercultural Training*, vol 1., D. Landis and R. W. Brislin, eds. (New York: Pergamon, 1983), pp. 176–202.

34. Individual members do instigate change and may, over time, cause a group to change some of its values. Still, at any given point, a group holds to certain values and beliefs.

35. See Dinges (1983), pp. 184–185, 197; and D. J. Kealey, *Cross-Cultural Effectiveness: A Study of Canadian Technical Advisors Overseas* (Hull, Quebec: Canadian International Development Agency, 1990), p. 53–54. At the same time, Church cautiously concluded in his extensive review of empirical research that effects of personality, interest, and value on performance in a foreign culture had not yet demonstrated strong relationships. See: Church (1982), p. 557.

36. This advice parallels the now widely supported solution for the classic negotiator's dilemma of needing to stand firm to achieve one's goals and needing to make concessions to sustain movement toward an agreement: namely, "be firm but conciliatory," firm with respect to means. See: Pruitt and Rubin (1986), p. 153.

37. Sometimes counterparts do not actually desire an agreement but some side effect. Thus their behavior may differ from that described here. See: F. C. Ikle, *How Nations Negotiate* (Millwood, New York: Kraus Reprint, 1976), pp. 43–58.

38. See "Universal Look of Contempt," *New York Times*, 22 December 1986, p. C3.

39. "Going International" film series, Copeland Griggs Productions, San Francisco.

40. A. Riding, *Distant Neighbors: A Portrait of Mexicans* (New York: Vintage Books, 1984), p. 487.

41. E. T. Hall, *Beyond Culture* (Garden City, New York: Anchor Press, 1977), p. 109.

42. The assertion concerning the predominance of one culture at a time was made by: Lewin (1948).

43. A. Taylor, "Why GM Leads the Pack in Europe," *Fortune,* 17 May 1993, p. 84.

# 12
# Managing Diversity

THE MULTICULTURAL ORGANIZATION
*Taylor Cox, Jr.*

VIVE LA DIFFÉRENCE? GENDER AND MANAGEMENT IN THE NEW WORKPLACE
*Gary N. Powell*

MOTIVATION, LEADERSHIP, AND ORGANIZATION:  DO AMERICAN THEORIES APPLY ABROAD?
*Geert Hofstede*

# THE MULTICULTURAL ORGANIZATION

*Taylor Cox, Jr.*

As we begin the 1990s, a combination of workforce demographic trends and increasing globalization of business has placed the management of cultural differences on the agenda of most corporate leaders. Organizations' workforces will be increasingly heterogeneous on dimensions such as gender, race, ethnicity and nationality.  Potential benefits of this diversity include better decision making, higher creativity and innovation, greater success in marketing to foreign and ethnic minority communities, and a better distribution of economic opportunity.  Conversely, cultural differences can also increase costs through higher turnover rates, interpersonal conflict, and communication breakdowns.

> *To capitalize on the benefits and minimize the costs of worker diversity, organizations of the '90s must be quite different from the typical organization of the past.  Specifically, consultants have advised organizations to become "multicultural."[1]  The term refers to the degree to which an organization values cultural diversity and is willing to utilize and encourage it.[2]*
> *Leaders are being charged to create the multicultural organization, but what does such an organization look like, and what are the specific ways in which it differs from the traditional organization?  Further, what tools and techniques are available to assist organizations in making the transition from the old to the new?*

This article addresses these questions.  I have used an adaptation of the societal-integration model developed by Milton Gordon, as well as available information on the early experience of American organizations with managing diversity initiatives, to construct a model of the multicultural organization.

*Source*: *Academy of Management Executive*, © 1991, Vol. 5, No. 2, pp. 34–47.

# CONCEPTUAL FRAMEWORK

In his classic work on assimilation in the United States, Milton Gordon argued that there are seven dimensions along which the integration of persons from different ethnic backgrounds into a host society should be analyzed.[3] I use "integration" to mean the coming together and mixing of people from different cultural identity groups in one organization. A cultural identity group is a group of people who (on average) share certain values and norms distinct from those of other groups. Although the boundaries of these groups may be defined along many dimensions, I am primarily concerned with gender, race, ethnicity, and national origin. Gordon's seven dimensions are:

1. Form of acculturation
2. Degree of structural assimilation
3. Degree of intergroup marriage
4. Degree of prejudice
5. Degree of discrimination
6. Degree of identification with the dominant group of the host society
7. Degree of intergroup conflict (especially over the balance of power)

Although Gordon's interest was in societal-level integration, I believe his model can be easily and usefully adapted for analysis of cultural integration for organizations. Therefore, an adaptation of his seven-point framework is used here as a basis for describing organizational models for integrating culturally divergent groups. Exhibit I shows my proposed six-dimensional adaptation of the Gordon framework along with definitions of each term.

Acculturation is the method by which cultural differences between the dominant (host) culture and any minority culture groups are resolved or treated. There are several alternatives, the most prominent being: 1. a unilateral process by which minority culture members adopt the norms and values of the dominant group in the organization (*assimilation*); 2. a process by which both minority and majority culture members adopt some norms of the other group (*pluralism*); and 3. a situation where there is little adaptation on either side (*cultural separatism*).[4] Pluralism also means that minority culture members are encouraged to enact behaviors from their alternative culture as well as from the majority culture. They are therefore able to retain a sense of identity with their minority-culture group. Acculturation is concerned with the cultural (norms of behavior) aspect of integration of diverse groups, as opposed to simply their physical presence in the same location.

EXHIBIT I    Conceptual Framework for Analysis of Organizational Capability for Effective Integration of Culturally Diverse Personnel

| Dimension | Definition |
| --- | --- |
| 1. Acculturation | Modes by which two groups adapt to each other and resolve cultural differences |
| 2. Structural Integration | Cultural profiles of organization members including hiring job placement, and job status profile |
| 3. Information Integration | Inclusion of minority-culture members in informal networks and activities outside of normal working hours |
| 4. Cultural Bias | Prejudice and discrimination |
| 5. Organizational Identification | Feelings of belonging, loyalty and commitment to the organization |
| 6. Inter-group Conflict | Friction, tension and power struggles between cultural groups |

*Structural integration* refers to the presence of persons from different cultural groups in a single organization. Workforce profile data has typically been monitored under traditional equal opportunity and affirmative action guidelines. However, to get a proper understanding of structural integration it is important to look beyond organization-wide profile data, and examine cultural mix by function, level, and individual workgroup. This is because it is commonplace in American companies for gaps of fifteen to thirty percentage points to exist between the proportion of minority members in the overall labor force of a firm, and their proportion at middle and higher levels of management.[5]

Even within levels of an organization, individual work groups may still be highly segregated. For example, a senior human resource manager for a Fortune 500 firm who is often cited as a leader in managing diversity efforts, recently told me that there are still many "white-male bastions" in his company. As an assistant vice-president with responsibility for equal opportunity, he indicated that breaking down this kind of segregation was a focal point of his current job.

The *informal integration* dimension recognizes that important work-related contacts are often made outside of normal working hours and in various social activities and organizations. This item looks at levels of inclusion of minority-culture members in lunch and dinner meetings, golf and other athletic outings, and social clubs frequented by organization leaders. It also addresses mentoring and other informal developmental relationships in organizations.

*Cultural bias* has two components. Prejudice refers to negative attitudes toward an organization member based on his/her culture group identity, and discrimination refers to observable adverse behavior for the same reason. Discrimination, in turn, may be either personal or institutional. The latter refers to ways that organizational culture and management practices may inadvertently disadvantage members of minority groups. An example is the adverse effect that emphasizing aggressiveness and self-promotion has on many Asians. Many managers that I have talked to are sensitive to the fact that prejudice is a cognitive phenomenon and therefore much more difficult than discrimination for organization managers to change. Nevertheless, most acknowledge the importance of reducing prejudice for long-range, sustained change.

Prejudice may occur among minority-culture members as well as among dominant-culture members. Putting the debate over whether rates of prejudice differ for different groups aside, it must be emphasized that the practical impact of prejudice by majority-culture members is far greater than that of minority-culture members because of their far greater decision-making power (except under extraordinary conditions, such as those of South Africa).

*Organizational identification* refers to the extent to which a person personally identifies with, and tends to define himself or herself as a member in the employing organization. Levels of organizational identification have historically been lower in the United States than in other countries (notably Japan). Indications are that recent changes in organizational design (downsizing and de-layering) have reduced organizational identification even further. Although levels of organizational identification may be low in general in the U.S. workforce, we are concerned here with comparative levels of identification for members of different cultural identity groups.

Finally, *inter-group* conflict refers to levels of culture-group-based tension and interpersonal friction. Research on demographic heterogeneity among group members suggests that communication and cohesiveness may decline as members of groups become dissimilar.[6] Also, in the specific context of integrating minority-group members into organizations, concerns have been raised about backlash from white males who may feel threatened by these developments. It is therefore important to examine levels of inter-group conflict in diverse workgroups.

EXHIBIT II   Organizational Types

| Dimension of Integration | Monolithic | Plural | Multicultural |
|---|---|---|---|
| Form of Acculturation | Assimilation | Assimilation | Pluralism |
| Degree of Structural Integration | Minimal | Partial | Full |
| Integration into Informal Org. | Virtually none | Limited | Full |
| Degree of Cultural Bias | Both prejudice and discrimination against minority-culture group is prevalent | Progress on both prejudice & discrimination but both continue to exist especially institutional discrimination | Both prejudice and discrimination are eliminated |
| Levels of Organizational Identification* | Large majority-minority gap | Medium to large majority-minority gap | No majority-minority gap |
| Degree of Intergroup Conflict | Low | High | Low |

*Defined as difference between organizational identification levels between minorities and majorities.

# TYPES OF ORGANIZATIONS

This six-factor framework will now be employed to characterize organizations in terms of stages of development on cultural diversity.[7]   Three organization types will be discussed: the monolithic organization, the plural organization and the multicultural organization.  The application of the six-factor conceptual framework to describe the three organization types appears in Exhibit II.

## Monolithic Organization

The most important single fact about the monolithic organization is that the amount of structural integration is minimal.  The organization is highly homogeneous.  In the United States, this commonly represents an organization characterized by substantial white male majorities in the overall employee population with few women and minority men in management jobs. In addition, these organizations feature extremely high levels of occupational segregation with women and racioethnic minority men (racially and/or culturally different from the majority) concentrated in low-status jobs such as secretary and maintenance.  Thus, the distribution of persons from minority-cultural backgrounds is highly skewed on all three components of function, level, and workgroup.

To a large extent, the specifications on the frameworks' other five dimensions follow from the structural exclusion of people from different cultural backgrounds.  Women, racioethnic minority men, and foreign nationals who do enter the organization must adopt the existing organizational norms, framed by the white male majority, as a matter of organizational survival.

*Ethnocentrism and other prejudices cause little, if any, adaptation of minority-culture norms by majority group members. Thus, a unilateral acculturation process prevails. The exclusionary practices of the dominant culture also apply to informal activities. The severe limitations on career opportunities for minority-culture members creates alienation, and thus the extent to which they identify with the organization can be expected to be low compared to the more fully enfranchised majority group.*

One positive note is that intergroup conflict based on culture-group identity is minimized by the relative homogeneity of the workforce. Finally, because this organization type places little importance on the integration of cultural minority group members, discrimination, as well as prejudice, are prevalent.

While the white-male dominated organization is clearly the prototypical one for the monolithic organization, at least some of its characteristics are likely to occur in organizations where another identity group is dominant. Examples include minority-owned businesses, predominantly Black and predominantly Hispanic colleges, and foreign companies operating in the United States.

Aside from the rather obvious downside implications of the monolithic model in terms of under-utilization of human resources and social equality, the monolithic organization is not a realistic option for most large employers in the 1990s. To a significant degree, large U.S. organizations made a transition away from this model during the '60s and '70s. This transition was spurred by a number of societal forces, most notably the civil-rights and feminist movements, and the beginnings of changes in workforce demographics, especially in the incidence of career-oriented women. Many organizations responded to these forces by creating the plural organization.

## Plural Organization

The plural organization differs from the monolithic organization in several important respects. In general, it has a more heterogeneous membership than the monolithic organization and takes steps to be more inclusive of persons from cultural backgrounds that differ from the dominant group. These steps include hiring and promotion policies that sometimes give preference to persons from minority-culture groups, manager training on equal opportunity issues (such as civil rights law, sexual harassment, and reducing prejudice), and audits of compensation systems to ensure against discrimination against minority group members. As a result, the plural organization achieves a much higher level of structural integration than the monolithic organization.

The problem of skewed integration across functions, levels, and workgroups, typical in the monolithic organization, is also present in the plural organization. For example, in many large U.S. organizations racioethnic minorities now make up twenty percent or more of the total workforce. Examples include General Motors, Chrysler, Stroh Brewery, Phillip Morris, Coca-Cola, and Anheuser-Busch. However, the representations of non-whites in management in these same companies average less than twelve percent.[8] A similar picture exists in workgroups. For example, while more than twenty percent of the clerical and office staffs at General Motors are minorities, they represent only about twelve percent of technicians and thirteen percent of sales workers. Thus, the plural organization features partial structural integration.

Because of the greater structural integration and the efforts (cited previously) which brought it about, the plural organization is also characterized by some integration of minority-group members into the informal network, substantial reductions in discrimination, and some moderation of prejudicial attitudes    The improvement in employment opportunities should also create greater identification with the organization among minority-group members.

The plural organization represents a marked improvement over the monolithic organization in effective management of employees of different racioethnic, gender, and nationality backgrounds. The plural organization form has been prevalent in the U.S. since the late 1960s, and in my judgment, represents the typical large firm as we enter the 1990s. These organizations emphasize affirmative action approach to managing diversity. During the 1980s increased evidence of resentment toward this approach among white males began to surface. They argue that such policies, in effect, discriminate against white males and therefore perpetuate the practice of using racioethnicity, nationality, or gender as a basis for making personnel decisions. In addition, they believe that it is not fair that contemporary whites be disadvantaged to compensate for management errors made in the past. This backlash effect, coupled with the increased number of minorities in the organization, often creates greater intergroup conflict in the plural organization than was present in the monolithic organization.

While the plural organization achieves a measure of structural integration, it continues the assimilation approach to acculturation which is characteristic of the monolithic organization. The failure to address cultural aspects of integration is a major shortcoming of the plural organization form, and is a major point distinguishing it from the multicultural organization.

## The Multicultural Organization

In discussing cultural integration aspects of mergers and acquisitions, Sales and Mirvis argue that an organization which simply contains many different cultural groups is a plural organization, but considered to be multicultural only if the organization values this diversity.[9] The same labels and definitional distinction is applied here. The meaning of the distinction between containing diversity and valuing it follows from an understanding of the shortcomings of the plural organization as outlined previously. The multicultural organization has overcome these shortcomings. Referring again to Exhibit II, we see that the multicultural organization is characterized by:

1. Pluralism
2. Full structural integration
3. Full integration of the informal networks
4. An absence of prejudice and discrimination
5. No gap in organizational identification based on cultural identity group
6. Low levels of intergroup conflict

I submit that while few, if any, organizations have achieved these features, it should be the model for organizations in the 1990s and beyond.

## CREATING THE MULTICULTURAL ORGANIZATION

As I have discussed issues of managing diversity with senior managers from various industries during the past year, I have observed that their philosophical viewpoints cover all three of the organizational models of Exhibit II. The few who are holding on to the monolithic model often cite geographic or size factors as isolating their organizations from the pressures of change.

*Some even maintain that because American white males will continue to be the single largest gender/race identity group in the U.S. workforce for many years, the monolithic organization is still viable today. I think this view is misguided. By understanding the generic implications of managing diversity (that is, skill at managing work groups which include members who are culturally distinct from the organization's dominant group), it becomes clear that virtually all organizations need to improve capabilities to manage diverse workforces.*

*Further, focusing too much attention on external pressures as impetus for change, misses the fact that gross under-utilization of human resources and failure to capitalize on the opportunities of workforce diversity, represent unaffordable economic costs.*

Fortunately, the monolithic defenders, at least among middle and senior managers seem to represent a minority view. Based on my observations, the majority of managers today are in plural organizations, and many are already convinced that the multicultural model is the way of the future. What these managers want to know is how to transform the plural organization into the multicultural organization. Although progress on such transformations is at an early stage, information on the tools that have been successfully used by pioneering American organizations to make this transformation is beginning to accumulate.

Exhibit III provides a list of tools that organizations have used to promote organization change toward a multicultural organization. The exhibit is organized to illustrate my analysis of which tools are most helpful for each of the six dimensions specified in Exhibit I.

## Creating Pluralism

Exhibit III identifies seven specific tools for changing organizational acculturation from a unilateral process to a reciprocal one in which both minority-culture and majority-culture members are influential in creating the behavioral norms, values, and policies of the organization. Examples of each tool are given below.

*Training and Orientation Programs.* The most widely used tool among leading organizations is managing or valuing cultural diversity training. Two types of training are most popular: awareness and skill-building . The former introduces the topic of managing diversity and generally includes information on workforce demographics, the meaning of diversity, and exercises to get participants thinking about relevant issues and raising their own self-awareness. The skill-building training provides more specific information on cultural norms of different groups and how they may affect work behavior. Often, these two types of training are combined. Such training promotes reciprocal learning and acceptance between groups by improving understanding of the cultural mix in the organization.

Among the many companies who have made extensive use of such training are McDonnell Douglas, Hewlett Packard, and Ortho Pharmaceuticals. McDonnell Douglas has a program ("Woman-Wise and Business Savvy") focusing on gender differences in work-related behaviors. It uses same-gender group meetings and mixed-gender role-plays. At its manufacturing plant in San Diego, Hewlett Packard conducted training on cultural differences between American-Anglos and Mexican, Indochinese, and Filipinos. Much of the content focused on cultural differences in communication styles. In one of the most thorough training efforts to date, Ortho Pharmaceuticals started its three-day training with small groups (ten to twelve) of senior managers and eventually trained managers at every level of the company.

Specific data on the effectiveness of these training efforts is hard to collect, but a study of seventy-five Canadian consultants found that people exposed to even the most rudimentary form of training on cultural diversity are significantly more likely to recognize the impact of cultural diversity on work behavior and to identify the potential advantages of cultural heterogeneity in organizations.[10]

In addition, anecdotal evidence from managers of many companies indicates that valuing and managing diversity training represents a crucial first step for organization change efforts.

New member orientation programs are basic in the hiring processes of many organizations. Some companies are developing special orientations as part of its managing diversity initiatives. Proctor and Gamble's "On Boarding" program, which features special components for women and minority hires and their managers, is one example.

| Model Dimension | Tools |
|---|---|
| I. Pluralism<br>Objective/s:Training<br>—create a two-way socialization process<br>—ensure influence of minority-culture perspective on core organization norms and values | 1. Managing/valuing diversity (MVD) training.<br>2. New member orientation program<br>3. Language training<br>4. Diversity in key committees<br>5. Explicit treatment of diversity in mission statements<br>6. Advisory groups to senior management<br>7. Create flexibility in norm systems |
| II. Full Structural Integration<br>Objective/s<br>—no correlation between culture-group identity and job status | 1. Education programs<br>2. Affirmative action programs<br>3. Targeted career development programs<br>4. Changes in manager performance appraisal and awards<br>5. HR policy and benefit changes |
| III. Integration in Informal Networks<br>Objective/s<br>—eliminate barriers to entry and participation | 1. Mentoring programs<br>2. Company sponsored social events |
| IV. Cultural Bias<br>Objective/s<br>—eliminate discrimination<br>—eliminate prejudice | 1. Equal Opportunity seminars<br>2. Focus groups<br>3. Bias reduction training<br>4. Research<br>5. Task Forces |
| V. Organizational Identification<br>—no correlation between identity group and levels of organization identification | 1. All items from the other five dimensions apply here |
| VI. Intergroup Conflict<br>Objective/s<br>—minimize interpersonal conflict based on group-identity<br>—minimize backlash by dominant group members | 1. Survey feedback<br>2. Conflict management training<br>3. MVD training<br>4. Focus groups |

Language training is important for companies hiring American Asians, Hispanics, and foreign nationals. To promote pluralism, it is helpful to offer second language training to Anglos as well as the minority-culture employees, and take other steps to communicate that languages other than English are valued. Leaders in this area include Esprit De Corp Economy Color Card, and Pace Foods. For many years, the women's clothier Esprit De Corp has offered courses in Italian and Japanese. At Economy Color Card, work rules are printed in both Spanish and English. Pace Foods, where thirty-five percent of employees are Hispanic, goes a step farther by printing company policies and also conducting staff meetings in Spanish and English. Motorola is a leader in the more traditional training for English as a second language where classes are conducted at company expense and on company time.

*Insuring Minority-Group Input and Acceptance.* The most direct and effective way to promote influence of minority-culture norms on organizational decision making is to achieve cultural diversity at all organization levels. However, an important supplemental method is through ensuring diversity on key committees. An example is the insistence of *USA Today* President Nancy Woodhull on having gender, racioethnic, educational, and geographic diversity represented in all daily news meetings. She attributes much of the company's success to this action.

Another technique is explicitly mentioning the importance of diversity to the organization in statements of mission and strategy. By doing this, organizations foster the mindset that increased diversity is an opportunity and not a problem. Examples of organizations that have done this are The University of Michigan and the Careers Division of the National Academy of Management. The latter group has fostered research addressing the impact of diversity on organizations by explicitly citing this as part of its interest.

Another way to increase the influence of minority-group members on organizational culture and policy is by providing specially composed minority advisory groups direct access to the most senior executives of the company. Organizations which have done this include Avon, Equitable Life Assurance, Intel, and U.S. West. At Equitable, committees of women, Blacks and Hispanics (called "Business Resource Groups") meet with the CEO to discuss important group issues and make recommendations on how the organizational environment might be improved. CEO John Carver often assigns a senior manager to be accountable for following up on the recommendations. U.S. West has a thirty-three member "Pluralism Council" which advises senior management on plans for improving the company's response to increased workforce diversity.

Finally, a more complex, but I believe potentially powerful, tool for promoting change toward pluralism is the development of flexible, highly tolerant climates that encourage diverse approaches to problems among all employees. Such an environment is useful to workers regardless of group identity, but is especially beneficial to people from nontraditional cultural backgrounds because their approaches to problems are more likely to be different from past norms. A company often cited for such a work environment is Hewlett Packard. Among the operating norms of the company which should promote pluralism are: 1. Encouragement of informality and unstructured work; 2. Flexible work schedules and loose supervision; 3. Setting objectives in broad terms with lots of individual employee discretion over how they are achieved; 4. A policy that researchers should spend at least ten percent of company time exploring personal ideas. I would suggest that Item 4 be extended to all management and professional employees.

## Creating Full Structural Integration

*Education Efforts.* The objectives of creating an organization where there is no correlation between one's culture-identity group and one's job status implies that minority-group members are well rep-resented at all levels, in all functions, and in all work groups. Achievement of this goal requires that skill and education levels be evenly distributed. Education statistics indicate that the most serious problems occur with Blacks and Hispanics.[11]

A number of organizations have become more actively involved in various kinds of education programs. The Aetna Life Insurance Company is a leader. It has initiated a number of programs including jobs in exchange for customized education taught by community agencies and private schools, and its own in-house basic education programs. The company has created an Institute for Corporate Education with a full-time director. Other companies participating in various new education initiatives include PrimAmerica, Quaker Oats, Chase Manhattan Bank, Eastman Kodak, and Digital Equipment. In Minnesota, a project headed by Cray Research and General Mills allows businesses to create schools of their own design. I believe that business community involvement in joint efforts with educational institutions and community leaders to promote equal achievement in education is critical to the future competitiveness of U.S. business. Business leaders should insist that economic support be tied to substantive programs which are jointly planned and evaluated by corporate representatives and educators

*Affirmative Action.* In my opinion, the mainstay of efforts to create full structural integration in the foreseeable future will continue to be affirmative action programs. While most large organizations have some kind of program already, the efforts of Xerox and Pepsico are among the standouts.

> *The Xerox effort, called "The Balanced Workforce Strategy," is noteworthy for several reasons including: an especially fast timetable for moving minorities up; tracking representation by function and operating unit as well as by level; and national networks for minority-group members (supported by the company) to provide various types of career support. Recently published data indicating that Xerox is well ahead of both national and industry averages in moving minorities into management and professional jobs, suggests that these efforts have paid off (Wall Street Journal, November 5, 1989).*

Two features of Pepsico's efforts which are somewhat unusual are the use of a "Black Managers Association" as a supplemental source of nominees for promotion to management jobs, and the practice of hiring qualified minorities directly into managerial and professional jobs.

*Career Development.* A number of companies including Mobil Oil, IBM, and McDonalds have also initiated special career development efforts for minority personnel. IBM's long standing "Executive Resource System" is designed to identify and develop minority talent for senior management positions. McDonald's "Black Career Development Program" provides career enhancement advice, and fast-track career paths for minorities. Company officials have stated that the program potentially cuts a fifteen year career path to regional manager by fifty percent.

*Revamping Reward Systems.* An absolutely essential tool for creating structural integration is to ensure that the organizations' performance appraisal and reward systems reinforce the importance of effective diversity management. Companies that have taken steps in this direction include The Federal National Mortgage (Fannie Mae), Baxter Health Care, Amtrak, Exxon, Coca-Cola, and Merck. Fannie Mae, Baxter, Coca-Cola, and Merck all tie compensations to manager performance on diversity management efforts. At Amtrak, manager promotion and compensation are tied to performance on affirmative action objectives, and at Exxon, evaluations of division managers must include a review of career development plans for at least ten women and minority men employees.

For this tool to be effective, it needs to go beyond simply including effective management of diversity among the evaluation and reward criteria. Attention must also be given to the amount of weight given to this criterion compared to other dimensions of job performance. How performance is measured is also important. For example, in addition to work-group profile statistics, subordinate evaluations of managers might be useful. When coded by cultural group, differences in perceptions based on group identity can be noted and used in forming performance ratings on this dimension.

*Benefits and Work Schedules.* Structural integration of women, Hispanics, and Blacks is facilitated by changes in human resource policies and benefit plans that make it easier for employees to balance work and family role demands. Many companies have made such changes in areas like child care, work schedules, and parental leave. North Carolina National Bank, Arthur Anderson, Levi Strauss, and IBM are examples of companies that have gone farther than most. NCNB's "select time" project allows even officers and professionals in the company to work part-time for several years and still be considered for advancement. Arthur Anderson has taken a similar step by allowing part-time accountants to stay "on-track" for partnership promotions. Levi Strauss has one of the most

362

comprehensive work-family programs in the country covering everything from paternity leave to part-time work with preservation of benefits. These companies are leaders in this area because attention is paid to the impact on advancement opportunities and fringe-benefits when employees take advantage of scheduling flexibility and longer leaves of absence. This kind of accommodation will make it easier to hire and retain both men and women in the '90s as parents struggle to balance work and home time demands. It is especially important for women, Hispanics, and Blacks because cultural traditions put great emphasis on family responsibilities. Organization change in this area will promote full structural integration by keeping more racioethnic minorities and white women in the pipeline.

## Creating Integration in Informal Networks

*Mentoring and Social Events.* One tool for including minorities in the informal networks of organizations is company-initiated mentoring programs that target minorities. A recent research project in which a colleague and I surveyed 800 MBAs indicated that racioethnic minorities report significantly less access to mentors than whites. If company-specific research shows a similar pattern, this data can be used to justify and bolster support among majority-group employees for targeted mentoring programs. Examples of companies which have established such targeted mentoring programs are Chemical Bank and General Foods.

A second technique for facilitating informal network integration is company-sponsored social events. In planning such events, multiculturalism is fostered by selecting both activities and locations with a sensitivity to the diversity of the workforce.

*Support Groups.* In many companies, minority groups have formed their own professional associations and organizations to promote information exchange and social support. There is little question that these groups have provided emotional and career support for members who traditionally have not been welcomed in the majority's informal groups. A somewhat controversial issue is whether these groups hinder the objective of informal-network integration. Many believe that they harm integration by fostering a "we-versus-they" mentality and reducing incentives for minorities to seek inclusion in informal activities of majority-group members. Others deny these effects, I'm not aware of any hard evidence on this point. There is a dilemma here in that integration in the informal networks is at best a long-term process and there is widespread skepticism among minorities as to its eventual achievement. Even if abolishing the minority-group associations would eventually promote full integration, the absence of a support network of any kind in the interim could be a devastating loss to minority-group members. Therefore, my conclusion is that these groups are more helpful than harmful to the overall multiculturalism effort.

## Creating a Bias-Free Organization

Equal opportunity seminars, focus groups, bias-reduction training, research, and task forces are methods that organizations have found useful in reducing culture-group bias and discrimination. Unlike prejudice, discrimination is a behavior and therefore more amenable to direct control or influence by the organization. At the same time, the underlying cause of discrimination is prejudice. Ideally, efforts should have at least indirect effects on the thought processes and attitudes of organization members. All of the tools listed, with the possible exception of task forces, should reduce prejudice as well as discrimination.

Most plural organizations have used equal opportunity seminars for many years. These include sexual harassment workshops, training on civil rights legislation, and workshops on sexism and racism.

*Focus Groups.* More recently, organizations like Digital Equipment have used "focus groups" as in-house, on-going mechanisms to explicitly examine attitudes, beliefs, and feelings about culture-group differences and their effects on behavior at work. At Digital, the centerpiece of its "valuing differences" effort is the use of small groups (called Core Groups) to discuss four major objectives: 1.) stripping away stereotypes; 2.) examining underlying assumptions about out-groups; 3.) building significant relationships with people one regards as different; 4.) raising levels of personal empowerment. Digital's experience suggests that a breakthrough for many organizations will be achieved by the simple mechanism of bringing discussion about group differences out in the open. Progress is made as people become more comfortable directly dealing with the issues.

*Bias-Reduction Training.* Another technique for reducing bias is through training specifically designed to create attitude change. An example is Northern Telecom's 16-hour program designed to help employees identify and begin to modify negative attitudes toward people from different cultural backgrounds. Eastman Kodak's training conference for its recruiters is designed to eliminate racism and sexism from the hiring process. This type of training often features exercises that expose stereotypes of various groups which are prevalent but rarely make explicit and may be subconscious. Many academics and consultants have also developed bias-reduction training. An example is the "Race Relation Competence Workshop," a program developed by Clay Alderfer and Robert Tucker of Yale University. They have found that participants completing the workshop have more positive attitudes toward Blacks and inter-race relations.

*Leveraging Internal Research.* A very powerful tool for reducing discrimination and (·to a smaller extent) prejudice, is to conduct and act on internal research on employment experience by cultural group. Time Inc. conducts an annual evaluation of men and women in the same jobs to ensure comparable pay and equal treatment. A second example comes from a large utility company which discovered that minority managers were consistently under-represented in lists submitted by line managers for bonus recommendations. As a result of the research, the company put pressure on the managers to increase the inclusion of minority managers. When that failed, the vice president of human resources announced that he would no longer approve the recommendations unless minorities were adequately represented. The keys to the organization change were, first obtaining the data identifying the problem and then acting on it. My experience suggests that this type of research-based approach is underutilized by organizations.

*Task Forces.* A final tool for creating bias-free organizations is to form task forces that monitor organizational policy and practices for evidence of unfairness. An example of what I consider to be a well-designed committee is the affirmative action committee used by Phillip Morris which is composed of senior managers and minority employees. This composition combines the power of senior executives with the insight into needed changes that the minority representatives can provide. Of course, minority culture-group members who are also senior managers are ideal but, unfortunately, such individuals are rare in most organizations.

## Minimizing Intergroup Conflict

Experts on conflict management have noted that a certain amount of interpersonal conflict is inevitable and perhaps even healthy in organizations.[12] However, conflict becomes destructive when it is excessive, not well managed, or rooted in struggles for power rather than the differentiation of ideas. We are concerned here with these more destructive forms of conflict which may be present with diverse workforces due to language barriers, cultural clash, or resentment by majority-group members of what they may perceive as preferential, and unwarranted treatment of minority-group members.

*Survey Feedback.* Probably the most effective tool for avoiding intergroup conflict (especially the backlash form that often accompanies new initiatives targeting minority groups of the organization) is the use of survey feedback. I will give three examples. As one of the most aggressive affirmative action companies of the past decade, Xerox has found that being very open with all employees about the specific features of the initiative as well the reasons for it, was helpful in diffusing backlash by whites. This strategy is exemplified by the high profile which Chairman David Kearns has taken on the company's diversity efforts.

A second example is Proctor and Gamble's use of data on the average time needed for new hires of various culture groups to become fully integrated into the organization. They found that "join-up" time varied by race and gender with white males becoming acclimated most quickly, and black females taking the longest of any group. This research led to the development of their "on-boarding program" referred to earlier.

A final example is Corning Glass Works' strategy of fighting white-male resistance to change with data showing that promotion rates of their group was indeed much higher than that of other groups. This strategy has also been used by U.S. West which recently reported on a 1987 study showing that promotion rates for white men were seven times higher than white women and sixteen times higher than non-white women.

The beauty of this tool is that it provides the double benefit of a knowledge base for planning change, and leverage to win employee commitment to implement the needed changes.

*Conflict-Resolution Training.* A second tool for minimizing intergroup conflict is management training in conflict resolution techniques. Conflict management experts can assist managers in learning and developing skill in applying alternative conflict management techniques such as mediation and superordinate goals. This is a general management skill which is made more crucial by the greater diversity of workforces in the '90s.

Finally, the managing and valuing diversity training and focus group tools discussed previously are also applicable here. AT&T is among the organizations which have explicitly identified stress and conflict reduction as central objectives of its training and focus group efforts.

## CONCLUSION

Increased diversity presents challenges to business leaders who must maximize the opportunities that it presents while minimizing its costs. To accomplish this, organizations must be transformed from monolithic or plural organizations to a multicultural model. The multicultural organization is characterized by pluralism, full integration of minority-culture members both formally and informally, an absence of prejudice and discrimination, and low levels of inter-group conflict; all of which should reduce alienation and build organizational identity among minority group members. The organization that achieves these conditions will create an environment in which all members can contribute to their maximum potential, and in which the "value in diversity" can be fully realized.

## ENDNOTES

1. See, for example, Lennie Copeland, "Valuing Workplace Diversity," *Personnel Administrator,* November 1988; Badi Foster et al., "Workforce Diversity and Business," *Training and Development Journal*, April 1988, 38–42; and R. Roosevelt Thomas, "From Affirmative Action to Affirming Diversity," *Harvard Business Review,* Vol. 2, 1990, 107–117.
2. This definition has been suggested by Afsavch Nahavandi and Ali Malekzadeh, "Acculturation in Mergers and Acquisitions," *Academy of Management Review*, Vol. 13, 83.

3. In his book, *Assimilation in American Life* (New York: Oxford University Press, 1964) Gordon uses the term assimilation rather than integration. However, because the term assimilation has been defined in so many different ways, and has come to have very unfavorable connotations in recent years for many minorities, I will employ the term integration here.
4. These definitions are loosely based on J. W. Berry, 1983, "Acculturation: A Comparative Analysis of Alternative Forms," in R. J. Samuda and S. L. Wood: *Perspectives in Immigrant and Minority Education*, 1983, 66–77.
5. This conclusion is based on data from nearly 100 large organizations as cited in "Best Places for Blacks to Work," *Black Enterprise*, February 1986 and February 1989 and in Zeitz and Dusky, *Best Companies for Women*, 1988.
6. Examples of this research include, Harry Triandis, "Some Determinants of Interpersonal Communication," *Human Relations*, Vol. 13, 1960, 279–287 and J. R. Lincoln and J. Miller, "Work and Friendship Ties in Organizations," *Administrative Science Quarterly*, Vol. 24, 1979, 181–199.
7. The concept of stages of development toward the multicultural organization has been suggested in an unpublished paper titled "Toward the Multicultural Organization" written by Dan Reigle and Jarrow Merenivitch of the Proctor and Gamble Company. I credit them with helping me to recognize the evolutionary nature of organizational responses to workforce diversity.
8. See note 5.
9. A. L. Sales and P. H. Mirvis, "When Cultures Collide: Issues of Acquisitions," in J. R. Kimberly and R. E. Quinn, *Managing Organizational Transition*, 1984, 107–133.
10. For details on this study see, Nancy J. Adler, *International Dimensions of Organizational Behavior* (Kent Publishing Co., 1986) 77–83.
11. For example, see the book by William Julius Wilson which reviews data on educational achievement by Blacks and Hispanics in Chicago, *The Truly Disadvantaged: Inner City, the Underclass and Public Policy* (The University of Chicago Press, 1987). Among the facts cited is that less than half of all Blacks and Hispanics in inner city schools graduate within four years of high school enrollment and only four in ten of those who do graduate read at the eleventh grade level or above.
12. For example, see *Organization Behavior: Conflict in Organizations*, by Gregory Northcraft and Margaret Neale (The Dryden Press, 1990), 221.

# VIVE LA DIFFERÉNCE?
# GENDER AND MANAGEMENT IN THE NEW WORKPLACE

*Gary N. Powell*

There has been a dramatic change in the "face" of management over the last two decades. That face is now female more than one-third of the time. What are the implications for the practice of management? Most of us are aware of traditional stereotypes about male-female differences, but how well do these stereotypes apply to the managerial ranks? Do female and male managers differ in their basic responses to work situations and their overall effectiveness (and if so, in what ways), or are they really quite similar?

*Note*: This chapter is reprinted with permission of the author. © Gary N. Powell. An earlier version appeared in *Academy of Management Executive*.

If you believe recent books and articles in business magazines, female and male managers bring very different personal qualities to their jobs. For example, Jan Grant, in an *Organizational Dynamics* article entitled "Women as Managers: What They Can Offer to Organizations,"[1] argued that women have unique qualities that make them particularly well-suited as managers. Instead of forcing women to fit the male model of managerial success, emphasizing such qualities as independence, competitiveness, forcefulness, and analytical thinking, Grant argues that organizations should place greater emphasis on such female qualities as affiliation and attachment, cooperativeness, nurturance, and emotionality.

Felice Schwartz's *Harvard Business Review* article, "Management Women and the New Facts of Life,"[2] triggered a national debate over the merits of "mommy tracks" (though she did not use this term herself). She proposed that corporations 1) distinguish between "career-primary women" who put their careers first and "career and family" women who seek a balance between career and family, 2) nurture the careers of the former group as potential top executives, and 3) offer flexible work arrangements and family supports to the latter group in exchange for lower opportunities for career advancement. Women were assumed to be more interested in such arrangements, and thereby less likely to be suitable top executives, than men; there has been less discussion over the merits of "daddy tracks."

Judy Rosener, in a Harvard Business Review article entitled "Ways Women Lead," concluded:

> The first female executives, because they were breaking new ground, adhered to many of the "rules of conduct" that spelled success for men. Now a second wave of women is making its way into top management, not by adopting the style and habits that have proved successful for men but by drawing on the skills and attitudes they developed from their shared experience as women. These second-generation managerial women are drawing on what is unique to their socialization as women and creating a different path to the top. They are seeking and finding opportunities in fast-changing and growing organizations to show that they can achieve results—in a different way. They are succeeding because of—not in spite of—certain characteristics generally considered to be "feminine" and inappropriate in leaders.[3]

Rosener labeled the leadership style more associated with women as "interactive leadership," because leaders who exhibit it actively promote positive interactions with subordinates by encouraging participation, sharing power and information, and stimulating excitement about work. In contrast, she labeled the leadership style more associated with men as "command-and-control leadership." Marilyn Loden, in a book entitled *Feminine Leadership, or How to Succeed in Business Without Being One of the Boys*, similarly concluded that female managers are more capable than male managers of exhibiting "feminine leadership," which she sees organizations as needing more than ever. She summarized her view about male-female differences in the managerial ranks in three words: "*Vive la différence!*"[4]

Women and men certainly differ in their success within the ranks of management. Although women have made great strides in entering management since 1970, with the overall proportion of women managers rising from 16% to 42%, the proportion of women who hold top management positions is less than 5%.[5] This could be due simply to the average male manager being older and more experienced than the average female manager. After all, managerial careers invariably start at the bottom. If there were no basic differences between male and female managers, it would be just a matter of time until the proportion of women was about the same at all managerial levels.

But *are* there basic differences between male and female managers? Traditional gender stereotypes state that males are more masculine (e.g., self-reliant, aggressive, competitive, decisive) and females more feminine, e.g., sympathetic, gentle, shy, sensitive to the needs of others).[6] Grant's Rosener's, and Loden's views of male-female differences mirror these stereotypes. However, there is disagreement over the applicability of these stereotypes to managers. Four distinct points of view have emerged:

1. *No differences.* Women who pursue the nontraditional career of manager reject the feminine stereotype and have goals, motives, personalities, and behaviors that are similar to those of men who pursue managerial careers.

2. *Stereotypical differences favoring men.* Female and male managers differ in ways predicted by gender stereotypes as a result of early socialization experiences that leave men better suited as managers.

3. *Stereotypical differences favoring women.* Female and male managers differ in accordance with gender stereotypes due to early socialization experiences, but femininity is particularly needed by managers in today's work world.

4. *Nonstereotypical differences.* Female and male managers differ in ways opposite to gender stereotypes because women managers have had to be exceptional to compensate for early socialization experiences that are different from those of men.

In this chapter, I briefly review the research evidence on gender differences in management that has been gathered since women managers were first noticed by researchers in the mid-1970s to determine the level of support for each of these points of view.[7] Possible differences are considered in personal traits, behavior, effectiveness, values, commitment, and subordinates' responses (see Exhibit I). Implications of the review are then discussed.

EXHIBIT I   Gender Differences in Management

| Dimension | Results |
| --- | --- |
| TRAITS | In AT&T study, offsetting gender differences in traits led to no gender difference in overall management potential. No difference in most other studies. However, when difference found, it tends to be a nonstereotypical difference favoring women. |
| BEHAVIOR | |
| Task style | No difference for actual managers. |
| Interpersonal style | No difference for actual managers. |
| Democratic versus autocratic leadership | Stereotypical difference. |
| EFFECTIVENESS | No difference. |
| VALUES | No difference. |
| COMMITMENT | No difference. |
| SUBORDINATES' RESPONSES | No difference in responses to actual managers. |

# DO FEMALE AND MALE MANAGERS DIFFER?

One of the most extensive research studies ever conducted of managers and their personal characteristics took place in the Bell System through its parent, the American Telephone and Telegraph Company (AT&T). Prior to the court-ordered 1984 divestiture of its regional operating companies, the Bell System was the nation's largest business enterprise. In the late 1970s and early 1980s, AT&T initiated a study of 344 lower-level managers who were considered to be representative of those managers from whom Bell's future middle and upper-level managers would come, nearly half of whom were women.[8]

These managers went through three days of assessment center exercises. Extensive comparisons were made in terms of background, work interests, personality, motivation, abilities, and overall management potential. Women had advantages in administrative ability, interpersonal skills and sensitivity, written communication skills, energy, and inner work standards. Men had advantages in company loyalty, motivation to advance within the company, and attentiveness to power structures. The greatest gender difference was that of masculinity/femininity: Men were more likely to have traditionally masculine interests, whereas women were more likely to have traditionally female interests. There were no gender differences in intellectual ability, leadership ability, oral communication skills, or stability of performance. When they took these tradeoffs into account, the assessors judged women and men as having similar management potential. Forty-five percent of the women and 39% of the men were judged to have the potential to attain middle management in the Bell System within 10 years. Douglas Bray, who directed the AT&T studies until he was succeeded by Ann Howard, concluded: "Vive la no différence!"

Other research on managers' personality and motivation generally has found few gender differences. Both male and female managers are high in their motivation to manage. Many researchers have found that women and men managers score essentially the same on psychological tests of needs and motives that are supposed to predict managerial success. When differences have been found in the relative strength of motives possessed by female and male managers, they have generally favored women and been contrary to gender stereotypes. In a study of nearly 2,000 managers that was similar to the AT&T study in scope but examined managers from different organizations, Susan Donnell and Jay Hall found that women managers reported lower basic needs and higher needs for self-actualization. Women were seen as exhibiting a "more mature and higher-achieving motivational profile" than their male counterparts, being more concerned with opportunities for growth, autonomy, and challenge and less concerned with work environment and pay.[9]

Most studies of gender differences in managerial or leader behavior have examined two aspects of leadership style. The first, called *task style*, refers to the extent to which the manager initiates work activity, organizes it, and defines the way work is to be done. The second, called *interpersonal style,* refers to the extent to which the manager engages in activities that tend to the morale and welfare of people in the work setting. Individuals' task and interpersonal styles of leadership are typically regarded as independent dimensions. That is, a manager may be high in both task and interpersonal style, low in both, or high in one but not the other. A third aspect of leadership style that has been frequently studied is the extent to which the leader exhibits *democratic leadership,* which allows subordinates to participate in decision-making, versus *autocratic leadership* which discourages such participation; these are considered to be opposite styles.

Although a "meta-analysis" of research studies found gender differences in each of these three dimensions of leadership style, the size of the difference and the circumstances under which it appeared varied. Small gender differences were found in task style and interpersonal style; however, these differences appeared only for subjects in laboratory experiments and for non-leaders who were assessed on how they would behave if they were actually leaders. There were no gender differences in the task and interpersonal styles of actual managers. In contrast, a more pronounced gender difference was found in individuals' democratic versus autocratic style. Women tended to be more democratic, less autocratic leaders than men, a difference that appeared for individuals in all settings—actual managers, non-managers, and subjects in laboratory experiments. These results offer support for both a no-differences and stereotypical-differences view.[10]

A separate meta-analysis found no sex difference in overall leader effectiveness. However, men fared better in male-dominated work environments such as the military, whereas women fared better in female-dominated work settings such as schools. These results support a no-differences view overall, but a stereotypical-differences view within work environments dominated by either sex.[11]

The values of managers, especially top executives, usually receive attention only when a corporate scandal takes place. Personal values have considerable influence on how managers handle the responsibilities of their jobs. Values may influence perceptions of others, solutions to problems, and the sense of what constitutes individual and organizational success. Values also influence what managers believe to be ethical and unethical behavior and whether they accept or resist organizational pressures and goals. Most evidence suggests that similarities outweigh differences in the value systems of male and female managers. With few exceptions, gender differences have not been found in the work values and personal business ethics of managers.[12]

The sense of commitment that managers bring to their work is also important, at least as far as their organizations are concerned. More committed managers might be expected to work longer hours when the need arises, to relocate when the organization wishes, and to place a greater importance on the interests of the organization than on personal interests when the two are in conflict. Managers who are less committed are more likely to believe that "a job is a job" and balk when they are asked to do anything that is outside of their normal routines. Gender stereotypes suggest that women lack the high level of commitment essential for a successful managerial career. However, a meta-analysis found no gender difference in commitment to either professional or nonprofessional jobs. Instead, commitment is best explained by other factors. For example, age and education are positively linked to commitment. Greater job satisfaction, more meaningful work, and greater utilization of skills are also associated with stronger commitment.[13]

Even if male and female managers did not differ in any respect, subordinates could still have different preferences for working with them or respond to them differently. General tendencies to prefer male managers to female managers are present in many workers. A survey of employed adult Americans found that almost half preferred a boss of a specific sex. Among those workers who expressed a preference, 85% of men and 65% of women said they would rather work for a male boss. In contrast, studies of actual managers and their subordinates have typically found that subordinates express similar satisfaction with male and female managers. Overall, subordinates do not appear to respond differently to male and female leaders for whom they have actually worked. Once subordinates have experienced both female and male managers, the effects of gender stereotypes tend to disappear and managers are treated more as individuals than as representatives of their sex.[14]

In summary, the title of this section of the chapter posed the question, "Do female and male managers differ?" The research evidence suggests the answer, "They differ in some ways and at some times, but, for the most part, they do not differ."

Although the AT&T study found several gender differences in managerial traits, these differences in motivational profiles found in other studies tend to favor female managers. Women and men do not differ in their effectiveness as leaders, although some situations favor women and others favor men. A stereotypical difference is present in the tendency to exhibit democratic versus autocratic leadership. In contrast, gender differences in task and interpersonal style are confined to laboratory studies and not present in the leadership styles of actual managers. Results suggest an absence of gender differences in values and commitment. Actual male and female managers provoke similar responses in subordinates. Thus, few gender differences favoring either men or women have been found.

Overall, this review supports the "no differences" view of gender differences in management. However, it does not necessarily mean that female and male managers are completely interchangeable. The leadership roles that women and men hold in organizations typically provide clear guidelines for acceptable behavior. Managers become socialized into their roles early in their careers. In addition, they are selected by their organizations to fill leadership roles because they are seen as meeting a specific set of attitudinal and behavioral criteria. These factors decrease the likelihood that female and male managers will differ substantially in the personal qualities they exhibit on their jobs, even if they are initially inclined to act differently. Because women remain in the minority in the managerial ranks, especially in the upper levers, they experience strong pressures to conform to standards based on a stereotypically masculine view of managerial effectiveness.

## IMPLICATIONS FOR ORGANIZATIONS

The implications of this review are clear: *If there are no differences between male and female managers, organizations should not act as if there are.* Instead, they should follow two principles in their actions:

1. To be gender-blind in how they fill open managerial positions, except when consciously trying to offset the effects of past discrimination.

2. To try to minimize differences in the job experiences of equally qualified male and female managers, so that artificial gender differences in managers' career patterns and success do not arise.

Grant, Rosener, and Loden based their recommendations on a "stereotypical differences favoring women" view. Although this view receives some support in my review, especially in women's greater tendency to exhibit democratic versus autocratic leadership, it is not supported by bulk of the research evidence. Nevertheless, it has been used as the basis for sweeping assertions. For example, Grant argued that organizations will benefit from placing greater value on women's special qualities as follows:[15]

> These "human resources" skills are critical in helping to stop the tide of alienation, apathy, cynicism, and low morale in organizations....If organizations are to become more humane, less alienating, and more responsive to the individuals who work for them, they will probably need to learn to value process as well as product. Women have an extensive involvement in the processes of our society—an involvement that derives from their greater participation in the reproductive process and their early experience of family life....Thus women may indeed be the most radical force available in bringing about organizational change.

Human resources skills are certainly essential to today's organizations. Corporations that are only concerned with getting a product out and pay little attention to their employees' needs are unlikely to have a committed work force or to be effective in the long run. However, women are at risk when corporations assume that they have a monopoly on human resources skills. The risk is that they will be placed exclusively in managerial jobs that particularly call for social sensitivity and interpersonal skills in dealing with individuals and special-interest groups, e.g., public relations, human resources management, consumer affairs, corporate social responsibility. These jobs are typically staff functions, peripheral to the more powerful line functions of finance, sales, and production and seldom regarded in exalted terms by line personnel. Women managers are disproportionately found in such jobs, outside the career paths that most frequently lead to top management jobs. Corporations that rely on Grant's assertions about women's special abilities could very well perpetuate this trend.

Thus it is very important that the facts about gender differences in management be disseminated to key decision makers. When individuals hold onto stereotypical views about gender differences that are not supported by the research evidence, either of two approaches may be tried:

1. Send them to programs such as cultural diversity workshops to make them aware of the ways in which biases related to gender (as well as race, age, etc.) can affect their decisions and to learn how to keep these biases from occurring. For example, Levi Strauss put all of its executives, including the president, through an intense three-day program designed to make them examine their attitudes toward women and minorities on the job. In Ortho Pharmaceuticals, Avon, and Citizens Insurance, every *employee* received diversity awareness training.[16]

2. Recognize that beliefs and attitudes are difficult to change and focus on changing behavior instead. If people are motivated to be gender-blind in their decision making by an effective performance appraisal and reward system backed by the CEO, they often come to believe in what they are doing.

Organizations should do whatever they can to equalize the job experiences of equally qualified female and male managers. This means abandoning the model of a successful career as an uninterrupted sequence of promotions to positions of greater responsibility heading toward the top ranks. All too often, any request to take time out from career for family reasons, either by a women or a man, is seen as evidence of lack of career commitment.

Schwartz based her recommendations on a real gender difference: More women than men leave work for family reasons due to the demands of maternity and the differing traditions and expectations of the sexes. However, her solution substitutes a different type of gender difference that such women remain at work with permanently reduced career opportunities. It does not recognize that women's career orientation may change during their careers. Women could temporarily leave the fast track for the mommy track, but then be ready and able to resume the fast track later. Once they were classified as "career-and-family," they would find it difficult to be reclassified as "career-primary" even if their career commitment returned to its original level.

More women and men are adopting a holistic approach to their careers and lives. By providing the opportunity for alternative work schedules and family supports for all employees, not just career-and-family women as Schwartz recommended, organizations can help women and men achieve their full potential for success. Firms that offer flexible work arrangements are not only more likely to retain their employees. They may also attract more qualified employees (even for less pay) who view the opportunity to take advantage of a flexible work arrangement as a worthwhile substitute for higher pay at another firm.[17]

Corporations could offer "parent tracks" rather than "mommy tracks" and accurately believe that they were treating their female and male employees alike. However, if women tended to opt for such programs more than men (as is often the case) and anyone who opted for one was held back in pursuing a future managerial career, the programs would contribute to a gender difference in access to top management positions. Automatic restrictions should not be placed on the later career prospects of individuals who choose alternative work arrangements. Those who wish to return to the fast track should be allowed to do so once they demonstrate the necessary skills and commitment.

Thus organizations need to create both standard and flexible career paths so *all* the needs of all their employees may be fully met. A firm that develops a flexible as well as a core work force may may find considerable advantages during downturns in the business cycle, as layoffs may be avoided in favor of "sabbaticals" for those who prefer a flexible career pattern. Organizations need to reorganize their work forces in this manner to better meet the needs of employees as well as business cycles.

There are other ways by which organizations can minimize gender differences in managers' job experiences. For example, the majority of both male and female top executives have had one or more mentors, and mentorship has been critical to their advancement and success. However, lower-level female managers have greater difficulty in finding mentors than male managers at equivalent levels, due to the smaller number of female top executives and the fact that people like to mentor people like themselves. This gives lower-level male managers an advantage in achieving career success.[18]

Some companies try to overcome barriers of gender by assigning highly placed mentors to promising lower-level managers. For example, at the Bank of America, senior executives are asked to serve as mentors to thee or four junior managers for a year at a time. Formal mentoring programs have also been implemented at the Jewel Companies, Aetna, Bell Labs, Merrill Lynch, Federal Express, and the U.S. General Accounting Office. However, good mentoring relationships cannot be engineered. They must emerge from the spontaneous and mutual involvement of two people who see value in relating to each other. If people feel coerced into or mismatched in mentoring relationships, the relationships are likely flounder. Instead, a better approach for organizations is to offer educational programs about mentoring and its role in career development, and then identify who is doing good mentoring and reward them for it.[19]

Companies also influence job experiences through the training and development programs that they encourage or require their managers to take. These programs contribute to a gender difference in job experiences if 1) men and women are systematically diagnosed to have different developmental needs and thereby go through different programs, or 2) men and women are deliberately segregated in such programs. However, female managers do not need to be sent off by themselves for "assertiveness training" as they were in the past. Instead, they need access to advanced training and development activities, such as executive MBAs or executive leadership workshops, just like male managers do.

Programs such as the Executive Women Workshop offered by the Center for Creative Leadership (CCL) are open only to women. In addition, some firms, such as Northwestern Bell, have their own executive leadership programs for women only. Such programs are intended "to give female managers the unique opportunity to understand their individual developmental needs and establish personal and career objectives," as the CCL's catalog puts it. In general, though, women and men should be recommended for training and development programs according to their individual needs rather than their sex. Almost half of the companies regarded as "the best companies for women" rely on training and workshops to develop their high-potential managerial talent. However, many of these companies, including Bidermann Industries, General Mills, Hewitt Associates, Neiman-Marcus, and PepsiCo, have no special programs for women; they simply assign the best and brightest people regardless of sex.[20]

In conclusion, organizations should not assume that male and female managers differ in personal qualities. They also should make sure that their policies, practices, and programs minimize the creation of gender differences in managers' experiences on the job. There is little reason to believe that either women or men make superior managers. Instead, there are likely to be excellent, average, and poor managerial performers within each sex. Success in today's highly competitive marketplace calls for organizations to make best use of the talent available to them. They need to identify, develop, encourage, and promote the most effective managers, regardless of sex. If they do so, what expression will best capture the difference between them and their less successful competitors? *Vive la différence!*

# REFERENCES

1. J. Grant, "Women as Managers: What They Can Offer to Organizations," *Organizational Dynamics*, 16 (No. 3, Winter 1988): 56–63.
2. F. N. Schwartz, "Management Women and the New Facts of Life," *Harvard Business Review*, 67 (No. 1, January/February 1989): 65–76.
3. J. B. Rosener, "Ways Women Lead," *Harvard Business Review*, 68 (No. 6, November/December 1990), pp. 119–120.
4. M. Loden, *Feminine Leadership, or How to Succeed in Business Without Being One of the Boys* (New York: Times Books, 1985), p. 79.
5. U.S. Department of Labor, Bureau of Labor Statistics, *Employment and Earnings,* 39 (No. 5, May 1992), computed from p. 29, table A–22; A. B. Fisher, "When Will Women Get to the Top?" *Fortune*, 126 (No. 6, 21 September 1992): 44–56.
6. For a review of research on gender stereotypes, see R. D. Ashmore, F. K. Del Boca , and A. J. Wohlers, "Gender Stereotypes," in *The Social Psychology of Female-Male Relations: A Critical Analysis of Central Concepts*, ed. R. D. Ashmore and F. K. Del Boca (Orlando: Academic Press, 1986).
7. For a more extensive report of this review with complete references, see G. N. Powell, Chapter 6, "Managing People," in *Women and Men in Management*, 2nd. ed. (Newbury Park, CA: Sage, 1993).
8. A. Howard and D. W. Bray, *Managerial Lives in Transition: Advancing Age and Changing Times* (New York: Guilford, 1988).
9. S. M. Donnell and J. Hall, "Men and Women as Managers: A Significant Case of No Significant Difference," *Organizational Dynamics,* 8 (No. 4, Spring 1980), p. 71.
10. A. H. Eagly and B. T. Johnson, "Gender and Leadership Style: A Meta-Analysis," *Psychological Bulletin,* 108 (1990): 233–256.
11. A. H. Eagly, "Gender and Leadership" (Presentation delivered at the Annual Meeting of the American Psychological Association, San Francisco, 1991).
12. C. Mottaz, "Gender Differences in Work Satisfaction, Work Related Rewards and Values, and the Determinants of Work Satisfaction," *Human Relations*, 39 (1986): 359–378; G. E. Stevens, "The Personal Business Ethics of Male and Female Managers: A Comparative Study" (Paper delivered at the Annual Meeting of the Academy of Management, Dallas, 1983).
13. F. F. Aven, Jr., B. Parker, and G. M. McEvoy, "Gender and Attitudinal Commitment to Organizations: A Meta-Analysis," *Journal of Business Research*, 26 (1993): 63–73; L. H. Chusmir, "Job Commitment and the Organizational Woman," *Academy of Management Review*, 7 (1982): 595–602.
14. M. B. Rubner, "More Workers Prefer a Man in Charge," *American Demographics*, 13 (No. 6, June 1991): 11; J. Adams, R. W. Rice, and D. Instone, "Follower Attitudes toward Women and Judgments Concerning Performance by Female and Male Leaders," *Academy of Management Journal*, 27 (1984): 636–643; H. F. Ezell, C. A. Odewahn, and J. D. Sherman, "The Effects of Having Been Supervised by a Woman on Perceptions of Female Managerial Competence: *Personnel Psychology*, 34 (1981): 291–299.
15. Grant, p. 62.
16. T. Cox, Jr., *Cultural Diversity in Organizations: Theory, Research and Practice* (San Francisco: Berrett-Koehler, 1993), pp. 236–237; B. Zeitz and L. Dusky, "Levi Strauss," in *The Best Companies for Women* (New York: Simon and Schuster, 1988).

17. M. A. Ferber and B. O'Farrell with L. R. Allen, eds., *Work and Family: Policies for a Changing Work Force* (Washington, DC: National Academy Press, 1991); D. E. Friedman and E. Galinsky, "Work and Family Issues: A Legitimate Business Concern," in *Work, Families, and Organizations*, ed. S. Zedeck (San Francisco: Jossey-Bass, 1992).

18. G. R. Roche, "Much Ado About Mentors," *Harvard Business Review*, 79 (No. 1, January/February 1979): 14–28; B. R. Ragins, "Barriers to Mentoring: The Female Manager's Dilemma," *Human Relations*, 42 (1989): 1–22.

19. K. E. Kram, "Mentoring in the Workplace," in *Career Development in Organizations*, ed. D. T. Hall and Associates (San Francisco: Jossey-Bass, 1986); M. Murray with M. A. Owen, *Beyond the Myths and Magic of Mentoring: How to Facilitate an Effective Mentoring Program* (San Francisco: Jossey-Bass, 1991).

20. Center for Creative Leadership, "Executive Women Workshop," in 1992 *Programs Catalog* (Greensboro, NC: Center for Creative Leadership, 1992), p. 8; Zeitz and Dusky.

# MOTIVATION, LEADERSHIP, AND ORGANIZATION: DO AMERICAN THEORIES APPLY ABROAD?

*Geert Hofstede*

A well-known experiment used in organizational behavior courses involves showing the class an ambiguous picture—one that can be interpreted in two different ways. One such picture represents either an attractive young girl or an ugly old woman, depending on the way you look at it. Some of my colleagues and I use the experiment, which demonstrates how different people in the same situation may perceive quite different things. We start by asking half of the class to close their eyes while we show the other half a slightly altered version of the picture—one in which only the young girl can be seen—for only five seconds. Then we ask those who just saw the young girl's picture to close their eyes while we give the other half of the class a five-second look at a version in which only the old woman can be seen. After this preparation we show the ambiguous picture to everyone at the same time.

The results are amazing—most of those "conditioned" by seeing the young girl first see only the young girl in the ambiguous picture, and those "conditioned" by seeing the old woman tend to see only the old woman. We then ask one of those who perceive the old woman to explain to one of those who perceive the young girl what he or she sees, and vice versa, until everyone finally sees both images in the picture. Each group usually finds it very difficult to get its views across to the other one and sometimes there's considerable irritation at how "stupid" the other group is.

*Source*: Reprinted from *Organizational Dynamics*, Summer 1980. © 1980, AMACOM, a division of American Management Associations. All rights reserved.

# CULTURAL CONDITIONING

I use this experiment to introduce a discussion on cultural conditioning. Basically, it shows that in five seconds I can condition half a class to see something different from what the other half sees. If this is so in the simple classroom situation, how much stronger should differences in perception of the same reality be between people who have been conditioned by different education and life experience—not for five seconds, but for twenty, thirty, or forty years?

I define culture as the collective mental programming of the people in an environment. Culture is not a characteristic of individuals; it encompasses a number of people who were conditioned by the same education and life experience. When we speak of the culture of a group, a tribe, a geographical region, a national minority, or a nation, culture refers to the collective mental programming that these people have in common; the programming that is different from that of other groups, tribes, regions, minorities or majorities, or nations.

Culture, in this sense of collective mental programming, is often difficult to change; if it changes at all, it does so slowly. This is so not only because it exists in the minds of the people but, if it is shared by a number of people, because it has become crystallized in the institutions these people have built together: their family structures, educational structures, religious organizations, associations, forms of government, work organizations, law, literature, settlement patterns, buildings and even, as I hope to show, scientific theories. All of these reflect common beliefs that derive from the common culture.

Although we are all conditioned by cultural influences at many different levels—family, social, group, geographical region, professional environment—this article deals specifically with the influence of our national environment: that is, our country. Most countries' inhabitants share a national character that's more clearly apparent to foreigners than to the nationals themselves; it represents the cultural mental programming that the nationals tend to have in common.

# NATIONAL CULTURE IN FOUR DIMENSIONS

The concept of national culture or national character has suffered from vagueness. There has been little consensus on what represents the national culture of, for example, Americans, Mexicans, French, or Japanese. We seem to lack even the terminology to describe it. Over a period of six years, I have been involved in a large research project on national cultures. For a set of 40 independent nations, I have tried to determine empirically the main criteria by which their national cultures differed. I found four such criteria, which I label dimensions; these are Power Distance, Uncertainty Avoidance, Individualism-Collectivism, and Masculinity-Femininity. To understand the dimensions of national culture, we can compare it with the dimensions of personality we use when we describe individuals' behavior. In recruiting, an organization often tries to get an impression of a candidate's dimensions of personality, such as intelligence (high-low); energy level (active-passive); and emotional stability (stable-unstable). These distinctions can be refined through the use of certain tests, but it's essential to have a set of criteria whereby the characteristics of individuals can be meaningfully described. The dimensions of national culture I use represent a corresponding set of criteria for describing national cultures.

Characterizing a national culture does not, of course, mean that every person in the nation has all the characteristics assigned to that culture. Therefore, in describing national cultures we refer to the common elements within each nation—the national norm—but we are not describing the individuals. This should be kept in mind when interpreting the four dimensions explained in the following paragraphs.

The four dimensions of national culture were found through a combination of theoretical reasoning and massive statistical analysis, in what is most likely the largest survey material ever obtained with a single questionnaire. This survey material was collected between 1967 and 1973 among employees of subsidiaries of one large U.S.-based multinational corporation (MNC) in 40 countries around the globe. The total data bank contains more than 116,000 questionnaires collected from virtually everyone in the corporation, from unskilled workers to research Ph.D.s and top managers. Moreover, data were collected twice—first during a period from 1967 to 1969 and a repeat survey during 1971 to 1973. Out of a total of about 150 different survey questions (of the precoded answer type), about 60 deal with the respondents' beliefs and values; these were analyzed for the present study. The questionnaire was administered in the language of each country; a total of 20 language versions had to be made. On the basis of these data, each of the 40 countries could be given an index score for each of the four dimensions.

I was wondering at first whether differences found among employees of one single corporation could be used to detect truly national culture differences. I also wondered what effect the translation of the questionnaire could have had. With this in mind, I administered a number of the same questions from 1971 to 1973 to an international group of about 400 managers from different public and private organizations following management development courses in Lausanne, Switzerland. This time, all received the questionnaire in English. In spite of the different mix of respondents and the different language used, I found largely the same differences between countries in the manager group that I found among the multinational personnel. Then I started looking for other studies, comparing aspects of national character across a number of countries on the basis of surveys using other questions and other respondents (such as students) or on representative public opinion polls. I found 13 such studies; these compared between 5 and 19 countries at a time. The results of these studies showed a statistically significant similarity (correlation) with one or more of the four dimensions. Finally, I also looked for national indicators (such as per capita national income, inequality of income distribution, and government spending on development aid) that could logically be supposed to be related to one or more of the dimensions. I found 31 such indicators—of which the values were available for between 5 and 40 countries—that were correlated in a statistically significant way with at least one of the dimensions. All these additional studies (for which the data were collected by other people, not by me) helped make the picture of the four dimensions more complete. Interestingly, very few of these studies had even been related to each other before, but the four dimensions provide a framework that shows how they can be fit together like pieces of a huge puzzle. The fact that data obtained within a single MNC have the power to uncover the secrets of entire national cultures can be understood when it's known that the respondents form well-matched samples from their nations: They are employed by the same firm (or its subsidiary); their jobs are similar (I consistently compared the same occupations across the different countries); and their age categories and sex compositions were similar—only their nationalities differed. Therefore, if we look at differences in survey answers between multinational employees in countries A, B, C, and so on, the general factor that can account for the differences in the answers is national culture.

# Power Distance

The first dimension of national culture is called *Power Distance*. It indicates the extent to which a society accepts the fact that power in institutions and organizations is distributed unequally. It's reflected in the values of the less powerful members of society as well as in those of the more powerful ones. A fuller picture of the difference between small Power Distance and large Power Distance societies is shown in Figure 1. Of course, this shows only the extremes; most countries fall somewhere in between.

FIGURE 1  The Power Distance Dimension

| Small Power Distance | Large Power Distance |
| --- | --- |
| Inequality in society should be minimized. | There should be an order of inequality in this world in which everybody has a rightful place: high and low are protected by this order. |
| All people should be interdependent. | A few people should be independent; most should be dependent. |
| Hierarchy means an inequality of roles, established for convenience. | Hierarchy means existential inequality. |
| Superiors consider subordinates to be "people like me." | Superiors consider subordinates to be a different kind of people. |
| Subordinates consider superiors to be "people like me" | Subordinates consider superiors to be a different kind of people. |
| Superiors are accessible. | Superiors are inaccessible. |
| The use of power should be legitimate and is subject to the judgment as to whether it is good or evil. | Power is a basic fact of society that antedates good or evil. Its legitimacy is irrelevant. |
| All should have equal rights. | Power-holders are entitled to privileges. |
| Those in power should try to look less powerful than they are. | Those in power should try to look as powerful as possible. |
| The system is to blame. | The underdog is to blame. |
| The way to change a social system is to redistribute power. | The way to change a social system is to dethrone those in power. |
| People at various power levels feel less threatened and more prepared to trust people. | Other people are a potential threat to one's power and can rarely be trusted. |
| Latent harmony exists between the powerful and the powerless. | Latent conflict exists between the powerful and the powerless. |
| Cooperation among the powerless can be based on solidarity. | Cooperation among the powerless is difficult to attain because of their low-faith-in-people norm. |

# Uncertainty Avoidance

The second dimension, *Uncertainty Avoidance*, indicates the extent to which a society feels threatened by uncertain and ambiguous situations and tries to avoid these situations by providing greater career stability, establishing more formal rules, not tolerating deviant ideas and behaviors, and believing in absolute truths and the attainment of expertise. Nevertheless, societies in which uncertainty avoidance is strong are also characterized by a higher level of anxiety and aggressiveness that creates, among other things, a strong inner urge in people to work hard. (See Figure 2.)

# Individualism-Collectivism

The third dimension encompasses *Individualism* and its opposite, *Collectivism*. Individualism implies a loosely knit social framework in which people are supposed to take care of themselves and of their immediate families only, while collectivism is characterized by a tight social framework in which people distinguish between in-groups and out-groups; they expect their ingroup (relatives, clan, organizations) to look after them, and in exchange for that they feel they owe absolute loyalty to it. A fuller picture of this dimension is presented in Figure 3.

FIGURE 2    The Uncertainty Avoidance Dimension

| Weak Uncertainty Avoidance | Strong Uncertainty Avoidance |
| --- | --- |
| The uncertainty inherent in life is more easily accepted and each day is taken as it comes. | The uncertainty inherent in life is felt as a continuous threat that must be fought. |
| Ease and lower stress are experienced. | Higher anxiety and stress are experienced. |
| Time is free. | Time is money. |
| Hard work, as such, is not a virtue. | There is an inner urge to work hard. |
| Aggressive behavior is frowned upon. | Aggressive behavior of self and others is accepted. |
| Less showing of emotions is preferred. | More showing of emotions is preferred. |
| Conflict and competition can be contained on the level of fair play and used constructively. | Conflict and competition can unleash aggression and should therefore be avoided. |
| More acceptance of dissent is entailed. | A strong need for consensus is involved. |
| Deviation is not considered threatening; greater tolerance is shown. | Deviant persons and ideas are dangerous; intolerance holds sway. |
| The ambiance is one of the less nationalism. | Nationalism is pervasive. |
| More positive feelings toward normal people are seen. | Younger people are suspect. |
| There is more willingness to take risks in life. | There is a great concern with security in life. |
| The accent is on relativism, empiricism. | The search is for ultimate, absolute truths and values. |
| There should be as few rules as possible. | There is a need for written rules and regulations. |
| If rules can not be kept, we should change them. | If rules can not be kept, we are sinners and should repent. |
| Belief is placed in generalists and common sense. | Beliefs is placed in experts and their knowledge. |
| The authorities are there to serve the citizens. | Ordinary citizens are incompetent compared with the authorities. |

FIGURE 3　The Individualism Dimension

| Collectivist | Individualist |
|---|---|
| In society, people are born into extended families or clans who protect them in exchange for loyalty. | In society, everybody is supposed to take care of himself /herself and his/her immediate family. |
| "We" consciousness holds sway. | "I" consciousness holds sway. |
| Identity is based on the social system. | Identity is based on the individual. |
| There is emotional dependence of individual on organizations and institutions. | There is emotional independence of individual from organizations or institutions. |
| The involvement with organizations is moral. | The involvement with organizations is calculative. |
| The emphasis is on belonging to organizations; membership is the ideal. | The emphasis is on individual initiative and achievement; leadership the ideal. |
| Private life is invaded by organizations and clans to which one belongs; opinions are predetermined. | Everybody has a right to a private life and opinion. |
| Expertise, order, duty, and security are provided by organization or clan. | Autonomy, variety, pleasure, and individual financial security are sought in the system. |
| Friendships are predetermined by stable social relationships, but there is need for prestige within these relationships. | The need is for specific friendships. |
| Belief is placed in group decisions. | Belief is placed in individual decisions. |
| Value standards differ for in-groups and out-groups (particularism). | Value standards should apply to all (universalism). |

## Masculinity

The fourth dimension is called *Masculinity* even though, in concept, it encompasses its opposite pole, *Femininity*. Measurements in terms of this dimension express the extent to which the dominant values in society are "masculine"—that is, assertiveness, the acquisition of money and things, and *not* caring for others, the quality of life, or people. These values were labeled "masculine" because, *within* nearly all societies, men scored higher in terms of the values' positive sense than of their negative sense (in terms of assertiveness, for example, rather than its lack)—even though the society as a whole might veer toward the "feminine" pole. Interestingly, the more an entire society scores to the masculine side, the wider the gap between its "men's" and "women's" values (see Figure 4).

FIGURE 4　The Masculinity Dimension

| Feminine | Masculine |
|---|---|
| Men needn't be assertive, but can also play nurturing roles. | Men should be assertive. Women should be nurturing. |
| Sex roles in society are more fluid. | Sex roles in society are clearly differentiated. |
| There should be equality between the sexes. | Men should dominate in society. |
| Quality of life is important. | Performance is what counts. |
| You work in order to live. | You live in order to work |
| People and environment are important. | Money and things are important. |
| Interdependence is the ideal. | Independence is the ideal. |
| Service provides the motivation. | Ambition provides the drive. |
| One sympathizes with the unfortunate. | One admires the successful achiever. |
| Small and slow are beautiful. | Big and fast are beautiful. |
| Unisex and androgyny are ideal. | Ostentatious manliness ("machismo") is appreciated. |

# A Set of Cultural Maps of the World

Research data were obtained by comparing the beliefs and values of employees within the subsidiaries of one large multinational corporation in 40 countries around the world. These countries represent the wealthy countries of the West and the larger, more prosperous of the Third World countries. The Socialist block countries are missing, but data are available for Yugoslavia (where the corporation is represented by a local, self-managed company under Yugoslavian law). It was possible, on the basis of mean answers of employees on a number of key questions, to assign an index value to each country on each dimension. As described in the box on page 377, these index values appear to be related in a statistically significant way to a vast amount of other data about these countries, including both research results from other samples and national indicator figures.

Because of the difficulty of representing four dimensions in a single diagram, the position of the countries on the dimensions is shown in Figures 5, 6, and 7 for two dimensions at a time. The vertical and horizontal axes and the circles around clusters of countries have been drawn subjectively, in order to show the degree of proximity of geographically or historically related countries. The three diagrams thus represent a composite set of cultural maps of the world.

Of the three "maps," those in Figure 5 (Power Distance x Uncertainty Avoidance) and Figure 7 (Masculinity x Uncertainty Avoidance) show a scattering of countries in all corners—that is, all combinations of index values occur. Figure 6 (Power Distance x Individualism), however, shows one empty corner: The combination of Small Power Distance and Collectivism does not occur. In fact, there is a tendency for Large Power Distance to be associated with Collectivism and for Small Power Distance with Individualism. However, there is a third factor that should be taken into account here: national wealth. Both Small Power Distance and Individualism go together with greater national wealth (per capita gross national product). The relationship between Individualism and Wealth is quite strong, as Figure 6 shows. In the upper part (Collectivist) we find only the poorer countries, with Japan as a borderline exception. In the lower part (Individualism), we find only the wealthier countries. If we look at the poorer and wealthier countries separately, there is no longer any relationship between Power Distance and Individualism.

The 40 Countries: Abbreviations Used in Figures 5, 6, and 7

| ARG | Argentina | FRA | France | JAP | Japan | SIN | Singapore |
|-----|-----------|-----|--------|-----|-------|-----|-----------|
| AUL | Australia | GBR | Great Britain | MEX | Mexico | SPA | Spain |
| AUT | Austria | GER | Germany (West) | NET | Netherlands | SWE | Sweden |
| BEL | Belgium | GRE | Greece | NOR | Norway | SWI | Switzerland |
| BRA | Brazil | HOK | Hong Kong | NZL | New Zealand | TAI | Taiwan |
| CAN | Canada | IND | India | PAK | Pakistan | THA | Thailand |
| CHL | Chile | IRA | Iran | PER | Peru | TUR | Turkey |
| COL | Colombia | IRE | Ireland | PHI | Philippines | USA | United States |
| DEN | Denmark | ISR | Israel | POR | Portugal | VEN | Venezuela |
| FIN | Finland | ITA | Italy | SAF | South Africa | YUG | Yugoslavia |

FIGURE 5   The Position of 40 Countries on the Power Distance and
Uncertainty Avoidance Scales

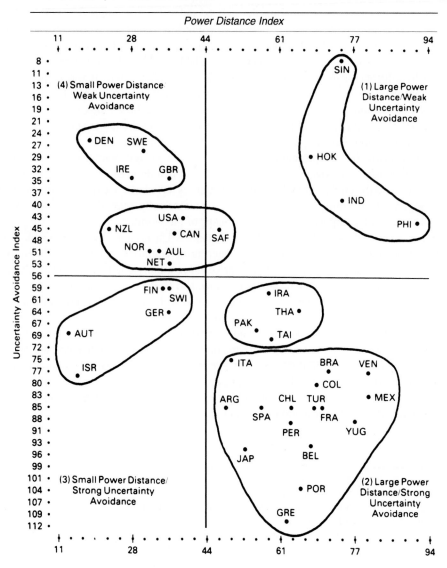

**FIGURE 6**   The Position of the 40 Countries on the Power Distance and Individualism Scales

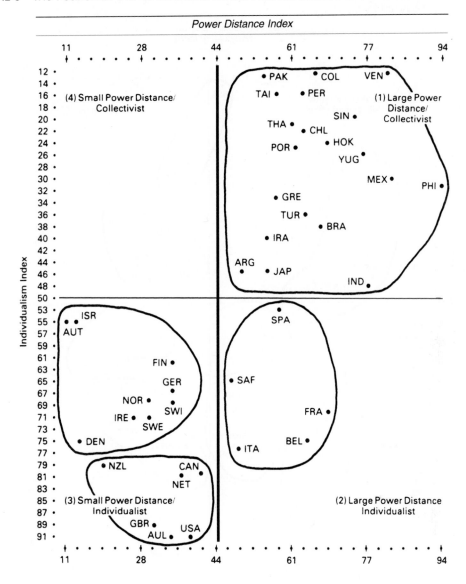

FIGURE 7 The Position of the 40 Countries on the Uncertainty Avoidance and Masculinity Scales

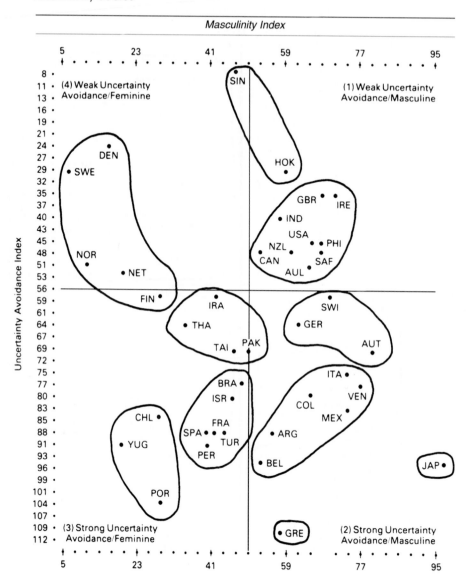

# THE CULTURAL RELATIVITY OF MANAGEMENT THEORIES

Of particular interest in the context of this discussion is the relative position of the United States on the four dimensions. Here is how the United States rates:

- On *Power Distance* at rank 15 out of the 40 countries (measured from below), it is below average but it is not as low as a number of other wealthy countries.
- On *Uncertainty Avoidance* at rank 9 out of 40, it is well below average.
- On *Individualism* at rank 40 out of 40, the United States is the single most individualist country of the entire set (followed closely by Australia and Great Britain).
- On *Masculinity* at rank 28 out of 40, it is well above average.

For about 60 years, the United States has been the world's largest producer and explorer of management theories covering such key areas as motivation, leadership, and organization. Before that, the centers of theorizing about what we now call "management" lay in the Old World. We can trace the history of management thought as far back as we want—at least to parts of the Old Testament of the Bible, and to ancient Greece (Plato's *The Laws* and *The Republic*, 350 B.C.). Sixteenth-century European "management" theorists include Niccolo Machiavelli (Italy) and Thomas More (Great Britain); early twentieth-century theorists include Max Weber (Germany) and Henri Fayol (France).

Today we are all culturally conditioned. We see the world in the way we have learned to see it. Only to a limited extent can we, in our thinking, step out of the boundaries imposed by our cultural conditioning. This applies to the author of a theory as much as it does to the ordinary citizen: Theories reflect the cultural environment in which they were written. If this is true, Italian, British, German, and French theories reflect the culture of Italy, Britain, Germany, and France of their day, and American theories reflect the culture of the United States of its day. Since most present-day theorists are middle-class intellectuals, their theories reflect a national intellectual middle-class culture background.

Now we ask the question: To what extent do theories developed in one country and reflecting the cultural boundaries of that country apply to other countries? Do American management theories apply in Japan? In India? No management theorist, to my knowledge, has ever explicitly addressed himself or herself to this issue. Most probably assume that their theories are universally valid. The availability of a conceptual framework built on four dimensions of national culture, in conjunction with the cultural maps of the world, makes it possible to see more clearly where and to what extent theories developed in one country are likely to apply elsewhere. In the remaining sections of this article I shall look from this viewpoint at most popular American theories of management in the areas of motivation, leadership, and organization.

# MOTIVATION

Why do people behave as they do? There is a great variety of theories of human motivation. According to Sigmund Freud, we are impelled to act by unconscious forces within us, which he called our id. Our conscious conception of ourselves—our ego—tries to control these forces, and an equally unconscious internal pilot—our superego—criticizes the thoughts and acts of our ego and causes feelings of guilt and anxiety when the ego seems to be giving in to the id. The superego is the product of early socialization, mainly learned from our parents when we were young children.

Freud's work has been extremely influential in psychology, but he is rarely quoted in the context of management theories. The latter almost exclusively refer to motivation theories developed later in the United States, particularly those of David McClelland, Abraham Maslow, Frederick Herzberg, and Victor Vroom. According to McClelland, we perform because we have a need to achieve (the achievement motive). More recently, McClelland has also paid a lot of attention to the power motive. Maslow has postulated a hierarchy of human needs, from more "basic" to "higher": most basic are physiological needs, followed by security, social needs, esteem needs, and, finally, a need for "self-actualization." The latter incorporates McClelland's theory of achievement, but is defined in broader terms. Maslow's theory of the hierarchy of needs postulates that a higher need will become active only if the lower needs are sufficiently satisfied. Our acting is basically a rational activity by which we expect to fulfill successive levels of needs. Herzberg's two-factor theory of motivation distinguishes between hygienic factors (largely corresponding to Maslow's lower needs—physiological, security, social) and motivators (Maslow's higher needs—esteem, self-actualization); the hygienic factors have only the potential to motivate negatively (demotivate—they are necessary but not sufficient conditions), while only the motivators have the potential to motivate positively. Vroom has formalized the role of "expectancy" in motivation; he opposes "expectancy" theories and "drive" theories. The former see people as being *pulled* by the expectancy of some kind of result from their acts, mostly consciously. The latter (in accordance with Freud's theories) see people as *pushed* by inside forces—often unconscious ones.

Let us now look at these theories through culture-conscious glasses. Why has Freudian thinking never become popular in U.S. management theory, as has the thinking of McClelland, Maslow, Herzberg, and Vroom? To what extent do these theories reflect different cultural patterns? Freud was part of an Austrian middle-class culture at the turn of the century. If we compare present-day Austria and the United States on our cultural maps, we find the following:

- Austria scores considerably lower on Power Distance.
- Austria scores considerably higher on Uncertainty Avoidance.
- Austria scores considerably lower on Individualism.
- Austria scores considerably higher on Masculinity.

We do not know to what extent Austrian culture has changed since Freud's time, but evidence suggests that cultural patterns change very slowly. It is, therefore, not likely to have been much different from today's culture. The most striking thing about present-day Austrian culture is that it combines a fairly high Uncertainty Avoidance with a very low Power Distance (see Figure 5). Somehow the combination of high Uncertainty Avoidance with high Power Distance is more comfortable (we find this in Japan and in all Latin and Mediterranean countries (see Figure 5). Having a powerful superior whom we can both praise and blame is one way of satisfying a strong need for avoiding uncertainty. The Austrian culture, however (together with the German, Swiss, Israeli, and Finnish cultures), cannot rely on an external boss to absorb its uncertainty. Thus Freud's superego acts naturally as an inner uncertainty-absorbing device, an internalized boss. For strong Uncertainty Avoidance countries like Austria, working hard is caused by an inner urge—it is a way of relieving stress (see Figure 2). The Austrian superego is reinforced by the country's relatively low level of Individualism (see Figure 6). The inner feeling of obligation to society plays a much stronger role in Austria than in the United States. The ultrahigh Individualism of the United States leads to a need to explain every act in terms of self-interest, and expectancy theories of motivation do provide this explanation—we always do something *because* we expect to obtain the satisfaction of some need.

The comparison between Austrian and U.S. culture has so far justified the popularity of expectancy theories of motivation in the United States. The combination in the United States of weak Uncertainty Avoidance and relatively high Masculinity can tell us more about why the achievement motive has become so popular in that country. David McClelland, in his book *The Achieving Society,* sets up scores reflecting how strong achievement need is in many countries by analyzing the content of children's stories used in those countries to teach the young to read. It now appears that there is a strong relationship between McClelland's need for achievement country scores and the combination of weak Uncertainty Avoidance and strong Masculinity charted in Figure 7. (McClelland's data were collected for two historic years—1925 and 1950—but only his 1925 data relate to the cultural map in Figure 7. It is likely that the 1925 stories were more traditional, reflecting deep underlying cultural currents; the choice of stories in 1950 in most countries may have been affected by modernization currents in education, often imported from abroad.)

Countries in the upper righthand corner of Figure 7 received mostly high scores on achievement need in McClelland's book; countries in the lower lefthand corner of Figure 7 received low scores. This leads us to the conclusion that the concept of the achievement motive presupposes two cultural choices—a willingness to accept risk (equivalent to weak Uncertainty Avoidance; see Figure 2) and a concern with performance (equivalent to strong Masculinity; see Figure 4). This combination is found exclusively in countries in the Anglo-American group and in some of their former colonies (Figure 7). One striking thing about the concept of achievement is that the word itself is hardly translatable into any language other than English; for this reason, the word could not be used in the questionnaire of the multinational corporation used in my research. The English-speaking countries all appear in the upper righthand corner of Figure 7.

If this is so, there is reason to reconsider Maslow's hierarchy of human needs in the light of the map shown in Figure 7. Quadrant I (upper righthand corner) in Figure 7 stands for *achievement motivation,* as we have seen (performance plus risk). Quadrant 2 distinguishes itself from quadrant I by strong Uncertainty Avoidance, which means *security motivation* (performance plus security). The countries on the feminine side of Figure 7 distinguish themselves by a focusing on quality of life rather than on performance and on relationships between people rather than on money and things (see Figure 4). This means *social motivation*: quality of life plus security in quadrant 3, and quality of life plus risk in quadrant 4. Now, Maslow's hierarchy puts self-actualization (achievement) plus esteem above social needs above security needs. This, however, is not the description of a universal human motivation process—it is the description of a value system, the value system of the U.S. middle class to which the author belonged. I suggest that if we want to continue thinking in terms of a hierarchy for countries in the lower righthand corner of Figure 7 (quadrant 2), security needs should rank at the top; for countries in the upper lefthand corner (quadrant 4), social needs should rank at the top, and for countries in the lower lefthand corner (quadrant 3) *both* security and social needs should rank at the top.

One practical outcome of presenting motivation theories is the movement toward humanization of work—an attempt to make work more intrinsically interesting to the workers. There are two main currents in humanization of work—one, developed in the United States and called *job enrichment*, aims at restructuring individual jobs. A chief proponent of job enrichment is Frederick Herzberg. The other current, developed in Europe and applied mainly in Sweden and Norway, aims at restructuring work into group work—forming, for example, such semiautonomous teams as those seen in the experiments at Volvo. Why the difference in approaches? What is seen as a "human" job depends on a society's prevailing model of humankind. In a more masculine society like the United States, humanization takes the form of masculinization, allowing individual performance. In the more feminine societies of Sweden and Norway, humanization takes the form of feminization—it is a means toward more wholesome interpersonal relationships in its de-emphasis of interindividual competition.

# LEADERSHIP

One of the oldest theorists of leadership in world literature is Machiavelli (1468–1527). He described certain effective techniques for manipulation and remaining in power (including deceit, bribery, and murder) that gave him a bad reputation in later centuries. Machiavelli wrote in the context of the Italy of his day, and what he described is clearly a large Power Distance situation. We still find Italy on the larger Power Distance side of Figure 5 (with all other Latin and Mediterranean countries), and we can assume from historical evidence that Power Distances in Italy during the sixteenth century were considerably larger than they are now. When we compare Machiavelli's work with that of his contemporary, Sir Thomas More (1478–1535), we find cultural differences between ways of thinking in different countries even in the sixteenth century. The British More described in *Utopia* a state based on consensus as a "model" to criticize the political situation of his day. But practice did not always follow theory, of course: More, deemed too critical, was beheaded by order of King Henry VIII, while Machiavelli the realist managed to die peacefully in his bed. The difference in theories is nonetheless remarkable.

In the United States a current of leadership theories has developed. Some of the best known were put forth by the late Douglas McGregor (Theory X versus Theory Y), Rensis Likert (System 4 management), and Robert R. Blake with Jane S. Mouton (the Management Grid®). What these theories have in common is that they all advocate participation in the manager's decisions by his/her subordinates (participative management); however, the initiative toward participation is supposed to be taken by the manager. In a worldwide perspective (Figure 5), we can understand these theories from the middle position of the United States on the Power Distance side (rank 15 out of 40 countries). Had the culture been one of larger Power Distance, we could have expected more "Machiavellian" theories of leadership. In fact, in the management literature of another country with a larger Power Distance index score, France, there is little concern with participative management American style, but great concern with who has the power. However, in countries with smaller Power Distances than the United States (Sweden, Norway, Germany, Israel), there is considerable sympathy for models of management in which even the initiatives are taken by the subordinates (forms of industrial democracy) and with which there's little sympathy in the United States. In the approaches toward "industrial democracy" taken in these countries, we notice their differences on the second dimension, Uncertainty Avoidance. In weak Uncertainty Avoidance countries like Sweden, industrial democracy was started in the form of local experiments and only later was given a legislative framework. In strong Uncertainty Avoidance countries like Germany, industrial democracy was brought about by legislation first and then had to be brought alive in the organizations ("Mitbestimmung").

The crucial fact about leadership in any culture is that it is a complement to subordinateship. The Power Distance Index scores in Figure 5 are, in fact, based on the values of people as *subordinates,* not on the values of superiors. Whatever a naive literature on leadership may give us to understand, leaders cannot choose their styles at will; what is feasible depends to a large extent on the cultural conditioning of a leader's subordinates. Along these lines, Figure 8 describes the type of subordinateship that, other things being equal, a leader can expect to meet in societies at three different levels of Power Distance—subordinateship to which a leader must respond. The middle level represents what is most likely found in the United States.

Neither McGregor, nor Likert, nor Blake and Mouton allow for this type of cultural proviso—all three tend to be prescriptive with regard to a leadership style that, at best, will work with U.S. subordinates and with those in cultures—such as Canada or Australia—that have not too different Power Distance levels (Figure 5). In fact, my research shows that subordinates in larger Power Distance countries tend to agree more frequently with Theory Y.

A U.S. theory of leadership that allows for a certain amount of cultural relativity, although indirectly, is Fred Fiedler's contingency theory of leadership. Fiedler states that different leader personalities are needed for "difficult" and "easy" situations, and that a cultural gap between superior and subordinates is one of the factors that makes a situation "difficult." However, this theory does not address the kind of cultural gap in question.

In practice, the adaptation of managers to higher Power Distance environments does not seem to present too many problems. Although this is an unpopular message—one seldom professed in management development courses—managers moving to a larger Power Distance culture soon learn that they have to behave more autocratically in order to be effective, and tend to do so; this is borne out by the colonial history of most Western countries. But it is interesting that the Western ex-colonial power with the highest Power Distance norm—France—seems to be most appreciated by its former colonies and seems to maintain the best postcolonial relationships with most of them. This suggests that subordinates in a large Power Distance culture feel even more comfortable with superiors who are real autocrats than with those whose assumed autocratic stance is out of national character.

FIGURE 8    Subordinateship for Three Levels of Power Distance

| Small Power Distance | Medium Power Distance (United States) | Large Power Distance |
|---|---|---|
| Subordinates have weak dependence need. | Subordinates have medium dependence needs. | Subordinates have strong dependence needs. |
| Superiors have weak dependence needs toward their superiors. | Superiors have medium dependence needs toward their superiors. | Superiors have strong dedependence needs toward their superiors. |
| Subordinates expert superiors to consult them and may rebel or strike if superiors are not seen as staying within their legitimate role. | Subordinates expect superiors to consult them but will accept autocratic behavior as well. | Subordinates expect superiors to act automatically. |
| Ideal superior to most is a loyal democratic. | Ideal superior to most is a resourceful democratic. | Ideal superior to most is a benevelont autocrat or paternalist. |
| Laws and rules apply to all and privileges for superiors are not considered. | Laws and rules apply to all, but a certain level of privileges for superiors is considered normal. | Everybody expects superiors to enjoy privileges; laws and subordinates. |
| Status symbols are frowned upon and will easily come under attack from subordinates. | Status symbols for superiors contribute moderately to their authority and will be accepted by subordinates. | Status symbols are important and contribute strongly to the superior's authority with the subordinates. |

The operation of a manager in an environment with a Power Distance norm lower than his or her own is more problematic. U.S. managers tend to find it difficult to collaborate wholeheartedly in the "industrial democracy" processes of such countries as Sweden, Germany, and even the Netherlands. U.S. citizens tend to consider their country as the example of democracy, and find it difficult to accept that other countries might wish to develop forms of democracy for which they feel no need and that make major inroads upon managers'(or leaders') prerogatives. However, the very idea of management prerogatives is not accepted in very low Power Distance countries. This is, perhaps, best illustrated by a remark a Scandinavian social scientist is supposed to have made to Herzberg in a seminar: "You are against participation for the very reason we are in favor of it—one doesn't know where it will stop. We think that is good."

One way in which the U.S. approach to leadership has been packaged and formalized is management by objectives (MBO), first advocated by Peter Drucker in 1955 in *The Practice of Management*. In the United States, MBO has been used to spread a pragmatic results orientation throughout the organization. It has been considerably more successful where results are objectively measurable than where they can only be interpreted subjectively, and, even in the United States, it has been criticized heavily. Still, it has been perhaps the single most popular management technique "made in U.S.A." Therefore, it can be accepted as fitting U.S. culture. MBO presupposes:

- That subordinates are sufficiently independent to negotiate meaningfully with the boss (not-too-large Power Distance).
- That both are willing to take risks (weak Uncertainty Avoidance).
- That performance is seen as important by both (high Masculinity).

Let us now take the case of Germany, a below-average Power Distance country. Here, the dialogue element in MBO should present no problem. However, since Germany scores considerably higher on Uncertainty Avoidance, the tendency toward accepting risk and ambiguity will not exist to the same extent. The idea of replacing the arbitrary authority of the boss with the impersonal authority of mutually agreed upon objectives, however, fits the small Power Distance/strong Uncertainty Avoidance cultural cluster very well. The objectives become the subordinates' "superego." In a book of case studies about MBO in Germany, Ian R. G. Ferguson states that "MBO has acquired a different flavor in the Germanspeaking area, not least because in these countries the societal and political pressure toward increasing the value of man in the organization on the right to codetermination has become quite clear. Thence, MBO has been transliterated into Management by Joint Goal Setting (Führung durch Zielvereinbarung)." Ferguson's view of MBO fits the ideological needs of the German-speaking countries of the moment. The case studies in his book show elaborate formal systems with extensive ideological justification; the stress on *team* objectives is quite strong, which is in line with the lower individualism in these countries.

The other area in which specific information on MBO is available is France. MBO was first introduced in France in the early 1960s, but it became extremely popular for a time after the 1968 student revolt. People expected that this new technique would lead to the long-overdue democratization of organizations. Instead of DPO (Direction par Objectifs), the French name for MBO became DPPO (Direction *Participative* par Objectifs). So in France, too, societal developments affected the MBO system. However, DPPO remained, in general, as much a vain slogan as did Liberté, Egalité, Fraternité (Freedom, Equality, Brotherhood) after the 1789 revolt. G. Frank wrote in 1973, "I think that the career of DPPO is terminated, or rather that it has never started, and it won't ever start as long as we continue in France our tendency to confound ideology and reality...." In a postscript to Frank's article, the editors of *Le Management* write: "French blue- and white-collar workers, lower-level and higher-level managers, and 'patrons' all belong to the same cultural system which maintains dependency relations from level to level. Only the deviants really dislike this system. The hierarchical structure protects against anxiety; DPO, however generates anxiety...." The reason for the anxiety in the French cultural context is that MBO presupposes a depersonalized authority in the form of internalized objectives; but French people, from their early childhood onward, are accustomed to large Power Distances, to an authority that is highly personalized. And in spite of all attempts to introduce Anglo-Saxon management methods, French superiors do not easily decentralize and do not stop short-circuiting intermediate hierarchical levels, nor do French subordinates expect them to. The developments of the 1970s have severely discredited DPPO, which probably does injustice to the cases in which individual French organizations or units, starting from less exaggerated expectations, have benefited from it.

In the examples used thus far in this section, the cultural context of leadership may look rather obvious to the reader. But it also works in more subtle, less obvious ways. Here's an example from the area of management decision making: A prestigious U.S. consulting firm was asked to analyze the decision making process in a large Scandinavian "XYZ" corporation. Their report criticized the corporation's decision-making style, which they characterized as being, among other things, "intuitive" and "consensus based." They compared "observations of traditional XYZ practices" with "selected examples of practices in other companies." These "selected examples," offered as a model, were evidently taken from their U.S. clients and reflect the U.S. textbook norm—"fact based" rather than intuitive management, and "fast decisions based on clear responsibilities" rather than the use of informal, personal contacts, and the concern for consensus.

Is this consulting firm doing its Scandinavian clients a service? It follows from Figure 7 that where the United States and the Scandinavian culture are wide apart is on the Masculinity dimension. The use of intuition and the concern for consensus in Scandinavia are "feminine" characteristics of the culture, well embedded in the total texture of these societies. Stressing "facts" and "clear responsibilities" fits the "masculine" U.S. culture. From a neutral viewpoint, the reasons for criticizing the U.S. decision-making style are as good as those for criticizing the Scandinavian style. In complex decision-making situations, "facts" no longer exist independently from the people who define them, so "fact-based management" becomes a misleading slogan. Intuition may not be a bad method of deciding in such cases at all. And if the implementation of decisions requires the commitment of many people, even a consensus process that takes more time is an asset rather than a liability. But the essential element overlooked by the consultant is that decisions have to be made in a way that corresponds to the values of the environment in which they have to be effective. People in this consulting firm lacked insight into their own cultural biases. This does not mean that the Scandinavian corporation's management need not improve its decision making and could not learn from the consultant's experience. But this can be done only through a mutual recognition of cultural differences, not by ignoring them.

## ORGANIZATION

The Power Distance x Uncertainty Avoidance map (Figure 5) is of vital importance for structuring organizations that will work best in different countries. For example, one U.S.-based multinational corporation has a worldwide policy that salary-increase proposals should be initiated by the employee's direct superior. However, the French management of its French subsidiary interpreted this policy in such a way that the superior's superior's superior—three levels above—was the one to initiate salary proposals. This way of working was regarded as quite natural by both superiors and subordinates in France. Other factors being equal, people in large Power Distance cultures prefer that decisions be centralized because even superiors have strong dependency needs in relation to their superiors; this tends to move decisions up as far as they can go (see Figure 8). People in small Power Distance cultures want decisions to be decentralized.

While Power Distance relates to centralization, Uncertainty Avoidance relates to formalization—the need for formal rules and specialization, the assignment of tasks to experts. My former colleague O. J. Stevens at INSEAD has done an interesting research project (as yet unpublished) with M.B.A. students from Germany, Great Britain, and France. He asked them to write their own diagnosis and solution for a small case study of an organizational problem—a conflict in one company between the sales and product development departments. The majority of the French referred the problem to the next higher authority (the president of the company); the Germans attributed it to the lack of a written policy, and proposed establishing one; the British attributed it to a lack of interpersonal communication, to be cured by some kind of group training.

Stevens concludes that the "implicit model" of the organization for most French was a pyramid (both centralized and formal); for most Germans, a well-oiled machine (formalized but not centralized); and for most British, a village market (neither formalized nor centralized). This covers three quadrants (2, 3, and 4) in Figure 5. What is missing is an "implicit model" for quadrant 1, which contains four Asian countries, including India. A discussion with an Indian colleague leads me to place the family (centralized, but not formalized) in this quadrant as the "implicit model" of the organization. In fact, Indian organizations tend to be formalized as far as relationships between people go (this is related to Power Distance), but not as far as workflow goes (this is Uncertainty Avoidance).

The "well-oiled machine" model for Germany reminds us of the fact that Max Weber, author of the first theory of bureaucracy, was a German. Weber pictures bureaucracy as a highly formalized system (strong Uncertainty Avoidance), in which, however, the rules protect the lower-ranking members against abuse of power by their superiors. The superiors have no power by themselves, only the power that their bureaucratic roles have given them as incumbents of the roles—the power is in the role, not in the person (small Power Distance).

The United States is found fairly close to the center of the map in Figure 5, taking an intermediate position between the "pyramid," "machine," and "market" implicit models—a position that may help explain the success of U.S. business operations in very different cultures. However, according to the common U.S. conception of organization, we might say that *hierarchy is not a goal by itself* (as it is in France) and that *rules are not a goal by themselves*. Both are means toward obtaining results, to be changed if needed. A breaking away from hierarchic and bureaucratic traditions is found in the development toward matrix organizations and similar temporary or flexible organization systems.

Another INSEAD colleague, André Laurent, has shown that French managers strongly disbelieve in the feasibility of matrix organizations, because they see them as violating the "holy" principle of unit of command. However, in the French subsidiary of a multinational corporation that has a long history of successful matrix management, the French managers were quite positive toward it; obviously, then, cultural barriers to organizational innovation can be overcome. German managers are not too favorably disposed toward matrix organizations either, feeling that they tend to frustrate their need for organizational clarity. This means that matrix organizations will be accepted *if* the roles of individuals within the organization can be defined without ambiguity.

The extreme position of the United States on the Individualism scale leads to other potential conflicts between the U.S. way of thinking about organizations and the values dominant in other parts of the world. In the U.S. Individualist conception, the relationship between the individual and the organization is essentially calculative, being based on enlightened self-interest. In fact, there is a strong historical and cultural link between Individualism and Capitalism. The capitalist system—based on self-interest and the market mechanism—was "invented" in Great Britain, which is still among the top three most Individualist countries in the world. In more Collectivist societies, however, the link between individuals and their traditional organizations is not calculative, but moral: It is based not on self-interest, but on the individual's loyalty toward the clan, organization, or society—which is supposedly the best guarantee of that individual's ultimate interest. "Collectivism" is a bad word in the United States, but "individualism" is as much a bad word in the writings of Mao Tse-tung, who writes from a strongly Collectivist cultural tradition (see Figure 6 for the Collectivist scores of the Chinese majority countries Taiwan, Hong Kong, and Singapore). This means that U.S. organizations may get themselves into considerable trouble in more Collectivist environments if they do not recognize their local employees' needs for ties of mutual loyalty between company and employee. "Hire and fire" is very ill perceived in these countries, if firing isn't prohibited by law altogether. Given the value position of people in more Collectivist cultures, it should not be seen as surprising if they prefer other types of economic order to capitalism—if capitalism cannot get rid of its Individualist image.

## CONSEQUENCES FOR POLICY

So far we have seriously questioned the universal validity of management theories developed in one country—in most instances here, the United States.

On a practical level, this has the least consequence for organizations operating entirely within the country in which the theories were born. As long as the theories apply within the United States, U.S. organizations can base their policies for motivating employees, leadership, and organization development on these policies. Still, some caution is due. If differences in environmental culture can be shown to exist between countries, and if these constrain the validity of management theories, what about the subcultures within the country? To what extent do the familiar theories apply when the organization employs people for whom the theories were not, in the first instance, conceived—such as members of minority groups with a different educational level, or belonging to a different generation? If culture matters, an organization's policies can lose their effectiveness when its cultural environment changes.

No doubt, however, the consequences of the cultural relativity of management theories are more serious for the multinational organization. The cultural maps in Figures 5, 6, and 7 can help predict the kind of culture difference between subsidiaries and mother company that will need to be met. An important implication is that identical personnel policies may have very different effects in different countries—and within countries for different subgroups of employees. This is not only a matter of different employee values; there are also, of course, differences in government policies and legislation (which usually reflect quite clearly the country's different cultural position). And there are differences in labor market situations and labor union power positions. These differences—tangible as well as intangible—may have consequences for performance, attention to quality, cost, labor turnover, and absenteeism. Typical universal policies that may work out quite differently in different countries are those dealing with financial incentives, promotion paths, and grievance channels.

The dilemma for the organization operating abroad is whether to adapt to the local culture or try to change it. There are examples of companies that have successfully changed local habits, such as in the earlier mention of the introduction of matrix organization in France. Many Third World countries want to transfer new technologies from more economically advanced countries. If they are to work at all, these technologies must presuppose values that may run counter to local traditions, such as a certain discretion of subordinates toward superiors (lower Power Distance) or of individuals toward ingroups (more Individualism). In such a case, the local culture has to be changed; this is a difficult task that should not be taken lightly. Since it calls for a conscious strategy based on insight into the local culture, it's logical to involve acculturated locals in strategy formulations. Often, the original policy will have to be adapted to fit local culture and lead to the desired effect. We saw earlier how, in the case of MBO, this has succeeded in Germany, but generally failed in France.

A final area in which the cultural boundaries of home-country management theories are important is the training of managers for assignments abroad. For managers who have to operate in an unfamiliar culture, training based on homecountry theories is of very limited use and may even do more harm than good. Of more importance is a thorough familiarization with the other culture, for which the organization can use the services of specialized cross-cultural training institutes or it can develop its own program by using host-country personnel as teachers.

## ACKNOWLEDGMENTS

This article is based on research carried out in the period 1973–78 at the European Institute for Advanced Studies in Management, Brussels. The article itself was sponsored by executive search consultants Berndtson International S.A., Brussels. The author acknowledges the helpful comments of Mark Cantley, André Laurent, Ernest C. Miller, and Jennifer Robinson on an earlier version of it.

## SELECTED BIBLIOGRAPHY

The first U.S. book about the cultural relativity of U.S. management theories is still to be written, I believe—which lack in itself indicates how difficult it is to recognize one's own cultural biases. One of the few U.S. books describing the process of cultural conditioning for a management readership is Edward T. Hall's *The Silent Language* (Fawcett, 1959, but reprinted since). Good reading also is Hall's article "The Silent Language in Overseas Business (*Harvard Business Review*, May–June 1960). Hall is an anthropologist and therefore a specialist in the study of culture. Very readable on the same subject are two books by the British anthropologist Mary Douglas, *Natural Symbols: Exploration in Cosmology* (Vintage, 1973) and the reader *Rules and Meanings: The Anthropology of Everyday Knowledge* (Penguin, 1973). Another excellent reader is Theodore D. Weinshall's *Culture and Management* (Penguin, 1977).

On the concept of national character, some well-written professional literature is Margaret Mead's "National Character," in the reader by Sol Tax, *Anthropology Today* (University of Chicago Press, 1962), and Alex Inkeles and D. J. Levinson's, "National Character," in Lindzey and Aronson's *Handbook of Social Psychology*, second edition, volume 4 (Addison-Wesley, 1969). Critique on the implicit claims of universal validity of management theories comes from some foreign authors: An important article is Michael Brossard and Marc Maurice's "Is There a Universal Model of Organization Structure?" (*International Studies of Management and Organization*, Fall 1976). This journal is a journal of translations from non-American American literature, based in New York, that often contains important articles on management issues by non-U.S. authors that take issue with the dominant theories. Another article is Gunnar Hjelholt's "Europe Is Different," in Geert Hofstede and M. Sami Kassem's reader, *European Contributions to Organization Theory* (Assen, Netherlands: Von Gorcum, 1976).

Some other references of interest: Ian R. G. Ferguson's *Management by Objectives in Deutschland* (Herder und Herder, 1973)(in German); G. Franck's "Epitaphepour la DPO," in *Le Management*, November 1973 (in French); and D. Jenkin's *Blue-and White-Collar Democracy* (Doubleday, 1973).

*Note*: Details of Geert Hofstede's study of national cultures have been published in his book, *Culture's Consequences: International Differences in Work-Related Values* (Beverly Hills: Sage Publications, 1980).

# 13
# Leadership

THE 4 COMPETENCIES OF LEADERSHIP
*Warren Bennis*

SUPERLEADERSHIP: BEYOND THE MYTH OF HEROIC LEADERSHIP
*Charles C. Manz*
*Henry P. Sims, Jr.*

FIRMS WITH A SUPERIOR LEADERSHIP CAPACITY: PRACTICES THAT
CREATE BETTER-THAN-AVERAGE MANAGEMENT TEAMS
*John P. Kotter*

# THE 4 COMPETENCIES OF LEADERSHIP

## *Warren Bennis*

For nearly five years I have been researching a book on leadership. During this period, I have traveled around the country spending time with 90 of the most effective, successful leaders in the nation; 60 from corporations and 30 from the public sector.

My goal was to find these leaders' common traits, a task that has required much more probing than I expected. For a while I sensed much more diversity than commonality among them. The group comprises both left-brain and right-brain thinkers; some who dress for success and some who don't; well-spoken, articulate leaders and laconic, inarticulate ones; some John Wayne types and some who are definitely the opposite. Interestingly, the group includes only a few stereotypically charismatic leaders.

Despite the diversity, which is profound and must not be underestimated, I identified certain areas of competence shared by all 90. Before presenting those findings, though, it is important to place this study in context, to review the mood and events in the United States just before and during the research.

## DECLINE AND MALAISE

When I left the University of Cincinnati late in 1977, our country was experiencing what President Carter called "despair" or "malaise." From 1960 to 1980, our institutions' credibility had eroded steadily. In an article about that period entitled, "Where Have All the Leaders Gone," I described how difficult the times were for leaders, including university presidents like myself.

The material in this article is developed further in W. Bennis & B. Nanus, *Leaders,* NY: Harper & Row, 1985. Used with permission of the author.

I argued that, because of the complexity of the times, leaders felt impotent. The assassinations of several national leaders, the Vietnam war, the Watergate scandal, the Iranian hostage crisis and other events led to a loss of trust in our institutions and leaderships.

I came across a quotation in a letter Abigail Adams wrote to Thomas Jefferson in 1790: "These are the hard times in which a genius would wish to live." If, as she believed, great necessities summon great leaders, I wanted to get to know the leaders brought forth by the current malaise. In a time when bumper stickers appeared reading "Impeach Someone," I resolved to seek out leaders who were effective under these adverse conditions.

At the same time that America suffered from this leadership gap, it was suffering from a productivity gap. Consider these trends:

- In the 1960s, the average GNP growth was 4.1 percent; in the 1970s, it was 2.9 percent; in 1982, it was negative.
- The U.S. standard of living, the world's highest in 1972, now ranks fifth.
- In 1960, when the economies of Europe and Japan had been rebuilt, the U.S. accounted for 25 percent of the industrial nations' manufacturing exports and supplied 98 percent of its domestic markets. Now, the U.S. has less than a 20 percent share of the world market, and that share is declining.
- In 1960, U.S. automobiles had a 96 percent market share; today we have about 71 percent. The same holds true for consumer electronics; in 1960 it was 94.4 percent, in 1980 only 49 percent. And that was before Sony introduced the Walkman!

In addition to leadership and productivity gaps, a subtler "commitment gap" existed, that is, a reluctance to commit to one's work or employer.

The Public Agenda's recent survey of working Americans shows the following statistics. Less than one out of four jobholders (23 percent) says he or she currently works at full potential. Nearly half say they do not put much effort into their jobs above what is required. The overwhelming majority, 75 percent, say they could be significantly more effective on their job than they are now. And nearly 6 in 10 working Americans believe that "most people do not work as hard as they used to."

A number of observers have pointed out the considerable gap between the number of hours people are paid to work and the number of hours they spend on productive labor. Evidence developed recently by the University of Michigan indicates the gap may be widening. They found the difference between paid hours and actual working hours grew 10 percent between 1970 and 1980.

This increasing commitment gap leads to the central question: How can we empower the work force and reap the harvest of human effort?

If I have learned anything from my research, it is this: The factor that empowers the work force and ultimately determines which organizations succeed or fail is the leadership of those organizations. When strategies, processes or cultures change, the key to improvement remains leadership.

## THE SAMPLE: 90 LEADERS

For my study, I wanted 90 effective leaders with proven track records. The final group contains 60 corporate executives, most, but not all, from Fortune 500 companies, and 30 from the public sector. My goal was to find people with leadership ability, in contrast to just "good managers"—true leaders who affect the culture, who are the social architects of their organizations and who create and maintain values.

Leaders are people who do the right thing; managers are people who do things right. Both roles are crucial, and they differ profoundly. I often observe people in top positions doing the wrong thing well.

Given my definition, one of the key problems facing American organizations and probably those in much of the industrialized world is that they are underfed and overmanaged. They do not pay enough attention to doing the right thing, while they pay too much attention to doing things right. Part of the fault lies with our schools of management; we teach people how to be good technicians and good staff people, but we don't train people for leadership.

The group of 60 corporate leaders was not especially different from any profile of top leadership in America. The median age was 56. Most were white males, with six black men and six women in the group. The only surprising finding was that all the CEOs not only were married to their first spouse, but also seemed enthusiastic about the institution of marriage. Examples of the CEOS are Bill Weschnick, chairman and CEO of Arco, and the late Ray Kroc of McDonald's restaurants.

Public-sector leaders included Harold Armstrong, a genuine all-American hero who happened to be at the University of Cincinnati; three elected officials; two orchestra conductors; and two winning athletics coaches. I wanted conductors and coaches because I mistakenly believed they were the last leaders with complete control over their constituents.

After several years of observation and conversation, I have defined four competencies evident to some extent in every member of the group. They are:

- management of attention;
- management of meaning;
- management of trust;
- management of self.

## MANAGEMENT OF ATTENTION

One of the traits most apparent in these leaders is their ability to draw others to them, because they have a vision, a dream, a set of intentions, an agenda, a time of reference. They communicate an extraordinary focus of commitment, which attracts people to them. One of these leaders was described as making people want to join in with him; he enrolls them in his vision.

Leaders, then, manage attention through a compelling vision that brings others to a place they have not been before. I came to this understanding in a roundabout way, as this anecdote illustrates.

One of the people I most wanted to interview was one of the few I couldn't seem to reach. He refused to answer my letters or phone calls. I even tried getting in touch with the members of the board. He is Leon Fleischer, a well-known child prodigy who grew up to become a prominent pianist, conductor and musicologist. What I did not know about him was that he had lost the use of his right hand and no longer performed.

When I called him originally to recruit him for the University of Cincinnati faculty, he declined and told me he was working with orthopedic specialists to regain the use of his hand. He did visit the campus, and I was impressed with his commitment to staying in Baltimore, near the medical institution where he received therapy.

Fleischer was the only person who kept turning me down for an interview, and finally I gave up. A couple of summers later I was in Aspen, Colorado while Fleischer was conducting the Aspen Music Festival. I tried to reach him again, even leaving a note on his dressing room door, but I got no answer.

One day in downtown Aspen, I saw two perspiring young cellists carrying their instruments and offered them a ride to the music tent. They hopped in the back of my jeep, and, as we rode, I questioned them about Fleischer.

"I'll tell you why he is so great," said one. "He doesn't waste our time."

Fleischer finally agreed not only to be interviewed but to let me watch him rehearse and conduct music classes. I linked the way I saw him work with that simple sentence, "He doesn't waste our time." Every moment Fleischer was before the orchestra, he knew exactly what sound he wanted. He didn't waste time because his intentions were always evident. What united him with the other musicians was their concern with intention and outcome.

When I reflected on my own experience, it struck me that when I was most effective, it was because I knew what I wanted. When I was ineffective, it was because I was unclear about it.

So, the first leadership competency is the management of attention through a set of intentions or a vision, not in a mystical or religious sense, but in the sense of outcome, goal or direction.

## MANAGEMENT OF MEANING

To make dreams apparent to others, and to align people with them, leaders must communicate their vision. Communication and alignment work together.

Consider, for example, the contrasting styles of Presidents Reagan and Carter. Ronald Reagan is called "the great communicator"; one of his speech writers said Reagan can read the phone book and make it interesting. The reason is that Reagan uses metaphors with which people can identify.

In his first budget message, for example, Reagan described a trillion dollars by comparing it to piling up dollar bills beside the Empire State Building. Reagan, to use one of Alexander Haig's coinages, "tangibilitated" the idea. Leaders make ideas tangible and real to others, so they can support them. For no matter how marvelous the vision, the effective leader must use a metaphor, a word or a model to make that vision clear to others.

In contrast, President Carter was boring. Carter was one of our best informed presidents; he had more facts at his finger tips than almost any other president. But he never made the meaning come through the facts.

I interviewed an assistant secretary of commerce appointed by Carter, who told me that after four years in his administration, she still did not know what Jimmy Carter stood for. She said that working for him was like looking through the wrong side of a tapestry; the scene was blurry and indistinct.

The leader's goal is not mere explanation or clarification but the creation of meaning. My favorite baseball joke is exemplary: In the ninth inning of a key playoff game, with a 3 and 2 count on the batter, the umpire hesitates a split second in calling the pitch. The batter whirls around angrily and says, "Well, what was it?" The umpire barks back, "It ain't *nothing* until I call it!"

The more far-flung and complex the organization, the more critical is the ability. Effective leaders can communicate ideas through several organizational layers, across great distances, even through the jamming signals of special interest groups and opponents.

When I was a university president, a group of administrators and I would hatch what we knew was a great idea. Then we would do the right thing: delegate, delegate, delegate. But when the product or policy finally appeared, it scarcely resembled our original idea.

This process occurred so often that I gave it a name: The Pinocchio Effect. (I am sure Geppetto had no idea how Pinocchio would look when he finished carving him.) The Pinocchio Effect leaves us surprised. Because of inadequate communication, results rarely resemble our expectations.

We read and hear so much about information that we tend to overlook the importance of meaning. Actually, the more bombarded a society or organization, the more deluged with facts and images, the greater its thirst for meaning. Leaders integrate facts, concepts and anecdotes into meaning for the public.

Not all the leaders in my group are word masters. They get people to understand and support their goals in a variety of ways.

The ability to manage attention and meaning comes from the whole person. It is not enough to use the right buzz word or a cute technique, or to hire a public relations person to write speeches.

Consider, instead, Frank Dale, publisher of the Los Angeles afternoon newspaper, *The Herald Examiner*. Dale's charge was to cut into the market share of his morning competitor, *The L.A. Times*. When he first joined the newspaper a few years ago, he created a campaign with posters picturing the *Herald Examiner* behind and slightly above the *Times*. The whole campaign was based on this potent message of how the *Herald Examiner* would overtake the *Times*.

I interviewed Dale at his office, and when he sat down at his desk and fastened around him a safety belt like those on airplanes, I couldn't suppress a smile. He did this to remind me and everybody else of the risks the newspaper entailed. His whole person contributed to the message.

No one is more cynical than a newspaper reporter. You can imagine the reactions that traveled the halls of the *Herald Examiner* building. At the same time, nobody forgot what Frank Dale was trying to communicate. And that is the management of meaning.

## MANAGEMENT OF TRUST

Trust is essential to all organizations. The main determinant of trust is reliability, what I call constancy. When I talked to the board members or staffs of these leaders, I heard certain phrases again and again: "She is all of a piece." "Whether you like it or not, you always know where he is coming from, what he stands for."

When John Paul II visited this country, he gave a press conference. One reporter asked how the Pope could account for allocating funds to build a swimming pool at the papal summer palace. He responded quickly: "I like to swim. Next question." He did not rationalize about medical reasons or claim he got the money from a special source.

A recent study showed people would much rather follow individuals they can count on, even when they disagree with their viewpoint, than people they agree with but who shift positions frequently. I cannot emphasize enough the significance of constancy and focus.

Margaret Thatcher's reelection in Great Britain is another excellent example. When she won office in 1979, observers predicted she quickly would revert to defunct Labor Party policies. She did not. In fact, not long ago a *London Times* article appeared headlined (parodying Christopher Fry's play) "The Lady's Not for Returning." She has not turned; she has been constant, focused and all of the piece.

## MANAGEMENT OF SELF

The fourth leadership competency is management of self, knowing one's skills and deploying them effectively. Management of self is critical; without it, leaders and managers can do more harm than good. Like incompetent doctors, incompetent managers can make life worse, make people sicker and less vital. (The term *iatrogenic,* by the way, refers to illness caused by doctors and hospitals.) Some managers give themselves heart attacks and nervous breakdowns; still worse, many are "carriers," causing their employees to be ill.

Leaders know themselves; they know their strengths and nurture them. They also have a faculty I think of as the Wallenda Factor.

The Flying Wallendas are perhaps the world's greatest family of aerialists and tightrope walkers. I was fascinated when, in the early 1970s, 71-year old Karl Wallenda said that for him living is walking a tightrope, and everything else is waiting. I was struck with his capacity for concentration on the intention, the task, the decision.

I was even more intrigued when, several months later, Wallenda fell to his death while walking a tightrope between two high-rise buildings in San Jaun. With a safety net, Wallenda fell, still clutching the balancing pole he warned his family never to drop lest it hurt somebody below.

Later, Wallenda's wife said that before her husband fell, for the first time since she had known him he was concentrating on falling, instead of on walking the tightrope. He personally supervised the attachment of the guide wires, which he never had done before.

Like Wallenda before his fall, the leaders in my group seemed unacquainted with the concept of failure. What you or I might call a failure, they referred to as a mistake. I began collecting synonyms for the word failure mentioned in the interviews, and I found more than 20: mistake, error, false start, bloop, flop, loss, miss, foul-up, stumble, botch, bungle...but not failure.

One CEO told me that if she had a knack for leadership, it was the capacity to make as many mistakes as she could as soon as possible, and thus get them out of the way. Another said that a mistake is simply "another way of doing things." These leaders learn from and use something that doesn't go well: it is not a failure but simply the next step.

When I asked Harold Williams, president of the Getty Foundation, to name the experience that most shaped him as a leader, he said it was being passed over for the presidency of Norton Simon. When it happened, he was furious and demanded reasons, most of which he considered idiotic. Finally, a friend told him that some of the reasons were valid and he should change. He did, and about a year and a half later became president.

Or consider coach Ray Meyer of DePaul University, whose team finally lost at home after winning 29 straight home games. I called him to ask how he felt. He said, "Great. Now we can start to concentrate on winning, not on *not* losing."

Consider Broadway producer Harold Prince, who calls a press conference the morning after his show opens, before reading the reviews, to announce his next play. Or Susan B. Anthony, who said, "Failure is impossible." Or Fletcher Byrum, who, after 22 years as president of Coopers, was asked about his hardest decision. He replied that he did not know what a hard decision was; that he never worried, that he accepted the possibility of being wrong. Byrum said that worry was an obstacle to clear thinking.

The Wallenda Factor is an approach to life; it goes beyond leadership and power in organizations. These leaders all have it.


## EMPOWERMENT: THE EFFECTS OF LEADERSHIP

Leadership can be felt throughout an organization. It gives pace and energy to the work and empowers the work force. Empowerment is the collective effect of leadership. In organizations with effective leaders, empowerment is most evident in four themes:

- *People feel significant.* Everyone feels that he or she makes a difference to the success of the organization. The difference may be small—prompt delivery of potato chips to a mom-and-pop grocery store or developing a tiny but essential part for an airplane. But where they are empowered, people feel that what they do has meaning and significance.

- *Learning and competence matter.* Leaders value learning and mastery, and so do people who work for leaders. Leaders make it clear that there is no failure, only mistakes that give us feedback and tell us what to do next.

- *People are part of a community.* Where there is leadership, there is a team, a family, a unity. Even people who do not especially like each other feel the sense of community. When Neil Armstrong talks about the Apollo explorations, he describes how a team carried out an almost unimaginably complex set of interdependent tasks. Until there were women astronauts, the men referred to this feeling as "brotherhood." I suggest they rename it "family."

- *Work is exciting.* Where there are leaders, work is stimulating, challenging, fascinating and fun. An essential ingredient in organizational leadership is pulling rather than pushing people toward a goal. A "pull" style of influence attracts and energizes people to enroll in an exciting vision of the future. It motivates through identification, rather than through rewards and punishments. Leaders articulate and embody the ideals toward which the organization strives.

People cannot be expected to enroll in just any exciting vision. Some visions and concepts have more staying power and are rooted more deeply in our human needs than others. I believe the lack of two such concepts in modern organizational life is largely responsible for the alienation and lack of meaning so many experience in their work.

One of these is the concept of quality. Modern industrial society has been oriented to quantity, providing more goods and services for everyone. Quantity is measured in money; we are a money-oriented society. Quality often is not measured at all, but is appreciated intuitively. Our response to quality is a feeling. Feelings of quality are connected intimately with our experience of meaning, beauty and value in our lives.

Closely linked to the concept of quality is that of dedication, even love, of our work. This dedication is evoked by quality and is the force that energizes high-performing systems. When we love our work, we need not be managed by hopes of reward or fears of punishment. We can create systems that facilitate our work, rather than being preoccupied with checks and controls of people who want to beat or exploit the system.

And that is what the human resources profession should care most about.


# SUPERLEADERSHIP:
# BEYOND THE MYTH OF HEROIC LEADERSHIP

*Charles C. Manz*
*Henry P. Sims, Jr.*

When most of us think of leadership, we think of one person doing something to another person. This is "influence," and a leader is someone who has the capacity to influence another. Words like "charismatic" and "heroic" are sometimes used to describe a leader. The word "leader" itself conjures up visions of a striking figure on a rearing white horse who is crying "Follow me!" The leader is the one who has either the power or the authority to command others.

Many historical figures fit this mold: Alexander, Caesar, Napoleon, Washington, Churchill. Even today, the turnaround of Chrysler Corporation by Lee Iacocca might be thought of as an act of contemporary heroic leadership. It's not difficult to think of Iacocca astride a white horse, and he is frequently thought of as "charismatic."

But is this heroic figure of the leader the most appropriate image of the organizational leader of today? Is there another model? We believe there is. In many modern situations, *the most appropriate leader is the one who can lead others to lead themselves.* We call this powerful new kind of leadership "SuperLeadership."

Reprinted, by permission of publisher, from *Organizational Dynamics*, Vol. 19, No.4. © Spring 1991. American Management Association, New York. All rights reserved.

Our viewpoint represents a departure from the dominant and, we think, incomplete view of leadership. Our position is that true leadership comes mainly from within a person, not from outside. At its best, external leadership provides a spark and supports the flame of the true inner leadership that dwells within each person. At its worst, it disrupts this internal process, causing damage to the person and the constituencies he or she serves.

Our focus is on a new form of leadership that is designed to facilitate the self-leadership energy within each person. This perspective suggests a new measure of a leader's strength—one's ability to maximize the contributions of others through recognition of their right to guide their own destiny, rather than the leader's ability to bend the will of others to his or her own. The challenge for organizations is to understand how to go about bringing out the wealth of talent that each employee possesses. Many still operate under a quasi-military model that encourages conformity and adherence rather than one that emphasizes how leaders can lead others to lead themselves.

## WHY IS SUPERLEADERSHIP AN IMPORTANT PERSPECTIVE?

This SuperLeadership perspective is especially important today because of several recent trends facing American businesses. First, the challenge to United States corporations from world competition has pressured companies to utilize more fully their human resources. Second, the workforce itself has changed a great deal in recent decades—for instance, "baby boomers" have carried into their organization roles elevated expectations and a need for greater meaning in their work lives.

As a consequence of these kinds of pressures, organizations have increasingly experimented with innovative work designs. Widespread introduction of modern management techniques, such as quality circles, self-managed work teams, Japanese business practices, and flatter organization structures, has led to the inherent dilemma of trying to provide strong leadership for workers who are being encouraged and allowed to become increasingly self-managed. The result is a major knowledge gap about appropriate new leadership approaches under conditions of increasing employee participation. The SuperLeadership approach is designed to meet these kinds of challenges.

Before presenting specific steps for becoming a SuperLeader, it is useful to contrast SuperLeadership with other views of leadership.

Viewpoints on what constitutes successful leadership in organizations have changed significantly over time. A simplified historical perspective on different approaches to leadership is presented in Figure 1. As it suggests, four different types of leader can be distinguished: the "strong man," the "transactor," the "visionary hero," and the "SuperLeader."

The strong-man view of leadership is perhaps the earliest dominant form in our culture. The emphasis with this autocrat view is on the strength of the leader. We use the masculine noun purposely because when this leadership approach was most prevalent it was almost a completely male-dominated process.

The strong-man view of leadership still exists today in many organizations (and is still widely reserved for males), although it is not as highly regarded as it once was.

The strong-man view of leadership creates an image of a John Wayne type who is not afraid to "knock some heads" to get followers to do what he wants done. The expertise for knowing what should be done rests almost entirely in the leader. It is he who sizes up the situation and, based on some seemingly superior strength, skill, and courage, delivers firm commands to the workers. If the job is not performed as commanded, inevitably some significant form of punishment will be delivered by the leader to the guilty party. The focus is on the leader whose power stems primarily from his position in the organization. He is the primary source of wisdom and direction—strong direction. Subordinates simply comply.

One would think that the day of the strong-man leader has passed, but one apparently managed to work his way up the corporate hierarchy at Kellogg Co. This venerable Battle Creek cereal maker recently terminated its president in an unusual action. Accounts printed in the *Wall Street Journal* described this person as "abrasive and often unwilling to listen,…very abrupt,…more inclined to manage without being questioned." He was known for deriding unimpressive presentations as a "CE"—career ending—performance. As another example, we suspect that the majority of employees at Eastern Airlines would describe CEO Frank Lorenzo as a prototypical strong man.

The second view of leadership is that of a *transactor.*

As time passed in our culture, the dominance of the strong-man view of leadership lessened somewhat. Women began to find themselves more frequently in leadership positions. With the development of knowledge of the power of rewards (such as that coming from research on behavior modification), a different view of influence began to emerge. With this view, the emphasis was increasingly placed on a rational exchange approach (exchange of rewards for work performed) in order to get workers to do their work. Even Taylor's views on scientific management, which still influence significantly many organizations in many industries, emphasized the importance of providing incentives to get workers to do work.

With the transactor type of leader, the focus is on goals and rewards; the leader's power stems from the ability to provide rewards for followers doing what the leader thinks should be done. The source of wisdom and direction still rests with the leader. Subordinates will tend to take a calculative view of their work. "I will do what he (or she) asks as long as the rewards keep coming."

Perhaps one of the most prototypical (and successful) transactor organizations in the world today is PEPSICO. *Fortune* described the company with phrases like "…boot camp,…sixty-hour weeks,…back breaking standards that are methodically raised." Those who can't compete are washed out. Those who do compete successfully are rewarded very handsomely—first-class air travel, fully loaded company cars, stock options, bonuses that can hit 90% of salary. Those who are comfortable and effective in this culture receive the spoils. Those who are not comfortable tend to leave early in their career.

Perhaps the ultimate transactor leader is Chairman Larry Phillips-Van Heusen, manufacturer of shirts, sweaters, and casual shoes. Phillips has set up a scheme whereby the 11 senior executives will each earn a \$1 million bonus if the company's earnings per share grow at a 35% compound annual rate during the four years ending in January 1992. Not surprisingly, company executives are actively absorbed in striving to meet this goal.

The next type of leader, which probably represents the most popular view today, is that of the *visionary hero.* Here the focus is on the leader's ability to create highly motivating and absorbing visions. The leader represents a kind of heroic figure who is somehow able to create an almost larger-than-life vision for the workforce to follow. The promise is that if organizations can just find those leaders that are able to capture what's important in the world and wrap it up into some kind of pur-poseful vision, then the rest of the workforce will have the clarifying beacon that will light the way to the promised land.

With the visionary hero, the focus is on the leader's vision, and the leader's power is based on followers' desire to relate to the vision and to the leader himself or herself. Once again, the leader represents the source of wisdom and direction. Followers, at least in theory, are expected to commit to the vision and the leader.

The notion of the visionary hero seems to have received considerable attention lately, but the idea has not gone without criticism. Peter Drucker, for example believes that charisma becomes the undoing of leaders. He believes they become inflexible, convinced of their own infallibility, and slow to really change. Instead, Drucker suggests that the most effective leaders are those not afraid of developing strength in their subordinates and associates. One wonders how Chrysler will fare when Iacocca is gone.

The final view of leadership included in our figure represents the focus of this article—the *SuperLeader*. We do not use the word "Super" to create an image of a larger-than-life-figure who has all the answers and is able to bend others' wills to his or her own. On the contrary, with this type of leader, the focus is largely on the followers. Leaders become "super"—that is, can possess the strength and wisdom of many persons—by helping to unleash the abilities of the "followers" (self-leaders) that surround them.

The focus of this leadership view is on the followers who become self-leaders. Power is more evenly shared by leaders and followers. The leader's task becomes largely that of helping followers to develop the necessary skills for work, especially self-leadership, to be able to contribute more fully to the organization. Thus, leaders and subordinates (that are becoming strong self-leaders) together represent the source of wisdom and direction. Followers (self-leaders), in turn, experience commitment and ownership of their work.

FIGURE 1

| | Strong Men | Transactor | Visionary Hero | SuperLeader |
|---|---|---|---|---|
| Focus | Commands | Rewards | Visions | Self-leadership |
| Type of power | Position/ authority | Rewards | Relational/ inspirational | Shared |
| Source of leader's wisdom and direction | Leader | Leader | Leader | Mostly followers (self-leaders) and then leaders |
| Followers' response | Fear-based compliance | Calculative compliance | Emotional commitment based on leader's vision | Commitment based on ownership |
| Typical leader behaviors | Direction/ command | Interactive goal setting | Communication of leader's vision | Becoming an effective self-leader |
| | Assigned goals | Contingent personal reward | Emphasis on leader's values | Modeling self-leadership |
| | Intimidation | Contingent material reward | Exhortation | Creating positive thought patterns |
| | Reprimand | Contingent reprimand | Inspirational persuasion | Developing self-leadership through reward & constructive reprimand |
| | | | | Promoting self-leading teams |
| | | | | Facilitating a self-leader leadership culture |

# SEVEN STEPS TO SUPERLEADERSHIP

For the SuperLeader, the essence of the challenge is to lead followers to discover the potentialities that lie within themselves. How can a SuperLeader lead others to become positive effective self-leaders? How can a SuperLeader lead others to lead themselves?

We will present seven steps to accomplish these ends. As we will see, some of the elements included in the other leadership views summarized above are a part of SuperLeadership (for instance, the use of rewards) but as Figure 1 indicates, the focus of the leadership process and the basis of power and the relationship of the SuperLeader with followers are very different.

# Step 1—Becoming a Self-Leader

Before learning how to lead others, it is important—make that essential—to first learn how to lead ourselves. Consequently, the first step to becoming a SuperLeader is to become an effective self-leader.

In a taped interview from the historical files of Hewlett-Packard, David Packard, co-founder of Hewlett-Packard, described how, as a young man, he used a daily schedule as a strategy to organize his own efforts. "I was resolved that I was going to have everything organized so, when I was a freshman, I had a schedule set for every day....what I was going to do every hour of the day....and times set up in the morning to study certain things...You did have to allocate your time…" At a very young age, David Packard was developing the self-leadership skills that became so critical to his later success as an executive.

Self-leadership is the influence we exert on ourselves to achieve the self-motivation and self-direction we need to perform. The process of self-leadership consists of an array of behavioral and cognitive strategies for enhancing our own personal effectiveness.

Self-leadership is also the essence of effective followership. As one Ford Motor Co. executive exclaimed to us, "We started participative management, but we didn't know what that meant for the subordinate!" What are the responsibilities of the follower? How does he or she behave in a participative management situation? Developing self-leadership skills is the answer to this question. From a SuperLeadership perspective, effective followers are leaders in their own right—they are skilled at leading themselves.

We will address two classes of self-leadership strategies. The first focuses mainly on effective behavior and action— "behavioral focused strategies"; the second focuses on effective thinking and feeling— "cognitive focused strategies." A summary of these strategies is provided in Figure 2.

*Behavioral focused strategies.* These self-leadership actions are designed to help individuals organize and direct their own work lives more effectively. Specifically, these strategies include self-observation, self-goal setting, cue management, self-reward, constructive self-punishment or self-criticism, and rehearsal.

The necessity for self-observation, for example, was dramatically brought forward at Harley Davidson, when the American motorcycle manufacturer instituted a Just-in-Time/employee involvement program. Management had to train workers to use statistical tools to monitor and control the quality of their own work—an effective prerequisite for helping employees to design and conduct their own self-observation system. The Harley story is a resounding success. This is one American company that has been extraordinarily successful in dealing with the Japanese incursion into their markets.

Each of these strategies, with the exception of self-criticism, when practiced consistently and effectively, has been found to be significantly related to higher performance. While self-criticism can at times serve a useful purpose, it tends to have a demoralizing and destructive impact when overused. Nevertheless, constructive self-criticism can sometimes send a signal to others that we are ready to accept responsibility for our own actions—and that we are sometimes human and make a mistake. Recently, basketball coach John Thompson of Georgetown University was ejected from a game when he protested too vigorously to game officials. Later he commented, "It was probably my fault more than the officials' fault. I have respect for all three of those men. I probably let my competitive juices overflow….I made a mistake." Thompson's willingness to recognize some of his own flaws is one reason he is so widely respected.

*Cognitive-focused strategies.* In addition to behaviorally focused strategies, we can help ourselves to become more effective through the application of self-leadership strategies that promote effective thinking.

First, effective self-leaders can both physically and mentally redesign their own tasks to make them more naturally rewarding; that is, they can create ways to do tasks so that significant natural

FIGURE 2    Self-Leadership Strategies

---

**Behavior-Focused Strategies**

*Self-Observation* – observing and gathering information about specific behavior that you have targeted
    for change

*Self-Set-Goals* – setting goals for your own work efforts

*Management of Cues* – arranging and altering cues in the work environment to facilitate your desired
    personal behaviors

*Rehearsal* – physical or mental practice of work activities before you actually perform them

*Self-Reward* – providing yourself with personally valued rewards for completing desirable behaviors

*Self-Punishment/Criticism* – administering punishments to yourself for behaving in undesirable ways

**Cognitive-Focused Strategies**

*Building Natural Rewards into Tasks* – self-redesign of where and how you do your work to increase the
    level of natural rewards in your job.  Natural rewards that are part of rather than separate from the
    work (*i.e.*, the work, like a hobby, becomes the reward) result from activities that cause you to feel:
    a sense of competence
    a sense of self-control
    a sense of purpose

*Focusing Thinking on Natural Rewards* – purposely focusing your thinking on the naturally rewarding
    features of your work

*Establishment of Effective Thought Patterns* – establishing constructive and effective habits or patterns
    in your thinking (*e.g.*, a tendency to search for opportunities rather than obstacles embedded in chal-
    lenges) by managing your:
    beliefs and assumptions
    mental imagery
    internal self-talk

---

reward value is obtained from the enjoyment of doing the job itself.  Natural rewards are derived from performing tasks in a way that allows us to experience 1) a sense of competence, 2) a sense of self-control, and 3) a sense of purpose.  An example of this notion is embodied in the reply of a young girl featured in a recent news story who was asked why she had made a rock collection, and why she had tried to understand all about rocks.  She replied, "Because it makes me feel good in my mind."

Other cognitive strategies help us by establishing constructive and effective habits or patterns of thinking—such as "opportunity thinking" as opposed to "obstacle thinking."  For example, by studying and managing our beliefs and assumptions, we can begin to develop the ability to find opportunities in each new work challenge.  Until managers began to believe that employees could be important participating partners in the success of American industry, much opportunity for progress was being wasted.

In summary, it's important to remember that if we want to lead others to be self-leaders, we must first practice self-leadership ourselves.  If you want to lead somebody, the first critical step is to lead yourself.

## Step 2—Modeling Self-Leadership

Once we have mastered self-leadership ourselves, the next step is to demonstrate these skills to sub-ordinate employees; that is, our own self-leadership behaviors serve as a model from which others can learn.  As Max DePree, chairman of Herman Miller, the office furniture maker, says, "It's not what you preach, but how you behave."

Modeling can be used to develop subordinate self-leadership on a day-to-day basis in two ways.  The first use is to establish new behaviors—specifically self-leadership behaviors.  The main point is that an employee can learn an entirely new behavior, especially self-leadership, without actually performing it. Executives that are self-starters and well-organized are likely to have subordinates who, in turn, are self-starters and well-organized. Executives, in particular, have a special responsibility to serve as the kind of self-leadership example that they wish subordinate employees to emulate.

The second use involves strengthening the probability of previously learned self-leadership behaviors. Self-leadership behaviors can be enhanced through observation of positive rewards received by others for desired behaviors. We observed, for example, an older woman react with delight when presented with a special achievement award for developing a new inspection procedure at Tandem Computer. She had developed this procedure using her own initiative—she had acted as a self-leader.

This incident served as a symbolic model for other employees at Tandem. Management made it clear that initiating the development of innovative cuing strategies (the inspection procedure) is desirable and that these types of actions are encouraged and rewarded. The hope and intention are that other employees will perceive innovative behavior to be desirable and potentially rewarding. Over time, the objective is to encourage and stimulate widespread incidents of innovative self-leadership.

The lesson from the Tandem incident is straightforward. Employees learn from and are motivated when they see rewards given to others for the performance of self-leadership behaviors. Public recognition to enhance a self-leadership model can be a powerful motivating force for others to initiate self-leadership actions.

Many learn the art of self-leadership from senior executives whom they admire and respect. The book *Eisenhower: Portrait of a Hero* by Peter Lyon (Little Brown, 1974) suggests that General Dwight Eisenhower formulated his own self-leadership style under the guidance of General George Marshall. "What General Marshall wanted most . . . were senior officers who would take the responsibility for action in their own areas of competence without coming to him for the final decision; officers who in their turn would have enough sense to delegate the details of their decisions to their subordinates." Learning to lead from those above him, Ike later carried this sense of delegation and control into his own military leadership style.

Sometimes a model of self-leadership can be inspiring. Who can forget the image of Jimmy Carter as he humbly went about building low-cost housing with his own hammer and nails. The sight of a former U.S. President actually engaging in a relatively minor self-leadership behavior had more influence than anything he could have said. Carter seems to be garnering more admiration as a former President than he acquired as a President.

## Step 3—Encouraging Self-Set Goals

Goal setting, in general, has been one of the most actively investigated aspects of employee behavior and performance. Several general principles have been derived from this extensive research.

First, virtually any kind of goal setting seems to be better than none at all. The mere existence of a goal serves to focus employee attention and energy. This is one of the most pervasive findings of all organizational psychological research. Further, specific goals seem to be better than ambiguous or "fuzzy" ones. Also, in general, more difficult goals result in higher performance—provided the goals are accepted by the employee.

Last but not least, many believe that participation in setting goals will also enhance performance. The logic is that if an employee sees the goal as his or her own, the employee is more likely to give the effort required to attain the goal. Of course, the idea of participation is very closely connected with the essence of SuperLeadership.

Since the main aim of the SuperLeader is to improve the performance of subordinates through the development of their own self-leadership capabilities, employee self-goal setting is a key element. An important point to note is that goal setting is a learned behavior; that is, it is a skill or sequence of actions that an employee can develop over a period of time, not an innate behavior that every new employee brings to the job. Since self-goal setting is something to be learned, the role of the SuperLeader is to serve as a model, coach, and teacher. The SuperLeader helps employees learn to effectively set specific challenging goals for themselves.

Among the more interesting and extreme examples of institutionalized self-set goals is the "Research Fellows" program at IBM. These high-status, high-performing scientists make their own decisions about how substantial resources will be allocated. Obviously, IBM believes its investment in the self-leadership capabilities of these eminent scientists will pay off in the long run. Other organizations would do well to learn from their example.

These ideas also have currency at the level of the shop floor. In a recent *Business Week* article (August 21, 1989), Alvin K. Allison, leader of a team of mechanics at Monsanto's Greenwood, South Carolina plant, says, "I knew 20 years ago that I could direct my own job, but nobody wanted to hear what I had to say." Today, Allison is a part of the upside-down revolution that seems to be driving dramatic improvements in quality and productivity at the Greenwood plant.

## Step 4—Create Positive Thought Patterns

Constructive thought patterns are an important element in successful self-leadership. Part of the SuperLeader role is to transmit positive thought patterns to subordinates. Especially important is the process of facilitating positive self-expectation in subordinates.

Sometimes, but especially in the early stages of a new job, employees do not have adequate natural habits of constructive thinking about themselves. They have doubts and fears—a general lack of confidence in themselves. At this stage, the actions of the SuperLeader are critical: His or her positive comments must serve as a temporary surrogate for the employee's own constructive thought patterns. As indicated in a recent *Fortune* article (March 26, 1990), Jack Welch, CEO of General Electric, thinks this issue is critical: "We need to drive self-confidence deep into the organization... We have to undo a 100-year-old concept and convince our managers that their role is not to control people and stay 'on top' of things but rather to guide, energize, and excite."

The notion of constructing positive thought patterns may also be particularly critical when things are not going well. In the book *Joe Paterno: Football My Way* by Hyman & White (Collier, 1971), the very successful football coach emphasized that enhancing self-esteem is an important part of the equation: "When the staff is down...when the squad is down...when they are starting to doubt themselves ...then it's gotta be a positive approach. The minute I have the feeling they have doubts concerning...[their] ability to do it... then I immediately want to jump in there and...talk about how good the kids are and what a great job they've done." He emphasizes confidence and pride: "A coach must be able to develop three things [in a team member]...pride, poise, and confidence in himself."

The SuperLeader creates productive thought patterns by carefully expressing confidence in the employee's ability to extend his or her present level of competence. Support and encouragement are necessary. In many ways, this expression of confidence is the essence of the "guided-participation" phase in which SuperLeaders teach each employee to lead himself or herself. We discuss this phase later in this article.

This SuperLeadership behavior is well founded in the results of research on the self-fulfilling prophecy: If a person believes something can be done, that belief makes it more likely that it *will* be done. Perhaps the SuperLeader plays "Professor Higgins" to an employee's "Eliza." Most of all, through expressions of confidence, the SuperLeader helps to create productive patterns of thinking— new constructive thought habits.

# Step 5—Develop Self-Leadership
# Through Reward and Constructive Reprimand

One of the SuperLeader's most potent strategies in developing employee self-leadership is reward and reinforcement. For the most part, conventional viewpoints about using organizational rewards tend to focus on so-called extrinsic rewards as a means of reinforcing performance. One example is incentive pay systems.

We are basically in sympathy with this behavioral-management viewpoint and generally believe that material rewards should be used to reinforce desirable job-related behaviors. However, rewards take on a new perspective when seen through the eyes of the SuperLeader. If the purpose of the SuperLeader is to lead others to self-leadership, then an essential ingredient is to teach employees how to reward themselves and to build natural rewards into their own work. The SuperLeader attempts to construct a reward system that emphasizes self-administered and natural rewards and, in a comparative sense, de-emphasizes externally administered rewards. Thus the focus shifts from material types of rewards to a stronger emphasis on natural rewards that stem more from the task itself and on self-administration of rewards.

This usually means that people need to have the freedom to do their jobs in the ways they most value and can thrive in; that is, in the ways that they find most naturally rewarding. In the book *Our Story So Far* (3M Co., 1977), William McKnight, former CEO of 3M Company during perhaps 3M's most critical years in becoming an organizational success story, was quoted on the need for employees to do their jobs the way they want to do them. He stated, "Those men and women to whom we delegate authority and responsibility, if they are good people, are going to want to do their jobs in their own way. These are characteristics we want and should be encouraging."

In addition, a new type of reprimand is appropriate to develop employee self-leadership. We know that reprimand, in the short term, can keep somebody's nose to the grindstone, but the effectiveness of this mode of behavior is limited. Author Ken Blanchard was quoted in the *Minneapolis Star and Tribune* (May 27, 1987) as saying, "Most managers can get things done when they are around to nag and push. However, the real test of leadership is when management isn't present ...which is about 70 percent of the time."

From a behavioral viewpoint, reprimand *should* be easy to understand. When an employee does something wrong, the manager provides a contingent aversive consequence, and the undesirable employee behavior *should* be reduced or eliminated. However, the long-term efficacy of reprimand is much more complex and leaves much to be desired. Most of all, a complex and sometimes confusing set of emotions typically accompanies reprimand, sometimes even leading to aggressive and disruptive behavior.

Reprimand is usually the opposite of what needs to be done to develop productive thought patterns in others. One objective of the SuperLeader is to encourage constructive self-confidence as an important part of the transition to self-leadership, but reprimand induces guilt and depression and diminishes self-confidence. On the other hand, if a SuperLeader treats a mistake as a learning opportunity, then employee self-esteem can be enhanced. After all, one sign of self-confidence is an individual objectively realizing that he has "made every mistake in the book" and has the experience and confidence to handle surprising situations.

We do recognize that reprimand is sometimes a necessary element in a SuperLeader's repertoire of behaviors, especially with careless or chronic underperformers. The most important lesson to remember is that the careless use of reprimand can be very discouraging to employees who are in their transition to self-leadership. The main focus should be to treat a mistake as a learning opportunity, to provide positive acceptance of the *person* despite the mistake, and to remember how the opportunity to make mistakes was a critical element in the SuperLeader's own development. Following these tips will result in a *constructive* feedback process that is more effective than the traditional use of reprimand and that positively influences employee self-leadership and long-term effectiveness.

## Step 6—Promote Self-Leadership Through Teamwork

One of the more interesting examples of self-leadership systems is the team-oriented system at Volvo. Volvo has considerable experience with team assembly concepts, which were pioneered at its Kalmar plant. Further, the automobile assembly approach has been completely scrapped in the design of the new $315 million plant at Uddevalla. The key organizational philosophy at this plant is the work team, and the technical system has been designed to match the team concept. As Peter Gyllenhammar, Volvo's CEO, says, "I want the people in a team to be able to go home at night and really say, 'I built that car.' "

In the U.S., the self-managing team concept has had a slow but steady start. More recent media interest seems to indicate that the team idea is about to take off. The dramatic success of the team approach at the GM-Toyota joint venture in Fremont, California has been instructive to the U.S. automotive industry in general. In our own research, we have documented the leader characteristics that are necessary to make a team effort successful, the core of which are the basic principles of SuperLeadership.

Top-management teams are also important, as represented by this quote that appeared in *Fortune* (August, 1987) from Tom Watson, Jr., former CEO of IBM: "My most important contribution to IBM was my ability to pick strong and intelligent men and then hold the team together...."

One of the more interesting indicators of a self-leadership culture is the presence of quite a few items. The types of teams (not all work groups are called teams) include product teams, top-executive teams, ad hoc teams, and shop-floor self-managing teams. Of course, teams require a good deal of self-leadership at the group level to function correctly.

> Teamwork is important at Hewlett-Packard when it comes to the precision timing and integration required for successful new product release. At H-P, a committee called "board of directors" serves to drive the process to completion. Representatives from every department involved in the project serve on these committees.

## Step 7—Facilitate a Self-Leadership Culture

A major factor in developing SuperLeadership is the challenge of designing an integrated organizational culture that is conducive to high performance. Organizations will find it difficult to obtain initiative and innovation from employees without providing a pervasive environment that facilitates those elements of self-leadership.

For the most part, we focus on the one-on-one relationship between a SuperLeader and an employee: How can an executive lead that employee to lead himself or herself? For an organization, however, the best results derive from a total integrated system that is deliberately intended to encourage, support, and reinforce self-leadership *throughout* the system. Most of all, this is an issue that addresses the question of how top executives can create self-leadership cultures.

One company that has shown demonstrable results of an effort to develop a self-leadership culture is Xerox Corporation, recent winner of the Malcolm Baldridge National Quality Award. The award recognized companies that attain preeminent leadership in quality control. At Xerox, the quality effort includes plant-level employee "family groups" that work with little direct supervision. But most of all, the award recognizes the effort of Xerox to build a total quality culture based on bottom-up employee involvement.

At another company, Dana Corporation, highly visible symbolic acts were instrumental in turning the organizational culture around. One of Rene McPherson's first concerns was to indicate the importance of giving discretion to make decisions down through the ranks. The most famous story is about one of his first actions: eliminating the procedures manual. According to one account, the procedures manual had risen to a height of 22.5 inches. McPherson was said to have dumped it in a wastebasket and replaced it with a one-page policy statement.

Rene McPherson used the following metaphor to describe his philosophy of a decentralized self-leadership culture at Dana as reported in an article in *Management Review* entitled "Hell Week—Or How Dana Makes its Managers Money Conscious" (1984). "You can control a business in one of two ways. You can institute a kind of martial law, with troops stationed in each hamlet or village standing guard; or you can sit back and let each village be self-governing....What we are after is to help that person [the division manager] to be [his own]...manager." McPherson said of his division managers, "We didn't tell the guys what they were gonna do—they came in and told us!"

Through his radical change in culture, McPherson has left a meaningful legacy for Dana Corporation. He transformed a top-heavy, bureaucratic, sluggish organization into one of the most successful and competitive manufacturing businesses in the United States today. Self-leadership was a key ingredient: Rene McPherson demonstrated a special capacity to lead others to lead themselves.

SuperLeadership at the top requires the creation of positive organizational cultures within which self-leadership can flourish. Such environments consist of a host of factors, some observable and concrete, others more subtle and symbolic. Culture becomes particularly important when it comes to balancing the needs of individualism with the needs for organized, coordinated effort. As Peter Drucker put it in the July 3, 1989 issue of *Fortune* "...it is important to build up the oboist as an oboist, but it is even more important to build up the oboist's pride in the performance of the orchestra...it puts a tremendous premium on having very clear goals and a very clear and demanding mission for the enterprise." Overreaching organizational values that support self-leadership are perhaps the most important factor.

Ford Motor Company, for example, has developed a set of guidelines that is widely circulated throughout the corporation and known as its "Mission, Values and Guiding Principles." Among other things, they identify employee involvement and teamwork as Ford's "core human values."

In addition, training and development efforts that equip employees with both task-performance and self-leadership capabilities are important means of stimulating cultures based on leading others to lead themselves. Thus the SuperLeader's challenge is not limited to direct one-on-one leadership; the SuperLeader must also foster an integrated world in which self-leadership can survive and grow; in which self-leadership becomes an exciting, motivating, and accepted way of life. At lower levels, the challenge for aspiring SuperLeaders is to develop subcultures within their own control that stimulate the unique self-leadership strengths of subordinates.

# THE TRANSITION TO SELF-LEADERSHIP

Three basic assumptions underlie our ideas on self-leadership. First, everyone practices self-leadership to some degree, but not everyone is an effective self-leader. Second, self-leadership can be learned, and thus is not restricted to people who are "born" to be self-starters or self-motivated. And third, self-leadership is relevant to executives, managers, and all employees—that is, to everyone who works.

Few employees are capable of highly effective self-leadership the moment they enter a job situation. Especially at the beginning, the SuperLeader must provide orientation, guidance, and direction. The need for specific direction at the beginning stages of employment stems from two sources. First, the new employee is unfamiliar with the objectives, tasks, and procedures of his or her position. He or she will probably not yet have fully developed task capabilities. But more pertinent, the new employee may not yet have an adequate set of self-leadership skills. For the SuperLeader, the challenge lies in shifting employees to self-leadership. Thus the role of the SuperLeader becomes critical: He or she must lead others to lead themselves.

Throughout the entire process of leading others to lead themselves, aspects of SuperLeadership are involved that do not necessarily represent a distinct step but that are nevertheless quite important. For example, *encouragement* of followers to exercise initiative, take on responsibility, and to use self-leadership strategies in an effective way to lead themselves, is an important feature that runs through the entire process. Also, a feature we call *guided participation* is very important to SuperLeadership. This involves facilitating the gradual shifting of followers from dependence to independent self-leadership through a combination of initial instruction, questions that stimulate thinking about self-leadership (e.g., What are you shooting for?...what is your goal. How well do you think you're doing?), and increasing participation of followers.

Consider the goal setting process as an example of how the transition to self-leadership unfolds. Teaching an employee how to set goals can follow a simple procedure: First, an employee is provided with a model to emulate; second, he or she is allowed guided participation; and finally, he or she assumes the targeted self-leadership skill, which in this case is goal setting. Once again modeling is an especially key element in learning this skill. Because of their formal position of authority, SuperLeaders have a special responsibility to personally demonstrate goal setting behavior that can be emulated by other employees. Furthermore, goals need to be coordinated among the different levels of the hierarchy. Subordinate goals, even those that are self-set, need to be consistent with superior and organizational goals.

A SuperLeader takes into account the employee's time and experience on the job, as well as the degree of the employee's skill and capabilities. For a new employee, whose job-related and self-leadership skills may yet be undeveloped, an executive may wish to begin with assigned goals, while modeling self-set goals for himself or herself. Within a short period of time, the SuperLeader endeavors to move toward interactive goals. Usually the best way to accomplish this is by "guided participation," which includes asking the employee to propose his or her own goals. At this stage, the SuperLeader still retains significant influence over goal setting, actively proposing and perhaps imposing some of the goals. Usually, this is the give and take that is typical of the traditional MBO approach.

Finally, for true self-leadership to develop and flourish, the SuperLeader will deliberately move toward employee self-set goals. In this situation, the SuperLeader serves as a source of information and experience, as a sounding board, and as the transmitter of overall organizational goals. In the end, in a true self-leadership situation, the employee is given substantial latitude to establish his or her own goals.

We have found that sharing goal setting with subordinates is frequently one of the most difficult transitions for traditional leaders to understand and accept on their road to effective SuperLeadership. Often, an executive is reluctant to provide the full opportunity for a subordinate to lead himself or herself because it seems the executive is losing control.

One of the most interesting aspects of Coach Joe Paterno is his ability to be introspective about this dilemma of overcontrol and undercontrol. Hyman and White quoted him as follows: "It's difficult" he candidly admits "for me to handle people in the way I think they want to be handled . . . because I have a tendency to want *complete* control....In the early part of my career,...I would plot every offensive and defensive move we would use in a ball game and try to devise the game play by myself...I felt that I had to have input in everything that went on every minute of the day and every day of the week." Paterno seems destined to deal with the classic dilemma between his natural "hands on" activist leadership style and the behaviors required of a SuperLeader. There seems to be a conflict between his emotional self, which has a strong desire to control—perhaps over-control— the situation, versus his intellectual self, which realizes the necessity and benefit of providing more opportunity for his assistant coaches. The "natural" self says, "Hey, I gotta get in there and do it myself," while the intellectual self says, "I have to stand back and give them an opportunity to do it." In the end, the important thing, he says, "is still keeping control but knowing when you don't have to have control."

Good leaders intuitively understand the effects on performance of "knowing where they are going." During subordinate employees' critical transition from traditional external leadership to self-leadership, previous dependency on superior authority needs to be unlearned. In its place, employees must develop a strong sense of confidence in their own abilities to set realistic and challenging goals on their own.

Frequently this transition is not very smooth, leaving the employee wondering why "the boss" is not providing more help, and the executive biting his lip to avoid telling the employee to do the "right thing." Employees need to have some latitude in making mistakes during this critical period.

Reprimand takes on special importance during the critical transition phase, when the superior-subordinate relationship is very delicate. Careless use of reprimand can seriously set back the employee's transition to self-leadership. The issue becomes especially salient when employees make mistakes—sometimes serious mistakes. In our experience, during the transition to self-leadership, some mistakes are inevitable and should be expected as an employee reaches out. The way the SuperLeader responds to the mistakes can ensure or thwart a successful transition. Again, in 3M's historical book *Our Story So Far*, former CEO William McKnight commented on the issue this way, "Mistakes will be made, but if a person is essentially right, the mistakes he or she makes are not as serious in the long run as the mistakes management will make if it is dictatorial and undertakes to tell those under its authority exactly how they must do their job....Management that is destructively critical when mistakes are made kills initiative and it is essential that we have many people with initiative if we're going to grow."

Andrew Grove, CEO of chip maker Intel Corporation, discussed the issue of how to react when an employee seems to be making a mistake. Reacting too soon or too harshly can result in a serious setback in efforts to develop employee self-leadership. According to Grove, the manager needs to consider the degree to which the error can be tolerated or not. For example, if the task is an analysis for internal use, the experience the employee receives may be well worth some wasted work and delay. However, if the error involves a shipment to a customer, the customer should not bear the expense of boosting the employee further down the learning curve.

Sometimes the SuperLeader might *deliberately* hold back goals or decisions that, at other times, in other places, he or she would be more than willing to provide. Self-led employees must learn to stand on their own.

Once through this critical transition phase, the effects on the self-led employee's performance can be remarkable. Effectively leading themselves produces a motivation and psychological commitment that energizes employees to greater and greater achievements. SuperLeaders who have successfully unleashed the power of self-led employees understand the ultimate reward and satisfaction of managing these individuals.

FIGURE 3    The Seven-Step Process of SuperLeadership

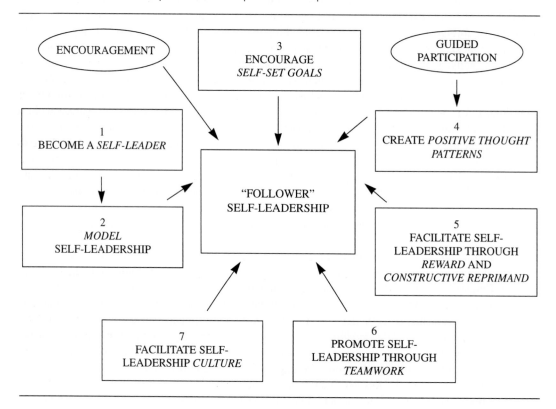

## SUPERLEADERSHIP: A COMPREHENSIVE FRAMEWORK

It should be clear by now that we are addressing a different approach to leadership, radically unlike many of the classic stereotypes of strong leadership. Most of all, we believe that SuperLeadership is a process that can be *learned*, that is not restricted to a few "special" individuals that are born with an unusual capability. Granted, some seem to have more to learn than others, but the potential for SuperLeadership seems to be almost universal.

Figure 3 is a representation of the separate components of SuperLeadership, brought together in an organized framework with self-leadership at the core. The logic is that each SuperLeadership component is of central importance to the development of the self-leadership system within each employee. The potential payoffs include increased employee performance and innovation flowing from enhanced commitment, motivation, and employee capability.

414

It seems clear that an essential ingredient to SuperLeadership is a boundless optimism about the potential of ordinary people to accomplish extraordinary things. In the March 26, 1990 issue of *Fortune*, Max DePree, Herman Miller chairman, put it this way: "Take a 33-year-old man who assembles chairs. He's been doing it several years. He has a wife and two children. He knows what to do when the children have earaches, and how to get them through school. He probably serves on a volunteer board, and when he comes to work we give him a supervisor....He doesn't need one." This positive viewpoint of man in general is a fairly common characteristic of SuperLeaders. They seem to have unlimited faith that, if given the opportunity to perform, most people will come through for them.

SuperLeadership is not all that unusual if we just know where to look for it. The Peace Corps, for example, has been an organization in the business of producing SuperLeaders for years, even though they don't use the term. Consider the young woman, Patty, who organizes health education events for the women and children of a third-world community. Eventually, the community decides itself to build community latrines, and within a year, 15 latrines have been constructed. Health improves. Now, building latrines doesn't sound much like the stuff of leadership, but this young Peace Corps volunteer was indeed a SuperLeader by leading others to lead themselves to accomplish something of critical importance to all those who were involved.

It's all too easy to underestimate the capability of seemingly ordinary people. Lincoln Electric, the highly successful welding manufacturer, found some special capabilities among its employees when its sales were sagging in 1982. Faced with a no-layoff policy, management asked its factory workers for some help. Fifty of their production workers volunteered to help out in sales.

After a quickie sales training course, the former production workers started calling on body shops all over the country. They concentrated on small shops that would be able to use the company's Model SP200, a small welder. The end of the story is that their efforts brought in $10 million in new sales and established the small arc welder as one of Lincoln's best-selling items.

Lincoln Electric was relying on the idea of the self-fulfilling prophecy. Like real SuperLeaders, they were willing to take a risk on people; and the risk frequently becomes self-fulfilling. Lincoln carries this philosophy throughout all parts of the organization. As one example, it manages to produce the lowest cost, highest quality welders in the industry with a supervisor to worker ratio of 1 to 100. Yes, that's right—one supervisor for every 100 workers. Clearly, this would not be possible unless every employee was considered to be a true self-leader. At Lincoln, every employee is evaluated on the ability to work without supervision.

Ideally, the SuperLeader comes to be surrounded by strong people—self-leaders in their own right—who pursue exceptional achievement because they love to. The SuperLeader's strength is greatly enhanced since it is drawn from the strength of many people who have been encouraged to grow, flourish, and become important contributors. The SuperLeader becomes "Super" through the talents and capabilities of others. As self-leadership is nurtured, the power for progress is unleashed. In the March 26, 1990 issue of *Fortune*, Colgate-Palmolive CEO Ruben Mark put it this way: "I see business moving away from the authoritarian approach and toward a shared decision-making approach. . . making partnership with our own people."

SuperLeadership offers the most viable mechanism for establishing exceptional self-leading followers. True excellence can be achieved by facilitating the self-leadership system that operates within each person—by challenging each person to reach deep inside for the best each has to offer. Employee compliance is not enough. Leading others to lead themselves is the key to tapping the intelligence, the spirit, the creativity, the commitment, and most of all the tremendous unique potential of each individual.

To us, the message is clear: Excellence is achievable, but only if leaders are dedicated to tapping the vast potential within each individual. Most of all, this does *not* mean that more so-called charismatic or transformational leaders are needed to influence followers to comply with and carry out the vision of the leader. Rather, the vision itself needs to reflect and draw upon the vast resources contained within individual employees.

The currently popular notion that excellent leaders need to be visionary and charismatic may be a trap if taken too far. Wisdom on leadership for centuries has warned us about this potential trap. Remember what Abraham Lincoln said, "You cannot help men permanently by doing for them what they could and should do for themselves." Remember, also, the timeless words, "Give a man a fish and he will be fed for a lifetime."

It is time to transcend the notion of leaders as heroes and to focus instead on leaders as hero-makers. Is the spotlight on the leader, or on the achievements of the followers? To discover this new breed of leader, look not at the leader but at the followers. SuperLeaders have SuperFollowers that are dynamic self-leaders. The SuperLeader leads others to lead themselves. Perhaps this spirit was captured most succinctly by Lao-tzu, a sixth-century B.C. Chinese philosopher, when he wrote the following:

A leader is best
When people barely know he exists,
Not so good when people obey and acclaim him.
Worse when they despise him.
But of a good leader, who talks little,
When his work is done, his aim fulfilled,
They will say:
We did it ourselves.


# FIRMS WITH A SUPERIOR LEADERSHIP CAPACITY: PRACTICES THAT CREATE BETTER-THAN-AVERAGE MANAGEMENT TEAMS

*John P. Kotter*


It is not entirely clear whether there are any firms today that do a truly exceptional job of attracting, developing, retaining, and motivating leadership talent. Nevertheless, some corporations clearly do achieve a level of success that is much superior (relatively) to others. Considerable evidence supports that conclusion—from the Executive Resources Questionnaire, the interviews done for this book, the *Fortune* Reputation Study, and elsewhere.

If we are to improve current practice related to creating a leadership capacity within management groups and help firms break out of the syndrome seen in the West Products case [*Mishandling and Losing Young Managers with Leadership Potential*], it would be useful to know what some corporations actually do to create those better-than-average management teams.

*Source*: Reprinted with permission of The Free Press, a Division of Macmillan, Inc., from *The Leadership Factor* by John P. Kotter. Copyright © 1988 by John P. Kotter, Inc.

# WHAT THE MANAGERIALLY STRONGER FIRMS DO DIFFERENTLY: EVIDENCE FROM THE QUESTIONNAIRE

A casual reading of management, leadership, and human resources literature can generate dozens of hypotheses regarding what is most important to creating a superior leadership capacity within management. Some writers imply that hiring standards are the key; bring in the right people, and everything else takes care of itself. Others focus on development; provide challenging job assignments to people early in their careers, and the leaders will emerge and grow. Some point to formal systems-succession planning, high potential identification, or compensation reviews. Others suggest that more informal practices, such as the amount of mentoring and coaching provided, are key.

The Executive Resources Questionnaire provides one basis for testing those hypotheses. The survey asks an overall question about the quality of a firm's management, as well as more specific questions about practices that affect the quality. Because there is a relatively broad range of responses to that first question (quality of management), we can see which (if any) of the more specific programs and practices seem to be associated with differences in that quality.

Tables 1 and 2 summarize the results of a very basic analysis of this sort. An examination of the first table shows that firms with superior managements are said to do a better job, on average, of attracting, developing, retaining, and motivating leadership talent (that is, *all four* aspects of the process). They achieve those results, the second table further suggests, by employing nothing less than dozens of more adequate practices.

More specifically, the detailed data (upon which Table 2 is based) say that those firms attract the people they need by having more adequate college recruiting efforts, programs for high potentials, training/educational opportunities, promotional opportunities, compensation, work environments, and reputations. They then hire the right people by having a more adequate sense of what they need to support business objectives, by keeping hiring standards high, and by having more hiring-level managers who can spot potential.

According to questionnaire data, those firms develop that talent by focusing scarce development resources on those who have the most potential. They spot that potential with more adequate performance appraisal processes, succession planning processes, and programs designed specifically to identify potential. They also tend to offer more opportunities to young people to get exposure to higher levels of management and have more executives at higher levels who can adequately spot young people with potential. They target development resources by more adequately identifying exactly what the development needs of those employees are. They then meet those needs in many ways, including adding responsibilities to jobs, creating special jobs, using inside and outside training, transferring people between functions and divisions, mentoring and coaching employees, giving those people feedback on development progress, and giving them instruction in how to manage their own development.

Firms with better-than-average management retain and motivate the people they develop, according to questionnaire data, by having more adequate practices for them in the areas of compensation, promotion opportunities, development opportunities, and training opportunities. They also provide them with more adequate information on job openings in the firm and have higher-quality career planning discussions with them. And they offer those people a considerably better work environment.

*In other words, the questionnaire data suggest that no single program or small set of practices is key to creating a stronger-than-average leadership capacity within management.* Good succession planning, excellent college recruiting, or superior economic incentives, by themselves, appear not to be sufficient. The firms with better-than-average management seem to do a more adequate job in dozens of areas that affect the hiring, development, and retention of talent.

TABLE 1　A Comparison of the "Stronger" Management Firms with All Others*

|  | Stronger Management Firms | All Other Firms |
|---|---|---|
| 1. How good a job is the company doing with respect to recruiting and hiring a sufficient number of people into the firm who have the potential of someday providing effective leadership in important management positions? | 2.8 (1 = excellent, 5 = poor) | 3.4 |
| 2. How good a job is the company doing with respect to developing employees with potential? | 3.0 | 3.0 |
| 3. How good a job is the company doing with respect to retaining and motivating those employees? | 2.8 | 3.4 |

* Only firms in which twenty or more executives completed the questionnaire are included in this analysis. Firm scores are the simple mean of all the executives' responses. This and the next table compare the four firms scoring highest on item 57 (the "Stronger Management Firms") with fourteen lower-scoring firms.

TABLE 2　A Comparison of Programs and Practices: From the Executive Resources Questionnaire

|  | Number of Areas in Which Stronger Firms Have: | | |
|---|---|---|---|
|  | More Adequate Practices | Equally Adequate Practices | Less Adequate Practices |
| 1. Regarding fifteen programs and practices that affect the recruitment and hiring of people with leadership potential | 14 | 1 | 0 |
| 2. Regarding nineteen programs and practices that affect the training and development of those people | 15 | 4 | 0 |
| 3. Regarding twelve programs and practices that affect the retention and motivation of such people | 12 | 0 | 0 |

# WHAT FIFTEEN FIRMS DO DIFFERENTLY: EVIDENCE FROM THE "BEST PRACTICES" STUDY

That questionnaire-based conclusion receives further support with information from a second source: a more in-depth study of fifteen firms.

Those firms were chosen using data from *Fortune*'s Reputation Study. The 1985 version of that survey asked hundreds of "experts" to rate 250 corporations on a number of dimensions, two of which were 1) the quality of the firms' management 2) the firms' success in attracting, developing and retaining talented employees. The twenty firms that were ranked the highest on those two dimensions are shown in Table 3. Fifteen of those firms were included in a "Best Practices" study as background for this book (the table identifies which fifteen). In using that procedure, it was not

418

assumed that the fifteen firms had managements that were excellent in any absolute sense, nor that they had the best leadership capacity within their managements in a relative sense (relative to all other firms). It was assumed *only* that the fifteen represented a good sample of corporations with better-than-average managements.

Eight or more top executives were interviewed in each of the fifteen firms, typically for an hour each. The two core questions that structured the discussions were: 1) What do you do to attract and retain people with some leadership potential? 2) What do you do to develop and broaden those people?

The responses from the 150 interviews are entirely consistent with the questionnaire data. There are no big "secrets to success." These firms just do a lot of little things differently from the norm in business today. For our purposes here, a discussion of all the practices will be grouped into five sessions relating to: a sophisticated recruiting effort, an attractive work environment, challenging opportunities, early identification, and planned development.

TABLE 3  Firms Rated Highest on Two Dimensions[a] in the 1985 *Fortune* Reputation Study

| Firm | Rating (1–10 Scale)[b] | Included in This Study |
|---|---|---|
| 1. IBM | 8.75 | Yes |
| 2. Dow Jones | 8.4 | Yes |
| 3. Hewlett-Packard | 8.4 | Yes |
| 4. Coca Cola | 8.35 | Yes |
| 5. Morgan Guaranty | 8.3 | Yes |
| 6. Anheuser-Busch | 8.3 | Yes |
| 7. 3M | 8.2 | Yes |
| 8. General Electric | 8.15 | Yes |
| 9. Boeing | 8.0 | No |
| 10. Citicorp | 7.9 | Yes |
| 11. Standard Oil of Indiana | 7.9 | No |
| 12. General Motors | 7.8 | Yes |
| 13. Du Pont | 7.75 | Yes |
| 14. Merck | 7.7 | Yes |
| 15. General Mills | 7.65 | Yes |
| 16. Johnson & Johnson | 7.6 | Yes |
| 17. Kodak | 7.55 | No |
| 18. Abbot | 7.55 | No |
| 19. Delta | 7.55 | No |
| 20. First Boston | 7.5 | Yes |

[a] "Quality of Management" and "Ability to Attract, Develop, and Keep Talented People."
[b] 10 = excellent. Mean score on the two dimensions combined.

# A SOPHISTICATED RECRUITING EFFORT

Interviews from the "Best Practices" study suggest, first of all, that the fifteen firms do a superior job of recruiting sufficient people who have the potential of providing them with leadership at some time in the future. They do so by using a half-dozen practices that are slightly different from the norm today in business.

The first practice is to let line management drive the recruiting effort. At these firms, human resource professionals aid in the process, providing coordination and administrative support, but they do not seem to run the process. Line management does, including some fairly senior people. At General Mills, for example, even the chairman sometimes visits key colleges. At First Boston, the managing director who heads the recruiting effort literally spends half his time on recruiting. At Mercke, the CEO himself devotes considerable time and effort to recruiting people who can help provide technical leadership in the firm. Although obviously expensive in terms of senior management time, most executives in these firms seem convinced it is necessary. A typical comment from one of those businessmen:

> Our current senior management is in the best position to know how many and what kind of people will be needed to run the business in the future; they understand where our business strategy is taking us better than anyone. They also are better able to spot the kind of quality minds and interpersonal abilities we want in young people; in a sense, it takes one to know one. And they are in a much better position to sell the company than are lower-level managers or personnel staff.

Second, many of these corporations target a limited number of colleges and universities that they feel are a good source of future leadership, and then they treat those schools much as they would major customers. Hewlett-Packard, for example, focuses on thirty schools for its corporate recruiting effort and works hard to develop good relationships with those schools by (among other things) networking with their faculties and donating computer equipment. When managed well, those efforts appear to pay off handsomely.

Third, most of these firms seem to work especially hard to keep hiring standards high across the entire company. IBM, for example, quantifies certain measures of the quality of incoming hires, sets targets on those measures, and then "inspects" on a regular basis how well each hiring department is doing. Merck brings all high-potential recruiting candidates to corporate headquarters to meet some senior managers who are thought to have a good sense of the firm's hiring standards. General Mills does that too, and if any of those senior executives vote "no" on a candidate, they seriously consider not making an offer despite plenty of "yes" votes. Morgan Guaranty brings all new recruits to a lengthy training program in New York; if any of its offices are diluting hiring standards, it becomes rather obvious by the end of the program. The exact practices vary from firm to firm, but the main objective seems to remain the same: Keep standards from slipping because of short-term economic pressures.

A fourth practice that appears to distinguish most of these firms is that they actually pay some attention to leadership potential when recruiting. Morgan Guaranty, for example, asks everyone who interviews candidates to fill out a one page "Prospective Employee-Interview Evaluation." The form gently reminds people to "keep in mind" four factors that have little to do with the technical components of banking; one of those factors is "leadership potential." "With all the well-educated and talented people we hire," an investment banker recently reported, "you'd think we would be guaranteed plenty of leadership and management potential. But it's not true. Unless we focus on that explicitly, we end up with a lot of smart technicians who often lack common sense and basic interpersonal skills."

420

A fifth practice commonly found at these firms might be called the well-managed "close." As one General Mills executive reported:

> When we find someone we really want, we work hard to close the sale. For example, if we meet such people at one of our informal wine and cheese gatherings, we'll immediately send a follow-up letter and invite them to Minneapolis. When they are here, we'll make sure they have lunch with a recent graduate of their school or someone from their home town. We will then make them an offer at the end of the day—no, "We'll get back to you in a few weeks" stuff. Then, if they don't accept immediately, we might fly them and their spouses back to corporate to see the community and meet the chairman. In between, there will be all the appropriate follow-up letters and calls.

Finally, these firms usually evaluate their overall recruiting at least once a year. Many generate statistics on offers made to offers accepted, or offers lost to key competitors, and then compare those statistics to historical averages. Some, like Du Pont, look at more indirect indices, such as how many relatively new hires are rated on the yearly performance appraisal as having high potential.

## ATTRACTIVE WORK ENVIRONMENT

A few years ago I visited a former student who works for Hewlett-Packard. By job standards, he was doing very well at the time. At age thirty-four, he was in charge of hundreds of people and a sizable budget. But by salary standards, he was making 25 percent less than the average person who graduated in his MBA class. When I questioned him about this, he admitted that he wished he made more money. He also volunteered that he had considered on several occasions leaving HP for startup ventures. But he hadn't. I asked why.

The long answer the young man provided basically boiled down to this: Hewlett-Packard has been a good place for a talented person to work. People are treated well. Competence is respected. Bureaucracy and political games are minimized. Individual initiative is recognized and rewarded. It is technically a very exciting place for people with engineering backgrounds, etc. etc.

What is so interesting about that response is that it is not at all unusual at the fifteen "Best Practice" firms. When one asks executives at those firms how they attract and retain good people, almost always they say "because it's a great place to work." Why they think it's a great place to work seems to vary somewhat from firm to firm and from individual to individual. What remains constant is their belief that it's "fun" for someone with leadership potential to work there.

Perhaps the most common answer regarding what makes a work environment fun is "lack of politics." By that, people typically mean the environment is friendly. ("When someone gets the knife out around here it is made of rubber.") They also mean that results are what count, not covert alliances or form. And they mean that people actually try to help each other. "I could get a job at (another prestigious newspaper)," a Dow Jones manager says, "but I'm not interested. Politics here are 10 percent of what they are over there. We don't have their warring factions. I mean, who wants to have to put up with that? It's not worth it."

Executives also often mention honesty or integrity as an important feature of a good work environment. Johnson & Johnson people, for example, often refer to the fact that they usually live up to the high ethical standards outlined in their "credo," and that makes J&J's environment very attractive. Executives at other firms sometimes talk about other corporate values, such as a dedication to quality (one hears that often at Dow Jones and Anheuser-Busch). They talk about the lack of bureaucracy or the informality. They talk about the quality of their fellow workers. They sometimes refer to the nice location of the workplace (e.g., 3M in Minneapolis, Coke in Atlanta) or the aesthetics of the work environment (Morgan Guaranty). And they often point out that "people are treated well around here."

For example, one of the frequent complaints one hears from lower-level managers in many firms is that they feel "trapped." Here is a very typical comment:

> I have almost no idea what job openings exist or will exist outside my department. That kind of information just doesn't circulate at my level. So my capacity to get a good opportunity in some other part of the company is almost completely under the control of my bosses. Unfortunately, they don't have much incentive to want to find those opportunities for me. So I'm trapped in a narrow and vertical career path, which in the long run won't be good for me. And the speed of my movement on this path is a function of strong forces I don't control. It's not a good situation. It's driving me to look for opportunities outside the company.

The fifteen firms studied here seem to do a much better job than average of minimizing that problem by providing high potentials (and often others too) with information on job openings throughout the company. Hewlett-Packard, for example, has worked to maintain a labor market inside the company that is at least as open and accessible as external markets. Most people really appreciate those efforts, and such practices facilitate lateral movement for development purposes (more on that later).

## CHALLENGING OPPORTUNITIES

Interviews at the fifteen "Best Practice" firms are replete with references to the importance of "challenging opportunities." One gets the sense that challenging entry-level jobs help attract good people in the first place, and challenging promotion opportunities help firms hold onto those people, because people with leadership potential love new challenges and hate old routines. The challenges, in turn, both stretch people and allow them, often early in their careers, to exercise some leadership. And that, of course, is at the heart of development.

Those interviewed say that challenging opportunities are created in a number of ways. In many firms, decentralization is the key. By definition, decentralization pushes responsibility lower in an organization and in the process creates more challenging jobs at lower levels. Johnson & Johnson, 3M, HP, General Electric, and a number of other well-known firms have used that approach quite successfully in the past.

Some of those same firms also have created as many small units as possible so there are lots of challenging little general management jobs available. Hewlett Packard, GE, and J&J are said to have benefited greatly over the years from that approach.

In a similar vein, many of the firms seem to develop additional challenging opportunities by stressing growth through new products: 3M has even had a policy over the years that at least 25 percent of its revenue should come from products introduced within the last five years. That encourages small new ventures, which in turn offer hundreds of opportunities to test and stretch young people with leadership potential.

Some of those same firms have also worked hard to minimize bureaucracy and rigid structures so that it's easier to enhance jobs with additional challenges. As an executive at Coca Cola recently put it:

> If I hire an MBA as a brand manager, because we are not highly compartmentalized and
> structured, he or she can make that job into almost anything. The person is not in a box.
> We can make the job as big and challenging as is necessary to really turn that person on.

In a similar way, more and more companies, like Du Pont, seem to be using task force assignments to generate additional challenge in jobs.

Other firms, including some that face limits to how much they can decentralize responsibility into small units, have created specific jobs to challenge people with leadership potential. Perhaps the most obvious example is administrative assistant (or executive assistant) jobs. Anheuser-Busch has created about thirty such jobs. IBM has even more, and has obviously benefited from the practice. The last few presidents and many of the current executive staff at IBM had AA jobs early in their careers.

When all of those techniques still do not produce enough opportunities, perhaps because the business (or part of the business) is not growing, these firms then (more often than the norm in business today) take the painful actions needed to free up promotion possibilities. That sometimes means making early retirement attractive to certain people. And it always means coming to grips with "blockers"—people who have no chance of further promotion, are a long way from retirement, and are not performing well in their current assignments.

## EARLY IDENTIFICATION

Equipping people with what they will need to provide effective leadership takes time, often lots of time. As such, it is not entirely surprising to find that the fifteen firms seem to do a far better job than average of identifying people with some leadership potential early in their careers and identifying just what will be needed to stretch and develop that potential.

The methods most of those firms use are surprisingly straightforward. They go out of their way to make young employees and people at lower levels in their organizations visible to senior management. Senior managers then judge for themselves who has potential and what the development needs of those people are. Executives then discuss their tentative conclusions openly and candidly, among themselves, in an effort to draw more and more accurate judgments. "Scientific" techniques seem to be rarely employed. The key is: look, talk, and think.

To make younger employees visible to senior management, a variety of techniques are said to be utilized. Here are the most common, each described by an executive whose firm uses that approach:

> We regularly take young people who someone thinks has potential and put them on special
> projects that conclude with presentations to senior management. I can still remember making a
> presentation when I was thirty years old to a group that included the chairman of the company.
>
> *An executive at Johnson & Johnson*

> Once a month, I have a luncheon with one of my key functional managers, and I always ask that
> he or she bring some high-potential employees along. At certain staff meetings, I do the same
> thing. This allows me to get to know a lot of young people and to draw my own conclusions
> about potential, strengths, and weaknesses.
>
> *An executive at Coca Cola*

We don't let the organizational structure constrain us. We always go right to the individual who has information we need. This puts us in contact with a lot of lower-level and more junior employees, and gives us a firsthand feeling for who they are and what they are good at.

*An executive at Dow Jones*

We have many recognition programs in this company. These programs often bring good people to the attention of senior management. They make good people more visible, which is very helpful.

*An executive at General Mills*

One of the things we do is to set up situations which allow our divisions to put their best people "on stage." And then we take a hard look. In this way, you can spot promising young people, and once you know their names, you can go out of your way to get to know them better.

*An executive at Hewlett-Packard*

Our top people make it a habit to get out to our plants on a regular basis. This gives them a chance to meet and to talk to younger employees. It makes folks visible to senior executives who would never meet them otherwise.

*An executive at Anheuser-Busch*

Those kinds of practices provide senior managers with information on people who might have leadership potential. Those executives then usually share and discuss that information among themselves, either informally or formally, on a regular basis.

The Management Council at Hewlett-Packard (the top twenty-eight people), for example, has had regular discussions about the middle management at the company, and the discussions are reported to be "very open." Large firms tend to try to do that sort of thing in a very systematic way. At Du Pont, for example, the sixteen senior department heads meet once a month for two hours. At a typical meeting, the agenda will include a discussion of the half-dozen people one of those executives thinks are "highly promotable." Before every meeting, a picture and biography for those six people are sent to all sixteen department heads. At the meeting, everyone who knows those people is expected to speak up, especially those who have concerns or questions about a person's potential (e.g., "When Harry worked for us five years ago, he only performed at an average level. What has happened to him recently that led you to think so highly of him?"). People who don't know the candidate being discussed are also expected to be aggressive in their questioning (e.g., "How does she compare to George Smith?" "How well did he do in his one staff assignment?").

## PLANNED DEVELOPMENT

Armed with a better-than-average sense of who has some leadership potential and what needs to be developed in those people, executives in the "Best Practices" firms then spend much more time than firms like West Products planning for that development. Sometimes that is done as a part of a formal succession planning or high-potential development process. Often it is done more informally. In either case, the key ingredient appears to be an intelligent assessment of what feasible development opportunities fit each candidate's needs.

424

"Developmental opportunities," in the sense that the term is being used here, include:

- New job assignments (promotions and lateral moves)
- Formal training (inside the firm, at a public seminar, or at a university)
- Task force or committee assignments
- Mentoring or coaching from a senior executive
- Attendance at meetings outside one's core responsibility
- Special projects
- Special developmental jobs (e.g., executive assistant jobs)

With the fifteen firms studied here, one finds those opportunities used more systematically than is the norm in business today. One finds (as this writer did) a Ph.D. organic chemist (at Coke) working as an executive's administrative assistant as part of a conscious strategy to broaden that person. One finds bankers (in Morgan and Citicorp) or functional heads (at J&J) systematically shipped off to foreign offices to give them international experience and a chance to run a small operation by themselves. One finds technically trained people (at Du Pont) moved from research to manufacturing to marketing to general management to corporate staff, and then into executive line jobs. One finds people (at IBM) regularly attending some type of educational experience. One finds, again and again, what appears to be considerable intelligent effort being expended to develop and broaden people so that they will someday have what it takes to provide leadership in complex executive jobs.

One also finds some effort in these firms not just to plan for development in a generic sense, but to plan for the kind of development that will support future business strategies. Sometimes that is done very formally (e.g., strategic business planning is somehow tied to succession planning). Often it is more informal. It is not clear how effective those efforts are, but some executives clearly think they are important.

And when formal training is used—and it seems to be used a great deal in these firms—it is never employed as a substitute for experience. Unlike in firms like West Products, where training is often used as a "quick fix," in these firms training both leverages past experiences (that is, it helps people to learn more from them) and prepares people to learn more from future assignments (in making them more aware of certain things).

## THE FINDINGS IN PERSPECTIVE

The findings in this chapter are consistent with Peters and Waterman's notion that successful firms do a lot of little things a little better, as well as the Center for Creative Leadership work on how effective executives are developed. Even more fundamentally...these findings have a certain logic to them. The business environment today is asking many people to help provide leadership. Doing that effectively is often extremely difficult. Indeed, the assets one needs to provide effective leadership in big jobs form a long list....Trying to find and equip many people with the tools they will need to provide that leadership might therefore logically be a large and very complicated task, one that should require a great effort in a lot of different areas. And that is essentially what the evidence in this chapter says...(as summarized in Exhibit I).

EXHIBIT I    How Practices Create a Leadership Capacity in Management

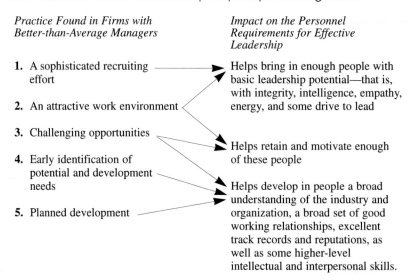

*Practice Found in Firms with*
*Better-than-Average Managers*

*Impact on the Personnel*
*Requirements for Effective*
*Leadership*

1. A sophisticated recruiting
   effort

2. An attractive work environment

3. Challenging opportunities

4. Early identification of
   potential and development
   needs

5. Planned development

Helps bring in enough people with
basic leadership potential—that is,
with integrity, intelligence, empathy,
energy, and some drive to lead

Helps retain and motivate enough
of these people

Helps develop in people a broad
understanding of the industry and
organization, a broad set of good
working relationships, excellent
track records and reputations, as
well as some higher-level
intellectual and interpersonal skills.

To put the magnitude of the task in perspective, let us remember that it seems to take all of this effort to produce what we have been calling "better-than-average" managements. That is, we have no evidence to suggest that any of the firms in the "Best Practices" study have managements that are, at least on the leadership dimension, excellent in any absolute sense. These firms simply have managements that are better able to supply leadership in competitively intense industries than is the norm today in business. Just imagine what might be required to produce truly excellent managements.

# 14

# Leadership and Organizational Culture

COMING TO A NEW AWARENESS OF ORGANIZATIONAL CULTURE
   *Edgar H. Schein*

EVOLUTION AND REVOLUTION AS ORGANIZATIONS GROW
   *Larry E. Greiner*

# COMING TO A NEW AWARENESS
# OF ORGANIZATIONAL CULTURE

*Edgar H. Schein*

## PREVIEW

A. Organizational culture can be defined in terms of a dynamic model of how culture is learned, passed on, and changed.
   1. Culture is the pattern of basic assumptions that a given group has invented, discovered, or developed in learning to cope with its problems of external adaptation and internal integration.
   2. The pattern of basic assumptions is the cultural paradigm on which the perceptions, thoughts, and feelings of organizational members are based.
   3. Culture exists in groups—sets of people who have shared significant problems, solved them, observed the effects of their solutions, and who have taken in new members.
   4. Basic assumptions inherent in a culture serve to stabilize the group and are highly resistant to change.
   5. Culture cannot serve its stabilizing function unless it is taught to new members.

B. Four approaches can be used in various combinations to decipher a culture's paradigm of assumptions.
   1. Interviews can analyze the process and content of socialization of new members.
   2. Interviewers can analyze responses to critical incidents in the organization's history.
   3. Beliefs, values, and assumptions of culture creators or carriers can be analyzed.
   4. Interviewers and organization members can jointly explore and analyze anomalies, or puzzling features, uncovered in interviews.
C. Cultures may serve different purposes at different stages in the development of an organization.
   1. Culture serves as a source of identity and strength for young and growing companies. Little chance exists for successfully changing culture at this stage.
   2. In organizational mid-life culture may be changed, but not without consideration of all sources of stability. Managers must decide whether to encourage diversity of subcultures to promote flexibility, or attempt to create a more homogeneous, stronger corporate culture.
   3. Maturity or decline resulting from excessive internal stability which prevents innovation may be combatted by changes in culture. This is a painful process, however, and one likely to elicit strong resistance.
   4. Attempts at culture management strategies must begin by considering the organizational life cycle.

The purpose of this article is to define the concept of organizational culture in terms of a dynamic model of how culture is learned, passed on, and changed. As many recent efforts argue that organizational culture is the key to organizational excellence, it is critical to define this complex concept in a manner that will provide a common frame of reference for practitioners and researchers. Many definitions simply settle for the notion that culture is a set of shared meanings that make it possible for members of a group to interpret and act upon their environment. I believe we must go beyond this definition: even if we knew an organization well enough to live in it, we would not necessarily know how its culture arose, how it came to be what it is, or how it could be changed if organizational survival were at stake.

The thrust of my argument is that we must understand the dynamic evolutionary forces that govern how culture evolves and changes. My approach to this task will be to lay out a formal definition of what I believe organizational culture is, and to elaborate each element of the definition to make it clear how it works.


## ORGANIZATIONAL CULTURE: A FORMAL DEFINITION

Organizational culture is the *pattern of basic assumptions* that a *given group* has *invented, discovered, or developed in learning to cope* with its *problems of external adaptation and internal integration*, and that have *worked well enough to be considered valid*, and, therefore, to be *taught to new members* as the correct way to *perceive, think, and feel* in relation to those problems.

# 1. Pattern of Basic Assumptions

Organizational culture can be analyzed at several different levels, starting with the *visible artifacts*—the constructed environment of the organization, its architecture, technology, office layout, manner of dress, visible or audible behavior patterns, and public documents such as charters, employee orientation materials, stories (see Figure 1). This level of analysis is tricky because the data are easy to obtain but hard to interpret. We can describe "how" a group constructs its environment and "what" behavior patterns are discernible among the members, but we often cannot understand the underlying logic—"why" a group behaves the way it does.

To analyze *why* members behave the way they do, we often look for the *values* that govern behavior, which is the second level in Figure 1. But as values are hard to observe directly, it is often necessary to infer them by interviewing key members of the organization or to content analyze artifacts such as documents and charters.[1] However, in identifying such values, we usually note that they represent accurately only the manifest or *espoused* values of a culture. That is, they focus on what people say is the reason for their behavior, what they ideally would like those reasons to be, and what are often their rationalizations for their behavior. Yet, the underlying reasons for their behavior remain concealed or unconscious.[2]

FIGURE 1   The Levels of Culture and Their Interaction

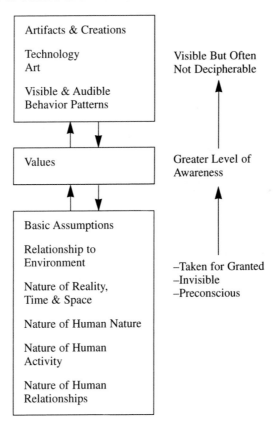

429

To really *understand* a culture and to ascertain more completely the group's values and overt behavior, it is imperative to delve into the *underlying assumptions*, which are typically unconscious but which actually determine how group members perceive, think, and feel.[3] Such assumptions are themselves learned responses that originated as espoused values. But, as a value leads to a behavior, and as that behavior begins to solve the problem which prompted it in the first place, the value gradually is transformed into an underlying assumption about how things really are. As the assumption is increasingly taken for granted, it drops out of awareness.

Taken-for-granted assumptions are so powerful because they are less debatable and con-frontable than espoused values. We know we are dealing with an assumption when we encounter in our informants a refusal to discuss something, or when they consider us "insane" or "ignorant" for bringing something up. For example, the notion that businesses should be profitable, that schools should educate, or that medicine should prolong life are assumptions, even though they are often considered "merely" values.

To put it another way, the domain of values can be divided into 1) ultimate, nondebatable, taken for granted values, for which the term "assumptions" is more appropriate; and 2) debatable, overt, espoused values, for which the term "values" is more applicable. In stating that basic assumptions are unconscious, I am not arguing that this is a result of repression. On the contrary, I am arguing that as certain motivational and cognitive processes are repeated and continue to work, they become unconscious. They can be brought back to awareness only through a kind of focused inquiry, similar to that used by anthropologists. What is needed are the efforts of both an insider who makes the unconscious assumptions and an outsider who helps to uncover the assumptions by asking the right kinds of questions.[4]

***Cultural Paradigms: A Need for Order and Consistency.*** Because of the human need for order and consistency, assumptions become patterned into what may be termed cultural "paradigms," which tie together the basic assumptions about humankind, nature, and activities. A cultural paradigm is a set of interrelated assumptions that form a coherent pattern. Not all assumptions are mutually compatible or consistent, however. For example, if a group holds the assumption that all good ideas and products ultimately come from individual effort, it cannot easily assume simultaneously that groups can be held responsible for the results achieved, or that individuals will put a high priority on group loyalty. Or, if a group assumes that the way to survive is to conquer nature and to manipulate its environment aggressively, it cannot at the same time assume that the best kind of relationship among group members is one that emphasizes passivity and harmony. If human beings do indeed have a cognitive need for order and consistency, one can then assume that all groups will eventually evolve sets of assumptions that are compatible and consistent.

To analyze cultural paradigms, one needs a set of logical categories for studying assumptions. Table 1 shows such a set based on the original comparative study of Kluckhohn and Strodtbeck.[5] In applying these categories broadly to cultures, Kluckhohn and Strodtbeck note that Western culture tends to be oriented toward an active mastery of nature, and is based on individualistic competitive relationships. It uses a future-oriented, linear, monochromic concept of time,[6] views space and resources as infinite, assumes that human nature is neutral and ultimately perfectible, and bases reality or ultimate truth on science and pragmatism.

**TABLE 1**  Basic Underlying Assumptions Around Which Cultural Paradigms Form

---

1. **The Organization's Relationship to Its Environment.** Reflecting even more basic assumptions about the relationship of humanity to nature, one can assess whether the key members of the organization view the relationship as one of dominance, submission, harmonizing, finding an appropriate niche, and so on.

2. **The Nature of Reality and Trust.** Here are the linguistic and behavioral rules that define what is real and what is not, what is "fact," how truth is ultimately to be determined, and whether truth is "revealed" or "discovered"; basic concepts of time as linear or cyclical, monochromic or polychronic; basic concepts such as space as limited or infinite and property as communal or individual; and so forth.

3. **The Nature of Human Nature.** What does it mean to be "human" and what attributes are considered intrinsic or ultimate? Is human nature good, evil, or neutral? Are human beings perfectible or not? Which is better, Theory X or Theory Y?

4. **The Nature of Human Activity.** What is the "right" thing for human beings to do, on the basis of the above assumptions about reality, the environment, and human nature: to be active, passive, self-developmental, fatalistic, or what? What is work and what is play?

5. **The Nature of Human Relationships.** What is considered to be the "right" way for people to relate to each other, to distribute power and love? Is life cooperative or competitive; individualistic, group, collaborative, or communal; based on traditional lineal authority, law, or charisma; or what?

---

*Source*: Reprinted, by permission of the publisher, from "The Role of the Founder in Creating Organizational Culture," by Edgar H. Schein, *Organizational Dynamics*, Summer 1983. © 1983 Periodicals Division, American Management Association. All rights reserved.

In contrast, some Eastern cultures are passively oriented toward nature. They seek to harmonize with nature and with each other. They view the group as more important than the individual, are present or past oriented, see time as polychronic and cyclical, view space and resources as very limited, assume that human nature is bad but improvable, and see reality as based more on revealed truth than on empirical experimentation.

In this light, organizational culture paradigms are adapted versions of broader cultural paradigms. For example, Dyer notes that the GEM Corporation operates on the interlocking assumptions that: 1) ideas come ultimately from individuals; 2) people are responsible, motivated, and capable of governing themselves; however, truth can only be pragmatically determined by "fighting" things out and testing in groups; 3) such fighting is possible because the members of the organization view themselves as a family who will take care of each other. Ultimately, this makes it safe to fight and be competitive.[7]

I have observed another organization that operates on the paradigm that 1) truth comes ultimately from older, wiser, better educated, higher status members; 2) people are capable of loyalty and discipline in carrying out directives; 3) relationships are basically lineal and vertical; 4) each person has a niche that is his or her territory that cannot be invaded; and 5) the organization is a "solidary unit" that will take care of its members.

Needless to say, the manifest behaviors in these two organizations are totally different. In the first organization, one observes mostly open office landscapes, few offices with closed doors, a high rate of milling about, intense conversations and arguments, and a general air of informality. In the second organization, there is a hush in the air: everyone is in an office and with closed doors. Nothing is done except by appointment and with a prearranged agenda. When people of different ranks are present, one sees real deference rituals and obedience, and a general air of formality permeates everything.

Nonetheless, these behavioral differences make no sense until one has discovered and deciphered the underlying cultural paradigm. To stay at the level of artifacts or values is to deal with the *manifestations* of culture, but not with the cultural essence.

## 2.  A Given Group

There cannot be a culture unless there is a group that "owns" it. Culture is embedded in groups, hence the creating group must always be clearly identified. If we want to define a cultural unit, therefore, we must be able to locate a group that is independently defined as the creator, host, or owner of that culture. We must be careful not to define the group in terms of the existence of a culture however tempting that may be, because we then would be creating a completely circular definition.

A given group is a set of people 1) who have been together long enough to have shared significant problems, 2) who have had opportunities to solve those problems and to observe the effects of their solutions, and 3) who have taken in new members. A group's culture cannot be determined unless there is such a definable set of people with a shared history.

The passing on of solutions to new members is required in the definition of culture because the decision to pass something on is itself a very important test of whether a given solution is shared and perceived as valid. If a group passes on with conviction elements of a way of perceiving, thinking, and feeling, we can assume that that group has had enough stability and has shared enough common experiences to have developed a culture. If, on the other hand, a group has not faced the issue of what to pass on in the process of socialization, it has not had a chance to test its own consensus and commitment to a given belief, value, or assumption.

***The Strength of a Culture.***    The "strength" or "amount" of culture can be defined in terms of 1) the *homogeneity* and *stability* of group membership and 2) the *length* and *intensity* of shared experiences of the group. If a stable group has had a long, varied, intense history (i.e., if it has had to cope with many difficult survival problems and has succeeded), it will have a strong and highly differentiated culture. By the same token, if a group has had a constantly shifting membership or has been together only for a short time and has not faced any difficult issues, it will, by definition, have a weak culture. Although individuals within that group may have very strong individual assumptions, there will not be enough shared experiences for the group as a whole to have a defined culture.

By this definition, one would probably assess IBM and the Bell System as having strong cultures, whereas very young companies or ones which have had a high turnover of key executives would be judged as having weak ones. One should also note that once an organization has a strong culture, if the dominant coalition or leadership remains stable, the culture can survive high turnover at lower ranks because new members can be strongly socialized into the organization as, for example, in elite military units.

It is very important to recognize that cultural strength may or may not be correlated with effectiveness. Though some current writers have argued that strength is desirable,[8] it seems clear to me that the relationship is far more complex. The actual content of the culture and the degree to which its solutions fit the problems posed by the environment seem like the critical variables here, not strength. One can hypothesize that young groups strive for culture strength as a way of creating an identity for themselves, but older groups may be more effective with a weak total culture and diverse subcultures to enable them to be responsive to rapid environmental change.

This way of defining culture makes it specific to a given group. If a total corporation consists of stable, functional, divisional, geographic, or rank-based subgroups, then that corporation will have multiple cultures within it. It is perfectly possible for those multiple cultures to be in conflict with each other, such that one could not speak of a single corporate culture. On the other hand, if there has been common corporate experience as well, then one could have a strong corporate culture on top of various subcultures that are based in subunits. The deciphering of a given company's culture then becomes an empirical matter of locating where the stable social units are, what cultures each of those stable units have developed, and how those separate cultures blend into a single whole. The total culture could then be very homogeneous or heterogeneous, according to the degree to which subgroup cultures are similar or different.

It has also been pointed out that some of the cultural assumptions in an organization can come from the occupational background of the members of the organization. This makes it possible to have a managerial culture, an engineering culture, a science culture, a labor union culture, etc., all of which coexist in a given organization.[9]

## 3. Invented, Discovered, or Developed

Cultural elements are defined as learned solutions to problems. In this section, I will concentrate on the nature of the learning mechanisms that are involved.

Structurally, there are two types of learning situations: 1) positive problem-solving situations that produce positive or negative reinforcement in terms of whether the attempted solution works or not; and 2) anxiety-avoidance situations that produce positive or negative reinforcement in terms of whether the attempted solution does or does not avoid anxiety. In practice, these two types of situations are intertwined, but they are structurally different and, therefore, they must be distinguished.

In the positive problem-solving situation, the group tries out various responses until something works. The group will then continue to use this response until it ceases to work. The information that it no longer works is visible and clear. By contrast, in the anxiety-avoidance situation, once a response is learned because it successfully avoids anxiety, it is likely to be repeated indefinitely. The reason is that the learner will not willingly test the situation to determine whether the cause of the anxiety is still operating. Thus all rituals, patterns of thinking or feeling, and behaviors that may originally have been motivated by a need to avoid a painful, anxiety-provoking situation are going to be repeated, even if the causes of the original pain are no longer acting, because the avoidance of anxiety is, itself, positively reinforcing.[10]

To fully grasp the importance of anxiety reduction in culture formation, we have to consider, first of all, the human need for cognitive order and consistency, which serves as the ultimate motivator for a common language and shared categories of perception and thought.[11] In the absence of such shared "cognitive maps, " the human organism experiences a basic existential anxiety that is intolerable— an anxiety observed only in extreme situations of isolation or captivity.[12]

Secondly, humans experience the anxiety associated with being exposed to hostile environmental conditions and to the dangers inherent in unstable social relationships, forcing groups to learn ways of coping with such external and internal problems.

A third source of anxiety is associated with occupational roles such as coal mining and nursing. For example, the Tavistock sociotechnical studies have shown clearly that the social structure and ways of operation of such groups can be conceptualized best as a "defense" against the anxiety that would be unleashed if work were done in another manner.[13]

If an organizational culture is composed of both types of elements—those designed to solve problems and those designed to avoid anxiety—it becomes necessary to analyze which is which if one is concerned about changing any of the elements. In the positive-learning situation, one needs innovative sources to find a better solution to the problem; in the anxiety-avoidance situation, one must first find the source of the anxiety and either show the learner that it no longer exists, or provide an alternative source of avoidance. Either of these is difficult to do.

In other words, cultural elements that are based on anxiety reduction will be more stable than those based on positive problem solving because of the nature of the anxiety reduction mechanism and the fact that human systems need a certain amount of stability to avoid cognitive and social anxiety.

Where do solutions initially come from? Most cultural solutions in new groups and organizations originate from the founders and early leaders of those organizations.[14] Typically, the solution process is an advocacy of certain ways of doing things  that are then tried out and either adopted or rejected, depending on how well they work out.  Initially, the founders have the most influence, but, as the group ages and acquires its own experiences, its members will find their own solutions.  Ultimately, the process of discovering new solutions will be more a result of interactive, shared experiences.  But leadership will always play a key role during these times when the group faces a new problem and must develop new responses to the situation.  In fact, one of the crucial functions of leadership is to provide guidance at precisely those times when habitual ways of doing things no longer work, or when a dramatic change in the environment requires new responses.

At those times, leadership must not only insure the invention of new and better solutions, but must also provide some security to help the group tolerate the anxiety of giving up old, stable responses, while new ones are learned and tested.  In the Lewinian change framework, this means that the "unfreezing stage" must involve both enough disconfirmation to motivate change and enough psychological safety to permit the individual or group to pay attention to the disconfirming data.[15]

## 4.   Problems of External Adaptation and Internal Integration

If culture is a solution to the problems a group faces, what can we say about the nature of those problems? Most group theories agree it is useful to distinguish between two kinds of problems: 1) those that deal with the group's basic survival, which has been labeled the primary task, basic function, or ultimate mission of the group; and 2) those that deal with the group's ability to function as a group. These problems have been labeled socioemotional, group building and maintenance, or integration problems.[16]

Homans further distinguishes between the *external system* and the *internal system* and notes that the two are interdependent.[17]  Even though one can distinguish between the external and internal problems, in practice both systems are highly interrelated.

*External Adaptation Problems.*   Problems of external adaptation are those that ultimately determine the group's survival in the environment.  While a part of the group's environment is "enacted," in the sense that prior cultural experience predisposes members to perceive the environment in a certain way and even to control that environment to a degree, there will always be elements of the environment (weather, natural circumstances, availability of economic and other resources, political upheavals) that are clearly beyond the control of the group and that will, to a degree, determine the fate of the group.[18] A useful way to categorize the problems of survival is to mirror the stages of the problem-solving cycle as shown in Table 2.[19]

TABLE 2  Problems of External Adaptation and Survival

| Strategy: | Developing consensus on the *primary task, core mission, or manifest and latent functions of the group.* |
|---|---|
| Goals: | Developing consensus of *goals*, such goals being the concrete reflection of the core mission. |
| Means for Accomplishing Goals: | Developing consensus of the *means to be used* in accomplishing the goals—for example, division of labor, organization structure, reward system, and so forth. |
| Measuring Performance: | Developing consensus on the criteria *to be used in measuring how well the group is doing against its goals and targets*–for example, information and control systems. |
| Correction: | Developing consensus on *remedial or repair strategies* as needed when the group is not accomplishing its goals. |

*Source*:  Reprinted by permission of the publisher, from "The Role of the Founder in Creating Organizational Culture," by Edgar H. Schein, *Organizational Dynamics*, Summer 1983. © 1983 Periodicals Division, American Management Association.  All rights reserved.

The basic underlying assumptions of the culture from which the founders of the organization come will determine to a large extent the initial formulations of core mission, goals, means, criteria, and remedial strategies, in that those ways of doing things are the only ones with which the group members will be familiar.  But as an organization develops its own life experience, it may begin to modify to some extent its original assumptions.  For example, a young company may begin by defining its core mission to be to "win in the marketplace over all competition" but may at a later stage find that "owning its own niche in the marketplace," "coexisting with other companies," or even "being a silent partner in an oligopolistic industry" is a more workable solution to survival.  Thus for each stage of the problem-solving cycle, there will emerge solutions characteristic of that group's own history, and those solutions or ways of doing things based on learned assumptions will make up a major portion of that group's culture.

***Internal Integration Problems.***  A group or organization cannot survive if it cannot manage itself as a group.  External survival and internal integration problems are, therefore, two sides of the same coin.  Table 3 outlines the major issues of internal integration around which cultural solutions must be found.

While the nature of the solutions will vary from one organization to another, by definition, every organization will have to face each of these issues and develop some kind of solution. However, because the nature of that solution will reflect the biases of the founders and current leaders, the prior experiences of group members, and the actual events experienced, it is likely that each organizational culture will be unique, even though the underlying issues around which the culture is formed will be common.[20]

TABLE 3    Problems of Internal Integration

| | |
|---|---|
| Language: | *Common language and conceptual categories.* If members cannot communicate with and understand each other, a group is impossible by definition. |
| Boundaries: | *Consensus on group boundaries and criteria for inclusion and exclusion.* One of the most important areas of culture is the shared consensus of who is in, who is out, and by what criteria one determines membership. |
| Power & Status: | Consensus on *criteria for the allocation of power and status.* Each organization must work out its pecking order and its rules for how one gets, maintains, and loses power. This area of consensus is crucial in helping members manage their own feelings of aggression. |
| Intimacy: | Consensus on *criteria for intimacy, friendship, and love.* Every organization must work out its rules of the game for peer relationships, for relationships between the sexes, and for the manner in which openness and intimacy are to be handled in the context of managing the organization's tasks. |
| Rewards & Punishments: | Consensus *on criteria for allocation of rewards and punishments.* Every group must know what its heroic and sinful behaviors are; what gets rewarded with property, status, and power; and what gets punished through the withdrawal of rewards and, ultimately, excommunication. |
| Ideology: | Consensus of *ideology and "religion."* Every organization, like every society, faces unexplainable events that must be given meaning so that members can respond to them and avoid the anxiety of dealing with the unexplainable and uncontrollable. |

An important issue to study across many organizations is whether an organization's growth and evolution follows an inherent evolutionary *trend* (e.g., developing societies are seen as evolving from that of a community to more of a bureaucratic, impersonal type of system). One should also study whether organizational cultures reflect in a patterned way the underlying technology, the age of the organization, the size of the organization, and the nature of the parent culture within which the organization evolves.

## 5. Assumptions That Work Well Enough To Be Considered Valid

Culture goes beyond the norms or values of a group in that it is more of an *ultimate* outcome, based on repeated success and a gradual process of taking things for granted. In other words, to me what makes something "cultural" is this "taken-for-granted" quality, which makes the underlying assumptions virtually undiscussable.

Culture is perpetually being formed in the sense that there is constantly some kind of learning going on about how to relate to the environment and to manage internal affairs. But this ongoing evolutionary process does not change those things that are so thoroughly learned that they come to be a stable element of the group's life. Since the basic assumptions that make up an organization's culture serve the secondary function of stabilizing much of the internal and external environment for the group, and since that stability is sought as a defense against the anxiety which comes with uncertainty and confusion, these deeper parts of the culture either do not change or change only very slowly.

## 6. Taught to New Members

Because culture serves the function of stabilizing the external and internal environment for an organization, it must be taught to new members. It would not serve its function if every generation of new members could introduce new perceptions, language, thinking patterns, and rules of interaction. For culture to serve its function, it must be perceived as correct and valid, and if it is perceived that way, it automatically follows that it must be taught to newcomers.

It cannot be overlooked that new members do bring new ideas and do produce culture change, especially if they are brought in at high levels of the organization. It remains to be settled empirically whether and how this happens. For example, does a new member have to be socialized first and accepted into a central and powerful position before he or she can begin to affect change? Or does a new member bring from the onset new ways of perceiving, thinking, feeling, and acting, which produce automatic changes through role innovation?[21] Is the manner in which new members are socialized influential in determining what kind of innovation they will produce?[22] Much of the work on innovation in organizations is confusing because often it is not clear whether the elements that are considered "new" are actually new assumptions, or simply new artifacts built on old cultural assumptions.

In sum, if culture provides the group members with a paradigm of how the world "is, " it goes without saying that such a paradigm would be passed on without question to new members. It is also the case that the very process of passing on the culture provides an opportunity for testing, ratifying, and reaffirming it. For both of these reasons, the process of socialization (i.e., the passing on of the group's culture) is strategically an important process to study if one wants to decipher what the culture is and how it might change.[23]

## 7. Perceive, Think, and Feel

The final element in the definition reminds us that culture is pervasive and ubiquitous. The basic assumptions about nature, humanity, relationships, truth, activity, time, and space cover virtually all human functions. This is not to say that a given organization's culture will develop to the point of totally "controlling" all of its members' perceptions, thoughts, and feelings. But the process of learning to manage the external and internal environment does involve all of one's cognitive and emotional elements. As cultural learning progresses, more and more of the person's responses will become involved. Therefore, the longer we live in a given culture, and the older the culture is, the more it will influence our perceptions, thoughts, and feelings.

By focusing on perceptions, thoughts, and feelings, I am also stating the importance of those categories relative to the category of *overt behavior*. Can one speak of a culture in terms of just the overt behavior patterns one observes? Culture is *manifested* in overt behavior, but the idea of culture goes deeper than behavior. Indeed, the very reason for elaborating an abstract notion like "culture" is that it is too difficult to explain what goes on in organizations if we stay at the descriptive behavioral level.

To put it another way, behavior is, to a large extent, a joint function of what the individual brings to the situation and the operating situational forces, which to some degree are unpredictable. To understand the cultural portion of what the individual brings to the situation (as opposed to the idiosyncratic or situational portions), we must examine the individual's pattern of perceptions, thoughts, and feelings. Only after we have reached a consensus at this inner level have we uncovered what is potentially *cultural*.

***The Study of Organizational Culture and Its Implications.*** Organizational culture as defined here is difficult to study. However, it is not as difficult as studying a different society where language and customs are so different that one needs to live in the society to get any feel for it at all. Organizations exist in a parent culture, and much of what we find in them is derivative from the assumptions of the parent culture. But different organizations will sometimes emphasize or amplify different elements of a parent culture. For example, in the two companies previously mentioned, we find in the first an extreme version of the individual freedom ethic, and in the second one, an extreme version of the authority ethic, both of which can be derived from U.S. culture.

The problem of deciphering a particular organization's culture, then, is more a matter of surfacing assumptions, which will be recognizable once they have been uncovered. We will not find alien forms of perceiving, thinking, and feeling if the investigator is from the same parent culture as the organization that is being investigated. On the other hand, the particular pattern of assumptions, which we call an organization's cultural paradigm, will not reveal itself easily because it is taken for granted.

How then do we gather data and decipher the paradigm? Basically, there are four approaches that should be used in combination with one another:

1. Analyzing the Process and Content of Socialization of New Members. By interviewing "socialization agents," such as the supervisors and older peers of new members, one can identify some of the important areas of the culture. But some elements of the culture will not be discovered by this method because they are not revealed to newcomers or lower members.

2. Analyzing Responses to Critical Incidents in the Organization's History. By constructing a careful "organizational biography" from documents, interviews, and perhaps even surveys of present and past key members, it is possible to identify the major periods of culture formation. For each crisis or incident identified, it is then necessary to determine what was done, why it was done, and what the outcome was. To infer the underlying assumptions of the organization, one would then look for the major themes in the reasons given for the actions taken.

3. Analyzing Beliefs, Values, and Assumptions of "Culture Creators or Carriers." When interviewing founders, current leaders, or culture creators or carriers, one should initially make an open-ended chronology of each person's history in the organization—his or her goals, modes of action, and assessment of outcomes. The list of external and internal issues found in Tables 2 and 3 can be used as a checklist later in the interview to cover areas more systematically.

4. Jointly Exploring and Analyzing with Insiders the Anomalies or Puzzling Features Observed or Uncovered in Interviews. It is the *joint inquiry* that will help to disclose basic assumptions and help determine how they may interrelate to form the cultural paradigm.

The insider must be a representative of the culture and must be interested in disclosing his or her *own* basic assumptions to test whether they are in fact cultural prototypes. This process works best if one acts from observations that puzzle the outsider or that seem like anomalies because the insider's assumptions are most easily surfaced if they are contrasted to the assumptions that the outsider initially holds about what is observed.

While the first three methods mentioned above should enhance and complement one another, at least one of them should systematically cover all of the external adaptation and internal integration issues. In order to discover the underlying basic assumptions and eventually to decipher the paradigm, the fourth method is necessary to help the insider surface his or her own cultural assumptions. This is done through the outsider's probing and searching.[24]

If an organization's total culture is not well developed, or if the organization consists of important stable subgroups, which have developed subcultures, one must modify the above methods to study the various subcultures.[25] Furthermore, the organizational biography might reveal that the organization is at a certain point in its life cycle, and one would hypothesize that the functions that a given kind of culture plays vary with the life-cycle stage.[26]

***Implications for Culture Management and Change.*** If we recognize organizational culture—whether at the level of the group or the total corporation—as a deep phenomenon, what does this tell us about when and how to change or manage culture? First of all, the evolutionary perspective draws our attention to the fact that the culture of a group may serve different functions at different times. When a group is forming and growing, the culture is a "glue"—a source of identity and strength. In other words, young founder-dominated companies need their cultures as a way of holding together their organizations. The culture changes that do occur in a young organization can best be described as clarification, articulation, and elaboration. If the young company's culture is genuinely maladaptive in relation to the external environment, the company will not survive anyway. But even if one identified needed changes, there is little chance at this stage that one could change the culture.

In organizational midlife, culture can be managed and changed, but not without considering all the sources of stability which have been identified above. The large diversified organization probably contains many functional, geographic, and other groups that have cultures of their own—some of which will conflict with each other. Whether the organization needs to enhance the diversity to remain flexible in the face of environmental turbulence, or to create a more homogeneous "strong" culture (as some advocate) becomes one of the toughest strategy decisions management confronts, especially if senior management is unaware of some of its own cultural assumptions. Some form of outside intervention and "culture consciousness raising" is probably essential at this stage to facilitate better strategic decisions.

Organizations that have reached a stage of maturity or decline resulting from mature markets and products or from excessive internal stability and comfort that prevents innovation[27] may need to change parts of their culture, provided they can obtain the necessary self-insight. Such managed change will always be a painful process and will elicit strong resistance. Moreover, change may not even be possible without replacing the large numbers of people who wish to hold on to all of the original culture.

No single model of such change exists: managers may successfully orchestrate change through the use of a wide variety of techniques, from outright coercion at one extreme to subtle seduction through the introduction of new technologies at the other extreme.[28]

## SUMMARY AND CONCLUSIONS

I have attempted to construct a formal definition of organizational culture that derives from a dynamic model of learning and group dynamics. The definition highlights that culture: 1) is always in the process of formation and change; 2) tends to cover all aspects of human functioning; 3) is learned around the major issues of external adaptation and internal integration; and 4) is ultimately embodied as an interrelated, patterned set of basic assumptions that deal with ultimate issues, such as the nature of humanity, human relationships, time, space, and the nature of reality and truth itself.

If we are to decipher a given organization's culture, we must use a complex interview, observation, and joint-inquiry approach in which selected members of the group work with the outsider to uncover the unconscious assumptions that are hypothesized to be the essence of the culture. I believe we need to study a large number of organizations using these methods to determine the utility of the concept of organizational culture and to relate cultural variables to other variables, such as strategy, organizational structure, and ultimately, organizational effectiveness.

If such studies show this model of culture to be useful, one of the major implications will be that our theories of organizational change will have to give much more attention to the opportunities and constraints that organizational culture provides. Clearly, if culture is as powerful as I argue in this article, it will be easy to make changes that are congruent with present assumptions, and very difficult to make changes that are not. In sum, the understanding of organizational culture would then become integral to the process of management itself.

## FOOTNOTES*

1. J. Martin and C. Sieln, "Organizational Culture and Counterculture: An Uneasy Symbiosis," *Organizational Dynamics*, Autumn 1983, pp. 52–64.
2. C. Argyris, "The Executive Mind and Double Loop Learning," *Organizational Dynamics*, Autumn 1982, pp. 5–22.
3. E. H. Schein, "Does Japanese Management Style Have a Message for American Managers?" *Sloan Management Review*, Fall 1981, pp. 55–68; E. H. Schein, "The Role of the Founder in Creating Organizational Culture," *Organizational Dynamics*, Summer 1983, pp. 13–28.
4. R. Evered and M. R. Louis, "Alternative Perspectives as the Organizational Sciences: 'Inquiry from the Inside' and 'Inquiry from the Outside,'" *Academy of Management Review* (1981): 385, 395,
5. F. R. Kluckholn and F. L. Strodtbeck, *Variations in Value Orientations* (Evanston, IL: Row Peterson, 1961). An application of these ideas to the study of organizations across cultures, as contrasted with the culture of organizations can be found in W. M. Evan, *Organization Theory* (New York: John Wiley & Sons, 1976), Ch. 15. Other studies of cross-cultural comparisons are not reviewed in detail here. See for example: G. Hofstede, *Culture's Consequences* (Beverly Hills, CA: Sage Publications, 1980); G. W. England, *The Manager and His Values* (Cambridge, MA: Ballinger, 1975).
6. E. T. Hall, *The Silent Language* (New York: Doubleday, 1969).
7. W. G. Dyer, Jr., *Culture in Organizations: A Case Study and Analysis* (Cambridge, MA: Sloan School of Management, MIT, Working Paper #1279-82, 1982).
8. T. E. Deal and A. A. Kennedy, *Corporate Culture* (Reading, MA: Addison-Wesley, 1982); T. J. Peters and R. H. Waterman, Jr., *In Search of Excellence* (New York: Harper & Row, 1982).
9. J. Van Maanen and S. R. Barley, "Occupational Communities: Culture and Control in Organizations" (Cambridge, MA: Sloan School of Management, November 1982); L. Bailyn, "Resolving Contradictions in Technical Careers," *Technology Review*, November–December 1982, pp. 40–47.
10. R. L. Solomon and L. C. Wynne, "Traumatic Avoidance Learning: The Principles of Anxiety Conservation and Partial Irreversibility," *Psychological Review* 61, 1954, p. 353.
11. D. O. Hebb, "The Social Significance of Animal Studies," in *Handbook of Social Psychology*, G. Lindzey (Reading, MA: Addison-Wesley, 1954).

*The research on which this article is based was supported by the Chief of Naval Research, Psychology of Sciences Division (Code 452). Organizational Effectiveness Research Programs, Office of Naval Research, Arlington, VA 22217, under Contract Number N(XX) 14 80-C-0905, NK 170-911.

Special thanks go to my colleagues Lotte Haydn, John Van Maanen, and Meryl Louis for helping me to think through this murky area; and to Gibb Dyer, Barbara Lawrence, Steve Barley, Jan Sanzchus, and Mary Nord whose research on organizational culture has begun to establish the utility of these ideas.

12. E. H. Schein, *Coercive Persuasion* (New York: Norton, 1961).

13. E. I. Trist and K. W. Bamforth, "Some Social and Psychological Consequences of the Long-Wall Method of Coal Getting," *Human Relations*, 1951, pp. 1–38; I. E. P. Menzies, "A Case Study in the Functioning of Social Systems as a Defense Against Anxiety," *Human Relations*, 1960, pp. 95–121.

14. A. M. Pettigrew, "On Studying Organizational Cultures," *Administrative Science Quarterly* (1979), pp. 570–581; Schein (Summer 1983), pp. 13–28.

15. Schein (1961); E. H. Scheinand and W. G. Bennis, *Personal and Organizational Change through Group Methods* (New York: John Wiley & Sons, 1965).

16. A. K. Rice, *The Enterprise and Its Environment* (London: Tavistock, 1963); R. F. Babes, *Interaction Process Analysis* (Chicago, IL: University of Chicago Press, 1950); T. Parsons, *The Social System* (Glencoe, IL: The Free Press, 1951).

17. G. Homans, *The Human Group* (New York: Harcourt Brace, 1950).

18. K. E. Weick, "Cognitive Processes in Organizations," in *Research in Organizational Behavior,* ed. B. Staw (Greenwich, CT: JAI Press, 1979), pp. 41–74; J. Van Maanen, "The Self, the Situation, and the Rules of Interpersonal Relations," in *Essays in Interpersonal Dynamics,* ed. W. G. Bennis, J. Van Maanen, E. H. Schein, and F. I. Steele (Homewood, IL: Dorsey Press, 1979).

19. E. H. Schein, *Process Consultation* (Reading, MA: Addison-Wesley, 1969).

20. When studying different organizations, it is important to determine whether the deeper paradigms that eventually arise in each organizational culture are also unique, or whether they will fit into certain categories such as those that the typological schemes suggest. For example, Handy describes a typology based on Harrison's work that suggests that organizational paradigms will revolve around one of four basic issues: 1) personal connections, power, and politics; 2) role structuring; 3) tasks and efficiency; or 4) existential here and now issues. See: C. Handy, *The Gods of Management* (London: Penguin, 1978); R. Harrison, "How to Describe Your Organization," *Harvard Business Review*, September–October 1972.

21. E. H. Schein, "The Role Innovator and His Education," *Technology Review,* October–November 1970, pp. 32–38.

22. J. Van Maanen and E. H. Schein, "Toward a Theory of Organizational Socialization," in *Research in Organizational Behavior*, Vol. 1, ed. B. Staw (Greenwich, CT: JAI Press, 1979).

23. Ibid.

24. Evered and Louis (1981).

25. M. R. Louis, "A Cultural Perspective on Organizations," *Human Systems Management* (1981): 246–258.

26. H. Schwartz and S. M. Davis, "Matching Corporate Culture and Business Strategy," *Organizational Dynamics,* Summer 1981, pp. 30–48; J. R. Kimberly and R. H. Miles, *The Organizational Life Cycle* (San Francisco: Jossey Bass, 1981).

27. R. Katz, "The Effects of Group Longevity of Project Communication and Performance," *Administrative Science Quarterly* (1982): 27, 81–194.

28. A fuller explication of these dynamics can be found in my forthcoming book on organizational culture.

# EVOLUTION AND REVOLUTION AS ORGANIZATIONS GROW

*Larry E. Greiner*

A small research company chooses too complicated and formalized an organization structure for its young age and limited size. It flounders in rigidity and bureaucracy for several years and is finally acquired by a larger company.

Key executives of a retail store chain hold on to an organization structure long after it has served its purpose, because their power is derived from this structure. The company eventually goes into bankruptcy.

A large bank disciplines a "rebellious" manager who is blamed for current control problems, when the underlying cause is centralized procedures that are holding back expansion into new markets. Many younger managers subsequently leave the bank, competition moves in, and profits are still declining.

The problems of these companies, like those of many others, are rooted more in past decisions than in present events or outside market dynamics. Historical forces do indeed shape the future growth of organizations. Yet management, in its haste to grow, often overlooks such critical developmental questions as: Where has our organization been? Where is it now? And what do the answers to these questions mean for where we are going? Instead, its gaze is fixed outward toward the environment and the future—as if more precise market projections will provide a new organizational identity.

Companies fail to see that many clues to their future success lie within their own organizations and their evolving states of development. Moreover, the inability of management to understand its organization development problems can result in a company becoming "frozen" in its present stage of evolution, or, ultimately, in failure, regardless of market opportunities.

My position in this article is that the future of an organization may be less determined by outside forces than it is by the organization's history. In stressing the force of history on an organization, I have drawn from the legacies of European psychologists (their thesis being that individual behavior is determined primarily by previous events and experiences, not by what lies ahead). Extending this analogy of individual development to the problems of organization development, I shall discuss a series of developmental phases through which growing companies tend to pass. But, first let me provide two definitions.

1. The term *evolution* is used to describe prolonged periods of growth where no major upheaval occurs in organization practices.
2. The term *revolution* is used to describe those periods of substantial turmoil in organizational life.

As a company progresses through developmental phases, each evolutionary period creates its own revolution. For instance, centralized practices eventually lead to demands for decentralization. Moreover, the nature of management's solution to each revolutionary period determines whether a company will move forward into its next stage of evolutionary growth. As I shall show later, there are at least five phases of organization development, each characterized by both an evolution and a revolution.

*Source*: Reprinted from the *Harvard Business Review*, July–August 1972, Copyright © 1972 by the President and Fellows of Harvard College; all rights reserved.

# KEY FORCES IN DEVELOPMENT

During the past few years a small amount of research knowledge about the phases of organization development has been building. Some of this research is very quantitative, such as time-series analyses that reveal patterns of economic performance over time.[1] The majority of studies, however, are case-oriented and use company records and interviews to reconstruct a rich picture of corporate development.[2] Yet both types of research tend to be heavily empirical without attempting more generalized statements about the overall process of development.

A notable exception is the historical work of Alfred D. Chandler, Jr., in his book *Strategy and Structure*.[3] This study depicts four very broad and general phases in the lives of four large U.S. companies. It proposes that outside market opportunities determine a company's strategy, which in turn, determines the company's organization structure. This thesis has a valid ring for the four companies examined by Chandler, largely because they developed in a time of explosive markets and technological advances. But more recent evidence suggests that organization structure may be less malleable than Chandler assumed; in fact, structure can play a critical role in influencing corporate strategy. It is this reverse emphasis on how organization structure affects future growth which is highlighted in the model presented in this article.

From an analysis of recent studies,[4] five key dimensions emerge as essential for building a model of organization development:

1. Age of the organization.
2. Size of the organization.
3. Stages of evolution.
4. Stages of revolution.
5. Growth rate of the industry.

I shall describe each of these elements separately, but first note their combined effect as illustrated in Exhibit I. Note especially how each dimension influences the other over time; when all five elements begin to interact, a more complete and dynamic picture of organizational growth emerges.

After describing these dimensions and their interconnections, I shall discuss each evolutionary revolutionary phase of development and show a) how each stage of evolution breeds its own revolution, and b) how management solutions to each revolution determine the next stage of evolution.

## Age of the Organization

The most obvious and essential dimension for any model of development is the life span of an organization (represented as the horizontal axis in Exhibit I). All historical studies gather data from various points in time and then make comparisons. From these observations, it is evident that the same organization practices are not maintained throughout a long time span. This makes a most basic point: management problems and principles are rooted in time. The concept of decentralization, for example, can have meaning for describing corporate practices at one time period but loses its descriptive power at another.

The passage of time also contributes to the institutionalization of managerial attitudes. As a result, employee behavior becomes not only more predictable but also more difficult to change when attitudes are outdated.

EXHIBIT I   Model of Organization Development

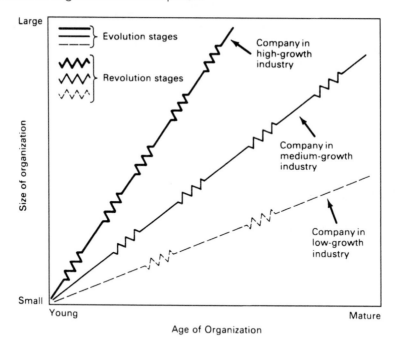

## Size of the Organization

This dimension is depicted as the vertical axis in Exhibit I. A company's problems and solutions tend to change markedly as the number of employees and sales volume increase. Thus, time is not the only determinant of structure; in fact, organizations that do not grow in size can retain many of the same management issues and practices over lengthy periods. In addition to increased size, however, problems of coordination and communication magnify, new functions emerge, levels in the management hierarchy multiply, and jobs become more interrelated.

## Stages of Evolution

As both age and size increase, another phenomenon becomes evident: the prolonged growth that I have termed the evolutionary period. Most growing organizations do not expand for two years and then retreat for one year; rather, those that survive a crisis usually enjoy four to eight years of continuous growth without a major economic setback or severe internal disruption. The term evolution seems appropriate for describing these quieter periods because only modest adjustments appear necessary for maintaining growth under the same overall pattern of management.

## Stages of Revolution

Smooth evolution is not inevitable; it cannot be assumed that organization growth is linear. *Fortune's* "500" list, for example, has had significant turnover during the last 50 years. Thus we find evidence from numerous case histories which reveals periods of substantial turbulence spaced between smoother periods of evolution.

I have termed these turbulent times the periods of revolution because they typically exhibit a serious upheaval of management practices. Traditional management practices, which were appropriate for a smaller size and earlier time, are brought under scrutiny by frustrated top managers and disillusioned lower-level managers. During such periods of crisis, a number of companies fail—those unable to abandon past practices and effect major organization changes are likely either to fold or to level off in their growth rates.

The critical task for management in each revolutionary period is to find a new set of organization practices that will become the basis for managing the next period of evolutionary growth. Interestingly enough, these new practices eventually sow their own seeds of decay and lead to another period of revolution. Companies therefore experience the irony of seeing a major solution in one time period become a major problem at a later date.

## Growth Rate of the Industry

The speed at which an organization experiences phases of evolution and revolution is closely related to the market environment of its industry. For example, a company in a rapidly expanding market will have to add employees rapidly; hence, the need for new organization structures to accommodate large staff increases is accelerated. While evolutionary periods tend to be relatively short in fast-growing industries, much longer evolutionary periods occur in mature or slowly growing industries.

Evolution can also be prolonged, and revolutions delayed, when profits come easily. For instance, companies that make grievous errors in a rewarding industry can still look good on their profit and loss statements; thus they can avoid a change in management practices for a longer period. The aerospace industry in its infancy is an example. Yet revolutionary periods still occur, as one did in aerospace when profit opportunities began to dry up. Revolutions seem to be much more severe and difficult to resolve when the market environment is poor.

## PHASES OF GROWTH

With the foregoing framework in mind, let us now examine in depth the five specific phases of evolution and revolution. As shown in Exhibit II, each evolutionary period is characterized by the dominant *management style* used to achieve growth, while each revolutionary period is characterized by the dominant *management problem* that must be solved before growth can continue. The patterns presented in Exhibit II seem to be typical for companies in industries with moderate growth over a long time period; companies in faster growing industries tend to experience all five phases more rapidly, while those in slower growing industries encounter only two or three phases over many years.

It is important to note that *each phase is both an effect of the previous phase and a cause for the next phase.* For example, the evolutionary management style in Phase 3 of the exhibit is "delegation," which grows out of, and becomes the solution to, demands for greater "autonomy" in the preceding Phase 2 revolution. The style of delegation used in Phase 3, however, eventually provokes a major revolutionary crisis that is characterized by attempts to regain control over the diversity created through increased delegation.

EXHIBIT II   The Five Phases of Growth

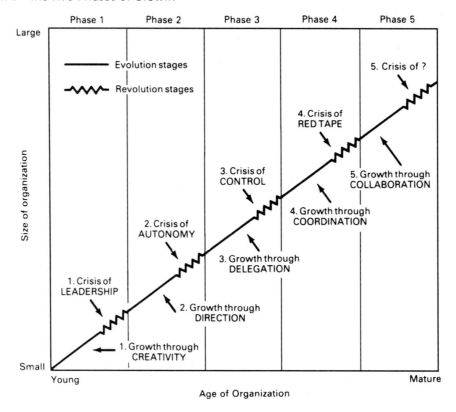

The principal implication of each phase is that management actions are narrowly prescribed if growth is to occur. For example, a company experiencing an autonomy crisis in Phase 2 cannot return to directive management for a solution—it must adopt a new style of delegation in order to move ahead.

## Phase 1: Creativity...

In the birth stage of an organization, the emphasis is on creating both a product and a market. Here are the characteristics of the period of creative evolution:

- The company's founders are usually technically or entrepreneurially oriented, and they disdain management activities; their physical and mental energies are absorbed entirely in making and selling a new product.
- Communication among employees is frequent and informal.
- Long hours of work are rewarded by modest salaries and the promise of ownership benefits.
- Control of activities come from immediate marketplace feedback; the management acts as the customers react.

***...& the leadership crisis:*** All of the foregoing individualistic and creative activities are essential for the company to get off the ground. But therein lies the problem. As the company grows, larger production runs require knowledge about the efficiencies of manufacturing. Increased numbers of employees cannot be managed exclusively through informal communication; new employees are not motivated by an intense dedication to the product or organization. Additional capital must be secured, and new accounting procedures are needed for financial control.

Thus the founders find themselves burdened with unwanted management responsibilities. So they long for the "good old days," still trying to act as they did in the past. And conflicts between the harried leaders grow more intense.

At this point a crisis of leadership occurs, which is the onset of the first revolution. Who is to lead the company out of confusion and solve the managerial problems confronting it? Quite obviously, a strong manager is needed who has the necessary knowledge and skill to introduce new business techniques. But this is easier said than done. The founders often hate to step aside even though they are probably temperamentally unsuited to be managers. So here is the first critical developmental choice—to locate and install a strong business manager who is acceptable to the founders and who can pull the organization together.

## Phase 2: Direction...

Those companies that survive the first phase by installing a capable business manager usually embark on a period of sustained growth under able and directive leadership. Here are the characteristics of this evolutionary period:

- A functional organization structure is introduced to separate manufacturing from marketing activities, and job assignments become more specialized.
- Accounting systems for inventory and purchasing are introduced.
- Incentives, budgets, and work standards are adopted.
- Communication becomes more formal and impersonal as a hierarchy of titles and positions builds.
- The new manager and his key supervisors take most of the responsibility for instituting direction, while lower-level supervisors are treated more as functional specialists than as autonomous decision-making managers.

***...& the autonomy crisis:*** Although the new directive techniques channel employee energy more efficiently into growth, they eventually become inappropriate for controlling a larger, more diverse and complex organization. Lower-level employees find themselves restricted by a cumbersome and centralized hierarchy. They have come to possess more direct knowledge about markets and machinery than do the leaders at the top; consequently, they feel torn between following procedures and taking initiative on their own.

Thus the second revolution is imminent as a crisis develops from demands for greater autonomy on the part of lower-level managers. The solution adopted by most companies is to move toward greater delegation. Yet it is difficult for top managers who were previously successful at being directive to give up responsibility. Moreover, lower-level managers are not accustomed to making decisions for themselves. As a result, numerous companies flounder during this revolutionary period, adhering to centralized methods while lower-level employees grow more disenchanted and leave the organization.

# Phase 3: Delegation...

The next era of growth evolves from the successful application of a decentralized organization structure. It exhibits these characteristics:

- Much greater responsibility is given to the managers of plants and market territories.
- Profit centers and bonuses are used to stimulate motivation.
- The top executives at headquarters restrain themselves to managing by exception, based on periodic reports from the field.
- Management often concentrates on making new acquisitions which can be lined up beside other decentralized units.
- Communication from the top is infrequent, usually by correspondence, telephone, or brief visits to field locations.

The delegation stage proves useful for gaining expansion through heightened motivation at lower levels. Decentralized managers with greater authority and incentive are able to penetrate larger markets, respond faster to customers, and develop new products.

*...& the control crisis:* A serious problem eventually evolves, however, as top executives sense that they are losing control over a highly diversified field operation. Autonomous field managers prefer to run their own shows without coordinating plans, money, technology, and manpower with the rest of the organization. Freedom breeds a parochial attitude.

Hence, the Phase 3 revolution is under way when top management seeks to regain control over the total company. Some top managements attempt a return to centralized management, which usually fails because of the vast scope of operations. Those companies that move ahead find a new solution in the use of special coordination techniques.

# Phase 4: Coordination...

During this phase, the evolutionary period is characterized by the use of formal systems for achieving greater coordination and by top executives taking responsibility for the initiation and administration of these new systems. For example:

- Decentralized units are merged into product groups.
- Formal planning procedures are established and intensively reviewed.
- Numerous staff personnel are hired and located at headquarters to initiate company-wide programs of control and review for line managers.
- Capital expenditures are carefully weighed and parceled out across the organization.
- Each product group is treated as an investment center where return on invested capital is an important criterion used in allocating funds.
- Certain technical functions, such as data processing, are centralized at headquarters, while daily operating decisions remain decentralized.
- Stock options and company-wide profit sharing are used to encourage identity with the firm as a whole.

All of these new coordination systems prove useful for achieving growth through more efficient allocation of a company's limited resources. They prompt field managers to look beyond the needs of their local units. While these managers still have much decision-making responsibility, they learn to justify their actions more carefully to a "watchdog" audience at headquarters.

*...& the red-tape crisis:*   But a lack of confidence gradually builds between line and staff, and between headquarters and the field.  The proliferation of systems and programs begins to exceed its utility; a red-tape crisis is created.  Line managers, for example, increasingly resent heavy staff direction from those who are not familiar with local conditions.  Staff people, on the other hand, complain about uncooperative and uninformed line managers.  Together both groups criticize the bureaucratic paper system that has evolved.  Procedures take precedence over problem solving, and innovation is dampened.  In short, the organization has become too large and complex to be managed through formal programs and rigid systems.  The Phase 4 revolution is under way.

## Phase 5: Collaboration...

The last observable phase in previous studies emphasizes strong interpersonal collaboration in an attempt to overcome the red-tape crisis.  Where Phase 4 was managed more through formal systems and procedures, Phase 5 emphasizes greater spontaneity in management action through teams and the skillful confrontation of interpersonal differences.  Social control and self-discipline take over from formal control.  This transition is especially difficult for those experts who created the old systems as well as for those line managers who relied on formal methods for answers.

The Phase 5 evolution, then, builds around a more flexible and behavioral approach to management. Here are its characteristics:

- The focus is on solving problems quickly through team action.
- Teams are combined across functions for task-group activity.
- Headquarters staff experts are reduced in number, reassigned, and combined in interdisciplinary teams to consult with, not to direct, field units.
- A matrix-type structure is frequently used to assemble the right teams for the appropriate problems.
- Previous formal systems are simplified and combined into single multipurpose systems.
- Conferences of key managers are held frequently to focus on major problem issues.
- Educational programs are utilized to train managers in behavioral skills for achieving better teamwork and conflict resolution.
- Real-time information systems are integrated into daily decision making.
- Economic rewards are geared more to team performance than to individual achievement.
- Experiments in new practices are encouraged throughout the organization.

*...& the ? crisis:*   What will be the revolution in response to this stage of evolution? Many large U.S. companies are now in the Phase 5 evolutionary stage, so the answers are critical.  While there is little clear evidence, I imagine the revolution will center around the "psychological saturation" of employees who grow emotionally and physically exhausted by the intensity of teamwork and the heavy pressure for innovative solutions.

My hunch is that the Phase 5 revolution will be solved through new structures and programs that allow employees to periodically rest, reflect, and revitalize themselves.  We may even see companies with dual organization structures: a "habit" structure for getting the daily work done, and a "reflective" structure for stimulating perspective and personal enrichment.  Employees could then move back and forth between the two structures as their energies are dissipated and refueled.

One European organization has implemented just such a structure. Five reflective groups have been established outside the regular structure for the purpose of continuously evaluating five task activities basic to the organization. They report directly to the managing director, although their reports are made public throughout the organization. Membership in each group includes all levels and functions, and employees are rotated through these groups on a six-month basis.

Other concrete examples now in practice include providing sabbaticals for employees, moving managers in and out of "hot spot" jobs, establishing a four-day workweek, assuring job security, building physical facilities for relaxation *during* the working day, making jobs more interchangeable, creating an extra team on the assembly line so that one team is always off for reeducation, and switching to longer vacations and more flexible working hours.

The Chinese practice of requiring executives to spend time periodically on lower-level jobs may also be worth a nonideological evaluation. For too long U.S. management has assumed that career progress should be equated with an upward path toward title, salary, and power. Could it be that some vice presidents of marketing might just long for, and even benefit from, temporary duty in the field sales organization?

## IMPLICATIONS OF HISTORY

Let me now summarize some important implications for practicing managers. First, the main features of this discussion are depicted in Exhibit III, which shows the specific management actions that characterize each growth phase. These actions are also the solutions which ended each preceding revolutionary period.

EXHIBIT III   Organization Practices during Evolution in the Five Phases of Growth

| Category | PHASE 1 | PHASE 2 | PHASE 3 | PHASE 4 | PHASE 5 |
|---|---|---|---|---|---|
| MANAGEMENT FOCUS | Make & Sell | Effciency of operations | Expansion of market | Consolidation of organization | Problem solving & innovation |
| MANAGEMENT FOCUS | Informal | Centralized & functional | Decentralized & geographical | Line-staff & product groups | Matrix of teams |
| TOP MANAGEMENT STYLE | Individualistic & entrepreneurial | Directive | Delegate | Watchdog | Participative |
| CONTROL SYSTEM | Market results | Standards & cost centers | Reports & profit centers | Plans & investment centers | Mutual goal setting |
| MANAGEMENT REWARD EMPHASIS | Ownership | Salary & merit increases | Individual bonus | Profit sharing & stock options | Team bonus |

In one sense, I hope that many readers will react to my model by calling it obvious and natural for depicting the growth of an organization. To me this type of reaction is a useful test of the model's validity.

But at a more reflective level I imagine some of these reactions are more hindsight than foresight. Those experienced managers who have been through a developmental sequence can empathize with it now, but how did they react when in the middle of a stage of evolution or revolution? They can probably recall the limits of their own developmental understanding at that time. Perhaps they resisted desirable changes or were even swept emotionally into a revolution without being able to propose constructive solutions. So let me offer some explicit guidelines for managers of growing organizations to keep in mind.

## Know Where You Are in the Developmental Sequence

Every organization and its component parts are at different stages of development. The task of top management is to be aware of these stages; otherwise, it may not recognize when the time for change has come, or it may act to impose the wrong solution.

Top leaders should be ready to work with the flow of the tide rather than against it; yet they should be cautious, since it is tempting to skip phases out of impatience. Each phase results in certain strengths and learning experiences in the organization that will be essential for success in subsequent phases. A child prodigy, for example, may be able to read like a teenager, but he cannot behave like one until he ages through a sequence of experiences.

I also doubt that managers can or should act to avoid revolutions. Rather, these periods of tension provide the pressure, ideas, and awareness that afford a platform for change and the introduction of new practices.

## Recognize the Limited Range of Solutions

In each revolutionary stage it becomes evident that this stage can be ended only by certain specific solutions; moreover, these solutions are different from those which were applied to the problems of the preceding revolution. Too often it is tempting to choose solutions that were tried before, which makes it impossible for a new phase of growth to evolve.

Management must be prepared to dismantle current structures before the revolutionary stage becomes too turbulent. Top managers, realizing that their own managerial styles are no longer appropriate, may even have to take themselves out of leadership positions. A good Phase 2 manager facing Phase 3 might be wise to find another Phase 2 organization that better fits his talents, either outside the company or with one of its newer subsidiaries.

Finally, evolution is not an automatic affair; it is a contest for survival. To move ahead, companies must consciously introduce planned structures that not only are solutions to a current crisis but also are fitted to the *next* phase of growth. This requires considerable self-awareness on the part of top management, as well as great interpersonal skill in persuading other managers that change is needed.

## Realize That Solutions Breed New Problems

Managers often fail to realize that organizational solutions create problems for the future (i.e., a decision to delegate eventually causes a problem of control). Historical actions are very much determinants of what happens to the company at a much later date.

An awareness of this effect should help managers to evaluate company problems with greater historical understanding instead of "pinning the blame" on a current development. Better yet, managers should be in a position to *predict* future problems, and thereby to prepare solutions and coping strategies before a revolution gets out of hand.

A management that is aware of the problems ahead could well decide *not* to grow. Top managers may, for instance, prefer to retain the informal practices of a small company, knowing that this way of life is inherent in the organization's limited size, not in their congenial personalities. If they choose to grow, they may do themselves out of a job and a way of life they enjoy.

And what about the management of very large organizations? Can they find new solutions for continued phases of evolution? Or are they reaching a stage where the government will act to break them up because they are too large?

## CONCLUDING NOTE

Clearly, there is still much to learn about processes of development in organizations. The phases outlined here are only five in number and are still only approximations. Researchers are just beginning to study the specific developmental problems of structure, control, rewards, and management style in different industries and in a variety of cultures.

One should not, however, wait for conclusive evidence before educating managers to think and act from a developmental perspective. The critical dimension of time has been missing for too long from our management theories and practices. The intriguing paradox is that by learning more about history we may do a better job in the future.

## FOOTNOTES

1. See, for example, William H. Starbuck, "Organizational Metamorphosis," in *Promising Research Directions,* eds. R. W. Millman and M. P. Hottenstein (Tempe, Ariz., Academy of Management, 1968), p. 113.
2. See, for example, The *Grangesberg* case series, prepared by C. Roland Christensen and Bruce R. Scott, Case Clearing House, Harvard Business School.
3. *Strategy and Structure: Chapters in the History of the American Industrial Enterprise* (Cambridge, Mass., The M.I.T. Press, 1962).
4. I have drawn on many sources for evidence: a) numerous cases collected at the Harvard Business School; b) *Organization Growth and Development*, ed. William H. Starbuck (Middlesex, England, Penguin Books, Ltd., 1971), where several studies are cited; and c) articles published in journals, such as Lawrence E. Fouraker and John M. Stopford, "Organization Structure and the Multinational Strategy," *Administrative Science Quarterly,* 1968, Vol. 13, No. 1, p. 47; and Malcolm S. Salter, "Management Appraisal and Reward Systems," *Journal of Business Policy,* 1971, Vol. 1, No. 4.

# 15
# Leadership and Decision Making

LEADERSHIP REVISITED
*Victor H. Vroom*

SPEED AND STRATEGIC CHOICE:  HOW MANAGERS ACCELERATE DECISION MAKING
*Kathleen M. Eisenhardt*

## LEADERSHIP REVISITED

*Victor H. Vroom*

### RESEARCH ON LEADERSHIP TRAITS

Early research on the question of leadership had roots in the psychology of individual differences and in the personality theory of that time.  The prevailing theory held that differences among people could be understood in terms of their traits—consistencies in behavior exhibited over situations.  Each person could be usefully described on such dimensions as honesty-dishonesty, introversion-extroversion or masculine-feminine.  In extrapolating this kind of theory to the study of leadership, it seemed natural to assume that there was such a thing as a trait of leadership, i.e., it was something that people possessed in different amounts.  If such differences existed, they must be measurable in some way.  As a consequence, psychologists set out, armed with a wide variety of psychological tests, to measure differences between leaders and followers.  A large number of studies were conducted including comparisons of bishops with clergymen, sales managers with salesmen and railway presidents with station agents.  Since occupancy of a leadership position may not be a valid reflection of the degree of leadership, other investigators pursued a different tack by looking at the relationship between personal traits of leaders and criteria for their effectiveness in carrying out their positions.

*Source*:  E. L. Case and F. G. Zimmer (eds.). *Man and Work in Society*.  New York: Van Nostrand Reinhold Company, 1975, pp. 221–233.  Reprinted by permission.

If this search for the measurable components of this universal trait of leadership had been effective, the implications for society would have been considerable. The resulting technology would have been of countless value in selecting leaders in all of our social institutions and would have eliminated errors inevitably found on the subjective assessments which typically guide this process. But the search was largely unsuccessful and the dream of its byproduct—a general technology of broader selection—was unrealized. The results, which have been summarized elsewhere (Bass, 1960; Gibb, 1969; Stogdill, 1948), cast considerable doubt on the usefulness of the concept of leadership as a personality trait. They do not imply that individual differences have nothing to do with leadership, but rather that their significance must be evaluated in relation to the situation.

Written more than 25 years ago, Stogdill's conclusions seem equally applicable today.

> The pattern of personal characteristics of the leader must bear some relevant relationship to the characteristics, activities and goals of the followers...It becomes clear that an adequate analysis of leadership involves not only a study of leaders, but also of situations. (1948, pp. 64–65)

The study of leadership based on personality traits had been launched on an oversimplified premise. But as Stogdill's conclusions were being written, social scientists at Ohio State University and at the University of Michigan were preparing to launch another and quite different attack on the problem of leadership. In these ventures, the focus was not on personal traits but on leader behavior and leadership style. Effective and ineffective leaders may not be distinguishable by a battery of psychological tests but may be distinguished by their characteristic behavior patterns in their work roles.

## RESEARCH ON EFFECTIVE LEADERSHIP METHODS

The focus on behavior of the leader rather than his personal traits was consistent with Lewin's classic dictum that behavior is a function of both person and environment (Lewin, 1951) and of growing recognition that the concept of trait provided little room for environmental or situational influences on behavior. Such a focus also envisioned a greater degree of consistency in behavior across situations than has been empirically demonstrated (Hartshorne and May, 1928; Mischel, 1968; Vroom and Yetton, 1973).

If particular patterns of behavior or leadership styles were found which consistently distinguished leaders of effective and ineffective work groups, the payoff to organizations and to society would have been considerable, but of a different nature than work based on the trait approach. Such results would have less obvious implications for leader selection but would have significant import for leader development and training. Knowledge of the behavior patterns which characterize effective leaders would provide a rational basis for the design of educational programs in an attempt to instill these patterns in actual or potential leaders.

Space does not permit a detailed account of the Ohio State and Michigan research or of its off-shoots in other institutions. It is fair to say, however, that the success of this line of inquiry in developing empirically based generalization about effective leadership styles is a matter of some controversy. There are some who see in the results a consistent pattern sufficient to constitute the basis of technologies or organization design or leader development. Likert (1967), reviewing the program of research at Michigan, finds support for what he calls System 4, a participative group-based conception of management. Similarly, Blake and Mouton (1964), with their conceptual roots in the Ohio State research program, argue that the effective leader exhibits concern for both production and employees (their 9-9 style) and have constructed a viable technology of management and organization development based on that premise.

454

On the other hand, other social scientists including the present writer (Korman, 1966; Sales, 1966; Vroom, 1964) have reviewed the evidence resulting from these studies and commented lamentably on the variability in results and the difficulty in making from them any definitive statements about effective leadership behavior without knowledge of the situation in which the behavior has been exhibited.

At first glance, these would appear to be two directly opposing interpretations of the same results, but that would probably be too strong a conclusion. The advocates of general leadership principles have stated these principles in such a way that they are difficult to refute by empirical evidence and at the same time provide considerable latitude for individual interpretation. To say that a leader should manage in such a way that personnel at all levels feel real responsibility for the attainment of the organization's goal (Likert, 1967) or alternatively that he should exhibit concern for both production and his employees (Blake and Mouton, 1964) are at best general blueprints for action rather than specific blueprints indicating how these objectives should be achieved. The need for adapting these principles to the demands of the situation is recognized by most social scientists. For example, Likert writes:

> Supervision is…always a relative process. To be effective and to communicate as intended, a leader must always adapt his behavior to take into account the expectations, values, and inter-personal skills of those with whom he is interacting.…There can be no specific rules of supervision which will work well in all situations. Broad principles can be applied in the process of supervision and furnish valuable guides to behavior. These principles, however, must be applied always in a manner that takes fully into account the characteristics of the specific situation and of the people involved. (1961, p. 95)

To this writer, the search for effective methods of supervision management and leadership has come close to foundering on the same rocks as the trait approach. It too has failed to deal explicitly with differences in situational requirements for leadership. If the behavioral sciences are to make a truly viable contribution to the management of the contemporary organization, they must progress beyond an advocacy of power equalization with appropriate caveats about the need for consideration of situational differences and attempt to come to grips with the complexities of the leadership process.

## INVESTIGATION ON LEADERSHIP STYLES

These convictions, whether right or wrong, provided the basis for a new approach to the investigation of leadership style—its determinants and consequences—launched about six years ago by the author and Phillip Yetton, then a graduate student at Carnegie Mellon University. We set ourselves two goals: 1) to formulate a normative or prescriptive model of leader behavior which incorporated situational characteristics in an explicit manner and which was consistent with existing empirical evidence concerning the consequences of alternative approaches; and 2) to launch an empirical attack on the determinants of leader behavior which would reveal the factors both within the person and in the situation which influence leaders to behave in various ways.

In retrospect, these goals were ambitious ones and the reader will have to judge for himself the extent to which either has been achieved. We attempted to make the task more manageable by focusing on one dimension of leader behavior—the degree to which the leader encourages the participation of his subordinates in decision-making. This dimension was chosen both because it was at the core of most prescriptive approaches to leadership and because a substantial amount of research had been conducted on it.

The first step was to review that evidence in detail. No attempt will be made here to repeat that review. (The reader interested in this question may consult Lowin, 1968; Vroom, 1964; or Wood, 1974.) Instead, we will restrict our attention to a summary of the major conclusions which appeared justifiable by the evidence.

1. Involvement of subordinates in "group decision-making" is costly in terms of time. Autocratic decision-making processes are typically faster (and thus of potential value in emergency or crisis situations) and invariably require less investment in man-hours of the group in the process of decision-making than methods which provide greater opportunities for participation by subordinates, particularly those decision processes which require consensus by the group.

2. Participation by subordinates in decision-making creates greater acceptance of decisions which in turn is reflected in better implementation. There is a wide range of circumstances under which "people support what they helped to build." Increasing the opportunity for subordinates to have a significant voice in decisions which affect them results in greater acceptance and commitment to the decisions, which will in turn be reflected in more effective and reliable implementation of the decision.

3. The effects of increased participation by subordinates in decision making on the quality or rationality of decisions tend to be positive, although the effects are likely to depend on several identifiable factors. Extensive research has been conducted on group and individual problem solving. Group decisions tend to be higher in quality when the relevant information is widely distributed among group members, when the problem is unstructured, and when there exists a mutual interest or common goal among group members.

4. Involvement of subordinates in decision making leads to growth and development of subordinates. This consequence of participation has been least researched and its assertion here is based primarily on theoretical rather than empirical grounds. It is different from the three previous factors (time, acceptance, and quality of decision) in its long-term nature.

From this general research foundation a normative model was constructed. The model utilized five decision processes which vary in the amount of opportunity afforded subordinates to participate in decision making. These processes are shown in Table 1.

---

TABLE 1  Types of Management Decision Styles

AI You solve the problem or make the decision yourself using information available to you at that time.

AII You obtain necessary information from subordinate(s) and then decide on a solution to the problem yourself. You may or may not tell subordinates what the problem is in getting the information from them. The role played by your subordinates in making the decision is clearly one of providing the necessary information to you, rather than generating or evaluating alternative solutions.

CI You share the problem with relevant subordinates individually, getting their ideas and suggestions without bringing them together as a group. Then you make the decision which may or may not reflect your subordinates' influence.

CII You share the problem with your subordinates as a group, collectively obtaining their ideas and suggestions. Then, you make the decision which may or may not reflect your subordinates' influence.

GII You share the problems with your subordinates as a group. Together you generate and evaluate alternatives and attempt to reach agreement (consensus) on a solution. Your role is much like that of chairman. You do not try to influence the group to adopt "your" solution and are willing to accept and implement any solution which has the support of the entire group.

---

The model to be described is a contingency model. It rests on the assumption that no one decision-making process is best under all circumstances, and that its effectiveness is dependent upon identifiable properties of the situation. However, it is different from other contingency models in the fact that the situational characteristics are attributes of the particular problem or decision rather than more general role characteristics. To distinguish this type of situational variable from others we have designated them as problem attributes. These attributers are the building blocks of the model and represent the means of diagnosing the nature of the problem or decision at hand so as to determine the optimal decision process.

The most recent form of the model is shown in Figure 1. It is expressed here in the form of a decision tree. The problem attributes are arranged along the top and are shown here in the form of yes-no questions. To use the model to determine the decision process, one starts at the left-hand side of the diagram and asks the question pertaining to attribute A. The answer (yes or no) will determine the path taken. When a second box is encountered, the question pertaining to that attribute is asked and the process continued until a terminal node is reached. At that node one will find a number (indicating problem type) and a feasible set of decision processes.

For some problem types only one decision process is shown; for others there are two, three, four or even all five processes. The particular decision processes shown are those that remain after a set of seven rules has been applied. The roles function to protect both the quality and the acceptance by eliminating methods that have a substantial likelihood of jeopardizing either of these two components of an effective decision. The interested reader should consult Vroom and Yetton (1973) for a detailed statement in both verbal and mathematical form, of these rules.

FIGURE 1  Decision-Process Flow Chart for Group Problems

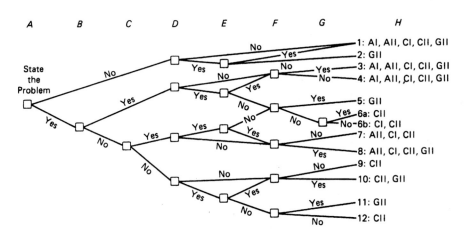

*A.* Is there a quality requirement such that one solution is likely to be more rational than another?
*B.* Do I have sufficient info to make a high quality decision?
*C.* Is the problem structured?
*D.* Is acceptance of decision by subordinates critical to effective implementation?
*E.* If I were to make the decision by myself, is it reasonably certain that it would be accepted by my subordinates?
*F.* Do subordinates share the organizational goals to be attained in solving this problem?
*G.* Is conflict among subordinates likely in preferred solutions? (This question is irrelevant to individual problems.)
*H.* Do subordinates have sufficient info to make a high quality decision?

457

If more than one alternative remains in the feasible set, there are a number of bases for choosing among them. One of them is time, the methods are arranged in ascending order of the time in man-hours which they require. Accordingly, a time minimizing model (which we have termed Model A) would select that alternative that is farthest to the left within the feasible set. An alternative to minimizing time is maximizing development of subordinates. This model (which we have termed Model B) would select that decision process which is farthest to the right within the feasible set.

While we have attempted to phrase the questions pertaining to the problem attributes in as meaningful a fashion as possible, the reader should keep in mind that they are really surrogates for more detailed specifications of the underlying variables. The reader interested in more information on the meaning of the attributes, the threshold for yes-no judgments or their rationale for inclusion in the model should consult Vroom and Yetton (1973). Illustrations of the models' application to concrete cases can be found in Vroom (1973); Vroom and Yetton (1973); and Vroom and Jago (1974).

The model shown in Figure 1 is intended to apply to a domain of managerial decision-making which Maier, Solem, and Maier (1957) refer to as group problems, i.e., problems which have potential effects on all or a substantial subset of the manager's subordinates. Recently, we have become interested in extending the model to "individual problems," i.e., those affecting only one subordinate. For these decisions, the first three decision processes shown in Table 1 represent potentially reasonable alternatives, but there are at least two other variable alternatives not yet represented. One of these we have called GI, which is a form of group decision involving only a single subordinate. (A GI manager shares the problem with the subordinate and together they analyze the problem and arrive at a mutually satisfactory solution.) The other, which we have designated as DI, consists of delegating the problem or decision to the subordinate.

Many of the considerations used in building the model for group problems—such as problem attributes and rules—could easily be adapted to the domain of individual problems. There remained, however, one major structural difference. For group problems, there was a tradeoff between the short-run consideration of time efficiency (which favored autocratic methods) and longer-range considerations involving subordinate development (which favored participative methods). The reader will recall that Model A and Model B represented two extreme modes of resolution of that tradeoff. For individual problems, the differences in time requirements of the five processes (AI, AII, CI, GI, DI) are not nearly as large and the alternative which provides the greatest amount of subordinate influence or participation, DI, can hardly be argued to be least time efficient. This difference in the correlation between time efficiency and participation for individual and group problems required an adjustment in the location of DI in the ordering of alternatives in terms of time. Model A and Model B retain their original meaning from the earlier model, but they are no longer polar opposites.

Figure 2 contains a model also expressed as a decision tree which purports to guide choices among decision processes for both individual and group problems. The only difference lies in the specifications of two feasible sets (one for group and one for individual problems) for each problem type.

Is the model in its present form an adequate guide to practice? Would managers make fewer errors in their choices of decision processes if they were to base them on the model? We would be less than honest if we said we knew the answers to such questions. Most managers who have had sufficient training in the use of the model to be able to use it reliably report that it is a highly useful guide, although there are occasionally considerations not presently contained in the model—such as geographical dispersion of subordinates—which prevent implementation of its recommendations. Some research has been conducted in an attempt to establish the validity of the model (see Vroom and Yetton, 1973: 182–84), but the results, while promising, are not conclusive. Perhaps the most convincing argument for the development of models of this kind is that they can serve as a guide for research that can identify their weaknesses and that superior models can later be developed.

458

FIGURE 2   Decision-Process Flow Chart for Both Individual and Group Problems

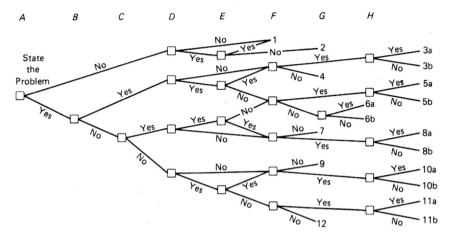

The feasible set is shown for each problem type for Group (G) and Individual (I) problems.

1 | G:  AI, AII, CI, CII, GII
  | I:  AI, DI, AII, CI, GI

2 | G:  GII
  | I:  DI, GI

3a | G:  AI, AII, CI, CII, GII
   | I:  AI, DI, AII, CI, GI

3b | G:  AI, AII, CI, CII, GII
   | I:  AI, AII, CI, GI

4 | G:  AI, AII, CI, CII
  | I:  AI, AII, CI

5a | G:  GII
   | I:  DI, GI

5b | G:  GII
   | I:  DI, GI

6a | G:  CII
   | I:  CI, GI

6b | G:  CI, CII
   | I:  CI, GI

7 | G:  AII, CI, CII
  | I:  CI, GI

8a | G:  AII, CI, CII, GII
   | I:  DI, AII, CI, GI

8b | G:  AII, CI, CII, GII
   | I:  AII, CI, GI

9 | G:  CII
  | I:  CI

10a | G:  CII, GII
    | I:  DI, CI, GI

10b | G:  CII, GII
    | I:  CI, GI

11a | G:  GII
    | I:  DI, GI

11b | G:  GII
    | I:  GI

12 | G:  CII
   | I:  CI, GI

A.  Is there a quality requirement such that one solution is likely to be more rational than another?
B.  Do I have sufficient info to make a high quality decision?
C.  Is the problem structured?
D.  Is acceptance of decision by subordinates critical to effective implementation?
E.  If I were to make the decision by myself, is it reasonably certain that it would be accepted by my subordinates?
F.  Do subordinates share the organizational goals to be attained in solving this problem?
G.  Is conflict among subordinates likely in preferred solutions? (This question is irrelevant to individual problems.)
H.  Do subordinates have sufficient info to make a high quality decision?

The reader will note that flexibility in leader behavior is one of the requirements of use of the model. To use it effectively, the leader must adapt his approach to the situation. But how flexible are leaders in the approaches they use? Do they naturally try and vary their approach with the situation? Is it possible to develop such flexibility through training? These questions were but a few of those which guided the next phase of our inquiry into how leaders do in fact behave and into the factors both within the leader himself and in the situations with which he deals which cause him to share decision-making power with his subordinates.

Two different research methods have been used in an attempt to answer questions such as these. The first investigation utilized a method that can be referred to as "recalled problems." Over 500 managers from 11 different countries representing a variety of firms were asked to provide a written description of a problem that they had recently had to solve. These varied in length from one paragraph to several pages and covered virtually every facet of managerial decision making. For each case, the

459

manager was asked to indicate which of the decision processes shown in Table 1 he used to solve the problem. Finally, each manager was asked to answer the questions corresponding to the problem attributes used in the normative model with his own case in mind.

These data made it possible to determine the frequency with which the managers' decision process was similar to that of the normative model and the factors in their description of the situation which were associated with the use of each decision process. This investigation provided results which were interesting but also led to the development of a second more powerful method for investigating the same questions. This method, which will be termed "standardized problems," used some of the actual cases, each of which depicts a manager faced with a problem to solve or decision to make. In each case, a leader would be asked to assume the role of the manager faced with the situation described and to indicate which decision process he would use if faced with that situation.

Several such sets of cases have been developed. In early research, each set consisted of thirty cases, but more recently longer sets of forty-eight and fifty four cases have been used. Composition of each set of standardized cases was in accordance with multifactorial experimental design. Cases varied in terms of each of the eight problem attributes used in the normative model, and variation in each attribute was independent of each other attribute. This feature permits the assessment of the effects of each of the problem attributes on the decision processes used by a given manager.

The cases themselves spanned a wide range of managerial problems including production scheduling, quality control, portfolio management, personnel allocation, and research and development project selection. To date, several thousand managers in the United States and abroad have been studied using this approach.

## RESULTS AND CONCLUSIONS

To summarize everything learned in the course of this research is well beyond the scope of this reading, but it is possible to discuss some of the highlights. Since the results obtained from the two research methods—recalled and standardized problems—are consistent, the major results can be presented independent of the method used.

Perhaps the most striking finding is the weakening of the widespread view that participativeness is a general trait that individual managers exhibit in different amounts. To be sure, there were differences among managers in their general tendencies to utilize participative methods as opposed to autocratic ones. On the standardized problems, these differences accounted for about 10 percent of the total variance in the decision processes observed. Furthermore, those managers who tended to use more participative methods such as CII and GII with group problems also tended to use more participative methods like delegation for dealing with individual problems.

However, these differences in behavior between managers were small in comparison with differences within managers. On the standardized problems, no manager has indicated that he would use the same decision process on all problems or decisions, and most use all methods under some circumstances. Taking managers' reports of their behavior in concrete situations, it is clear that they are striving to be flexible in their approaches to different situations.

Some of this variance in behavior within managers can be attributed to widely shared tendencies to respond to some situations by sharing power and others by retaining it. It makes more sense to talk about participative and autocratic situations than it does to talk about participative and autocratic managers. In fact, on the standardized problems, the variance in behavior across problems or cases is from three to five times as large as the variance across managers.

What are the characteristics of an autocratic as opposed to a participative situation? An answer to this question would constitute a partial descriptive model of this aspect of the decision-making process and has been the goal of much of the research conducted. From observations of behavior on both recalled problems and on standardized problems, it is clear that the decision-making process employed by a typical manager is influenced by a large number of factors, many of which also show up in the normative model. Following are several conclusions substantiated by the results on both recalled and standardized problems.

Managers use decision processes providing less opportunity for participation 1) when they possess all the necessary information rather than when they lack some of the needed information; 2) when the problem they face is well-structured rather than unstructured; 3) when their subordinates' acceptance of the decision is not critical for the effective implementation of the decision or when the prior probability of acceptance of an autocratic decision is high; and 4) when the personal goals of their subordinates are not congruent with the goals of the organization as manifested in the problem.

These findings concern relatively common or widely shared ways of dealing with organizational problems. The results also strongly suggest that managers have ways of "tailoring" their decision process to the situation that distinguish one manager from another. Theoretically, these can be thought of as differences among managers in decision rules that they employ about when to encourage participation.

Consider, for example, two managers who have identical distributions of the use of the five decision processes shown in Table 1 on a set of thirty cases. In a sense, they are equally participative (or autocratic). However, the situation in which they permit or encourage participation in decision making on the part of their subordinates may be very different. One may restrict the participation of his subordinates to decisions without a quality requirement, whereas the other may restrict their participation to problems with a quality requirement. The former would be more inclined to use participative decision processes (like GI) on such decisions as what color the walls should be painted or when the company picnic should be held. The latter would be more likely to encourage participation in decision making on decisions that have a clear and demonstrable impact on the organization's success in achieving its external goals.

Use of the standardized problem set permits the assessment of such differences in decision rules that govern choices among decision-making processes. Since the cases are selected in accordance with an experimental design, they can indicate differences in the behavior of managers attributable not only to the existence of a quality requirement in the problem but also in the effects of acceptance requirements, conflict, information requirements, and the like.

The research using both recalled and standardized problems has also permitted the examination of similarities and differences between the behavior of the normative model and the behavior of a typical manager. Such an analysis reveals, at the very least, what behavioral changes could be expected if managers began using the normative model as the basis for choosing their decision-making processes.

A typical manager says he would (or did) use exactly the same decision process as that shown in Figure 1 in about 40 percent of the group problems. In two-thirds of the situations, his behavior is consistent with the feasible set of methods proposed in the model. However, in the remaining one-third of the situations, his behavior violates at least one of the seven rules underlying the model. Results show significantly higher agreement with the normative model for individual problems than for group problems.

The rules designed to protect the acceptance or commitment of the decision have substantially higher probabilities of being violated than do the rules designed to protect the quality or rationality of the decision. Assuming for the moment that these two sets of rules have equal validity, these findings strongly suggest that the decisions made by typical managers are more likely to prove ineffective due to deficiencies of acceptance by subordinates than due to deficiencies in decision quality.

461

Another striking difference between the behavior of the model and of the typical manager lies in the fact that the former shows far greater variance with the situation. If a typical manager voluntarily used the model as the basis for choosing his methods of making decisions, he would become both more autocratic and more participative. He would employ autocratic methods more frequently in situations in which his subordinates were unaffected by the decision and participative methods more frequently when his subordinates' cooperation and support were critical and/or their information and expertise were required.

It should be noted that the typical manager to whom we have been referring is merely a statistical average of the several thousand who have been studied over the last three or four years. There is a great deal of variation around that average. As evidenced by their behavior on standardized problems, some managers are already behaving in a manner that is highly consistent with the model, while others' behavior is clearly at variance with it.

The research program that has been summarized was conducted in order to shed new light on the causes and consequences of decision-making processes used by leaders in formal organizations. In the course of research, it was realized that the data collection procedures, with appropriate additions and modifications, might also serve a useful function in leadership development. From this realization evolved an important byproduct of the research activities—a new approach to leadership training based on the concepts in the normative model and the empirical methods of the descriptive research.

A detailed description of this training program and of initial attempts to evaluate its effectiveness may be found in Vroom and Yetton (1973, chap. 8). It is based on the premise that one of the critical skills required of all leaders is the ability to adapt their behavior to the demands of the situation and that a component of this skill involves selecting the appropriate decision-making process for each problem or decision they confront. The purpose of the program is not to "train" managers to use the model in their everyday decision-making activities. Instead the model serves as a device for encouraging managers to examine their leadership styles and for coming to a conscious realization of their own, often implicit, choices among decision processes, including their similarity and dissimilarity with the model. By helping managers to become aware of their present behavior and of alternatives to it, the training provides a basis for rethinking their leadership style to be more consistent with goals and objectives. Succinctly, the training is intended to transform habits into choices rather than to program a leader with a particular method of making choices.

A fundamental part of the program in its present form is the use of a set of standardized cases previously described in connection with the descriptive phase of the research. Each participant specifies the decision process he would employ if he were the leader described in the case. His responses to the entire set of cases are processed by computer, which generates a highly detailed analysis of his leadership style. The responses for all participants in a single course are typically processed simultaneously, permitting the calculation of differences between the person and others in the same program.

In its latest form, a single computer printout for a person consists of seven 15" by 11" pages, each filled with graphs and tables highlighting different features of his behavior. Understanding the results requires a detailed knowledge of the concepts underlying the model, something already developed in one of the previous phases of the training program. The printout is accompanied by a manual that aids in explaining the results and provides suggested steps to be followed in extracting the full meaning from the printout.

Following are a few of the questions that the printout answers:

1. How autocratic or participative am I in my dealings with subordinates in the program?
2. What decision processes do I use more or less frequently than the average?

3. How close does my behavior come to that of the model? How frequently does my behavior agree with the feasible set? What evidence is there that my leadership style reflects the pressure of time as opposed to a concern with the development of my subordinates? How do I compare in these respects with other participants in the program?
4. What rules do I violate most frequently and least frequently? On what cases did I violate these rules? Does my leadership style reflect more concern with getting decisions that are high in quality or with getting decisions that are accepted?

When a typical manager receives his printout, he immediately goes to work trying to understand what it tells him about himself. After most of the major results have been understood, he goes back to the set of cases to reread those on which he has violated rules. Typically, managers show an interest in discussing and comparing their results with others in the program. Gatherings of four to six people comparing their results and their interpretations of them, often for several hours at a stretch, were such a common feature that they have recently been institutionalized as part of the procedure.

It should be emphasized that this method of providing feedback on their leadership style is just one part of the total training experience which encompasses over thirty hours over a period of three successive days. To date, no longterm evaluations of its effectiveness has been undertaken, but initial results appear quite promising.

## SUMMARY

How far has the understanding of leadership progressed in the 50 years since the Hawthorne Studies? The picture that has been painted in this reading is one of false starts stemming from oversimplified conceptions of the process. An encouraging sign, however, is the increased interest in contingency theories or models incorporating both leader and situational variables. In this reading I have spent much time describing one kind of contingency model; Professor Fiedler, who accompanies me on this panel, has developed another form of contingency model.

These two models share a number of qualities, but are different in several important aspects. I believe that Professor Fiedler sees much greater consistency and less flexibility in leader behavior than is required by the normative model or exhibited in managers' statements of how they would behave on the problem set. I suspect that we also have substantially different views on the potential for modification of leadership style through training and development.

Both of these are fascinating and important questions, and I for one would enjoy exploring them during our later discussion. But there is one prediction about which I feel quite confident. Fifty years from now, both contingency models will be found wanting in detail if not in substance. If either Professor Fiedler or I am remembered at that time, it will be for the same reason that we meet to commemorate the Hawthorne Studies this week—the kinds of questions we posed rather than the specific answers we provided.

## REFERENCES

Bass, B. M. *Leadership, Psychology and Organizational Behavior.* New York: Harper, 1960.
Blake, R., and Mouton, J. *The Managerial Grid*, Houston: Gulf, 1964.
Gibb, C. A. "Leadership," in *Handbook of Social Psychology*, edited by G. Lindzey and E. Aronson, vol. 4. Reading, Mass.: Addison-Wesley, 1969.
Hartshone, H., and May, M. A. *Studies in Deceit.* New York: Macmillan, 1928.

Korman, A. K. "'Consideration,' 'Initiating Structure,' and Organizational Criteria—A Review," *Personnel Psychology* 19 (1966).

Lewin, K. *Field Theory in Social Science*, edited by D. Cartwright. New York: Harper, 1941.

Likert, R. *New Patterns of Management*. New York: McGraw-Hill, 1961.

Likert, R. *The Human Organization*. New York: McGraw-Hill, 1967.

Lowin, A. "Participative Decision-Making: A Model, Literature Critique, and Prescriptions for Research." *Organizational Behavior and Human Performance* 3 (1968).

Maier, N. R. F.; Solem, A. R.; and Maier, A. A. *Supervisory and Executive Development: A Manual for Role Playing*. New York: Wiley, 1954.

Mischel, W. *Personality and Assessment*. New York: Wiley, 1968.

Sales, S. M. "Supervisory Style and Productivity: Review and Theory." *Personnel Psychology* 19 (1966).

Stogdill, R. M. "Personal Factors Associated with Leadership: A Survey of the Literature. *Journal of Psychology* 25 (1948).

Vroom, V. H. *Work and Motivation*. New York: Wiley, 1964.

Vroom, V. H. "A New Look at Management Decision-Making." *Organizational Dynamics* 1 (1973).

Vroom, V. H. , and Jago, A. G. "Decision-Making as a Social Process: Normative and Descriptive Models of Leader Behavior." *Decision Science* (1974).

Vroom, V. H. , and Yetton, P. W. "A Normative Model of Leadership Style. In *Readings in Managerial Psychology,* edited by H. J. Leavitt and L. Pondy, 2d ed. Chicago: University of Chicago Press, 1973.

Wood, M. J. "Power Relationships and Group Decision Making in Organizations." *Psychological Bulletin* (1974).

# SPEED AND STRATEGIC CHOICE: HOW MANAGERS ACCELERATE DECISION MAKING

## Kathleen M. Eisenhardt

*Strategy making has changed. The carefully conducted industry analysis or the broad-ranging strategic plan is no longer a guarantee of success. The premium now is on moving fast and keeping pace. More than ever before, the best strategies are irrelevant if they take too long to formulate.* Rather, especially where technical and competitive change are rapid, fast strategic decision making is essential.

But, how do people make fast choices? Conventional wisdom suggests several strategies. One strategy is to skimp on analysis. That is, managers could look at limited information, consider only one or two alternatives, or gather data from only a few sources. Yes, this is fast. But the obvious problem is that such skimping seriously compromises the quality of the choice. A more subtle concern is whether decision makers will actually have enough confidence to make major choices with so little information and analysis to bolster their decisions.

Another strategy suggested by conventional wisdom is to limit conflict. Conflict drags outs decision making, and the more powerful the combatants, the longer this conflict is likely to persist. So, minimizing conflict seems likely to accelerate choice. But, how can managers actually go about repressing real conflict among key executives? And if it can be suppressed, will managers support decisions if their opinions have been ignored? Most importantly, is it possible to make high-quality decisions without conflict? A wide spectrum of research indicates that high conflict yields more innovative, thorough decision making.

Conventional wisdom also suggests a third strategy to accelerate choices. Be an autocrat—make bold and rapid unilateral moves. While such a leader can move quickly, the era of swashbucklers is over. Such leaders often become isolated. This means poor information for making important choices, lack of support once those choices are made, and disabling anxiety which plagues people attempting to make major decisions alone.

Thus, at first glance, conventional wisdom offers strategies which appear to accelerate choices. More often, they are ineffective because they fail to deal with important realities. How can decision makers formulate high-quality choices when information and analysis are limited? How can they maintain a committed group if conflict and debate are suppressed? How can they avoid the natural tendency to procrastinate, especially when information is poor and stakes are high? The purpose of this article is to explore how managers actually do make fast, yet high-quality, strategic decisions.

## RESEARCH BASE

The ideas described here partially rest on data which I collected with a colleague, Jay Bourgeois. Our motivation was to study how executives coped with strategic decision making in fast-moving, high-technology environments. Past research on choice processes had neglected such environments in favor of studying large bureaucracies in stable settings. We tracked decision-making processes in 12 microcomputer firms. We relied on extensive interviews with each member of the top management team of every firm, plus questionnaires, observations of group meetings, and various secondary data. I then followed up the microcomputer study with contacts with numerous Silicon Valley firms and their key executives.

These field data suggest striking differences in the pace of strategic decision making across firms. Some decision makers are fast. They make decisions on critical issues such as product innovations, strategic alliances, and strategic redirection within several months. Others are slow. They spend 6 months, more often 12 to 18 months, on decisions that the fast decision makers can execute in 2 to 4 months.

The ideas in this article are bolstered by recent psychological research. Writings on artificial intelligence and problem solving under time pressure are useful for understanding how people accelerate cognitive processing by more efficient use of information.[1] Work on the effects of emotion on decision making is also germane. Particularly relevant are findings about how individuals cope with anxiety and stress when dealing with high uncertainty.[2] Finally, the psychological literature provides insight into how groups build cohesive interactions and ensure perceptions of equality when resolving conflict situations.[3] Thus, the combination of field study plus related psychological research led to the portrait of fast, yet high-quality, decision making that follows.

Overall, fast decision makers use simple, yet powerful tactics to accelerate choices (see Table 1). They maintain constant watch over real time operating information and rely on fast, comparative analysis of multiple alternatives to speed cognitive processing. They favor approaches to conflict resolution which are quick and yet maintain a cohesive group process. Lastly, their use of advice and integration of decisions and tactics creates the self-confidence needed to make a fast choice, even when information is limited and stakes are high.

At the other end of the spectrum slow decision makers become bogged down by the fruitless search for information, excessive development of alternatives, and paralysis in the fact of conflict and uncertainty.

## TRACKING REAL TIME INFORMATION

One of the myths of fast strategic decision making is that limiting information saves time. That is, slashing the amount of information, the number of information sources, and the depth of analysis accelerates choice. But, is this what fast decision makers actually do? The answer is "no." They do just the opposite. They use as much, and sometimes more, information than do their slower counterparts.

However, there is a crucial difference in the kind of information. Slow decision makers rely on planning and futuristic information. They spend time tracking the likely path of technologies, markets, or competitor actions, and then develop plans In contrast, the fast decision makers look to real time information—that is, information about current operations and current environment which is reported with little or no time lag.

Fast decision makers gather real time information in several ways. One critical source is operational measures of internal performance. Fast decision makers typically examine a wide variety of operating measures on a monthly, weekly, and even daily basis. They prefer indicators such as bookings, backlog, margins, engineering milestones, cash, scrap, and work-in-process to more refined, accounting-based indicators such as profitability. The key finance manager often has a critical role in the fast decision-making organization. This executive typically is charged with providing this "constant pulse" of what is happening. In comparison with the classic big-company view, fast decision makers keep the key financial manager close to operations, and not in a watch-dog, staff role.

For less quantitative data, fast decision makers emphasize frequent operational meetings—2 or 3 such meetings per week are not unusual. And, the intensity of such meetings is high, with each being a "must" on all calendars. Typically, these meetings cover "what's happening" with sales, engineering schedules, releases, or whatever comprises the critical operating information of the organization. But, these meetings are not limited to internal information. Fast decision makers also relay to each other external real time information such as new product introductions by competitors, competition at key accounts, and technical developments within the industry.

A good example is Zap Computers (a fictitious name for an actual firm). Zap's top management team is known for rapid decisions. Typically, they execute, in 2 or 3 months, decisions which elsewhere often drag on for a year or more. How do they do it? The popular press highlights their "laid back" and "fun-loving" California culture. A closer inspection reveals slavish dedication to real time information.

Zap executives claim to "over-MBA it," to "measure everything." They come close. Zap executives review bookings, scrap, inventory, cash flow, and engineering milestones on a weekly and sometimes daily basis. The monthly review is more comprehensive, emphasizing ratios such as revenue per employee and margins. Firm executives maintain fixed targets for margins and key expense categories. These targets themselves are not so unusual, but what is striking is the number of people who can recite them. Zap executives also attend three regularly scheduled operations meetings each week. One is a staff meeting for general topics while another is for products and the third is a review of engineering schedules. The tone is emotional, intense, and vocal.

TABLE 1    Fast versus Slow Strategic Decision Making

| Fast | Implications |
|---|---|
| • Track real time information on firm operations and the competitive environment | • Acts as a warning system to spot problems and opportunities early on |
| | • Builds a deep, intuitive grasp of the business |
| • Build multiple, simultaneous alternatives | • Permits quick, comparative analysis |
| | • Bolsters confidence that the best alternatives have been considered |
| | • Adds a fallback position |
| • Seek the advice of experienced counselors | • Emphasizes advice from the most useful managers |
| | • Provides a safe forum to experiment with ideas and options |
| | • Boosts confidence in the choice |
| • Use "consensus with qualification" | • Offers proactive conflict resolution which recognizes its inevitability in many situations |
| | • Is a popular approach which balances managers' desires to be heard with the need to make a choice |
| • Integrate the decision with other decisions and tactics | • "Actively" copes with the stress of choice when information is poor and stakes are high |
| | • Signals possible mismatches with other decisions and tactics in the future |

| Slow | Implications |
|---|---|
| • Focus on planning and futuristic information, keeping a loose grip on current operations and environment | • Can be time-consuming to develop |
| | • Quickly obsolete in fast changing situations |
| • Develop a single alternative, while moving to a second only if the first fails | • Obscures real preferences |
| | • Limits confidence that the best alternatives have been considered |
| | • Eliminates a fallback position |
| • Solicit advice haphazardly or from less experienced counselors | • Fails to take best advantage of the advice of experienced executives |
| • Use of consensus of deadlines to resolve conflicts | • Consensus is often wishful thinking in complex business decisions |
| | • Deadlines may not exist and so decisions can be postponed indefinitely. |
| • Consider the decision as a single choice in isolation from other choices | • Increases stress by keeping the decision in the abstract |
| | • Risks the chance that the decision will conflict with other choices |

The Zap top management team plays an important role in gathering real time data. The VP Finance, described as "having a good understanding of business" and years of experience, oversees more than just the usual treasury and accounting functions. He is responsible for the financial model of the firm which is run at least weekly. The model itself is simple, but it allows Zap executives to translate possible decisions into their impact on basic operating results. His group also provides updated operational data, usually available on a daily basis.

Other executives are also essential to the real time information network at Zap. For example, the VP Marketing is charged with tracking the moves of competitors as they occur. This means constant phone calls and frequent travel. The VP R&D also works the phone to maintain a complex web of university and business contacts which keep him cognizant of the latest technical developments.

Zap executives also favor electronic mail or fact-to-face meetings. As they described it, "We e-mail constantly." They are also frequently in and out of each others' offices. On the other hand, Zap executives avoid time delayed media such as memos. They are seen as too slow and too dated. Overall, dedication to real time information gives Zap executives an extraordinary grasp of the details of their business.

In contrast, slow decision makers have a much looser grip on current operations and the competitive environment. For example, decision makers in the slower firms track few operational measures and they review them less frequently than do their faster counterparts. Their emphasis is on future, not current, information.

The lack of real time information is also evident in the use of group meetings. In the micro-computer study, slow decision makers had few, if any, weekly operations meetings. Several firms did not have VP Finance or else relied on a less experienced executive. For example, one used an ex-engineer, claimed by all to be "weak" in financial matters. At another firm, the VP Finance had left the firm and there were no current plans to replace him.

Instead of real time data, these executives prefer planning information. For example, executives at one corporation spent close to a year doing a technology study of various operating systems for microprocessors as a prelude to a new product decision. At another firm, executives responded to a performance decline by spending 6 months developing a technology forecast for the industry. The elapsed decision-making time in both firms was over a year.

Why does real time information speed decision making? An obvious reason is that the continual tracking allows mangers to spot opportunities and problems sooner. Real time information acts as an early warning system so that managers can respond before situations become too problematic. When crises do arise, such managers can go right to the problem, rather than groping about for relevant information.

However, a more subtle explanation comes from artificial intelligence. Research on the development of intuition suggests that the basis of intuition is experience.[4] For example, chess players develop their intuition by playing chess over and over again. This repeated practice allows the chess player to play the game using what lay people term "intuition." In fact, intuitive chess players have actually learned to process information in patterns or blocks. Because they recognize and manipulate information in blocks, they can process information much faster than others who think only in single items of information.

Consistent with this view, managers who track real time information are actually developing their intuition. Aided by intuition, they can then react quickly and accurately to changing events. Indeed, in the microcomputer study, the executives who were most attuned to real time data were also those most described as intuitive. For example, one executive was described as a "numbers" person and claimed to "over-MBA it." Yet, he was also described by his colleagues as "intuitive," "a lateral thinker," and as having "the best sense of everything in the business." Another also claimed to be a

468

"numbers guy." His VP Finance praised "the quality of his understanding" and frequent use of operating data. This executive was also described as having "an immense instinctive feel" and a superior "grasp of the business."

In contrast, slow strategic decision makers emphasize planning and forecasting information. They look to the future and attempt to predict it. Or, they hope that, by waiting, the future will become clear. Yet, their faster counterparts maintain that this is foolish. They claim that extensive planning wastes time. Why? It's difficult to predict what will happen and impossible to predict who will do it and when. As one fast-moving executive claimed, "No company can know how things will evolve. You can only monitor the outside world and direct the evolving strategy at what you see." Overall, it appears that real time information—which gives executives an intimate knowledge of their business—speeds choice, but planning information—which attempts to predict the future—does not.

# BUILDING MULTIPLE, SIMULTANEOUS ALTERNATIVES

A second myth is that fast decision makers save time by focusing on only one or two alternatives. The underlying logic is that fewer alternatives are faster to analyze than more. But, in fact, fast decision makers do the reverse. They explicitly search for and debate multiple alternatives, often working several options at once. At the extreme, some fast decision makers will support alternatives that they oppose if doing so furthers debate, and they will even introduce alternatives which they do not actually support.

A good example of multiple alternatives occurred at one of the microcomputer firms. Here, a new CEO was faced with improving the lackluster performance of the firm. New products were slow in coming out and there was pressure from investors to do something. This new CEO launched a fact-gathering exercise. Almost simultaneously firm executives began to develop a rough set of alternatives. As the fact-gathering continued, so did the shaping of alternatives. In less than 2 months, the executives had developed 4 options. They considered selling some of their technology—there were willing buyers, especially from overseas. They also considered a major strategic redirection of the firm which would involve using the base technology to enter a new market. A third option involved various tactical changes in the form of redeployment of some engineering resources and adjustments to the marketing approach. The final option was extreme—liquidation of the firm.

Executives at the firm admitted that this decision strategy was ambiguous and complicated. Why did they do it? As one executive claimed, they and the CEO, in particular, liked to have multiple options, "a larger set of options than most people do." There was a preference for "working a multiple array of possibilities instead of just a couple."

At another firm, the problem was cash flow. The business was prospering, but the cash flow was not keeping pace. These executives also developed multiple alternatives. One executive negotiated with banks to extend credit lines. Others developed several strategic alliance alternatives with both U.S. and foreign firms. A third set of executives planned a major equity financing. With rough details of each option in hand, firm executives chose the strategic alliance for flexibility and marketing reasons. When the first choice alliance partner backed out, firm executives quickly cut a deal with the second. The credit and equity plans were waiting on the shelf, if the alliance option had failed.

In contrast, surprisingly, slow decision makers work with fewer, not more, alternatives. They typically develop and analyze a single alternative, and only seriously consider other alternatives if the first becomes infeasible. Thus, slow decision makers favor a highly sequential approach to alternatives—and, one which emphasizes depth of analysis over breadth of options.

A new product decision at one of the microcomputer firms illustrates this process. These executives wanted to develop a new product which made greater use of VLSI technology. The rationale was that increased integration would lower product costs. Firm executives explored the possibility of in-house development for several months. When they concluded that the firm lacked sufficient expertise, they then migrated to a second alternative, a strategic alliance with a major U.S. firm. They spent about six months getting to know the personnel of their would-be partner and negotiating the terms of the deal. However, the deal fell through when the two parties could not reach a final agreement. At this point, firm executives then had to search several months for another partner. After further delay, they eventually closed the deal with this second firm.

This same pattern of single, sequential alternatives is characteristic of many slow decisions. At another firm, executives were also interested in developing a new product. They too explored the in-house route to a new product for several months. When they determined that in-house development would be too slow, they belatedly went outside for a product source. It took several more months to locate a suitable partner. At another firm, executives noted increasing competition in their marketplace. They spent almost a year deciding whether they needed a new strategy. Only after they decided that the old strategy was no longer workable did they then seriously consider what that new strategy should be.

Why are multiple, simultaneous alternatives fast? One reason is that multiple alternatives (at least, in the range of 3 to 5) are faster to analyze than 1 or 2. Why? The reason is comparison. Comparative analysis sharpens preferences. For example, car buyers often find it difficult to understand their preferences in the abstract. Rather, actually driving cars and then comparing across cars helps prospective buyers to decide whether they prefer a leather or plush interior, a standard or rally suspension package, one make over another, and so forth. Comparative analysis is also fast because it allows decision makers to use rankings to assess alternatives. The superiority of an alternative is often apparent in comparison, even if its superiority cannot be readily quantified.

Multiple alternatives also speed decision making because they are confidence building. With multiple alternatives, decision makers are more likely to feel that they have not missed a superior alternative. Again, to use the car buying example, it is difficult to buy a car without seeing others because buyers often cannot overcome the feeling that they may be missing something better elsewhere.

Finally, multiple alternatives are fast because they provide a fall back position. When one option falls through, decision makers can quickly move on to a second. Although a first choice option sometimes prevails, situations can change rapidly and dramatically. So, the odds are good that adjustments will be needed. In the illustrations above, the firms which pursued multiple alternatives simultaneously had fallback positions when one or more options proved infeasible. In contrast, the firms pursuing sequential alternatives lost time because they waited until an option failed before looking for a new one.

Overall, there is a fundamental difference in how fast and slow decision makers treat alternatives. Fast decision makers develop multiple alternatives, but analyze them rapidly. They rely primarily on quick, comparative analysis, which reveals relative rankings and sharpens preferences. Theirs is a "breadth-not-depth" strategy. Recent laboratory research indicates that this is the efficient cognitive processing approach when the decision maker is under time pressure.[5]

In contrast, slow decision makers emphasize depth of analysis. They analyze few alternatives, but do so in greater depth. And so, they often conduct a similar amount of analysis, but without gaining the confidence in their choice that multiple alternatives bring and without gaining the advantage of fallback positions.

# RELYING ON THE ADVICE OF COUNSELORS

A third critical aspect of fast strategic decision making is the judicious use of advice. Most fast decision makers rely on a two-tier advice process in which all executives offer some advice, but the key decision maker focuses on the advice provided by one or two of the most experienced executives in the group, who are termed "counselors." By contrast, slow decision makers typically have no one in this counselor role.

What do these counselors do? Typically, they work in the background advising the key decision maker about a wide range of issues. They also serve as an early and confidential sounding board for ideas. For example, at one firm, the counselor played an important role in a new product decision. The situation was triggered by an unexpected new product introduction by an important competitor. In private, the counselor alerted the CEO to the imminent introduction. The two then conferred, with the counselor helping the CEO to shape and test alternatives. Even after the CEO brought the issue to the attention of the entire top management team, the counselor continued to work behind the scenes with the CEO. As the CEO described, "Our interaction is more general than just sales....When I talk with Joe it's often about company issues."

A striking feature of the counselor role is the consistent demographic profile of these individuals. The counselor is typically an older and more experienced person, who is recognized as "savvy"or "street smart" by colleagues. For example, the counselors at one firm were 10 to 20 years older than the rest of the top management team. One of these executives had been a senior manager at a major, international firm. He was described as "the best manager" on the top management team. The other had been a senior executive at two important firms in the industry. He was credited with being the "most knowledgeable about the outside world." Counselors are also frequently on a career plateau, with their aspirations no longer centering on the fast-track to the top. Rather, they relish the personal challenge. As one counselor claimed, "It's fun to build an organization again."

What do fast decision makers do when they have no colleague who fits the counselor profile? In one such case, a consultant was hired to play the role. This consultant had extensive industry contacts, had been a senior executive at two other firms, and had known the CEO for many years. This executive was credited with an important advisory role to the CEO as well as to several other executives.

In contrast, slow strategic decision makers typically have no executive who acts as a counselor. These decision makers usually do not develop any kind of a close, advisory relationship with another colleague. Or, if they do, that colleague often is a poor choice. For example, the counselor to a CEO in a slow decision making firm was considered to be "bright," but "young." He was in his early 30s and had only functional staff experience. Given his modest background, his ability to be an effective counselor was limited.

Why do experienced counselors accelerate choices? Clearly, one reason is that these individuals can provide high-quality advice to decision makers more readily than less experienced colleagues. They have simply seen more and done more. Not surprisingly, they can usually assess situations more rapidly and offer better advice than less experienced people.

Second, they are excellent sounding boards. They combine strong experience with a trustworthiness that comes with limited personal ambition and often long acquaintance with the key decision maker. These are people who understand discretion and the subtle exercise of power.

Perhaps most importantly, counselors can boost the confidence of decision makers to decide. One of the highest barriers to fast decision making is anxiety. Big stakes decision making with high uncertainty is stressful, and so it is extraordinarily tempting simply to procrastinate. However, conversations with an experienced confidante can counteract this tendency to delay by bolstering decision makers' confidence to make difficult choices.

# RESOLVING CONFLICT

Another myth of fast strategic decision making is that conflict slows down the pace of choice. Obviously, conflict can have this effect. But, fast decision makers know how to gain the advantages of conflict without extensive delays in their decision process. The key is conflict resolution.

Fast decision makers typically use a two step process, termed "consensus with qualification" by one executive, to resolve deadlocks among individuals. This process works as follows. First, executives talk over an issue and attempt to gain consensus. If consensus occurs, the choice is made. However, if consensus is not forthcoming, the key manager and most relevant functional head make the choice, guided by the input from the rest of the group. As one executive told us, "Most of the time we reach consensus, but if not Randy makes the choice."

A description of decision making at Forefront (a fictitious name for an actual firm) serves as an illustration. Forefront was faced with a major challenge in its principal market from an important competitor. This firm had unexpectedly announced a new machine which appeared to challenge Forefront's leadership in its primary area of business. Forefront executives confronted the problem, and substantial disagreement was apparent. Several executives wanted to shift R&D resources to counter this competitive move. The price was diverting significant engineering talent from a more innovative product currently in design. Others argued that a simple extension of an existing product was appropriate. Under this plan, Forefront would simply repackage an existing product with a few new features from its stable of modest technical improvements. A third set of executives perceived that the threat was not all that important and that Forefront should continue with current plans, making no response.

The team held a series of meetings over several weeks. Consensus was not in the cards. Given the stalemate, the CEO and his marketing VP simply made the choice. Not all agreed with their selection, but everyone had a voice in the process. As the CEO claimed, "The functional heads do the talking...I pull the trigger."

The approach to conflict used by fast decision makers, such as the executives at Forefront, contrasts markedly with that used by the slow decision makers. Sometimes slow decision makers wait for consensus. They forage for an option which satisfies everyone. However, since conflict is common in decision making, the search for consensus often drags on for months. For example, the decision makers at one firm debated the specifications of a new product for about a year. Finally, consensus came—after several executives who opposed one of the options left the firm.

Sometimes slow decision makers wait for deadlines, which then energize them to make a choice. For example, the annual meeting triggered a decision at one firm. The CEO had worked for almost a year on a proposal to develop a new market. Others in the group felt that such a project would stretch sales and engineering resources too much. The CEO was unwilling to do nothing and yet also unwilling to decide. So, he continually refined his proposal in the hopes of gaining others' agreement. What was the result? Each refinement improved the proposal, but also stiffened the opposition. This pattern might have dragged on indefinitely except for the annual meeting. Frustrated by repeated rejections and facing the impending deadline, the CEO came up with a new alternative and as he claimed, "shoved it down their throats."

Why is consensus with qualification rapid? One reason is that it takes a realistic view of conflict. Conflict is seen as natural, valuable, and almost always inevitable. Therefore, fast decision makers recognize that choices must be made even if there is disagreement. The other reason that consensus with qualification is rapid is its popularity. Managers like it. Most people want a voice in the decision-making process, but are willing to accept that their opinions may not prevail. Consensus with qualification gives people this voice, and goes one better by giving them added influence when the choice particularly affects their part of the organization.

In contrast, slow decision makers are stymied by conflict. They delay in the hopes that uncertainty will magically become certain. Or, they look for consensus. But unfortunately, consensus is often wishful thinking in most complex business situations. People are likely to have differing opinions, especially regarding big and important choices. Although consensus sometimes emerges, often it does not. Rather, as one executive described, "We found that operating by consensus essentially gave everyone veto power. There was no structure. Nothing got accomplished." Overall, many managers dislike a strictly consensual approach to choice and prefer simply to "get on with it."

## INTEGRATING DECISIONS AND TACTICS

The final key to fast decision making is the integration of the focal decision with other key choices and tactical plans. In effect, fast strategic decision makers fit any single decision into a web of interlocking choices. This decision integration does not imply any sort of elaborate planning. In fact, frequently there is no written plan. Rather, fast decision makers maintain a cognitive map which they can readily describe or sketch on a piece of paper. At most, fast decision makers stitch together a 5 to 10 page document describing the relationship among choices and tactics.

A good example of decision integration occurred at Triumph (a fictitious name for an actual firm). The decision began with the arrival of a new CEO. The firm was struggling in the wake of the highly mercurial, former CEO. The new CEO spent several weeks learning about people and products. He and other executives also began developing options for how to energize the firm. In the process of defining and refining these options, the executive group also decided on the specifications for a new product, scheduled three new product releases, reprioritized engineering assignments, and rebudgeted the firm for the year. All of this occurred in about 2 months.

These decisions contrast with a similar one executed by a slower team. These executives also faced deteriorating financial performance. However, their response was a technology forecasting project. This project was completed several months later. Firm executives then spent the next several months debating whether to change the firm strategy or to execute the existing approach more effectively. Key firm executives were seriously split on the issue. Finally, after several opponents left the firm and the financial situation had deteriorated to the point that the existing strategy could no longer be salvaged, the CEO chose to alter the strategy. Only then did the executives think about what the new strategy would be. Five more months passed before the new strategic direction was set. And, there were still tactical plans such as engineering assignments to be made.

The contrast with the Triumph case is striking. Triumph executives made a similar decision on strategic redirection—plus they chose a new product, scheduled 3 new product releases, reassigned engineering priorities and rebudgeted the firm—in less than 2 months, compared to the 18-month period of the second company.

Why does decision integration accelerate decision making? On the surface, it appears time-consuming to link together decisions and tactics. However, this surface view neglects the value of decision integration for building the confidence of decision makers. Anxiety is a major impediment to fast choice. Making choices, when information is poor and stakes are high, is paralyzing. The psychological literature indicates that a key to efficacy in such stressful situations is proactive and structuring behavior—that is, formulation of concrete action steps to structure one's unstable world.[6] Such "active coping" enhances feelings of competence and control which, in turn, boost the confidence to decide. Consistent with this view, managers who integrate decisions and tactics are actually engaging in active coping. Aided by enhanced feelings of competence and control, they can make choices more quickly and confidently in high stress and information poor situations.

Secondly, decision integration does more than simply give a psychological illusion of control. The process also provides better understanding of alternatives and potential conflicts with other decisions. By linking together decisions and tactics at the outset, managers can avoid many of the delays that occur when executing one action has unanticipated consequences for other actions.

In contrast, slow decision makers treat each decision as a separate event detached from other major choices and from tactics of implementation. In effect, they employ a linear view of decision making. Unfortunately, such an approach does nothing to diminish anxiety. Decisions remain in the abstract, unattached to other activities within the organization. Evidence from several firms confirms that anxiety looms large for slow decision makers. For example, one slow decision maker worried that "we don't know if we have the confidence to do it." A second executive lamented, "Maybe we saw too much mystery. Maybe we needed more gut." His conclusion was simple: "You don't know any more even though you wait." Overall, slow decision makers see decisions as very large, discrete, and anxiety-provoking events whereas fast decision makers see individual decisions as a smaller part of an overarching pattern of choices.

## MANAGERIAL IMPLICATIONS

Strategy making is changing. Strategies that may have been viable in the past are no longer feasible if they take too long to formulate. The field data echo this point. For example, the microcomputer study revealed that fast strategic decision makers led either high performing organizations or organizations that achieved performance turnarounds.[7] These fast decision makers also explicitly linked the speed of their strategic decision making to success. They claimed: "you have to keep up with the train," "you've got to catch the big opportunities," "simply do *something*," and so on.

In contrast, the slow strategic decision makers managed mediocre organizations, some of which have since failed. These decision makers usually recognized that speed was important, but they did not understand how to be fast. As a result, they missed opportunities and lost the learning that comes with making frequent choices. As one described, "The company wound up doing a random walk. Our products were too late and they were too expensive."

How do managers actually make fast, yet high-quality, strategic decisions? This article has identified five key tactics for accelerating decision making. They involve simple behaviors which decision makers in a variety of settings can use. To summarize:

- Before decisions arise, track real time information to develop a deep and intuitive grasp of the business. Focus on both operating parameters and critical environmental variables to hone your intuition.

- During the decision process, immediately begin to build multiple alternatives using your intuitive grasp of the business. Be certain to analyze the alternatives quickly and in comparison with one another. Possibly even begin execution of several before settling on a final choice.

- Ask everyone for advice, but depend on one or two counselors. Be selective in your choice of counselors. Look for savvy, trustworthy, and discreet colleagues.

- When it's time to decide, involve everyone. Try for consensus. But, if it doesn't emerge, don't delay. Make the choice yourself or better yet, with the others most affected by the decision. Delaying won't make you popular and won't make you fast.

- Ensure that you have integrated your choice with other decisions and tactical moves. You'll feel more confident and you will have avoided many of the headaches of mismatched decisions down the road.

# CONCLUSION

Previous scholarly research on decision making has ignored speed in favor of topics such as the breakdown of rationality and the difficulty of identifying goals. It has also emphasized the study of large bureaucracies in stable settings, rather than the high velocity environments which many decision makers actually face.

However, most managers have recognized that speed matters. A slow strategy is as ineffective as the wrong strategy. So, fast strategic decision making has emerged as a crucial competitive weapon. But, knowing how to be fast is difficult. The process involves accelerating information processing, building up the confidence to decide, and yet maintaining the cohesiveness of the decision-making group. Should managers learn how to be fast? One executive summarized the prevailing reality in many industries: "No advantage is long-term because our industry isn't static. The only competitive advantage is in moving quickly."

# REFERENCES

1.  J. Hayes, *The Complete Problem Solvers* (Philadelphia, PA: Franklin Press, 1981); H. Simon, "Making Management Decisions," *Academy of Management Executive* (1987); J. Payne, J. Bettman, and E. Johnson, "Adaptive Strategy Selection in Decision Making," *Journal of Experimental Psychology* (1988).
2.  R. Gal and R. Lazarus, "The Role of Activity in Anticipating Stressful Situations," *Journal of Human Stress* (1975); E. Langer, "Illusion of Control," *Journal of Personality and Social Psychology* (1975).
3.  P. C. Earley and E. A. Lind, "Procedural Justice and Participation in Task Selection: The Role of Control in Mediating Justice Judgments," *Journal of Personality and Social Psychology* (1987).
4.  Simon, op. cit.
5.  Payne et al., op. cit.
6.  Gal and Lazarus, op. cit.
7.  K. Eisenhardt, "Making Fast Strategic Decisions in High Velocity Environments," *Academy of Management Journal*, 28/3 (1989).

# 16

# Leadership, Power, and Influence

## THE LEADERSHIP CHALLENGE—A CALL FOR THE TRANSFORMATIONAL LEADER

*Noel M. Tichy*
*David O. Ulrich*

Some optimists are heralding in the age of higher productivity, a transition to a service economy, and a brighter competitive picture for U.S. corporations in world markets. We certainly would like to believe that the future will be brighter, but our temperament is more cautious. We feel that the years it took for most U.S. companies to get "fat and flabby" are not going to be reversed by a crash diet for one or two years. Whether we continue to gradually decline as a world competitive economy will largely be determined by the quality of leadership in the top echelons of our business and government organizations. Thus, it is our belief that now is the time for organizations to change their corporate lifestyles.

To revitalize organizations such as General Motors, American Telephone and Telegraph, General Electric, Honeywell, Ford, Burroughs, Chase Manhattan Bank, Citibank, U.S. Steel, Union Carbide, Texas Instruments, and Control Data—just to mention a few companies currently undergoing major transformations—a new brand of leadership is necessary. Instead of managers who continue to move organizations along historical tracks, the new leaders must transform the organizations and head them down new tracks. What is required of this kind of leader is an ability to help the organization develop a vision of what it can be, to mobilize the organization to accept and work toward achieving the new vision, and to institutionalize the changes that must last over time. Unless the creation of this breed of leaders becomes a national agenda, we are not very optimistic about the revitalization of the U.S. economy.

We call these new leaders transformational leaders, for they must create something new out of something old: out of an old vision, they must develop and communicate a new vision and get others not only to see the vision but also to commit themselves to it. Where transactional managers make only minor adjustments in the organization's mission, structure, and human resource management, transformational leaders not only make major changes in these areas but they also evoke fundamental changes in the basic political and cultural systems of the organization. The revamping of the political and cultural systems is what most distinguishes the transformational leader from the transactional one.

## LEE IACOCCA: A TRANSFORMATIONAL LEADER

One of the most dramatic examples of transformational leadership and organizational revitalization in the early 1980s has been the leadership of Lee Iacocca, the chairman of Chrysler Corporation. He provided the leadership to transform a company from the brink of bankruptcy to profitability. He created a vision of success and mobilized large factions of key employees toward enacting that vision while simultaneously downsizing the workforce by 60,000 employees. As a result of Iacocca's leadership, by 1984 Chrysler had earned record profits, had attained high levels of employee morale, and had helped employees generate a sense of meaning in their work.

Until Lee Iacocca took over at Chrysler, the basic internal political structure had been unchanged for decades. It was clear who reaped what benefits from the organization, how the pie was to be divided, and who could exercise what power. Nonetheless, Mr. Iacocca knew that he needed to alter these political traditions, starting with a new definition of Chrysler's link to external stakeholders. Therefore, the government was given a great deal of control over Chrysler in return for the guaranteed loan that staved off bankruptcy. Modification of the political system required other adjustments, including the "trimming of fat" in the management ranks, limiting financial rewards for all employees, and receiving major concessions for the UAW. An indicator of a significant political shift was the inclusion of Douglas Frazer on the Chrysler Board of Directors as part of UAW concessions.

Equally dramatic was the change in the organization's cultural system. First, the company had to recognize its unique status as a recipient of a federal bailout. This bailout came with a stigma, thus Mr. Iacocca's job was to change the company's cultural values from a loser's to a winner's feeling. Still, he realized that employees were not going to be winners unless they could, in cultural norms, be more efficient and innovative than their competitors. The molding and shaping of the new culture was clearly and visibly led by Mr. Iacocca, who not only used internal communication as a vehicle to signal change but also used his own personal appearance in Chrysler ads to reinforce these changes. Quickly, the internal culture was transformed to that of a lean and hungry team looking for victory. Whether Chrysler will be able to sustain this organizational phenomenon over time remains to be seen. If it does, it will provide a solid corporate example of what Burns referred to as a transforming leader.[1]

Lee Iacocca's high visibility and notoriety may be the *important* missing elements in management today: there seems to be a paucity of transformational leader role models at all levels of the organization.

# ORGANIZATIONAL DYNAMICS OF CHANGE

## Assumption One: Trigger Events
## Indicate Change Is Needed

Organizations do not change unless there is a trigger which indicates change is needed. This trigger can be as extreme as the Chrysler impending bankruptcy or as moderate as an abstract future-oriented fear that an organization may lose its competitiveness. For example, General Electric's trigger for change is a view that by 1990 the company will not be world competitive unless major changes occur in productivity, innovation, and marketing. Thus, Chairman Jack Welch sees his role as that of transforming GE even though it does not face imminent doom. Nonetheless, the trick for him is to *activate* the trigger; otherwise, complacency may prevail. Similarly, for AT&T, technological, competitive, and political forces have led it to undertake its massive transformation. For General Motors, economic factors of world competition, shifting consumer preferences, and technological change have driven it to change.

In a decade of increased information, international competition, and technological advances, triggers for change have become commonplace and very pressing. However, not all potential trigger events lead to organizational responses, and not all triggers lead to change. Nonetheless, the trigger must create a felt need in organizational leaders. Without this *felt* need, the "boiled frog phenomenon" is likely to occur.

*The Boiled Frog.* This phenomenon is based on a classic experiment in biology. A frog which is placed in a pan of cold water but which still has the freedom to jump out can be boiled if the temperature change is gradual, for it is not aware of the barely detectable changing heat threshold. In contrast, a frog dropped in a pot of boiling water will immediately jump out: it has a felt need to survive. In a similar vein, many organizations that are insensitive to gradually changing organizational thresholds are likely to become "boiled frogs"; they act in ignorant bliss of environmental triggers and eventually are doomed to failure. This failure, in part, is a result of the organization having no felt need to change.

## Assumption Two: A Change
## Unleashes Mixed Feelings

A felt need for change unleashes a mix of forces, both a positive impetus for change as well as a strong negative individual and organizational resistance. These forces of resistance are generated in each of three interrelated systems—technical, political, cultural—which must be managed in the process of organizational transitions (see Table 1).[2] Individual and organizational resistance to change in these three systems must be overcome if an organization is to be revitalized.[3] Managing technical systems refers to managing the coordination of technology, capital, information, and people in order to produce products or services desired and used in the external marketplace, Managing political systems refers to managing the allocation of organizational rewards such as money, status, power, and career opportunities and to exercise power so employees and departments perceive equity and justice. Managing cultural systems refers to managing the set of shared values and norms which guides the behavior of members of the organization.

TABLE 1  A List of Technical, Political, and Cultural System Resistances

**Technical System Resistances include:**

Habit and inertia. Habit and inertia cause task-related resistance to change. Individuals who have always done things one way may not be politically or culturally resistant to change, but may have trouble, for technical reasons, changing behavior patterns. Example: some office workers may have difficulty shifting from electric typewriters to word processors.

Fear of the unknown or loss of organizational predictability. Not knowing or having difficulty predicting the future creates anxiety and hence resistance in many individuals. Example: the introduction of automated office equipment has often been accompanied by such resistances.

Sunk costs. Organizations, even when realizing that there are potential payoffs from a change, are often unable to enact a change because of the sunk costs of the organization's resources in the old way of doing things.

**Political System Resistances include:**

Powerful coalitions. A common threat is found in the conflict between the old guard and the new guard. One interpretation of the exit of Archie McGill, former president of the newly formed AT&T American Bell, is that the backlash of the old-guard coalition exacted its price on the leader of the new-guard coalition.

Resource limitations. In the days when the economic pie was steadily expanding and resources were much less limited, change was easier to enact as every part could gain—such was the nature of labor management agreements in the auto industry for decades. Now that the pie is shrinking decisions need to be made as to who shares a smaller set of resources. These zero-sum decisions are much more politically difficult. As more and more U.S. companies deal with productivity, downsizing, and divesture, political resistance will be triggered.

Indictment quality of change. Perhaps the most significant resistance to change comes from leaders having to indict their own past decisions and behaviors to bring out a change. Example: Roger Smith, chairman and CEO of GM, must implicitly indict his own past behavior as a member of senior management when he suggests changes in GM's operations. Psychologically, it is very difficult for people to change when they were party to creating the problems they are trying to change. It is much easier for a leader from the outside, such as Lee Iacocca, who does not have to indict himself every time he says something is wrong with the organization.

**Cultural System Resistances include:**

Selective perception (cultural filters). An organization's culture may highlight certain elements of the organization, making it difficult for members to conceive of other ways of doing things. An organization's culture channels that which people perceive as possible; thus, innovation may come from outsiders or deviants who are not as channeled in their perceptions.

Security based on the past. Transition requires people to give up the old ways of doing things. There is security in the past, and one of the problems is getting people to overcome the tendency to want to return to the "good old days." Example: today, there are still significant members of the white-collar workforce at GM who are waiting for the "good old days" to return.

Lack of climate for change. Organizations often vary in their conduciveness to change. Cultures that require a great deal of conformity often lack much receptivity to change. Example: GM with its years of internally developed managers must overcome a limited climate for change.

## FIGURE 1 Transformational Leadership

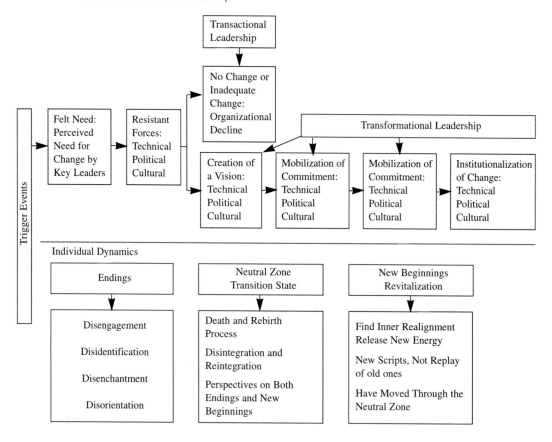

When a needed change is perceived by the organizational leaders, the dominant group in the organization must experience a dissatisfaction with the status quo. For example, in the late 1970s John DeButts, chairman and chief executive officer of AT&T, was not satisfied with the long-term viability of AT&T as a regulated telephone monopoly in the age of computers and satellite communication systems. Likewise, when Roger Smith became CEO at General Motors in the early 1980s, he could hardly be satisfied with presiding over GM's first financial loss since the depression. In these two cases, the felt need provided the impetus for transition; yet, such impetus is not uniformly positive.

The technical, political, and cultural resistances are most evident during early stages of an organizational transformation. At GM the early 1980s were marked by tremendous uncertainty concerning many technical issues such as marketing strategy, production strategy, organization design, factory automation, and development of international management. Politically, many powerful coalitions were threatened. The UAW was forced to make wage concessions and accept staffing reductions. The white-collar workers saw their benefits being cut and witnessed major layoffs within the managerial ranks. Culturally, the once dominant managerial style no longer fit the environmental pressures for change: the "GM way" was no longer the right way.

One must be wary of these resistances to change as they can lead to organizational stagnation rather than revitalization. In fact, some managers at GM in late 1983 were waiting for "the good old days" to return. Such resistance exemplifies a dysfunctional reaction to the felt need. As indicated in Figure 1, a key to whether resistant forces will lead to little or inadequate change and hence organizational decline or revitalization lies in an organization's leadership. Defensive, transactional leadership will not rechannel the resistant forces. A case in point is International Harvester which appears to have had a defensive transactional leadership. Thus, in the early 1980s, International Harvester lacked a new vision which would inspire employees to engage in new behaviors. In contrast, Lee Iacocca has been a transformational leader at Chrysler by creating a vision, mobilizing employees, and working toward the institutionalization of Chrysler's transition.

## Assumption Three: Quick-Fix Leadership Leads to Decline

Overcoming resistance to change requires transformational leadership, not defensive, transactional managers who are in search of the one minute quick fix. The transformational leader needs to avoid the trap of simple, quick-fix solutions to major organizational problems. Today, many versions of this quick-fix mentality abound: the book, *One Minute Manager*, has become a best seller in companies in need of basic transformation.[4] Likewise, *In Search of Excellence* has become a cookbook for change.[5] In fact, a number of CEOs have taken the eight characteristics of the "excellent" companies and are trying to blindly impose them on their organizations without first examining their appropriateness. For example, many faltering organizations try to copy such company practices at Hewlett Packard's (HP) statement of company values. Because they read that HP has a clearly articulated statement of company values—the HP equivalent of the ten commandments—they want to create their list of ten commandments. The scenario which has been carried out in many major U.S. firms in the past year goes something like this: the CEO wants to develop the company value statement, so he organizes an off-site meeting in order to spend a couple of days developing the company XYZ corporate value statement. The session is usually quite enlightening—managers become quite thoughtful, and soul-searching takes place. At the end of the session, the group is able to list the XYZ company's "ten commandments." The CEO is delighted that they are now well on the way to a major cultural change. He brings the ten commandments back to the corporation and calls in the staff to begin the communication program so that all company employees can learn the new cultural values. This about ends the transformational process.

The problem with the ten-commandments quick fix is that the CEOs tend to overlook the lesson Moses learned several thousand years ago—namely, getting the ten commandments written down and communicated is the easy part; getting them implemented is the challenge. How many thousands of years has it been since Moses received the ten commandments, and yet today there still seems to be an implementation challenge. Transformational leadership is different from defensive, transactional leadership. Lee Iacocca did not have to read about what others did to find a recipe for his company's success.

## Assumption Four: Revitalization Requires Transformational Leadership

There are three identifiable programs of activity associated with transformational leadership.

*1. Creation of a Vision.* The transformational leader must provide the organization with a vision of a desired future state. While this task may be shared with other key members of the organization, the vision remains the core responsibility of the transformational leader. The leader needs to integrate analytic, creative, intuitive, and deductive thinking. Each leader must create a vision which gives direction to the organization while being congruent with the leader's and the organization's philosophy and style.

For example, in the early 1980s at GM, after several years of committee work and staff analysis, a vision of the future was drafted which included a mission statement and eight objectives for the company. This statement was the first articulation of a strategic vision for General Motors since Alfred Sloan's leadership. This new vision was developed consistently with the leadership philosophy and style of Roger Smith. Many people were involved in carefully assessing opportunities and constraints for General Motors. Meticulous staff work culminated in committee discussions to evoke agreement and commitment to the mission statement. Through this process a vision was created which paved the way for the next phases of the transformation at GM.

At Chrysler, Lee Iacocca developed a vision without committee work or heavy staff involvement. Instead, he relied more on his intuitive and directive leadership, philosophy, and style. Both GM and Chrysler ended up with a new vision because of transformational leaders proactively shaping a new organization mission and vision. The long-term challenge to organizational revitalization is not "how" the visions are created but the extent to which the visions correctly respond to environmental pressures and transitions within the organization.

*2. Mobilization of Commitment.* Here, the organization, or at least a critical mass of it, accepts the new mission and vision and makes it happen. At General Motors, Roger Smith took his top 900 executives on a five-day retreat to share and discuss the vision. The event lasted five days not because it takes that long to share a one-paragraph mission statement and eight objectives, but because the process of evolving commitment and mobilizing support requires a great deal of dialogue and exchange. It should be noted that mobilization of commitment must go well beyond five-day retreats; nevertheless, it is in this phase that transformational leaders get deeper understanding of their *followers*. Maccoby acknowledges that leaders who guide organizations through revitalization are distinct from previous leaders and gamesmen who spearheaded managers to be winners in the growth days of the 1960s and early 1970s. Today, Maccoby argues:

> The positive traits of the gamesman, enthusiasm, risk taking, meritocratic fairness, fit America
> in a period of unlimited economic growth, hunger for novelty, and an unquestioned career ethic.
> The negative traits for manipulation, seduction, and the perpetual adolescent need for adventure
> were always problems, causing distrust and unnecessary crises. The gamesman's daring, the
> willingness to innovate and take risks are still needed. Companies that rely on conservative
> company men in finance to run technically based organizations (for example, auto and steel)
> lose the competitive edge. But unless their negative traits are transformed or controlled, even
> gifted gamesmen become liabilities as leaders in a new economic reality. A period of limited
> resources and cutbacks, when the team can no longer be controlled by the promise of more, and
> one person's gains may be another's loss, leadership with values of caring and integrity and a
> vision of self-development must create the trust that no one will be penalized for cooperation
> and that sacrifice as well as rewards are equitable.[6]

After transformational leaders create a vision and mobilize commitment, they must determine how to institutionalize the new mission and vision.

*3. Institutionalization of Change.* Organizations will not be revitalized unless new patterns of behavior within the organization are adopted. Transformational leaders need to transmit their vision into reality, their mission into action, their philosophy into practice. New realities, action, and practices must be shared throughout the organization. Alterations in communication, decision making, and problem-solving systems are tools through which transitions are shared so that visions become a reality. At a deeper level, institutionalization of change requires shaping and reinforcement of a new culture that fits with the revitalized organization. The human resource systems of selection, development, appraisal, and reward are major levers for institutionalizing change.

# INDIVIDUAL DYNAMICS OF CHANGE

The previous section outlined requisite processes for organizational revitalization. Although organizational steps are necessary, they are not sufficient in creating an implementing change. In managing transitions, a more problematic set of forces which focuses on individual psychodynamics of change must be understood and managed. Major transitions unleash powerful conflicting forces in people. The change invokes simultaneous positive and negative personal feelings of fear and hope, anxiety and relief, pressure and stimulation, leaving the old and accepting a new direction, loss of meaning and new meaning, threat to self-esteem and new sense of value. The challenge for transformational leaders is to recognize these mixed emotions, act to help people move from negative to positive emotions, and mobilize and focus energy that is necessary for individual renewal and organizational revitalization.

Figure 1 provides a set of concepts for understanding the individual dynamics of transitions. The concepts, drawn from the work by Bridges, propose a three-phase process of individual change: first come endings, followed by neutral zones, and then new beginnings.[7] During each of these phases, an identifiable set of psychological tasks can be identified which individuals need to successfully complete in order to accept change.

# THE THREE-PHASE PROCESS

*Endings.* All individual transitions start with endings. Endings must be accepted and understood before transitions can begin. Employees who refuse to accept the fact that traditional behaviors have ended will be unable to adopt new behaviors. The first task is to disengage, which often accompanies a physical transaction. For example, when transferring from one job to another, individuals must learn to accept the new physical setting and disengage from the old position: when transferred employees continually return to visit former colleagues, this is a sign that they have inadequately disengaged. The second task is to disidentify. Individual self-identity is often tied to a job position in such a way that when a plant manager is transferred to corporate staff to work in the marketing department, he or she must disidentify with the plant and its people and with the self-esteem felt as a plant manager. At a deeper personal level, individual transactions require disenchantment. Disenchantment entails recognizing that the enchantment or positive feelings associated with past situations will not be possible to replicate in the future. Chrysler, GM, AT&T, or U.S. Steel employees who remember the "good old days" need to become disenchanted with those feelings: the present reality is different and self-worth cannot be recaptured by longing for or thinking about the past. A new enchantment centered on new circumstances needs to be built. Finally, individuals need to experience and work through disorientation which reflects the loss of familiar trappings. As mature organizations become revitalized, individuals must disengage, disidentify, disenchant, and disorient with past practices and discover in new organizations a new sense of worth or value.

To help individuals cope with endings, transformational leaders need to replace past glories with future opportunities. However, leaders must also acknowledge individual resistances and senses of loss in a transitional period while encouraging employees to face and accept failures as learning opportunities. Holding on to past accomplishments and memories without coming to grips with failure and the need to change may be why companies such as W. T. Grant, International Harvester, and Braniff were unsuccessful at revitalization. There is a sense of dying in all endings, and it does not help to treat transactions as if the past can be buried without effort. Yet, one should see the past as providing new directions.

*Neutral Zone.*   The key to individuals being able to fully change may be in the second phase which Bridges terms the neutral zone.[8]  This phase can be interpreted as a seemingly unproductive "time out" when individuals feel disconnected from people and things of the past and emotionally unconnected with the present.  In reality, this phase is a time of reorientation where individuals complete endings and begin new patterns of behavior.  Often Western culture, especially in the U.S., avoids this experience and treats the neutral zone like a busy street, to be crossed as fast as possible and certainly not a place to contemplate and experience.  However, running across the neutral zone too hurriedly does not allow the ending to occur nor the new beginning to properly start.  A death and rebirth process is necessary so that organizational members can work through the disintegration and reintegration.  To pass through the neutral zone requires taking the time and thought to gain perspective on both the ending—what went wrong, why it needs to be changed, and what must be overcome in both attitude and behavioral change—and the new beginning—what the new priorities are, why they are needed, and what new attitudes and behaviors will be required.  It is in this phase that the most skillful transformational leadership is called upon.

A timid, bureaucratic leader who often reels in the good old days will not provide the needed support to help individuals cross through the neutral zone.  On the other hand, the militaristic dictatorial leader who tries to force a "new beginning" and does not allow people to work through their own feelings and emotions may also fail to bring about change.  The purported backlash toward the "brash" Archie McGill at American Bell in June 1983 may have been an example of trying to force people through the neutral zone in order to get to a new beginning.  Archie McGill was known to rant and rave about the stodgy, old fashioned, and noninnovative "bell-shaped men" at AT&T.  While he was trying to help and lead individuals to become innovative and marketing orientated, he may not have allowed them to accept the endings inherent in the transition.  Although his enthusiasm may have been well placed, he may have lacked the sensitivity to individual endings and neutral phases of transactions.

Failure to lead individuals through the neutral zone may result in aborted new beginnings.  In 1983, International Harvester appeared to be stuck in the neutral zone.  In order for International Harvester to make a new beginning, it must enable people to find a new identification with the future organization while accepting the end of the old organization.  Such a transformation has successfully occurred at Chrysler Corporation where morale and esprit de corps grew with the new vision implanted by Lee Iacocca.  In the end, organizational revitalization can only occur if individuals accept past failures and engage in new behaviors and attitudes.

*New Beginnings.*   After individuals accept endings by working through neutral zones, they are able to work with new enthusiasm and commitment.  New beginnings are characterized by employees learning from the past rather than reveling in it, looking for new scripts rather than acting out old ones, and being positive and excited about current and future work opportunities rather than dwelling on past successes or failures.  When Mr. Iacocca implemented his vision at Chrysler, many long-term employees discovered new beginnings.  They saw the new Chrysler as an opportunity to succeed, and they worked with a renewed vigor.

# WHAT QUALITIES DO
# TRANSFORMATIONAL LEADERS POSSESS?

So what does it take to transform an organization's technical, political, and cultural systems? The transformational leader must possess a deep understanding, whether it be intuitive or learned, of organizations and their place both in society at large and in the lives of individuals. The ability to build a new institution requires the kind of political dialogue our founding fathers had when Jefferson, Hamilton, Adams, and others debated issues of justice, equity, separation of powers, checks and balances, and freedom. This language may sound foreign to corporate settings but when major organization revitalization is being undertaken, all of these concepts merit some level of examination. At Chrysler, issues of equity, justice, power, and freedom underlay many of Mr. Iacocca's decisions. Thus, as a start, transformational leaders need to understand concepts of equity, power, freedom, and the dynamics of decision making. In addition to modifying systems, transformational leaders must understand and realign cultural systems.

In addition to managing political and cultural systems, transformational leaders must make difficult decisions quickly. Leaders need to know when to push and when to back off. Finally, transformational leaders are often seen as creators of their own luck. These leaders seize opportunities and know when to act so that casual observers may perceive luck as a plausible explanation for their success; whereas, in reality it is a transformational leader who knows when to jump and when not to jump. Again, Mr. Iacocca can be viewed either as a very lucky person or as the possessor of a great ability to judge when to act and when not to act.

# THE SIGNIFICANCE OF CORPORATE CULTURES

Much has been written about organizational cultures in recent years.[9] We suggest that every organization has a culture, or a patterned set of activities that reflects the organization's underlying values. Cultures don't occur randomly. They occur because leaders spend time on and reward some behaviors and practices more than others. These practices become the foundation of the organization's culture. At HP, for example, Bill Hewlett and Dave Packard spent time wandering around, informally meeting with and talking to employees. Such leadership behavior set the HP cultural tone of caring about and listening to people. Similarly, Tom Watson, Sr., at IBM spent a great deal of time with customers. His practice led to a company culture of commitment to customers. Indeed, corporate cultures exist. Leaders can shape cultures by carefully monitoring where and how they spend their time and by encouraging and rewarding employees to behave in certain ways.

Culture plays two central roles in organizations. First, it provides organizational members with a way of understanding and making sense of events and symbols. Thus, when employees are confronted with certain complex problems, they "know" how to approach them the "right" way. Like the Eskimos, who have a vocabulary that differentiates the five types of snow, organizations create vocabularies to describe how things are done in the organization. At IBM, it is very clear to all insiders how to form a task force and to solve problems since task forces and problem solving are a way of life in IBM's culture.

Second, culture provides meaning. It embodies a set of values which helps justify why certain behaviors are encouraged at the exclusion of other behaviors. Companies with strong cultures have been able to commit people to the organization and have them identify very personally and closely with the organization's success. Superficially, this is seen in the "hoopla" activities associated with an IBM sales meeting, a Tupperware party, or an Amway distributor meeting. Outsiders often ridicule such activities, yet they are part of the process by which some successful companies manage cultural meaning. On one level, corporate culture is analogous to rituals carried out in religious groups. The key point in assessing culture is to realize that in order to transform an organization the culture that provides meaning must be assessed and revamped. The transformational leader needs to articulate new values and norms and then to use multiple change levers ranging from role modeling, symbolic acts, creation of rituals, and revamping of human resource systems and management processes to support new cultural messages.

## CONCLUSION

Based on the premise that the pressures for basic organizational change will intensify and not diminish, we strongly believe that transformational leadership, not transactional management, is required for revitalizing our organizations. Ultimately, it is up to our leaders to choose the right kind of leadership and corporate lifestyle.

## REFERENCES

1. See J. M. Burns, *Leadership* (New York: Harper & Row, 1978).
2. See N. M. Tichy, *Managing Strategic Change: Technical, Political and Cultural Dynamics* (New York: John Wiley & Sons, 1983).
3. Ibid.
4. See K. H. Blanchard and S. Johnson, *The One Minute Manager* (New York: Berkeley Books, 1982).
5. See T. J. Peters and R. J. Waterman, Jr., *In Search of Excellence* (New York: Harper & Row, 1982).
6. See M. Maccoby, *The Leader* (New York: Ballentine Books, 1981).
7. See W. Bridges, *Making Sense of Life's Transitions* (New York: Addison-Wesley, 1980).
8. Ibid.
9. See T. E. Deal and A. A. Kennedy, *Corporate Cultures* (Reading, MA: Addison-Wesley, 1982); "Corporate Culture: The Hard-to-Change Values That Spell Success or Failure," *Business Week*, 27 October 1980, pp. 148–160; W. Ulrich, "HRM and Culture: History, Rituals, and Myths," *Human Resource Management* (23/2) Summer 1984.

# WHO GETS POWER—AND HOW THEY HOLD ON TO IT: A STRATEGIC CONTINGENCY MODEL OF POWER

*Gerald R. Salancik*
*Jeffrey Pfeffer*

Power is held by many people to be a dirty word or, as Warren Bennis has said, "It is the organization's last dirty secret."

This article will argue that traditional "political" power, far from being a dirty business, is, in its most naked form, one of the few mechanisms available for aligning an organization with its own reality. However, institutionalized forms of power—what we prefer to call the cleaner forms of power: authority, legitimization, centralized control, regulations, and the more modern "management information systems"—tend to buffer the organization from reality and obscure the demands of its environment. Most great states and institutions declined, not because they played politics, but because they failed to accommodate to the political realities they faced. Political processes, rather than being mechanisms for unfair and unjust allocations and appointments, tend toward the realistic resolution of conflicts among interests. And power, while it eludes definition, is easy enough to recognize by its consequences—the ability of those who possess power to bring about the outcomes they desire.

The model of power we advance is an elaboration of what has been called strategic-contingency theory, a view that sees power as something that accrues to organizational subunits (individuals, departments) that cope with critical organizational problems. Power is used by subunits, indeed, used by all who have it, to enhance their own survival through control of scarce critical resources, through the placement of allies in key positions, and through the definition of organizational problems and policies. Because of the processes by which power develops and is used, organizations become both more aligned and more misaligned with their environments. This contradiction is the most interesting aspect of organizational power, and one that makes administration one of the most precarious of occupations.

## WHAT IS ORGANIZATIONAL POWER?

You can walk into most organizations and ask without fear of being misunderstood, "Which are the powerful groups or people in this organization?" Although many organizational informants may be *unwilling* to tell you, it is unlikely they will be *unable* to tell you. Most people do not require explicit definitions to know what power is.

Power is simply the ability to get things done the way one wants them to be done. For a manager who wants an increased budget to launch a project that he thinks is important, his power is measured by his ability to get that budget. For an executive vice-president who wants to be chairman, his power is evidenced by his advancement toward his goal.

People in organizations not only know what you are talking about when you ask who is influential but they are likely to agree with one another to an amazing extent. Recently, we had a chance to observe this in a regional office of an insurance company. The office had 21 department managers; we asked ten of these managers to rank all 21 according to the influence each one had in the organization. Despite the fact that ranking 21 things is a difficult task, the managers sat down and began arranging the names of their colleagues and themselves in a column. Only one person bothered to ask, "What do you mean by influence?" When told "power," he responded, "Oh," and went on. We compared the rankings of all ten managers and found virtually no disagreement among them in the managers ranked among the top five or the bottom five. Differences in the rankings came from department heads claiming more influence for themselves than their colleagues attributed to them.

Such agreement on those who have influence, and those who do not, was not unique to this insurance company. So far we have studied over 20 very different organizations—universities, research firms, factories, banks, retailers, to name a few. In each one we found individuals able to rate themselves and their peers on a scale of influence or power. We have done this both for specific decisions and for general impact on organizational policies. Their agreement was unusually high, which suggests that distributions of influence exist well enough in everyone's mind to be referred to with ease—and we assume with accuracy.

## WHERE DOES ORGANIZATIONAL POWER COME FROM?

Earlier we stated that power helps organizations become aligned with their realities. This hopeful prospect follows from what we have dubbed the strategic-contingencies theory of organizational power. Briefly, those subunits most able to cope with the organization's critical problems and uncertainties acquire power. In its simplest form, the strategic-contingencies theory implies that when an organization faces a number of lawsuits that threaten its existence, the legal department will gain power and influence over organizational decisions. Somehow other organizational interest groups will recognize its critical importance and confer upon it a status and power never before enjoyed. This influence may extend beyond handling legal matters and into decisions about product design, advertising production, and so on. Such extensions undoubtedly would be accompanied by appropriate, or acceptable, verbal justifications. In time, the head of the legal department may become the head of the corporation, just as in times past the vice-president for marketing had become the president when market shares were a worrisome problem and, before him, the chief engineer, who had made the production line run as smooth as silk.

Stated in this way, the strategic-contingencies theory of power paints an appealing picture of power. To the extent that power is determined by the critical uncertainties and problems facing the organization and, in turn, influences decisions in the organization, the organization is aligned with the realities it faces. In short, power facilitates the organization's adaptation to its environment—or its problems.

We can cite many illustrations of how influence derives from a subunit's ability to deal with critical contingencies. Michel Crozier described a French cigarette factory in which the maintenance engineers had a considerable say in the plantwide operation. After some probing he discovered that the group possessed the solution to one of the major problems faced by the company, that of troubleshooting the elaborate, expensive, and irascible automated machines that kept breaking down and dumbfounding everyone else. It was the one problem that the plant manager could in no way control.

The production workers, while troublesome from time to time, created no insurmountable problems; the manager could reasonably predict their absenteeism or replace them when necessary. Production scheduling was something he could deal with since, by watching inventories and sales, the demand for cigarettes was known long in advance. Changes in demand could be accommodated by slowing down or speeding up the line. Supplies of tobacco and paper were also easily dealt with through stockpiles and advance orders.

The one thing that management could neither control nor accommodate to, however, was the seemingly happenstance breakdowns. And the foremen couldn't instruct the workers what to do when emergencies developed since the maintenance department kept its records of problems and solutions locked up in a cabinet or in its members' heads. The breakdowns were, in truth, a critical source of uncertainty for the organization, and the maintenance engineers were the only ones who could cope with the problem.

The engineers' strategic role in coping with breakdowns afforded them a considerable say on plant decisions. Schedules and production quotas were set in consultation with them. And the plant manager, while formally their boss, accepted their decisions about personnel in their operation. His submission was to his credit, for without their cooperation he would have had an even more difficult time in running the plant.

## Ignoring Critical Consequences

In this cigarette factory, sharing influence with the maintenance workers reflected the plant manager's awareness of the critical contingencies. However, when organizational members are not aware of the critical contingencies they face, and do not share influence accordingly, the failure to do so can create havoc. In one case, an insurance company's regional office was having problems with the performance of one of its departments, the coding department. From the outside, the department looked like a disaster area. The clerks who worked in it were somewhat dissatisfied; their supervisor paid little attention to them, and they resented the hard work. Several other departments were critical of this manager, claiming that she was inconsistent in meeting deadlines. The person most critical was the claims manager. He resented having to wait for work that was handled by her department, claiming that it held up his claims adjusters. Having heard the rumors about dissatisfaction among her subordinates, he attributed the situation to poor supervision. He was second in command in the office and therefore took up the issue with her immediate boss, the head of administrative services. They consulted with the personnel manager and the three of them concluded that the manager needed leadership training to improve her relations with her subordinates. The coding manager objected, saying it was a waste of time, but agreed to give more priority to the claims department's work. Within a week after the training, the results showed that her workers were happier but that the performance of her department had decreased, save for the people serving the claims department.

About this time, we began, quite independently, a study of influence in this organization. We asked the administrative services director to draw up flow charts of how the work of one department moved on to the next department. In the course of the interview, we noticed that the coding department began or interceded in the work flow of most of the other departments and casually mentioned to him. "The coding manager must be very influential." He said "No, not really. Why would you think so?" Before we could reply he recounted the story of her leadership training and the fact that things were worse. We then told him that it seemed obvious that the coding department would be influential from the fact that all the other departments depended on it. It was also clear why productivity had fallen. The coding manager took the training seriously and began spending more time raising her workers' spirits than she did worrying about the problems of all the departments that depended on her. Giving priority to the claims area only exaggerated the problem, for their work was getting done at the expense of the work of the other departments. Eventually the company hired a few more clerks to relieve the pressure in the coding department and performance returned to a more satisfactory level.

Originally we got involved with this insurance company to examine how the influence of each manager evolved from his or her department's handling of critical organizational contingencies. We reasoned that one of the most important contingencies faced by all profit-making organizations was that of generating income. Thus we expected managers would be influential to the extent to which they contributed to this function. Such was the case. The underwriting managers, who wrote the policies that committed the premiums, were the most influential; the claims managers who kept a lid on the funds flowing out, were a close second. Least influential were the managers of functions unrelated to revenue, such as mailroom and payroll managers. And contrary to what the administrative services manager believed, the third most powerful department head (out of 21) was the woman in charge of the coding function, which consisted of rating, recording, and keeping track of the codes of all policy applications and contracts. Her peers attributed more influence to her than could have been inferred from her place on the organization chart. And it was not surprising, since they all depended on her department. The coding department's records, their accuracy and the speed with which they could be retrieved, affected virtually every other operating department in the insurance office. The underwriters depended on them in getting the contracts straight; the typing department depended on them in preparing the formal contract document; the claims department depended on them in adjusting claims; and accounting depended on them for billing. Unfortunately, the "bosses" were not aware of these dependencies, for unlike the cigarette factory, there were no massive breakdowns that made them obvious, while the coding manager, who was a hardworking but quiet person, did little to announce her importance.

The cases of this plant and office illustrate nicely a basic point about the source of power in organizations. The basis for power in an organization derives from the ability of a person or subunit to take or not take actions that are desired by others. The coding manager was seen as influential by those who depended on her department, but not by the people at the top. The engineers were influential because of their role in keeping the plant operating. The two cases differ in these respects: The coding supervisor's source of power was not as widely recognized as that of the maintenance engineers, and she did not use her source of power to influence decisions; the maintenance engineers did. Whether power is used to influence anything is a separate issue. We should not confuse this issue with the fact that power derives from a social situation in which one person has a capacity to do something and another person does not, but wants it done.

## POWER SHARING IN ORGANIZATIONS

Power is shared in organizations; and it is shared out of necessity more than out of concern for principles of organizational development or participatory democracy. Power is shared because no one person controls all the desired activities in the organization. While the factory owner may hire people to operate his noisy machines, once hired they have some control over the use of the machinery. And thus they have power over him in the same way he has power over them. Who has more power over whom is a mooter point than that of recognizing the inherent nature of organizing as a sharing of power.

Let's expand on the concept that power derives from the activities desired in an organization. A major way of managing influence in organizations is through the designation of activities. In a bank we studied, we saw this principle in action. This bank was planning to install a computer system for routine credit evaluation. The bank, rather progressive-minded, was concerned that the change would have adverse effects on employees and therefore surveyed their attitudes.

The principal opposition to the new system came, interestingly, not from the employees who performed the routine credit checks, some of whom would be relocated because of the change, but from the manager of the credit department. His reason was quite simple. The manager's primary function was to give official approval to the applications, catch any employee mistakes before giving approval, and arbitrate any difficulties the clerks had in deciding what to do. As a consequence of his role, others in the organization, including his superiors, subordinates, and colleagues, attributed considerable importance to him. He, in turn, for example, could point to the low proportion of credit approvals, compared with other financial institutions, that resulted in bad debts. Now, to his mind, a wretched machine threatened to transfer his role to a computer programmer, a man who knew nothing of finance and who, in addition, had ten years less seniority. The credit manager eventually quit for a position at a smaller firm with lower pay, but one in which he would have more influence than his redefined job would have left him with.

Because power derives from activities rather than individuals, an individual's or subgroup's power is never absolute and derives ultimately from the context of the situation. The amount of power an individual has at any one time depends, not only on the activities he or she controls, but also on the existence of other persons or means by which the activities can be achieved and on those who determine what ends are desired and, hence, on what activities are desired and critical for the organization. One's own power always depends on other people for these two reasons. Other people, or groups or organizations, can determine the definition of what is a critical contingency for the organization and can also undercut the uniqueness of the individual's personal contribution to the critical contingencies of the organization.

Perhaps one can best appreciate how situationally dependent power is by examining how it is distributed. In most societies, power organizes around scarce and critical resources. Rarely does power organize around abundant resources. In the United States, a person doesn't become powerful because he or she can drive a car. There are simply too many others who can drive with equal facility. In certain villages in Mexico, on the other hand, a person with a car is accredited with enormous social status and plays a key role in the community. In addition to scarcity, power is also limited by the need for one's capacities in a social system. While a racer's ability to drive a car around a 90° turn at 80 mph may be sparsely distributed in a society, it is not likely to lend the driver much power in the society. The ability simply does not play a central role in the activities of the society.

The fact that power revolves around scarce and critical activities, of course, makes the control and organization of those activities a major battleground in struggles for power. Even relatively abundant or trivial resources can become the bases for power if one can organize and control their allocation and the definition of what is critical. Many occupational and professional groups attempt to do just this in modern economies. Lawyers organize themselves into associations, regulate the entrance requirements for novitiates, and then get laws passed specifying situations that require the services of an attorney. Workers had little power in the conduct of industrial affairs until they organized themselves into closed and controlled systems. In recent years, women and blacks have tried to define themselves as important and critical to the social system, using law to reify their status.

In organizations there are obviously opportunities for defining certain activities as more critical than others. Indeed, the growth of managerial thinking to include defining organizational objectives and goals has done much to foster these opportunities. One sure way to liquidate the power of groups in the organization is to define the need for their services out of existence. David Halberstam presents a description of how just such a thing happened to the group of correspondents that evolved around Edward R. Murrow, the brilliant journalist, interviewer, and war correspondent of CBS News. A close friend of CBS chairman and controlling stockholder William S. Paley, Murrow, and the news department he directed, were endowed with freedom to do what they felt was right. He used it to create some of the best documentaries and commentaries ever seen on television. Unfortunately, television became too large, too powerful, and too suspect in the eyes of the federal government that licensed it. It thus became, or at least the top executives believed it had become, too dangerous to have in-depth, probing commentary on the news. Crisp, dry, uneditorializing headliners were considered safer. Murrow was out and Walter Cronkite was in.

The power to define what is critical in an organization is no small power. Moreover, it is the key to understanding why organizations are either aligned with their environments or misaligned. If an organization defines certain activities as critical when in fact they are not critical, given the flow of resources coming into the organization, it is not likely to survive, at least in its present form.

Most organization managers evolve a distribution of power and influence that is aligned with the critical realities they face in the environment. The environment, in turn, includes both the internal environment, the shifting situational contexts in which particular decisions get made, and the external environment that it can hope to influence but is unlikely to control.

## THE CRITICAL CONTINGENCIES

The critical contingencies facing most organizations derive from the environmental context within which they operate. This determines the available needed resources and thus determines the problems to be dealt with. That power organizes around handling these problems suggests an important mechanism by which organizations keep in tune with their external environments. The strategic contingencies model implies that subunits that contribute to the critical resources of the organization will gain influence in the organization. Their influence presumably is then used to bend the organization's activities to the contingencies that determine its resources. This idea may strike one as obvious. But its obviousness in no way diminishes its importance. Indeed, despite its obviousness, it escapes the notice of many organizational analysts and managers, who all too frequently think of the organization in terms of a descending pyramid, in which all the departments in one tier hold equal power and status. This presumption denies the reality that departments differ in the contributions they are believed to make to the overall organization's resources, as well as to the fact that some are more equal than others.

Because of the importance of this idea to organizational effectiveness, we decided to examine it carefully in a large Midwestern university. A university offers an excellent site for studying power. It is composed of departments with nominally equal power and is administered by a central executive structure much like other bureaucracies. However, at the same time it is a situation in which the departments have clearly defined identities and face diverse external environments. Each department has its own bodies of knowledge, its own institutions, its own sources of prestige and resources. Because the departments operate in different external environments, they are likely to contribute differentially to the resources of the overall organization. Thus a physics department with close ties to NASA may contribute substantially to the funds of the university; and a history department with a renowned historian in residence may contribute to the intellectual credibility or prestige of the whole university. Such variations permit one to examine how these various contributions lead to obtaining power within the university.

We analyzed the influence of 29 university departments throughout an 18-month period in their history. Our chief interest was to determine whether departments that brought more critical resources to the university would be more powerful than departments that contributed fewer or less critical resources.

To identify the critical resources each department contributed, the heads of all departments were interviewed about the importance of seven different resources to the university's success. The seven included undergraduate students (the factor determining size of the state allocations by the university), national prestige, administrative expertise, and so on. The most critical resource was found to be contract and grant monies received by a department's faculty for research or consulting services. At this university, contract and grants contributed somewhat less than 50 percent of the overall budget, with the remainder primarily coming from state appropriations. The importance attributed to contract and grant monies, and the rather minor importance of undergraduate students, was not surprising for this particular university. The university was a major center for graduate education; many of its departments ranked in the top ten of their respective fields. Grant and contract monies were the primary source of discretionary funding available for maintaining these programs of graduate education, and hence for maintaining the university's prestige. The prestige of the university itself was critical both in recruiting able students and attracting top-notch faculty.

From university records it was determined what relative contributions each of the 29 departments made to the various needs of the university (national prestige, outside grants, teaching). Thus, for instance, one department may have contributed to the university by teaching 7 percent of the instructional units, bringing in 2 percent of the outside contracts and grants, and having a national ranking of 20. Another department, on the other hand, may have taught one percent of the instructional units, contributed 12 percent to the grants, and be ranked the third best department in its field within the country.

The question was: Do these different contributions determine the relative power of the departments within the university? Power was measured in several ways; but regardless of how measured, the answer was "Yes." Those three resources together accounted for about 70 percent of the variance in subunit power in the university.

But the most important predictor of departmental power was the department's contribution to the contracts and grants of the university. Sixty percent of the variance in power was due to this one factor, suggesting that the power of departments derived primarily from the dollars they provided for graduate education, the activity believed to be the most important for the organization.

# THE IMPACT OF ORGANIZATIONAL POWER ON DECISION MAKING

The measure of power we used in studying this university was an analysis of the responses of the department heads we interviewed. While such perceptions of power might be of interest in their own right, they contribute little to our understanding of how the distribution of power might serve to align an organization with its critical realities. For this we must look to how power actually influences the decisions and policies of organizations.

While it is perhaps not absolutely valid, we can generally gauge the relative importance of a department of an organization by the size of the budget allocated to it relative to other departments. Clearly it is of importance to the administrators of those departments whether they get squeezed in a budget crunch or are given more funds to strike out after new opportunities. And it should also be clear that when those decisions are made and one department can go ahead and try new approaches while another must cut back on the old, then the deployment of the resources of the organization in meeting its problems is most directly affected.

Thus our study of the university led us to ask the following questions. Does power lead to influence in the organization? To answer this question, we found it useful first to ask another one, namely: Why should department heads try to influence organizational decisions to favor their own departments to the exclusion of other departments? While this second question may seem a bit naive to anyone who has witnessed the political realities of organizations, we posed it in a context of research on organizations that sees power as an illegitimate threat to the neater rational authority of modern bureaucracies. In this context, decisions are not believed to be made because of the dirty business of politics but because of the overall goals and purposes of the organization. In a university, one reasonable basis for decision making is the teaching workload of departments and the demands that follow from that workload. We would expect, therefore, that departments with heavy student demands for courses would be able to obtain funds for teaching. Another reasonable basis for decision making is quality. We would expect, for that reason, that departments with esteemed reputations would be able to obtain funds both because their quality suggests they might use such funds effectively and because such funds would allow them to maintain their quality. A rational model of bureaucracy intimates, then, that the organizational decisions taken would favor those who perform the stated purposes of the organization—teaching undergraduates and training professional and scientific talent—well.

The problem with rational models of decision making, however, is that what is rational to one person may strike another as irrational. For most departments, resources are a question of survival. While teaching undergraduates may seem to be a major goal for some members of the university, developing knowledge may seem so to others; and to still others, advising governments and other institutions about policies may seem to be the crucial business. Everyone has his own idea of the proper priorities in a just world. Thus goals rather than being clearly defined and universally agreed upon are blurred and contested throughout the organization. If such is the case, then the decisions taken on behalf of the organization as a whole are likely to reflect the goals of those who prevail in political contests, namely, those with power in the organization.

Will organizational decisions always reflect the distribution of power in the organization? Probably not. Using power for influence requires a certain expenditure of effort, time, and resources. Prudent and judicious persons are not likely to use their power needlessly or wastefully. And it is likely that power will be used to influence organizational decisions primarily under circumstances that both require and favor its use. We have examined three conditions that are likely to affect the use of power in organizations: scarcity, criticality, and uncertainty. The first suggests that subunits will try to exert influence when the resources of the organization are scarce. If there is an abundance of resources, then a particular department or a particular individual has little need to attempt influence. With little effort, he can get all he wants anyway.

The second condition, criticality, suggests that a subunit will attempt to influence decisions to obtain resources that are critical to its own survival and activities. Criticality implies that one would not waste effort, or risk being labeled obstinate, by fighting over trivial decisions affecting one's operations.

An office manager would probably balk less about a threatened cutback in copying machine usage than about a reduction in typing staff. An advertising department head would probably worry less about losing his lettering artist than his illustrator. Criticality is difficult to define because what is critical depends on people's beliefs about what is critical. Such beliefs may or may not be based on experience and knowledge and may or may not be agreed upon by all. Scarcity, for instance, may itself affect conceptions of criticality. When slack resources drop off, cutbacks have to be made—those "hard decisions," as congressmen and resplendent administrators like to call them. Managers then find themselves scrapping projects they once held dear.

The third condition that we believe affects the use of power is uncertainty: When individuals do not agree about what the organization should do or how to do it, power and other social processes will affect decisions. The reason for this is simply that, if there are no clear-cut criteria available for resolving conflicts of interest, then the only means for resolution is some form of social process, including power, status, social ties, or some arbitrary process like flipping a coin or drawing straws. Under conditions of uncertainty, the powerful manager can argue his case on any grounds and usually win it. Since there is no real consensus, other contestants are not likely to develop counter arguments or amass sufficient opposition. Moreover, because of his power and their need for access to the resources he controls, they are more likely to defer to his arguments.

Although the evidence is slight, we have found that power will influence the allocations of scarce and critical resources. In the analysis of power in the university, for instance, one of the most critical resources needed by departments is the general budget. First granted by the state legislature, the general budget is later allocated to individual departments by the university administration in response to requests from the department heads. Our analysis of the factors that contribute to a department getting more or less of this budget indicated that subunit power was the major predictor, overriding such factors as student demand for courses, national reputations of departments, or even the size of a department's faculty. Moreover, other research has shown that when the general budget has been cut back or held below previous uninflated levels, leading to monies becoming more scarce, budget allocations mirror departmental powers even more closely.

Student enrollment and faculty size, of course, do themselves relate to budget allocations, as we would expect since they determine a department's need for resources, or at least offer visible testimony of needs. But departments are not always able to get what they need by the mere fact of needing them. In one analysis it was found that high-power departments were able to obtain budget without regard to their teaching loads and, in some cases, actually in inverse relation to their teaching load. In contrast, low-power departments could get increases in budget only when they could justify the increases by a recent growth in teaching load, and then only when it was far in excess of norms for other departments.

General budget is only one form of resources that is allocated to departments. There are others such as special grants for student fellowships or faculty research. These are critical to departments because they affect the ability to attract other resources, such as outstanding faculty or students. We examined how power influenced the allocations of four resources department heads had described as critical and scarce.

When the four resources were arrayed from the most to the least critical and scarce, we found that departmental power best predicted the allocations of the most critical and scarce resources. In other words, the analysis of how power influences organizational allocations leads to this conclusion. Those subunits most likely to survive in times of strife are those that are more critical to the organization. Their importance to the organization gives them power to influence resource allocations that enhance their own survival.

## HOW EXTERNAL ENVIRONMENT IMPACTS EXECUTIVE SELECTION

Power not only influences the survival of key groups in an organization, it also influences the selection of individuals to key leadership positions, and by such a process further aligns the organization with its environmental context.

We can illustrate this with a recent study of the selection and tenure of chief administrators in 57 hospitals in Illinois. We assumed that since the critical problems facing the organization would enhance the power of certain groups at the expense of others, then the leaders to emerge should be those most relevant to the context of the hospitals. To assess this we asked each chief administrator about his professional background and how long he had been in office. The replies were then related to the hospitals' funding, ownership, and competitive conditions for patients and staff.

One aspect of a hospital's context is the source of its budget. Some hospitals, for instance, are run much like other businesses. They sell bed space, patient care, and treatment services. They charge fees sufficient both to cover their costs and to provide capital for expansion. The main source of both their operating and capital funds is patient billings. Increasingly, patient billings are paid for, not by patients, but by private insurance companies. Insurers like Blue Cross dominate and represent a potent interest group outside a hospital's control but critical to its income. The insurance companies, in order to limit their own costs, attempt to hold down the fees allowable to hospitals, which they do effectively from their positions on state rate boards. The squeeze on hospitals that results from fees increasing slowly while costs climb rapidly more and more demands the talents of cost accountants or people trained in the technical expertise of hospital administration.

By contrast, other hospitals operate more like social service institutions, either as government healthcare units (Bellevue Hospital in New York City and Cook County Hospital in Chicago, for example) or as charitable institutions. These hospitals obtain a large proportion of their operating and capital funds, not from privately insured patients, but from government subsidies or private donations. Such institutions rather than requiring the talents of a technically efficient administrator are likely to require the savvy of someone who is well integrated into the social and political power structure of the community.

Not surprisingly, the characteristics of administrators predictably reflect the funding context of the hospitals with which they are associated. Those hospitals with larger proportions of their budget obtained from private insurance companies were most likely to have administrators with backgrounds in accounting and least likely to have administrators whose, professions were business or medicine. In contrast, those hospitals with larger proportions of their budget derived from private donations and local governments were most likely to have administrators with business or professional backgrounds and least likely to have accountants. The same held for formal training in hospital management. Professional hospital administrators could easily be found in hospitals drawing their incomes from private insurance and rarely in hospitals dependent on donations or legislative appropriations.

As with the selection of administrators, the context of organizations has also been found to affect the removal of executives. The environment, as a source of organizational problems, can make it more or less difficult for executives to demonstrate their values to the organization. In the hospitals we studied, long-term administrators came from hospitals with few problems. They enjoyed amicable and stable relations with their local business and social communities and suffered little competition for funding and staff. The small city hospital director who attended civic and Elks meetings while running the only hospital within a 100-mile radius, for example, had little difficulty holding on to his job. Turnover was highest in hospitals with the most problems, a phenomenon similar to that observed in a study of industrial organizations in which turnover was highest among executives in industries with competitive environments and unstable market conditions. The interesting thing is that instability characterized the industries rather than the individual firms in them. The troublesome conditions in the individual firms were attributed, or rather misattributed, to the executives themselves.

It takes more than problems, however, to terminate a manager's leadership. The problems themselves must be relevant and critical. This is clear from the way in which an administrator's tenure is affected by the status of the hospital's operating budget. Naively we might assume that all administrators would need to show a surplus. Not necessarily so. Again, we must distinguish between those hospitals that depend on private donations for funds and those that do not. Whether an endowed budget shows a surplus or deficit is less important than the hospital's relations with benefactors. On the other hand, with a budget dependent on patient billing, a surplus is almost essential; monies for new equipment or expansion must be drawn from it, and without them quality care becomes more difficult and patients scarcer. An administrator's tenure reflected just these considerations. For those hospitals dependent upon private donations, the length of an administrator's term depended not at all on the status of the operating budget but was fairly predictable from the hospital's relations with the business community. On the other hand, in hospitals dependent on the operating budget for capital financing, the greater the deficit the shorter was the tenure of the hospital's principal administrators.

## CHANGING CONTINGENCIES AND ERODING POWER BASES

The critical contingencies facing the organization may change. When they do, it is reasonable to expect that the power of individuals and subgroups will change in turn. At times the shift can be swift and shattering, as it was recently for powerholders in New York City. A few years ago it was believed that David Rockefeller was one of the ten most powerful people in the city, as tallied by *New York* magazine, which annually sniffs out power for the delectation of its readers. But that was before it was revealed that the city was in financial trouble, before Rockefeller's Chase Manhattan Bank lost some of its own financial luster, and before brother Nelson lost some of his political influence in Washington. Obviously David Rockefeller was no longer as well positioned to help bail the city out. Another loser was an attorney with considerable personal connections to the political and religious leaders of the city. His talents were no longer in much demand. The persons with more influence were the bankers and union pension fund executors who fed money to the city; community leaders who represent blacks and Spanish-Americans, in contrast, witnessed the erosion of their power bases.

One implication of the idea that power shifts with changes in organizational environments is that the dominant coalition will tend to be that group that is most appropriate for the organization's environment, as also will the leaders of an organization. One can observe this historically in the top executives of industrial firms in the United States. Up until the early 1950s, many top corporations were headed by former production line managers or engineers who gained prominence because of their abilities to cope with the problems of production. Their success, however, only spelled their demise. As production became routinized and mechanized, the problem of most firms became one of selling all those goods they so efficiently produced. Marketing executives were more frequently found in corporate boardrooms. Success outdid itself again, for keeping markets and production steady and stable requires the kind of control that can only come from acquiring competitors and suppliers or the invention of more and more appealing products—ventures that typically require enormous amounts of capital. During the 1960s, financial executives assumed the seats of power. And they, too, will give way to others. Edging over the horizon are legal experts, as regulation and antitrust suits are becoming more and more frequent in the 1970s, suits that had their beginnings in the success of the expansion generated by prior executives. The more distant future, which is likely to be dominated by multinational corporations, may see former secretaries of state and their minions increasingly serving as corporate figureheads.

## THE NONADAPTIVE CONSEQUENCES OF ADAPTATION

From what we have said thus far about power aligning the organization with its own realities, an intelligent person might react with a resounding ho-hum, for it all seems too obvious. Those with the ability to get the job done are given the job to do.

However, there are two aspects of power that make it more useful for understanding organizations and their effectiveness. First, the "job" to be done has a way of expanding itself until it becomes less and less clear what the job is. Napoleon began by doing a job for France in the war with Austria and ended up Emperor, convincing many that only he could keep the peace. Hitler began by promising an end to Germany's troubling postwar depression and ended up convincing more people than is comfortable to remember that he was destined to be the savior of the world. In short, power is a capacity for influence that extends far beyond the original bases that created it. Second, power tends to take on institutionalized forms that enable it to endure well beyond its usefulness to an organization.

There is an important contradiction in what we have observed about organizational power. On the one hand we have said that power derives from the contingencies facing an organization and that when those contingencies change so do the bases for power. On the other hand we have asserted that subunits will tend to use their power to influence organizational decisions in their own favor, particularly when their own survival is threatened by the scarcity of critical resources. The first statement implies that an organization will tend to be aligned with its environment since power will tend to bring to key positions those with capabilities relevant to the context. The second implies that those in power will not give up their positions so easily; they will pursue policies that guarantee their continued domination. In short, change and stability operate through the same mechanism, and, as a result, the organization will never be completely in phase with its environment or its needs.

The study of hospital administrators illustrates how leadership can be out of phase with reality. We argued that privately funded hospitals needed trained technical administrators more so than did hospitals funded by donations. The need as we perceived it was matched in most hospitals, but by no means in all. Some organizations did not conform with our predictions. These deviations imply that some administrators were able to maintain their positions independent of their suitability for those positions. By dividing administrators into those with long and short terms of office, one finds that the characteristics of longer-termed administrators were virtually unrelated to the hospital's context. The shorter-termed chiefs on the other hand had characteristics more appropriate for the hospital's problems. For a hospital to have a recently appointed head implies that the previous administrator had been unable to endure by institutionalizing himself.

One obvious feature of hospitals that allowed some administrators to enjoy a long tenure was a hospital's ownership. Administrators were less entrenched when their hospitals were affiliated with and dependent upon larger organizations, such as governments or churches. Private hospitals offered more secure positions for administrators. Like private corporations, they tend to have more diffused ownership, leaving the administrator unopposed as he institutionalizes his reign. Thus he endures, sometimes at the expense of the performance of the organization. Other research has demonstrated that corporations with diffuse ownership have poorer earnings than those in which the control of the manager is checked by a dominant shareholder. Firms that overload their boardrooms with more insiders than are appropriate for their context have also been found to be less profitable.

A word of caution is required about our judgment of "appropriateness." When we argue some capabilities are more appropriate for one context than another, we do so from the perspective of an outsider and on the basis of reasonable assumptions as to the problems the organization will face and the capabilities they will need. The fact that we have been able to predict the distribution of influence and the characteristics of leaders suggests that our reasoning is not incorrect. However, we do not think that all organizations follow the same pattern. The fact that we have not been able to predict outcomes with 100 percent accuracy indicates they do not.

# MISTAKING CRITICAL CONTINGENCIES

One thing that allows subunits to retain their power is their ability to name their functions as critical to the organization when they may not be. Consider again our discussion of power in the university. One might wonder why the most critical tasks were defined as graduate education and scholarly research, the effect of which was to lend power to those who brought in grants and contracts. Why not something else? The reason is that the more powerful departments argued for those criteria and won their case, partly because they were more powerful.

In another analysis of this university, we found that all departments advocate self-serving criteria for budget allocation. Thus a department with large undergraduate enrollments argued that enrollments should determine budget allocations, a department with a strong national reputation saw prestige as the most reasonable basis for disturbing funds, and so on. We further found that advocating such self-serving criteria actually benefited a department's budget allotments but, also, it paid off more for departments that were already powerful.

Organizational needs are consistent with a current distribution of power also because of a human tendency to categorize problems in familiar ways. An accountant sees problems with organizational performance as cost accountancy problems or inventory flow problems. A sales manager sees them as problems with markets, promotional strategies, or just unaggressive sales people. But what is the truth? Since it does not automatically announce itself, it is likely that those with prior credibility, or those with power, will be favored as the enlightened. This bias, while not intentionally self-serving, further concentrates power among those who already possess it, independent of changes in the organization's context.

# INSTITUTIONALIZING POWER

A third reason for expecting organizational contingencies to be defined in familiar ways is that the current holders of power can structure the organization in ways that institutionalize themselves. By institutionalization we mean the establishment of relatively permanent structures and policies that favor the influence of a particular subunit. While in power, a dominant coalition has the ability to institute constitutions, rules, procedures, and information systems that limit the potential power of others while continuing their own.

The key to institutionalizing power always is to create a device that legitimates one's own authority and diminishes the legitimacy of others. When the "Divine Right of Kings" was envisioned centuries ago it was to provide an unquestionable foundation for the supremacy of royal authority. There is generally a need to root the exercise of authority in some higher power. Modern leaders are no less affected by this need. Richard Nixon, with the aid of John Dean, reified the concept of executive privilege, which meant in effect that what the President wished not to be discussed need not be discussed.

In its simpler form, institutionalization is achieved by designating positions or roles for organizational activities. The creation of a new post legitimizes a function and forces organization members to orient to it. By designating how this new post relates to older, more established posts, moreover, one can structure an organization to enhance the importance of the function in the organization. Equally, one can diminish the importance of traditional functions. This is what happened in the end with the insurance company we mentioned that was having trouble with its coding department. As the situation unfolded, the claims director continued to feel dissatisfied about the dependency of his functions on the coding manager. Thus he instituted a reorganization that resulted in two coding departments.

In so doing, of course, he placed activities that affected his department under his direct control, presumably to make the operation more effective. Similarly, consumer-product firms enhance the power of marketing by setting up a coordinating role to interface production and marketing functions and then appoint a marketing manager to fill the role.

The structures created by dominant powers sooner or later become fixed and unquestioned features of the organization. Eventually, this can be devastating. It is said that the battle of Jena in 1806 was lost by Frederick the Great, who died in 1786. Though the great Prussion leader had not direct hand in the disaster, his imprint on the army was so thorough, so embedded in its skeletal underpinnings, that the organization was inappropriate for others to lead in different times.

Another important source of institutionalized power lies in the ability to structure information systems. Setting up committees to investigate particular organizational issues and having them report only to particular individuals or groups, facilitates their awareness of problems by members of those groups while limiting the awareness of problems by the members of other groups. Obviously, those who have information are in a better position to interpret the problems of an organization, regardless of how realistically they may, in fact, do so.

Still another way to institutionalize power is to distribute rewards and resources. The dominant group may quiet competing interest groups with small favors and rewards. The credit for this artful form of cooptation belongs to Louis XIV. To avoid usurpation of his power by the nobles of France and the Fronde that had so troubled his father's reign, he built the palace at Versailles to occupy them with hunting and gossip. Awed, the courtiers basked in the reflected glories of the "Sun King" and the overwhelming setting he had created for his court.

At this point, we have not systematically studied the institutionalization of power. But we suspect it is an important condition that mediates between the environment of the organization and the capabilities of the organization for dealing with that environment. The more institutionalized power is within an organization, the more likely an organization will be out of phase with the realities it faces. President Richard Nixon's structuring of his White House is one of the better documented illustrations. If we go back to newspaper and magazine descriptions of how he organized his office from the beginning in 1968, most of what occurred subsequently follows almost as an afterthought. Decisions flowed through virtually only the small White House staff; rewards, small presidential favors of recognition, and perquisites were distributed by this staff to the loyal; and information from the outside world—the press, Congress, the people on the streets—was filtered by the staff and passed along only if initialed "bh." Thus it was not surprising that when Nixon met war protesters in the early dawn, the only thing he could think to talk about was the latest football game, so insulated had he become from their grief and anger.

One of the more interesting implications of institutionalized power is that executive turnover among the executives who have structured the organization is likely to be a rare event that occurs only under the most pressing crisis. If a dominant coalition is able to structure the organization and interpret the meaning of ambiguous events like declining sales and profits or lawsuits, then the "real" problems to emerge will easily be incorporated into traditional molds of thinking and acting. If opposition is designed out of the organization, the interpretations will go unquestioned. Conditions will remain stable until a crisis develops, so overwhelming and visible that even the most adroit rhetorician would be silenced.

# IMPLICATIONS FOR THE MANAGEMENT
# OF POWER IN ORGANIZATIONS

While we could derive numerous implications from this discussion of power, our selection would have to depend largely on whether one wanted to increase one's power, decrease the power of others, or merely maintain one's position. More important, the real implications depend on the particulars of an organizational situation. To understand power in an organization one must begin by looking outside it—into the environment—for those groups that mediate the organization's outcomes but are not themselves within its control.

Instead of ending with homilies, we will end with a reversal of where we began. Power, rather than being the dirty business it is often made out to be, is probably one of the few mechanisms for reality testing in organizations. And the cleaner forms of power, the institutional forms, rather than having the virtues they are often credited with, can lead the organization to become out of touch. The real trick to managing power in organizations is to ensure somehow that leaders cannot be unaware of the realities of their environments and cannot avoid changing to deal with those realities. That, however, would be like designing the "self-liquidating organization," an unlikely event since anyone capable of designing such an instrument would be obviously in control of the liquidation.

Management would do well to devote more attention to determining the critical contingencies of their environments. For if you conclude, as we do, that the environment sets most of the structure influencing organizational outcomes and problems, and that power derives from the organization's activities that deal with those contingencies, then it is the environment that needs managing, not power. The first step is to construct an accurate model of the environment, a process that is quite difficult for most organizations. We have recently started a project to aid administration in systematically understanding their environments. From this experience, we have learned that the most critical blockage to perceiving an organization's reality accurately is a failure to incorporate those with the relevant expertise into the process. Most organizations have the requisite experts on hand but they are positioned so that they can be comfortably ignored.

One conclusion you can, and probably should, derive from our discussion is that power—because of the way it develops and the way it is used—will always result in the organization suboptimizing its performance. However, to this grim absolute, we add a comforting caveat: If any criteria other than power were the basis for determining an organization's decisions, the results would be even worse.

# SELECTED BIBLIOGRAPHY

The literature on power is at once both voluminous and frequently empty of content. Some is philosophical musing about the concept of power, while other writing contains popularized palliatives for acquiring and exercising influence. Machiavelli's *The Prince*, if read carefully, remains the single best prescriptive treatment of power and its use. Most social scientists have approached power descriptively, attempting to understand how it is acquired, how it is used, and what its effects are. Meyer Zald's edited collection *Power in Organizations* (Vanderbilt University Press, 1970) is one of the more useful sets of thoughts about power from a sociological perspective, while James Tedeschi's edited book, *The Social Influences Processes* (Aldine Atherton, 1972) represents the social psychological approach to understanding power and influence. The strategic contingencies' approach with its emphasis on the importance of uncertainty for understanding power in organizations, is described by David Hickson and his colleagues in "A Strategic Contingencies Theory of Intraorganizational Power" (*Administrative Science Quarterly*, December 1971, pp. 216–229).

Unfortunately, while many have written about power theoretically, there have been few empirical examinations of power and its use. Most of the work has taken the form of case studies. Michel Crozier's *The Bureaucratic Phenomenon* (University of Chicago Press, 1964) is important because it describes a group's source of power as control over critical activities and illustrates how power is not strictly derived from hierarchical position. J. Victor Baldridge's *Power and Conflict in the University* (John Wiley & Sons, 1971) and Andrew Pettigrew's study of computer purchase decisions in one English firm (*Politics of Organizational Decision Making*, Tavistock, 1973) both present insights into the acquisition and use of power in specific instances. Our work has been more empirical and comparative, testing more explicitly the ideas presented in this article. The study of university decision making is reported in articles in the June 1974, pp. 135–151, and December 1974, pp. 453–473, issues of the *Administrative Science Quarterly,* the insurance firm study in J. G. Hunt and L. L. Larson's collection, *Leadership Frontiers* (Kent State University Press, 1975), and the study of hospital administrator succession will appear in 1977 in the *Academy of Management Journal.*

# INFLUENCE WITHOUT AUTHORITY:
# THE USE OF ALLIANCES, RECIPROCITY, AND
# EXCHANGE TO ACCOMPLISH WORK

*Allan R. Cohen*
*David L. Bradford*

Bill Heatton is the director of research at a $250 million division of a large West Coast Company. The division manufactures exotic telecommunications components and has many technical advancements to its credit. During the past several years, however, the division's performance has been spotty at best; multimillion dollar losses have been experienced in some years despite many efforts to make the division more profitable. Several large contracts have resulted in major financial losses, and in each instance the various parts of the division blamed the others for the problems. Listen to Bill's frustration as he talks about his efforts to influence Ted, a colleague who is marketing director, and Roland, the program manager who reports to Ted.

> Another program is about to come through. Roland is a nice guy, but he knows nothing and never will. He was responsible for our last big loss, and now he's in charge of this one. I've tried to convince Ted, his boss, to get Roland off the program, but I get nowhere. Although Ted doesn't argue that Roland is capable, he doesn't act to find someone else. Instead, he comes to me with worries about my area.
>
> I decided to respond by changing my staffing plan, assigning to Roland's program the people they wanted. I had to override my staff's best judgment about who should be assigned. Yet I'm not getting needed progress reports from Roland, and he's never available for planning. I get little argument from him, but there's no action to correct the problem. That's bad because I'm responding but not getting any response.

*Source*: Reprinted, by permission of publisher, from *Organizational Dynamics*, Winter 1989. © 1989 American Management Association, New York. All rights reserved.

There's no way to resolve this. If they disagree, that's it. I could go to a tit-for-tat strategy, saying that if they don't do what I want, we'll get even with them next time. But I don't know how to do that without hurting the organization, which would feel worse than getting even!

Ted, Roland's boss, is so much better than his predecessor that I hate to ask that he be removed. We could go together to our boss, the general manager, but I'm very reluctant to do that. You've failed in a matrix organization if you have to go to your boss. I have to try hard because I'd look bad if I had to throw it in his lap.

Meanwhile, I'm being forceful, but I'm afraid it's in a destructive way. I don't want to wait until the program has failed to be told it was all my fault.

Bill is clearly angry and frustrated, leading him to behave in ways that he does not feel good about. Like other managers who very much want to influence an uncooperative co-worker whom they cannot control, Bill has begun to think of the intransigent employee as the enemy. Bill's anger is narrowing his sense of what is possible; he fantasizes revenge but is too dedicated to the organization to actually harm it. He is genuinely stuck.

Organizational members who want to make things happen often find themselves in this position. Irrespective of whether they are staff or line employees, professionals or managers, they find it increasingly necessary to influence colleagues and superiors. These critical others control needed resources, possess required information, set priorities on important activities, and have to agree and cooperate if plans are to be implemented. They cannot be ordered around because they are under another area's control and can legitimately say no because they have many other valid priorities. They respond only when they choose to. Despite the clear need and appropriateness of what is being asked for (certainly as seen by the person who is making the request), compliance may not be forthcoming.

All of this places a large burden on organizational members, who are expected not only to take initiatives but also to respond intelligently to requests made of them by others. Judgment is needed to sort out the value of the many requests made of anyone who has valuable resources to contribute. As Robert Kaplan argued in his article "Trade Routes: The Manager's Network of Relationships" (*Organizational Dynamics*, Spring 1984), managers must now develop the organizational equivalent of "trade routes" to get things done. Informal networks of mutual influence are needed. In her book *The Change Masters* (Simon & Schuster, 1983) Rosabeth Moss Kanter showed that developing and implementing all kinds of innovations require coalitions to be built to shape and support new ways of doing business.

A key current problem, then, is finding ways to develop mutual influence without the formal authority to command. A peer can not "order" a colleague to change priorities, modify an approach, or implement a grand new idea. A staff member cannot "command" his or her supervisor to back a proposal, fight top management for greater resources, or allow more autonomy. Even Bill Heatton, in dealing with Roland (who was a level below him in the hierarchy but in another department), could not dictate that Roland provide the progress reports that Bill so desperately wanted.

## EXCHANGE AND THE LAW OF RECIPROCITY

The way influence is acquired without formal authority is through the "law of reciprocity"—the almost universal belief that people should be paid back for what they do, that one good (or bad) deed deserves another. This belief is held by people in primitive and not-so-primitive societies all around the world, and it serves as the grease that allows the organizational wheel to turn smoothly. Because people expect that their actions will be paid back in one form or another, influence is possible.

In the case of Bill Heatton, his inability to get what he wanted from Roland and Ted stemmed from his failure to understand fully how reciprocity works in organizations. He therefore was unable to set up mutually beneficial exchanges. Bill believed that he had gone out of his way to help the marketing department by changing his staffing patterns, and he expected Roland to reciprocate by providing regular progress reports. When Roland failed to provide the reports, Bill believed that Ted was obligated to remove Roland from the project. When Ted did not respond, Bill became angry and wanted to retaliate. Thus Bill recognized the appropriateness of exchange in making organizations work. However, he did not understand how exchange operates.

Before exploring in detail how exchange can work in dealing with colleagues and superiors, it is important to recognize that reciprocity is the basic principle behind all organizational transactions. For example, the basic employment contract is an exchange ("an honest day's work for an honest day's pay"). Even work that is above and beyond what is formally required involves exchange. The person who helps out may not necessarily get (or expect) immediate payment for the extra effort requested, but some eventual compensation is expected.

Think of the likely irritation an employee would feel if his or her boss asked him or her to work through several weekends, never so much as said thanks, and then claimed credit for the extra work. The employee might not say anything the first time this happened, expecting or hoping that the boss would make it up somehow. However, if the effort were never acknowledged in any way, the employee, like most people, would feel that something important had been violated.

Exchanges enable people to handle the give-and-take of working together without strong feelings of injustice arising. They are especially important during periods of rapid change because the number of requests that go far beyond the routine tends to escalate. In those situations, exchanges become less predictable, more free-floating, and spontaneous. Nevertheless, people still expect that somehow or other, sooner or later, they will be (roughly) equally compensated for the acts they do above and beyond those that are covered by the formal exchange agreements in their job. Consequently, some kind of "currency" equivalent needs to be worked out, implicitly if not explicitly, to keep the parties in the exchange feeling fairly treated.

## CURRENCIES: THE SOURCE OF INFLUENCE

If the basis of organizational influence depends on mutually satisfactory exchanges, then people are influential only insofar as they can offer something that others need. Thus power comes from the ability to meet others' needs.

A useful way to think of how the process of exchange actually works in organizations is to use the metaphor of "currencies." This metaphor provides a powerful way to conceptualize what is important to the influencer and the person to be influenced. Just as many types of currencies are traded in the world financial market, many types are "traded" in organizational life. Too often people think only of money or promotion and status. Those "currencies," however, usually are available only to a manager in dealing with his or her employees. Peers who want to influence colleagues or employees who want to influence their supervisors often feel helpless. They need to recognize that many types of payments exist, broadening the range of what can be exchanged.

Some major currencies that are commonly valued and traded in organizations are listed in Exhibit I. Although not exhaustive, the list makes evident that a person does not have to be at the top of an organization or have hands on the formal levers of power to command multiple resources that others may value.

Part of the usefulness of currencies comes from their flexibility. For example, there are many ways to express gratitude and to give assistance. A manager who most values the currency of appreciation could be paid through verbal thanks, praise, a public statement at a meeting, informal comments to his peers, and/or a note to her boss. However, the same note of thanks seen by one person as a sign of appreciation may be seen by another person as an attempt to brownnose or by a third person as a cheap way to try to repay extensive favors and service. Thus currencies have value not in some abstract sense but as defined by the receiver.

Although we have stressed the interactive nature of exchange, "payments" do not always have to be made by the other person. They can be self-generated to fit beliefs about being virtuous, benevolent, or committed to the organization's welfare. Someone may respond to another person's request because it reinforces cherished values, a sense of identity, or feelings of self-worth. The exchange is interpersonally stimulated because the one who wants influence has set up conditions that allow this kind of self-payment to occur by asking for cooperation to accomplish organizational goals. However, the person who responds because "it is the right thing to do" and who feels good about being the "kind of person who does not act out of narrow self-interest" is printing currency (virtue) that is self-satisfying.

Of course, the five categories of currencies listed in Exhibit I are not mutually exclusive. When the demand from the other person is high, people are likely to pay in several currencies across several categories. They may, for example, stress the organizational value of their request, promise to return the favor at a later time, imply that it will increase the other's prestige in the organization, and express their appreciation.

## ESTABLISHING EXCHANGE RATES

What does it take to pay back in a currency that the other party in an exchange will perceive as equivalent? In impersonal markets, because everything is translated into a common monetary currency, it generally is easy to say what a fair payment is. Does a ton of steel equal a case of golfclubs? By translating both into dollar equivalents, a satisfactory deal can be worked out.

In interpersonal exchanges, however, the process becomes a bit more complicated. Just how does someone repay another person's willingness to help finish a report? Is a simple thank-you enough? Does it also require the recipient to say something nice about the helper to his or her boss? Whose standard of fairness should be used? What if one person's idea of fair repayment is very different from the other's?

Because of the natural differences in the way two parties can interpret the same activity, establishing exchanges that both parties will perceive as equitable can be problematic. Thus it is critical to understand what is important to the person to be influenced. Without a clear understanding of what that person experiences and values, it will be extremely difficult for anyone to thread a path through the minefield of creating mutually satisfactory exchanges.

Fortunately, the calibration of equivalent exchanges in the interpersonal and organizational worlds is facilitated by the fact that approximations will do in most cases. Occasionally, organizational members know exactly what they want in return for favors of help, but more often they will settle for very rough equivalents (providing that there is reasonable goodwill).

# THE PROCESS OF EXCHANGE

To make the exchange process effective, the influencer needs to 1) think about the person to be influenced as a potential ally, not an adversary; 2) know the world of the potential ally, including the pressures as well as the person's needs and goals; 3) be aware of key goals and available resources that may be valued by the potential ally; and 4) understand the exchange transaction itself so that win-win outcomes are achieved. Each of these factors is discussed below.

## Potential Ally, Not Adversary

A key to influence is thinking of the other person as a potential ally. Just as many contemporary organizations have discovered the importance of creating strategic alliances with suppliers and customers, employees who want influence within the organization need to create internal allies. Even though each party in an alliance continues to have freedom to pursue its own interests, the goal is to find areas of mutual benefit and develop trusting, sustainable relationships. Similarly, each person whose cooperation is needed inside the organization is a potential ally. Each still has self-interests to pursue, but those self-interests do not preclude searching for and building areas of mutual benefit.

Seeing other organizational members as potential allies decreases the chance that adversarial relationships will develop—an all-too-frequent result (as in the case of Bill Heatton) when the eager influencer does not quickly get the assistance of cooperation needed. Assuming that even a difficult person is a potential ally makes it easier to understand that person's world and thereby discover what that person values and needs.

## The Potential Ally's World

We have stressed the importance of knowing the world of the potential ally. Without awareness of what the ally needs (what currencies are valued), attempts to influence that person can only be haphazard. Although this conclusion may seem self-evident, it is remarkable how often people attempt to influence without adequate information about what is important to the potential ally. Instead, they are driven by their own definition of "what should be" and "what is right" when they should be seeing the world from the other person's perspective.

For example, Bill Heatton never thought about the costs to Ted of removing Roland from the project. Did Ted believe he could coach Roland to perform better on this project? Did Ted even agree that Roland had done a poor job on the previous project, or did Ted think Roland had been hampered by other departments' shortcomings? Bill just did not know.

Several factors can keep the influencer from seeing the potential ally clearly. As with Bill Heatton, the frustration of meeting resistance from a potential ally can get in the way of really understanding the other person's world. The desire to influence is so strong that only the need for cooperation is visible to the influencer. As a result of not being understood, the potential ally digs in, making the influencer repeat an inappropriate strategy or back off in frustration.

When a potential ally's behavior is not understandable ("Why won't Roland send the needed progress reports?"), the influencer tends to stereotype that person. If early attempts to influence do not work, the influencer is tempted to write the person off as negative, stubborn, selfish, or "just another bean counter/whiz kid/sales-type" or whatever pejorative label is used in that organizational culture to dismiss those organizational members who are different.

EXHIBIT I   Commonly Traded Organizational Currencies

### Inspiration-Related Currencies

| | |
|---|---|
| Vision | Being involved in a task that has larger significance for the unit, organization, customers, or society. |
| Excellence | Having a chance to do important things really well. |
| Moral/Ethical Correctness | Doing what is "right" by a higher standard than efficiency. |

### Task-Related Currencies

| | |
|---|---|
| Resources | Lending or giving money, budget increases, personnel, space, and so forth. |
| Assistance | Helping with existing projects or undertaking unwanted tasks. |
| Cooperation | Giving task support, providing quicker response time, approving a project, or aiding implementation. |
| Information | Providing organizational as well as technical knowledge. |

### Position-Related Currencies

| | |
|---|---|
| Advancement | Giving a task or assignment that can aid in promotion. |
| Recognition | Acknowledging effort, accomplishment, or abilities. |
| Visibility | Providing chance to be known by higher-ups or significant others in the organization. |
| Reputation | Enhancing the way a person is seen. |
| Importance/Insiderness | Offering a sense of importance, of "belonging." |
| Network/Contacts | Providing opportunities for linking with others. |

### Relationship-Related Currencies

| | |
|---|---|
| Acceptance/Inclusion | Providing closeness and friendship. |
| Personal support | Giving personal and emotional backing. |
| Understanding | Listening to others' concerns and issues. |

### Personal-Related Currencies

| | |
|---|---|
| Self-Concept | Affirming one's values, self-esteem, and identity. |
| Challenge/Learning | Sharing tasks that increase skills and abilities. |
| Ownership/Involvement | Letting others have ownership and influence. |
| Gratitude | Expressing appreciation or indebtedness. |

Although some stereotypes may have a grain of truth, they generally conceal more than they reveal. The actuary who understands that judgment, not just numbers, is needed to make decisions disappears as an individual when the stereotype of "impersonal, detached number machine" is the filter through which he or she is seen. Once the stereotype is applied, the frustrated influencer is no longer likely to see what currencies that particular potential ally actually values.

Sometimes, the lack of clear understanding about a potential ally stems from the influencer's failure to appreciate the organizational forces acting on the potential ally. To a great extent, a person's behavior is a result of the situation in which that person works (and not just his or her personality). Potential allies are embedded in an organizational culture that shapes their interests and responses. For example, one of the key determinants of anyone's behavior is likely to be the way the person's performance is measured and rewarded. In many instances, what is mistaken for personal orneriness is merely the result of the person's doing something that will be seen as good performance in his or her function.

The salesperson who is furious because the plant manager resists changing priorities for a rush order may not realize that part of the plant manager's bonus depends on holding unit costs down—a task made easier with long production runs. The plant manager's resistance does not necessarily reflect his or her inability to be flexible or lack of concern about pleasing customers or about the company's overall success.

Other organizational forces that can affect the potential ally's behavior include the daily time demands on that person's position; the amount of contact the person has with customers, suppliers, and other outsiders; the organization's information flow (or lack of it); the style of the potential ally's boss; the belief and assumptions held by that person's co-workers; and so forth. Although some of these factors cannot be changed by the influencer, understanding them can be useful in figuring out how to frame and time requests. It also helps the influencer resist the temptation to stereotype the noncooperator

## Self-Awareness of the Influencer

Unfortunately, people desiring influence are not always aware of precisely what they want. Often their requests contain a cluster of needs (a certain product, arranged in a certain way, delivered at a specified time). They fail to think through which aspects are more important and which can be jettisoned if necessary. Did Bill Heatton want Roland removed, or did he want the project effectively managed? Did he want overt concessions from Ted, or did he want better progress reports?

Further, there is a tendency to confuse and intermingle the desired end goal with the means of accomplishing it, leading to too many battles over the wrong things. In *The Change Masters*, Kanter reported that successful influencers in organizations were those who never lost sight of the ultimate objective but were willing to be flexible about means.

Sometimes influencers underestimate the range of currencies available for use. They may assume, for example, that just because they are low in the organization they have nothing that others want. Employees who want to influence their boss are especially likely not to realize all of the supervisor's needs that they can fulfill. They become so caught up with their feelings of powerlessness that they fail to see the many ways they can generate valuable currencies.

In other instances, influencers fail to be aware of their preferred style of interaction and its fit with the potential ally's preferred style. Everyone has a way of relating to others to get work done. However, like the fish who is unaware of the water, many people are oblivious of their own style of interaction or see it as the only way to be. Yet interaction style can cause problems with potential allies who are different.

508

For example, does the influencer tend to socialize first and work later? If so, that style of interaction will distress a potential ally who likes to dig right in to solve the problem at hand and only afterward chat about sports, family, or office politics. Does the potential ally want to be approached with answers, not problems? If so, a tendency to start influence attempts with open-ended, exploratory problem solving can lead to rejection despite good intentions.

## Nature of the Exchange Transaction

Many of the problems that occur in the actual exchange negotiation have their roots in the failure to deal adequately with the first three factors outlined above. Failure to treat other people as potential allies, to understand a potential ally's world, and to be self-aware are all factors that interfere with successful exchange. In addition, some special problems commonly arise when both parties are in the process of working out a mutually satisfactory exchange agreement.

- *Not knowing how to use reciprocity.* Using reciprocity requires stating needs clearly without "crying wolf," being aware of the needs of an ally without being manipulative, and seeking mutual gain rather than playing "winner takes all." One trap that Bill Heatton fell into was not being able to "close on the exchange." That is, he assumed that if he acted in good faith and did his part, others would automatically reciprocate. Part of his failure was not understanding the other party's world; another part was not being able to negotiate cleanly with Ted about what each of them wanted. It is not even clear that Ted realized Bill was altering his organization as per Ted's requests, that Ted got what he wanted, or that Ted knew Bill intended an exchange of responses.

- *Preferring to be right rather than effective.* This problem is especially endemic to professionals of all kinds. Because of their dedication to the "truth" (as their profession defines it), they stubbornly stick to their one right way when trying to line up potential allies instead of thinking about what will work given the audience and conditions. Organizational members with strong technical backgrounds often chorus the equivalent of "I'll be damned if I'm going to sell out and become a phone salesman, trying to get by on a shoeshine and smile." The failure to accommodate to the potential ally's needs and desires often kills otherwise sound ideas.

- *Overusing what has been successful.* When people find that a certain approach is effective in many situations, they often begin to use it in many situations, they often begin to use it in places where it does not fit. By overusing the approach, they block more appropriate methods. Just as a weight lifter becomes muscle-bound from overdeveloping particular muscles at the expense of others, people who have been reasonably successful at influencing other people can diminish that ability by overusing the same technique.

For example, John Brucker, the human resources director at a medium-size company, often cultivated support for new programs by taking people out to fancy restaurants for an evening of fine food and wine. He genuinely derived pleasure from entertaining, but at the same time he created subtle obligations. One time, a new program he wanted to introduce required the agreement of William Adams, head of engineering. Adams, an old-timer, perceived Brucker's proposal as an unnecessary frill, mainly because he did not perceive the real benefits to the overall organization. Brucker responded to Adams's negative comments as he always did in such cases—by becoming more friendly and insisting that they get together for dinner soon. After several of these invitations, Adams became furious. Insulted by what he considered to be Brucker's attempts to buy him off, he fought even harder to kill the proposal. Not only did the program die, but Brucker lost all possibility of influencing Adams in the future. Adams saw Brucker's attempts at socializing as a sleazy and crude way of trying to soften him up. For his part, Brucker was totally puzzled by Adams' frostiness and assumed that he was against all progress. He never realized that Adams had a deep sense of integrity and a real commitment to the good of the organization. Thus Brucker lost his opportunity to sell a program that, ironically, Adams would have found valuable had it been implemented.

As the case above illustrates, a broad repertoire of influence approaches is needed in modern organizations. Johnny-one-notes soon fall flat.

## THE ROLE OF RELATIONSHIPS

All of the preceding discussion needs to be conditioned by one important variable: the nature of the relationship between both parties. The greater the extent to which the influencer has worked with the potential ally and created trust, the easier the exchange process will be. Each party will know the other's desired currencies and situational pressures, and each will have developed a mutually productive interaction style. With trust, less energy will be spent on figuring out the intentions of the ally, and there will be less suspicion about when and how the payback will occur.

A poor relationship (based on previous interactions, on the reputation each party has in the organization, and/or on stereotypes and animosities between the functions or departments that each party represents) will impede an otherwise easy exchange. Distrust of the goodwill, veracity, or reliability of the influencer can lead to the demand for "no credit; cash up front," which constrains the flexibility of both parties.

The nature of the interaction during the influencer process also affects the nature of the relationship between the influencer and the other party. The way that John Brucker attempted to relate to William Adams not only did not work but also irreparably damaged any future exchanges between them.

Few transactions within organizations are one-time deals. (Who knows when the other person may be needed again or even who may be working for him or her in the future?) Thus in most exchange situations two outcomes matter: success in achieving task goals and success in improving the relationship so that the next interaction will be even more productive. Too often, people who want to be influential focus only on the task and act as if there is no tomorrow. Although both task accomplishment and an improved relationship cannot always be realized at the same time, on some occasions the latter can be more important than the former. Winning the battle but losing the war is an expensive outcome.

## INCONVERTIBLE CURRENCIES

We have spelled out ways organizational members operate to gain influence for achieving organizational goals. By effectively using exchange, organizational members can achieve their goals and at the same time help others achieve theirs. Exchange permits organizational members to be assertive without being antagonistic by keeping mutual benefit a central outcome.

In many cases, organizational members fail to acquire desired influence because they do not use all of their potential power. However, they sometimes fail because not all situations are amenable to even the best efforts at influencing. Not everything can be translated into compatible currencies. If there are fundamental differences in what is valued by two parties, it may not be possible to find common ground, as illustrated in the example below.

The founder and chairman of a high-technology company and the president he had hired five years previously were constantly displeased with one another. The president was committed to creating maximum shareholder value, the currency he valued most as a result of his M.B.A. training, his position, and his temperament. Accordingly, he had concluded that the company was in a perfect position to cash in by squeezing expenses to maximize profits and going public. He could see that the company's product line of exotic components was within a few years of saturating its market and would require massive, risky investment to move to sophisticated end-user products.

The president could not influence the chairman to adopt this direction, however, because the chairman valued a totally different currency, the fun of technological challenge. An independently wealthy man, the chairman had no interest in realizing the $10 million or so he would get if the company maximized profits by cutting research and selling out. He wanted a place to test his intuitive, creative research hunches, not a source of income.

Thus the president's and chairman's currencies were not convertible into one another at an acceptable exchange rate. After they explored various possibilities but failed to find common ground, they mutually agreed that the president should leave—on good terms and only after a more compatible replacement could be found. Although this example acknowledges that influence through alliance, currency conversion, and exchange is not always possible, it is hard to be certain that any situation is hopeless until the person desiring influence has fully applied all of the diagnostic and interpersonal skills we have described.

Influence is enhanced by using the model of strategic alliances to engage in mutually beneficial exchanges with potential allies. Even though it is not always possible to be successful, the chances of achieving success can be greatly increased In a period of rapid competitive, technological, regulative, and consumer change, individuals and their organizations need all the help they can get.

# 17
# Empowerment and Coaching

THE EMPOWERMENT OF SERVICE WORKERS: WHAT, WHY, HOW, AND WHEN
> *David E. Bowen*
> *Edward E. Lawler III*

MANAGEMENT DIALOGUES: TURNING ON THE MARGINAL PERFORMER
> *John R. Schermenhorn, Jr.*
> *William L. Gardner*
> *Thomas N. Martin*

## THE EMPOWERMENT OF SERVICE WORKERS: WHAT, WHY, HOW, AND WHEN

*David E. Bowen*
*Edward E. Lawler III*

Empowering service workers has acquired almost a "born again" religious fervor. Tom Peters calls it "purposeful chaos." Robert Waterman dubs it "directed autonomy." It has also been called the "art of improvisation."

Yet in the mid-1970s, the production-line approach to service was the darling child of service gurus. They advocated facing the customer with standardized, procedurally driven operations. Should we now abandon this approach in favor of empowerment?

Unfortunately, there is no simple, clear-cut answer. In this article we try to help managers think about the question of whether to empower by clarifying its advantages and disadvantages, describing three forms that empower employees to different degrees, and presenting five contingencies that managers can use to determine which approach best fits their situation. We do not intend to debunk empowerment, rather we hope to clarify why to empower (there are costs, as well as benefits), how to empower (there are alternatives), and when to empower (it really does depend on the situation).

# THE PRODUCTION-LINE APPROACH

In two classic articles, the "Production-Line Approach to Service" and the "Industrialization of Service," Theodore Levitt described how service operations can be made more efficient by applying manufacturing logic and tactics.[1] He argued:

> *Manufacturing thinks technocratically, and that explains its success...By contrast, service looks for solutions in the performer of the task. This is the paralyzing legacy of our inherited attitudes: the solution to improved service is viewed as being dependent on improvements in the skills and attitudes of the performers of that service.*
>
> *While it may pain and offend us to say so, thinking in humanistic rather than technocratic terms ensures that the service sector will be forever inefficient and that our satisfaction will be forever marginal.[2]*

He recommended 1) simplification of tasks, 2) clear division of labor, 3) substitution of equipment and systems for employees, and 4) little decision-making discretion afforded to employees. In short, management designs the system, and employees execute it.

McDonald's is a good example. Workers are taught how to greet customers and ask for their order, including a script for suggesting additional items. They learn a set procedure for assembling the order (for example, cold drinks first, then hot ones), placing items on the tray, and placing the tray where customers need not reach for it. There is a script and a procedure for collecting money and giving change. Finally, there is a script for saying thank you and asking the customer to come again.[3] This production-line approach makes customer-service interactions uniform and gives the organization control over them. It is easily learned; workers can be quickly trained and put to work.

What are the gains from a production-line approach? Efficient, low-cost, high-volume service operations, with satisfied customers.

# THE EMPOWERMENT APPROACH

Ron Zemke and Dick Schaaf, in *The Service Edge: 101 Companies That Profit from Customer Care*, note that empowerment is a common theme running through many, even most, of their excellent service businesses, such as American Airlines, Marriott, American Express, and Federal Express. To Zemke and Schaaf, empowerment means "turning the front line loose," encouraging and rewarding employees to exercise initiative and imagination: "Empowerment in many ways is the reverse of doing things by the book."[4]

The humanistic flavor of empowerment pervades the words of advocates such as Tom Peters:

> *It is necessary to "dehumiliate" work by eliminating the policies and procedures (almost always tiny) of the organization that demean and belittle human dignity. It is impossible to get people's best efforts, involvement, and caring concern for things you believe important to your customers and the long-term interests of your organization when we write policies and procedures that treat them like thieves and bandits.[5]*

And from Jan Carlzon, CEO of Scandinavian Airlines Systems (SAS):

*To free someone from rigorous control by instructions, policies, and orders, and to give that person freedom to take responsibility for his ideas, decisions, and actions is to release hidden resources that would otherwise remain inaccessible to both the individual and the organization.*[6]

In contrast to the industrialization of service, empowerment very much looks to the "performer of the tasks" for solutions to service problems. Workers are asked to suggest new services and products and to solve problems creatively and effectively.

What, then, does it really mean—beyond the catchy slogans—to empower employees? We define empowerment as sharing with frontline employees four organizational ingredients: 1) information about the organization's performance, 2) rewards based on the organization's performance, 3) knowledge that enables employees to understand and contribute to organizational performance, and 4) power to make decisions that influence organizational direction and performance. We will say more about these features later. For now, we can say that with a production-line approach, these features tend to be concentrated in the hands of senior management; with an empowerment approach, they tend to be moved downward to frontline employees.

## WHICH APPROACH IS BETTER?

In 1990, Federal Express became the first service organization to win the Malcolm Baldridge National Quality Award. The company's motto is "people, service, and profits." Behind its blue, white, and red planes and uniforms are self-managing work teams, gainsharing plans, and empowered employees seemingly consumed with providing flexible and creative service to customers with varying needs.

At UPS, referred to as "Big Brown" by its employees, the philosophy was stated by founder Jim Casey: "Best service at low rates." Here, too, we find turned-on people and profits. But we do not find empowerment. Instead we find controls, rules, a detailed union contract, and carefully studied work methods. Nor do we find a promise to do all things for customers, such as handling off-schedule pickups and packages that don't fit size and weight limitations. In fact, rigid operational guidelines help guarantee the customer reliable, low-cost service.

Federal Express and UPS present two different faces to the customer, and behind these faces are different management philosophies and organizational cultures. Federal Express is a high-involvement, horizontally coordinated organization that encourages employees to use their judgment above and beyond the rulebook. UPS is a top-down, traditionally controlled organization, in which employees are directed by policies and procedures based on industrial engineering studies of how all service delivery aspects should be carried out and how long they should take.

Similarly, at Disney theme parks, ride operators are thoroughly scripted on what to say to "guests," including a list of preapproved "ad libs"! At Club Med, however, CEO Jacques Giraud fervently believes that guests must experience real magic, and the resorts' GOs (*gentils organisateurs*, "congenial hosts") are set free to spontaneously create this feeling for their guests. Which is the better approach? Federal Express or UPS? Club Med or Disney?

At a recent executive education seminar on customer service, one of us asked, "Who thinks that it is important for their business to empower their service personnel as a tool for improving customer service?" All twenty-seven participants enthusiastically raised their hands. Although they represented diverse services—banking, travel, utilities, airlines, and shipping—and they disagreed on most points, they all agreed that empowerment is key to customer satisfaction. But is it?

# EMPOWERING SERVICE EMPLOYEES: WHY, HOW, AND WHEN

## Why to Empower: The Benefits

What gains are possible from empowering service employees?

- *Quicker On-Line Responses to Customer Needs during Service Delivery.*  Check-in time at the hotel begins at 2 p.m., but a guest asks the desk clerk if she can check in at 1:30 p.m.  An airline passenger arrives at the gate at 7:30 a.m., Friday, for a 7:45 a.m. departure and wants to board the plane with a travel coupon good Monday through Thursday, and there are empty seats on the plane.  The waitress is taking an order in a modestly priced family restaurant; the menu says no substitutions, but the customer requests one anyway.

The customer wants a quick response.  And the employee would often like to be able to respond with something other than "No, it is against our rules" or "I will have to check with my supervisor."  Empowering employees in these situations can lead to the sort of spontaneous, creative rule-breaking that can turn a potentially frustrated or angry customer into a satisfied one.  This is particularly valuable when there is little time to refer to a higher authority, as when the plane is leaving in fifteen minutes.  Even before greeting customers, empowered employees are confident that they have all the necessary resources at their command to provide customers with what they need.

- *Quicker On-Line Responses to Dissatisfied Customers during Service Recovery.*  Customer service involves both delivering the service, such as checking a guest into a hotel room, and recovering from poor service, such as relocating him from a smoking floor to the nonsmoking room he originally requested.  Although delivering good service may mean different things to different customers, all customers feel that service businesses ought to fix things when service is delivered improperly.  Figure 1 depicts the relationships among service delivery, recovery, and customer satisfaction.

Fixing something after doing it wrong the first time can turn a dissatisfied customer into a satisfied, even loyal, customer.  But service businesses frequently fail in the act of recovery because service employees are not empowered to make the necessary amends with customers.  Instead, customers hear employees saying, "Gee, I wish there was something I could do, but I can't," "It's not my fault," or "I could check with my boss, but she's not here today."  These employees lack the power and knowledge to recover, and customers remain dissatisfied.

FIGURE 1    Possible Outcomes during Service Delivery and Recovery

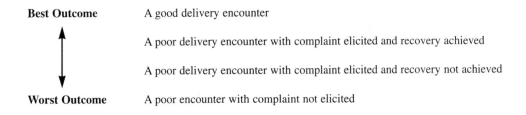

• *Employees Feel Better about Their Jobs and Themselves.*   Earlier we mentioned Tom Peters' thinking on how strict rules can belittle human dignity.  Letting employees call the shots allows them to feel "ownership" of the job; they feel responsible for it and find the work meaningful. Think of how you treat your car as opposed to a rented one.  Have you ever washed a rental car?  Decades of job design show that when employees have a sense of control and of doing meaningful work they are more satisfied.  This leads to lower turnover, less absenteeism, and fewer union organizing drives.

• *Employees Will Interact with Customers with More Warmth and Enthusiasm.*   Research now supports our long-standing intuition that customers' perceptions of service quality are shaped by the courtesy, empathy, and responsiveness of service employees.[7]  Customers want employees to appear concerned about their needs. Can empowerment help create this?  One of us has done customer service researching branch banks that showed that when the tellers reported feeling good about how they were supervised, trained, and rewarded, customers thought more highly of the service they received.[8]  In short, when employees felt that management was looking after their needs, they took better care of the customer.

In service encounters, employees' feelings about their jobs will spill over to affect how customers feel about the service they get.  This is particularly important when employee attitudes are a key part of the service package.  In banking, where the customer receives no tangible benefits in the exchange other than a savings deposit slip, a sour teller can really blemish a customer's feelings about the encounter.

• *Empowered Employees Can Be a Great Source of Service Ideas.*   Giving frontline employees a voice in "how we do things around here" can lead to improved service delivery and ideas for new services.  The bank study showed that the tellers could accurately report how customers viewed overall service quality and how they saw the branches' service climate (e.g., adequacy of staff and appearance of facilities).[9]

Frontline employees are often ready and willing to offer their opinion.  When it comes to market research, imagine the difference in response rates from surveying your employees and surveying your customers.

• *Great Word-of-Mouth Advertising and Customer Retention.*   Nordstrom's advertising budget is 1.5 percent of sales, whereas the industry average is 5 percent.  Why?  Their satisfied-no-matter-what customers spread the word about their service and become repeat customers.

## The Costs

What are the costs of empowerment?

• *A Greater Dollar Investment in Selection and Training.*   You cannot hire effective, creative problem solvers on the basis of chance or mere intuition.  Too bad, because the systematic methods necessary to screen out those who are not good candidates for empowerment are expensive.  For example, Federal Express selects customer agents and couriers on the basis of well-researched profiles of successful performers in those jobs.

Training is an even greater cost.  The production-line approach trains workers easily and puts them right to work.  In contrast, new hires at SAS are formally assigned a mentor to help them learn the ropes; Nordstrom department managers take responsibility for orienting and training new members of the sales team; customer service representatives at Lands' End and L.L. Bean spend a week in training before handling their first call.  They receive far more information and knowledge about their company and its products than is the norm.

The more labor intensive the service, the higher these costs. Retail banking, department stores, and convenience stores are labor intensive, and their training and selection costs can run high. Utilities and airlines are far less labor intensive.

• *Higher Labor Costs.* Many consumer service organizations, such as department stores, convenience stores, restaurants, and banks, rely on large numbers of part-time and seasonal workers to meet their highly variable staffing needs. These employees typically work for short periods of time at low wages. To empower these workers, a company would have to invest heavily in training to try to quickly inculcate the organization's culture and values. This training would probably be unsuccessful, and the employees wouldn't be around long enough to provide a return on the investment. Alternatively, the organization could pay higher wages to full-time, permanent employees, but they would be idle when business was slow.

• *Slower or Inconsistent Service Delivery.* Remember the hotel guest wanting to check in early and the airline passenger requesting special treatment at the gate? True, there is a benefit to empowering the employee to bend the rules, but only for the person at the front of the line! Customers at the back of the line are grumbling and checking their watches. They may have the satisfaction of knowing that they too may receive creative problem solving when and if they reach the counter, but it is small consolation if the plane has already left.

Based on our experiences as both researchers and customers, we believe that customers will increasingly value speed in service delivery. Purposeful chaos may work against this. We also believe that many customers value "no surprises" in service delivery. They like to know what to expect when they revisit a service business or patronize different outlets of a franchise. When service delivery is left to employee discretion, it may be inconsistent.

The research data show that customers perceive reliability—"doing it right the first time"—as the most important dimension of service quality. It matters more than employees' responsiveness, courtesy, or competency, or the attractiveness of the service setting.[10] Unfortunately, in the same research, a sample of large, well-known firms was more deficient on reliability than on these other dimensions. Much of the touted appeal of the production-line approach was that procedurally and technocratically driven operations could deliver service more reliably and consistently than service operations heavily dependent upon the skills and attitudes of employees. The production-line approach was intended to routinize service so that customers would receive the "best outcome" possible from their service encounters—service delivery with no glitches in the first place.

We feel that service managers need to guard against being seduced into too great a focus on recovery, at the expense of service delivery reliability. We say "seduced" because it is possible to confuse good service with inspiring stories about empowered employees excelling at the art of recovery. Recovery has more sex appeal than the nitty-gritty detail of building quality into every seemingly mundane aspect of the service delivery system, but an organization that relies on recovery may end up losing out to firms that do it right the first time.

• *Violations of "Fair Play."* A recent study of how service businesses handle customer complaints revealed that customers associate sticking to procedures with being treated fairly.[11] Customers may be more likely to return to a business if they believe that their complaint was handled effectively because of company policies rather than because they were lucky enough to get a particular employee. In other words, customers may prefer procedurally driven acts of recovery. We suspect that customers' notions of fairness may be violated when they see employees cutting special deals with other customers.

• **Giveaways and Bad Decisions.**   Managers are often reluctant to empower their employees for fear they will give too much away to the customer.  Perhaps they have heard the story of Willie, the doorman at a Four Seasons Hotel, who left work and took a flight to return a briefcase left behind by a guest.  Or they have heard of too many giveaways by empowered Nordstrom employees.  For some services, the costs of giveaways are far outweighed by enhanced customer loyalty, but not for others.

Sometimes creative rule breaking can cause a major problem for an organization.  There may be a good reason why no substitutions are allowed or why a coupon cannot be used on a certain day (e.g., an international airfare agreement).  If so, having an empowered employee break a rule may cause the organization serious problems, of which the employee may not even be aware.

These are some of the costs and benefits of empowerment.  We hope this discussion will help service businesses use empowerment knowledgeably, not just because it is a fad.  But we must add one more caveat: There is still precious little research on the consequences of empowerment. We have used anecdotal evidence, related research (e.g., in job design), and our work on service.  More systematic research must assess whether this array of costs and benefits fully captures the "whys" (and "why nots") of empowerment.

## How to Empower:  Three Options

Empowering service employees is less understood than industrializing service delivery.  This is largely because the production-line approach is an example of the well-developed control model of organization design and management, whereas empowerment is part of the still evolving "commitment" or "involvement" model.  The latter assumes that most employees can make good decisions if they are properly socialized, trained, and informed.  They can be internally motivated to perform effectively, and they are capable of self-control and self-direction.  This approach also assumes that most employees can produce good ideas for operating the business.[12]

The control and involvement models differ in that four key features are concentrated at the top of the organization in the former and pushed down in the organization in the latter.  As we have discussed above, these features are the following: 1) information about organizational performance (e.g., operating results and competitor performance); 2) rewards based on organizational performance (e.g., profit sharing and stock ownership); 3) knowledge that enables employees to understand and contribute to organizational performance (e.g., problem-solving skills); and 4) power to make decisions that influence work procedures and organizational direction (e.g., through quality circles and self-managing teams).

FIGURE 2   Levels of Empowerment

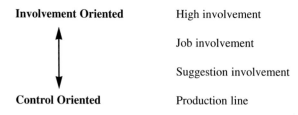

518

Three approaches to empowering employees can be identified (see Figure 2).[13] They represent increasing degrees of empowerment as additional knowledge, information, power, and rewards are pushed down to the front line. Empowerment, then, is not an either/or alternative, but rather a choice of three options:

**1. Suggestion Involvement** represents a small shift away from the control model. Employees are encouraged to contribute ideas through formal suggestion programs or quality circles, but their day-to-day work activities do not really change. Also, they are only empowered to recommend; management typically retains the power to decide whether or not to implement.

Suggestion involvement can produce some empowerment without altering the basic production-line approach. McDonald's, for example, listens closely to the front line. The Big Mac, Egg McMuffin, and McDLT all were invented by employees as was the system of wrapping burgers that avoids leaving a thumbprint in the bun. As another example, Florida Power and Light, which won the Deming quality award, defines empowerment in suggestion involvement terms.

**2. Job Involvement** represents a significant departure from the control model because of its dramatic "opening up" of job content. Jobs are redesigned so that employees use a variety of skills. Employees believe their tasks are significant, they have considerable freedom in deciding how to do the work, they get more feedback, and they handle a whole, identifiable piece of work. Research shows that many employees find enriched work more motivating and satisfying, and they do higher-quality work.[14]

Often job involvement is accomplished through extensive use of teams. Teams are often appropriate in complex service organizations such as hospitals and airlines because individuals cannot offer a whole service or handle a customer from beginning to end of service delivery. Teams can empower back-office workers in banks and insurance companies as well.

Employees in this environment require training to deal with the added complexity. Supervisors, who now have fewer shots to call, need to be reoriented toward supporting the front line, rather than directing it. Despite the heightened level of empowerment it brings, the job involvement approach does not change higher-level strategic decisions concerning organization structure, power, and the allocation of awards. These remain the responsibility of senior management.

**3. High-Involvement** organizations give their lowest-level employees a sense of involvement not just in how they do their jobs or how effectively their group performs, but in the total organization's performance. Virtually every aspect of the organization is different from that of a control-oriented organization. Business performance information is shared. Employees develop skills in teamwork, problem solving, and business operations. They participate in work-unit management decisions. There is profit sharing and employee ownership.

High-involvement designs may be expensive to implement. Perhaps most troublesome is that these management techniques are relatively undeveloped and untested. People Express tried to operate as a high-involvement airline, and the ongoing struggle to learn and develop this new organizational design contributed to its operating problems.

Today, America West is trying to make the high-involvement design work. New hires spend 25 percent of their first year's salary on company stock. All employees receive annual stock options. Flight attendants and pilots develop their own work procedures and schedules. Employees are extensively cross-trained to work where they are needed. Only time will tell if America West can make high-involvement work as it struggles with its financial crisis stemming from high fuel costs and rapid growth.

Federal Express displays many high-involvement features. A couple of years ago, it began a company-wide push to convert to teams, including the back office. It organized its 1,000 clerical workers in Memphis into superteams of five to ten people and gave them the authority and training to manage themselves. These teams helped the company cut customer service problems, such as incorrect bills and lost packages, by 13 percent in 1989.

## When to Empower: A Contingency Approach

Management thought and practice frequently have been seduced by the search for the "one best way to manage." Unfortunately, business does not lend itself to universal truths, only to "contingency theories" of management. For example, early job enrichment efforts in the 1960s assumed that all employees would prefer more challenging work and more autonomy. By the early 1970s it was clear that only those employees who felt the need to grow at work responded positively to job enrichment.[15] As the research on it is still thin, it is at least possible that empowerment is a universal truth, but historical evidence weighs against its being the best way to manage in all situations.

We believe that both the empowerment and production-line approaches have their advantages, and that each fits certain situations. The key is to choose the management approach that best meets the needs of both employees and customers.

Table 1 presents five contingencies that determine which approach to adopt. Each contingency can be rated on a scale of 1 to 5 to diagnose the quality of fit between the overall situation and the alternative approaches. The following propositions suggest how to match situations and approaches. Matching is not an exact science, but the propositions suggest reasonable rules of thumb.

**Proposition 1:** The higher the rating of each contingency (5 being the highest), the better the fit with an empowerment approach; the lower the rating (1 being the lowest), the better the fit with a production-line approach.

**Proposition 2:** The higher the total score from all five contingencies, the better the fit with an empowerment approach; the lower the total score, the better the fit with a production-line approach. A production-line approach is a good fit with situations that score in the range of 5 to 10. For empowerment approaches, suggestion involvement is a good fit with situations that score in the range of 11 to 15, job involvement with scores that range from 16 to 20, and high involvement with scores that range from 21 to 25.

**Proposition 3:** The higher the total score, the more the benefits of increasing empowerment will outweigh the costs.

TABLE 1    The Contingencies of Empowerment

| Contingency | Production-Line Approach | Empowerment | |
|---|---|---|---|
| Basic business strategy | Low cost, high volume | 1 2 3 4 5 | Differentiation, customized, personalized |
| Tie to customer | Transaction, short time period | 1 2 3 4 5 | Relationship, long time period |
| Technology | Routine, simple | 1 2 3 4 5 | Nonroutine, complex |
| Business Environment | Predictable, few surprises | 1 2 3 4 5 | Unpredictable, many surprises |
| Types of people | Theory X managers, employees with low growth needs, low social needs, and weak interpersonal skills | 1 2 3 4 5 | Theory Y managers, employees with high growth needs, high social needs, and strong interpersonal skills |

In what follows, we describe each contingency's implications for a production-line or empowerment approach.

*Basic Business Strategy.*  A production-line approach makes the most sense if your core mission is to offer high-volume service at the lowest cost. "Industrializing" service certainly leverages volume. The question is: what is the value-added from spending the additional dollars on employee selection, training, and retention necessary for empowerment? This question is especially compelling in labor-intensive services (e.g., fast food, grocery stores, and convenience stores) and those that require part-time or temporary employees.

These customers prefer a production-line approach. A recent study of convenience stores actually found a negative relationship between store sales and clerks being friendly with customers.[16] Customers wanted speed, and friendly clerks slowed things down. The point is that customers themselves may prefer to be served by a nonempowered employee.

At Taco Bell, counter attendants are expected to be civil, but they are not expected or encouraged to be creative problem solvers. Taco Bell wants to serve customers who want low-cost, good quality, fast food. Interestingly, the company believes that as more chains move to customized, service-oriented operations, it has more opportunities in the fast, low-price market niche.

The production-line approach does not rule out suggestion involvement As mentioned earlier, employees often have ideas even when much of their work is routinized. Quality circles and other approaches can capture and develop them.

An empowerment approach works best with a market segment that wants the tender loving care dimension more than speed and cost. For example, SAS targets frequent business travelers (who do not pay their own way). The SAS strategy was to differentiate itself from other airlines on the basis of personalized service. Consequently, the company looked at every ingredient of its service package to see if it fit this segment's definition of service quality, and, if so, whether or not customers would pay for it.

*Tie to the Customer.*  Empowerment is the best approach when service delivery involves managing a relationship, as opposed to simply performing a transaction. The service firm may want to establish relationships with customers to build loyalty or to get ideas for improving the service delivery system or offering new services. A flexible, customized approach can help establish the relationship and get the ideas flowing.

The returns on empowerment and relationship building are higher with more sophisticated services and delivery systems. An employee in the international air freight industry is more likely to learn from a customer relationship than is a gasoline station attendant.

The relationship itself can be the principle valued commodity that is delivered in many services. When no tangibles are delivered, as in estate planning or management consulting, the service provider often is the service to the customer, and empowerment allows the employee to customize the service to fit the customer's needs.

The more enduring the relationship, and the more important it is in the service package, the stronger the case for empowerment. Remember the earlier comparison between Disney, which tightly scripts its ride operators, and Club Med, which encourages its GOs to be spontaneous? Giraud, Club Med's CEO, explains that Disney employees relate to their guests in thousands of brief encounters; GOs have week-long close relationships with a limited number of guests. The valuable service they sell is "time."

*Technology.*  It is very difficult to build challenge, feedback, and autonomy into a telephone operator's job, given the way the delivery technology has been designed. The same is true of many fast-food operations. In these situations. the technology limits empowerment to only suggestion involvement and ultimately may almost completely remove individuals from the service delivery process, as has happened with ATMs.

When technology constrains empowerment, service managers can still support frontline employees in ways that enhance their satisfaction and the service quality they provide. For example, managers can show employees how much their jobs matter to the organization's success and express more appreciation for the work they do. In other words, managers can do a better job of making the old management model work!

Routine work can be engaging if employees are convinced that it matters. Volunteers will spend hours licking envelopes in a fundraising campaign for their favorite charity. Disney theme park employees do an admirable job of performing repetitive work, partly because they believe in the values, mission, and show business magic of Disney.

*Business Environment.* Businesses that operate in unpredictable environments benefit from empowerment. Airlines face many challenges to their operations: bad weather, mechanical breakdowns, and competitors' actions. They serve passengers who make a wide variety of special requests. It is simply impossible to anticipate many of the situations that will arise and to "program" employees to respond to them. Employees trained in purposeful chaos are appropriate for unpredictable environments.

Fast-food restaurants, however, operate in stable environments. Operations are fairly fail-safe; customer expectations are simple and predictable. In this environment, the service business can use a production-line approach. The stability allows, even encourages, management with policies and procedures, because managers can predict most events and identify the best responses.

*Types of People.* Empowerment and production-line approaches demand different types of managers and employees. For empowerment to work, particularly in the high-involvement form, the company needs to have Theory Y managers who believe that their employees can act independently to benefit both the organization and its customers. If the management ranks are filled with Theory X types who believe that employees only do their best work when closely supervised, then the production-line approach may be the only feasible option unless the organization changes its managers. Good service can still be the outcome. For example, most industry observers would agree that Delta and American Airlines are managed with a control orientation rather that a strong empowerment approach.

Employees will respond positively to empowerment only if they have strong needs to grow and to deepen and test their abilities—at work. Again, a checkered history of job enrichment efforts has taught us not to assume that everyone wants more autonomy, challenge, and responsibility at work. Some employees simply prefer a production-line approach.

Lastly, empowerment that involves teamwork requires employees who are interested in meeting their social and affiliative needs at work. It also requires that employees have good interpersonal and group process skills.

## THE FUTURE OF SERVICE WORK

How likely is it that more and more service businesses will choose to face the customer with empowered employees? We would guess that far more service organizations operate at the production-line end of our continuum than their business situations call for. A recent survey of companies in the "Fortune 1000" offers some support for this view.[17] This survey revealed that manufacturing firms tend to use significantly more employee-involvement practices than do service firms. Manufacturing firms use quality circles, participation groups, and self-managing work teams far more that service firms.

Why is this so? We think that the intense pressure on the manufacturing sector from global competition has created more dissatisfaction with the old control-oriented way of doing things. Also, it can be easier to see the payoffs from different management practices in manufacturing than in service. Objective measures of productivity can more clearly show profitability than can measures of customer perceptions of service quality. However, these differences are now blurring as service competition increases and service companies become more sophisticated in tracking the benefits of customer service quality.

As service businesses consider empowerment, they can look at high-involvement manufacturing organizations as labs in which the various empowerment approaches have been tested and developed. Many lessons have been learned in manufacturing about how to best use quality circles, enriched jobs, and so on. And the added good news is that many service businesses are ideally suited to applying and refining these lessons. Multisite, relatively autonomous service operations afford their managers an opportunity to customize empowerment programs and then evaluate them.

In summary, the newest approaches to managing the production line can serve as role models for many service businesses, but perhaps not all. Before service organizations rush into empowerment programs, they need to determine whether and how empowerment fits their situation.

## REFERENCES

1. T. Levitt, "Production-Line Approach to Service," *Harvard Business Review*, September–October 1972, pp. 41–52; and T. Levitt, "Industrialization of Service," *Harvard Business Review*, September–October 1976, pp. 63–74.
2. Levitt (1972).
3. D. Tansik, "Managing Human Resources Issues for High-Contact Service Personnel," in *Service Management Effectiveness,* eds. D. Bowen, R. Chase, and T. Cummings (San Francisco: Jossey-Bass, 1990).
4. R. Zemke and D. Schaaf, *The Service Edge: 101 Companies That Profit from Customer Care* (New York: New American Library, 1989), p. 68.
5. As quoted in Zemke and Schaaf (1989), p. 68.
6. J. Carlzon, *Moments of Truth* (New York: Ballinger, 1987).
7. V. Zeithaml, A. Parasuraman, and L. L. Berry, *Delivering Quality Service: Balancing Customer Perceptions and Expectations* (New York: The Free Press, 1990). See also: B. Schneider and D. Bowen, "Employee and Customer Perceptions of Service in Banks: Replication and Extension," *Journal of Applied Psychology* 70 (1985): 423–433.
8. Schneider and Bowen (1985).
9. Ibid.
10. Zeithaml, Parasuraman, and Berry (1990).
11. C. Goodwin and I. Ross, "Consumer Evaluations of Responses to Complaints: What's Fair and Why," *Journal of Services Marketing* 4 (1990): 53–61.
12. See E. E. Lawler III, *High-Involvement Management* (San Francisco: Jossey-Bass, 1986).
13. See E. E. Lawler III, "Choosing an Involvement Strategy," *Academy of Management Executive* 2 (1988): 197–204.
14. See for example J. R. Hackman and G. R. Oldham, *Work Redesign* (Reading, Massachusetts: Addison-Wesley, 1980).
15. Ibid.
16. R. J. Sutton and A. Rafaeli, "Untangling the Relationship between Displayed Emotions and Organizational Sales: The Case of Convenience Stores," *Academy of Management Journal* 31 (1988): 461–487.
17. E. E. Lawler III, G. E. Ledford, Jr., and S. A. Mohrman, *Employee Involvement in America: A Study of Contemporary Practice* (Houston: American Productivity & Quality Center, 1989).

# MANAGEMENT DIALOGUES:
# TURNING ON THE MARGINAL PERFORMER

*John R. Schermerhorn, Jr.*
*William L. Gardner*
*Thomas N. Martin*

Bob is an employee in the R&D laboratory of a large high-technology firm. He was hired by the lab supervisor, Fred, after a thorough recruitment and selection process. Both men were enthusiastic about the appointment. Bob had excellent technical credentials, was glad to be hired by the lab, and really liked Fred. Fred was confident in Bob's abilities and sure that Bob was just the person the lab needed. He passed by Bob's work station during Bob's first day on the job. Here's the way things started off:

*Fred*:  Hi, Bob. First full day on the job, I see?
*Bob:*  Yes, and I'm ready to go to work.
*Fred*:  Good. I just thought I'd stop by first thing to say hi and remind you we're expecting good results. You'll be pretty much on your own here, so it will be your responsibility to stay on top of things.
*Bob:*  Well, that shouldn't be a problem.
*Fred:*  I hope not. But if you hit any snags, don't be afraid to call me.
*Bob:*  All right.
*Fred*:  Good enough, Bob. See you later.

Everything seemed in order with this brief but positive exchange between a manager and his new employee. The two men talked easily with each other. Fred quite specifically reminded Bob of his expectations and pledged his support. Bob expressed confidence in his ability to fulfill Fred's expectations, and he acknowledged the offer of support.

But six months later, things had changed dramatically. For example, consider one of Bob's typical workdays. He arrived late for work and looked at the clock, which read 8:55. "Little late this morning," he thought to himself. "Oh well, no big deal. Fred's not around anyway." Later in the day he noted that he had "come up short again" in his work. "But not too bad," he said. "This ought to be enough to keep Fred off my back." Finally, just before quitting time he considered getting a jump on the next day's schedule. But after thinking just a moment, he concluded, "Ah, why sweat it? I'll do it tomorrow."

People like Bob show up in most work sites. Although they initially seem capable and highly motivated, they become marginal performers—workers who do just enough to get by. Many frustrated managers simply consider these people unfortunate employment mistakes that must be tolerated. By contrast, we believe managers can "turn around" many marginal performers and thereby produce large productivity gains for their organization. Such *high-performance management* gets the best from each and every individual contributor.

Let's go back to the opening vignette to determine what went wrong in Fred and Bob's relationship and what could have been done about it. Why did Bob, a capable and motivated person, become a marginal performer? What could Fred have done to turn the situation around so that Bob's high-performance potential would have been realized?

*Source*:  Reprinted, by permission of publisher, from *Organizational Dynamics*, Spring 1990. © 1990 American Management Association, New York. All rights reserved.

# A COMPREHENSIVE APPROACH
# TO INDIVIDUAL PERFORMANCE

The answers can be found in a management framework based on what we call the *individual performance equation: Performance = Ability x Support x Effort.* Central to the equation is the principle that high levels of work performance result from the combination of a person's job-related abilities, various forms of organizational support, and individual work efforts. The multiplication signs indicate that all three factors must exist for high performance to occur. Take any one or more away, and performance will be compromised. High-performance management starts with the following implications of the individual performance equation.

1. *Performance begins with ability.* Individual abilities are the skills and other personal characteristics we use in a job. for someone to perform well, he or she must have the skills and abilities required to complete the work. If the person lacks the requisite baseline abilities, it will be very difficult for even extraordinary effort and support to produce high performance.

Because ability is a prerequisite for performance, it is the first factor to consider when searching for explanations of marginal work. Initially, managers must determine whether employees have the skills and aptitudes necessary to succeed. The best way to ensure that they do is to develop selection procedures that properly match individual talents and job demands. In cases where employees lack essential skills, managers should use training and development programs to help them acquire these skills. The manger may also consider replacing or reassigning personnel to achieve a better match of individual abilities with job requirements.

In addition, as Victor Vroom's expectancy theory of motivation points out, individuals must believe in their abilities if they are to exhibit high performance. A person may have the right abilities but may fail to develop the expectation that by using these skills, he or she will achieve the desired performance levels. Thus part of a manager's job is to help build self-confidence among the individual contributors—to help them realize that they have the abilities required to meet high-performance expectations.

2. *Performance requires support.* The second but frequently overlooked high-performance factor is support. Even the most hard-working and highly capable individuals will be unable to maximize their performance if they do not have the necessary support.

In searching for the causes of marginal performance, managers need to examine two major dimensions of support. First, they must ask if they have done their part to create a physical work setting that supplies employees with broad opportunities to fully use their abilities. A supportive work environment provides appropriate technologies, tools, facilities, and equipment; offers adequate budgets; includes clearly defined task goals; gives autonomy without the burden of too much red tape and other performance obstacles; and pays a market-competitive base wage or salary. Deficiencies in these areas impose situational constraints that too often frustrate employees' performance efforts.

Second, managers must give proper attention to the social aspects of the work environment. Recent research into job stress, for example, suggests that social support is critical for *sustained* high performance. Emotional support from a person's supervisor and co-workers, as well as from non-job sources (i.e., spouse, family, and friends), can have long-term positive effects on job performance. Indeed, empathy can help a worker better handle such work stresses as skill underutilization, high workloads, and role ambiguity.

A manager's responsibility thus includes providing every individual contributor with the maximum opportunity to perform at a high level. This advice echoes Robert House's path-goal theory of leadership. Path-goal theory suggests that effective managers use various management styles—directive, supportive, achievement oriented, and participative—as necessary to ensure that employees have clear "paths" as they seek to accomplish their goals. That is, good managers use leadership behaviors that maximize the amount of situational support available to others.

**3. *Performance involves effort.*** Effort is the final, and perhaps most commonly emphasized, individual performance factor. Here, effort refers to the amount of energy (physical and/or mental) a person applies to perform a task. In other words, it represents someone's willingness to work hard.

Effort is necessary to achieve high-performance results. Capable, well-supported, but uninspired employees are no more likely to succeed than are hard-working persons who lack ability and/or support. Yet unlike the other performance factors, which are subject to direct managerial control, the decision to exert or withhold one's effort rests solely with the individual contributor. To understand why employees sometimes decide *not* to work as hard as possible, it is again useful to consider Vroom's expectancy theory of motivation. According to this perspective, the motivation to work is the product of expectancy, instrumentality, and valence: *Expectancy* is the individual's assessment of the likelihood that his or her work effort will lead to task performance; *instrumentality* is the individual's belief that a given level of performance will lead to certain work outcomes; and *valence* is the value the person attaches to these outcomes. If the level of any one of these factors is low, motivation is likely to suffer. To avoid motivational deficits, managers are advised to make sure individual contributors see clear linkages between how hard they work, their performance results, and their rewards.

## BOB, THE MARGINAL PERFORMER

Let's return to the opening vignette and begin to apply the individual performance equation. All three elements of the equation—ability, support, and effort—appear to exist. Fred set the stage for Bob's high performance by 1) hiring a technically competent person, 2) indicating his intention to provide support, and 3) encouraging Bob to work hard and use his ability to good advantage. Our first clues as to what went wrong are found in a conversation that took place after Bob had been on the job about a month.

Fred happened to pass by Bob's area and noticed Bob was working hard. He thought to himself how fortunate he was to have a dependable go-getter like Bob in his department. Bob noticed Fred approaching and wondered whether Fred would mention his good performance from the past week.

*Fred:* Hi, Bob. It sure is good weather, wouldn't you say?

*Bob:* Yes, it sure is.

*Fred:* I was just passing through the building on another matter. While I'm here, I thought I'd show you some new schedule changes.

*Bob:* Oh yes, Darlene (the project manager) told me all about them. Say, how'd we end up last week anyway?

*Fred:* Pretty good, pretty good. If you have any questions about those schedule changes, just call the project manager. Well, I've got to run. See you later, Bob.

In this interaction Bob obviously wanted Fred's praise. What he got was a lukewarm "Pretty good, pretty good" followed by "I've got to run." Fred passed up a perfect opportunity to recognize directly Bob's accomplishments. From an expectancy theory perspective, this oversight could prove costly. Bob's expectation was probably quite high—he had already shown he could do the job when he wanted to. The valence he attached to possible work outcomes, such as praise, also was probably high. But Bob's instrumentality may have become low because he sensed little or no relationship between performing well and receiving the desired supervisory recognition. The positive reinforcement he both desired and needed was just not there. As a result, his motivation to work hard was reduced.

Things could have gotten better if the motivational dynamics had improved in later interactions between Fred and Bob. Unfortunately, as we'll now see, they didn't. Several weeks later while reading the weekly lab reports, Fred noticed a decline in Bob's performance. This was a serious problem, so Fred decided to chat with Bob right away. Bob had met high performance standards in the past and should still have been able to reach them. When Fred stopped by Bob's work station, they engaged in the following conversation.

> *Fred*: Hi, Bob, how's it going?
> *Bob:* Pretty good.
> *Fred:* Say, I wanted to check with you about your performance figures for the past couple of weeks. They've been down a little, you know.
> *Bob:* Well, I got stuck on a couple of things that threw me off. But I think I'm back on track now.
> *Fred:* The only reason I'm bringing it up is that you've busted the charts in the past. I know you can do it when you put your mind to it. You're one of our top performers. I figured if you were off on the numbers there must be a reason.
> *Bob:* Well, I'm sure my performance results will be back up this week.
> *Fred:* Okay, good, Bob, Take care now.

Reviewing this interaction, Fred thought it had been right to let Bob know he wasn't happy with his performance. But in this developing scheme, we have an indication that the only time Bob got the desired personal attention from Fred was when he did poorly. As social-learning theorists will tell us, Bob was essentially "learning" through reinforcement to work below his actual performance potential. By giving attention only when Bob turned in marginal, rather than high, performance, Fred was positively reinforcing the wrong behaviors and neglecting critical opportunities to positively reinforce the right ones. As long as this pattern continued, Bob was likely to remain a marginal performer. And, as we will see, a manager's frustrations with this situation can all too easily lead him or her to adopt ever more punitive approaches.

A few weeks later Fred noted that Bob's performance still wasn't back up to standard. While he was not the worst performer in the lab, he surely could have been doing a lot better; Bob's past record was proof positive. Being even more concerned now, Fred went to Bob's work area to discuss things with him.

> *Fred:* Bob, I want to talk to you.
> *Bob:* Hi, Fred, what's on your mind?
> *Fred*: Your lousy performance, that's what! Your output has been down again for the past two weeks. Look, Bob, I know you can hit the numbers, but you're just not putting out. I need someone in here who can get the job done. If it is not you, I'll get someone else. I hope I won't have to do that. Now let's get to it?
> *Bob*: (No response.)

Theorists advise us that Fred's threats reveal a number of shortcomings. For example, behaviors targeted for punishment frequently receive positive reinforcement from another source—like peers and co-workers or even the supervisor's inadvertent actions. For another, managers who use punishment often come to be viewed negatively by the recipients of the punishment. At the very least, then, we can expect that Fred had set the stage for potentially irreparable damage to his working relationship with Bob! Unfortunately, Fred made a common mistake. He focused only on what the employee might have been doing wrong while overlooking other possible causes for the marginal performance.

One thing is clear from the above episode. Fred was telling Bob that it was *Bob's* responsibility to find out what had gone wrong over the past couple of weeks, then take steps to correct it. Implicitly he was also attributing Bob's marginal performance to one or more things that might be wrong—with Bob! Unfortunately, Fred made a common mistake: He focused only on what the employee might have been doing wrong while overlooking other possible causes for the marginal performance.

## ATTRIBUTION ERRORS IN PERFORMANCE MANAGEMENT

Take a look at the data in Exhibit I. It summarizes how managers from the health care and banking industries responded to two questions :1) "What is the most frequent cause of poor performance by your employees?" and 2) "What is the most frequent cause of poor performance by yourself?" The exhibit shows quite different patterns of responses: When employees' performance deficiencies were at issue, the managers tended to attribute the problem to employees' lack of ability and/or effort; when the manager's own performance deficiencies were at issue, the problem was overwhelmingly viewed as a lack of outside support. But, we must ask, if managers need better support to achieve higher performance, doesn't the same hold true for their employees?

Responses such as these are of no great surprise to those familiar with an area of management research known as attribution theory. When dealing with marginal performers like Bob, the theory predicts that managers like Fred are more likely to "attribute" any performance problems to some deficiency within the individual—that is, to a lack of ability or lack of effort—rather than to a deficiency in the work situation, like a lack of organizational or managerial support. Given that Bob was considered technically competent when he was hired (thus satisfying the ability factor), Fred probably assumed that Bob's reduced performance resulted from a lack of motivation (a problem with the effort factor).

Managers who view performance problems in such a manner will spend valuable time and money trying to find ways to increase their employees' motivation directly and immediately. When these initial efforts fail, the threatening and punitive approach that Fred used in the last episode is likely to follow.

EXHIBIT I   Marginal Performance: Attributions Given by Managers and by Employees Themselves

| Number of Responses to the Question: Most common cause of poor performance by your employees? | Attribution | Number of Responses to the Question: Most common cause of poor performance by yourself? |
|:---:|:---|:---:|
| 22 | Lack of Ability | 2 |
| 15 | Lack of Support | 66 |
| 36 | Lack of Effort | 6 |

The fact that employees tend to attribute deficiencies in their performance to external causes, such as inadequate support, rather than to the internal causes their managers favor further complicates such situations. Bob, for example, is more likely to attribute his mediocre performance to a lack of supervisory recognition (an external cause) than to his own laziness (an internal cause)—which Fred seems to assume *is* the case. When such gaps between attributions exist, employees like Bob typically resent the harsh and punitive responses their managers use. On the other hand, managers get increasingly frustrated because they cannot understand the employee's failure to perform.

If this cycle of mismatched manager-employee attributions is allowed to continue, a worst-case scenario, in the form of what social psychologists call "learned helplessness," may occur. This term refers to the tendency for people who are exposed to repeated punishment or failure to believe they do not possess the skills needed to succeed at their job. As a result they become passive in their work, and they tend to remain so even after situational changes occur that make success once again possible. A feeling that outcomes are beyond one's control, when in fact they are not, is the essence of learned helplessness. People become convinced that they are doomed to fail no matter what they do. As a consequence, employees who experience learned helplessness will usually continue to exhibit passive and maladaptive behavior long after changes (such as increased support or the arrival of a new manager) occur that make success possible

In Bob's case, learned helplessness resulting from Fred's punitive responses may cause Bob eventually to doubt the very abilities that led to his hiring and early successes. While learned helplessness is a worst-case scenario, it exemplifies the serious complications that can arise if managers fail to address marginal performance in a constructive way. The approach that we recommend for dealing more positively with the marginal performer is outlined below.

## DEALING WITH BOB—A BETTER WAY

Many marginal performers, like Bob, are aware that they are not working up to their potential—and they know why. Given a positive environment for dialogue, they are often willing able to pinpoint the causes—both personal and situational—of their performance problems. They are also willing to assume their share of the responsibility for correcting them. Toward this end, we suggest the following managerial strategy for "turning around" a marginal performer.

- Bring the performance gap to the marginal performer's attention.
- Ask in a nonthreatening manner for an explanation.
- Describe the implications of the marginal performer's substandard work.
- Restate the original and still-desirable performance objectives.
- Offer the external support necessary for the marginal performer to improve his or her performance.
- Express confidence that the marginal performer will respond as expected.
- Agree on an appropriate time frame for jointly evaluating future performance in terms of the agreed-upon standards.
- Continue the process until it succeeds or the individual admits to an employment mismatch that can be reconciled only by a job change.

To illustrate how these steps can be followed, let's go back in time and pick up our vignette at the point where Fred first noticed that Bob's performance had dropped off. We'll assume he was prepared to adopt this more positive approach to the situation. As Fred's dialogue with Bob develops, we'll occasionally interject some discussion of his actions and Bob's responses. This will help illustrate the steps and potential benefits of the recommended approach.

Fred noticed that Bob's performance had been down for two weeks. After thinking it over, he realized that a capable person like Bob should have been consistently performing at a higher level—but he may have needed some help. Fred decided to walk to Bob's work station and talk to him about the matter at once.

> *Fred:* Bob? I'd like to talk with you a bit. This last production report shows you came in below standard again the past week.
> *Bob:* Yeah, I guess I was a bit behind.

Immediately, Fred brought the performance gap to Bob's attention. He did this politely, but specifically and face-to-face. Bob readily admitted he had fallen behind.

> *Fred:* How do you feel about falling behind?
> *Bob:* Well, every time I get rolling I get hit with a schedule change. Sometimes they make sense, sometimes they don't. I'm not always clear about what to do. I didn't want to say much. So I just tried to struggle through on my own.

In the above exchange, Fred gave Bob a chance to express his feelings without putting him on the defensive. His next step was to try to identify the causes for Bob's substandard performance. To do this, Fred asked in a nonthreatening manner for an explanation.

> *Fred:* There certainly have been a lot of schedule changes lately. Which ones are giving you the most problems?
> *Bob:* Mostly the changes with the Series J designs. I'm just not clear on how to handle them.
> *Fred:* Yeah, they can be tricky. Have you asked anyone about them?
> *Bob:* Well, I realize the project manager has a lot on her mind. I just didn't want to bother her with my own problems. And…
> *Fred:* And?
> *Bob:* Uh…I just didn't want her to think I couldn't do the job.

This back-and-forth talk revealed Bob's belief that his performance suffered from unclear schedule changes, something beyond his control. Fred listened to the content of Bob's message and tried to understand his feelings. He also asked Bob to clarify certain points, such as the types of schedule changes he had the most problems with and the reasons why he didn't ask for help. By remaining open-minded and avoiding common attribution errors, Fred learned a lot about the possible causes of Bob's poor performance. In fact, his active listening revealed that Bob feared he would look incompetent if he brought his problems with the design changes to the project manager's attention. Next, Fred provided Bob with some immediate support to reassure him that he was viewed as a capable and trustworthy worker.

> *Fred:* You shouldn't worry about it, Bob. She thinks highly of you. In fact, she said having you here is really going to make things a lot easier. And your part of the process really counts. The project manager needs your help to meet the deadlines.
> *Bob:* Well, I thought I could work it out, even if it took extra time.
> *Fred:* I'm sure you could, Bob, with your technical skills. But on this project time counts, and there are other people here to help you when needed. It's important that you understand completely what happens when you don't make your numbers because of confusion over the schedule changes. You slow down the next process, and that compounds the schedule changes down the line. Then our standards fall off, and we risk missing the target dates. So you see, your work directly affects the overall performance of the unit.
> *Bob:* Yes, I can see where it would.

After reassuring Bob that he was viewed as a highly capable and dependable worker, Fred made sure Bob understood the implications of his substandard work. Fred explained to Bob what happened when he slowed down on the job and stressed that his performance affected the entire project. This reminded Bob that others depended on his work being done well and on time so they could meet their performance objectives. It highlighted not only the significance of his job in general, but also the significance of high performance in that job. From the perspective of House's path-goal theory, Fred clarified the path Bob needed to follow to achieve the desired goal of high performance. But Fred wasn't finished yet.

*Fred*: Bob, before going further, let's review the performance objectives we established for you. They are …(*Fred and Bob review objectives.*).

*Bob*: Yes, Fred, they're clear to me.

*Fred*: Well look, Bob, the next schedule change you get hit with, I want you to talk to the project manager or to me before it throws you behind. In the meantime, let's discuss ways of dealing with schedule changes for the Series J designs so that you know how to handle them. Then I'm sure your performance will be back up to the standard level where it belongs. Okay?

*Bob:* Okay, I'll sure feel better when things are back on track.

During this exchange Fred once again stated Bob's original and still-desired performance objectives. By doing this face-to-face, Fred reinforced the personal dimensions of their relationship, further heightened Bob's commitment to improve, and increased Bob's sense of accountability to Fred. In addition, Fred offered the support necessary for Bob to improve his performance. He urged Bob to ask for help when he ran into problems, something Bob had previously considered an unwelcome intrusion on the project manager. He further suggested that the two of them discuss how to deal with the Series J schedule changes. This was an offer of immediate help for dealing with a perceived job constraint. Finally, Fred expressed confidence that Bob would respond as expected. Bob readily agreed that he would be able to do so.

Following this discussion, Bob probably felt pretty good. Fred then made one more effort to ensure that Bob would get back on and stay on the high-performance track.

*Fred:* I feel real good about our conversation, Bob. You're a capable guy, and I know you'll be right back on top soon. Just to make sure things go okay, though, let's talk again after next week's reports are in. What do you think?

*Bob*: I'll look forward to it. It'll give us a chance to touch base.

Fred established an appropriate time frame and standards for evaluating Bob's future performance. By adding this control, he helped ensure that the promised improvements in productivity would become a reality. Bob was assured that Fred was interested in his ongoing performance and that productivity gains would receive attention. He also saw that a failure to obtain the desired results would require an explanation. By formally scheduling further meetings with Bob, Fred assured himself of opportunities to recognize performance improvements. If such improvements did not occur, the meetings would ensure that Bob's marginal performance would receive further attention before too much time had elapsed. At that point Fred could continue the process with Bob or, if he believed the job was a true mismatch, work with Bob to develop an alternative solution. Thus, the stage seemed set once again for Bob to become the high performer everyone expected him to be.

*Questions to Ask About Ability*

Has the individual performed at a higher level in the past?

Is the performance deficiency total, or is it confined to particular tasks?

How well do the individual's capabilities match the job's selection criteria?

Has the individual been properly trained for current task requirements?

*Questions to Ask About Support*

Have clear and challenging task goals been set?

Are other employees having difficulty with the same tasks?

Is the job properly designed to achieve a "best fit" with the individual's capabilities?

Do any policies and/or procedures inhibit task performance?

Is the manager providing adequate feedback?

Is the individual being fairly compensated?

Is the work environment comfortable?

Is the manager providing sufficient empathy and emotional support?

Are the individual's co-workers providing sufficient emotional support?

Has the manager actually encouraged high performance?

*Questions to Ask About Effort*

Does the individual lack enthusiasm for work in general? For the assigned tasks in particular?

Are individuals with similar abilities performing at higher levels?

Has the individual been properly recognized for past accomplishments?

Are rewards and incentives provided on a performance-contingent basis?

Is the individual aware of possible rewards and incentives?

Does the individual have an appropriate role model?

# BROAD-BASED HIGH-PERFORMANCE MANAGEMENT

Our continuing example offers managers a starting point for developing personal and situation-specific strategies for dealing with marginal performers. Of course the exact nature of the marginal performance will vary from one person to the next. Our example has dealt with only one type—the capable individual whose work efforts have declined over time. From the individual performance equation, however, we know that marginal performance can arise from a lack of ability, effort, or support, or from some combination of these factors. To deal with the uniqueness of each situation, we suggest asking the diagnostic questions listed in Exhibit II. The following guidelines also highlight useful actions.

## To Maximize Ability

The manager's task is to achieve and maintain an appropriate match between the capabilities of the marginal performer and the job he or she is asked to do. Depending on the nature of the job and the person, one of several options may be selected. In some cases the individual's abilities can be developed through training; in other cases the job may have to be changed so it better fits the individual; and in still others, individuals may have to be replaced with more capable workers. In all cases a job vacancy must be recognized for what it is—perhaps the manager's greatest opportunity to build high-performance potential into a system by hiring a person whose talents and interests match the job's requirements.

Earlier we noted that repeated exposure to failure and punishment can lead to learned helplessness. Because the ability deficits are more imagined than real, however, individuals suffering from learned helplessness will need help in refocusing their concerns toward other performance factors. Take, for example, the case of a newly appointed manager who inherits a team of marginal performers who had received little or no support from their previous supervisor. To restore their feelings of competence, the manager must first help them understand that any past performance problems were not due to a lack of ability. This is the first step of a "turnaround" strategy.

## To Maximize Support

The manager's task here is to 1) help marginal performers secure the resources they need to achieve high levels of job performance, and 2) help remove any and all obstacles that inhibit high performance. Success with this factor sometimes requires a dramatic change in the way managers view their responsibilities. Rather than simply being the person who directs and controls the work of others, an effective manager always acts to facilitate their accomplishments. This involves doing much more than telling employees what to do and then following up on them. The truly effective manager creates a supportive work environment by clarifying performance expectations, changing job designs, providing immediate feedback, fostering better interpersonal relations, and eliminating unnecessary rules, procedures, and other job constraints.

Consider again the case of the newly appointed supervisor. Support is an especially critical component of an effort to alleviate learned helplessness. Once marginal performers are convinced through attributional training that they do have the ability required to perform, they must be further persuaded that they will receive the support required to excel. The manager should engage marginal performers in dialogues that identify the types of external support needed to help them apply their abilities to best advantage. Ideally initial task assignments will then be created to produce successful experiences that further bolster employees' newfound self-confidence.

## To Maximize Effort

Basic principles of motivation and positive reinforcement should be applied whenever managers deal with marginal performers. First, the marginal performer should be made aware whenever his or her performance falls below standard. He or she should also be told how substandard performance adversely impacts other workers, subunits, and the organization as a whole. Immediate positive reinforcement should follow performance improvements and all above-standard achievements. Punishment should be avoided. By serving as an enthusiastic role model, a supervisor can further help marginal performers become high achievers.

For the new supervisor dealing with a group of marginal performers, strategies to correct ability and support deficits must be accompanied by assurances that high performance will lead to desired outcomes. The most powerful means of persuasion are successful experiences clearly followed by positive reinforcement—praise, recognition, and other valued rewards. It is also helpful to provide positive role models who obtain desired rewards through skilled utilization and task accomplishment.

Finally, it is important to note that managers' motivational attempts gain leverage from ability and support efforts. The key is what psychologists call the *effectance motive,* a natural motivation that occurs from feelings of self-efficacy. When people feel competent in their work, the argument goes, they can be expected to work harder at it. Competence, in turn, comes from ability and the feeling that one's skills and aptitudes are equal to the tasks at hand. Competence also comes from support and the feeling that one's work environment helps, rather than hinders, task accomplishment.

It is said that the very best motivation is that which comes from within. Thus, managers can gain additional motivational impact by investing in ability and support factors. To the extent that greater perceived ability and support enhance one's sense of competence, internal motivation is a likely consequence. Rather than concentrating only on motivational strategies designed to encourage more work effort externally, managers should make sure they take full advantage of the improved internal motivation that may be derived when ability and support factors are addressed.

## A VAST POOL OF RESOURCES

Marginal performers present significant challenges to their managers—but they also represent a vast pool of human resources with the potential to offer major productivity gains to their organizations. To capitalize on this potential, managers must be committed to working with marginal performers to identify the causes of their problems and take positive actions to move them toward greater accomplishments. The individual performance equation can provide managers with the insight they need to tap the true potential of the marginal performer. Specifically, it directs a manager's attention toward three major factors that influence individual performance—the often neglected support factor as well as the more commonly recognized ability and effort factors. Guided by this action framework, managers can take advantage of every interaction and every conversation with marginal performers to pursue their turnaround strategies. In the final analysis, the foundations for high-performance management rest with the managers themselves. To achieve the desired results, managers must:

• *Recognize that marginal performers are potential sources of major productivity gains for organizations.* At the very least, they must be considered just as important as any other human resource within the organization.

• *Recognize the need to implement positive turnaround strategies for dealing with marginal performers.* Systematic and well-considered attention, rather than outright neglect and even punishment, is the order of the day—every day of a manager's workweek.

• *Be ready to accept at least partial responsibility for the fact that a subordinate has become a marginal performer.* Many workers learn to be marginal performers from the way they are treated in the workplace—they don't start out to be that way. Bob, for one, sure didn't.

## ACKNOWLEDGMENT

The case setting for this article was developed from a vignette presented in Wilson Learning Corporation's instructional video "Dealing with the Marginal Performer" (*Building Leadership Skills*, New York: Wiley, 1986) and examined in William L. Gardner's accompanying instructor's guide. The initial four dialogues reported here are loosely adapted from the video. We are indebted to Wilson Learning Corporation and John Wiley & Sons for allowing us to build upon this case framework.

# 18

# Performance Appraisal

PERFORMANCE APPRAISAL REVISITED
 *Edward E. Lawler III*
 *Allan M. Mohrman, Jr.*
 *Susan M. Resnick*

ON THE FOLLY OF REWARDING A, WHILE HOPING FOR B
 *Steven Kerr*

## PERFORMANCE APPRAISAL REVISITED

*Edward E. Lawler III*
*Allan M. Mohrman, Jr.*
*Susan M. Resnick*

For decades performance appraisal has been a much discussed and studied practice. It is also one that has produced a great deal of frustration and a never-ending search for the "right" system. As part of this search, organizations seem to be regularly changing their systems in the hope that they will find the answer. Our study reports on the results of one company's search and suggests that the system may not be the solution.

One of the most influential series of studies was done by the General Electric (GE) Company during the early 1960s. Publication of these results in a *Harvard Business Review* article in 1965 led a number of corporations to revise their performance appraisal practices, and in important respects changed the way appraisal is conceptualized by researchers and managers (Meyer, Kay and French, 1965). Among the key recommendations in this article were to separate pay discussions from performance appraisal and to use a process called *work planning and review*. In this process, specific objectives are identified in advance of a performance period; then, at the end of the period, results are reviewed against these objectives.

*Source*: Reprinted by permission of the publisher, from *Organizational Dynamics*, Summer 1984. © 1984 American Management Association, New York. All rights reserved.

The years since the publication of the seminal GE study have seen performance appraisal emerge as an increasingly important issue in organizations. Growing concern about productivity and legal issues surrounding age, sex, and race discrimination have brought the performance appraisal practices of organizations into even sharper focus. In addition, current thinking about effective human resources management more and more places performance appraisal at the center of integrated human resources management systems. For example, it is often noted that performance appraisal needs to be very clearly related to the pay system, the career-development system, and the selection system and, in turn, needs to flow from the way job design is approached in the organization.

Finally, it is important that the appraisal system measure and reward behaviors that support the organization's strategic objectives. Thus, if an organization wishes to have an integrated human resources management system that supports its business plan, performance appraisal of some form or another is a necessity, not an option. Further, it is something that should not be done poorly. Its inputs are so vital to the successful operation of other human resources management systems that, if it is done poorly, the overall human resources management system is destined to be ineffective.

At least two perspectives must be accounted for in assessing any performance appraisal system. There is 1) the effectiveness of the system as judged by the management or the appraisers and there is 2) the effectiveness of the system as judged by the subordinate employees or the appraisers. Ideally, performance appraisal should meet the needs of both. If it is to meet the needs of employees, it must help them know the organization's official view of their work, their chances for advancement and salary increases within the organization, and ways they can improve their performance to better meet their own and the organization's goals. If it is to meet the typical goals of the organization, performance appraisal must help the organization utilize the skills of its employees, and motivate and develop them to perform effectively.

Although increased interests in performance appraisals has led to a great deal of research, much of it has focused only on the mechanics of measurement and the appraisal forms. Research, for example, has compared the advantages of five-point versus seven-point scales versus management by objectives system, and so on. For years we have suspected that research focusing on the form itself and on the mechanics of appraisal is missing many important issues involved in designing and managing performance appraisal systems.

Thus, when the General Electric Company asked us if we would be interested in doing a study on the impact and the organizational role of their performance appraisal practices, we were delighted. It promised the opportunity to look at a corporation that for several decades has seriously studied and worked on performance appraisal, and a chance to go beyond focusing only on the nuts and bolts of the performance appraisal system in the context of an organization and its jobs and to test emerging notions of the multiple functions of performance appraisal.

After briefly describing the study, we will discuss what managers and employees believed the performance appraisal system should be like and should accomplish; then we will discuss actual performance appraisal practices and some determinants of appraisal effectiveness. Finally, we make recommendations for organizations that are considering changing their performance appraisal systems. Our recommendations are not based solely on our GE experience, however. We have since done similar research in a number of other organizational settings. Our findings continue to confirm the patterns first noted at GE.

# STUDY DESCRIPTION

Interviews, questionnaires, and personnel records served as the major data sources for the study. We interviewed personnel executives and other top level executives, with numerous manager-subordinate pairs among them. In addition, we collected questionnaire data from 700 manager-subordinate pairs from all levels of management and all functional areas in the "exempt" population. In half the cases, the person being appraised was also responsible for appraising the performance of others. Half of the pairs we studied completed questionnaires both before and after a performance appraisal while other pairs completed questionnaires only after the event. This was done in order to eliminate from our results any effects of filling out a questionnaire before the appraisal. Interestingly, this proved unnecessary as the results were the same for both groups. Therefore, the results reported in Exhibits I–V, while based on a sample size of 320 manager-subordinate pairs who filled out the "before" and "after" questionnaires, also reflect the responses of the 400 pairs who filled out an "after only" version of the questionnaire.

Often, researchers question whether research findings from a single organization can be generalized. This study minimized such concerns by including many different types of organizations within the General Electric Corporation. We intentionally picked nine very different businesses in the company. This is exemplified by the fact that performance appraisal was done in widely varying ways in these sites. For example, performance appraisal was conducted at regular intervals at eight sites, but only sometimes at one site. We found more than 50 different performance appraisal forms in use across the nine sites, along with variations in such features as how often and when the performance appraisal was done. (One organization even gave its appraisers a booklet containing ten different forms and told them to pick the one they preferred.) Additional variations involved whether and how appraisal was linked with pay, manpower planning, promotion, and the job itself.

When studied 20 years ago, few GE employees could cite any examples of constructive action— or even significant improvement—that stemmed from suggestions received in a performance appraisal interview with their boss. Today, as Exhibit I shows, managers and subordinates believe that appraisal practices do indeed make a difference to the organization as a whole by fostering motivation, productive changes in behavior, and increased understanding. Both groups believe that their appraisals provide accurate feedback and are based on general agreement about performance criteria (although subordinates were considerably less sanguine than the managers). But, like their colleagues 20 years ago, only a minority in each group thought these practices would occur if they were not organizational requirements.

In addition to documenting attitudes, the earlier General Electric study made recommendations about the appropriate practice of performance appraisal. One recommendation was that appraisal should be based on mutually agreed-upon goals. Interestingly, when asked about specific practices that should be part of the appraisal process, the GE employees now mention that performance appraisal should be based on goals previously agreed to by the appraiser and the subordinate. And, in the spirit of the earlier recommendations, today's appraisers and subordinates believe that an employee's self-appraisal should be an important part of performance appraisal. In contrast to the recommendations of the earlier study, there is strong support for the proposition that performance evaluation should be integrated with other human resources systems. The GE respondents believed evaluations should be done for more than developmental purposes and should be an important determinant of salary and promotions.

Appraisers and subordinates had differing beliefs in three areas concerning the purposes of performance appraisal (see Exhibit II). Appraisers, more than subordinates, believed that one purpose of performance appraisal should be to allow subordinates to have input on the definition of work;

subordinates, more than appraisers, believed that a purpose was to explain and communicate pay decisions and to mutually plan future work goals. These discrepancies in beliefs suggest the differing needs appraisers and subordinates bring to performance appraisal. For example, because employees look to the performance appraisal session to let them know how they stand vis-à-vis the other human resources systems ,and what the future holds for them, the discussion of pay is more salient to them than to management.

EXHIBIT I   General Beliefs About Performance Appraisal[1]

|  |  | Disagree | Neutral | Agree |
|---|---|---|---|---|
| 1. PA *should* be done *only* for the subordinate's | appraisers | 78 | 7 | 15 |
| personal development. | subordinates | 71 | 9 | 20 |
| 2. Salary and promotion decisions *should* be | appraisers | 5 | 3 | 92 |
| based on PA results. | subordinates | 12 | 3 | 85 |
| 3. Salary and promotion decisions are based on | appraisers | 24 | 8 | 68 |
| PA results. | subordinates | 41 | 10 | 49 |
| 4. PA practices provide accurate feedback to the | appraisers | 22 | 6 | 72 |
| the subordinate and superiors and subordinates | subordinates | 36 | 8 | 55 |
| agree on what constitutes good or poor |  |  |  |  |
| performance. |  |  |  |  |
| 5. PA makes a difference. It motivates | appraisers | 17 | 9 | 74 |
| employees, leads to more productive behavior, | subordinates | 25 | 13 | 62 |
| and increases understanding about the |  |  |  |  |
| subordinate's role. |  |  |  |  |
| 6. Superiors and subordinates carry out PA | appraisers | 35 | 8 | 57 |
| activities only because the organization | subordinates | 28 | 9 | 63 |
| requires it. |  |  |  |  |
| 7. Subordinate's PA *should* be based on goals | appraisers | 4 | 3 | 93 |
| previously agreed to by the superior and | subordinates | 8 | 5 | 87 |
| subordinate. |  |  |  |  |
| 8. A subordinate's self-appraisal *should* be an | appraisers | 6 | 4 | 90 |
| important part of PA. | subordinates | 8 | 6 | 86 |

[1]Percents of those answering the questions are reported.

Overall, the data from General Electric show a fairly consistent and well-developed set of beliefs about performance appraisal. Despite the fact that a variety of practices and procedures are used within the company, the overall view is clear that performance appraisal should be done, that it has an organizational impact, that it needs to be organizationally required, that it should be based on goals, and that it should determine such things as pay and promotion. The data also highlight the fact that appraisers and subordinates bring different needs and hopes to the appraisal event.

EXHIBIT II   Possible Instrumental Purposes of Performance Appraisal: Extent to Which
They Should Be Fulfilled

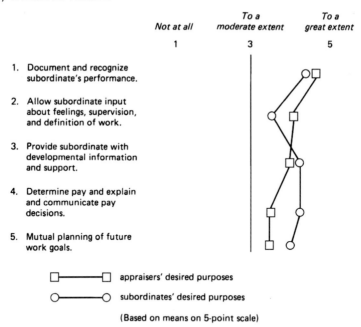

|  | Not at all | To a moderate extent | To a great extent |
|---|---|---|---|
|  | 1 | 3 | 5 |

1. Document and recognize subordinate's performance.

2. Allow subordinate input about feelings, supervision, and definition of work.

3. Provide subordinate with developmental information and support.

4. Determine pay and explain and communicate pay decisions.

5. Mutual planning of future work goals.

□————□   appraisers' desired purposes

○————○   subordinates' desired purposes

(Based on means on 5-point scale)

## THE PRACTICE OF PERFORMANCE APPRAISAL

Having looked at what appraisers and subordinates believe should happen in performance appraisal, we now turn to a discussion of what they actually experience.

In general, performance appraisal interviews were called on short notice and took less than an hour. These results seem to indicate a rather casual approach to performance appraisal and thus are of some significance in and of themselves. They become more interesting, however, when we compare the participants' views about what occurred in the appraisal and their reactions to the event.

Overall, the subordinates' attitude toward the appraisal event was much more negative than that of the appraisers. Although appraisers tended to know about the appraisal in advance, subordinates were more often surprised. Appraisers also tended to see the appraisal meeting as lasting much longer than did the subordinates. In general appraisers were satisfied with the duration of time while subordinates would have liked more. Subordinates also saw more distractions and interruptions and generally felt the appraisal did not get the time that it warranted.

On the positive side, both parties at least agreed that the appraisal took place. In other companies we have studied, there is sometimes no agreement on whether the appraisal has taken place! The superior typically reports that it has, while the subordinate says it hasn't. One director of human resources, frustrated by employees' complaints that they hadn't received performance appraisals and by their managers' insistence on having given the appraisals, suggested that managers keep a banner in their upper left-hand drawer—a banner that reads, "This is your performance appraisal." The banner can be unfurled and placed over their desk at the appropriate time. In addition to this solution, there are other, less theatrical and more effective ones for improving the practice of performance appraisal in the eyes of the subordinate.

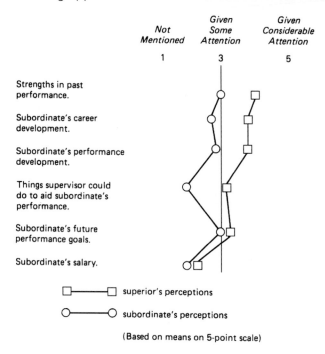

(Based on means on 5-point scale)

Appraisers were quite clear that things really important to them were discussed in the appraisal event. For example, 82 percent said that such matters were discussed to a great extent. The situation was quite different with respect to subordinates: Only 46 percent of them felt that things important to them were discussed to a great extent.

With respect to decision making, subordinates (much more than appraisers) saw the most important decisions as being made primarily by the appraisers. Similarly, with respect to communication, the subordinates saw communication as coming mostly from their appraiser; appraisers saw the communication patterns as more balanced.

As mentioned earlier, both appraisers and their subordinates were in agreement that performance appraisals should be based on previously agreed-to goals and subordinates' self-appraisals. In practice, however, these expectations were not always fulfilled. Self-appraisals, for example, were used to only a moderate extent or less in about half the appraisals. While slightly over half the appraisers believed that the appraisal was based on predetermined goals to more than a moderate extent, only one-third of the subordinates corroborated these observations.

Earlier we noted that, in order to meet the needs of the subordinate *and* the organization, the appraisal had to deal with a number of issues. Exhibit III shows the reported content of the discussion during the performance appraisal session. In general, appraisers report giving more attention to each topic than do subordinates. Nevertheless, they do tend to agree on which areas get the most attention and which get the least. Both agree that strengths in past performance got the most attention while salary received the least.

This is quite consistent with respondents' beliefs that the primary purpose of performance appraisal is to document a subordinate's performance. It is also consistent with the recommendations of the earlier GE study to separate discussion of salary from the performance appraisal session.

However, it is in conflict with what needs to happen if the appraisal is to meet the needs of the subordinate and to provide the kind of data that link it to other human resources management systems.

In summary, although there are significant disagreements between managers and employees about what goes on during performance appraisal, some general conclusions can be reached. Performance appraisals seem to be events that focus on performance and content important to appraisers, take place in a relatively short period of time, and are not, according to subordinates, necessarily scheduled in advance. In addition, they usually do not include an employee's self-appraisal or a discussion of salary—and, depending on whom you ask, they may or may not be based on mutually agreed-to goals.

## EFFECTIVENESS OF THE APPRAISAL PROCESS

Both appraisers and subordinates were asked to judge the extent to which the five possible purposes shown in Exhibit II were accomplished by their appraisal. Exhibit IV shows the responses for appraisers and Exhibit V shows them for the appraisers' subordinates. As can be seen, appraisers were generally more satisfied that the appraisal met their purposes than the subordinates were that it met theirs. The overall pattern suggests that existing performance appraisal practices were most effective in documenting performance and recognizing it. But the appraisal clearly failed to deal with pay, planning, and developmental issues as fully as the subordinates would have liked. In other words, the performance appraisal system is falling short in meeting the employees' needs.

In interviews with manager-subordinate pairs, a discrepancy commonly arises. Managers feel that they have spent time discussing the larger picture of the subordinate's career and life within the organization. Yet when subordinates are asked about the amount of time spent discussing their development and career, they frequently say they would have liked more, or that it was not discussed at all, or that it was discussed only in passing.

At first, these opposite reactions surprised us. In fact, there was an initial question on whether the interview schedule was correct—whether the two people involved really were an appraiser-subordinate pair. Then we considered the amount of time spent on the subordinate's development at work in general. In the hustle-bustle of the work day, a subordinate's development is often forgotten. So subordinates often look forward to the performance appraisal session as a time to focus on *their* work and *their* development. Their managers, however, have a different perspective: one of managing a unit, having their own performance judged (one H. R. director commented, "After all, we are all subordinates, aren't we?"), and being unsure of what their own career path or future in the organization looks like; thus they have generally offered all that they know (which may not be much) or that they are comfortable sharing. It is not surprising, then, that we interviewed subordinates who hungered for information about their career development in the organization, or out of the organization, and felt shortchanged by their appraisal in this regard. Nor is it surprising that this hunger tends to come particularly from younger employees, generally in their twenties; from women returning to work; or from employees of all ages in companies undergoing reorganization.

These unmet needs are reflected in the subordinates' satisfaction—or dissatisfaction—with the appraisal system. Only about half of them report being satisfied with the appraisal or feeling good about the way it was conducted. In comparison, over 80 percent of the appraisers report being satisfied or feeling good about the event.

EXHIBIT IV   Appraisers' Desired Instrumental Purposes vs. Perceived Occurrences

|  | Not at all | To a moderate extent | To a great extent |
|---|---|---|---|
|  | 1 | 3 | 5 |

1. Document and recognize subordinate's performance.

2. Allow subordinate input about feelings, supervision, and definition of work.

3. Provide subordinate with developmental information and support.

4. Determine pay and explain and communicate pay decisions.

5. Mutual planning of future work goals.

☐————☐   appraisers' desired purposes

○————○   subordinates' desired purposes

(Based on means on 5-point scale)

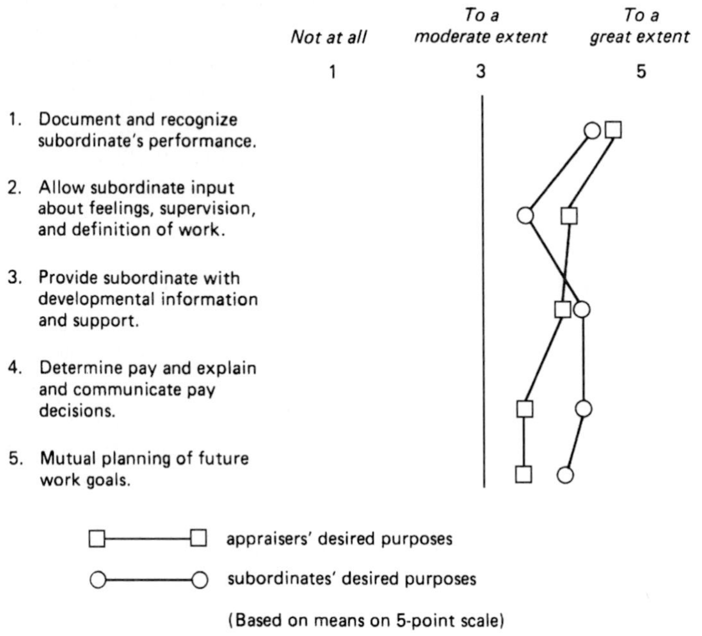

EXHIBIT V  Subordinates' Desired Instrumental Purposes vs. Perceived Occurrences

1. Document and recognize subordinate's performance.

2. Allow subordinate input about feelings, supervision, and definition of work.

3. Provide subordinate with developmental information and support.

4. Determine pay and explain and communicate pay decisions.

5. Mutual planning of future work goals.

☐————☐   subordinates' desired purposes

○————○   subordinate's perceptions of actuality

542

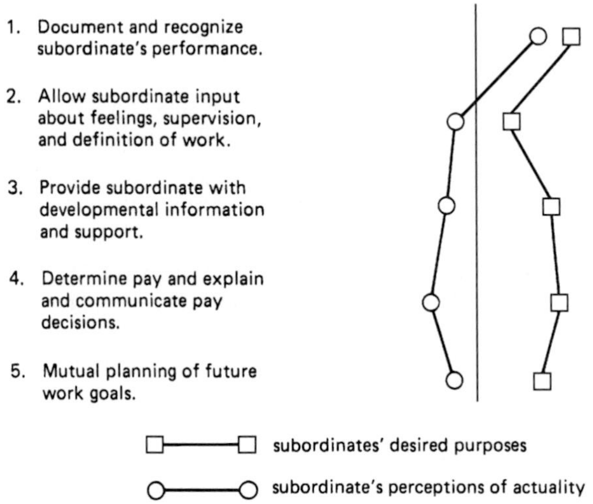

Other data collected to test the effectiveness of the appraisal process also showed great differences between appraisers and subordinates. Not only do a substantial majority of appraisers report learning from the event themselves, they also feel that the appraisal gave subordinates a clearer understanding of their duties and responsibilities, a clearer idea of what is expected of them, and other useful information.

The subordinates were much less likely to see these positive results from the appraisal event. For example: Although 53 percent of the managers reported that the employees' behavior improved after the appraisal, only 41 percent of the employees felt that this was the case.

With respect to the subordinate's overall performance rating, a familiar pattern appeared. That is, subordinates tended to rate their own performance much higher than did the appraisers. Our study of this issue, however, did not stop with simply asking appraisers and subordinates to rate the subordinates' performance. We also asked them both before and after the appraisal to estimate what they thought each other's appraisal of the subordinate's performance was. Interestingly, we found that both before and after the appraisal the subordinate had a clear, generally accurate perception of the appraiser's point of view. The superior was not as accurate about the subordinate's view, but was aware that an important discrepancy existed. Thus, although they disagreed on the absolute level of the subordinate's performance, they were both aware that some disagreement existed, and the subordinates knew rather accurately the nature and extent of the disagreement. This is a particularly important point because it suggests that although appraisers are frequently going to be in the position of delivering a negative message, the message typically does not come as a surprise to the subordinate.

In summary, the appraisal process gets very different marks depending on whether the perspective is that of appraisers or that of subordinates. Appraisers, who of course are largely in control of the event, feel that it generally meets their needs. On the other hand, subordinates recognize the importance of the process, but feel that it falls short of meeting their needs.

# DETERMINANTS OF PERFORMANCE APPRAISAL EFFECTIVENESS

Given these differing views of performance appraisal and the need for it to serve the purposes of both parties, we decided to determine both 1) the characteristics that leave both appraisers and subordinates with a perception of positive outcomes from the appraisal process and 2) those that merely lead subordinates to feel their needs are met (since our research suggests that if either party's needs are likely to go unmet it is the subordinates'). In looking for these characteristics we focused on the organizational context and the processes and procedures of the performance appraisal system.

## Climate

The general climate of the organization seemed to have a significant impact on how well the performance appraisal process went. When the climate was one of high trust, support, and openness, appraisers and subordinates alike saw performance appraisal as going better. In these instances both reported greater emphasis on the subordinate's development, greater participation and contribution by the subordinate, and a higher degree of trust, openness, and constructiveness during the appraisal interview. In other words, in an environment of high trust the performance appraisal system is more likely to meet the individual subordinate's developmental needs.

Another organization studied illustrates how the climate or culture of the organization created its own definition for mutual goal setting. The organization was highly autocratic and hierarchical; subordinates had rarely been asked their opinion about anything, particularly their own performance. (In fact, these subordinates were so unused to stating their opinions that when an attitude survey was administered which asked what they thought should be accomplished by performance appraisal systems, there was an inordinate amount of missing data.) In interviews of several manager-and-subordinate pairs about a new appraisal system based on mutual goal setting, the managers typically reported that mutual goal setting took place, while the subordinates typically reported being "goaled." This organization's culture leads its people to conclude that mutual goal setting occurs when the subordinate is present while the manager presents the goals.

## Job Content

The content of the subordinate's job was another important factor in determining how the appraisal went. In general, jobs that met the characteristics of being enriched tended to have better performance appraisals. Enriched tasks exhibit these characteristics: 1) people performing them have a whole piece of work to do and are responsible for the methods and procedures used in carrying out this whole piece of work and 2) the jobs themselves allow feedback—that is, subordinates know from the work itself whether or not they accomplished their tasks and the precise results of their labors. Specifically, subordinates who thought of their jobs as being enriched were more satisfied and enthusiastic about the appraisal; felt they had participated and contributed; and felt the atmosphere to have been trusting, friendly, and open. On the other hand, there was no evidence that appraisers saw the outcome of the appraisal process more favorably when the content of the subordinate's job was enriched.

Subordinates also rated the degree to which their jobs were clear, well specified, and well defined. When subordinates saw well-defined job procedures, goals, priorities, and responsibilities, they felt not only that the appraisal achieved the same qualities perceived by those with enriched jobs, but also that it led to a higher degree of learning, more focus on development, more discussion of ways to improve weaknesses, more discussion of future goals, and more discussion of how managers could aid employees. In short, well-specified jobs led to constructive appraisal events. As was the case with enriched jobs, appraisers did not tend to report more favorable outcomes when jobs were well specified.

In sum, subordinates who view their jobs as enriched or well-specified are more likely to perceive the performance appraisal as meeting their needs. Job content, however, seemed to have little impact on the appraiser's reaction.

## Pay Discussion

Having discussed contextual issues and their relationship to performance appraisal, we now turn our attention to a discussion of procedural issues and their impact. As mentioned, an important recommendation of the initial General Electric study was the separation of pay and performance appraisal discussions. Earlier we mentioned the employees' desire for pay discussions and the fact that salary was infrequently discussed during the appraisal session. A natural question then becomes, "Does the discussion of pay during the performance appraisal make a difference to the effectiveness of the appraisal?"

As the earlier General Electric study suggested, we found that the discussion of pay does make a difference. However, implications of the data are different from what the earlier study suggested. Discussion of salary change seemed to make the event go slightly but significantly better for both parties, particularly in the employee's eyes. A number of reasons for this suggest themselves—including the fact that discussing pay makes the event a more serious one and thus causes better preparation. In addition, the information content needed to justify a salary action gives the employee something to which he or she can respond. Finally, as already stressed, subordinates feel that a pay discussion *should* be part of the appraisal event. Therefore, the discussion of pay helps subordinates fulfill their needs.

## Appraisal Forms

The design of appraisal systems almost always begins (and often ends) with the design of the appraisal form to be used. As indicated, we found more than 50 different forms being used in the nine GE organizations. We even found managers who secretly used forms they had developed or brought with them from other companies. Many forms were hybrids, combinations, and recombinations of one another and of almost all prominent approaches to appraisal forms in general use. Overall, we found that form content had little if any effect on the actual appraisal event.

## Work Planning

Another major recommendation of the initial General Electric study was the use of a work planning and review process. Performance appraisal research has long held that the use of such a *process* will lead to performance improvement. Nevertheless, many system administrators have painstakingly designed a form and assumed a process would ensue. Fortunately, this study gave us the opportunity to investigate not only the impact of work planning, but also the impact a form can have on the way the appraisal is done.

When we compared appraisals using forms with work-planning components and those not mentioning work planning, we found no difference in the extent to which work planning and associated practices such as goal setting took place. Form content had no effect on perceptions of whether work planning actually took place. We have found many superiors in GE and elsewhere who are expert at getting the form filled out and signed without having *the process* take place. Nevertheless, when the process of work planning was done it lead to performance improvement and to a generally more successful appraisal in the eyes of both parties.

## Subordinate Input

Although the form had no effect, two procedures did affect perceptions of work planning. If the subordinate compiled information before the review, or if the appraisal form was completed during or after the appraisal session, both manager and employee perceived that work planning took place. In addition to affecting perceptions of work planning, these procedures led to a greater feeling of ownership by subordinates for the performance appraisal event. These findings, combined with several others, tend to confirm the validity of the point made in numerous articles on performance appraisals—namely, that the more active the subordinate is and the more influence the subordinate has on the appraisal process, the more likely it is that the appraisal process will meet all its objectives.

# RECOMMENDATIONS

Our results suggest some general advice that can be given to any organization. First, they suggest that performance appraisal should be a key link in the overall human resources management strategy. Both managers and subordinates think that it should have an important overall role and that it should accomplish a number of objectives vital to organizational effectiveness. These include defining work roles, motivating performance, and aiding the subordinate's development. In order to accomplish all these, a performance appraisal cannot be a casual activity. It must be an important part of the culture and activities in the organization. The tone set by appraisal has important ramifications throughout all other processes of human resource management. General Electric, as a result of the research, decided to continue to put a strong emphasis on performance appraisal as a management tool rather than to diminish their focus on it.

Our data strongly suggest that the answer to doing a performance appraisal well lies in focusing on the process of the appraisal and on the organizational context in which the event takes place, not on the form or system. This recommendation is in direct contrast to the emphasis usually placed on the form.

Issues like culture, job design, the relationship between pay and performance, the timing of career-development discussions, and the degree to which the process encourages subordinates to become equal partners all seem to be more important than the form used. Let us briefly comment on what may need to be done in each of these areas.

1. In the area of culture, appraisal seems to be influenced by a number of larger trends and factors that cannot be treated here, but some specifics are worth mentioning. At the very least, top management needs to take performance appraisal seriously, to explicitly fit it to the prevailing culture and human resource strategy, to evaluate how well it does fit, to encourage practices that do fit, and to reward superiors and subordinates who do it well. All this has a decided impact on whether supervisors take it seriously and spend the time and effort needed to do it well. It is also important that superiors at higher managerial levels model the type of appraisal behavior they wish superiors lower down in the organization to demonstrate. In short, appraisal needs to be real and effective at higher organizational levels.

2. It seems clear that poor job designs can make performance appraisals ineffective. This suggests that a strong emphasis be placed on early definition of the nature of the job for which a subordinate is to be held accountable and on how performance on that job is going to be measured. Here, work on job enrichment seems appropriate and, as such, should be an integral part of the job definition process. In the absence of well-defined and well-designed jobs, the appraisal process is doomed from the beginning. To the extent that jobs cannot be predefined—and there are good reasons to legitimately expect this in some settings—the appraisal system needs to recognize that the appraisal itself will in part need to function as a process of job definition. If both parties are to agree on the definition and design of the job, then the appraisal process will benefit from mutual participation.

3. Our data suggest that pay actions and consequences should be a natural part of the appraisal discussion. Efforts to separate them seem to be more counterproductive than productive, no matter how well intentioned—especially in organizational contexts that stress pay for performance. Thus our recommendation is that they be made an important part of the appraisal process.

4. Our data suggest that the area that gets the least attention—yet is very important to subordinates—is career development. Some parts of General Electric successfully handled this as a different process. Our suggestion is that other organizations should do this as well. That is, at a different time and as part of a different system, organizations should put into place a joint process in which superiors and subordinates work through the kind of career opportunities that exist, the kind of developmental

needs the subordinates have, and the kind of career track that a subordinate can reasonably aspire to. This is, appropriately, part of another future-oriented system that is integrated into the overall human resources management system. Nevertheless, as in the case of pay, past performance is an important element in career discussions and vice versa. Superiors should therefore talk about such connections during the appraisal event. This should be particularly emphasized when a merit promotion policy is in effect.

5. Specific steps should be built into the procedure to assure that the subordinate is an active partner in defining the performance appraisal process. We found appraisals more effective, for example, when the subordinate shared a self-appraisal of his or her performance with the supervisor before a final appraisal judgment was reached. For this to happen, it is important that the subordinate participate in defining the job and pinpointing the measures that will be used in the performance appraisal. In short, if the appraisal process is to be of mutual benefit, it must be a mutual process; therefore, anything that encourages this two-way exchange of information is desirable. This is, of course, one way to get the manager out of the role of judge so that he or she can help the subordinate take responsibility for the outcome of the overall process. If subordinates are to become an active part of the appraisal process, *they* (and not just the appraisers) need training and orientation for this role.

## CONCLUSIONS

Overall, the study results point out just how complex the performance appraisal process is and emphasize the importance of doing it well. It is not an optional activity for organizations that want to have an effective human resources management system. It is significant that a corporation like General Electric, which has spent decades improving its performance appraisal process, is still questioning how well it is doing performance appraisals. Somewhat discouragingly, the data show a considerable gap between what their system might accomplish and what it actually accomplishes. GE's willingness to take an objective look at such an important part of their human resources management system is greatly to GE's credit. It is also to their credit that they acted upon the study results and made important changes in their corporate policy. In many respects, General Electric can serve as a model for other corporations.

Finally, with respect to the specifics of performance appraisal, several important messages emerge. Quick fixes that make alterations in forms are no more likely to be successful here than are quick fixes in other areas. Performance appraisal in an organization is only as good as its overall human resources climate, strategy, and policies, and especially its processes of fitting it to these. It is unrealistic to expect to have an effective performance appraisal system where jobs are poorly designed, the culture is negative, and subordinates are asked to be passive and do what they are told.

Performance appraisal is both a personal event between two people who have an ongoing relationship and a bureaucratic event that is needed to maintain an organization's human resource management system. Therefore, it is a major mechanism for integrating the individual and the organization. As such, it will always be subject to contradictory purposes, misperceptions, miscommunications, and some ineffectiveness. On the other hand, our data suggest that there are some ways to make it go better and that it is worth investing time and effort to do it well. At best, it's two people sharing their perceptions of each other, their relationships, their work, and their organization—sharing that results in better performance, better feelings, and a more effective organization. At its worst, it is one person in the name of the organization trying to force his or her will on another with the result of miscommunication, misperception, disappointment, and alienation. The best is achievable, but only with considerable effort, careful design, constant attention to process, and support by top management.

## SELECTED BIBLIOGRAPHY

The following is offered as suggested reading for those interested in pursuing the topic of performance appraisal:

D. L. DeVries, A. M. Morrison, S. L. Shullman, and M. L. Geriach's *Performance Appraisal on the Line* (Wiley-Interscience, 1981).

G. P. Latham and K. N. Wexley's *Increasing Productivity Through Performance Appraisal* (Addison-Wesley, 1981).

E. E. Lawler's *Pay and Organization Development* (Addison-Wesley, 1981).

H. H. Meyer, E. Kay, and J. R. P. French's "Split Roles in Performance Appraisal" (*Harvard Business Review*, January–February 1965).

A. M. Mohrman and E. E. Lawler's "Motivation and Performance Appraisal Behavior," a chapter in *Performance Measurement and Theory*, F. Landy and S. Zedeck (eds.) (Erlbaum, 1983).

# ON THE FOLLY OF REWARDING A, WHILE HOPING FOR B

*Steven Kerr*

Whether dealing with monkeys, rats, or human beings, it is hardly controversial to state that most organisms seek information concerning what activities are rewarded, and then seek to do (or at least pretend to do) those things, often to the virtual exclusion of activities not rewarded. The extent to which this occurs of course will depend on the perceived attractiveness of the rewards offered, but neither operant nor expectancy theorists would quarrel with the essence of this notion.

Nevertheless, numerous examples exist of reward systems that are fouled up in that behaviors which are rewarded are those which the rewarder is trying to *discourage*, while the behavior he desires is not being rewarded at all.

In an effort to understand and explain this phenomenon, this paper presents examples from society, from organizations in general, and from profit-making firms in particular. Data from a manufacturing company and information from an insurance firm are examined to demonstrate the consequences of such reward systems for the organizations involved, and possible reasons why such reward systems continue to exist are considered.

## SOCIETAL EXAMPLES

### Politics

Official goals are "purposely vague and general and do not indicate...the host of decisions that must be made among alternative ways of achieving official goals and the priority of multiple goals..." (8, p. 66). They usually may be relied on to offend absolutely no one, and in this sense can be considered high-acceptance, low-quality goals. An example might be "build better schools." Operative goals are

*Source*: Reprinted from *Academy of Management Journal,* 1975, vol. 18, pp. 769–83.

higher in quality but lower in acceptance, since they specify where the money will come from, what alternative goals will be ignored, etc.

The American citizenry supposedly wants its candidates for public office to set forth operative goals, making their proposed programs "perfectly clear," specifying sources and uses of funds, etc. However, since operative goals are lower in acceptance, and since aspirants to public office need acceptance (from at least 50.1 percent of the people), most politicians prefer to speak only of official goals, at least until after the election. They of course would agree to speak at the operative level if "punished" for not doing so. The electorate could do this by refusing to support candidates who do not speak at the operative level.

Instead, however, the American voter typically punishes (withholds support from) candidates who frankly discuss where the money will come from, rewards politicians who speaks only of official goals, but hopes that candidates (despite the reward system) will discuss the issues operatively. It is academic whether it was moral for Nixon, for example, to refuse to discuss his 1968 "secret plan" to end the Vietnam war, his 1972 operative goals concerning the lifting of price controls, the reshuffling of his cabinet, etc. The point is that the reward system made such refusal rational.

It seems worth mentioning that no manuscript can adequately define what is "moral" and what is not. However, examination of costs and benefits, combined with knowledge of what motivates a particular individual, often will suffice to determine what for him is "rational."[1] If the reward system is so designed that it is irrational to be moral, this does not necessarily mean that immorality will result. But is this not asking for trouble?

## War

If some oversimplification may be permitted, let it be assumed that the primary goal of the organization (Pentagon, Luftwaffe, or whatever) is to win. Let it be assumed further that the primary goal of most individuals on the front lines is to get home alive. Then there appears to be an important conflict in goals—personally rational behavior by those at the bottom will endanger goal attainment by those at the top.

But not necessarily! It depends on how the reward system is set up. The Vietnam war was indeed a study of disobedience and rebellion, with terms such as "fragging" (killing one's own commanding officer) and "search and evade" becoming part of the military vocabulary. The difference in subordinates' acceptance of authority between World War II and Vietnam is reported to be considerable, and veterans of the Second World War often have been quoted as being outraged at the mutinous actions of many American soldiers in Vietnam.

Consider, however, some critical differences in the reward system in use during the two conflicts. What did the GI in World War II want? To go home. And when did he get to go home? When the war was won! If he disobeyed the orders to clean out the trenches and take the hills, the war would not be won and he would not go home. Furthermore, what were his chances of attaining his goal (getting home alive) if he obeyed the orders compared to his chances if he did not? What is being suggested is that the rational soldier in World War II, *whether patriotic or not,* probably found it expedient to obey.

Consider the reward system in use in Vietnam. What did the man at the bottom want? To go home. And when did he get to go home? When his tour of duty was over! This was the case *whether or not the war was won.* Furthermore, concerning the relative chance of getting home alive by obeying orders compared to the chance if they were disobeyed, it is worth noting that a mutineer in

---

[1]In Simon's (10, pp. 76–77) terms, a decision is "subjectively rational" if it maximizes an individual's valued outcomes so far as his knowledge permits. A decision is "personally rational" if it is oriented toward the individual's goals.

Vietnam was far more likely to be assigned rest and rehabilitation (on the assumption that fatigue was the cause) than he was to suffer any negative consequence.

In his description of the "zone of indifference," Barnard stated that "a person can and will accept a communication as authoritative only when…at the time of his decision, he believes it to be compatible with his personal interests as a whole" (1, p. 165). In light of the reward system used in Vietnam, would it not have been personally irrational for some orders to have been obeyed? Was not the military implementing a system which *rewarded* disobedience, while *hoping* that soldiers (despite the reward system) would obey orders?

## Medicine

Theoretically, a physician can make either of two types of error, and intuitively one seems as bad as the other. A doctor can pronounce a patient sick when he is actually well, thus causing him needless anxiety and expense, curtailment of enjoyable foods and activities, and even physical danger by subjecting him to needless medication and surgery. Alternately, a doctor can label a sick person well, and thus avoid treating what may be a serious, even fatal ailment. It might be natural to conclude that physicians seek to minimize both types of error.

Such a conclusion would be wrong.[2] It is estimated that numerous Americans are presently afflicted with iatrogenic (physician *caused*) illnesses (9). This occurs when the doctor is approached by someone complaining of a few stray symptoms. The doctor classifies and organizes these symptoms, gives then a name, and obligingly tells the patient what further symptoms may be expected. This information often acts as a self-fulfilling prophecy, with the result that from that day on the patient for all practical purposes is sick.

Why does this happen? Why are physicians so reluctant to sustain a type 2 error (pronouncing a sick person well) that they will tolerate many type 1 errors? Again, a look at the reward system is needed. The punishments for a type 2 error are real: guilt, embarrassment, and the threat of lawsuit and scandal. On the other hand, a type 1 error (labeling a well person sick) "is sometimes seen as sound clinical practice, indicating a healthy conservative approach to medicine" (9, p. 69). Type 1 errors also are likely to generate increased income and a stream of steady customers who, being well in a limited physiological sense, will not embarrass the doctor by dying abruptly.

Fellow physicians and the general public therefore are really *rewarding* type 1 errors and at the same time *hoping* fervently that doctors will try not to make them.

## GENERAL ORGANIZATIONAL EXAMPLES

### Rehabilitation Centers and Orphanages

In terms of the prime beneficiary classification (2, p. 42) organizations such as these are supposed to exist for the "public-in-contact," that is, clients. The orphanage therefore theoretically is interested in placing as many children as possible in good homes. However, often orphanages surround themselves with so many rules concerning the adoption that it is nearly impossible to pry a child out of the place. Orphanages may deny adoption unless the applicants are a married couple, both of the same religion as the child, without history of emotional or vocational instability, with a specified minimum income and a private room for the child, etc.

---

[2]In one study (4) of 14,867 films for signs of tuberculosis, 1,216 positive readings turned out to be clinically negative; only 24 negative readings proved clinically active, a ratio of 50 to 1.

If the primary goal is to place children in good homes, then the rules ought to constitute means toward that goal. Goal displacement results when these "means become ends-in-themselves that displace the original goals" (2, p. 229).

To some extent these rules are required by law. But the influence of the reward system on the orphanage's management should not be ignored. Consider, for example, that the:

1. Number of children enrolled often is the most important determinant of the size of the allocated budget.
2. Number of children under the director's care also will affect the size of his staff.
3. Total organizational size will determine largely the director's prestige at the annual conventions, in the community, etc.

Therefore, to the extent that staff size, total budget, and personal prestige are valued by the orphanage's executive personnel, it becomes rational for them to make it difficult for children to be adopted. After all, who wants to be the director of the smallest orphanage in the state?

If the reward system errs in the opposite direction, paying off only for placements, extensive goal displacement again is likely to result. A common example of vocational rehabilitation in many states, for example, consists of placing someone in a job for which he has little interest and few qualifications, for two months or so, and then "rehabilitating" him again in another position. Such behavior is quite consistent with the prevailing reward system, which pays off for the number of individuals placed in any position for 60 days or more. Rehabilitation counselors also confess to competing with one another to place relatively skilled clients, sometimes ignoring persons with few skills who would be harder to place. Extensively disabled clients find that counselors often prefer to work with those whose disabilities are less severe.[3]

## Universities

Society *hopes* that teachers will not neglect their teaching responsibilities but *rewards* them almost entirely for research and publications. This is most true at the large and prestigious universities. Clichés such as "good research and good teaching go together" notwithstanding, professors often find that they must choose between teaching and research-oriented activities when allocating their time. Rewards for good teaching usually are limited to outstanding teacher awards, which are given to only a small percentage of good teachers and which usually bestow little money and fleeting prestige. Punishments for poor teaching also are rare.

Rewards for research and publications, on the other hand, and punishments for failure to accomplish these, are commonly administered by universities at which teachers are employed. Furthermore, publication-oriented resumés usually will be well received at other universities, whereas teaching credentials, harder to document and quantify, are much less transferable. Consequently it is rational for university teachers to concentrate on research, even if to the detriment of teaching and at the expense of their students.

By the same token, it is rational for students to act based upon the goal displacement which has occurred within universities concerning what they are rewarded for. If it is assumed that a primary goal of a university is to transfer knowledge from teacher to student, then grades become identifiable as a means toward that goal, serving as motivational, control, and feedback devices to expedite the knowledge transfer. Instead, however, the grades themselves have become much more important for entrance to graduate school, successful employment, tuition refunds, parental respect, etc., than the knowledge or lack of knowledge they are supposed to signify.

[3]Personal interviews conducted during 1972–73.

It therefore should come as no surprise that information has surfaced in recent years concerning fraternity files for examinations, term-paper writing services, organized cheating at the service academics, and the like. Such activities constitute a personally rational response to a reward system which pays off for grades rather than knowledge.

## BUSINESS-RELATED EXAMPLES

### Ecology

Assume that the president of XYZ Corporation is confronted with the following alternatives:

1. Spend $11 million for antipollution equipment to keep from poisoning fish in the river adjacent to the plant; or
2. Do nothing, in violation of the law, and assume a one in ten chance of being caught, with a resultant $1 million fine plus the necessity of buying the equipment.

Under this not unrealistic set of choices it requires no linear program to determine that XYZ Corporation can maximize its probabilities by flouting the law. Add the fact that XYZ's president is probably being rewarded (by creditors, stockholders, and other salient parts of his task environment) according to criteria totally unrelated to the number of fish poisoned, and his probable course of action becomes clear.

### Evaluation of Training

It is axiomatic that those who care about a firm's well-being should insist that the organization get fair value for its expenditures. Yet it is commonly known that firms seldom bother to evaluate a new GRID, MBO, job enrichment program, or whatever, to see if the company is getting its money's worth. Why? Certainly it is not because people have not pointed out that this situation exists; numerous practitioner-oriented articles are written each year to just this point.

The individuals (whether in personnel, manpower planning, or wherever) who normally would be responsible for conducting such evaluations are the same ones often charged with introducing the change effort in the first place. Having convinced top management to spend the money, they usually are quite animated afterwards in collecting rigorous vignettes and anecdotes about how successful the program was. The last thing many desire is a formal systematic and revealing evaluation. Although members of top management may actually *hope* for such systematic evaluation, their reward systems continue to *reward* ignorance in this area. And if the personnel department abdicates its responsibility, who is to step into the breach? The change agent himself? Hardly! He is likely to be too busy collecting anecdotal "evidence" of his own, for use with his next client.

### Miscellaneous

Many additional examples could be cited of systems which in fact are rewarding behaviors other than those supposedly desired by the rewarder. A few of these are described briefly below.

Most coaches disdain to discuss individual accomplishments, preferring to speak of teamwork, proper attitude, and a one-for-all spirit. Usually, however, rewards are distributed according to individual performance. The college basketball player who feeds his teammates instead of shooting will not compile impressive scoring statistics and is less likely to be drafted by the pros. The ballplayer who hits to right field to advance the runners will win neither the batting nor home run titles, and will be offered smaller raises. It therefore is rational for players to think of themselves first, and the team second.

In business organizations where rewards are dispensed for unit performance or for individual goals achieved, without regard for overall effectiveness, similar attitudes often are observed. Under most Management by Objectives (MBO) systems, goals in areas where quantification is difficult often go unspecified. The organization therefore often is in a position where it *hopes* for employee effort in the areas of team building, interpersonal relations, creativity, etc., but it formally *rewards* none of these. In cases where promotions and raises are formally tied to MBO, the system itself contains a paradox in that it "asks employees to set challenging, risky goals, only to face smaller paychecks and possibly damaged careers if these goals are not accomplished" (5, p. 40).

It is *hoped* that administrators will pay attention to long-run costs and opportunities and will institute programs which will bear fruit later on. However, many organizational reward systems pay off for short-run sales and earnings only. Under such circumstances it is personally rational for officials to sacrifice long-term growth and profit (by selling off equipment and property, or by stifling research and development) for short-term advantages. This probably is most pertinent in the public sector, with the result that many public officials are unwilling to implement programs which will not show benefits by election time.

As a final, clear-cut example of a fouled-up reward system, consider the costplus contract or its next of kin, the allocation of next year's budget as a direct function of this year's expenditures. It probably is conceivable that those who award such budgets and contracts really hope for economy and prudence in spending. It is obvious, however, that adopting the proverb "to him who spends shall more be given," rewards not economy, but spending itself.

## TWO COMPANIES' EXPERIENCES

### A Manufacturing Organization

A midwest manufacturer of industrial goods had been troubled for some time by aspects of its organizational climate it believed dysfunctional. For research purposes, interviews were conducted with many employees and a questionnaire was administered on a company-wide basis, including plants and offices in several American and Canadian locations. The company strongly encouraged employee participation in the survey, and made available time and space during the workday for completion of the instrument. All employees in attendance during the day of the survey completed the questionnaire. All instruments were collected directly by the researcher, who personally administered each session. Since no one employed by the firm handled the questionnaires, and since respondent names were not asked for, it seems likely that the pledge of anonymity given was believed.

A modified version of the Expect Approval scale (7) was included as part of the questionnaire. The instrument asked respondents to indicate the degree of approval or disapproval they could expect if they performed each of the described actions. A seven-point Likert scale was used, with 1 indicating that the action would probably bring strong disapproval and 7 signifying likely strong approval.

Although normative data for this scale from studies of other organizations are unavailable, it is possible to examine fruitfully the data obtained from this survey in several ways. First, it may be worth noting that the questionnaire data corresponded closely to information gathered through interviews. Furthermore, as can be seen from the results summarized in Table 1, sizable differences between various work units, and between employees at different job levels within the same work unit, were obtained. This suggests that response bias effects (social desirability in particular loomed as a potential concern) are not likely to be severe.

Most importantly, comparisons between scores obtained on the Expect Approval scale and a statement of problems which were the reason for the survey revealed that the same behaviors which managers in each division thought dysfunctional were those which lower level employees claimed were rewarded. As compared to job levels 1 to 8 in Division B (see Table 1), those in Division A claimed a much higher acceptance by management of "conforming" activities. Between 31 and 37 percent of Division A employees at levels 1–8 stated that going along with the majority, agreeing with the boss, and staying on everyone's good side brought approval; only once (level 5–8 responses to one of the three items) did a majority suggest that such actions would generate disapproval.

Furthermore, responses from Division A workers at levels 1–4 indicate that behaviors geared toward risk avoidance were as likely to be rewarded as to be punished. Only at job levels 9 and above was it apparent that the reward system was positively reinforcing behaviors desired by top management. Overall, the same "tendencies toward conservatism and apple-polishing at the lower levels" which divisional management had complained about during the interviews were those claimed by subordinates to be the most rational course of action in light of the existing reward system. Management apparently was not getting the behaviors it was *hoping* for, but it certainly was getting the behaviors it was perceived by subordinates to be *rewarding*.

## An Insurance Firm

The Group Health Claims Division of a large eastern insurance company provides another rich illustration of a reward system which reinforces behaviors not desired by top management.

Attempting to measure and reward accuracy in paying surgical claims, the firm systematically keeps track of the number of returned checks and letters of complaint received from policyholders. However, underpayments are likely to provoke cries of outrage from the insured, while overpayments often are accepted in courteous silence. Since it often is impossible to tell from the physician's statement which of two surgical procedures, with different allowable benefits, was performed, and since writing for clarifications will interfere with other standards used by firm concerning "percentage of claims paid within two days of receipt," the new hire in more than one claims section is soon acquainted with the informal norm: "When in doubt, pay it out!"

The situation would be even worse were it not for the fact that other features of the firm's reward system tend to neutralize those described. For example, annual "merit" increases are given to all employees, in one of the following three amounts:

1. If the worker is "outstanding" (a select category, into which no more than two employees per section may be placed): 5 percent

2. If the worker is "above average" (normally all workers not "outstanding" are so rated): 4 percent

3. If the worker commits gross acts of negligence and irresponsibility for which he might be discharged in many other companies: 3 percent.

TABLE 1 Summary of Two Divisions' Data Relevant to Conforming and Risk-Avoidance Behaviors (extent to which subjects expect approval)

| Dimension | Item | Division and Sample | Total Responses | Percentage of Workers Responding | | |
|---|---|---|---|---|---|---|
| | | | | 1, 2, or 3 (Disapproval) | 4 | 5, 6, or 7 (Approval) |
| Risk avoidance | Making a risky decision based on the best information available at the time, but which turns out wrong. | A, levels 1–4 (lowest) | 127 | 61 | 25 | 14 |
| | | A, levels 5–8 | 172 | 46 | 31 | 23 |
| | | A, levels 9 and above | 17 | 41 | 30 | 30 |
| | | B, levels 1–4 (lowest) | 31 | 56 | 26 | 16 |
| | | B, levels 5–8 | 19 | 42 | 41 | 16 |
| | | B, levels 9 and above | 10 | 50 | 20 | 30 |
| Risk | Setting extremely high and challenging standards and goals, and then narrowly failing to make them. | A, levels 1–4 | 122 | 47 | 28 | 25 |
| | | A, levels 5–8 | 168 | 33 | 26 | 41 |
| | | A, levels 9+ | 17 | 24 | 6 | 70 |
| | | B, levels 1–4 | 31 | 48 | 23 | 29 |
| | | B, levels 5–8 | 18 | 17 | 33 | 50 |
| | | B, levels 9+ | 10 | 30 | 0 | 70 |

TABLE 1 (continued)

| Dimension | Item | Division and Sample | Total Responses | Percentage of Workers Responding | | |
|---|---|---|---|---|---|---|
| | | | | 1, 2, or 3 (Disapproval) | 4 | 5, 6, or 7 (Approval) |
| Setting goals which are extremely easy to make and then making them. | | A, levels 1–4 | 124 | 35 | 30 | 35 |
| | | A, levels 5–8 | 171 | 47 | 27 | 26 |
| | | A, levels 9+ | 17 | 70 | 24 | 6 |
| | | B, levels 1–4 | 31 | 58 | 26 | 16 |
| | | B, levels 5–8 | 19 | 63 | 16 | 21 |
| | | B, levels 9+ | 10 | 80 | 9 | 20 |
| Being a "yes man" and always agreeing with the boss. | | A, levels 1–4 | 126 | 46 | 17 | 37 |
| | | A, levels 5–8 | 180 | 54 | 14 | 31 |
| | | A, levels 9+ | 17 | 88 | 12 | 0 |
| | | B, levels 1–4 | 32 | 53 | 28 | 19 |
| | | B, levels 5–8 | 19 | 68 | 21 | 11 |
| | | B, levels 9+ | 10 | 80 | 10 | 10 |

TABLE 1 *(continued)*

| Dimension | Item | Division and Sample | Total Responses | Percentage of Workers Responding | | |
|---|---|---|---|---|---|---|
| | | | | 1, 2, or 3 (Disapproval) | 4 | 5, 6, or 7 (Approval) |
| | Always going along with the majority. | A, levels 1–4 | 125 | 40 | 29 | 35 |
| | | A, levels 5–8 | 170 | 47 | 31 | 32 |
| | | A, levels 9+ | 17 | 70 | 12 | 18 |
| | | B, levels 1–4 | 31 | 61 | 23 | 16 |
| | | B, levels 5–8 | 19 | 68 | 11 | 21 |
| | | B, levels, 9+ | 10 | 80 | 10 | 10 |
| | Being careful to stay on the good side of everyone, so that everyone agrees that you are a great guy. | A, levels 1–4 | 127 | 45 | 18 | 37 |
| | | A, levels 5–8 | 173 | 45 | 22 | 33 |
| | | A, levels 9+ | 17 | 64 | 6 | 30 |
| | | B, levels 1–4 | 31 | 54 | 23 | 23 |
| | | B, levels 5–8 | 19 | 73 | 22 | 16 |
| | | B, levels 9+ | 10 | 80 | 10 | 10 |

Now, since *a*) the difference between the 5 percent theoretically attainable through hard work and the 4 percent attainable merely by living until the review data is small and *b*) since insurance firms seldom dispense much of a salary increase in cash (rather, the worker's insurance benefits increase, causing him to be further overinsured), many employees are rather indifferent to the possibility of obtaining the extra one percent reward and therefore tend to ignore the norm concerning indiscriminant payments.

However, most employees are not indifferent to the rule which states that, should absences or latenesses total three or more in any six-month period, the entire 4 or 5 percent due at the next "merit" review must be forfeited. In this sense the firm may be described as *hoping* for performance, while *rewarding* attendance. What it gets, of course, is attendance. (If the absence-lateness rule appears to the reader to be stringent, it really is not. The company counts "times" rather than "days" absent, and a ten-day absence therefore counts the same as one lasting two days. A worker in danger of accumulating a third absence within six months merely has to remain ill (away from work) during his second absence until his first absence is more than six months old. The limiting factor is that at some point his salary ceases, and his sickness benefits take over. This usually is sufficient to get the younger workers to return, but for those with 20 or more years' service, the company provides sickness benefits of 90 percent of normal salary, tax-free! Therefore....)

## CAUSES

Extremely diverse instances of systems which reward behavior A although the rewarder apparently hopes for behavior B have been given. These are useful to illustrate the breadth and magnitude of the phenomenon, but the diversity increases the difficulty of determining commonalities and establishing causes. However, four general factors may be pertinent to an explanation of why fouled-up reward systems seem to be so prevalent.

### Fascination with an "Objective" Criterion

It has been mentioned elsewhere that:

> Most "objective" measures of productivity are objective only in that their subjective elements are a) determined in advance, rather than coming into play at the time of the formal evaluation, and b) well concealed on the rating instrument itself. Thus industrial firms seeking to devise objective rating systems first decide, in an arbitrary manner, what dimensions are to be rated,...usually including some items having little to do with organizational effectiveness while excluding others that do. Only then does Personnel Division churn out official-looking documents on which all dimensions chosen to be rated are assigned point values, categories, or whatever (6, p. 92).

Nonetheless, many individuals seek to establish simple, quantifiable standards against which to measure and reward performance. Such efforts may be successful in highly predictable areas within an organization, but are likely to cause goal displacement when applied anywhere else. Overconcern with attendance and lateness in the insurance firm and with number of people placed in the vocational rehabilitation division may have been largely responsible for the problems described in those organizations.

## Overemphasis on Highly Visible Behaviors

Difficulties often stem from the fact that some parts of the task are highly visible while other parts are not. For example, publications are easier to demonstrate than teaching, and scoring baskets and hitting home runs are more readily observable than feeding teammates and advancing base runners. Similarly, the adverse consequences of pronouncing a sick person well are more visible than those sustained by labeling a well person sick. Team-building and creativity are other examples of behaviors which may not be rewarded simply because they are hard to observe.

## Hypocrisy

In some of the instances described the rewarder may have been getting the desired behavior, notwithstanding claims that the behavior was not desired. This may be true, for example, of management's attitude toward apple polishing in the manufacturing firm (a behavior which subordinates felt was rewarded, despite management's avowed dislike of the practice). This also may explain politicians' unwillingness to revise the penalties for disobedience of ecology laws, and the failure of top management to devise reward systems which would cause systematic evaluation of training and developing programs.

## Emphasis on Morality or Equity
## Rather than Efficiency

Some consideration of other factors prevents the establishment of a system which rewards behaviors desired by the rewarder. The felt obligation of many Americans to vote for one candidate or another, for example, may impair their ability to withhold support from politicians who refuse to discuss the issues. Similarly, the concern for spreading the risks and costs of wartime military service may outweigh the advantage to be obtained by committing personnel to combat until the war is over.

It should be noted that only with respect to the first two causes are reward systems really paying off for other than desired behaviors. In the case of the third and fourth causes the system *is* rewarding behaviors desired by the rewarder, and the systems are fouled up only from the standpoints of those who believe the rewarder's public statements (cause 3), or those who seek to maximize efficiency rather than other outcomes (cause 4).

## CONCLUSIONS

Modern organization theory requires a recognition that the members of organizations and society possess divergent goals and motives. It therefore is unlikely that managers and their subordinates will seek the same outcomes. Three possible remedies for this potential problem are suggested.

## Selection

It is theoretically possible for organizations to employ only those individuals whose goals and motives are wholly consonant with those of management. In such cases the same behaviors judged by subordinates to be rational would be perceived by management as desirable. State-of-the-art reviews of selection techniques, however, provide scant grounds for hope that such an approach would be successful (for example, see 12).

## Training

Another theoretical alternative is for the organization to admit those employees whose goals are not consonant with those of management and then, through training, socialization, or whatever, alter employee goals to make them consonant. However, research on the effectiveness of such training programs, though limited, provides further grounds for pessimism (for example, see 3).

## Altering the Reward System

What would have been the result if:

1. Nixon had been assured by his advisors that he could not win reelection except by discussing the issues in detail?
2. Physicians' conduct was subjected to regular examination by review boards for type 1 errors (calling healthy people ill) and to penalties (fines, censure, etc.) for errors of either type?
3. The President of XYZ Corporation had to choose between (a) spending $11 million for antipollution equipment, and (b) incurring a 50-50 chance of going to jail for five years?

Managers who complain that their workers are not motivated might do well to consider the possibility that they have installed reward systems which are paying off for behaviors other than those they are seeking. This, in part, is what happened in Vietnam, and this is what regularly frustrates societal efforts to bring about honest politicians, civic-minded managers, etc. This certainly is what happened in both the manufacturing and the insurance companies.

A first step for such managers might be to find out what behaviors currently are being rewarded. Perhaps an instrument similar to that used in the manufacturing firm could be useful for this purpose. Chances are excellent that these managers will be surprised by what they find—that their firms are not rewarding what they assume they are. In fact, such undesirable behavior by organizational members as they have observed may be explained largely by the reward systems in use.

This is not to say that all organizational behavior is determined by formal rewards and punishments. Certainly it is true that in the absence of formal reinforcement some soldiers will be patriotic, some presidents will be ecology minded, and some orphanage directors will care about children. The point, however, is that in such cases the rewarder is not *causing* the behaviors desired but is only a fortunate bystander. For an organization to *act* upon its members, the formal reward system should positively reinforce desired behaviors, not constitute an obstacle to be overcome.

It might be wise to underscore the obvious fact that there is nothing really new in what has been said. In both theory and practice these matters have been mentioned before. Thus in many states Good Samaritan laws have been installed to protect doctors who stop to assist a stricken motorist. In states without such laws it is commonplace for doctors to refuse to stop, for fear of involvement in a subsequent lawsuit. In college basketball additional penalties have been instituted against players who foul their opponents deliberately. It has long been argued by Milton Friedman and others that penalties should be altered so as to make it irrational to disobey the ecology laws, and so on.

By altering the reward system the organization escapes the necessity of selecting only desirable people or of trying to alter undersirable ones. In Skinnerian terms (as described in 11, p. 704), "As for responsibility and goodness—as commonly defined—no one…would want or need them. They refer to a man's behaving well despite the absence of positive reinforcement that is obviously sufficient to explain it. Where such reinforcement exists, 'no one needs goodness.'"

## REFERENCES

1. Barnard, Chester I. *The Functions of the Executive*. Cambridge, Mass.: Harvard University Press, 1964.
2. Blau, Peter M., and W. Richard Scott. *Formal Organizations*. San Francisco: Chandler, 1962.
3. Fiedler, Fred E. "Predicting the Effects of Leadership Training and Experience from the Contingency Model," *Journal of Applied Psychology*, vol. 56 (1972), pp. 114–19.
4. Garland, L. H. "Studies of the Accuracy of Diagnostic Procedures," *American Journal Roentgenological Radium Therapy Nuclear Medicine,* vol. 82 (1959), pp. 25–38.
5. Kerr, Steven. "Some Modifications in MBO as an OD Strategy," *Academy of Management Proceedings*, 1973, pp. 39–42.
6. Kerr, Steven. "What Price Objectivity?" *American Sociologist,* vol. 8 (1973), pp. 92–93.
7. Litwin, G. H., and R. A. Stringer, Jr. *Motivation and Organizational Climate*. Boston: Harvard University Press, 1968.
8. Perrow, Charles. "The Analysis of Goals in Complex Organizations," in A. Etzioni, ed., *Readings on Modern Organizations*. Englewood Cliffs, N.J.: Prentice-Hall, 1969.
9. Scheff, Thomas J. "Decision Rules, Types of Error, and Their Consequences in Medical Diagnosis," in F. Massarik and P. Ratoosh, eds., *Mathematical Explorations in Behavioral Science*. Homewood, Ill.: Irwin, 1965.
10. Simon, Herbert A. *Administrative Behavior.* New York: Free Press, 1957.
11. Swanson, G. E. "Review Symposium: Beyond Freedom and Dignity," *American Journal of Sociology*, vol. 78 (1972), pp. 702–05.
12. Webster, E. *Decision Making in the Employment Interview.* Montreal: Industrial Relations Center, McGill University, 1964.

# 19

# Organizational Analysis

A CONGRUENCE MODEL FOR DIAGNOSING ORGANIZATIONAL BEHAVIOR
> *David A. Nadler*
> *Michael Tushman*

STRUCTURE IS NOT ORGANIZATION
> *Robert H. Waterman, Jr.*
> *Thomas J. Peters*
> *Julien R. Phillips*

# A CONGRUENCE MODEL FOR DIAGNOSING ORGANIZATIONAL BEHAVIOR

*David A. Nadler*
*Michael Tushman*

Managers perform their jobs within complex social systems called organizations.  In many senses, the task of the manager is to influence behavior in a desired direction, usually toward the accomplishment of a specific task or performance goal.  Given this definition of the managerial role, skills in the diagnosis of patterns of organizational behavior become vital.  Specifically, the manager needs to be able to *understand* the patterns of behavior that are observed, to *predict* in what direction behavior will move (particularly in the light of managerial action), and to use this knowledge to *control* behavior over the course of time.

The understanding, prediction, and control of behavior by managers occurs, of course, in organizations every day.  The problem with managerial control of behavior as frequently practiced is that the understanding-prediction-control sequence is based on the intuition of the individual manager.  This intuitive approach is usually based on models of behavior or organization which the manager carries around in his/her head—models that are often naive and simplistic.  One of the aims of this paper will be to develop a model of organizations, based on behavioral science research, that is both systematic and useful.

The model to be discussed in this paper will serve two ends.  It will provide a way of systematically thinking about behavior in organizations as well as provide a framework within which the results of research on organizational behavior can be expressed.

*Source*:  Reprinted by permission of the authors.

Effective managerial action requires that the manager be able to diagnose the system she/he is working in. Since all elements of social behavior cannot be dealt with at once, the manager facing this "blooming-buzzing" confusion must simplify reality—that is, develop a model of organizational functioning. The diagnostic model will present one way of simplifying social reality that still retains the dynamic nature of organizations. The model will focus on a set of key organizational components (or variables) and their relationships as the primary determinants of behavior. The diagnosis of these key components will provide a concise snapshot of the organization. However, organizations do not stand still. The diagnostic model will preserve the changing nature of organizations by evaluating the effects of feedback on the nature of the key components and their relationships. In all, the diagnostic model will provide a way of thinking about organizations by focusing on a set of key variables and their relationships over time. The model will therefore not consider all the complexity of organizational behavior. To be useful in real settings, insight from the model must be supplemented with clinical data and managerial insight.

Besides as a way of thinking about organizational behavior, the diagnostic model can also serve as a vehicle to organize a substantial portion of research on organizational behavior. An increased awareness of the research results concerning the relationships between the key components should help the manager make the link between diagnosing the situation and making decisions for future action. The model, then, cannot only help the manager to diagnose and describe organizational behavior, but it can provide an effective way to organize and discuss behavioral science research results that may be of use to managers.

While the diagnostic model is a potentially powerful managerial tool, it must be seen as a developing tool. Parts of the model are less well developed than others (e.g., the informal organization). As research in organizational behavior advances, so, too, should the development of this diagnostic model. Finally, no claim is made that this model is the most effective way of organizing reality. It is suggested, however, that models of organizational behavior are important and that they ought to 1) deal with several variables and their relationships, and 2) take into account the dynamic nature of organizations.

In conclusion, the premise of this article is that effective management requires that the manager be able to systematically diagnose, predict, and control behavior. The purpose of this paper is to present a research-based (as opposed to intuitive) model of organizational behavior that can be used to diagnose organizations as well as to integrate behavioral science research results. The model should therefore be of use to practitioners in organizations as well as to students in the classroom.

## BASIC ASSUMPTIONS OF THE MODEL

The diagnostic model that will be discussed here is based on a number of assumptions about organizational life. These assumptions are as follows:

1. *Organizations are dynamic entities.* Organizations exist over time and space, and the activities that make up organizations are dynamic. There are many definitions of organizations, such as Schein's (1970) statement that

> an organization is the rational coordination of the activities of a number of people for the achievement of some common explicit purpose or goal, through division of labor and function, and through a hierarchy of authority and responsibility.

While definitions like this are adequate to define what an organization is, they are static in nature and do not enable one to grasp how the different components of organization interact with each other over time. An adequate model of organizations must reflect the dynamic nature of organizational behavior.

2. *Organizational behavior exists at multiple levels.*   There are different levels of abstraction at which organizational behavior can be examined.  Specifically, behavior occurs at the individual, the group, and the organizational systems' levels.  Behavior that is attributable to each of these levels can be identified and isolated (that is, one can see the behavior of individuals as different from the behavior of groups or of organizations themselves).  At the same time, these three levels interact with each other, organizational-level behavior being affected by the behavior of individuals, group-level behavior being affected by the organizational-level phenomena, and so on.

3. *Organizational behavior does not occur in a vacuum.*   Organizations are made up of both social and technical components and thus have been characterized as sociotechnical systems (Emery and Trist, 1960).  The implication of this is that any approach to looking at behavior must also take into account the technical components of the organization—such issues as the nature of the task and the technology.  Since the organization is dependent on inputs, knowledge, and feedback from the environment, our model must also take into account the constraints of the organization's task environment (e.g., to what extent the market is changing).

4. *Organizations have the characteristics of open social systems.*   Organizations have the characteristics of systems that are composed of interrelated components and conduct transactions with a larger environment.  Systems have a number of unique behavioral characteristics, and thus a model of organizational behavior must take into account the systemic nature of organizations.


## OPEN-SYSTEMS THEORY

The point made above about open-systems theory is a crucial one which needs to be explored in more depth.  The basic premise is the characteristics of systems that are seen in both the physical and social sciences (Von Bertalanffy, 1962; Buckley, 1967) are particularly valuable when looking at organizations.  Social organizations, it is claimed, can be viewed as systems (Katz and Kahn, 1966) with a number of key systems characteristics.

What is a system and what are systems characteristics? In the simplest of terms, a system is a "set of interrelated elements." These elements are interdependent such that changes in the nature of one component may lead to changes in the nature of the other components.  Further, because the system is embedded with larger systems, it is dependent on the larger environment for resources, information, and feedback.  Another way of looking at a system is to define it as a mechanism that imports some form of energy input from the environment, which submits that input to some kind of transformation process, and which produces some kind of energy output back to the environment (Katz and Kahn, 1966).  The notion of open systems also implies the existence of some boundary differentiating the system from the larger environment in which it is embedded.  These system boundaries are usually not rigid.  This familiar view of a system can be seen in Figure 1. Closed systems, on the other hand, are not dependent on the environment and are more deterministic in nature.  Closed systems tend to have more rigid boundaries and all transactions take place within the system, guided by unitary goals and rationality. (An example approaching a closed system would be a terrarium, completely self-contained and insulated from the larger environment.)

A more extensive definition of open systems has been presented by Katz and Kahn (1966) in the form of a listing of characteristics of open social systems. An adapted list of these characteristics is as follows:

1. *Importation of energy.* A system functions by importing energy (information, products, materials, etc.) from the larger environment.

2. *Throughput.* Systems move energy through them, largely in the form of transformation processes. These are often multiple processes (i.e., decisions, material manipulation, etc.)

3. *Output.* Systems send energy back to the larger environment in the form of products, services, and other kinds of outcomes which may or may not be intended.

4. *Cycles of events over time.* Systems function over time and thus are dynamic in nature. Events tend to occur in natural repetitive cycles of input, throughput, and output, with events in sequence occurring over and over again.

5. *Equilibrium seeking.* Systems tend to move toward the state where all components are in equilibrium—where a steady state exists. When changes are made that result in an imbalance, different components of the system move to restore the balance.

6. *Feedback.* Systems use information about their output to regulate their input and transformation processes. These informational connections also exist between system components, and thus changes in the functioning of one component will lead to changes in other system components (second-order effects).

7. *Increasing differentiation.* As systems grow, they also tend to increase their differentiation; more components are added, more feedback loops, more transformation processes. Thus, as systems get larger, they also get more complex.

8. *Equifinality.* Different system configurations may lead to the same end point, or conversely, the same end state may be reached by a variety of different processes.

9. *System survival requirements.* Because of the inherent tendency of systems to "run down" or dissipate their energy, certain functions must be performed (at least at minimal levels) over time. These requirements include (a) goal achievement, and (b) adaptation (the ability to maintain balanced successful transactions with the environment).

FIGURE 1   The Elementary Systems Model

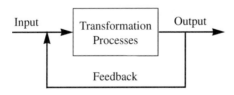

# A SPECIFIC SYSTEMS MODEL

Open-systems theory is a general framework for conceptualizing organizational behavior over time. It sensitizes the manager to a basic model of organizations (i.e., input-throughput-output-feedback) as well as to a set of basic organizational processes (e.g., equilibrium, differentiation, equifinality). While systems concepts are useful as an overall perspective, they do not help the manager systematically diagnose specific situations or help him/her apply research results to specific problems. A more concrete model must be developed that takes into account system-theory concepts and processes and helps the manager deal with organizational reality.

According to Figure 1, organizations (or some other unit of interest, e.g., a department or factory) take some set of inputs, work on these inputs through some sort of transformation process, and produce output that is evaluated and responded to by the environment. While managers must attend to the environment and input considerations, they must specifically focus on what the organization does to produce output. That is, managers are intimately involved in what systems theory terms the transformation processes. It is the *transformation processes*, then, that the model will specifically focus on. Given the cycle of processes from input to feedback, the model will focus on the more specific variables and processes that affect how the organization takes a given set of inputs and produces a set of organizational outputs (e.g., productivity, innovation, satisfaction). While the diagnostic model will specifically focus on the determinants of the transformation processes and their relationships to outputs, it must be remembered that these processes are part of a more general model of organizational behavior that takes inputs, outputs, and the environment into account (see Figure 1).

The model focuses on the critical system characteristic of dependence. Organizations are made up of components or parts that interact with each other. These components exist in states of relative balance, consistency, or "fit" with each other. The different parts of the organization can fit well together and thus function effectively; or fit poorly, leading to problems. Given the central nature of fit in the model, we shall talk about it as a *congruence model* of organizational behavior, since effectiveness is a function of the congruence of the various components.

This concept of congruence between organizational components is not a new one. Leavitt (1965), for example, identifies four major components of organization as being people, tasks, technology, and structure. The model presented here builds on this view and also draws from models developed and used by Seiler (1967), Lawrence and Lorsch (1969), and Lorsch and Sheldon (1972).

What we are concerned about is modeling the *behavioral system* of the organization—the system of elements that ultimately produce patterns of behavior. In its simplest form, what inputs does the system have to work with, what are the major components of the system and the nature of their interactions, and what is the nature of the system output?

The congruence model is based on the system's assumptions outlined above. The inputs to the system (see Figure 2) are those factors that at any one point in time are relatively fixed or given. Three major classes of inputs can be identified: 1) the environment of the system, 2) the resources available to the system, and 3) the organizational strategies that are developed over time.

The transformation process of the system is seen as the interaction between four major components of the organizational system. These components are 1) the tasks of the organization, 2) the individuals in the organizational system, 3) the organizational arrangements, and 4) the informal organization.

The outputs are the results of the interactions among the components, given the inputs. Several major outputs can be identified, including individual affect and behavior, group behavior, and the effectiveness of total system functioning. Looking at the total system, particular attention is paid to the system's ability to attain its goals, to utilize available resources, and to successfully adapt over time. Explicit in the model are feedback loops running from the outputs and the transformation process. The loops represent information flow about the nature of the system output and the interaction of system components. The information is available for use to make modifications in the nature of systems inputs or components.

FIGURE 2    The Systems Model as Applied to Organizational Behavior

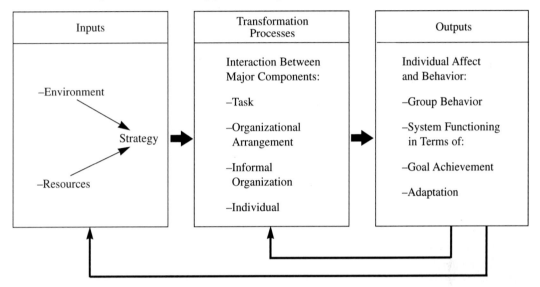

In understanding the model, it is therefore important to understand what makes up the system inputs, components, and outputs and how they relate to each other. In particular, it is important for the manager to understand how system components relate to each other since these relationships are particularly critical for influencing behavior.

## The Nature of Inputs

Inputs are important since at any point in time they are the fixed or given factors that influence organizational behavior. The inputs provide both constraints and opportunities for managerial action. While the diagnosis of organizational behavior is focused primarily on the understanding of the interactions among system components, an understanding of the nature of the inputs is still important. The major classes of inputs that constrain organizational behavior are listed in Table 1. A brief description of these inputs is as follows:

1. *Environmental inputs.*   Organizations as open systems carry on constant transactions with the environment. Specifically, three factors in the environment of the specific organization are important. First, there are the various groups, organizations, and events that make up the external environment. This includes the functioning of product, service, and capital markets; the behavior of competitors and suppliers; governmental regulation; and the effect of the larger culture. Second, the organization may be embedded within another larger formal system. For example, a factory that is being considered may be part of a larger multinational corporation or of a larger corporate division. These larger "supra-systems" form an important part of the environment of the organization. Third, both the internal and external environment can be described according to a number of dimensions that appear to impact the functioning of organizations (Emery and Trist, 1965). Specifically, the issues of stability and homogeneity of the environment are important.

567

TABLE 1    Dimension of System Inputs

| Environment | Resources | Strategy |
| --- | --- | --- |
| External environment | Capital | Critical decisions in the past |
|   Markets | Raw materials | Identification of environmental |
|   Government | Technologies |   opportunities and distinctive |
|   Financial institutions | People |   competencies |
|   Competitors | Intangibles | Organizational mission |
|   Suppliers | | Long-range and short-range goals |
|   Labor unions | | Plans |
|   The larger culture, etc. | | |
| Internal environment | | |
|   Immediate supra-systems | | |
| Environmental characteristics | | |
|   Stability | | |
|   Homogeneity | | |

2. *Resources.*    Another important input is composed of the resources that are available to the organization. Any organization has a range of resources available as inputs. Major categories for classifying resources would include capital resources (including liquid capital, physical plant, property, etc.), raw materials (the material on which the organization will perform the transformation process), technologies (approaches or procedures for performing the transformation), people, and various intangible resources.

3. *Strategy.*    Over time, organizations develop ways of utilizing their resources that deal effectively with the constraints, demands, and opportunities of the environment. They develop plans of action that centrally define what the organization will attempt to do in relation to the larger systems in which it is embedded. These plans of action are called strategies and are another major input.

While all three inputs are important, one, however, has a very critical primary effect upon the nature of one of the components, and therefore it ultimately affects all the components and their interactions. This input is strategy.

As has been said, an organization as an open system functions within a larger environment. That environment provides opportunities for action, it provides constraints on activities, and it makes demands upon the organization's capacities. The organization faces the environment with a given set of resources of various kinds: human, technological, managerial, and so on. The process of determining how those resources can best be used to function within the environment is generally called strategy determination (see Newman and Logan, 1976, or Andrews, 1971). The organization identifies opportunities in the environment where its distinctive competence or unique set of resources will provide it with a competitive advantage.

Some organizations develop strategies through formalized and complex processes of long-range strategic planning, while other organizations may give no or little conscious attention to strategy at all. Further, the process of strategy formulation can itself be seen as the output of intraorganizational processes (e.g., Bower, 1970; Mintzberg, 1973). The point is, however, that organizations have strategies, whether they be implicit or explicit, formal or informal. The point for organizational behavior is that the strategy of an organization is probably the single most important input (or constraint set) to the behavioral system. The strategy and the elements of that strategy (goals or plans) essentially define the *task* of the organization, one of the major components of the behavioral system (see Figure 3).  From one perspective, all organizational behavior is concerned with implementation of strategies through the performance of tasks.  Individuals, formal organizational arrangements, and informal organizational arrangements are all important because of their relationship to the tasks that need to be performed.

FIGURE 3    The Role of Strategy as the Primary Input to the Model

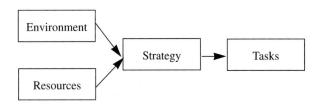

The inputs listed above therefore provide opportunities, provide constraints, and may even make demands upon the organization.  Given these inputs, the issue of how the organization functions to make use of the opportunities and constraints provided by the inputs is perhaps the most central issue of managerial and organizational behavior.

## The Nature of Organizational Components

Assuming a set of inputs, the transformation process occurs through the interaction of a number of basic components of organization.  The major components (listed with their subdimensions in Table 2) are as follows:

1. *Task component.*   This component concerns the nature of the tasks or jobs that must be performed by the organization, by groups, and by individuals.  Major dimensions of tasks include the extent and nature of interdependence between task performers, the level of required skills, the degree of autonomy, the extent of feedback, the variability of the task, the potential meaningfulness of the task, and the types of information needed to adequately perform the task.

2. *Individuals component.*   This component obviously refers to the individuals who are members of the organization.  The major dimensions of this component relate to the systematic differences in individuals which have relevance for organizational behavior.  Such dimensions include background or demographic variables such as skill levels, levels of education, and so on, and individual differences in need strength, personality, or perceptual biases.

3. *Organizational arrangements.*   This includes all the formal mechanisms used by the organization to direct structure or control behavior.  Major dimensions include leadership practices, microstructure (how specific jobs, systems, or subcomponents are structured), and macrostructure (how whole units, departments, and organizations are structured).

4. *Informal organization.*   In addition to the formal prescribed structure that exists in the system, there is an informal social structure that tends to emerge over time.  Relevant dimensions of the informal organization include the functioning of informal group structures, the quality of intergroup relations, and the operation of various political processes throughout the organization.

Organizations can therefore be looked at as a set of components, including the task, the individuals, the organizational arrangements, and the informal organization. (For the complete model, see Figure 4.) To be useful, however, the model must go beyond the simple listing and description of these components and describe the dynamic relationship that exists among the various components.

TABLE 2   Basic Characteristics of Behavioral System Components

| Tasks | Individuals | Organizational Arrangements | Informal Organization |
|---|---|---|---|
| Organizational tasks | Response capabilities | Subunits | Small-group functioning |
| Complexity | Intelligence | Grouping of tasks and roles | Norms |
| Predictability | Skills and abilities | Unit composition | Informal goals |
| Required interdependence | Experience | Unit design | Communication patterns |
| | Training | Formal leadership in the unit | Cohesiveness |
| | | Physical arrangements, etc. | Informal group structures |
| Subunit and individual tasks | Psychological differences | Coordination and control | Intergroup relations |
| Complexity | Need strength | Goals | Conflict/cooperation |
| Predictability | Attitudes | Plans | Information flows |
| Required interdependence | Perceptual biases | Hierarchy | Perceptions |
| Autonomy | Expectations | Reward systems | Organizational level |
| Feedback | Background differences | Personnel systems | Networks, cliques, and |
| Task variety | | Control systems | coalitions |
| Task identity | | Integrator roles and groups | Conflicting interest groups |
| Task meaningfulness | | | Power distribution |
| Task skill demands | | | Ideology and values |

***The Concept of Fit.*** Between each pair of inputs there exists a degree of congruence, or "fit." Specifically, the congruence between two components is defined as follows:

> The degree to which the needs, demands, goals, objectives and/or structures of one component are consistent with the needs, demands, goals, objectives and/or structures of another component.

Thus fit (indicated by the double-headed arrows in Figure 4) is a measure of the congruence between pairs of components. Because components cover a range of different types of phenomena, however, fit can be more clearly defined only by referring to specific fits between specific pairs of components. In each case research results can be used as a guide to evaluate whether the components are in a state of high consistency or high inconsistency. An awareness of these fits is critical since inconsistent fits will be related to dysfunctional behavior.

Specific definitions of congruence and examples of research on the nature of these fits is presented in Table 3. For each of the six fits among the components, more information is provided about the specific issues that need to be examined to determine the level of consistency between the components. Citations are given for examples of the research relevant to each of these relationships.

***The Congruence Hypothesis.*** Just as each pair of components has a degree of high or low congruence, so does the aggregate model display a relatively high or low total system congruence. Underlying the model is a basic hypothesis about the nature of its and their relationship to behavior. This hypothesis is as follows:

> Other things being equal, the greater the total degree of congruence of fit between the various components, the more effective will be organizational behavior at multiple levels. Effective organizational behavior is defined as behavior which leads to higher levels of goal attainment, utilization of resources, and adaptation.

FIGURE 4 A Congruence Model for Diagnosing Organizational Behavior

Feedback

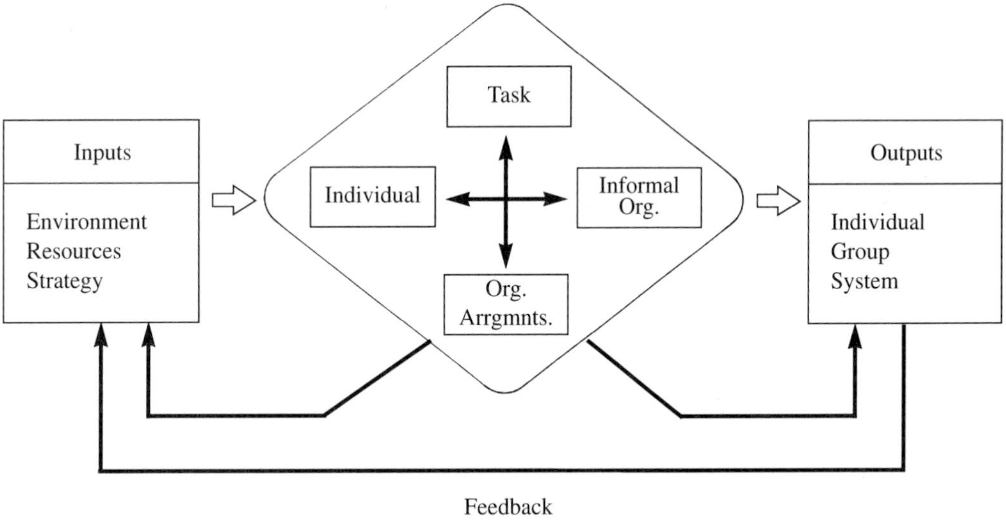

The implications of the congruence hypothesis in this model is that the manager needs to adequately diagnose the system, determine the location and nature of inconsistent fits, and plan courses of action to change the nature of those fits without bringing about dysfunctional second-order effects. The model also implies that different configurations of the key components can lead to effective behavior (consistent with the system characteristics of equifinality). Therefore, the question is not finding the "one best way" of managing, but of determining effective combinations of inputs that will lead to congruent fits.

This process of diagnosing fit and identifying combinations of inputs to produce congruence is not necessarily an intuitive process. A number of situations that lead to consistent fits have been defined in the research literature (for example, see some of the research cited in Table 3). Thus, in many cases fit is something that can be defined, measured, and quantified in many organizational systems. The basic point is that goodness of fit is based upon theory and research rather than intuition. In most cases, the theory provides considerable guidance about what leads to congruence relationships (although in some areas the research is more abundant than others; the research on informal organization, for example, has been sparse in recent years). The implication is that the manager who is attempting to diagnose behavior needs to become familiar with critical findings of the relevant research so that she/he can evaluate the nature of fits in a particular system.

TABLE 3   Definitions of Fits and Examples of Research

| Fit | The Issues | Examples of Research on the Fits |
|---|---|---|
| Individual-organization | To what extent individual needs are met by the organizational arrangements; to what extent individuals hold clear or distorted perceptions of organizational structures; the convergence of individual and organizational goals. | Argyris (1957), Vroom (1959), Tannenbaum, Allport, and Schein (1970) |
| Individual-task | To what extent the needs of individuals are met by the tasks; to what extent individuals have skills and abilities to meet task demands. | Turner and Lawerence (1965), Hackman and Lawler (1971), Hackman and Oldham (1975) |
| Individual-informal organization | To what extent individual needs are met by the informal organization; to what extent the informal organization makes use of individual resources, consistent with informal goals. | Whyte (1955), Hackman and Morris (1976), Gouldner (1954), Crozier (1964), Trist and Bamforth (1951) |
| Task-organization | Whether the organizational arrangements are adequate to meet the demands of the task; whether organizational arrangements tend to motivate behavior consistent with task demands. | Burms and Stalker (1961), Woodward (1965), Lawrence and Lorsch (1969), Vroom and Yetton (1973) |
| Task-informal | Whether the informal organization structure facilitates task performance or not; whether it hinders or promotes meeting the demands of the task. | Blake, Shepard, and Mouton (1964), Blau (1956), Trist and Bamforth (1951), Burns and Stalker (1961), Gouldner (1954) |
| Organization-informal organization | Whether the goals, rewards, and structures of the organization are consistent with those of the informal organization. | Roethlisberger and Dickson (1939), Dalton (1959), Likert (1967), Crozier (1964), Strauss (1962) |

# The Nature of Outputs

The model indicates that the outputs flow out of the interaction of the various components. Any organizational system produces a number of different outputs. For general diagnostic purposes, however, three major classes of outputs are particularly important:

1. *Individual behavior and effect.* A crucial issue is how individuals behave, specifically with regard to their organizational membership behavior (for example, absenteeism, lateness, turnover) and with regard to performance of designated tasks. Individuals also have effective responses to the work environment (levels of satisfaction, for example) which also are of consequence. Other individual behavior such as nonproductive behavior, drug usage, off-the-job activities, and so on, are also outputs of the organization in many cases.

2. *Group and intergroup behavior.* Beyond the behavior of individuals, the organization is also concerned with the performance of groups or departments. Important considerations would include intergroup conflict or collaboration and the quality of intergroup communication.

3. *System-functioning.* At the highest level of abstraction is the question of how well the system as a whole is functioning. The key issues here include 1) how well is the system attaining its desired goals of production, output, return on investment, etc.; 2) how well the organization is utilizing available resources; and 3) how well is the organization adapting (i.e., maintaining favorable transactions with the environment over time).

# USING THE DIAGNOSTIC MODEL

Given the diagnostic model, the final question to be addressed here is how the model can be put to use. A number of authors have observed that the conditions facing organizations are always changing and that managers must therefore continually engage in problem identification and problem-solving activities (e.g., Schein, 1970)). These authors suggest that managers must gather data on the performance of their organization, compare the ideal to the actual performance levels, develop and choose action plans, and then implement and evaluate these action plans. These problem-solving phases link together to form a *problem-solving process* if the evaluation phase is seen as the beginning of the next diagnostic phase. For long-term organizational viability, this problem-solving process must be continually reaccomplished (Schein, 1970; Weick, 1969). The basic phases of this problem-solving process are outlined in Figure 5.

How does the diagnostic model relate to this problem-solving process? The problem-solving process requires diagnosis, the generation of action plans, and the evaluation of the action plans. *Each of these steps requires a way of looking at organizations to guide the analysis.* To the extent that the diagnostic model integrates system-theory concepts and presents a specific model of organizations, the model can be used as the core of the problem-solving process. The model can therefore be used as a framework to guide the diagnosis, the evaluation of alternative actions, and the evaluation and feedback of the results of a managerial action. Further, to the extent that the manager is familiar with the research results bearing on the different fits in the model, s/he will be better able to both diagnose the situation and evaluate alternative action plans. In short, the problem-solving process, along with the research-based use of the diagnostic model, can be used as an effective managerial tool.

Given the problem-solving process and the diagnostic model, it is possible to identify and describe a number of discrete steps in the problem-solving cycle. These steps can be organized into three phases: 1) diagnosis, 2) alternative solutions-action, and 3) evaluation-feedback. The basic phases and their component steps will be outlined here.

FIGURE 5    Basic Phases of Using the Diagnostic Model

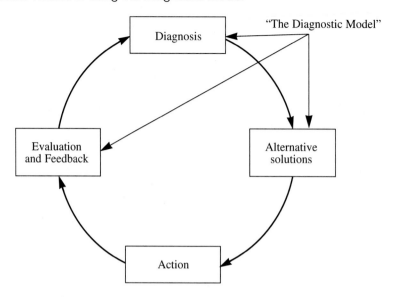

## The Diagnostic Phase

This phase is premised on the idea that any managerial action must be preceded by a systematic diagnosis of the system under investigation. This phase can be broken into four distinct, but related, steps.

1. *Identify the system.*    Before any detailed analysis can begin it is important to identify the system being considered. The unit of analysis must be clearly specified (i.e., project, division, organization). The boundaries of the focal unit, its membership, and what other units constitute the layer system should be considered.

2. *Determine the nature of the key variables.*    Having defined the system, the next step is to use the data in the situation (or case) to determine the nature of the inputs and the four key components. The analyst should focus on the underlying dimensions of each variable. The diagnosis should focus not on an exhaustive description of each component but on the dimensions the analyst considers most important in the particular situation. The question could be phrased: In this situation, what are the most salient characteristics of the key components that are affecting the observed behavior?

3. *Diagnose the state of fits and their relationship to behaviors (i.e., outputs).*    This step is the most critical in the diagnosis phase. It really involves two related stages: a) diagnosing fits between the components, and b) considering the link between the fits and system output.

   a. Using experience, observations, and relevant research knowledge, the manager must evaluate each of the fit lines in the model. The analyst must focus on the extent to which the key components are consistent (or fit) with each other. For instance, to what extent are the organizational arrangements consistent with the demands of the task?

   b. Fits (or lack of fits) between the key components have consequences in terms of system behavior. This step makes the fit-to-behavior link explicit. That is, given the diagnoses of the various fits, the analyst must then relate the fits to behaviors observed in the system (e.g., conflict, performance, stress, satisfaction). This is a particular key step since managerial action will be directed at the inconsistent fits to improve some aspect of the organization's behavior.

4. *Identifying critical system problems.*    Based on the diagnosis of fits and their behavioral con-sequences, the final diagnostic step is to relate the set of behaviors to system outputs (goal achieve-ment, resource utilization, and adaptation).   Given these outputs, the manager must then evaluate which system behaviors require managerial attention and action.

The diagnostic phase forces the analyst to make a set of decisions.   The analyst must decide the unit of analysis, make decisions as to the most salient characteristics of each of the key variables, make decisions as to the relationships between the key components and their effects on behavior, and relate the observed behaviors to system outputs and decide on the system's most pressing problems. None of these decisions are clear cut—each involves managerial discretion.   It follows that there is no one best diagnosis of any set of organizational conditions.   The final point to be made in the diagnosis phase is that diagnosis makes a difference.   The manager's diagnosis must lead to a set of actions.   Different diagnoses will therefore usually lead to different actions.

## Alternative Solutions-Action Plan Phase

Diagnosis leads to a consideration of potential managerial actions.   This alternative action phase can be separated into three stages.

5. *Generate alternative solutions.*   Having identified critical problems and the relationship between fits and behavior, the next step is to generate a range of possible managerial actions.   These actions or interventions will be directed at the inconsistent fits, which will in turn affect the behaviors under consideration.

Action plans for a particular situation may differ.   There may be different diagnoses or there may be a number of interventions or organizational arrangements leading to the same end point (following from the system characteristic of equifinality).   In short, there is not likely to be one most appropriate set of managerial actions to deal with a particular set of conditions.

6. *Evaluating alternative strategies.*   While there usually is not one single most appropriate managerial action to deal with a particular situation, the various alternatives can be evaluated for their relative merits.   To what extent do the solutions deal with the inconsistent fits? Does one solution deal with the inconsistent fits more comprehensively? Are there dysfunctional second-order (i.e., latent) consequences of the action—for instance, will changing the task dimensions deal with an inconsistent task-informal organization fit but adversely affect the task-individual fit? In short, given the highly interdependent nature of open systems, the manager must systematically evaluate the alternative actions.   Based on theory, research, and experience, the manager must make predictions about the possible effects of different strategies.   The manager should therefore focus on the extent to which the intervention deals with the critical system problem *as well* as with the possibilities of latent consequences of the intervention.   This exercise of prediction should provide a way of evaluating the relative strengths and weaknesses of the alternative actions.

7. *Choice of strategies to be implemented*   Given the explicit evaluation of the different approaches, the final step in this phase is to weigh the various advantages and disadvantages of the alternative actions and choose an action plan to be implemented.

## Evaluation and Feedback Phase

The diagnosis and alternative solution-action phases leave the manager with an action plan to deal with the critical system problem(s).   The final phase in using the diagnostic model deals with the implementation of the action plan and with the importance of evaluation, feedback, and adjustment of strategy to meet emergent system requirements.

8. *Implementation of strategies.* This step deals explicitly with issues that arise in introducing change into an ongoing system. This step recognizes the need to deal with the response of organizations to change. To what extent will the intervention be accepted and worked on as opposed to resisted and sabotaged? There is an extensive literature dealing with the implementation of change programs (e.g., Walton, 1975; Rogers and Shoemaker, 1971; French and Bell, 1973). While these considerations cannot be dealt with here, it is important to highlight the potential problems of translating plans and strategies into effective action.

9. *Evaluation and feedback.* After implementing a strategy, it is important to continue the diagnostic activity and to explicitly evaluate the actual vs. the ideal (or predicted) impact of the intervention on the system. Feedback concerning the organization's or the environment's response to the action can then be used to adjust the intervention to better fit the system's requirements and/or deal with any unanticipated consequences of the change. In a sense, then, step 9 closes the loop and starts the diagnosis-alternatives-action-evaluation cycle again (see Figure 5).

In conclusion, we have discussed a number of discrete, though related, steps for using the diagnostic model. The model provides a way of systematically diagnosing organizations. This diagnosis can then be used as an integral part of a problem-solving strategy for the organization. Further, the model can assist the manager in evaluating alternative solutions (i.e., what fits are dealt with) as well as evaluating the effects of the managerial actions (i.e., what fits were affected). Since organizations are made up of processes that must recur over time, the manager must continually go through the kind of problem-solving strategy indicated in Figure 5. If this adaptive-coping kind of scheme is critical for organizational viability over time (see Schein, 1970), the diagnostic model can be seen as a concrete research-based tool to facilitate the diagnosis of the system and to provide a base for evaluating alternative actions and the consequences of those actions.

The diagnostic model and the problem-solving cycle are ways of structuring and dealing with the complex reality of organizations. Given the indeterminate nature of social systems, there is no one best way of handling a particular situation. The model and problem-solving cycle do, however, force the manager to make a number of decisions and to think about the consequences of those decisions. If the diagnostic model and problem-solving process have merit, it is up to the manager to use these tools along with his/her experiences to make the appropriate set of diagnostic, evaluative, and action decisions over time.

## SUMMARY

This article has attempted to briefly outline a model for diagnosing organizational behavior. The model is based on the assumption that organizations are open social systems and that an interaction of inputs leads to behavior and various outputs. The model presented is one based on the theory and research literature in organizational behavior and thus assumes that the manager using the model has some familiarity with the concepts coming out of this literature. Together with a process for its use, the model provides managers with a potentially valuable tool in the creation of more effective organizations.

# REFERENCES

Andrews, K. R. *The concept of corporate strategy.* Homewood, Ill.: Dow Jones-Irwin, 1971.

Argyris. C. *Personality and organization: The conflict between system and the individual.* New York: Harper & Row, 1957.

Blake, R. R., Shephard, H. A., and Mouton, J. S. *Managing intergroup conflict in industry.* Houston, Tex.: Gulf, 1964.

Blau, P. M. *The dynamics of bureaucracy.* Chicago: University of Chicago Press, 1955.

Bower, J. L. *Managing the resource allocation process.* Cambridge, Mass.: Harvard University Graduate School of Business Administration, Division of Research, 1970.

Buckley, W. *Sociology and modern systems theory.* Englewood Cliffs, N.J.: Prentice-Hall, 1967.

Burns, T., and Stalker, G. M. *The management of innovation.* London: Tavistock Publications, 1961.

Crozier, R. *The bureaucratic phenomenon.* Chicago: University of Chicago Press, 1964.

Dalton, M. *Men who manage.* New York: Wiley, 1959.

Duncan, R. Characteristics of organizational environments. *Administrative Science Quarterly*, 1972, *17*, 313–327.

Emery. F. E., and Trist, E. L. Socio-technical systems. In *Management sciences models and techniques,* Vol. II. London: Pergamon Press, 1960.

Emery, F. E., and Trist, E. L. The causal texture of organizational environments. *Human Relations,* 1965, *18*, 21–32.

French, W. L., and Bell, C. H. *Organization development.* Englewood Cliffs, N.J.: Prentice-Hall, 1973.

Gouldner, A. *Patterns of industrial bureaucracy.* New York: Free Press, 1954.

Katz, D., and Kahn, R. L. *The social psychology of organizations.* New York: John Wiley & Sons, 1966.

Hackman, J. R., and Lawler, E. E. Employee reactions to job characteristics. *Journal of Applied Psychology,* 1971, *55*, 259–286.

Hackman, J. R., and Morris, C. G. Group tasks, group interaction process and group performance effectiveness: A review and proposed integration. In L. Berkowitz (ed.), *Advances in experimental social psychology.* New York: Academic Press, 1976.

Hackman, J. R., and Oldham, G. R. Development of the job diagnostic survey. *Journal of Applied Psychology*, 1975, *60*, 159–170.

Lawrence, P. R., and Lorsch, J. W. *Organization and environment: Managing differentiation and integration.* Homewood, Ill.: Richard D. Irwin, 1969.

Leavitt, H. J. Applied organizational change in industry. In J. G. March (ed.), *Handbook of organizations.* Chicago: Rand McNally, 1965, 1144–1170.

Likert, R. *The human organization: Its management and value.* New York: McGraw-Hill, 1967.

Lorsch, J. W., and Sheldon, A. The individual in the organization: A systems view. In J. W. Lorsch and P. R. Lawrence (eds.), *Managing group and intergroup relations.* Homewood, Ill.: Irwin-Dorsey, 1972.

Mintzberg, H. *The nature of managerial work.* New York: Harper & Row, 1973.

Newman, W. H., and Logan, J. P. *Strategy, policy, and central management,* 7th ed. Cincinnati, Ohio: South-Western Publishing Co., 1976.

Roethlisberger, F. J., and Dickson, W. J. *Management and the worker.* Cambridge, Mass.: Harvard University Press, 1939 (also New York: Wiley, 1964).

Rogers, E. M., and Shoemaker, F. F. *Communication of innovations: A cross-cultural approach.* New York: Free Press, 1971.

Schein, E. H. *Organizational psychology.* Englewood Cliffs, N.J.: Prentice-Hall, 1970.

Seiler, J. A. *Systems analysis in organizational behavior.* Homewood, Ill.: Irwin-Dorsey, 1967.

Strauss, G. Tactics of lateral relationships. *Administrative Science Quarterly*, 1962, *7*, 161–186.

Tannenbaum, A. S., and Allport, F. H. Personality structure, and group structure: An interpretative study of their relationship through an event structure hypothesis. *Journal of Abnormal and Social Psychology,* 1956, *53*, 272–280.

Trist, E. L., and Bamforth, R. Some social and psychological consequences of the long wall method of coal-getting. *Human Relations*, 1951, *4*, 3–38.

Turner, A. N., and Lawrence, P. R. *Industrial jobs and the worker.* Boston: Harvard University School of Business Administration, 1965.

Von Bertalanffy, L. *General systems theory: Foundations, development, applications*, rev. ed. New York: Braziller, 1968.

Vroom, V. H. Some personality determinants of the effects of participation. *Journal of Abnormal and Social Psychology*, 1959, *59*, 322–327.

Vroom, V. H., and Yetton, P. W. *Leadership and decision making.* Pittsburgh, Pa.: University of Pittsburg Press, 1973.

Walton, R. E. The diffusion of new work structures: Explaining why success didn't take. *Organizational Dynamics,* 1975 (Winter), 3–22.

Weick, K. E. *The social psychology of organizing.* Reading, Mass.: Addison-Wesley, 1969.

Whyte, W. F. (ed.). *Money and motivation. An analysis of incentives in industry.* New York: Harper & Row, 1955.

Woodward, J. *Industrial organization: Theory and practice.* New York: Oxford University Press, 1965.

# STRUCTURE IS NOT ORGANIZATION

*Robert H. Waterman, Jr.*
*Thomas J. Peters*
*Julien R. Phillips*

The Belgian surrealist René Magritte painted a series of pipes and titled the series *Ceci n'est pas une pipe*: This is not a pipe. The picture of the thing is not the thing. In the same way, a structure is not an organization. We all know that, but like as not, when we reorganize what we do is to restructure. Intellectually all managers and consultants know that much more goes on in the process of organizing than the charts, boxes, dotted lines, position descriptions, and matrices can possibly depict. But all too often we behave as though we didn't know it; if we want change we change the structure.

Early in 1977, a general concern with the problems of organization effectiveness, and a particular concern about the nature of the relationship between structure and organization, led us to assemble

*Source:* Reprinted from *Business Horizons*, June 1980. Copyright 1980 by the Foundation for the School of Business at Indiana University. Used with permission.

The authors want to offer special acknowledgement and thanks to Anthony G. Athos of Harvard University, who was instrumental in the development of the 7-S framework and who, in his capacity as our consultant, helped generally to advance our thinking on organization effectiveness.

an internal task force to review our client work. The natural first step was to talk extensively to consultants and client executives around the world who were known for their skill and experience in organization design. We found that they too were dissatisfied with conventional approaches. All were disillusioned about the usual structural solutions, but they were also skeptical about anyone's ability to do better. In their experience, the techniques of the behavioral sciences were not providing useful alternatives to structural design. True, the notion that structure follows strategy (get the strategy right and the structure follows) looked like an important addition to the organizational tool kit; yet strategy rarely seemed to dictate unique structural solutions. Moreover, the main problem in strategy had turned out to be execution: getting it done. And that, to a very large extent, meant *organization*. So the problem of organization effectiveness threatened to prove circular. The dearth of practical additions to old ways of thought was painfully apparent.

## OUTSIDE EXPLORATIONS

Our next step was to look outside for help. We visited a dozen business schools in the United States and Europe and about as many superbly performing companies. Both academic theorists and business leaders, we found, were wrestling with the same concerns.

Our timing in looking at the academic environment was good. The state of theory is in great turmoil but moving toward a new consensus. Some researchers continue to write about structure, particularly its latest and most modish variant, the matrix organization. But primarily the ferment is around another stream of ideas that follow from some startling premises about the limited capacity of decision makers to process information and reach what we usually think of as "rational" decisions.

The stream that today's researchers are tapping is an old one, started in the late 1930s by Fritz Roethlisberger and Chester Barnard, then both at Harvard (Barnard had been president of New Jersey Bell). They challenged rationalist theory, first—in Roethlisberger's case—on the shop floors of Western Electric's Hawthorne plant. Roethlisberger found that simply *paying attention* provided a stimulus to productivity that far exceeded that induced by formal rewards. In a study of workplace hygiene, they turned the lights up and got an expected productivity increase. Then to validate their results they turned the lights down. But something surprising was wrong: productivity went up again. Attention, they concluded, not working conditions per se, made the difference.

Barnard, speaking from the chief executive's perspective, asserted that the CEO's role is to harness the social forces in the organization, to shape and guide values. He described good value-shapers as *effective* managers, contrasting them with the mere manipulators of formal rewards who dealt only with the narrower concept of *efficiency*.

Barnard's words, though quickly picked up by Herbert Simon (whom we'll come back to later), lay dormant for thirty years while the primary management issues focused on decentralization and structure—the appropriate and burning issue of the time.

But then, as the decentralized structure proved to be less than a panacea for all time, and its substitute, the matrix, ran into worse trouble, Barnard's and Simon's ideas triggered a new wave of thinking. On the theory side, it is exemplified by the work of James March and Karl Weick, who attacked the rational model with a vengeance. Weick suggests that organizations learn—and adapt—very slowly. They pay obsessive attention to internal cues long after their practical value has ceased. Important business assumptions are buried deep in the minutiae of organizational systems and other habitual routines whose origins have been long obscured by time. March goes further. He introduced, only slightly facetiously, the garbage can as an organizational metaphor. March pictures organizational learning and decision making as a stream of choices, solutions, decision makers, and opportunities interacting almost randomly to make decisions that carry the organization toward the future. His observations about large organizations parallel Truman's about the presidency: "You issue orders from this office and if you can find out what happens to them after that, you're a better man that I am."

Other researchers have accumulated data which support this unconventional view. Henry Mintzberg made one of the few rigorous studies of how senior managers actually use time. They don't block out large chunks of time for planning, organizing, motivating, and controlling as some suggest they should. Their time, in fact, is appallingly but perhaps necessarily fragmented. Andrew Pettigrew studied the politics of strategic decision and was fascinated by the inertial properties of organizations. He showed that organizations frequently hold onto faulty assumptions about their world for as long as a decade, despite overwhelming evidence that it has changed and they probably should too.

In sum, what the researchers tell us is: "We can explain why you have problems." In the face of complexity and multiple competing demands, organizations simply can't handle decision making in a totally rational way. Not surprisingly, then, a single blunt instrument-like structure is unlikely to prove the master tool that can change organizations with best effect.

Somewhat to our surprise, senior executives in the top-performing companies that we interviewed proved to be speaking very much the same language. They were concerned that the inherent limitations of structural approaches could render their companies insensitive to an unstable business environment marked by rapidly changing threats and opportunities from every quarter—competitors, governments, and unions at home and overseas. Their organizations, they said, had to learn how to build capabilities for rapid and flexible response. Their favored tactic was to choose a temporary focus, facing perhaps one major issue this year and another next year or the year after. Yet at the same time, they were acutely aware of their peoples' needs for a stable, unifying value system—a foundation for long-term continuity. Their task, as they saw it, was largely one of preserving internal stability while adroitly guiding the organization's responses to fast-paced external change.

Companies such as IBM, Kodak, Hewlett-Packard, GM, Du Pont, and P&G, then, seem obsessive in their attention to maintaining a stable culture. At the same time, these giants are more responsive than their competitors. Typically, they do not seek responsiveness through major structural shifts. Instead, they seem to rely on a series of temporary devices to focus the attention of the entire organization for a limited time on a single priority goal or environmental threat.

## SIMON AS EXEMPLAR

Thirty years ago, in *Administrative Behavior*, Herbert Simon (a 1977 Nobel laureate) anticipated several themes that dominate much of today's thinking about organization. Simon's concepts of "satisficing" (settling for adequate instead of optimal solutions) and "the limits of rationality" were, in effect, nails in the coffin of economic man. His ideas, if correct, are crucial. The economic man paradigm has not only influenced the economists but has also influenced thought about the proper organization and administration of most business enterprises—and, by extension, public administration. Traditional thought has it that economic man is basically seeking to maximize against a set of fairly clear objectives. For organization planners the implications of this are that one can specify objectives, determine their appropriate hierarchy, and then logically determine the "best" organization.

Simon labeled this the "rational" view of the administrative world and said, in effect, that it was all right as far as it went but that it had decided limits. For one, most organizations cannot maximize—the goals are really not that clear. Even if they were, most business managers do not have access to complete information, as the economic model requires, but in reality operate with a set of relatively simple decision rules in order to *limit* the information they really need to process to make most decisions. In other words, the rules we use in order to get on with it in big organizations limit our ability to optimize anything.

Suppose the goal is profit maximization. The definition of profit and its maximization varies widely even within a single organization. Is it earnings growth, quality of earnings, maximum return on equity, or the discounted value of the future earnings stream—and if so, at what discount rate? Moreover, business organizations are basically large social structures with diffuse power. Most of the individuals who make them up have different ideas of what the business ought to be. The few at the top seldom agree entirely on the goals of their enterprise, let alone on maximization against one goal. Typically they will not push their views so hard as to destroy the social structure of their enterprise and, in turn, their own power base.

All this leaves the manager in great difficulty. While the research seems valid and the message of complexity rings true, the most innovative work in the field is descriptive. The challenge to the manager is how to organize better. His goal is organization effectiveness. What the researchers are saying is that the subject is much more complex than any of our past prescriptive models have allowed for. What none has been able to usefully say is, "OK, here's what to do about it."

## THE 7-S FRAMEWORK

After a little over a year and a half of pondering this dilemma, we began to formulate a new framework for organizational thought. As we and others have developed it and tested it in teaching, in workshops, and in direct problem solving over the past year, we have found it enormously helpful. It has repeatedly demonstrated its usefulness both in diagnosing the causes of organizational malaise and in formulating programs for improvement. In brief, it seems to work.

Our assertion is that productive organization change is not simply a matter of structure, although structure is important. It is not so simple as the interaction between strategy and structure, although strategy is critical too. Our claim is that effective organizational change is really the relationship between structure, strategy, systems, style, skills, staff, and something we call superordinate goals. (The alliteration is intentional: it serves as an aid to memory.)

Our central idea is that organization effectiveness stems from the interaction of several factors— some not especially obvious and some underanalyzed. Our framework for organization change, graphically depicted in the following exhibit, suggests several important ideas:

- First is the idea of a multiplicity of factors that influence an organization's ability to change and its proper mode of change. Why pay attention to only one or two, ignoring the others? Beyond structure and strategy, there are at least five other identifiable elements. The division is to some extent arbitrary, but it has the merit of acknowledging the complexity identified in the research and segmenting it into manageable parts.

- Second, the diagram is intended to convey the notion of the interconnectedness of the variables—the idea is that it's difficult, perhaps impossible, to make significant progress in one area without making progress in the others as well. Notions of organization change that ignore its many aspects or their interconnectedness are dangerous.

- In a recent article on strategy, *Fortune* commented that perhaps as many as 90 percent of carefully planned strategies don't work. If that is so, our guess would be that the failure is a failure in execution, resulting from inattention to the other S's. Just as a logistics bottleneck can cripple a military strategy, inadequate systems or staff can make paper tigers of the best-laid plans for clobbering competitors.

- Finally, the shape of the diagram is significant. It has no starting point or implied hierarchy. A priori, it isn't obvious which of the seven factors will be the driving force in changing a particular organization at a particular point in time. In some cases, the critical variable might be strategy. In others, it could be systems or structure.

A New View of Organization

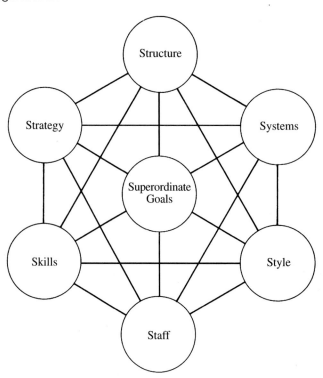

## Structure

To understand this model of organization change better, let us look at each of its elements, beginning—as most organization discussions do—with structure. What will the new organization of the 1980s be like? If decentralization was the trend of the past, what is next? Is it matrix organization? What will "Son of matrix" look like? Our answer is that those questions miss the point.

To see why, let's take a quick look at the history of structural thought and development. The basic theory underlying structure is simple. Structure divides tasks and then provides coordination. It trades off specialization and integration. It decentralizes and then recentralizes.

The old structural division was between production and sales. The chart showing this was called a functional organization. Certain principles of organization, such as one-man/one-boss, limited span of control, grouping of like activities, and commensurate authority and responsibility, seemed universal truths.

What happened to this simple idea? Size and complexity. A company like General Electric has grown over a thousandfold in both sales and earnings in the past eighty years. Much of its growth has come through entry into new and diverse businesses. At a certain level of size and complexity, a functional organization, which is dependent on frequent interaction among all activities, breaks down. As the number of people or businesses increases arithmetically, the number of interactions required to make things work increases geometrically. A company passing a certain size and complexity threshold must decentralize to cope.

Among the first to recognize the problem and explicitly act on it was Du Pont in 1921. The increasing administrative burden brought about by its diversification into several new product lines ultimately led the company to transform its highly centralized, functionally departmental structure into a decentralized, multidivisional one. Meanwhile, General Motors, which has been decentralized from the outset, was learning how to make a decentralized structure work as more than just a holding company.

However, real decentralization in world industry did not take place until much later. In 1950, for example, only about 20 percent of the *Fortune* 500 companies were decentralized. By 1970, 80 percent were decentralized. A similar shift was taking place throughout the industrialized world.

Today three things are happening. First, because of the portfolio concept of managing a business, spun off from General Electric research (which has now become PIMS), companies are saying, "We can do more with our decentralized structure than control complexity. We can shift resources, act flexibly—that is, manage strategically."

Second, the dimensions along which companies want to divide tasks have multiplied. Early on, there were functional divisions. Then came product divisions. Now we have possibilities for division by function, product, market, geography, nation, strategic business unit, and probably more. The rub is that as the new dimensions are added, the old ones don't go away. An insurance company, for example, can organize around market segments, but it still needs functional control over underwriting decisions. The trade-offs are staggering if we try to juggle them all at once.

Third, new centralist forces have eclipsed clean, decentralized divisions of responsibility. In Europe, for example, a company needs a coherent union strategy. In Japan, especially, companies need a centralized approach to the government interface. In the United States, regulation and technology force centralization in the interest of uniformity.

This mess has produced a new organization form: the matrix, which purports, at least in concept, to reconcile the realities of organizational complexity with the imperatives of managerial control. Unfortunately, the two-dimensional matrix model is intrinsically too simple to capture the real situation. Any spatial model that really did capture it would be incomprehensible.

Matrix does, however, have one well-disguised virtue: it calls attention to the central problem in structuring today. That problem is not the one on which most organization designers spend their time-that is, how to divide up tasks. It is one of emphasis and coordination—how to make the whole thing work. The challenge lies not so much in trying to comprehend all the possible dimensions of organization structure as in developing the ability to focus on those dimensions which are currently important to the organization's evolution—and to be ready to refocus as the crucial dimensions shift. General Motors' restless use of structural change—most recently the project center, which led to their effective downsizing effort—is a case in point.

The General Motors solution has a critical attribute—the use of a temporary overlay to accomplish a strategic task. IBM, Texas Instruments, and others have used similar temporary structural weapons. In the process, they have meticulously preserved the shape and spirit of the underlying structure (e.g., the GM division or the TI Product Customer Center). We regularly observe those two attributes among our sample of top performers: the use of the temporary and the maintenance of the simple underlying form.

We speculate that the effective "structure of the eighties" will more likely be described as "flexible" or "temporary"; this matrix-like property will be preserved even as the current affair with the formal matrix structure cools.

## Strategy

If structure is not enough, what is? Obviously, there is strategy. It was Alfred Chandler who first pointed out that structure follows strategy, or more precisely, that a strategy of diversity forces a decentralized structure.[1] Throughout the past decade, the corporate world has given close attention to the interplay between strategy and structure. Certainly, clear ideas about strategy make the job of structural design more rational.

By "strategy" we mean those actions that a company plans in response to or anticipation of changes in its external environment—its customers, its competitors. Strategy is the way a company aims to improve its position vis-à-vis competition—perhaps through low-cost production or delivery, perhaps by providing better value to the customer, perhaps by achieving sales and service dominance. It is, or ought to be, an organization's way of saying: "Here is how we will create unique value."

As the company's chosen route to competitive success, strategy is obviously a central concern in many business situations—especially in highly competitive industries where the game is won or lost on share points. But "structure follows strategy" is by no means the be-all and end-all of organization wisdom. We find too many examples of large, prestigious companies around the world that are replete with strategy and cannot execute any of it. There is little if anything wrong with their structures; the causes of their inability to execute like in other dimensions of our framework. When we turn to nonprofit and public-sector organizations, moreover, we find that the whole meaning of "strategy" is tenuous—but the problem of organizational effectiveness looms as large as ever.

Strategy, then, is clearly a critical variable in organization design—but much more is at work.

## Systems

By systems we mean all the procedures, formal and informal, that make the organization go, day by day and year by year: capital budgeting systems, training systems, cost accounting procedures, budgeting systems. If there is a variable in our model that threatens to dominate the others, it could well be systems. Do you want to understand how an organization really does (or doesn't) get things done? Look at the systems. Do you want to change an organization without disruptive restructuring? Try changing the systems.

A large consumer goods manufacturer was recently trying to come up with an overall corporate strategy. Textbook portfolio theory seemed to apply: Find a good way to segment the business, decide which segments in the total business portfolio are most attractive, invest most heavily in those. The only catch: Reliable cost data by segment were not to be had. The company's management information system was not adequate to support the segmentation.

Again, consider how a bank might go about developing a strategy. A natural first step, it would seem, would be to segment the business by customer and product to discover where the money is made and lost and why. But in trying to do this, most banks almost immediately come up against an intractable costing problem. Because borrowers are also depositors, because transaction volumes vary, because the balance sheet turns fast, and because interest costs are half or more of total costs

[1]Alfred D. Chandler, Jr., *Strategy and Structure: Chapters in the History of the American Industrial Enterprise* (Cambridge, Mass.: MIT Press, 1962).

and unpredictable over the long term, costs for various market segments won't stay put. A strategy based on today's costs could be obsolete tomorrow.

One bank we know has rather successfully sidestepped the problem. Its key to future improvement is not strategy but the systems infrastructure that will allow account officers to negotiate deals favorable to the bank. For them the system is the strategy. Development and implementation of a superior account profitability system, based on a return-on-equity tree, has improved their results dramatically. "Catch a fish for a man and he is fed for a day; teach him to fish and he is fed for life": The proverb applies to organizations in general and to systems in particular.

Another intriguing aspect of systems is the way they mirror the state of an organization. Consider a certain company we'll call International Wickets. For years management has talked about the need to become more market oriented. Yet astonishingly little time is spent in their planning meetings on customers, marketing, market share, or other issues having to do with market orientation. One of their key systems, in other words, remains *very* internally oriented. Without a change in this key system, the market orientation goal will remain unattainable no matter how much change takes place in structure and strategy.

To many business managers the word "systems" has a dull, plodding, middle-management sound. Yet it is astonishing how powerfully systems changes can enhance organizational effectiveness—without the disruptive side effects that so often ensue from tinkering with structure.

## Style

It is remarkable how often writers, in characterizing a corporate management for the business press, fall back on the word "style." Tony O'Reilly's style at Heinz is certainly not AT&T's, yet both are successful. The trouble we have with style is not in recognizing its importance, but in doing much about it. Personalities don't change, or so the conventional wisdom goes.

We think it important to distinguish between the basic personality of a top-management team and the way that team comes across to the organization. Organizations may listen to what managers say, but they believe what managers do. Not words, but patterns of actions are decisive. The power of style, then, is essentially manageable.

One element of a manager's style is how he or she chooses to spend time. As Henry Mintzberg has pointed out, managers don't spend their time in the neatly compartmentalized planning, organizing, motivating, and controlling modes of classical management theory.[2] Their days are a mess—or so it seems. There's a seeming infinity of things they might devote attention to. No top executive attends to all of the demands on his time; the median time spent on any one issue is nine minutes.

What can a top manager do in nine minutes? Actually, a good deal. He can signal what's on his mind; he can reinforce a message; he can nudge people's thinking in a desired direction. Skillful management of his inevitably fragmented time is, in fact, an immensely powerful change lever.

By way of example, we have found differences beyond anything attributable to luck among different companies' success rations in finding oil or mineral deposits. A few years ago, we surveyed a fairly large group of the finders and nonfinders in mineral exploration to discover what they were doing differently. The finders almost always said their secret was "top-management attention." Our reaction was skeptical: "Sure, that's the solution to most problems." But subsequent hard analysis showed that their executives *were* spending more time in the field, *were* blocking out more time for exploration discussions at board meetings, and *were* making more room on their own calendars for exploration-related activities.

[2]Henry Mintzberg, "The Manager's Job: Folklore and Fact," *Harvard Business Review,* July/August 1975: 49–61.

Another aspect of style is symbolic behavior. Taking the same example, the successful finders typically have more people on the board who understand exploration or have headed exploration departments. Typically they fund exploration more consistently (that is, their year-to-year spending patterns are less volatile). They define fewer and more consistent exploration targets. Their exploration activities typically report at a higher organizational level. And they typically articulate better reasons for exploring in the first place.

A chief executive of our acquaintance is fond of saying that the way you recognize a marketing-oriented company is that "everyone talks marketing." He doesn't mean simply that an observable preoccupation with marketing is the end result, the final indication of the company's evaluation toward the marketplace. He means that it can be the lead. Change in orientation often starts when enough people talk about it before they really know what "it" is. Strategic management is not yet a crisply defined concept, but many companies are taking it seriously. If they talk about it enough, it will begin to take on specific meaning for their organizations—and those organizations will change as a result.

This suggests a second attribute of style that is by no means confined to those at the top. Our proposition is that a corporation's style, as a reflection of its culture, has more to do with its ability to change organization or performance than is generally recognized. One company, for example, was considering a certain business opportunity. From a strategic standpoint, analysis showed it to be a winner. The experience of others in the field confirmed that. Management went ahead with the acquisition. Two years later it backed out of the business, at a loss. The acquisition had failed because it simply wasn't consistent with the established corporate culture of the parent organization. It didn't fit their view of themselves. The will to make it work was absent.

Time and again strategic possibilities are blocked—or slowed down—by cultural constraints. One of today's more dramatic examples is the Bell System, where management has undertaken to move a service-oriented culture toward a new and different kind of marketing. The service idea, and its meaning to AT&T, is so deeply embedded in the Bell System's culture that the shift to a new kind of marketing will take years.

The phenomenon at its most dramatic comes to the fore in mergers. In almost every merger, no matter how closely related the businesses, the task of integrating and achieving eventual synergy is a problem no less difficult than combining two cultures. At some level of detail, almost everything done by two parties to a merger will be done differently. This helps explain why the management of acquisitions is so hard. If the two cultures are not integrated, the planned synergies will not accrue. On the other hand, to change too much too soon is to risk uprooting more tradition than can be replanted before the vital skills of the acquiree wither and die.

## Staff

Staff (in the sense of people, not line/staff) is often treated in one of two ways. At the hard end of the spectrum, we talk of appraisal systems, pay scales, formal training programs, and the like. At the soft end, we talk about morale, attitude, motivation, and behavior.

Top management is often, and justifiably, turned off by both these approaches. The first seems too trivial for their immediate concern ("Leave it to the personnel department"), the second too intractable ("We don't want a bunch of shrinks running around, stirring up the place with more attitude surveys").

Our predilection is to broaden and redefine the nature of the people issue. What do the top-performing companies do to foster the process of developing managers? How, for example, do they shape the basic values of their management cadre? Our reason for asking the question at all is simply that no serious discussion of organization can afford to ignore it (although many do). Our reason for framing the question around the development of managers is our observation that the superbly performing companies pay extraordinary attention to managing what might be called the socialization process in their companies. This applies especially to the way they introduce young recruits into the mainstream of their organizations and to the way they manage their careers as the recruits develop into tomorrow's managers.

The process for orchestrating the early careers of incoming managers, for instance, at IBM, Texas Instruments, P&G, Hewlett-Packard, or Citibank is quite different from its counterpart in many other companies we know around the world. Unlike other companies, which often seem prone to sidetrack young but expensive talent into staff positions or other jobs out of the mainstream of the company's business, these leaders take extraordinary care to turn young managers' first jobs into first opportunities for contributing in practical ways to the nuts and-bolts of what the business is all about. If the mainstream of the business is innovation, for example, the first job might be in new-products introduction. If the mainstream of the business is marketing, the MBA's first job could be sales or product management.

The companies who use people best rapidly move their managers into positions of real responsibility, often by the early- to mid-thirties. Various active support devices like assigned mentors, fast-track programs, and carefully orchestrated opportunities for exposure to top management are hallmarks of their management of people.

In addition, these companies are all particularly adept at managing, in a special and focused way, their central cadre of key managers. At Texas Instruments, Exxon, GM, and GE, for instance, a number of the very most senior executives are said to devote several weeks of each year to planning the progress of the top few hundred.

These, then, are a few examples of practical programs through which the superior companies manage people as aggressively and concretely as others manage organization structure. Considering people as a pool of resources to be nurtured, developed, guarded, and allocated is one of the many ways to turn the "staff" dimension of our 7-S framework into something not only amenable to, but worthy of practical control by senior management.

We are often told, "Get the structure 'right' and the people will fit" or "Don't compromise the 'optimum' organization for people considerations." At the other end of the spectrum we are earnestly advised, "The right people can make any organization work." Neither view is correct. People do count, but staff is only one of our seven variables.

## Skills

We added the notion of skills for a highly practical reason: It enables us to capture a company's crucial attributes as no other concept can do. A strategic description of a company, for example, might typically cover markets to be penetrated or types of products to be sold. But how do most of us characterize companies? Not by their strategies or their structures, We tend to characterize them by what they do best. We talk of IBM's orientation to the marketplace, its prodigious customer service capabilities, or its sheer market power. We talk of Du Pont's research prowess, Procter & Gamble's product management capability, ITT's financial controls, Hewlett-Packard's innovation and quality, and Texas Instruments' project management. These dominating attributes, or capabilities, are what we mean by skills.

Now why is this distinction important? Because we regularly observe that organizations facing big discontinuities in business conditions must do more than shift strategic focus. Frequently they need to add a new capability, that is to say, a new skill. The Bell System, for example, is currently striving to add a formidable new array of marketing skills. Small copier companies, upon growing larger, find that they must radically enhance their service capabilities to compete with Xerox. Meanwhile Xerox needs to enhance its response capability in order to fend off a host of new competition. These dominating capability needs, unless explicitly labeled as such, often get lost as the company "attacks a new market" (strategy shift) or "decentralizes to give managers autonomy" (structure shift).

Additionally, we frequently find it helpful to *label* current skills, for the addition of a new skill may come only when the old one is dismantled. Adopting a newly "flexible and adaptive marketing thrust," for example, may be possible only if increases are accepted in certain marketing or distribution costs. Dismantling some of the distracting attributes of an old "manufacturing mentality" (that is, a skill that was perhaps crucial in the past) may be the only way to insure the success of an important change program. Possibly the most difficult problem in trying to organize effectively is that of weeding out old skills—and their supporting systems, structures, etc.—to ensure that important new skills can take root and grow.

## Superordinate Goals

The word "superordinate" literally means "of higher order." By superordinate goals, we mean guiding concepts—a set of values and aspirations, often unwritten, that goes beyond the conventional formal statement of corporate objectives.

Superordinate goals are the fundamental ideas around which a business is built. They are its main values. But they are more as well. They are the broad notions of future direction that the top management team wants to infuse throughout the organization. They are the way in which the team wants to express itself, to leave its own mark. Examples would include Theodore Vail's "universal service" objective, which has so dominated AT&T; the strong drive to "customer service" which guides IBM's marketing; GE's slogan, "Progress is our most important product," which encourages engineers to tinker and innovate throughout the organization; Hewlett-Packard's "innovative people at all levels in the organization"; Dana's obsession with productivity, as a total organization, not just a few at the top; and 3M's dominating culture of "new products."

In a sense, superordinate goals are like the basic postulates in a mathematical system. They are the starting points on which the system is logically built, but in themselves are not logically derived. The ultimate test of their value is not their logic but the usefulness of the system that ensues. Everyone seems to know the importance of compelling superordinate goals. The drive for their accomplishment pulls an organization together. They provide stability in what would otherwise be a shifting set of organization dynamics.

Unlike the other six S's, superordinate goals don't seem to be present in all, or even most, organizations. They are, however, evident in most of the superior performers.

To be readily communicated, superordinate goals need to be succinct. Typically, therefore, they are expressed at high levels of abstraction and may mean very little to outsiders who don't know the organization well. But for those inside, they are rich with significance. Within an organization, superordinate goals, if well articulated, make meanings for people. And making meanings is one of the main functions of leadership.

# CONCLUSION

We have passed rapidly through the variables in our framework. What should the reader have gained from the exercise?

We started with the premise that solutions to today's thorny organizing problems that invoke only structure—or even strategy and structure—are seldom adequate. The inadequacy stems in part from the inability of the two-variable model to explain why organizations are so slow to adapt to change. The reasons often lie among our other variables: systems that embody outdated assumptions, a management style that is at odds with the stated strategy, the absence of a superordinate goal that binds the organization together in pursuit of a common purpose, the refusal to deal concretely with "people problems" and opportunities.

At its most trivial, when we merely use the framework as a checklist, we find that it leads into new terrain in our efforts to understand how organizations really operate or to design a truly comprehensive change program. At a minimum, it gives us a deeper bag in which to collect our experiences.

More importantly, it suggests the wisdom of taking seriously the variables in organizing that have been considered soft, informal, or beneath the purview of top management interest. We believe that style, systems, skills, superordinate goals can be observed directly, even measured—if only they are taken seriously. We think that these variables can be at least as important as strategy and structure in orchestrating major change; indeed, that they are almost critical for achieving necessary, or desirable, change. A shift in systems, a major retraining program for staff, or the generation of top-to-bottom enthusiasm around a new superordinate goal could take years. Changes in strategy and structure, on the surface, may happen more quickly. But the pace of real change is geared to all seven S's.

At its most powerful and complex, the framework forces us to concentrate on interactions and fit. The real energy required to redirect an institution comes when all the variables in the model are aligned. One of our associates looks at our diagram as a set of compasses. "When all seven needles are all pointed the same way," he comments, "you're looking at an *organized* company."

# 20
# Organization Design

---

MANAGING INNOVATION: CONTROLLED CHAOS
> *James Brian Quinn*

RESTORING AMERICAN COMPETITIVENESS:
LOOKING FOR NEW MODELS OF ORGANIZATIONS
> *Tom Peters*

MANAGING 21ST CENTURY NETWORK ORGANIZATIONS
> *Charles C. Snow*
> *Raymond E. Miles*
> *Henry J. Coleman, Jr.*

---

# MANAGING INNOVATION: CONTROLLED CHAOS

## *James Brian Quinn*

Management observers frequently claim that small organizations are more innovative than large ones. But is this commonplace necessarily true? Some large enterprises are highly innovative. How do they do it? Can lessons from these companies and their smaller counterparts help other companies become more innovative?

This article proposes some answers to these questions based on the initial results of an ongoing 2 1/2 year worldwide study. The research sample includes both well-documented small ventures and large U.S., Japanese, and European companies and programs selected for their innovation records. More striking than the cultural differences among these companies are the similarities between innovative small and large organizations and among innovative organizations in different countries. Effective management of innovation seems much the same, regardless of national boundaries or scale of operations.

There are, of course, many reasons why small companies appear to produce a disproportionate number of innovations. First, innovation occurs in a probabilistic setting. A company never knows whether a particular technical result can be achieved and whether it will succeed in the marketplace.

*Source*: Reprinted by permission of *Harvard Business Review* (July–Aug., 1975). Copyright 1975 by The President and Fellows of Harvard College; all rights reserved.

For every new solution that succeeds, tens to hundreds fail. The sheer number of attempts—most by small scale entrepreneurs—means that some ventures will survive. The 90% to 99% that fail are distributed widely throughout society and receive little notice.

On the other hand, a big company that wishes to move a concept from invention to the market-place must absorb all potential failure costs itself. This risk may be socially or managerially intolerable, jeopardizing the many other products, projects, jobs, and communities the company supports. Even if its innovation is successful, a big company may face costs that newcomers do not bear, like converting existing operations and customer bases to the new solution.

By contrast, a new enterprise does not risk losing an existing investment base or cannibalizing customer franchises built at great expense. It does not have to change an internal culture that has successfully supported doing things another way or that has developed intellectual depth and belief in the technologies that led to past successes. Organized groups like labor unions, consumer advocates, and government bureaucracies rarely monitor and resist a small company's moves as they might a big company's. Finally, new companies do not face the psychological pain and the economic costs of laying off employees, shutting down plants and even communities, and displacing supplier relationships built with years of mutual commitment and effort. Such barriers to change in large organizations are real, important, and legitimate.

The complex products and systems that society expects large companies to undertake further compound the risks. Only big companies can develop new ships or locomotives; telecommunication networks; or systems for space, defense, air traffic control, hospital care, mass foods delivery, or nationwide computer interactions. These large-scale projects always carry more risk than single-product introductions. A billion-dollar development aircraft, for example, can fail if one inexpensive part in its 100,000 components fails.

Clearly, a single enterprise cannot by itself develop or produce all the parts needed by such large new systems. And communications among the various groups making design and production decisions on components are always incomplete. The probability of error increases exponentially with complexity, while the system innovator's control over decisions decreases significantly—further escalating potential error costs and risks. Such forces inhibit innovation in large organizations. But proper management can lessen these effects.

## OF INVENTORS & ENTREPRENEURS

A close look at innovative small enterprises reveals much about the successful management of innovation. Of course, not all innovations follow a single pattern. But my research—and other studies in combination—suggest that the following factors are crucial to the success of innovative small companies.

### Need Orientation

Inventor-entrepreneurs tend to be "need or achievement oriented."[1] They believe that if they "do the job better," rewards will follow. They may at first focus on their own view of market needs. But lacking resources, successful small entrepreneurs soon find that it pays to approach potential customers early, test their solutions in users' hands, learn from these interactions, and adapt designs rapidly. Many studies suggest that effective technological innovation develops hand-in-hand with customer demand.[2]

1David McClelland, *The Achieving Society* (New York: Halsted Press, 1976); Gene Bvlinksy, *The Innovation Millionaires* (New York: Scribner's, 1976).

2Eric von Hippel, "Get New Products From Customers," *HBR,* March–April 1982, p. 117.

## Experts and Fanatics

Company founders tend to be pioneers in their technologies and fanatic when it comes to solving problems. They are often described as "possessed" or "obsessed," working toward their objectives to the exclusion even of family or personal relationships. As both experts and fanatics, they perceive probabilities of success as higher than others do. And their commitment allows them to persevere despite the frustrations, ambiguities, and setbacks that always accompany major innovations.

## Long Time Horizons

Their fanaticism may cause inventor-entrepreneurs to underestimate the obstacles and length of time to success. Time horizons for radical innovations make them essentially "irrational" from a present value viewpoint. In my sample, delays between invention and commercial production ranged from 3 to 25 years.[3] In the late 1930s, for example, industrial chemist Russell Marker was working on steroids called sapogenins when he discovered a technique that would degrade one of these, diosgenin, into the female sex hormone progesterone. By processing some ten tons of Mexican yams in rented and borrowed lab space, Marker finally extracted about four pounds of diosgenin and started a tiny business to produce steroids for the laboratory market. But it was not until 1962, over 23 years later, that Syntex, the company Marker founded, obtained FDA approval for its oral contraceptive.

For both psychological and practical reasons, inventor-entrepreneurs generally avoid early formal plans, proceed step-by-step, and sustain themselves by other income and the momentum of the small advances they achieve as they go along.

## Low Early Costs

Innovators tend to work in homes, basements, warehouses, or low-rent facilities whenever possible. They incur few overhead costs; their limited resources go directly into their projects. They pour nights, weekends, and "sweat capital" into their endeavors. They borrow whatever they can. They invent cheap equipment and prototype processes, often improving on what is available in the marketplace. If one approach fails, few people know; little time or money is lost. All this decreases the costs and risks facing a small operation and improves the present value of its potential success.

## Multiple Approaches

Technology tends to advance through a series of random—often highly intuitive—insights frequently triggered by gratuitous interactions between the discoverer and the outside world. Only highly committed entrepreneurs can tolerate (and even enjoy) this chaos. They adopt solutions wherever they can be found, unencumbered by formal plans or PERT charts that would limit the range of their imaginations. When the odds of success are low, the participation and interaction of many motivated players increase the chance that one will succeed.

---

[3]A study at Battelle found an average of 19.2 years between invention and commercial production. Battelle Memorial Laboratories, "Science, Technology, and Innovation," Report to the National Science Foundation, 1973; R. C. Dean, "The Temporal Mismatch: Innovation's Pace vs. Management's Time Horizon," *Research Management*, May 1974, p. 13.

A recent study of initial public offerings made in 1962 shows that only 2% survived and still looked like worthwhile investments 20 years later.[4] Small-scale entrepreneurship looks efficient in part because history only records the survivors.

## Flexibility and Quickness

Undeterred by committees, board approvals, and other bureaucratic delays, the inventor-entrepreneur can experiment, test, recycle, and try again with little time lost. Because technological progress depends largely on the number of successful experiments accomplished per unit of time, fast-moving small entrepreneurs can gain both timing and performance advantages over clumsier competitors. This responsiveness is often crucial in finding early markets for radical innovations where neither innovators, market researchers, nor users can quite visualize a product's real potential. For example, Edison's lights first appeared on ships and in baseball parks; Astroturf was intended to convert the flat roofs and asphalt of playgrounds of city schools into more humane environments; and graphite and boron composites designed for aerospace unexpectedly found their largest markets in sporting goods. Entrepreneurs quickly adjusted their entry strategies to market feedback.

## Incentives

Inventor-entrepreneurs can foresee tangible personal rewards if they are successful. Individuals often want to achieve a technical contribution, recognition, power, or sheer independence, as much as money. For the original, driven personalities who create significant innovations, few other paths offer such clear opportunities to fulfill all their economic, psychological, and career goals at once. Consequently, they do not panic or quit when others with solely monetary goals might.

## Availability of Capital

One of America's great competitive advantages is its rich variety of sources to finance small, low-probability ventures. If entrepreneurs are turned down by one source, other sources can be sought in myriads of creative combinations.

Professionals involved in such financings have developed a characteristic approach to deal with the chaos and uncertainty of innovation. First, they evaluate a proposal's conceptual validity: If the technical problems can be solved, is there a real business there for someone and does it have a large upside potential? Next, they concentrate on people: Is the team thoroughly committed and expert? Is it the best available? Only then do these financiers analyze specific financial estimates in depth. Even then, they recognize that actual outcomes generally depend on subjective factors, not numbers.[5]

Timeliness, aggressiveness, commitment, quality of people, and the flexibility to attack opportunities not at first perceived are crucial. Downside risks are minimized, not by detailed controls, but by spreading risks among multiple projects, keeping early costs low, and gauging the tenacity, flexibility, and capability of the founders.

[4]Business Economics Group, W. R. Grace & Co., 1983.

[5]Christina C. Pence, *How Venture Capitalists Make Venture Decisions* (Ann Arbor, Mich.: UMI Research Press, 1982).

# BUREAUCRATIC BARRIERS TO INNOVATION

Less innovative companies and, unfortunately, most large corporations operate in a very different fashion. The most notable and common constraints on innovation in larger companies include:

## Top Management Isolation

Many senior executives in big companies have little contact with conditions on the factory floor or with customers who might influence their thinking about technological innovation. Since risk perception is inversely related to familiarity and experience, financially oriented top managers are likely to perceive technological innovations as more problematic than acquisitions that may be just as risky but that will appear more familiar.[6]

## Intolerance of Fanatics

Big companies often view entrepreneurial fanatics as embarrassments or troublemakers. Many major cities are now ringed by companies founded by these "nonteam" players—often to the regret of their former employers.

## Short Time Horizons

The perceived corporate need to report a continuous stream of quarterly profits conflicts with the long time spans that major innovations normally require. Such pressures often make publicly owned companies favor quick marketing fixes, cost cutting, and acquisition strategies over process, product, or quality innovations that would yield much more in the long run.

## Accounting Practices

By assessing all its direct, indirect, overtime, and service costs against a project, large corporations have much higher development expenses compared with entrepreneurs working in garages. A project in a big company can quickly become an exposed political target, its potential net present value may sink unacceptably, and an entry into small markets may not justify its sunk costs. An otherwise viable project may soon founder and disappear.

## Excessive Rationalism

Managers in big companies often seek orderly advance through early market research studies or PERT planning. Rather than managing the inevitable chaos of innovation productively, these managers soon drive out the very things that lead to innovation in order to prove their announced plans.

---

[6]Robert H. Hayes and David A. Garvin, "Managing As If Tomorrow Mattered," *HBR,* May–June 1982, p. 70; Robert H. Hayes and William J. Abernathy, "Managing Our Way to Economic Decline," *HBR,* July–August 1980, p. 67.

## Excessive Bureaucracy

In the name of efficiency, bureaucratic structures require many approvals and cause delays at every turn. Experiments that a small company can perform in hours may take days or weeks in large organizations. The interactive feedback that fosters innovation is lost, important time windows can be missed, and real costs and risks rise for the corporation.

## Inappropriate Incentives

Reward and control systems in most big companies are designed to minimize surprises. Yet innovation, by definition, is full of surprises. It often disrupts well-laid plans, accepted power patterns, and entrenched organizational behavior at high costs to many. Few large companies make millionaires of those who create such disruptions, however profitable the innovations may turn out to be. When control systems neither penalize opportunities missed nor reward risks taken, the results are predictable.

# HOW LARGE INNOVATIVE COMPANIES DO IT

Yet some big companies are continuously innovative. Although each such enterprise is distinctive, the successful big innovators I studied have developed techniques that emulate or improve on their smaller counterparts' practices. What are the most important patterns?

## Atmosphere and Vision

Continuous innovation occurs largely because top executives appreciate innovation and manage their company's value system and atmosphere to support it. For example, Sony's founder, Masaru Ibuka, stated in the company's "Purposes of Incorporation" the goal of a "free, dynamic, and pleasant factory…where sincerely motivated personnel can exercise their technological skills to the highest level." Ibuka and Sony's chairman, Akio Morita, inculcated the "Sony spirit" through a series of unusual policies: hiring brilliant people with nontraditional skills (like an opera singer) for high management positions, promoting young people over their elders, designing a new type of living accommodation for workers, and providing visible awards for outstanding technical achievements.

Because familiarity can foster understanding and psychological comfort, engineering and scientific leaders are often those who create atmospheres supportive of innovation, especially in a company's early life. Executive vision is more important than a particular management background—as IBM, Genentech, AT&T, Merck, Elf Aquitaine, Pilkington, and others in my sample illustrate. CEOs of these companies value technology and include technical experts in their highest decision circles.

Innovative managements—whether technical or not—project clear long-term visions for their organizations that go beyond simple economic measures. As Intel's chairman, Gordon Moore, says: "We intend to be the outstandingly successful innovative company in this industry: We intend to continue to be a leader in this revolutionary (semiconductor) technology that is changing the way this world is run." Genentech's original plan expresses a similar vision: "We expect to be the first company to commercialize the [rDNA] technology, and we plan to build a major profitable corporation by manufacturing and marketing needed products that benefit mankind. The future uses of genetic engineering are far reaching and many. Any product produced by a living organism is eventually within the company's reach."

Such visions, vigorously supported, are not "management fluff," but have many practical implications. They attract quality people to the company and give focus to their creative and entrepreneurial drives. When combined with sound internal operations, they help channel growth by concentrating attention on the actions that lead to profitability, rather than on profitability itself. Finally, these visions recognize a realistic time frame for innovation and attract the kind of investors who will support it.

## Orientation to the Market

Innovative companies tie their visions to the practical realities of the marketplace. Although each company uses techniques adapted to its own style and strategy, two elements are always present: a strong market orientation at the very top of the company and mechanisms to ensure interactions between technical and marketing people at lower levels. At Sony, for example, soon after technical people are hired, the company runs them through weeks of retail selling. Sony engineers become sensitive to the ways retail sales practices, product displays, and nonquantifiable customer preferences affect success. Similarly, before AT&T's recent divestiture, Bell Laboratories had an Operating Company Assignment Program to rotate its researchers through AT&T and Western Electric development and production facilities. And it had a rigorous Engineering Complaint System that collected technical problems from operating companies and required Bell Labs to specify within a few weeks how it would resolve or attack each problem.

From top to bench levels in my samples most innovative companies, managers focus primarily on seeking to anticipate and solve customers' emerging problems.

## Small, Flat Organizations

The most innovative large companies in my sample try to keep the total organization flat and project teams small. Development teams normally include only six or seven key people. This number seems to constitute a critical mass of skills while fostering maximum communication and commitment among members. According to research done by my colleague, Victor McGee, the number of channels of communication increases as $n[2(n-1)-1]$. Therefore:

| For team size = | 1 | 2 | 3 | 4 | 5 | 6 | 7 | 8 | 9 | 10 | 11 |
|---|---|---|---|---|---|---|---|---|---|---|---|
| Channels = | 1 | 2 | 9 | 28 | 75 | 186 | 441 | 1016 | 2295 | 5110 | 11253 |

Innovative companies also try to keep their operating divisions and total technical units small—below 400 people. Up to this number, only two layers of management are required to maintain a span of control over 7 people. In units much larger than 400, people quickly lose touch with the concept of their product or process, staffs and bureaucracies tend to grow, and projects may go through too many formal screens to survive. Since it takes a chain of yesses and only one no to kill a project, jeopardy multiplies as management layers increase.

## Multiple Approaches

At first one cannot be sure which of several technical approaches will dominate a field. The history of technology is replete with accidents, mishaps, and chance meetings that allowed one approach or group to emerge rapidly over others. Leo Baekelund was looking for a synthetic shellac when he found Bakelite and started the modem plastics industry. At Syntex, researchers were not looking for

596

an oral contraceptive when they created 19-norprogesterone, the precursor to the active ingredient in half of all contraceptive pills. And the microcomputer was born because Intel's Ted Hoff "happened" to work on a complex calculator just when Digital Equipment Corporation's PDP8 architecture was fresh in his mind.

Such "accidents" are involved in almost all major technological advances, When theory can predict everything, a company has moved to a new stage, from development to production. Murphy's law works because engineers design for what they can foresee; hence what fails is what theory could not predict. And it is rare that the interactions of components and subsystems can be predicted over the lifetime of operations. For example, despite careful theoretical design work, the first high performance jet engine literally tore itself to pieces on its test stand, while others failed in unanticipated operating conditions (like an Iranian sandstorm).

Recognizing the inadequacies of theory, innovative enterprises seem to move faster from paper studies to physical testing than to noninnovative enterprises. When possible, they encourage several prototype programs to proceed in parallel. Sony pursued 10 major options in developing its videotape recorder technology. Each option had two to three subsystem alternatives. Such redundancy helps the company cope with uncertainties in development, motivates people through competition, and improves the amount and quality of information available for making final choices on scale-ups or introductions.

## Developmental Shoot-Outs

Many companies structure shoot-outs among competing approaches only after they reach the prototype stages. They find this practice provides more objective information for making decisions, decreases risk by making choices that best reflect marketplace needs, and helps ensure that the winning option will move ahead with a committed team behind it. Although many managers worry that competing approaches may be inefficient, greater effectiveness in choosing the right solution easily outweighs duplication costs when the market rewards higher performance or when large volumes justify increased sophistication. Under these conditions, parallel development may prove less costly because it both improves the probability of success and reduces development time.

Perhaps the most difficult problem in managing competing projects lies in reintegrating the members of the losing team. If the company is expanding rapidly or if the successful project creates a growth opportunity, losing team members can work on another interesting program or sign on with the winning team as the project moves toward the marketplace. For the shoot-out system to work continuously, however, executives must create a climate that honors high-quality performance whether a project wins or loses, reinvolves people quickly in their technical specialties or in other projects, and accepts and expects rotation among tasks and groups.

At Sony, according to its top R&D manager, the research climate does not penalize the losing team: "We constantly have several alternative projects going. Before the competition is over, before there is a complete loss, we try to smell the potential outcome and begin to prepare for that result as early as possible. Even after we have consensus, we may wait for several months to give the others a chance. Then we begin to give important jobs (on the other programs) to members of the losing groups. If your team doesn't win, you may still be evaluated as performing well. Such people have often received my 'crystal award' for outstanding work. We never talk badly about these people. Ibuka's principle is that doing something, even if it fails, is better than doing nothing. A strike-out at Sony is OK, but you must not just stand there. You must swing at the ball as best you can."

# Skunkworks

Every highly innovative enterprise in my research sample emulated small company practices by using groups that functioned in a skunkworks style. Small teams of engineers, technicians, designers, and model makers were placed together with no intervening organizational or physical barriers to developing a new product from idea to commercial prototype stages. In innovative Japanese companies, top managers often worked hand-in-hand on projects with young engineers. Surprisingly, *ringi* decision making was not evident in these situations. Soichiro Honda was known for working directly on technical problems and emphasizing his technical points by shouting at his engineers or occasionally even hitting them with wrenches!

The skunkworks approach eliminates bureaucracies, allows fast, unfettered communications, permits rapid turnaround times for experiments, and instills a high level of group identity and loyalty. Interestingly, few successful groups in my research were structured in the classic "venture group" form, with a careful balancing of engineering, production, and marketing talents. Instead they acted on an old truism: introducing a new product or process to the world is like raising a healthy child—it needs a mother (champion) who loves it, a father (authority figure with resources) to support it, and pediatricians (specialists) to get it through difficult times. It may survive solely in the hands of specialists, but its chances of success are remote.

# Interactive Learning

Skunkworks are as close as most big companies can come to emulating the highly interactive and motivating learning environment that characterizes successful small ventures. But the best big innovators have gone even farther. Recognizing that the random, chaotic nature of technological change cuts across organizational and even institutional lines, these companies tap into multiple outside sources of technology as well as their customers' capabilities. Enormous external leverages are possible. No company can spend more than a small share of the world's $200 billion devoted to R&D. But like small entrepreneurs, big companies can have much of that total effort cheaply if they try.

In industries such as electronics, customers provide much of the innovation on new products. In other industries, such as textiles, materials or equipment suppliers provide the innovation. In still others, such as biotechnology, universities are dominant, while foreign sources strongly supplement industries such as controlled fusion. Many R&D units have strategies to develop information for trading with outside groups and have teams to cultivate these sources.[7] Large Japanese companies have been notably effective at this. So have U.S. companies as diverse as Du Pont, AT&T, Apple Computer, and Genentech.

An increasing variety of creative relationships exist in which big companies participate—as joint ventures, consortium members, limited partners, guarantors of first markets, major academic funding sources, venture capitalists, spin-off equity holders, and so on. These rival the variety of inventive financing and networking structures that individual entrepreneurs have created.

Indeed, the innovative practices of small and large companies look even more alike. This resemblance is especially striking in the interactions between companies and customers during development. Many experienced big companies are relying less on early market research and more on interactive development with lead customers. Hewlett-Packard, 3M, Sony, and Raychem frequently introduce

---

[7]In *Managing the Flow of Technology* (Cambridge: MIT Press, 1977), Thomas J. Allen illustrates the enormous leverage provided such technology accessors (called "gatekeepers") in R&D organizations.

radically new products through small teams that work closely with lead customers. These teams learn from their customers' needs and innovations, and rapidly modify designs and entry strategies on this information.

Formal market analyses continue to be useful for extending product lines, but they are often misleading when applied to radical innovations. Market studies predicted that Haloid would never sell more than 5,000 xerographic machines, that Intel's microprocessor would never sell more than 100% as many units as there were minicomputers, and that Sony's transistor radios and miniature television sets would fail in the marketplace. At the same time, many eventual failures such as Ford's Edsel, IBM's FS system, and the supersonic transport were studied and planned exhaustively on paper, but lost contact with customers' real needs.

## A STRATEGY FOR INNOVATION

The flexible management practices needed for major innovations often pose problems for established cultures in big companies. Yet there are reasonable steps managers in these companies can take. Innovation can be bred in a surprising variety of organizations, as many examples show. What are its key elements?

### An Opportunity Orientation

In the 1981–1983 recession, many large companies cut back or closed plants as their "only available solution." Yet I repeatedly found that top managers in these companies took these actions without determining firsthand why their customers were buying from competitors, discerning what niches in their markets were growing, or tapping the innovations their own people had to solve problems. These managers foreclosed innumerable options by defining the issue as cost cutting rather than opportunity seeking. As one frustrated division manager in a manufacturing conglomerate put it: "If management doesn't actively seek or welcome technical opportunities, it sure won't hear about them."

By contrast, Intel met the challenge of the last recession with its "20% solution." The professional staff agreed to work one extra day a week to bring innovations to the marketplace earlier than planned. Despite the difficult times, Intel came out of the recession with several important new products ready to go—and it avoided layoffs.

Entrepreneurial companies recognize that they have almost unlimited access to capital and they structure their practices accordingly. They let it be known that if their people come up with good ideas, they can find the necessary capital—just as private venture capitalists or investment bankers find resources for small entrepreneurs.

### Structuring for Innovation

Managers need to think carefully about how innovation fits into their strategy and structure their technology, skills, resources, and organizational commitments accordingly. A few examples suggest the variety of strategies and alignments possible:

- Hewlett-Packard and 3M develop product lines around a series of small, discrete, freestanding products. These companies form units that look like entrepreneurial start-ups. Each has a small team, led by a champion, in low-cost facilities. These companies allow many different proposals to come forward and test them as early as possible in the market-place. They design control systems to spot significant losses on any single entry quickly. They look for high gains on a few winners and blend less successful, smaller entries into prosperous product lines.

- Other companies (like AT&T or the oil majors) have had to make large system investments to last for decades. These companies tend to make long-term needs forecasts. They often start several programs in parallel to be sure of selecting the right technologies. They then exten-sively test new technologies in use before making systemwide commitments. Often they sacrifice speed of entry for long-term low cost and reliability.

- Intel and Dewey & Almy, suppliers of highly technical specialties to OEM, develop strong technical sales networks to discover and understand customer needs in depth. These companies try to have technical solutions designed into customers' products. Such companies have flexible applied technology groups working close to the marketplace. They also have quickly expandable plant facilities and a cutting-edge technology (not necessarily basic research) group that allows rapid selection of currently available technologies.

- Dominant producers like IBM or Matsushita are often not the first to introduce new technolo-gies. They do not want to disturb their successful product lines any sooner than necessary. As market demands become clear, these companies establish precise price-performance windows and form overlapping project teams to come up with the best answer for the marketplace. To decrease market risks, they use product shoot-outs as close to the market as possible. They develop extreme depth in production technologies to keep unit costs low from the outset. Finally, depending on the scale of the market entry, they have project teams report as close to the top as necessary to secure needed management attention and resources.

- Merck and Hoffman-LaRoche, basic research companies, maintain laboratories with better facilities, higher pay, and more freedom than most universities can afford. These companies leverage their internal spending through research grants, clinical grants, and research relation-ships with universities throughout the world. Before they invest $20 million to $50 million to clear a new drug, they must have reasonable assurance that they will be first in the market-place. They take elaborate precautions to ensure that the new entry is safe and effective, and that it cannot be easily duplicated by others. Their structures are designed to be on the cutting edge of science, but conservative in animal testing, clinical evaluation, and production control.

These examples suggest some ways of linking innovation to strategy. Many other examples, of course, exist. Within a single company, individual divisions may have different strategic needs and hence different structures and practices. No single approach works well for all situations.

## Complex Portfolio Planning

Perhaps the most difficult task for top managers is to balance the needs of existing lines against the needs of potential lines. This problem requires a portfolio strategy much more complex than the popular four-box Boston Consulting Group matrix found in most strategy texts. To allocate resources for innovation strategically, managers need to define the broad, long-term actions within and across divisions necessary to achieve their visions. They should determine which positions to hold at all costs, where to fall back, and where to expand initially and in the more distant future.

A company's strategy may often require investing most resources in current lines. But sufficient resources should also be invested in patterns that ensure intermediate and long-term growth; provide defenses against possible government, labor, competitive, or activist challenges; and generate needed organizational, technical, and external relations flexibilities to handle unforeseen opportunities or threats. Sophisticated portfolio planning within and among divisions can protect both current returns and future prospects—the two critical bases for that most cherished goal, high price-earnings ratios.

## AN INCREMENTALIST APPROACH

Such managerial techniques can provide a strategic focus for innovation and help solve many of the timing, coordination, and motivation problems that plague large, bureaucratic organizations. Even more detailed planning techniques may help in guiding the development of the many small innovations that characterize any successful business. My research reveals, however, that few, if any, major innovations result from highly structured planning systems. Within the broad framework I have described, major innovations are best managed as incremental, goal-oriented, interactive learning processes.[8]

Several sophisticated companies have labeled this approach "phased program planning." When they see an important opportunity in the marketplace (or when a laboratory champion presses them), top managers outline some broad, challenging goals for the new programs: "to be the first to prove whether rDNA is commercially feasible for this process," or "to create an economic digital switching system for small country telephone systems." These goals have few key timing, cost, or performance numbers attached. As scientists and engineers (usually from different areas) begin to define technical options, the programs' goals become more specific—though managers still allow much latitude in technical approaches.

As options crystallize, managers try to define the most important technical sequences and critical decision points. They may develop "go, no go" performance criteria for major program phases and communicate these as targets for project teams. In systems innovations, for example, performance specifications must be set to coordinate the interactions of subsystems. Successful companies leave open for as long as possible exactly how these targets can be achieved.

While feeding resources to the most promising options, managers frequently keep other paths open. Many of the best concepts and solutions come from projects partly hidden or "bootlegged" by the organization. Most successful managers try to build some slack or buffers into their plans to hedge their bets, although they hesitate to announce these actions widely. They permit chaos and replication in early investigations, but insist on much more formal planning and controls as expensive development and scale-up proceed. But even at these later stages, these managers have learned to maintain flexibility and to avoid the tyranny of paper plans. They seek inputs from manufacturing, marketing, and customer groups early. Armed with this information, they are prepared to modify their plans even as they enter the marketplace. A European executive describes this process of directing innovation as "a somewhat orderly tumult that can be managed only in an incremental fashion."

### Why Incrementalism?

The innovative process is inherently incremental. As Thomas Hughes says, "Technological systems evolve through relatively small steps marked by an occasional stubborn obstacle and by constant random breakthroughs interacting across laboratories and borders."[9] A forgotten hypothesis of Einstein's

---

[8]For a further discussion of incrementalism, see James Brian Quinn, "Managing Strategies Incrementally," *Omega* 10, no. 6 (1982), p. 613; and *Strategies for Change: Logical Incrementalism* (Homewood, Ill.: Dow Jones-Irwin, 1980).

[9]Thomas Hughes, "The Inventive Continuum," *Science 84*, November 1984, p. 83.

became the laser in Charles Townes's mind as he contemplated azaleas in Franklin Square. The structure of DNA followed a circuitous route through research in biology, organic chemistry, X-ray crystallography, and mathematics toward its Nobel Prize-winning conception as a spiral staircase of amino acids and bases. Such rambling trails are characteristic of virtually all major technological advances.

At the outset of the attack on a technical problem, an innovator often does not know whether his problem is tractable, what approach will prove best, and what concrete characteristics the solution will have if achieved. The logical route, therefore, is to follow several paths—though perhaps with varying degrees of intensity—until more information becomes available. Not knowing precisely where the solution will occur, wise managers establish the widest feasible network for finding and assessing alternative solutions. They keep many options open until one of them seems sure to win. Then they back it heavily.

Managing innovation is like a stud poker game, where one can play several hands. A player has some idea of the likely size of the pot at the beginning, knows the general but not the sure route to winning, buys one card (a project) at a time to gain information about probabilities and the size of the pot, closes hands as they become discouraging, and risks more only late in the hand as knowledge increases.

## Political & Psychological Support

Incrementalism helps deal with the psychological, political, and motivational factors that are crucial to protect success. By keeping goals broad at first, a manager avoids creating undue opposition to a new idea. A few concrete goals may be projected as a challenge. To maintain flexibility, intermediate steps are not developed in detail. Alternate routes can be tried and failures hidden. As early problems are solved, momentum, confidence, and identity build around the new approach. Soon a project develops enough adherents and objective data to withstand its critics' opposition.

As it comes more clearly into competition for resources, its advocates strive to solve problems and maintain its viability. Finally, enough concrete information exists for nontechnical managers to compare the programs fairly with more familiar options. The project now has the legitimacy and political clout to survive which might never have happened if its totality has been disclosed or planned in detail at the beginning. Many sound technical projects have died because their managers did not deal with the politics of survival.

## Chaos Within Guidelines

Effective managers of innovation channel and control its main directions. Like venture capitalists, they administer primarily by setting goals, selecting key people, and establishing a few critical limits and decision points for intervention rather than by implementing elaborate planning or control systems. As technology leads or market needs emerge, these managers set a few—most critical—performance targets and limits. They allow their technical units to decide how to achieve these, subject to defined constraints and reviews at critical junctures.

Early bench-scale project managers may pursue various options, making little attempt at first to integrate each into a total program. Only after key variables are understood—and perhaps measured and demonstrated in lab models—can more precise planning be meaningful. Even then, many factors may remain unknown; chaos and competition can continue to thrive in the pursuit of the solution. At defined review points, however, only those options that can clear performance milestones may continue.

Choosing which projects to kill is perhaps the hardest decision in the management of innovation. In the end, the decision is often intuitive, resting primarily on a manager's technical knowledge and familiarity with innovation processes. Repeatedly, successful managers told me, "Anyone who thinks he can quantify this decision is either a liar or a fool....There are too many unknowables, variables... Ultimately, one must use intuition, a complex feeling, calibrated by experience....We'd be foolish not to check everything, touch all the bases. That's what the models are for. But ultimately it's a judgment about people, commitment, and probabilities....You don't dare use milestones too rigidly."

Even after selecting the approaches to emphasize, innovative managers tend to continue a few others as smaller scale "side bets" or options. In a surprising number of cases, these alternatives prove winners when the planned option fails.

Recognizing the many demands entailed by successful programs, innovative companies find special ways to reward innovators. Sony gives "a small but significant" percentage of a new product's sales to its innovating teams. Pilkington, IBM, and 3M's top executives are often chosen from those who have headed successful new product entries. Intel lets its Magnetic Memory Group operate like a small company, with special performance rewards and simulated stock options. GE, Syntex, and United Technologies help internal innovators establish new companies and take equity positions in "nonrelated" product innovations.

Large companies do not have to make their innovators millionaires, but rewards should be visible and significant. Fortunately, most engineers are happy with the incentives that Tracy Kidder calls "playing pinball"—giving widespread recognition to a job well done and the right to play in the next exciting game.[10] Most innovative companies provide both, but increasingly they are supplementing these with financial rewards to keep their most productive innovators from jumping outside.


## MATCH MANAGEMENT TO THE PROCESS

Management practices in innovative companies reflect the realities of the innovation process itself. Innovation tends to be individually motivated, opportunistic, customer responsive, tumultuous, non-linear, and interactive in its development. Managers can plan overall directions and goals, but surprises are likely to abound. Consequently, innovative companies keep their programs flexible for as long as possible and freeze plans only when necessary for strategic purposes such as timing. Even then they keep options open by specifying broad performance goals and allowing different technical approaches to compete for as long as possible.

Executives need to understand and accept the tumultuous realities of innovation, learn from the experiences of other companies, and adapt the most relevant features of these others to their own management practices and cultures. Many features of small company innovators are also applicable in big companies. With top-level understanding, vision, a commitment to customers and solutions, a genuine portfolio strategy, a flexible entrepreneurial atmosphere, and proper incentives for innovative champions, many more large companies can innovate to meet the severe demands of global competition.

[10]Tracy Kidder, *The Soul of a New Machine* (Boston: Little, Brown, 1981).

# RESTORING AMERICAN COMPETITIVENESS: LOOKING FOR NEW MODELS OF ORGANIZATIONS

*Tom Peters*

Every day brings new reports of lousy American product or service quality, vis-à-vis our foremost overseas competitors. The news of buyers rejecting our products pours in from Des Moines; Miami; Santa Clara County, California; Budapest; Zurich; and even Beijing. Industry after industry is under attack—old manufacturers and new, as well as the great hope of the future, the service industry. Change on an unimagined scale is a must, and islands of good news—those responding with alacrity—are available for our inspection. But it is becoming increasingly clear that the response is not coming fast enough. For instance, even the near-freefall of the dollar does not seem to be enough to make our exports attractive or reduce our passion for others' imports.

"Competitiveness is a macroeconomic issue," the chairman of Toyota Motors stated recently. By and large, I agree. There are things that Washington, Bonn, Tokyo, Sacramento, Harrisburg, and Albany can do to help. But most of the answers lie within—that is, within the heads and hearts of our own managers.

## NEEDED: NEW MODELS

If we are to respond to wildly altered business and economic circumstances, we need entirely new ways of thinking about organizations. The familiar "military model"—the hierarchical, or "charts and boxes" structure—is not bearing up. It is a structure designed for more placid settings, and derived in times when you knew who the enemy was (not today's nameless or faceless Libyan terrorists or religious fanatics led by an old man in Teheran), and had time to prepare a response to your problems. (It took us Americans several years to gear up to win World War II—a luxury we can no longer afford in this era of nuclear capability.)

Likewise, peacetime economic wars of yore were marked by near certainty. Americans brought cheap energy to the fray, and were blessed by a vast "free trade" market at home. And for the first six decades of this century, we knew who our competitors were—a few big, domestic concerns. We knew where their leaders went to school, what cereals they ate for breakfast. Today, almost every U.S. industry has its competitors, from low-cost Malaysia to high-cost Switzerland, topped off by scores of tiny domestic competitors. Every industry now has—and keeps getting—new, unknown competitors. Moreover, the reality of exchange rates, interest rates, rates of inflation, prices of energy, and the ever-reconfigured microprocessor means that all of everything is up for grabs, unknown, constantly gyrating.

But remember that the American colonists broke away from their British masters in a war that featured the use of guerilla tactics. Popular mythology has it that the British insisted on lining up in rigid, straight-line formations to do battle, sorting bright red coats. By contrast, Ethan Allen and his fabled Green Mountain Boys eschewed formations, hid behind trees, and used their skill as crack shots while victoriously scampering through icy woods of the Hampshire Grants (now Vermont).

*Source*: Reprinted from *The Academy of Management Executive*, 1988, with the permission of the author and publisher.

Perhaps we again need organizations that evince the spunk and agility of the Green Mountain Boys rather than the formality of the British—a formality that was out of touch, with the new competitive reality in 18th century colonial wars and is out of touch, now, with the reality of the new economic wars.

Pictures, so it is said, are worth a thousand words. I believe that, and this article is devoted to describing two pictures, or "organizational maps." Neither looks much like a traditional organization chart: there is no square box at the top labeled "Chairman" (or "Vice-Chairman," or "Chief Executive Officer," or "President," and so on). Both charts break tradition in that they include customers, suppliers, distributors, and franchisees. The layouts are circular, moving from customers in toward the corporate chieftains at the circle's center. But beyond the circular scheme, the two bear little resemblance to one another.

## EXHIBIT I: THE INFLEXIBLE, RULE-DETERMINED, MASS PRODUCER OF THE PAST

Let's begin with an assessment of Exhibit I. Start with *a*, the corporate center policy. This is the traditional, invisible, impersonal, generally out-of-touch corporate hub. The tininess of the circle representing the corporate center suggests both tightness and narrowness of scope; communication

EXHIBIT I    The Inflexible, Rule-determined, Mass Producer of the Past: All Persons Know Their Place

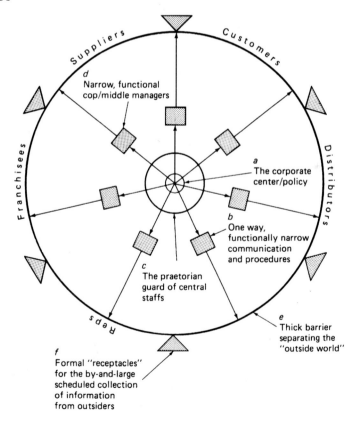

to the outside world (in or beyond the firm's official boundary) is usually via formal declaration—the policy manual or the multivolume plan, by and large determined on high and communicated via the chain of command (i.e., downward). Within this tiny circle lie the "brains of the organization." It is here, almost exclusively, that the long-term thinking, planning, and peering into the future takes place.

Move on to *b*—one-way, functionally narrow communication via rules and procedures. Most communication in this generic organization type is highly channeled (hence the straight line) and top-down (note the direction of the arrowheads). So communication and "control" are principally via rulebook, procedure manual, union contract, or the endless flow of memos providing guidance and demanding an endless stream of microinformation from the line. Moreover, the communication rarely "wobbles" around the circle (look ahead to Exhibit II for a dramatic contrast); that is, the lion's share of the communicating is restricted to the narrow functional specialty (operations, engineering, marketing, etc.), more or less represented by the individual arrows.

Then comes *c*, the praetorian guard of central corporate staffs. The corporate center is tightly protected (note the thick line) by a phalanx of brilliant, MBA-trained, virgin (no line-operating experience), analysis-driven staffs. If the isolation of the corporate chieftains in their plush-carpeted executive suites were not enough, this group seals them off once and for all. It masticates any input from below (i.e., the field) into 14-color desktop-published graphics, with all the blood, sweat, tears, and frustrated customer feedback drained therefrom. On those occasions when the senior team attempts to reach out directly, the staff is as good at cutting its superiors off ("Don't bother, we'll do a study of that marketplace—no need to visit") as it is at cutting off unexpurgated flow from below to the chief and his or her most senior cohorts.

Next, per *d*, are the functionally narrow cop/middle managers. My graphic description is a lumpy (substantial) square, located in the midst of the linear communication flow between the top and the bottom (the bottom, as in last and least—the first line of supervision and the front line). The middle manager, as his or her role is traditionally conceived, sits directly athwart the virtually sole communication channel between the top and the bottom. He or she is, first and foremost, the guardian of functional turf and prerogatives and the *next* block in the communication channel— remember that the praetorian guard was substantial block #1. The "cop" notion is meant to be represented by both the solidity of the block and its direct positioning in the downward communication flow. The middle manager is a filter of data, coming both from the bottom (infrequently) and from the top (much more frequently). The middle manager's job, as depicted here, is seen as vertically oriented (largely confined to the function in question and to passing things up and down) rather than horizontally oriented.

A thick, opaque barrier—*e*—marks the transition from the firm to the outside world of suppliers, customers, distributors, franchisees, reps, and so on. The barrier is very impermeable. Communication, especially informal communication, does not flow readily across it, either from the customer "in" or from the front line of the organization "out."

Which leads directly to the idea of *f*—formal "receptacles" from the scheduled collection of information from outsiders. Of course the old, inflexible organization does communicate with the outside world. But the communication tends to be formal, coming mainly from market research or from orderly interaction via salespeople. Both the timing and the format of the communication is predetermined. Even competitive analysis is rigid, hierarchical, and focused—a formal competitive analysis unit that audits known competitors, mainly on a scheduled basis.

These six attributes are hardly an exhaustive examination of the old-style organization, but they do capture many of its outstanding attributes and orientation—static, formal, top-down oriented, and rule-and-policy determined. It is orderly to a fault (a dandy trait in a different world). To be sure, this depiction is stylized and therefore somewhat unfair, but my observations argue that it captures a frightening amount of the truth in today's larger organizations.

606

# EXHIBIT II: THE FLEXIBLE, POROUS, ADAPTIVE, FLEET-OF-FOOT ORGANIZATION OF THE FUTURE

It takes but a glance to appreciate the radically different nature of Exhibit II—it's a mess! So, welcome to the real world in today's more innovative businesses: start-ups, mid-size firms, and the slimmed-down business units of bigger firms. To the world of The Limited, Benetton, or the Gap in retailing. To the world of Compaq, Sun Microsystems, or the ASIC divisions of Intel or Motorola in computer systems. To the world of steelmakers Worthington Industries, Chaparral, and Nucor. To the world of Weaver Popcorn, Johnsonville Sausage, Neutrogena, ServiceMaster, and University National Bank & Trust of Palo Alto, California. To the world of somewhat ordered chaos, somewhat purposeful confusion; the world, above all, of flexibility, adaptiveness, and action. Or to a new world violently turned upside down.

Begin with *a*—the new-look corporate guidance system, a vital vision, philosophy, set of core values, and an out-and-about senior management team (see b and c below). First, the innermost circle depicting the corporate center in Exhibit II is obviously bigger than its counterpart in Exhibit I. My point is frightfully difficult to describe. I pictured the traditional corporate center in Exhibit I as out of touch, shrivelled, formalistic, and ruled by very tight policy and a constraining rather than opportunistic plan, with contacts inside and outside the enterprise conveyed in written format, usually via brisk, impatient, and bloodless staffers (the praetorian guard). But the visual image that comes to mind for the center of Exhibit II is of a glowing, healthy, breathing corporate center. People from below regularly wander in without muss or fuss, and those at the top are more often than not out wandering. Customers and suppliers are as likely to be members of the executive floor (which, happily, doesn't really exist as a physical entity) as are the members of the senior team. But above all, the glow comes from management's availability, informality, energy, hustle, and the clarity of (and excitement associated with) the competitive vision, philosophy, or core values. Rule here is not written, but by example, by role model, by spirited behavior, and by fun—the vigorous pursuit of a worthwhile competitive idea, whether the firm is a bank, local insurance agency, or superconductor outfit.

Next, as previously anticipated, comes *b*—top management "wandering" across functional barriers and out to the front line in the firm. First, all the communication lines in Exhibit II are portrayed as zigzagging and wavy, with reason: To be as flexible and adaptive as required by tomorrow's competitive situation demands the wholesale smashing of traditional barriers and functional walls, both up and down and from side to side. So, this particular wavy line not only depicts the chief and his or her senior cohorts wandering about, but it shows them purposefully disrespecting those functional spokes (in fact, there are no formal functional spokes in this organization chart). And, of course, the even more significant point is that the chiefs' (and their lieutenants') wandering regularly takes them to where the action is—at the front line, in the distribution center at 2 a.m., at the reservation center, at the night clerk's desk, in the factory, in the lab, or on the operations center floor.

Top management's "somewhat aimless ambling," as I like to call it, is not just restricted to the inside portion of the chart. Therefore, *c* depicts top management "wandering" with customers. Of course, the primary point is that top management is out and about—hanging out in the dealerships, with suppliers, and in general with customers, both big and small. But, again, the waviness of the line suggests a clarification; that is, the senior management visit here is not restricted to the stilted, formal "visit a customer a day" sort of affairs that mark all too many traditional top-management teams. Instead, it is the semi-unplanned visit; the drop-in to the dealer, supplier, or customer; or the largely unscheduled "ride around" with a salesperson on his or her normal, daily route.

EXHIBIT II    The Flexible, Porous, Adaptive, Fleet-of-Foot Organization of the Future:  Every
Is "Paid" to Be Obstreperous, a Disrespecter of Formal Boundaries, to Hustle and
to               Be Engaged Fully with Engendering Swift Action, Constantly Improving Everything

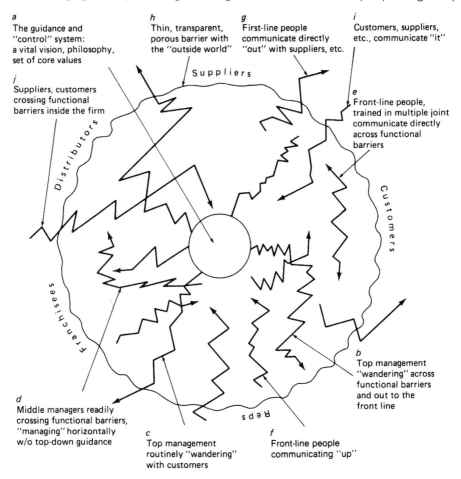

*a*
The guidance and
"control" system:
a vital vision, philosophy,
set of core values

*h*
Thin, transparent,
porous barrier with
the "outside world"

*g*
First-line people
communicate directly
"out" with suppliers, etc.

*i*
Customers, suppliers,
etc., communicate "it"

*j*
Suppliers, customers
crossing functional
barriers inside the firm

Suppliers

*e*
Front-line people,
trained in multiple joint
communicate directly
across functional
barriers

Distributors

Customers

Franchisees

*b*
Top management
"wandering" across
functional barriers
and out to the
front line

*d*
Middle managers readily
crossing functional barriers,
"managing" horizontally
w/o top-down guidance

Reps

*c*
Top management
routinely "wandering"
with customers

*f*
Front-line people
communicating "up"

As important as any of the contrasts between Exhibits I and II is *d*—middle managers routinely crossing functional barriers and managing horizontally without specific top-down guidance. Moving fast to implement anything, particularly engaging in fast-paced new product and service development, demands much faster, much less formal, and much less defensive communication across traditional organization boundaries. Thus, the chief role for the middle manager of the future (albeit much fewer in number than in today's characteristically bloated middle-management ranks) is horizontal management rather than vertical management. The latter, as suggested in Exhibit I, principally involves guarding the sanctity of the functional turf, providing any number of written reasons why function *x* is already overburdened and can't help function *y* at this particular juncture. In the new arrangement, the middle manager is paid proactively to grease skids between functions; that is, to be out of the office working with other functions to accomplish, not block, swift action taking. Once more, the zigzag nature of the line is meant to illustrate an essential point: Communication across functional barriers should be natural, informal, proactive, and helpful, not defensive and not preceded by infinite checking with the next layer(s) of management.

Perhaps the biggest difference involves *e*—frontline people, trained in multiple jobs, also routinely communicating across previously impenetrable functional barriers. The frontline person in Exhibit I has not only been cut off from the rest of the world by the button-down chieftains, praetorian guards, and turf-guarding middle managers, but also by a lack of training and cross-training, a history of not being listened to, and a last layer of cop—an old-school, Simon Legree, firstline supervisor. The role of the new-look frontline person sets all this on its ear. First, he or she is "controlled" not by a supervisor, middle management, or procedure book, but rather by the clarity and excitement of the vision, its daily embodiment by wandering senior managers, an extraordinary level of training, the obvious respect she or he is given, and the self-discipline that almost automatically accompanies exceptional grants of autonomy.

Not only is the frontline person encouraged to learn numerous jobs within the context of the work team, but she or he is also encouraged, at the frontline, to cross functional boundaries. Only regular frontline boundary crossing, in a virtually uninhibited fashion, will bring forth the pace of action necessary for survival today. More formally, in the new regime you would expect to see frontline people as members of quality or productivity improvement teams that involve four or five functions. Informally, you would routinely observe the frontline person talking with the purchasing officer, a quality expert, or an industrial engineer (who she or he called in for advice, not vice versa) or simply chatting with members of the team 75 feet down the line—always at work on improvement projects that disdain old divisions of labor/task.

Move on to *f* and *g*, which take this frontline person two nontraditional steps further. First, *f*—frontline people communicating "up." The key to unlocking extraordinary productivity and quality improvements lies within the heads of the persons who live with the task, the persons on the firing line. Thus, in the newlook organization it becomes more commonplace for the frontline person to be communicating up, perhaps even two or three levels of management up (and one prays that there are no more than that in total) or all the way to the top on occasion.

And then—virtually unheard of outside sales and service departments today—the "average" person, per *g*, will routinely be out and about; that is, frontline people communicating directly with suppliers, customers, etc. Who is the person who best knows the problem with defective supplier material? Obviously, it's the frontline person who lives with it eight hours a day. With a little bit of advice and counsel from team members, and perhaps some occasional help from a middle manager (and following a bunch of perpetual training), who is the best person to visit the supplier—yes, take on a multiday visit that includes discussions with senior supplier management? Answer: It's again obvious—the first-line person or persons who suffer daily at the scene of the supplier's crime.

Now let's turn to the boundary, *h*—a thin, transparent permeable barrier to the outside world. This is yet another extraordinary distinction between the old look and the new-look outfit. Recall Exhibit I: The external barrier was thick, impermeable, and penetrated only at formal "receptacles." The new barrier is thin and wavy. Both the thinness and the imprecision are meant to suggest that there will be regular movement across it, in both directions. Frontline people, and senior people without prior notification, will be heading out with only semiplanned routines. Likewise, "external" colleagues will be regularly hanging out inside the firm (see *i* and *j* below). To be sure, the firm does exist as a legal entity: it is incorporated, and people are on its payroll. But more than any other factor, the idea of the firm turned inside out—the tough, recalcitrant hide that separates from "them" (customers, suppliers, etc.) ripped off—is the image I'm trying to convey. NIH (not invented here) in no longer tolerable. The firm must be permeable to (that it listen to with ease and respect and act upon) ideas from competitors, both small and large, foreign and domestic from interesting noncompetitors; from suppliers, customers, franchisees, reps, dealers, frontline people, and suppliers' frontline persons; and from joint venture partners. It must become virtually impossible to put one's finger on the outside organization boundary. Flow to and fro, by virtually everyone, all the time, and largely informally (i.e., leading to fast improvement without muss, fuss, and memos) must become the norm.

Next we move to *i*—customers, suppliers, etc. communicating (talking, hanging out, and participating "in"). The movement from adversarial to new nonadversarial/partnership relations with outsiders of all stripes is one of the biggest shifts required of American firms. Right now, the big (or small) business organization is typically the site of unabated warfare: top management versus lower management, management versus franchisees, company versus dealers and, above all, company versus suppliers. This must stop—period. Cleaning out the bulk of the distracting praetorian guard and middle management will obviously help, but achieving an attitude of partnership is at the top of the list of requirements, truly "living" a permeable organizational barrier. Customers and suppliers (and their people at all levels) must be part of any new product or service design teams. Even more routinely, customers, suppliers, franchisees, and reps ought to be part of day-to-day productivity and quality improvement teams. Once again, to compete today means to improve constantly, to invest fast; stripping away the impermeable barriers is the sine qua non of speedy implementation.

Which leads directly to *j*—suppliers, customers, etc., crossing functional barriers to work, and help, inside the firm. The idea of *i* was fine and dandy, but not enough. Customers shouldn't just be in the firm; they must be part of its most strategic internal dealings. The supplier shouldn't be shunted off to the purchasing person. Rather, he should be working with cost accountants, factory or operations center people, marketing teams, and new product and service design teams. Moreover, the wavy line suggests that the communication will be informal, not stilted.

There is no doubt that Exhibit II, taken as a whole, appears anarchic. To a large extent, this must be so. To move faster in the face of radical uncertainty (competitors; energy, money, and currency costs; revolutionary technologies; and world instability) means that more chaos, more anarchy is required.[1] But that is only half the story. Return to Exhibit II, idea *a*—the corporate guidance system in the new-look firm. Recall my halting effort to describe it as a glowing sun, an energy center. In fact, the control in Exhibit II may be much tighter than in the traditional Exhibit I organization. Instead of a bunch of stilted, formalistic baloney and out-of-touch leaders, the new control as noted is the energy, excitement, spirit, hustle, and clarity of the competitive vision that emanates from the corporate center. So when the newly empowered frontline person goes out to experiment—for example, to work with a supplier or with a multifunction team on quality or productivity improvement—she or he is, in fact, tightly controlled or guided by the attitudes, beliefs, energy, spirit, and so on, of the vital competitive vision. Moreover, that frontline person is extraordinarily well trained, unlike in the past, and remarkably well informed (for example, almost no performance information is kept secret from him or her). So, it's not at all a matter of tossing people out into a supplier's operation and saying, "We gotta be partners, now." The frontline person "out there" is someone who has seen senior management face to face (and smelled their enthusiasm); a person who has served on numerous multifunction teams; a person whose learning and training is continuous; a person who has just seen last month's divisional P&L in all its gory (or glorious) detail, following a year-long accounting course for all frontline "hands." Thus, there can be an astonishing high degree of controlled flexibility and informality, starting with the frontline and outsiders, in our new-look (Exhibit II) organization.

---

[1] See R. C. Conant and R. W. Ashby, "Every Good Regulator of a System Must Be a Model of That System." *International Journal of Systems Science*, 1970, 1(2), 89–97. There is a compelling theoretical as well as pragmatic basis for the idea. In 1970, Conant and Ashby posited the Law of Requisite Variety, which has become the cornerstone of information theory. In layman's terms, it means that you have to be as messy as the surrounding situation. In a volatile world, we must have more sensors, processing information faster and leading to faster (and by definition more informal) action taking.

But there is also an astonishing amount of hard work required—perpetually clarifying the vision, living the vision, wandering, chatting, listening, *and* providing extraordinary and continuous training, for example—that must precede and/or accompany all this. So, perhaps "purposeful chaos," or something closely akin, is the best description of the Exhibit II new-look firm.

The ultimate point that underlies this brief contrast between and description of the two models is the nonoptional nature of the Exhibit II approach. Americans are getting kicked, battered, and whacked about in industry after industry. We must change, and change fast. The two charts discussed here are radically different, and although I'm not sure that Exhibit II is entirely "correct," I am sure that the radical difference between the two is spot on.

# MANAGING 21ST CENTURY NETWORK ORGANIZATIONS

*Charles C. Snow*
*Raymond E. Miles*
*Henry J. Coleman, Jr.*

*A new form of organization—delayered, downsized, and operating through a network of market-sensitive business units—is changing the global business terrain. What does the growth of these new "network organizations" mean for the training and selection of tomorrow's managers?*

What began quietly, more than a decade ago, has become a revolution. In industry after industry, multilevel hierarchies have given way to clusters of business units coordinated by market mechanisms rather than by layers of middle-management planners and schedulers.

These market-guided entities are now commonly called "network organizations," and their displacement of centrally managed hierarchies has been relentless, though hardly painless—particularly to the million or so managers whose positions have been abolished. Our descriptions of emerging network structures in the late 1970s helped identify this organizational form. Since then, awareness and acceptance have spread rapidly throughout the business community, and recent authors have heralded the network as the organizational form of the future.

The widespread changeover is producing a new agenda for both managers and scholars. To this point, there is growing agreement about the basic characteristics of the network organization, the forces that have shaped it, and some of the arenas for which the network organization appears to be ideally suited, and in which it has achieved major success. What is much less clear, however, is how networks are designed and operated, and where their future applications lie. Most troublesome, perhaps, is the question of how the managers of tomorrow's network organizations should be selected and trained.

*Source*: Reprinted, by permission of publisher, from *Organizational Dynamics*, Spring/1992 © 1993. American Management Association, New York. All rights reserved.

In this article, we first review the progress of the network form and the factors affecting its deployment across the developed and newly industrializing countries of the world. Next, we discuss the major varieties of the network organization, describing and illustrating three specific types of networks: stable, dynamic, and internal. Finally, we identify three managerial roles (architect, lead operator, and caretaker) critical to the success of every network, and we speculate on how managers may be educated to carry out these roles.

## NETWORK STRUCTURES—CAUSES AND EFFECTS

The large, vertically integrated companies that dominated the U.S. economy during the first three quarters of this century arose to serve a growing domestic market for efficiently produced goods. These companies then used their advantages of scale and experience to expand into overseas markets served by less efficient or war-damaged competitors.

Then, during the 1980s in particular, markets around the world changed dramatically, as did the technologies available to serve those markets. Today, competitive pressures demand both efficiency *and* effectiveness. Firms must adapt with increasing speed to market pressures and competitors' innovations, simultaneously controlling and even lowering product or service costs.

Confronted by these demands, the large enterprises designed for the business environment of the 1950s and 1960s—firms that typically sought scale economies through central planning and control mechanisms—understandably faltered. The declining effectiveness of traditionally organized firms produced a new business equation. Instead of advocating resource accumulation and control, this equation linked competitive success to doing fewer things better, with less. Specifically, managers who want their companies to be strong competitors in the 21st century are urged to:

- Search globally for opportunities and resources.
- Maximize returns on all the assets dedicated to a business—whether owned by the managers's firm or by other firms.
- Perform only those functions for which the company has, or can develop, expert skill.
- Outsource those activities that can be performed quicker, more effectively, or at lower cost, by others.

Not surprisingly, firms following these prescriptions frequently find themselves organizing into networks. One firm in the network may research and design a product, another may engineer and manufacture it, a third may handle distribution, and so on. (See Exhibit I.) When numerous designers, producers, and distributors interact, they bring competitive forces to bear on each element of the product or service value chain, and market factors heavily influence resource-allocation decisions. By using a network structure, a firm can operate an ongoing business both efficiently and innovatively, focusing on those things it does well and contracting with other firms for the remaining resources. Alternatively, it can enter new business with minimal financial exposure and at an optimal size, given its unique competencies.

Exhibit II summarizes both the competitive realities facing today's firms and the organizational imperatives these realities produce. The benefits of the network structure in meeting these imperatives, as well as some of the possible costs associated with networks, are discussed below.

# Globalization and Technological Change

Globalization today is a compelling reality, with at least 70 to 85 percent of the U.S. economy feeling the impact of foreign competition. In growing strength and numbers, foreign competitors reduce profit margins on low-end goods to the barest minimum, and they innovate across high-end products and services, at ever-increasing rates.

Moreover, foreign competitors are technologically sophisticated. Around the world, technology is changing at a faster rate than ever before. Perhaps more important, technological innovations are transferring from one industry to another and across international borders at increasing speed. Firms thus find it difficult to build barriers of either technology or location around their businesses.

As a response to increasing globalization and the ease of technology transfer, many U.S. firms are focusing on only those things they do especially well, outsourcing a growing roster of goods and services and ridding themselves of minimally productive assets. Such delayered companies are not only less costly to operate, they are more agile. By limiting operations and performing them expertly, firms require less planning and coordination, and they can accelerate product and service innovations to keep pace with marketplace changes.

For these smaller, more adaptive companies, the global economy contains not only an increasing number of competitors but also more candidates for outsourcing and partnering relationships. Indeed, alliances of various kinds have given rise to the "stateless" corporation in which people, assets, and transactions move freely across international borders. As the world economy continues to concentrate into three regional centers (Europe, North America, and the Pacific Rim), companies scramble for presence in each of these huge markets—something most cannot do single-handedly.

Thus, whether the objective is to extend distribution reach, increase manufacturing efficiency and adaptability, add design capacity, or whatever, the global economy is full of opportunities for networking. Of course, the opportunities available to one firm are probably equally accessible to others, raising concern that the outsourcing firm may not find a manufacturer, supplier, distributor, or designer when one is needed. Further, there are oft-expressed concerns about quality assurance in geographically far-flung networks and worries that extensive outsourcing will increase the likelihood of innovative products being copied (and improved) as technological competence spreads.

# Deregulation

Changing regulatory processes in the U.S. and abroad are a corollary of more sophisticated global competition. Financial deregulation, in particular, has caused an explosion of international profit-seeking activity. For example, the development of overseas capital markets has vaulted formerly minor functions, such as cash management, into the strategic limelight. Many U.S. companies now sweep excess cash from their accounts every afternoon and deposit the funds in overnight money market accounts somewhere in the world.

Frequently, firms find the rules of the game being rewritten after they have placed their bets. Cross-national differences and changes in tax laws, investment credits, and currency exchange rates force companies to constantly re-evaluate how they report profits and invest excess cash.

Essentially, deregulation unleashes entrepreneurial behavior, which in turn raises the level of competition. Often deregulation creates new outsourcing opportunities—as seen, for example, in the increased privatization of public corporations and agencies in many countries. Most important, deregulation reduces margins, and this requires companies to maximize returns on all assets—those they control as well as those their vendors and partners control.

EXHIBIT I   Network Organization Structure

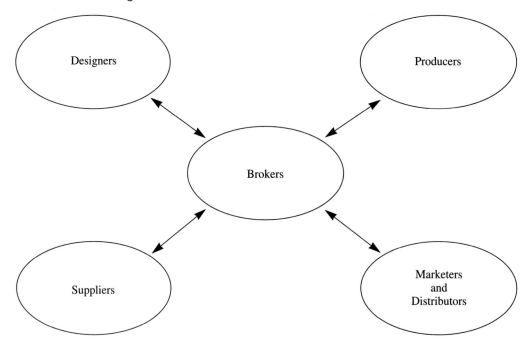

## Work Force Demographics

Changes in the composition of the U.S. work force are also driving companies to abandon the old business equation. Our work force is becoming older, and its growth is slowing. Seventy-five percent of the people who will be in the work force in the year 2000 are already working. As the work force matures, human resource costs will rise, in part because older employees draw more heavily on their companies' health-care and pension benefits. Because older workers are less inclined to move or to be retrained, flexibility and mobility for this segment of the work force will decline. Rising costs and decreasing flexibility are stimulating U.S. companies to search globally for new human resources and to develop empowerment schemes that generate greater returns from their current stock of human capital. Increasingly, so-called minorities will become a larger majority. Women already form a sizable and growing segment of the work force. Immigration from non-English-speaking countries will likely continue (and perhaps expand), adding to training requirements at a time when U.S. public education is in a troubled state.

Given these demographic trends, the network and its operating mechanisms offer some distinct advantages. First, as older workers and some women with small children seek shorter working hours, firms already skilled in outsourcing will invent new means of accommodating these employees' requests for part-time and telecommuting work. Second, firms retain as small a permanent work force as possible, turning more frequently to consulting firms and other resources for temporary employees. Third, more and more firms will allow their employees to make their services available to other firms on a contractual basis.

EXHIBIT II   Organizational Responses to the New Business Environment

---

**The New Competitive Reality**

---

**Driving Forces**
Globalization
Strong new players at every stage of the value
chain (upstream and downstream)
Competition has reduced all margins—no
slack left in most economic systems

Technological Change and Technology Transfer
Shorter product life cycles
Lower barriers to entry
Economies of scope as well as scale

**Interactive Forces**
Deregulation
Legal and policy changes produce
uncertainty and increase competition
Public services are being privatized

Changing Workforce Demographics
Domestic workforce is becoming more mature,
diverse, and less well trained and educated
Global workforce is becoming more mobile

Facilitating Forces
CAD/CAM and other manufacturing advances
Faster, lower cost communications and
computer technologies
More social and political freedom

**Organizational Imperatives**

---

**Product and Service Demands**
Focus on distinctive competence
Reduce costs and accelerate innovation
Hold only productive assets
Reduce overall cycle time

**Managerial Requirements**
Build smaller, better trained, permanent
workforces
Develop and use links to part-time and
temporary human resources
Develop and use links to global
technological resources

---

Although the network form allows for a smaller permanent work force, it requires that work force to be highly trained. In fact, it is the ability of the various network components to apply their expertise to a wide range of related activities that provides the overall network with agility and cost efficiency. For their permanent employees, network firms must be prepared to make large and continuing investments in training and development. Most employees in these companies will need to know how to perform numerous operations, and demonstrate an in-depth understanding of the firms's technologies.

## Communications and Computer Technologies

Network organizations cannot operate effectively unless member firms have the ability to communicate quickly, accurately, and over great distances. Advances in fiber optics, satellite communications, and facsimile machines have made it much easier for managers to communicate within international network organizations. In addition, microcomputers now offer managers and employees all the computational capacity they need, 24 hours a day. And the micros can follow their users wherever they go. Moreover, the cost of data transmission has been declining consistently since the early 1970s, and the decline shows no signs of slowing down. In short, information-processing capacity and geographic distance are no longer major constraints in designing an organization.

Even more important in the long run, computers are changing the traditional concept of product design and production. Today's computer-aided product engineer can quickly produce a multitude of designs or modifications, each complete with parts and components specifications. To evaluate the design of smaller components, an engineer can use stereo lithography, a computer-aided design/laser hookup that "grows" a prototype in a vat, thus achieving a first stage of "desktop manufacturing." Moreover, computer-controlled, general-purpose plant equipment can manufacture directly from computer-stored specifications. Thus, a single manufacturing site can serve several product designers,, using their instructions to guide expensive, but usually fully loaded, equipment. Organizationally speaking, we are at the point where capital investments in complex general-purpose machinery can provide a manufacturing component with the ability to serve numerous partners in a network arrangement.

To summarize, globalization and technological change, coupled with deregulation and changing work force demographics, have created a new competitive reality. Taken together, these forces are placing heavy demands on firms to be simultaneously efficient and adaptive. Global competition and deregulation have squeezed most of the slack out of the U.S. economy, and firms can afford to hold only fully employed, flexible resources. Fortunately, however, network structures permit both high utilization and flexibility. Relying on computer-aided communications, product design, and manufacturing, companies can now forge sophisticated linkages—quickly.

## TYPES OF NETWORK ORGANIZATIONS

As firms turned to some form of network organization to meet competitive challenges, three types of structures became prominent: internal, stable, and dynamic. Though similar in purpose, each type is distinctly suited to a particular competitive environment. (See Exhibit III.)

### Internal Network

An internal network typically arises to capture entrepreneurial and market benefits without having the company engage in much outsourcing. The internal-network firm owns most or all of the assets associated with a particular business. Managers who control these assets are encouraged (if not required) to expose them to the discipline of the market. The basic logic of the internal network is that if internal units have to operate with prices set by the market (instead of artificial transfer prices), then they will constantly seek innovations that improve their performance.

The General Motors' components business provides a good example of an internal network.[1] Through a series of reorganizations and consolidations (mostly in the the 1980s), GM reduced the number of its components divisions to eight. Each of the eight divisions pursues its own specialty; together, they create what has been called a "specialization consortium."

Turning GM's formerly rigid and inefficient components divisions into a group of coordinated and flexible subcontractors required two more actions. First, the parent corporation established clear performance measures for each of the divisions so that their behavior could be legitimately compared

---

[1]The General Motors and BMW examples used in this article to illustrate internal and stable networks, respectively, were drawn from Charles Sabel, Horst Kern, and Gary Herrigel, "Collaborative Manufacturing: New Supplier Relations in the Automobile Industry and the Redefinition of the Industrial Corporation" (Working Paper, Massachusetts Institute of Technology, 1989).

EXHIBIT III   Common Network Types

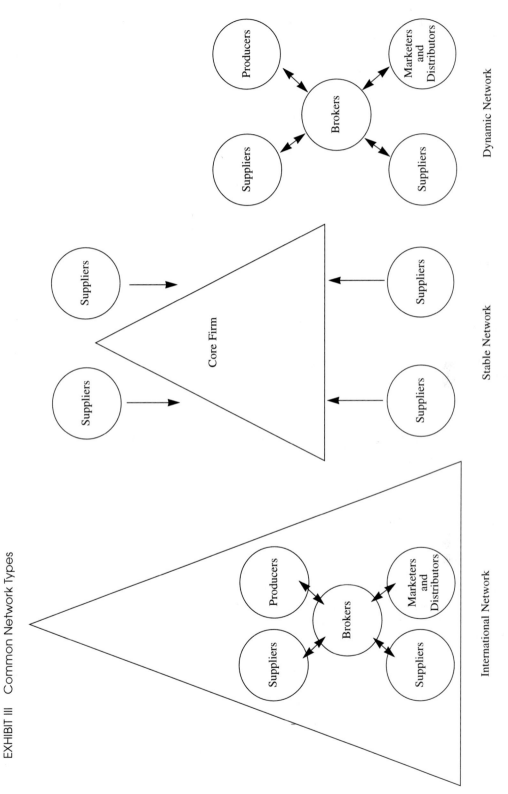

to that of external suppliers. Usually, this meant converting each components facility into a business unit that was encouraged to sell its products on the open market. Second, each division was assigned (or retained) an area of expertise related to a particular automotive system or subassembly. Each division was to be *the* expert at providing its product and to cooperate with other divisions in the consortium whenever appropriate.

To cite a specific example, the AC-Rochester Division was formed in 1988 by merging the former AC Spark Plugs Division and the Rochester Products Division. The combined division specializes in products that govern the flow of air and fluids into and out of the automobile (filters, fuel and exhaust systems, and so forth). The division is organized into several business units, each a specialist, just as AC-Rochester itself is a specialist within the consortium of components divisions. The various business units of AC-Rochester sell their products to GM, of course, but they also sell to Mitsubishi Motors (Japan), Daewoo (Korea), Opel (Europe), and other manufacturers.

If this organizational arrangement were to be extended throughout General Motors, then the parent corporation would eventually evolve toward the brokering function shown in Exhibit I. That is, corporate headquarters would become a holding company that maintained an interest in a broad array of specialization consortia, each of which possessed the ability to complete favorably in international markets. It would seek, through subsidies, taxes, loans, and investments, to keep the "internal economy" healthy, focused, and renewing.

Multinational resource-based companies also gravitate toward internal networks. For example, an international oil company would likely find it too costly to hold resources for exploration, extraction, refining, and distribution in every country in which it operates. Nor is deployment from a central location very practical. No matter where its resources were concentrated, the firm could not allocate them quickly and efficiently with a central planning mechanism. Instead, an internal network is constructed. For the network to operate properly, each of its nodes must interact regularly with outsiders—trading, buying, or selling products and raw materials to other firms in order to bring real prices to bear on internal transactions. Thus, inside the company, clusters of business units, grouped by region and product category, can be seen buying and selling from one another as well as from outside firms.

A well-conceived internal network can reduce resource redundancy and decrease response time to market opportunities. Such a network achieves total resource utilization. But there are pitfalls. Internal networks may sometimes fall victim to corporate politics. Instead of exchanging goods or services at verifiable market prices, divisions transfer goods at administered prices that do not reflect external realities—and bad decisions result.

## Stable Network

The stable network typically employs partial outsourcing and is a way of injecting flexibility into the overall value chain. In the stable network, assets are owned by several firms, but dedicated to a particular business. Often, a set of vendors is nestled around a large "core" firm, either providing inputs to the firm or distributing its outputs. (Again, see Exhibit III.)

BMW, for example, is organized as a stable network. In principle, any part of a BMW is a candidate for outsourcing, and somewhere between 55 and 75 percent of total production costs at BMW come from outsourced parts. As at GM, various internal BMW operating units are obligated to prove their competence according to market standards. Beyond this, however, BMW keeps pace with developments in a variety of relevant product and process technologies through its own subsidiaries, and by partnering with other firms. Three subsidiaries concentrate on technologically advanced forms of automobile development and production: BMW Motor Sports Group, Advanced Engineering Group, and the Motorcycle Group. Each of these subsidiaries, especially Motor Sports and Advanced Engineering, focuses on extending the boundaries of knowledge related to automobile engineering and design. The basic objective of these research groups is to understand enough about a particular technology to know who among potential outside vendors would be the best provider. Further, BMW engages in joint ventures and uses its own venture capital fund to participate financially in the operations of other firms. Currently, four areas are closely monitored: new product materials, new production technologies (e.g., with Cecigram in France), electronics (with Leowe Opta), and basic research in several related fields.

Thus, we can see different forms of network operation within the same industry. In its components business, GM is almost entirely an internal network, whereas BMW relies to a greater extent on outsourcing and partnering.

A stable network spreads asset ownership and risk across independent firms. In bad times, however, the "parent" firm may have to protect the health of smaller "family members." The benefits of stability are the dependability of supply or distribution, as well as close cooperation on scheduling and quality requirements. The "costs" of stability are mutual dependence and some loss of flexibility.

## Dynamic Network

In faster-paced or discontinuous competitive environments, some firms have pushed the network form to the apparent limits of its capabilities. Businesses such as fashion, toys, publishing, motion pictures, and biotechnology may require or allow firms to outsource extensively. (See Exhibit III.) In such circumstances, the lead firm identifies and assembles assets owned largely (or entirely) by other companies. Lead firms typically rely on a core skill such as manufacturing (e.g., Motorola), R&D/design (e.g., Reebok), design/assembly (e.g., Dell Computer), or, in some cases, pure brokering.

An example of a broker-led dynamic network is Lewis Galoob Toys. Only a hundred or so employees run the entire operation. Independent inventors and entertainment companies conceive most of Galoob's products, while outside specialists do most of the design and engineering. Galoob contracts for manufacturing and packaging with a dozen or so vendors in Hong Kong, and they, in turn, pass on the most labor-intensive work to factories in China. When the toys arrive in the U.S., Galoob distributes through commissioned manufacturers' representatives. Galoob does not even collect its accounts. It sells its receivables to Commercial Credit Corporation, a factoring company that also sets Galoob's credit policy. In short, Galoob is the chief broker among all of these independent specialists.

Dynamic networks can provide both specialization and flexibility. Each network node practices its particular expertise, and, if brokers are able to package resources quickly, the company achieves maximum responsiveness. However, dynamic networks run the risk of quality variation across firms, of needed expertise being temporarily unavailable, and of possible exploitation of proprietary knowledge or technology. The dynamic network operates best in competitive situations where there are myriad players, each guided by market pressures to be reliable and to stay at the leading edge of its specialty. The dynamic network is also appropriate in settings where design and production cycles are short enough to prevent knockoffs or where proprietary rights can be protected by law or by outsourcing only standard parts and assemblies.

## THE BROKER'S ROLE

In hierarchically organized firms, the fundamental role of management is to plan, organize, and control resources that are held in-house. In many network firms, however, certain key managers operate *across* rather than *within* hierarchies, creating and assembling resources controlled by outside parties. These managers, therefore, can be thought of as brokers. Three broker roles are especially important to the success of network organizations: architect, lead operator, and caretaker.

EXHIBIT IV   A Value Chain Grid of Firms and Three Operating Networks

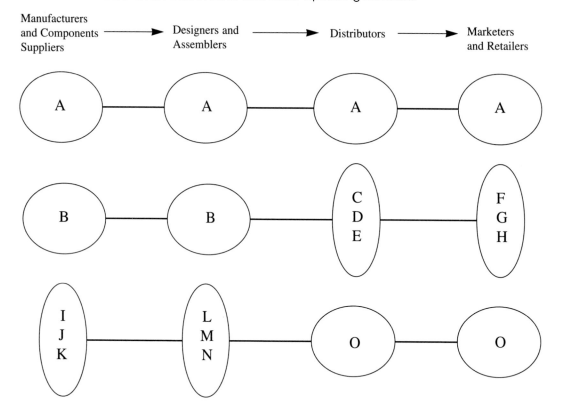

## Architect

Managers who act as architects facilitate the emergence of specific operating networks. Entrepreneurial behavior of this sort has been going on for centuries. For example, beginning in the 13th century, some early network architects fueled the rapid growth of the European cottage textile industry by designing a "putting out" system that organized an army of rural workers who spun thread and wove cloth in their homes. The architects of this system financed the network by providing workers with raw materials to be paid for when the finished goods were delivered. In some cases, brokers also supplied product designs and special equipment suitable for cottage production.

A network architect seldom has a clear or complete vision of all the specific operating networks that may ultimately emerge from his or her efforts. Frequently, the architect has in mind only a vague concept of the product and of the value chain required to offer it. This business concept is then brought into clearer focus as the broker seeks out firms with desirable expertise, takes an equity position in a firm to coax it into the value chain, helps create new groups that are needed in specialized support roles, and so on.

In designing an internal network, it may be relatively easy to identify the appropriate organizational units for each stage of the value chain. In the early years at General Motors, for example, Alfred Sloan envisioned an internal network of automotive suppliers, assemblers, producers, and distributors that could be assembled from among the various firms that William Durant had acquired. The internal network that GM uses today is the modern-day result of a similar process.

In both stable and dynamic networks, the architect's role is likely to be more complicated, because the resources that must be organized are not contained entirely within the firm. The managers who designed BMW's stable network, for example, had to identify several outside firms who would be suitable partners for long-term R&D relationships. When partners and relationships change frequently, as in dynamic networks, certain managers must devote ongoing effort to the architect's role.

The overall result of the architect's efforts can be portrayed as a grid of firms and value-chain elements, such as that shown in Exhibit IV. A grid can be developed entirely within an industry, or it can cut across established industry boundaries. The critical factor is that all firms recognize that they are part of the grid and are at least minimally committed to supporting it. Under these conditions, a number of specific operating networks may emerge.

The personal computer business, for example, is organized in large part around three types of operating networks. One type, perhaps best represented by Tandy Corporation (Radio Shack) offers a product that is mostly designed, manufactured, and sold in-house. Thus, Tandy by itself performs all of the major functions along the value chain. A second network type, represented by Apple Computer, looks much like the Tandy network at the upstream (manufacturing) end, but it contains more distributors and retailers downstream. The third type of network, of which there are many examples, has as its center of gravity the distribution and retailing portion of the value chain. Here distributor-retailers buy off-the-shelf components from various manufacturers, then assemble and sell customized packages of computer hardware and software to specialized market segments.

## Lead Operator

As the grid of firms clustered around a particular business evolves, emphasis shifts from design to decisions about operation. Managers who act primarily as lead operators take advantage of the groundwork laid by manager-architects (although the two roles may overlap considerably and may be played by the same person or group). Essentially, this means that the lead operator formally connects specific firms together into an operating network. At Galoob Toys, for example, a handful of key executives perform this role. They select from a known set of potential partners those individuals and firms needed to design, manufacture, and sell children's toys. The firm outsources virtually every operating activity, choosing to perform only the brokering role in-house.

The lead-operator role is often played by a firm positioned downstream in the value chain. Brokers in the lead firm rely on their negotiating and contracting skills to hook together firms into more-or-less permanent alliances. Nike, an R&D and marketing company, operates this way. However, the lead-operator role is not limited to downstream firms. For example, some large semiconductor manufacturers, such as Intel, have formed alliances with particular assemblers and distributors to promote the sale of new memory and operating chips. These firms advertise their new designs to potential end-users, and major exhibitions are staged to showcase the latest hardware and software developments.

## Caretaker

Networks require continual enhancement if they are to operate smoothly and effectively. Thus, the process of network development is ongoing. Managers who focus on enhancement activity could be called caretakers. The caretaker role is multifaceted and may be just as important as the architect and lead-operator roles to the ultimate success of a network.

A caretaker may have to monitor a large number of relationships with respect to the specific operating network as well as to the larger grid of firms from which it came. In the operating network, this means sharing information among firms about how the network runs, as well as information on recent technological and marketing developments, schedules, and so on. Downstream firms in the value chain need to be kept abreast of new manufacturing capabilities, and upstream firms need an awareness and understanding of coming changes in the marketplace. Thus, the caretaker does more than help the network plan; managers who play this role also help the network learn.

With regard to the grid of potential network firms, the caretaker may engage in nurturing and disciplinary behavior. For example, a caretaker may notice that a particular firm appears to be falling behind technologically, or in some other way devaluing its usefulness to the grid. Appropriate actions could be taken to rectify the situation. An even more troublesome case occurs when a firm exploits its position in the grid—for example, by obtaining some short-run gain at the expense of its actual or potential partners. Here the caretaker's challenge is to point out the dysfunctional effects of such behavior on the overall system and teach the offending firm how to behave more appropriately for the common good.

## IMPLICATIONS FOR BROKER SELECTION AND DEVELOPMENT

If, as seems likely, network organizations continue to spread, it is important to consider how managers with broker skills will be selected and developed. Positions labeled network architect, operator, or caretaker are not commonly found on organization charts, and no career paths are obvious. Nevertheless, it seems that many corporate experiences, and even some university courses, may be vehicles for developing needed skills. Some examples are discussed below.

### Network Design

Many business experiences have characteristics related to network design. For example, in consumer packaged goods firms, product and brand managers learn to build informal networks among the various designers, producers, distributors, and marketers involved in the offering of their product. Similarly, project managers in matrix organizations develop network-building skills as they work across the functional boundaries of their firms and with outside contractors.

Network designers are essentially entrepreneurs, not only pulling together the skills and equipment needed to produce a new product or service, but also, on occasion, arranging the financing. Indeed, many of the network organizations found today in the personal computer, biotechnology, fashion, and entertainment businesses are the joint product of numerous entrepreneurs who originally created a piece of the overall value-chain grid.

However, in most corporations only a limited number of managers are individuals with direct entrepreneurial experience that can be drawn on as a resource. Therefore, firms like 3M and Texas Instruments practice "intrapreneuring"—rewarding their employees for turning ideas into prototype products or services, frequently with limited resources. In fact, one Swedish consulting firm (the Foresight Group) helps firms select and develop intrapreneurs. Interestingly, these consultants accept only volunteers, and they require them to work on their chosen projects while carrying out their regular duties (some limited financial support is also provided). Volunteers are encouraged to "scrounge" for needed resources—both inside and outside the organization. This process has developed many new products, complete with their own internal or external network already in place. The characteristics of intrapreneuring—individual initiative, cross-functional team building, resource acquisition, and so on—are very consistent with the development of successful networks.

Many business schools now offer courses or workshops in entrepreneurship, and most of these cover product and project management, intrapreneuring, and the writing of business plans. While coursework is not a direct substitute for hands-on experience, these courses, often relying on guest lecturers, give students opportunity to explore many aspects of network design and operation.

## Network Operation

The task of putting a network into operation by linking all the value-chain components needed for a given product or service involves not only conceptual and organizational skills but also the skill to negotiate mutually beneficial returns for the contributions of all participants. Here one might look to purchasing or sales as a likely breeding ground for negotiations knowledge and skill. However, experience in such arenas as construction or engineering management may be even more relevant, in that the process of subcontracting is closely akin to network operation. "Partnering" is now common in the construction industry, a process whereby the various parties involved in a project meet in a team-building session to uncover mutual interests and to create the mechanisms and build the trust necessary for resolving the inevitable disputes and inequities.

Again, many business schools now offer courses in negotiation strategies and skills, with emphasis on collaboration and ethical behavior. Understanding the processes of (and the responsibilities involved in) collaborative negotiation is an essential characteristic of the lead operator. The quest is not for an airtight legal contract guaranteeing one's own rights, but for an objective, clearly understood relationship that protects all parties' interests.

Increasingly, as networks extend across international borders, both the network architect and lead operator will require extensive international knowledge and experience. Architects must keep abreast of available skills and resources around the world, and operators must understand how cross-cultural relationships are forged and maintained. It seems likely that courses exploring general international similarities and differences will be helpful, as will courses focused on specific skills, such as those involved in countertrade. Japanese companies are noted for both their ability to build lasting relationships and for their extensive programs for assuring that managers gain hands-on experience across their organizations and various operating regions. Few U.S. firms appear to be as dedicated to such cross-training and experience, and few are as adept at building effective internal and external relationships.

## Networks Caretaking

In some ways, the function of caretaking—maintaining and enhancing an existing network—is both the least understood and the most challenging of the three broker roles. One aspect of caretaking is simply taking care of one's self—for example, by being an active member of a trade association. A more important purpose of the caretaking function is to develop a sense of community among the members of a network. Networks operate effectively when member firms voluntarily behave as if they are all part of a broader organization sharing common objectives and rewards. This sense of community may be easier to instill in an internal network, where assets are held by a single firm, than in a dynamic network, where assets are spread across changeable combinations of designers, manufacturers, suppliers, and so on. Nevertheless, in either case, the network somehow must create an organization "culture" that transcends ownership and national borders.

Clearly, brokers involved in the task of nurturing networks will benefit from team-building skills. General Electric's Workout Program, for example, is designed in part to bring GE's managers, customers, and vendors together to form effective working relationships. Once more, business school courses may be helpful in this area, but theory lags practice. That is, courses in organization development and change contain many useful concepts, but most are oriented toward developing the single firm, not the set of firms that constitutes a network.

In sum, the job of broker, with its attendant roles of architect, lead operator, and caretaker, is unlikely to be filled by managers from any particular part of today's corporation. Individuals from product management, sales, and purchasing may possess some of the knowledge and skills required by the effective network broker. However, none of these functions appears to be the sole source of future brokers. Further, the broker's job is far too complex to lend itself to the use of any available selection instruments. Consequently, as is often the case, a manager's track record may be the best selection and placement device. In any case, however they are chosen, managers must be found for an increasing number of broker positions in the next century.

## THE FUTURE

The forces currently pushing many American companies toward network forms of organization are likely to continue unabated. In fact, the recent emergence of Eastern Europe as a significant factor in the global economy will add to the turbulence currently found in many industries. New foreign producers will add to competitive pressures, and emerging foreign markets will offer opportunities for flexible first movers. In short, it is difficult to imagine any industry ever returning to a form of competition in which traditional pyramidical organizations can survive.

In the future, network organizations will emerge in a variety of circumstances. Dynamic networks, for example, will appear on the fringes of those mature industries that are in danger of stagnation. The ability of networks to generate new products with lower levels of investment will help to invigorate these industry segments. Also, dynamic networks will continue to operate in emerging industries where the pace of new product development and overall market demand cannot be accurately predicted. Alternatively, the efficiency-oriented stable network will become the dominant organizational form in mature, healthy industries. Lastly, an internal network will develop in situations where firms find it is difficult to create a new set of suppliers, but are unwilling to risk the potential inflexibility associated with wholly self-contained units.

Global competition in the 21st century will force every firm to become, at least to some extent, a network designer, operator, and caretaker. And as competition intensifies, companies will find themselves constantly subjecting virtually every internal asset to market tests in order to justify its ownership. However, the most successful firms will not only maximize the utilization of their assets, they will also learn how to market and deploy those assets to other firms. For example, firms will share or lease physical assets (e.g., more than one firm will use the same plant), their skilled staff groups (e.g., logistics units will sell services to other firms), and even their line work teams (e.g., autonomous work groups will be loaned on credit to other firms during slack periods).

Ultimately, every firm may have to decide whether it should create (or join), a cost-based or investment-based network. Eventually, cost-based global networks, which rely on inexpensive labor (or base plants in locales where there is minimal concern for ecological conditions, thus lowering environmental costs) will approach an equilibrium from which it will be difficult to extract further competitive advantages. Investment-driven networks, on the other hand, can be self-renewing. These networks will be constructed around those firms that are prepared to make continual capital expenditures—either for the most-advanced technology or for additional training and development of top-quality people.

# 21
# Job Design and Job Involvement

FROM CONTROL TO COMMITMENT IN THE WORKPLACE
> *Richard E. Walton*

A NEW STRATEGY FOR JOB ENRICHMENT
> *J. Richard Hackman*
> *Greg Oldham*
> *Robert Janson*
> *Kenneth Purdy*

DEMING'S REDEFINITION OF MANAGEMENT
> *Myron Tribus*

# FROM CONTROL TO COMMITMENT IN THE WORKPLACE

*Richard E. Walton*

The larger shape of institutional change is always difficult to recognize when one stands right in the middle of it. Today, throughout American industry, a significant change is underway in long-established approaches to the organization and management of work. Although this shift in attitude and practice takes a wide variety of company-specific forms, its larger shape—its overall pattern—is already visible if one knows where and how to look.

Consider, for example, the marked differences between two plants in the chemical products division of a major U.S. corporation. Both make similar products and employ similar technologies, but that is virtually all they have in common.

The first, organized by businesses with an identifiable product or product line, divides its employees into self-supervising 10- to 15-person work teams that are collectively responsible for a set of related tasks. Each team member has the training to perform many or all of the tasks for which the team is accountable, and pay reflects the level of mastery of required skills. These teams have received assurances that management will go to extra lengths to provide continued employment in any economic downturn. The teams have also been thoroughly briefed on such issues as market share, product costs, and their implications for the business.

*Source*: Reprinted by permission of *Harvard Business Review* (March–April, 1985). Copyright 1985 by The President and Fellows of Harvard College; all rights reserved.

Not surprisingly, this plant is a top performer economically and rates well on all measures of employee satisfaction, absenteeism, turnover, and safety. With its employees actively engaged in identifying and solving problems, it operates with fewer levels of management and fewer specialized departments than do its sister plants. It is also one of the principal suppliers of management talent for these other plants and for the division manufacturing staff.

In the second plant, each employee is responsible for a fixed job and is required to perform up to the minimum standard defined for that job. Peer pressure keeps new employees from exceeding the minimum standards and from taking other initiatives that go beyond basic job requirements. Supervisors, who manage daily assignments and monitor performance, have long since given up hope for anything more than compliance with standards, finding sufficient difficulty in getting their people to perform adequately most of the time. In fact, they and their workers try to prevent the industrial engineering department, which is under pressure from top plant management to improve operations, from using changes in methods to "jack up" standards.

A recent management campaign to document an "airtight case" against employees who have excessive absenteeism or sub-par performance mirrors employees' low morale and high distrust of management. A constant stream of formal grievances, violations of plant rules, harassment of supervisors, wildcat walkouts, and even sabotage has prevented the plant from reaching its productivity and quality goals and has absorbed a disproportionate amount of division staff time. Dealings with the union are characterized by contract negotiations on economic matters and skirmishes over issues of management control.

No responsible manager, of course, would ever wish to encourage the kind of situation at this second plant, yet the determination to understand its deeper causes and to attack them at their root does not come easily. Established modes of doing things have an inertia all their own. Such an effort is, however, in process all across the industrial landscape. And with that effort comes the possibility of a revolution in industrial relations every bit as great as that occasioned by the rise of mass production the better part of a century ago. The challenge is clear to those managers willing to see it— and the potential benefits, enormous.

## APPROACHES TO WORK-FORCE MANAGEMENT

What explains the extraordinary differences between the plants just described? Is it that the first is new (built in 1976) and the other old? Yes and no. Not all new plants enjoy so fruitful an approach to work organization; not all older plants have such intractable problems. Is it that one plant is unionized and the other not? Again, yes and no. The presence of a union may institutionalize conflict and lackluster performance, but it seldom causes them.

At issue here is not so much age or unionization but two radically different strategies for managing a company's or a factory's work force, two incompatible views of what managers can reasonably expect of workers and of the kind of partnership they can share with them. For simplicity, I will speak of these profound differences as reflecting the choice between a strategy based on imposing *control* and a strategy based on eliciting *commitment*.

### The "Control" Strategy

The traditional—or control-oriented—approach to work-force management took shape during the early part of this century in response to the division of work into small, fixed jobs for which individuals could be held accountable. The actual definition of jobs, as of acceptable standards of performance, rested on "lowest common denominator" assumptions about workers' skill and motivation. To monitor and control effort of this assumed caliber, management organized its own responsibilities into a hierarchy of specialized roles buttressed by a top-down allocation of authority and by status symbols attached to positions in the hierarchy.

For workers, compensation followed the rubric of "a fair day's pay for a fair day's work" because precise evaluations were possible when individual job requirements were so carefully prescribed. Most managers had little doubt that labor was best thought of as a variable cost, although some exceptional companies guaranteed job security to head off unionization attempts.

In the traditional approach, there was generally little policy definition with regard to employee voice unless the work force was unionized, in which case damage control strategies predominated. With no union, management relied on an opendoor policy, attitude surveys, and similar devices to learn about employees' concerns. If the work force was unionized, then management bargained terms of employment and established an appeal mechanism. These activities fell to labor relations specialists, who operated independently from line management and whose very existence assumed the inevitability and even the appropriateness of an adversarial relationship between workers and managers. Indeed, to those who saw management's exclusive obligation to be to a company's shareowners and the ownership of property to be the ultimate source of both obligation and prerogative, the claims of employees were constraints, nothing more.

At the heart of this traditional model is the wish to establish order, exercise control, and achieve efficiency in the application of the work force. Although it has distant antecedents in the bureaucracies of both church and military, the model's real father is Frederick W. Taylor, the turn-of-the-century "father of scientific management," whose views about the proper organization of work have long influenced management practice as well as the reactive policies of the U.S. labor movement.

Recently, however, changing expectations among workers have prompted a growing disillusionment with the apparatus of control. At the same time, of course, an intensified challenge from abroad has made the competitive obsolescence of this strategy clear. A model that assumes low employee commitment and that is designed to produce reliable if not outstanding performance simply cannot match the standards of excellence set by world-class competitors. Especially in a high-wage country like the United States, market success depends on a superior level of performance, a level that, in turn, requires a deep commitment, not merely the obedience—if you could obtain it—of workers. And as painful experience shows, this commitment cannot flourish in a work-place dominated by the familiar model of control.

## The "Commitment" Strategy

Since the early 1970s, companies have experimented at the plant level with a radically different workforce strategy. The more visible pioneers—among them, General Foods at Topeka, Kansas; General Motors at Brookhaven, Mississippi; Cummins Engine at Jamestown, New York; and Proctor & Gamble at Lima, Ohio—have begun to show how great and productive the contribution of a truly committed work force can be. For a time, all new plants of this sort were nonunion, but by 1980 the success of efforts undertaken jointly with unions—GM's cooperation with the UAW at the Cadillac plant in Livonia, Michigan, for example—was impressive enough to encourage managers of both new and existing facilities to rethink their approach to the work force.

Stimulated in part by the dramatic turnaround at GM's Tarrytown assembly plant in the mid-1970s, local managers and union officials are increasingly talking about common interests, working to develop mutual trust, and agreeing to sponsor quality-of-work-life (QWL) or employee involvement (EI) activities. Although most of these ventures have been initiated at the local level, major exceptions include the joint effort between the Communication Workers of America and AT&T to promote QWL throughout the Bell System and the UAW-Ford EI program centrally directed by Donald Ephlin of the UAW and Peter Pestillo of Ford. In the nonunion sphere, the spirit of these new initiatives is evident in the decision by workers of Delta Airlines to show their commitment to the company by collecting money to buy a new plane.

More recently, a growing number of manufacturing companies has begun to remove levels of plant hierarchy, increase managers' spans of control, integrate quality and production activities at lower organizational levels, combine production and maintenance operations, and open up new career possibilities for workers. Some corporations have even begun to chart organizational renewal for the entire company. Cummins Engine, for example, has ambitiously committed itself to inform employees about the business, to encourage participation by everyone, and to create jobs that involve greater responsibility and more flexibility.

In this new commitment-based approach to the work force, jobs are designed to be broader than before, to combine planning and implementation, and to include efforts to upgrade operations, not just maintain them. Individual responsibilities are expected to change as conditions change, and teams, not individuals, often are the organizational units accountable for performance. With management hierarchies relatively flat and differences in status minimized, control and lateral coordination depend on shared goals, and expertise rather than formal position determines influence.

People Express, to cite one example, started up with its management hierarchy limited to three levels, organized its work force into three- or four-person groups, and created positions with exceptionally broad scope. Every full-time employee is a "manager": flight managers are pilots who also perform dispatching and safety checks; maintenance managers are technicians with other staff responsibilities; customer service managers take care of ticketing, security clearance, passenger boarding, and in-flight service. Everyone, including the officers, is expected to rotate among functions to boost all workers' understanding of the business and to promote personal development.

Under the commitment strategy, performance expectations are high and serve not to define minimum standards but to provide "stretch objectives," emphasize continuous improvement, and reflect the requirements of the marketplace. Accordingly, compensation policies reflect less the old formulas of job evaluation than the heightened importance of group achievement, the expanded scope of individual contribution, and the growing concern for such questions of "equity" as gain sharing, stock ownership, and profit sharing. This principle of economic sharing is not new. It has long played a role in Dana corporation, which has many unionized plants, and is a fundamental part of the strategy of People Express, which has no union. Today, Ford sees it as an important part of the company's transition to a commitment strategy.

Equally important to the commitment strategy is the challenge of giving employees some assurance of security, perhaps by offering them priority in training and retraining as old jobs are eliminated and new ones created. Guaranteeing employees access to due process and providing them the means to be heard on such issues as production methods, problem solving, and human resource policies and practices is also a challenge. In unionized settings, the additional tasks include making relations less adversarial, broadening the agenda for joint problem solving and planning, and facilitating employee consultation.

Underlying all these policies is a management philosophy, often embodied in a published statement, that acknowledges the legitimate claims of a company's multiple stakeholders—owners, employees, customers, and the public. At the center of this philosophy is a belief that eliciting employee commitment will lead to enhanced performance. The evidence shows this belief to be well-grounded. In the absence of genuine commitment, however, new management policies designed for a committed work force may well leave a company distinctly more vulnerable than would older policies based on the control approach. The advantages—and risks—are considerable.

# THE COSTS OF COMMITMENT

Because the potential leverage of a commitment-oriented strategy on performance is so great, the natural temptation is to assume the universal applicability of that strategy. Some environments, however, especially those requiring intricate teamwork, problem solving, organizational learning, and self-monitoring, are better suited than others to the commitment model. Indeed, the pioneers of the deep commitment strategy—a fertilizer plant in Norway, a refinery in the United Kingdom, a paper mill in Pennsylvania, a pet-food processing plant in Kansas—were all based on continuous process technologies and were all capital and raw material intensive. All provided high economic leverage to improvements in workers' skills and attitudes, and all could offer considerable job challenge.

Is the converse true? Is the control strategy appropriate whenever—as with convicts breaking rocks with sledgehammers in a prison yard—work can be completely prescribed, remains static, and calls for individual, not group, effort? In practice, managers have long answered yes. Mass production, epitomized by the assembly line, has for years been thought suitable for old-fashioned control. But not any longer. Many mass producers, not least the automakers, have recently been trying to reconceive the structure of work and to give employees a significant role in solving problems and improving methods. Why? For many reasons, including to boost in-plant quality, lower warranty costs, cut waste, raise machine utilization and total capacity with the same plant and equipment, reduce operating and support personnel, reduce turnover and absenteeism, and speed up implementation of change. In addition, some managers place direct value on the fact that the commitment policies promote the development of human skills and individual self-esteem.

The benefits, economic and human, of worker commitment extend not only to continuous-process industries but to traditional manufacturing industries as well. What, though, are the costs? To achieve these gains, managers have had to invest extra effort, develop new skills and relationships, cope with higher levels of ambiguity and uncertainty, and experience the pain and discomfort associated with changing habits and attitudes. Some of their skills have become obsolete, and some of their careers have been casualties of change. Union officials, too, have had to face the dislocation and discomfort that inevitably follow any upheaval in attitudes and skills. For their part, workers have inherited more responsibility and, along with it, greater uncertainty and a more open-ended possibility of failure.

Part of the difficulty in assessing these costs is the fact that so many of the following problems inherent to the commitment strategy remain to be solved.

## Employment Assurances

As managers in heavy industry confront economic realities that make such assurances less feasible and as their counterparts in fiercely competitive high-technology areas are forced to rethink early guarantees of employment security, pointed questions await.

Will managers give lifetime assurances to the few, those who reach, say, 15 years' seniority, or will they adopt a general no-layoff policy? Will they demonstrate by policies and practices that employment security, though by no means absolute, is a higher priority item than it was under the control approach? Will they accept greater responsibility for outplacement?

## Compensation

In one sense, the more productive employees under the commitment approach deserve to receive better pay for their better efforts, but how can managers balance this claim on resources with the harsh reality that domestic pay rates have risen to levels that render many of our industries uncompetitive internationally? Already, in such industries as trucking and airlines, new domestic competitors have placed companies that maintain prevailing wage rates at a significant disadvantage. Experience shows, however, that wage freezes and concession bargaining create obstacles to commitment, and new approaches to compensation are difficult to develop at a time when management cannot raise the overall level of pay.

Which approach is really suitable to the commitment model is unclear. Traditional job classifications place limits on the discretion of supervisors and encourage workers' sense of job ownership. Can pay systems based on employees' skill levels, which have long been used in engineering and skilled crafts, prove widely effective? Can these systems make up in greater mastery, positive motivation, and workforce flexibility what they give away in higher average wages?

In capital-intensive businesses, where total payroll accounts for a small percentage of costs, economics favor the move toward pay progression based on deeper and broader mastery. Still, conceptual problems remain with measuring skills, achieving consistency in pay decisions, allocating opportunities for learning new skills, trading off breadth and flexibility against depth, and handling the effects of "topping out" in a system that rewards and encourages personal growth.

There are also practical difficulties. Existing plants cannot, for example, convert to a skill-based structure overnight because of the vested interests of employees in the higher classifications. Similarly, formal profit- or gain-sharing plans like the Scanlon Plan (which shares gains in productivity as measured by improvements in the ratio of payroll to the sales value of production) cannot always operate. At the plant level, formulas that are responsive to what employees can influence, that are not unduly influenced by factors beyond their control, and that are readily understood, are not easy to devise. Small stand-alone businesses with a mature technology and stable markets tend to find the task least troublesome, but they are not the only ones trying to implement the commitment approach.

Yet another problem, very much at issue in the Hyatt-Clark bearing plant, which employees purchased from General Motors in 1981, is the relationship between compensation decisions affecting salaried managers and professionals, on the one hand, and hourly workers, on the other. When they formed the company, workers took a 25% pay cut to make their bearings competitive but the managers maintained and, in certain instances increased, their own salaries in order to help the company attract and retain critical talent. A manager's ability to elicit and preserve commitment, however, is sensitive to issues of equity, as became evident once again when GM and Ford announced huge executive bonuses in the spring of 1984 while keeping hourly wages capped.

## Technology

Computer-based technology can reinforce the control model or facilitate movement to the commitment model. Applications can narrow the scope of jobs or broaden them, emphasize the individual nature of tasks or promote the work of groups, centralize or decentralize the making of decisions, and create performance measures that emphasize learning or hierarchical control.

To date, the effects of this technology on control and commitment have been largely unintentional and unexpected. Even in organizations otherwise pursuing a commitment strategy, managers have rarely appreciated that the side effects of technology are not somehow "given" in the nature of things or that they can be actively managed. In fact, computer-based technology may be the least deterministic, most flexible technology to enter the workplace since the industrial revolution. As it becomes less hardware-dependent and more software-intensive and as the cost of computer power declines, the variety of ways to meet business requirements expands, each with a different set of human implications. Management has yet to identify the potential role of technology policy in the commitment strategy, and it has yet to invent concepts and methods to realize that potential.

EXHIBIT I  Work-force strategies

| | Control | Transitional | Commitment |
|---|---|---|---|
| Job design principles | Individual attention limited to performing individual job. | Scope of individual responsibility extended to upgrading system performance, via participative problem-solving groups in QWL, EI, and quality circle programs. | Individual responsibility extended to upgrading system performance. |
| | Job design deskills and fragments work and separates doing and thinking. | No change in traditional job design or accountability. | Job design enhances content of work, emphasizes whole task, and combines doing and thinking. |
| | Accountability focused on individual. | | Frequent use of teams as basis accountable unit. |
| | Fixed job definition. | | Flexible definition of duties, contingent on changing conditions. |
| Performance expectations | Measured standards define minimum performance. Stability seen as desirable. | | Emphasis placed on higher, "stretch objectives," which tend to be dynamic and oriented to the marketplace. |
| Management organization: structure systems and style | Structure tends to be layered, with top-down controls. | No basis changes in approaches to structure, control, or authority. | Flat organization structure with mutual influence systems. |
| | Coordination and control rely on rules and procedures. | | Coordination and control based more on shared goals, values, and traditions. |
| | More emphasis on prerogatives than positional authority. | | Management emphasis on problem solving and relevant information and expertise. |
| | Status symbols distributed to reinforce hierarchy. | A few visible symbols change. | Minimum status differentials to deemphasize inherent hierarchy. |

EXHIBIT I  Work-force strategies (continued)

| | Control | Transitional | Commitment |
|---|---|---|---|
| Compensation policies | Variable pay where feasible to provide individual incentive. | Typically no basis changes in compensation concepts. | Variable rewards to create equity and to reinforce group achievements: gain sharing, profit sharing. |
| | Individual pay geared to job evaluation. | | Individual pay linked to skills and mastery. |
| | In downturn, cuts concentrated on hourly payroll. | Equality of sacrifice among employee groups. | Equality of sacrifice. |
| Employment assurances | Employees regarded as variable costs. | Assurances that participation will not result in job loss. | Assurances that participation will not result in loss of job. |
| | | Extra effort to avoid layoffs | High commitment to avoid or assist in reemployment. |
| | | | Priority for training and retaining existing work force. |
| Employee voice policies | Employee input allowed on relatively narrow agenda. Attendant risks emphasized. Method include open-door policy, attitude surveys, grievance procedures, and collective bargaining in some organizations. | Addition of limited, ad hoc consultation mechanisms. No change in corporate governance. | Employee participation encouraged on wide range of issues. Attendant benefits emphasized. New concepts of corporate governance. |
| | Business information distributed on strictly defined "need to know" basis. | Additional sharing of information. | Business data shared widely. |
| Labor-management relations | Adversarial labor relations; emphasis on interest conflict. | Thawing of adversarial attitudes; joint sponsorship of QWL or EI; emphasis on common fate. | Mutuality in relations; joint planning and problem solving on expanded agenda. |
| | | | Unions, management, and workers redefine their respective roles. |

## Supervisors

The commitment model requires first-line supervisors to facilitate rather than direct the work force, to impart rather than merely practice their technical and administrative expertise, and to help workers develop the ability to manage themselves. In practice, supervisors are to delegate away most of their traditional functions—often without having received adequate training and support for their new team-building tasks or having their own needs for voice, dignity, and fulfillment recognized.

These dilemmas are even visible in the new titles many supervisors carry—"team advisers" or "team consultants," for example—most of which imply that supervisors are not in the chain of command, although they are expected to be directive if necessary and assume functions delegated to the work force if they are not being performed. Part of the confusion here is the failure to distinguish the behavioral style required of supervisors from the basic responsibilities assigned them. Their ideal style may be advisory, but their responsibilities are to achieve certain human and economic outcomes. With experience, however, as first-line managers become more comfortable with the notion of delegating what subordinates are ready and able to perform, the problem will diminish.

Other difficulties are less tractable. The new breed of supervisors must have a level of interpersonal skill and conceptual ability often lacking in the present supervisory work force. Some companies have tried to address this lack by using the position as an entry point to management for college graduates. This approach may succeed where the work force has already acquired the necessary technical expertise, but it blocks a route of advancement for workers and sharpens the dividing line between management and other employees. Moreover, unless the company intends to open up higher level positions for these college-educated supervisors, they may well grow impatient with the shift work of first-line supervision.

Even when new supervisory roles are filled—and filled successfully—from the ranks, dilemmas remain. With teams developed and functions delegated, to what new challenges do they turn to utilize fully their own capabilities? Do those capabilities match the demands of the other managerial work they might take on? If fewer and fewer supervisors are required as their individual span of control extends to a second and a third work team, what promotional opportunities exist for the rest? Where do they go?

## Union-Management Relations

Some companies, as they move from control to commitment, seek to decertify their unions and, at the same time, strengthen their employees' bond to the company. Others—like GM, Ford, Jones & Laughlin, and AT&T—pursue cooperation intensified in the late 1970s, as improved work-force effectiveness could not by itself close the competitive gap in many industries and wage concessions became necessary. Based on their own analysis of competitive conditions, unions sometimes agreed to these concessions but expanded their influence over matters previously subject to management control.

These developments open up new questions. Where companies are trying to preserve the nonunion status of some plants and yet promote collaborative union relations in others, will unions increasingly force the company to choose? After General Motors saw the potential of its joint QWL program with the UAW, it signed a neutrality clause (in 1976) and then an understanding about automatic recognition in new plants (in 1979). If forced to choose, what will other managements do? Further, where union and management have collaborated in promoting QWL, how can the union prevent management from using the program to appeal directly to the workers about issues, such as wage concessions, that are subject to collective bargaining?

And if, in the spirit of mutuality, both sides agree to expand their joint agenda, what new risks will they face? Do union officials have the expertise to deal effectively with new agenda items like investment, pricing, and technology? To support QWL activities, they already have had to expand their skills and commit substantial resources at a time when shrinking employment has reduced their membership and thus their finances.

## THE TRANSITIONAL STAGE

Although some organizations have adopted a comprehensive version of the commitment approach, most initially take on a more limited set of changes, which I refer to as a "transitional" stage or approach. The challenge here is to modify expectations, to make credible the leaders' stated intentions for further movement, and to support the initial changes in behavior. These transitional efforts can achieve a temporary equilibrium, provided they are viewed as part of a movement toward a comprehensive commitment strategy.

The cornerstone of the transitional stage is the voluntary participation of employees in problem-solving groups like quality circles. In unionized organizations, union-management dialogue leading to a jointly sponsored program is a condition for this type of employee involvement, which must then be supported by additional training and communication and by a shift in management style. Managers must also seek ways to consult employees about changes that affect them and to assure them that management will make every effort to avoid, defer, or minimize layoffs from higher productivity. When volume-related layoffs or concessions on pay are unavoidable, the principle of "equality of sacrifice" must apply to all employee groups, not just the hourly work force.

As a rule, during the early stages of transformation, few immediate changes can occur in the basic design of jobs, the compensation system, or the management system itself. It is easy, of course, to attempt to change too much too soon. A more common error, especially in established organizations, is to make only "token" changes that never reach a critical mass. All too often managers try a succession of technique-oriented changes one by one: job enrichment, sensitivity training, management by objectives, group brainstorming, quality circles, and so on. Whatever the benefits of these techniques, their value to the organization will rapidly decay if the management philosophy—and practice-does not shift accordingly.

A different type of error—"overreaching"—may occur in newly established organizations based on commitment principles. In one new plant, managers allowed too much peer influence in pay decisions; in another, they underplayed the role of first-line supervisors as a link in the chain of command; in a third, they overemphasized learning of new skills and flexibility at the expense of mastery in critical operations. These design errors by themselves are not fatal, but the organization must be able to make mid-course corrections.

## RATE OF TRANSFORMATION

How rapidly is the transformation in work-force strategy, summarized in the *Exhibit*, occurring? Hard data are difficult to come by, but certain trends are clear. In 1970, only a few plants in the United States were systematically revising their approach to the work force. By 1975, hundreds of plants were involved. Today, I estimate that at least a thousand plants are in the process of making a comprehensive change and that many times that number are somewhere in the transitional stage.

In the early 1970s, plant managers tended to sponsor what efforts there were. Today, company presidents are formulating the plans. Not long ago, the initiatives were experimental; now they are policy. Early change focused on the blue-collar work force and on those clerical operations that most closely resemble the factory. Although clerical change has lagged somewhat—because the control model has not produced such overt employee disaffection, and because management has been slow to recognize the importance of quality and productivity improvement—there are signs of a quickened pace of change in clerical operations.

Only a small fraction of U.S. workplaces today can boast of a comprehensive commitment strategy, but the rate of transformation continues to accelerate, and the move toward commitment via some explicit transitional stage extends to a still larger number of plants and offices. This transformation may be fueled by economic necessity, but other factors are shaping and pacing it—individual leadership in management and labor, philosophical choices, organizational competence in managing change, and cumulative learning from change itself.

## SUGGESTED READINGS

Irving Bluestone, "Labor's Stake in Improving the Quality of Working Life," *The Quality of Working Life and the 1980s,* ed. Harvey Kolodny and Hans van Beinum (New York: Praeger, 1983).

Robert H. Guest, "Quality of Work Life—Learning from Tarrytown," *HBR,* July–August 1979, p. 76.

Janice A. Klein, "Why Supervisors Resist Employee Involvement," *HBR,* September–October 1984, p. 87.

John F. Runcie, " 'By Days I Make the Cars' " *HBR,* May–June 1980, p. 106.

W. Earl Sasser and Frank S. Leonard, "Let First-Level Supervisors Do Their Job," *HBR,* March–April 1980, p. 113.

Leonard A. Schlesinger and Janice A. Klein, "The First-Line Supervisor: Past, Present and Future," *Handbook of Organizational Behavior,* ed. Jay W. Lorsch (Englewood Cliffs, N.J.: Prentice-Hall, 1983).

Richard E. Walton, "Work Innovations in the United States," *HBR,* July–August 1979, p. 88; "Improving the Quality of Work Life," *HBR,* May–June 1974, p. 12; "How to Counter Alienation in the Plant," *HBR,* November–December 1972, p. 70.

Richard E. Walton and Leonard A. Schlesinger, "Do Supervisors Thrive in Participative Work Systems?" *Organizational Dynamics,* Winter 1979, p. 25.

Richard E. Walton and Wendy Vittori, "New Information Technology: Organizational Problem or Opportunity?" *Office: Technology and People,* No. 1, 1983, p. 249.

# A NEW STRATEGY FOR JOB ENRICHMENT

*J. Richard Hackman*
*Greg Oldham*
*Robert Janson*
*Kenneth Purdy*

We present here a new strategy for going about the redesign of work. The strategy is based on three years of collaborative work and cross-fertilization among the authors—two of whom are academic researchers and two of whom are active practitioners in job enrichment. Our approach is new, but it has been tested in many organizations. It draws on the contributions of both management practice and psychological theory, but it is firmly in the middle ground between them. It builds on and complements previous work by Herzberg and others, but provides for the first time a set of tools for diagnosing existing jobs—and a map for translating the *diagnostic* results into specific action steps for change. What we have, then, is the following:

1. A theory that specifies when people will get personally "turned on" to their work. The theory shows what kinds of jobs are most likely to generate excitement and commitment about work, and what kinds of employees it works best for.

2. A set of action steps for job enrichment based on the theory, which prescribe in concrete terms what to do to make jobs more motivating for the people who do them.

3. Evidence that the theory holds water and that it can be used to bring about measurable—and sometimes dramatic—improvements in employee work behavior, in job satisfaction, and in the financial performance of the organizational unit involved.

## THE THEORY BEHIND THE STRATEGY

### What Makes People Get Turned on to Their Work?

For workers who are really prospering in their jobs, work is likely to be a lot like play. Consider, for example, a golfer at a driving range, practicing to get rid of a hook. His activity is *meaningful* to him; he has chosen to do it because he gets a "kick" from testing his skills by playing the game. He knows that he alone is *responsible* for what happens when he hits the ball. And he has *knowledge of the results* within a few seconds.

Behavioral scientists have found that the three "psychological states" experienced by the golfer in the above example also are critical in determining a person's motivation and satisfaction on the job.

***Experienced Meaningfulness.*** The individual must perceive his work as worthwhile or important by some system of values he accepts.

***Experienced Responsibility.*** He must believe that he personally is accountable for the outcomes of his efforts.

***Knowledge of Results.*** He must be able to determine, on some fairly regular basis, whether or not the outcomes of his work are satisfactory.

*Source*: *California Management Review*, Summer 1975, pp. 57–71.

When these three conditions are present, a person tends to feel very good about himself when he performs well. And those good feelings will prompt him to try to continue to do well—so he can continue to earn the positive feelings in the future. That is what is meant by "internal motivation"—being turned on to one's work because of the positive internal feelings that are generated by doing well, rather than being dependent on external factors (such as incentive pay or compliments from the boss) for the motivation to work effectively.

What if one of the three psychological states is missing? Motivation drops markedly. Suppose, for example, that our golfer has settled in at the driving range to practice for a couple of hours. Suddenly a fog drifts in over the range. He can no longer see if the ball starts to tail off to the left a hundred yards out. The satisfaction he got from hitting straight down the middle—and the motivation to try to correct something whenever he didn't—are both gone. If the fog stays, it's likely that he soon will be packing up his clubs.

The relationship between the three psychological states and on-the-job outcomes is illustrated in Figure 1. When all three are high, then internal work motivation, job satisfaction, and work quality are high, and absenteeism and turnover are low.

## What Job Characteristics Make It Happen?

Recent research has identified five "core" characteristics of jobs that elicit the psychological states described above.[1-3] These five core job dimensions provide the key to objectively measuring jobs and to changing them so that they have high potential for motivating people who do them.

FIGURE 1    Relationships Among Core Job Dimensions, Critical Psychological States, and On-the-Job Outcomes

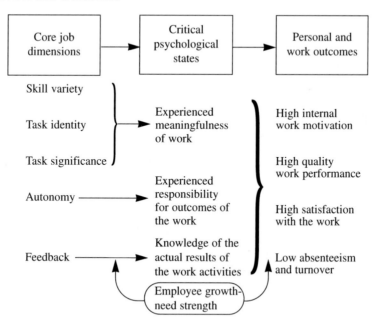

[1]A. N. Turner and P. R. Lawrence, *Industrial Jobs and the Worker* (Cambridge, Mass.: Harvard Graduate School of Business Administration, 1965).

[2]J. R. Hackman and E. E. Lawler, "Employee Reactions to Job Characteristics," *Journal of Applied Psychology Monograph*, 1971, pp. 259–286.

[3]J. R. Hackman and G. R. Oldham, *Motivation Through the Design of Work: Test of a Theory*, Technical Report No. 6 (New Haven, Conn.: Department of Administrative Sciences, Yale University, 1974).

*Toward Meaningful Work.*    Three of the five core dimensions contribute to a job's meaningfulness for the worker:

1. Skill variety. The degree to which a job requires the worker to perform activities that challenge his skills and abilities. When even a single skill is involved, there is at least a seed of potential meaningfulness. When several are involved, the job has the potential of appealing to the monotony of performing the same task repeatedly, no matter how much skill it may require.

2. Task identity. The degree to which the job requires completion of a "whole" and identifiable piece of work—doing a job from beginning to end with a visible outcome. For example, it is clearly more meaningful to an employee to build complete toasters than to attach electrical cord after electrical cord, especially if he never sees a completed toaster. (Note that the whole job, in this example, probably would involve greater skill variety as well as task identity.)

3. Task significance. The degree to which the job has a substantial and perceivable impact on the lives of other people, whether in the immediate organization or the world at large. The worker who tightens nuts on aircraft brake assemblies is more likely to perceive his work as significant than the worker who fills small boxes with paper clips—even though the skill levels involved may be comparable.

Each of these three jobs dimensions represents an important route to experienced meaningfulness. If the job is high in all three, the worker is quite likely to experience his job as very meaningful. It is not necessary, however, for a job to be very high in all three dimensions. If the job is low in any one of them, there will be a drop in overall experienced meaningfulness. But even when two dimensions are low the worker may find the job meaningful if the third is high enough.

*Toward Personal Responsibility.*    A fourth core dimension leads a worker to experience increased responsibility in his job. This is *autonomy*, the degree to which the job gives the worker freedom, independence, and discretion in scheduling work and determining how he will carry it out. People in highly autonomous jobs know that they are personally responsible for successes and failures. To the extent that their autonomy is high, then, how the work goes will be felt to depend more on the individual's own efforts and initiatives—rather than on detailed instructions from the boss or from a manual of job procedures.

*Toward Knowledge of Results.*    The fifth and last core dimension is *feedback*. This is the degree to which a worker, in carrying out the work activities required by the job, gets information about the effectiveness of his efforts. Feedback is most powerful when it comes directly from the work itself—for example, when a worker has the responsibility for gauging and otherwise checking a component he has just finished, and learns in the process that he has lowered his reject rate by meeting specifications more consistently.

*The Overall "Motivating Potential" of a Job.*    Figure 1 shows how the five core dimensions combine to affect the psychological states that are critical in determining whether or not an employee will be internally motivated to work effectively. Indeed, when using an instrument to be described later, it is possible to compute a "motivating potential score" (MPS) for any job. The MPS provides a single summary index of the degree to which the objective characteristics of the job will prompt high internal work motivation. Following the theory outlined above, a job high in motivating potential must be high in at least one (and hopefully more) of the three dimensions that lead to experienced meaningfulness and high in both autonomy and feedback as well. The MPS provides a quantitative index of the degree to which this is in fact the case (see Appendix for detailed formula). As will be seen later, the MPS can be very useful in diagnosing jobs and in assessing the effectiveness of job-enrichment activities.

# Does the Theory Work for Everybody?

Unfortunately not. Not everyone is able to become internally motivated in his work, even when the motivating potential of a job is very high indeed.

Research has shown that the *psychological needs* of people are very important in determining who can (and who cannot) become internally motivated at work. Some people have strong needs for personal accomplishment, for learning and developing themselves beyond where they are now, for being stimulated and challenged, and so on. These people are high in "growth-need strength."

Figure 2 shows diagrammatically the proposition that individual growth needs have the power to moderate the relationship between the characteristics of jobs and work outcomes. Many workers with high growth needs will turn on eagerly when they have jobs that are high in the core dimensions. Workers whose growth needs are not so strong may respond less eagerly—or, at first, even balk at being "pushed" or "stretched" too far.

Psychologists who emphasize human potential argue that everyone has within him at least a spark of the need to grow and develop personally. Steadily accumulating evidence shows, however, that unless that spark is pretty strong, chances are it will get snuffed out by one's experiences in typical organizations. So, a person who has worked for 20 years in stultifying jobs may find it difficult or impossible to become internally motivated overnight when given the opportunity.

We should be cautious, however, about creating rigid categories of people based on their measured growth-need strength at any particular time. It is true that we can predict from these measures who is likely to become internally motivated on a job and who will be less willing or able to do so. But what we do not know yet is whether or not the growth-need "spark" can be rekindled for those individuals who have had their growth needs dampened, by years of growth-depressing experience in their organizations.

Since it is often the organization that is responsible for currently low levels of growth desires, we believe that the organization also should provide the individual with the chance to reverse that trend whenever possible, even if that means putting a person in a job where he may be "stretched" more than he wants to be. He can always move back later to the old job—and in the meantime the embers of his growth needs just might burst back into flame, to his surprise and pleasure, and for the good of the organization.

FIGURE 2   The Moderating Effect of Employee Growth-Need Strength

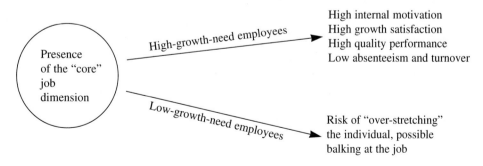

# FROM THEORY TO PRACTICE:
# A TECHNOLOGY FOR JOB ENRICHMENT

When job enrichment fails, it often fails because of inadequate diagnosis of the target job and employees' reactions to it. Often, for example, job enrichment is assumed by management to be a solution to "people problems" on the job and is implemented even though there has been no diagnostic activity to indicate that the root of the problem is in fact how the work is designed. At other times, some diagnosis is made—but it provides no concrete guidance about what specific aspects of the job require change. In either case, the success of job enrichment may wind up depending more on the quality of the intuition of the change agent—or his luck—than on a solid base of data about the people and the work.

In the paragraphs to follow, we outline a new technology for use in job enrichment which explicitly addresses the diagnostic as well as the action components of the change process. The technology has two parts: 1) a set of diagnostic tools that are useful in evaluating jobs and people's reactions to them prior to change and in pinpointing exactly what aspects of specific jobs are most critical to a successful change attempt; and 2) a set of "implementing concepts" that provide concrete guidance for action steps in job enrichment. The implementing concepts are tied directly to the diagnostic tools; the output of the diagnostic activity specifies which action steps are likely to have the most impact in a particular situation.

## The Diagnostic Tools

Central to the diagnostic procedure we propose is a package of instruments to be used by employees, supervisors, and outside observers in assessing the target job and employees' reactions to it.[4] These instruments gauge the following:

1. The objective characteristics of the jobs themselves, including both an overall indication of the "motivating potential" of the job as it exists (that is, the MPS score) and the score of the job on each of the five core dimensions described previously. Because knowing the strengths and weaknesses of the job is critical to any work redesign effort, assessments of the job are made by supervisors and outside observers as well as the employees themselves—and the final assessment of a job uses data from all three sources.

2. The current levels of motivation, satisfaction, and work performance of employees on the job. In addition to satisfaction with the work itself, measures are taken of how people feel about other aspects of the work setting, such as pay, supervision, and relationships with co-workers.

3. The level of growth-need strength of the employees. As indicated earlier, employees who have strong growth needs are more likely to be more responsive to job enrichment than employees with weak growth needs. Therefore, it is important to know at the outset just what kinds of satisfactions the people who do the job are (and are not) motivated to obtain from their work. This will make it possible to identify which persons are best to start changes with, and which may need help in adapting to the newly enriched job.

---

[4]J. R. Hackman and G. R. Oldham, "Development of the Job Diagnostic Survey," *Journal of Applied Psychology*, 1975, pp. 159–70.

What, then, might be the actual steps one would take in carrying out a job diagnosis using these tools? Although the approach to any particular diagnosis depends upon the specifics of the particular work situation involved, the sequence of questions listed below is fairly typical.

## Step 1. Are Motivation and Satisfaction Central to the Problem?

Sometimes organizations undertake job enrichment to improve the work motivation and satisfaction of employees when in fact the real problem with work performance lies elsewhere—for example, in a poorly designed production system, in an error-prone computer, and so on. The first step is to examine the scores of employees on the motivation and satisfaction portions of the diagnostic instrument. (The questionnaire taken by employees is called the Job Diagnostic Survey and will be referred to hereafter as the JDS.) If motivation and satisfaction are problematic, the change agent would continue to Step 2; if not, he would look to other aspects of the work situation to identify the real problem.

## Step 2. Is the Job Low in Motivating Potential?

To answer this question, one would examine the motivating potential score of the target job and compare it to the MPS's of other jobs to determine whether or *not the job itself* is a probable cause of the motivational problems documented in Step 1. If the job turns out to be low on the MPS, one would continue to Step 3; if it scores high, attention should be given to other possible reasons for the motivational difficulties (such as the pay system, the nature of supervision, and so on).

## Step 3. What Specific Aspects of the Job Are Causing the Difficulty?

This step involves examining the job on each of the five core dimensions to pinpoint the specific strengths and weaknesses of the job as it is currently structured. It is useful at this stage to construct a "profile" of the target job, to make visually apparent where improvements need to be made. An illustrative profile for two jobs (one "good" job and one job needing improvement) is shown in Figure 3.

Job A is an engineering maintenance job and is high on all of the core dimensions; the MPS of this job is a very high 260. (MPS scores can range from 1 to about 350; an "average" score would be about 125.) Job enrichment would not be recommended for this job; if employees working on the job were unproductive and unhappy, the reasons are likely to have little to do with the nature or design of the work itself.

Job B, on the other hand, has many problems. This job involves the routine and repetitive processing of checks in the "back room" of a bank. The MPS is 30, which is quite low—and indeed, would be even lower if it were not for the moderately high task significance of the job. (Task significance is moderately high because the people are handling large amounts of other people's money, and therefore the quality of their efforts potentially has important consequences for their unseen clients.) The job provides the individuals with very little direct feedback about how effectively they are doing it; the employees have little autonomy in how they go about doing the job; and the job is moderately low in both skill variety and task identity.

For Job B, then, there is plenty of room for improvement—and many avenues to examine in planning job changes. For still other jobs, the avenues for change often turn out to be considerably more specific: for example, feedback and autonomy may be reasonably high, but one or more of the core dimensions that contribute to the experienced meaningfulness of the job (skill variety, task identity, and task significance) may be low. In such a case, attention would turn to ways to increase the standing of the job on these latter three dimensions.

FIGURE 3  The JDS Diagnostic Profile for a "Good" and a "Bad" Job

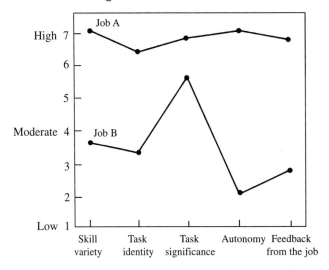
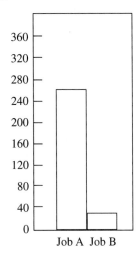

## Step 4. How "Ready" Are the Employees for Change?

Once it has been documented that there is need for improvement in the job—and the particularly troublesome aspects of the job have been identified—then it is time to begin to think about the specific action steps which will be taken to enrich the job. An important factor in such planning is the level of growth needs of the employees, since employees high on growth needs usually respond more readily to job enrichment than do employees with little need for growth. The JDS provides a direct measure of the growth-need strength of the employees. This measure can be very helpful in planning how to introduce the changes to the people (for instance, cautiously versus dramatically), and in deciding who should be among the first group of employees to have their jobs changed.

In actual use of the diagnostic package, additional information is generated which supplements and expands the basic diagnostic questions outlined above. The point of the above discussion is merely to indicate the kinds of questions which we believe to be most important in diagnosing a job prior to changing it. We now turn to how the diagnostic conclusions are translated into specific job changes.

## The Implementing Concepts

Five "implementing concepts" for job enrichment are identified and discussed below.[5] Each one is a specific action step aimed at improving both the quality of the working experience for the individual and his work productivity. They are: 1) forming natural work units; 2) combining tasks; 3) establishing client relationships; 4) vertical loading; 5) opening feedback channels.

The links between the implementing concepts and the core dimensions are shown in Figure 4—which illustrates our theory of job enrichment, ranging from the concrete action steps through the core dimensions and the psychological states to the actual personal and work outcomes.

[5]R. W. Walters and Associates, *Job Enrichment for Results* (Cambridge, Mass.: Addison-Wesley Publishing Co. Inc., 1975).

After completing the diagnosis of a job, a change agent would know which of the core dimensions were most in need of remedial attention. He could then turn to Figure 4 and select those implementing concepts that specifically deal with the most troublesome parts of the existing job. How this would take place in practice will be seen below.

FIGURE 4    The Full Model: How Use of the Implementing Concepts Can Lead to Positive Outcomes

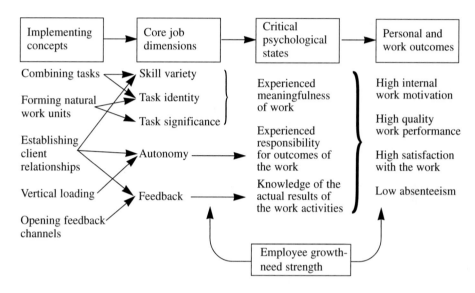

***Forming Natural Work Units.***    The notion of distributing work in some logical way may seem to be an obvious part of the design of any job. In many cases, however, the logic is one imposed by just about any consideration except jobholder satisfaction and motivation. Such considerations include technological dictates, level of worker training or experience, "efficiency" as defined by industrial engineering, and current workload. In many cases the cluster of tasks a worker faces during a typical day or week is natural to anyone *but* the worker.

For example, suppose that a typing pool (consisting of one supervisor and ten typists) handles all work for one division of a company. Jobs are delivered in rough draft or dictated form to the supervisor, who distributes them as evenly as possible among the typists. In such circumstances the individual letters, reports, and other tasks performed by a given typist in one day or week are randomly assigned. There is no basis for identifying with the work or the person or department for whom it is performed, or for placing any personal value upon it.

The principle underlying natural units of work, by contrast, is "ownership"—a worker's sense of continuing responsibility for an identifiable body of work. Two steps are involved in creating natural work units. The first is to identify the basic work items. In the typing pool, for example, the items might be "pages to be typed." The second step is to group the items in natural categories. For example, each typist might be assigned continuing responsibility for all jobs requested by one or several specific departments. The assignments should be made, of course, in such a way that workloads are about equal in the long run. (For example, one typist might end up with all the work from one busy department, while another handles jobs from several smaller units.)

At this point we can begin to see specifically how the job-design principles relate to the core dimensions (cf., Figure 4). The ownership fostered by natural units of work can make the difference between a feeling that work is meaningful and rewarding and the feeling that it is irrelevant and boring. As the diagram shows, natural units of work are directly related to two of the core dimensions: task identity and task significance.

A typist whose work is assigned naturally rather than randomly—say, by departments—has a much greater chance of performing a whole job to completion. Instead of typing one section of a large report, the individual is likely to type the whole thing, with knowledge of exactly what the product of the work is (task identity). Furthermore, over time the typist will develop a growing sense of how the work affects co-workers in the department serviced (task significance).

***Combining Tasks.*** The very existence of a pool made up entirely of persons whose sole function is typing reflects a fractionalization of jobs that has been a basic precept of "scientific management." Most obvious in assemblyline work, fractionalization has been applied to nonmanufacturing jobs as well. It is typically justified by efficiency, which is usually defined in terms of either low costs or some time-and-motion type of criteria.

It is hard to find fault with measuring efficiency ultimately in terms of cost effectiveness. In doing so, however, a manager should be sure to consider *all* the costs involved. It is possible, for example, for highly fractionalized jobs to meet all the time-and-motion criteria of efficiency, but if the resulting job is so unrewarding that performing it day after day leads to high turnover, absenteeism, drugs and alcohol, and strikes, then productivity is really lower (and costs higher) than data on efficiency might indicate.

The principle of combining tasks, then, suggests that whenever possible existing and fractionalized tasks should be put together to form new and larger modules of work. At the Medfield, Massachusetts, plant of Corning Glass Works the assembly of a laboratory hot plate has been redesigned along the lines suggested here. Each hot plate now is assembled from start to finish by one operator, instead of going through several separate operations that are performed by different people.

Some tasks, if combined into a meaningfully large module of work, would be more than an individual could do by himself. In such cases, it is often useful to consider assigning the new larger task to a small *team* of workers—who are given great autonomy for its completion. At the Racine, Wisconsin plant of Emerson Electric, the assembly process for trash disposal appliances was restructured this way. Instead of a sequence of moving the appliance from station to station, the assembly now is done from start to finish by one team. Such teams include both men and women to permit switching off the heavier and more delicate aspects of the work. The team responsible is identified on the appliance. In case of customer complaints, the team often drafts the reply.

As a job-design principle, task combination, like natural units of work, expands the task identity of the job. For example, the hot-plate assembler can see and identify with a finished product ready for shipment, rather than a nearly invisible junction of solder. Moreover, the more tasks that are combined into a single worker's job, the greater the variety of skills he must call on in performing the job. So task combination also leads directly to greater skill variety—the third core dimension that contributes to the overall experienced meaningfulness of the work.

***Establishing Client Relationships.*** One consequence of fractionalization is that the typical worker has little or no contact with (or even awareness of) the ultimate user of his product or service. By encouraging and enabling employees to establish direct relationships with the clients of their work, improvements often can be realized simultaneously on three of the case dimensions. Feedback increases because of additional opportunities for the individual to receive praise or criticism of his work outputs directly. Skill variety often increases because of the necessity to develop and exercise one's interpersonal skills in maintaining the client relationship. And autonomy can increase because the individual often is given personal responsibility for deciding how to manage his relationships with the clients of his work.

Creating client relationships is a three-step process. First, the client must be identified. Second, the most direct contact possible between the worker and the client must be established. Third, criteria must be set up by which the client can judge the quality of the product or service he receives. And whenever possible, the client should have a means of relaying his judgments directly back to the worker.

The contact between worker and client should be as great as possible and as frequent as necessary. Face-to-face contact is highly desirable, at least occasionally. Where that is impossible or impractical, telephone and mail can suffice. In any case, it is important that the performance criteria by which the worker will be rated by the client must be mutually understood and agreed upon.

*Vertical Loading.* Typically the split between the "doing" of a job and the "planning" and "controlling" of the work has evolved along with horizontal fractionalization. Its rationale, once again, has been "efficiency through specialization." And once again, the excess of specialization that has emerged has resulted in unexpected but significant costs in motivation, morale, and work quality. In vertical loading, the intent is to partially close the gap between the doing and the controlling parts of the job—and thereby reap some important motivational advantages.

Of all the job-design principles, vertical loading may be the single most crucial one. In some cases, where it has been impossible to implement any other changes, vertical loading alone has had significant motivational effects.

When a job is vertically loaded, responsibilities and controls that formerly were reserved for high levels of management are added to the job. There are many ways to accomplish this:

- Return to the job holder greater discretion in settling schedules, deciding on work methods, checking on quality, and advising or helping to train less experienced workers.

- Grant additional authority. The objective should be to advance workers from a position of no authority or highly restricted authority to positions of reviewed, and eventually, near-total authority for his own work,

- Time management. The job holder should have the greatest possible freedom to decide when to start and stop work, when to break, and how to assign priorities

- Troubleshooting and crisis decisions. Workers should be encouraged to seek problem solutions on their own, rather than calling immediately for the supervisor.

- Financial controls. Some degree of knowledge and control over budgets and other financial aspects of a job can often be highly motivating. However, access to this information frequently tends to be restricted. Workers can benefit from knowing something about the costs of their jobs, the potential effect upon profit, and various financial and budgetary alternatives.

When a job is vertically loaded it will inevitably increase in *autonomy*. And as shown in Figure 4, this increase in objective personal control over the work will also lead to an increased feeling of personal responsibility for the work, and ultimately to higher internal work motivation.

- Opening feedback channels. In virtually all jobs there are ways to open channels of feedback to individuals or teams to help them learn whether their performance is improving, deteriorating, or remaining at a constant level. While there are numerous channels through which information about performance can be provided, it generally is better for a worker to learn about his performance *directly as he does his job*—rather than from management on an occasional basis.

Job-provided feedback usually is more immediate and private than supervisor-supplied feedback, and it increases the worker's feelings of personal control over his work in the bargain. Moreover, it avoids many of the potentially disruptive interpersonal problems that can develop when the only way a worker has to find out how he is doing is through direct messages or subtle cues from the boss.

Exactly what should be done to open channels for job-provided feedback will vary from job to job and organization to organization. Yet in many cases the changes involve simply removing existing blocks that isolate the worker from naturally occurring data about performance—rather than generating entirely new feedback mechanisms. For example:

- Establishing direct client relationships often removes blocks between the worker and natural external sources of data about his work.

- Quality-control efforts in many organizations often eliminate a natural source of feedback. The quality check on a product or service is done by persons other than those responsible for the work. Feedback to the workers—if there is any—is belated and diluted. It often fosters a tendency to think of quality as "someone else's concern." By placing quality control close to the worker (perhaps even in his own hands), the quantity and quality of data about performance available to him can dramatically increase.

- Tradition and established procedure in many organizations dictate that records about performance be kept by a supervisor and transmitted up (not down) in the organizational hierarchy. Sometimes supervisors even check the work and correct any errors themselves. The worker who made the error never knows it occurred—and is denied the very information that could enhance both his internal work motivation and the technical adequacy of his performance. In many cases it is possible to provide standard summaries of performance records directly to the worker (as well as to his superior), thereby giving him personally and regularly the data he needs to improve his performance.

- Computers and other automated operations sometimes can be used to provide the individual with data now blocked from him. Many clerical operations, for example, are now performed on computer consoles. These consoles often can be programmed to provide the clerk with immediate feedback in the form of a CRT display or a printout indicating that an error has been made. Some systems even have been programmed to provide the operator with a positive feedback message when a period of error-free performance has been sustained.

Many organizations simply have not recognized the importance of feedback as a motivator. Data on quality and other aspects of performance are viewed as being of interest only to management. Worse still, the *standards* for acceptable performance often are kept from workers as well. As a result, workers who would be interested in following the daily or weekly ups and downs of their performance, and in trying accordingly to improve, are deprived of the very guidelines they need to do so. They are like the golfer we mentioned earlier, whose efforts to correct his hook are stopped dead by fog over the driving range.

## THE STRATEGY IN ACTION: HOW WELL DOES IT WORK?

So far we have examined a basic theory of how people get turned on to their work; a set of core dimensions of jobs that create the conditions for such internal work motivation to develop on the job; and a set of five implementing concepts that are the action steps recommended to boost a job on the core dimensions and thereby increase employee motivation, satisfaction, and productivity.

The remaining question is straightforward and important: *Does it work?* In reality, that question is twofold. First, does the theory itself hold water, or are we barking up the wrong conceptual tree? And second, does the change strategy really lead to measurable differences when it is applied in an actual organizational setting?

This section summarizes the findings we have generated to date on these questions.

## Is the Job-Enrichment Theory Correct?

In general, the answer seems to be yes. The JDS instrument has been taken by more than 1,000 employees working on about 100 diverse jobs in more than a dozen organizations over the last two years. These data have been analyzed to test the basic motivational theory—and especially the impact of the core job dimensions on worker motivation, satisfaction, and behavior on the job. An illustrative overview of some of the findings is given below.[6]

1. People who work on jobs high on the core dimensions are more motivated and satisfied than are people who work on jobs that score low on the dimensions. Employees with jobs high on the core dimensions (MPS scores greater than 240) were compared to those who held unmotivating jobs (MPS scores less than 40). As shown in Figure 5, employees with high MPS jobs were higher on  a) the three psychological states,  b) internal work motivation,  c) general satisfaction, and  d) "growth" satisfaction.

FIGURE 5  Employee Reactions to Jobs High and Low in Motivating Potential for Two Banks and a Steel Firm

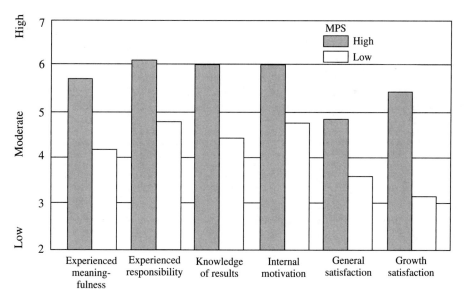

[6]Hackman and Oldham, *Motivation.*

2. Figure 6 shows that the same is true for measures of actual behavior at work—absenteeism and performance effectiveness—although less strongly so for the performance measure.

FIGURE 6   Absenteeism and Job Performance for Employees with Jobs High and Low in Motivating Potential

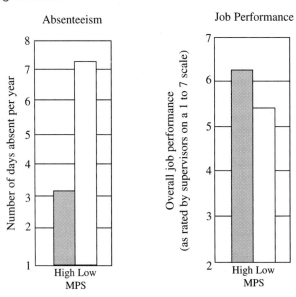

3. Responses to jobs high in motivating potential are more positive for people who have strong growth needs than for people with weak needs for growth.  In Figure 7 the linear relationship between the motivating potential of a job and employees' level of internal work motivation is shown, separately for people with high versus low growth needs as measured by the JDS.  While both groups of employees show increases in internal motivation as MPS increases, the rate of increase is significantly greater for the group of employees who have strong needs for growth.

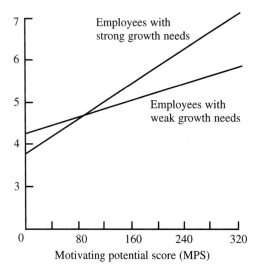

FIGURE 7 Relationship Between the Motivating Potential of a Job and the Internal Work Motivation of Employees (shown separately for employees with strong versus weak growth-need strength)

## How Does the Change Strategy Work in Practice?

The results summarized above suggest that both the theory and the diagnostic instrument work when used with real people in real organizations. In this section, we summarize a job-enrichment project conducted at The Travelers Insurance Companies, which illustrates how the change procedures themselves work in practice.

The Travelers project was designed with two purposes in mind. One was to achieve improvements in morale, productivity, and other indicators of employee well-being. The other was to test the general effectiveness of the strategy for job enrichment we have summarized in this article.

The work group chosen was a keypunching operation. The group's function was to transfer information from printed or written documents onto punched cards for computer input. The work group consisted of 98 keypunch operators and verifiers (both in the same job classification), plus seven assignment clerks. All reported to a supervisor who, in turn, reported to the assistant manager and manager of the data-input division.

The size of individual punching orders varied considerably, from a few cards to as many as 2,500. Some work came to the work group with a specified delivery date, while other orders were to be given routine service on a predetermined schedule assignment clerks received the jobs from the user departments. After reviewing the work for obvious errors, omissions, and legibility problems, the assignment clerk parceled out the work in batches expected to take about one hour. If the clerk found the work not suitable for punching it went to the supervisor, who either returned the work to the user department or cleared up problems by phone. When work went to operators for punching, it was with the instruction, "Punch only what you see. Don't correct errors, no matter how obvious they look."

Because of the high cost of computer time, keypunched work was 100 percent verified—a task that consumed nearly as many manhours as the punching itself. Then the cards went to the supervisor, who screened the jobs for due dates before sending them to the computer. Errors detected in verification were assigned to various operators at random to be corrected.

The computer output from the cards was sent to the originating department, accompanied by a printout of errors. Eventually the printout went back to the supervisor for final correction.

A great many phenomena indicated that the problems being experienced in the work group might be the result of poor motivation. As the only person performing supervisory functions of any kind, the supervisor spent most of his time responding to crisis situations, which recurred continually. He also had to deal almost daily with employees' salary grievances or other complaints. Employees frequently showed apathy or outright hostility toward their jobs.

Rates of work output, by accepted work-measurement standards, were inadequate. Error rates were high. Due dates and schedules frequently were missed. Absenteeism was higher than average, especially before and after weekends and holidays.

The single, rather unusual exception was turnover. It was lower than the company-wide average for similar jobs. The company has attributed this fact to a poor job market in the base period just before the project began, and to an older, relatively more settled work force—made up, incidentally, entirely of women.

## The Diagnosis

Using some of the tools and techniques we have outlined, a consulting team from the Management Services Department and from Roy W. Walters & Associates concluded that the keypunch-operator's job exhibited the following serious weaknesses in terms of the core dimensions.

*Skill Variety.* There was none. Only a single skill was involved—the ability to punch adequately the data on the batch of documents.

*Task Identity.* Virtually nonexistent. Batches were assembled to provide an even workload, but not whole identifiable jobs.

*Task Significance.* Not apparent. The keypunching operation was a necessary step in providing service to the company's customers. The individual operator was isolated by an assignment clerk and a supervisor from any knowledge of what the operation meant to the using department, let alone its meaning to the ultimate customer.

*Autonomy.* None. The operators had no freedom to arrange their daily tasks to meet schedules, to resolve problems with the using department, or even to correct, in punching, information that was obviously wrong.

*Feedback.* None. Once a batch was out of the operator's hands, she had no assured chance of seeing evidence of its quality or inadequacy.

## Design of the Experimental Trial

Since the diagnosis indicated that the motivating potential of the job was extremely low, it was decided to attempt to improve the motivation and productivity of the work group through job enrichment. Moreover, it was possible to design an experimental test of the effects of the changes to be introduced: the results of changes made in the target work group were to be compared with trends in a control work group of similar size and demographic make-up. Since the control group was located more than a mile away, there appeared to be little risk of communication between members of the two groups.

A base period was defined before the start of the experimental trial period, and appropriate data were gathered on the productivity, absenteeism, and work attitudes of members of both groups. Data also were available on turnover, but since turnover was already below average in the target group, prospective changes in this measure were deemed insignificant.

An educational session was conducted with supervisors, at which they were given the theory and implementing concepts and actually helped to design the job changes themselves. Out of this session came an active plan consisting of about 25 change items that would significantly affect the design of the target jobs.

## The Implementing Concepts and the Changes

Because the job as it existed was rather uniformly low on the core job dimensions, all five of the implementing concepts were used in enriching it.

*Natural Units of Work.* The random batch assignment of work was replaced by assigning to each operator continuing responsibility for certain accounts—either particular departments or particular recurring jobs. Any work for those accounts now always goes to the same operator.

*Task Combination.* Some planning and controlling functions were combined with the central task of keypunching. In this case, however, these additions can be more suitably discussed under the remaining three implementing concepts.

*Client Relationships.* Each operator was given several channels of direct contact with clients. The operators, not their assignment clerks, now inspect their documents for correctness and legibility. When problems arise, the operator, not the supervisor, takes them up with the client.

*Feedback.*  In addition to feedback from client contact, the operators were provided with a number of additional sources of data about their performance.  The computer department now returns incorrect cards to the operators who punched them, and operators correct their own errors.  Each operator also keeps her own file of copies of her errors.  These can be reviewed to determine trends in error frequency and types of errors.  Each operator receives weekly a computer printout of her errors and productivity, which is sent to her directly, rather than given to her by the supervisor.

*Vertical Loading.*  Besides consulting directly with clients, operators now have the authority to correct obvious coding errors on their own.  Operators may set their own schedules and plan their daily work, as long as they meet schedules.  Some competent operators have been given the option of not verifying their work and making their own program changes.

## Results of the Trial

The results were dramatic.  The number of operators declined from 90 to 60.  This occurred partly through attrition and partly through transfer to other departments.  Some of the operators were promoted to higher-paying jobs in departments whose cards they had been handling—something that had never occurred before.  Some details of the results are given below.

*Quantity of Work.*  The control group, with no job changes made, showed an increase in productivity of 8.1 percent during the trial period.  The experimental group showed an increase of 39.6 percent.

*Error rates.*  To assess work quality, error rates were recorded for about 40 operators in the experimental group.  All were experienced, and all had been in their jobs before the job-enrichment program began.  For two months before the study, these operators had a collective error rate of 1.53 percent.  For two months toward the end of the study, the collective error rate was 0.99 percent.  By the end of the study the number of operators with poor performance had dropped from 11.1 percent to 5.5 percent.

*Absenteeism.*  The experimental group registered a 24.1 percent decline in absences.  The control group, by contrast, showed a 29 percent *increase.*

*Attitudes Toward the Job.*  An attitude survey given at the start of the project showed that the two groups scored about average, and nearly identically, in nine different areas of work satisfaction.  At the end of the project the survey was repeated.  The control group showed an insignificant 0.5 percent improvement, while the experimental group's overall satisfaction score rose 16.5 percent.

*Selective Elimination of Controls.*  Demonstrated improvements in operator proficiency permitted them to work with fewer controls.  Travelers estimates that the reduction of controls had the same effect as adding seven operators—a saving even beyond the effects of improved productivity and lowered absenteeism.

*Role of the Supervisor.*  One of the most significant findings in the Travelers experiment was the effect of the changes on the supervisor's job, and thus on the rest of the organization.  The operators took on many responsibilities that had been reserved at least to the unit leaders and sometimes to the supervisor.  The unit leaders, in turn, assumed some of the day-to-day supervisory functions that had plagued the supervisor.  Instead of spending his days supervising the behavior of subordinates and dealing with crises, he was able to devote time to developing feedback systems, setting up work modules and spearheading the enrichment effort—in other words, managing.  It should be noted, however, that helping supervisors change their own work activities when their subordinates' jobs have been enriched is itself a challenging task. And if appropriate attention and help are not given to supervisors in such cases, they rapidly can become disaffected—and a job-enrichment "backlash" can result.[7]

## SUMMARY

By applying work-measurement standards to the changes wrought by job enrichment—attitude and quality, absenteeism, and selective administration of controls—Travelers was able to estimate the total dollar impact of the project. Actual savings in salaries and machine rental charges during the first year totaled $64,305. Potential savings by further application of the changes were put at $91,937 annually. Thus, by almost any measure used—from the work attitudes of individual employees to dollar savings for the company as a whole—the Travelers' test of the job-enrichment strategy proved a success.

## CONCLUSIONS

In this article we have presented a new strategy for the redesign of work in general and for job enrichment in particular. The approach has four main characteristics:

1. It is grounded in a basic psychological theory of what motivates people in their work.
2. It emphasizes that planning for job changes should be done on the basis of *data* about the jobs and the people who do them—and a set of diagnostic instruments is provided to collect such data.
3. It provides a set of specific implementing concepts to guide actual job changes, as well as a set of theory-based rules for selecting which action steps are likely to be most beneficial in a given situation.
4. The strategy is buttressed by a set of findings showing that the theory holds water, that the diagnostic procedures are practical and informative, and that the implementing concepts can lead to changes that are beneficial both to organizations and to the people who work in them.

We believe that job enrichment is moving beyond the stage where it can be considered "yet another management fad." Instead, it represents a potentially powerful strategy for change that can help organizations achieve their goals for higher quality work—and at the same time further the equally legitimate needs of contemporary employees for a more meaningful work experience. Yet there are pressing questions about job enrichment and its use that remain to be answered.

Prominent among these is the question of employee participation in planning and implementing work redesign. The diagnostic tools and implementing concepts we have presented are neither designed nor intended for use only by management. Rather, our belief is that the effectiveness of job enrichment is likely to be enhanced when the tasks of diagnosing and changing jobs are undertaken *collaboratively* by managing and by the employees whose work will be affected.

[7]E. E. Lawler III, J. R. Hackman, and S. Kaufman, "Effects of Job Redesign: A Field Experiment," *Journal of Applied Social Psychology*, 1973, pp. 49–62.

Moreover the effects of work redesign on the broader organization remain generally unchartered. Evidence now is accumulating that when jobs are changed, turbulence can appear in the surrounding organization—for example, in supervisory-subordinate relationships, in pay and benefit plans, and so on. Such turbulence can be viewed by management either as a problem with job enrichment, or as an opportunity for further and broader organizational development by teams of managers and employees. To the degree that management takes the latter view, we believe, the oft-espoused goal of achieving basic organizational change through the redesign of work may come increasingly within reach.

The diagnostic tools and implementing concepts we have presented are useful in deciding on and designing basic changes in the jobs themselves. They do not address the broader issues of who plans the changes, how they are carried out, and how they are followed up. The way these broader questions are dealt with, we believe, may determine whether job enrichment will grow up—or whether it will die an early and unfortunate death, like so many other fledgling behavioral science approaches to organizational change.

## APPENDIX

For the algebraically inclined, the Motivating Potential Score is computed as follows:

$$MPS = \left[ \frac{\text{Skill + Task identity + Task significance}}{3} \times \text{Autonomy} + \text{Feedback} \right]$$

It should be noted that in some cases the MPS score can be too high for positive job satisfaction and effective performance–in effect overstimulating the person who holds the job. This paper focuses on jobs which are toward the low end of the scale—and which potentially can be improved through job enrichment.

Acknowledgements. The authors acknowledge with great appreciation the editorial assistance of John Hickey in the preparation of this paper, and the help of Kenneth Brousseau, Daniel Feldman, and Linda Frank in collecting the data that are summarized here. The research activities reported were supported in part by the Organizational Effectiveness Research Program of the Office of Naval Research, and the Manpower Administration of the U.S. Department of Labor, both through contracts to Yale University.

# DEMING'S REDEFINITION OF MANAGEMENT

*Myron Tribus*

Recent publications in the *Harvard Business Review* and the popular press have indicated American management practices as the principal reason behind America's decline in international competitiveness. The problem seems to lie in the self-image of managers. Everyone, of course, has an image of what his or her job requires. People need self-images; they help them decide how to behave in different circumstances. It seems that many managers do not have images that correspond to their true responsibilities.

I was inspired to this line of inquiry by a conversation with Dr. W. Edwards Deming, well known for his contributions to Japanese productivity and quality of manufacture. I asked him, "Suppose I were the president of a major corporation and I became convinced of the superiority of your methods. What would you advise me to do, if I wanted to take advantage of them, starting tomorrow?"

Dr. Deming leaned forward, looked me straight in the eye in his unique way, and said: "Oh! You want someone to explain your job to you, is that it?"

Subsequently, I went to the library to look for definitions of the manager's job. A great deal has been written about management, but very few authors have defined the job operationally.

Many people define the manager's job something like this: The manager has to see that everything gets done that should be done and prevent things that shouldn't happen from happening. More succinctly, Harry Truman had a small sign on his desk that said, "The Buck Stops Here." That description is accurate, for in the end the manager is responsible for everything that goes on in his or her domain. Such broad definitions are not useful.

A more useful approach is to ask: "What are the essential responsibilities that a manager may not delegate?" These responsibilities define the core of the manager's job.

Dr. Deming has prepared a list containing fourteen points, which, in his experience, are essential to quality and productivity and cannot be delegated by a manager. This paper starts from Dr. Deming's fourteen points (although not in the order he gives). It is only a beginning on the task of defining the job of a manager. At the end I shall return to the question of what needs to be done to complete the definition. Deming's points are discussed extensively in his new book, *Quality, Productivity, and Competitive Position*, and several of his publications.

## PROVIDE CONTINUITY
## AND CONSISTENCY OF PURPOSE

No one but the manager can set the goals and aspirations of the organization. Sometimes it is said, "We have to decide what business we are in." This is not enough. The manager must decide what kind of organization the company is to become. The manager must articulate the goals and strategies of the company in such a way that the public, the employees, the vendors, and the customers understand what to expect from the company.

*Source:* Reprinted from Massachusetts Institute of Technology Center for Advanced Engineering Study.

At the entrance to the Newport News Shipyards there stood a sign:

*"We shall build great ships.*
*At a profit if we can*
*At a loss if we must*
*but we shall build great ships."*

When the shipyard was purchased by a conglomerate, the sign was removed with the statement: "We do not intend to build at a loss!' Later the sign was restored.

The manager who removed the sign articulated the goals of the company. But managers should realize that the goals will be interpreted by the workers at all levels and will determine how they behave. Goals that invite the workers to cut corners will not lead to high-quality, competitive products.

The manager's behavior sets the style for others to follow. Only the manager can decide if the performance of the organization is satisfactory. Only the manager can make the decision to improve it.

The manager must not only articulate a purpose for the organization. The manager must also do whatever is required to ensure that the purpose is followed with integrity, altering it as circumstances dictate.

The statement of purpose must be credible, operational, and inspirational. It should provide a basis for everyone in the organization to want to work for a common purpose.

Two executives stand out in my mind as examples of the two extremes. The late Joe Wilson, founder of the Xerox Corporation, was extraordinarily able in setting forth what he wanted the company to be. His death led to a discontinuity in this ability, which, in my opinion, has led to some of the difficulties experienced by that organization today.

At the other extreme, I recall a CEO who made the following statement to an assembly of his managers:

*"Never forget, gentlemen: The purpose of this company is to make money."*

Not only is such a statement inadequate as a guide to decision making, it is an invitation to everyone to put his or her own career aspirations first, to jump ship at the earliest good opportunity, and to look outside the company for life's nonmonetary rewards. It is inadequate because it does not address the question, Are profits today more important than in the future? How are the employees to regard the company's future competitive position?

This way of providing guidance to a company can have unfortunate consequences, some of which have been discussed elsewhere.


## DETERMINE THAT EVERYONE IN THE ORGANIZATION UNDERSTANDS WHAT THE CUSTOMERS WANT

The manager may delegate to someone in the organization the marketing function and the task of gathering information about customer preferences, marketability, and so forth. But no one else can see that the results of such studies are diffused throughout the organization and actually put to use. Only the manager can judge if the information provided is appropriate and appropriately used.

Too many managers think of the system for which they are responsible as operation in a *linear fashion*:

DESIGN IT      MAKE IT      TRY TO SELL IT

A more accurate image of how the system should work is taken from computer programming. The manager should think of the system as being in an endless *DO LOOP*:

START:   DESIGN IT
         MAKE IT
         TEST IT
         SELL IT
         TEST IT IN THE MARKETPLACE
         FIND OUT WHAT THE CUSTOMERS WANT
         GO TO START

The manager must be *involved in these judgments*. They cannot be delegated.


## IMPROVE THE QUALITY OF THE OUTPUT OF THE SYSTEM

This is probably the most misunderstood aspect of the manager's job in America today.

The workers work *in* a system. The job of the manager is to work *on* the system, to improve it and thereby to improve the quality of the output and decrease its cost. The quality of the output is determined by:

The quality of the inputs
    The information
    The materials
    The supplies
    The delivery
    The storage
    The handling

The design and operation of the system
    The relation between engineering and manufacturing
    The relation between sales and manufacturing
    The relation between purchasing and manufacturing
    The relation between marketing and engineering
    In short:
    The relations among all parts of the system

The training and education of all employees
    On-the-job training
    Supervisory training
    Professional training

Statistical control of quality
    Inspection methods
    Feedback and control for quality
    Materials acceptability

Many of these aspects may be delegated, of course, but only the manager can take the responsibility to *harmonize* the activities of the different parts of the system. Only the manager can judge the adequacy of the answers to such questions as these:

> Are the specifications to the purchasing department adequate? Is the reward system for purchasing agents driving them to the lowest bidder regardless of quality? Are the purchased materials, instruments, supplies always the best for the job? Why not? Is the information on which product specifications are based adequate? If the information is inadequate, who should take action? If the information is inadequate, who knows and acts?

One of the more common errors is to confuse quality of product with quality of process. It is often possible to obtain a high-quality product from a low-quality process, just by inspecting thoroughly enough and rejecting enough of the output. Of course, costs will rise under such a system. On the other hand, a high-quality process will produce high-quality output at a lower cost simply because there will be fewer delays, less rework, less wasted human effort, less wasted space, and less wasted material. In a high-quality *process* everything works right the first time. The work goes smoothly and productivity rises; not just the productivity of labor but also of capital and of management.

Another error is to fail to distinguish between high technology products and high technology production processes. In the manufacture of tissue paper, to cite an obviously low technology product, the manufacturing equipment of successfully competing companies will be of very high quality and technology. To compete in a market in which the cost of the raw material is a substantial fraction of the cost of the finished *product*, it is essential to run it efficiently, with statistical quality control. Otherwise the productivity of the capital investment will be too low to compete.

Unfortunately, this confusion between quality of product and quality of process causes many managers to believe that higher quality means higher cost. In their search for cost savings, they often indulge in false economies. It is especially unfortunate when the manager can say, truthfully, "We have no complaints on the quality of our product." The issue is quality of *process*, not quality of *product*.

The worst case of all is when it is said, "People have always complained about that."


# ENSURE THAT EVERYONE IN THE COMPANY, FROM THE CHAIRMAN OF THE BOARD TO THE LOWEST LEVEL EMPLOYEE, UNDERSTANDS STATISTICAL REASONING AND CAN USE ELEMENTARY STATISTICS

Of all Dr. Deming's points, this one is the most resisted at first and endorsed most solidly in the end.

> "Those who fear sin the most,
> are those who have the least acquaintance with it."
> >                                        Anon.

Modern systems of people and machines used for production, sales, distribution, and managing are subject to many disturbances. Any quantity that can be measured in connection with these processes will be found to vary. These variations combine in ways that can only be described and understood through the use of statistics.

It should go without saying that managerial decisions should be based on valid, relevant *data*. Managers, and all who are involved with gathering, discussing, and deciding on data, should be able to reason statistically. Is the drop in sales this month meaningful? With what is it to be correlated? Is the sudden increase in orders attributable to the new advertising or the weather? Is the increase in orders sufficient basis for working an extra shift? What faith shall we put into a proposed correlation between defects and material purchased from a vendor who swears he is not at fault? People who do not understand even how to *discuss* such issues are a menace in these systems. Understanding variation is at the very heart of understanding the application of statistics to business.

Consider, for example, the related problems of inventory control, number of employees, and getting orders out on time. When an order is filled, each part of the organization will estimate the time required. This time estimate will be set at a level that gives a reasonable probability for meeting it. Just how much cushion is included will depend very much on the penalties for failure and the rewards for success.

For a delivery to occur "on time," the following events must each occur "on time":

The order must be written up—on time.
The items to be made must be described—on time.
Materials must be ordered—on time.
Materials must be delivered—on time.
Instructions to the workers must be given—on time.
Machines must be ready—on time.
Workers must be ready—on time.
Parts must be inspected—on time.
The completed system must be inspected—on time.
The system must be packaged for shipment—on time.
The product must be delivered—on time.

If the product is to be produced on time, each step should be done on time. Unless each job is watched over very carefully and priorities in each department changed on a daily basis, if the probability of achieving the schedule at each stage is 0.95, for the eleven steps taken together the probability that the schedule will be met is:

$$(0.95)^{11} = 0.57$$

If each organization sets its own schedule at a more comfortable level, one in which 99 percent of the tasks are done on time, the probability of completing the entire task on time still only rises to 0.89.

If the quality of the process is defined to include the ability to meet schedules, it is clear why increasing the quality of the process reduces cost. The gains from getting control over the time of the process are much greater than indicated by just the throughput.

Inventory, floor space, record keeping, conferences of people spending time to fix things up are all reduced.

The essence of gaining such control is understanding the *statistics of variation*. No company could afford the army of statisticians it would take to study, in fine detail, all of the industrial processes of a company. Even if such an army were available, it could not possibly persuade the workers to adopt the changes that would be suggested from an analysis done by "outsiders. " On the other hand, if the workers are themselves part of the observing team and participants in the analysis of the data, both the cost of observation and of implementation will be reduced. Managers must first be instilled with the belief that current levels of variation are unacceptable, and they can and must be substantially improved.

Too many people believe that these ideas apply only to the factory floor. But, as Lester Thurow keeps pointing out, the factory floor employs fewer and fewer workers and their productivity is a constant source of inquiry. On average the productivity of American factory workers is higher than the workers in Japan, though the Japanese are said to be gaining. Where we have a disadvantage is in the size of the office staff used to support the factory. Unless the productivity of these workers is addressed, the overall productivity of the organization will not increase. The concepts of statistical quality control used to increase productivity have been applied to banks, for example. They may be used in the service industries as well as factories. As economists, such as Lester Thurow, keep pointing out, the work force is now more engaged in the production of services than of goods. Since it is goods we export, the inefficiencies in the service sector are added to the cost of what we sell. Therefore, the most rewarding applications of these ideas are likely to be in administrative areas.

The level of statistics that needs to be taught to the workers is not high. Based on Japanese and American experience, it probably will suffice if *everyone* understands the following statistical techniques:

1. How to read and construct a histogram.
2. How to read a process flow chart.
3. How to construct an Ishekawa ("fishbone") chart.
4. How to understand a Pareto chart.
5. How to read x-bar and R-bar charts.
6. Scatter plots (correlating x and y).

Each of these techniques may be taught in a short time, as part of on-the-job problem solving. Of course, these elementary tools are not enough. They should be supported by higher level abilities from consulting statisticians, either in-house or from outside.


## INVITE EMPLOYEES TO BE
## PARTNERS IN SYSTEM IMPROVEMENT

Although the manager is responsible for the improvement of the *system,* the job cannot be done by the manager alone. To the extent that everyone in the organization understands statistical reasoning, the manager can make everyone else in the system a partner in the improvement process. The responsibility to observe and gather data can be delegated to the lowest possible levels. Suggestions for improvements will result, and where they can be adopted at the lower levels, the manager should install procedures to allow people at these levels to implement them. But the manager must remain involved in the process because proposed changes will often involve procedures that cut across departmental lines. If the tools for the job are inadequate or the materials are inappropriate, purchasing may need to change its policies or practices.

The workers are *in* the system. They can observe it and propose changes. Only the manager works *on* the system and can judge and implement the changes.

Improvements will not come without management involvement. They will be made on a project-by-project basis. Management must provide leadership or the workers will not be able to participate. When the workers discover "common causes" (as Dr. Deming calls those causes of defects that are in the system itself), they will need the help of management to remove them. And only the managers can initiate those actions that reveal the special causes, in which workers may need more training or better supervision.

There are many benefits that flow from this responsibility. The modern movement toward "quality of work life" improvements fall naturally into place. But most of all, it will be possible to reach the record-breaking productivities that have been achieved only if the manager involves the employees as partners in improving the system, and not just the work.

## REPLACE MASS INSPECTION
## WITH QUALITY CONTROL

Only the manager can make the policy decision to place responsibility for quality on the workers and not on an army of inspectors. Sometimes, of course, there are legal requirements for inspection, as in some aspects of federal procurement. Wherever it is possible to do so, the inspection procedure should be delegated to the workers involved with the product, and they should be trained to carry out this function.

This philosophy should extend from purchasing through manufacturing, sales, delivery, and maintenance. It should be applied in the office as well. The office is already a complex system of people and machines. It, too, can be improved by this approach.

If everyone waits until something has gone wrong, the time to figure out what went wrong and how to fix it will be excessive and expensive. If time is spent seeing that things do not go wrong, time will not have to be spent fixing things. It is that simple.

Quality control procedures require a deeper understanding of each and every step of an industrial process. To commit to statistical quality control in place of mass inspection is to begin a never-ending search for improvement. Ultimately it will involve everyone in the observation and measurement of the statistical variations of the work under their control.

The first benefits will be the transfer of inspectors to the work force, the reduction of wasted effort, improved quality, and greater productivity.

## MAKE CONTINUOUS IMPROVEMENTS A GOAL
## OF THE COMPANY

## STOP USING NUMERICAL TARGETS AND
## SLOGANS TO "MOTIVATE" THE WORKERS

This is probably the hardest practice for American managers to give up. American managers are habituated to using slogans ("Zero Defects") and to "negotiating" performance improvements ("Managing by Objectives"). It appears heretical to suggest that the practice is itself counterproductive.

The technique does not bear up under scrutiny, however. As every soldier knows, the only target to which one should make a commitment is one that is clearly attainable. And once attained, it will be foolish to exceed it. Next time demands will be raised.

The reason most managers seem to like these methods is that they have an air of crispness and authority about them that sets the boss apart from the worker. "I gave my people tough targets, and by God, they met them. Shows what they can do when you put the pressure on."

"I did my part. I set a goal. Now you do your part and meet it."

The output of a system is just that, the output of a system. Very few activities are entirely under the control of the workers in the system. The manager is (or should be) part of the system, not apart from it.

The slogan "Zero Defects" has no meaning for people searching out and correcting causes of defects. In general the people do not cause defects. The system causes them. Management can remove them; sloganeering cannot.

## TEACH THE EMPLOYEES TO BE PROBLEM SOLVERS: SET AN EXAMPLE

The manager should be able to identify the barriers to quality improvement (and cost reduction—they amount to the same thing). The manager cannot do this alone and should teach subordinates to help with this process. This means the manager must be capable of being a "problem finder" and "problem solver" and teaching others how to define and solve problems. A good manager knows how to interpret statistical information to determine when the solution is to be sought in design of the product, maintenance, machines for production, training for workers, testing, materials handling, shipping, records keeping, marketing, sales, order handling, inventory control, or information systems. Possibilities for improvement exist in all of these activities (and more) and in the interfaces between them.

One of the important side benefits from teaching everyone to be a "problem finder and solver" (at their level) is that the organization becomes ready for innovation. As Utterback has shown, as an industry matures, its production processes tend to become fixed. There is greater and greater commitment to fixed hardware, fixed choices of materials, fixed procedures, fixed organizations, fixed processes, practices, and protocols. Everyone settles into a routine, bureaucracies are formed. When circumstances force a change, everyone resists.

On the other hand, if the organization is *habituated* to the constant search for improvement, for better ways, it will be much less resistant to the introduction of new ideas. Such a major cultural change in an organization takes years. Do not expect results overnight. It took the Japanese twenty to thirty years.

# INSTITUTE TRAINING:
# EVALUATE THE ADEQUACY OF TRAINING

All too often workers are presumed adequately trained if no one complains.  On the other hand, it may also be mistakenly assumed that more training is needed when in fact the process is not in control. In such cases the added training may not accomplish anything worthwhile.

Modern methods of training involve evaluation as well as instruction.  This means determining:

If the workers understand how the characteristics of their output affect customer satisfaction and company cost.

If the workers can use statistical methods at the appropriate level.

If the workers understand the technology they are using  (welding, glueing, machining, measuring, word processing, and so on).

If the workers are able to work together in groups.  If the workers are capable problem solvers.

Modern methods are aimed not at sorting out the "good" from the "bad" and setting pay rates but rather at finding out whether additional training would be beneficial, and if so, of what kind.

# ESTABLISH A "QUALITY PHILOSOPHY"

Only the manager can decide what level of quality is adequate.

In the emerging era of international competition, the levels of performance of products will be continually raised.  Consumers will not accept defective workmanship, unsuited materials, poor maintenance, unreliability, delays, mistakes in handling and order filling, and unresponsiveness. Organizations that do not meet this challenge will simply disappear.

Everyone in the organization must believe that the management is devoted to quality, or the organization will not produce quality output.  Cost cutting in maintenance as a way to bolster a quarterly dividend will send an unmistakable message throughout the organization.

It takes time to build quality habits into an organization.  It takes education and training.  It takes managerial example.  The concept must be translated into action at every level of the organization. The example must flow through the various levels of management.  Therefore the top management must be involved in training the intermediate and lower levels of management and in seeing the reward mechanisms (promotions and salary) are consistent with this objective.

Because so many American managers neglect this responsibility in favor of the quarterly dividend, it will be an especially difficult challenge to change their habits.  In my judgment we should learn to recognize their approach to management for what it is: *bad management.*

Why some boards of directors pay such huge salaries to executives who obviously, by their words and actions, have no interest in this part of their responsibilities is, for me, one of the great dilemmas of our time.

The workers must feel that they are in a genuine partnership with the management in the quest of high quality.

# STOP THE PRACTICE OF BUYING
# FROM THE LOWEST BIDDER

The practice of purchasing from the lowest bidder as a means to stimulate competition among vendors is destructive to the quest for high quality. Only the manager can investigate and change these practices, for the behavior of the purchasing agents is determined by the reward system within which they work.

Purchasing agents should purchase on quality as well as price. Quality can be judged by examining the statistical quality control charts that should accompany every purchase. Such charts show the variability in the manufacturing process and therefore give an indication of how suited the purchased goods will be to the production process into which they go. This information should be the basis for joint discussions involving the vendor, manufacturing, engineering, and, on some occasions, the research staff (and often the company statistician) seeking opportunities for improvement. A smaller number of vendors involved in a cooperative effort to reduce costs and improve quality is much better than a swarm of vendors intent only on reducing costs and with no long-term interest in the success of the purchaser.

# DRIVE OUT FEAR

If the workers believe that increased productivity means they will be fired, they will certainly resist productivity increases. Not until the company is demonstrably on the verge of bankruptcy will they accept changes. The only way for the management to enlist the workers' help will be to form a genuine partnership in which everyone—workers, supervisors, managers—everyone has the same job security. Only the management can determine the priority it attaches to responsibilities to its four constituencies:

> The stockholders
> The customers
> The public
> The workers

In my opinion, the responsibilities should be in this order:

> The public
> The workers
> The customers
> The stockholders

The order in which these are regulated will be understood from the actions of management, and the workers will react accordingly.

The manager should strive toward a method of pay and rewards that helps the workers identify with the prosperity of the company. They should not only be unafraid of improving productivity, they should see, in a tangible way, how it benefits them.

# CONCLUSION

In my opinion it is time to define anew what we mean by "good management." The idea that management is to be judged from the quarterly or even the annual bottom line is too simplistic. It represents an abdication of responsibility. Chrysler's problems this year were laid down a decade ago, when the bottom line looked quite favorable. The whole system of rewards for executives needs to be reconsidered. Ideas like Thurow's who suggests that retirement benefits for executives should be keyed to profits *after* retirement deserves careful consideration. The rewards will reflect how well we think they are doing their jobs, and this calls for better definitions than we now have. I believe that most executives would welcome a change in the system, which rewards them for building something that has a good chance of outlasting them, and to their credit.

Today, under the pressure of Japanese competition, we can sense in American managers a renewed interest in productivity and quality. It is said in many quarters that not only must American managers change their ways, they must also change their attitudes, especially toward labor. Today's managers come mostly from colleges and universities and do not have experience on the factory floor. Nor do they often have experience at the lowest levels of the firm and with the people who work there. The ultimate levels of quality and productivity will be achieved only by people who know how to work as a team, and that means having respect for one another. Years of adversarial relations must now be overcome, and this will require new initiatives on the part of leaders of both management and labor. It begins with a new respect for one another. But in the end, respect will not be enough.

The degree of trust and confidence required for people to participate in productivity and quality improvements requires more than mere trust. It requires caring and genuine affection. This may be the hardest change in self-image required. America may have to wait for a new generation of managers, for those who grew up and became successful under the old rules may not be able to change. Time is precious. Those who can make the transition should be helped to do so, now.

# 22
# Managing Change

WHY CHANGE PROGRAMS DON'T PRODUCE CHANGE
*Michael Beer*
*Russell A. Eisenstat*
*Bert Spector*

MANAGING THE HUMAN SIDE OF CHANGE
*Rosabeth Moss Kanter*

RULES OF THUMB FOR CHANGE AGENTS
*Herbert A. Shepard*

## WHY CHANGE PROGRAMS DON'T PRODUCE CHANGE

*Michael Beer*
*Russell A. Eisenstat*
*Bert Spector*

In the mid-1980s, the new CEO of a major international bank—call it U.S. Financial—announced a companywide change effort. Deregulation was posing serious competitive challenges—challenges to which the bank's traditional hierarchical organization was ill-suited to respond. The only solution was to change fundamentally how the company operated. And the place to begin was at the top.

The CEO held a retreat with his top 15 executives, where they painstakingly reviewed the bank's purpose and culture. He published a mission statement and hired a new vice president for human resources from a company well known for its excellence in managing people. And in a quick succession of moves, he established companywide programs to push change down through the organization: a new organizational structure, a a performance appraisal system, a pay-for-performance compensation plan, training programs to turn managers into "change agents," and quarterly attitude surveys to chart the progress of the change effort.

As much as these steps sound like a textbook case in organizational transformation, there was one big problem: two years after the CEO launched the change program, virtually nothing in the way of actual changes in organizational behavior had occurred. What had gone wrong?

From *Harvard Business Review*, November–December 1990, pp. 158–66. Copyright © 1990 by the President and Fellows of Harvard College. All rights reserved.

The answer is "everything." Every one of the assumptions the CEO made—about who should lead the change effort, what needed changing, and how to go about doing it—was wrong.

U.S. Financial's story reflects a common problem. Faced with changing markets and increased competition, more and more companies are struggling to reestablish their dominance, regain market share, and, in some cases, ensure their survival. Many have come to understand that the key to competitive success is to transform the way they function. They are reducing reliance on managerial authority, formal rules and procedures, and narrow divisions of work. And they are creating teams, sharing information, and delegating responsibility and accountability far down the hierarchy. In effect, companies are moving from the hierarchical and bureaucratic model of organization that has characterized corporations since Work War II to what we call the "task-driven organization," where what has to be done governs who works with whom and who leads.

But while senior managers understand the necessity of change to cope with new competitive realities, they often misunderstand what it takes to bring it about. They tend to share two assumptions with the CEO of U.S. Financial: that promulgating companywide programs—mission statements, "corporate culture" programs, training courses, quality circles, and new pay-for-performance systems—will transform organizations, and that employee behavior is changed by altering a company's formal structure and systems.

In a four-year study of organizational change at six large corporations (see the boxed insert, "Tracking Corporate Change"; the names are fictitious), we found that exactly the opposite is true: the greatest obstacle to revitalization is the idea that it comes about through companywide change programs, particularly when a corporate staff group, such as human resources, sponsors them. We call this "the fallacy of programmatic change." Just as important, formal organization structure and systems cannot lead a corporate renewal process.

While in some companies, wave after wave of programs rolled across the landscape with little positive impact, in others, more successful transformations did take place. They usually started at the periphery of the corporation in a few plants and divisions far from corporate headquarters. And they were led by the general managers of those units, not by the CEO or corporate staff people.

The general managers did not focus on formal structures and systems; they created ad hoc organizational arrangements to solve concrete business problems. By aligning employee roles, responsibilities, and relationships to address the organization's most important competitive task—a process we call "task alignment"—they focused energy for change on the work itself, not on abstractions such as "participation" or "culture." Unlike the CEO at U.S. Financial, they didn't employ massive training programs or rely on speeches and mission statements. Instead, we say that general managers carefully developed the change process through a sequence of six basic managerial interventions.

Once general managers understand the logic of this sequence, they don't have to wait for senior management to start a process of organizational revitalization. There is a lot they can do even without support from the top. Of course, having a CEO or other senior managers who are committed to change does make a difference—and when it comes to changing an entire organization, such support is essential. But top management's role in the change process is very different from that which the CEO played at U.S. Financial.

Grass-roots change presents managers with a paradox: directing a "nondirective" change process. The most effective senior managers in our study recognized their limited power to mandate corporate renewal from the top. Instead, they defined their roles as creating a climate for change, then spreading the lessons of both successes and failures. Put another way, they specified the general direction in which the company should move without insisting on specific solutions.

## Tracking Corporate Change

Which strategies for corporate change work, and which do not? We sought the answers in a comprehensive study of 12 large companies where top management was attempting to revitalize the corporation. Based on preliminary research, we identified six for in-depth analysis: five manufacturing companies and one large international bank. All had revenues between $4 billion and $10 billion. We studied 26 plants and divisions in these six companies and conducted hundreds of interviews with human resource managers; line managers engaged in change efforts at plants, branches, or business units; workers and union leaders; and, finally, top management.

Based on this material, we ranked the six companies according to the success with which they had managed the revitalization effort. Were there significant improvements in interfunctional coordination, decision making, work organization, and concern for people? Research has shown that in the long term, the quality of these four factors will influence performance. We did not define success in terms of improved financial performance because, in the short run, corporate financial performance is influenced by many situational factors unrelated to the change process.

To corroborate our rankings of the companies, we also administered a standardized questionnaire in each company to understand how employees viewed the unfolding change process. Respondents rated their companies on a scale of 1 to 5. A score of 3 meant that no change had taken place; a score below 3 meant that, in the employee's judgment, the organization had actually gotten worse. As the table suggests, with one exception—the company we call Livingston Electronics—employees' perceptions of how much their companies had changed were identical to ours. And Livingston's relatively high standard of deviation (which measures the degree of consensus among employees about the outcome of the change effort) indicates that within the company there was considerable disagreement as to just how successful revitalization had been.

Researchers and Employees—Similar Conclusions

### Extent of Revitalization

| Company | Ranked by Researchers | Rated by Employees | |
|---|---|---|---|
| | | Average | Standard Deviation |
| General Products | 1 | 4.04 | 0.35 |
| Fairweather | 2 | 3.58 | 0.45 |
| Livingston Electronics | 3 | 3.61 | 0.76 |
| Scranton Steel | 4 | 3.30 | 0.65 |
| Continental Glass | 5 | 2.96 | 0.83 |
| U.S. Financial | 6 | 2.78 | 1.07 |

In the early phases of a companywide change process, any senior manager can play this role. Once grass-roots change reaches a critical mass, however, the CEO has to be ready to transform his or her own work unit as well—the top team composed of key business heads and corporate staff heads. At this point, the company's structure and system must be put into alignment with the new management practices that have developed at the periphery. Otherwise, the tension between dynamic units and static top management will cause the change process to break down.

We believe that an approach to change based on task alignment, starting at the periphery and moving steadily toward the corporate core, is the most effective way to achieve enduring organizational change. This is not to say that change can *never* start at the top, but it is uncommon and too risky as a deliberate strategy. Change is about learning. It is a rare CEO who knows in advance the fine-grained details of organizational change that the many diverse units of a large corporation demand. Moreover, most of today's senior executives developed in an era in which top-down hierarchy was the primary means for organizing and managing. They must learn from innovative approaches coming from younger unit managers closer to the action.

## THE FALLACY OF PROGRAMMATIC CHANGE

Most change programs don't work because they are guided by a theory of change that is fundamentally flawed. The common belief is that the place to begin is with the knowledge and attitudes of individuals. Changes in attitudes, the theory goes, lead to changes in individual behavior. And changes in individual behavior, repeated by many people, will result in organizational change. According to this model, change is like a conversion experience. Once people "get religion," changes in their behavior will surely follow.

This theory gets the change process exactly backward. In fact, individual behavior is powerfully shaped by the organizational roles that people play. The most effective way to change behavior, therefore, is to put people into a new organizational context, which imposes new roles, responsibilities, and relationships on them. This creates a situation that, in a sense, "forces" new attitudes and behaviors on people. (See the table, "Contrasting Assumptions about Change.")

One way to think about this challenge is in terms of three interrelated factors required for corporate revitalization. *Coordination* or teamwork is especially important if an organization is to discover and act on cost, quality, and product development opportunities. The production and sale of innovative, high-quality, low-cost products (or services) depend on close coordination among marketing, product design, and manufacturing departments, as well as between labor and management. High levels of *commitment* are essential for the effort, initiative, and cooperation that coordinated action demands. New *competencies*, such as knowledge of the business as a whole, analytical skills, and interpersonal skills, are necessary if people are to identify and solve problems as a team. If any of these elements are missing, the change process will break down.

The problem with most companywide change programs is that they address only one or, at best, two of these factors. Just because a company issues a philosophy statement about teamwork doesn't mean its employees necessarily know what teams to form or how to function within them to improve coordination. A corporate reorganization may change the boxes on a formal organization chart but not provide the necessary attitudes and skills to make the new structure work. A pay-for-performance system may force managers to differentiate better performers from poorer ones, but it doesn't help them internalize new standards by which to judge subordinates' performances. Nor does it teach them how to deal effectively with performance problems. Such programs cannot provide the cultural context (role models from whom to learn) that people need to develop new competencies, so ultimately they fail to create organizational change.

Similarly, training programs may target competence, but rarely do they change a company's patterns of coordination. Indeed, the excitement engendered in a good corporate training program frequently leads to increased frustration when employees get back on the job only to see their new skills go unused in an organization in which nothing else has changed. People end up seeing training as a waste of time, which undermines whatever commitment to change a program may have roused in the first place.

When one program doesn't work, senior managers, like the CEO at U.S. Financial, often try another, instituting a rapid progression of programs. But this only exacerbates the problem. Because they are designed to cover everyone and everything, programs end up covering nobody and nothing particularly well. They are so general and standardized that they don't speak to the day-to-day realities of particular units. Buzzwords like "quality," "participation," "excellence," "empowerment," and "leadership" become a substitute for a detailed understanding of the business.

And all these change programs also undermine the credibility of the change effort. Even when managers accept the potential value of a particular program for others—quality circles, for example, to solve a manufacturing problem—they may be confronted with another, more pressing business problem, such as new product development. One-size-fits-all change programs take energy away from efforts to solve key business problems—which explains why so many general managers don't support programs, even when they acknowledge that their underlying principles may be useful.

## Contrasting Assumptions about Change

| *Programmatic Change* | *Task Alignment* |
|---|---|
| Problems in behavior are a function of individual knowledge, attitudes, and beliefs. | Individual knowledge, attitudes, and beliefs are shaped by recurring patterns of behavioral interactions. |
| The primary target of renewal should be the content of attitudes and ideas; actual behavior should be secondary. | The primary target of renewal should be behavior; attitudes and ideas should be secondary. |
| Behavior can be isolated and changed individually. | Problems in behavior come from a circular pattern, but the effects of the organizational system on the individual are greater than those of the individual on the system. |
| The target for renewal should be at the individual level. | The target for renewal should be at level of roles, responsibilities, and relationships. |

This is not to state that training, changes in pay systems or organizational structure, or a new corporate philosophy are always inappropriate. All can play valuable roles in supporting an integrated change effort. The problems come when such programs are used in isolation as a kind of "magic bullet" to spread organizational change rapidly through the entire corporation. At their best, change programs of this sort are irrelevant. At their worst, they actually inhibit change. By promoting skepticism and cynicism, programmatic change can inoculate companies against the real thing.

## Six Steps to Effective Change

Companies avoid the shortcomings of programmatic change by concentrating on "task alignment"—reorganizing employee roles, responsibilities, and relationships to solve specific business problems. Task alignment is easiest in small units—a plant, department, or business unit—where goals and tasks are clearly defined. Thus, the chief problem for corporate change is how to promote task-aligned changed across many diverse units.

We saw that general managers at the business unit or plant level can achieve task alignment through a sequence of six overlapping but distinctive steps, which we call the *critical path*. This path develops a self-reinforcing cycle of commitment, coordination, and competence. The sequence of steps is important because activities appropriate at one time are often counterproductive if started too early. Timing is everything in the management of change.

1. *Mobilize commitment to change through joint diagnosis of business problems*. As the term *task alignment* suggests, the starting point of any effective change effort is a clearly defined business problem. By helping people develop a shared diagnosis of what is wrong in an organization and what can and must be improved, a general manager mobilizes the initial commitment that is necessary to begin the change process.

Consider the case of a division we call Navigation Devices, a business unit of about 600 people set up by a large corporation to commercialize a product originally designed for the military market. When the new general manager took over, the division had been in operation for several years without ever making a profit. It had never been able to design and produce a high-quality, cost-competitive product. This was due largely to an organization in which decisions were made at the top, without proper involvement of or coordination with other functions.

The first step the new general manager took was to initiate a broad review of the business. Where the previous general manager had set strategy with the unit's marketing director alone, the new general manager included his entire management team. He also brought in outside consultants to help him and his managers function more effectively as a group.

Next, he formed a 20-person task force representing all the stakeholders in the organization—managers, engineers, production workers, and union officials. The group visited a number of successful manufacturing organizations in an attempt to identify what Navigation Devices might do to organize more effectively. One high-performance manufacturing plant in the task force's own company made a particularly strong impression. Not only did it highlight the problems at Navigation Devices but it also offered an alternative organizational model, based on teams, that captured the group's imagination. Seeing a different way of working helped strengthen the group's commitment to change.

The Navigation Devices task force didn't learn new facts from this process of joint diagnosis; everyone already knew the unit was losing money. But the group came to see clearly the organizational roots of the unit's inability to compete and, even more important, came to share a common understanding of the problem. The group also identified a potential organizational solution: to redesign the way it worked, using ad hoc teams to integrate the organization around the competitive task.

2. *Develop a shared vision of how to organize and manage for competitiveness.* Once a core group of people is committed to a particular analysis of the problem, the general manager can lead employees toward a task-aligned vision of the organization that defines new roles and responsibilities. These new arrangements will coordinate the flow of information and work across interdependent functions at all levels of the organization. But since they do not change formal structures and systems like titles or compensation, they encounter less resistance.

At Navigation Devices, the 20-person task force became the vehicle for this second stage. The group came up with a model of the organization in which cross-functional teams would accomplish all work, particularly new product development. A business-management team composed of the general manager and his staff would set the unit's strategic direction and review the work of lower-level teams. Business-area teams would develop plans for specific markets. Product-development teams would manage new products from initial design to production. Production-process teams composed of engineers and production workers would identify and solve quality and cost problems in the plant. Finally, engineering-process teams would examine engineering methods and equipment. The teams got to the root of the unit's problems—functional and hierarchical barriers to sharing information and solving problems.

To create a consensus around the new vision, the general manager commissioned a still larger task force of about 90 employees from different levels and functions, including union and management, to refine the vision and obtain everyone's commitment to it. On a retreat away from the workplace, the group further refined the new organizational model and drafted a values statement, which it presented later to the entire Navigation Devices work force. The vision and the values statement made sense to Navigation Devices employees in a way many corporate mission statements never do—because it grew out of the organization's own analysis of real business problems. And it was built on a model for solving those problems that key stakeholders believed would work.

3. *Foster consensus for the new vision, competence to enact it, and cohesion to move it along.* Simply letting employees help develop a new vision is not enough to overcome resistance to change—or to foster the skills needed to make the new organization work. Not everyone can help in the design, and even those who do participate often do not fully appreciate what renewal will require until the new organization is actually in place. This is when strong leadership from the general manager is crucial. Commitment to change is always uneven. Some managers are enthusiastic; others are neutral or even antagonistic. At Navigation Devices, the general manager used what his subordinates termed the "velvet glove." One made it clear that the division was going to encourage employee involvement and the team approach. To managers who wanted to help him, he offered support. To those who did not, he offered outplacement and counseling.

Once an organization has defined new roles and responsibilities, people need to develop the competencies to make the new setup work. Actually, the very existence of the teams with their new goals and accountabilities will force learning. The changes in roles, responsibilities, and relationships foster new skills and attitudes. Changed patterns of coordination will also increase employee participation, collaboration, and information sharing.

But management also has to provide the right supports. At Navigation Devices, six resource people—three from the corporate headquarters—worked on the change project. Each team was assigned one internal consultant, who attended every meeting, to help people be effective team members. Once employees could see exactly what kinds of new skills they needed, they asked for formal training programs to develop those skills further. Since these courses grew directly out of the employee's own experiences, they were far more focused and useful than traditional training programs.

Some people, of course, just cannot or will not change, despite all the direction and support in the world. Step 3 is the appropriate time to replace those managers who cannot function in the new organization—after they have had a chance to prove themselves. Such decisions are rarely easy, and sometimes those people who have difficulty working in a participatory organization have extremely valuable specialized skills. Replacing them early in the change process, before they have worked in the new organization, is not only unfair to individuals, it can be demoralizing to the entire organization and can disrupt the change process. People's understanding of what kind of manager and worker the new organization demands grows slowly and only from the experience of seeing some individuals succeed and others fail.

Once employees have bought into a vision of what's necessary and have some understanding of what the new organization requires, they can accept the necessity of replacing or moving people who don't make the transition to the new way of working. Sometimes people are transferred to other parts of the company where technical expertise, rather than the new competencies, is the main requirement. When no alternatives exist, sometimes they leave the company through early retirement programs, for example. The act of replacing people can actually reinforce the organization's commitment to change by visibly demonstrating the general manager's commitment to the new way.

Some of the managers replaced at Navigation Devices were high up in the organization—for example, the vice president of operations, who oversaw the engineering and manufacturing departments. The new head of manufacturing was far more committed to change and skilled in leading a critical path change process. The result was speedier change throughout the manufacturing function.

4. *Spread revitalization to all departments without pushing it from the top.* With the new ad hoc organization for the unit in place, it is time to turn to the functional and staff departments that must interact with it. Members of teams cannot be effective unless the department from which they come is organized and managed in a way that supports their roles as full-fledged participants in team decisions. What this often means is that these departments will have to rethink their roles and authority in the organization.

At Navigation Devices, this process was seen most clearly in the engineering department. Production department managers were the most enthusiastic about the change effort; engineering managers were more hesitant. Engineering had always been king at Navigation Devices; engineers designed products to the military's specifications without much concern about whether manufacturing could easily build them or not. Once the new team structure was in place, however, engineers had to participate on product development with production workers. This required them to reexamine their roles and rethink their approaches to organizing and managing their own department.

The impulse of many general managers faced with such a situation would be to force the issue—to announce, for example, that now all parts of the organization must manage by teams. The temptation to force newfound insights on the rest of the organization can be great, particularly when rapid change is needed, but it would be the same mistake that senior managers make when they try to push programmatic change throughout a company. It short-circuits the change process.

It's better to let each department "reinvent the wheel"—that is, to find its own way to the new organization. At Navigation Devices, each department was allowed to take the general concepts of coordination and teamwork and apply them to its particular situation. Engineering spent nearly a year agonizing over how to implement the team concept. The department conducted two surveys, held off-site meetings, and proposed, rejected, then accepted a matrix management structure before it finally got on board. Engineering's decision to move to matrix management was not surprising; but because it was its own choice, people committed themselves to learning the necessary new skills and attitudes.

5. *Institutionalize revitalization through formal policies, systems and structures.* There comes a point where general managers have to consider how to institutionalize change so the process continues even after they've moved on to other responsibilities. Step 5 is the time: the new approach has become entrenched, the right people are in place, and the team organization is up and running. Enacting changes in structures and systems any earlier tends to backfire. Take information systems. Creating a team structure means new information requirements. Why not have the MIS department create new systems that cut across traditional functional and departmental lines early in the change process? The problem is that, without a well-developed understanding of information requirements, which can best be obtained by placing people on task-aligned teams, managers are likely to resist new systems as an imposition by the MIS department. Newly formed teams can often pull together enough information to get their work done without fancy new systems. It's better to hold off until everyone understands what the team's information needs are.

What's true for information systems is even more true for other formal structures and systems. Any formal system is going to have some disadvantages; none is perfect. These imperfections can be minimized, however, once people have worked in an ad hoc team structure and learned what interdependencies are necessary. Then employees will commit to them, too.

Again, Navigation Devices is a good example. The revitalization of the unit was highly successful. Employees changed how they saw their roles and responsibilities and became convinced that change could actually make a difference. As a result, there were dramatic improvements in value added per employee, scrap reduction, quality, customer service, gross inventory per employee, and profits. And all this happened with almost no formal changes in reporting relationships, information systems, evaluation procedures, compensation, or control systems.

When the opportunity arose, the general manager eventually did make some changes in the formal organization. For example, when he moved the vice president of operations out of the organization, he eliminated the position altogether. Engineering and manufacturing reported directly to him from that point on. For the most part, however, the changes in performance at Navigation Devices were sustained by the general manager's expectations and the new norms for behavior.

6. *Monitor and adjust strategies in response to problems in the revitalization process.* The purpose of change is to create an asset that did not exist before—a learning organization capable of adapting to a changing competitive environment. The organization has to know how to continually monitor its behavior—in effect, to learn how to learn.

Some might say that this is the general manager's responsibility. But monitoring the change process needs to be shared just as analyzing the organization's key business problem does.

At Navigation Devices, the general manager introduced several mechanisms to allow key constituents to help monitor the revitalization. An oversight team—composed of some crucial managers, a union leader, a secretary, an engineer, and an analyst from finance—kept continual watch over the process. Regular employee attitude surveys monitored behavior patterns. Planning teams were formed and reformed in response to new challenges. All these mechanisms created a long-term capacity for continual adaptation and learning.

The six-step process provides a way to elicit renewal without imposing it. When stakeholders become committed to a vision, they are willing to accept a new pattern of management—here the ad hoc team structure—that demands changes in their behavior. And as the employees discover that the new approach is more effective (which will happen only if the vision aligns with the core task), they have to grapple with personal and organizational changes they might otherwise resist. Finally, as improved coordination helps solve relevant problems, it will reinforce team behavior and produce a desire to learn new skills. This learning enhances effectiveness even further and results in an even stronger commitment to change. This mutually reinforcing cycle of improvements in commitment, coordination, and competence creates a growing sense of efficacy. It can continue as long as the ad hoc team structure is allowed to expand its role in running the business.

## THE ROLE OF TOP MANAGEMENT

To change an entire corporation, the change process we have described must be applied over and over again in many plants, branches, departments, and divisions. Orchestrating this companywide change process is the first responsibility of senior management. Doing so successfully requires a delicate balance. Without explicit efforts by top management to promote conditions for change in individual units, only a few plants or divisions will attempt change and those that do will remain isolated. The best senior manager leaders we studied held their subordinates responsible for starting a change process without specifying a particular approach.

*Create a market for change.* The most effective approach is to set demanding standards for all operations and then hold managers accountable to them. At our best-practice company, which we call General Products, senior managers developed ambitious product and operating standards. General managers unable to meet these product standards by a certain date had to scrap their products and take a sharp hit to their bottom lines. As long as managers understand that high standards are not arbitrary but are dictated by competitive forces, standards can generate enormous pressure for better performance, a key ingredient in mobilizing energy for change.

But merely increasing demands is not enough. Under pressure, most managers will seek to improve business performance by doing more of what they have always done—overmanage—rather than alter the fundamental way they organize. So, while senior managers increase demands, they should also hold managers accountable for fundamental changes in the way they use human resources.

For example, when plant managers at General Products complained about the impossibility of meeting new business standards, senior managers pointed them to the corporate organization-development department within human resources and emphasized that the plant managers would be held accountable for moving revitalization along. Thus, top management had created a demand system for help with the new way of managing, and the human resource staff could support change without appearing to push a program.

*Use successfully revitalized units as organizational models for the entire company.* Another important strategy is to focus the company's attention on plants and divisions that have already begun experimenting with management innovations. These units become developmental laboratories for further innovation.

There are two ground rules for identifying such models. First, innovative units need support. They need the best managers to lead them, and they need adequate resources—for instance, skilled human resource people and external consultants. In the most successful companies that we studied, senior managers saw it as their responsibility to make resources available to leading-edge units. They did not leave it to the human resource function.

Second, because resources are always limited and the costs of failure high, it is crucial to identify those units with the likeliest chance of success. Successful management innovations can appear to be failures when the bottom line is devastated by environmental factors beyond the unit's control. The best models are in healthy markets.

Obviously, organizational models can serve as catalysts for change only if others are aware of their existence and are encouraged to learn from them. Many of our worst-practice companies had plants and divisions that were making substantial changes. The problem was, nobody knew about them. Corporate management had never bothered to highlight them as examples to follow. In the leading companies, visits, conferences, and educational programs facilitated learning from model units.

*Develop career paths that encourage leadership development.* Without strong leaders, units cannot make the necessary organizational changes, yet the scarcest resource available for revitalizing corporations is leadership. Corporate renewal depends as much on developing effective change leaders as it does on developing effective organizations. The personal learning associated with leadership development—or the realization by higher management that a manager does not have this capacity—cannot occur in the classroom. It only happens in an organization where the teamwork, high commitment, and new competencies we have discussed are already the norm.

The only way to develop the kind of leaders a changing organization needs is to make leadership an important criterion for promotion, and then manage people's careers to develop it. At our best-practice companies, managers were moved from job to job and from organization to organization based on their learning needs, not on their position in the hierarchy. Successful leaders were assigned to units that had been targeted for change. People who needed to sharpen their leadership skills were moved into the company's model units, where those skills would be demanded and, therefore, learned. In effect, top management used leading-edge units as hothouses to develop revitalization leaders.

But what about the top management team itself? How important is it for the CEO and his or her direct reports to practice what they preach? It is not surprising—indeed, it's predictable—that, in the early years of a corporate change effort, top managers' actions are often not consistent with their words. Such inconsistencies don't pose a major barrier to corporate change in the beginning, though consistency is obviously desirable. Senior managers can create a climate for grassroots change without paying much attention to how they themselves operate and manage. And unit managers will tolerate this inconsistency so long as they can freely make changes in their own units in order to compete more effectively.

There comes a point, however, when addressing the inconsistencies becomes crucial. As the change process spreads, general managers in the ever-growing circle of revitalized units eventually demand changes from corporate staff groups and top management. As they discover how to manage differently in their own units, they bump up against constraints of policies and practices that corporate staff and top management have created. They also begin to see opportunities for better coordination between themselves and other parts of the company over which they have little control. At this point, corporate organization must be aligned with corporate strategy, and coordination between related but hitherto independent businesses improved for the benefit of the whole corporation.

None of the companies we studied had reached this "moment of truth." Even when corporate leaders intellectually understood the direction of change, they were just beginning to struggle with how they would change themselves and the company as a whole for a total corporate revitalization.

This last step in the process of corporate renewal is probably the most important. If the CEO and his or her management team do not ultimately apply to themselves what they have been encouraging their general managers to do, the whole process can break down. The time to tackle the tough challenge of transforming companywide systems and structures comes finally at the end of the corporate change process.

At this point, senior managers must make an effort to adopt the team behavior, attitudes, and skills that they have demanded of others in earlier phases of change. Their struggle with behavior change will help sustain corporate renewal in three ways. It will promote the attitudes and behavior needed to coordinate diverse activities in the company; it will lend credibility to top management's continued espousal of change; and it will help the CEO identify and develop a successor who is capable of learning the new behaviors. Only such a manager can lead a corporation that can renew itself continually as competitive forces change.

Companies need a particular mindset for managing change: one that emphasizes process over specific content, recognizes organization change as a unit-by-unit learning process, rather than a series of programs, and acknowledges the payoffs that result from persistence over a long time as opposed to quick fixes. This mindset is difficult to maintain in an environment that presses for quarterly earnings, but we believe it is the only approach that will bring about successful renewal.

# MANAGING THE HUMAN SIDE OF CHANGE

*Rosabeth Moss Kanter*

This is a time of historically unprecedented change for most corporations. The auto and steel industries are in turmoil because of the effects of foreign competition. Financial services are undergoing a revolution. Telecommunications companies are facing profound and dramatic changes because of the breakup of AT&T and greater competition from newly organized long-distance carriers. Health care organizations are under pressure to cut costs and improve services in the face of government regulation and the growth of for-profit hospital chains.

Change, and the need to manage it well, has always been with us. Business life is punctuated by necessary and expected changes: the introduction of new toothpastes, regular store remodelings, changes in information systems, reorganizations of the office staff, announcements of new benefits programs, radical rethinking of the fall product line, or a progression of new senior vice-presidents.

But as common as change is, the people who work in an organization may still not like it. Each of those "routine" changes can be accompanied by tension, stress, squabbling, sabotage, turnover, subtle undermining, behind-the-scenes footdragging, work slowdowns, needless political battles, and a drain on money and time—in short, symptoms of that ever-present bugaboo resistance to change.

If even small and expected changes can be the occasion for decrease in organizational effectiveness, imagine the potential for disaster when organizations try to make big changes, such as developing a new corporate culture, restructuring the business to become more competitive, divesting losing operations and closing facilities, reshuffling product divisions to give them a market orientation, or moving into new sales channels.

Because the pace of change has speeded up, mastering change is increasingly a part of every manager's job. All managers need to know how to guide people through change so that they emerge at the other end with an effective organization. One important key is being able to analyze the reasons people resist change. Pinpointing the source of the resistance makes it possible to see what needs to be done to avoid resistance, or convert it into commitment to change.

*Source*: Reprinted from *Managing Change—The Human Dimension*, Goodmeasure, Inc., 1984 with permission of the author and publisher.

As a consulting firm, Goodmeasure has worked with the change-related problems of over a hundred major organizations. We have distilled a list of the ten most common reasons managers encounter resistance to change, and tactics for dealing with each.

## 1. LOSS OF CONTROL

How people greet a change has to do with whether they feel in control of it or not. Change is exciting when it is done *by us*, threatening when it is done *to us*.

Most people want and need to feel in control of the event around them. Indeed, behind the rise of participative management today is the notion that "ownership" counts in getting commitment to actions, that if people have a chance to participate in decisions, they feel better about them. Even involvement in details is better than noninvolvement. And the more choices that are left to people, the better they feel about the changes. If all actions are imposed upon them from outside, however, they are more likely to resist.

Thus, the more choices we can give people the better they'll feel about the change. But when they feel out of control and powerless, they are likely not only to feel stress, but also to behave in defensive, territorial ways. I proposed in my *1977 Men and Women of the Corporation* that, in organizations at least, it is powerlessness that "corrupts," not power. When people feel powerless, they behave in petty, territorial ways. They become rules-minded, and they are over-controlling, because they're trying to grab hold of some little piece of the world that they *do* control and then overmanage it to death. (One way to reassert control is to resist everyone else's new ideas.) People do funny things when they feel out of control, but giving people chances for involvement can help them feel more committed to the change in question.

## 2. EXCESS UNCERTAINTY

A second reason people resist change is what I call the "Walking Off A Cliff Blindfolded Problem"— too much uncertainty. Simply not knowing enough about what the next step is going to be or feel like makes comfort impossible. If people don't know where the next step is going to take them, whether it is the organizational equivalent of off a cliff or under a train, change seems dangerous. Then they resist change, because they reason, "It's safer to stay with the devil you know than to commit yourself to the devil you don't."

Managers who do not share enough information with their employees about exactly what is happening at every step of a change process, and about what they anticipate happening next, and about when more information will be coming, make a mistake, because they're likely to meet with a great deal of resistance. Information counts in building commitment to a change, especially step-by-step scenarios with timetables and milestones. Dividing a big change into a number of small steps can help make it seem less risky and threatening. People can focus on one step at a time, but not a leap off the cliff; they know what to do next.

Change requires faith that the new way will indeed be the right way. If the leaders themselves do not appear convinced, then the rest of the people will not budge. Another key to resolving the discomfort of uncertainty is for leaders to demonstrate their commitment to change. Leaders have to be the first over the cliff if they want the people they manage to follow suit. Information, coupled with the leaders' actions to make change seem safer, can convert resistance to commitment.

# 3. SURPRISE, SURPRISE!

A third reason people resist change is the surprise factor. People are easily shocked by decisions or requests suddenly sprung on them without groundwork or preparation. Their first response to something totally new and unexpected, that they have not had time to prepare for mentally, is resistance.

Companies frequently make this mistake when introducing organizational changes. They wait until all decisions are made, and then spring them on an unsuspecting population. One chemical company that has had to reorganize and frequently lay people off is particularly prone to this error. A manager might come into work one day to find on her desk a list of people she is supposed to inform, immediately, that their jobs are changing or being eliminated. Consequently, that manager starts to wonder whether she is on somebody *else's* list, and she feels so upset by the surprise that her commitment to the organization is reduced. The question, "Why couldn't they trust me enough to even hint that this might happen?" is a legitimate one.

Decisions for change can be such a shock that there is no time to assimilate or absorb them, or see what might be good about those changes. All we can do is feel threatened and resist—defend against the new way or undermine it.

Thus, it is important to not only provide employees with information to build a commitment to change, but also to arrange the timing of the information's release. Give people advance notice, a warning, and a chance to adjust their thinking.


# 4. THE "DIFFERENCE" EFFECT

A fourth reason people resist change is the effect of "difference"—the fact that change requires people to become conscious of, and to question, familiar routines and habits.

A great deal of work in organizations is simply habitual. In fact, most of us could not function very well in life if we were not engaged in a high proportion of "mindless" habitual activities—like turning right when you walk down the corridor to work, or handling certain forms, or attending certain meetings. Imagine what it would be like if, every day you went to work, your office was in an entirely different place and the furniture was rearranged. You would stumble around, have trouble finding things, feel uncomfortable, and need to expend an additional amount of physical and emotional energy. This would be exhausting and fatiguing. Indeed, rapidly growing high-technology companies often present people with an approximation of this new-office-every-day nightmare, because the addition of new people and new tasks is ubiquitous, while established routines and habitual procedures are minimal. The overwork syndrome and "burn-out" phenomenon are accordingly common in the industry.

One analogy comes from my work on the introduction of a person who is "different" (an "O") in a group formerly made up of only one kind of person (the "X's"), the theme of Goodmeasure's production, *A Tale of "O."* When a group of X's has been accustomed to doing things a certain way, to having habits and modes of conversation and jokes that are unquestioned, they are threatened by the presence of a person who seems to require operating in a different way. The X's are likely to resist the introduction of the O, because the difference effect makes them start feeling self-conscious, requires that they question even the habitual things that they do, and demands that they think about behavior that used to be taken for granted. The extra effort required to "reprogram" the routines is what causes resistance to the change.

Thus, an important goal in managing change is to minimize or reduce the number of "differences" introduced by the change, leaving as many habits and routines as possible in place. Sometimes managers think they should be doing just the opposite—changing everything else they can think of to symbolize that the core change is really happening. But commitment to change is more likely to occur when the change is not presented as a wild difference but rather as continuous with tradition. Roger Smith, the chairman of General Motors, launched what I consider one of the most revolutionary periods of change in the company's history by invoking not revolution, but tradition: "I'm going to take this company back to the way Alfred Sloan intended it to be managed."

Not only do many people need or prefer familiar routines, they also like familiar surroundings. Maintaining some familiar sights and sounds, the things that make people feel comfortable and at home, is very important in getting employees' commitment to a change.

## 5. LOSS OF FACE

If accepting a change means admitting that the way things were done in the past was wrong, people are certain to resist. Nobody likes losing face or feeling embarrassed in front of their peers. But sometimes making a commitment to a new procedure, product, or program carries with it the implicit assumption that the "old ways" must have been wrong, thereby putting all the adherents of the "old ways" in the uncomfortable position of either looking stupid for their past actions or being forced to defend them—and thereby arguing against any change.

The great sociologist Erving Goffman showed that people would go to great lengths to save face, even engaging in actions contrary to their long-term interest to avoid embarrassment.

---

### BUILDING COMMITMENT TO CHANGE

- Allow room for participation in the planning of the change.
- Leave choices within the overall decision to change.
- Provide a clear picture of the change, a "vision" with details about the new state.
- Share information about change plans to the fullest extent possible.
- Divide a big change into more manageable and familiar steps; let people take a small step first.
- Minimize surprises; give people advance warning about new requirements.
- Allow for digestion of change requests—a chance to become accustomed to the ideas of change before making a commitment.
- Repeatedly demonstrate your own commitment to the change.
- Make standards and requirements clear—tell exactly what is expected of people in the change.
- Offer positive reinforcement for competence; let people know they can do it.
- Look for and reward pioneers, innovators, and early successes to serve as models.
- Help people find or feel compensated for the extra time and energy change requires.
- Avoid creating obvious "losers" from the change. (But if there are some, be honest with them—early on.)
- Allow expressions of nostalgia and grief for the past—then create excitement about the future.

*—Rosabeth Moss Kanter and the staff of Goodmeasure, Inc.*

I have seen a number of new chief executives introduce future strategies in ways that "put down" the preceding strategies, thus making automatic enemies of the members of the group that had formulated and executed them. The rhetoric of their speeches implies that the new way gains strength only in contrast to the failures and flaws of the old way—a kind of Maoist "cultural revolution" mentally in business. "The way we've been managing is terrible," one CEO says routinely. He thus makes it hard for people who lived the old ways to shed them for the new, because to do so is to admit they must have been "terrible" before. While Mao got such confessions, businesses do not.

Instead, commitment to change is ensured when past actions are put in perspective—as the apparently right thing to do then, but now times are different. This way people do not lose face for changing; just the opposite. They look strong and flexible. They have been honored for what they accomplished under the old conditions, even if it is now time to change.

## 6. CONCERNS ABOUT FUTURE COMPETENCE

Sometimes people resist change because of personal concerns about their future ability to be effective after the change: Can I do it? How will I do it? Will I make it under the new conditions? Do I have the skills to operate in a new way? These concerns may not be expressed out loud, but they can result in finding many reasons why change should be avoided.

In local telephone companies, employees have been told for years that they would be promoted for one set of reasons, and the workers had developed one set of skills and competencies. It is very threatening for many employees to be told that, all of a sudden, the new world demands a new set of competencies, a new set of more market-oriented entrepreneurial skills. Nobody likes to look inadequate. And nobody, especially people who have been around a long time, wants to feel that he or she has to "start over again" in order to feel competent in the organization.

It is essential, when managing a change, to make sure that people *do* feel competent, that there is sufficient education and training available so that people understand what is happening and know that they can master it—that they *can* indeed do what is needed. Positive reinforcement is even more important in managing change than it is in managing routine situations.

In addition to education and training, people also need a chance to practice the new skills or actions without feeling that they are being judged or that they are going to look foolish to their colleagues and peers. They need a chance to get comfortable with new routines or new ways of operating without feeling stupid because they have questions to ask. Unfortunately, many corporations I know have spent a lot of time making executives and managers feel stupid if they have questions; they're the ones that are supposed to have the *answers*.

We have to be sensitive enough to the management of change to make sure that nobody feels stupid, that everyone can ask questions, and that everybody has a chance to be a learner, to come to feel competent in the new ways.

## 7. RIPPLE EFFECTS

People may resist change for reasons connected to their own activities. Change does sometimes disrupt other kinds of plans or projects, or even personal and family activities that have nothing to do with the job, and anticipation of those disruptions causes resistance to change.

Changes inevitably send ripples beyond their intended impact. The ripples may also negate promises the organization has made. Plans or activities seemingly unrelated to the core of the change can be very important to people. Effective "change masters" are sensitive to the ripples changes cause. They look for the ripples and introduce the change with *flexibility* so that, for example, people who have children can finish out the school year before relocating, or managers who want to finish a pet project can do so, or departments can go through a transition period rather than facing an abrupt change. That kind of sensitivity helps get people on board and makes them feel committed, rather than resistant, to the change.

## 8. MORE WORK

One reasonable source of resistance to change is that change is simply *more work*. The effort it takes to manage things under routine circumstances needs to be multiplied when things are changing. Change requires more energy, more time, and greater mental preoccupation.

Members of project teams creating innovation put in a great deal of overtime on their own, because of the demands—and the hire—of creating something new. During the breakup of the Bell System, many managers worked 60 or 70 hour weeks during the process, not seeing their families, simply because of the work involved in moving such a large system from one state to another. And the pattern is repeated in corporation after corporation.

Change does require above-and-beyond effort. It cannot be done automatically, it cannot be done without extra effort, and it takes time. There is ample reason to resist change, if people do not want to put in the effort. They need support and compensation for the extra work of change in order to move from resistance to commitment.

Managers have options for providing that support. They can make sure that families are informed and understanding about the period of extra effort. They can make sure that people are given credit for the effort they are putting in and rewarded for the fact that they are working harder than ever before—rewards ranging from cash bonuses to special trips or celebrations. They can recognize that the extra effort is voluntary and not take it for granted, but thank people by providing recognition, as well as the additional support or facilities or comfort they need. While an employee is working harder, it certainly helps to know that your boss is acknowledging that extra effort and time.

## 9. PAST RESENTMENTS

The ninth reason people resist change is negative, but it is a reality of organizational life—those cobwebs of the past that get in the way of the future. Anyone who has ever had a gripe against the organization is likely to resist the organization telling them that they now have to do something new.

The conspiracy of silence, that uneasy truce possible as long as everything remains the same and people can avoid confrontations, is broken when you ask for change. Unresolved grievances from the past rise up to entangle and hamper the change effort. One new plant manager at Honeywell was surprised by resistance to a quality-of-work-life program, which he thought the workers would like because of the direct benefits to them. Then he discovered that the workers were still angry at management for failing to get them a quiet air-conditioning system despite years of complaints about summer noise levels in the factory. Until he listened to them and responded to their grievance, he could not get their commitment to his change plans.

Sweeping away the cobwebs of the past is sometimes a necessity for overcoming resistance to change. As long as they remain aggrieved, people will not want to go along with something we want. Going forward can thus mean first going back—listening to past resentments and repairing past rifts.

## 10. SOMETIMES THE THREAT IS REAL

The last reason people resist change is, in many ways, the most reasonable of all: *Sometimes the threat posed by the change is a real one.*

Sometimes a change does create winners and losers. Sometimes people do lose status, clout, or comfort because of the change. It would be naive to imagine otherwise. In fact, managing change well means recognizing its political realities.

The important thing here is to avoid pretense and false promises. If some people *are* going to lose something, they should hear about it early, rather than worrying about it constantly and infecting others with their anxiety or antagonism. And if some people are going to be let go or moved elsewhere, it is more humane to do it fast.

We all know the relief that people feel, even people who are being told the worst, at finally knowing that the thing they have feared is true. Now they can go ahead and plan their life. Thus, if some people are threatened by change because of the realities of their situations, managers should not pretend this is not so. Instead, they should make a clean break or a clean cut—as the first step in change, rather than leaving it to the end.

Of course, we all lose something in change, even the winners. Even those of us who are exhilarated about the opportunity it represents, or who are choosing to participate in a new era that we think is going to be better for our careers, more productive and technologically exciting, as many of the changes in American corporations promise to be.

Change is never entirely negative; it is also a tremendous opportunity. But even in that opportunity there is some small loss. It can be a loss of the past, a loss of routines, comforts, and traditions that were important, maybe a loss of relationships that became very close over time. Things will not, in fact, be the same any more.

Thus, we all need a chance to let go of the past, to "mourn" it. Rituals of parting help us say goodbye to the people we have been close to, rather than just letting those relationships slip away. "Memorial services," "eulogies," or events to honor the past help us let go. Unfortunately, those kinds of ceremonies and rituals are not legitimate in some companies. Instead, people are in one state, and the next day they have to move to another state without any acknowledgement of the loss that is involved. But things like goodbye parties or file-burning ceremonies or tacking up the company's history on bulletin boards are not just frills or luxuries; they are rituals that make it easier for people to move into the future because their loss is acknowledged and dealt with.

Resistance to change is not irrational; it stems from good and understandable concerns. Managers who can analyze the sources of resistance are in the best position to invent the solutions to it—and to manage change smoothly and effectively.

There may be no skill more important for the challenging times ahead.

# RULES OF THUMB FOR CHANGE AGENTS

*Herbert A. Shepard*

The following aphorisms are not so much bits of advice (although they are stated that way) as things to think about when you are being a change agent, a consultant, an organization or community development practitioner—or when you are just being yourself trying to bring about something that involves other people.

## RULE I: STAY ALIVE

This rule counsels against self-sacrifice on behalf of a cause that you do not wish to be your last.

Two exceptionally talented doctoral students came to the conclusion that the routines they had to go through to get their degrees were absurd, and decided they would be untrue to themselves to conform to an absurd system. That sort of reasoning is almost always self-destructive. Besides, their noble gesture in quitting would be unlikely to have any impact whatever on the system they were taking a stand against.

This is not to say that one should never take a stand, or a survival risk. But such risks should be taken as part of a purposeful strategy of change and appropriately timed and targeted. When they are taken under such circumstances, one is very much alive.

But Rule I is much more than a survival rule. The rule means that you should let your whole being be involved in the undertaking. Since most of us have never been in touch with our whole beings, it means a lot of putting together of parts that have been divided, of using internal communications channels that have been closed or were never opened.

Staying alive means loving yourself. Self-disparagement leads to the suppression of potentials, to a win-lose formulation of the world, and to wasting life in defensive maneuvering.

Staying alive means staying in touch with your purpose. It means using your skills, your emotions, your labels and positions, rather than being used by them. It means not being trapped in other people's games. It means turning yourself on and off, rather than being dependent on the situation. It means choosing with a view to the consequences as well as the impulse. It means going with the flow even while swimming against it. It means living in several worlds without being swallowed up in any. It means seeing dilemmas as opportunities for creativity. It means greeting absurdity with laughter while trying to unscramble it. It means capturing the moment in the light of the future. It means seeing the environment through the eyes of your purpose.

## RULE II: START WHERE THE SYSTEM IS

This is such ancient wisdom that one might expect its meaning had been fully explored and apprehended. Yet in practice the rule—and the system—are often violated.

The rule implies that one should begin by diagnosing the system. But systems do not necessarily *like* being diagnosed. Even the *term* "diagnosis" may be offensive. And the system may be even less

*Source*: Reprinted by permission of the publisher and author from the *OD Practitioner*, December 1984. Organization Development Network, Portland, Oregon.

ready for someone who calls himself or herself a "change agent!" It is easy for the practitioner to forget that the use of jargon which prevents laymen from understanding the professional mysteries is a hostile act.

Starting where the system is can be called the Empathy Rule. To communicate effectively, to obtain a basis for building sound strategy, the change agent needs to understand how the client sees himself and his situation, and needs to understand the culture of the system. Establishing the required rapport does not mean that the change agent who wants to work in a traditional industrial setting should refrain from growing a beard. It does mean that, if he has a beard, the beard is likely to determine where the client is when they first meet, and the client's curiosity needs to be dealt with. Similarly, the rule does not mean that a female change agent in a male organization should try to act like one of the boys, or that a young change agent should try to act like a senior executive. One thing it does mean is that sometimes where the client is, is wondering where the change agent is.

Rarely is the client in any one place at any one time. That is, she or he may be ready to pursue any of several paths. The task is to walk together on the most promising path.

Even unwitting or accidental violations of the Empathy Rule can destroy the situation. I lost a client through two violations in one morning. The client group spent a consulting day at my home. They arrived early in the morning, before I had my empathy on. The senior member, seeing a picture of my son in the livingroom said, "What do you do with boys with long hair?" I replied thoughtlessly, " I think he's handsome that way." The small chasm thus created between my client and me was widened and deepened later that morning when one of the family tortoises walked through the butter dish.

Sometimes starting where the client is, which sounds both ethically and technically virtuous, can lead to some ethically puzzling situations. Robert Frost* described a situation in which a consultant was so empathetic with a king who was unfit to rule that the king discovered his own unfitness and had himself shot, whereupon the consultant became king.

Empathy permits the development of a mutual attachment between client and consultant. The resulting relationship may be one in which their creativities are joined, a mutual growth relationship. But it can also become one in which the client becomes dependent and is manipulated by the consultant. The ethical issues are not associated with starting where the system is, but with how one moves with it.

# RULE III: NEVER WORK UPHILL

This is a comprehensive rule, and a number of other rules are corollaries or examples of it. It is an appeal for an organic rather than a mechanistic approach to change, for a collaborative approach to change, for building strength and building on strength. It has a number of implications that bear on the choices the change agent makes about how to use him/herself, and it says something about life.

## Corollary 1: Don't Build Hills As You Go

This corollary cautions against working in a way that builds resistance to movement in the direction you have chosen as desirable. For example, a program which has a favorable effect on one portion of a population may have the opposite effect on other portions of the population. Perhaps the commonest error of this kind has been in the employment of T-group training in organizations: turning on the participants and turning off the people who didn't attend, in one easy lesson.

*Robert Frost, "How Hard It Is To Keep From Being King When It's in You and in The Situation," *In the Clearing,* pp. 74–84 (New York: Holt, Rinehart and Winston, 1962).

## Corollary 2: Work in the Most Promising Arena

The physician-patient relationship is often regarded as analogous to the consultant-client relationship. The results for system change of this analogy can be unfortunate. For example, the organization development consultant is likely to be greeted with delight by executives who see in his specialty the solution to a hopeless situation in an outlying plant. Some organization development consultants have disappeared for years because of the irresistibility of such challenges. Others have whiled away their time trying to counteract the Peter Principle by shoring up incompetent managers.

## Corollary 3: Build Resources

Don't do anything alone that could be accomplished more easily or more certainly by a team. Don Quixote is not the only change agent whose effectiveness was handicapped by ignoring this rule. The change agent's task is an heroic one, but the need to be a hero does not facilitate team building. As a result, many change agents lose effectiveness by becoming spread too thin. Effectiveness can be enhanced by investing in the development of partners.

## Corollary 4: Don't Overorganize

The democratic ideology and theories of participative management that many change agents possess can sometimes interfere with common sense. A year or two ago I offered a course to be taught by graduate students. The course was oversubscribed. It seemed that a data-based process for deciding whom to admit would be desirable, and that participation of the graduate students in the decision would also be desirable. So I sought data from the candidates about themselves, and xeroxed their responses for the graduate students. Then the graduate students and I held a series of meetings. Then the candidates were informed of the decision. In this way we wasted a great deal of time and everyone felt a little worse than if we had used an arbitrary decision rule.

## Corollary 5: Don't Argue If You Can't Win

Win-lose strategies are to be avoided because they deepen conflict instead of resolving it. But the change agent should build her or his support constituency as large and deep and strong as possible so that she or he can continue to risk.

## Corollary 6: Play God a Little

If the change agent doesn't make the critical value decisions, someone else will be happy to do so. Will a given situation contribute to your fulfillment? Are you creating a better world for yourself and others, or are you keeping a system in operation that should be allowed to die? For example, the public education system is a mess. Does that mean that the change agent is morally obligated to try to improve it, destroy it, or develop a substitute for it? No, not even if he or she knows how. But the change agent does need a value perspective for making choices like that.

# RULE IV: INNOVATION REQUIRES A GOOD IDEA, INITIATIVE AND A FEW FRIENDS

Little can be accomplished alone, and the effects of social and cultural forces on individual perception are so distorting that the change agent needs a partner, if only to maintain perspective and purpose.

The quality of the partner is as important as the quality of the idea. Like the change agent, partners must be relatively autonomous people. Persons who are authority-oriented—who need to rebel or need to submit—are not reliable partners: the rebels take the wrong risks and the good soldiers don't take any. And rarely do they command the respect and trust from others that is needed if an innovation is to be supported.

The partners need not be numerous. For example, the engineering staff of a chemical company designed a new process plant using edge-of-the-art technology. The design departed radically from the experience of top management, and they were about to reject it. The engineering chief suggested that the design be reviewed by a distinguished engineering professor. The principal designers were in fact former students of the professor. For this reason he accepted the assignment, charged the company a large fee for reviewing the design (which he did not trouble to examine) and told the management that it was brilliantly conceived and executed. By this means the engineers not only implemented their innovations, but also grew in the esteem of their management.

A change agent experienced in the Washington environment reports that he knows of only one case of successful interdepartmental collaboration in mutually designing, funding and managing a joint project. It was accomplished through the collaboration of himself and three similarly-minded young men, one from each of four agencies. They were friends, and met weekly for lunch. They conceived the project, and planned strategies for implementing it. Each person undertook to interest and influence the relevant key people in his own agency. The four served one another as consultants and helper in influencing opinion and bringing the decision-makers together.

An alternative statement of Rule IV is as follows: Find the people who are ready and able to work, introduce them to one another, and work with them. Perhaps because many change agents have been trained in the helping professions, perhaps because we have all been trained to think bureaucratically, concepts like organization position, representatives or need are likely to guide the change agent's selection of those he or she works with.

A more powerful beginning can sometimes be made by finding those persons in the system whose values are congruent with those of the change agent, who possess vitality and imagination, who are willing to work overtime, and who are eager to learn. Such people are usually glad to have someone like the change agent join in getting something important accomplished, and a careful search is likely to turn up quite a few. In fact, there may be enough of them to accomplish general system change, if they can team up in appropriate ways.

In building such teamwork the change agent's abilities will be fully challenged, as he joins them in establishing conditions for trust and creativity; dealing with their anxieties about being seen as subversive; enhancing their leadership, consulting, problem-solving, diagnosing and innovating skills; and developing appropriate group norms and policies.

# RULE V: LOAD EXPERIMENTS FOR SUCCESS

This sounds like counsel to avoid risk taking. But the decision to experiment always entails risk. After that decision has been made, take all precautions.

The rule also sounds scientifically immoral. But whether an experiment produces the expected results depends upon the experimenter's depth of insight into the conditions and processes involved. Of course, what is experimental is what is new to the system; it may or may not be new to the change agent.

Build an umbrella over the experiment. A chemical process plant which was to be shut down because of the inefficiency of its operations undertook a union management cooperation project to improve efficiency, which involved a modified form of profit-sharing. Such plans were contrary to company policy, but the regional vice president was interested in the experiment, and successfully concealed it from his associates. The experiment was successful; the plant became profitable. But in this case, the umbrella turned out not to be big enough. The plant was shut down anyway.

Use the Hawthorne effect. Even poorly conceived experiments are often made to succeed when the participants feel ownership. And conversely, one of the obstacles to the spread of useful innovations is that the groups to which they are offered do not feel ownership of them.

For example, if the change agent hopes to use experience-based learning as part of his/her strategy, the first persons to be invited should be those who consistently turn all their experiences into constructive learning. Similarly, in introducing team development processes into a system, begin with the best functioning team.

Maintain voluntarism. This is not easy to do in systems where invitations are understood to be commands, but nothing vital can be built on such motives as duty, obedience, security-seeking or responsiveness to social pressure.

# RULE VI: LIGHT MANY FIRES

Not only does a large, monolithic development or change program have high visibility and other qualities of a good target, it also tends to prevent subsystems from feeling ownership of, and consequent commitment to the program.

The meaning of this rule is more orderly than the random prescription—light many fires—suggests. Any part of a system is the way it is partly because of the way the rest of the system is. To work towards change in one subsystem is to become one more determinant of its performance. Not only is the change agent working uphill, but as soon as he turns his back, other forces in the system will press the subsystem back towards its previous performance mode.

If many interdependent subsystems are catalyzed, and the change agent brings them together to facilitate one another's efforts, the entire system can begin to move.

Understanding patterns of interdependency among subsystems can lead to a strategy of fire-setting. For example, in public school systems, it requires collaboration among politicians, administrators, teachers, parents and students to bring about significant innovation, and active opposition on the part of only one of these groups to prevent it. In parochial school systems, on the other hand, collaboration between the administration and the church can provide a powerful impetus for change in the other groups.

# RULE VII: KEEP AN OPTIMISTIC BIAS

Our society grinds along with much polarization and cruelty, and even the helping professions compose their world of grim problems to be "worked through." The change agent is usually flooded with the destructive aspects of the situations he enters. People in most systems are impressed by one another's weaknesses, and stereotype each other with such incompetencies as they can discover.

This rule does not advise ignoring destructive forces. But its positive prescription is that the change agent be especially alert to the constructive forces which are often masked and suppressed in a problem-oriented, envious culture.

People have as great an innate capacity for joy as for resentment, but resentment causes them to overlook opportunities for joy. In a workshop for married couples, a husband and wife were discussing their sexual problem and how hard they were working to solve it. They were not making much progress, since they didn't realize that sex is not a problem, but an opportunity.

Individuals and groups locked in destructive kinds of conflict focus on their differences. The change agent's job is to help them discover and build on their commonalities, so that they will have a foundation of respect and trust which will permit them to use their differences as a source of creativity. The unhappy partners focus on past hurts, and continue to destroy the present and future with them. The change agent's job is to help them change the present so that they will have a new past on which to create a better future.

# RULE VIII: CAPTURE THE MOMENT

A good sense of relevance and timing is often treated as though it were a "gift" or "intuition" rather than something that can be learned, something spontaneous rather than something planned. The opposite is nearer the truth. One is more likely to "capture the moment" when everything one has learned is readily available.

Some years ago my wife and I were having a very destructive fight. Our nine-year-old daughter decided to intervene. She put her arms around her mother and asked: "What does Daddy do that bugs you?" She was an attentive audience for the next few minutes while my wife told her, ending in tears. She then put her arms around me: "What does Mommy do that bugs you?" and listened attentively to my response, which also ended in tears. She then went to the record player and put on a favorite love song ("If Ever I Should Leave You"), and left us alone to make up.

The elements of my daughter's intervention had all been learned. They were available to her, and she combined them in a way that could make the moment better.

Perhaps it's our training in linear cause-and-effect thinking and the neglect of our capacities for imagery that makes us so often unable to see the multiple potential of the moment. Entering the situation "blank" is not the answer. One needs to have as many frameworks for seeing and strategies for acting available as possible. But it's not enough to involve only one's head in the situation; one's heart has to get involved too. Cornelia Otis Skinner once said that the first law of the stage is to love your audience. You can love your audience only if you love yourself. If you have relatively full access to your organized experience, to yourself and to the situation, you will capture the moment more often.